italian

Italian · English
English · Italian

Isopel May, B.A., Ph.D.

Collins
London and Glasgow

General Editor
W. T. McLeod

First published 1954
Latest Reprint 1979

ISBN 0 00 458623 9

© William Collins Sons & Co. Ltd. 1954

Printed in Great Britain by
Collins Clear-Type Press

I am happy to have the opportunity to thank all the Italian friends who helped me with advice and criticism and especially my Florentine friend, Miss Franca Parenti, without whose precious collaboration this work would never have been finished.

ISOPEL MAY

Con piacere colgo l'occasione di ringraziare tutti gli amici italiani che con i loro consigli e le loro critiche mi hanno aiutata. In modo speciale ringrazio la mia amica fiorentina, Signorina Franca Parenti, senza la di cui preziosa collaborazione questo lavoro non sarebbe mai stato terminato.

ISOPEL MAY

CONTENTS

FOREWORD

THIS is the third volume of a series which now comprises four bi-lingual dictionaries ; the first, French–English and English–French ; the second, German–English and English–German ; and the fourth, Spanish–English and English–Spanish Each volume has been compiled by a scholar with special qualifications for the task and the greatest pains have been taken to ensure that these dictionaries, though small shall be thoroughly reliable as far as they go.

A pocket dictionary is intended, in the first place, to meet all the needs of ordinary, everyday life. It is particularly handy for the traveller and must therefore contain all the words he will normally require in trains, in the customs, in hotels and in shops. It is, besides, intended to help the reader of Italian novels, reviews and papers, as well as those writing letters or making translations of a non-technical character. The dictionary must therefore be both general and practical. All the different branches of modern activities must be taken into consideration, as far as limitations of space permit, and above all the dictionary must be up to date. A few of the terms most commonly used in aviation, broadcasting, television, sport, motoring and commerce are therefore included, but for everything beyond the bare essentials of these different subjects a technical dictionary is indispensable.

Moreover, it is frequently the case that a single English word has several Italian equivalents, and *vice versa*. It then becomes necessary to make a selection whenever possible, among the different words which in one language express the different ideas of the other. This has, in fact, been done ; but it has often been impossible, in such a small volume to give *all* the translations which exist.

PREFAZIONE

QUESTO è il terzo volumetto d'una serie che attualmente comprende 4 dizionari bilingui : il primo francese–inglese, inglese–francese, il secondo tedesco–inglese inglese–tedesco, e il quarto spagnuolo–inglese. inglese–spagnuolo. Ciascun volume è stato compilato da uno studioso con particolare competenza in materia, e ogni cura è stata messa affinché i dizionari riescano completi e diano il massimo affidamento,

Un dizionario tascabile è ideato principalmente per sopperire alle necessità della semplice vita di ogni giorno. E'il *vade mecum* del viaggiatore, e pertanto contiene i vocaboli di cui egli avrà bisogno in treno, alla dogana, nei negozi e negli alberghi. Deve inoltre servire al lettore di romanzi, riviste e giornali inglesi. Il dizionario deve quindi avere carattere generale e pratico. Tutti i vari settori dell' attività moderna vanno anche presi in considerazione e il vocabolario, dev'essere sopratutto aggiornato. Alcuni termini piu comuni usati per l'aviazione, per la radio-diffusione, per la televisione, per lo sport, per l'automobilismo e per il commercio sono dunque inclusi, ma è chiaro che non sarà possibile oltrepassare i limiti molto ristretti ; chi vuol approfondirsi in questi vari argomenti dovrà sempre ricorrere ai vocabolari tecnici.

Inoltre, può darsi che un solo vocabolo inglese abbia diversi equivalenti italiani, e vice versa ; è quindi necessario fare una selezione, quando questo è possibile, fra le varie parole che in una lingua esprimono i diversi concetti dell'altra. Questo è stato fatto ; ma non è possibile, in un volume cosi piccolo, dare sempre *tutte* le traduzioni che esistono.

ABBREVIATIONS

a.	adjective.	*mus.*	music.
ad.	adverb.	*n.*	noun.
Am.	American.	*nf.*	noun feminine.
an.	anatomy.	*nm.*	noun masculine.
arch.	architecture.	*naut.*	nautical.
aut.	automobile	*ph.*	philosophy.
avia.	aviation.	*phot.*	photography.
bot.	botany.	*pl.*	plural.
com.	commercial.	*pn.*	pronoun.
con.	conjunction.	*poet.*	poetical.
dem. pn.	demonstrative pronoun.	*pr.*	preposition.
eccl.	ecclesiastic.	*rad.*	radio.
elec.	electricity.	*rel. pn.*	relative pronoun.
fam.	familiar	*rly.*	railway.
fig.	figurative.	*tech.*	technical.
gram.	grammar.	*theat.*	theatrical.
int.	interjection.	*typ.*	typographical.
leg.	legal.	*vi.*	intransitive verb.
mech.	mechanical.	*v. imp.*	impersonal verb.
med.	medical.	*vr.*	reflexive verb.
mil.	military.	*vt.*	transitive verb.

THE ITALIAN ALPHABET

The Italian language possesses twenty-two letters, of which **a, e, i, o, u** are vowels, **vocali**; the others are consonants, **consonanti**.

A,	ah.	**G,**	gee.	**N,**	ennay.	**T,**	tee.
B,	bee.	**H,**	ahk-kah.	**O,**	o.	**U,**	oo.
C,	chee.	**I,**	ee.	**P,**	pee.	**V,**	vee.
D,	dee.	**J,**	ee loong-goh	**Q,**	koo.	**Z,**	zay-tah.
E,	ay.	**L,**	ellay.	**R,**	erray.		
F,	effay.	**M,**	emmay.	**S,**	essay.		

The letters **k, w, x, y** do not exist in Italian. The **x** is found in some Latin expressions, and also in **Xanto**, the river Xanthus, to distinguish it from **Santo**, saint.

Pronunciation of Vowels

A is sounded broad like the *a* in *rather*, *art*, as: **amare, to** love; **andare**, to go; **lana**, wool; **mano**, hand.

E has a close and an open sound, the first like *Mary*, as: **fede**, faith; **penna**, pen; **sera**, evening; the second like *were* as **trofeo**, trophy; **sette**, seven; **era**, was.

I is pronounced like the English *ea* in *mean*, as: **venire,** to come; **sentire**, to hear; **finire**, to finish.

O sounds close and open. It is open, as in the English *tropic*, ex.; **povero**, poor; **nota**, note; **oggi**, to-day. It is close as in *own*, ex.; **ombra**, shade: **pozzo**, well; **ordine**, order.

U is pronounced like *oo* in English, ex.; **luna**, moon, **uno**, one; **tutto**, all. In diphthongs each vowel must be pronounced separately ex.: **Europa**, Europe; **buono,** good; **pieno**, full; **miei**, my.

Pronunciation of Consonants

The consonants **b, d, f, l, m, n, p, t, v** are always pronounced as in English; when the same consonant occurs twice, each letter is distinctly sounded, as: **bello**, beautiful; **birra**, beer.

c before **a, o, u** and before consonants is pronounced like the English *k*: **calamaio**, inkstand; **cosa,** thing; **cuore**, heart; **culla**, cradle; **chiesa,**

church; **occhio**, eye; **chiave**, key; **chiamare**, to call.

c   before **e** or **i** sounds as in the English *cha* in *chase*, *chee* in *cheese*; **cena**, supper; **città**, city; **cielo**, sky; **cibo**, food; **civile**, civil; **bacio**, kiss; **cecità**, blindness; **cioccolata**, chocolate.

cc   before **e** or **i** sounds like *tch*; **faccia**, face; **accento**, accent; **eccellanza**, excellency.

g   before **a**, **o**, **u** is pronounced hard like the English *God*; **galante**, gallant; **gallo**, cock; **governatore**, governor; **gufo**, owl.

g   before **e** or **i** sounds softly as in *general*; **gente**, people; **genio**, genius; **gentile**, gentle; **gigante**, giant; **ginocchio**, knee.

gg   before **e** or **i** is pronounced like *dg*; **coraggio**, courage; **raggio**, ray; **oggetto**, object.

ghe, ghi   sound as in *guess*, *guilt*; **ghinea**, guinea; **ghiaccio**, ice; **ghiottone**, glutton; **alberghi**, hotels.

gl   followed by **a**, **e**, **o**, **u** is pronounced like *gl* in *gland*; **glandula**, gland; **gleba**, glebe; **gloria**, glory

gli   sounds like *lli* in *brilliant*; **egli**, he; **maglio**, better; **aglio**, garlic; **giglio**, lily; **figlio**, son. The words **Anglia**, England; **glicerina**, glycerine; **negligere**, to neglect, are pronounced as in English.

gn   is pronounced more like the *ni* in *opinion*, *companion*; **campagna**, country; **agnello**, lamb; **magnifico**, magnificent.

h   is never pronounced.

q   which is always followed by **u**, is pronounced as in *question*; **quattro**, four; **questo**, this; **quindici**, fifteen; **nacque**, was born.

r   must be very distinctly pronounced; **raro**, rare; **arte**, art; **ramo**, branch; **tortura**, torture.

s   sounds as in English; **sensibile**, sensible; **simpatia**, liking; **servo**, servant; **seta**, silk.

s   between two vowels sounds as in *rose* **mese**, month; **asino**, donkey; **offesa**, offence; **esilio**, exile.

sce, sci   sound like *sh* in *shell*; **scendere**, to go down; **scena**, scene; **scettro**, sceptre; **scienza**, science.

z   sometimes sounds soft like *ds*; **zelo**, zeal;

NUMERAL ADJECTIVES

bronzo, bronze, **canzone**, song; sometimes sharp like *ts*; **zio** uncle; **zitto**, hush; **zampa**, paw.

NUMERAL ADJECTIVES

Cardinal Numbers

1 uno		32	trentadue
2 due		40	quaranta
3 tre		50	cinquanta
4 quattro		60	sessanta
5 cinque		70	settanta
6 sei		80	ottanta
7 sette		90	novanta
8 otto		100	cento
9 nove		101	centuno
10 dieci		102	cento due
11 undici		200	duecento
12 dodici		300	trecento
13 tredici		400	quattrocento
14 quattordici		500	cinquecento
15 quindici		1,000	mille
16 sedici		1,100	mille e cento
17 diciassette		1,200	mille e duecento
18 diciotto		2,000	duemila
19 diciannove		3,000	tremila
20 venti		10,000	diecimila
21 ventuno		100,000	centomila
22 ventidue		1,000,000	un milione
23 ventitre, etc.	**two millions**		due milioni
30 trenta	**a milliard**		un miliardo
31 trentuno	**two milliards**		due miliardi

Ordinal Numbers

1st primo		20th	ventesimo
2nd secondo		21st	ventesimoprimo
3rd terzo		22nd	ventesimosecondo
4th quarto			etc.
5th quinto		30th	trentesimo
6th sesto		40th	quarantesimo
7th settimo		50th	cinquantesimo
8th ottavo		60th	sessantesimo

THE AUXILIARY VERBS

9th	nono	70th	settantesimo
10th	decimo	80th	ottantesimo
11th	undecimo / undicesimo	90th	novantesimo
		100th	centesimo
12th	duodecimo / dodicesimo	101st	centesimoprimo
		150th	centocinquantesimo
13th	tredicesmo / decimo terzo	190th	centonovantesimo
		200th	dugentesimo
14th	decimo quarto	1,000th	millesimo
15th	decimo quinto	2,000th	duemillesimo
16th	decimo sesto	10 000th	diecimillesimo
17th	decimo settimo	100,000th	centomillesimo
18th	decimo ottavo	1,000,000th	milionesimo
19th	decimo nono	1,000,000,000th	miliardesimo

THE AUXILIARY VERBS

Essere, to be
Avere, to have

PRESENT INDICATIVE

I am.	*I have.*
io sono.	io ho.
tu sei.	tu hai.
egli } è	egli } ha.
essa	essa
noi siamo.	noi abbiamo.
voi siete.	voi avete.
essi } sono.	essi } hanno.
esse	esse

IMPERFECT

I was.	*I had.*
io ero.	io avevo.
tu eri.	tu avevi.
egli era.	egli aveva.
noi eravamo.	noi avevamo.
voi eravate.	voi avevate.
essi erano.	essi avevano.

PAST DEFINITE

I was.	*I had.*
io fui.	io ebbi.
tu fosti.	tu avesti.

x

THE AUXILIARY VERBS

PERFECT CONDITIONAL

I should have been.	*I should have had.*
Io sarei stato.	io avrei avuto.
tu saresti stato.	tu avresti avuto.
egli sarebbe stato. ⎫	egli ⎫ avrebbe avuto.
essa sarebbe stata. ⎭	essa ⎭
noi saremmo stati.	noi avremmo avuto.
voi saresti stati.	voi avreste avuto.
essi sarebbero stati. ⎫	essi ⎫ avrebbero avuto.
esse sarebbero state. ⎭	esse ⎭

PERFECT INFINITIVE

to have been	*to have had*
essere stato.	avere avuto.
essere stata.	avere avuta.

PERFECT GERUND

having been.	*having had.*
essendo stato.	avendo avuto.
essendo stata.	avendo avuta.

PRESENT

that I be.	*that I have.*
ch'io sia.	ch'io abbia.
che tu sia.	che tu abbia.
che egli sia.	che egli abbia.
che noi siamo.	che noi abbiamo.
che voi siate.	che voi abbiate.
che essi siano.	che essi abbiano.

IMPERFECT

if I were	*if I had.*
se io fossi.	se io avessi.
se tu fossi.	se tu avessi.
se egli fosse.	se egli avesse.
se noi fossimo.	se noi avessimo.
se voi foste.	se voi aveste.
se essi fossero.	se essi avessero.

PERFECT

that I have been.	*that I have had.*
ch'io sia stato.	ch'io abbia avuto.
che tu sia stato.	che tu abbia avuto.

che egli sia stato.	che egli	
che essa sia stata.	che essa	} abbia avuto.
che noi siamo stati.	che noi abbiamo avuto.	
che voi siate stati.	che voi abbiate avuto.	
che essi siano stati.	che essi	
che esse siano state.	che esse	} abbiano avuto.

PLUPERFECT

if I had been.	*if I had had.*
se io fossi stato.	se io avessi avuto.
se tu fossi stato.	se tu avessi avuto.
se egli fosse stato.	se egli avesse avuto.
se essa fosse stata. }	se essa avesse avuto. }
se noi fossimo stati.	se noi avessimo avuto.
se voi foste stati.	se voi aveste avuto.
se essi fossero stati. }	se essi avessero avuto. }
se esse fossero state.	se esse avessero avuto.

REGULAR VERBS

Conjugation 1	**Conjugation 2**	**Conjugation 3**

INFINITIVE

Parlare, to speak.   **Temére**, to fear.   **Sentire**, to hear.

PRESENT INDICATIVE

I speak	*I fear*	*I hear*
io parl-o.	tem-o.	sent-o.
tu parl-i.	tem-i.	sent-i.
egli parl-a.	tem-e.	sent-e.
noi parl-iamo.	tem-iamo.	sent-iamo.
voi parl-ate.	tem-ete.	sent-ite.
essi parl-ano.	tem-ono.	sent-ono.

IMPERFECT

I used to speak	*I used to fear.*	*I used to hear.*
io parl-avo.	tem-evo.	sent-ivo.
tu parl-avi.	tem-evi.	sent-ivi.
egli parl-ava.	tem-eva.	sent-iva.
noi parl-avamo.	tem-evamo.	sent-ivamo.
voi parl-avate.	tem-evate.	sent-ivate
essi parl-avano.	tem-evano.	sent-ivano.

REGULAR VERBS

PAST DEFINITE

I spoke	*I feared*	*I heard.*
io parl-ai.	tem-ei.	sent-ii.
tu parl-asti.	tem-esti.	sent-isti.
egli parl-ò.	tem-è.	sent-i.
noi parl-ammo.	tem-emmo.	sent-immo.
voi parl-aste.	tem-este.	sent-iste.
essi parl-arono.	tem-erono.	sent-irono.

FUTURE

I shall speak.	*I shall fear.*	*I shall hear.*
io parl-erò.	tem-erò.	sent-irò.
tu parl-erai.	tem-erai.	sent-irai.
egli parl-erà.	tem-erà.	sent-irà.
noi parl-eremo.	tem-eremo.	sent-iremo.
voi parl-erete.	tem-erete.	sent-irete.
essi parl-eranno.	tem-eranno.	sent-iranno.

CONDITIONAL

I should speak.	*I should fear*	*I should hear.*
io parl-erei.	tem-erei.	sent-irei.
tu parl-eresti.	tem-eresti.	sent-iresti.
egli parl-erebbe.	tem-erebbe.	sent-irebbe.
noi parl-eremmo.	tem-eremmo.	sent-iremmo.
voi parl-ereste.	tem-ereste.	sent-ireste.
essi parl-erebbero.	tem-erebbero.	sent-irebbero.

IMPERATIVE

speak	*fear.*	*hear.*
parl-a.	tem-i.	sent-i.
parl-i.	tem-a.	sent-a.
parl-iamo.	tem-iamo.	sent-iamo.
parl-ate.	tem-ete.	sent-ite.
parl-ino.	tem-ano.	sent-ano.

PRESENT INFINITIVE

parl-are, *to speak.*   tem-ere, *to fear.*   sent-ire, *to hear.*

PRESENT PARTICIPLE

parl-ante, *speaking.*   tem-ente, *fearing.*   sent-ente, *hearing.*

REGULAR VERBS

GERUND

parl-ando, *speaking.*   tem-endo, *fearing.*   sent-endo. *hearing.*

PAST PARTICIPLE

parl-ato, *spoken.*   tem-uto, *feared.*   sent-ito, *heard.*

Subjunctive

PRESENT

that I speak.	*that I fear.*	*that I hear.*
ch'io parl-i.	ch'io tem-a.	ch'io sent-a.
che tu parl-i.	che tu tem-a.	che tu sent-a.
ch'egli parl-i.	ch'egli tem-a.	ch'egli sent-a.
che noi parl-iamo.	che noi tem-iamo.	che noi sent-iamo.
che voi parl-iate.	che voi tem-iate.	che voi sent-iate.
ch'essi parl-ino.	che essi tem-ano.	ch'essi sent-ano.

IMPERFECT

If I spoke.	*if I feared.*	*if I heard.*
se io parl-assi.	tem-essi.	sent-issi.
se tu parl-assi.	tem-essi.	sent-issi.
se egli parl-asse.	tem-esse.	sent-isse.
se noi parl-assimo.	tem-essimo.	sent-issimo.
se voi parl-aste.	tem-este.	sente-iste.
se essi parl-assero.	tem-essero.	sent-issero.

Compound Tenses

Perfect	io ho	parlato,	*I have*	*spoken.*
Pluperfect	io avevo		*I had*	
2nd Pluperf.	io ebbi		*I had*	
2nd Future	io avrò	or	*I shall have*	or
2nd Condit.	io avrei		*I should*	
Subj. Perfect.	ch'io abbia	temuto,	*have*	*feared.*
Subj. Pluperf.	se io avessi		*that I have*	
Past Infin.	aver(e)	or	*if I had*	or
Past Gerund	avendo	sentito,	*to have*	*heard.*
		having		

xvi

Progressive Form

The English progressive forms *I am speaking, I was speaking*, are rendered in Italian, either by the ordinary present or imperfect, or by the present and imperfect of the indicative of the verb **stare**,[1] followed by the gerund:

[1] When the act implies motion, *andare* is used instead of *stare*.

PRESENT	IMPERFECT
io sto parlando.	io stavo parlando.
tu stai parlando.	tu stavi parlando.
egli sta parlando.	egli stava parlando.
noi stiamo parlando.	noi stavamo parlando.
voi state parlando.	voi stavate parlando.
essi stanno parlando.	essi stavano parlando.

Semi-Irregularities of some Verbs in *ARE*

1. Verbs ending in **care** and **gare**, as: **pagare**, to pay; **cercare**, to look for; **pregare**, to pray; **mancare**, to fail; **giudicare**, to judge, when the **c** or **g** is followed by **e** or **i**, take an **h** in order to preserve the hard sound of the consonant.

io pago.	ch'io paghi.
tu paghi.	che tu paghi.
egli paga.	ch'egli paghi.
noi paghiamo.	che noi paghiamo.
voi pagate.	che voi paghiate.
essi pagano.	ch'essi paghino.

2. In the future they make—**paghero, pregherò, cercherò, mancherò,** etc.;

egli pagherà il suo conto,   *he will pay his account.*
noi pregheremo per lei,   *we shall pray for you.*

3. Verbs in **ciare** and in **giare** or **sciare**, as: **cominciare**, to begin; **lasciare**, to leave; **mangiare**, to eat, drop the **i** before **e** or **i**

io mangio.	io comincio.
tu mangi.	tu cominci.
Fut. mangerò.	comincerò.

4. Verbs in **iare** having a stress on the **i**, as; **spiare, to spy; inviare**, to send; **obliare**, to forget, retain the **i**, even before the other **i** of the 2nd singular person of the present of the indicative

tu invii una lettera.	*thou sendest a letter.*
noi non vi oblieremo.	*we shall not forget you.*

5. Verbs in **chaire, gliare**, and **oiare**, as; **pigliare, to take; invecchiare**, to grow old; **annoiare**, to bore: drop the **i** when followed by another **i**:—

	io pigliò.	io annoio.
	tu pigli.	tu annoi.
Fut.	piglierò.	annoierô.

Peculiarities of some Verbs in
ERE

Some verbs of the 2nd conjugation have two distinct terminations for the 1st and 3rd person singular, and for the 3rd plural of the past definite

io credei.	io credetti.
tu credesti.	
egli credè.	egli credette.
noi credemmo.	
voi credeste.	
essi crederono.	essi credettero.

Semi-Irregularities of some Verbs in
IRE

1. The verb **cucire**, to sew, and **sdruceir**, to rend, take an i whenever the **c** precedes an **a** or an **o**

io cucio.	io sdrucio.
tu cuci.	tu sdruci.
egli cuce.	egli sdruce.
noi cuciamo.	noi sdruciamo.
voi cucite.	voi sdrucite.
essi cuciono.	essi sdruciono.

2. A large number of the verbs in **ire** in the 1st, 2nd, and 3rd sing., and in the 3rd plural of the indicative, take the terminations **isco**, **isci**, **isce**, **iscono**, instead of the regular forms. A similar change takes place in the present subjunctive and in the imperative

I understand	*that I understand*
io capisco.	ch'io capisca.
tu capisci.	che tu capisca.
egli capisce.	ch'egli capisca.
noi capiamo.	che noi capiamo.
voi capite.	che voi capiate.
essi capiscono.	ch'essi capiscano.

3. The following verbs are conjugated like **capire**

finire,	*to finish*	costituire,	*to constitute.*
preferire,	*to prefer.*	digerire,	*to digest.*
riverire,	*to revere.*	esibire	*to exhibit.*
florire,	*to flourish.*	suggerire,	*to suggest.*
ferire,	*to wound.*	abbellire,	*to beautify.*
definire,	*to define.*	appassire,	*to fade.*
demolire,	*to demolish.*	punire,	*to punish.*
patire,	*to suffer.*	ardire,	*to dare.*
arrossire,	*to blush.*	costruire,	*to construct.*
restituire,	*to restore.*	compatire,	*to pity.*
ubbidire,	*to obey.*	progredire,	*to progress.*
colpire,	*to strike.*	inpallidire	*to become pale.*

Table of the Conjugations

FIRST CONJUGATION

ends in are, as parlare, *to speak*

INFINITIVE MOOD.	*Present*		ends in are, as parlare, *to speak*				
	Gerund		ando				
	Participle		ato				
INDICATIVE MOOD.	*Present*	o	i	a	iamo	ate	ano
	Imperfect	avo	avi	ava	avamo	avate	avano
	Past Definite	ai	asti	ò	ammo	aste	arono
	Future	erò	erai	erà	eremo	erete	eranno
	Conditional	erei	eresti	erebbe	eremmo	ereste	erebbero
SUBJUNCTIVE MOOD.	*Present*	i	i	i	iamo	iate	ino
	Imperfect	assi	assi	asse	assimo	aste	assero
IMPERATIVE MOOD.		—	a	i	iamo	ate	ino

SECOND CONJUGATION

ends in ere, as temere, *to fear.*

INFINITIVE MOOD.	*Present*		ends in ere, as temere, *to fear.*				
	Gerund		endo				
	Participle		uto				
INDICATIVE MOOD.	*Present*	o	i	e	iamo	ete	ono
	Imperfect	evo	evi	eva	evamo	evate	evano
	Past Definite	ei	esti	è	emmo	este	erono
	Future	erò	erai	erà	eremo	erete	eranno
	Conditional	erei	eresti	erebbe	eremmo	ereste	erebbero
SUBJUNCTIVE MOOD.	*Present*	a	a	a	iamo	iate	ano
	Imperfect	essi	essi	esse	essimo	este	essero
IMPERATIVE MOOD.		—	i	a	iamo	ete	ano

TABLE OF THE CONJUGATIONS

THIRD CONJUGATION

Infinitive Mood.						
Present : ends in ire, as *sentire, to feel.*						
Gerund :	endo					
Participle :	ito					

Indicative Mood.	io	tu	egli	noi	voi	loro
Present :	o	i	e	iamo	ite	ono
Imperfect :	ivo	ivi	iva	ivamo	ivate	ivano
Past Definite :	ii	isti	ì	immo	iste	irono
Future :	irò	irai	irà	iremo	irete	iranno
Conditional :	irei	iresti	irebbe	iremmo	ireste	irebbero

Subjunctive Mood.						
Present :	a	i	a	iamo	iate	ano
Imperfect :	issi	issi	isse	issimo	iste	issero

Imperative Mood.						
		i	a	iamo	ite	ano

THIRD CONJUGATION

Infinitive Mood.						
Present : ends in ire, as *finire, to finish.*						
Gerund :	endo					
Participle :	ito					

Indicative Mood.	io	tu	egli	noi	voi	loro
Present :	isco	isci	isce	iamo	ite	iscono
Imperfect :	ivo	ivi	iva	ivamo	ivate	ivano
Past Definite :	ii	isti	ì	immo	iste	irono
Future :	irò	irai	irà	iremo	irete	iranno
Conditional :	irei	iresti	irebbe	iremmo	ireste	irebbero

Subjunctive Mood.						
Present :	isca	isca	isca	iamo	iate	iscano
Imperfect :	issi	issi	isse	issimo	iste	issero

Imperative Mood.						
		isci	isca	iamo	ite	iscano

ALPHABETICAL LIST OF THE IRREGULAR VERBS

		Pres.	Def.	Fut.	P.p.
Accendere,	to light, to set on fire.	accendo	accesi	accenderò	acceso.
Accorgersi,	to perceive.	m'accorgo	m'accorsi	m'accorgerò	accorto.
Addurre,	to bring.	adduco	addussi	addurrò	addotto.
Affliggere,	to afflict.	affliggo	afflissi	affliggerò	afflitto.
Algere,	to freeze.	—	alsi (only **1, 2, 3 pers. sing.**)	—	(P.pr. algente.)
Andare,	to go.	vado	andai	andrò	andato.
Annettere,	to annex.	annetto	annessi	annetterò	annesso.
Apparire,	to appear.	apparisco	apparì (apparvi) (apparsi)	apparirò	apparso.
Aprire,	to open.	apro	aprii (apersi)	aprirò	aperto.
Ardere,	to burn.	ardo	arsi	arderò	arso.
Assistere,	to assist.	assisto	assistei	assisterò	assistito.
Assolvere,	to absolve.	assolvo	assolsi	assolverò	assoluto.
Assumere,	to assume.	assumo	assunsi	assumerò	assunto.
Bere.	to drink.	bevo	bevetti (bevvi)	berrò	bevuto.
Cadere,	to fall.	cado	caddi	cadrò	caduto.
Calére,	to care for.	mi cale	mi calse	—	caluto.
Cedere,	to cede, to yield.	cedo	cedei (cedetti)	cederò	ceduto (cesso).
Chiedere,	to ask.	chiedo	chiesi	chiederò	chiesto.
Chiudere,	to shut.	chiudo	chiusi	chiuderò	chiuso.
Cingere (Cignere).	to gird.	cingo (cigno)	cinsi	cingerò (cignerò)	cinto.

xxii

ALPHABETICAL LIST OF THE IRREGULAR VERBS

		Pres. colgo (coglio)	Def. colsi	Ful. coglierò (corro)	P.p. colto.
Cogliere (Corre),	to gather.	colgo, cole	colsi		—
Colere,	to revere.	cole			
Condurre,	to lead.	conduco	condussi	condurrò	condotto.
Conoscere,	to know.	conosco	conobbi	conoscerò	conosciuto.
Coprire,	to cover.	copro	coprii	coprirò	coperto.
Correggere,	to correct.	correggo	coressi	correggerò	corretto.
Correre,	to run.	corro	corsi	correrò	corso.
Crescere,	to grow.	cresco	crebbi	crescerò	cresciuto.
Cuocere,	to cook.	cuocio	cossi	cuocerò	cotto.
Dare,	to give.	do	diedi	darò	dato.
Deprimere,	to depress.	deprimo	depressi	deprimerò	depresso.
Difendere,	to defend.	difendo	difesi	difenderò	difeso.
Dire,	to say, to tell.	dico	dissi	dirò	detto.
Dirigere,	to direct.	dirigo	diressi	dirigerò	diretto.
Distinguere,	to distinguish.	distinguo	distinsi	distinguerò	distinto.
Dividere,	to divide.	divido	divisi	dividerò	diviso.
Dolère,	to smart, to ail.	dolgo (doglio)	dolsi	dorrò	doluto.
Dovère,	to be obliged.	devo (debbo)	dovei (dovetti)	dovrò	dovuto.
Elidere,	to elide.	elido	elisi	eliderò	eliso.
Eludere,	to elude.	eludo	elusi	eluderò	eluso.
Erigere, (Erigere),	to erect.	erigo	eressi	erigerò	eretto.
Escludere,	to exclude.	escludo	esclusi	escluderò	escluso.
Esigere,	to require.	esigo	esigei (esigetti)	esigerò	esatto.
Esistere,	to exist.	esisto	esistei (esistetti)	esisterò	esistito.

		Pres.	Def.	Fut.	P.p.
Espellere,	*to expel.*	espello	espulsi	espellerò	espulso,
Esprimere,	*to express.*	esprimo	espressi	esprimerò	espresso,
Evadere,	*to evade.*	evado	evasi	evaderò	evaso,
Fare,	*to do, to make.*	fo (faccio)	feci	farò	fatto,
Figgere,	*to fix.*	figgo	fissi	figgerò	fisso, fitto,
Fingere,	*to feign.*	fingo	finsi	fingerò	finto,
Fondere,	*to cast.*	fondo	fusi	fonderò	fuso,
Frangere,	*to break.*	frango	fransi	frangerò	franto,
		(fragno)		(fragnerò)	
Friggere,	*to fry.*	friggo	frissi	friggerò	fritto,
Giacère,	*to lie.*	giaccio	giacqui	giacerò	giaciuto,
Gire,	*to go.*	—	gii	girò	gito,
Giungere,	*to arrive.*	giungo	giunsi	giungerò	giunto.
		(giugno)		(giugnerò)	
Incidere,	*to enrave.*	incido	incisi	inciderò	inciso,
Influire,	*to influence.*	influisco	influssi	influirò	influsso,
Intridere,	*to temper, to dilute.*	intrido	intrisi	intriderò	intriso,
Intrudere,	*to intrude.*	intrudo	intrusi	intruderò	intruso,
Invadere,	*to invade.*	invado	invasi	invaderò	invaso,
Istruire,	*to instruct.*	istruisco	istruii	istruirò	istruito
			(istrussi)		(istrutto)
Ledere,	*to wound, to hurt*	ledo	lesi	lederò	leso,
Leggere,	*to read.*	leggo	lessi	leggerò	letto.
Lucere,	*to shine.*	luce (3 pers.)	lussi	lucerò	—
Mergere.	*to immerse.*	mergo	mersi	mergerò	merso,
(Immergere).					

xxiv

ALPHABETICAL LIST OF THE IRREGULAR VERBS

		Pres.	Def.	Fut.	P. p.
Mescere,	to mix.	mesco	mescei	mescerò	misto (mesciuto) poured in
Mettere,	to put.	metto	misi	metterò	messo.
Mordere,	to bite.	mordo	morsi	morderò	morso.
Morire,	to die.	muoio	morii	morrò	morto.
Mungere (Mugnere)	to milk.	mungo	munsi	mungerò (mugnerò)	munto.
Muovere (Movere)	to move.	muovo (movo)	mossi	muoverò (moverò)	mosso.
Nascere,	to be born.	nasco	nacqui	nascerò	nato.
Nascondere,	to hide.	nascondo	nascosi	nasconderò	nascosto.
Negligere,	to neglect.	negligo	neglessi	negligerò	negletto.
Nuocere,	to damage, to hurt.	nuocio	nocqui	nuocerò	nociuto.
Offrire,	to offer.	offro	offrii (offersi)	offrirò	offerto.
Opprimere,	to oppress.	opprimo	oppressi	opprimerò	oppresso.
Parere,	to seem.	paio	parvi	parrò	paruto (parso),
Percuotere,	to strike.	percuoto	percossi	percuoterò	percosso.
Persua.iere,	to persuade.	persuado	persuasi	persuaderò	persuaso.
Piacere,	to please.	piaccio	piacqui	piacerò	piaciuto.
Pingere (Pignere)	to paint.	pingo	pinsi	pingerò	pinto.
Piangere,	to weep.	piango	piansi	piangerò	pianto.
Piovere,	to rain.	piove	piovve	pioverà	piovuto.
Porgere,	to hand, to offer.	porgo	porsi	porgerò	porto.
Porre (ponere)	to lay.	pongo	posi	porrò	posto.
Potère,	to be able.	posso	poter	potrò	potuto.

ALPHABETICAL LIST OF THE IRREGULAR VERBS

		Pres.	*Def.*	*Fut.*	*P.p.*
Premere,	to press.	premo	premei	premerò	premuto (presso).
Prendere,	to take.	prendo	presi	prenderò	preso.
Proferire,	to utter.	proferisco	proferii	proferirò (profirirò)	proferito.
Propendere,	to be inclined.	propendo	propendei	propenderò	propenso,
Proteggere,	to protect.	proteggo	protessi	proteggerò	protetto.
Pungere,	to prick, to be pungent.	pungo	punsi	pungerò	punto.
Radere,	to shave.	rado	rasi	raderò	raso.
Ravvedersi,	to amend, toalter one's behaviour.	mi ravvedo	mi ravvidi	mi ravvedrò	ravveduto (ravvisto).
Recidere,	to clip.	recido	recisi	reciderò	reciso,
Redimere,	to redeem.	redimo	redensi	redimerò	redento.
Reggere,	to reign, to govern, to lead.	reggo	ressi	reggerò	retto.
Rendere,	to render, to give back.	rendo	resi	renderò	reso
Repellere,	to repel.	repello	repulsi	repellerò	repulso,
Reprimere,	to repress.	reprimo	repressi (reprimei)	reprimerò	represso,
Rescindere,	to rescind.	rescindo	rescissi	rescinderò	reciso,
Ridere,	to laugh.	rido	risi	riderò	riso.
Rimanére,	to remain.	rimango	rimasi	rimarrò	rimasto
Rincrescere,	to regret.	rincresce	rincrebbe	rincrescerò	rincresciuto.
Risorgere,	to rise again.	risorgo	risorsi	risorgerò	risorto.
Rispondere,	to answer.	rispondo	risposi	risponderò	risposto.
Rodere,	to gnaw.	rodo	rosi	roderò	roso.

		Pres.	Def.	Fut.	P.p.
Rompere,	to break.	rompo	ruppi	romperò	rotto.
Salire,	to ascend.	salgo	salii	salirò	salito.
Sapère,	to know.	so	seppi	saprò	saputo.
Scegliere,	to choose.	scelgo	scelsi	sceglierò	scelto.
Scendere,	to descend.	scendo	scesi	scenderò	sceso.
Scindere,	to cleave.	scindo	scissi	scinderò	scisso.
Sciogliere,	to untie.	sciolgo	sciolsi	scioglierò	sciolto.
Scrivere,	to write.	scrivo	scrissi	scriverò	scritto.
Scuotere,	to shake.	scuoto	scossi	scuoterò	scosso.
Sedere,	to sit.	siedo (seggo, seggio)	sedei	sederò (sedrò)	seduto.
Seppelire,	to bury.	seppellisco	seppellii	seppellirò	seppellito (sepolto).
Solere,	to use, to be accustomed	soglio	—	—	solito.
Solvere,	to solve.	solvo	solsi	solverò	soluto (solto).
Sorgere,	to rise.	sorgo	sorsi	sorgerò	sorto.
Spandere,	to shed.	spando	spandei	spanderò	spanduto (spanso).
Spegnere,	to extinguish.	spegno	spensi	spegnerò	spento.
Spendere,	to spend.	spendo	spesi	spenderò	speso.
Spergere,	to disperse, to waste.	spergo	spersi	spergerò	sperso.
Spingere (Spignere).	to drive, to thrust.	spingo	spinsi	spingerò	spinto.
Stare,	to stand.	sto	stetti	starò	stato.
Stringere (Strignere).	to contract, to press.	stringo (strigno)	strinsi	stringerò	stretto.

ALPHABETICAL LIST OF THE IRREGULAR VERBS

		Pres.	*Def.*	*Fut.*	*P.p.*
Struggere,	*to dissolve.*	struggo	strussi	struggerò	strutto.
Tacére,	*to be silent.*	taccio	tacqui	tacerò	taciuto.
Tendere,	*to spread.*	tendo	tesi	tenderò	teso.
Tenere,	*to hold.*	tengo	tenni	terrò	tenuto.
Tergere,	*to wipe.*	tergo	tersi	tergerò	terso.
Tingere	*to dye.*	tingo (tigno)	tinsi	tingerò (tignerò)	tinto.
(Tignere),					
Tondere,	*to shear.*	tondo	tondei	tonderò	tonduto (tonso).
Torcere,	*to twist.*	torco	torsi	torcerò	torto.
Torre	*to take off.*	tolgo (toglio)	tolsi	toglierò (torrò)	tolto.
(Togliere),					
Trarre (traere),	*to draw.*	traggo	trassi	trarrò	tratto.
Uccidere,	*to kill.*	uccido	uccisi	ucciderò	ucciso.
Udire,	*to hear.*	odo	udii	udirò	udito.
Ungere,	*to annoint.*	ungo (ugno)	unsi	ungerò (ugnerò)	unto.
Uscire,	*to go out.*	esco	uscii	uscirò	uscito.
Valére,	*to be worth.*	valgo	valsi	varrò	valuto (valso).
Vedére,	*to see.*	vedo	vidi	vedrò	veduto (visto).
Venire,	*to come.*	vengo	venni	verrò	venuto.
Vilipendere,	*to despise.*	vilipendo	vilipesi	vilipenderò	vilipeso.
Vincere,	*to vanquish.*	vinco	vinsi	vincerò	vinto.
Vivere,	*to live.*	vivo	vissi	viverò (vivrò)	vissuto (vivuto).
Volere,	*to be willing.*	voglio	volli	vorrò	voluto.
Volgere (Volvere),	*to turn to, revolve.*	volgo	volsi	volgerò	volto.

ITALIAN-ENGLISH DICTIONARY

A [ah] *pr.* at, to, by, for, on.

Abbacinare [ahb-bah-chee-nah'ray] *vt.* to blind, dazzle, bewilder.

Abbagliamento [ahb-bahl-yah-men'toh] *nm.* dazzling, dimness of sight.

Abbaglia/re [ahb-bahl-yah'ray] *vt.* to dazzle, blind with light; —rsi *vr.* to be dazzled, bewildered.

Abbaiare [ahb-bah-ee-ah'ray] *vi.* to bark.

Abbaino [ahb-bah-ee'noh] *nm.* sky-light.

Abballare [ahb-bahl-lah'ray] *vt.* to pack up.

Abbandona/re [ahb-bahn-doh-nah'ray] *vt.* to leave, quit, abandon; —rsi *vr.* to give oneself up to, despair.

Abbandono [ahb-bahn-doh'noh] *nm.* abandonment, desertion.

Abbarbagliare [ahb-bahr-bahl-yah'ray] *vt.* to dazzle.

Abbarbica/re [ahb-bahr-bee-kah'ray] *vi.* to take root; —rsi *vr.* to cling (as ivy).

Abbassamento [ahb-bahs-sah-men'toh] *nm.* humiliation, lowering.

Abbassa/re [ahb-bahs-sah'ray] *vt.* to abase, humble, lower, lessen; —rsi *vr.* to humble oneself, fall.

Abbasso [ahb-bahs'soh] *ad.* below; *int.* down! down with.

Abbastanza [ahb-bah-stah-nt'zah] *ad.* enough.

Abbattere [ahb-baht'tay-ray] *vt.* to throw down, depress, slaughter; to shoot down (a plane, etc.).

Abbattimento [ahb-baht-tee-men'toh] *nm.* depression, overthrow.

Abbattuto [abh-baht-too'toh] *a.* depressed, cast-down.

Abbazia [ahb-bah-tsee'ah] *nf.* abbey.

Abbecedario [ahb-bay-chay-dah'ree-oh] *nm.* spelling-book.

Abbelli/re [ahb-bell-lee'ray] *vt.* to adorn, embellish; —rsi *vr.* to adorn oneself.

Abbeverare [ahb-bay-vay-rah'ray] *vt.* to water (animals).

Abbiatici [ahb-bee-ah'tee-chee] *nm. (pl.)* grandchildren.

Abbicci [ahb-beech-chee'] *nm.* alphabet.

Abbiente [ahb-bee-en'tay] *nm.* well-to-do-person.

Abbietto [ahb-yet'toh] *a.* abject, base.

Abbiezione [ahb-yet-see-oh'nay] *nf.* abjectness, baseness.

Abbigliamento [ahb-beel-yah-men'toh] *nm.* adornment, finery.

Abbiglia/re [ahb-beel-yah'ray] *vt.* to deck, dress; —rsi *vr.* to deck oneself, dress up.

Abbindola/re [ahb-been-doh-lah'ray] *vt.* to wind (skeins) cheat, trick; —rsi *vr.* to be puzzled.

Abbisognare [ahb-bee-sohn-yah'ray] *vt.* to need, want.

abb 2 abi

Abboccamento [ahb-bock-kah-men'toh] *nm.* interview, conference.

Abbocca/re [ahb-bock-kah'ray] *vt.* to fill up to the brim; —**rsi** *vr.* to have an interview with, confer.

Abboccato [ahb-bock-kah'toh] *a.* brimful, nice (in speech), sweet (of wine).

Abbonaccia/re [ahb-boh-nahch-chah'ray] *vt.* to calm, pacify; —**rsi** *vr.* to grow calm (of the sea).

Abbonamento [ahb-boh-nah-men'toh] *nm.* subscription, discount.

Abbona/re [ahb-boh-nah'ray] *vt.* (com.) to deduct, pass (a doubtful account); —**rsi** *vr.* to subscribe.

Abbonato [ahb-boh-nah'toh] *nm.* subscriber.

Abbondante [ahb-bon-dahn'tay] *a.* abundant, plentiful.

Abbondanza [ahb-bon-dahnt'zah] *nf.* abundance, plenty.

Abbonda/re [ahb-bon-dah'ray] *vi.* to abound.

Abborda/re [ahb-borr-dah'ray] *vt.* to board (a ship), accost; —**rsi** *vr.* (*mar.*) to collide (at sea).

Abbordo [ahb-borr'doh] *nm.* boarding (a ship), approach, collision (at sea).

Abbottonare [ahb-boht-toh-nah'ray] *vt.* to button.

Abbozzamento [ahb-bohd-zah-men'toh], **Abbozzo** [ahb-bohd'zoh] *nm.* rough draught, sketch.

Abbozzare [ahb-bohd-zah'ray] *vt.* to outline, sketch.

Abbracciamento [ahb-brahch-chah-men'toh], **Abbraccio** [ahb-brahch'choh] *nm.* embrace.

Abbracciare [ahb-brahch-chah'ray] *vt.* to embrace,

contain, choose (a profession, etc.).

Abbranca/re [ahb-brahng-kah'ray] *vt.* to grasp, seize; —**rsi** *vr.* to cling to, grasp.

Abbreviamento [ahb-bray-vee-ah-men'toh] *nm.* abridgement.

Abbreviare [ahb-bray-vee-ah'ray] *vt.* to abridge, shorten.

Abbreviazione [ahb-bray-vee-ah-tsee-oh'nay] *nf.* abbreviation.

Abbronzamento [ahb-brond-zah-men'toh] *nm.* sunburn, scorching, bronzing.

Abbronzare [ahb-brond-zah'ray] *vt.* to sunburn, tan, scorch, bronze.

Abbruciacchiare [ahb-broo-chahk-yah'ray] *vt.* to scorch, burn slightly.

Abbruciare [ahb-broo-tchah'ray] *vt.* to burn.

Abbruna/re [ahb-broo-nah'ray] *vt.* to brown, darken; —**rsi** *vr.* to go into mourning.

Abbrustoli/re [ahb-broo-stoh-lee'ray] *vt.* to toast, crisp; —**rsi** *vr.* to turn brown.

Abbrutire [ahb-broo-tee'ray] *vt.* to brutalize.

Abbruttire [ahb-broot-tee'ray] *vi.* to grow ugly.

Abbuia/re [ahb-boo-yah'ray] *vt.* to hide, conceal; —**rsi** *vr.* to grow dark, cloud over.

Abbuono [ahb-boo-oh'noh] *nm.* discount, deduction.

Abburattare [ahb-boo-raht-tah'ray] *vt.* to bolt, sift.

Abdicare [ahb-dee-kah'ray] *vi.* to abdicate.

Abdicazione [ahb-dee-kah-tsee-oh'nay] *nf.* abdication.

Aberrazione [ahb-behr-rah-dee-oh'nay] *nf.* aberration, deviation.

Abete [ah-bay'tay] *nm.* fir-tree.

Abile [ah'bee-lay] *a.* able, capable, clever, skilful.

Abilità [ah-bee-lee-tah'] nf. ability, dexterity, skill.

Abilitare [ah-bee-lee-tah'ray] vt. to enable, qualify.

Abilitazione [ah-bee-lee-tah-tsee-oh'nay] nf. qualifying (for a post, etc.).

Abisso [ah-bees'soh] nm. abyss, gulf, hell.

Abitabile [ah-bee-tah'bee-lay] a. habitable.

Abitante [ah-bee-tahn'tay] nm. inhabitant.

Abitare [ah-bee-tah'ray] vt. to inhabit, live in.

Abitato [ah-bee-tah'toh] nm. inhabited place.

Abitazione [ah-bee-tah-tsee-oh'nay] nf. habitation, house.

Abito [ah'bee-toh] nm. dress, clothes, suit, habit, custom; **a.borghese** [bor-gay'zay] mufti.

Abituale [ah-bee-too-ah'iay] a. habitual.

Abitua/re [ah-bee-too-ah'ray] vt. to accustom; —rsi vr. to get accustomed.

Abitudine [ah-bee-too'dee-nay] nf. habit, custom.

Abiura(zione) [ahb-yoo'rah, ahb-yoo-rah-tsee-oh'nay] nf. abjuration, recantation.

Abiurare [ahb-yoo-rah'ray] vt. to abjure, recant.

Ablativo [ah-blah-tee'voh] nm. ablative case.

Abluzione [ah-bloo-tsee-oh'nay] nf. ablution, purification.

Abnegare [ahb-nay-gah'ray] vt. to renounce, give up, deny (oneself).

Abnegazione [ahb-nay-gah-tsee-oh'nay] nf. self-denial, abnegation.

Abolire [ah-boh-lee'ray] vt. to abolish, annul.

Abolizione [ah-boh-lee-tsee-oh'nay] nf. abolition.

Abominare [ah-boh-mee-nah'ray] vt. to abominate, detest.

Abominazione [ahb-boh-mee-nah-tsee-oh'nay] nf. abomination, detestation.

Aborigini [ah-boh-ree'jee-nee] nm. (pl.) natives (pl.).

Aborrire [ah-borr-ree'ray] vt. to abhor.

Abortire [ah-borr-tee'ray] vi. to miscarry, abort.

Aborto [ah-borr'toh] nm. miscarriage, abortion, still-born child.

Abrasione [ah-brah-zee-oh'nay] nf. bruise.

Abrogare [ah-broh-gah'ray] vt. to abrogate, repeal.

Abrogazione [ah-broh-gah-tsee-oh'nay] nf. abrogation, repeal.

Abside [ahb'see-day] nm. arch, apse.

Abusare [ah-boo-sah'ray] vt. to abuse, misuse, trespass on.

Abusivo [ah-boo-see'voh] a. abusive, improper.

Abuso [ah-boo'soh] nm. abuse, misuse, infringement (of the law).

A. C. [ah'chee'] = **Avanti Cristo** [ah-vahn'tee kree'stoh] av. B.C.

Acacia [ah-kah'chah] nf. acacia-tree.

Accademia [ahk-kah-day'mee-ah] nf. academy, university.

Accademico [ahk-kah-day'mee-koh] nm. academician; a. academic.

Accadere [ahk-kah-day'ray] imp. to happen, occur.

Accadimento [ahk-kah-dee-men'toh] nm. happening.

Accaduto [ahk-kah-doo'toh] nm. event.

Accaglia/re [ahk-kahl-yah'ray] vi. —rsi vr. to curdle.

Accalappiare [ahk-kah-lap-pee-ah'ray] vt. to catch, ensnare, inveigle.

Accalcare [ahk-kahl-kah'ray] vt. to crowd.

Accaldato [ahk-kahl-dah'toh] a. heated (with running, etc.).

Accalora/re [ahk-kah-loh-rah'ray] vt. to heat; —rsi vr. to get heated.

Accampamento [ahk-kahm-pah-men'toh] nm. encampment, camp.

Accampa/re [ahk-kahm-pah'ray] vi. to camp; vt. to adduce (reasons, etc.); —rsi vr. to pitch a camp.

Accanimento [ahk-kah-nee-men'toh] nm. fury, ardour.

Accani/re [ahk-kah-nee'ray] vt. to enrage; —rsi vr. to fly into a passion.

Accanito [ahk-kah-nee'toh] a. furious, eager.

Accanto [ahk-kahn'toh] ad. beside, near.

Accantonare [ahk-kahn-toh-nah'ray] vt. to billet.

Accaparramento [ahk-kah-pahr-rah-men'toh] nm. earnest money.

Accaparrare [ahk-kah-pahr-rah'ray] vt. to conclude (a bargain) by paying earnest money.

Accapatoio [ahk-kah-pah-toh'yoh] nm. bath-robe, dressing-gown.

Accappona/re [ahk-kahp-poh-nah'ray] vt. to make capons; —rsi la pelle [lah pell'lay] vr. to shiver.

Accarezzamento [ahk-kah-ret-zah-men'toh] nm. caress.

Accarezzare [ahk-kah-ret-zah'ray] vt. to caress.

Accartocciare [ahk-kahr-tohch-chah'ray] vt. to roll up in paper.

Accasa/re [ahk-kah-zah'ray] vt. to marry; —rsi vr. to marry, set up house.

Accasciamento [ahk-kah-shah-men'toh] nm. weakness, debility.

Accascia/re [ahk-kah-shah'ray] vt. to weaken; —rsi vr. to grow weak.

Accattabrighe [ahk-kaht-tah-bree'gay] nm. quarrelsome fellow.

Accattamento [ahk-kaht-tah-men'toh] nm. beggary.

Accattare [ahk-kaht-tah'ray] vi. to beg.

Accattino [ahk-kaht-tee'noh] nm. beggar.

Accattonaggio [ahk-kaht-toh-nah'djoh] nm. begging, mendicity.

Accattone [ahk-kaht-toh'nay] nm. beggar, impostor.

Accavalcare [ahk-kah-vahl-kah'ray] vt. to climb over, mount upon. v. Scavalcare.

Accavalciare [ahk-kah-vahl-chah'ray] vt. to ride, bestride.

Accavalcioni [ahk-kah-vahl-choh'nee] ad. astride.

Accecamento [ahch-chay-kah-men'toh] nm. blindness.

Accecare [ahch-chay-kah'ray] vt. and i. to (become) blind.

Accedere [ahch-chay'day-ray] vi. to approach, enter.

Accelera/re [ahch-chay-lay-rah'ray] vt. to accelerate;—rsi vr. to hurry, make haste.

Accelerato [ahch-chay-lay-rah'toh] nm., treno [tray'noh] a.—nm. slow train, stopping train.

Accende/re [ahch-chehn'day-ray] vt. to light, kindle; —rsi vr. to catch fire, grow angry.

Accenditoio [ahch-chehn-dee-toh'yoh] nm. lighter.

Accennare [ahch-chen-nah'ray] vi. to hint, mention.

Accenno [ahch-chen'noh] nm. hint, signal.

Accensione [ahch-chehn-see-oh'nay] nf. ignition (aut.), kindling, conflagration.

Accento [ahch-chehn'toh] *nm.* accent.

Accentuare [ahch-chehn-too-ah'ray] *vt.* to accent(uate).

Accerchiamento [ahch-chehrr-kee-ah-men'toh] *nm.* encirclement.

Accerchiare [ahch-chehrr-kee-ah'ray] *vt.* to encircle, surround.

Accertamento [ahch-chehrr-tah-men'toh] *nm.* confirmation, assurance.

Accerta/re [ahch-chehrr-tah'ray] *vt.* to confirm, assure; —rsi *vr.* to find out.

Accessibile [ahch-chess-see'bee-lay] *a.* accessible, approachable.

Accesso [ahch-chess'soh] *nm.* access, fit, paroxysm.

Accessorio [ahch-chess-soh'ree-oh] *nm. and a.* accessory.

Accetta [ahch-chet'tah] *nf.* hatchet, axe.

Accettabile [ahch-chet-tah'bee-lay] *a.* acceptable.

Accettare [ahch-chet-tah'ray] *vt.* to accept, receive.

Accettazione [ahch-chet-tah-tsee-oh'nay] *nf.* acceptance.

Accetto [ahch-chet'toh] *a.* acceptable, welcome.

Accheta/re [ah-kay-tah'ray] *vt.* to quieten, hush, calm; —rsi *vr.* to calm down.

Acchiappare [ahk-kee-ahp-pah'ray] *vt.* to catch, cheat.

Accia [ahch'chah] *nf.* axe, thread.

Acciabattare [ahch-chah-baht-tah'ray] *vt.* to cobble.

Acciaccare [ahch-chahk-kah'ray] *vt.* to bruise, pound.

Acciacco [ahch-chahk'koh] *nm.* infirmity, misfortune.

Acciaieria [ahch-chah-yay-ree'ah] *nf.* steel foundry.

Acciaio [ahch-chah'yoh] *nm.* steel.

Acciarpare [ahch-chahr-pah'ray] *vt.* to cobble, botch.

Accidentale [ahch-chee-den-tah'lay] *a.* accidental, casual.

Accidentato [ahch-chee-dehn-tah'toh] *a.* apoplectic, broken (of ground).

Accidente [ahch-chee-dehn'tay] *nm.* accident, misfortune.

Accidenti! [ahch-chee-dehn'tee] *int.* my goodness!

Accidia [ahch-chee'dee-ah] *nf.* idleness, sloth.

Accidioso [ahch-chee-dee-oh'soh] *a.* idle, slothful.

Accigliamento [ahch-cheel-yah-men'toh] *nm.* frown, sullen air.

Acciglia/re [ahch-cheel-yah'ray] *vt.* —rsi *vr.* to frown, look sullen.

Accigliato [ahch-cheel-yah'toh] *a.* a frowning, sullen.

Accingersi [ahch-cheen'jehr-see] *vr.* to set about, prepare oneself.

Acciò [ahch-choh'], **Acciochè** [ahch-choh-kay'] *con.* in order that.

Acciuffare [ahch-choof-fah'ray] *vt.* to seize by the hair, grasp. [anchovy.

Acciuga [ahch-choo'gah] *nf.*

Acclamare [ahk-klah-mah'ray] *vt.* to acclaim; *vi.* to clap hands.

Acclimare [ahk-klee-mah'ray] *vt.* to acclimatize.

Acclimatarsi [ahk-klee-mah-tahr'see] *vr.* to grow acclimatized.

Acclive [ahk-klee'vay] *a.* sloping, steep.

Acclività [ahk-klee-vee-tah'] *nf.* slope, steepness.

Accludere [ahk-kloo'day-ray] *vt.* to enclose (letter, etc.).

Acclusa [ahk-kloo'sah] *nf.* enclosure.

Accoccolarsi [ahch-kock-koh-lahr'see] *vr.* to crouch, squat.

Accoglienza [ahk-kohl-yent′zah] *nf.* reception, welcome.

Accoglie/re [ahk-kohl′yay-ray] *vt.* to receive, welcome, collect; **—rsi** *vr.* to meet, assemble; [*nm.* acolyte.

Accolito [ahk-koh′lee-toh]

Accolla/re [ahk-koll-lah′ray] *vt.* to yoke, cover up to the neck; **—rsi** *vr.* to undertake, be responsible for.

Accollo [ahk-koll′loh] *nm.* (com.) tender.

Accoltellare [ahk-koll-tell-lah′ray] *vt.* to stab, knife.

Accomandante [ahk-koh-mahn-dahn′tay] *nm.* (com.) sleeping partner.

Accomandatario [ahk-koh-mahn-dah-tah′ree-oh] *nm.* (com.) active partner.

Accomandita [ahk-koh-mahn′dee-tah] *nf.* (com.) partnership, company.

Accomiata/re [ahk-koh-mee-ah-tah′ray] *vt.* to dismiss; **—rsi** *vr.* to take leave.

Accomoda/re [ahk-koh-moh-dah′ray] *vt.* to adjust, arrange, mend; **—rsi** *vr.* to reconcile oneself, sit down, take a seat, (com.) come to an agreement; **s'accomodi** [sahk-koh′moh-dee], take a seat, please.

Accomodatura [ahk-koh-moh-dah-too′rah] *nf.* adjustment, agreement.

Accompagnamento [ahk-kom-pahn-yah-men′toh] *nm.* accompaniment, retinue.

Accompagna/re [ahk-kom-pahn-yah′ray] *vt.* to accompany, escort; **—rsi** *vr.* to join with, take a companion.

Acconcia/re [ahk-kon-chah′ray] *vt.* to fit, settle, arrange, dress (the hair), punish severely; **—rsi** *vr.* to deck oneself.

Acconciatura [ahk-kon-chah-too′rah] *vt.* style of hair-dressing.

Acconcio [ahk-kon′choh] *a.* fitted, dressed, suitable.

Accondiscendere [ahk-kon-dee-shehn′day-ray] *vi.* to condescend.

Acconsentire [ahk-kon-sehn-tee′ray] *vi.* to consent, approve.

Accontentare [ahk-kon-ten-tah′ray] *vt.* to content.

Acconto [ahk-kon′toh] *nm.* (com.) part payment.

Accoppia/re [ahk-kop-pee-ah′ray] *vt.* to couple, pair, yoke; **—rsi** *vr.* to join together.

Accoramento [ahk-koh-rah-men′toh] *nm.* grief, affliction.

Accora/re [ahk-koh-rah′ray] *vt.* to grieve deeply; **—rsi** *vr.* to be grieved to the heart.

Accorcia/re [ahk-korr-chah′ray] *vt.* to shorten, abbreviate; **—rsi** *vr.* to grow shorter, shrivel, contract.

Accorda/re [ahk-korr-dah′ray] *vt.* to tune (instruments), reconcile; *vi.* to agree; **—rsi** *vr.* to be in harmony, agree.

Accordo [ahk-korr′doh] *nm.* agreement, harmony, arrangement, essere d'a—[ess′say-ray dahk-korr′-doh] to agree.

Accorgersi [ahk-korr′jenr-see] *vr.* to perceive.

Accorgimento [ahk-korr-jee-men′toh] *nm.* circumspection, prudence.

Accorrere [ahk-korr′ray-ray] *vi.* to run up, to go to one's help.

Accortezza [ahk-korr-tet′zah] *nf.* prudence, sagacity, cunning.

Accorto [ahk-korr′toh] *a* wary, circumspect, prudent.

Accosta/re [ahk-koh-stah′ray] *vt.* to advance, bring near, push to (a door, etc.); **—rsi** *vr.* to approach, draw near, accost.

Accosto [ahk-koh'stoh] *ad.* beside, hard by.

Accostuma/re [ahk-koh-stoo-mah'ray] *vt.* to get, accustom; —**rsi** *vr.* to get accustomed.

Accovacciarsi [ahk-koh-vahch-char'see] *vr.* to cower down, crouch.

Accredita/re [ahk-kray-dee-tah'ray] *vt.* to give credit to, bring into repute; —**rsi** *vr.* to get a name.

Accrescere [ahk-kray'shay-ray] *vt. and i.* to increase.

Accrescimento [ahk-kray-shee-men'toh] *nm.* increase, growth.

Accudire [ahk-koo-dee'ray] *vi.* to look after, apply oneself to.

Accumula/re [ahk-koo-moo-lah'ray] *vt.* to accumulate, heap up; —**rsi** *vr.* to accumulate.

Accumulatore [ahk-koo-moo-lah-toh'ray] *nm.* (*tech.*) accumulator; —**caricare un a.** [kah-ree-kah'ray oon a] to charge an accumulator.

Accumulazione [ahk-koo-moo-lah-tsee-oh'nay] *nf.* accumulation.

Accuratezza [ahk-koo-rah-tet'zah] *nf.* accuracy, diligence.

Accurato [ahk-koo-rah'toh] *a.* accurate, diligent, neat.

Accusa [ahk-koo'zah] *nf.* accusation, charge.

Accusa/re [ahk-koo-zah'ray] *vt.* to accuse, charge, blame; —**rsi** *vr.* to accuse oneself, confess.

Accusato [ahk-koo-zah'toh] *nm.* accused, defendant.

Accusatore [ahk-koo-zah-toh'ray] *nm.* accuser, plaintiff.

Acerbezza [ah-cherr-bet'zah] *nf.* acerbity, asperity.

Acerbire [ah-cherr-bee'ray]

vt. and i. to exasperate, turn sour.

Acerbità [ah-cherr-bee-tah'] *nf.* acerbity, asperity.

Acerbo [ah-cherr'boh] *a.* sour, unripe.

Acero [ah'chay-roh] *nm.* maple-tree. [gar.

Aceto [ah-chay'toh] *nm.* vine-

Acetoso [ah-chay-toh'soh] *a.* vinegary, sourish.

Acidità [ah-chee-dee-tah'] *nf* acidity, sourness.

Acido [ah'chee-doh] *nm. and a.* acid; **a. fenico** [fay'nee-koh] carbolic acid.

Acino [ah'chee-noh] *nm.* grape, grape-stone.

Acqua [ahk'kwah] *nf.* water; **a. corrente** [korr-ren'tay], running water; **a. dolce** [doll'chay] fresh water; **a. minerale** [mee-nay-rah'lay], mineral water; **a. potabile** [poh-tah'bee-lay], drinking water; **a. di seltz** [dee seltz], soda-water.

Acquaforte [ahk-kwah-forr'tay] *nf.* etching.

Acquaio [ahk-kwah-ee'oh] *nm.* sink, conduit.

Acquaiolo [ahk-kwah-ee-oh'loh] *nm.* water-carrier.

Acquario [ahk-kwah'ree-oh] *nm.* aquarium.

Acquartiera/re [ahk-kwa-hrr-tee-ay-rah'ray] *vt.* to quarter; —**rsi** *vr.* to take up quarters.

Acquata [ahk-kwah'tah] *nf.* heavy shower.

Acquatico [ahk-kwah-tee-koh] *a.* aquatic.

Acquavite [ahk-kwah-vee'tay] *nf.* brandy (of inferior quality).

Acquazzone [ahk-kwaht-zoh'nay] *nm.* sudden and heavy shower, downpour.

Acquedotto [ahk-kway-dot'toh] *nm.* aqueduct.

Acquerellista [ahk-kway-rell-lee′stah] *nm.* painter in water-colours.

Acquerello [ahk-kway-rell′loh] *nm.* water colour, water-colour painting.

Acquidoccio [ahk-kwee-doh′choh] *nm.* ditch, sewer.

Acquietamento [ahk-kwee-ay-tah-men′toh] *nm.* appeasement, pacification.

Acquietare [ahk-kwee-ay-tah′ray] *vt.* to appease, pacify.

Acquirente [ahk-kwee-rehn′tay] *nm.* acquirer, buyer.

Acquisire [ahk-kwee-zee′ray] *vt.* to acquire, buy.

Acquistare [ahk-kwee-stah′ray] *vt.* to acquire, buy.

Acquisto [ahk-kwee′stoh] *nm.* acquisition purchase.

Acquitrinoso [ahk-kwee-tree-noh′soh] *a.* marshy, boggy.

Acquoso [ahk-kwoh′soh] *a.* watery.   [harsh.

Acre [ah′kray] *a.* sharp, sour,

Acredine [ah-kray′dee-nay] *nf.* acrimony, sharpness.

Acrimonia [ah-kree-moh′nee-ah] *nf.* acrimony, sharpness.

Acrimonioso [ah-kree-moh-nee-oh′soh] *a.* acrimonious, harsh.

Acrobata [ah-kroh′bah-tah] *nm.* acrobat.

Acuire [ah-koo-ee′ray] *vt.* to sharpen, whet.

Acuità [ah-koo-ee-tah′] *nf.* sharpness, acuteness.

Acume [ah-koo′may] *nf.* sharp point, quickness of wit, acumen.

Acuminare [ah-koo-mee-nah′ray] *vt.* to point, sharpen.

Acustica [ah-koo′stee-kah] *nf.* acoustics (*pl.*).

Acutezza [ah-koo-tet′zah] *nf.* acuteness, wit, penetration.   [sharp, pointed.

Acuto [ah-koo′toh] *a.* acute,

Adacquare [ah-dahk-kwah′ray] *vt.* to water, irrigate.

Adagiare [ah-dah-jah′ray] *vt.* to lay down, make comfortable; —**rsi** *vr.* to arrange oneself comfortably.

Adagio [ah-dah′joh] *ad.* slowly, softly, at leisure.

Adattabile [ah-daht-tah′bee-lay] *a.* adaptable, applicable.

Adattabilità [ah-daht-tah-bee-lee-tah′] *nf.* adaptability.

Adatta/re [ah-daht-tah′ray] *vt.* to fit, adapt, adjust; —**rsi** *vr.* to adapt oneself.

Adatto [ah-daht′toh] *a.* fit, proper, right, suitable.

Addebitare [ahd-day-bee-tah′ray] *vt.* to debit.

Addensa/re [ahd-den-sah′ray] *vt.* to condense, make thick; —**rsi** *vr.* to grow dense, thicken.

Addentrare [ahd-den-trah′ray] *vt.* to drive in.

Addentro [ahd-den′troh] *ad.* within, inside.

Addestra/re [ahd-dess-trah′ray] *vt.* to train, drill, instruct, break in (a horse); —**rsi** *vr.* to train oneself, practise.

Addetto [ahd-det′toh] *a.* attached, addicted; *a.* *ad* un′ambasciata [ahd oon ahm-bah-shah′tah], attaché at an embassy.

Addietro [ahd-dee-ay′troh] *ad.* behind, back(wards).

Addio [ahd-dee′oh] *ad.*, *nm.* good-bye (*fam.*).

Addirittura [ahd-dee-reet-too′rah] *ad.* downright, immediately, outright.

Addirsi [ahd-deer′see] *vr.* *imp.* to suit, become.

Additare [ahd-dee-tah′ray] *vt.* to point out, show to indicate.

Addizionare [ahd-dee-tsee-oh-nah′ray] *vt.* to add (up).

Addizione [ahd-dee-tsee-oh′nay] *nf.* addition, supplement.

Addobbare [ahd-dob-bah′

ray] *vt.* to furnish, decorate, set off.

Addobbo [ahd-dob'boh] *nm.* decorative furnishing, finery.

Addolcire [ahd-doll-chee'ray] *vt.* to sweeten, soften, alleviate.

Addolora/re [ahd-doh-loh-rah'ray] *vt.* to afflict, grieve; —**rsi** *vr.* to be grieved.

Addome [ahd-doh'may] *nm.* abdomen.

Addomestica/re [ahd-doh-mess-tee-kah'ray] *vt.* to tame, treat as one of the family; —**rsi** *vr.* to feel at home.

Addormenta/re [ahd-dorr-men-tah'ray] *vt.* to lull to sleep; —**rsi** *vr.* to fall asleep.

Addossa/re [ahd-doss-sah'ray] *vt.* to take upon one's back, charge, load, entrust; —**rsi** *vr.* to undertake charge oneself with.

Addosso [ahd-doss'soh] *ad.* on (one), about (one); avere [ah-vay'ray] addosso, to have about one.

Addurre [ahd-door'ray] *vt.* to adduce, cite.

Adduzione [ahd-doo-tsee-oh'nay] *nf.* quotation.

Adeguare [ah-day-gwah'ray] *vt.* to equalise, balance, compare.   [*a.* sufficient.

Adeguato [ah-day-gwah'toh] *a.* sufficient.

Adempiere [ah-demp'yay-ray], **adempi/re** [ah-dem-pee'ray] *vt.* to execute, fulfil, grant; —**rsi** *vr.* to come to pass.

Adempimento [ah-dem-pee-men'toh] *nm.* fulfilment, execution.

Adentro [ah-den'trod] *ad.* inwardly. *v.* **Dentro**.

Aderente [ah-day-ren'tay[*nm.* and *a.* adherent.

Aderenza [ah-day-rent'zah] *nf.* adherence, acceptance.

Aderire [ah-day-ree'ray] *vt.* to adhere, follow (a party).

Adesione [ah-day-zee-oh'nay] *nf.* adhesion, adherence, consent.

Adesivo [ah-day-zee'voh] *a.* adhesive.

Adesso [ah-dess'soh] *ad.* now, at present.

Adetto [ah-det'toh] *a.* adept.

Adiacente [ahd-yah-chen'tay] *a.* adjacent, next.

Adiacenza [ahd-yah-chent'zah] *nf.* adjacency, vicinity.

Adianto [ahd-yahn'toh] *nm.* maidenhair fern.

Adibir [ah-dee-bee'ray] *vt.* to adapt.   [grease.

Adipe [ah dee-pay] *nm.* fat, **Adiposità** [ah-dee-poh-see-tah] *nf.* fatness, plumpness.

Adiposo [ah-dee-poh'soh] *a.* fat, plump.

Adira/re [ah-dee-rah'ray] *vt.* to make angry, provoke; —**rsi** *vr.* to get angry.   [access.

Adito [ah'dee-toh] *nm.* entry, **Adocchiare** [ahd-dock-kee-ah'ray] *vt.* to eye, stare at.

Adolescente [ah-doh-lay-shen'tay] *nm.* and *a.* adolescent.

Adolescenza [ah-doh-lay-shent'zah] *nf.* adolescence, youth.

Adombra/re [ah-dom-brah'ray] *vt.* to overshadow, shade, fancy, symbolise, hide; —**rsi** *vr.* to become suspicious.

Adopera/re [ah-doh-pay-rah'ray] *vt.* to use, employ; —**rsi** *vr.* to exert oneself, endeavour, contribute.

Adorare [ah-doh-rah'ray] *vt.* to adore, worship.

Adorazione [ah-doh-rah-tsee-oh'nay] *nf.* adoration, worship.

Adorna/re [ah-dorr-nah'ray] *vt.* to adorn, deck, set off; —**rsi** *vr.* to adorn oneself.

Adorno [ah-dorr'noh] *a.* adorned, set off.

Adottare [ah-dot-tah´ray] vt. to adopt.

Adottivo [ah-dot-tee´voh] a. adoptive, adopted.

Adozione [ah-doh-tsee-oh´nay] nf. adoption.

Adulare [ah-doo-lah´ray] vt. to flatter.

Adulatorio [ah-doo-lah-toh´ree-oh] a. adulatory, flattering.

Adulazione [ah-doo-lah-tsee-oh´nay] nf. adulation, flattery.

Adulterare [ah-dool-tay-rah´ray] vt. to adulterate, mix, blend.

Adulteratore [ah-dool-tay-rah-toh´ray] nm. adulterer.

Adulterio [ah-dool-tay´ree-oh] nm. adultery.

Adultero [ah-dool´tay-roh] nm. adulterer.

Adulto [ah-dool´toh] nm. and a. adult, grown-up.

Adunanza [ah-doo-nahnt´zah] nf. meeting, assembly.

Aduna/re [ah-doo-nah´ray] vt. to assemble, bring together, convoke; —rsi vr. to come together, assemble, (mil.) fall-in.

Adunata [ah-doo-nah´tah] nf. (mil.), fall-in.

Adunco [ah-doong´koh] a. hooked, curved.

Adunque [ah-doong´kway] ad. then, therefore.

Adusto [ah-doo´stoh] a. scorched, dry. (air.

Aere [ah´ay-ray] nm. (poet.)

Aereo [ah-ay´ray-oh] a. aerial, airy.

Aerodromo [ah-ay-roh-dro´moh] nm. aerodrome.

Aeronautica [ah-ay-roh-now´tee-kah] nf. air force; regia [ray´jah] a., royal air force.

Aeroplano [ah-ay-roh-plah´noh] nm. aeroplane; a. di caccia (dee kahch´chah), fighter plane.

Aeroporto [ah-ay-roh-porr´toh] nm. airport.

Afa [ah´fah] nf. sultry heat.

Affabile [ahf-fah´bee-lay] a. affable, civil.

Affabilità [ahf-fah-bee-lee-tah´] nf. affability, civility.

Affacciarsi [ahf-fahch-chahr´see] vr. to look out, show oneself.

Affaccendarsi [ahf-fah-chehn-dahr´see] vr. to occupy oneself, be very busy.

Affaccendato [ahf-fah-chehn-dah´toh] a. busy.

Affamare [ahf-fah-mah´ray] vt. to famish, starve.

Affamato [ahf-fah-mah´toh] a. hungry, famished, starving.

Affannamento [ahf-fahn-nah-men´toh] nm. shortness of breath (rare). v. Affanno.

Affanna/re [ahf-fahn-nah´ray] vt. to grieve, trouble; vi. to feel suffocated, be grieved; —rsi vr. to endeavour, be uneasy, grieved.

Affanno [ahf-fahn´noh] nm. shortness of breath, asthma, trouble, anxiety.

Affannoso [ahf-fahn-noh´soh] a. suffocating, troublesome, vexatious.

Affare [ahf-fah´ray] nm. business, affair; uomo d'affari [oo-oh´moh dahf-fah´ree], business man.

Affascinare [ahf-fah-shee-nah´r y] vt. to fascinate; to tie up in faggots.

Affaticare [ahf-fah-tee-kah´ray] vt. to tire, harass; vi. and —rsi vr. to toil, strive.

Affatto [ahf-faht´toh] ad. entirely, at all.

Affermare [ahf-fehr-mah´ray] vt. to affirm; —rsi vr. to strengthen oneself, be confirmed.

Afferrare [ahf-fehr-rah´ray] vt. to seize, grasp, comprehend

Affettare [ahf-feht-tah'ray] vt. to cut in slices; vt. and i. to affect, be affected, pretend, influence.

Affettazione [ahf-fet-tah-tsee-oh'nay] nf. affectation.

Affetto [ahf-fet'toh] nm. affection, love, wish; a. affected, afflicted.

Affettuoso [ahf-fet-too-oh'soh] a. affectionate.

Affezionare [ahf-fet-see-oh-nah'ray] vt. to make fond; —rsi vr. to become fond of, attached to.

Affezione [ahf-fet-see-oh'nay] nf. affection, attachment.

Affiatarsi [ahf-fee-ah-tahr'see] vr. to get on well together, (mus.) to be in tune.

Affibbiare [ahf-feeb-bee-ah'ray] vt. to buckle, clasp.

Affibbiatura [ahf-feeb-bee-ah-too'rah] nf. buckle, clasp.

Affidare [ahf-fee-dah'ray] vt. to confide, entrust; —rsi vr. to trust, rely on.

Affievolire [ahf-fee-ay-voh-lee'ray] vt. and i. to make (grow) weak.

Affiggere [ahf-fee'djay-ray] vt. to affix, stick (bills, etc.), attach.

Affilare [ahf-fee-lah'ray] vt. to whet, grind, set in rows; —rsi vr. to march in file, become thin.

Affiliare [ahf-fee-lee-ah'ray] vt. to affiliate; —rsi vr. to become a member, join.

Affiliazione [ahf-fee-lee-ah-tsee-oh'nay] nf. affiliation.

Affinare [ahf-fee-nah'ray] vt. to refine, sharpen, streamline, purify (by fire); —rsi vr. to become refined.

Affinatoio [ahf-fee-nah-toh'yoh] nm. crucible, melting-pot.

Affinché [ahf-feeng-kay'] con. so that, in order that.

Affine [ahf-fee'nay] a. akin, kindred.

Affinità [ahf-fee-nee-tah'] nf. affinity.

Affiocato [ahf-fee-oh-kah'toh] a. hoarse.

Affiochimento [ahf-fee-oh-kee-men'toh] nm. hoarseness.

Affiorare [ahf-fee-oh-rah'ray] vi. to come to the surface.

Affissare [ahf-fees-sah'ray] vt. to affix, gaze at, stick (bills).

Affissione [ahf-fees-see-oh'nay] nf. bill-posting; vietata l'af. [vee-ay-tah'tah lahf] stick no bills.

Affisso [ahf-fees'soh] nm. placard, bill posted up; a. fixed, stuck.

Affittare [ahf-feet-tah'ray] vi. to let, rent, hire, lease.

Affitto [ahf-feet'toh] nm. rent, dare in a. [dah'ray een a.] to let; prendere in a. [pren'day-ray een a.] to rent

Affliggere [ahf-flee'djay-ray] vt. to afflict, torment; —rsi vr. to be grieved.

Afflitto [ahf-fleet'toh] a. afflicted, sad.

Afflizione [ahf-flee-tsee-oh'nay] nf. affliction.

Affluenza [ahf-floo-ent'zah] nf. crowd, large audience.

Affluire [ahf-floo-ee'ray] vi. to flow, flock.

Affogare [ahf-foh-gah'ray] vt. and i. to suffocate, stifle, drown; vr. to drown oneself, be stifled; uovo affogato [oo-oh'voh ahf-foh-gah'toh], poached egg.

Affollare [ahf-foll-lah'ray] vt. to crowd, throng; —rsi vr. to crowd together.

Affondare [ahf-fon-dah'ray] vt. and i. to sink, founder, ruin; —rsi vr. to sink, founder, go to the bottom.

Affossamento [ahf-foss-sah-men'toh] *nm.* trench, intrenchment, sinking.

Affranca/re [ahf-frahng-kah'ray] *vt.* to free, exempt, stamp (a letter); —**rsi** *vr.* to be freed, grow strong.

Affrancatura [ahf-frahng-kah-too'rah] *nf.* postage (prepaid).

Affranto [ahf-frahn'toh] *a.* broken, crushed, overcome.

Affratellarsi [ahf-frah-tell-lahr'see] *vr.* to fraternise, live like brothers.

Affresco [ahf-fress'koh] *nm.* fresco.

Affretta/re [ahf-fret-tah'ray] *vt.* to hasten, speed; —**rsi** *vr.* to hurry, make haste.

Affronta/re [ahf-fron-tah'ray] *vt.* to affront, face, attack; —**rsi** *vr.* to meet face to face, fight.

Affronto [ahf-fron'toh] *nm.* affront, insult.

Affumica/re [ahf-foo-mee-kah'ray] *vt.* to fumigate, smoke-dry, blacken; —**rsi** *vr.* to be smoked, grow black.

Affusto [ahf-foo'stoh] *nm.* (*mil.*) gun-carriage.

Afoso [ah-foh'soh] *a.* sultry, heavy.

Agente [ah-jen'tay] *nm.* agent, factor, manager; a. di polizia [.. dee poh-leet-zee'ah], policeman.

Agenzia [ah-jent-zee'ah] *nf.* agency; a. di turismo [.. dee too-rees'moh], travel-agency.

Agevolare [ah-jay-voh-lah'ray] *vt.* to facilitate, make easy, help.

Agevole [ah-jay'voh-lay] *a.* easy, manageable.

Agganciare [ahg-gahn-chah'ray] *vt.* to hook (up).

Aggeggio [ah-djay'djoh] *nm.* gadget, nick-nack, trifle, any small object of little value.

Agghiaccia/re [ahg-ghee-

aht-chah'ray] *vt.* to freeze, turn to ice; —**rsi** *vr.* to freeze, grow cold.

Aggiogare [ah-djoh-gah'ray] *vt.* to yoke.

Aggiorna/re [ah-djorr-nah'ray] *vt.* to postpone, bring up to date.

Aggiotaggio [ah-djoh-tah'djoh] *nm.* stock-jobbing.

Aggira/re [ah-djee-rah'ray] *vt.* to turn, deceive; *vi.* to turn round, go about; —**rsi** *vr.* to turn (round), ramble.

Aggiunge/re [ah-djoon'jay-ray] *vt.* to add, join, unite; —**rsi** *vr.* to join, meet together.

Aggiunta [ah-djoon'tah] *nf.* addition.

Aggiunto [ah-djoon'toh] *nm.* adjunct, assistant; *a.* added, additional.

Aggiusta/re [ah-djoo-stah'ray] *vt.* to adjust, regulate, set to rights, tidy, settle (bills); —**rsi** *vr.* to adjust oneself, tidy oneself, agree.

Aggrandi/re [ahg-grahn-dee'ray] *vt.* to enlarge, increase, exaggerate; —**rsi** *vr.* to augment. *See also* **Ingrandire.**

Aggrappa/re [ahg-grahp-pah'ray] *vt.* to grapple, grasp; —**rsi** *vr.* to cling to, lay hold (of).

Aggrava/re [ahg-grah-vah'ray] *vt.* to aggravate, weigh upon, oppress; —**rsi** *vr.* to grow heavy, lean heavily, grow worse (of illnesses).

Aggredire [ahg-gray-dee'ray] *vt.* to attack, assault, vilify.

Aggregare [ahg-gray-gah'ray] *vt.* to aggregate.

Aggregato [ahg-gray-gah'toh] *nm.* employee transferred to a different office.

Aggregazione [ahg-gray-gah-tsee-oh'nay] *nf.* aggregation, association.

Aggressione [ahg-gress-see-

oh'nay] *nf.* aggression, attack.
Aggressore [ahg-gress-soh'ray] *nm.* aggressor, assailant.
Aggrinzare [ahg-greent-zah'ray] *vt.* to wrinkle, shrivel.
Aggrottarsi le ciglia [ahg-grot-tahr'see lay cheel'yah] *vr.* to frown, knit one's brows.
Aggrumarsi [ahg-groo-mahr'see] *vi.* to curdle, clot.
Aggruppa/re [ahg-groop-pah'ray] *vt.* to group, collect, gather; **—si** *vr.* to form a group.
Aggruzzolare [ahg-groot-zoh-lah'ray] *vt.* to gather, hoard. *v.* **Raggruzzolare.**
Agguaglio [ahg-gwahl'yoh] *nm.* comparison.
Agguantare [ahg-gwahn-tah'ray] *vt.* to seize.
Agguato [ahg-gwah'toh] *nm.* ambush.
Agiatezza [ah-jah-tet'tzah] *nf.* ease, comfort, easy circumstances (*pl.*).
Agiato [ah-jah'toh] *a.* in easy circumstances, well-off, comfortable.
Agile [ah'jee-lay] *a.* agile, nimble.
Agilità [ah-jee-lee-tah'] *nf.* agility, nimbleness.
Agio [ah'joh] *nm.* ease, comfort, leisure.
Agire [ah-jee'ray] *vi.* to act.
Agita/re [ah-jee-tah'ray] *vt.* to agitate, upset, excite; **—rsi** *vr.* to get agitated.
Agitazione [ah-jee-tah-tsee-oh'nay] *nf.* agitation, excitement.
Aglio [ahl'yoh] *nm.* garlic.
Agnello [ahn-yell'loh] *nm.* lamb.
Agnizione [ahn-yee-tsee-oh'nay] *nf.* recognition.
Ago [ah'goh] *nm.* needle.
Agognare [ah-gohn-yah'ray] *vt.* to yearn for, covet.

Agone [ah-goh'nay] *nm.* large needle.
Agonia [ah-goh-nee'ah] *nf.* agony, anguish.
Agonizzare [ah-goh-need-zah'ray] *vi.* to be in agony, at the point of death.
Agosto [ah-goss'toh] *nm.* August (month).
Agrario [ah-grah'ree-oh] *a.* agrarian.
Agreste [ah-gress'tay] *a.* rustic, rural, clownish.
Agrezza [ah-gret'zah] *nf.* sourness, tartness.
Agricolo [ah-gree'koh-loh] *a.* agricultural.
Agricoltura [ah-gree-kohl-too'rah] *nf.* agriculture.
Agrifoglio [ah-gree-fohl'yoh] *nm.* holly.
Agrimensore [ah-gree-men-soh'ray] *nm.* land-surveyor.
Agro [ah'groh] *a.* sour, sharp, severe.
Agrodolce [ah-groh-dohl'chay] *nm.* bitter-sweet sauce. *a.* bitter-sweet.
Agrumi [ah-groo'mee] *nm.* (*pl.*) acid fruit.
Aguzzare [ah-goot-zah'ray] *vt.* to whet, sharpen, point; **—a l'occhio** [lock'ee-oh] to strain one's eyes.
Aguzzo [ah-goot'zoh] *a.* sharp-pointed.
Ahi [ah'ee] *int.* oh!
Ahimè [ah-ee-may'] *int.* alas!
Aia [ah'ee-ah] *nf.* threshing-floor.
Aire [ah-ee'ray] *nm.* going, direction; **prendere l'aire** [pren'day-ray lah-ee'ray] to start off (running or flying).
Aita [ah-ee'tah] *nf.* (*poet.*) help. [(flower-bed)
Aiuola [ah-ee-oo-oh'lah] *nf.*
Aiutante [ah-yoo-tahn'tay] *nm.* helper, assistant; *a.* **di campo** [dee kahm'poh], aide-de-camp.

Aiuta/re [ah-yoo-tah'ray] vt. to help, assist, lend a hand; —rsi vr. to make use of.

Aiuto [ah-yoo'toh] nm. help, assistance.

Aizzare [ah-eet-zah'ray] vt. to stir up, instigate, enrage, set on (dogs).

Ala [ah'lah] nf. wing.

Alabastro [ah-lah-bahs'troh] nm. alabaster.

Alacre [ah'lah-kray] a. willing, quick.

Alacrità [ah-lah-kree-tah'] nf. alacrity, quickness. [tiff.

Alano [ah-lah'noh] nm. mastiff.

Alare [ah-lah'ray] nm. andiron, fire-dog.

Alato [ah-lah'toh] a. winged.

Alba [ahl'bah] nf. dawn.

Albagia [ahl-bah-jee'ah] nf. vanity, conceit.

Albagioso [ahl-bah-joh'soh] a. vain, conceited.

Albatro [ahl'bah-troh] nm. arbutus (tree), albatros.

Albeggiare [ahl-bay-djah'ray] vi. to dawn.

Albergare [ahl-behr-gah'ray] vt. and i. to lodge, harbour.

Albergatore [ahl-behr-gah-toh'ray] nm. innkeeper, host.

Albergo [ahl-behr'goh] nm. inn, hotel.

Albero [ahl'bay-roh] nm. tree, ship's mast.

Albicocca [ahl-bee-kock'kah] nf. apricot.

Albore [ahl-boh'ray] nm. dawn.

Albume [ahl-boo'may] nm. albumen, white of an egg.

Alcalizzare [ahl-kah-leed-zah'ray] vt. to alkalise.

Alce [ahl'chay] nm. elk.

Alchimia [ahl-kee'mee-ah] nf. alchemy.

Alchimista [ahl-kee-mee'stah] nm. alchemist.

Alcool [ahl-koh'ohl] nm. alcohol.

Alcuno [ahl-koo'noh] pr. somebody, anybody, (preceded by non) nobody; a. any, (preceded by non) no; alcuni [ahl-koo'nee] a. and pr. (pl.) some, a few (pl.).

Aleggiare [ah-lay-djah'ray] vi. to flutter, try to fly.

Aletta [ah-let'tah] nf. flap.

Alettone [ah-let-toh'nay] nm. aileron.

Alfabeto [ahl-fah-bay'toh] nm. alphabet.

Alfiere [ahl-fee-ay'ray] nm. ensign (bearer), bishop (at chess).

Alfine [ahl-fee'nay] ad. at last.

Alga [ahl'gah] nf. seaweed.

Aliante [ah-lee-ahn'tay] nm. glider.

Alice [ah-lee'chay] nf. anchovy.

Aliena/re [ah-lee-ay-nah'ray] vt. to alienate, estrange; —rsi vr. to be estranged.

Alienato [ah-lee-ay-nah'toh] nm. mentally deranged person; a. mentally deranged, crazy.

Alienazione [ah-lee-ay-nah-tsee-oh'nay] nf. alienation, estrangement, mental derangement.

Alieno [ah-lee-ay'noh] a. alien, adverse.

Alimentare [ah-lee-men-tah'ray] vt. to feed, nourish; a. alimentary.

Alimento [ah-lee-men'toh] nm. food, nourishment.

Alisei [ah-lee-zay'ee], **venti alisei** [ven'tee] nm. (pl.) trade-winds (pl.).

Alito [ah'lee-toh] nm. breath, breathing, breeze.

Allacciare [ahl-lahch-chah'ray] vt. to lace, connect, entangle.

Allagamento [ahl-lah-gah-men'toh] nm. inundation.

Allagare [ahl-lah-gah'ray] vt.

to inundate, overflow. submerge.

Allampanato [ahl-lahm-pah-nah'toh] *a.* emaciated.

Allargare [ahl-lahr-gah'ray] *vt.* to enlarge extend, widen.

Allarma/re [ahl-lahr-mah'ray] *vt.* to alarm, disturb; —rsi *vr.* to be alarmed.

Allarme [ahl-lahr'may] *nm.* alarm, alert.

Allato [ahl-lah'toh] *ad.* beside.

Allattare [ahl-laht-tah'ray] *vt.* to suckle, breast-feed.

Alleanza [ahl-lay-ahnt'zah] *nf.* alliance, league.

Allearsi [ahl-lay-ahr'see] *vr.* to make an alliance.

Alleato [ahl-lay-ah'toh] *nm.* ally; *a.* allied.

Allegare [ahl-lay-gah'ray] *vt.* to allege, cite, annex.

Allegazione [ahl-lay-gah-tsee-oh'nay] *nf.* allegation.

Alleggeri/re [ahl-lay-djay-ree'ray] *vt.* to lighten, relieve; —rsi *vr.* to put on lighter clothing.

Allegoria [ahl-lay-goh-ree'ah] *nf.* allegory.

Allegrezza [ahl-lay-gret'zah] *nf.* gaiety, cheerfulness.

Allegria [ahl-lay-gree'ah] *nf.* mirth, gladness.

Allegro [ahl-lay'groh] *a.* gay, cheerful, merry.

Allenamento [ahl-lay-nah-men'toh] *nm.* training, breathing.

Allenare [ahl-lay-nah'ray] *vt.* to train, strengthen, invigorate; *vi.* to take breath.

Allenta/re [ahl-len-tah'ray] *vt.* to slacken; —rsi *vr.* to get slack, unlace or undo one's clothing.

Allesti/re [ahl-less-tee'ray] *vt.* to prepare, make ready; —rsi *vr.* to get ready.

Allettamento [ahl-let-tah-men'toh] *nm.* allurement.

Alletta/re [ahl-let-tah'ray] *vt.* to allure, entice; —rsi *vr.* to take to one's bed (in illness).

Allevamento [ahl-lay-vah-men'toh] *nm.* bringing-up, breeding.

Allevare [ahl-lay-vah'ray] *vt.* to bring up, breed.

Alleviare [ahl-lay-vee-ah'ray] *vt.* to alleviate.

Allibire [ahl-lee-bee'ray] *vi.* to be amazed.

Allietare [ahl-lee-ay-tah'ray] *vt.* to gladden.

Allievo [ahl-lee-ay'voh] *nm.* pupil, foster-child.

Allignare [ahl-leen-yah'ray] *vi.* to take root, grow.

Allineare [ahl-lee-nay-ah'ray] *vi.* to align, set in rows.

Allocuzione [ahl-loh-koo-tsee-oh'nay] *nf.* allocution.

Allodola [ahl-loh'doh-lah] *nf.* skylark.

Alloggiare [ahl-loh-djah'ray] *vt. and i.* to lodge, stay, billet.

Alloggio [ahl-loh'djoh] *nm.* lodgings (*pl.*), billet, inn.

Allontanamento [ahl-lon-tah-nah-men'toh] *nm.* removal, remoteness.

Allontana/re [ahl-lon-tah-nah'ray] *vt.* to remove, send away; —rsi *vr.* to remove, go away, withdraw.

Allora [ahl-loh'rah] *ad.* then, at that time.

Allorchè [ahl-lorr-kay'] *con.* when, whilst, provided.

Alloro [ahl-loh'roh] *nm.* laurel.

Allucina/re [ahl-loo-chee-nah'ray] *vt.* to hallucinate; —rs *vr.* to suffer from hallucinations.

Alludere [ahl-loo-day-ray] *vi.* to allude, refer, hint.

Alluminio [ahl-loo-mee'nee-oh] *nm.* aluminium.

Allunga/re [ahl-loong-gah'ray] *vt.* to lengthen, prolong, water (wine, etc.), pass, hand;

—**rsi** *vr.* to grow longer, stretch oneself.

Allusione [ahl-loo-zee-oh'nay] *nf.* allusion.

Alma [ahl'mah] *nf.* (*poet.*) soul, spirit.

Almanaccare [ahl-mah-nahk-kah'ray] *vi.* to fancy, build castles in the air, puzzle one's brain.

Almanacco [ahl-mah-nahk'koh] *nm.* almanack, calendar.

Almeno [ahl-may'noh] *ad.* at least.

Alno [ahl'noh] *nm.* alder-tree.

Alone [ah-loh'nay] *nm.* halo.

Alpestre [ahl-pess'tray] *a.* mountainous, wild.

Alpigiano [ahl-pee-jah'noh] *nm.* inhabitant of a hilly district, mountaineer.

Alpinismo [ahl-pee-ness'moh] *nm.* mountaineering.

Alpino [ahl-pee'noh] *nm.* soldier of a special Italian Alpine division; *a.* Alpine.

Alquanto [ahl-kwahn'toh] *ad.* somewhat, up to a point.

Altalena [ahl-tah-lay'nah] *nf.* swing, see-saw.

Altare [ahl-tah'ray] *nm.* altar; **a. maggiore** [mah-djoh'ray], high-altar.

Altera/re [ahl-tay-rah'ray] *vt.* to alter, change; —**rsi** *vr.* to get angry.

Alterezza [ahl-tay-ret'zah], **alterigia** [ahl-tay-ree'jah] *nf.* haughtiness, pride, insolence.

Alternare [ahl-tehr-nah'ray] *vt.* to alternate.

Alternativa [ahl-tehr-nah-tee'vah] *nf.* alternative, choice.

Alternativo [ahl-tehr-nah-tee'voh] *a.* alternate, alternative.

Altezza [ahl-tet'zah] *nf.* height, width, depth, highness; **a. reale** [ray-ah'lay], Royal Highness.

Alticcio [ahl-teech'choh] *a.* tipsy, (haughty).

Alt(i)ero [ahl-(tee)ay'roh] *a.*

Altipiano [ahl-tee-pee-ah'noh] *nm.* plateau, table-land.

Altitudine [ahl-tee-too'dee-nay] *nf.* altitude, height.

Alto [ahl'toh] *a.* high, tall, loud, deep, wide; **ad alta voce** [ahd ahl'tah voh'chay], aloud.

Altoparlante [ahl-toh-pahr-lahn'tay] *nm.* loud-speaker.

Altresì [ahl-tray-see'] *ad.* likewise too.

Altrettanto [ahl-tret-tahn'toh] *ad.* equally, as much (again); *in.* the same to you!

Altri [ahl'tree] *pr.* (*sing. and pl.*) someone, another, some (*pl.*).

Altrieri, l' [lahl-tree-ay'ree] *ad.* a day or two ago.

Altrimenti [ahl-tree-men'tee] *ad.* otherwise.

Altro [ahl'troh] *pr. and a.* (an)other, different, next; (something) else; *int.* not at all! **per altro** [pehr ahl'troh], anyhow.

Altronde, d' [dahl-tron'day] *ad.* besides, on the other hand.

Altrove [ahl-troh'vay] *ad.* elsewhere, somewhere else.

Altrui [ahl-troo'ee] *pr.* others, other people (*pl.*); **l'altrui** [lahl-troo'ee] *nm.* other people's property.

Altura [ahl-too'rah] *nf.* height, elevation.

Alunno [ah-loon'noh] *nm.* pupil, school-boy.

Alveare [ahl-vay-ah'ray] *nm.* beehive.

Alveo [ahl'vay-oh] *nm.* channel, bed of a river.

Alza/re [ahlt-zah'ray] *vt.* to raise, lift, build; **a. le carte** [lay kahr'tay], to cut the cards; **a. le spalle** [lay spahl'lay], to shrug one's shoulders; —**rsi** *vr.* to get up, rise.

Alzata [ahl-zah′tah] *nf.* rise, elevation, shrug.

Amabile [ah-mah′bee-lay] *a.* amiable, kind, agreeable.

Amabilità [ah-mah-bee-lee-tah′] *nf.* amiability, kindness.

Amalgamare [ah-mahl-gah-mah′ray] *vt.* to amalgamate.

Amante [ah-mahn′tay] *nm.* lover, sweetheart; *a.* loving, fond.

Amare [ah-mah′ray] *vt.* to love, like, be fond of.

Amareggiare [ah-mah-ray-djah′ray] *vt.* to embitter; *vi.* to grow bitter.

Amarezza [ah-mah-ret′zah] *nf.* bitterness.

Amaritudine [ah-mah-ree-too′dee-nay] *nf.* bitterness, grief.

Amaro [ah-mah′roh] *a.* bitter, grievous, cruel.

Amarrare [ah-mahr-rah′ray] *vt.* to moor.

Amazzone [ah-mahd′zoh-nay] *nf.* Amazon, horse-woman.

Ambasceria [ahm-bah-shay-ree′ah] *nf.* embassy, deputation, diplomatic mission.

Ambascia [ahm-bah′shah] *nf.* shortness of breath, anxiety.

Ambasciata [ahm-bah-shah′tah] *nf.* embassy, message, commission.

Ambasciatore [ahm-bah-shah-toh′ray] *nm.* ambassador.

Ambedue [ahm-bay-doo′ay] *pr.* (*pl.*) both (*pl.*).

Ambiente [ahm-bee-en′tay] *nm.* atmosphere, circle, environment, room; *a.* ambient

Ambiguità [ahm-bee-goo-ee-tah′] *nf.* ambiguity, doubt.

Ambire [ahm-bee′ray] *vt.* to long for, covet.

Ambizione [ahm-bee-tsee-oh′nay] *nf.* ambition, love of finery, vanity.

Ambizioso [ahm-bee-tsee-oh′soh] *a.* ambitious, vain, fond of finery.

Ambra [ahm′brah] *nf.* amber.

Ambulante [ahm-boo-lahn′tay] *a.* ambulant, walking.

Ambulanza [ahm-boo-lahnt′zah] *nf.* ambulance.

Ambulare [ahm-boo-lah′ray] *vi.* to run away. *v.* Andare via.

Ambulatorio [ahm-boo-lah-toh′ree-oh] *nm.* out-patients' department, first-aid post.

Amenità [ah-may-nee-tah′] *nf.* amenity, agreeableness.

Ameno [ah-may′noh] *a.* pleasant, agreeable.

Amica [ah-mee′kah] *nf.* (woman) friend, mistress.

Amichevole [ah-mee-kay′voh-lay] *a.* friendly, amiable.

Amicizia [ah-mee-chee′tsee-ah] *nf.* friendship.

Amico [ah-mee′koh] *nm.* friend, lover; *a.* friendly.

Amido [ah-mee′doh] *nm.* starch.

Ammacca/re [ahm-mahk-kah′ray] *vt.* to bruise, crush; **—rsi** *vr.* to get bruised.

Ammaestramento [ahm-mah-ess-trah-men′toh] *nm.* teaching, instruction, training of animals.

Ammaestrare [ahm-mah-ess-trah′ray] *vt.* to teach, instruct, train (animals).

Ammainare [ahm-mah-ee-nah′ray] *vt.* to lower, furl (sails).

Ammala/re [ahm-mah-lah′ray] *vi.* **—rsi** *vr.* to fall sick, sicken.

Ammalato [ahm-mah-lah′toh] *nm.* patient; *a.* sick, ill.

Ammaliare [ahm-mah-lee-ah′ray] *vt.* to bewitch.

Ammansare [ahm-mahn-sah′ray], **ammansire** [ahm-mahn-see′ray] *vt.* to make tame, gentle; **—rsi** *vr.* to grow tame, gentle.

Ammarraggiare [ahm-mahr-rah-djah′ray] *vi.* to light on the water (of a seaplane).

Ammarraggio [ahm-mahr-rah′djoh] *nm.* lightning on the water (of a seaplane).

Ammassa/re [ahm-mahs-sah′ray] *vt.* to amass, heap up; —rsi *vr.* to come together, meet.

Ammasso [ahm-mahs′soh] *nm.* heap, accumulation.

Ammattire [ahm-maht-tee′ray] *vt. and i.* to make (go) mad.

Ammazza/re [ahm-maht-zah′ray] *vt.* to kill, murder; —rsi *vr.* to kill oneself, toil hard.

Ammazzatoio [ahm-maht-zah-toh′yoh] *nm.* slaughter-house.

Ammenda [ahm-men′dah] *nf.* amends (*pl.*), fine.

Ammenda/re [ahm-men-dah′ray] *vt.* to amend, reform; —rsi *vr.* to improve, get better.

Ammettere [ahm-met′tay-ray] *vt.* to admit, allow, receive.

Ammezzare [ahm-med-zah′ray] *vt.* to halve.

Ammiccare [ahm-meek-kah′ray] *vt.* to wink, beckon, make a sign (with the eyes).

Amministrare [ahm-mee-nee-strah′ray] *vt.* to administer, rule.

Amministrazione [ahm-mee-nee-strah-tsee-oh′nay] *nf.* administration, government, trusteeship.

Ammirabile [ahm-mee-rah′bee-lay] *a.* admirable, wonderful.

Ammiragliato [ahm-mee-rah-lyah′toh] *nm.* admiralty.

Ammiraglio [ahm-mee-rahl′yoh] *nm.* admiral.

Ammirare [ahm-mee-rah′ray] *vt.* to admire.

Ammirazione [ahm-mee-rah-tsee-oh′nay] *nf.* admiration wonder.

Ammissibile [ahm-mees-see′bee-lay] *a.* admissible.

Ammissione [ahm-mees-see-oh′nay] *nf.* admission; tassa d'a. [tass′sah] entrance-fee.

Ammobiliare [ahm-moh-bee-lee-ah′ray] *vt.* to furnish.

Ammodo [ahm-moh′doh] *a.* nice-mannered, respectable; *ad.* nicely, carefully.

Ammoglia/re [ahm-mohl-yah′ray] *vt.* to give a wife to; —rsi *vr.* to take a wife.

Ammolla/re [ahm-moll-lah′ray] *vt.* to steep, soak, soften; —rsi *vr.* to be soaked, get wet.

Ammolli/re [ahm-moll-lee′ray] *vt.* to soften, move (to compassion); —rsi *vr.* to get soft.

Ammoniaca [ahm-moh-nee′ah-kah] *nf.* ammonia.

Ammonimento [ahm-moh-nee-men′toh] *nm.* admonition, warning.

Ammonire [ahm-moh-nee′ray] *vi.* to admonish, warn, advise.

Ammonizione [ahm-moh-nee-tsee-oh′nay] *nf.* admonition, reproof, warning.

Ammorbidi/re [ahm-morr-bee-dee′ray] *vt.* to soften, calm; —rsi *vr.* to grow soft.

Ammortire [ahm-morr-tee′ray] *vt.* to weaken, deaden.

Ammortizzare [ahm-morr-teed-zah′ray] *vt.* to redeem (a debt), mortgage.

Ammorzare [ahm-morr-zah′ray] *vt.* to extinguish, put out.

Ammostare [ahm-moss-tah′ray] *vt.* to tread (grapes).

Ammostatoio [ahm-moss-tah-toh′yoh] *nm.* wine-press.

egli fu.	egli ebbe.
noi fummo.	noi avemmo.
voi foste.	voi aveste.
essi furono.	essi ebbero

FUTURE

I shall be.	*I shall have.*
io sarò.	io avrò.
tu sarai.	tu avrai.
egli sarà.	egli avrà.
noi saremo.	noi avremo.
voi sarete.	voi avrete.
essi saranno.	essi avranno.

CONDITIONAL

I should be.	*I should have.*
io sarei.	io avrei.
tu saresti.	tu avresti.
egli sarebbe.	egli avrebbe.
noi saremmo.	noi avremmo
voi sareste.	voi avreste.
essi sarebbero.	essi avrebbero.

IMPERATIVE

be.	*have.*
sii.	abbi.
sia.	abbia.
siano	abbiamo.
siate.	abbiate.
siano.	abbiano.

INFINITIVE

essere, *to be*	avere, *to have.*

GERUND

essendo, *being.*	avendo, *having.*

PAST PARTICIPLE

stato, stata, stati, state,	} been.	avuto, avuta, avuti, avute,	} had.

Compound Tenses

PERFECT

I have been.
io sono stato.
tu sei stato.
egli è stato
essa è stata.
noi siamo stati.
voi siete stati.
essi sono stati
esse sono state.

I have had.
io ho avuto.
tu hai avuto.
egli
essa } ha avuto.
noi abbiamo avuto.
voi avete avuto.
essi hanno avuto.
esse hanno avuto.

PLUPERFECT

I had been.
io ero stato.
tu eri stato.
egli era stato,
essa era stata.
noi eravamo stati.
voi eravate stati.
essi erano stati.
esse erano state.

I had had.
io avevo avuto.
tu avevi avuto.
egli
essa } aveva avuto.
noi avevamo avuto.
voi avevate avuto.
essi
esse } avevano avuto.

SECOND PLUPERFECT

I had been.
io fui stato.
tu fosti stato.
egli fu stato.
essa fu stata.
voi fummo stati.
voi foste stati.
essi furono stati.
esse furono state.

I had had.
io ebbi avuto.
tu avesti avuto.
egli
essa } ebbe avuto.
noi avemmo avuto.
voi aveste avuto.
essi
esse } ebbero avuto

FUTURE PERFECT

I shall have been.
io sarò stato.
tu sarai stato.
egli sarà stato.
essa sarà stata.
noi saremo stati.
voi sarete stati.
essi saranno stati.
esse saranno state.

I shall have had.
io avrò avuto.
tu avrai avuto.
egli
essa } avrà avuto.
noi avremo avuto.
voi avrete avuto.
essi
esse } avranno avuto.

Ammucchiare [ahm-mook-kee-ah'ray] *vt.* to heap up.

Ammuffire [ahm-moof-fee'ray] *vi.* to grow stale.

Ammutinamento [ahm-moo-tee-nah-men'toh] *nm.* mutiny, revolt.

Ammutinarsi [ahm-moo-tee-nahr'see] *vr.* to mutiny, revolt.

Amnistia [ahm-nee-stee'ah] *nf.* amnesty. [bait.

Amo [ah'moh] *nm.* fish- hook,

Amore [ah-moh'ray] *nm.* love, affection; **a. proprio** [proh'pree-oh], self-esteem; **per l'a di** [pehr lah-moh'ray dee], for the sake of.

Amoreggiare [ah-moh-ray-djah'ray] *vi.* to make love, flirt.

Amorevole [ah-moh-ray'voh-lay] *a.* loving, kind.

Amoroso [ah-moh-roh'soh] *nm.* lover, gallant; *a.* loving.

Ampiezza [ahm-pee-et'zah] *nf.* amplitude, extension.

Ampio [ahm'pee-oh] *a.* ample, wide, spacious.

Amplesso [ahm-pless'soh] *nm.* embrace.

Amplia/re [ahm-plee-ah'ray] *vt.* to enlarge, extend; **—rsi** *vr.* to stretch, dilate.

Amplificare [ahm-plee-fee-kah'ray] *vt.* to amplify, exaggerate.

Amplificatore [ahm-plee-fee-kah-toh'ray] *nm.* ampli-fier, loud-speaker.

Amplitudine [ahm-plee-too'dee-nay] *nf.* amplitude, capaciousness.

Ampolla [ahm-poll'lah] *nf.* phial, ampoule.

Ampollosità [ahm-poll-loh-see-tah'] *nf.* bombast.

Ampolloso [ahm-poll-loh'soh] *a.* bombastic.

Amputare [ahm-poo-tah'ray] *vt.* to amputate.

Amputazione [ahm-poo-tah-tsee-oh'nay] *nf.* amputa-tion.

Amuleto [ah-moo-lay'toh] *nm.* amulet, talisman.

Anacoreta [ah-nah-koh-ray'tah] *nm.* anchorite, hermit.

Anagrafe [ah-nah'grah-fay] *nf.* census.

Analfabeto [ah-nahl-fah-bay'toh] *nm.* one who can neither read nor write; *a.* illiterate. [analysis.

Analisi [ah-nah'lee-zee] *nf.*

Analizzare [ah-nah-leed-zah'ray] *vt.* to analyse.

Analogia [ah-nah-loh-jee'ah] *nf.* analogy.

Ananasso [ah-nah-nahs'soh] *nm.* pine-apple.

Anarchia [ah-nahr-kee'ah] *nf.* anarchy.

Anarchico [ah-nahr'kee-koh] *nm.* anarchist; *a.* anarchic.

Anatomia [ah-nah-toh-mee'ah] *nf.* anatomy.

Anatomizzare [ah-nah-toh-meed-zah'ray] *vt.* to ana-tomize, dissect.

Anatra [ah'nah-trah] *nf.* duck.

Anca [ahng'kah] *nf.* hip, haunch.

Ancella [ahn-chell'lah] *nf.* maid(-servant).

Anche [ahng'kay] *ad.* also, too, even.

Ancora [ahng'koh-rah] *nf.* anchor.

Ancora [ahng-koh'rah] *ad.* yet, still, again, even, also.

Ancoraggio [ahng-koh-rah'djoh] *nm.* anchorage.

Ancorare [ahng-koh-rah'ray] *vi.* to anchor.

Ancudine [ahng-koo'dee-nay] *nf.* anvil.

Andamento [ahn-dah-men'toh] *nm.* gait, carriage, trend.

Andante [ahn-dahn'tay] *a.* going, current, fair (price), flowing (style).

Andare [ahn-dah'ray] vi. to go, march, proceed, please, suit; a. a piedi [ah pee-ay'dee], to go on foot; andarsene [ahn-dahr'say-nay], to go away. [nf. gait.

Andatura [ahn-dah-too'rah]

Andazzo [ahn-daht'zoh] nm. trend, passing fashion.

Andirivieni [ahn-dee-ree-vee-ay'nee] nm. (pl.) coming and going of people, digressions, windings (pl.).

Andito [ahn'dee-toh] nm. passage, entrance.

Androne [ahn-droh'nay] nm. portal, entrance(-hall).

Aneddoto [ah-ned'doh-toh] nm. anecdote.

Anelare [ah-nay-lah'ray] vt. to long for; vi. to pant, be breathless.

Anello [ah-nell'loh] nm. ring, ringlet, thimble, link (of a chain).

Anemia [ah-nay-mee'ah] nf. anemia.

Anemico [ah-nay'mee-koh] a. anemic.

Anestetica [ah-ness-tay'tee-kah] nf. anesthetic.

Anfibio [ahn-fee'bee-oh] a. amphibious.

Anfiteatro [ahn-fee-tay-ah'troh] nm. amphitheatre.

Angariare [ahng-gah-ree-ah'ray] vt. to vex, harass, ill-treat.

Angelico [ahn-jay'lee-koh] a. angelic.

Angelo [ahn'jay-loh], angiolo [ahn'joh-loh] nm. angel.

Angheria [ahng-gay-ree'ah] nf. vexation, oppression, ill-treatment.

Angina [ahn-jee'nah] nf. sore throat.

Angiporto [ahn-jee-porr'toh] nm. blind alley.

Anglicano [ahng-glee-kah'noh] a. Anglican, Protestant.

Angolare [ahng-goh-lah'ray] a. angular.

Angolo [ahng'goh-loh] nm. angle, corner.

Angoscia [ahng-goh'shah] nf. anguish, affliction.

Angoscioso [ahng-goh-shoh'soh] a. afflicted, grievous.

Anguilla [ahng-gweel'lah] nf eel.

Angustia [ahng-goo'stee-ah] nf. narrowness, want, distress.

Angustia/re [ahng-goo-stee-ah'ray] vt. to grieve, vex, harass; —rsi vr. to be distressed.

Angusto [ahng-goo'stoh] a. narrow. [seed.

Anice [ah'nee-chay] nm. ani-

Anima [ah'nee-mah] nf. soul, spirit, person.

Animale [ah-nee-mah'lay] nm. and a. animal.

Anima/re [ah-nee-mah'ray] vt. to animate, enliven; —rsi vr. to grow animated.

Animella [ah-nee-mell'lah] nf. sweet-bread.

Animo [ah'nee-moh] nm. mind, heart, courage; farsi [fahr'see] a. to pluck up courage; perdersi d'a. [pehr'dehr-see dah'nee-moh] to lose heart.

Animosità [ah-nee-moh-see-tah'] nf. animosity.

Animoso [ah-nee-moh'soh] a. courageous, valiant.

Anisetta [ah-nee-set'tah] nm. anise-water.

Anitra [ah'nee-trah] nf. duck.

Anitroccolo [ah-nee-trock'koh-loh] nm. duckling.

Annacquare [ahn-nahk-kwah'ray] vt. to mix with water.

Annaffiare [ahn-nahf-fee-ah'ray] vt. to water, sprinkle.

Annaffiatoio [ahn-nahf-fee-ah-toh'yoh] nm. watering-can.

Annali [ahn-nah'lee] nm. (pl.) annals (pl.).

tah'ray] vt. to annihilate, bring to nothing; —**rsi** vr. to come to nothing.

Anniversario [ahn-nee-vehr-sah'ree-oh] nm. and a. anniversary.

Anno [ahn'noh] nm. year; **capo d'a.** [kah'poh dahn'noh] New Year ('s Day).

Annoia/re [ahn-noh-yah'ray] vt. to bore, vex, tease; —**rsi** vr. to get tired, be bored.

Annona [ahn-noh'nah] nf. victuals, provisions (pl.).

Annonario [ahn-noh-nah'ree-oh] a. connected with provisions. (ancient).

Annoso [ahn-noh'soh] a. old.

Annotare [ahn-noh-tah'ray] vt. to note, annotate.

positive pole.

Anomalia [ah-noh-mah-lee'ah] nf. anomaly.

Anomalo [ah-noh'mah-loh] a. anomalous.

Anonimo [ah-noh'nee-moh] a. anonymous.

Anormale [ah-norr-mah'lay] a. abnormal.

Anormalità [ah-norr-mah-lee-tah'] nf. abnormality.

Ansa [ahn'sah] nf. handle, pretext.

Ansare [ahn-sah'ray] vi. to pant.

Ansia [ahn'see-ah] nf. anxiety.

Ansietà [ahn-see-ay-tah'] nf. anxiety, trouble.

Ansimare [ahn-see-mah'ray] vi. to pant.

Antidiluviano [ahn-tee-dee-loo-vee-ah'noh] a. antediluvian.

Antidoto [ahn-tee'doh-toh] nm. antidote.

Ansioso [ahn-see-oh'soh] a. anxious.

Antagonismo [ahn-tah-goh-nees'moh] nm. antagonism.

An...tico [ahn-tah'tee-koh]

Annata [ahn-nah'tah] *nf.* year, year's profits (*pl.*), produce, etc.

Annebbia/re [ahn-neb-bee-ah'ray] *vt.* to cloud, dim, darken; —rsi *vr.* to grow dim, be overcast.

Annega/re [ahn-nay-gah'ray] *vt.* to drown; *vi.* to be drowned; —rsi *vr.* to drown oneself.

Anneghittire [ahn-nay-gheet-tee'ray] *vt. and i.* to make (grow) lazy.

Annerire [ahn-nay-ree'ray] *vt.* to blacken, tarnish.

Annessione [ahn-ness-see-oh'nay] *nf.* annexation.

Annestare [ahn-ness-tah'ray] *vt.* to graft. v. Inncstare.

Annettere [ahn-net'tay-ray] *vt.* to annex.

Annichilire [ahn-nee-kee-lee'ray] *vt.* to annihilate.

Annida/re [ahn-nee-dah'ray] *vi.* to build a nest, settle; —rsi *vr.* to nestle, settle oneself.

Annicntamento [ahn-nee-en-tah-men'toh] *nm.* annihilation, reduction to nothing.

Annotta/re [ahn-not-tah'ray] *vi.*—rsi *vr.* to grow dark.

Annoverare [ahn-noh-vay-rah'ray] *vt.* to number, count.

Annuale [ahn-noo-ah'lay] *a.* annual, yearly.

Annuire [ahn-noo-ee'ray] *vi.* to nod.

Annualità [ahn-noo-ah-lee-tah'] *nf.* annuity.

Annullamento [ahn-nool-lah-men'toh] *nm.* abolition, repeal.

Annullare [ahn-nool-lah'ray] *vt.* to abolish, repeal.

Annunziare [ahn-noon-tsee-ah'ray] *vt.* to announce, predict.

Annunziata [ahn-noon-tsee-ah'tah] *nf.* Our Lady of the Annunciation.

Annunzio [ahn-noon'tsee-oh] *nm.* announcement, advertisement.

Annuo [ahn'noo-oh] *a.* annual, yearly.

Annusare [ahn-noo-sah'ray] *vi.* to sniff, smell.

Anodino [ah-noh-dee'noh] *nm. and a.* anodyne.

ray] vt. to value, rate, appreciate.

Approccio [ahp-prohch'choh] nm. approach.

Approdare [ahp-proh-dah'ray] vi. to come to shore, land.

Approdo [ahp-proh'doh] nm. landing-place.

Approfittare [ahp-proh-feet-tah'ray] vi. to profit.

Approfon/dare [ahp-proh-fon-dah'ray]; —dire [dee'ray] vt. to dig, deepen, search out, go into thoroughly.

Appropria/re [ahp-proh-pree-ah'ray] vt. to use properly, adapt; —rsi vr. to appropriate to oneself.

Approssima/re [ahp-pross-see-mah'ray] vt. to place near; —rsi vr. to approach, draw near.

Approvare [ahp-proh-vah'ray] vt. to approve, confirm.

Approvazione [ahp-proh-vah-tsee-oh'nay] nf. approvation.

Approvvigionare [ahp-prov-vee-joh-nah'ray] vt. to victual, provision.

Appuntamento [ahp-poon-tah-men'toh] nm. appointment.

Appuntare [ahp-poon-tah'ray] vt. to point, sharpen, pin, tack.

Appuntino [ahp-poon-tee'noh] nm. (com.) bill of exchange, receipt; ad. just in time, exactly, neatly.

Appunto [ahp-poon'toh] nm. note; ad. precisely, exactly.

Appurare [ahp-poo-rah'ray] vt. to purify, verify, make clear.

Aprile [ah-pree'lay] nm. April.

Apri/re [ah-pree'ray] vt. to open, discover, disclose; —rsi vr. to open, expand.

Aquila [ah'kwee-lah] nf. eagle, great genius.

Aquilone [ah-kwee-loh'nay] nm. North wind, kite (toy).

Aragosta [ah-rah-goss'tah] nf. lobster.

Araldica [ah-rahl'dee-kah] nf. heraldry.

Araldo [ah-rahl'doh] nm. herald, harbinger.

Arancia [ah-rahn'chah] nf. orange.

Aranciata [ah-rahn-chah'tah] nf. orangeade.

Arancio [ah-rahn'choh] nm. orange tree; a. orange (colour).

Arare [ah-rah'ray] vt. to plough, cultivate.

Aratore [ah-rah-toh'ray] nm. ploughman.

Aratro [ah-rah'troh] nm. plough. [tapestry.

Arazzo [ah-raht'zoh] nm.

Arbitraggio [ahr-bee-trah'djoh] nm. speculation on the Exchange.

Arbitrare [ahr-bee-trah'ray] vi. to arbitrate, judge.

Arbitrario [ahr-bee-trah'ree-oh] a. arbitrary, despotic.

Arbitrio [ahr-bee'tree-oh] nm. free-will, absolute power.

Arbitro [ahr'bee-troh] nm. arbiter, umpire, referee.

Arboreo [ahr-boh'ray-oh] a. arboreous.

Arboreto [ahr-boh-ray'toh] nm. grove.

Arboscello [ahr-boh-shell'loh] nm. small tree, shrub.

Arbusto [ahr-boo'stoh] nm. shrub.

Arca [ahr-kah] nf. chest, coffer, tomb; a. di Noè [dee noh-ay'], Noah's Ark.

Arcaico [ahr-kah-ee-koh] a. archaic.

Arcaismo [ahr-kah-ees'moh] nm. archaism.

Arcangelo [ahr-kahn'jay-loh] nm. archangel.

Arcano [ahr-kah'noh] *nm.* mystery; *a.* secret, mysterious.

Archeologia [ahr-kay-oh-loh-jee'ah] *nf.* archeology.

Archetto [ahr-ket'toh] *nm.* small arch, violin bow.

Architettare [ahr-kee-teht-tah'ray] *vt.* to build, contrive.

Architetto [ahr-kee-teht'toh] *nm.* architect, contriver.

Architettura [ahr-kee-teht-too'rah] *nf.* architecture.

Archivio [ahr-kee'vee-oh] *nm.* archives (*pl.*), record-office.

Archivista [ahr-kee-vee'stah] *nm.* recorder.

Arciduca [ahr-chee-doo'kah] *nm.* archduke.

Arciduchessa [ahr-chee-doo-kess'sah] *nf.* archduchess.

Arcigno [ahr-cheen'yoh] *a.* sharp, harsh, gruff.

Arcipelago [ahr-chee-pay'lah-goh] *nm.* archipelago.

Arciprete [ahr-chee-pray'tay] *nm.* senior priest (in a country parish).

Arcivescovado [ahr-chee-vess-koh-vah'doh] *nm.* archbishopric.

Arcivescovo [ahr-chee-vess'koh-voh] *nm.* archbishop.

Arco [ahr'koh] *nm.* bow, arch.

Arcobaleno [ahr-koh-bah-lay'noh] *nm.* rainbow.

Ardente [ahr-den'tay] *a.* burning, ardent, eager, spirited.

Ardere [ahr'day-ray] *vi.* to burn, glow, be on fire, shine.

Ardesia [ahr-day'zee-ah] *nf.* slate.

Ardimento [ahr-dee-men'toh] *nm.* boldness, daring.

Ardire [ahr-dee'ray] *vi.* to dare, be bold; *nm.* daring, valour.

Arditezza [ahr-dee-tet'zah] *nf.* daring, hardihood, confidence.

Ardito [ahr-dee'toh] *a.* daring, hardy, confident.

Ardore [ahr-doh'ray] *nm.* ardour, enthusiasm.

Arduo [ahr'doo-oh] *a.* arduous, difficult, dangerous.

Area [ah'ray-ah] *nf.* area, surface.

Arena [ah-ray'nah] *nf.* sand, amphitheatre.

Arena/re [ah-ray-nah'ray] *vi.* to run aground; —rsi *vr.* to stick fast, be in difficulties.

Areoplano [ah-ray-oh-plah'noh] *nm.* aeroplane.

Argenteria [ahr-jen-tay-ree'ah] *nf.* silver-plate.

Argentiera [ahr-jen-tee-ay'rah] *nf.* silver-mine.

Argentiere [ahr-jen-tee-ay'ray] *nm.* silversmith.

Argentino [ahr-jen-tee'noh] *a.* silvery.

Argento [ahr-jen'toh] *nm.* silver; *a.* vivo [vee'voh] mercury, quick-silver.

Argilla [ahr-jeel'lah] *nf.* argil, potter's clay.

Argilloso [ahr-jeel-loh'soh] *a.* clayey.

Arginare [ahr-jee-nah'ray] *vt.* to dam, dike, embank.

Argine [ahr'jee-nay] *nm.* bank, dam, embankment.

Argomenta/re [ahr-goh-men-tah'ray] *vi.* to argue, reason; —rsi *vr.* to presume, imagine.

Argomento [ahr-goh-men'toh] *nm.* argument, reason, subject.

Arguire [ahr-gwee'ray] *vi.* to infer.

Argutezza [ahr-goo-tet'zah] *nf.* finesse, quibble, witticism.

Arguto [ahr-goo'toh] *a.* subtle, witty, ingenious.

Arguzia [ahr-goot'zee-ah] *nf.* subtlety, piquancy, joke.

Aria [ah'ree-ah] *nf.* air, wind, appearance, song.

Aridità [ah-ree-dee-tah'] *nf.* aridity, barrenness.

Arido [ah'ree-doh] *a.* arid, barren, dry.

Arieggiare [ah-ree-ay-djah'ray] *vt. and i.* to air.

Aringa [ah-reeng'gah] *nf.* herring.

Arioso [ah-ree-oh'soh] *a.* airy.

Aristocratico [ah-ree-stoh-krah'tee-koh] *a.* aristocratic.

Aristocrazia [ah-ree-stoh-kraht-zee'ah] *nf.* aristocracy.

Aritmetica [ah-reet-may'tee-kah] *nf.* arithmetic.

Aritmetico [ah-reet-may'tee-koh] *nm.* arithmetician; *a.* arithmetical.

Arlecchino [ahr-leck-kee'noh] *nm.* harlequin, buffoon.

Arma [ahr'mah] *nf.* (*mil.*) branch (of the services), service; weapon.

Armadio [ahr-mah'dee-oh] *nm.* cupboard, wardrobe.

Armaiuolo [ahr-mah-ee'oo-oh'loh] *nm.* gunsmith, armourer.

Armamento [ahr-mah-men'toh] *nm.* armament, arming, weapons (*pl.*).

Arma/re [ahr-mah'ray] *vt.* to arm, equip, provide;—**rsi** *vr.* to arm oneself, take up arms.

Armata [ahr-mah'tah] *nf.* army, navy; **corpo d'armata** [kohr'poh dahr-mah'tah] army corps.

Armatura [ahr-mah-too'rah] *nf.* armour, armouring.

Arme [ahr'may] *nf.* arms, weapons (*pl.*), armour; **armi da fuoco** [ahr-mee dah foo-oh'koh] (*pl.*), fire-arms (*pl.*).

Armento [ahr-men'toh] *nm.* herd of cattle.

Armistizio [ahr-mee-stee'tsee-oh] *nm.* armistice.

Armonia [ahr-moh-nee'ah] *nf.* harmony, concord.

Armonizzare [ahr-moh-need zah'ray] *vt. and i.* to harmonise.

Arnese [ahr-nay'say] *nm.* harness, utensil.

Arnia [ahr'nee-ah] *nf.* beehive.

Aro [ah'roh] *nm.* 100 square metres.

Aroma [ah-roh'mah] *nf.* aroma, fragrance.

Arpa [ahr'pah] *nf.* harp.

Arpeggiare [ahr-pay-djah'ray] *vi.* to play the harp, play in arpeggios.

Arpia [ahr-pee'ah] *nf.* harpy.

Arpione [ahr-pee-oh'nay] *nm.* hinge, hook.

Arra [ahr'rah] *nf.* earnest-money, pledge.

Arrabbia/re [ahr-rahb-bee-ah'ray] *vt.* to make angry; —**rsi** *vr.* to get angry.

Arrabbiato [ahr-rahb-bee-ah'toh] *a.* furious.

Arrampicarsi [ahr-rahm-pee-kahr'see] *vr.* to climb.

Arrecare [ahr-ray-kah'ray] *vt.* to bring, cause.

Arredamento [ahr-ray-dah-men'toh] *nm.* furnishing, outfitting.

Arredare [ahr-ray-dah'ray] *vt.* to fit out, furnish.

Arredo [ahr-ray'doh] *nm.* furniture.

Arrena/re [ahr-ray-nah'ray] *vt.* to polish with sand-paper; *vi. and* —**rsi** *vr.* to run aground, be in difficulties.

Arrendersi [ahr-ren'dehr-see] *vr.* to surrender, yield, submit.

Arresta/re [ahr-ress-tah'ray] *vt.* to stop, seize, arrest; —**rsi** *vr.* to stop.

Arresto [ahr-ress'toh] *nm.* arrest, delay; **in a.**, under arrest; **mettere agli arresti** [met'tay-ray ahl'yee ahr-ress'tee] *vt.* (*mil.*) to arrest.

Arretrarsi [ahr-ray-trahr´-
see] *vr.* to flinch, recoil.
Arretrati [ahr-ray-trah´tee]
nm. (*pl.*) arrears (*pl.*).
Arricchi/re [ahr-reek-kee´-
ray] *vt.* to enrich, embellish;
vi. and —**rsi** *vr.* to grow rich,
thrive.
Arricciare [ahr-reech-chah´-
ray] *vi.* to stand on end (of
hair); *vt.* to curl, frizzle.
Arridere [ahr-ree´day-ray] *vi.*
to smile upon.
Arringa [ahr-reeng´gah] *nf.*
harangue, speech.
Arringare [ahr-reeng-gah´-
ray] *vi.* to harangue.
Arrischia/re [ahr-ree-skee-
ah´ray] *vt.* to risk, hazard; *vi.*
and —**rsi** *vr.* to run the risk.
Arrischiato [ahr-ree-skee-
ah´toh] *a.* hazardous, risky.
Arrivare [ahr-ree-vah´ray]
vi. to arrive, get to happen,
understand; **non ci arrivo**
[nonn chee ahr-ree´voh], it is
beyond my comprehension.
Arrivo [ahr-ree´voh] *nm.*
arrival, coming.
Arrogante [ahr-roh-gahn´-
tay] *a.* arrogant, proud.
Arrola/re [ahr-roh-lah´ray]
vt. to enrol, register; —**rsi** *vr.*
to enrol oneself, enlist.
Arrossire [ahr-ross-see´ray]
vi. to blush, be ashamed.
Arrostire [ahr-ross-tee´ray]
vt. to roast, toast.
Arrosto [ahr-ross´toh] *nm.*
roast meat.
Arrotare [ahr-roh-tah´ray] *vt.*
to whet, grind, wear smooth.
Arrotino [ahr-roh-tee´noh]
nm. knife-grinder.
Arrotolare [ahr-roh-toh-lah´-
ray] *vt.* to roll.
Arrovella/re [ahr-roh-vell-
lah´ray] *vt.* to irritate, make
mad; —**rsi** *vr.* to get angry.
Arroventare [ahr-roh-ven-
tah´ray] *vt.* to make red-hot.

Arrovescia/re [ahr-roh-vay-
shah´ray] *vt.* to turn inside
out, overthrow; —**rsi** *vr.* to
get upset, turn over.
Arrovescio [ahr-roh-vay´-
shoh] *ad.* against the grain,
on the wrong side, the reverse
way.
Arruffa/re [ahr-roof-fah´ray]
vt. to ruffle, tousle, confuse;
—**rsi** *vr.* to get ruffled, confused.
Arruggini/re [ahr-roo-djee-
nee´ray] *vi.*; —**rsi** *vr.* to rust,
grow rusty.
Arsella [ahr-sell´lah] *nf.*
mussel (shellfish).
Arsenale [ahr-say-nah´lay]
nm. arsenal.
Arsura [ahr-soo´rah] *nf.*
burning heat, drought.
Arte [ahr´tay] *nf.* art, artifice,
craft.
Artefice [ahr-tay´fee-chay]
nm. artificer, artisan.
Arteria [ahr-tay´ree-ah] *nf.*
artery.
Artico [ahr´tee-koh] *a.*
Arctic, Northern.
Articolare [ahr-tee-koh-
lah´ray] *vt.* to articulate, pronounce; *a.* articular.
Articolo [ahr-tee´koh-loh]
nm. article, clause; a. di fondo
[dee fon´doh], leading article
(in newspapers).
Artificiale [ahr-tee-fee-chah´-
lay] *a.* artificial.
Artificio [ahr-tee-fee´choh]
nm. artifice, deceit.
Artificioso [ahr-tee-fee-choh´-
soh] *a.* artful, crafty, sly.
Artigianato [ahr-tee-jah-
nah´toh] *nm.* artisans (*pl.*),
arts and crafts (*pl.*).
Artigiano [ahr-tee-jah´noh]
nm. artisan, craftsman; *a.* of
a workman.
Artigliere [ahr-teel-yay´ray]
nm. gunner, artilleryman.
Artiglieria [ahr-teel-yay-

ree'ah] *nf.* (*mil.*) **artillery,** ordnance.

Artiglio [ahr-teel'yoh] *nm.* claw, talon, clutch.

Artista [ahr-tee-stah] *nm. and f.* actor, actress, singer.

Arto [ahr'toh] *nm.* (*an.*), limb, member.

Arzigogolare [ahrd-zee-goh-goh-lah'ray] *vi.* to fancy.

Arzigogolo [ahrd-zee-goh'-goh-loh] *nm.* conceit, fancy, whim.

Arzillo [ahrd-zeel'loh] *a.* sprightly, nimble.

Ascella [ah-shell'lah] *nf.* arm-pit.

Ascendenza [ah-shen-dent'-zah] *nf.* ancestors (*pl.*), ascendancy.

Ascendere [ah-shen'day-ray] *vt.* to climb, ascend; *vi.* to amount to.

Ascenzione [ah-shen-tsee-oh'nay] *nf.* ascent, ascension, Ascension Day.

Ascensore [ah-shen-soh'ray] *nm.* lift.

Ascesa [ah-shay'sah] *nf.* ascent. [abscess.

Ascesso [ah-shess'soh] *nm.*

Asceta [ah-shay'tah] *nm.* ascetic, recluse.

Ascetico [ah-shay'tee-koh] *a.* ascetic.

Ascetismo [ah-shay-tees'-noh] *nm.* asceticism.

Ascia [ah'shah] *nf.* axe, hatchet.

Asciugamano [ah-shoo-gah-mah'noh] *nm.* towel.

Asciugare [ah-shoo-gah'ray] *vt.* to dry, wipe.

Asciutto [ah-shoot'toh] *a.* dry, thin, blunt.

Ascoltare [ah-skohl-tah'ray] *vt.* to listen, attend, (*med.*) auscultate.

Ascoltatore [ah-skohl-tah-toh'ray] *nm.* listener, hearer.

Ascoltazione [ah-skohl-tah-

tsee-oh'nay] *nf.*, **ascolto** [ah-skohl'toh] *nm.* listening, hearing, (*med.*) auscultation; **stare in** [stah'ray een] **ascolto,** to listen, **dare** [dah'ray] **ascolto,** to lend an ear.

Asello [ah-sell'loh] *nm.* whiting (fish). [asphalt.

Asfalto [ah-sfahl'toh] *nm.*

Asfissia [ah-sfees-see'ah] *nf.* asphyxia.

Asfissiare [ah-sfees-see-ah'ray] *vt. and i.* to asphyxiate.

Asilo [ah-zee'loh] *nm.* refuge.

Asina [ah'see-nah] *nf.* she-ass.

Asino [ah'see-noh] *nm.* ass.

Asma [ahs'mah] *nf.* asthma.

Asmatico [ahs-mah'tee-koh] *a.* asthmatic.

Asparago [ah-spah'rah-goh] *nm.* asparagi [ah-spah'rah-jee] *nm.* (*pl.*) asparagus.

Aspergere [ah-spehr'jay-ray] *vt.* to sprinkle.

Asperità [ah-spay-ree-tah'] *nf.* roughness, severity.

Aspetta/re [ah-spet-tah'ray] *vt.* to wait for, await; **—rsi** *vr.* to expect, look for.

Aspettativa [ah-spet-tah-tee'vah], **aspettazione** [ah-spet-tah-tsee-oh'nay] *nf.* expectation, hope; **in** [een] **a.** *ad.* on the reserve-list.

Aspetto [ah-spet'toh] *nm.* air, aspect, appearance, delay, waiting; **sala d'aspetto** [sah'lah dah'spet'toh] *nf.* waiting-room.

Aspirante [ah-spee-rahn'tay] *nm.* candidate, competitor; *a.* aspiring to, sucking up.

Aspirare [ah-spee-rah'ray] *vt.* to aspire to, be a candidate for, suck up.

Aspiratore (di polvere) [ah-spee-rah-toh'ray dee pohl'vay-ray] *nm.* vacuum cleaner.

Aspirina [ah-spee-ree'nah] *nf.* aspirin.

Asportabile [ah-sporr-tah'-

bee-lay'] *a.* fit to be removed, transportable.

Asportare [ah-sporr-tah'ray] *vt.* to carry away, remove, transport.

Asportazione [ah-sporr-taht-see-oh'nay] *nf.* removal.

Asprezza [ah-spret'zah] *nf.* bitterness, harshness, roughness, sharpness.

Asprigno [ah-spreen'yoh] *a.* sourish.

Asprità [ah-spree-tah'] *nf.* sharpness. *v.* **Asprezza.**

Aspro [ah'sproh] *a.* bitter, rough, sharp, severe, sour, uneven.

Assaggiamento [ahs-sah-djah-men'toh] *nm.* assay, tasting, trial.

Assaggiare [ahs-sah-djah'ray] *vt.* to assay, taste, try.

Assaggio [ahs-sah'djoh] *nm.* taste, trial.

Assai [ahs-sah'ee] *nm.* plenty; *ad.* much, very, enough, copiously.

Assalire [ahs-sah-lee'ray] *vt.* to assail, attack.

Assaltare [ahs-sahl-tah'ray] *vt.* to assault, attack.

Assalto [ahs-sahl'toh] *nm.* assault, attack, onset.

Assassinare [ahs-sahs-see-nah'ray] *vt.* to assassinate, murder, destroy.

Assassinio [ahs-sahs-see'nee-oh] *nm.* assassination, murder.

Assassino [ahs-sahs-see'noh] *nm.* assassin, murderer.

Asse [ahs'say] *nm.* axis; *nf.* board, plank.

Assecondare [ahs-say-kon-dah'ray] *vt.* to second, support.

Assediare [ahs-say-dee-ah'ray] *vt.* to besiege, shut up.

Assedio [ahs-say'dee-oh] *nm.* siege, blockade.

Assegnamento [ahs-sayn-yah-men'toh] *nm.* allowance,

assignment, transfer, special task (journalese).

Assegnare [ahs-sayn-yah'-ray] *vt.* to allow, assign, consign, fix (time).

Assegnazione [ahs-sayn-yah-tsee-oh'nay] *nf.* assignment, allowance.

Assegno [ahs-sayn'yoh] *nm.* allowance, fixed income; a. bancario [bahng-kah'ree-oh] (*com.*) draft; a. postale [posstah'lay], money order.

Assemblea [ahs-sem-blay'ah] *nf.* assembly.

Assennatezza [ahs-sen-nah-tet'zah] *nf.* good sense, judgment.

Assennato [ahs-sen-nah'toh] *a.* sensible, judicious.

Assenso [ahs-sen'soh] *nm.* assent, consent.

Assente [ahs-sen'tay] *nm.* absentee; *a.* absent.

Assentimento [ahs-sen-tee-men'toh] *nm.* assent, consent.

Assentire [ahs-sen-tee'ray] *vi.* to assent, consent, allow.

Assenza [ahs-sent'zah] *nf.* absence.

Assenzio [ahs-sent'zee-oh] *nm.* absinthe.

Asserire [ahs-say-ree'ray] *vt.* to assert, affirm.

Asseraglia/re [ahs-say-rahl-yah'ray] *vt.* to barricade; —rsi *vr.* to barricade oneself.

Asserzione [ahs-serr-tsee-oh'nay] *nf.* assertion, declaration.

Assessore [ahs-sess-soh'ray] *nm.* assessor, magistrate.

Assestamento [ahs-sess-tah-men'toh], **assesto** [ahs-sess'toh] *nm.* arrangement, settlement.

Assestare [ahs-sess-tah'ray] *vt.* to arrange, settle, set in order, adjust, deliver (a blow).

Assetato [ahs-say-tah'toh] *a.* dry, eager, thirsty.

Assetta/re [ahs-set-tah′ray] vt. to adjust, arrange, trim; —rsi vr. to adorn onself, to put oneself to rights; a. i capelli [ee kah-pell′lee] to do one's hair.

Assetto [ahs-set′toh] nm. arrangement, settlement, decoration (for festivals); mettere [met′tay-ray] in a., to put in order, tidy.

Asseverare [ahs-say-vay-rah′ray] vi. to assert, asseverate.

Assicura/re [ahs-see-koo-rah′ray] vt. to secure, protect, certify, insure, make sure, register (letters, etc.); —rsi vr. to insure, secure, guard oneself.

Assicurazione [ahs-see-koo-rah-tsee-oh′nay] nf. assurance, insurance.

Assideramento [ash-see-day-rah-men′toh] nm. assiderazione [ahs-see-day-rah-tsee-oh′nay] nf. numbness, freezing.

Assiderare [ahs-see-day-rah′ray] vt. and i, to chill, benumb, be benumbed (with cold), freeze.

Assiduità [ahs-see-doo-ee-tah′] nf. assiduity, diligence.

Assiduo [ahs-see′doo-oh] a. assiduous, diligent.

Assieme [ahs-see-ay′may] ad. together.

Assillare (di domande) [ahs-seel-lah′ray dee doh-mahn′day] vt. to bombard with questions, heckle.

Assimilare [ahs-see-mee-lah′ray] vt. to assimilate.

Assimilazione [ahs-see-mee-lah-tsee-oh′nay] nf. assimilation.

Assisa [ahs-see′zah] nf. livery, uniform; corte d'assise [korr′tay dahs-see′zay] nf. assizes (pl.).

Assistente [ahs-sees-ten′tay] nm. attendant, assistant, by-stander.

Assistenza [ahs-sees-tent′zah] nf. assistance, aid, help.

Assistere [ahs-sees′tay-ray] vt. to assist, help; vi. to be present.

Asso [ahs′soh] nm. ace (at cards or dice).

Associa/re [ahs-soh-chah′ray] vt. to associate, join, take into partnership; —rsi vr. to join, become a partner.

Assoggetta/re [ahs-soh-djet-tah′ray] vt. to subject, subdue; —rsi vr. to subject oneself, submit.

Assolato [ahs-soh-lah′toh] a. exposed to the sun, sunny.

Assolda/re [ahs-soll-dah′ray] vt. to recruit; —rsi vr. to enlist.

Assolto [ahs-soll′toh] a. acquitted, absolved, released.

Assoluto [ahs-soh-loo′toh] a. absolute, positive.

Assoluzione [ahs-soh-loo-tsee-oh′nay] nf. absolution, acquittal.

Assolvere [ahs-soll′vay-ray] vt. to acquit, absolve, release.

Assomiglia/re [ahs-soh-meel-yah′ray] vt. to compare, make a comparison; —rsi vr. to be like, resemble.

Assonnacchiato [ahs-sohn-nahk-kee-ah′toh] a. drowsy, sleepy.

Assopi/re [ahs-soh-pee′ray] vi. —rsi vr. to become drowsy, doze off.

Assorbente [ahs-sorr-ben′tay] a. absorbent; a. igienico [ee-jay′nee-koh] nm. sanitary towel.

Assorbire [ahs-sorr-bee′ray] vt. to absorb, suck up.

Assordamento [ahs-sorr-dah-men′toh] nm. stunning, deafening.

Assordare [ahs-sor-dah′ray] vt. to stun, deafen; vi. to grow deaf.

Assortimento [ahs-sorr-tee-men′toh] nm. assortment, lot.

Assortire [ahs-sorr-tee′ray] vt. to sort, match.

Assorto [ahs-sorr′toh] a. absorbed.

Assottiglia/re [ahs-sot-teel-yah′ray] vt. to sharpen, refine, subtilise; —rsi vr. to grow thin, diminish.

Assuefa/re [ahs-soo-ay-fah′ray] vt. to accustom, inure; —rsi vr. to grow accustomed, inured.

Assumere [ahs-soo′may-ray] vt. to assume, undertake, take up.

Assunto [ahs-soon′toh] nm. assumption, charge, office.

Assunzione [ahs-soon-tsee-oh′nay] nf. assumption, elevation.

Assurdità [ahs-soor-dee-tah′] nf. absurdity, incongruity.

Assurdo [ahs-soor′doh] nm. absurdity, nonsense; a. absurd, incongruous.

Asta [ah′stah] nf. pole, staff, rod, lance, part of a letter above or below the line; vendere all'asta [venn′day-ray ahl lah-stah] vt. to sell by auction.

Astante [ah-stahn′tay] nm. assistant, bystander; a. present, standing-by.

Astemio [ah-stay′mee-oh] nm. abstainer; a. abstemious.

Astenersi [ah-stay-nehr′see] vr. to abstain.

Astensione [ah-sten-see-oh′nay] nf. abstention.

Astia/re [ah-stee-ah′ray] vt. to envy, grudge; —rsi vr. to hate each other, bear a mutual grudge.

Astinente [ah-stee-nen′tay] a. abstinent, temperate.

Astinenza [ah-stee-nent′zah] nf. abstinence, temperance.

Astio [ah′stee-oh] nm. envy, grudge, spite.

Astioso [ah-stee-oh′soh] a. envious, spiteful.

Astrar/re [ah-strahr′ray] vt. to abstract; —rsi vr. to turn one's mind from.

Astratto [ah-straht′toh] a. abstract, abstracted.

Astrazione [ah-strah-tsee-oh′nay] nf. abstraction, separation.

Astringente [ah-streen-jen′tay] a. astringent, costive.

Astringere [ah-streen′jay-ray] vt. to compel, force.

Astro [ah-stroh] nm. star.

Astrologia [ah-stroh-loh-jee′ah] nf. astrology.

Astrologico [ah-stroh-loh′jee-koh] a. astrological.

Astrologo [ah-stroh′loh-goh] nm. astrologer.

Astronomia [ah-stroh-noh-mee′ah] nf. astronomy.

Astronomico [ah-stroh-noh′mee-koh] a. astronomical.

Astronomo [ah-stroh′noh-moh] nm. astronomer.

Astruso [ah-stroo′zoh] a. abstruse, obscure.

Astuccio [ah-stooch′choh] nm. box, case, sheath.

Astutezza [ah-stoo-tet′zah] nf. cunning, artifice, deceit.

Astuto [ah-stoo′toh] a. crafty, cunning, deceitful.

Astuzia [ah-stoot′zee-ah] nf. craft, cunning, art.

Ateismo [ah-tay-ees′moh] nm. atheism.

Ateista [ah-tay-ee′stah], **Ateo** [ah′tay-oh] nm. atheist.

Ateistico [ah-tay-ees′tee-koh] a. atheistic.

Ateneo [ah-tay-nay′oh] nm. athenæum, university.

Atlante [aht-lahn′tay] nm. atlas.

Atlantico [aht-lahn'tee-koh] *nm.* Atlantic; *a* herculean.

Atleta [aht-lay'tah] *nm.* athlete, wrestler.

Atmosfera [aht-moh-sfay'rah] *nf.* atmosphere.

Atomico [ah-toh'mee-koh] *a.* atomic.

Atomo [ah'toh-moh] *nm.* atom, corpuscle.

Atonia [ah-toh-nee'ah] *nf.* atony.

Atono [ah'toh-noh] *a.* unstressed.

Atrio [ah'tree-oh] *nm.* porch, vestibule.

Atro [ah'troh] *a.* black, dreadful.

Atroce [ah-troh'chay] *a.* atrocious, frightful.

Atrocità [ah-troh-chee-tah'] *nf.* atrocity.

Atrofia [ah-troh-fee'ah] *nf.* atrophy.

Atrofizzare [ah-troh-feet-zah'ray] *vi.* to atrophy. waste away.

Attaccabottone [aht-tahk-kah-bot-toh'nay] *nm.* great talker.

Attaccamento [aht-tahk-kah-men'toh] *nm.* attachment.

Attaccapanni [aht-tahk-kah-pahn'nee] *nm.* hat-stand.

Attacca/re [aht-tahk-kah'ray] *vt.* to stick, tie, fasten, sew on, attack, put to (horses); *a.* un bottone [oon bot-toh'nay] to buttonhole someone; —rsi *vr.* to stick to, become attached to, quarrel.

Attacco [aht-tahk'koh] *nm.* attack, assault; (*elec.*) connection, plug.

Attecchire [aht-teck-kee'ray] *vi.* to grow, thrive.

Atteggiamento [aht-tay-djah-men'toh] *nm.* attitude, posture.

Atteggia/re [aht-tay-djah'-]

ray] *vt.* to animate, give the right expression to; —rsi *vr.* to strike the right attitude.

Attempato [aht-tem-pah'toh] *a.* elderly.

Attendare [aht-ten-dah'ray] *vt. and i.* to encamp.

Attendente [aht-ten-den'tay] *nm.* (*mil.*) soldier-servant, batman.

Attendere [aht-ten'day-ray] *vt. and i.* to await, expect, attend to.

Attenta/re [aht-ten-tah'ray] *vt.* to attempt, venture; —rsi *vr.* to expose oneself, dare.

Attentato [aht-ten-tah'toh] *nm.* criminal attempt, crime.

Attenti! [aht-ten'tee] *int.* (*mil.*) attention!

Attento [aht-ten'toh] *a.* attentive, careful.

Attenuante [aht-tay-noo-ahn'tay] *nm.* palliating circumstance; *a.* attenuating.

Attenuare [aht-tay-noo-ah'ray] *vt.* to attenuate, lessen.

Attenzione [aht-ten-tsee-oh'nay] *nf.* attention, application.

Atterraggio [aht-tehr-rah'djoh] *nm.* landing (of aircraft).

Atterrare [aht-tehr-rah'ray] *vt.* to cast down, overthrow; *vi.* to land (of aircraft or by parachute).

Atterri/re [aht-tehr-ree'ray] *vt.* to frighten, terrify; —rsi *vr.* to be afraid, terrified.

Attesa [aht-tay'sah] *nf.* expectation.

Atteso [aht-tay'soh] *a.* awaited, expected.

Attestato [aht-tess-tah'toh] *nm.* attestation, certificate.

Attestazione [aht-tess-tah-tsee-oh'nay] *nf.* attestation, testimony.

Attiguità [aht-tee-goo-ee-tah'] *nf.* contiguity.

Attiguo [aht-tee'goo-oh] a. contiguous, adjacent, next.

Attillarsi [aht-teel-lahr'see] vr. to dress smartly, dress so as to show off one's figure.

Attillato [aht-teel-lah'toh] a. smartly dressed, close-fitting.

Attimo [aht'tee-moh] nm. moment, instant.

Attinente [aht-tee-nen'tay] a. contiguous, belonging to.

Attinenza [aht-tee-nent'zah] nf. affinity, relationship.

Attingere [aht-teen'jay-ray] vt. to draw (water, etc.), to get (information, etc.).

Attira/re [aht-tee-rah'ray] vt. —rsi vr. to attract, draw, obtain.

Attitudine [aht-tee-too'dee-nay] nf. skill, aptitude, attitude.

Attivare [aht-tee-vah'ray] vt. to put (set) in motion.

Attività [aht-tee-vee-tah'] nf. activity, influence, assets (pl.).

Attivo [aht-tee'voh] a. active, enterprising; debiti attivi [day' bee-tee aht-tee'vee] nm. (pl.) (com.) outstanding credits.

Attizzare [aht-teet-zah'ray] vt. to stir up, poke the fire, irritate.

Attizzatoio [aht-teet-zah-toh'yoh] nm. poker.

Atto [aht'toh] nm. act, deed, gesture, sign; a. fit, proper, suitable.

Attonito [aht-toh'nee-toh] a. astonished, amazed.

Attorcere [aht-torr'chay-ray], **attorcigliare** [aht-torr-cheel-yah'ray] vt. to twist, wring.

Attorcigliamento [aht-torr-cheel-yah-men'toh] nm. twisting.

Attore [aht-toh'ray] nm. actor.

Attorniare [aht-torr-nee-ah'ray] vt. to enclose, surround.

Attorno [aht-torr'noh] pr. about, round; ad. round-about.

Attossicare [aht-toss-see-kah'ray] vt. to poison.

Attossicazione [aht-toss-see-kah-tsee-oh'nay] nf. poisoning.

Attraente [aht-trah-en'tay] a. attractive.

Attrappire [aht-trahp-pee'ray] vt. to numb.

Attrarre [aht-trahr'ray] vt. to attract, allure.

Attratti/va [aht-traht-tee' vah] nf. —vo [-voh] nm. attraction.

Attraversa/re [aht-trah-vehr-sah'ray] vt. to cross, traverse, thwart; —rsi vt. to oppose oneself to.

Attraverso [aht-trah-vehr' soh] ad. across, through; wrong.

Attrazione [aht-trah-tsee-oh'nay] nf. attraction, inducement.

Attrezzare [aht-tret-zah' ray] vt. to rig, equip.

Attrezzo [aht-tret'zoh] nm. tool, instrument.

Attribui/re [aht-tree-boo-ee'ray] vt. to ascribe, attribute, impute; —rsi vr. to claim.

Attributo [aht-tree-boo'toh] nm. attribute, essential quality.

Attrice [aht-tree'chay] nf. actress.

Attrupparsi [aht-troop-pahr'see] vr. to gather in crowds, flock together.

Attuabile [aht-too-ah'bee-lay] a. practicable, feasible.

Attuabilità [aht-too-ah-bee-lee-tah'] nf. feasibility.

Attuale [aht-too-ah'lay] a. topical, present, effective, real, actual.

Attualità [aht-too-ah-lee-tah'] nf. reality, topicality

Attuare [aht-too-ah´ray] *vt.* to effect, execute, perform, realise.

Attuazione [aht-too-ah-tsee-oh´nay] *nf.* actuation.

Attuffa/re [aht-toof-fah´ray] *vt.* to dip, immerse, plunge; —**rsi** *vr.* to dive, plunge into the water.

Attuosità [aht-too-oh-see-tah´] *nf.* " pure act."

Attutire [aht-too-tee´ray] *vt.* to calm, ease, silence, still.

Audace [ow-dah´chay] *a.* audacious, bold.

Auditore [ow-dee-toh´ray] *nm.* auditor, hearer.

Audizione [ow-dee-tsee-oh´nay] *nf.* audition.

Auge [ow´jay] *nm.* apogee; **essere in** [ess´say-ray een] *a. vi.* to be at the zenith of one's fortune.

Augurare [ow-goo-rah´ray] *vt. and i.* to wish, augur, foretell.

Augurio [ow-goo´ree-oh] *nm.* good wish, augury, omen.

Augusto [ow-goo´stoh] *a.* august, royal.

Aula [ow´lah] *nf.* hall, classroom, royal palace.

Aumentare [ow-men-tah´ray] *vt.* to augment, extend, increase.

Aumento [ow-men´toh] *nm.* growth, increase.

Aura [ow´rah] *nf.* (*poet.*) air, gentle breeze.

Aureo [ow´ray-oh] *a.* golden, gilded.

Aureola [ow-ray´oh-lah] *nf.* halo, glory. [dawn.

Aurora [ow-roh´rah] *nf.*

Ausiliare [ow-zee-lee-ah´ray] *a.* auxiliary.

Ausilio [ow-zee´lee-oh] *nm.* help, assistance.

Auspicio [ow-spee´choh] *nm.* auspice, protection, patronage.

Auspicioso [ow-spee-choh´soh] *a.* (*poet.*) auspicious.

Austerità [ow-stay-ree-tah´] *nf.* austerity, severity.

Austero [ow-stay´roh] *a.* austere, severe.

Autenticare [ow-ten-tee-kah´ray] *vt.* to authenticate, prove.

Autenticità [ow-ten-tee-chee-tah´] *nf.* authenticity.

Autentico [ow-ten´tee-koh] *a.* authentic.

Autista [ow-tee´stah] *nm.* driver, chauffeur.

Auto [ow´toh] *nf.* motor-car; a. **pubblica** [poob´blee-kah] taxi.

Autobiografia [ow-toh-bee-oh-grah-fee´ah] *nf.* autobiography.

Autoblinda [ow-toh-bleen´dah], **auto blindata** [bleen-dah´tah] *nf.* armoured car.

Autobus [ow-toh´boos] *nm.* bus, omnibus.

Autocorriera [ow-toh-korr-ree-ay´rah] *nf.* long-distance bus (which carries the mail).

Autocrazia [ow-toh-kraht-zee´ah] *nf.* autocracy.

Autografia [ow-toh-grah-fee´ah] *nf.* autography.

Autografo [ow-toh´grah-foh] *nm.* autograph; *a.* autographic.

Automa [ow-toh´mah] *nm.* automaton.

Automatico [ow-toh-mah´tee-koh] *a.* automatic.

Automobile [ow-toh-moh´bee-lay] *nm. and f.* motor-car; **a. di piazza** [dee-peeaht´zah], taxi.

Autonomia [ow-toh-noh-mee´ah] *nf.* autonomy, self-government, (*mil.*) range.

Autonomo [ow-toh´noh-moh] *a.* autonomous, self-governing.

Autopsia [ow-top-see´ah] *nf.* autopsy. [author.

Autore [ow-toh´ray] *nm.*

Autorevole [ow-toh-ray´voh-lay] _a._ authoritative, competent.

Autorimessa [ow-toh-ree-mess'sah] _nf._ garage.

Autorità [ow-toh-ree-tah'] _nf._ authority.

Autorizzare [ow-toh-reed-zah'ray] _vt._ to authorise.

Autorizzazione [ow-toh-reed-zah-tsee-oh'nay] _nf._ authorisation, permit.

Autostrada [ow-toh-strah'dah] _nf._ main road (specially made for motor-traffic).

Autrice [ow-tree'chay] _nf._ authoress.

Autunnale [ow-toon-nah'lay] _a._ autumnal.

Autunno [ow-toon'noh] _nm._ autumn.

Avambraccio [ah-vahm-brahch'choh] _nm._ fore-arm.

Avanguardia [ah-vahn-gwahr'dee-ah] _nf._ vanguard.

Avanti [ah-vahn'tee] _ad. and pr._ before, forward, in front of, rather; _int._ forward!

Avantieri [ah-vahn-tee-ay'ree] _ad._ the day before yesterday.

Avanzamento [ah-vahnt-zah-men'toh] _nm._ advancement, promotion, progress.

Avanza/re [ah-vahnt-zah'ray] _vt._ to advance, promote, augment, improve, save, put by, have owing to one; _vi._ to be over, remain; —rsi _vr._ to get on, improve.

Avanzata [ah-vahnt-zah'tah] _nf._ advance.

Avanzo [ah-vahnt'zoh] _nm._ remainder, remnant, residue, ancient ruin; d'avanzo, _ad._ over and above.

Avaria [ah-vah-ree'ah] _nf._ damage (from accident).

Avaria/re [ah-vah-ree-ah'ray] _vi._ —rsi _vr._ to sustain damage.

Avarizia [ah-vah-ree'tsee-ah] _nf._ avarice, niggardliness.

Avaro [ah-vah'roh] _nm._ miser; _a._ avaricious, miserly.

Ave! [ah'vay] _int._ hail!

Avena [ah-vay'nah] _nf._ oats.

Avere [ah-vay'ray] _vt. and aux._ to have, hold, possess; _nm._ property, wealth, inheritance.

Aviatore [ah-vee-ah-toh'ray] _nm._ airman, flyer.

Aviazione [ah-vee-ah-tsee-oh'nay] _nf._ aviation.

Avidità [ah-vee-dee-tah'] _nf._ avidity, greed.

Avido [ah'vee-doh] _a._ avid, greedy.

Aviolinea [ah-vee-oh-lee'nay-ah] _nf._ air company, air-line.

Aviorimessa [ah-vee-oh-ree-mess'sah] _nf._ hangar.

Avorio [ah-voh'ree-oh] _nm._ ivory.

Avvallamento [ah-vahl-lah-men'toh] _nm._ cavity, subsidence, falling-in.

Avvalla/re [ah-vahl-lah'ray] _vt._ to let down; _vi. and_ —rsi _vr._ to fall in, subside.

Avvalora/re [ah-vahl-loh-rah'ray] _vt._ to strengthen, animate; —rsi _vr._ to take courage.

Avvampa/re [ah-vahm-pah'ray] _vi._ to burn, be on fire, be inflamed; —rsi _vr._ to blaze up, grow red with anger.

Avvantaggia/re [ah-vahn-tah-djah'ray] _vt._ to advantage; —rsi _vr._ to better oneself, derive advantage.

Avvantaggio [ah-vahn-tah'djoh] _nm._ advantage, profit.

Avvedersi [ahv-vay-dehr'see] _vr._ to perceive, find.

Avvedutezza [ah-vay-doo-tet'zah] _nf._ foresight, sagacity.

Avveduto [ahn-vay-doo'toh] _a._ cautious, provident, sagacious.

Avvegnacchè [ahv-vayn-yahk-kay'] _con._ although.

Avvelenamento [ahv-vay-lay-nah-men'toh] *nm.* poisoning.

Avvelenare [ahv-vay-lay-nah'ray] *vt.* to poison.

Avvenente [ahv-vay-nen'tay] *a.* agreeable, attractive.

Avvenenza [ahv-vay-nent'zah] *nf.* attractiveness, grace.

Avvenimento [ahv-vay-nee-men'toh] *nm.* event, accident, accession (to the throne).

Avvenire [ahv-vay-nee'ray] *v. imp.* to happen; *nm.* future.

Avventato [ahv-ven-tah'toh] *a.* imprudent, rash.

Avventizio [ahv-ven-teet'tsee-oh] *a.* adventitious.

Avvento [ahv-ven'toh] *nm.* advent, arrival.

Avventore [ahv-ven-toh'ray] *nm.* customer, purchaser.

Avventura [ahv-ven-too'rah] *nf.* adventure, chance.

Avventura/re [ahv-ven-too-rah'ray] *vt.* to risk, hazard; —**rsi** *vr.* to run the risk.

Avventuriere [ahv-ven-too-ree-ay'ray] *nm.* adventurer.

Avventuroso [ahv-ven-too-roh'soh] *a.* lucky, fortunate.

Avvera/re [ahv-vay-rah'ray] *vt.* to confirm; —**rsi** *vr.* to come true.

Avverbio [ahv-vehr'bee-oh] *nm.* adverb.

Avversare [ahv-vehr-sah'ray] *vt.* to oppose, resist, thwart.

Avversario [ahv-vehr-sah'ree-oh] *nm.* adversary; *a.* adverse, contrary.

Avversione [ahv-vehr-see-oh'nay] *nf.* aversion, dislike.

Avversità [ahv-vehr-see-tah'] *nf.* adversity.

Avverso [ahv-vehr'soh] *a.* adverse, bad for; *pr.* against, facing.

Avvertente [ahv-vehr-ten'tay] *a.* careful, circumspect.

Avvertenza [ahv-vehr-tent'zah] *nf.* circumspection, pre-

caution, preface, warning note.

Avvertimento [ahv-vehr-tee-men'toh] *nm.* advice, warning.

Avvertire [ahv-vehr-tee'ray] *vt.* to advise, inform, perceive, warn; *vi.* to mind, pay attention to.

Avvezzo [ahv-vet'zoh] *a.* accustomed, used.

Avviamento [ahv-vee-ah-men'toh] *nm.* setting-out, beginning, start.

Avvia/re [ahv-vee-ah'ray] *vt.* to set going, prepare, begin, start (an engine); —**rsi** *vr.* to get going, bend one's steps.

Avviato [ahv-vee-ah'toh] *a.* prosperous.

Avvicenda/re [ahv-vee-chen-dah'ray] *vi.* to alternate; —**rsi** *vr.* to change by turns, take turns.

Avvicina/re [ahv-vee-chee-nah'ray] *vt.* to put near; —**rsi** *vr.* to approach, draw near.

Avvilimento [ahv-vee-lee-men'toh] *nm.* humiliation, discouragement.

Avvili/re [ahv-vee-lee'ray] *vt.* to abase, humiliate; —**rsi** *vr.* to humiliate oneself, lose courage.

Avviluppa/re [ahv-vee-loop-pah'ray] *vt.* to entangle, wrap up; —**rsi** *vr.* to get bewildered.

Avvisaglia [ahv-vee-zahl'yah] *nf.* skirmish.

Avvisa/re [ahv-vee-zah'ray] *vt.* to advise, inform, warn, judge; —**rsi** *vr.* to think, imagine.

Avvisato [ahv-vee-zah'toh] *a.* cautious, prudent.

Avviso [ahv-vee'zoh] *nm.* advice, news, bill, advertisement, announcement, warning; **a mio** [ah mee'oh] **a.,** in my opinion.

Avvitare [ahv-vee-tah'ray] *vt.* to screw.

Avviticchia/re [ahv-vee-teek-kee-ah'ray] *vt.* to twine, twist; —**rsi** *vr.* to be entwined.

Avvizzire [ahv-veet-zee'ray] *vi.* to fade, wither.

Avvocato [ahv-voh-kah'toh] *nm.* lawyer, advocate, solicitor, defender.

Avvolge/re [ahv-voll'jay-ray] *vt.* to wrap round, entwine; —**rsi** *vr.* to wrap oneself, get involved in.

Avvolta/re [ahv-voll-tah'ray] *vt.* to wrap up, turn round; —**rsi** *vr.* to wind round.

Avvoltoio [ahv-voll-toh'yoh] *nm.* vulture.

Azienda [ah-tzee-en'dah] *nf.* management, business, firm.

Azione [ah-tzee-oh'nay] *nf.* action, deed, battle, movement, share.

Azionista [ah-tzee-oh-nee'stah] *nm.* share-holder, stock-holder.

Azzannare [aht-zahn-nah'ray] *vt.* to seize with the teeth.

Azzarda/re [ahd-zahr-dah'ray] *vt.* to hazard; risk; —**rsi** *vr.* to run the risk.

Azzardo [ahd-zahr'doh] *nm.* hazard, risk; giuoco [joo-oh'koh] d'a. game of chance.

Azzardoso [ahd-zahr-doh'soh] *a.* hazardous, risky.

Azzeccare [aht-zeck-kah'ray] *vt.* to hit the mark, guess, chance on.

Azzima [ahd'zee-mah] *nf.* unleavened bread.

Azzimo [ahd-zee-moh] *a.* unleavened.

Azzuffarsi [aht-zoof-fahr'see] *vr.* to come to blows, scuffle.

Azzurro [ahd-zoor'roh] *a.* blue, azure.

B

Babbeo [bahb-bay'oh] *nm.* blockhead.

Babbo [bahb'boh] *nm.* (*fam.*) Daddie.

Babbuccia [bahb-booch'chah] *nf.* slipper.

Babbuino [bahb-boo-ee'noh] *nm.* baboon, monkey.

Babordo [bah-borr'doh] *nm.* (*naut.*) larboard.

Bacare [bah-kah'ray[*vi.* to be worm-eaten.

Bacca [bahk'kah] *nf.* berry.

Baccalà [bahk-kah-lah'] *nm.* stock-fish, cod dried and salted.

Baccano [bahk-kah'noh] *nm.* great noise, tumult.

Baccellierato [bahch-chell-lee-ay-rah'toh] *nm.* bachelor's degree.

Baccelliere [bahch-chell-lee-ay'ray] *nm.* bachelor (academic).

Baccello [bahch-chell'loh] *nm.* husk, pod, shell.

Bacchetta [bahk-ket'tah] *nf.* rod, staff, stick, wand, mahlstick.

Bacherozzo [bah-kay-roht'zoh] *nm.* grub, worm.

Bacia/re [bah-chah'ray] *vt.* to kiss; —**rsi** *vr.* to exchange a kiss.

Bacile [bah-chee'lay] *nm.* [basin.

Bacillo [bah-cheel'loh] *nm.* bacillus.

Bacinetto [bah-chee-net'toh] *nm.* helmet, casket.

Bacino [bah-chee'noh] *nm.* basin, wash-hand basin; (*an.*) pelvis.

Bacio [bah'choh] *nm.* kiss.

Baco [bah'koh] *nm.* worm, silk-worm hankering, fancy.

Bada, tenere a [tay-nay'ray ah bah'dah] *vt.* to keep waiting, put off with promises.

Badare [bah-dah'ray] *vt.* to mind, pay attention to, take care of.

Badessa [bah-dess'sah] *nf.* abbess.

Badia [bah-dee'ah] *nf.* abbey.

Baff/o [bahf'foh] *nm.* moustache;—i [ee] (*pl.*) whiskers; **coi** [koh'ee]—i, *ad.* (*fam.*) elegant, smart.

Baffuto [bahf-foo'toh] *a.* heavily moustached.

Bagagliaio [bah-gahl-yah'yoh] *nm.* luggage-van, guard's van.

Bagaglio [bah-gahl'yoh] *nm.* **bagagli** [bah-gahl-yee] *nm.* (*pl.*) luggage.

Bagattella [bah-gaht-tell'lah] *nf.* trifle, small matter.

Bagliore [bah-lyoh'ray] *nm.* flash of light, lightning.

Bagnante [bahn-yahn'tay] *nm. and f.* bather.

Bagna/re [bahn-yah'ray] *vt.* to moisten, wet, bath;—**rsi** *vr.* to bathe.

Bagnatura [bahn-yah-too'rah] *nf.* bathing, bathing-season.

Bagnino [bahn-yee'noh] *nm.* bath-attendant.

Bagno [bahn'yoh] *nm.* bath, tank.

Bagordo [bah-gorr'doh] *nm.* orgy, revelling, riot.

Baia [bah'yah] *nf.* bay; joke, banter.

Baio [bah'yoh] *a.* bay, chestnut-colour.

Baionetta [bah-ee-oh-net'tah] *nf.* bayonet.

Balaustrata [bahl-ow-strah'tah] *nf.* balustrade.

Balbettare [bahl-bet-tah'ray] *vi.* to stammer, stutter.

Balbettio [bahl-bet-tee'oh] *nm.*, **balbuzie** [bahl-boot'zee-ay] *nf.* stammer(ing).

Balbuziente [bahl-boot-zee-en'tay] *a.* stammering, stuttering.

Balcone [bahl-koh'nay] *nm.* balcony, french window.

Baldanza [bahl-dahnt'zah] *nf.* boldness, haughtiness.

Baldanzoso [bahl-dahnt-zoh'soh] *a.* bold, valiant.

Baldo [bahl'doh] *a.* bold, haughty.

Baldoria [bahl-doh'ree-ah] *nf.* bonfire; **fare** [fah-ray] **b.** *vi.* to feast, make merry.

Balena [bah-lay'nah] *nf.* whale.

Balenare [bah-lay-nah'ray] *vi.* to flash, lighten.

Baleniera [bah-lay-nee-ay'rah] *nf.* whaling, whaler (ship).

Balenio [bah-lay-nee'oh] *nm.* continuous lightning.

Baleno [bah-lay'noh] *nm.* lightning; **in un** [een oon] **b.** *ad.* immediately.

Balia [bah'lyah] *nf.* wet-nurse.

Balìa [bah-lee'ah] *nf.* power, authority.

Balla [bahl'lah] *nf.* bale, bundle, pack.

Ballabile [bahl-lah'bee-lay] *a.* that may be danced to (music, etc.).

Ballare [bahl-lah'ray] *vi.* to dance.

Ballata [bahl-lah'tah] *nf.* dancing-song, ballad.

Ballatoio [bahl-lah-toh'yoh] *nm.* gallery, platform.

Ballerina [bahl-lay-ree'nah] *nf.* dancer, dancing-girl, ballet-dancer.

Ballerino [bahl-lay-ree'noh] *nm.* dancer, dancing partner.

Balletto [bahl-let'toh] *nm.* ballet, interlude.

Ballo [bahl'loh] *nm.* ball, dance.

Ballonzolare [bahl-lont-zoh-lah'ray] *vi.* to dance a little, hop about.

Ballotta [bahl-lot'tah] *nf.* boiled chestnut.

Ballottare [bahl-lot-tah'ray] vi. to ballot, vote.

Balneario [bahl-nay-ah'ree-oh] a. bathing.

Balocca/re [bah-lock-kah'ray] vt. to amuse; —rsi vr. to amuse oneself, dally, toy with.

Balocco [bah-lock'koh] nm. plaything, toy.

Balordaggine [bah-lorr-dah'djee-nay] nf. stupidity.

Balordo [bah-lorr'doh] nm. fool, numskull; a. stupid.

Balsamo [bahl'sah-moh] nm. balm, balsam.

Baluardo [bah-loo-ahr'doh] nm. bastion, bulwark.

Balza [bahlt'zah] nf. cliff, rock; flounce.

Balzare [bahlt-zah'ray] vi. to bounce, jump, spring.

Balzo [bahlt'zoh] nm. jump, spring.

Bambagia [bahm-bah'jah] nf. cotton-wool.

Bambina [bahm-bee'nah] nf. little girl.

Bambinaia [bahm-bee-nah'yah] nf. children's nurse.

Bambinesco [bahm-bee-ness'koh] a. childish.

Bambino [bahm-bee'noh] nm. little boy.

Bambola [bahm'boh-lah] nf. doll.

Bambù [bahm-boo'] nm. bamboo.

Banale [bah-nah'lay] a. common, trivial.

Banalità [bah-nah-lee-tah'] nf. commonplace, vulgarity.

Banano [bah-nah'noh] nm. banana-(tree).

Banca [bahng'kah] nf. bank.

Bancario [bahng-kah'ree-oh] a. pertaining to a bank.

Bancarotta [bahng-kah-rot'tah] nf. fraudulent bank failure, bankruptcy; fare [fah'ray] b. vi. to go bankrupt.

Bancarottiere [bahng-kah-rot-tee-ay'ray] nm. bankrupt.

Banchetto [bahng-ket'toh] nm. banquet.

Banchiere [bahng-kee-ay'ray] nm. banker.

Banchina [bahng-kee'nah] nf. small bench, quay, wharf, platform (at a station).

Banco [bahng'koh] nm. bench, counter, desk, office, bank, stall; b. di sabbia [dee sahb'bee-ah], sand-bank, shoal.

Bancogiro [bahng-koh-jee'roh] nm. (com.) clearing, transfer.

Banconota [bahng-koh-noh'tah] nf. banknote.

Banda [bahn'dah] nf. band, side, stripe, gang; da [dah] b. ad. aside.

Banderuola [bahn-day-roo-oh'lah] nf. pennon, vane, weather-cock.

Bandiera [bahn-dee-ay'rah] nf. banner, flag.

Bandi/re [bahn-dee'ray] vt. to banish, proclaim; —rsi vr. to go away.

Bandista [bahn-dee'stah] nm. bandsman.

Bandita [bahn-dee'tah] nf. privileged place, preserve.

Bandito [bahn-dee'toh] nm. bandit, outlaw; a. outlawed, exiled.

Banditore [bahn-dee-toh'ray] nm. public crier.

Bando [bahn'doh] nm. ban, banishment.

Bandolo [bahn'doh-loh] nm. head of a skein.

Bara [bah'rah] nf. bier, coffin, litter.

Baracca [bah-rahk'kah] nf. booth, stall, barrack, hut.

Baraonda [bah-rah-on'dah] nf. confusion, disorder, tumult.

Barare [bah-rah'ray] vi. to cheat (at play).

Baratro [bah'rah-troh] nm. abyss, gulf.

Barattare [bah-raht-tah'ray]

vt. to barter, chaffer, exchange, take another's property by mistake.

Baratteria [bahr-raht-tay-ree'ah] *nf.* embezzlement, swindling.

Barattiere [bah-raht-tee-ay'ray] *nm.* barterer, embezzler, swindler.

Barattolo [bah-raht'toh-loh] *nm.* small tin or jar.

Barba [bahr'bah] *nf.* beard, root; **fare la** [fah'ray lah] **b.** *vi.* to shave.

Barbabietola [bahr-bah-bee-ay'toh-lah] *nf.* beetroot.

Barbagianni [bahr-bah-jahn'nee] *nm.* owl, simpleton.

Barbaglio [bahr-bahl'yoh] *nm.* dazzle.

Barbarico [bahr-bah'ree-koh], **barbaro** [bahr'bah-roh] *a.* barbarous, cruel.

Barbarie [bahr-bah'ree-ay], **barbarità** [bahr-bah-ree-tah'] *nf.* barbarity.

Barbicare [bahr-bee-kah'ray] *vi.* to take root.

Barbiera [bahr-bee-ay'rah] *nf.* barber's shop (old-fashioned).

Barbiere [bahr-bee-ay'ray] *nm.* barber.

Barbone [bahr-boh'nay] *nm.* grey-beard; poodle.

Barbugliare [bahr-bool-yah'ray] *vi.* to stammer, stutter.

Barbuglio [bahr-bool'yoh] *nm.* stammering, stuttering.

Barbuto [bahr-boo'toh] *a.* bearded, rooted.

Barca [bahr'kah] *nf.* boat, ferry-boat, business, affair, pile (of hay, wood, etc.).

Barcaccia [bahr-kahch'chah] *nf.* launch, barge; (*theat.*) stage-box.

Barcaiuolo [bahr-kah-ee-oo-oh'loh] *nm.* boatman, ferryman.

Barcamenare [bahr-kah-may-nah'ray] *vi.* to manage cleverly, steer a middle course.

Barcarola [bahr-kah-roh'lah] *nf.* gondolier's song.

Barchett/a [bahr-ket'tah] *nf.* **-o** [oh] *nm.* small boat, skiff.

Barcollare [bahr-koll-lah'ray] *vi.* to rock, sway, totter, waver.

Barcollio [bahr-koll-lee'oh] *nm.* rocking.

Barcone [bahr-koh'nay] *nm.* barge, large boat.

Bardare [bahr-dah'ray] *vt.* to caparison, harness.

Bardo [bahr'doh] *nm.* bard, poet.

Barella [bahr-rell'lah] *nf.* hand-barrow, stretcher.

Bargello [bahr-jell'loh] *nm.* sheriff, spy; prison (in Florence).

Barile [bah-ree'lay] *nm.* barrel, hogshead.

Barlume [bahr-loo'may] *nm.* gleam, glimmer.

Baro [bah'roh] *nm.* cheat, sharper.

Barocciaio [bah-rohch-chah'yoh] *nm.* carter, wagoner, hawker.

Baroccino [bah-rohch-chee'noh] *nm.* small cart, hand-cart.

Baroccio [bah-rohch'choh] *nm.* cart, wagon.

Barocco [bah-rock'koh] *a.* baroque, grotesque.

Barometro [bah-roh'may-troh] *nm.* barometer.

Barone [bah-roh'nay] *nm.* baron.

Barraggio [bahr-rah'djoh] *nm.* barrage.

Barrare [bahr-rah'ray] *vt.* to bar. *v* **Sbarrare**.

Barricare [bahr-ree-kah'ray] *vt.* to barricade.

Barricata [bahr-ree-kah'tah] *nf.* barricade.

Barriera [bahr-ree-ay'rah] *nf.* barrier, palisade.

Baruffa [bah-roof'fah] *nf.* altercation, fray.

Barzelletta [bahrd-zell-let'tah] *nf.* joke, funny story.

Basa/re [bah-zah'ray] *vt.* to base, ground; **—rsi** *vr.* to take one's stand.

Base [bah'zay] *nf.* base, basis, ground; **b. aerea** [ah-ay'ray-ah] air base.

Basett/a [bah-zet'tah] *nf.* moustache; **—e** [ay] (*pl.*) whiskers.

Basilica [bah-zee'lee-kah] *nf.* basilica, cathedral.

Basilico [bah-zee'lee-koh] *nm.* sweet basil.

Bassezza [bahs-set'zah] *nf.* baseness, meanness.

Basso [bahs'soh] *a.* base, low, mean, cheap (price), narrow (stuff).

Bassofondo [bahs-soh-fon'doh] *nm.* (*naut.*) shallow.

Bassorilievo [bahs-soh-ree-lee-ay'voh] *nm.* bas-relief.

Bassotto [bahs-sot'toh] *nm.* tubby man, terrier.

Bassura [bahs-soo'rah] *nf.* low ground.

Basta! [bah'stah] *int.* enough, stop, that will do.

Bastardo [bah-stahr'doh] *nm. and a.* bastard, illegitimate.

Bastare [bah-stah'ray] *v. imp.* to be enough, suffice.

Bastimento [bah-stee-men'toh] *nm.* ship, vessel.

Bastione [bah-stee-oh'nay] *nm.* bastion, rampart.

Bastonare [bah-stoh-nah'ray] *vt.* to beat, cudgel, thrash.

Bastonatura [bah-stoh-nah-too'rah] *nf.* beating, thrashing.

Bastoncino [bah-ston-chee'noh] *nm.* walking-stick.

Bastone [bah-stoh'nay] *nm.* cudgel, stick, truncheon.

Batosta [bah-toh'stah] *nf.* blow (to health), misfortune.

Battaglia [baht-tahl'yah] *nf.* battle.

Battagliare [baht-tahl-yah'ray] *vi.* to combat, fight.

Battagliero [baht-tahl-yay'roh] *a.* fighting, warlike.

Battaglio [baht-tahl'yoh] *nm.* bell-clapper.

Battaglione [baht-tahl-yoh'nay] *nm.* battalion.

Battelliere [baht-tell-lee-ay'ray] *nm.* boatman, waterman.

Battello [baht-tell'loh] *nm.* boat; **b. a vapore** [ah vah-poh'ray], steamer.

Battente [baht-ten'tay] *nm.* leaf (of a door), screen; door-knocker.

Batte/re [baht'tay-ray] *vt.* to beat, knock, thrash, throb, wash (of waves), strike (of clocks); **b. bandiera** [bahn-dee-ay'rah], to sail under colours; **b. cassa** [kahs'sah], to collect money for charity; **b. i denti** [ee den'tee], to chatter (with cold); **b. le mani** [lay mah'nee], to clap; **b. moneta** [moh-nay'tah], to mint money; *vi.* to knock against, insist; **—rsi** *vr.* to fight a duel; **battersela** [baht-tehr'say-lah] *vr.* to run away.

Batteria [baht-tay-ree'ah] *nf.* battery, kitchen utensils (*pl.*).

Battesimale [baht-tay-zee-mah'lay] *a.* baptismal.

Battesimo [baht-tay'zee-moh] *nm.* baptism, christening.

Battezzare [baht-ted-zah'ray] *vt.* to baptise, christen.

Battibecco [baht-tee-beck'koh] *nm.* quarrel.

Batticuore [baht-tee-kwoh'ray] *nm.* fear, palpitation.

Battistero [baht-tee-stay'roh] *nm.* baptistery, font.

Battito [baht'tee-toh] *nm.* beating, palpitation, throbbing.

Battitore [baht-tee-toh'ray] *nm.* beater.

Battuta [baht-too'tah] *nf.* beating, (*mus.*) beat.

Battuto [baht-too'toh] *nm.* floor, stuffing (food); *a.* beaten, trodden.

Battuffolo [baht-toof'foh-loh] *nm.* small wad (of wool, etc.).

Baule [bah-oo'lay] *nm.* trunk, travelling-chest.

Bava [bah'vah] *nf.* foam, froth, slaver; floss-silk.

Bavaglino [bah-vahl-yee'noh] *nm.* child's bib.

Bavaglio [bah-vahl'yoh] *nm.* gag.

Bavero [bah'vay-roh] *nm.* coat-collar, cape of a cloak.

Bavoso [bah-voh'soh] *a.* slavering.

Bazza [bahd'zah] *nf.* jutting chin, person with a jutting chin.

Bazzecola [bahd-zay'koh-lah] *nf.* nonsense, trifle.

Bazzicare [baht-zee-kah'ray] *vt.* to frequent, visit.

Bea/re [bay-ah'ray] *vt.* (*poet.*) to bless; —**rsi** *vr.* to take delight in.

Beatificare [bay-ah-tee-fee-kah'ray] *vt.* to beatify, bless, praise.

Beatificazione [bay-ah-tee-fee-kah-tsee-oh'nay] *nf.* beatification.

Beatitudine [bay-ah-tee-too'dee-nay] *nf.* beatitude, bliss.

Beato [bay-ah'toh] *a.* blessed, fortunate.

Beccaccia [beck-kahch'chah] *nf.* wood-cock.

Beccaio [beck-kah'yoh] *nm.* butcher.

Beccamorti [beck-kah-morr'tee] *nm.* grave-digger.

Becca/re [beck-kah'ray] *vt.* to peck; —**rsi il cervello** [eel chehr-vel'loh] *vr.* to puzzle one's brains (*rare*).

Beccheggiare [beck-kay-djah'ray] *vi.* (*naut.*) to pitch.

Beccheggio [beck-kay'djoh] *nm.* (*naut.*) pitching.

Becchime [beck-kee'may] *nm.* bird-feed.

Becchino [beck-kee'noh] *nm.* sexton.

Becco [beck'koh] *nm.* beak.

Beccuccio [beck-kooch'choh] *nm.* gullet, spout.

Becero [bay'chay-roh] *nm.* (*fam.*) low fellow, rascal.

Becerume [bay-chay-roo'may] *nm.* set of rascals, rogues' meeting-place.

Befana [bay-fah'nah] *nf.* Epiphany; old woman taking the place of Father Christmas in Italian tales; witch, ugly deformed woman.

Beffa [bef'fah] *nf.* jest, mockery, trick.

Beffardo [bef-fahr'doh] *nm.* jester.

Beffa/re [bef-fah'ray] *vt.* to laugh at, ridicule; —**rsi** *vr.* to deride, make game of.

Beffeggiare [bef-fay-djah'ray] *vt.* to deride, mock.

Beghin/a [bay-ghee'nah] *nf.*, —**o** [oh] *nm.* bigot, pietist.

Belare [bay-lah'ray] *vi.* to bleat.

Belletta [bell-let'tah] *nf.* filth, mud. *v.* **Fango**.

Belletto [bell-let'toh] *nm.* paint, rouge.

Bellezza [bell-let'zah] *nf.* beauty.

Bellico [bell'lee-koh], **bellicoso** [bell-lee-koh'soh] *a.* warlike, belligerent.

Bellimbusto [bell-leem-boo'stoh] *nm.* dandy, fop.

Bellino [bell-lee'noh] *a.* nice, pretty.

Bello [bell'loh] *nm.* beauty, the Beautiful; *a.* beautiful, fine, handsome, nice; *ad.* finely, nicely; **il b. è** [eel bell'loh ay] the best of it is that . . .

Beltà [bell-tah'] *nf.* beauty.

Belva [bell'vah] *nf.* wild beast.

Belvedere [bell-vay-day'ray] *nm.* terrace.

Benchè [beng-kay'] *con.* although.

Benda [ben'dah] *nf.* band, bandage, fillet.

Bendare [ben-dah'ray] *vt.* to blindfold.

Bene [bay'nay] *nm.* property, wealth; **beni mobili** [bay-nee moh'bee-lee] *nm. (pl.)* movable property; **beni stabili** [bay-nee stah'bee-lee] real estate; *ad.* well, quite, right; **per [pehr] b.** *a.*, decent, respectable; **voler b. a.** [voh-lehr' bay'nay ah] *vt.* to like, be fond of.

Benedettino [bay-nay-det-tee'noh] *nm.* and *a.* Benedictine.

Benedetto [bay-nay-det'toh] *a.* blessed.

Benedire [bay-nay-dee'ray] *vt.* to bless, consecrate.

Benedizione [bay-nay-dee-tsee-oh'nay] *nf.* benediction, blessing.

Beneducato [bay-nay-doo-kah'toh] *a.* well-bred.

Benefattore [bay-nay-faht-toh'ray] *nm.* benefactor.

Benefattrice [bay-nay-faht-tree'chay] *nf.* benefactress.

Beneficare [bay-nay-fee-kah'ray] *vt.* to benefit, do good to.

Beneficenza [bay-nay-fee-chent'zah] *nf.* beneficence.

Beneficio [bay-nay-fee'choh], **benefizio** [bay-nay-fee'tsee-oh] *nm.* benefice, benefit, living, profit.

Benefico [bay-nay'fee-koh] *a.* beneficent, generous.

Benemerenza [bay-nay-may-rent'zah] *nf.* desert, merit.

Benemerito [bay-nay-may'ree-toh] *a.* deserving, meritorious.

Beneplacito [bay-nay-plah'chee-toh] *nm.* approval, consent, convenience, option.

Benestante [bay-ness-tan'tay] *a.* wealthy, well-to-do.

Benessere [bay-ness'say-ray] *nm.* well-being.

Benestare [bay-nay-stah'ray] *nm.* approval, endorsement.

Benevolenza [bay-nay-voh-lent'zah] *nf.* benevolence, liking.

Benevolo [bay-nay'voh-loh] *a.* benevolent, kind.

Benignità [bay-neen-yee-tah'] *nf.* benignity, goodness.

Benigno [bay-neen'yoh] *a.* benignant, kindly, obliging.

Benino [bay-nee'noh] *ad.* pretty well.

Beninteso [bay-neen-tay'soh] *a.* agreed, understood.

Benone [bay-noh'nay] *ad.* splendidly, very well.

Benportante [behn-porr-tahn'tay] *a.* in good health.

Bensì [behn-see'] *ad.* but, certainly.

Bentornato [behn-torr-nah'toh], **benvenuto** [behn-vay-noo'toh] *nm.* and *a.* welcome.

Benvolere [behn-voh-lay'ray] *vt.* and *vi.* to like, wish well; **farsi** [fahr'see] **b.** *vr.* to make oneself liked, win popularity; *nm.* benevolence, affection.

Benzina [bend-zee'nah] *nf.* benzine, petrol.

Ber/e [bay'ray] *vt.* to absorb, drink; **—rsi una cosa** [oo'nah koh'sah] *vr.* to believe implicitly.

Berlina [behr-lee'nah] *nf.* pillory, berlin.

Berlingaccio [behr-leen-gahch'choh] *nm.* last Thursday before Shrove Tuesday.

Bernesco [behr-ness'koh] *a.* burlesque.

Bernoccolo [behr-nock'koh-loh] *nm.* boss, bump, knob, lump.

Bernoccoluto [behr-nock-koh-loo'toh] *a.* full of bosses or knobs.

Berretta [behr-ret'tah] *nf.* —o [oh] *nm.* bonnet, cap.

Bersagliare [behr-sah-lyah'ray] *vt.* to shoot at a mark.

Bersagliere [behr-sah-lyay'ray] *nm.* sharpshooter.

Bersaglio [behr-sah'lyoh] *nm.* aim, butt, mark, target.

Bertuccia [behr-tooch'chah] *nf.* monkey, ugly woman.

Bestemmia [bess-tem'mee-ah] *nf.* blasphemy, imprecation.

Bestemmiare [bess-tem-mee-ah'ray] *vi.* to blaspheme, swear.

Bestia [bess'tee-ah] *nf.* animal, beast, brute, idiot.

Bestiale [bess-tee-ah'lay] *a.* bestial, brutal, stupid.

Bestialità [bess-tee-ah-lee-tah'] *nf.* bestiality, stupidity.

Bestiame [bess-tee-ah'may] *nm.* cattle.

Bettola [bet'toh-lah] *nf.* ale-house, tavern.

Betulla [bay-tool'lah] *nf.* birch-tree.

Bevanda [bay-vahn'dah] *nf.* drink, potion.

Beveraggio [bay-vay-rah'djoh] *nm.* beverage.

Beveratoio [bay-vay-rah-toh'yoh] *nm.* horse-trough, watering-place.

Bevibile [bay-vee'bee-lay] *a.* drinkable.

Bevitore [bay-vee-toh'ray] *nm.* drinker.

Bevuta [bay-voo'tah] *nf.* draught, drink, drinking-bout.

Bezzica/re [bet-zee-kah'ray] *vt.* to peck, scold; **—rsi** *vr.* to quarrel.

Biacca [bee-ahk'kah] *nf.* white lead, paint.

Biacco [bee-ahk'koh] *nm.* adder, snake.

Biada [bee-ah'dah] *nf.* standing corn, oats.

Biancastro [bee-ahng-kah'stroh], **bianchetto** [bee-ahng-ket'toh] *a.* whitish.

Biancheggiare [bee-ahng-kay-djah'ray] *vi.* to grow white, show white.

Biancheria [bee-ahng-kay-ree'ah] *nf.* linen; clothing and articles made of linen.

Bianchezza [bee-ahng-ket'zah] *nf.*, **biancore** [bee-ahng-koh'ray] *nm.* whiteness, paleness.

Bianco [bee-ahng'koh] *nm.* white(ness), whitewash, blank; **lasciare in** [lah-shah'ray-een] **b.** *vt.* to leave blank; **di punto in** [dee poon'toh een] **b.** *ad.* point-blank; *a.* white, hoary, pale.

Biancospino [bee-ahng-koh-spee'noh] *nm.* hawthorn.

Biancume [bee-ahng-koo'may] *nm.* mass of whitish things.

Biascia [bee-ah'shah] *nf.* saliva, slaver. *v.* Saliva.

Biasi/mabile [bee-ah-zee-mah'bee-lay], **—mevole** [may'voh-lay] *a.* blameworthy, reprehensible.

Biasimare [bee-ah-zee-mah'ray] *vt.* to blame, reprove.

Biasimo [bee-ah'zee-moh] *nm.* blame, reproof.

Bibbia [beeb'bee-ah] *nf.* Bible.

Bibita [bee'bee-tah] *nf.* draught, drink.

Bibliografia [bee-blee-oh-grah-fee'ah] *nf.* bibliography.

Bibliografo [bee-blee-oh'grah-foh] *nm.* bibliographer.

Bibliologia [bee-blee-oh-loh-jee'ah] *nf.* bibliology.

Biblioteca [bee-blee-oh-tay'-kah] *nf.* library.

Bibliotecario [bee-blee-oh-tay-kah'ree-oh] *nm.* librarian.

Bicchiere [beek-kee-ay'ray] *nm.* drinking-glass, tumbler.

Bicchierino [beek-kee-ay-ree'noh] *nm.* small glass.

Bicicletta [bee-chee-klet'tah] *nf.* bicycle.

Bidello [bee-dell'loh] *nm.* beadle, janitor, porter, usher.

Bidone [bee-doh'nay] *nm.* receptacle (tin).

Bieco [bee-ay'koh] *a.* grim, squinting; *ad.* askance.

Biennale [bee-en-nah'lay] *a.* biennial.

Biennio [bee-en'nee-oh] *nm.* space of two years.

Bietola [bee-ay'toh-lah] *nf.* beet.

Bifolco [bee-foll'koh] *nm.* boor, ploughman, rustic.

Biforcarsi [bee-forr-kahr'see] *vr.* to divide, fork.

Bigamia [bee-gah-mee'ah] *nf.* bigamy.

Bigamo [bee'gah-moh] *nm.* bigamist.

Bighellonare [bee-ghell-loh-nah'ray] *vi.* to idle, loaf, lounge.

Bighellone [bee-ghell-loh'nay] *nm.* idler, loafer.

Bigio [bee'joh] *a.* grey.

Biglietteria [beel-yet-tay-ree'ah] *nf.* booking-hall, ticket-office.

Bigliettaio [beel-yet-ah'-yoh] *nm.* booking-clerk, conductor (on bus, etc.).

Biglietto [beel-yet'toh] *nm.* card, letter, note, ticket; b. andata e ritorno [ahn-dah'tah ay ree-torr'noh], return ticket.

Bigottismo [bee-goht-tees'moh] *nm.* bigotry.

Bigotto [bee-goht'toh] *nm.* bigot, hypocrite.

Bilancia [bee-lahn'chah] *nf.* balance, pair of scales.

Bilanciare [bee-lahn-chah'ray] *vt.* to ponder, weigh.

Bilanciere [bee-lahn-chay'ray] *nm.* pendulum, balance-wheel.

Bilancio [bee-lahn'choh] *nm.* (com.) balance-sheet.

Bilaterale [bee-lah-tay-rah'lay] *a.* bilateral.

Bile [bee'lay] *nf.* anger, bile, wrath.

Biliardo [bee-lee-ahr'doh] *nm.* billiards, billiard-room, billiard-table.

Bilico [bee'lee-koh] *nm.* equipoise, hinge, pivot.

Bilingue [bee-leeng'gway] *a.* bilingual, deceitful.

Bilioso [bee-lee-oh'soh] *a.* bilious, irascible.

Bimbo [beem'bah] *nf.—o* [oh] *nm.* small child.

Bimestrale [bee-may-strah'lay] *a.* bi-monthly.

Binario [bee-nah'ree-oh] *nm.* rail, railway-track; unico [oo'nee-koh] b. single-track; doppio [dop'pee-oh] b., double-track; *a.* binary, double.

Bindoleria [been-doh-lay-ree'ah] *nf.* artifice, trick.

Bindolo [been'doh-loh] *nm.* reel, winder, drum (for raising and discharging water); cheater.

Binoccolo [bee-nock'koh-loh] *nm.* field-glass, opera-glass.

Bioccolo [bee-ock'koh-loh] *nm.* flock of wool.

Biografia [bee-oh-grah-fee'ah] *nf.* biography.

Biografo [bee-oh'grah-foh] *nm.* biographer.

Biologia [bee-oh-loh-jee'ah] *nf.* biology.

Biondeggiare [bee-on-day-djah'ray] *vi.* to grow yellow (of corn).

Biondezza [bee-on-det'zah] *nf.* fairness, flaxen colour.

Biondo [bee-on'doh] a. blond, fair, flaxen.

Bipartizione [bee-pahr-tee-tsee-oh'nay] nf. division into two parts.

Bipede [bee'pay-day] a. biped, two-legged.

Biplano [bee-plah'noh] nm. biplane.

Birbante [beer-bahn'tay] nm. rogue, dishonest fellow.

Birbonata [beer-boh-nah'tah] nf. roguish act.

Birbone [beer-boh'nay] nm. bad fellow, rascal; **freddo** [fred'doh] b., bitter cold.

Birboneria [beer-boh-nay-ree'ah] nf. knavery, roguery.

Bircio [beer'choh] a. short-sighted. v. Miope.

Birichinata [bee-ree-kee-nah'tah] nf. mischievous trick.

Birichino [bee-ree-kee'noh] nm. little scamp, urchin; a. mischievous, roguish.

Birilli [bee-reel'lee] nm. (pl.) ninepins (pl.).

Biroccino [bee-rohch-chee'noh] nm. small cart, barrow.

Biroccio [bee-rohch'choh] nm. cart, trap.

Birra [beer'rah] nf. beer.

Birraio [beer-rah'yoh] nm. brewer, beer-seller.

Birreria [beer-ray-ree'ah] nf. beer-shop, brewery, beer-garden.

Birro [beer'roh] nm. police-man (contemptuous).

Bis! [beez] int. encore.

Bisaccia [bee-zahch'chah] nf. knapsack.

Bisbetico [bees-bay'tee-koh] a. hot-tempered, shrewish.

Bisbigliare [bees-beel-yah'ray] vi. to whisper.

Bisbiglio [bees-beel'yoh] nm. whisper, rumour.

Bisca [bees'kah] nf. gaming-house, gaming-den.

Biscaiuolo [bees-kah-ee-oo-oh'loh] nm. gamester.

Biscia [bee'shah] nf. adder, snake.

Biscottino [bees-koht-tee'noh] nm. biscotto [bees-koht'toh] nm. biscuit.

Bisestile [bee-zess-tee'lay] a. bissextile; **anno** [ahn'noh] b., leap-year.

Bislacco [bees-lahk'koh] a. capricious, whimsical.

Bislungo [bees-loong'goh] a. oblong. [bismuth.

Bismuto [bees-moo'toh] nm. **Bisogna** [bee-zohn'yah] nf. business.

Bisognare [bee-zohn-yah'ray] v. imp. to need, want.

Bisognevole [bee-zohn-yay'voh-lay] nm. requisite, what is necessary; a. needful, necessary.

Bisognoso [bee-zohn-yoh'soh] a. indigent, needy.

Bistecca [bee-steck'kah] nf. beef-steak.

Bisticcia/re [bee-steech-chah'ray] vi., —rsi vr. to dispute, quarrel.

Bistrattare [bee-straht-tah'ray] vt. to ill-treat, offend, wrong.

Bisunto [bee-zoon'toh] a. very greasy.

Bitorzolo [bee-tort'zoh-loh] nm. knob, pimple, wart.

Bitorzoluto [bee-tort-zoh-loo'toh] a. gnarled, knotty, pimply.

Bitume [bee-too'may] nm. bitumen.

Bivaccare [bee-vahk-kah'ray] vi. to bivouac.

Bivacco [bee-vahk'koh] nm. bivouac. [bivalve.

Bivalvo [bee-vahl'voh] a. **Bivio** [bee'vee-oh] nm. cross-roads (pl.).

Bizantino [beet-zahn-tee'noh] a. Byzantine.

Bizza [beed'zah] *nf.* choler, rage.

Bizzarro [beed-zahr'roh] *a.* bizarre, odd, queer.

Bizzeffe, a [ah beed-zef'fay] *ad.* galore, in quantity.

Bizzoso [beed-zoh'soh] *a.* angry, choleric.

Blandizie [blahn-dee-tsee-ay] *nf.* (*pl.*) blandishments (*pl.*), wheedling.

Blando [blahn'doh] *a.* affable, bland, wheedling.

Blasone [blah-zoh'nay] *nm.* blazonry.

Blesare [blay-zah'ray] *vi.* to lisp (in pronunciation).

Bleso [blay'zoh] *a.* lisping.

Blindamento [bleen-dah-men'toh] *nm.* **blindatura** [bleen-dah-too'rah] *nf.* armour-plating.

Blindare [bleen-dah'ray] *vt.* to armour-plate.

Bloccare [block-kah'ray] *vt.* to block, blockade.

Blocco [block'koh] *nm.* block, blockade.

Blù [bloo] *a.* blue.

Bluastro [bloo-ah'stroh] *a.* bluish.

Blusa [bloo'zah] *nf.* blouse.

Boa [boh'ah] *nf.* boa (serpent), boa (for the neck); (*naut.*) buoy.

Boato [boh-ah'toh] *nm.* bellowing, thundering.

Bocca [bock'kah] *nf.* mouth, aperture, opening; *a.* [ah] **b.** *ad.* by word of mouth; **a b. aperta** [ah-pehr'tah] *ad.* open-mouthed.

Boccale [bock-kah'lay] *nm.* decanter.

Boccata [bock-kah'tah] *nf.* mouthful.

Boccheggiare [bock-kay-djah'ray] *vi.* to gasp for air.

Bocchino [bock-kee'noh] *nm.* cigarette-holder, mouth-piece.

Boccia [bohch-chah] *nf.* bud, sprout, water-bottle; **bocce**

[bohch'chay] *nf.* (*pl.*) bowls (*pl.*).

Bocciare [bohch-chah'ray] *vt.* and *i.* to fail (in an exam.).

Bocciatura [bohch-chah-too'rah] *nf.* failure (in an exam.).

Boccio [bohch'choh] *nm.* bud.

Bocciolo [bohch-choh'loh] *nm.* bud, reed.

Bocconcino [bock-kon-chee'noh] *nm.* tit-bit.

Boccone [bock-koh'nay] *nm.* mouthful, bribe.

Bocconi [bock-koh'nee] *ad.* prone, face-downwards.

Bofonchiare [boh-fong-kee-ah'ray] *vi.* to grumble, mutter.

Boia [boh'yah] *nm.* executioner, hangman.

Boicottaggio [boh-ee-kot-tah'djoh], **boicotto** [boh-ee-kot'toh] *nm.* boycotting.

Boicottare [boh-ee-kot-tah'ray] *vt.* to boycott.

Bolgetta [boll-jet'tah] *nf.* attache-case, brief-case.

Bolgia [boll'jah] *nf.* dark hole, pit; portmanteau.

Bolide [boh'lee-day] *nm.* meteor, thunder-bolt.

Bolla [boll'lah] *nf.* blister, bubble, papal bull, seal.

Bollare [boll-lah'ray] *vt.* to confirm, mark, seal, stamp.

Bollatura [boll-lah-too'rah] *nf.* sealing, stamping.

Bollente [boll-len'tay] *a.* boiling, fiery.

Bolletta [boll-let'tah] *nf.* bill, certificate, note, receipt.

Bollettino [boll-let-tee'noh] *nm.* bulletin, schedule; **b. meteorologico** [may-tay-oh-roh-loh'jee-koh], weather-forecast, weather-report.

Bollicina [boll-lee-chee'nah] *nf.* small bubble, pimple.

Bollire [boll-lee'ray] *vt.* to boil; *vi.* to boil, bubble up.

Bollitura [boll-lee-too'rah] *nf.* boiling, bubbling.

Bollo [boll'loh] *nm.* seal, stamp.

Bollore [boll-loh'ray] *nm.* boiling, excessive heat.

Bolsaggine [boll-sah'djee-nay] *nf.* pursiness, shortness of wind.

Bolso [boll'soh] *a.* asthmatical.

Bomba [bom'bah] *nf.* bomb, shell; b. a mano [ah mah'noh], hand-grenade; b. a scoppio ritardato [ah skop'pee-oh ree-tahr-dah'toh], delayed-action bomb; b. chimica [kee'mee-kah], gas-bomb; b. esplosiva [ay-sploh-zee'vah], high-explosive bomb; b. fumogena [foo-moh'jay-nah] smoke-bomb; b. incendiaria [een-chen-dee-ah'ree-ah], incendiary bomb.

Bombardamento [bom-bahr-dah-men'toh] *nm.* bombardment, bombing.

Bombardare [bom-bahr-dah'ray] *vt.* to bombard, bomb.

Bonaccia [bo-nahch'chah] *nf.* calm (at sea), tranquillity.

Bonaccione [bo-nahch-choh'nay] *nm.* good-humoured fellow.

Bonarietà [boh-nah-ree-ay-tah'] *nf.* good-humour, good-nature.

Bonario [boh-nah'ree-oh] *a.* good-humoured.

Bongustaio [bon-goo-stah'yoh] *nm.* gourmand.

Bonifica [boh-nee'fee-kah] *nf.* land reclamation.

Bonificare [boh-nee-fee-kah'ray] *vt.* to reclaim land, put under cultivation.

Bontà [bon-tah'] *nf.* goodness, kindness.

Bontempone [bon-tem-poh'nay] *nm.* free-liver.

Borbogliare [borr-bohl-yah'ray] *vi.* to mutter, rumble.

Borboglio [borr-bohl'yoh] *nm.* rumbling.

Borbottamento [borr-bot-tah-men'toh], borbottio [borr-bot-tee'oh] *nm.* grumbling, muttering.

Borbottare [borr-bot-tah'ray] *vi.* to grumble, mutter.

Borchia [borr'kee-ah] *nf.* boss, stud.

Bordo [borr'doh] *nm.* border, (*naut.*) board; a. [ah] b. ad. on board.

Borea [boh'ray-ah] *nm.* North wind.

Borgata [borr-gah'tah] *nf.* small cluster of houses, hamlet.

Borghese [borr-gay'zay] *nm.* citizen, civilian; a. bourgeois, civilian.

Borghesia [borr-gay-zee'ah] *nf.* the middle classes; citizenship.

Borghetto [borr-ghet'toh] *nm.* small village.

Borgo [borr'goh] *nm.* village (usually on a hill and often walled).

Borioso [boh-ree-oh'soh] *a.* arrogant, vainglorious.

Borraccia [borr-rahch'chah] *nf.* leather bottle, canteen.

Borraccina [borr-rahch-chee'nah] *nf.* kind of moss.

Borro [borr'roh] *nm.* ravine.

Borsa [borr'sah] *nf.* bag, purse, brief-case, Exchange; b. di studio [dee stoo'dee-oh], bursary, scholarship.

Borsaiuolo [borr-sah-ee-oo-oh'loh] *nm.* cut-purse, pick-pocket.

Borseggiare [borr-say-djah'ray] *vt.* to rob, pick one's pocket.

Borseggio [borr-say'djoh] *nm.* bag-snatching, robbery.

Borsellino [borr-sell-lee'noh] *nm.* fob, purse, small pocket.

Borsista [borr-see′stah] *nm.* stock-broker.

Boscaglia [boss-kahl′yah] *nf.* woods (*pl.*), forest.

Boscaiuolo [boss-kah-ee-oo-oh′loh] *nm.* wood-cutter, wood-man.

Boschereccio [boss-kay-rehch′choh] *a.* sylvan, woody.

Boschetto [boss-ket′toh] *nm.* grove, small wood.

Boschivo [boss-kee′voh] *a.* woody.

Bosco [boss′koh] *nm.* wood, forest.

Boscoso [boss-koh′soh] *a.* wooded.

Bosso [boss′soh], **bossolo** [boss′soh-loh] *nm.* box-plant, box-wood.

Botanica [boh-tah′nee-kah] *nf.* botany.

Botola [boh′toh-lah] *nf.* trap-door.

Botta [bot′tah] *nf.* toad, blow.

Bottaio [bot-tah′yoh] *nm.* cooper.

Botte [bot′tay] *nf.* barrel, cask, pipe (of wine).

Bottega [bot-tay′gah] *nf.* shop, work-shop.

Bottegaio [bot-tay′gah-yoh] *nm.* shop-keeper, shopman.

Botteghino [bot-tay-ghee′noh] *nm.* small shop, ticket-office.

Bottiglia [bot-teel′yah] *nf.* bottle.

Bottiglieria [bot-teel-yay-ree′ah] *nf.* bar, wine-shop.

Bottino [bot-tee′noh] *nm.* booty, pillage.

Botto [bot′toh] *nm.* blow; di [dee] *b. ad.* suddenly, directly.

Bottone [bot-toh′nay] *nm.* bud, button, cuff-link.

Bove [boh′vay] *nm.* ox.

Bovile [boh-vee′lay] *nm.* ox-stall, byre.

Bozza [bod′zah] *nf.* rough draught, proof sheet, sketch.

Bozzetto [bod-zet′toh] *nm.* outline, sketch.

Bozzo [bod′zoh] *nm.* pool.

Bozzolo [bot′zoh-loh] *nm.* cocoon.

Braccetto [brahch-chet′toh] *nm.* small arm; a [ah] *b. ad.* arm-in-arm.

Bracciale [brahch-chah′lay] *nm.* armlet.

Braccialetto [brahch-chah-let′toh] *nm.* bracelet.

Bracciante [brahch-chahn′tay] *nm.* labourer.

Bracciata [brahch-chah′tah] *nf.* armful.

Braccio [brahch′choh] *nm.* arm, branch, inlet; might.

Bracciuolo [brahch-choo-oh′loh] *nm.* elbow-rest, hand-rail; sedia a bracciuoli [say′dee-ah ah brahch-choo-oh′lee] *nf.* arm-chair.

Bracco [brahk′koh] *nm.* hound, hunting-dog.

Brace [brah′chay] *nf.* embers (*pl.*), coke.

Brache [brah′kay] *nf.* (*pl.*) breeches (*pl.*).

Braciere [brah-chay′ray] *nm.* brazier, warming-pan.

Braciola [brah-choh′lah] *nf.* chop, cutlet, steak.

Braitare [brah-ee-tah′ray] *vi.* to cry, shout. *v.* **Sbraitare.**

Brama [brah′mah] *nf.* desire, eagerness, longing.

Bramare [brah-mah′ray] *vt.* to desire, long for.

Bramosia [brah-moh-see′ah] **bramosità** [brah-moh-see-tah′] *nf.* longing.

Bramoso [brah-moh′soh] *a.* eager, longing.

Branchie [brahng′kee-ay] *nf.* (*pl.*) gills of fishes (*pl.*).

Branco [brahng′koh] *nm.* band, flock, herd.

Brancolare [brahng-koh-lah′ray] *vi.* to grope.

Brancolone [brahng-koh-loh'nay]—i [ee] *ad.* groping.

Branda [brahn'dah] *nf.* cot, hammock.

Brandello [brahn-dell'loh] *nm.* fragment, rag, tatter.

Brandire [brahn-dee'ray] *vt.* to brandish.

Brano [brah'noh] *nm.* extract, passage, piece.

Bravare [brah-vah'ray] *vt.* to brave, defy.

Braveggiare [brah-vay-djah'ray] *vi.* to bluster, swagger.

Braveria [brah-vay-ree'ah] *nf.* bravado, boastful threat.

Bravo [brah'voh] *nm.* cutthroat; *a.* brave, clever, honest.

Bravura [brah-voo'rah] *nf.* bravery, spirit.

Breccia [brehch'chah] *nf.* breach.

Brefotrofio [bray-foh-troh'-fee-oh] *nm.* orphanage.

Bretelle [bray-tell'lay] *nf.* (*pl.*) braces (*pl.*).

Breve [bray'vay] *nm.* brief; *a.* brief, concise, short; in [een] b. *ad.* in short.

Brevettare [bray-vet-tah'ray] *vt.* to license, patent.

Brevetto [bray-vet'toh] *nm.* license, patent.

Breviario [bray-vee-ah'ree-oh] *nm.* breviary.

Brevità [bray-vee-tah'] *nf.* brevity, conciseness.

Brezza [bred'zah] *nf.* breeze.

Bricco [breek'koh] *nm.* coffee-pot, jug.

Bricconata [breek-koh-nah'-tah], **bricconeria** [breek-koh-nay-ree'ah] *nf.* roguery, trick.

Briccone [breek-koh'nay] *nm.* rascal, rogue; *a.* rascally.

Briciola [bree'choh-lah] *nf.* crumb, bit of bread.

Briga [bree'gah] *nf.* affair, business, quarrel, trouble; attaccare [aht-tahk-kah'ray] b. *vi.* to quarrel; darsi

[dahr'see] b. *vi.* to take pains.

Brigadiere [bree-gah-dee-ay'ray] *nm.* brigadier.

Brigantaggio [bree-gahn-tah'djoh] *nm.* brigandage.

Brigante [bree-gahn'tay] *nm.* brigand.

Brigantesco [bree-gahn-tess'koh] *a.* of a brigand.

Brigare [bree-gah'ray] *vt.* to solicit; *vi.* to busy oneself, strive.

Brigata [bree-gah'tah] *nf.* brigade, company, party.

Briglia [breel'yah] *nf.* bridle, reins (*pl.*).

Brillante [breel-lahn'tay] *nm.* diamond; *a.* bright, brilliant.

Brillare [breel-lah'ray] *vi.* to glitter, shine, sparkle.

Brillo [breel'loh] *a.* merry, tipsy.

Brina [bree'nah], **brinata** [bree-nah'tah] *nf.* hoar-frost, rime.

Brinare [bree-nah'ray] *v. imp.* to be white with frost.

Brindare [breen-dah'ray] *vi.* to drink one's health, toast.

Brindello [breen-dell'loh] *nm.* rag, tatter.

Brindisi [breen'dee-zee] *nm.* health, toast.

Brio [bree'oh] *nm.* fire, spirit, vivacity.

Brioso [bree-oh'soh] *a.* lively, spirited, vivacious.

Brivido [bree'vee-doh] *nm.* shiver, shudder.

Brizzolato [breet-zoh-laht'toh] *a.* speckled, spotted.

Brocca [brock'kah] *nf.* jar, jug, pitcher.

Broccato [brock-kah'toh] *nm.* brocade.

Broccolo [brock'koh-loh] *nm.* broccoli, sprout, tendril.

Brodo [broh'doh] *nm.* broth, soup.

Brogliare [brohl-yah'ray] *vt.* to intrigue.

Broglio [broh'lyoh] nm. intrigue.

Bromo [broh'moh], **bromuro** [broh-moo'roh] nm. bromide.

Bronchite [brong-kee'tay] nf. bronchitis.

Broncio [bron'choh] nm. anger, sulkiness;—tenere il [tay-nay'ray eel] b. vi. to sulk.

Bronco [brong'koh] nm. stem, trunk; bronchi [brong'kee] (pl.) bronchi (pl.).

Brontolare [bron-toh-lah'ray] vi. to grumble.

Bronzo [brond'zoh] nm. bronze.

Brucare [broo-kah'ray] vt. to browse.

Bruciacchiare [broo-chahk-kee-ah'ray] vt. to scorch, burn.

Bruciapelo, a [ah broo-chah-pay'loh] ad. at point-blank range, suddenly.

Bruciare [broo-chah'ray] vt. to burn.

Bruciata [broo-chah'tah] nf. roast chestnut.

Brucio [broo'choh], **bruco** [broo'koh] nm. caterpillar, grub.

Bruciore [broo-choh'ray] nm. itch, smart.

Brughiera [broo-ghee-ay'rah] nf. heath.

Brulicame [broo-lee-kah'may] nm. swarm.

Brulicare [broo-lee-kah'ray] vi. to crowd, swarm.

Brulichio [broo-lee-kee'oh] nm. buzzing, swarming.

Brullo [brool'loh] a. bare, sterile.

Bruma [broo'mah] nf. midwinter.

Bruno [broo'noh] nm. mourning; a. brown, dark, gloomy.

Bruschezza [broos-ket'zah] nf. brusqueness, rudeness.

Brusco [broos'koh] a. brusque, rude, tart.

Brutale [broo-tah'lay] a. brutal, rough.

Brutalità [broo-tah-lee-tah'] nf. brutality, roughness.

Bruto [broo'toh] nm. animal, brute; a. brutal, unreasoning.

Brutta/re [broot-tah'ray] vt. to dirty, soil, stain;—rsi vr. to get dirty.

Bruttezza [broot-tet'zah] nf. ugliness.

Brutto [broot'toh] a. dirty, nasty, ugly.

Buaggine [boo-ah'djee-nay] nf. stupidity.

Bubbola [boob'boh-lah] nf. peewit, idle tale.

Bubbolo [boob'boh-loh] nm. little bell.

Bubbone [boob-boh'nay] nm. (med.) bubo.

Bubbonico [boob-boh'nee-koh] a. bubonic.

Buca [boo'kah] nf. cave, hole; b. delle lettere (dell'lay let-tay-ray], letter-box.

Bucaneve [boo-kah-nay'vay] nf. snowdrop.

Bucare [boo-kah'ray] vt. to bore, pierce, tap (a cask).

Bucato [boo-kah'toh] nm. wash(ing), clean linen.

Buccia [boot'chah] nf. bark, husk, peel, rind, skin.

Buccola [book'koh-lah] nf. earring, pendant.

Bucherellare [boo-kay-rell-lah'ray] vt. to bore holes in.

Buco [boo'koh] nm. hole, round opening.

Budellame [boo-dell-lah'may] nm. bowels, entrails (pl.).

Budello [boo-dell'loh] nm. bowels (pl.), gut, intestine.

Bue [boo'ay] nm. ox, dunce.

Bufera [boo-fay'rah] nf. hurricane, whirlwind.

Buffa [boof'fah] nf. hood.

Buffare [boof-fah'ray] vi. to blow. v. Sbuffare, Soffiare.

Buffetto [boof-fet'toh] *nm.* buffet (restaurant).
Buffo [boof'foh] *nm.* comedian, puff, whiff; *a.* comic, droll, funny, queer.
Buffonata [boof-foh-nah'tah] *nf.* silly trick.
Buffone [boof-foh'nay] *nm.* buffoon, jester.
Bugia [boo-jee'ah] *nf.* lie, flat-candlestick.
Bugiardo [boo-jahr'doh] *nm.* liar; *a.* lying.
Bugigattolo [boo-jee-gaht'toh-loh] *nm.* very small room, cubby-hole.
Buio [boo'ee-oh] *nm.* darkness, obscurity; *a.* dark, obscure; essere al [ess'say-ray ahl] b. *vi.* to be ignorant of.
Bulbo [bool'boh] *nm.* bulb.
Bulino [boo-lee'noh] *nm.* (*tech.*) graver.
Bulletta [bool-let'tah] *nf.* permit, small nail.
Bullettino [bool-let-tee'noh] *nm.* bulletin. [bolt.
Bullone [bool-loh'nay] *nm.*
Buongusto [b(oo-)on-goo'stoh] *nm.* good taste, judgment.
Buono [boo-oh'noh] *nm.* bond, coupon; *a.* able, fit, good, kind; a buon mercato [ah boo'on mehr-kah'toh] *ad.* cheap; di buon'ora [dee boo'oh noh'rah] *ad.* early.
Burattino [boo-raht-tee'noh] *nm.* puppet, flighty person.
Burbanza [boor-bahnt'zah] *nf.* arrogance, insolent bearing.
Burbero [boor'bay-roh] *a.* crabbed, morose.
Burchiello [boor-kee-ell'loh], **burchio** [boor'kee-oh] *nm.* ferry-boat.
Burla [boor'lah] *nf.* banter, joke, trick; per [pehr] b. *ad.* in fun.

Burla/re [boor-lah'ray] *vt. and i.* to jest, ridicule; —rsi *vr.* to laugh at, make fun of.
Burlesco [boor-less'koh] *a.* burlesque, ludicrous.
Burletta [boor-let'tah] *nf.* farce, jest, joke.
Burlevole [boor-lay'voh-lay] *a.* laughable, ludicrous.
Burlone [boor-loh'nay] *nm.* jester, joker.
Burocratico [boo-roh-krah'tee-koh] *nm.* bureaucrat; *a.* bureaucratic.
Burocrazia [boo-roh-kraht-zee'ah] *nf.* bureaucracy.
Burrasca [boor-rahs'kah] *nf.* storm, tempest.
Burrascoso [boor-rahs-koh'soh] *a.* stormy, tempestuous.
Burro [boor'roh] *nm.* butter.
Burrone [boor-roh'nay] *nm.* ravine. [search.
Busca [boos'kah] *nf.* quest,
Busca/re [boos-kah'ray] *vt.* to earn, gain; —rsi *vr.* to bring upon oneself.
Busillis [boo-zeel'lees] *nm.* chief difficulty, trouble.
Bussare [boos-sah'ray] *vt.* to beat, knock.
Busse [boos'say] *nf.* (*pl.*) beating, blows (*pl.*).
Bussola [boos'soh-lah] *nf.* mariner's compass, sedan-chair; perdere la [pehr'day-ray lah] b. *vi.* to be at one's wits-ends.
Bussolotto [boos-soh-lot'toh] *nm.* dice-box.
Busta [boo'stah] *nf.* case, cover, envelope.
Bustaia [boo-stah'yah] *nf.* corset-maker.
Busto [boo'stoh] *nm.* bust, corset, stays (*pl.*).
Butta/re [boot-tah'ray] *vt.* to throw; b. all'aria [ahl lah'ree-ah] *vt.* to throw up, upset; —rsi *vr.* to throw oneself, give oneself up to.

Buttero [boot'tay-roh] nm. pock-mark.

B.V. [bee vee] = Beata Vergine [bay-ah'tah Vehr'jee-nay] nf. the Blessed Virgin.

C

Cabina [kah-bee'nah] nf. cabin; c. telefonica [tay-lay-foh'nee-kah] call-box.

Cablografare [kah-bloh-grah-fah'ray] vi. to cable.

Cablogramma [kah-bloh-grahm'mah] nm. cablegram.

Cacao [kah-kah'oh] nm. cocoa, cocoa-tree.

Caccia [kahch'chah] nf. chase, hunt, pursuit, shooting; andare a [ahn-dah'ray-ah] c. vi. to go shooting.

Cacciagione [kahch-chah-joh'nay] nf. game, venison.

Caccia/re [kahch-chah'ray] vt. to chase, hunt, go hunting, pursue, thrust; c. un grido [oon gree'doh], to utter a cry; —rsi vr. to intrude, thrust one's way into.

Cacciatore [kahch-chah-toh'ray] nm. hunter, sportsman.

Cacciatorpediniera [kahch-chah-torr-pay-dee-nee-ay'rah] nf. (torpedo-boat) destroyer.

Cacciavite [kahch-chah-vee'tay] nf. screw-driver.

Cacio [kah'choh] nm. cheese.

Cadavere [kah-dah'vay-ray] nm. corpse, carcass.

Cadaverico [kah-dah-vay'ree-koh] a. cadaverous, corpselike.

Cadente [kah-den'tay] a. falling.

Cadenzato [kah-dent-zah'toh] a. measured, rhythmical.

Cadere [kah-day'ray] vi. to fall.

Cadetto [kah-det'toh] nm. cadet; a. younger.

Caducità [kah-doo-chee-tah'] nf. decay, frailty.

Caduco [kah-doo'koh] a. frail, infirm, old.

Caduta [kah-doo'tah] nf. fall, ruin. [café.

Caffè [kahf-fay'] nm. coffee.

Caffettiera [kahf-fet-tee-ay'rah] nf. coffee-pot.

Caffettiere [kahf-fet-tee-ay'ray] nm. café proprietor.

Cagionare [kah-joh-nah'ray] vt. to cause, occasion.

Cagione [kah-joh'nay] nf. cause, pretext, reason; a [ah] c. di [dee] pr. on account of.

Cagionevole [kah-joh-nay'voh-lay] a. sickly, weak.

Caglio [kahl'yoh] nm. rennet.

Cagna [kahn'yah] nf. bitch.

Cagnesco [kahn-yess'koh] a. currish, surly.

Cagnolino [kahn-yoh-lee'noh] nm. pretty little dog.

Calabrone [kah-lah-broh'nay] nm. hornet.

Calamaio [kah-lah-mah'yoh] nm. ink-stand, cuttle-fish.

Calamità [kah-lah-mee-tah'] nf. calamity, misfortune.

Calamita [kah-lah-mee'tah] nf. loadstone.

Calamitare [kah-lah-mee-tah'ray] vt. to magnetise.

Calamitoso [kah-lah-mee-toh'soh] a. calamitous, miserable.

Calamo [kah-lah-moh] nm. pen, reed.

Calare [kah-lah'ray] vt. to let down, lower; vi. to decrease, descend, fall (of prices).

Calca [kahl'kah] nf. crowd, throng.

Calcagno [kahl-kahn'yoh] nm. heel.

Calcare [kahl-kah'ray] vt.

to lay stress on, trace (a drawing), tread on.

Calce [kahl'chay] *nf.* lime; *nm.* bottom, foot; in [een] **c. a** [ah] *ad.* at the foot.

Calciare [kahl-chah'ray] *vt. and i.* to kick.

Calciatore [kahl-chah-toh'ray] *nm.* player (at football).

Calcina [kahl-chee'nah] *nf.* lime, mortar.

Calcinaio [kahl-chee-nah'yoh] *nm.* lime-kiln.

Calcinare [kahl-chee-nah'ray] *vt.* to calcine.

Calcio [kahl'choh] *nm.* calcium, kick, stock (of a gun); giuoco del [joo-oh'koh del] **c.** football.

Calcitrante [kahl-chee-trahn'tay] *a.* restive.

Calcolabile [kahl-koh-lah' bee-lay] *a.* calculable.

Calcolare [kahl-koh-lah'ray] *vt.* to calculate, reckon.

Calcolatore [kahl-koh-lah-toh'ray] *nm.* accountant, calculator, reckoner.

Calcolo [kahl'koh-loh] *nm.* calculation, reckoning, (med.) gravel stone in the bladder.

Caldaia [kahl-dah'yah] *nf.* boiler, cauldron.

Caldeggiare [kahl-day-djah'ray] *vt.* to favour, foster, protect.

Calderino [kahl-day-ree' noh] *nm.* goldfinch.

Caldezza [kahl-det'zah] *nf.* heat, v. **Caldo.**

Caldo [kahl'doh] *nm.* heat; *a.* ardent, hot.

Calduccio [kahl-dooch'choh] *nm.* moderate heat; *a.* warmish.

Calendario [kah-len-dah' ree-oh] *nm.* almanac, calendar.

Calere [kah-lay'ray] *v.imp.* to concern, interest; non me ne cale [nonn may nay kah' lay] it doesn't interest me.

Calesse [kah-less'say] *nm.* carriage, chaise.

Calia [kah-lee'ah] *nf.* gold filings (*pl.*), old-fashioned thing, querulous person.

Calibro [kah-lee'broh] *nm.* calibre.

Calice [kah'lee-chay] *nm.* chalice, glass.

Caligine [kah-lee'jee-nay] *nf.* darkness, murk, obscurity.

Caliginoso [kah-lee-jee-noh' soh] *a.* dark, murky.

Calle [kahl'lay] *nf.* path, narrow lane.

Calligrafia [kah-lee-grah-fee'ah] *nf.* calligraphy, handwriting.

Callo [kahl'loh] *nm.* corn, hard skin.

Callosità [kahl-loh-see-tah'] *nf.* callosity.

Calloso [kahl-loh'soh] *a.* callous, hard.

Calma [kahl'mah] *nf.* calm, coolness, quietness.

Calmante [kahl-mahn'tay] *nm.* sedative; *a.* soothing.

Calma/re [kahl-mah'ray] *vt.* to appease, calm, soften; —rsi *vr.* to calm down.

Calmo [kahl'moh] *a.* calm, tranquil.

Calo [kah'loh] *nm.* descent, lowering (of price or weight).

Calore [kah-loh'ray] *nm.* heat, warmth.

Caloroso [kah-loh-roh'soh] *a.* eager, hot.

Caloscia [kah-loh'shah] *nf.* galosh.

Calpestare [kahl-pay-stah' ray] *vt.* to oppress, trample on.

Calpestio [kahl-pay-stee'oh] *nm.* clattering, stamping (with the feet).

Calunnia [kah-loon'nee-ah] *nf.* calumny.

Calunniare [kah-loon-nee-ah'ray] *vt.* to calumniate, slander.

Calunnioso [kah-loon-nee-oh'soh] *a.* calumnious, slanderous.

Calvario [kahl-vah'ree-oh] *nm.* Calvary, wayside shrine.

Calvizie [kahl-veet'zee-ay] *nf.* baldness.

Calvo [kahl'voh] *a.* bald, hairless.

Calza [kahlt'zah] *nf.* stocking, wick (for lamps); fare la [fah'ray lah] *c. vi.* to knit.

Calzatura [kahlt-zah-too'rah] *nf.* boots, shoes, stockings (*pl.*). (sock.)

Calzino [kahlt-zee'noh] *nm.*

Calzolaio [kahlt-zoh-lah'yoh] *nm.* bootmaker, shoemaker.

Calzoleria [kahlt-zoh-lay-ree'ah] *nf.* shoemaker's shop.

Calzoni [kahlt-zoh'nee] *nm.* (*pl.*) breeches, trousers (*pl.*); c. corti [korr'tee] shorts (*pl.*).

Cambiabile [kahm-bee-ah'bee-lay] *a.* changeable, fickle.

Cambiale [kahm-bee-ah'lay] *nf.* (*com.*) bill of exchange.

Cambiamento [kahm-bee-ah-men'toh] *nm.* change.

Cambia/monete [kahm-bee-ah-moh-nay'tay], —valute [vah-loo'tay] *nm.* money changer.

Cambia/re [kahm-bee-ah'ray] *vt.* to alter, change, turn; —rsi *vr.* to change.

Cambio [kahm'bee-oh] *nm.* change, exchange, (*tech.*) gear.

Camera [kah'may-rah] *nf.* chamber, room; c. da letto [dah let'toh], bed-room; c. dei comuni [day koh-moo'nee], House of Commons; c. dei pari [day'ee pah'ree], House of Lords.

Camerata [kah-may-rah'tah] *nm.* comrade.

Camerie/ra [kah-may-ree-ay'rah] *nf.* maid, servant, waitress; —re [ray] *nm.* waiter, man-servant.

Camerino [kah-may-ree'noh] *nm.* (*theat.*) dressing-room.

Camicetta [kah-mee-chet'tah] *nf.* blouse.

Camicia [kah-mee'chah] *nf.* chemise, shirt.

Caminetto [kah-mee-net'toh] *nm.* fireplace.

Camino [kah-mee'noh] *nm.* chimney, fireplace.

Camion [kah'mee-on] *nm.* lorry.

Camioncino [kah-mee-on-chee'noh] *nm.* small van, tradesman's delivery van.

Cammello [kahm-mell'loh] *nm.* camel.

Cammeo [kahm-may'oh] *nm.* cameo.

Camminamento [kahm-mee-nah-men'toh] *nm.* (*mil.*) communication trench.

Camminare [kahm-mee-nah'ray] *vi.* to go, march, walk.

Cammino [kahm-mee'noh] *nm.* journey, road, way; cammin facendo [kahm'meen fah-chen'doh] *ad.* on the way.

Camorra [kah-morr'rah] *nf.* clique, Italian secret society.

Camoscio [kah-moh'shoh] *nm.* chamois, shammy.

Campagna [kahm-pahn'yah] *nf.* campaign, country.

Campagnuolo [kahm-pahn-yoo-oh'loh] *nm.* countryman, villager.

Campale [kahm-pah'lay] *a.* (of the) field; battaglia [baht-tahl'yah] *c. nf.* pitched battle.

Campana [kahm-pah'nah] *nf.* bell.

Campanello [kahm-pah-nell'loh] *nm.* bell (in the house).

Campanile [kahm-pah-nee'lay] *nm.* belfry, bell-tower.

Campanilismo [kahm-pah-nee-lees'moh] *nm.* local patriotism.

Campare [kahm-pah'ray] *vt.* to keep, maintain; *vi.* to exist, live.

Campeggiare [kahm-pay-djah'ray] *vi.* to camp, stand out (from a background).

Campestre [kahm-pess'ray] *a.* rural, rustic.

Campionario [kahm-pee-oh-nah'ree-oh] *nm.* (*com.*) pattern-book, sample-case; *a.* sample.

Campionato [kahm-pee-oh-nah'toh] *nm.* championship.

Campione [kahm-pee-oh'nay] *nm.* champion, (*com.*) sample.

Campo [kahm'poh] *nm.* camp, field; c. d'aviazione [dah-vee-ah-tsee-oh'nay], airfield; c. di fortuna [dee forr-too'nah], emergency landing-ground; mettere in [met'tay-ray een] c. *vt.* to bring forward, propose.

Camposanto [kahm-poh-sahn'toh] *nm.* burial-ground, cemetery.

Canaglia [kah-nah'lyah] *nf.* mob, rabble, riff-raff, rogue.

Canale [kah-nah'lay] *nm.* canal, channel.

Canalizzare [kah-nah-leet-zah'ray] *vt.* to channel.

Canapa [kah'nah-pah] *nf.* hemp.

Canapè [kah-nah-pay'] *nm.* couch, sofa.

Canarino [kah-nah-ree'noh] *nm.* canary; *a.* canary-coloured.

Cancellare [kahn-chell-lah'ray] *vt.* to cancel, erase, repeal.

Cancelleria [kahn-chell-lay-ree'ah] *nf.* chancellor's office, chancery.

Cancelliere [kahn-chell-lee-ay'ray] *nm.* chancellor, registrar.

Cancello [kahn-chell'loh] *nm.* chancel-bar, gate, railing.

Cancrena [kahng-kray'nah] *nf.* gangrene.

Cancro [kahng'kroh] *nm.* cancer, crab.

Candela [kahn-day'lah] *nf.* candle, (*tech.*) sparking plug.

Candeliere [kahn-dell-lee-ay'ray] *nm.* candle-stick.

Candelora [kahn-day-loh'rah], —**lara** [lah'rah] *nf.* Candlemas.

Candidato [kahn-dee-dah'toh] *nm.* candidate.

Candidatura [kahn-dee-dah-too'rah] *nf.* candidature.

Candidezza [kahn-dee-det'zah] *nf.* candidness, whiteness.

Candido [kahn'dee-doh] *a.* candid, sincere, white.

Candire [kahn-dee'ray] *vt.* to candy.

Candore [kahn-doh'ray] *nm.* candour, whiteness.

Cane [kah'nay] *nm.* dog, cock (of a gun), c. da caccia [dah kahch'chah], hound.

Canestro [kah-ness'troh] *nm.* basket, hamper.

Canfora [kahn'foh-rah] *nf.* camphor.

Cangiabile [kahn-jah'bee-lay] *a.* changeable, fickle.

Cangiare [kahn-jah'ray] *vt. and i.* to alter, change.

Canicola [kah-nee'koh-lah] *nf.* Dog-Star, dog days (*pl.*).

Canile [kah-nee'lay] *nm.* kennel.

Canizie [kah-neet'zee-ay] *nf.* white hair, old age.

Canna [kahn'nah] *nf.* barrel (of a gun), cane, reed, tube.

Cannella [kahn-nell'lah] *nf.* cock, spigot, tap.

Cannellare, *q.v.* **scannellare**.

Cannibale [kahn-nee'bah-lay] *nm.* cannibal.

Cannocchiale [kahn-nock-kee-ah'lay] *nm.* opera-glass, telescope.

Cannonata [kahn-noh-nah'tah] *nf.* cannon-shot, cannonade.

Cannone [kahn-noh'nay] *nm.* cannon, gun; c. anticarro [ahn-tee-kahr'roh], anti-tank gun; c. controaereo [kon-troh-ah-ay'ray-oh], A.-A. gun.

Cannoneggiamento [kahn-noh-nay-djah-men'toh] *nm.* cannonade, cannonading.

Cannoneggiare [kahn-noh-nay-djah'ray] *vt. and i.* to cannonade.

Cannoniera [kahn-noh-nee-ay'rah] *nf.* gun-boat.

Cannoniere [kahn-noh-nee-ay'ray] *nm.* cannoneer, gunner.

Canone [kah'noh-nay] *nm.* canon, church-law.

Canonica [kah-noh'nee-kah] *nf.* presbytery, priest's house.

Canonico [kah-noh'nee-koh] *nm.* canon; *a.* canonical.

Canonizzare [kah-noh-need-zah'ray] *vt.* to canonise.

Canonizzazione [kah-noh-need-zah-tsee-oh'nay] *nf.* canonization. [canoe

Canotto [kah-not'toh] *nm.*

Canova [kah'noh-vah] *nf.* retail shop for wine, etc.

Canovaccio [kah-noh-vahch'choh] *nm.* dish-cloth.

Cantante [kahn-tahn'tay] *nm. and f.* singer; *a.* singing.

Cantare [kahn-tah'ray] *vt. and i.* to sing.

Canta/tore [kahn-tah-toh'ray] *nm.* —**trice** [tree'chay] *nf.* singer.

Canterellare [kahn-tay-rell-lah'ray], **canticchiare** [kahn-teek-kee-ah'ray] *vi.* to hum, warble.

Cantica [kahn'tee-kah] *nf.* song.

Cantiere [kahn-tee-ay'ray] *nm.* dock-yard, ship-building yard.

Cantilena [kahn-tee-lay'nah] *nf.* monotonous song, sing-song intonation.

Cantina [kahn-tee'nah] *nf.* cellar.

Canto [kahn'toh] *nm.* angle, corner, side, singing, song.

Cantonata [kahn-toh-nah'tah] *nf.* angle, corner.

Cantone [kahn-toh'nay] *nm.* canton, corner.

Cantoniere [kahn-toh-nee-ay'ray] *nm.* maintenance-man on roads, railways, etc.

Cantuccio [kahn-tooch'choh] *nm.* biscuit, corner.

Canuto [kah-noo'toh] *a.* grey-headed, hoary.

Canzonare [kahnt-zoh-nah'ray] *vt.* to make fun of, tease.

Canzonatorio [kahnt-zoh-nah-toh'ree-oh] *a.* mocking, teasing.

Canzonatura [kahnt-zoh-nah-too'rah] *nf.* mockery, teasing.

Canzone [kahnt-zoh'nay] *nf.* ballad, song.

Canzoniere [kahnt-zoh-nee-ay'ray] *nm.* collection of songs, song-book. [fusion.

Caos [kah'oss] *nm.* chaos, con-

Capace [kah-pah'chay] *a.* able, capable, capacious.

Capacità [kah-pah-chee-tah'] *nf.* ability, capacity.

Capacitarsi [kah-pah-chee-tarr'see] *vr.* to make out, understand.

Capan/na [kah-pahn'nah] *nf.* —**no** [noh] *nm.* hut.

Caparbietà [kah-pahr-bee-ay-tah'] *nf.* obstinacy, stubbornness.

Caparbio [kah-pahr'bee-oh] *a.* obstinate, stubborn.

Caparra [kah-pahr'rah] *nf.* advance payment, earnest money.

Caparrare [kah-pahr-rah'ray] *vt.* to secure by paying a deposit. *v.* **Accaparrare.**

Capel/lo [kah-pell'loh] *nm.* —li [lee] (*pl.*) hair.

Capelluto [kah-pell-loo'toh] *a.* hairy. [contain.

Capere [kah'pay-ray] *vt.* to

Capestro [kap-pess'troh] *nm.* halter, rope.

Capezzale [kah-pet-zah'lay] *nm.* bolster, pillow.

Capezzolo [kah-pet'zoh-loh] *nm.* nipple.

Capigliatura [kah-peel-yah-too'rah] *nf.* hair, head of hair.

Capire [kah-pee'ray] *vt.* to comprehend, contain, understand.

Capitale [kah-pee-tah'lay] *nm.* capital, principal, stock; *a.* main, principal.

Capitanare [kah-pee-tah-nah'ray] *vt.* to captain, head.

Capitaneria [kah-pee-tah-nay-ree'ah] *nf.* coastal region; c. di porto [dee porr'toh] harbour-master's office.

Capitano [kah-pee-tah'noh] *nm.* captain, commander.

Capitare [kah-pee-tah'ray] *vi.* to happen, occur, turn up.

Capitolare [kah-pee-toh-lah'ray] *vi.* to capitulate; *a.* capitulary.

Capitolo [kah-pee'toh-loh] *nm.* chapter.

Capitombolare [kah-pee-tom-boh-lah'ray] *vi.* to tumble.

Capitombolo [kah-pee-tom'boh-loh] *nm.* somersault, tumble.

Capo [kah'poh] *nm.* beginning, cape, chief, end, head, summit; da [dah] c. *ad.* again; in [een] c. a [ah] *vr.* at the end of; venire a [vay-nee'ray ah] c. *vt.* to make out, reason out.

Capobanda [kah-poh-bahn'dah] *nm.* bandmaster, gangleader.

Capocchia [kah-pock'kee-ah] *nf.* head of a nail, pin, etc.

Capocomico [kah-poh-koh'mee-koh] *nm.* (*theat.*) managing director.

Capofitto, a [ah kah-poh-feet'toh] *ad.* head downwards, head-foremost.

Capogiro [pah-poh-jee'roh] *nm.* dizziness, giddiness.

Capolavoro [kah-poh-lah-voh'roh] *nm.* masterpiece.

Capolino [kah-poh-lee'noh] *nm.* small head; fare [fah'ray] c. *vi.* to peep in.

Capoluogo [kah-poh-loo-oh'goh] *nm.* chief town in a district.

Capomastro [kah-poh-mah'stroh] *nm.* master-builder, overseer.

Caponaggine [kah-poh-nah'djee-nay] *nf.* obstinacy.

Capone [kah-poh'nay] *nm.* obstinate man.

Caporale [kah-poh-rah'lay] *nm.* corporal.

Caporione [kah-poh-ree-oh'nay] *nm.* ring-leader.

Caposaldo [kah-poh-sahl'doh] *nm.* essential point of a speech, etc.

Capostazione [kah-poh-stah-tsee-oh'nay] *nm.* stationmaster.

Capotreno [kah-poh-tray'noh] *nm.* guard (on a train).

Capoverso [kah-poh-vehr'soh] *nm.* beginning of a verse or paragraph.

Capovolge/re [kah-poh-voll'jay-ray] *vt.* to overturn, upset; —rsi *vr.* to capsize, be upset.

Cappa [kahp'pah] *nf.* cape, cloak, cope; the letter k.

Cappella [kahp-pell'lah] *nf.* chapel.

Cappellano [kahp-pell-lah'noh] *nm.* chaplain.

Cappelliera [kahp-pell-lee-ay'rah] *nf.* hat-box.

Cappello [kahp-pell'loh] *nm.* cap, hat.

Capperi! [kahp'pay-ree] *int.* goodness!

Cappero [kahp'pay-roh] *nm.* caper, caper-bush.

Cappone [kahp-poh'nay] *nm.* capon.

Cappot/ta [kahp-pot'tah] *nf.* —**to** [toh] *nm.* cloak, overcoat.

Cappuccino [kahp-pooch-chee'noh] *nm.* Capuchin friar, coffee with a dash of milk.

Cappuccio [kahp-pooch'choh] *nm.* cowl, hood.

Capra [kah'prah] *nf.* she-goat.

Capretto [kah-pret'toh] *nm.* kid, young goat.

Capriccio [kah-preech'choh] *nm.* caprice, whim.

Capriccioso [kah-preech-choh'soh] *a.* capricious, whimsical.

Caprifoglio [kah-pree-foll'yoh] *nm.* honeysuckle.

Capriola [kah-pree-oh'lah] *nf.* caper, capriole, doe, roe.

Capriolo [kah-pree-oh'loh] *nm.* roe-buck.

Capro [kah'proh] *nm.* he-goat; c. espiatorio [ay-spee-ah-toh'ree-oh], scape-goat.

Capsula [kahp'soo-lah] *nf.* capsule, husk, pod.

Carabina [kah-rah-bee'nah] *nf.* carbine.

Carabiniere [kah-rah-bee-nee-ay'ray] *nm.* carabineer, member of a special military police force.

Caraffa [kah-rahf'fah] *nf.* decanter.

Caramella [kah-rah-mell'lah] *nf.* caramel, monocle.

Carattere [kah-raht'tay-ray] *nm.* character, quality, style, *(typ.)* type.

Caratteristi/ca [kah-raht-tay-ree'stee-kah] *nf.* —**co** [koh] *a.* characteristic.

Caratterizzare [kah-raht-tay-reed-zah'ray] *vt.* to characterise.

Carbonaio [kahr-boh-nah'yoh] *nm.* coalman.

Carbonchio [kahr-bong'kee-oh] *nm.* carbuncle.

Carbone [kahr-boh'nay] *nm.* coal; c. fossile [foss'see-lay], pit-coal.

Carbonio [kahr-boh'nee-oh] *nm.* carbon.

Carbonizzare [kahr-boh-need-zah'ray] *v.t.* to carbonise.

Carburatore [kahr-boo-rah-toh'ray] *nm.* carburettor.

Carcame [kahr-kah'may] *nm.* carcassa [kahr-kahs'sah] *nf.* carcass.

Carcerare [kahr-chay-rah'ray] *vt.* to imprison.

Carcerato [kahr-chay-rah'toh] *nm.* prisoner.

Carcerazione [kahr-chay-rah-tsee-oh'nay] *nf.* imprisonment.

Carcere [kahr'chay-ray] *nm.* jail, prison.

Carceriere [kahr-chay-ree-ay'ray] *nm.* jailer.

Carciofo [kahr-choh'foh] *nm.* artichoke.

Cardare [kahr-dah'ray] *vt.* to card.

Cardellino [kahr-dell-lee'noh] *nm.* gold-finch.

Cardiaco [kahr-dee'ah-koh] *a.* cardiac.

Cardinale [kahr-dee-nah'lay] *nm.* cardinal, door-post, jamb; *a.* cardinal, principal.

Cardine [kahr'dee-nay] *nm.* hinge, pole.

Cardo [kahr'doh] *nm.* carder's comb, thistle.

Carena [kah-ray'nah] *nf.* keel (of a ship).

Carenare [kah-ray-nah'ray] *vt. (naut.)* to careen, caulk.

Carestia [kah-ress-tee'ah] *nf.* dearth, famine.

Carezza [kah-ret'zah] *nf.* caress, high price.

Carezzare [kah-ret-zah'ray] *vt.* to caress, fondle.

Carezzevole [kah-ret-zay'voh-lay] *a.* caressing, flattering.

Cariare [kah-ree-ah'ray] *vt. and i.* to decay, rot.

Carica [kah'ree-kah] *nf.* charge, load, position, post.

Caricare [kah-ree-kah'ray] *vt.* to charge, exaggerate, load, over-burden; c. un orologio [oon oh-roh-loh'joh] to wind up a clock.

Caricatura [kah-ree-kah-too'rah] *nf.* caricature.

Carico [kah'ree-koh] *nm.* charge, freight, load; *a.* charged, loaded.

Carie [kah'ree-ay] *nf.* rottenness.

Carino [kah-ree'noh] *a.* dear, nice, pretty, sweet.

Carità [kah-ree-tah'] *nf.* charity; per (pehr) c. *int.* for Heaven's sake.

Caritatevole [kah-ree-tah-tay'voh-lay] *a.* charitable.

Carlona, alla [ahl'lah kahr-loh'nah] *ad.* in a slovenly manner.

Carmelitano [kahr-may-lee-tah'noh] *nm.* Carmelite friar.

Carnagione [kahr-nah-joh'nay] *nf.* carnato [kahr-nah'toh] *nm.* complexion.

Carnale [kahr-nah'lay] *a.* carnal, sensual.

Carnalità [kahr-nah-lee-tah'] *nf.* carnality, sensuality.

Carne [kahr'nay] *nf.* flesh, meat.

Carnefice [kahr-nay'fee-chay] *nm.* executioner.

Carnevale [kahr-nay-vah'lay] *nm.* carnival.

Carnificina [kahr-nee-fee-chee'nah] *nf.* carnage, slaughter.

Carnivoro [kahr-nee'voh-roh] *a.* carnivorous.

Carnoso [kahr-noh'soh] *a.* fleshy.

Caro [kah'roh] *nm.* dearness (of price); *ad.* dearly, at a high price; *a.* beloved, dear, expensive; tener [tay'nehr] c. *vt.* to esteem, value.

Carogna [kah-rohn'yah] *nf.* carrion.

Carota [kah-roh'tah] *nf.* carrot.

Carovana [kah-roh-vah'nah] *nf.* caravan, convoy.

Carpentiere [kahr-pen-tee-ay'ray] *nm.* carpenter, cartwright.

Carpione [kahr-pee-oh'nay] *nm.* carp (fish).

Carpire [kahr-pee'ray] *vt.* to seize, snatch.

Carpone [kahr-poh'nay] carponi [kahr-poh'nee] *ad.* on all fours.

Carreggiabile [kahr-ray-djah'bee-lay] *a.* practicable for carts.

Carrello [kahr-rell'loh] *nm. (tech.)* bogie, undercarriage.

Carretta [kahr-ret'tah] *nf.* cart.

Carrettata [kahr-ret-tah'tah] *nf.* cart-load.

Carrettiere [kahr-ret-tee-ay'ray] *nm.* carrier, carter.

Carretto [kahr-ret'toh] *nm.* hand-cart.

Carriera [kahr-ree-ay'rah] *nf.* career, course, race.

Carriola [kahr-ree-oh'lah] *nf.* wheel-barrow.

Carro [kahr'roh] *nm.* car.

truck, (*astr.*) Great Bear; c. armato [ahr-mah'toh] (*mil.*) tank; c. leggero [lay-djay'roh] (*mil.*) light tank.

Carrozza [kahr-rot'zah] *nf.* carriage, coach.

Carrozzabile [kahr-rot-zah'-bee-lay] *a.* practicable for carriages.

Carrozzeria [kahr-rot-zay-ree'ah] *nf.* body of a car, car-making firm.

Carrozzina [kahr-rot-zee'-nah] *nf.* perambulator.

Carrozzino [kahr-rot-zee'-noh] *nm.* small carriage drawn by one horse.

Carrub(i)o [kahr-roo'b(ee)-oh] *nm.* carob (tree).

Carta [kahr'tah] *nf.* document, map, paper, playing-card; c. d'identità [dee-den-tee-tah'] identity card; c. igienica [ee-jay'nee-kah] toilet-paper.

Cartaccia [kahr-tahch'chah], cartastraccia [kahr-tah-strahch'chah] *nf.* waste-paper.

Cartaio [kahr-tah'yoh] *nm.* paper-maker, playing-card manufacturer.

Cartapecora [kahr-tah-pay'-koh-rah] *nf.* parchment.

Cartapesta [kahr-tah-pay'-stah] *nf.* papier-mâché.

Cartello [kahr-tell'loh] *nm.* bill, label, sign-board.

Cartellone [kahr-tell-loh'-nay] *nm.* placard, play-bill.

Cartiera [kahr-tee-ay'rah] *nf.* paper-mill.

Cartilagine [kahr-tee-lah'-jee-nay] *nf.* cartilage, gristle.

Cartoccio [kahr-tohch'choh] *nm.* cornet, paper-bag.

Cartolaio [kahr-toh-lah'yoh] *nm.* stationer.

Cartoleria [kahr-toh-lay-ree'ah] *nf.* stationer's shop.

Cartolina [kahr-toh-lee'nah] *nf.* card; c. illustrata [eel-loo-strah'tah], picture post-card; c. postale [poh-stah'lay] post-card.

Cartone [kahr-toh'nay] *nm.* cardboard, cartoon.

Cartuccia [kahr-tooch'chah] *nf.* cartridge.

Casa [kah'sah] *nf.* family, house; c. di salute [dee sah-loo'tay], nursing-home.

Casaccio [kah-zahch'choh] *nm.* accident; a. [ah] c. *ad.* at random, hap-hazard.

Casale [kah-sah'lay] *nm.* hamlet, village.

Casalingo [kah-sah-leeng'-goh] *a.* domestic, household.

Casamento [kah-sah-men'-toh] *nm.* tenement-house.

Casata [kah-sah'tah] *nf.* family, race.

Casato [kah-sah'toh] *nm.* surname.

Cascaggine [kahs-kah'djee-nay] *nf.* drowsiness.

Cascare [kahs-kah'ray] *vi.* to fall.

Cascata [kahs-kah'tah] *nf.* cascade, fall.

Cascina [kah-shee'nah] *nf.* dairy, dairy-farm.

Caseggiato [kah-say-djah'-toh] *nm.* block of houses.

Caseificio [kah-zay-ee-fee'-choh] *nm.* dairy.

Casella [kah-sell'lah] *nf.* compartment, division, pigeon-hole.

Casellante [kah-sell-lahn'-tay] *nm.* level-crossing keeper, signalman.

Casellario [kah-sell-lah'ree-oh] *nm.* case with pigeon-holes.

Caserma [kah-zehr'mah] *nf.* barracks (*pl.*).

Caset/ta [kah-set'tah],—**tina** [tee'nah] *nf.* cottage, small house.

Casino [kah-see'noh] *nm.*

club, gaming-house, house of ill-fame.
Caso [kah'zoh] *nm.* accident, case, chance; **a** [ah] **c. ad.** at random.
Casolare [kah-soh-lah'ray] *nm.* hamlet.
Cassa [kahs'sah] *nf.* case, chest, coffer, coffin, drum, stock (of a gun); **c. forte** [forr'tay], safe; **c. di risparmio** [dee rees-pahr'mee-oh] savings bank.
Cassapanca [kahs-sah-pahng'kah] *nf.* wooden chest in the form of a bench.
Cassazione [kahs-sah-tsee-oh'nay] *nf.* annulling, cassation; **corte di** [korr'tay dee] **c.** (*jur.*), court of cassation.
Casserola [kahs-say-roh'lah] *nf.* saucepan.
Cassetta [kahs-set'tah] *nf.* box-seat, cash-box, collection-box, drawer, letter-box.
Cassettone [kahs-set-toh'nay] *nm.* chest of drawers.
Cassiere [kahs-see-ay'ray] *nm.* cashier.
Casta [kah'stah] *nf.* caste.
Casta/gna [kah-stahn'yah] *nf.* chestnut; —**gno** [yoh] *nm.* chestnut-tree.
Castellano [kah-stell-lah'noh] *nm.* castellan, lord of a manor.
Castello [kah-stell'loh] *nm.* castle, fortress.
Castigare [kah-stee-gah'ray] *vt.* to chastise, punish.
Castigo [kah-stee'goh] *nm.* chastisement, punishment.
Castità [kah-stee-tah'] *nf.* chastity, purity. [pure.
Casto [kah'stoh] *a.* chaste,
Castoro [kah-stoh'roh] *nm.* beaver, castor.
Castrato [kah-strah'toh] *nm.* mutton.
Casuale [kah-zoo-ah'lay] *a.* accidental, casual.

Casualità [kah-zoo-ah-lee-tah'] *nf.* chance, hazard.
Casupola [kah-soo'poh-lah] *nf.* hovel.
Cataclisma [kah-tah-kleez'mah] *nm.* cataclysm.
Catacomba [kah-tah-kom'bah] *nf.* catacomb.
Catalessia [kah-tah-less-see'ah] *nf.* catalepsy.
Catalogare [kah-tah-loh-gah'ray] *vt.* to catalogue.
Catalogo [kah-tah'loh-goh] *nm.* catalogue, list.
Catapecchia [kah-tah-peck'kee-ah] *nf.* hovel.
Cataplasma [kah-tah-plahz'mah] *nm.* poultice.
Catarro [kah-tahr'roh] *nm.* catarrh.
Catasta [kah-tah'stah] *nf.* wood-pile.
Catastare [kah-tah-stah'ray] *vt.* to pile up.
Catasto [kah-tah'stoh] *nm.* tax, tax-book.
Catastrofe [kah-tah'stroh-fay] *nf.* catastrophe.
Catechismo [kah-tay-kees'moh] *nm.* catechism.
Categoria [kah-tay-goh-ree'ah] *nf.* category.
Categorico [kah-tay-goh'ree-koh] *a.* categorical.
Catena [kah-tay'nah] *nf.* chain, fetter, range (of hills); **c. cingolata** [cheeng - goh - lah'tah] (*mil.*) caterpillar track.
Catenaccio [kah-tay-nahch'choh] *nm.* door-chain.
Cateratta [kah-tay-raht'tah] *nf.* cataract, sluice.
Catinel/la [kah-tee-nell'lah] *nf.* wash-hand basin; **piovere a—le** [pee-oh'vay-ray ah—lay] *vi.* to rain cats and dogs.
Catino [kah-tee'noh] *nm.* basin, bowl.
Catrame [kah-trah'may] *nm.* tar.

Cattedra [kaht'tay-drah) *nf.* teacher's or professor's chair.

Cattedrale [kaht-tay-drah'lay] *nf.* cathedral.

Cattiva/re [kaht-tee-vah'ray] *vt.* to captivate; —**rsi** *vr.* to win (love, favour, etc.).

Cattiveria [kaht-tee-vay'ree-ah] *nf.* naughtiness, wickedness.

Cattività [kaht-tee-vee-tah'] *nf.* captivity.

Cattivo [kaht-tee'voh] *a.* bad, naughty, wicked.

Cattolicismo [kaht-toh-lee-chees'moh] *nm.* Catholic faith.

Cattolicità [kaht-toh-lee-chee-tah'] *nf.* Catholicism, Catholic countries (*pl.*).

Cattolico [kaht-toh'lee-koh] *nm. and a.* Catholic.

Cattura [kaht-too'rah] *nf.* capture, arrest; **mandato di** [mahn-dah'toh dee] *c. nm.* (*jur.*) warrant of arrest.

Catturare [kaht-too-rah'ray] *vt.* to arrest, capture.

Caucciù [kowch-choo'] *nm.* india-rubber.

Causa [kow'zah] *nf.* cause, origin, reason, (*jur.*) law-suit.

Causare [kow-zah'ray] *vt.* to cause, occasion.

Causticità [kow-stee-chee-tah'] *nf.* causticity.

Caustico [kow'stee-koh] *nm.* caustic; *a.* burning, caustic.

Cautela [kow-tay'lah] *nf.* caution, wariness, (*jur.*) bail, security.

Cauto [kow'toh] *a.* cautious, wary.

Cauzione [kow-tsee-oh'nay] *nf.* caution, (*jur.*) bail, security.

Cava [kah'vah] *nf.* cave, quarry.

Cavalcare [kah-vahl-kah'ray] *v.t.* to mount (a horse, etc.); *vi.* to ride.

Cavalcata [kah-vahl-kah'tah] *nf.* cavalcade, ride.

Cavalcavia [kah-vahl-kah-vee'ah] *nm.* bridge across (or under) a street or railway.

Cavaliere [kah-vah-lee-ay'ray] *nm.* cavalier, horseman, knight, partner (at a dance).

Cavalla [kah-vahl'lah] *nf.* mare.

Cavalleresco [kah-vahl-lay-ress'koh] *a.* chivalrous, knightly, noble.

Cavalleria [kah-vahl-lay-ree'ah] *nf.* cavalry, chivalry, horse (*pl.*).

Cavalleriz/za [kah-vahl-lay-reet'zah] *nf.* riding-school; —**zo** [zoh] *nm.* horse-breaker, riding-master.

Cavalletta [kah-vahl-let'tah] *nf.* grasshopper.

Cavalletto [kah-vahl-let'toh] *nm.* small horse, easel, trestle.

Cavallina [kah-vahl-lee'nah] *nf.* filly; **correre la** [korr'ray-ray lah] *c. vi.* to sow one's wild oats.

Cavallo [kah-vahl'loh] *nm.* horse, knight (at chess); **c. vapore** [vah-poh'ray] horse-power.

Cava/re [kah-vah'ray] *vt.* to dig, draw, extract, free, take out; —**rsi** *vr.* to get out of.

Cavatappi [kah-vah-tahp'pee] *nm.* cork-screw.

Caverna [kah-vehr'nah] *nf.* cave, cavern.

Caviale [kah-vee-ah'lay] *nm.* caviar.

Caviglia [kah-veel'yah] *nf.* ankle (-bone).

Cavillare [kah-veel-lah'ray] *vi.* to carp, cavil, split hairs.

Cavillo [kah-veel'loh] *nm.* cavil, quibble.

Cavilloso [kah-veel-loh'soh] *a.* cavilling, quibbling.

Cavità [kah-vee-tah′] *nf.* cavity, hole.

Cavo [kah′voh] *nm.* (*naut.*) cable, rope; c. di ormeggio [dee orr-may′djoh], mooring-cable; *a.* concave, hollow.

Cavolfiore [kah-vohl-fyoh′ray] *nm.* cauliflower.

Cavolo [kah′voh-loh] *nm.* cabbage. [pea.

Cece [chay′chay] *nm.* chick-

Cecità [chay-chee-tah′] *nf.* blindness, ignorance.

Cedere [chay′day-ray] *vt. and i.* to cede, give up, yield.

Cedevole [chay-day′voh-lay] *a.* flexible, yielding.

Cedibile [chay-dee′bee-lay] *a.* transferable.

Cedola [chay′doh-lah] *nf.* coupon, interest-warrant.

Cedro [chay′droh] *nm.* cedar, citron.

Cefalo [chay′fah-loh] *nm.* mullet (fish). [snout.

Ceffo [chef′foh] *nm.* muzzle,

Cela/re [chay-lah′ray] *vt.* to disguise, hide; —rsi *vr.* to hide oneself.

Celebrante [chay-lay-brahn′tay] *nm.* officiating priest.

Celebrare [chay-lay-brah′ray] *vt.* to celebrate, praise.

Celebre [chay′lay-bray] *a.* celebrated, famous.

Celebrità [chay-lay-bree-tah′] *nf.* celebrity.

Celere [chay′lay-ray] *a.* nimble, rapid, swift.

Celerità [chay-lay-ree-tah′] *nf.* celerity, swiftness.

Celeste [chay-less′tay] *a.* celestial, divine, heavenly, sky-blue. [joke.

Celia [chay′lee-ah] *nf.* jest,

Celibato [chay-lee-bah′toh] *nm.* celibacy.

Celibe [chay′lee-bay] *nm.* bachelor; *a.* unmarried.

Cella [chell′lah] *nf.* cell, cellar.

Cellulare [chell-loo-lah′ray] *nm.* jail, prison; *a.* cellular, honey-combed.

Cementare [chay-men-tah′ray] *vt.* to cement.

Cemento [chay-men′toh] *nm.* cement.

Cena [chay′nah] *nf.* supper.

Cenacolo [chay-nah′koh-loh] *nm.* supper-room, picture, of the Last Supper. [sup.

Cenare [chay-nah′ray] *vi.* to sup.

Cencia/ia [chen-chah′yah] *nf.* —io [yoh] *nm.* rag-picker.

Cencio [chen′choh] *nm.* dish-clout, rag.

Cencioso [chen-choh′soh] *a.* ragged, in tatters.

Cenere [chay′nay-ray] *nf.* ashes, cinders (*pl.*); giorno delle ceneri [jorr′noh-dell′lay chay′nay-ree] *nm.* Ash Wednesday.

Cenno [chen′noh] *nm.* hint, nod, sign, signal, wave (of the hand); far [fahr] c. *vi.* to beckon, nod.

Cenobita [chay-noh-bee′tah] *nm.* friar, monk.

Censimento [chen-see-men′toh] *nm.* census.

Censire [chen-see′ray] *vt.* to take the census.

Censo [chen′soh] *nm.* income, property-qualification to vote. [censor.

Censore [chen-soh′ray] *nm.*

Censorio [chen-soh′ree-oh] *a.* censorious.

Censuare [chen-soo-ah′ray] *vt.* to assess (for taxes).

Censura [chen-soo′rah] *nf.* censure, censorship.

Censurare [chen-soo-rah′ray] *vt.* to blame, censor, censure.

Centenario [chen-tay-nah′ree-oh] *nm.* centenarian, centenary; *a.* centenary, centennial.

Centesimale [chen-tay-zee-mah'lay] *a.* centesimal, hundredth.

Centesimo [chen-tay'zee-moh] *nm.* centime (hundredth part of a lira).

Centigrado [chen-tee'grah-doh] *a.* centigrade.

Centigrammo [chen-tee-grahm'moh] *nm.* centigramme.

Centimetro [chen-tee'may-troh] *nm.* centimetre.

Centinaio [chen-tee-nah'yoh] *nm.* hundred; a centinaia [ah chen-tee-nah'yah] *ad.* by hundreds.

Cento [chen'toh] *a.* hundred.

Centrale [chen-trah'lay] *nf.* exchange, station; c. elettrica [ay-let'tree-kah] power-station; c. telefonica [tay-lay-foh'nee-kah], telephone-exchange; *a.* central, main.

Centralizzare [chen-trah-leet-zah'ray] *vt.* to centralise.

Centro [chen'troh] *nm.* centre, heart, middle.

Centuplo [chen'too-ploh] *a.* centuple, hundredfold.

Centuria [chen-too-ree'ah] *nf.* century. a hundred.

Ceppaia [chep-pah'yah] *nf.* rooty stump.

Ceppo [chep'poh] *nm.* block, origin, stock, stump; ceppi [chep'pee] (*pl.*), chains, fetters (*pl.*).

Cera [chay'rah] *nf.* face, mien, wax, wax-candle.

Ceralacca [chay-rah-lahk'kah] *nf.* sealing-wax.

Ceramica [chay-rah'mee-kah] *nf.* ceramics (*pl.*).

Cerca [chehr'kah] *nf.* quest, search.

Cercare [chehr-kah'ray] *vt.* to look for, seek, strive, try.

Cerchia [chehr'kee-ah] *nf.* circle, encircling-walls (*pl.*).

Cerchiare [chehr-kee-ah'ray] *vt.* to hoop, surround.

Cerchio [chehr'kee-oh] *nm.* circle, enclosure, group, garland, hoop, tyre.

Cereale [chay-ray-ah'lay] *nm. and a.* cereal.

Cerebrale [chay-ray-brah'lay] *a.* cerebral.

Cereo [chay'ray-oh] *a.* waxen, waxy.

Cerimonia [chay-ree-moh'nee-ah] *nf.* ceremony.

Cerimoniale [chay-ree-moh-nee-ah'lay] *nm.* ceremonial; *a.* ceremonial, formal.

Cerimonioso [chay-ree-moh-nee-oh'soh] *a.* ceremonious.

Cerino [chay-ree'noh] *nm.* wax-light, wax match.

Cerniera [chehr-nee-ay'rah] *nf.* frame, hinge, mount (of a bag, purse, etc.).

Cernita [chehr'nee-tah] *nf.* choice. [candle.

Cero [chay'roh] *nm.* church

Cerotto [chay-rot'toh] *nm.* botch, bungle, tedious person; sticking plaster. [oak.

Cerro [chehr'roh] *nm.* green

Certezza [chehr-tet'zah] *nf.* assurance, certainty.

Certificare [chehr-tee-fee-kah'ray] *vt.* to certify, confirm.

Certificato [chehr-tee-fee-kah'toh] *nm.* certificate.

Certo [chehr'toh] *a.* certain, positive, sure; *ad.* certainly, of course.

Certosa [chehr-toh'zah] *nf.* Carthusian monastery.

Certosino [chehr-toh-zee'noh] *nm.* Carthusian monk.

Certuni [chehr-too'nee] *pr.* (*pl.*) a few, some (*pl.*).

Cerva [chehr'vah] *nf.* female deer, hind.

Cervellino [chehr-vell-lee'noh] *nm.* hare-brained person; *a.* giddy, queer.

Cervello [chehr-vell'loh] *nm.* brain, brains (*pl.*), genius, judgment, sense.

Cervellotico [chehr-vell-loh'tee-koh] *a.* fantastic, queer.

Cervo [chehr'voh] *nm.* hart, stag; **c. volante** [voh-lahn'tay] stag-beetle.

Cesellare [chay-zell-lah'ray] *vt.* to chisel, engrave.

Cesello [chay-zell'loh] *nm.* chisel, graver.

Cesoie [chay-zoh'yay] *nf.* (*pl.*) shears (*pl.*).

Cespuglio [chess-pool'yoh] *nm.* bush, thicket.

Cessare [chess-sah'ray] *vt. and i.* to cease, end, stop.

Cesso [chess'soh] *nm.* water-closet. [hamper.

Cesta [chess'tah] *nf.* basket.

Cestinare [chess-tee-nah'ray] *vt.* to throw into the waste-paper basket.

Cestino [chess-tee'noh] *nm.* small basket, waste-paper basket.

Cesto [chess'toh] *nm.* box-ing-glove, bush, tuft.

Ceto [chay'toh] *nm.* class, rank. [cithern, harp.

Cetra [chay'trah] *nf.* (*mus.*)

Cetriolo [chay-tree-oh'loh] *nm.* cucumber.

Che [kay] *con.* because, than, that, whether; *pn.* that, what, which, who; **che c'è?** [kay chay], what's the matter? *nm.* matter, thing; **non gran** [grahn] **c.** nothing much; **non . . . che** *ad.* but, only.

Checchessia [keck-kess-see'ah] *pn.* (anything) whatever.

Chermisi [kehr'mee-zee] *nm. and a.* crimson.

Cheta/re [kay-tah'ray] *vt.* to quiet, silence; —**rsi** *vr.* to grow quiet, silent.

Chetichella, alla [ahl'lah kay-tee-kell'lah] *ad.* quietly, secretly.

Cheto [kay'toh] *a.* quiet, silent.

Chi [kee] *pn.* who, whom, he who, anyone, whoever, some (*pl.*).

Chiacchiera [kee-ahk'yay-rah] *nf.* gossip, prattle, tittle-tattle.

Chiacchierare [kee-ahk-yay-rah'ray] *vi.* to gossip.

Chiacchierio [kee-ahk-yay-ree'oh] *nm.* chattering.

Chiacchiero/na [kee-ahk-yay-roh'nah] *nf.* —**ne** [nay] *nm.* babbler, prattler.

Chiama [kee-ah'mah] *nf.* roll-call.

Chiama/re [kee-ah-mah'ray] *vt.* to call, name; —**rsi** *vr.* to be called; **come si chiama?** [koh'may see kee-ah'mah], what is your name?

Chiamata [kee-ah-mah'tah] *nf.* call, summons.

Chiappare [kee-ahp-pah'ray] *vt.* to catch, seize.

Chiarezza [kee-ah-ret'zah] *nf.* brightness, clearness.

Chiarificare [kee-ah-ree-fee-kah'ray] *vt.* to clarify, clear up.

Chiari/re [kee-ah-ree'ray] *vt.* to clarify, explain; —**rsi** *vr.* to become clear, clear up (of the weather).

Chiaro [kee-ah'roh] *nm.* light colour; *a.* bright, clear, illustrious.

Chiarore [kee-ah-roh'ray] *nm.* brightness, light.

Chiaroveggente [kee-ah-roh-vay-djen'tay] *a.* clair-voyant.

Chiaroveggenza [kee-ah-roh-vay-djent'zah] *nf.* clair-voyance.

Chiasso [kee-ahs'soh] *nm.* alley, lane, noise, uproar.

Chiassoso [kee-ahs-soh'soh] *a.* noisy.

Chiatta [kee-aht'tah] *nf.* ferry-boat, lighter (boat).

Chiatto [kee-aht'toh] *a.* flat, flat-bottomed.

Chiavarda [kee-ah-vahr'dah] *nf.* bolt, screw.

Chiave [kee-ah'vay] *nf.* key, stop-cock, tuning-key, (*mus.*) clef.

Chiavistello [kee-ah-vee-stell'loh] *nm.* bolt.

Chiazza [kee-aht'zah] *nf.* spot, stain. [*nf.* cup.

Chicchera [keek'kay-rah]

Chicchessia [keek-kess-see'ah] *pn.* whoever.

Chicco [keek'koh] *nm.* coffee-bean, grain, pip, seed.

Chiedere [kee-ay'day-ray] *vt.* to ask, beg, enquire.

Chierico [kee-ay'ree-koh] *nm.* clerk, priest.

Chiesa [kee-ay'zah] *nf.* church.

Chiglia [keel'yah] *nf.* (*naut.*) keel.

Chilo [kee'loh] *nm.* chyle; fare il [fah'ray eel] *c. vi.* to rest after a meal.

Chilo (grammo) [kee-loh-grahm'moh] *nm.* kilogramme.

Chilometro [kee-loh'may-troh] *nm.* kilometre.

Chimera [kee-may'rah] *nf.* chimera, illusion.

Chimica [kee'mee-kah] *nf.* chemistry.

Chimico [kee'mee-koh] *nm.* chemist; *a.* chemical.

China [kee'nah] *nf.* declivity, slope, Peruvian bark.

China/re [kee-nah'ray] *vt.* to bend, bow; **—rsi** *vr.* to bow down, stoop, submit.

Chincaglie [keeng-kahl'yay] *nf.* (*pl.*) chincaglieria [keeng-kahl-yay-ree'ah] *nf.* hardware, ironmongery.

Chincagliere [keeng-kahl-yay'ray] *nm.* ironmonger.

Chinino [kee-nee'noh] *nm.* quinine. [*cast.*

Chino [kee'noh] *a.* bent, down-

Chiocciola [kee-och'choh-lah] *nf.* female-screw, snail; scala a [skah'lah ah] *c.* winding-stair.

Chiodo [kee-oh'doh] *nm.* nail; roba da chiodi [roh'bah dah kee-oh'dee], dishonest thing or person, badly done (or made) thing; piantare i chiodi [pee-ahn-tah'ray ee kee-oh'dee] *vi.* to run up debts.

Chioma [kee-oh'mah] *nf.* foliage (of trees), head of hair.

Chiosare [kee-oh-zah'ray] *vt.* to comment, gloss.

Chiosco [kee-oss'koh] *nm.* kiosk.

Chio/stra [kee-oh'strah] *nf.* **—stro** [stroh] *nm.* cloister, convent. [silent.

Chiotto [kee-ot'toh] *a.*

Chiozzo [kee-ot'zoh] *nm.* gudgeon (fish).

Chirurgia [kee-roor-jee'ah] *nf.* surgery.

Chirurgo [kee-roor'goh] *nm.* surgeon. [knows!

Chissà [kees-sah'] *int.* who

Chiude/re [kee-oo'day-ray] *vt.* to close, enclose, fence, shut (up), turn off; **—rsi** *vr.* to shut, shut oneself up.

Chiunque [kee-oong'kway] *pn.* anyone who, whoever.

Chiusa [kee-oo'sah] *nf.* dam, fence, lock, weir.

Chiusura [kee-oo-soo'rah] *nf.* closing, enclosure, conclusion, lock.

Ci [chee] *pn.* us, to us; *ad.* here, there.

Ciabattino [chah-baht-tee'noh] *nm.* botcher, cobbler.

Cialda [chahl'dah] *nf.* cialdone [chahl-doh'nay] *nm.* biscuit, wafer.

Cialtrona [chahl-troh'nah] *nf.* slut.

Cialtrone [chahl-troh'nay] *nm.* blackguard, dirty fellow.

Cialtroneria [chahl-troh-nay-ree'ah] *nf.* slatternliness, sluttishness.

Ciambella [chahm-bel'lah] *nf.* ring-shaped cake; name given to many objects similarly shaped, as an air-cushion, life-belt, etc.

Ciambellano [chahm-bell-lah'noh] *nm.* chamberlain.

Ciampicare *v.* **inciampicare.**

Cianciare [chahn-chah'ray] *vi.* to prate, tattle.

Cianfrusaglia [chahn-froo-zah'lyah] *nf.* trash, odds and ends.

Ciarla [chahr'lah] *nf.* nonsense, talkativeness.

Ciarlare [chahr-lah'ray] *vi.* to talk a lot.

Ciarlataneria [chahr-lah-tah-nay-ree'ah] *nf.* ciarlatanismo [chahr-lah-tah-nees'moh] humbug, quackery.

Ciarlatano [chahr-lah-tah'noh] *nm.* humbug, quack.

Ciascheduno [chah-skay-doo'noh] *pn.* each, everyone.

Ciascuno [chee-skoo'noh] *a. and pn.* each, every, each one, everyone.

Ciba/re [chee-bah'ray] *vt.* to feed, give food; —rsi *vr.* to eat, feed upon.

Cibaria [chee-bah'ree-ah] *nf.* food, victuals (*pl.*).

Cibo [chee'boh] *nm.* food.

Cicala [chee-kah'lah] *nf.* cicada, grasshopper.

Cicatrice [chee-kah-tree'chay] *nf.* scar.

Cicatrizzare [chee-kah-treed-zah'ray] *vi.* to cicatrize, heal up.

Cicca [cheek'kah] *nf.* cigar-butt, cigarette-end, quid.

Cicerone [chee-chay-roh'nay] *nm.* cicerone, guide.

Cicisbeo [chee-chees-bay'oh] *nm.* gallant, spark.

Ciclamino [chee-klah-mee'noh] *nm.* cyclamen.

Ciclismo [chee-klees'moh] *nm.* cycling.

Ciclista [chee-klee'stah] *nm.* cyclist.

Ciclone [chee-kloh'nay] *nm.* cyclone, depression.

Cicogna [chee-kohn'yah] *nf.* stork.

Cicoria [chee-koh'ree-ah] *nf.* chicory, succory.

Cicuta [chee-koo'tah] *nf.* hemlock.

Cieco [chay'koh] *nm.* blind man; *a.* blind.

Cielo [chay'loh] *nm.* climate, Heaven, sky.

Cifra [chee'frah] *nf.* cypher, figure, number.

Cifrare [chee-frah'ray] *vt.* to write in cypher.

Ciglio [cheel'yoh] *nm.* eye-brow.

Ciglione [cheel-yoh'nay] *nm.* bank, edge (of a ditch, etc.).

Cigno [cheen'yoh] *nm.* swan.

Cigolare [chee-goh-lah'ray] *vi.* to creak, squeak.

Cigolio [chee-goh-lee'oh] *nm.* creaking, squeaking.

Cilecca [chee-leck'kah] *nf.* disappointment, failure.

Cilicio [chee-lee'choh], cilizio [chee-leet'zee-oh] *nm.* hair-shirt, sack-cloth.

Cilie/gia [chee-lee-ay'jah] *nf.* cherry; —gio [joh] *nm.* cherry-tree.

Cilindro [chee-leen'droh] *nm.* cylinder, roller.

Cima [chee'mah] *nf.* eminence, summit, top.

Cimelio [chee-may'lee-oh] *nm.* antique, relic of ancient art.

Cimenta/re [chee-men-tah'ray] *vt.* to put to the test, risk, try; —rsi *vr.* to enter into contest with, expose oneself.

Cimento [chee-men'toh] *nm.* experience, hazard, risk.

Cimice [chee'mee-chay] *nm.* bug, bed-bug, drawing-pin.

Cimitero [chee-mee-tay'roh] *nm.* cemetery.

Cimurro [chee-moor'roh] *nm.* glanders (*pl.*); distemper (dogs).

Cinciallegra [cheen-chahl-lay'grah] *nf.* tit.

Cinematografare [chee-nay-mah-toh-grah-fah'ray] *vt.* to film.

Cinematografo [chee-nay-mah-toh'grah-foh] *nm.* cinema(tograph), picture-house.

Cinge/re [cheen'jay-ray] *vt.* to encircle, gird, surround; —rsi *vr.* to gird on.

Cinghia [cheeng'ghee-ah] *nf.* belt, strap.

Cinghiale [cheeng-ghee-ah'lay] *nm.* wild boar.

Cingolo [cheen'goh-loh] *nm.* girdle, (*tech.*) caterpillar.

Cinguettare [cheeng-gwet-tah'ray] *vi.* to chirp, twitter.

Cinico [chee'nee-koh] *nm.* cynic; *a.* cynical.

Cinismo [chee-nees'moh] *nm.* cynicism.

Cinquanta [cheeng-kwahn'tah] *a.* fifty.

Cinquantesimo [cheeng-kwahn-tay'see-moh] *a.* fiftieth.

Cinquantina [cheeng-kwahn-tee'nah] *nf.* some fifty (things).

Cinque [cheeng'kway] *a.* five.

Cinquecentista [cheeng-kway-chen-tee'stah] *nm.* artist or writer of the 16th century.

Cinquecento [cheeng-kway-chen'toh] *nm.* 16th century; *a.* five hundred.

Cinquennio [cheeng-kwen'nee-oh] *nm.* period of 5 years.

Cinta [cheen'tah] *nf.* circuit, circumference, city walls (*pl.*).

Cinto [cheen'toh] *nm.* belt;

c. erniario [ehr-nee-ah'ree-oh], truss; *a.* girded.

Cintura [cheen-too'rah] *nf.* belt, waist; c. di salvataggio [dee-sahl-vah-tah'djoh] life-belt.

Ciò [choh] *pn.* that, this, what, which.

Ciocca [chock'kah] *nf.* cluster, lock (of hair), tuft.

Ciocco [chock'koh] *nm.* billet of wood, block, log.

Cioccolata [chock-koh-lah'tah] *nf.* chocolate.

Cioccolattini [chock-koh-laht-tee'nee] *nm.* (*pl.*) chocolates (*pl.*).

Cioè [choh-ay'] *ad.* i.e., namely, that is.

Ciondolare [chon-doh-lah'ray] *vi.* to dangle, swing.

Ciondolo [chon'doh-loh] *nm.* pendant, trinket.

Ciondoloni [chon-doh-loh'nee] *ad.* dangling.

Ciotola [choh'toh-lah] *nf.* bowl.

Ciottolo [chot'toh-loh] *nm.* (pebble).

Cipiglio [chee-peel'yoh] *nm.* frown, scowl.

Cipolla [chee-poll'lah] *nf.* bulb, onion.

Cipollino [chee-poll-lee'noh] *nm.* chive, shallot.

Cippo [cheep'poh] *nm.* half column, mile-stone.

Cipresso [chee-press'soh] *nm.* cypress.

Cipria [chee'pree-ah] *nf.* powder (for face, hair, etc.).

Circa [cheer'kah] *ad.* about, nearly; *pr.* as to, concerning, with regard to.

Circo [cheer'koh] *nm.* amphitheatre, circus.

Circolare [cheer-koh-lah'ray] *vi.* to circulate, go round; *nm.* and *a.* circular.

Circolazione [cheer-koh-lah-tsee-oh'nay] *nf.* circulation, rotation.

Circolo [cheer'koh-loh] nm. circle, circuit, club.

Circoncisione [cheer-kon-chee-zee-oh'nay] nf. circumcision.

Circondare [cheer-kon-dah'ray] vt. to border, enclose, surround.

Circonferenza [cheer-kon-fay-rent'zah] nf. circumference.

Circonlocuzione [cheer-kon-loh-koo-tsee-oh'nay] nf. circumlocution, periphrasis.

Circonvenire [cheer-kon-vay-nee'ray] vt. to circumvent, deceive.

Circoscrivere [cheer-koh-skree'vay-ray] vt. to circumscribe, limit.

Circoscrizione [cheer-koh-skree-tsee-oh'nay] nf. limitation, limits (pl.).

Circospetto [cheer-koh-spet'toh] a. circumspect.

Circospezione [cheer-koh-spay-tsee-oh'nay] nf. circumspection.

Circostante [cheer-koh-stahn'tay] a. encircling, surrounding.

Circostanza [cheer-koh-stahnt'zah] nf. circumstance.

Circuire [cheer-koo-ee'ray] vt. to surround.

Circuito [cheer-koo-ee'toh] nm. circuit, compass; corto [korr'toh] c. (tech.) short circuit.

Cireneo [chee-ray-nay'oh] nm. scape-goat.

Cispità [chee-spoh-see-tah'] nf. blear-eyedness.

Cisposo [chee-spoh'soh] a. blear-eyed, rheumy.

Ciste [chee'stay] nf. cyst.

Cisterna [chee-stehr'nah] nf. cistern, tank.

Citare [chee-tah'ray] vt. to cite, quote, summon.

Citazione [chee-tah-tsee-oh'nay] nf. citation, quotation, summons; (jur.) writ.

Citeriore [chee-tay-ree-oh'ray] a. hither, nearer.

Citrato [chee-trah'toh] nm. citrate. [town.

Città [cheet-tah'] nf. city,

Cittadella [cheet-tah-dell'lah] nf. citadel.

Cittadinanza [cheet-tah-dee-nahnt'zah] nf. citizenship, naturalisation, citizens (pl.).

Cittadino [cheet-tah-dee'noh] nm. citizen, townsman; a. of a town.

Ciuco [choo'koh] nm. donkey.

Ciuffare [choof-fah'ray] vt. to catch v. **Acciuffare**.

Ciuffo [choof'foh] nm. forelock, top-knot, tuft.

Ciurma [choor-mah] nf. (naut.) ship's crew.

Ciurmaglia [choor-mahl'yah] nf. mob, rabble.

Civaie [chee-vah'yay] nf. (pl.) all kinds of pulse.

Civetta [chee-vet'tah] nf. coquette, flirt, screech-owl.

Civettare [chee-vet-tah'ray] vi. to coquet, flirt.

Civico [chee'vee-koh] a. civic.

Civile [chee-vee'lay] a. civil, civilised.

Civilizzare [chee-vee-leed-zah'ray] vt. to civilise.

Civiltà [chee-veel-tah'] nf. civility, civilisation.

Civismo [chee-vees'moh] nm. civic feeling.

Clamore [klah-moh'ray] nm. clamour, outcry.

Clamoroso [klah-moh-roh'soh] a. clamorous, noisy.

Classe [klahs'say] nf. class, form, rank.

Classico [klahs'see-koh] nm and a. clasisc, classical.

Classificare [klahs-see-fee-kah'ray] vt. to classify.

Classificazione [klahs-see-

fee-kah-tsee-oh'nay] nf. classification.   [clause.
Clausola [klow'zoh-lah] nf.
Claustrale [klow-strah'lay]
a. cloistral.
Clausura [klow-zoo'rah] nf.
seclusion.
Clava [klah'vah] nf. club.
Clavicembalo [klah-vee-
chem'bah-loh] nm. (mus.)
harpsichord.
Clavicola [klah-vee'koh-lah]
nf. collar-bone.
Clemente [klay-men'tay] a.
clement, merciful.
Clemenza [klay-ment'zah]
nf. clemency, mercy.
Clericale [klay-ree-kah'lay]
a. clerical.
Clericato [klay-ree-kah'toh]
nm. holy orders (pl.). priesthood.
Clero [klay'roh] nm. clergy.
Cliente [klee-en'tay] nm.
client, customer.
Clientela [klee-en-tay'lah]
nf. clients, customers (pl.).
patronage, practice.
Clima [klee'mah] nm.
climate, region.
Climaterico [klee-mah-tay-
ree-koh] nm. and a. clim-
acteric.
Climati/co [klee-mah'tee-
koh] a. climatic; stazione
[stah-tsee-oh'nay]—ca [kah]
nf. health-resort.
Clinica [klee'nee-kah] nf.
clinical medicine, nursing-
home.
Clinico [klee'nee-koh] nm.
clinical doctor; a. clinical.
Clistere [klee-stay'ray] nm.
clyster, enema.
Clivo [klee'voh] nm. declivity,
slope. v Collina, Pendio.
Cloaca [kloh-ah'kah] nf.
drain, sewer.
Coabitare [koh-ah-bee-tah'-
ray] vi. to live together.
Coabitazione [koh-ah-bee-

tah-tsee-oh'nay] nf. living
together.
Coadiuvare [koh-ahd-yoo-
vah'ray] vt. to assist, help.
Coagulare [koh-ah-goo-lah'-
ray] vi. and i. to coagulate.
Coalizione [koh-ah-lee-tsee-
oh'nay] nf. coalition.
Coazione [koh-ah-tsee-oh'-
nay] nf. compulsion.
Cocca [kock'kah] nf. arrow,
darling, hem (of an apron,
etc.).
Coccarda [kock-kahr'dah]
nf. cockade.
Cocchiere [kock-kee-ay'ray]
nm. coachman, driver.
Cocchio [kock'yoh] nm.
carriage, coach.
Cocciniglia [kohch-chee-
neel'yah] nf. cochineal.
Coccio [kohch'choh] nm.
earthenware pot, potsherd.
Cocciutaggine [kohch-
choo-tah'djee-nay] nf. obsti-
acy.
Cocciuto [kohch-choo'toh]
a. obstinate.
Cocco [kock'koh] nm. cocoa-
nut.
Coccodrillo [kock-koh-dreel'-
loh] nm. crocodile.
Coccola [kock'koh-lah] nf.
berry.
Coccola/re [kock-koh-lah'-
ray] vt. to fondle; —rsi vr. to
make oneself snug, nestle.
Cocente [koh-chen'tay] a.
burning, sharp.
Cocitura [koh-chee-too'rah]
nf. cooking.
Cocolla [koh-koll'lah] nf.
cowl, hood.
Cocomero [koh-koh'may-
roh] nm. watermelon.
Cocuzzolo [koh-koot'zoh-
loh] nm. crown of the head,
summit, top.
Coda [koh'dah] nf. end, file,
queue, tail; fare la [fah'ray
lah] c. vi. to queue.

Codardia [koh-dahr'dee-ah] *nf.* cowardice.

Codardo [koh-dahr'doh] *nm. and a.* coward(ly).

Codazzo [koh-daht'zoh] *nm.* swarm (of beggars, etc.).

Codesto [koh-dess'toh] *pn. and a.* that, this.

Codice [koh'dee-chay] *nm.* code.

Codicillo [koh-dee-cheel'loh] *nm.* codicil.

Codificare [koh-dee-fee-kah'ray] *vt.* to codify.

Codino [koh-dee'noh] *nm.* conservative, small tail, pigtail. [*nm.* rump.

Codione [koh-dee-oh'nay]

Coeguale [koh-ay-gwah'lay] *a.* co-equal.

Coerede [koh-ay-ray'day] *nm. and f.* co-heir(ess).

Coerente [koh-ay-ren'tay] *a.* coherent, logical.

Coerenza [koh-ay-rent'zah] *nf.* coherency.

Coesione [koh-ay-zee-oh'nay] *nf.* cohesion.

Coesistere [koh-ay-zee'stay-ray] *vi.* to coexist.

Coetaneo [koh-ay-tah'nay-oh] *a.* contemporary.

Coevo [koh-ay'voh] *a.* coeval.

Cofano [koh'fah-noh] *nm.* bonnet (of a car), case, coffer.

Cogitare [koh-jee-tah'ray] *vi.* to cogitate. *v.* **Ponderare.**

Cogli [kohl'yee]=con gli *pr. and art. m.* (*pl.*) with the.

Cogliere [kohl'yay-ray] *vt.* to catch, gather, hit, strike.

Cogna/ta [kohn-yah'tah] *nf.* sister-in-law; **—to** [toh] *nm.* brother-in-law.

Cognito [kohn'yee-toh] *a.* known.

Cognizione [kohn-yee-tsee-oh'nay] *nf.* knowledge, notion.

Cognome [kohn-yoh'may] *nm.* surname.

Coi [koh'ee]=con i *pr. and art. m.* (*pl.*) with the.

Coiaio [koh-ee-ah'yoh] *nm.* currier, leather dresser, tanner.

Coiame [koh-ee-ah'may] *nm.* hides (*pl.*), leather.

Coincidenza [koh-een-chee-dent'zah] *nf.* coincidence, connection (of trains).

Coincidere [koh-een-chee'day-ray] *vi.* to coincide.

Coinquilino [koh-een-kweel-lee'noh] *nm.* fellow-tenant.

Coinvolgere [koh-een-voll'jay-ray] *vt.* to involve.

Col [kohl]=con il *pr. and art. m.* with the.

Cola [koh'lah] *nf.* filter, strainer.

Colà [koh-lah'] *ad.* there.

Colaggiù [koh-lah-djoo'] *ad.* below, down there. *v.* **Laggiù.**

Colare [koh-lah'ray] *vt.* to cast (metals), riddle, strain; *vi.* to drop, leak, sink.

Colassù [koh-lahs-soo'] *ad.* up there. *v.* **Lassù.**

Colazione [koh-lah-tsee-oh'nay] *nf.* lunch; **prima** [pree'mah] c. breakfast.

Colei [koh-lay'ee] *pn.* she.

Colera [koh-lay'rah] *nf.* cholera.

Coleroso [koh-lay-roh'soh] *nm.* cholera-patient.

Colibrì [koh-lee-bree'] *nm.* humming-bird.

Colica [koh'lee-kah] *nf.* colic.

Colla [koll'lah] *nf.* glue.

Colla [koll'lah]=con la *pr. and art. f.* with the.

Collaborare [koll-lah-boh-rah'ray] *vi.* to collaborate.

Collana [koll-lah'nah] *nf.* collection (of books), necklace.

Collare [koll-lah'ray] *nm.* collar.

Collaudare [koll-low-dah'ray] *vt.* to test, try out.

Collaudo [koll-low′doh] *nm.* test, trial-flight, trial-run.

Collazionare [koll-lah-zee-oh-nah′ray] *vt.* to collate, compare.

Colle [koll′lay]—con le *vr. and art. f.* (*pl.*) with the.

Collega [koll-lay′gah] *nm. and f.* colleague, fellow.

Collega/re [koll-lay-gah′ray] *vt.* to connect, join; —rsi *vr.* to league, unite.

Collegio [koll-lay′joh] *nm.* boarding-school, college.

Collera [koll′lay-rah] *nf.* anger, wrath.

Collerico [koll-lay′ree-koh] *a.* choleric, irascible.

Colletta [koll-let′tah] *nf.* collect (prayer), collection, gathering.

Collezione [koll-lay-tsee-oh′nay] *nf.* collection.

Collezionista [koll-lay-tsee-oh-nee′stah] *nm.* collector.

Collimare [koll-lee-mah′ray] *vi.* to agree, tally.

Collina [koll-lee′nah] *nf.* hill.

Collinoso [koll-lee-noh′soh] *a.* hilly.

Collirio [koll-lee′ree-oh] *nm.* eye-wash.

Collisione [koll-lee-see-oh′nay] *nf.* clash, collision.

Collo [koll′loh] *nm.* neck, piece of luggage; **c. del piede** [dell pee-ay′day], instep.

Collo [koll′loh]—con lo *vr. and art. m.* with the.

Collocamento [koll-loh-kah-men′toh] *nm.* investment, employment, placing, situation; **ufficio di** [oof-fee′choh dee] **c.** registry-office.

Colloca/re [koll-loh-kah′ray] *vt.* to give in marriage, invest, place; —rsi *vr.* to get a position, settle down.

Colloquio [koll-loh′kwee-oh] *nm.* conversation, interview.

Colmare [koll-mah′ray] *vt.*

to fill to overflowing, load, overwhelm.

Colmo [koll′moh] *nm.* culminating point; *a.* brimming, full, loaded.

Colo [koh′loh] *nm.* sieve, strainer.

Colom/ba [koh-lom′bah] *nf.* —bo [boh] *nm.* pigeon;—**c. viaggiatore** [vee-ah-djah-toh′ray], carrier-pigeon.

Colombaia [koh-lom-bah′yah] *nf.* dovecote.

Colonia [koh-loh′nee-ah] *nf.* colony, settlers (*pl.*).

Colonizzare [koh-loh-neet-zah′ray] *vt.* to colonise.

Colonna [koh-lon′nah] *nf.* column, file, pillar.

Colonnello [koh-lon-nell′loh] *nm.* colonel.

Colono [koh-loh′noh] *nm.* colonist, farmer, peasant.

Colo/rare [koh-loh-rah′ray] —rire [ree′ray] *vt.* to colour, dye.

Colore [koh-loh′ray] *nm.* colour, dye, pretext, suit (at cards).

Colorito [koh-loh-ree′toh] *nm.* colouring, complexion.

Coloro [koh-loh′roh] *pn.* they, those.

Colosso [koh-loss′soh] *nm.* colossus.

Colpa [koll′pah] *nf.* crime, fault, offence, sin.

Colpabilità [koll-pah-bee-lee-tah′] *nf.* culpability.

Colpevole [koll-pay′voh-lay] *a.* culpable, guilty.

Colpire [koll-pee′ray] *vt.* to hit, strike.

Colpo [koll′poh] *nm.* blow, stroke, wound; **ad un** [ahd oon] **c., di** [dee] **c.** *ad.* all at once.

Colta [koll′tah] *nf.* collection, gathering. (rare). *v.* Raccolta.

Coltellata [koll-tell-lah′tah] *nf.* cut, stab (with a knife).

Coltellinaio [koll-tell-lee-nah'yoh] *nm.* cutler.

Coltellino [koll-tell-lee'noh] *nm.* small knife.

Coltello [koll-tell'loh] *nm.* dagger, knife.

Coltivare [koll-tee-vah'ray] *vt.* to cultivate, improve, till.

Colto [koll'toh] *a.* cultivated cultured, educated, improved

Coltre [koll'tray] *nm.* counterpane, coverlet.

Coltrone [koll-troh'nay] *nm.* quilt.

Coltura [koll-too'rah] *nf.* [culture.

Colui [koh-loo'ee] *pn.* he, that fellow.

Comandante [koh-mahn-dahn'tay] *nm.* commander, chief; c. in seconda [een say-kon'dah] second-in-command.

Comandare [koh-mahn-dah'ray] *vt.* to command, order.

Comando [koh-mahn'doh] *nm.* command, (mil.) H.Q., (avia.) control.

Combaciare [koh-bah-chah'ray] *vi.* to fit, tally.

Combattente [kom-baht-ten'tay] *nm.* combatant, soldier; *a.* fighting.

Combattere [kom-baht'tay-ray] *vt. and i.* to fight, oppose, resist.

Combinare [kom-bee-nah'-ray] *vt.* to arrange, assemble, combine, conclude, settle; *vi.* to agree.

Combinazione [kom-bee-nah-tsee-oh'nay] *nf.* agreement, arrangement, combination, chance.

Combriccola [kom-breek'koh-lah] *nf.* band, gang.

Combustibile [kom-boo-stee'bee-lay] *nm.* fuel; *a.* combustible.

Combutta [een kom-boot'tah] *ad.* in a heap.

Come [koh'may] *ad.* almost,

as, how, like, when, why; *int.* what! c. sta? [stah], how do you do?

Comicità [koh-mee-chee-tah'] *nf.* amusing side.

Comico [koh'mee-koh] *nm.* comic actor, writer of comedies; *a.* comic, droll, funny.

Cominciare [koh-meen-chah'ray] *vt. and i.* to begin.

Comitato [koh-mee-tah'toh] *nm.* committee.

Comitiva [koh-mee-tee'vah] *nf.* company, party.

Comizio [koh-meet'zee-oh] *nm.* assembly (political).

Commedia [kom-may'dee-ah] *nf.* comedy, play.

Commediografo [kom-may-dee-oh'grah-foh] *nm.* writer of comedies.

Commemorare [kom-may-moh-rah'ray] *vt.* to commemorate.

Commemorazione [kom-may-moh-rah-tsee-oh'nay] *nf.* commemoration.

Commenda [kom-men'dah] *nf.* allowance, living, civic honour given in Italy.

Commen/dabile [kom-men-dah'bee-lay]—**devole** [day'voh-lay] *a.* commendable, praiseworthy.

Commendare [kom-men-dah'ray] *vt.* to commend, praise.

Commendatore [kom-men-dah-toh'ray] *nm.* special title given in Italy for civic merit.

Commendazione [kom-men-dah-tsee-oh'nay] *nf.* commendation. *v.* Lode.

Commentare [kom-men-tah'ray] *vt.* to comment.

Commento [kom-men'toh] *nm.* comment.

Commerciale [kom-mehr-chah'lay] *a.* commercial.

Commerciante [kom-mehrchahn'tay] *nm.* dealer, merchant, trader.

Commerciare [kom-mehr-chah'ray] *vi.* to deal, trade, traffic.

Commercio [kom-mehr'choh] *nm.* commerce, trade.

Commesso [kom-mess'soh] *nm.* clerk, shop-assistant; **c. viaggiatore** [vee-ah-djah-toh'ray], commercial traveller, representative.

Commestibi/le [kom-may-stee'bee-lay] *a.* eatable, edible; **—li** [lee] *nm. (pl.)* eatables *(pl.).*

Commettere[kom-met'tay-ray] *vt.* to commit, entrust.

Commiatare [kom-mee-ah-tah'ray] *vi.* to say good-bye.

Commiato [kom-mee-ah'toh] *nm.* dismissal, leave, parting.

Comminare [kom-mee-nah'ray] *vt.* to threaten.

Comminazione [kom-mee-nah-tsee-oh'nay] *nf.* threat.

Commiserazione [kom-mee-zay-rah-tsee-oh'nay] *nf.* compassion, pity.

Commissariato [kom-mee-sah-ree-ah'toh] *nm. (mil.)* commissariat, commissary's office, police-station.

Commissario [kom-mees-sah'ree-oh] *nm.* commissary, commissioner.

Commission/e [kom-mees-see-oh'nay] *nf.* board, commission, errand, message; **fare delle** [fah'ray dell-lay], **—i** [ee] *vi.* to do errands, go shopping.

Commosso [kom-moss'soh] *a.* affected, moved, touched.

Commovente [kom-moh-ven'tay] *a.* affecting, moving, touching.

Commozione [kom-moh-tsee-oh'nay] *nf.* emotion.

Commuove/re [kom-moo-

oh'vay-ray] *vt.* to affect, touch; **—rsi** *vr.* to be moved, touched.

Commutare [kom-moo-tah'ray] *vt.* to change, commute.

Comodino [koh-moh-dee'noh] *nm.* comode, night-table.

Comodità [koh-moh-dee-tah'] *nf.* comfort, convenience, opportunity.

Comodo [koh'moh-doh] *nm.* convenience, ease, leisure; **a suo** [ah soo'oh] **c.** *ad.* at your convenience; *a.* comfortable, convenient, useful, well-to-do.

Compaesano [kom-pah-ay-zah'noh] *nm.* fellow-countryman.

Compaginare [kom-pah-jee-nah'ray] *vt.* to join.

Compagine [kom-pah'jee-nay] *nf.* connection, joining of parts.

Compagna [kom-pahn'yah] *nf.* female companion, wife.

Compagnia [kom-pahn-yee'ah] *nf.* company, society.

Compagno [kom-pahn'yoh] *nm.* companion, comrade, mate, partner; *a.* like, similar.

Companatico [kom-pah-nah'tee-koh] *nm.* food eaten with bread.

Comparare [kom-pah-rah'ray] *vt.* to compare.

Comparazione [kom-pah-rah-tsee-oh'nay] *nf.* comparison, similitude.

Comparire [kom-pah-ree'ray] *vi.* to appear.

Comparsa [kom-pahr'sah] *nf.* appearance, summons, *(theat.)* super.

Compartecipare [kom-pahr-tay-chee-pah'ray] *vi.* to share (in).

Compartimento [kom-pahr-tee-men'toh] *nm.* compartment, division.

Compartire [kom-pahr-tee′ray] *vt.* to divide, share.

Gompassato [kom-pahs-sah′toh] *a.* reserved, stiff.

Compassionare [kom-pahs-see-oh-nah′ray] *vt.* to pity.

Compassione [kom-pahs-see-oh′nay] *nf.* compassion, pity.

Compassionevole [kom-pahs-see-oh-nay′voh-lay] *a.* exciting or feeling pity, pitiful.

Compasso [kom-pahs′soh] *nm.* compasses (*pl.*).

Compatibile [kom-pah-tee′bee-lay] *a.* excusable, pardonable.

Compatimento [kom-pah-tee-men′toh] *nm.* compassion, excuse, forbearance.

Compatire [kom-pah-tee′ray] *vt.* to excuse, pity.

Compatriota [kom-pah-tree-oh′tah] *nm.* compatriot.

Compatto [kom-paht′toh] *a.* compact, solid.

Compendiare [kom-pen-dee-ah′ray] *vt.* to abridge.

Compendio [kom-pen′dee-oh] *nm.* abridgement, compendium.

Compensare [kom-pen-sah′ray] *vt.* to compensate, indemnify.

Compenso [kom-pen′soh] *nm.* compensation, reward; in [een] c. *ad.* in return.

Compera: *v.* **Compra.**

Competente [kom-pay-ten′tay] *a.* competent, fit, qualified.

Competen/za [kom-pay-ten′tzah] *nf.* authority, competence; —ze [zay] (*pl.*), fees (*pl.*).

Competere [kom-pay′tay-ray] *vi.* to be due to, compete.

Compiacente [kom-pee-ah-chen′tay] *a.* complaisant, polite.

Compiacenza [kom-pee-ah-chent′zah] *nf.* complaisance, satisfaction.

Compiace/re [kom-pee-ah-chay′ray] *vt.* to comply with, please; —rsi *vr.* to condescend, be pleased to.

Compiangere [kom-pee-ahn′jay-ray] *vt.* to be sorry for, lament, pity.

Compicciare [kom-peech-chah′ray] *vt.* to succeed in something.

Compiere [komp′yay-ray] *vt.* to accomplish, complete, fulfil, finish.

Compilare [kom-pee-lah′ray] *vt.* to compile, compose.

Compilazione [kom-pee-lah-tsee-oh′nay] *nf.* compilation.

Compimento [kom-pee-men′toh] *nm.* accomplishment, completion, fulfilment.

Compire: *v.* **Compiere.**

Compitare [kom-pee-tah′ray] *vt.* to spell.

Compitezza [kom-pee-tet′tzah] *nf.* courtesy, politeness.

Compito [kom′pee-toh] *nm.* home-work, task.

Compito [kom-pee′toh] *a.* courteous, polite.

Compiuto [komp-yoo′toh] *a.* accomplished, ended.

Compleanno [kom-play-ahn′noh] *nm.* birthday.

Complementare [kom-play-men-tah′ray] *a.* additional, complementary.

Complessione [kom-pless-see-oh′nay] *nf.* constitution.

Complessità [kom-pless-see-tah′] *nf.* complexity.

Complessivo [kom-pless-see′voh] *a.* comprehensive, total.

Complesso [kom-pless′soh] *nm.* mass, set, whole; in [een] c. *ad.* in general, on the whole; *a.* complex, robust, strong.

Completare [kom-play-tah′ray] *vt.* to complete.

Completo [kom-play'toh] *a.* complete, whole.

Complica/re [kom-plee-kah'ray] *vt.* to complicate, make intricate; —rsi *vr.* to become complicated, difficult.

Complicazione [kom-plee-kah-tsee-oh'nay] *nf.* complication.

Complice [kom'plee-chay] *nm.* accomplice.

Complimentare [kom-plee-men-tah'ray] *vt.* to compliment.

Complimen/to [kom-plee-men'toh] *nm.* compliment; —ti [tee] (*pl.*) congratulations (*pl.*); senza [sent'zah] —ti *ad.* frankly, without ceremony.

Complimentoso [kom-plee-men-toh'soh] *a.* complimentary, obsequious.

Complotto [kom-plot'toh] *nm.* conspiracy, plot.

Componente [kom-poh-nen'tay] *nm. and f.* component, ingredient.

Componimento [kom-poh-nee-men'toh] *nm.* arrangement, composition.

Compor/re [kom-porr'ray] *vt.* to arrange, compose, conciliate, (*typ.*) set up (type); —rsi *vr.* to consist of, (*jur.*) compound with one's creditors.

Comportabile [kom-porr-tah'bee-lay] *a.* bearable, tolerable.

Comporta/re [kom-porr-tah'ray] *vt.* to bear, tolerate; —rsi *vr.* to act, behave.

Comporto [kom-porr'toh] *nm.* delay, indulgence, respite.

Compositore [kom-poh-zee-toh'ray] *nm.* composer, (*typ.*) compositor.

Composizione [kom-poh-zee-tsee-oh'nay] *nj.* agreement, arrangement, composition.

Compostezza [kom-poh-

stet'zah] *nf.* composure, sen. possession.

Composto [kom-poh'stoh] *nm.* compound, mixture; *a.* composed, sedate, self-possessed.

Compra [kom'prah] *nf.* purchase; a prezzo di [ah pret'zoh dee] *c. ad.* at cost price.

Comprare [kom-prah'ray] *vt.* to buy, purchase.

Comprendere [kom-pren'day-ray] *vt.* to comprehend, comprise, include, understand.

Comprendonio [kom-pren-doh'nee-oh] *nm.* understanding.

Comprensibile [kom-pren-see'bee-lay] *a.* comprehensible, intelligible.

Comprensibilità [kom-pren-see-bee-lee-tah'] *nf.* comprehensibility.

Comprensione [kom-pren-see-oh'nay] *nf.* comprehension, perception.

Compreso [kom-pray'soh] *a.* full, included, including.

Compressa [kom-press'sah] *nf.* compress.

Compresso [kom-press'soh] *a.* close, compressed, restrained.

Comprimente [kom-pree-men'tay] *a.* compressing, restraining.

Comprimere [kom-pree'may-ray] *vt.* to compress, restrain.

Compromettente [kom-proh-met-ten'tay] *a.* compromising.

Compromettere [kom-proh-met'tay-ray] *vt.* to compromise, expose, involve, risk.

Comprovamento [kom-proh-vah-men'toh] *nm.* proof.

Comprovare [kom-proh-vah'ray] *vt.* to bring evidence, prove.

Compunto [kom-poon'toh] *a.* contrite, sorry.

Compunzione [kom-poon-tsee-oh'nay] *nf.* compunction, contrition.

Computare [kom-poo-tah'ray] *vt.* to compute, reckon.

Computista [kom-poo-tee'stah] *nm.* accountant, book-keeper, computor, reckoner.

Computisteria [kom-poo-tee-stay-ree'ah] *nf.* accountant's office, bookkeeping.

Computo [kom'poo-toh] *nm.* account, reckoning.

Comunale [koh-moo-nah'lay] *a.* communal, municipal.

Comune [koh-moo'nay] *nm.* community, municipality, town-hall; *a.* common, mutual, ordinary.

Comunica/re [koh-moo-nee-kah'ray] *vt.* to administer the Sacrament, announce, communicate; —**rsi** *vr.* to take the Sacrament.

Comunicativa [koh-moo-nee-kah-tee'vah] *nf.* facility in explaining and instructing.

Comunicazione [koh-moo-nee-kah-tsee-oh'nay] *nf.* communication, connection, message.

Comunione [koh-moo-nee-oh'nay] *nf.* communion, Sacrament.

Comunque [koh-moong'kway] *ad.* anyhow, however.

Con [kon] *pr.* by, with.

Conato [koh-nah'toh] *nm.* attempt, effort.

Conca [kong'kah] *nf.* cavity, hollow, wash-tub.

Concatenare [kong-kah-tay-nah'ray] *vt.* to interlink.

Concavo [kong'kah-voh] *nm.* hollow; *a.* concave.

Concedere [kon-chay'day-ray] *vt.* to allow, concede.

Concedibile [kon-chay-dee'bee-lay] *a.* allowable.

Concedimento [kon-chay-dee-men'toh] *nm.* concession, consent.

Concentramento [kon-chen-trah-men'toh] *nm.* concentrazione [kon-chen-trah-tsee-oh'nay] *nf.* concentration; **campo di** [kahm-poh dee]—mento, concentration camp.

Concentrare [kon-chen-trah'ray] *vt.* to concentrate.

Concepibile [kon-chay-pee'bee-lay] *a.* conceivable.

Concepimento [kon-chay-pee-men'toh] *nm.* conception.

Concepire [kon-chay-pee'ray] *vt.* to conceive, imagine.

Concernere [kon-chehr'nay-ray] *vt.* to concern, relate.

Concerta/re [kon-chehr-tah'ray] *vt.* to arrange, concert, plan; —**rsi** *vr.* to agree, be agreed.

Concertista [kon-chehr-tee'stah] *nm. and f.* concert-artist.

Concerto [kon-chehr'toh] *nm.* agreement, concert; **di** [dee] *c. ad.* unanimously.

Concessione [kon-chess-see-oh'nay] *nf.* concession, permission.

Concetto [kon-chet'toh] *nm.* conceit, conception, fancy, opinion.

Concettoso [kon-chet-toh'soh] *a.* full of ideas, sententious.

Concezione [kon-chay-tsee-oh'nay] *nf.* conception, thought.

Conchiglia [kong-keel'yah] *nf.* conch, sea-shell.

Concia [kon'chah] *nf.* tan, tanning.

Conciare [kon-chah'ray] *vt.* to dress (skins), tan; **c. la terra** [lah-tehr'rah], to dress the ground.

Conciatore [kon-chah-toh'ray] *nm.* currier, tanner.

Conciatura [kon-chah-too'-rah] *nf.* dressing, tanning.

Conciliabile [kon-chee-lee-ah'bee-lay] *a.* reconcilable.

Conciliabolo [kon-chee-lee-ah'boh-loh] *nm.* conventicle, meeting.

Concilia/re [kon-chee-lee-ah'ray] *vt.* to conciliate, reconcile; —rsi *vr.* to agree, win (affection, etc.).

Conciliazione [kon-chee-lee-ah-tsee-oh'nay] *nf.* conciliation, reconciliation.

Concilio [kon-cheel'yoh] *nm.* council.

Concimare [kon-chee-mah'ray] *vt.* to manure.

Concime [kon-chee'may] *nm.* compost, dung, manure.

Concio [kon'choh] *nm.* dung, manure.

Conciossiachè [kon-choss-see-ah-kay'] *con.* because.

Concisione [kon-chee-see-oh'nay] *nf.* conciseness.

Conciso [kon-chee'soh] *a.* concise, short.

Concitamento [kon-chee-tah-men'toh] *nm.* excitement, tumult.

Concitare [kon-chee-tah'ray] *vt.* to excite, rouse, stir up.

Concitazione [kon-chee-tah-tsee-oh'nay] *nf.* emotion, excitement.

Concittadino [kon-cheet-tah-dee'noh] *nm.* fellow-citizen.

Concludente [kong-kloo-den'tay], **conclusivo** [kong-kloo-zee'voh] *a.* conclusive, decisive.

Concludere [kong-kloo'day-ray] *vt.* to conclude, decide, end, infer.

Conclusione [kong-kloo-zee-oh'nay] *nf.* conclusion, end, summing-up; **in** [een] **c.** *ad.* finally.

Concordare [kong-korr-dah'ray] *vt.* to reconcile; *vi.* to agree.

Concordato [kong-korr-dah'toh] *nm.* agreement, concordat; *a.* agreed.

Concordevole [kong-korr-day'voh-lay] *a.* agreeable, conformable.

Concordia [kong-korr-dee-ah] *nf.* harmony, unanimity.

Concorrente [kong-korr-ren'tay] *nm.* competitor, rival; *a.* concurrent.

Concorrenza [kong-korr-rent'zah] *nf.* competition, rivalry, concurrence.

Concorrere [kong-korr-ray-ray] *vi.* to rival, compete, concur.

Concorso [kong-korr'soh] *nm.* competition, competitive examination, concourse, throng.

Concretare [kong-kray-tah'ray] *vt.* to conclude, settle, sum up.

Concreto [kong-kray'toh] *a.* concrete, positive.

Concubina [kong-koo-bee'nah] *nf.* concubine.

Concupiscenza [kong-koo-pee-shent'zah] *nf.* concupiscence, lust.

Concussione [kong-koos-see-oh'ray] *nf.* concussion, extortion.

Condanna [kon-dahn'nah] *nf.* condemnation, sentence.

Condannare [kon-dahn-nah'ray] *vt.* to condemn, sentence.

Condensa/re [kon-den-sah'ray] *vt.* to condense, thicken; —rsi *vr.* to condense, grow thick.

Condimento [kon-dee-men'toh] *nm.* relish, seasoning.

Condire [kon-dee'ray] *vt.* to dress, season.

Condiscendente [kon-dee-shen-den'tay] *a.* affable, condescending.

Condiscendenza [kon-dee-shen-dent'zah] *nf.* condescension.

Condiscendere [kon-dee-shen'day-ray] *vi.* to condescend, yield.

Condiscepolo [kon-dee-shay'poh-loh] *nm.* fellow-disciple, school-fellow.

Condito [kon-dee'toh] *a.* flavoured, seasoned.

Condividere [kon-dee-vee'day-ray] *vt.* to partake, share.

Condizionare [kon-dee-tsee-oh-nah'ray] *vt.* to condition.

Condizione [kon-dee-tsee-oh'nay] *nf.* condition, position, rank, situation; **a** [ah] **c.** *ad.* upon condition.

Condoglianza [kon-dohl-yahnt'zah] *nf.* condolence.

Condolersi [kon-doh-lehr'see] *vr.* to condole, grieve.

Condominio [kon-doh-mee'nee-oh] *nm.* joint-dominion.

Condonare [kon-doh-nah'ray] *vt.* to condone, excuse, pardon.

Condonazione [kon-doh-nah-tsee-oh'nay] *nf.* forgiveness.

Condotta [kon-dot'tah] *nf.* behaviour, conduct, conduit.

Condotto [kon-dot'toh] *nm.* conduit, pipe, trough, way; *a.* conducted, done.

Condur/re [kon-door'ray] *vt.* to conduct, lead; **—rsi** *vr.* to act, behave.

Conduttore [kon-doot-toh'ray] *nm.* conductor, driver, guide, leader.

Confabulare [kon-fah-boo-lah'ray] *vi.* to confabulate.

Confacente [kon-fah-chen'tay] *a.* convenient, suitable.

Confacimento [kon-fah-chee-men'toh] *nm.* fitness, suitableness.

Confarsi [kon-fahr'see] *vr.* to agree, become, fit, suit.

Confederarsi [kon-fay-day-rahr'see] *vr.* to confederate, form an alliance.

Conferenza [kon-fay-rent'zah] *nf.* conference, lecture.

Conferenziere [kon-fay-rent-zee-ay'ray] *nm.* lecturer.

Conferimento [kon-fay-ree-men'toh] *nm.* bestowal, conferment.

Conferire [kon-fay-ree'ray] *vt.* to bestow, confer, contribute; *vi.* to confer (with).

Conferma [kon-fehr'mah] *nf.* confirmation.

Confermare [kon-fehr-mah'ray] *vt.* to confirm, strengthen.

Confessa/re [kon-fess-sah'ray] *vt.* to acknowledge, confess; **—rsi** *vr.* to go to confession.

Confessione [kon-fess-see-oh'nay] *nf.* confession, faith.

Confessore [kon-fess-soh'ray] *nm.* confessor.

Confetto [kon-fet'toh] *nm.* bonbon, sweet. [*nf.* jam.

Confettura [kon-fet-too'rah]

Confezionare [kon-fay-tsee-oh-nah'ray] *vt.* to confect, make.

Confezione [kon-fay-tsee-oh'nay] *nf.* dress, manufacture, outfit.

Conficcare [kon-feek-kah'ray] *vt.* to drive in, thrust.

Confida/re [kon-fee-dah'ray] *vt.* to confide, trust; **—rsi** *vr.* to confide in.

Confidente [kon-fee-den'tay] *nm. and f.* confidant; *a.* confident.

Confidenza [kon-fee-dent'zah] *nf.* assurance, confidence, intimacy.

Configgere [kon-fee'djay-ray] *vt.* to nail, thrust.

Configurare [kon-fee-goo-rah'ray] *vt.* to form, shape.

Confinante [kon-fee-nahn'tay] *a.* bordering, contiguous.

Confina/re [kon-fee-nah'ray] *vt.* to confine, set bounds; *vi.* to border upon;—**rsi** *vr.* to confine oneself, retire.

Confine [kon-fee'nay] *nm.* border, frontier, limit.

Confino [kon-fee'noh] *nm.* confinement.

Confisca(zione) [kon-fees-kah-tsee-oh'nay] *nf.* confiscation, forfeiture.

Conflitto [kon-fleet'toh] *nm.* combat, conflict.

Confluire [kon-floo-ee'ray] *vi.* to flow together.

Confonde/re [kon-fon'day-ray] *vt.* to abash, confound, confuse, mistake (one for another); —**rsi** *vr.* to get confused, worry.

Conforma/re [kon-forr-mah'ray] *vt.* to conform; —**rsi** *vr.* to comply (with).

Conforme [kon-forr'may] *a.* conforming, suitable.

Conforta/re [kon-forr-tah'ray] *vt.* to comfort, console, encourage, fortify; —**rsi** *vr.* to console oneself, take courage.

Conforto [kon-forr'toh] *nm.* comfort, consolation, ease.

Confratello [kon-frah-tell'loh] *nm.* colleague, fellow-member.

Confraternità [kon-frah-tehr-nee-tah'] *nf.* brotherhood, confraternity.

Confrontare [kon-fron-tah'ray] *vt.* to compare, confront.

Confronto [kon-fron'toh] *nm.* comparison.

Confusione [kon-foo-zee-oh'nay] *nf.* confusion, (mental) disorder, shame.

Confuso [kon-foo'zoh] *a.* abashed, confused, embarrassed, indistinct.

Confutare [kon-foo-tah'ray] *vt.* to confute, disprove.

Congeda/re [kon-jay-dah'-

ray] *vt.* to dismiss, grant leave to, send away; —**rsi** *vr.* to resign, take leave.

Congedo [kon-jay'doh] *nm.* discharge, leave; in [een] **c.** *ad.* on leave.

Congegnare [kon-jayn-yah'-ray] *vt.* to put together, set up.

Congegno [kon-jayn'yoh] *nm.* appliance, gear.

Congelare [kon-jay-lah'ray] *vi.* to congeal, freeze.

Congenere [kon-jay'nay-ray] *a.* (com.) similar.

Congenito [kon-jay'nee-toh] *a.* congenital.

Congerie [kon-jay'ree-ay] *nf.* heap, mass.

Congestionare [kon-jay-stee-oh-nah'ray] *vt.* to congest, crowd.

Congettura [kon-jet-too'-rah] *nf.* conjecture, guess.

Congetturare [kon-jet-too-rah'ray] *vt.* and *i.* to conjecture.

Congiunge/re [kon-joon'-jay-ray] *vt.* to connect, join, unite, weld; —**rsi** *vr.* to join, marry.

Congiuntivo [kon-joon-tee'-voh] *nm.* (*gram.*) subjunctive; *a.* conjunctive.

Congiunto [kon-joon'toh] *nm.* kinsman, relative; *a.* joined, related.

Congiuntura [kon-joon-too'rah] *nf.* circumstance, conjuncture, emergency.

Congiura [kon-joo'rah] *nf.* conspiracy, plot.

Congiurare [kon-joo-rah'ray] *vi.* to conspire.

Conglomerare [kong-gloh-may-rah'ray] *vt.* to conglomerate.

Conglutinare [kong-gloo-tee-nah'ray] *vt.* to conglutinate.

Congratula/re [kong-grah-too-lah'ray] *vi.* —**rsi** *vr.* to congratulate.

Congrega [kong-gray'gah] *nf.* congregation, gathering.

Congrega/re [kong-gray-gah'ray] *vt.* to assemble, call together; —**rsi** *vr.* to congregate.

Congresso [kong-gress'soh] *nm.* congress, meeting.

Congruente [kong-groo-en'tay] *a.* congruent, suitable.

Congruo [kong'groo-oh] *a.* congruous, fit, suitable.

Conguaglia/re [kong-gwahl-yah'ray] *vt.* to balance, equalise; —**rsi** *vr.* to become equal.

Coniare [kohn-yah'ray] *vt.* to coin, strike (a medal).

Conigliera [koh-neel-yay'rah] *nf.* rabbit-warren.

Coniglio [koh-neel'yoh] *nm.* rabbit.

Conio [kohn'yoh] *nm.* brand, coinage, die.

Coniugare [kohn-yoo-gah'ray] *vt.* to conjugate; —**rsi** *vr.* to marry.

Coniugazione [kohn-yoo-gah-tsee-oh'nay] *nf.* conjugation.

Coniu/ge [kohn'yoo-jay] *nm.* husband; *nf.* wife; —**gi** [jee] (*pl.*) married couple.

Connazionale [kon-nah-tsee-oh-nah'lay] *nm.* and *f.* compatriot; *a.* of the same nation.

Connettere [kon-net'tay-ray] *vt.* to connect, join; **non c.** *vi.* to talk at random.

Connivente [kon-nee-ven'tay] *nm.* conniver; *a.* conniving.

Connivenza [kon-nee-vent'zah] *nf.* connivance.

Connota/to [kon-noh-tah'toh] *nm.* distinctive mark; —**ti** [tee] (*pl.*) description (of a person).

Connubio [kon-noo'bee-oh] *nm.* marriage, union.

Conocchia [koh-nock'kee-ah] *nf.* distaff.

Conoscente [koh-noh-shen'tay] *nm.* and *f.* acquaintance.

Conoscenza [koh-noh-shent'zah] *nf.* acquaintance, consciousness, knowledge.

Conosce/re [koh-noh'shay-ray] *vt.* to be acquainted with, know, recognise; **farsi c.** [fahr' see] *c.* *vi.* to make oneself known; —**rsi** *vr.* to know oneself, know each other.

Conoscibile [koh-noh-shee'bee-lay] *a.* knowable, recognisable.

Conoscimento [koh-noh-shee-men'toh] *nm.* knowledge, sense.

Conoscitore [koh-noh-shee-toh'ray] *nm.* connoisseur, good judge.

Conquista [kong-kwee'stah] *nf.* acquisition, conquest.

Conquistare [kong-kwee-stah'ray] *vt.* to conquer.

Consacrare [kon-sah-krah'ray] *vt.* to consecrate, dedicate, devote, ordain.

Consacrazione [kon-sah-krah-tsee-oh'nay] *nf.* consecration, ordination.

Consanguineo [kon-sahng-gwee'nay-oh] *a.* consanguineous, closely related.

Consapevole [kon-sah-pay'voh-lay], **conscio** [kon-shoh] *a.* acquainted, aware, conscious.

Consapevolezza [kon-sah-pay-voh-let'zah] *nf.* consciousness, knowledge.

Consegna [kon-sayn'yah] *nf.* consignment, delivery; **lasciare in** [lah-shah'ray een] *c.* *vi.* to deposit.

Consegnare [kon-sayn-yah'ray] *vt.* to consign, deliver.

Conseguente [kon-say-gwen'tay] *a.* consequent, ensuing, following.

Conseguenza [kon-say-gwent'zah] *nf.* consequence.

Conseguimento [kon-say-gwee-men'toh] *nm.* acquisition, attainment.

Conseguire [kon-say-gwee'ray] *vt.* to attain, obtain, reach; *vi.* to follow, result.

Consenso [kon-sen'soh] *nm.* assent, consent.

Consentire [kon-sen-tee'ray] *vi.* to agree, consent.

Consenziente [kon-sen-zee-en'tay] *a.* approving, consenting.

Conserva [kon-sehr'vah] *nf.* conserve, jam, preserve, reservoir, store-room.

Conserva/re [kon-sehr-vah'ray] *vt.* to keep, preserve; —rsi *vr.* to keep in good health, last.

Conservazione [kon-sehr-vah-tsee-oh'nay] *nf.* conservation, preservation.

Consesso [kon-sess'soh] *nm.* assembly, meeting.

Considerabile [kon-see-day-rah'bee-lay] *a.* important.

Considera/re [kon-see-day-rah'ray] *vt.* to consider, look at, reflect on; —rsi *vr.* to consider oneself.

Considerazione [kon-see-day-rah-tsee-oh'nay] *nf.* consideration, esteem.

Considerevole [kon-see-day-ray'voh-lay] *a.* considerable, pretty large.

Consiglia/re [kon-seel-yah'ray] *vi.* to advise, counsel; —rsi *vr.* to ask advice, consult.

Consigliere [kon-seel-yay'ray] *nm.* councillor, counsellor.

Consiglio [kon-seel'yoh] *nm.* council, counsel.

Consimile [kon-see'mee-lay] *a.* like, similar.

Consistenza [kon-see-stent'zah] *nf.* consistence, consistency, solidity.

Consistere [kon-see'stay-ray] *vi.* to consist.

Consocio [kon-soh'choh] *nm.* associate, partner.

Consola/re [kon-soh-lah'ray] *vt.* to comfort, console; —rsi *vr.* to get over, take comfort.

Consolare [kon-soh-lah'ray] *a.* consular.

Consolato [kon-soh-lah'toh] *nm.* consulate, consulship; *a.* comforted, consoled.

Console [kon'soh-lay] *nm.* consul.

Consolida/re [kon-soh-lee-dah'ray] *vt.* to consolidate, strengthen; —rsi *vr.* to grow firm.

Consonanza [kon-soh-nahnt'zah] *nf.* conformity, consonance.

Consonare [kon-soh-nah'ray] *vi.* to harmonise.

Consono [kon'soh-noh] *a.* agreeing, consonant.

Consorteria [kon-sorr-tay-ree'ah] *nf.* clique, set.

Consorzio [kon-sort'zee-oh] *nm.* syndicate, trust.

Constare [kon-stah'ray] *vi.* to appear, be evident, be made of, consist.

Constatare [kon-stah-tah'ray] *vt.* to ascertain, confirm, verify.

Consueto [kon-soo-ay'toh] *a.* habitual, usual.

Consuetudine [kon-soo-ay-too'dee-nay] *nf.* custom, habit, practise.

Consulta [kon-sool'tah] *nf.* council.

Consulta/re [kon-sool-tah'ray] *vt.* to consult, examine; *vi.* to deliberate; —rsi *vr.* to confer with, seek advice.

Consulto [kon-sool'toh] *nm.*

consultation, opinion (legal or medical).

Consuma/re [kon-soo-mah'ray] *vt.* to accomplish, consume, consummate, wear out; —rsi *vr.* to pine away, wear out.

Consumazione [kon-soo-mah-tsee-oh'nay] *nf.* consumption, consummation, drink or food (in a café, etc.).

Consumo [kon-soo'moh] *nm.* consumption, necessary quantity (of food, etc.), use.

Consunzione [kon-soon-tsee-oh'nay] *nf.* consumption (disease).

Contabile [kon-tah'bee-lay] *nm.* accountant, bookkeeper, clerk.

Contabilità [kon-tah-bee-lee-tah'] *nf.* bookkeeping.

Contadi/na [kon-tah-dee'nah] *nf.*—no [noh] *nm.* peasant.

Contadinesco [kon-tah-dee-nay'skoh] *a.* clownish, rural, rustic.

Contado [kon-tah'doh] *nm.* country (round a town).

Contagio [kon-tah'joh] *nm.* contagion.

Contagioso [kon-tah-joh'soh] *a.* catching, contagious.

Contagocce [kon-tah-gohch'chay] *nm.* dropper.

Contaminare [kon-tah-mee-nah'ray] *vt.* to contaminate.

Contante [kon-tahn'tay] *a.* counting, prompt, ready; denaro [day-nah'roh] *c.* *nm.* cash, ready money.

Contare [kon-tah'ray] *vt. and i.* to be esteemed, count, relate, rely on; ciò che conta [choh kay kon'tah], what matters.

Contatore [kon-tah-toh'ray] *nm.* meter (gas, etc.), reckoner.

Conte [kon'tay] *nm.* count, earl.

Contea [kon-tay'ah] *nf.* county, shire.

Conteggiare [kon-tay-djah'ray] *vt.* to cast up, compute.

Conteggio [kon-tay'djoh] *nm.* account, computation.

Contegno [kon-tayn'yoh] *nm.* behaviour, dignity, gravity.

Contegnoso [kon-tayn-yoh'soh] *a.* dignified, grave, staid.

Contemperare [kon-tem-pay-rah'ray] *vt.* to proportion, temper.

Contemplare [kon-tem-plah'ray] *vt.* to contemplate.

Contemporaneità [kon-tem-poh-rah-nay-ee-tah'] *nf.* contemporaneousness.

Contemporaneo [kon-tem-poh-rah'nay-oh] *nm. and a.* contemporary.

Contendente [kon-ten-den'tay] *nm.* contender, contestant; *a.* contending.

Contende/re [kon-ten'day-ray] *vt.* to contest; *vi.* to contend, quarrel; —rsi *vr.* to contend, be rivals for.

Contene/re [kon-tay-nay'ray] *vt.* to contain, hold, restrain; —rsi *vr.* to abstain, control oneself.

Contenta/re [kon-ten-tah'ray] *vt.* to content, gratify; —rsi *vr.* to be pleased, satisfied.

Contentatura [kon-ten-tah-too'rah] *nf.* contentment; di facile [dee fah'chee-lay] *c.* *ad.* easy to please.

Contentezza [kon-ten-tet'zah] *nf.* contentment, satisfaction.

Contento [kon-ten'toh] *nm.* contentment, happiness; *a.* content, glad, satisfied.

Contenuto [kon-tay-noo'toh] *nm.* contents (*pl.*), subject; *a.* contained.

Contenzione [kon-ten-tsee-oh'nay] *nf.* contention, strife.

Contenzioso [kon-ten-tsee-oh'soh] *a.* contentious, quarrelsome.

Contesa [kon-tay'sah] *nf.* contest, dispute.

Contessa [kon-tess'sah] *nf.* countess.

Contestare [kon-tay-stah'ray] *vt.* to contest, deny.

Contestazione [kon-tay-stah-tsee-oh'nay] *nf.* contest, denial, dispute.

Contesto [kon-tay'stoh] *nm.* context, text. [knowledge.

Contezza [kon-tet'zah] *nf.*

Contiguità [kon-tee-gwee-tah'] *nf.* contiguity.

Contiguo [kon-tee'gwoh] *a.* contiguous.

Continentale [kon-tee-nen-tah'lay] *a.* continental.

Continente [kon-tee-nen'tay] *nm.* continent; *a.* continent, temperate.

Continenza [kon-tee-nent'zah] *nf.* continence, self-restraint.

Contingenza [kon-teen-jent'zah] *nf.* contingency, emergency.

Continuare [kon-tee-noo-ah'ray] *vt.* to continue, pursue; *vi.* to go on, last.

Continuazione [kon-tee-noo-ah-tsee-oh'nay], **continuità** [kon-tee-noo-ee-tah'] *nf.* continuity, continuation, duration.

Continuo [kon-tee'noo-oh] *a.* continuous, lasting.

Conto [kon'toh] *nm.* account, bill, computation, reckoning, worth.

Contorcere [kon-torr'chay-ray] *vt.* —**rsi** *vr.* to twist, wring, writhe.

Contornare [kon-torr-nah'ray] *vt.* to outline, surround.

Contorno [kon-torr'noh] *nm.* contour, outline, vegetables served with a dish of meat.

Contorsione [kon-torr-see-oh'nay] *nf.* contortion, convulsion.

Contra [kon'trah] *pr.* against, opposite. *v.* Contro.

Contrabbandiere [kon-trahb-bahn-dee-ay'ray] *nm.* smuggler.

Contrabbando [kon-trahb-bahn'doh] *nm.* contraband goods (*pl.*), smuggling.

Contraccambiare [kon-trahk-kahm-bee-ah'ray] *vt.* to exchange, return.

Contraccambio [kon-trahk-kahm'bee-oh] *nm.* exchange, return.

Contraccolpo [kon-trahk-koll'poh] *nm.* rebound, recoil.

Contrada [kon-trah'dah] *nf.* countryside, district, street.

Contraddire [kon-trahd-dee'ray] *vt.* to contradict.

Contraddistinguere [kon-trahd-dee-steeng'gway-ray] *vt.* to distinguish, recognise, signalise.

Contra(d)dizione [kon-trah(d)-dee-tsee-oh'nay] *nf.* contradiction.

Contraffare [kon-trahf-fah'ray] *vt.* to counterfeit, forge, imitate; —**rsi** *vr.* to disguise oneself.

Contraffatto [kon-trahf-faht'toh] *a.* counterfeit, disguised.

Contraffazione [kon-trahf-fah-tsee-oh'nay] *nf.* counterfeiting, forgery.

Contrammiraglio [kon-trahm-mee-rahl'yoh] *nm.* Rear-Admiral.

Contrappelo [kon-trahp-pay'loh] *ad.* wrong-way.

Contrappeso [kon-trahp-pay'soh] *nm.* counter-balance, counterpoise.

Contrapporre [koh-trahp-porr'ray] *vt.* to compare, oppose; —**rsi** *vr.* to cross, oppose.

Contrappunto [kon-trahp-poon'toh] *nm.* (*mus.*) counterpoint.

Contrariare [kon-trah-ree-ah'ray] *vt.* to contradict, gainsay, thwart.

Contrario [kon-trah'ree-oh] *nm.* contrary; *a.* adverse, contrary; **al** [ahl] *c. ad.* on the contrary.

Contrar/re [kon-trahr'ray] *vt.* to contract; **—rsi** *vr.* to shrink.

Contrassegno [kon-trahs-sayn'yoh] *nm.* badge, countersign.

Contrastante [kon-trah-stahn'tay] *a.* conflicting, contradictory.

Contrasta/re [kon-trah-stah'ray] *vt.* to contest, oppose, resist; *vi.* to wrangle, be conflicting; **—rsi** *vr.* to contend for.

Contrasto [kon-trah'stoh] *nm.* contrast, opposition, strife

Contrattacco [kon-traht-tahk'koh] *nm.* counter-attack.

Contrattare [kon-traht-tah'ray] *vt. and i.* to contract, negotiate, stipulate.

Contrattempo [kon-traht-tem'poh] *nm.* contretemps, hitch, misfortune, (*mus.*) different time.

Contratto [kon-traht'toh] *nm.* agreement, contract.

Contravveleno [kon-trahv-vay-lay'noh] *nm.* antidote.

Contravvenire [kon-trahv-vay-nee'ray] *vi.* to contravene, infringe.

Contravvenzione [kon-trahv-ven-tsee-oh'nay] *nf.* contravention, fine, infringement, penalty; **fare una** [fah'ray oo'nah] *c. vi.* to impose a fine.

Contrazione [kon-trah-tsee-oh'nay] *nf.* contraction.

Contribuente [kon-tree-boo-en'tay] *nm.* tax-payer; *a.* contributing.

Contribuire [kon-tree-boo-ee'ray] *vt. and i.* to contribute, help, share.

Contrista/re [kon-tree-stah'ray] *vt.* to afflict, sadden; **—rsi** *vr.* to be afflicted, grieve.

Contrito [kon-tree'toh] *a.* contrite, penitent.

Contro [kon'troh] *pr.* against, opposite.

Controfirmare [kon-troh-feer-mah'ray] *vt.* to countersign.

Controllare [kon-troll-lah'ray] *vt.* to check, control, direct (traffic), verify.

Controllo [kon-troll'loh] *nm.* check, control.

Controllore [kon-troll-loh'ray] *nm.* controller, ticket-collector.

Controporta [kon-troh-porr'tah] *nf.* double-door.

Contrordine [kon-trorr'dee-nay] *nm.* counter-order.

Controsenso [kon-troh-sen'soh] *nm.* misinterpretation, nonsense.

Controstomaco [kon-troh-stoh'mah-koh] *ad.* unwillingly.

Controverso [kon-troh-vehr'soh] *a.* controversial, doubtful.

Controvertere [kon-troh-vehr'tay-ray] *vt.* to controvert, dispute.

Contumace [kon-too-mah'chay] *a.* contumacious.

Contumelia [kon-too-may'lee-ah] *nf.* contumely, outrage.

Contumelioso [kon-too-may-lee-oh'soh] *a.* contumelious, outrageous.

Contundente [kon-toon-den'tay] *a.* bruising.

Contundere [kon-toon'day-ray] *vt.* to bruise, contuse.

Conturba/re [kon-toor-bah-ray] *vt.* to disturb, trouble; —rsi *vr.* to be agitated, fret.

Contusione [kon-too-zee-oh'nay] *nf.* bruise, contusion.

Contuttochè [kon-toot-toh-kay'] *con.* although.

Contuttociò [kon-toot-toh-choh'] *ad.* however, still.

Convalescente [kon-vah-lay-shen'tay] *nm. and a.* convalescent.

Convalescenza [kon-vah-lay-shent'zah] *nf.* convalescence.

Convalidare [kon-vah-lee-dah'ray] *vt.* to confirm, corroborate.

Convegno [kon-vayn'yoh] *nm.* meeting(-place).

Convenevole [kon-vay-nay'voh-lay] *nm.* propriety; *a.* convenient, fit, proper, suitable.

Convenevolezza [kon-vay-nay-voh-let'zah] *nf.* propriety, suitability.

Conveniente [kon-vay-nee-en'tay] *a.* convenient, decent, fit, suitable.

Convenienza [kon-vay-nee-ent'zah] *nf.* advantage, convenience, decency, profit, propriety.

Convenire [kon-vay-nee'ray] *vi.* to agree, be better, be necessary, meet together, suit.

Convento [kon-ven'toh] *nm.* convent, monastery.

Convenuto [kon-vay-noo'toh] *nm.* (*jur.*) defendant; *a.* agreed (on), fixed, summoned.

Convenzionale [kon-ven-tsee-oh-nah'lay] *a.* conventional.

Convenzione [kon-ven-tsee-oh'nay] *nf.* convention, covenant.

Convergenza [kon-vehr-jent'zah] *nf.* convergence.

Convergere [kon-vehr'jay-ray] *vi.* to converge.

Conversa [kon-vehr'sah] *nf.* lay-sister (in a convent).

Conversare [kon-vehr-sah'ray] *vi.* to converse, talk.

Conversazione [kon-vehr-sah-tsee-oh'nay] *nf.* conversation, talk.

Converso [kon-vehr'soh] *nm.* lay-brother (in a monastery).

Converti/re [kon-vehr-tee'ray] *vt.* to convert; —rsi *vr.* to be converted, change's one religion.

Convertita [kon-vehr-tee'tah] *nm. and f.* convert.

Convessità [kon-vess-see-tah'] *nf.* convexity.

Convincere [kon-veen'chay-ray] *vt.* to convince, persuade.

Convincimento [kon-veen-chee-men'toh] *nm.* **convinzione** [kon-veen-tsee-oh'nay] *nf.* conviction, persuasion.

Convitato [kon-vee-tah'toh] *nm.* guest.

Convito [kon-vee'toh] *nm.* banquet, feast.

Convitto [kon-veet'toh] *nm.* day-school where the pupils get meals.

Convivente [kon-vee-ven'tay] *a.* living together.

Convivenza [kon-vee-vent'zah] *nf.* living together, (*jur.*) cohabitation.

Convocare [kon-voh-kah'ray] *vt.* to convoke, summon.

Convogliare [kon-voll-yah'ray] *vt.* to convoy, direct.

Convoglio [kon-voll'yoh] *nm.* convoy, train.

Convulsione [kon-vool-see-oh'nay] *nf.* convulsion, spasm.

Convulsivo [kon-vool-see'voh] *a.* convulsive, spasmodic.

Convulso [kon-vool'soh] *a.* convulsed, jerky.

Cooperare [koh-oh-pay-rah'ray] *vi.* to co-operate.

Cooperativa [koh-oh-pay

rah-tee'vah] *nf.* (com.) co-operative society.

Cooperazione [koh-oh-pay-rah-tsee-oh'nay] *nf.* co-operation.

Coordinare [koh-orr-dee-nah'ray] *vt.* to arrange, co-ordinate.

Coperchiare [koh-pehr-kee-ah'ray] *vt.* to cover.

Coperchio [koh-pehr'kee-oh] *nm.* cover, lid.

Coperta [koh-pehr'tah] *nf.* cover covering, coverlet, (naut.) deck.

Copertina [koh-pehr-tee'nah] *nf.* bedspread, book-cover.

Coperto [koh-pehr'toh] *nm.* cover, covert, place at table, safety; *a.* covered, hidden, overcast (of the sky).

Copertura [koh-pehr-too'rah] *nf.* covering.

Copia [koh'pee-ah] *nf.* copy, plenty, quantity.

Copiare [koh-pee-ah'ray] *vt.* to copy, imitate, transcribe.

Copiativo [koh-pee-ah-tee'voh] *a.* copying.

Copiatura [koh-pee-ah-too'rah] *nf.* copying, transcription.

Copioso [koh-pee-oh'soh] *a.* abundant, copious.

Copista [koh-pee'stah] *nm.* copyist.

Copisteria [koh-pee-stay-ree'ah] *nf.* copying-office.

Coppa [kop'pah] *nf.* bowl, cup.

Coppellare [kop-pell-lah'ray] *vt.* to assay, test (metals).

Coppia [kop'pee-ah] *nf.* couple, pair.

Coprifuoco [koh-pree-foo-oh'koh] *nm.* curfew.

Copri/re [koh-pree'ray] *vt.* to cover, hide, hold (a post), protect, shelter; —**rsi** *vr.* to put on one's hat, wrap oneself up.

Coraggio [koh-rah'djoh] *nm.* courage, valour.

Coraggioso [koh-rah-djoh'soh] *a.* courageous, valiant.

Corallo [koh-rahl'loh] *nm.* coral.

Corame [koh-rah'may] *nm.* all sorts of leather.

Corazza [koh-raht'zah] *nf.* armour-plate, cuirass.

Corazzare [koh-raht-zah'ray] *vt.* to armour-plate.

Corazziere [koh-raht-zee-ay'ray] *nm.* cuirassier.

Corba [korr-bah] *nf.* basket, kreel.

Corbellare [korr-bell-lah'ray] *vt.* to make a fool of, make fun of.

Corbelleria [korr-bell-lay-ree'ah] *nf.* foolish act.

Corbello [korr-bell'loh] *nm.* (small) basket.

Corbezzo/la [korr-bet'zoh-lah] *nf.* arbute-berry; —**lo** [loh] *nm.* arbute-tree.

Corda [korr'dah] *nf.* cord, rope, string (of an instrument).

Cordame [korr-dah'may] *nm.* (naut.) cordage, ropes (pl.).

Cordiale [korr-dee-ah'lay] *nm.* cordial, restorative; *a.* affectionate, cordial, hearty.

Cordicella [korr-dee-chell'lah] *nf.* **cordoncino** [korr-don-chee'noh] *nm.* fine cord.

Cordoglio [korr-dohl'yoh] *nm.* grief, mourning, sorrow.

Cordone [korr-doh'nay] *nm.* cord, cordon.

Coriando/lo [koh-ree-ahn'doh-loh] *nm.* paper-streamer; **li** [lee] (pl.) confetti.

Corica/re [koh-ree-kah'ray] *vt.* to lay down; —**rsi** *vr* to go to bed, lie down.

Corista [koh-ree'stah] *nm.* chorister.

Cornacchia [korr-nahk'kee-ah] *nf.* crow.

Cornamusa [korr-nah-moozah] *nf.* (*mus.*) bagpipes (*pl.*).

Cornetta [korr-net'tah] *nf.* (*mus.*) cornet, horn.

Cornetto [korr-net'toh] *nm.* ear-trumpet, small horn.

Cornice [korr-nee'chay] *nf.* frame.

Corniciare [korr-nee-chah' ray] *vt.* to frame.

Cornicione [korr-nee-choh' nay] *nm.* cornice.

Corno [korr'noh] *nm.* bump, horn. [horned.

Cornuto [korr-noo'toh] *a.*

Coro [koh'roh] *nm.* choir, chorus.

Corona [koh-roh'nah] *nf.* chaplet, crown, wreath.

Coronare [koh-roh-nah'ray] *vt.* to crown, perfect.

Coronazione [koh-roh-nah-tsee-oh'nay] *nf.* coronation.

Corpacciuto [korr-pahch-choo'toh] *a.* burly, corpulent.

Corpetto [korr-pet'toh] *nm.* bodice, waistcoat.

Corpo [korr'poh] *nm.* body, corps, mass.

Corporale [korr-poh-rah'lay] *a.* bodily, corporal, corporeal.

Corporatura [korr-poh-rah-too'rah] *nf.* size.

Corporazione [korr-poh-rah-tsee-oh'nay] *nf.* corporation.

Corporeo [korr-poh'ray-oh] *a.* corporeal.

Corpulento [korr-poo-len'toh] *a.* corpulent.

Corpulenza [korr-poo-lent' zah] *nf.* corpulence.

Corredare [korr-ray-dah' ray] *vt.* to equip, fit up, outfit.

Corredino [korr-ray-dee' noh] *nm.* baby's layette.

Corredo [korr-ray'doh] *nm.* equipment, furniture, kit, outfit, trousseau.

Corregge/re [korr-ray'djay-ray] *vt.* to chastise, correct,

revise, upbraid; —**rsi** *vr.* to improve, mend one's ways.

Correlazione [korr-ray-lah-tsee-oh'nay] *nf.* correlation.

Corrente [korr-ren'tay] *nm.* current, draught, fashion, stream; **tenere al** [tay-nay'ray ahl] *c.* *vt.* to keep informed; *a.* current, fluent, flowing, usual.

Correre [korr'ray-ray] *vi.* to be current, circulate, flow, pass (of time). run.

Correttezza [korr-ret-tet' zah] *nf.* correctness, propriety.

Corretto [korr-ret'toh] *a.* correct, exact, upright, well-bred.

Corret/tore [korr-ret-toh' ray] *nm.* —**trice** [tree'chay] *nf.* c. corrector, (*typ.*) proof-reader.

Correzione [korr-ray-tsee-oh' nay] *nf.* correction, reform.

Corridoio [korr-ree-doh'yoh] *nm.* corridor, passage.

Corridore [korr-ree-doh'ray] *nm.* racer, runner.

Corriera [korr-ree-ay'rah] *nf.* mail-boat, mail-bus, mail-coach.

Corriere [korr-ree-ay'ray] *nm.* courier, messenger; **a volta di** [ah voll'tah dee] *c.* *ad.* by return of post.

Corrispettivo [korr-ree-spet-tee'voh] *nm.* recompense; *a.* correspondent.

Corrispondente [korr-ree-spon-den'tay] *nm.* correspondent; *a.* correspondent, corresponding.

Corrispondere [korr-ree-spon'day-ray] *vi.* to correspond, return.

Corrivo [korr-ree'voh] *a.* easy-going.

Corroborare [korr-roh-boh-rah'ray] *vt.* to corroborate, strengthen.

Corrode/re [korr-roh'day-ray] *vt.* to corrode, eat away.

wear away; **—rsi** *vr.* to corrode, waste away.

Corrompe/re [korr-rom'-pay-ray] *vt.* to bribe, corrupt, pollute, seduce; **—rsi** *vr.* to become corrupt, rot.

Corrosivo [korr-roh-zee'voh] *a.* caustic, corrosive.

Corrotto [korr-rot'toh] *a.* corrupt(ed).

Corruccia/re [korr-rooch-chah'ray] *vi.* **—rsi** *vr.* to be angry, get angry.

Corruccio [korr-rooch'choh] *nm.* anger, wrath.

Corruccioso [korr-rooch-choh'soh] *a.* angry.

Corrugare [korr-roo-gah'ray] *vt.* to corrugate, frown, knit (one's brows), wrinkle.

Corruscare [korr-roo-skah'ray] *vi.* to scintillate.

Corruttela [korr-root-tay'lah] *nf.* corruption.

Corruttibilità [korr-root-tee-bee-lee-tah'] *nf.* corruptibility.

Corruttivo [korr-root-tee'voh] *a.* corruptive.

Corruzione [korr-roo-tsee-oh'nay] *nf.* corruption, perversion.

Corsa [korr'sah] *nf.* career, course, heat, race.

Corsaro [korr-sah'roh] *nm.* corsair, pirate.

Corsia [korr-see'ah] *nf.* current, passage, ward (in a hospital).

Corsivo [korr-see'voh] *nm.* (*typ.*) italics (*pl.*); *a.* flowing, running.

Corso [korr'soh] *nm.* course, flow, main street, tide.

Corte [korr'tay] *nf.* court, hall, tribunal, yard.

Corteccia [korr-tech'chah] *nf.* bark, crust.

Corteggiamento [korr-tay-djah-men'toh] *nm.* courtship, wooing.

Corteggiare [korr-tay-djah'ray] *vt.* to court, woo.

Corteggio [korr-tay'djoh] *nm.* attendants (*pl.*), retinue.

Corteo [korr-tay'oh] *nm.* procession, train.

Cortese [korr-tay'zay] *a.* courteous, kind, polite.

Cortesia [korr-tay-zee'ah] *nf.* courtesy, politeness.

Cortezza [korr-tet'zah] *nf.* deficiency, dullness.

Cortigiano [korr-tee-jah'noh] *nm.* courtier.

Cortile [korr-tee'lay] *nm.* court, courtyard.

Cortina [korr-tee'nah] *nf.* curtain.

Corto [korr'toh] *a.* brief, concise, deficient, short; **essere a** [ess'say-ray ah] **c.** *vi.* to be short of, lack.

Corvetta [korr-vet'tah] *nf.* curvet, (*naut.*) corvette.

Corvo [korr'voh] *nm.* raven.

Cosa [koh'sah] *nf.* business, matter, thing; **che** [kay] **cosa?** what?

Coscia [koh'shah] *nf.* haunch, thigh.

Coscienza [koh-shent'zah] *nf.* conscience, consciousness.

Coscienzioso [koh-shent-zee-oh'soh] *a.* conscientious.

Cosciotto [koh-shot'toh] *nm.* leg (of meat).

Coscritto [koh-skreet'toh] *nm. and a.* conscript.

Coscrizione [koh-skree-tsee-oh'nay] *nf.* conscription.

Così [koh-see'] *ad.* as, so, thus; **cosi, cosi,** so-so; **per** [per] **c. dire** [dee'ray] so to speak.

Cosicchè [koh-see-kay'] *con.* so that.

Cosidetto [koh-see-det'toh] *a.* so-called.

Cosmetico [koss-may'tee-koh] *nm. and a.* cosmetic.

Cosmopolita [koss-moh-poh-lee'tah] *nm. and a.* cosmopolitan.

Coso [koh'soh] *nm.* thing, thingummy (word used instead of the real name of something).

Cospargere [koh-spahr'jay-ray] *vt.* to sprinkle, strew.

Cospetto [koh-spet'toh] *nm.* presence.

Cospicuo [koh-spee'koo-oh] *a.* conspicuous.

Cospirare [koh-spee-rah'ray] *vi.* to conspire, plot.

Cospirazione [koh-spee-rah-tsee-oh'nay] *nf.* conspiracy.

Costa [koh'stah] *nf.* coast, declivity.

Costà [koh-stah'] *ad.* there, thither, in that place.

Costaggiù [koh-stah-djoo'] *ad.* down there, there below.

Costante [koh-stahn'tay] *a.* constant, firm.

Costanza [koh-stahnt'zah] *nf.* constancy, firmness, perseverance.

Costare [koh-stah'ray] *vt.* to cost.

Costatare *v.* constatare.

Costato [koh-stah'toh] *nm.* flank, ribs (*pl.*), side.

Costeggiare [koh-stay-djah'ray] *vt.* to coast, lie along, run along by.

Costei [koh-stay'ee] *pr.* she, this woman.

Costerna/re [koh-stehr-nah'ray] *vt.* to appal, dismay, terrify; —**rsi** *vr.* to be dismayed.

Costì [koh-stee'] *ad.* there, in that place.

Costiera [koh-stee-ay'rah] *nf.* coast, shore.

Costipa/re [koh-stee-pah'ray] *vt.* to constipate, give a cold to; —**rsi** *vr.* to become costive, catch a cold.

Costipato [koh-stee-pah'toh] *a.* costive, having a cold.

Costitui/re [koh-stee-too-ee'ray] *vt.* to appoint, constitute, elect; —**rsi** *vr.* to constitute oneself, give oneself up, surrender.

Costituzione [koh-stee-too-tsee-oh'nay] *nf.* constitution.

Costo [koh'stoh] *nm.* cost, price.

Costola [koh'stoh-lah] *nf.* back (of a book), rib.

Costoletta [koh-stoh-let'tah] *nf.* chop, cutlet.

Costoro [koh-stoh'roh] *pr.* (*pl.*) they, these (those) people.

Costoso [koh-stoh'soh] *a.* costly, expensive.

Costringere [koh-streen'jay-ray] *vt.* to compel, constrain, force.

Costrizione [koh-stree-tsee-oh'nay] *nf.* compulsion, constraint.

Costruire [koh-stroo-ee'ray] *vt.* to build, construct.

Costrutto [koh-stroot'toh] *nm.* construction, profit; *a.* built, constructed.

Costruzione [koh-stroo-tsee-oh'nay] *nf.* building, construction.

Costui [koh-stoo'ee] *pr.* he, this man.

Costumare [koh-stoo-mah'ray] *v. imp.* to be usual, be the fashion.

Costumatezza [koh-stoo-mah-tet'zah] *nf.* good manners (*pl.*), politeness.

Costumato [koh-stoo-mah'toh] *a.* civil, polite.

Costume [koh-stoo'may] *nm.* custom, fancy dress, habit.

Cosuccia [koh-sooch'chah] *nf.* little thing of no value, trifle.

Cotale [koh-tah'lay] *pr. and a.* such, such a one.

Cotanto [koh-tahn'toh] *a.* as much; *ad.* so long, so much.

Cotenna [koh-ten'nah] *nf.* pigskin, scalp.

Cotesto [koh-tay'stoh] *pr. and a.* that, this.

Cotidiano [koh-tee-dee-ah'-noh] a. daily.

Coto/gna [koh-tohn'yah] nf. quince; —gno [yoh] nm. quince-tree.

Cotognata [koh-tohn-yah'-tah] nf. quince marmalade.

Cotoletta: v. **costoletta.**

Cotone [koh-toh'nay] nm. cotton, cotton-plant; c. idrofilo [ee-droh'fee-loh], cotton-wool.

Cotonificio [koh-toh-nee-fee'choh] nm. cotton-mill.

Cotta [kot'tah] nf. baking, surplice; prendere una [pren'day-ray oo'nah] c. vi. to fall madly in love with, get tipsy.

Cottimo [kot'tee-moh] nm. job-work, piece-work; lavorare a [lah-voh-rah'ray ah] c. vi. to do piece-work.

Cotto [kot'toh] a. cooked, madly in love, tipsy.

Cottura [kot-too'rah] nf. cooking.

Covare [koh-vah'ray] vt. to brood, foment, hatch, hide.

Covata [koh-vah'tah] nf. brood, covey, batch.

Covile [koh-vee'lay] nm. burrow, hole.

Covo [koh'voh] nm. cave, den.

Covone [koh-voh'nay] nm. sheaf (of corn).

Cozzare [kot-zah'ray] vt. and i. to butt against, knock against, run into.

Cozzo [kot'zoh] nm. butting, collision, shock.

Crac [krahk] nm. crash, failure (financial).

Crampo [krahm'poh] nm. cramp.

Cranio [krah'nee-oh] nm. skull.

Crapulare [krah-poo-lah'ray] vi. to eat and drink to excess, lead a debauched life.

Crasso [krahs'soh] a. crass, gross.

Cratere [krah-tay'ray] nm. crater.

Cravatta [krah-vaht'tah] nf. cravat, stock, tie.

Creanza [kray-ahnt'zah] nf. breeding, manners (pl.).

Creare [kray-ah'ray] vt. to appoint, create.

Creato [kray-ah'toh] nm. creation, universe.

Creatore [kray-ah-toh'ray] nm. creator.

Creatura [kray-ah-too'rah] nf. child, creature.

Creazione [kray-ah-tsee-oh'nay] nf. appointment, creation, election.

Credente [kray-den'tay] nm. and f. believer; a. believing.

Credenza [kray-dent'zah] nf. belief, credit, faith, sideboard.

Crede/re [kray'day-ray] vt. and i. to believe, think, trust; —rsi vr. to believe oneself.

Credibile [kray-dee-bee'lay] a. believable, credible.

Credito [kray'dee-toh] nm. credit, esteem, trust.

Credo [kray'doh] nm. creed.

Credulo [kray'doo-loh] a. credulous.

Crema [kray'mah] nf. custard, élite (of society).

Cremare [kray-mah'ray] vt. to cremate.

Cremazione [kray-mah-tsee-oh'nay] nf. cremation.

Cremisi [kray-mee'zee] nm. and a. crimson.

Crepa [kray'pah] nf. chink, crack (in a wall, etc.).

Crepaccio [kray-pahch'choh] nm. crevasse, large crack.

Crepacuore [kray-pah-kwoh'ray] nm. grief, heart-break.

Crepare [kray-pah'ray] vi. to burst, crack, split.

Crepitare [kray-pee-tah'ray] vi. to crackle, patter.

Crepitio [kray-pee-tee'oh] nm. crackling, pattering.

Crepuscolo [kray-poo'skoh-loh] *nm.* dusk, gloaming, twilight.

Crescenza [kray-shent'zah] *nf.* growth, increase, rise (of water-level).

Crescere [kray'shay-ray] *vi.* to grow, increase, rise (of prices or water-level), wax (of the moon).

Crescione [kray-shoh'nay] *nm.* watercress.

Crescita [kray'shee-tah] *nf.* growth, rise.

Cresima [kray'zee-mah] *nf.* chrism, confirmation.

Cresima/re [kray-zee-mah'ray] *vt.* to confirm; **—rsi** *vr.* to be confirmed.

Crespare [kress-pah'ray] *vt.* to pleat. [clay.

Creta [kray'tah] *nf.* chalk,

Cretineria [kray-tee-nay-ree'ah] *nf.* foolish act.

Cretinismo [kray-tee-nees'moh] *nm.* cretinism, idiocy.

Cretino [kray-tee'noh] *nm. and a.* cretin, idiot(ic).

Cribro [kree'broh] *nm.* sieve.

Cricca [kreek'kah] *nf.* flush (of cards), gang.

Cricco [kreek'koh] *nm.* (*tech.*) lifting-jack.

Crimine [kree'mee-nay] *nm.* crime, offence.

Cri/ne [kree'nay], **—no** [noh] *nm.* horse-hair.

Criniera [kree-nee-ay'rah] *nf.* mane.

Cripta [kreep'tah] *nf.* crypt.

Crisantemo [kree-zahn-tay'moh] *nm.* chrysanthemum.

Crisi [kree'zee] *nf.* crisis.

Crisma [kreez'mah] *nm.* chrism, consecrated oil.

Cristallame [kree-stahl-lah'may] *nm.* crystal ware, glass ware.

Cristallizza/re [kree-stahl-leed-zah'ray] *vt.* **—rsi** *vr.* to crystallise.

Cristallo [kree-stahl'loh] *nm.* crystal, glass.

Cristianesimo [kree-stee-ah-nay'zee-moh] *nm.* Christianity.

Cristianità [kree-stee-ah-nee-tah'] *nf.* Christendom.

Cristiano [kree-stee-ah'noh] *nm. and a.* Christian.

Criterio [kree-tay'ree-oh] *nm.* criterion, judgment.

Critica [kree'tee-kah] *nf.* censure, criticism, critique.

Criticare [kree-tee-kah'ray] *vt.* to censure, criticise.

Critico [kree'tee-koh] *nm.* critic; *a.* censorious, critical.

Crocchio [krock'yoh] *nm.* gathering, group, number (of people).

Croce [kroh'chay] *nf.* affliction, cross.

Crocerossina [kroh-chay-ross-see'nah] *nf.* Red Cross nurse.

Crocevia [kroh-chay-vee'ah] *nf.* cross-roads.

Crociata [kroh-chah'tah] *nf.* crusade.

Crociato [kroh-chah'toh] *nm.* crusader; *a.* crossed.

Crocicchio [kroh-cheek'yoh] *nm.* cross-roads. [cruise.

Crociera [kroh-chay'rah] *nf.*

Crocifiggere [kroh-chee-feed'djay-ray] *vt.* to crucify.

Crocifissione [kroh-chee-fees-see-oh'nay] *nf.* crucifixion.

Crocifisso [kroh-chee-fees'soh] *nm.* crucifix; *a.* crucified.

Croco [kroh'koh] *nm.* crocus, saffron.

Crogiuolo [kroh-joo-oh'loh] *nm.* crucible.

Crollare [kroll-lah'ray] *vt.* to shake; *vi.* to collapse, fall in, subside, totter.

Crollo [kroll'loh] *nm.* collapse, fall, ruin, shake.

Cromatico [kroh-mah'tee-koh] *a.* chromatic.

Cronaca [kroh'nah-kah] *nf.* chronicle, report.

Cronico [kroh'nee-koh] *a.* (*med.*) chronic.

Cronista [kroh-nee'stah] *nm.* chronicler, reporter.

Crosciare [kroh-shah'ray] *vi.* to pour (with rain).

Crosta [kroh'stah] *nf.* crust, scab.

Crostaceo [kroh-stah'chay-oh] *nm.* crustacean; *a.* crustaceous.

Crostino [kroh-stee'noh] *nm.* snippet of toast.

Crostoso [kroh-stoh'soh] *a.* crusty.

Crotalo [kroh'tah-loh] *nm.* rattle-snake.

Cruccia/re [krooch-chah'ray] *vt.* to irritate, worry; —rsi *vr.* to be troubled, worry.

Cruccio [krooch'choh] *nm.* trouble, worry.

Cruciare [kroo-chah'ray] *vt.* to torment.

Crudele [kroo-day'lay] *a.* cruel.

Crudezza [kroo-det'zah] *nf.* crudeness, rawness.

Crudo [kroo'doh] *a.* crude, harsh, raw, unripe.

Cruento [kroo-en'toh] *a.* bloody, dreadful.

Crusca [kroo'skah] *nf.* bran, freckles (*pl.*).

Cubito [koo'bee-toh] *nm.* cubit, elbow, forearm.

Cubo [koo'boh] *nm.* cube, die.

Cuccagna [kook-kahn'yah] *nf.* land flowing with milk and honey, cockaigne.

Cuccetta [kooch-chet'tah] *nf.* berth, bunk.

Cucchiaiata [kook-kee-ah-yah'tah] *nf.* spoonful.

Cucchiaino [kook-kee-ah-ee'noh] *nm.* small spoon, tea-spoon.

Cucchiaio [kook-kee-ah'yoh] *nm.* spoon.

Cuccia [kooch'chah] *nf.* dog's bed.

Cucciolo [kooch'choh-loh] *nm.* puppy.

Cucco [kook'koh] *nm.* darling, pet.

Cucina [koo-chee'nah] *nf.* cooking, kitchen.

Cucinare [koo-chee-nah'ray] *vt.* to cook, dress (food).

Cucire [koo-chee'ray] *vt.* to sew, stitch.

Cucitrice [koo-chee-tree'chay] *nf.* seamstress.

Cucitura [koo-chee-too'rah] *nf.* seam, sewing.

Cuculo [koo'koo-loh] *nm.* cuckoo.

Cuffia [koof'yah] *nf.* bonnet, cap, (*rad.*) ear-phone.

Cugi/na [koo-jee'nah] *nf.* —no [noh] *nm.* cousin.

Cui [koo'ee] *pn.* which, whom, whose.

Culinaria, arte [koo-lee-nah'ree-ah ahr'tay] *nf.* cookery.

Culla [kool'lah] *nf.* cradle.

Cullare [kool-lah'ray] *vt.* to lull, rock (a cradle).

Culminare [kool-mee-nah'ray] *vi.* to culminate.

Culmine [kool'mee-nay] *nm.* apex, top.

Culo [koo'loh] *nm.* buttocks (*pl.*) rump.

Culto [kool'toh] *nm.* cult, worship.

Cultura [kool-too'rah] *nf.* cultivation, culture.

Cumulare [koo-moo-lah'ray] *vt.* to accumulate.

Cumulo [koo'moo-loh] *nm.* accumulation, heap, pile.

Cuneo [koo'nay-oh] *nm.* wedge.

Cuo/ca [koo-oh'kah] *nf.* —co [koh] *nm.* cook.

Cuocere [koo-oh'chay-ray] *vt.* to boil, cook.

Cuoiaio [koo-oh-ee-ah'yoh] *nm.* currier.

Cuoio [koo-oh'yoh] *nm.* leather, skin.

Cuore [kwoh'ray] *nm.* centre, courage, heart.

Cupidigia [koo-pee-dee'jah], **cupidità** [koo-pee-dee-tah'] *nf.* cupidity, covetousness, greed.

Cupido [koo'pee-doh] *a.* covetous, eager, greedy.

Cupo [koo'poh] *a.* dark, deep, hollow.

Cupola [koo'poh-lah] *nf.* cupola, dome.

Cupone [koo-poh'nay] *nm.* coupon.

Cura [koo'rah] *nf.* care, cure, parish, (*med.*) treatment.

Curante, medico [may'dee-koh koo-rahn'tay] *nm.* doctor in charge of a case.

Cura/re [koo-rah'ray] *vt.* to care, take care of, (*med.*) treat; —**rsi** *vr.* to take care of oneself, mind.

Curato [koo-rah'toh] *nm.* curate, parish-priest.

Curatore [koo-rah-toh'ray] *nm.* trustee.

Curiosare [koo-ree-oh-sah'ray] *vi.* to be curious about, pry into.

Curioso [koo-ree-oh'soh] *a.* curious, inquisitive.

Curva [koor'vah] *nf.* bend, curve.

Curva/re [koor-vah'ray] *vt.* —**rsi** *vr.* to bend, curve.

Curvatura [koor-vah-too'rah] *nf.* bending, (*tech.*) camber, curvature.

Curvo [koor'voh] *a.* bent, crooked, curved.

Cuscinetto [koo-shee-net'toh] *nm.* (*tech.*) bearing; small cushion.

Cuscino [koo-shee'noh] *nm.* (*tech.*) buffer; cushion.

Custode [koo-stoh'day] *nm.* attendant, custodian, janitor, porter.

Custodia [koo-stoh-dee-ah] *nf.* care, case, custody, keeping.

Custodi/re [koo-stoh-dee'ray] *vt.* to guard, keep; —**rsi** *vr.* to take care of oneself.

Cute [koo'tay] *nf.* skin (human).

Cuticola [koo-tee'koh-lah] *nf.* cuticle.

Czeco [chay'koh] *nm. and a.* Czech.

D

Da [dah] *pr.* at, by from, off, out of, since, to; *ad.* as, like.

Dabbasso, da basso [dah(b)-bahs'soh] *ad.* below, down there, downstairs.

Dabbenaggine [dahb-bay-nah'djee-nay] *nf.* ingenuousness, simplicity, stupidity.

Dabbene [dahb-bay'nay] *a.* good, honest, upright.

Daccanto, da canto [dah(k)-kahn'toh] *ad. and pr.* by, close, near.

Daccapo, da capo [dah(k)-kah'poh] *ad.* again, once more, over again.

Dacché [dahk-kay'], **da che** [dah kay] *con.* seeing that, since.

Dado [dah'doh] *nm.* cube, die, (*mech.*) nut.

Daffare, da fare [dah(f)-fah'ray] *nm.* occupation, work; **un gran** (con grahn) **d.** a great to-do.

Dagli [dahl'yee]=da gli *pr. and art. m.* (*pl.*) by the, etc.

Dai [dah'ee]=da i, *pr. and art. m.* (*pl.*) by the, etc.

Dal [dahl]=da il, *pr. and art. m.* (*sing.*) by the, etc.

Dalla [dahl'lah]=da la, *pr. and art. f.* (*sing.*) by the, etc.

Dalle [dahl'lay]=da le, *pr. and art. f.* (*pl.*) by the, etc.

D'altronde [dahl-tron'day] *ad.* on the other hand, moreover.

Dama [dah'mah] *nf.* draughts (game), lady, noblewoman.

Damigiana [dah-mee-jah'nah] *nf.* demijohn, large jar.

Danaro: *v.* denaro.

Danna/re [dahn-nah'ray] *vt.* to damn; —rsi *vr.* to damn oneself.

Danneggiare [dahn-nay-djah'ray] *vt.* to damage, harm, impair, injure, spoil.

Danno [dahn'noh] *nm.* damage, hurt, injury.

Dannoso [dahn-noh'soh] *a.* damaging, hurtful, prejudicial.

Danzare [dahnt-zah'ray] *vi.* to dance.

Dappertutto [dahp-pehr-toot'toh] *ad.* everywhere.

Dappocaggine [dahp-poh-kah'djee-nay] *nf.* silliness, worthlessness.

Dappoco [dahp-poh'koh] *a.* good-for-nothing, silly.

Dappoi [dahp-poh'ee] *ad.* afterwards, then.

Dappresso [dahp-press'soh] *ad.* by, close by, near.

Dapprima, da prima [dah(p)-pree'mah] *ad.* at first, first of all, to begin with.

Da/re [dah'ray] *vt.* to give, produce, yield; —rsi *vr.* to devote oneself, give oneself.

Dare [dah'ray] *nm.* (com.) debit, liabilities (pl.).

Darsena [dahr'say-nah] *nf.* basin, wet-dock.

Data [dah'tah] *nf.* date.

Datare [dah-tah'ray] *vi.* to date.

Da/tore [dah-toh'ray] *nm.* —trice [tree'chay] *nf.* giver; d. di lavoro [dee lah-voh'roh], employer.

Dattero [daht'tay-roh] *nm.* date, date-tree.

Dattilografare [daht-tee-loh-grah-fah'ray] *vt. and i.* to type.

Dattilogra/fo [daht-tee-loh'grah-foh] *nm.*—fa [fah] *nf.* typist.

Dattorno, da torno [dah(t)-torr'noh] *ad.* around.

Davanti [dah-vahn'tee] *ad.* before; *pr.* before, in front of, opposite.

Davanzale [dah-vahnt-zah'lay] *nm.* window-sill.

Davanzo, d'avanzo [dah-vahnt'zoh] *ad.* more than enough, over.

Davvero, da vero [dah(v)-vay'roh] *ad.* indeed, really, truly; per [pehr] d. in earnest.

Dazio [dah'tsee-oh] *nm.* customs duty, excise, toll.

Dea [day'ah] *nf.* goddess.

Debilitare [day-bee-lee-tah'ray] *vt.* to debilitate, weaken.

Debito [day'bee-toh] *nm.* debt; *a.* due, needful.

Debi/tore [day-bee-toh'ray] *nm.*—trice [tree'chay] *nf.* debtor.

Debole [day'boh-lay] *nm.* partiality, weakness; *a.* feeble, weak.

Debolezza [day-boh-let'zah] *nf.* feebleness, weakness.

Debuttare [day-boot-tah'ray] *vi.* to make one's début.

Debutto [day-boot'toh] *nm.* début, first appearance on the stage.

Decadere [day-kah-day'ray] *vi.* to become obsolete, decay, have seen better days.

Decano [day-kah'noh] *nm.* dean.

Decantare [day-kahn-tah'ray] *vt.* to extol, praise.

Decapitare [day-kah-pee-tah'ray] *vt.* to behead, decapitate.

Decapitazione [day-kah-pee-tah-tsee-oh'nay] *nf.* beheading.

Decarburare [day-kahr-boo-rah'ray] *vt.* to decarbonise.

Deceduto [day-chay-doo'toh] *a.* deceased, late.

Decenne [day-chen'nay] *a.* ten years old.

Decennio [day-chen'nee-oh] *nm.* decade, period of ten years.

Decente [day-chen'tay] *a.* decent, seemly.

Decentra/re [day-chen-trah'ray] *vt.*; —**rsi** *vr.* to decentralise.

Decenza [day-chent'zah] *nf.* decency, seemliness.

Decesso [day-chess'soh] *nm.* death, decease; **atto di** [aht'toh dee] d. death-certificate.

Decide/re [day-chee'day-ray] *vt.* to decide, settle; —**rsi** *vr.* to decide, make up one's mind.

Decima [day'chee-mah] *nf.* tenth part, tithe.

Decimare [day-chee-mah'ray] *vt.* to decimate, tithe.

Decimo [day'chee-moh] *a.* tenth.

Decina [day-chee'nah] *nf.* half a score.

Decisione [day-chee-zee-oh'nay] *nf.* decision, resolution.

Deciso [day-chee'zoh] *a.* decided, determined, resolute.

Declamare [day-klah-mah'ray] *vt.* and *i.* to declaim.

Declamatore [day-klah-mah-toh'ray] *nm.* declaimer, tub-thumper.

Declinare [day-klee-nah'ray] *vt.* to decline, refuse; **d. le proprie generalità** [lay proh'pree-ay jay-nay-rah-lee-tah'], to give an account of oneself; *vi.* to decline, fall off, slope.

Declivio [day-klee'vee-oh] *nm.* declivity, slope.

Decollare [day-koll-lah'ray] *vt.* to behead; *vi.* (*avia.*) to take off.

Decollo [day-koll'loh] *nm.* (*avia.*) taking-off.

Decompor/re [day-kom-porr'ray] *vt.* to decompose; —**rsi** *vr.* to decompose, putrefy.

Decorare [day-koh-rah'ray] *vt.* to confer a title on, decorate, embellish.

Decoratore [day-koh-rah-toh'ray] *nm.* decorator.

Decorazione [day-koh-rah-tsee-oh'nay] *nf.* decoration, ornament.

Decoro [day-koh'roh] *nm.* decorum, honour.

Decoroso [day-koh-roh'soh] *a.* decorous, seemly.

Decorrere [day-korr'ray-ray] *vi.* to date, elapse, expire, run (of time).

Decorso [day-korr'soh] *nm.* course, period; *a.* expired, last (of time).

Decrepitezza [day-kray-pee-tet'zah] *nf.* decrepitude.

Decrepito [day-kray'pee-toh] *a.* decrepit, worn out.

Decrescere [day-kray'shay-ray] *vi.* to decrease, fall, wane.

Decretare [day-kray-tah'ray] *vt.* to award, decree.

Decreto [day-kray'toh] *nm.* decree.

Decuplo [day'koo-ploh] *nm. and a.* ten times, tenfold.

Dedica [day'dee-kah] *nf.* dedication (written).

Dedica/re [day-dee-kah'ray] *vt.* to consecrate, dedicate, devote; —**rsi** *vr.* to devote oneself, take to.

Dedito [day'dee-toh] *a.* addicted, devoted, prone.

Dedizione [day-dee-tsee-oh'nay] *nf.* dedication, devotion.

Dedurre [day-door'ray] *vt.* to deduce, infer.

Deferente [day-fay-ren'tay] *a.* deferent, respectful.

Deferenza [day-fay-rent'zah] *nf.* deference, respect.

Deferire [day-fay-ree'ray] *vt. and i.* to commit, defer, put off.

Defezione [day-fay-tsee-oh'nay] *nf.* defection, desertion.

Deficiente [day-fee-chen'tay] *a.* deficient, wanting, weak-minded.

Deficienza [day-fee-chent'zah] *nf.* deficiency, weak-mindedness.

Definire [day-fee-nee'ray] *vt.* to define, settle.

Definito [day-fee-nee'toh] *a.* definite.

Definizione [day-fee-nee-tsee-oh'nay] *nf.* definition, settlement.

Deforma/re [day-forr-mah'ray] *vt.* to deface, deform, spoil the shape of; **—rsi** *vr.* to get deformed, lose one's shape.

Deforme [day-forr'may] *a.* deformed, shapeless, ugly.

Deformità [day-forr-mee-tah'] *nf.* deformity.

Defunto [day-foon'toh] *a.* deceased, late.

Degenerare [day-jay-nay-rah'ray] *vi.* to degenerate, get worse.

Degenerazione [day-jay-nay-rah-tsee-oh'nay] *nf.* degeneration.

Degenere [day-jay'nay-ray] *a.* degenerate.

Degente [day-jen'tay] *nm. and f.* in-patient; *a.* bed-ridden, confined to bed.

Degli [dayl'yee]=di gli *pr. and art. m. (pl.)* of the.

Degna/re [dayn-yah'ray] *vt.* to hold worthy; *vi.* to be affable; **—rsi** *vr.* to deign.

Degnazione [dayn-yah-tsee-oh'nay] *nf.* condescension.

Degno [dayn'yoh] *a.* deserving, worthy.

Degrada/re [day-grah-dah'-ray] *vt.* to degrade, disgrace; **—rsi** *vr.* to abase oneself, degrade oneself.

Degustare [day-goo-stah'ray] *vt.* to sample, taste.

Degustazione [day-goo-stah-tsee-oh'nay] *nf.* sample (of food, etc.), sampling, tasting.

Dei [day'ee] *nm. (pl.)* gods *(pl.)*.

Dei [day'ee]=di i, *pr. and art. m. (pl.)* of the.

Deificare [day-ee-fee-kah'ray] *vt.* to deify.

Del [dell]=di il, *pr. and art. m. (sing.)* of the.

Dela/tore [day-lah-toh'ray] *nm.* **—trice** [tree-chay] *nf.* accuser, informer.

Delazione [day-lah-tsee-oh'nay] *nf.* accusation, information.

Delega [day'lay-gah] *nf.* delegation (of authority, etc.), power.

Delegare [day-lay-gah'ray] *vt.* to delegate, depute.

Delegazione [day-lay-gah-tsee-oh'nay] *nf.* committee, delegation.

Deleterio [day-lay-tay'ree-oh] *a.* deleterious, harmful.

Delfino [dell-fee'noh] *nm.* Dauphin, dolphin (fish).

Deliberare [day-lee-bay-rah'ray] *vt.* to deliberate, pass (a resolution).

Deliberazione [day-lee-bay-rah-tsee-oh'nay] *nf.* deliberation, resolution.

Delicatezza [day-lee-kah-tet'zah] *nf.* delicateness, delicacy, nicety, sense of propriety.

Delicato [day-lee-kah'toh] *a.* delicate, fastidious, nice.

Delimitare [day-lee-mee-tah'ray] *vt.* to fix the boundaries.

Delineare [day-lee-nay-ah'ray] *vt.* to delineate, outline, sketch.

Delinquente [day-leeng-kwen'tay] *nm.* and *a.* delinquent, criminal.

Delinquere [day-leeng-kway-ray] *vi.* to commit a crime.

Deliquio [day-lee'kwee-oh] *nm.* faint, swoon.

Delirare [day-lee-rah'ray] *vi.* to be delirious, rave.

Delirio [day-lee'ree-oh] *nm.* delirium, raving.

Delitto [day-leet'toh] *nm.* crime.

Delittuoso [day-leet-too-oh'soh] *a.* criminal.

Delizia [day-leet'see-ah] *nf.* charm, delight, pleasure.

Delizia/re [day-lee-tsee-ah'ray] *vt.* to charm, delight; —**rsi** *vr.* to delight in, take pleasure in.

Delizioso [day-lee-tsee-oh'soh] *a.* charming, delightful.

Della [dell'lah]=di la, *pr.* and *art.* f. (*sing.*) of the.

Delle [dell'lay]=di le, *pr.* and *art.* f. (*pl.*) of the.

Dello [dell'loh]=di lo, *pr.* and *art.* m. (*sing.*) of the.

Delucidare [day-loo-chee-dah'ray] *vt.* to explain.

Deludere [day-loo'day-ray] *vt.* to delude, disappoint, impose on.

Delusione [day-loo-zee-oh'nay] *nf.* delusion, disappointment.

Demente [day-men'tay] *nm.* and f. lunatic; *a.* demented, insane, out of one's mind.

Demenza [day-ment'zah] *nf.* insanity, lunacy.

Demeritare [day-may-ree-tah'ray] *vt.* and *i.* to forfeit (one's good opinion), be unworthy of.

Democratico [day-moh-krah'tee-koh] *a.* democratic.

Democrazia [day-moh-krah-tsee'ah] *nf.* democracy.

Demolire [day-moh-lee'ray] *vt.* to demolish, raze.

Demone [day'moh-nay], demonio [day-moh'nee-oh] *nm.* demon.

Demoniaco [day-moh-nee'ah-koh] *a.* demoniac(al).

Demoralizzare [day-moh-rah-leed-zah'ray] *vt.* to corrupt, demoralise.

Denaro [day-nah'roh] *nm.* money.

Denaroso [day-nah-roh'soh] *a.* moneyed, wealthy.

Denigrare [day-nee-grah'ray] *vt.* to detract, disparage.

Denigrazione [day-nee-grah-tsee-oh'nay] *nf.* disparagement.

Denominare [day-noh-mee-nah'ray] *vt.* to denominate, name.

Denotare [day-noh-tah'ray] *vt.* to denote, signify.

Densità [den-see-tah'] *nf.* density, thickness [thick.

Denso [den'soh] *a.* dense,

Dentare [den-tah'ray] *vt.* (*tech.*) to cog, indent, tooth.

Dentato [den-tah'toh] *a.* cogged, toothed.

Dentatura [den-tah-too'rah] *nf.* (set of) teeth.

Dente [den'tay] *nm.* fang, prong, tooth.

Dentellare [den-tell-lah'ray] *vt.* to indent, notch.

Dentice [den'tee-chay] *nm.* a kind of fish.

Dentiera [den-tee-ay'rah] *nf.* dental plate, false teeth (*pl.*).

Dentifricio [den-tee-free'choh] *nm.* tooth-paste.

Dentista [den-tee'stah] *nm.* dentist.

Dentizione [den-tee-tsee-oh'nay] *nf.* dentition, teething.

Dentro [den'troh] *ad.* and *pr.* inside, within.

Denudare [day-noo-dah'ray] *vt.* to denude, strip.

6

Denuncia [day-noon'chah] *nf.* declaration, denunciation.

Denunciare [day-noon-chah'ray] *vt.* to declare, denounce.

Denutrito [day-noo-tree'toh] *a.* underfed.

Deperimento [day-pay-reemen'toh] *nm.* decay, deterioration, pining away.

Deperire [day-pay-ree'ray] *vi.* to decay, perish, pine away.

Depilare [day-pee-lah'ray] *vt.* to depilate, remove hairs.

Depilatorio [day-pee-lahtoh'ree-oh] *nm. and a.* depilatory.

Deplorare [day-ploh-rah'ray] *vt.* to deplore, lament regret.

Deplorevole [day-ploh-ray'voh-lay] *a.* deplorable, lamentable, pitiable.

Depopolare [day-poh-pohlah'ray] *vt.* to depopulate.

Deporre [day-porr'ray] *vt.* to depose, lay aside, lay down; *vi.* to bear witness, depone.

Deportare [day-porr-tah'ray] *vt.* to deport, transport.

Deportato [day-porr-tah'toh] *nm.* deportee, criminal condemned to transportation; *a.* deported, transported.

Depositare [day-poh-zeetah'ray] *vt.* to bank, deposit, lodge.

Depositario [day-poh-zeetah'ree-oh] *nm.* depository.

Deposito [day-poh'zee-toh] *nm. (mil.)* depôt; deposit, warehouse.

Deprava/re [day-prah-vah'ray] *vt.* to corrupt, deprave; **—rsi** *vr.* to become depraved.

Deprecare [day-pray-kah'ray] *vt.* to deprecate, disapprove.

Depredamento [day-praydah-men'toh] *nm.* **depredazione** [day-pray-dah-tsee-oh'nay] *nf.* depredation, pillage.

Depredare [day-pray-dah'ray] *vt.* to depredate, pillage.

Depresso [day-press'soh] *a.* depressed, low-spirited.

Deprezzare [day-pret-zah'ray] *vt.* to depreciate, disparage, slight, undervalue.

Deprimente [day-pree-men'tay] *nm. (med.)* sedative; *a.* depressing.

Depurare [day-poo-rah'ray] *vt.* to purify, refine.

Deputare [day-poo-tah'ray] *vt.* to appoint, delegate, depute.

Deputato [day-poo-tah'toh] *nm.* delegate, deputy; *a.* delegated, deputed.

Deputazione [day-poo-tahtsee-oh'nay] *nf.* committee, deputation.

Deragliamento [day-rahl-yah-men'toh] *nm.* derailment, leaving the rails.

Deragliare [day-rahl-yah'ray] *vt.* to derail; *vi.* to be derailed, leave the rails.

Derelitto [day-ray-leet'toh] *a.* abandoned, derelict.

Deridere [day-ree'day-ray] *vt.* to deride, laugh at, ridicule.

Derisione [day-ree-zee-oh'nay] *nf.* derision, ridicule.

Deriva [day-ree'vah] *nf. (naut.)* drift, lee-way; **alla** [ahl'lah] d. *ad.* adrift, astray.

Derivare [day-ree-vah'ray] *vt.* to deduce, derive, trace; *vi.* to be caused by, result from.

Derivazione [day-ree-vah-tsee-oh'nay] *nf.* derivation.

Deroga [day'roh-gah] *nf.* derogation.

Derogare [day-roh-gah'ray] *vi.* to depart, derogate, fall below.

Derogazione [day-roh-gah-tsee-oh'nay] *nf.* derogation.

Derrata [dehr-rah'tah] *nf.* edible commodity.

Derubamento [day-roo-bah-men'toh] *nm.* robbery.

Derubare [day-roo-bah'ray] *vt.* to rob.

Desco [dess'koh] *nm.* butcher's slab, dinner table.

Descrivere [dess-kree'vay-ray] *vt.* to describe, relate.

Descrizione [dess-kree-tsee-oh'nay] *nf.* description.

Deserto [day-zehr'toh] *nm.* desert; *a.* deserted, desolate, lonely.

Deserzione [day-zehr-tsee-oh'nay] *nf.* desertion.

Desiderare [day-see-day-rah'ray] *vt.* to desire, long for, want; farsi [fahr'see] d. *vi.* to be missed, keep people waiting.

Desiderio [day-see-day'ree-oh] *nm.* desire, wish.

Desideroso [day-see-day-roh'soh] *a.* eager, longing for.

Designare [day-seen-yah'ray] *vt.* to appoint, design, designate, name.

Desinare [day-zee-nah'ray] *vi.* to dine; *nm.* main meal.

Desinenza [day-zee-nent'zah] *nf.* ending, termination.

Desistere [day-see'stay-ray] *vi.* to desist, give up, leave off.

Desolare [day-zoh-lah'ray] *vt.* to desolate, devastate, ravage.

Desolato [day-zoh-lah'toh] *a.* desolate, very sorry.

Desolazione [day-zoh-lah-tsee-oh'nay] *nf.* desolation, devastation.

Despota [dess'poh-tah] *nm.* despot.

Des/sa [dess'sah] *pr.* she; —so [soh] *pr.* he.

Desta/re [dess-tah'ray] *vt.* to (a)wake, excite, rouse, stir up; —rsi *vr.* to (a)wake, be roused.

Destinare [dess-tee-nah'ray] *vt.* to apply, appoint, destine, fix.

Destino [dess-tee'noh] *nm.* destiny, fate.

Destituire [dess-tee-too-ee'ray] *vt.* to dismiss, remove (from office).

Destituito [dess-tee-too-ee'toh] *a.* deprived of, removed from, void of, destitute.

Destituzione [dess-tee-too-tsee-oh'nay] *nf.* dismissal, removal.

Desto [dess'toh] *a.* awake, quick, watchful.

Destra [dess'trah] *nf.* right, right hand, right side, (*naut.*) starboard.

Destreggia/re [dess-tray-djah'ray] *vi.* to act skilfully, be skilful; —rsi *vr.* to manage, manoeuvre, steer one's course.

Destrezza [dess-tret'zah] *nf.* dexterity, skill.

Destro [dess'troh] *nm.* opportunity, right moment; cogliere il [koll'yay-ray eel] d. *vi.* to seize the chance; *a.* clever, dexterous, right.

Desumere [day-soo'may-ray] *vt.* to deduce, infer.

Detenere [day-tay-nay'ray] *vt.* to detain, keep back, withhold.

Detenuto [day-tay-noo'toh] *nm.* prisoner; *a.* kept back, withheld.

Detenzione [day-ten-tsee-oh'nay] *nf.* detention, imprisonment.

Deteriora/re [day-tay-ree-oh-rah'ray] *vt.* to deteriorate, make worse; —rsi *vr.* to deteriorate, get worse.

Determinare [day-tehr-mee-nah'ray] *vt. and i.* to decide, determine.

Detersivo [day-tehr-see'voh] *a.* cleansing.

Detestare [day-tess-tah'ray] *vt.* to detest, hate, loathe.

Detestazione [day-tess-tah-tsee-oh'nay] *nf.* detestation, loathing. (*rare*) *v.* Odio.

Detonare [day-toh-nah'ray] vt. and i. to detonate.

Detrarre [day-trahr'ray] vt. to deduct.

Detrat/tore [day-traht-toh'ray] nm.—**trice** [tree'chay] nf. detractor, slanderer.

Detrazione [day-trah-tsee-oh'nay] nf. deduction, detraction, slander.

Detrito [day-tree'toh] nm. rubbish, sweepings (pl.).

Detronizzare [day-troh-need-zah'ray] vt. to dethrone.

Detta [det'tah] nf. saying, what they say; a [ah] d. di [dee] ad. according to.

Dettagliare [det-tahl-yah'ray] vt. to detail.

Dettaglio [det-tahl'yoh] nm. detail, particular; **commercio al** [kom-mehr'choh ahl] d. (com.), retail trade.

Dettame [det-tah'may] nm. dictate, suggestion. [dictate.

Dettare [det-tah'ray] vt. to

Dettato [det-tah'toh] nm. **dettatura** [det-tah-too'rah] nf. dictation.

Detto [det'toh] nm. by-word, saying; a. called, named, said.

Deturpare [day-toor-pah'ray] vt. to deface, disfigure.

Devastare [day-vah-stah'ray] vt. to devastate, ravage.

Devastazione [day-vah-stah-tsee-oh'nay] nf. devastation.

Deviamento [day-vee-ah-men'toh] nm. deviation, derailment, diversion (of traffic, etc.).

Deviare [day-vee-ah'ray] vt. and i. to deviate, be diverted, stray, swerve.

Deviatoio [day-vee-ah-toh'yoh] nm. (tech.) points (pl.), switch.

Devoluzione [day-voh-loo-tsee-oh'nay] nf. devolution, transfer.

Devolvere [day-voll'vay-ray] vt. to assign, devolve, transfer.

Devoto [day-voh'toh] nm. devotee; a. devout.

Devozione [day-voh-tsee-oh'nay] nf. devotion, piety.

Di [dee] pr. at, by, of, on, with.

Di [dee] nm. day.

Diabolico [dee-ah-boh'lee-koh] a. diabolic(al).

Diabolo [dee-ah'boh-loh] nm. devil. v. **Diavolo**.

Diacono [dee-ah'koh-noh] nm. deacon.

Diafano [dee-ah'fah-noh] a. diaphanous.

Diagnosi [dee-ahn'yoh-zee] nf. diagnosis.

Diagnosti/ca [dee-ahn-yoh'stee-kah] nf. diagnostics (pl.). —**co** [koh] a. diagnostic.

Diagramma [dee-ah-grahm'mah] nm. chart, diagram.

Dialettale [dee-ah-let-tah'lay] a. dialectal, dialectical.

Dialetto [dee-ah-let'toh] nm. dialect.

Dialogo [dee-ah'loh-goh] nm. dialogue.

Diamante [dee-ah-mahn'tay] nm. diamond.

Diamine! [dee-ah'mee-nay] int. the deuce! of course!

Diana [dee-ah'nah] nf. morning-star, reveille.

Dianzi [dee-ahnt'zee] ad. just now, not long ago.

Diario [dee-ah're-oh] nm. diary.

Diarrea [dee-ahr-ray'ah] nf. diarrhoea.

Diavolo [dee-ah'voh-loh] nm. devil.

Dibatte/re [dee-baht'tay-ray] vt. to argue, discuss; —**rsi** vr. to struggle.

Dicastero [dee-kah'stay-roh] nm. (higher) government office.

Dicembre [dee-chem'bray] nm. December.

Diceria [dee-chay-ree'ah] *nf.* hearsay, rumour.

Dicevole [dee-chay'voh-lay] *a.* becoming, fit, proper.

Dicevolezza [dee-chay-voh-let'zah] *nf.* becomingness, propriety.

Dichiara/re [dee-kee-ah-rah'ray] *vt.* to declare, state; —rsi *vr.* to declare oneself.

Dicianno/ve [dee-chahn-noh'vay] *a.* nineteen; —vesimo [vay'zee-moh] *a.* nineteenth.

Diciasset/te [dee-chahs-set'tay] *a.* seventeen; —tesimo [tay'zee-moh] *a.* seventeenth.

Dicibile [dee-chee'bee-lay] *a.* that may be said, tellable.

Diciot/to [dee-chot'toh] *a.* eighteen; —tesimo [tay'zee-moh] *a.* eighteenth.

Dici/tore [dee-chee-toh'ray] *nm.*—trice [tree'chay] *nf.* (*rad.*) announcer, speaker, teller.

Dicitura [dee-chee-too'rah] *nf.* delivery, diction, elocution.

Didascalia [dee-dah-skahl'yah] *nf.* caption.

Didentro [dee-den'troh] *ad.* inside.

Dieci [dee-ay'chee] *a.* ten.

Diecina [dee-ay-chee'nah] *nf.* half-score, ten.

Dieta [dee-ay'tah] *nf.* assembly, diet, regimen.

Dietreggiare: *v.* **indietreggiare**.

Dietro [dee-ay'troh] *nm.* back; *ad.* and *pr.* after, behind; **essere** [ess'say-ray] d. *vi.* to be busy.

Difende/re [dee-fen'day-ray] *vt.* to defend, guard, protect; —rsi *vr.* to defend oneself.

Difensiva [dee-fen-see'vah] *nf.* defensive.

Difensivo [dee-fen-see'voh] *a.* defensive.

Difesa [dee-fay'sah] *nf.* defence.

Difettare [dee-fet-tah'ray]

vi. to be deficient in, destitute of, lack.

Difet/tivo [dee-fee-tee'voh] —toso [toh'soh] *a.* defective, lacking.

Difetto [dee-fet'toh] *nm.* defect, flaw, lack.

Diffamare [deef-fah-mah'ray] *vt.* to defame, libel.

Diffamazione [deef-fah-mah-tsee-oh'nay] *nf.* defamation.

Differenza [deef-fay-rent'zah] *nf.* difference.

Differenzia/re [deef-fay-rent-zee-ah'ray] *vt.* to differentiate, distinguish (between); —rsi *vr.* to differ (from), be different.

Differimento [deef-fay-ree-men'toh] *nm.* adjournment, deferment.

Differire [deef-fay-ree'ray] *vt.* to adjourn, defer, postpone; *vi.* to be different, to differ, disagree.

Difficile [deef-fee'chee-lay] *a.* arduous, difficult, hard, hard to please.

Difficoltà [deef-fee-koll-tah'] *nf.* difficulty, objection.

Difficoltoso [deef-fee-koll-toh'soh] *a.* full of difficulties.

Diffida [deef-fee'dah] *nf.* intimation, notice.

Diffidare [deef-fee-dah'ray] *vt.* to serve a notice; *vi.* to distrust, suspect.

Diffidenza [deef-fee-dent'zah] *nf.* diffidence, distrust, suspicion.

Diffonde/re [deef-fon'day-ray] *vt.* to diffuse, pour, spread; —rsi *vr.* to be diffused, dwell on, spread.

Diffusione [deef-foo-zee-oh'nay] *nf.* diffusion.

Difilato [dee-fee-lah'toh] *ad.* at once, forthwith.

Difterite [deef-tay-ree'tay] *nf.* diphtheria.

Diga [dee'gah] *nf.* breakwater, dyke.

Digeribile [dee-jay-ree'bee-lay] *a.* digestible.

Digerire [dee-jay-ree'ray] *vt.* to digest, swallow.

Digiunare [dee-joo-nah'ray] *vi.* to fast.

Digiuno [dee-joo'noh] *nm.* fast; *a.* fasting.

Dignità [deen-yee-tah'] *nf.* dignity.

Dignitoso [deen-yee-toh'soh] *a.* dignified.

Digradare [dee-grah-dah'ray] *vt.* to shade (colours); *vi.* to slope gently.

Digrassare [dee-grahs-sah'ray] *vt.* to remove the fat, skim.

Digressione [dee-gress-see-oh'nay] *nf.* digression.

Digrignare [dee-green-yah'ray] *vt.* to gnash, grind (one's teeth).

Digrossare [dee-gross-sah'ray] *vt.* to chip, rough-hew.

Dilacerare [dee-lah-chay-rah'ray), **dilaniare** [dee-lah-nee-ah'ray] *vt.* to tear (to pieces).

Dilagare [dee-lah-gah'ray] *vi.* to overflow, spread.

Dilapidare [dee-lah-pee-dah'ray] *vt.* to dilapidate, squander.

Dilatabile [dee-lah-tah'bee-lay] *a.* dilatable, extensible.

Dilata/re [dee-lah-tah'ray] *vt.*, **—rsi** *vr.* to dilate, expand.

Dilatazione [dee-lah-tah-tsee-oh'nay] *nf.* dilation, expansion.

Dilatorio [dee-lah-toh'ree-oh] *a.* delaying, dilatory.

Dilazionare [dee-lah-tsee-oh-nah'ray] *vt.* to adjourn, postpone.

Dilazione [dee-lah-tsee-oh'nay] *nf.* delay, respite.

Dileggiare [dee-lay-djah'ray] *vt.* to mock, ridicule.

Dileggio [dee-lay'djoh] *nm.* derision, mockery.

Dileguamento [dee-lay-gwah-men'toh] *nm.* disappearance.

Dilegua/re [dee-lay-gwah'ray] *vt.* to disperse, dissipate; **—rsi** *vr.* to dissolve, fade away, vanish.

Diletta/re [dee-let-tah'ray] *vt.* to charm, delight; **—rsi** *vr.* to delight in, take pleasure in.

Dilettevole [dee-let-tay'voh-lay] *a.* charming, delightful.

Diletto [dee-let'toh] *nm.* delight; *a.* beloved, darling.

Diligenza [dee-lee-jent'zah] *nf.* diligence, stage-coach.

Dilucidare [dee-loo-chee-dah'ray] *vt.* to elucidate.

Diluire [dee-loo-ee'ray] *vt.* to dilute, water.

Dilungarsi [dee-loong-gahr'see] *vr.* to dwell (on).

Dilungo [dee-loong'goh] *ad.* straight away.

Diluviare [dee-loo-vee-ah'ray] *vt.* to flood; *vi.* to pour, deluge, rain in torrents.

Diluvio [dee-loo'vee-oh] *nm.* deluge, flood.

Dima/grare, —grire [dee-mah-grah'ray, —gree'ray] *vt.* to make thin ; *vi.* to grow thin.

Dimena/re [dee-may-nah'ray] *vt.* to shake, wag (a tail); **—rsi** *vr.* to fidget, toss.

Dimensione [dee-men-see-oh'nay] *nf.* dimension, size.

Dimenticanza [dee-men-tee-kahnt'zah] *nf.* forgetfulness, oblivion.

Dimentica/re [dee-men-tee-kah'ray] *vt.* to forget; **—rsi** *vr.* to forget oneself.

Dimesso [dee-mess'soh] *a.* humble, modest.

Dimesticare: *v.* **addomesticare.**

Dimestichezza [dee-mess-tee-ket'zah] *nf.* familiarity.

Dimette/re [dee-met'tay-ray] *vt.* to dismiss, forgive, remove; —**rsi** *vr.* to resign.

Dimezzare [dee-med-zah'ray] *vt.* to halve.

Diminuire [dee-mee-noo-ee'ray] *vt.* to abate, diminish, lessen, reduce; *vi.* to abate, decline, decrease, get lower.

Diminuzione [dee-mee-noo-tsee-oh'nay] *nf.* diminution, fall, reduction.

Dimissio/ne [dee-mees-see-oh'nay] *nf.* resignation; **dare le** [dah'ray lay]—**ni** [nee] *vi.* to resign.

Dimodochè [dee-moh-doh-kay'], **di modo che** [dee moh'doh kay] *con.* in such a way that, so that.

Dimora [dee-moh'rah] *nf.* abode, dwelling, stay; **senza fissa** [sent'zah fees'sah] *d. a.* homeless, vagabond.

Dimostra/re [dee-moh-strah'ray] *vt.* to demonstrate, prove, show; —**rsi** *vr.* to appear, show oneself.

Dinamica [dee-nah'mee-kah] *nf.* dynamics (*pl.*).

Dinamite [dee-nah-mee'tay] *nf.* dynamite.

Dinanzi [dee-nahnt'zee] *ad.* and *pr.* before, opposite.

Dinastia [dee-nah-stee'ah] *nf.* dynasty.

Diniego [dee-nee-ay'goh] *nm.* denial.

Dinoccolato [dee-nock-koh-lah'toh] *a.* disjointed, loose-limbed, shambling.

Dintor/no [deen-torr'noh] *ad.* and *pr.* about, (a)round; —**ni** [nee] *nm.* (*pl.*) neighbourhood.

Dio [dee'oh] *nm.* God.

Diocesi [dee-oh'chay-zee] *nf.* diocese.

Dipartimento [dee-pahr-tee-men'toh] *nm.* department, district.

Dipartirsi [dee-pahr-teer'see] *vr.* to depart, go away.

Dipartita [dee-pahr-tee'tah] *nf.* (*poet.*) death, departure.

Dipendente [dee-pen-den'tay] *nm.* and *f.* dependant; *a.* dependent.

Dipendenza [dee-pen-dent'zah] *nf.* dependence, dependency.

Dipendere [dee-pen'day-ray] *vi.* to be dependent, depend (on), rest (with).

Dipinge/re [dee-peen'jay-ray] *vt.* to depict, paint; —**rsi** *vr.* to be painted, paint oneself.

Dipinto [dee-peen'toh] *nm.* painting, picture; *a.* painted.

Diplomazia [dee-ploh-mah-tsee'ah] *nf.* diplomacy.

Dipoi, di poi [dee-poh'ee] *ad.* after(wards).

Diporto [dee-porr'toh] *nm.* amusement, walk.

Diradamento [dee-rah-dah-men'toh] *nm.* thinning (out).

Dirada/re [dee-rah-dah'ray] *vt.* to thin out; —**rsi** *vr.* to get thin (of hair, etc.).

Dirama/re [dee-rah-mah'ray] *vt.* to lop, prune, send out; —**rsi** *vr.* to branch out, ramify, spread.

Dire [dee'ray] *vt.* and *i.* to say, speak, tell; *nm.* saying.

Direttissimo [dee-ret-tees-see-moh] *nm.* express train.

Diret/to [dee-ret'toh] *nm.* fast train; *a.* bound for, direct, right, straight; **carrozza** [kahr-rot'zah]—**ta** *nf.* through coach (on a train).

Diret/tore [dee-ret-toh'ray] *nm.*—**trice** [tree'chay] *nf.* director, directress, headmaster, headmistress, manager(ess).

Direzione [dee-ray-tsee-oh'nay] *nf.* direction, management, office, (*tech.*) steering-gear.

Dirige/re [dee-ree'jay-ray]

vt. to address, direct, dispose, manage, regulate; —**rsi** *vr.* to apply, go towards, make for.

Dirigibile [dee-ree-jee′bee-lay] *nm.* air-ship.

Dirimpetto [dee-reem-pet′toh] *ad.* opposite, over the way.

Diritta [dee-reet′tah] *nf.* right, right hand, right side.

Diritto [dee-reet′toh] *nm.* claim, law, right, title; *a.* erect, plumb, right, straight; *ad.* directly, straight (on).

Dirittura [dee-reet-too′rah] *nf.* straightness, uprightness; a [ih] *d.* ad. outright.

Drizza/re [dee-reet-zah′ray] *vt.* to prick up (one's ears), straighten; —**rsi** *vr.* to draw oneself up.

Dirocca/re [dee-rock-kah′ray] *vt.* to demolish, dismantle; —**rsi** *vr.* to fall in ruins.

Dirot/to [dee-rot′toh] *a.* heavy; **pianto** [pee-ahn′toh] **d.** flood of tears; **pioggia** [pee-oh′djah]—**ta** [tah] *nf.* heavy rain.

Dirozza/re [dee-rod-zah′ray] *vt.* to civilise, polish, roughhew; —**rsi** *vr.* to become civilised, refined.

Dirupamento [dee-roo-pah-men′toh] *nm.* fall of rock, landslide.

Dirupo [dee-roo′poh] *nm.* rocky precipice.

Dis– [deez] common prefix indicating reversal, usually equivalent to Eng. *dis-, im-, in-, un-,* etc.

Disabitato [deez-ah-bee-tah′toh] *a.* uninhabited.

Disabitua/re [deez-ah-bee-too-ah′ray] *vt.* to disaccustom; —**rsi** *vr.* to lose the habit.

Disaccordo [deez-ak-korr′doh] *nm.* disagreement, discord.

Disadatto [deez-ah-daht′toh] *a.* improper, unbecoming, unfit.

Disadorno [deez-ah-dorr′noh] *a.* bare, simple, unadorned.

Disagevole [deez-ah-jay′voh-lay] *a.* difficult, uncomfortable, uneasy.

Disagevolezza [deez-ah-jay-voh-let′zah] *nf.* difficulty, discomfort, uneasiness.

Disaggradevole [deez-ahg-grah-day′voh-lay] *a.* disagreeable.

Disagiato [deez-ah-jah′toh] *a.* uncomfortable.

Disagio [deez-ah′joh] *nm.* discomfort, uneasiness; **sentirsi a** [sen-teer′see ah] **d.** *vi.* to feel uncomfortable.

Disappetenza [deez-ahp-pay-tent′zah] *nf.* lack of appetite.

Disapprovare [deez-ahp-proh-vah′ray] *vt.* to blame, disapprove.

Disappunto [deez-ahp-poon′toh] *nm.* disappointment.

Disarmare [deez-ahr-mah′ray] *vt.* to disarm, dismantle, (*naut.*) lay up (a ship).

Disarmo [deez-ahr′moh] *nm.* disarming, disarmament.

Disastrato [deez-ah-strah′toh] *a.* become poor.

Disastro [deez-ah′stroh] *nm.* accident, disaster.

Disattenzione [deez-aht-ten-tsee-oh′nay] *nf.* inattention, inattentiveness.

Disattrezzare [deez-aht-tret-zah′ray] *vt.* (*naut.*) to dismantle.

Disavanzo [deez-ah-vahnt′zoh] *nm.* deficiency, deficit, discredit.

Disavvedutezza [deez-ahv-vay-doo-tet′zah], **disavvertenza** [deez-ahv-vehr-tent′zah] *nf.* inadvertency.

Disavventura [deez-ahv-ven-too'rah] *nf.* misfortune, mishap.

Disavvezzare [deez-ahv-vet-zah'ray] *vt.* to disaccustom.

Disborso [dees-borr'soh] *nm.* disbursement, outlay.

Disbriga/re [dees-bree-gah'ray] *vt.—rsi vr.* to clear off, dispatch, manage.

Disbrigo [dees-bree'goh] *nm.* dispatch, settlement.

Discapito [dees-kah'pee-toh] *nm.* damage, detriment.

Discendenza [dee-shen-dent'zah] *nf.* descent, issue, offspring.

Discendere [dee-shen'day-ray] *vi.* to descend, fall, go down, spring from.

Discepolo [dee-shay'poh-loh] *nm.* disciple, pupil.

Discernere [dee-shehr'nay-ray] *v.t.* to discern, distinguish.

Discernimento [dee-shehr-nee-men'toh] *nm.* discernment, judgment.

Discesa [dee-shay'sah] *nf.* abatement, descent, fall.

Disciòglie/re [dee-sholl'yay-ray] *vt.* to disband, melt, untie; *—rsi vr.* to dissolve, melt.

Disciplina [dee-shee-plee'nah] *nf.* discipline.

Disciplinare [dee-shee-plee-nah'ray] *vt.* to discipline; *a.* disciplinary.

Discolo [dee'skoh-loh] *nm.* rogue; *a.* undisciplined, unruly, wild.

Discolpa/re [dee-skoll-pah'ray] *vt.* to defend, excuse, justify; *—rsi vr.* to defend oneself, justify oneself.

Disconoscenza [dees-skoh-noh-shent'zah] *nf.* ingratitude.

Disconoscere [dees-skoh-noh'shay-ray] *vt.* to disavow, fail to appreciate, slight.

Disconvenienza [dee-skon-

vay-nee-ent'zah] *nf.* inconveniency, impropriety.

Discordare [dee-skorr-dah'ray] *vi.* to disagree, (*mus.*) be out of tune.

Discorde [dee-skorr'day] *a.* conflicting, discordant.

Discordia [dee-skorr'dee-ah] *nf.* discord, dissension, strife.

Discorrere [dee-skorr'ray-ray] *vi.* to discourse, talk.

Discorso [dee-skorr'soh] *nm.* discourse, speech, talk.

Discosto [dee-skoh'stoh] *a.* distant, far.

Discredita/re [dee-skray-dee-tah'ray] *vt.* to discredit, disgrace, speak ill of; *—rsi vr.* to damage one's reputation.

Discrepanza [dee-skray-pahnt'zah] *nf.* discrepancy.

Discretezza [dee-skray-tett'zah] *nf.* discretion, moderation.

Discretiva [dee-skray-tee'vah] *nf.* power of discernment.

Discreto [dee-skray'toh] *a.* discreet, moderate, passable, reasonable.

Discrezione [dee-skray-tsee-oh'nay] *nf.* discretion; a [ah] d. *ad.* as much as one wants.

Discriminare [dee-skree-mee-nah'ray] *vt.* to discriminate.

Discussione [dee-skoos-see-oh'nay] *nf.* debate, discussion, dispute.

Discutere [dee-skoo'tay-ray] *vt. and i.* to argue, discuss.

Disdegnare: *v.* sdegnare.

Disdegno [deez-dayn'yoh] *nm.* contempt, scorn.

Disdegnoso [deez-dayn-yoh'soh] *a.* contemptuous, scornful.

Disdetta [deez-det'tah] *nf.* mishap, misfortune, notice.

Disdi/re [deez-dee'ray] *vt.* to annul, cancel, contradict, revoke, unsay; *v.imp.* to be unbecoming; *—rsi vr.* to go back on one's word.

Disdoro [deez-doh'roh] *nm.* dishonour.

Disegnare [dee-sayn-yah'ray] *vt.* to draw, plan.

Disegno [dee-sayn'yoh] *nm.* design, drawing, plan, purpose.

Diseredare [deez-ay-ray-dah'ray] *vt.* to disinherit.

Disertare [dee-zehr-tah'ray] *vt.* to desert, lay waste, ruin.

Diserzione [dee-zehr-tsee-oh'nay] *nf.* desertion.

Disfacimento [deez-sfah-chee-men'toh] *nm.* decay, destruction, ruin.

Disfa/re [dee-sfah'ray] *vt.* to break up, take to pieces, undo, untie; —**rsi** *vr.* to dispose of, get rid of.

Disfatta [dee-sfaht'tah] *nf.* defeat.

Disfida [dee-sfee'dah] *nf.* defiance.

Disgelare [dees-jay-lah'ray] *vi.* to thaw.

Disgrado [dee-sgrah'doh] *nm.* dislike. *v.* Antipatia.

Disgrazia [dee-sgrah'tsee-ah] *nf.* accident, ill-luck, misfortune.

Disgraziato [dee-sgrah-tsee-ah'toh] *nm. and a.* unfortunate, unlucky (man).

Disguido [dee-sgwee'doh] *nm.* miscarriage, going astray (of post).

Disgusta/re [dee-sgoo-stah'ray] *vt.* to disgust, dislike, vex; —**rsi** *vr.* to take a disgust, dislike.

Disgusto [dee-sgoo'stoh] *nm.* disgust, dislike, loathing.

Disillude/re [dee-zeel-loo'day-ray] *vt.* to disillusion, undeceive; —**rsi** *vr.* to lose one's illusions.

Disimpegna/re [deez-zeem-payn-yah'ray] *vt.* to carry out, fulfil, redeem (a pledge); —**rsi** *vr.* to free oneself, manage one's own affairs.

Disimpegno [dee-zeem-payn'yoh] *nm.* disengagement, release.

Disincagliare [dee-zeeng-kah-lyah'ray] *vt.* (*naut.*) to float (a stranded ship).

Disinfettante [dee-zeen-fet-tahn'tay] *nm. and a.* disinfectant.

Disinfettare [dee-zeen-fet-tah'ray] *vt.* to disinfect.

Disinfezione [dee-zeen-fay-tsee-oh'nay] *nf.* disinfection.

Disingannare [dee-zeeng-gahn-nah'ray] *vt.* to disillusion, undeceive.

Disinganno [dee-zeeng-gahn'noh] *nm.* disillusionment, undeceiving.

Disinteressa/re [dee-zeen-tay-ress-sah'ray] *vt.* (*com.*) to buy out, indemnify; —**rsi** *vr.* to disinterest oneself.

Disinteresse [dee-zeen-tay-ress'say] *nm.* disinterest, unselfishness.

Disinvolto [dee-zeen-voll'toh] *a.* easy, free, sure of oneself, unconstrained.

Disinvoltura [dee-zeen-voll-too'rah] *nf.* ease, nonchalance, self-possession.

Disistimare [dee-zee-stee-mah'ray] *vt.* not to esteem.

Dislivello [dee-slee-vell'loh] *nm.* inequality, difference in height (geographical).

Dislocare [dee-sloh-kah'ray] *vt.* to transfer.

Dismisura, a [ah dee-smee-soo'rah] *a.* immoderately.

Disobbediente [dee-zob-bay-dee-en'tay] *a.* disobedient.

Disobbedienza [dee-zob-bay-dee-ent'zah] *nf.* disobedience.

Disobbedire [dee-zob-bay-dee'ray] *vt.* to disobey.

Disobbligare [dee-zob-blee-gah'ray] *vt.* to free from obligation.

Disoccupato [dee-zock-koo-pah'toh] a. free, out of work, unemployed.

Disonestà [dee-zoh-ness-tah'] nf. dishonesty.

Disonorare [dee-zoh-noh-rah'ray] vt. to disgrace, dishonour.

Disonore [dee-zoh-noh'ray] nm. disgrace, dishonour, shame.

Disopra [dee-soh'prah] nm. top, upper side; ad. and pr. above, on, over, upon, upstairs; al di [ahl dee] s. di [dee] pr. beyond.

Disordinare [dee-zorr-dee-nah'ray] vt. to cancel (an order).

Disordinato [dee-zorr-dee-nah'toh] a. disorderly, untidy.

Disordine [dee-zorr'dee-nay] nm. disorder disturbance, riot.

Disorganizzare [dee-zorr-gah-need-zah'ray] vt. to disorganise.

Disorienta/re [dee-zoh-reeen-tah'ray] vt. to confuse, disconcert, lead astray, mislead; —rsi vr. to be at a loss, not know where one is.

Disotto [dee-sot'toh] nm. bottom, lower side; ad. and pr. below, downstairs, under (neath); al [ahl] di [dee] ad. inferior to.

Dispaccio [dee-spahch'choh] nm. dispatch, telegram.

Disparato [dee-spah-rah'toh] a. different, disparate, incongruous, unequal.

Dispari [dee'spah-ree] a. odd, uneven, (numbers, etc.).

Disparire [dee-spah-ree'ray] vi. to disappear, vanish.

Disparizione [dee-spah-reet-see-oh'nay] nf. disappearance.

Disparte, in [een dee-spahr'tay] ad. aloof, apart, aside.

Dispendio [dee-spen'dee-oh] nm. expense, outlay, waste.

Dispendioso [dee-spen-dee-oh'soh] a. expensive, wasteful.

Dispensa [dee-spen'sah] nf. dispensation, distribution, exemption, number (of a publication), pantry.

Dispensare [dee-spen-sah'ray] vt. to dispense, distribute, exempt.

Dispensario [dee-spen-sah'ree-oh] nm. dispensary.

Dispera/re [dee-spay-rah'ray] vi. to despair; —rsi vr. to be in despair, lose all hope.

Disperato [dee-spay-rah'toh] a. desperate, hopeless, in despair.

Disperazione [dee-spay-rah-tsee-oh'nay] nf. despair, desperation, hopelessness.

Disperde/re [dee-spehr'day-ray] vt. to dispel, disperse, scatter, waste; —rsi vr. to be scattered, disperse, get lost.

Disperso [dee-spehr'soh] nm. (mil.) missing (man); a. dispersed, lost, scattered.

Dispetto [dee-spet'toh] nm. grudge, pique, spite.

Dispettoso [dee-spet-toh'soh] a. spiteful, teasing.

Dispiacere [dee-spee-ah-chay'ray] vt. to displease; v. imp. to be sorry, mind; mi dispiace [mee dee-spee-ah'chay], I am sorry; nm. displeasure, dissatisfaction, grief, regret.

Disponibile [dee-spoh-nee'bee-lay] a. available, free.

Dispor/re [dee-sporr'ray] vt. to arrange, direct, dispose, order, regulate; vi. to dispose; —rsi vr. to get ready.

Disposizione [dee-spoh-zee-tsee-oh'nay] nf. arrangement, disposal, inclination, order; avere [ah-vay'ray] d. per [pehr] to have a talent for; alla sua [ahl'lah soo'ah] d. ad. at your disposal.

Disposto [dee-spoh'stoh] *a.* arranged, disposed, inclined, willing.

Dispregiare, etc.: *v.* **disprezzare**, etc.

Disprezzabile [dee-spret-zah'bee-lay] *a.* contemptible, despicable, negligible.

Disprezzare [dee-spret-zah'ray] *vt.* to despise, scorn.

Disprezzo [dee-spret'zoh] *nm.* contempt, scorn.

Disputa [dee'spoo-tah] *nf.* dispute, quarrel.

Disputa/re [dee-spoo-tah'ray] *vt. and i.* to argue, contend, debate, dispute, quarrel; **—rsi** *vr.* to contend (for).

Dissanguare [dees-sahng-gwah'ray] *vt.* to bleed, let blood.

Dissanguato [dees-sahng-gwah'toh] *a.* exhausted from loss of blood.

Dissapore [dees-sah-poh'ray] *nm.* difference, dissension, rancour.

Disseminare [dees-say-mee-nah'ray] *vt.* to disseminate, propagate, scatter, sow.

Dissennatezza [dees-sen-nah-tet'zah] *nf.* inconsiderateness, precipitancy, rashness.

Dissenso [dees-sen'soh] *nm.* difference of opinion, dissent.

Dissenteria [dees-sen-tay-ree'ah] *nf.* dysentery.

Dissentire [dees-sen-tee'ray] *vi.* to disagree (with).

Disseppellimento [dees-sep-pell-lee-men'toh] *nm.* disinterment, exhumation.

Disseppellire [dees-sep-pell-lee'ray] *vt.* to disinter.

Dissertare [dees-sehr-tah'ray] *vi.* to discourse.

Dissestato [dees-sess-tah'toh] *a.* in financial straits, badly off.

Dissesto [dees-sess'toh] *nm.* disorder, financial trouble.

Dissetarsi [dees-say-tahr'see] *vr.* to quench one's thirst.

Dissezione [dees-say-tsee-oh'nay] *nf.* dissection.

Dissidente [dees-see-den'tay] *nm. and f.* dissenter, dissident; *a.* dissentient.

Dissiggellare [dees-see-djell-lah'ray] *vt.* to unseal.

Dissimile [dees-see'mee-lay] *a.* unlike.

Dissimilitudine [dees-see-mee-lee-too'dee-nay] *nf.* dissimilarity, unlikeness.

Dissimula/re [dees-see-moo-lah'ray] *vt.* to dissemble, dissimulate, 'conceal *vi.* to feign, pretend; **—rsi** *vr.* to conceal from oneself.

Dissipa/re [dees-see-pah'ray] *vt.* to clear up, dissipate, remove; **—rsi** *vr.* to disappear, vanish.

Dissodare [dees-soh-dah'ray] *vt.* to clear (land), till.

Dissolubilità [dees-soh-loo-bee-lee-tah'] *nf.* dissolubility.

Dissolutezza [dees-soh-loo-tet'zah] *nf.* dissoluteness, licentiousness.

Dissolutivo [dees-soh-loo-tee'voh] *a.* dissolvent.

Dissolve/re [dees-soll'vay-ray] *vt.* **—rsi** *vr.* to dissolve, melt.

Dissomiglianza [dees-soh-meel-yahnt'zah] *nf.* dissimilarity.

Dissonante [dees-soh-nahn'tay] *a.* at variance.

Dissotterrare [dees-sot-tehr-rah'ray] *vt.* to disinter.

Dissuadere [dees-swah'day-ray] *vt.* to deter, dissuade.

Dissuetudine [dees-soo-ay-too'dee-nay] *nf.* disuse.

Distaccamento [dee-stahk-kah-men'toh] *nm.* (*mil.*) detachment.

Distacca/re [dee-stahk-kah'ray] *vt.* to cut off, detach, separate, sever; —rsi *vr.* to become detached, break off.

Distacco [dee-stahk'koh] *nm.* absence, separation.

Distante [dee-stahn'tay] *a.* distant, far, remote.

Distare [dee-stah'ray] *vi.* to be distant.

Distende/re [dee-sten'day-ray] *vt.* to extend, lay (out), spread; —rsi *vr.* to extend, stretch (oneself).

Distendimento [dee-sten-dee-men'toh] *nm.* distensione [dee-sten-see-oh'nay] *nf.* distension, extension, spreading.

Distesa [dee-stay'sah] *nf.* extent, expanse, length.

Distilla/re [dee-steel-lah'ray] *vt.* to distil; —rsi *vr.* to be distilled.

Distilleria [dee-steel-lay-ree'ah] *nf.* distillery.

Distingue/re [dee-steeng'gway-ray] *vt.* to distinguish; —rsi *vr.* to become famous, distinguish oneself.

Distinta [dee-steen'tah] *nf.* catalogue, price-list.

Distintivo [dee-steen-tee'voh] *nm.* badge, (mil.) stripe; *a.* distinctive.

Distinzione [dee-steen-tsee-oh'nay] *nf.* discrimination, distinction.

Distoglie/re [dee-stoll'yay-ray] *vt.* to deter, dissuade, distract; —rsi *vr.* to let one's attention wander.

Distrar/re [dee-strahr'ray] *vt.* to amuse, distract, divert; —rsi *vr.* to amuse oneself, let one's attention wander.

Distratto [dee-straht'toh] *a.* absent-minded, confused.

Distrazione [dee-strah-tsee-oh'nay] *nf.* absence of mind, confusion. [district.

Distretto [dee-stret'toh] *nm.*

Distribuire [dee-stree-boo-ee'ray] *vt.* to arrange, assign, distribute, share.

Districa/re, distriga/re [dee-stree-kah(gah)'ray] *vt.* to disentangle, unravel; —rsi *vr.* to extricate oneself, free oneself.

Distrugge/re [dee-strooʒdjay-ray] *vt.* to destroy, ruin; —rsi *vr.* to destroy oneself (each other).

Distruzione [dee-stroo-tsee-oh'nay] *nf.* destruction.

Disturba/re [dee-stoor-bah'ray] *vt.* to disturb, interrupt, trouble; —rsi *vr.* to put oneself out, take trouble.

Disturbo [dee-stoor'boh] *nm.* annoyance, anxiety, trouble, upset.

Disubbediente, etc.: *v.* dis-obbediente, etc.

Disuguaglianza [dee-zoo-gwahl-yahnt'zah] *nf.* disparity, inequality.

Disuguale [dee-zoo-gwah'lay] *a.* unequal.

Disumano [dee-zoo-mah'noh] *a.* inhuman.

Disunione [dee-zoo-nee-oh'nay] *nf.* discord, disunion.

Disunire [dee-zoo-nee'ray] *vt.* to disjoin, disunite.

Disusare [dee-zoo-zah'ray] *vt.* to cease using.

Disuso [dee-zoo'zoh] *nm.* desuetude; cadere in [kah-day'ray een] d. *vi.* to become obsolete.

Ditale [dee-tah'lay] *nm.* finger-stall, thimble.

Dito [dee'toh] *nm.* finger, toe.

Ditta [deet'tah] *nf.* firm, house (commercial).

Dittatura [deet-tah-too'rah] *nf.* dictatorship.

Diurno [dee-oor'noh] *a.* daily, diurnal; albergo [ahl-behr'goh] d. *nm.* public baths and toilette rooms.

Diva [dee-vah] *nf.* goddess, great actress or singer.

Divaga/re [dee-vah-gah'ray] *vi.* to amuse, divert; *vi.* to wander; —**rsi** *vr.* to amuse oneself, relax.

Divampare [dee-vahm-pah'ray] *vi.* to blaze, flare.

Divano [dee-vah'noh] *nm.* couch, divan.

Divenire [dee-vay-nee'ray], **diventare** [dee-ven-tah'ray] *vi.* to become, get, grow, turn.

Diverbio [dee-vehr'bee-oh] *nm.* altercation, dispute.

Divergente [dee-vehr-jen'tay] *a.* divergent, diverging.

Divergere [dee-vehr'jay-ray] *v.* to divert; *vi.* to diverge, wander from.

Diversificare [dee-vehr-see-fee-kah'ray] *vi.* to be different, differ.

Diversione [dee-vehr-see-oh'nay] *nf.* diversion, turning.

Diversità [dee-vehr-see-tah'] *nf.* diversity.

Diver/so [dee-vehr'soh] *a.* different; —**si** *a. and pn.* (*pl.*) divers, several, sundry, various.

Divertimento [dee-vehr-tee-men'toh] *nm.* amusement, entertainment, recreation.

Diverti/re [dee-vehr-tee'ray] *vi.* to amuse, entertain; —**rsi** *vr.* to amuse oneself, have a good time.

Divezzar/e [dee-vet-zah'ray] *vt.* to disaccustom, wean; —**rsi** *vr.* to disaccustom oneself.

Divide/re [dee-vee'day-ray] *vi.* to divide, part, share; —**rsi** *vr.* to be divided, separate.

Divieto [dee-vee-ay'toh] *nm.* prohibition; d. d'affissione [dahf-fees-see-oh'nay], " stick no bills "; d. di sosta [dee soh'stah], " no parking."

Divinare [dee-vee-nah'ray] *vt.* to divine, foretell.

Divincolarsi [dee-veeng-koh-lahr'see] *vr.* to struggle, writhe.

Divinità [dee-vee-nee-tah'] *nf.* divinity.

Divino [dee-vee'noh] *a.* divine.

Divisa [dee-vee'zah] *nf.* coat of arms, livery, parting (of the hair), uniform; d. estera [ess'tay-rah], foreign bill of exchange.

Divisare [dee-vee-zah'ray] *vi.* to devise, plan, resolve.

Divisione [dee-vee-zee-oh'nay] *nf.* dividing, division.

Divisorio [dee-vee-zoh'ree-oh] *a.* dividing, separating; muro [moo'roh] d. *nm.* partition wall.

Divorare [dee-voh-rah'ray] *vt.* to devour, eat up.

Divorzia/re [dee-vorr-tsee-ah'ray] *vt. and i.*, —**rsi** *vr.* to be divorced, divorce, get a divorce.

Divulgar/e [dee-vool-gah'ray] *vi.* to divulge, spread; —**rsi** *vr.* to spread.

Dizionario [dee-tsee-oh-nah'ree-oh] *nm.* dictionary.

Dizione [dee-tsee-oh'nay] *nf.* diction.

Doccia [dohch'chah] *nf.* douche, (water)-pipe, shower-(bath); fare la [fah'ray lah] d. *vi.* to take a douche, (or shower).

Docciare [dohch-chah'ray] *vi.* to (give a) douche.

Docente [doh-chen'tay] *nm. and f.* teacher.

Docenza [doh-chent'zah] *nf.* teacher's diploma.

Docilità [doh-chee-lee-tah'] *nf.* docility, meekness.

Documentare [doh-koo-men-tah'ray] *vt.* to bring documentary evidence, document.

Documentario [doh-koo-men-tah'ree-oh] *nm.* news-reel; *a.* documentary.

Documento [doh-koo-men'-toh] *nm.* document, *(jur.)* instrument.

Dodicenne [doh-dee-chen'-nay] *a.* twelve years old.

Dodicesimo [doh-dee-chay'-zee-moh] *a.* twelfth.

Dodici [doh'dee-chee] *a.* twelve.

Dogana [doh-gah'nah] *nf.* Customs, Customs office.

Doganale [doh-gah-nah'lay] *a.* Customs.

Doganiere [doh-gah-nee-ay'-ray] *nm.* Customs officer.

Doglia [doll'yah] *nf.* ache, pain.

Dogma [dog'mah] *nm.* dogma, principle.

Dolce [doll'chay] *nm.* pudding, sweet; *a.* soft, sweet.

Dolcezza [doll-chet'zah] *nf.* softness, sweetness.

Dolciumi [doll-choo'mee] *nm. (pl.)* sweets *(pl.)*.

Dole/re [doh-lay'ray] *vi.* to ache; —**rsi** *vr.* to be sorry, complain, grieve, lament, regret.

Dolo [doh-loh] *nm.* fraud.

Dolore [doh-loh'ray] *nm.* ache, grief, pain, regret.

Doloroso [doh-loh-roh'soh] *a.* grievous, painful, sorrowful.

Doloso [doh-loh'soh] *a.* fraudulent.

Domanda [doh-mahn'dah] *nf.* demand, enquiry, question, request; **fare una** [fah'ray oo'nah] d. *vi.* to ask a question, make a request.

Domanda/re [doh-mahn-dah'ray] *vt.* to ask, demand, request; —**rsi** *vr.* to ask oneself, wonder.

Domani [doh-mah'nee] *nm.* and *ad.* next day, the day after, tomorrow; d. l'altro [lahl'troh] *ad.* the day after to-morrow.

Domare [doh-mah'ray] *vt.*

to break (horses), conquer, extinguish, subdue, overcome, tame.

Domatura [doh-mah-too'-rah] *nf.* breaking (of horses), taming.

Domenica [doh-may'nee-kah] *nf.* Sunday.

Domenicale [doh-may-nee-kah'lay] *a.* (of) Sunday.

Domenicano [doh-may-nee-kah'noh] *nm.* and *a.* a Dominican.

Domestica [doh-mess'tee-kah] *nf.* maid, servant.

Domestichezza [doh-mess-tee-ket'zah] *n* domesticity, familiarity, intimacy.

Domestico [doh-mess'tee-koh] *nm.* domestic, servant; *a.* domestic, familiar, homely.

Domicilia/re [doh-mee-chee-lee-ah'ray] *vt.* to domiciliate, house; —**rsi** *vr.* to live, settle, take up one's abode.

Domicilio [doh-mee-chee'-lee-oh] *nm.* abode, domicile.

Domina/re [doh-mee-nah'-ray] *vt.* to command, dominate, govern, overlook, rule;—**rsi** *vr.* to control oneself, master oneself.

Dominazione [doh-mee-nah-tsee-oh'nay] *nf.* domination, rule.

Dominio [doh-mee'nee-oh] *nm.* authority, dominion, power, territory.

Dona/re [doh-nah'ray] *vt.* to bestow, confer, grant; *vi.* to be becoming, suit; —**rsi** *vr.* to devote oneself.

Donde [don'day] *ad.* hence, from where, whence.

Dondolamento [don-doh-lah-men'toh], **dondolo** [don'doh-loh] *nm.* rocking, swaying, swinging.

Dondola/re [don-doh-lah'-ray] *vt.* —**rsi** *vr.* to rock, sway, swing.

Dondoloni [don-doh-loh'nee] *ad.* dangling.

Donna [don'nah] *nf.* woman.

Donnaiuolo [don-nah-ee-oo-oh'loh] *nm.* admirer of the fair sex.

Donnesco [don-ness'koh] *a.* womanish, womanly.

Donnola [don'noh-lah] *nf.* weasel.

Dono [doh'noh] *nm.* gift, present, talent.

Dopo [doh'poh] *ad. and pr.* after, afterwards, next, then; e [ay] *d.?* what next?

Dopochè [doh-poh-kay'] *con.* after, when.

Dopoguerra [doh-poh-gwehr'rah] *nm.* the post-war period.

Doppiaggio [dop-pee-ah'-djoh] *nm.* version of a talking film in a foreign language.

Doppiare [dop-pee-ah'ray] *vt.* to double.

Doppiezza [dop-pee-et'zah] *nf.* double-dealing, duplicity.

Doppio [dop'pee-oh] *nm.* copy, double, duplicate; *a.* double, duplicate, two-fold.

Doppione [dop-pee-oh'nay] *nm.* duplicate.

Dorare [doh-rah'ray] *vt.* to gild, glaze (in cooking).

Dormicchiare [dorr-meek-kee-ah'ray] *vi.* to doze.

Dormiglione [dorr-meel-yoh'nay] *nm.* sleepy fellow, lie-a-bed.

Dormire [dorr-mee'ray] *vi.* to sleep; *nm.* sleep.

Dormitorio [dorr-mee-toh'ree-oh] *nm.* dormitory.

Dormiveglia [dorr-mee-vayl'yah] *nf.* (state) between sleeping and waking.

Dorso [dorr'soh] *nm.* back.

Dosare [doh-zah'ray] *vt.* to dose.

Dose [doh'zay] *nf.* dose.

Dosso [doss'soh] *nm.* back.

Dotare [doh-tah'ray] *vt.* to endow, give a dowry.

Dote [doh'tay] *nf.* dowry, gift, talent.

Dotto [dot'toh] *nm.* learned man, scholar; *a.* learned.

Dottorato [dot-toh-rah'toh] *nm.* doctor's degree.

Dottore [dot'toh-ray] *nm.* doctor, physician (at the University it corresponds to the English *Bachelor*).

Dottrina [dot-tree'nah] *nf.* catechism, doctrine, learning.

Dove [doh'vay] *ad.* where, whither.

Dovere [doh-vay'ray] *vi.* to be obliged, have to, must, ought, should, be indebted, owe; *nm.* duty, home-work, task.

Doveroso [doh-vay-roh'soh] *a.* due, right.

Dovizia [doh-vee'tsee-ah] *nf.* abundance, plenty, wealth.

Dovunque [doh-voong'kway] *ad.* anywhere, everywhere, wherever.

Dozzina [dod-zee'nah] *nf.* board (pension) dozen (number).

Dozzinale [dod-zee-nah'lay] *a.* common, ordinary.

Dozzinante [dod-zee-nahn'tay] *nm. and f.* boarder.

Draga [drah'gah] *nf.* (naut.) dredge.

Dragamina [drah-gah-mee'nah] *nf.* (naut.) minesweeper.

Dragare [drah-gah'ray] *vt.* (naut.) to dredge.

Drago [drah'goh] *nm.* dragon.

Dramma [drahm'mah] *nf.* drachm(a); *nm.* drama.

Drammatica [drahm-mah'tee-kah] *nf.* dramatic art.

Drammatico [drahm-mah'tee-koh] *a.* dramatic.

Drammaturgo [drahm-mah-toor'goh] *nm.* dramatist.

Drappello [drahp-peil'loh] *nm.* band, party, troop.

Drapperia [drahp-pay-ree′ah] *nf.* drapery, silk stuffs (*pl.*).
Drappo [drahp′poh] *nm.* silk material.
Drenaggio [dray-nah′djoh] *nm.* drainage.
Drenare [dray-nah′ray] *vt.* to drain.
Droga [droh′gah] *nf.* spice.
Drogare [droh-gah′ray] *vt.* to spice.
Drogheria [droh-gay-ree′ah] *nf.* grocer's shop.
Droghiere [droh-ghee-ay′ray] *nm.* grocer.
Dubbiezza [doob-bee-et′zah] *nf.* doubt, uncertainty.
Dubbio [doob′bee-oh] *nm.* doubt, suspense; **essere in** [ess′say-ray-een] d. *vi.* to be doubtful; **mettere in** [met′tay-ray een] d. *vt.* to question; *a.* doubtful, dubious.
Dubitare [doo-bee-tah′ray] *vt. and i.* to doubt, question, wonder.
Duca [doo′kah] *nm.* duke.
Ducato [doo-kah′toh] *nm.* ducat, duchy.
Duce [doo′chay] *nm.* chief, leader.
Duchessa [doo-kess′sah] *nf.* duchess.
Due [doo′ay] *a.* two.
Duecento [doo-ay-chen′toh] *nm.* the thirteenth century; *a.* two hundred.
Ducentista [doo-chen-tee′stah], **dugentista** [doo-jen-tee′stah] *nm.* painter or writer of the thirteenth century.
Duellare [doo-ell-lah′ray] *vi.* to fight a duel.
Duello [doo-ell′loh] *nm.* duel. [sand-hill.
Duna [doo′nah] *nf.* dune.
Dunque [doong′kway] *ad. and int.* consequently, then, well! what! what about it?
Duodecimo [doo-oh-day′chee-moh] *a.* twelfth.

Duomo [doo-oh′moh] *nm.* cathedral.
Duplicare [doo-plee-kah′ray] *vt.* to double, duplicate.
Duplice [doo′plee-chay] *a.* double, twofold.
Durabile [doo-rah′bee-lay] *a.* durable, lasting.
Durante [doo-rahn′tay] *pr.* during.
Durare [doo-rah′ray] *vi.* to continue, go on, last.
Durata [doo-rah′tah] *nf.* duration, period.
Duraturo [doo-rah-too′roh], **durevole** [doo-ray′voh-lay] *a.* durable, lasting.
Durezza [doo-ret′zah] *nf.* hardness, harshness.
Duro [doo′roh] *nm.* hardness; *a.* hard, harsh, rough (of wine), stale (of food).
Duttile [doot′tee-lay] *a.* ductile.

E

E [ay], **ed** [ed] *con.* and; **e . . . e** *con.* either . . . or.
Ebanista [ay-bah-nee′stah] *nm.* cabinet-maker.
Ebano [ay′bah-noh] *nm.* ebony.
Ebbene [eb-bay′nay] *ad.* well, well then, what about it?
Ebbrezza [eb-bret′zah] *nf.* drunkenness, intoxication, rapture.
Ebbro [eb′broh] *a.* drunk, intoxicated.
Ebete [ay′bay-tay] *nm.* dullard, fool, imbecile; *a.* dull, stupid.
Ebetismo [ay-bay-tees′moh] *nm.* dullness, stupidity.
Ebollizione [ay-boll-lee-tsee-oh′nay] *nf.* boiling, ebullition.
Ebre/a [ay-bray′ah] *nf.* —o [oh] *nm.* Hebrew, Jew; *a.* Hebrew, Jewish.

Eburneo [ay-boor'nay-oh] *a.* of ivory, ivory-white.

Eccedente [etch-chay-den'tay] *a.* exceeding, excessive.

Eccedenza [etch-chay-dent'zah] *nf.* excess, superfluity, surplus.

Eccedere [etch-chay-day'ray] *vt.* to exceed, outdo; *vi.* to exaggerate, go beyond, go too far.

Eccellente [etch-chell-len'tay] *a.* excellent, superior.

Eccellere [etch-chell'lay-ray] *vi.* to excel.

Eccelso [etch-chell'soh] *a.* lofty.

Eccentricità [etch-chen-tree-chee-tah'] *nf.* eccentricity, queerness, strangeness.

Eccepire [etch-chay-pee'ray] *vt.* to except, object.

Eccesso [etch-chess'soh] *nm.* excess.

Eccetera [etch-chay'tay-rah] *nf.* etcetera.

Eccetto [etch-chet'toh] *ad. and pr.* except(ing), save, unless.

Eccettuare [etch-chet-too-ah'ray] *vt.* to except.

Eccezionale [etch-chay-tsee-oh-nah'lay] *a.* exceptional.

Eccezione [etch-chay-tsee-oh'nay] *nf.* exception.

Eccidio [etch-chee'dee-oh] *nm.* massacre, slaughter.

Eccitabile [etch-chee-tah'bee-lay] *a.* excitable.

Eccitamento [etch-chee-tah-men'toh] *nm.* eccitazione [etch-chee-tah-tsee-oh'nay] *nf.* excitement.

Eccita/re [etch-chee-tah'ray] *vt.* to excite, rouse, stimulate; —rsi *vr.* to get excited.

Ecclesiastico [ek-klay-see-ah'stee-koh] *nm. and a.* ecclesiastic(al).

E(c)clissa/re [ay(k)-klees-sah'ray] *vt.* to eclipse, obscure,

outdo; —rsi *vr.* to be eclipsed, disappear, slip away.

Ecclissi [ek-klees'see] *nf.* eclipse.

Ecco [ek'koh] *ad.* here, there, here is, here are, etc.

Echeggiare [ay-kay-djah'ray] *vi.* to echo, resound.

Eco [ay'koh] *nm. and f.* echo.

Economato [ay-koh-noh-mah'toh] *nm.* stewardship, steward's office, treasurership, treasurer's office.

Economi/a [ay-koh-noh-mee'ah] *nf.* economy, saving, thrift; fare delle [fah'ray dell'lay] e—e *vi.* to retrench.

Economico [ay-koh-noh'mee-koh] *a.* economical, thrifty.

Economizzare [ay-koh-noh-meed-zah'ray] *vt.* to economise, husband, save, use sparingly.

Economo [ay-koh'noh-moh] *nm.* bursar, steward, treasurer.

Edera [ay'day-rah] *nf.* ivy.

Edicola [ay-dee'koh-lah] *nf.* news-stand, small chapel.

Edificante [ay-dee-fee-kahn'tay] *a.* edifying, exemplary.

Edificare [ay-dee-fee-kah'ray] *vt.* to build, edify.

Edificio [ay-dee-fee'choh] *nm.* building, edifice.

Edilizio [ay-dee-lee'tsee-oh] *a.* building.

Edito [ay'dee-toh] *a.* edited, published.

Editore [ay-dee-toh'ray] *nm.* editor, publisher.

Edizione [ay-dee-tsee-oh'nay] *nf.* edition.

Edotto [ay-dot'toh] *a.* acquainted (with), aware (of), informed (of).

Educare [ay-doo-kah'ray] *vt.* to bring up, rear, train.

Educato [ay-doo-kah'toh] *a.* bred, brought up, polite; ben [behn] e. well-bred; mal [mahl] e. ill-bred.

Educazione [ay-doo-kah-tsee-oh'nay] *nf.* breeding, manners (*pl.*), upbringing.

Effe [ef'fay] the letter F.

Effeminatezza [ef-fay-mee-nah-tet'zah] *nf.* effeminacy.

Efferatezza [ef-fay-rah-tet'zah] *nf.* brutality, ferocity.

Efferato [ef-fay-rah'toh] *a.* brutal, ferocious.

Effervescente [ef-fehr-vay-shen'tay] *a.* effervescent.

Effettivi [ef-fet-tee'vee] *nm.* (*pl.*) (*mil.*) effectives, man-power.

Effettività [ef-fet-tee-vee-tah'] *nf.* effectiveness, efficiency. (*rare*) *v.* **Efficienza**.

Effettivo [ef-fet-tee'voh] *a.* actual, effective, efficient, real.

Effetto [ef-fet'toh] *nm.* consequence, effect, end, result.

Effettone [ef-fet-toh'nay] *nm.* great impression, great success.

Effettuale [ef-fet-too-ah'lay] *a.* effectual. *v.* **Effettivo**.

Effettua/re [ef-fet-too-ah'ray] *vt.* to carry out, effect, execute, make, produce; —**rsi** *vr.* to be effected, fulfilled, produced.

Effettuazione [ef-fet-too-ah-tsee-oh'nay] *nf.* execution, fulfilment, performance.

Efficace [ef-fee-kah'chay] *a.* effectual, efficacious.

Efficacia [ef-fee-kah'chah] *nf.* efficacy, efficaciousness.

Efficiente [ef-fee-chen'tay] *a.* effective, efficient.

Efficienza [ef-fee-chent'zah] *nf.* effectiveness, efficiency.

Effigiare [ef-fee-jah'ray] *vt.* to image, make an effigy of, portray, represent.

Effigie [ef-fee'jay] *nf.* effigy.

Effimero [ef-fee'may-roh] *a.* ephemeral, fleeting.

Efflorescente [ef-floh-ray-shen'tay] *a.* efflorescent.

Efflusso [ef-floos'soh] *a.* effluxion, flow.

Effluvio [ef-floo'vee-oh] *nm.* effluvium, stink.

Effondere [ef-fon'day-ray] *vt.* to pour out, vent; —**rsi** *vr.* to break out into, burst, flow, spread.

Effusione [ef-foo-zee-oh'nay] *nf.* effusion, outpouring.

Egiziano [ay-jee-tsee-ah'noh] *nm.* and *a.* Egyptian.

Egida [ay'jee-dah] *nf.* protection, shelter, shield.

Egli [ayl'yee] *pn.* he.

Eglino [ayl'yee-noh] *pr.* (*m.pl.*) they (*old-fashioned*).

Egoista [ay-goh-ee'stah] *nm.* egoist; *a.* egoistic(al).

Egregio [ay-gray'joh] *a.* egregious, exceptional, remarkable.

Eguaglianza [ay-gwah-lyahnt'zah] *nf.* equality.

Eguagliare [ay-gwah-lyah'ray] *vt.* and *i.* to be (make) equal, level.

Eguale [ay-gwah'lay] *a.* equal, even, like, uniform.

Egualità [ay-gwah-lee-tah'] *nf.* equality, evenness, uniformity.

Elaborare [ay-lah-boh-rah'ray] *vt.* to elaborate, plan, work out.

Elargire [ay-lahr-jee'ray] *vt.* to give liberally, grant, lavish.

Elargizione [ay-lahr-jee-tsee-oh'nay] *nf.* donation, generous contribution, gift, grant.

Elasticità [ay-lah-stee-chee-tah'] *nf.* buoyancy, elasticity, light-heartedness.

Elastico [ay-lah'stee-koh] *nm.* elastic; *a.* buoyant elastic, light-hearted.

Elce [ell'chay] *nm.* evergreen oak.

Elefante [ay-lay-fahn'tay] *nm.* elephant.

Elegante [ay-lay-gahn´tay] *a.* elegant, fine, graceful.

Eleggere [ay-lay´djay-ray] *vt.* to choose, elect.

Eleggibile [ay-lay-djee´bee-lay] *a.* eligible, qualified.

Elegia [ay-lay-jee´ah] *nf.* elegy.

Elementare [ay-lay-men-tah´ray] *a.* elementary.

Elemento [ay-lay-men´toh] *nm.* element, principle.

Elemosina [ay-lay-moh´zee-nah] *nf.* alms (*pl.*). charity

Elemosinare [ay-lay-moh-zee-nah´ray] *vt.* to beg.

Elemosiniera [ay-lay-moh-zee-nee-ay´rah] *nf.*—**re** [ray] *nm.* almoner, alms-giver; *a.* charitable.

Elencare [ay-leng-kah´ray] *vt.* to draw up a statement, make an inventory.

Elenco [ay-leng´koh] *nm.* inventory, specification.

Eletto [ay-let´toh] *a.* chosen, elect, elected.

Elettorale [ay-let-toh-rah´lay] *a.* electoral.

Elet/tore [ay-let-toh´ray] *nm.* elector; —**trice** [tree´chay] *nf.* electress.

Elettricista [ay-let-tree-chee´stah] *nm.* electrician.

Elettricità [ay-let-tree-chee-tah´] *nf.* electricity.

Elettrizzare [ay-let-treed-zah´ray] *vt.* to electrify.

Eleva/re [ay-lay-vah´ray] *vt.* to elevate, erect, lift, raise; —**rsi** *vr.* to make one's way, raise oneself.

Elevatezza [ay-lay-vah-tet´zah] *nf.* elevation, loftiness, nobility.

Elevatore [ay-lay-vah-toh´ray] *nm.* (*tech.*) elevator.

Elica [ay´lee-kah] *nf.* propeller, screw.

Elide/re [ay-lee´day-ray] *vt.* to elide, suppress; —**rsi** *vr.* to be elided.

Elimina/re [ay-lee-mee-nah´ray] *vt.* to eliminate, leave out; —**rsi** *vr.* to be eliminated.

Eliminazione [ay-lee-mee-nah-tsee-oh´nay] *nf.* elimination, removal.

Elisione [ay-lee-zee-oh´nay] *nf.* elision.

Elisi [ay-lee´zee] *nm.* Elysium;—**so** [zoh] *a.* Elysian, elided, suppressed.

Ella [ell´lah] *pn.* she.

Elle [ell´lay], the letter L.

Elleboro [ell-lay´boh-roh] *nm.* Christmas rose, hellebore.

Elleno [ell-lay´noh] *pn.* (*f.pl.*) they (*old-fashioned*).

Ellera: *v.* edera.

Ellisse [ell-lees´say] *nf.* ellipse, omission.

Elmo [ell´moh] *nm.* helmet.

Elocuzione [ay-loh-koo-tsee-oh´nay] *nf.* elocution.

Elogiare [ay-loh-jah´ray] *vt.* to commend, eulogise, praise.

Elogio [ay-loh´joh] *nm.* commendation, eulogy.

Eloquente [ay-loh-kwen´tay] *a.* eloquent, fluent.

Eloquio [ay-loh´kwee-oh] *nm.* speech.

Elsa [ell´sah] *nf.* hilt (of a sword).

Eludere [ay-loo´day-ray] *vt.* to avoid, elude, escape.

Elusione [ay-loo-zee-oh´nay] *nf.* (*rare*)elusion, evasion.

Emaciarsi [ay-mah-chahr´see] *vr.* to become emaciated.

Emaciazione [ay-mah-chah-tsee-oh´nay] *nf.* emaciation.

Emanare [ay-mah-nah´ray] *vt.* to issue, publish; *vi.* to emanate, flow, spring.

Emanazione [ay-mah-nah-tsee-oh´nay] *nf.* emanation, origin.

Emancipa/re [ay-mahn-chee-pah´ray] *vt.* to emancipate, free; —**rsi** *vr.* to be emancipated, free oneself.

Emblema [em-blay'mah] *nm.* emblem, symbol.

Embolismo [em-boh-lees'moh] *nm.* embolism.

Embrione [em-bree-oh'nay] *nm.* embryo.

Emenda [ay-men'dah] *nf.* amendment, correction.

Emenda/re [ay-men-dah'ray] *vt.* to amend, emend, mend; —**rsi** *vr.* to correct oneself, mend one's ways.

Emergenza [ay-mehr-jent'-zah] *nf.* critical period, emergency, exigency.

Emergere [ay-mehr'jay-ray] *vi.* to appear, crop up, emerge, stand out.

Emesso [ay-mess'soh] *a.* emitted, issued, put out.

Emettere [ay-met'tay-ray] *vt.* to emit, express, give out, issue.

Emicrania [ay-mee-krah'nee-ah] *nf.* headache.

Emigrante [ay-mee-grahn'-tay] *nm.* and *f.* and *a.* emigrant.

Emigrare [ay-mee-grah'ray] *vi.* to emigrate.

Eminente [ay-mee-nen'tay] *a.* eminent.

Eminenza [ay-mee-nent'zah] *nf.* eminence, eminency.

Emissario [ay-mees-sah'ree-oh] *nm.* emissary.

Emissione [ay-mees-see-oh'nay] *nf.* discharge, emission, issue.

Emittente [ay-meet-ten'tay] *nm.* issuer; *a.* issuing; banca [bahng'kah] e. *nf.* bank of issue; stazione [stah-tsee-oh'-nay] e. *nf.* (rad., etc.) sending station. [M.

Emme [em'may], the letter

Emorroidi [ay-morr-roh'ee-dee] *nm.* (pl.) (med.) piles (pl.).

Emozionante [ay-moh-tsee-oh-nahn'tay] *a.* exciting, thrilling.

Emozionare [ay-moh-tsee-

oh-nah'ray] *vt.* to excite, thrill.

Emozione [ay-moh-tsee-oh'-nay] *nf.* emotion, excitement.

Empiastro [em-pee-ah'stroh] *nm.* plaster, (fig.) bore.

Empiere: *v.* **empire**.

Empietà [em-pee-ay-tah'] *nf.* impiety.

Empio [em'pee-oh] *a.* impious.

Empire [em-pee'ray] *vt.* to cram, fill (up).

Empirico [em-pee'ree-koh] *nm.* empiric, quack.

Empirismo [em-pee-rees'-moh] *nm.* empiricism, quackery.

Emporio [em-poh'ree-oh] *nm.* emporium, mart.

Emulare [ay-moo-lah'ray] *vt.* to emulate, vie (with).

Emulazione [ay-moo-lah-tsee-oh'nay] *nf.* emulation, rivalry.

Emulo [ay'moo-loh] *nm.* competitor; *a.* emulous.

Enciclica [en-chee'klee-kah] *nf.* and *a.* encyclic(al).

Enciclopedia [en-chee-kloh-pay-dee'ah] *nf.* encyclopedia.

Encomiabile [en-koh-mee-ah'bee-lay] *a.* commendable, praiseworthy.

Encomio [en-koh'mee-oh] *nm.* encomium, praise; e. solenne [soh-len'nay] (mil.) mention in dispatches.

Endivia [en-dee'vee-ah] *nf.* endive. [energy.

Energia [ay-nehr-jee'ah] *nf.*

Energico [ay-nehr'jee-koh] *a.* energetic, powerful.

Energumeno [ay-nehr-goo'-may-noh] *nm.* demoniac, madman, one possessed.

Enfasi [en'fah-zee] *nf.* emphasis, stress.

Enfiagione [en-fee-ah-joh'-nay] *nf.* bloatedness, swelling.

Enfia/re [en-fee-ah'ray] *vt.*

and i. to swell; —**rsi** *vr.* to be puffed up, swollen.

Enigma [ay-neeg'mah] *nm.* enigma, riddle.

Enorme [ay-norr'may] *a.* enormous, huge, incredible.

Enormità [ay-norr-mee-tah'] *nf.* enormity, nonsense.

Ente [en'tay] *nm.* being.

Enterico [en-tay'ree-koh] *a.* enteric.

Enterite [en-tay-ree'tay] *nf.* (*med.*) enteritis.

Entità [en-tee-tah'] *nf.* entity, existence.

Entrambi [en-trahm'bee] *pn.* and *a.* (*pl.*) both (*pl.*).

Entrante [en-trahn'tay] *a.* forward, pushing.

Entrare [en-trah'ray] *vi.* to come in, enter, go in.

Entrata [en-trah'tah] *nf.* admittance, (*com.*) assets (*pl.*), entering, entrance, income.

Entro [en'troh] *pn.* within.

Entusiasma/re [en-too-zee-ah-smah'ray] *vt.* to enrapture, make enthusiastic; —**rsi** *vt.* to become enthusiastic.

Entusiasmo [en-too-zee-ah'smoh] *nm.* enthusiasm, rapture.

Entusiastico [en-too-zee-ah'stee-koh] *a.* enthusiastic.

Enumerare [ay-noo-may-rah'ray] *vt.* to detail, enumerate.

Enunciare [ay-noon-chah'ray] *vt.* to enunciate, state, utter.

Epatico [ay-pah'tee-koh] *a.* (*med.*) hepatic, of the liver.

Epicureismo [ay-pee-koo-ray-ees'moh] *nm.* epicureanism.

Epicureo [ay-pee-koo-ray'oh] *a.* epicurean.

Epidemia [ay-pee-day-mee'ah] *nf.* epidemic.

Epidermide [ay-pee-dehr'mee-day] *nf.* (*med.*) epidermis, outer skin.

Epifania [ay-pee-fah-nee'ah] *nf.* Epiphany.

Epigrafe [ay-pee'grah-fay] *nf.* epigraph, inscription.

Epigramma [ay-pee-grahm'mah] *nm.* epigram.

Epilessia [ay-pee-less-see'ah] *nf.* (*med.*) epilepsy.

Epilettico [ay-pee-let'tee-koh] *nm.* and *a.* epileptic.

Epilogare: *v.* **riepilogare**

Epilogo [ay-pee'loh-goh] *nm.* epilogue.

Episcopale [ay-pees-koh-pah'lay] *a.* episcopal.

Episcopato [ay-pees-koh-pah'toh] *nm.* episcopacy, episcopate.

Episodio [ay-pee-soh'dee-oh] *nm.* digression, episode.

Epistola [ay-pee'stoh-lah] *nf.* epistle.

Epiteto [ay-pee'tay-toh] *nm.* epithet.

Epoca [ay'poh-kah] *nf.* epoch, time.

Eppure [ep-poo'ray] *ad.* and *con.* and yet, however, nevertheless.

Epura/re [ay-poo-rah'ray] *vt.* to clarify, clear up, purify, refine, remove; —**rsi** *vr.* to be made clear, be refined, grow purer.

Epurazione [ay-poo-rah-tsee-oh'nay] *nf.* clarification, refining, removal (from office).

Equanime [ay-kwah'nee-may] *a.* calm, tranquil, well-balanced.

Equatore [ay-kwah-toh'ray] *nm.* equator.

Equestre [ay-kwess-tray] *nm.* and *f.* and *a.* equestrian.

Equilibra/re [ay-kwee-lee-brah'ray] *vt.* to balance, poise; —**rsi** *vr.* to balance (each other).

Equilibrio [ay-kwee-lee'bree-oh] *nm.* balance, equilibrium.

Equilibrista [ay-kwee-lee-bree'stah] *nm.* rope-dancer.

Equinozio [ay-kwee-noh'-tsee-oh] *nm.* equinox.

Equipaggiare [ay-kwee-pah-djah'ray] *vt.* to equip, fit out.

Equipaggio [ay-kwee-pah'-djoh] *nm.* (*mar.*) crew, effects (*pl.*), equipage.

Equiparare [ay-kwee-pah-rah'ray] *vt.* to balance, make equal.

Equipollente [ay-kwee-poll-len'tay] *a.* equal, equivalent.

Equità [ay-kwee-tah'] *nf.* equity, fairness, impartiality, justice.

Equitazione [ay-kwee-tah-tsee-oh'nay] *nf.* equitation, horsemanship.

Equivalente [ay-kwee-vah-len'tay] *nm. and a.* equivalent.

Equivocare [ay-kwee-voh-kah'ray] *vt. and i.* to make a mistake, misunderstand.

Equivoco [ay-kwee'voh-koh] *nm.* misunderstanding; *a.* equivocal, of ill-fame.

Equo [ay'kwoh] *a.* equitable, fair, impartial, just.

Erario [ay-rah'ree-oh] *nm.* exchequer, public treasury.

Erba [ehr'bah] *nf.* grass, herb; in [een] e. a. inexperienced, in embryo.

Erbaggio [ehr-bah'djoh] *nm.* pot herbs (*pl.*).

Erbaiolo [ehr-bah-ee-oh'loh] *nm.* herbalist.

Erbivendolo [ehr-bee-ven'doh-loh] *nm.* greengrocer.

Erbeso [ehr-boh'soh] *a.* grassy.

Erede [ay-ray'day] *nm.* heir.

Eredità [ay-ray-dee-tah'] *nf.* heritage, inheritance.

Ereditare [ay-ray-dee-tah'ray] *vt.* to inherit.

Ereditario [ay-ray-dee-tah'ree-oh] *a.* hereditary; **principe**

[preen'chee-pay] **e.** *nm.* crown-prince.

Ereditiera [ay-ray-dee-tee-ay'rah] *nf.* heiress.

Eremitaggio [ay-ray-mee-tah'djoh], **eremo** [ay'ray-moh] *nm.* hermitage.

Eresia [ay-ray-zee'ah] *nf.* heresy.

Eretico [ay-ray'tee-koh] *nm. and a.* heretic(al).

Erezione [ay-ray-tsee-oh'nay] *nf.* erection.

Ergastolo [ehr-gah'stoh-loh] *nm.* galleys (*pl.*), life-sentence.

Erica [ay'ree-kah] *nf.* heath, heather.

Erige/re [ay-ree'jay-ray] *vt.* to erect, institute, raise; —**rsi** *vr.* to raise oneself, set up for.

Ermellino [ehr-mell-lee'noh] *nm.* ermine.

Ermo [ehr'moh] *a.* lonely, solitary (*poet.*); *v.* Solitario.

Ernia [ehr'nee-ah] *nf.* (*med.*) hernia, rupture.

Eroe [ay-roh'ay] *nm.* hero.

Erogare [ay-roh-gah'ray] *vt.* to bestow, lay out.

Eroico [ay-roh'ee-koh] *a.* heroic. [heroine.

Eroina [ay-roh-ee'nah] *nf.*

Erompere [ay-rom'pay-ray] *vi.* to break out, burst out, flow, rush out.

Erosione [ay-roh-zee-oh'nay] *nf.* eating away, erosion.

Erotico [ay-roh'tee-koh] *a.* erotic.

Erpice [ehr'pee-chay] *nm.* harrow.

Errante [ehr-rahn'tay] *a.* errant, wandering.

Errare [ehr-rah'ray] *vi.* to be mistaken, blunder, err, roam, rove, wander.

Erre [ehr'ray], the letter R.

Erroneo [ehr-roh'nay-oh] *a.* erroneous, faulty, incorrect.

Errore [ehr-roh'ray] *nm.* blunder, error, mistake.

Erta [ehr-tah] *nf.* slope, steep ascent.

Erto [ehr'toh] *a.* steep.

Erudi/re [ay-roo-dee'ray] *vt.* to instruct, teach; —**rsi** *vr.* to acquire knowledge, become learned.

Erudito [ay-roo-dee'toh] *nm.* scholar; *a.* erudite, learned.

Esacerba/re [ay-zah-chehr-bah'ray] *vt.* to aggravate, embitter, exacerbate, provoke; —**rsi** *vr.* to become embittered, grow worse.

Esagerare [ay-zah-jay-rah'ray] *vt. and i.* to exaggerate.

Esagerazione [ay-zah-jay-rah-tsee-oh'nay] *nf.* exaggeration.

Esalare [ay-zah-lah'ray] *vt.* to exhale, give out.

Esalazione [ay-zah-lah-tsee-oh'nay] *nf.* exhalation.

Esalta/re [ay-zahl-tah'ray] *vt.* to exalt, praise; —**rsi** *vr.* to get excited.

Esaltato [ay-zahl-tah'toh] *nm.* lunatic; *a.* crazy, excited.

Esame [ay-zah'may] *nm.* examination, investigation; **commissione di** [kom-mees-see-oh-nay dee] **e.** *nf.* Board of Examiners.

Esaminare [ay-zah-mee-nah'ray] *vt.* to examine, inspect, investigate, survey, test.

Esangue [ay-zahng'gway] *a.* bloodless.

Esanime [ay-zah'nee-may] *a.* dead, lifeless.

Esaspera/re [ay-zahs-pay-rah'ray] *vt.* to exasperate; —**rsi** *vr.* to get exasperated.

Esattezza [ay-zaht-tet'zah] *nf.* accuracy, exactness, exactitude, punctuality.

Esatto [ay-zaht'toh] *a.* accurate, exact, precis punctual.

Esattore [ay-zaht-toh'ray] *nm.* collector (of taxes, etc.).

Esaudire [ay-zow-dee'ray] *vt.* to assent, consent, grant, listen favourably.

Esauriente [ay-zow-ree-en'tay] *a.* exhausting, exhaustive.

Esaurimento [ay-zow-ree-men'toh] *nm.* exhaustion, failure; **e. nervoso** [nehr-voh'soh], nervous breakdown.

Esauri/re [ay-zow-ree'ray] *vt.* to exhaust, use up, wear out; —**rsi** *vr.* to be out of print, be sold out, exhaust oneself.

Esausto [ay-zow'stoh] *a.* exhausted.

Esautorare [ay-zow-toh-rah'ray] *vt.* to deprive of authority, discredit.

Esazione [ay-zah-tsee-oh'nay] *nf.* collection, exaction.

Esca [ess'kah] *nf.* bait, decoy, enticement, tinder (for a lighter).

Escandescente [ess-kahn-day-shen'tay] *a.* choleric, hot-tempered.

Escandescenza [ess-kahn-day-shen'zah] *nf.* outburst, sudden burst of rage.

Escavazione [ess-kah-vah-tsee-oh'nay] *nf.* excavation.

Escire, etc.; *v.* **uscire,** etc.

Esclamare [ess-klah-mah'ray] *vi.* to cry out exclaim.

Esclamazione [ess-klah-mah-tsee-oh'nay] *nf.* exclamation.

Escludere [ess-kloo'day-ray] *vt.* to except, exclude, leave out.

Esclusione [ess-kloo-zee-oh'nay] *nf.* exclusion, omission.

Escogitare [ess-koh-jee-tah'ray] *vt.* to concert, contrive, devise, excogitate.

Escoriare [ess-koh-ree-ah'ray] *vt.* to excoriate, scratch.

Escursione [ess-koor-see-oh'nay] *nf.* excursion, trip.

Escursionista [ess-koor-see-oh-nee'stah] *nm.* and *f.* and *a.* excursionist.

Esecrare [ay-zay-krah'ray] *vt.* to execrate.

Esecrazione [ay-zay-krah-tsee-oh'nay] *nf.* execration.

Esecutivo [ay-zay-koo-tee'-voh] *a.* executive, executory, working.

Esecutore [ay-zay-koo-toh'-ray] *nm.* doer, executant, (*mus.*) executant, (*jur.*) executor, executioner, performer.

Esecuzione [ay-zay-koo-tsee-oh'nay] *nf.* eseguimento [ay-zay-gwee-men'toh] *nm.* execution, performance.

Eseguire [ay-zay-gwee'ray] *vt.* to accomplish, carry out, execute, fulfil, perform.

Esempio [ay-zem'pee-oh] *nm.* example, instance, pattern, precedent.

Esemplare [ay-zem-plah'-ray] *nm.* copy, model, pattern, specimen; *a.* exemplary.

Esemplificare [ay-zem-plee-fee-kah'ray] *vt.* to exemplify.

Esenta/re [ay-zen-tah'ray] *vt.* to excuse, exempt, exonerate, free; —rsi *vr.* to free oneself.   [empt, free.

Esente [ay-zen'tay] *a.* ex-

Esenzione [ay-zen-tsee-oh'-nay] *nf.* (*eccl.*) dispensation, exemption.

Esequie [ay-zay'kwee-ay] *nf.* (*pl.*) burial, funeral, obsequies (*pl.*).

Esercente [ay-zehr-chen'tay] *nm.* dealer, shopkeeper, trader; *a.* carrying on, keeping, practising.

Esercire [ay-zehr-chee'ray] *vt.* to carry on, keep, practise; non e. più [pee-oo'] *vi.* to have retired (from business or practice).

Esercita/re [ay-zehr-chee-tah'ray] *vt.* to drill, exercise,

exert, practise, train; —rsi *vr.* to practise.

Esercito [ay-zehr'chee-toh] *nm.* army.

Esercizio [ay-zehr-chee'tsee-oh] *nm.* exercise, function, office.

Esibi/re [ay-zee-bee'ray] *vt.* to display, exhibit, show; —rsi *vr.* to offer oneself, show oneself.

Esibizione [ay-zee-bee-tsee-oh'nay] *nf.* exhibition, show.

Esibizionista [ay-zee-bee-tsee-oh-nee'stah] *a.* fond of showing off.

Esigente [ay-zee-jen'tay] *a.* exacting, exigent, hard to please.

Esigere [ay-zee'jay-ray] *vt.* to demand, exact, require.

Esiguità [ay-zee-goo-ee-tah'] *nf.* exiguity, scantiness.

Esiguo [ay-zee'goo-oh] *a.* exiguous, scanty, slender.

Esilara/re [ay-zee-lah-rah'-ray] *vt.* to cheer up, enliven, exhilarate; —rsi *vr.* to become merry, cheer up.

Esile [ay-zee-lay] *a.* delicate, slender, slim.

Esilia/re [ay-zee-lee-ah'ray] *vt.* to banish, exile; —rsi *vr.* to exile oneself, withdraw from.

Esiliato [ay-zee-lee-ah'toh] *nm.* exile (person); *a.* exiled.

Esilio [ay-zee'lee-oh] *nm.* exile (state).

Esilità [ay-zee-lee-tah'] *nf.* delicacy, slenderness.

Esime/re [ay-zee'may-ray] *vt.* to excuse, exempt, exonerate; —rsi *vr.* to excuse oneself, evade, free oneself.

Esimio [ay-zee'mee-oh] *a.* excellent, famous.

Esistenza [ay-zees-tent'zah] *nf.* being, existence, life.

Esistere [ay-zees'tay-ray] *vi.* to be, exist, live.

Esitare [ay-zee-tah'ray] *vt.*

(com.) to retail, sell; *vi.* to demur, hesitate, waver.

Esito [ay'zee-toh] *nm.* issue, result, *(com.)* sale.

Esiziale [ay-zee-tsee-ah'lay] *a.* baneful, fatal.

Esodo [ay'zoh-doh] *nm.* departure, exodus.

Esonerare [ay-zoh-nay-rah'ray] *vt.* to exempt, exonerate, free, release, relieve.

Esonero [ay-zoh'nay-roh] *nm.* dispensation, exemption, exoneration.

Esorcizzare [ay-zorr-cheed-zah'ray] *vt.* to exorcise.

Esordio [ay-zorr'dee-oh] *nm.* beginning, exordium, preamble.

Esordire [ay-zorr-dee'ray] *vt. and i.* to begin, start.

Esortare [ay-zorr-tah'ray] *vt.* to admonish, exhort.

Esortazione [ay-zorr-tah-tsee-oh'nay] *nf.* exhortation.

Esoso [ay-zoh'zoh] *a.* hateful, odious, uncongenial.

Espande/re [ess-pahn'day-ray] *vt.* to spread; **—rsi** *vr.* to expand, open one's heart.

Espansione [ess-pahn-see-oh'nay] *nf.* demonstration of affection, expansion.

Espatriare [ess-pah-tree-ah'ray] *vt.* to exile, expatriate, banish.

Espatrio [ess-pah'tree-oh] *nm.* expatriation.

Espediente [ess-pay-dee-en'tay] *nm.* expedient, makeshift; *a.* expedient, fit, proper.

Esperienza [ess-pay-ree-en'zah] *nf.* experience, experiment.

Esperimentare [ess-pay-ree-men-tah'ray] *vt.* to experience, experiment, go through, try.

Esperimento [ess-pay-ree-men'toh] *nm.* experiment, proof, test, trial.

Esperto [ess-pehr'toh] *nm.* expert; *a.* experienced, expert, skilled.

Espettazione [ess-pet-tah-tsee-oh'nay] *nf.* expectancy. *(rare). v.* Aspettazione.

Espettorare [ess-pet-toh-rah'ray] *vt.* to cough up, expectorate.

Espiare [ess-pee-ah'ray] *vt.* to atone, expiate, make amends for.

Espiazione [ess-pee-ah-tsee-oh'nay] *nf.* amends *(pl.)*, atonement, expiation.

Esplicare [ess-plee-kah'ray] *vt.* to develop, display, explain.

Esplicazione [ess-plee-kah-tsee-oh'nay] *nf.* explanation.

Esplicito [ess-plee'chee-toh] *a.* clear, explicit, express, formal.

Esplodere [ess-ploh'day-ray] *vi.* to blow up, burst out, explode.

Esplorare [ess-ploh-rah'ray] *vt.* to examine, explore, *(mil.)* reconnoitre, search.

Esploratore [ess-ploh-rah-toh'ray] *nm.* explorer, *(mil.)* scout.

Esplorazione [ess-ploh-rah-tsee-oh'nay] *nf.* exploration, *(mil.)* reconnaissance.

Esplosione [ess-ploh-zee-oh'nay] *nf.* blowing up, discharge, explosion.

Esponente [ess-poh-nen'tay] *nm.* exponent, expounder.

Espor/re [ess-porr'ray] *vt.* to detail, exhibit, explain, expose, risk, show; **—rsi** *vr.* to expose oneself, run the risk.

Esportare [ess-porr-tah'ray] *vt.* to export.

Esportazione [ess-porr-tah-tsee-oh'nay] *nf.* export, exportation.

Esposizione [ess-poh-zee-tsee-oh'nay] *nf.* exhibition, exposition, statement.

Esposto [ess-poh'stoh] *nm.* (written) application for a post; *a.* exhibited, exposed, expressed.

Espressione [ess-press-see-oh'nay] *nf.* expression.

Espresso [ess-press'soh] *nm.* express letter; *a.* express, expressed, precise.

Esprimere [ess-pree'may-ray] *vt.* to declare, express, signify, utter.

Espropriare [ess-proh-pree-ah'ray] *vt.* to expel, expropriate.

Espugnare [ess-poon-yah'ray] *vt.* to (take by) storm.

Espulsione [ess-pool-see-oh'nay] *nf.* banishment, expulsion.

Espurgare [ess-poor-gah'ray] *vt.* to expurgate.

Espurgazione [ess-poor-gah-tsee-oh'nay] *nf.* expurgation.

Essa [ess'sah] *pn.* she.

Essenza [ess-sent'zah] *nf.* essence, nature.

Essenziale [ess-sen-tsee-ah'lay] *a.* essential, main, principal.

Essere [ess'say-ray] *vi.* to be, exist, happen, occur; **e. di** [dee], to belong to; **e. per** [pehr], to be on the point of.

Essicca/re [ess-seek-kah'ray] *vt.* to dry; —rsi *vr.* to dry up.

Esso [ess'soh] *pn.* he.

Estasi [ess'tah-zee] *nf.* ecstasy, rapture.

Estasiarsi [ess-tahr-zee-ahr'see] *vr.* to be in raptures.

Estate [ess-tah'tay] *nf.* summer.

Estende/re [ess-ten'day-ray] *vt.* to extend, stretch; —rsi *vr.* to diffuse, extend.

Estenua/re [ess-tay-noo-ah'ray] *vt.* to exhaust; —rsi *vr.* to become exhausted, weak.

Estenuazione [ess-tay-noo-ah-tsee-oh'nay] *nf.* exhaustion.

Esteriore [ess-tay-ree-oh'ray] *nm.* exterior; *a.* exterior, external, outward.

Esterminare [ess-tehr-mee-nah'ray] *vt.* to exterminate.

Esterna/re [ess-tehr-nah'ray] *vt.* to disclose, express, open; —rsi *vr.* to open one's heart.

Esterno [ess-tehr'noh] *nm. ad. and pr.* outside; *a* external, outer, outside.

Estero [ess'tay-roh] *nm.* foreign country; **all'e.** [ahl] *ad.* abroad; *a.* foreign.

Esterrefatto [ess-tehr-ray-faht'toh] *a.* frightened, terrified.

Esteso [ess-tay'soh] *a.* diffuse, extended, extensive, wide.

Estetica [ess-tay'tee-kah] *nf.* æsthetics (*pl.*).

Estimo [ess'tee-moh] *nm.* appraisement, valuation.

Estingue/re [ess-teeng'gway-ray] *vt.* to cancel (a debt), extinguish, put out; —rsi *vr.* to become dim, fade away, go out.

Estinto [ess-teen'toh] *nm. and a.* deceased; *a.* extinguished, put out.

Estinzione [ess-teen-tsee-oh'nay] *nf.* cancelling (of a debt), extinction, putting out.

Estirpare [ess-teer-pah'ray] *vt.* to extirpate, pull up, root up.

Estirpazione [ess-teer-pah-tsee-oh'nay] *nf.* extirpation, rooting up.

Estorcere [ess-torr'chay-ray] *vt.* to extort.

Estorsione [ess-torr-see-oh'nay] *nf.* extortion.

Estradizione [ess-trah-dee-tsee-oh'nay] *nf.* extradition.

Estraneo [ess-trah'nay-oh] *nm.* outsider, stranger; *a* extraneous, not related, unknown.

Estrarre [ess-trahr'ray] *vt.* to dig out, draw out, extract.

Estratto [ess-traht'toh] *nm.* certificate, extract; *a.* drawn out, extracted.

Estremità [ess-tray-mee-tah'] *nf.* end, extreme, extremity.

Estremo [ess-tray'moh] *nm.* excess, extreme, extremity; *a.* farthest, extreme, last.

Estrinsecare [ess-treen-say-kah'ray] *vt.* to express, manifest.

Estrinseco [ess-treen'say-koh] *a.* extrinsic.

Estro [ess'troh] *nm.* caprice, freak, inspiration.

Estroso [ess-troh'soh] *a.* capricious, freakish, whimsical.

Estuario [ess-too-ah'ree-oh] *nm.* estuary, mouth.

Esuberante [ay-zoo-bay-rahn'tay] *a.* exuberant, overflowing.

Esulare [ay-zoo-lah'ray] *vi.* to go into exile.

Esulcerare [ay-zool-chay-rah'ray] *vt.* to produce sores.

Esule [ay'zoo-lay] *nm.* and *f.* exile (person); *a.* exiled.

Esultante [ay-zool-tahn'tay] *a.* exultant, joyful.

Esultare [ay-zool-tah'ray] *vi.* to exult, rejoice.

Esumazione [ay-zoo-mah-tsee-oh'nay] *nf.* exhumation.

Età [ay-tah'] *nf.* age.

Etere [ay'tay-ray] *nm.* ether.

Etereo [ay-tay'ray-oh] *a.* airy, ethereal, impalpable.

Eterna/re [ay-tehr-nah'ray] *vt.* to eternalise, make endless; —rsi *vr.* to become eternal, last for ever.

Eternità [ay-tehr-nee-tah'] *nf.* eternity.

Eterno [ay-tehr'noh] *a.* eternal, everlasting.

Etica [ay'tee-kah] *nf.* ethics (*pl.*).

Etichetta [ay-tee-ket'tah] *nf.* etiquette, forms (*pl.*), label.

Etico [ay'tee-koh] *a.* ethical, (*med.*) hectic.

Etimologia [ay-tee-moh-loh-jee'ah] *nf.* etymology.

Etisia [ay-tee-zee'ah] *nf.* (*med.*) consumption.

Etnico [et'nee-koh] *a.* ethnic(al).

Ettaro [et'tah-roh] *nm.* hectare.

Eucaristia [ay-oo-kah-ree-stee'ah] *nf.* Eucharist.

Eufemia [ay-oo-fay-mee'ah] *nf.* euphemism.

Eufonia [ay-oo-foh-nee'ah] *nf.* euphony.

Eunuco [ay-oo-noo'koh] *nm.* eunuch.

Evacuare [ay-vah-koo-ah'ray] *vt.* to clear out, evacuate.

Evadere [ay-vah'day-ray] *vt.* to evade; *vi.* to escape.

Evangelizzare [ay-vahn-jay-leed-zah'ray] *vt.* to evangelise.

Evangelo [ay-vahn-jay'loh] *nm.* gospel.

Evaporare [ay-vah-poh-rah'ray] *vi.* to evaporate.

Evasione [ay-vah-zee-oh'nay] *nf.* escape, evasion.

Evenienza [ay-vay-nee-ent'zah] *nf.* contingency, emergency, need, occurrence.

Evento [ay-ven'toh] *nm.* adventure, event, incident, occurrence; in ogni caso [in ohn'yee] *e. ad.* at all events.

Eventuale [ay-ven-too-ah'lay] *a.* eventual, incidental.

Evidente [ay-vee-den'tay] *a.* clear, evident, obvious, plain.

Evidenza [ay-vee-dent'zah] *nf.* clearness, evidence, obviousness.

Evitabile [ay-vee-tah'bee-lay] *a.* avoidable, preventable

Evita/re [ay-vee-tah'ray] *vt.* to avoid, prevent, shun; **—rsi** *vr.* to be avoided.

Evo [ay'voh] *nm.* age, period, time.

Evocare [ay-voh-kah'ray] *vt.* to call up, conjure, evoke.

Evoluzione [ay-voh-loo-tsee-oh'nay] *nf.* evolution.

Evviva [ev-vee'vah] *int.* hurrah! long live!

Eziandio [ay-tsee-ahn-dee'oh] *ad.* also, even. *v.* Anche, Pure.

F

Fa [fah] *ad.* ago; *nm.* (*mus.*) fourth note in sol-fa notation.

Fabbisogno [fahb-bee-zohn'yoh] *nm.* estimate of expenditure, requirements (*pl.*), what is needed.

Fabbrica [fahb'bree-kah] *nf.* factory, manufactory, works (*pl.*).

Fabbricare [fahb-bree-kah'ray] *vt.* to build, fabricate, make, manufacture.

Fabbricato [fahb-bree-kah'toh] *nm.* building, premises (*pl.*); *a.* built, made, manufactured.

Fabbricazione [fahb-bree-kah-tsee-oh'nay] *nf.* fabrication, manufacture, manufacturing.

Fabbro (fahb'broh] *nm.* blacksmith, smith; **f. ferraio** [fehr-rah'yoh] locksmith.

Faccenda [fahch-chen'dah] *nf.* affair, business, matter, thing.

Facchinaggio [fahk-kee-nah'djoh] *nm.* porterage.

Facchino [fahk-kee'noh] *nm.* porter.

Faccia [fahch'chah] *nf.* face; **f. tosta** [toss'tah] impudence.

Facciata [fahch-chah'tah] *nf.* façade, front, side (of a page).

Faceto [fah-chay'toh] *a.* facetious.

Facezia [fah-chay'tsee-ah] *nf.* jest, joke, witticism.

Facile [fah'-chee-lay] *a.* easy.

Facilità [fah-chee-lee-tah'] *nf.* ease, easiness, facility.

Facilitare [fah-chee-lee-tah'ray] *vt.* to facilitate, make easy.

Facoltà [fah-koll-tah'] *nf.* authority, faculty, power, talent.

Facoltativo [fah-koll-tah-tee'voh] *a.* optional.

Facoltoso [fah-koll-toh'soh] *a.* wealthy, well-to-do.

Facondia [fah-kon'dee-ah] *nf.* eloquence, fluency.

Facondo [fah-kon'doh] *a.* eloquent, fluent, talkative.

Faggio [fah'djoh] *nm.* beech-tree.

Fagiano [fah-jah'noh] *nm.* pheasant.

Fagiolo [fah-joh'loh] *nm.* kidney-bean.

Fagotto [fah-got'toh] *nm.* (*mus.*) bassoon, bundle; **fare** [fah'ray] **f.** *vi.* to pack up.

Faina [fah-ee'nah] *nf.* pole-cat.   [sickle.

Falce [fahl'chay] *nf.* scythe,

Falciare [fahl-chah'ray] *vt.* to cut down, mow.

Falco [fahl'koh], **falcone** [fahl-koh'nay] *nm.* falcon, hawk.

Falda [fahl'dah] *nf.* base (of a hill), brim (of a hat), flake (of snow), fold, layer, sheet (of metal), tail (of a coat).

Falegname [fah-layn-yah'may] *nm.* carpenter, joiner.

Falena [fah-lay'nah] *nf.* ashes (*pl.*), moth.

Fallace [fahl-lah'chay] *a.* deceptive, fallacious.

Fallare [fahl-lah'ray] *vi.* to make a mistake.

Fallibile [fahl-lee'bee-lay] *a.* fallible, liable to error.

Fallimento [fahl-lee-men'toh] *nm.* bankruptcy, failure, insolvency.

Fallire [fahl-lee'ray] *vt.* to miss; *vi.* to fail, go bankrupt.

Fallito [fahl-lee'toh] *nm.* bankrupt; *a.* failed, missed.

Fallo [fahl-loh] *nm.* defect, fault. [fire, bonfire.

Falò [fah-loh'] *nm.* beacon-

Falsare [fahl-sah'ray] *vt.* to alter, distort, falsify.

Falsario [fahl-sah'ree-oh] *nm.* forger.

Falsificare [fahl-see-fee-kah'ray] *vt.* to falsify, forge, mis-represent.

Falsità [fahl-see-tah'] *nf.* duplicity, falsehood, untruth.

Falso [fahl'soh] *nm.* untruth; *a.* counterfeit, false, forged, fraudulent, wrong.

Fama [fah'mah] *nf.* fame, renown, reputation.

Fame [fah'may] *nf.* hunger; avere [ah-vay'ray] f. *vi.* to be hungry.

Famelico [fah-may'lee-koh] *a.* famishing, starving.

Famigerato [fah-mee-jay-rah'toh] *a.* notorious.

Famiglia [fah-meel'yah] *nf.* family, household.

Familiare [fah-mee-lee-ah'ray] *nm.* and *f.* member of the family or household, or intimate friend; *a.* familiar, intimate.

Familiarità [fah-mee-lee-ah-ree-tah'] *nf.* familiarity, intimacy.

Familiarizza/re [fah-mee-lee-ah-reed-zah'ray] *vt.* to familiarise; —rsi *vr.* to become familiar.

Famoso [fah-moh'soh] *a.* famous, renowned, well-known.

Fanale [fah-nah'lay] *nm.* headlight, lamp, light, light-house.

Fanatico [fah-nah'tee-koh] *nm.* and *a.* fanatic.

Fanciul/la [fahn-chool'lah] *nf.* young girl; —lo [loh] *nm.* young boy.

Fanciullaggine [fahn-chool-làh'djee-nay] *nf.* childishness.

Fanciullesco [fahn-chool-less'koh] *a.* childish, child's.

Fanciullezza [fahn-chool-let'zah] *nf.* childhood.

Fandonia [fahn-doh'nee-ah] *nf.* hoax, idle story, tall tale.

Fango [fahng'goh] *nm.* mire, mud, vice. [miry, muddy.

Fangoso [fahng-goh'soh] *a.*

Fannullone [fahn-nool-loh'nay] *nm.* idler, lazy-bones.

Fantasia [fahn-tah-zee'ah] *nf.* caprice, fancy, imagination.

Fantasticare [fahn-tah-stee-kah'ray] *vi.* to build castles in the air.

Fante [fahn'tay] *nm.* foot-soldier, jack (at cards), man-servant; *nf.* woman-servant.

Fanteria [fahn-tay-ree'ah] *nf.* infantry. [jockey.

Fantino [fahn-tee'noh] *nm.*

Fantoccio [fahn-tohch'choh] *nm.* doll, lay-figure, puppet.

Fardello [fahr-dell'loh] *nm.* bundle, burden.

Fa/re [fah'ray] *vt.* and *i.* to do, make; f. attenzione [ahtten-tsee-oh'nay] to pay attention; f. bel tempo [bell tem'poh] to be fine; f. il bagno [eel bahn'yoh] to take a bath; f. il medico [eel may'dee-koh] to be a doctor; f. fare una cosa [fah'ray oo'nah koh'sah] to have a thing done; f. lavorare una persona [lah-yoh-rah'**ray** oo'nah pehr-soh'nah] to make a person work; —rsi *vr.* to become, grow, make oneself, turn; f. frate [frah'tay] to turn monk; f. capire [kah-pee'ray] to make oneself understood; f. vedere

[vay-day´ray] to show oneself.
Fare [fah´ray] *nm.* behaviour, doing, making, manner.
Farfalla [fahr-fahl´lah] *nf.* butterfly.
Farina [fah-ree´nah] *nf.* flour, meal.
Farinoso [fah-ree-noh´soh] *a.* floury, mealy.
Farmaceutica [fahr-mah-chay-oo´tee-kah] *nf.* pharmaceutics (*pl.*).
Farmacia [fahr-mah-chee´ah] *nf.* chemist's shop, pharmacy.
Farmacista [fahr-mah-chee´stah] *nm.* chemist.
Farneticare [fahr-nay-tee-kah´ray] *vi.* to be delirious, rave.
Faro [fah´roh] *nm.* lighthouse.
Farragine [fahr-rah´jee-nay] *nf.* medley.
Farsa [fahr´sah] *nf.* farce, interlude.
Fascia [fah´shah] *nf.* band, bandage, cover, swaddling band.
Fasciame [fah-shah´may] *nm.* (*tech.*) plating, planking.
Fasciare [fah-shah´ray] *vt.* to bandage, swaddle, wrap.
Fascicolo [fah-shee´koh-loh] *nm.* number (of a publication), papers (concerning a case, etc.)
Fascina [fah-shee´nah] *nf.* fagot, (*mil.*) fascine.
Fascino [fah´shee-noh] *nm.* charm, fascination.
Fascio [fah´shoh] *nm.* bundle, fasces (*pl.*), pencil (of rays), (*mil.*) pile, sheaf.
Fase [fah´zay] *nf.* phase, stage.
Fastello [fah-stell´loh] *nm.* bundle (of wood), fagot.
Fastidiare: *v.* **infastidire.**
Fastidio [fah-stee´dee-oh] *nm.* annoyance, tediousness, trouble.
Fastidioso [fah-stee-dee-oh´-

soh] *a.* annoying, tedious, troublesome.
Fasto [fah´stoh] *nm.* display, ostentation, splendour, show.
Fastoso [fah-stoh´soh] *a.* gorgeous, ostentatious, splendid.
Fata [fah´tah] *nf.* fairy.
Fatale [fah-tah´lay] *a.* fated inevitable, unavoidable.
Fatalità (fah-tah-lee-tah´) *nf.* destiny, fatality, fate.
Fatica [fah-tee´kah] *nf.* difficulty, fatigue, labour, toil; **a** [ah] **f.** *ad.* with difficulty.
Faticare [fah-tee-kah´ray] *vt.* to exhaust, fatigue; *vi.* to overwork, toil, work hard.
Faticoso [fah-tee-koh´soh] *a.* exhausting, fatiguing.
Fato [fah´toh] *nm.* destiny, doom, fate, lot.
Fatta [faht´tah] *nf.* kind, nature, sort, species.
Fattezze [faht-tet´zay] *nf.* (*pl.*) features (*pl.*).
Fattibile [faht-tee´bee-lay] *a.* feasible, practicable.
Fattivo [faht-tee´voh] *a.* active, efficient.
Fatto [faht´toh] *nm.* act, action, deed, fact; *a.* done, grown-up, made.
Fattore [faht-toh´ray] *nm.* creator, doer, factor, maker, steward.
Fattoria [faht-toh-ree´ah] *nf.* farm.
Fattorino [faht-toh-ree´noh] *nm.* conductor (of a tram, etc.), message-boy, messenger.
Fattura [faht-too´rah] *nf.* (*com.*) bill, invoice, make, making, workmanship.
Fatuo [fah´too-oh] *a.* conceited, fatuous; **fuoco** [foo-oh´koh] **f.** *nm.* will-o'-the-wisp.
Fausto [fow´stoh] *a.* fortunate, happy, lucky.
Fau/tore [fow-toh´ray] *nm.*

—trice [tree'chay] *nf.* favourer, partizan, supporter.

Fava [fah'vah] *nf.* bean.

Favella [fah-vell'lah] *nf.* language, speech, tongue.

Favellare [fah-vell-lah'ray] *vi.* to speak, talk.

Favilla [fah-veel'lah] *nf.* spark. [comb.

Favo [fah'oh] *nm.* honey-

Favola [fah'voh-lah] *nf.* fable, plot (of a play).

Favoloso [fah-voh-loh'soh] *a.* fabulous.

Favore [fah-voh'ray] *nm.* benefit, civility, (*com.*) credit, favour, kindness.

Favoreggiare [fah-voh-ray-djah'ray] *vt.* to back, favour, support.

Favorevole [fah-voh-ray'voh-lay] *a.* favourable, propitious.

Favorire [fah-voh-ree'ray] *vt.* to favour, foster, oblige, promote.

Favorito [fah-voh-ree'toh] *nm.* favourite. *a.* favourite, preferred.

Fazione [fah-tsee-oh'nay] *nf.* faction, party.

Fazioso [fah-tsee-oh'soh] *nm.* mutineer, rebel; *a.* factious.

Fazzoletto [faht-zoh-let'toh] *nm.* handkerchief.

Febbraio [feb-brah'yoh] *nm.* February.

Febbre [feb'bray] *nf.* fever, temperature; avere la [ah-vay'ray lah] i. *vi.* to have (run) a temperature.

Febbricitare [feb-bree-chee-tah'ray] *vi.* to be feverish.

Feccia [fech'chah] *nf.* dregs (*pl.*), scum, sediment.

Fecondare [fay-kon-dah'ray] *vt.* to fecundate, fertilise.

Fecondo [fay-kon'doh] *a.* fecund, fertile, fruitful.

Fede [fay'day] *nf.* belief, certificate, creed, faith,

fidelity, trust, wedding-ring; f. di nascita [dee nah'shee-tah] birth certificate.

Fedele [fay-day'lay] *nm.* and *f.* faithful follower, true believer; *a.* faithful, loyal, true.

Fedeltà [fay-dell-tah'] *nf.* fidelity, loyalty.

Federa [fay'day-rah] *nf.* pillow-case.

Federazione [fay-day-rah-tsee-oh'nay] *nf.* (con)federacy

Fedina [fay-dee'nah] *nf.* whisker; f. penale [pay-nah'lay], police record, clean conduct sheet.

Fegato [fay'gah-toh] *nm.* courage, guts (*pl.*), (*anat.*) liver.

Felce [fell'chay] *nf.* fern.

Felice [fay-lee'chay] *a.* glad, happy, lucky.

Felicità [fay-lee-chee-tah'] *nf.* happiness, prosperity.

Felicitare [fay-lee-chee-tah'ray] *vt.* to congratulate.

Felicitazione [fay-lee-chee-tah-tsee-oh'nay] *nf.* congratulation.

Feltro [fell'troh] *nm.* felt.

Femmina [fem'mee-nah] *nf.* female, woman (contemptuous).

Femmineo [fem-mee'nay-oh] *a.* female, woman's.

Femminile [fem-mee-nee'lay] *a.* feminine, womanly.

Fende/re [fen'day-ray] *vt.* to cleave, cut open, split; —rsi *vr.* to burst, crack, split.

Fenditura [fen-dee-too'rah] *nf.* cleft, crack, split.

Fenice [fay-nee'chay] *nf.* phoenix, rarity.

Fenomeno [fay-noh'may-noh] *nm.* phenomenon.

Ferace [fay-rah'chay] *a.* fertile, fruitful.

Ferale [fay-rah'lay] *a.* of death, tragic.

Feretro [fay´ray-troh] *nm.* bier, litter.

Feria [fay´ree-ah] *nf.* holiday, vacation.

Feriale [fay-ree-ah´lay] *a.* business, working.

Feri/re [fay-ree´ray] *vt.* to hurt, wound; —**rsi** *vr.* to hurt oneself, wound oneself.

Ferita [fay-ree´tah] *nf.* hurt, injury, wound.

Ferma [fehr´mah] *nf.* (*mil.*) service, term of service.

Fermaglio [fehr-mahl´yoh] *nm.* buckle, clip.

Ferma/re [fehr-mah´ray] *vt.* to attract, check, fix, hinder, stop; —**rsi** *vr.* to dwell on, stay, stop.

Fermata [fehr-mah´tah] *nf.* halt, stop.

Fermento [fehr-men´toh] *nm.* commotion, ferment, tumult.

Fermezza [fehr-met´zah] *nf.* firmness, resolution, steadiness.

Fermo [fehr´moh] *a.* firm, steady, still; **f. in posta** [een poh´stah] *ad.* "poste restante."

Feroce [fay-roh´chay] *a.* ferocious, fierce.

Ferocia [fay-roh´chah] *nf.* ferocity, fierceness, savagery.

Ferragosto [fehr-rah-goh´stoh] *nm.* August holidays (Aug. 15th).

Ferramenta [fehr-rah-men´tah] *nf.* (*pl.*) iron fittings (*pl.*), iron tools (*pl.*).

Ferramento [fehr-rah-men´toh] *nm.* iron tool.

Ferrare [fehr-rah´ray] *vt.* to add iron fittings, shoe (a horse).

Ferrat/o [fehr-rah´toh] *a.* iron-plated, shod; **strada** [strah´dah] **f—a** *nf.* railway.

Ferreo [fehr´ray-oh] *a.* hard, inflexible, (of) iron.

Ferro [fehr´roh] *nm.* iron;

f. da calza [dah kahlt´zah], knitting-needle; **f. da stiro** [dah stee´roh], iron (for ironing).

Ferrovia [fehr-roh-vee´ah] *nf.* railway.

Ferroviario [fehr-roh-vee-ah´ree-oh] *a.* (of the) railway; **orario** [oh-rah´ree-oh] **f.** *nm.* time-table.

Ferroviere [fehr-roh-vee-ay´ray] *nm.* railway-man.

Fertile [fehr´tee-lay] *a.* fertile, fruitful, prolific.

Fertilizzare [fehr-tee-leed-zah´ray] *vt.* to fertilise.

Fervente [fehr-ven´tay] *a.* eager, fervent.

Fervere [fehr´vay-ray] *vi.* to be hot, boil.

Fervido [fehr´vee-doh] *a.* ardent, fervid, impetuous.

Fervore [fehr-voh´ray] *nm.* ardour, fervour, zeal.

Fesso [fess´soh] *nm.* fool; *a.* cleft, cracked.

Fessura [fess-soo´rah] *nf.* crack, crevice, fissure, split.

Festa [fess´tah] *nf.* birthday, feast, festivity, holiday, merry-making.

Festeggiare [fess-tay-djah´ray] *vt.* to celebrate, feast, give a feast for, solemnise, welcome.

Festevole [fess-tay´voh-lay] *a.* festive, joyous.

Festino [fess-tee´noh] *nm.* entertainment, party.

Festività [fess-tee-vee-tah´] *nf.* festivity, gaiety.

Festivo [fess-tee´voh] *a.* festive.

Festoso [fess-toh´soh] *a.* festive, gay, merry.

Feto [fay´toh] *nm.* fœtus.

Fetta [fet´tah] *nf.* cut, fillet, rasher, slice.

Feudale [fay-oo-dah´lay] *a.* feudal.

Fiaba [fee-ah´bah] *nf.* fairy-tale, story.

Fiacca/re [fee-ahk-cah'ray] vt. to exhaust, fatigue, wear out; —rsi vr. to become tired, weak.

Fiaccheraio [fee-ahk-kay-rah'yoh] nm. cabby, driver.

Fiacchere [fee-ahk'cay-ray] nm. cab, hackney-carriage.

Fiacchezza [fee-ahk-ket'zah] nf. fatigue, lassitude, weakness, weariness.

Fiacco [fee-ahk'koh] a. exhausted, feeble, tired. weary.

Fiaccola [fee-ahk'koh-lah] nf. flambeau, torch.

Fiamma [fee-ahm'mah] nf. blaze, flame, glare, (naut.) pennant.

Fiammeggiare [fee-ahm-may-djah'ray] vi. to blaze, flame, shine.

Fiammifero [fee-ahm-mee'fay-roh] nm. match.

Fiammingo [fee-ahm-meeng'goh] nm. Fleming; a. Flemish.

Fiancheggiare [fee-ahng-kay-djah'ray] vt. to border, flank, help, support.

Fianco [fee-ahng'koh] nm. flank, side.

Fiasca [fee-ah'skah] nf. flask.

Fiaschetteria [fee-ah-sket-tay-ree'ah] nf. tavern, wineshop.

Fiasco [fee-ah'skoh] nm. failure, fiasco, flask; fare [fah'ray] f. i. to fail.

Fiatare [fee-ah-tah'ray] vi. to breathe, whisper.

Fiato [fee-ah'toh] nm. breath.

Fibbia [feeb'bee-ah] nf. buckle.

Fibra [fee'brah] nf. constitution, fibre.

Ficca/re [feek-cah'ray] vt. to drive in, nail, thrust in; —rsi vr. to force one's way in, intrude. meddle.

Fico [fee'koh] nm. fig, fig-tree.

Fidanzamento [fee-dahnt-zah-men'toh] nm. betrothal, engagement.

Fidanza/re [fee-dahnt-zah'ray] vt. to betroth; —rsi vr. to become engaged.

Fida/re [fee-dah'ray] vt. to entrust; —rsi vr. to confide, rely, trust.

Fidato [fee-dah'toh], fido [feo'doh] a. faithful, trusty.

Fido [fee'doh] nm. (com.) credit.

Fiducia [fee-doo'chah] nf. confidence, trust.

Fiele [fee-ay'lay] nm. bitterness, gall, rancour.

Fienile [fee-ay-nee'lay] nm. hay-loft.

Fieno [fee-ay'noh] nm. hay.

Fiera [fee-ay'rah] nf. exhibition, fair, wild beast.

Fierezza [fee-ay-ret'zah] nf. boldness, fierceness, hardihood, pride.

Fiero [fee-ay'roh] a. bold, fierce, hardy, proud.

Figlia [feel'yah] nf. daughter. (com.) counterfoil.

Figlio [feel'yoh] nm. child, son.

Figlias/tra [feel-yahs'trah] nf. step-daughter; —tro [troh] nm. step-son.

Figlioc/cia [feel-yohch'chah] nf. god-daughter; —cio [choh] nm. god-son.

Figura [fee-goo'rah] nf. appearance, figure, shape.

Figura/re [fee-goo-rah'ray] vt. and i. to figure, look well, represent, symbolize; —rsi vr. to fancy, imagine, picture to oneself.

Figurino [fee-goo-ree'noh] nm. fashion-plate, pattern.

Fila [fee'lah] nf. line, queue, row.

Filanda [fee-lahn'dah] nf. spinning-mill.

Filantropia [fee-lahn-troh-pee'ah] *nf.* philanthropy.

Filare [fee-lah'ray] *vt.* to spin; *vi.* to run away, take oneself off; *nm.* row (of trees, etc.).

Filarmonica [fee-lahr-moh'-nee-kah] *nf.* philharmonic society.

Filarmonico [fee-lahr-moh'-nee-koh] *nm.* music-lover.

Filastrocca [fee-lah-strok'-kah] *nf.* nonsense-rhyme, rigmarole.

Filatoio [fee-lah-toh'yoh] *nm.* jenny, spinning-machine.

Fila/tore [fee-lah-toh'ray] *nm.* —**trice** [tree-chay] *nf.* spinner.

Filetto [fee-let'toh] *nm.* fillet, thin thread.

Filiale [fee-lee-ah'lay] *nm.* branch, branch-house or office; *a.* filial.

Filiazione [fee-lee-ah-tsee-oh'nay] *nf.* filiation.

Filo [fee'loh] *nm.* clue, thread, trickle, wire; **f. spinato** [spee-nah'toh], barbed wire.

Filologia [fee-loh-loh-jee'ah] *nf.* philology.

Filosofia [fee-loh-zoh-fee'ah] *nf.* philosophy.

Filovia [fee-loh-vee'ah] *nf.* trolley-bus.

Filtrare [feel-trah'ray] *vt. and i.* to filter, percolate.

Filtro [feel'troh] *nm.* filter, philtre, strainer.

Filugello [fee-loo-jell'loh] *nm.* silk-worm.

Filza [feelt'zah] *nf.* collection, row, series, string.

Finalità [fee-nah-lee-tah'] *nf.* finality.

Fin/anche [feen-ahng'kay], —**anco** [ahng'koh] *ad.* also, even.

Finanza [fee-nahnt'zah] *nf.* finance, means.

Finanziario [fee-nahn-tsee-ah'ree-oh] *a.* financial.

Finanziere [fee-nahn-tsee-ay'ray] *nm.* financier.

Finchè [feeng-kay'] *con.* as long as; **f. non** [nonn] *con.* till, until.

Fine [fee'nay] *nm.* aim, end, object, view; *nf.* close, conclusion, end; *a.* delicate, fine, thin. [window.

Finestra [fee-ness'trah] *nf.*

Finezza [fee-net'zah] *nf.* fineness, finesse, politeness, shrewdness.

Finge/re [feen'jay-ray] *vi.* —**rsi** *vr.* to dissemble, feign, pretend.

Finimondo [fee-nee-mon'-doh] *nm.* end of the world, great uproar, utter ruin.

Finire [fee-nee'ray] *vt.* to bring to an end, conclude, finish; *vi.* to be over, end, finish, give up.

Finlandese [feen-lahn-day'-zay] *nm.* Finn; *a.* Finnish.

Fino [fee'noh] *a.* delicate, fine, thin; *pr.* as far as, to, till, until. [*nm.* fennel.

Finocchio [fee-nock'kee-oh]

Finora [fee-noh'rah] *ad.* hitherto, so far, up to now.

Finta [feen'tah] *nf.* artifice, deceit, feint; **fare** [fah'ray] **f.** *vi.* to pretend.

Finzione [feen-tsee-oh'nay] *nf.* art, artifice, deceit, fiction, sham.

Fio [fee'oh] *nm.* penalty.

Fiocaggine [fee-oh-kah'djee-nay] *f.* hoarseness.

Fioccare [fee-ock-kah'ray] *vi.* to abound, snow in large flakes.

Fiocco [fee-ock'koh] *nm.* flake (of snow), flock (of wool), knot, tassel; **coi fiocchi** [koh'ee fee-ock'kee] *ad.* excellent, first-rate.

Fioco [fee-oh'koh] *a.* dim, feeble (of light), hoarse.

Fiora/ia [fee-oh-rah'yah] *nf.* —**io** [yoh] *nm.* flower-seller.

Fiore [fee-oh'ray] nm. bloom, blossom, club (at cards), flower; f. di latte [dee laht'tay] cream; f. di quattrini [kwaht-tree'nee], a lot of money; a pelo d'acqua [dahk'kwah] ad. on the surface.

Fiorire [fee-oh-ree'ray] vt. to adorn with flowers; vi. to flourish, flower, thrive.

Fiorista [fee-oh-ree'stah] nm. and f. maker of artificial flowers.

Fiorito [fee-oh-ree'toh] a. flowery, full of flowers.

Fiotto [fee-ot'toh] nm. surge, wave. [ture.

Firma [feer'mah] nf. signa-

Firmamento [feer-mah-men'toh] nm. firmament.

Firmare [feer-mah'ray] vt. to sign, underwrite.

Fischiare [fees-kee-ah'ray] vt. to hiss; vi. to whistle.

Fischio [fees'kee-oh] nm. buzzing (in the ears), hiss, whistle.

Fisco [fees'koh] nm. Exchequer, fisc.

Fisica [fee'zee-kah] nf. physics (pl.).

Fisico [fee'zee-koh] nm. physical constitution, physique, physicist; a. physical.

Fisiologia [fee-zee-oh-loh-jee'ah] nf. physiology.

Fis(i)onomia [fees-z(ee)-oh-noh-mee'ah] nf. countenance, physiognomy.

Fiso [fee'zoh] a. attentive, straight, fixed; ad. attentively, fixedly.

Fissa/re [fees-sah'ray] vt. to appoint, arrange, establish, settle, stare at; —rsi vr. to be obstinate, fixed, settle, think constantly.

Fissazione [fees-sah-tsee-oh'nay] nf. fixed idea, mania.

Fisso [fees'soh] a. effective, fixed, settled, stationary, on the staff; ad. attentively, fixedly.

Fittizio [feet-tee'tsee-oh] a. fictitious.

Fitto [feet'toh] nm. depth, thickness; a. dense, thick; a capo [ah kah'poh] f. headlong.

Fiumana [fee-oo-mah'nah] nf. flood, stream (of people), swollen river, torrent.

Fiume [fee-oo'may] nm. flood, river.

Fiutare [fee-oo-tah'ray] vt. to detect, scent, smell, suspect.

Fiuto [fee-oo'toh] nm. scent, (sense of) smell.

Flagellare [flah-jell-lah'ray] vt. to flagellate, scourge.

Flagello [flah-jell'loh] nm. calamity, scourge, whip.

Flagrante [flah-grahn'tay] a. flagrant. [flannel.

Flanella [flah-nell'lah] nf.

Flebile [flay'bee-lay] a. mournful, plaintive.

Flemma [flem'mah] nf. phlegm.

Flessibile [fless-see'bee-lay] a. flexible, pliable, pliant.

Flessione [fless-see-oh'nay] nf. bend, flexion.

Flessuoso [fless-soo-oh'soh] a. flexuous, pliant.

Flettere [flet'tay-ray] vt. to bend, flex.

Floridezza [floh-ree-det'zah] nf. floridness, prosperity.

Florido [floh'ree-doh] a. florid, flourishing, prosperous.

Floscio [floh'shoh] a. flabby, flaccid.

Flotta [flot'tah] nf. fleet, navy.

Flottiglia [flot-teel'yah] nf. flotilla.

Fluidezza [floo-ee-det'zah], **fluidità** [floo-ee-dee-tah'] nf. fluidity. [a. fluid.

Fluido [floo'ee-doh] nm. and

Fluire [floo-ee-ray'] vi. to flow, gush, run.

Flusso [floos'soh] nm. diarrhœa, (med.) discharge, flood tide, flux.

Flutto [floot'toh] nm. breaker, surge, wave.

Fluttuare [floot-too-ah-ray'] vi. to fluctuate, waver.

Fluttuoso [floot-too-oh'soh] a. stormy.

Fluviale [floo-vee-ah'lay] a. fluvial, river.

Foca [foh'kah] nf. seal (fish).

Focaccia [foh-kahch'chah] nf. kind of cake.

Foce [foh'chay] nf. river-mouth.

Focolare [foh-koh-lah'ray] nm. fireplace, hearth.

Focoso [foh-koh'soh] a. fiery.

Fodera [foh'day-rah] nf. lining, sheeting (with metal).

Foderare [foh-day-rah'ray] vt. to line, sheet.

Foga [foh'gah] nf. impetuosity.

Foggia [foh'djah] nf. fashion, form, manner, way.

Foggiare [foh-djah'ray] vt. to fashion, form, shape.

Foglia [foll'yah] nf. blade (of corn), foil, leaf.

Fogliame [foll-yah'may] nm. foliage, leafage.

Foglio [foll'yoh] nm. roll, sheet of paper.

Fogna [fohn'yah] nf. drain, sewer.

Folgorare [foll-goh-rah'ray] vi. to flash, strike.

Folgore [foll'goh-ray] nm. thunder-bolt.

Folla [foll'lah] nf. crowd, multitude, throng.

Folle [foll'lay] nm. and f. lunatic, maniac; a. crazed, insane, mad.

Folletto [foll-let'toh] nm. elf, goblin.

Follia [foll-lee'ah] nf. folly, insanity, madness.

Folto [foll'toh] nm. thick(ness); a. dense, thick.

Fomentare [foh-men-tah'ray] vt. to foment, incite, stir up.

Fomento [foh-men'toh] nm. (med.) fomentation.

Fomite [foh'mee-tay] nm. cause, source.

Fondaco [fon'dah-koh] nm. store, warehouse.

Fondamento [fon-dah-men'toh] nm. base, foundation, ground.

Fonda/re [fon-dah'ray] vt. to build, found, ground, rest; —rsi vr. to be built, founded, rely on.

Fondazione [fon-dah-tsee-oh'nay] nf. foundation, institution.

Fondere [fon'day-ray] vt. to cast, fuse melt, smelt.

Fonderia [fon-day-ree'ah] nf. foundry.

Fondiaria [fon-dee-ah'ree-ah] nf. ground-tax.

Fonditore [fon-dee-toh'ray] nm. caster, founder, smelter.

Fondo [fon'doh] nm. bottom, capital, depth, fund, grounds (pl.); articolo di [ahr-tee'koh-loh dee] i. leading article.

Fonetica [foh-nay'tee-kah] nf. phonetics (pl.).

Fonetico [foh-nay'tee-koh] nm. phonetician; a. phonetic.

Fonografo [foh-noh'grah-foh] nm. phonograph.

Fonologia [foh-noh-loh-jee'ah] nf. phonology.

Fontana [fon-tah'nah] nf. fountain, source, spring.

Fonte [fon'tay] nf. fountain, spring; nm. font.

Foraggio [foh-rah'djoh] nm. fodder, forage.

Forame [foh-rah'may] nm. a number of holes.

Forare [foh-rah′ray] vt. to bore, pierce.

Forbici [forr′bee-chee] nf. (pl.) claws (of a crab, etc.) (pl.). scissors (pl.).

Forbire [forr-bee′ray] vt. to furbish, polish, rub up.

Forbitezza [forr-bee-tet′zah] nf. elegance (of style), neatness.

Forca [forr′kah] nf. gallows (pl.), pitchfork.

Forcella [forr-chell′lah], **forcina** [forr-chee′nah] nf. hairpin.

Forchetta [forr-ket′tah] nf. (table-)fork.

Forcuto [forr-koo′toh] a. forked.

Forense [foh-ren′say] a. forensic.

Foresta [foh-ress′tah] nf. forest.

Forestie/re, —ro [foh-resstee-ay′ray/roh] nm. man from another town, stranger, visitor, foreigner; a. outside, strange, unknown.

Forfora [forr′foh-rah] nf. dandruff, scurf.

Forgia [forr′jah] nf. forge.

Foriere [foh-ree-ay′ray] nm. forerunner, harbinger, precursor.

Foriero [foh-ree-ay′roh] a. forerunning, presaging.

Forma [forr′mah] nf. conformation, figure, form, formality, mould, shape.

Formaggio [forr-mah′djoh] nm. cheese.

Formale [forr-mah′lay] a. formal, solemn.

Formalità [forr-mah-leetah′] nf. formality.

Forma/re [forr′mah-ray] vt. to fashion, form, mould, shape; —rsi vr. to build, form, win (an opinion).

Formato [forr-mah′toh] nm. shape, size; a. formed.

Formica [forr-mee′kah] nf. ant.

Formicolare [forr-mee-kohlah′ray] vi. to crawl with, swarm with, tingle.

Formidabile [forr-mee-dah′bee-lay] a. alarming, dreadful, formidable.

Formoso [forr-moh′soh] a. big-built, shapely.

Formulare [forr-moo-lah′ray] vt. to draw up, formulate, word, work out.

Fornace [forr-nah′chay] nf. furnace, kiln.

Fornaio [forr-nah′yoh] nm. baker.

Fornello [forr-nell′loh] nm. kitchen-stove.

Forni/re [forr-nee′ray] vt. to fit out, furnish, provide, stock, supply; —rsi vr. to provide oneself.

Forni/tore [forr-nee-toh′ray] nm.—**trice** [tree′chay] nf. contractor, purveyor, supplier.

Fornitura [forr-nee-too′rah] nf. stock, supplies (pl.).

Forno [forr′noh] nm. furnace, oven.

Foro [foh′roh] nm. forum, hole.

Forse [forr′say] ad. perhaps.

Forsennato [forr-sen-nah′toh] nm. madman; a. crazy, mad.

Forte [forr′tay] nm. forte, strong point; a. forcible, heavy, high, loud, sour (wine), strong, sturdy; ad. strongly, loudly; powerfully.

Fortezza [forr-tet′zah] nf. fortitude, fortress.

Fortifica/re [forr-tee-feekah′ray] vt. to fortify, strengthen; —rsi vr. to acquire strength, grow stronger.

Fortuito [forr-too′ee-toh] a. casual, fortuitous.

Fortuna [forr-too′nah] nf. chance, fortune, luck, risk.

Fortunale [forr-too-nah'lay] *nm.* storm at sea.

Fortunato [forr-too-nah'toh] *a.* fortunate, lucky.

Foruncolo [foh-roong'koh-loh] *nm. (med.)* boil.

Forviare [forr-vee-ah'ray] *vt.* to lead astray, mislead, misguide.

Forza [forrt'zah] *nf.* force, power, strength.

Forzare [forrt-zah'ray] *vt.* to compel, force.

Forzato [forrt-zah'toh] *nm.* convict; *a.* forced.

Forziere [forr-tsee-ay'ray] *nm.* safe, strong-box.

Foschia [foss-kee'ah] *nf.* mist, murk.

Fosco [foss'koh] *a.* dark, dull, gloomy, sombre.

Fosforescente [foss-foh-ray-shen'tay] *a.* phosphorescent.

Fossa [foss'sah] *nf.* grave, hole, pit. [dimple.

Fossetta [foss-set'tah] *nf.*

Fossile [foss'see-lay] *nm. and a.* fossil.

Fossilizza/re [foss-see-leed-zah'ray] *vt.* —rsi *vr.* to fossilise. [trench.

Fosso [foss'soh] *nm.* ditch.

Fotografare [foh-toh-grah-fah'ray] *vt.* to photograph.

Fotografia [foh-toh-grah-fee'ah] *nf.* photograph, photography; f. istantanea [ee-stahn-tah'nay-ah] snap-shot.

Fotografo [foh-toh'grah-foh] *nm.* photographer.

Fra [frah] *pr.* among, amid, between (two), in (time).

Fracassa/re [frah-kahs-sah'ray] *vt.* —rsi *vr.* to break in pieces, smash.

Fracasso [frah-kahs'soh] *nm.* crash, fracas, uproar.

Fracido [frah'chee-doh] *a.* rotten, wet.

Fradicio [frah'dee-choh] *a.* wet, (sometimes used with other adjectives to emphasise them).

Fradiciume [frah-dee-choo'may] *nm.* wet(ness).

Fragile [frah'jee-lay] *a.* brittle, fragile, frail.

Fragola [frah'goh-lah] *nf.* strawberry(-plant).

Frago/re [frah-goh'ray], —**rio** [ree'oh] *nm.* crash, din.

Fragoroso [frah-goh-roh'soh] *a.* roaring, very noisy.

Fragrante [frah-grahn'tay] *a.* fragrant, sweet-smelling.

Fraintendere [frah-een-ten'day-ray] *vt.* to misunderstand.

Frainteso [frah-een-tay'soh] *nm.* misunderstanding; *a.* misunderstood.

Frammassone [frahm-mahs-soh'nay] *nm.* Freemason.

Frammassoneria [frahm-mahs-soh-nay-ree'ah] *nf.* Freemasonry.

Frammento [frahm-men'toh] *nm.* fragment, scrap.

Frammette/re [frahm-met'tay-ray] *vt.* to insert, interpose; —rsi *vr.* to interfere, interpose, intrude, meddle.

Frana [frah'nah] *nf.* frana**mento** [frah-nah-men'toh] *nm.* fall of earth or rock, landslip, subsidence.

Franare [frah-nah'ray] *vi.* to fall, sink, slip (earth, etc.).

Francare [frahng-kah'ray] *vt.* to frank, put on stamps.

Francescano [frahn-chess-kah'noh] *nm. and a.* Franciscan.

Francese [frahn-chay'zay] *nm.* Frenchman; *nf.* Frenchwoman; *a.* French.

Franchezza [frahng-ket'zah] *nf.* candidness, frankness, openness.

Franchigia [frahng-kee'jah] *nf.* exemption, franchise, privilege.

Franco [frahng-koh] *nm.*

franc; *a.* candid, frank, open, plain, unreserved.

Francobollo [frahng-koh-boll'loh] *nm.* (postage) stamp.

Frange/re [frahn'jay-ray] *vt.* to break to pieces, crush; —rsi *vr.* to break.

Frangitura [frahn-jee-too'rah] *nf.* extraction of oil from olives.

Frantoio [frahn-toh'yoh] *nm.* oil-presser (for olives), stone-crusher.

Frantumare [frahn-too-mah'ray] *vt.* to break, smash.

Frantumi [frahn-too'mee] *nm.* (*pl.*) fragments (*pl.*), pieces (*pl.*), rubbish.

Frasario [frah-zah'ree-oh] *nm.* collection of phrases, phrase-book, vocabulary.

Frasca [frahs'kah] *nf.* inn-sign, spray, twig.

Frase [frah'zay] *nf.* phrase, sentence.

Fraseologia [frah-zay-oh-loh-jee'ah] *nf.* phraseology.

Frassino [frahs'see-noh] *nm.* ash, ash-tree.

Frastornare [frah-storr-nah'ray] *vt.* to disturb, interrupt, trouble.

Frastuono [frah-stoo-oh'noh] *nm.* din, hubbub.

Frate [frah'tay] *nm.* brother (*pl.* brethren), friar.

Fratellanza [frah-tell-lahnt'zah] *nf.* brotherhood.

Fratellastro [frah-tell-lah'stroh] *nm.* half-brother.

Fratello [frah-tell'loh] *nm.* brother.

Fraterno [frah-tehr'noh] *a.* brotherly, fraternal.

Fratricida [frah-tree-chee'dah] *nm.* fratricide (person); *a.* fratricidal.

Fratricidio [frah-tree-chee'dee-oh] *nm.* fratricide (crime).

Fratta [fraht'tah] *nf.* briar-patch, hedge.

Frattanto [fraht-tahn'toh] *ad.* in the meantime, meanwhile.

Frattempo [fraht-tem'poh] *nm.* interval; nel [nell] f. *ad.* meanwhile.

Frattura [fraht-too'rah] *nf.* (*geol.*) fault, (*med.*) fracture.

Fratturare [fraht-too-rah'ray] *vt.* to break, fracture.

Fraudare [frow-dah'ray] *vt.* to defraud.

Fraude [frow'day] *nf.* artifice, fraud.

Frazione [frah-tsee-oh'nay] *nf.* district, fraction, section.

Freccia [frehch'chah] *nf.* arrow, (*arch.*) spire.

Fredda/re [fred-dah'ray] *vt.* to cool, kill, make cold; —rsi *vr.* to grow cold, cool.

Freddezza [fred-det'zah] *nf.* coldness, coolness, indifference.

Freddo [fred'doh] *nm.* chill, chilliness, cold; avere [ah-vay'ray] f. *vi.* to be cold; *a.* chilly, cold, cool, indifferent.

Freddoloso [fred-doh-loh'soh] *a.* chilly, sensitive to cold.

Freddura [fred-doo'rah] *nf.* cold, nonsense, silly story.

Frega/re [fray-gah'ray] *vt.* to draw a line, rub; —rsene [say'nay] *vr.* to laugh at, not care about.

Fregata [fray-gah'tah] *nf.* rubbing, (*naut.*) frigate.

Fregia/re [fray-jah'ray] *vt.* to adorn, trim; —rsi *vr.* to adorn oneself.

Fregio [fray'joh] *nm.* frieze, ornament.

Fremere [fray'may-ray] *vi.* to boil, quiver, shiver.

Fremito [fray'mee-toh] *nm.* quiver, shiver.

Frena/re [fray-nah'ray] *vt.* to brake, curb, hinder, repress, restrain; —rsi *vr.* to keep one's temper, refrain from, restrain oneself.

Frenesia [fray-nay-zee'ah] nf. frenzy, insanity.

Frenetico [fray-nay'tee-koh] a. frantic, raving.

Freno [fray'noh] nm. brake, bridle, curb, restraint.

Frenologia [fray-noh-loh-jee'ah] nf. phrenology.

Frequentare [fray-kwen-tah'ray] vt. to attend, frequent, haunt, resort.

Frequente [fray-kwen'tay] a. frequent, quick.

Frequenza [fray-kwent'zah] nf. attendance, frequency, quickness.

Fresco [fress'koh] nm. coolness, freshness; a. cool, fresh.

Frescura [fress-koo'rah] nf. freshness, sharpness (of air).

Fretta [fret'tah] nf. haste, hurry; avere [ah-vay'ray] f. vi. to be in a hurry.

Frettoloso [fret-toh-loh'soh] a. hasty, hurried.

Friggere [freed'jay-ray] vt. to fry.

Frigidezza [free-jee-det'zah] frigidità [free-jee-dee-tah'] nf. frigidness, frigidity.

Frigido [free'jee-doh] a. frigid.

Frigorifero [free-goh-ree'fay-roh] nm. refrigerator.

Frittata [freet-tah'tah] nf. omelet.

Frittella [freet-tell'lah] nf. fritter, pancake.

Fritto [freet'toh] nm. dish of fried food, fry; a. fried, (fig.) lost, ruined.

Frivolezza [free-voh-let'zah] nf. frivolity, frivolousness.

Frivolo [free'voh-loh] a. flimsy, frivolous, petty, shallow, trifling.

Frizione [free-tsee-oh'nay] nf. friction, rubbing.

Frizzante [freed-zahn'tay] a. lively, piquant, pricking, pungent, sparkling, stinging.

Frizzare [freed-zah'ray] vi. to prick, smart, sparkle, sting.

Frizzo [freed'zoh] nm. witticism. [etc.

Frodare, etc.: v. fraudare.

Frodo [froh'doh] nm. poaching, smuggling.

Frollo [froll'loh] a. exhausted, flaky (pastry), high (game, etc.).

Fronda [fron'dah] nf. leafy bough. [leafy.

Frondoso [fron-doh'soh] a.

Frontale [fron-tah'lay] nm. front, frontal; a. frontal.

Fronte [fron'tay] nf. forehead, front; far [fahr] f. a [ah] vt. to cope with, face, meet.

Frontespizio [fron-tay-spee'tsee-oh] nm. frontispiece.

Frontiera [fron-tee-ay'rah] nf. border, frontier.

Fronzolo [frond'zoh-loh] nm. ribbon, tassel.

Frotta [frot'tah] nf. crowd, throng.

Frottola [frot'toh-lah] nf. nonsense, old wives' tale.

Frugale [froo-gah'lay] a. frugal.

Fruga/re [froo-gah'ray] vt. to grope, poke, rummage; —rsi vr. to search one's pockets.

Fruire [froo-ee'ray] vt. to enjoy, receive, use.

Fruizione [froo-ee-tsee-oh'nay] nf. enjoyment, fruition.

Frumento [froo-men'toh] nm. wheat.

Fruscio [froo-shee'oh] nm. rustle, rustling.

Frusta [froo'stah] nf. lash, scourge, whip.

Frustagno [froo-stahn'yoh] nm. fustian.

Frustare [froo-stah'ray] vt. to lash, scourge, whip.

Frutta [froot'tah] nf. fruit (of plants).

Fruttare [froot-tah'ray] *vt.* to fructify, pay, produce, yield. [orchard.

Frutteto [froot-tay'toh] *nm.*

Fruttifero [froot-tee'fay-roh] *a.* paying, fruit-bearing.

Fruttificare [froot-tee-fee-kah'ray] *vt. and i.* to fructify.

Fruttivendolo [froot-tee-ven'doh-loh] *nm.* fruiterer.

Frutto [froot'toh] *nm.* benefit, fruit, profit, result, revenue.

Fu [foo] *a.* deceased, late.

Fucilare [foo-chee-lah'ray] *vt.* to shoot.

Fucilazione [foo-chee-lah-tsee-oh'nay] *nf.* execution, shooting. [rifle.

Fucile [foo-chee'lay] *nm.* gun,

Fucina [foo-chee'nah] *nf.* forge, smithy.

Fucinare [foo-chee-nah'ray] *vt.* to forge.

Fuga [foo'gah] *nf.* escape, flight, (*mus.*) fugue.

Fugace [foo-gah'chay] *a.* fleeting, transient.

Fugare [foo-gah'ray] *vt.* to put to flight, rout.

Fuggevole [foo-djay'voh-lay] *a.* fleeting, flying.

Fuggiasco [foo-djahs'koh] *nm.* fugitive, runaway; *a.* fugitive.

Fuggi-fuggi [foo'djee foo'djee] *nm.* headlong flight, panic, stampede.

Fuggire [foo-djee'ray] *vt.* to avoid, shun; *vi.* to flee, run away, take to flight.

Fulgido [fool'jee-doh] *a.* brilliant, fulgid.

Fulgore [fool-goh'ray] *nm.* blaze, dazzling light.

Fuliggine [foo-lee'djee-nay] *nf.* soot.

Fulminare [fool-mee-nah'ray] *vt.* to strike dumb, strike with lightning; *vi.* to flash, lighten.

Fulmine [fool'mee-nay] *nm.* lightning, thunder, thunderbolt.

Fulmineo [fool-mee'nay-oh] *a.* quick as lightning, sudden.

Fulvo [fool'voh] *a.* reddish, tawny.

Fumaiuolo [foo-mah-ee-oo-oh'loh] *nm.* chimney-pot.

Fumare [foo-mah'ray] *vt.* to smoke; vietato [vee-ay-tah'toh] f. "no smoking."

Fumigeno [foo-mee'jay-noh] *a.* smoke-producing.

Fumo [foo'moh] *nm.* fume, reek, smoke.

Fumoso [foo-moh'soh] *a.* smoky.

Funamb/olo, -ulo [foo-nahm'boh(boo)-loh] *nm.* rope-dancer. [rope.

Fune [foo'nay] *nf.* cable,

Funebre [foo'nay-bray] *a.* funeral, funereal.

Funerale [foo-nay-rah'lay] *nm.* funeral.

Funestare [foo-ness-tah'ray] *vt.* to desolate, distress, sadden.

Funesto [foo-ness'toh] *a.* baneful, disastrous, distressing.

Fungere [foon'jay-ray] *vi.* to act as, officiate as.

Fungo [foong'goh] *nm.* fungus, mushroom, toadstool.

Funicolare [foo-nee-koh-lah'ray] *nf. and a.* funicular.

Funzionare [foon-tsee-oh-nah'ray] *vi.* to act, function, run, work.

Funzionario [foon-tsee-oh-nah'ree-oh] *nm.* functionary, official.

Funzione [foon-tsee-oh'nay] *nf.* appointment, function, office, service (in church).

Fuochista [foo-oh-kee'stah] *nm.* fireman, stoker.

Fuoco [foo-oh'koh] *nm.* fire; f. d'artifizio [dahr-tee-fee'tsee-oh], fire-work; f. di sbarramento [sbahr-rah-men'toh] (*mil.*) barrage-fire.

Fuorchè [foo-orr-kay'] *con.* but, except, save.

Fuori [foo-oh'ree] *ad. and pr.* out, outside.

Fuoruscito [foo-oh-roo-shee'toh] *nm.* exile, outlaw.

Furberia [foor-bay-ree'ah] *nf.* art, cunning, slyness.

Furbesco [foor-bess'koh], **furbo** [foor'boh] *a.* artful, cunning, sly, wily.

Furente: *v.* **furibondo**.

Furetto [foo-ret'toh] *nm.* ferret.

Furfante [foor-fahn'tay] *nm.* rascal, scamp.

Furgone [foor-goh'nay], **furgoncino** [foor-gon-chee'noh] *nm.* van.

Furia [foo'ree-ah] *nf.* fury, fury, hurry, precipitancy, rage; **avere** [ah-vay'ray] **f.** *vi.* to be in a hurry.

Furibondo [foo-ree-bon'doh], **furioso** [foo-ree-oh'soh] *a.* furious, raging.

Furore [foo-roh'ray] *nm.* frenzy, fury, rage; **fare** [fah'ray] **f.** *vi.* to be much admired.

Furtivo [foor-tee'voh] *a.* furtive, sly, stealthy.

Furto [foor'toh] *nm.* burglary, stealing, theft.

Fuscellino [foo-shell-lee'noh] *nm.* blade, mote, bit of straw.

Fusione [foo-zee-oh'nay] *nf.* casting, fusion, melting.

Fuso [foo'zoh] *nm.* spindle; *a.* cast, fused, melted; **fare le fusa** [fah'ray lay foo'zah] *vi.* to purr. [fustian.

Fustagno [foo-stahn'yoh] *nm.*

Fustigare [foo-stee-gah'ray] *vt.* to beat, scourge.

Fusto [foo'stoh] *nm.* barrel, cask, frame (of a bed, etc.), stem, trunk (of a plant).

Futile [foo'tee-lay] *a.* flimsy, futile, trifling.

Futuro [foo-too'roh] *nm. and a.* future.

G

Gabba/re [gahb-bah'ray] *vt.* to deceive, mock, swindle; **—rsi** *v.* to make fun of.

Gabba/tore [gahb-bah-toh'ray] *nm.* **—trice** [tree'chay] *nf.* deceiver, impostor, swindler.

Gabbia [gahb'bee-ah] *nf.* cage, coop, jail.

Gabbiano [gahb-bee-ah'noh] *nm.* sea-gull.

Gabbo [gahb'boh] *nm.* jeering, mocking; **farsi** [fahr'see] **g. di** [dee] *vr.* to mock.

Gabella [gah-bell'lah] *nf.* custom, duty, tax (on goods entering a town).

Gabellabile [gah-bell-lah'bee-lay] *a.* dutiable.

Gabellare [gah-bell-lah'ray] *vt.* to impose (levy) duty, tax.

Gabelliere [gah-bell-lee-ay'ray] *nm.* customs officer.

Gabinetto [gah-bee-net'toh] *nm.* cabinet, closet, consulting-room (of dentist or doctor), reading-room, w.c.

Gagliardo [gahl-yahr'doh] *a.* bold, strong, sturdy.

Gaglioffo [gahl-yoff'foh] *nm.* dolt, lout.

Gaiezza [gah-yet'zah] *nf.* gaiety, gaudiness (colours), sprightliness.

Gaio [gah'yoh] *a.* gaudy, gay, sprightly.

Gala [gah'lah] *nf.* finery, gala; **tenuta di** [tay-noo'tah dee] **g.** (*mil.*) full-dress uniform.

Galante [gah-lahn'tay] *nm.* beau, gallant; *a.* brave, elegant, gallant.

Galanteggiare [gah-lahn-tay-djah'ray] *vi.* to play the gallant.

Galanteria [gah-lahn-tay-ree'ah] *nf.* bravery, finery, gallantry.

Galantina [gah-lahn-tee'nah] *nf.* galantine.

Galantuomo [gah-lahn-too-oh'moh] *nm.* honest man, man of honour.

Galateo [gah-lah-tay'oh] *nm.* code of manners.

Galea [gah-lay'ah] *nf.* galley, helmet.

Galeotto [gah-lay-ot'toh] *nm.* convict, galley-slave.

Galera [gah-lay'rah] *nf.* galley, jail.

Galla [gahl'lah] *nf.* blister, bubble; a [ah] *g. ad.* afloat.

Galleggiante [gahl-lay-djahn'tay] *nm.* (*tech.*) float; *a.* floating.

Galleggiare [gahl-lay-djah'ray] *vi.* to be buoyant, float.

Galleria [gahl-lay-ree'ah] *nf.* gallery, tunnel.

Gallina [gahl-lee'nah] *nf.* hen.

Gallinaccio [gahl-lee-nahch'choh] *nm.* turkey-cock.

Gallinaio [gahl-lee-nah'yoh] *nm.* poultry-thief.

Gallo [gahl'loh] *nm.* cock, Gaul.

Gallonare [gahl-loh-nah'ray] *vt.* to braid.

Gallone [gahl-loh'nay] *nm.* braid, gallon (measure).

Galoppare [gah-lop-pah'ray] *vi.* to gallop.

Galoppata [gah-lop-pah'tah] *nf.* gallopade.

Galoppino [gah-lop-pee'noh] *nm.* errand boy, messenger.

Galoppo [gah-lop'poh] *nm.* gallop.

Galvanico [gahl-vah'nee-koh] *a.* galvanic.

Galvanizzare [gahl-vah-need-zah'ray] *vt.* to galvanise.

Gamba [gahm'bah] *nf.* leg; essere in [ess'say-ray een] *g. vi.* to be fit.

Gambacorta [gahm-bah-korr'tah] *nm.* lame man.

Gambale [gahm-bah'lay] *nm.* legging.

Gambata [gahm-bah'tah] *nf.* kick.

Gambero [gahm'bay-roh] *nm.* crayfish.

Gambo [gahm'boh] *nm.* stalk, stem.

Gamma [gahm'mah] *nf.* gamut, range, scale.

Ganascia [gah-nah'shah] *nf.* jaw, jaw-bone.

Gancio [gahn'choh] *nm.* claw, hook.

Gangherare [gahng-gay-rah'ray] *vt.* to hinge, set on hinges.

Ganghe/ro [gahng'gay-roh] *nm.* hinge; fuori dei [foo-oh'ree day'ee] g—ri *ad.* furious.

Gara [gah'rah] *nf.* competition, match, rivalry.

Garante [gah-rahn'tay] *nm.* guarantor, surety.

Garantire [gah-rahn-tee'ray] *vt.* to guarantee, stand surety for.

Garanzia [gah-rahnt-zee'ah] *nf.* guarantee, surety, warrant.

Garbare [gahr-bah'ray] *vi.* to be agreeable, to be to one's liking, please, suit.

Garbatezza [gahr-bah-tet'zah] *nf.* favour, politeness.

Garbato [gahr-bah'toh] *a.* civil, polite.

Garbo [gahr'boh] *nm.* courtesy, grace, manner, politeness; a [ah] *g. ad.* gracefully, politely.

Garbuglio [gahr-bool'yoh] *nm.* confusion, disorder, intrigue.

Garbuglione [gahr-bool-yoh'nay] *nm.* intriguer.

Gareggiare [gah-ray-djah'ray] *vi.* to compete, vie.

Garetta [gah-ret'tah] *nf.* sentry-box.

Garetto [gah-ret'toh] *nm.* ham, hough, shin.

Garganella, bere a [bay'ray ah gahr-gah-nell'lah] *vt.* to gulp down, toss off.

Gargarizzare [gahr-gah-reed-zah'ray] vi. to gargle.

Garibaldino [gah-ree-bahl-dee'noh] nm. and a. (one who) fought under Garibaldi.

Garofano [gah-roh'fah-noh] nm. carnation, clove pink.

Garrire [gahr-ree'ray] vi. to chatter, chirp, warble.

Garrulità [gahr-roo-lee-tah'] nf. garrulity.

Garrulo [gahr'roo-loh] a. garrulous.

Garza [gahrd'zah] nf. gauze.

Garzone [gahrd-zoh'nay] nm. farm-servant, shop-boy.

Gas [gahs] nm. gas; fornello a [forr-nell'loh ah] g. gas-cooker.

Gassista [gahs-see'stah] nm. gas-fitter, gas-man.

Gassosa [gahs-soh'sah] nf. effervescing drink, mineral water.

Gassoso [gahs-soh'soh] a. effervescent, gassy.

Gastrico [gah'stree-koh] a. gastric; succo [sook'koh] g. nm. gastric juice.

Gastrite [gah-stree'tay] nf. (med.) gastritis.

Gastronomia [gah-stroh-noh-mee'ah] nf. gastronomy.

Gastronomico [gah-stroh-noh'mee-koh] a. gastronomic(al).

Gatta [gaht'tah] nf. she-cat; dare una [dah'ray oo'nah] g. a pelare [ah pay-lah'ray] vi. to give a lot of trouble.

Gattabuia [gaht-tah-boo'yah] nf. jail, prison.

Gattesco [gaht-tess'koh] a. cat-like. [kitten.

Gattino [gaht-tee'noh] nm.

Gat/to [gaht'toh] nm. cat; essere quattro [ess'say-ray kwaht'troh] g-ti vi. to be very few people.

Gatto/ne [gaht-toh'nay] nm. tom-cat; —ni [nee] (pl.) (med.) mumps.

Gaudente [gow-den'tay] nm. and f. reveller; a. rejoicing.

Gaudio [gow'dee-oh] nm. joy, revelry.

Gaudioso [gow-dee-oh'soh] a. joyful, jubilant.

Gavazzare [gah-vaht-zah'ray] vi. to revel.

Gazza [gahd'zah] nf. magpie, (fig.) babbler, chatterer.

Gazzarra [gahd-zahr'rah] nf. turmoil, uproar.

Gazzella [gahd-zell'lah] nf. gazelle.

Gazzetta [gahd-zet'tah] nf. gazette, newspaper.

Gelare [jay-lah'ray] vt. and i. to freeze.

Gelatina [jay-lah-tee'nah] nf. gelatine, jelly.

Gelato [jay-lah'toh] nm. ice-(cream); a. frozen.

Gelido [jay'lee-doh] a. chilly, frozen, gelid.

Gelo [jay'loh] nm. freezing weather, frost, ice.

Gelone [jay-loh'nay] nm. chilblain.

Gelosia [jay-loh-see'ah] nf. jealousy, Venetian blind.

Geloso [jay-loh'soh] a. jealous. [(-tree).

Gelso [jell'soh] nm. mulberry

Gelsomino [jell-soh-mee'noh] nm. jasmine, jessamine.

Gemebondo [jay-may-bon'doh] a. doleful, plaintive.

Gemel/lo [jay-mell'loh] nm. and a. twin; —li [lee] (pl.) twins (pl.) cuff-links (pl.).

Gemere [jay'may-ray] vi. to drip, groan, moan, trickle.

Gemito [jay'mee-toh] nm. groan, moan.

Gemma [jem'mah] nf. bud, gem, precious stone.

Gemmare [jem-mah'ray] vi. to bud.

Gemmato [jem-mah'toh] a

full of buds. studded with gems.

Gendarme [jen-dahr'may] *nm.* gendarm, policeman.

Gendarmeria [jen-dahr-may-ree'ah] *nf.* gendarmerie, police.

Genealogia [jay-nay-ah-loh-jee'ah] *nf.* genealogy.

Generale [jay-nay-rah'lay] *nm. and a.* general.

Generalità [jay-nay-rah-lee-tah'] *nf.* generality (used in plural to indicate data for identifying a person).

Generalizzare [jay-nay-rah-leed-zah'ray] *vt. and i.* to generalise.

Generare [jay-nay-rah'ray] *vt.* to beget, breed, cause, engender, generate, produce.

Generatore [jay-nay-rah-toh'ray] *nm.* generator.

Generazione [jay-nay-rah-tsee-oh'nay] *nf.* age, breed, generation, race.

Gene/re [jay'nay-ray] *nm.* gender, kind, sex, sort; in [een] g. *ad.* in general; —ri (pl.) articles, goods (pl.); g. di prima necessità [dee pree'mah nay-chess-see-tah'] necessaries (pl.). [son-in-law.

Genero [jay'nay-roh] *nm.*

Generosità [jay-nay-roh-see-tah'] *nf.* generosity.

Generoso [jay-nay-roh'soh] *a.* generous.

Gengiva [jen-jee'vah] *nf.* gum (in the mouth).

Geniale [jay-nee-ah'lay] *a.* genial, of genius, talented.

Genialità [jay-nee-ah-lee-tah'] *nf.* geniality, talent.

Genio [jay'nee-oh] *nm.* genius, talent, taste; arma del [ahr'mah dell] g. *nf.* (*mil.*) engineers; andare a [ahn-dah'-ray ah] g. *vi.* to be to one's liking. [genital.

Genitale [jay-nee-tah'lay] *a.*

Genito [jay'nee-toh] *a.* born, generated.

Geni/tore [jay-nee-toh'ray] *nm.* father; —trice [tree'chay] *nf.* mother; —tori [toh'ree] (pl.) parents (pl.).

Gennaio [jen-nah'yoh] *nm.* January.

Gen/taccia [jen-tahch'chah], —taglia [tah'lyah] *nf.* mob, rabble. [(pl.)

Gente [jen'tay] *nf.* folk, people

Gentildonna [jen-teel-don'nah] *nf.* gentlewoman, lady of quality.

Gentile [jen-tee'lay] *nm.* Gentile, heathen, pagan; *a.* courteous, kind, polite.

Gentilezza [jen-tee-let'zah] *nf.* civility, kindness, politeness.

Gentilizio [jen-tee-lee'tsee-oh] *a.* aristocratic, gentleborn; stemma [stem'mah] g. *nm.* coat of arms.

Gentiluomo [jen-teel-oo-oh'moh] *nm.* gentleman, nobleman.

Genuflessione [jay-noo-fless-see-oh'nay] *nf.* genuflection.

Genuflettersi [jay-noo-flet'-tehr-see] *vr.* to genuflect.

Genuinità [jay-noo-ee-nee-tah'] *nf.* genuineness.

Genuino [jay-noo-ee'noh] *a.* authentic, genuine.

Genziana [jent-zee-ah'nah] *nf.* gentian.

Geografia [jay-oh-grah-fee'ah] *nf.* geography.

Geologia [jay-oh-loh-jee'ah] *nf.* geology.

Geometra [jay-oh'may-trah] *nm.* geometer, surveyor.

Geometria [jay-oh-may-tree'ah] *nf.* geometry.

Geranio [jay-rah'nee-oh] *nm.* geranium.

Gerarca [jay-rahr'kah] *nm.* hierarch.

Gerarchia [jay-rahr-kee'ah] *nf.* hierarchy.

Gerente [jay-ren'tay] *nm.* confidential clerk, manager.

Gerenza [jay-rent'zah] *nf.* management.

Gergo [jehr'goh] *nm.* jargon, slang.

Germe [jehr'may] *nm.* germ, shoot, sprout.

Germinare [jehr-mee-nah'ray] *vi.* to germinate.

Germogliare [jehr-mohl-yah'ray] *vi.* to bud, sprout.

Germoglio [jehr-mohl'yoh] *nm.* bud, shoot.

Geroglifico [jay-roh-glee'fee-koh] *nm* and *a.* hieroglyph(ic).

Gesso [jess'soh] *nm.* chalk, gypsum, plaster of Paris.

Gesta [jess'tah] *nf.* (*pl.*) deeds, exploits, feats (*pl.*).

Gestante [jess-tahn'tay] *nf.* expectant mother.

Gestazione [jess-tah-tsee-oh'nay] *nf.* gestation, pregnancy.

Gesticolare [jess-tee-koh-lah'ray] *vi.* to gesticulate.

Gesticolazione [jess-tee-koh-lah-tsee-oh'nay] *nf.* gesticulation.

Gestione [jess-tee-oh'nay] *nf.* management.

Gestire [jess-tee'ray] *vt.* to manage.

Gesto [jess'toh] *nm.* gesture, (*fig.*) exploit (*v.* gesta).

Gestore [jess-toh'ray] *nm.* head clerk, manager.

Gesuita [jay-zoo-ee'tah] *nm.* and *a.* Jesuit.

Getta/re [jet-tah'ray] *vt.* to cast, fling, mould, throw; —rsi *vr.* to jump, throw oneself.

Gettito [jet'tee-toh] *nm.* (*naut.*) jettison.

Getto [jet'toh] *nm.* casting, throw, water-spout; **a** [ah]

g. continuo [kon-tee'noo-oh] *ad.* without a break.

Gettone [jet-toh'nay] *nm.* counter, token.

Ghermire [ghehr-mee'ray] *vt.* to claw, collar, seize.

Ghetta [ghet'tah] *nf.* gaiter.

Ghetto [ghet'toh] *nm.* ghetto, Jews' quarter.

Ghiacciaia [ghee-ahch-chah'yah] *nf.* ice-box, refrigerator.

Ghiacciaio [ghee-ahch-chah'yoh] *nm.* glacier.

Ghiaccia/re [ghee-ahch-chah'ray] *vt.* and *i.* —rsi *vr.* to freeze. [*nm.* ice.

Ghiaccio [ghee-ahch'choh] *nm.*

Ghiacciuolo [ghee-ahch-choo-oh'loh] *nm.* icicle.

Ghiaia [ghee-ah'yah] *nf.* gravel. [acorn.

Ghianda [ghee-ahn'dah] *nf.*

Ghiandaia [ghee-ahn-dah'yah] *nf.* jackdaw, jay.

Ghibellino [ghee-bell-lee'noh] *nm.* and *a.* Ghibelline.

Ghigliottina [gheel-yot-tee'nah] *nf.* guillotine.

Ghigna [gheen'yah] *nf.* evil face. [*vi.* to sneer.

Ghignare [gheen-yah'ray]

Ghigno [gheen'yoh] *nm.* grin, sneer. [guinea.

Ghinea [ghee-nay'ah] *nf.*

Ghingheri, in [een gheeng'gay-ree] *ad.* finely dressed.

Ghiotto [ghee-ot'toh] *a.* gluttonous, greedy.

Ghiottone [ghee-ot-toh'nay] *nm.* glutton.

Ghiottoneria [ghee-ot-toh-nay-ree'ah] *nf.* dainty, gluttony, titbit.

Ghiribizzo [ghee-ree-beed'zoh] *nm.* freak, whim.

Ghiribizzoso [ghee-ree-beed-zoh'soh] *a.* freakish, whimsical.

Ghirlanda [gheer-lahn'dah] *nf.* garland, wreath.

Ghiro [ghee'roh] *nm.* dormouse.

Ghisa [ghee'zah] *nf.* cast-iron, pig-iron.

Già [jah] *ad.* already, before, formerly, once; *int.* of course, yes.

Giacca [jahk'kah] *nf.* jacket.

Giacchè [jahk-kay'] *con.* as, seeing that, since.

Giacenza [jah-chent'zah] *nf.* stoppage, unproductiveness.

Giacere [jah-chay'ray] *vi.* to be situated, lie.

Giaciglio [jah-cheel'yoh] *nm.* bed, lair, place for lying.

Giacinto [jah-cheen'toh] *nm.* hyacinth.

Giaggiolo [jah-djoh'loh] *nm.* Florentine iris.

Giaguaro [jah-gwah'roh] *nm.* jaguar.

Giallastro [jahl-lah'stroh], **giallognolo** [jahl-lohn'yoh-loh] *a.* yellowish.

Giallo [jahl'loh] *nm.* and *a.* yellow; g. d'uovo [doo-oh'voh] *nm.* yolk (of an egg).

Giambo [jahm'boh] *nm.* iambus.

Giammai [jahm-mah'ee] *ad.* never.

Giapponese [jahp-poh-nay'zay] *nm.* and *f.* and *a.* Japanese.

Giardiniere [jahr-dee-nee-ay'ray] *nm.* gardener.

Giardino [jahr-dee'noh] *nm.* garden.

Giarrettiera [jahr-ret-tee-ay'rah] *nf.* garter.

Gibboso [jeeb-boh'soh] *a.* humped, hump-backed.

Giberna [jee-behr'nah] *nf.* cartridge-box, pouch.

Gibetto [jee-bet'toh] *nm.* gibbet. *v.* **Forca.** [hat.

Gibus [jee'boos] *nm.* opera-

Gigante [jee-gahn'tay] *nm.* giant; *a.* giant, gigantic.

Giganteggiare [jee-gahn-

tay-djah'ray] *vi.* to be gigantic, loom, tower.

Gigantesco [jee-gahn-tess'-koh] *a.* gigantic.

Gigantessa [jee-gahn-tess'-sah] *nf.* giantess.

Giglio [jeel'yoh] *nm.* lily.

Gilè [jee-lay'] *nm.* waistcoat.

Ginecologia [jee-nay-koh-loh-jee'ah] *nf.* gynæcology.

Ginecologo [jee-nay-koh'-loh-goh] *nm.* gynæcologist.

Ginepraio [jee-nay-prah'-yoh] *nm.* peck of troubles, thicket of junipers.

Ginepro [jee-nay'proh] *nm.* gin, juniper.

Ginestra [jee-ness'trah] *nf.* broom, gorse.

Gingilla/re [jeen-jeel-lah'-ray] *vi.* —rsi *vr.* to dawdle, play, trifle.

Gingillino [jeen-jeel-lee'noh] *nm.* small pretty person.

Gingillo [jeen-jeel'loh] *nm.* nick-nack, trifle.

Gingillone [jeen-jeel-loh'-nay] *nm.* dawdler.

Ginnasiale [jeen-nah-zee-ah'lay] *a.* gymnasial.

Ginnasio [jeen-nah'zee-oh] *nm.* gymnasium, middle school.

Ginnastica [jeen-nah'stee-kah] *nf.* gymnastics (*pl.*).

Ginocchio [jee-nock'kee-oh] *nm.* knee.

Ginocchioni, in [een jee-nock-kee-oh'nee] *ad.* on one's knees.

Gioca/re [joh-kah'ray], **giuo-care** [joo-oh-kah'ray] *vt.* and *i.* to make a fool of, play, stake; —rsi *vr.* to make a fool of.

Gioca/tore [joh-kah-toh'ray] *nm.* —trice [tree'chay] *nf.* player.

Giocattolo [joh-kaht'toh-loh] *nm.* plaything, toy.

Giocherellare [joh-kay-rell-lah'ray] *vi.* to amuse oneself, play.

Gioco: v. giuoco.

Giocoforza, essere [ess' say-ray joh-koh-fort'zah] v. imp. to be necessary.

Giocoliere [joh-koh-lee-ay' ray] nm. juggler.

Giocondità [joh-kon-dee-tah'] nf. gaiety, jocundity.

Giocondo [joh-kon'doh] a. gay, jocund.

Giocoso [joh-koh'soh] a. facetious, jocose.

Giogaia [joh-gah'yah] nf. chain of mountains.

Giogo [joh'goh] nm. peak, slavery, yoke.

Gioia [joh'yah] nf. delight, jewel, joy, pleasure.

Gioielleria [joh-yell-lay-ree' ah] nf. jewelry.

Gioielliere [joh-yell-lee-ay' ray] nm. jeweller. [jewel.

Gioiello [joh-yell'loh] nm.

Gioioso [joh-yoh'soh] a. joyful, merry.

Gioire [joh-ee'ray] vi. to be glad, rejoice.

Giornalaio [jorr-nah-lah'yoh] nm. newsagent, newsboy.

Giornale [jorr-nah'lay] nm. diary, journal, (news)paper.

Giornaliero [jorr-nah-lee-ay'roh] a. daily.

Giornalismo [jorr-nah-lees'moh] nm. journalism.

Giornalista [jorr-nah-lee' stah] nm. journalist.

Giornata [jorr-nah'tah] nf. day, day's work; vivere alla [vee'vay-ray ahl'lah] g. vi. to live from hand to mouth.

Giorno [jorr'noh] nm. day; essere a [ess'say-ray ah] g. di [dee] vt. to be informed of.

Giostra [joss'trah] nf. joust, merry-go-round, roundabout.

Giostrare [joss-trah'ray] vi. to joust, tilt.

Giovamento [joh-vah-men'toh] nm. advantage, benefit, improvement.

Giovane [joh'vah-nay], gio-vine [joh'vee-nay] nm. young man, youth; nf. young woman; a. young.

Giovanile [joh-vah-nee'lay] a. juvenile, youthful.

Giovanotto [joh-vah-not' toh] nm. young man.

Giova/re [joh'vah'ray] vi. to be of use, serve; —rsi vr. to avail oneself of, make use of.

Giovedì [joh-vay-dee'] nm. Thursday.

Gioven/ca [joh-veng'kah] nf. heifer; —co [koh] nm. bullock, steer.

Gioventù [joh-ven-too'], giovinezza [joh-vee-net'zah] nf. young people, youth.

Giovevole [joh-vay'voh-lay] a. beneficial, good, profitable.

Gioviale [joh-vee-ah'lay] a. jolly, jovial.

Giovialità [joh-vee-ah-lee-tah'] nf. joviality.

Giovinet/ta [joh-vee-net'tah] nf. young girl; —to [toh] nm. lad, young fellow.

Giraffa [jee-rahf'fah] nf. giraffe.

Giramento [jee-rah-men' toh] nm. turning; g. di testa [dee tess'tah], dizziness.

Girandola [jee-rahn'doh-lah] nf. Catherine wheel.

Girante [jee-rahn'tay] nm. endorser; a. revolving.

Gira/re [jee-rah'ray] vt. and i. to travel, turn; —rsi vr. to turn round.

Girarrosto [jee-rahr-ross' toh] nm. roasting-jack, spit, turnspit.

Girasole [jee-rah-soh'lay] nm. sunflower.

Girata [jee-rah'tah] nf. endorsement, walk.

Giratorio [jee-rah-toh'ree-oh] a. gyratory, revolving.

Giravolta [jee-rah-voll'tah]

nf. change of front, turning, twirl.

Gire [jee'ray] *vi. (poet.)* to go.

Girellare [jee-rel-lah'ray] *vi.* to saunter, stroll.

Girevole [jee-ray'voh-lay] *a.* revolving, turning.

Girino [jee-ree'noh] *nm.* tadpole.

Giro [jee'roh] *nm.* ride, round, tour, turn; **fare un** [fah'ray oon] g. *vi.* to go for a ride, take a turn.

Gironzolare [jee-rond-zoh-lah'ray] *vi.* to stroll.

Girovagare [jee-roh-vah-gah'ray] *vi.* to roam, rove, wander.

Girovago [jee-roh'vah-goh] *nm.* rover, wanderer; *a.* roving, wandering.

Gita [jee'tah] *nf.* excursion, trip.

Gitante [jee-tahn'tay] *nm. and f.* excursionist.

Gittare: *v.* gettare.

Giù [joo] *ad.* down; **su per** [soo pehr] g. approximately, roughly; **g. per** [pehr] *pr.* down. [jacket.

Giubba [joob'bah] *nf.* coat,

Giubilare [joo-bee-lah'ray] *vi.* to exult, jubilate.

Giubileo [joo-bee-lay'oh] *nm.* jubilee.

Giubilo [joo'bee-loh] *nm.* jubilation, rejoicing.

Giudaico [joo-dah'ee-koh] *a.* Judaic.

Giudaismo [joo-dah-ees'moh] *nm.* Judaism.

Giudeo [joo-day'oh] *nm.* Jew, Judean; *a.* Jewish.

Giudicare [joo-dee-kah'ray] *vt. and i.* to consider, judge, think.

Giudice [joo'dee-chay] *nm.* judge, justice (title).

Giudizi/ale [joo-dee-tsee-ah'lay], **—ario** [ah'ree-oh] *a.* judicial.

Giudizio [joo-dee'tsee-oh] *nm.* decision, decree, judgment; **aver** [ah-vehr'] g. *vi.* to be sensible; **dente del** [den' tay dell] g. *nm.* wisdom tooth.

Giudizioso [joo-dee-tsee-oh'soh] *a.* judicious, sensible, wise.

Giugno [joon'yoh] *nm.* June.

Giulivo [joo-lee'voh] *a.* gay, joyful.

Giullare [jool-lah'ray] *nm.* minstrel. [mare.

Giumenta [joo-men'tah] *nf.*

Giuncaia [joong-kah'yah] *nf.* giuncheto [joong-kay'toh] *nm.* reed-bed.

Giunchiglia [joong-keel' yah] *nf.* jonquil.

Giunco [joong'koh] *nm.* reed, rush.

Giungere [joon'jay-ray] *vt. and i.* to fold (one's hands), arrive, get to, reach.

Giungla [joong'glah] *nf.* jungle.

Giunta [joon'tah] *nf.* addition, council, increase, make-weight; **per** [pehr] g. *ad.* in addition, moreover.

Giuntare [joon-tah'ray] *vt.* to join, sew together.

Giuntura [joon-too'rah] *nf.* articulation, joint.

Giuocare: *v.* giocare.

Giuoco [joo-oh'koh] *nm.* game, play, trick.

Giuramento [joo-rah-men' toh] *nm.* oath.

Giurare [joo-rah'ray] *vt. and i.* to swear, take an oath.

Giurato [joo-rah'toh] *nm.* juryman; *a.* sworn.

Giureconsulto [joo-ray-kon-sool'toh] *nm.* jurisconsult.

Giuri [joo-ree'] *nm.* giuria [joo-ree'ah] *nf.* jury.

Giuridico [joo-ree'dee-koh] *a.* juridical.

Giurisdizione [joo-rees-dee-tsee-oh'nay] *nf.* jurisdiction.

Giurisprudenza [joo-rees-proo-dent'zah] *nf.* jurisprudence, law. [jurist.

Giurista [joo-ree'stah] *nm.*

Giusta [joo'stah] *pr.* according to.

Giustezza [joo-stet'zah] *nf.* exactness, propriety.

Giustifica/re [joo-stee-fee-kah'ray] *vt.* to justify; —rsi *vr.* to excuse oneself, justify oneself.

Giustificazione [joo-stee-fee-kah-tsee-oh'nay] *nf.* excuse, justification.

Giustizia [joo-stee'tsee-ah] *nf.* justice.

Giustiziare [joo-stee-tsee-ah'ray] *vt.* to execute, put to death.

Giustiziere [joo-stee-tsee-ay'ray] *nm.* avenger, executioner.

Giusto [joo'stoh] *a.* fair, just, lawful, proper, right; *ad.* just.

Glaciale [glah-chah'lay] *a.* glacial, icy.

Gladiatore [glah-dee-ah-toh'ray] *nm.* gladiator.

Glandula [glahn'doo-lah] *nf.* gland.

Glandulare [glahn-doo-lah'ray] *a.* glandular.

Glanduloso [glahn-doo-loh'soh] *a.* glandulous.

Glauco [glow'koh] *a.* glaucous, greyish blue or green.

Gleba [glay'bah] *nf.* earth, glebe, ground; servo della [sehr'voh dell'lah] *g. nm.* serf.

Gli [lyee] *art. m.* (*pl.*) the; *pr. m.* (*dat.*) to him.

Glicerina [glee-chay-ree'nah] *nf.* glicerin.

Glicine [glee'chee-nay] *nf.* wistaria.

Globale [gloh-bah'lay] *a.* round, total; spesa [spay'zah] *g. nf.* total expenditure.

Globo [gloh'boh] *nm.* globe; g. dell'occhio [dell-lock'kee-oh] eye-ball.

Globulo [gloh'boo-loh] *nm.* globule. [glory.

Gloria [gloh'ree-ah] *nf.*

Gloriare [gloh-ree-ah'ray] *vt.* to glorify; —rsi *vr.* to boast of, be proud of, pride oneself on.

Glorificamento [gloh-ree-fee-kah-men'toh] *nm.* glorificazione [gloh-ree-fee-kah-tsee-oh'nay] *nf.* glorification.

Glorificare [gloh-ree-fee-kah'ray] *vt.* to glorify.

Glorioso [gloh-ree-oh'soh] *a.* glorious, proud.

Glossare [gloss-sah'ray] *vt.* to gloss.

Glossario [gloss-sah'ree-oh] *nm.* glossary.

Gnaulare [nyow-lah'ray] *vi.* to mew.

Gnocco [nyock'koh] *nm.* kind of small dumpling.

Gnomo [nyoh'moh] *nm.* gnome, goblin.

Gnosticismo [nyoss-tee-chees'moh] *nm.* gnosticism.

Gnostico [nyoss'stee-koh] *a.* gnostic.

Gobba [gob'bah] *nf.* hump, hump-backed woman.

Gobbo [gob'boh] *nm.* hump-backed man; *a.* hump-backed, hunch-backed; mettere in [met'tay-ray een] *g. vt.* to pawn.

Goccia [gohch'chah], gocciola [gohch-choh-lah] *nf.* drop.

Gocciolamento [gohch-choh-lah-men'toh] *nm.* gocciolatura [gohch-choh-lah-too'rah] *nf.* dripping, trickling.

Gocciolare [gohch-choh-lah'ray] *vi.* to drip, drop, trickle.

Gode/re [goh-day'ray] *vt. and i.* to be happy, enjoy; —rsi, —rsela *vr.* to enjoy oneself.

Godereccio [goh-day-rehch'choh] a. enjoyable.

Godimento [goh-dee-men'toh] nm. enjoyment, pleasure, possession, use.

Goffaggine [gof-fah'djee-nay] nf. awkwardness, clumsiness.

Goffo [gof'foh] a. awkward, clumsy.

Gola [goh'lah] nf. gorge, throat; far [fahr] g. vi. to be a temptation.

Golfo [goll'foh] nm. gulf.

Goliardo [goh-lee-ahr'doh] nm. University student.

Golosità [goh-loh-see-tah'] nf. gluttony, greed.

Goloso [goh-loh'soh] a. gluttonous, greedy.

Golpe [goll'pay] nf. blight, mildew.

Gomena [goh'may-nah] nf. (naut.) cable, hawser.

Gomito [goh'mee-toh] nm. elbow.

Gomitolo [goh-mee'toh-loh] nm. ball (of thread, etc.).

Gomma [gom'mah] nf. gum, resin, tyre.

Gondola [gon'doh-lah] nf. gondola.

Gondoliere [gon-doh-lee-ay'ray] nm. gondolier.

Gonfalone [gon-fah-loh'nay] nm. flag, standard.

Gonfaloniere [gon-fah-loh-nee-ay'ray] nm. standard-bearer.

Gonfiagione [gon-fee-ah-joh'nay] nf. swelling.

Gonfia/re [gon-fee-ah'ray] vt. to inflate, puff up, swell; —rsi vr. to swell (up).

Gonfiatura [gon-fee-ah-too'rah] nf. inflation (of balloons, etc.).

Gonfiezza [gon-fee-et'zah] nf. swelling.

Gonfio [gon'fee-oh] a. inflated, puffed up, swollen.

Gongolare [gong-goh-lah'ray] vi. to be very happy.

Gon/na [gon'nah], **—nella** [nell'lah] nf. skirt.

Gonzo [gond'zoh] nm. blockhead; a. stupid.

Gora [goh'rah] nf. channel, conduit.

Gorgheggiare [gorr-gay-djah'ray] vi. to trill, warble.

Gorgheggio [gorr-gay'djoh] nm. trilling, warbling.

Gorgo [gorr'goh] nm. abyss, whirlpool.

Gorgogliare [gorr-gohl-yah'ray] vi. to gurgle.

Gorgoglio [gorr-gohl'yoh] nm. gurgling.

Gorilla [goh-reel'lah] nm. gorilla.

Gota [goh'tah] nf. cheek.

Gotico [goh'tee-koh] a. Gothic.

Gotta [got'tah] nf. gout.

Gottoso [got-toh'soh] a. gouty.

Governante [goh-vehr-nahn'tay] nf. governess, housekeeper; a. governing, ruling.

Governare [goh-vehr-nah'ray] vt. to feed (animals), govern, rule over, steer (a boat).

Governativo [goh-vehr-nah-tee'voh] a. government(al).

Governatore [goh-vehr-nah-toh'ray] nm. governor, ruler.

Governo [goh-vehr'noh] nm. government, rule; g. della casa [dell'lah kah'sah], housekeeping.

Gozzo [got'zoh] nm. bird's crop, goitre.

Gozzovigliare [got-zoh-veel-yah'ray] vi. to revel.

Gracchi/a [grahk'kee-ah] nf. -o [oh] nm. crow.

Gracchiare [grahk-kee-ah'ray] vi. to caw.

Gracidare [grah-chee-dah'ray] vi. to croak.

Gracile [grah′chee-lay] a. delicate, feeble, weak.

Gracilità [grah-chee-lee-tah′] nf. delicacy, weakness.

Gradasso [grah-dahs′soh] nm. blusterer, braggart.

Gradazione [grah-dah-tsee-oh′nay] nf. arrangement, gradation.

Gradevole [grah-day′voh-lay] a. agreeable, pleasant.

Gradimento [grah-dee-men′toh] nm. approval, enjoyment, liking, pleasure.

Gradino [grah-dee′noh] nm. step.

Gradire [grah-dee′ray] vt. to accept, approve, find pleasant, like.

Gradito [grah-dee′toh] a. agreeable, pleasant, welcome.

Grado [grah′doh] nm. degree, pleasure, rank, will; essere in [ess′say-ray een] g. vi. to be able.

Graduale [grah-doo-ah′lay] a. gradual.

Graduare [grah-doo-ah′ray] vt. to confer (a degree or rank), graduate.

Graduato [grah-doo-ah′toh] nm. graduate, (mil.) N.C.O.

Graduatoria [grah-doo-ah-toh′ree-ah] nf. classification, pass-list.

Graduazione [grah-doo-ah-tsee-oh′nay] nf. graduation.

Graffiare [grahf-fee-ah′ray] vt. to scratch.

Graffiatura [grahf-fee-ah-too′rah] nf. scratch.

Graffio [grahf′fee-oh] nm. scratch, (naut.) grapnel.

Grafia [grah-fee′ah] nf. spelling, writing.

Gragnola [grahn-yoh′lah] nf. hail (fig.).

Gramaglia [grah-mahl′yay] nf. (pl.) deep mourning.

Gramigna [grah-meen′yah] nf. couch-grass, weed.

Grammatica [grahm-mah′tee-kah] nf. grammar.

Grammaticale [grahm-mah-tee-kah′lay] a. grammatical. [gramme.

Grammo [grahm′moh] nm.

Gramo [grah′moh] a. miserable, poor, wretched.

Grana [grah′nah] nf. grain, Parmesan cheese.

Granaglie [grah-nahl′yay] nf. (pl.) corn, grain.

Granaio [grah-nah′yoh] nm. barn, granary.

Granata [grah-nah′tah] nf. broom, brush, grenade.

Granatiere [grah-nah-tee-ay′ray] nm. grenadier.

Grancassa [grahn-kahs′sah] nf. bass-drum.

Granchio [grahng′kee-oh] nm. crab; prendere un [pren′day-ray oon] g. vi. to make a mistake.

Gran(de) [grahn′day] a. big, great, grown-up, high, tall, wide; i grandi [ee grahn′dee] nm. (pl.) grown-ups. (pl.)

Grandeggiare [grahn-day-djah′ray] vi. to rise to a great height, tower above.

Grandezza [grahn-det′zah] nf. grandeur, greatness, size.

Grandinare [grahn-dee-nah′ray] vi. to hail.

Grandine [grahn′dee-nay] nf. hail.

Grandioso [grahn-dee-oh′soh] a. grand, grandiose.

Granduca [grahn-doo′kah] nm. grand-duke.

Granello [grah-nell′loh] nm. grain, seed.

Granfia [grahn′fee-ah] nf. claw, clutch.

Granifero [grah-nee′fay-roh] a. graniferous.

Granire [grah-nee′ray] vt. to cut (teeth); vi. to seed.

Granito [grah-nee′toh] nm. granite.

Grano [grah'noh] *nm.* bead (of a rosary), corn, grain, wheat.

Granoso [grah-noh'soh] *a.* grainy.

Granturco [grahn-toor'koh] *nm.* Indian corn, maize.

Granulazione [grah-noo-lah-tsee-oh'nay] *nf.* granulation.

Granuloso [grah-noo-loh'soh] *a.* granulous.

Grappolo [grahp'poh-loh] *nm.* bunch, cluster.

Grassatore [grahs-sah-toh'ray] *nm.* highwayman.

Grassazione [grahs-sah-tsee-oh'nay] *nf.* highway robbery.

Grassezza [grahs-set'zah] *nf.* fatness, fertility, stoutness.

Grasso [grahs'soh] *a.* fat, fertile, stout; **martedì** [marr-tay-dee'] g. *nm.* Shrove Tuesday.

Grassoccio [grahs-sohch'choh] *a.* plump.

Grassume [grahs-soo'may] *nm.* fat substance.

Grata [grah'tah] *nf.* grating.

Graticola [grah-tee'koh-lah] *nf.* grating, grill.

Gratificare [grah-tee-fee-kah'ray] *vt.* to gratify.

Gratificazione [grah-tee-fee-kah-tsee-oh'nay] *nf.* bonus, gratification, gratuity.

Gratis [grah'tees] *ad.* free, gratis.

Gratitudine [grah-tee-too'dee-nay] *nf.* gratitude.

Grato [grah'toh] *a.* grateful, obliged, thankful.

Grattacapo [graht-tah-kah'poh] *nm.* problem, trouble.

Grattacielo [graht-tah-chay'loh] *nm.* skyscraper.

Grattare [graht-tah'ray] *vt.* to scrape, scratch.

Grattugia [graht-too'jah] *nf.* grater.

Grattugiare [graht-too-jah'ray] *vt.* to grate.

Gratuito [grah-too'ee-toh] *a.* free, gratuitous.

Gravame [grah-vah'may] *nm.* burden, duty, tax.

Grava/re [grah-vah'ray] *vt.* to burden, load, weigh on; **—rsi** *vr.* to burden oneself, saddle oneself.

Grave [grah'vay] *nm.* body, weight; *a.* grave, heavy, serious; **essere** [ess'say-ray] g. *vi.* to be seriously ill.

Gravezza [grah-vet'zah] *nf.* gravity, heaviness, tax.

Gravidanza [grah-vee-dahnt'zah] *nf.* pregnancy.

Gravido [grah'vee-doh] *a.* full, loaded, pregnant.

Gravità [grah-vee-tah'] *nf.* gravity, seriousness, weight.

Gravitare [grah-vee-tah'ray] *vi.* to gravitate.

Gravitazione [grah-vee-tah-tsee-oh'nay] *nf.* gravitation.

Gravosità [grah-voh-see-tah'] *nf.* heaviness, oppressiveness.

Gravoso [grah-voh'soh] *a.* grievous, heavy, oppressive.

Grazia [grah'tsee-ah] *nf.* favour, grace, mercy.

Graziare [grah-tsee-ah'ray] *vt.* to pardon.

Grazie [grah'tsee-ay] *int.* thanks, thank you.

Grazioso [grah-tsee-oh'soh] *a.* dainty, gracious, pretty.

Grecista [gray-chee'stah] *nm.* Hellenist.

Greco [gray'koh] *nm. and a.* Greek.

Gregario [gray-gah'ree-oh] *nm.* follower, private soldier.

Gregge [gray'djay] *nm.* flock, herd.

Greggio [gray'djoh], **grezzo** [gred'zoh] *a.* raw (of materials).

Grembiule [grem-bee-oo'lay] *nm.* apron.

Grembo [grem'boh] *nm.* lap, (*fig.*) bosom.

Gremi/re [gray-mee'ray] *vt.* to crowd, fill; —**rsi** *vr.* to fill up, get crowded.

Gremito [gray-mee'toh] *a.* crowded, packed.

Greppia [grep'pee-ah] *nf.* crib, manger, rack. [bank.

Greppo [grep'poh] *nm.* cliff, rock.

Greto [gray'toh] *nm.* pebbly

Grettezza [gret-tet'zah] *nf.* meanness, stinginess.

Gretto [gret'toh] *a.* mean, niggardly, stingy.

Greve [gray'vay] *a.* grievous, heavy.

Gridare [gree-dah'ray] *vi.* to call, cry, shout, scream.

Grido [gree'doh] *nm.* cry, shout, scream; **di** [dee] **g.** *a.* fashionable.

Grifone [gree-foh'nay] *nm.* griffin, griffon. [grey.

Grigio [gree'joh] *nm. and a.*

Griglia [greel'yah] *nf.* grating, grill.

Grilletto [greel-let'toh] *nm.* trigger.

Grillo [greel'loh] *nm.* cricket, grasshopper, whim.

Grinza [greent'zah] *nf.* crease, wrinkle.

Grinzoso [greent-zoh'soh] *a.* creased, wrinkled.

Groenlandese [groh-en-lahn-day'zay] *nm. and f.* Greenlander; *a.* of Greenland.

Gronda [gron'dah] *nf.* eaves (*pl.*). [gutter.

Grondaia [gron-dah'yah] *nf.*

Grondare [gron-dah'ray] *vi.* to drip, gush, stream.

Groppa [grop'pah] *nf.* back, rump. [(12 dozen).

Grossa [gross'sah] *nf.* gross

Grossezza [gross-set'zah] *nf.* bigness, size, thickness.

Grossista [gross-see'stah] *nm.* wholesale dealer.

Grosso [gross'soh] *nm.* main body; *a.* big, thick; **pezzo** [pet'zoh] **g.** *nm.* big-wig.

Grossolanità [gross-soh-lah-nee-tah'] *nf.* coarseness, grossness.

Grossolano [gross-soh-lah'noh] *a.* coarse, gross, rude.

Grotta [grot'tah] *nf.* cave, grotto.

Grottesco [grot-tess'koh] *nm.* grotesqueness; *a.* grotesque.

Gru/e [groo'ay] *nf.* crane.

Gruccia [grooch'chah] *nf.* coathanger, crutch.

Grugnire [groon-yee'ray] *vi.* to grunt.

Grugno [groon'yoh] *nm.* muzzle, snout.

Grullo [grool'loh] *nm.* fool; *a.* foolish, silly.

Grumo [groo'moh] *nm.* clot.

Grumoso [groo-moh'soh] *a.* clotted.

Gruppo [groop'poh] *nm.* group, knot.

Gruzzolo [groot'zoh-loh] *nm.* hoard, savings (*pl.*).

Guadabile [gwah-dah-bee'lay] *a.* fordable, wadable.

Guadagna/re [gwah-dahn-yah'ray] *vt. and i.* —**rsi** *vr.* to acquire, deserve, earn, gain, get, win.

Guada/gno [gwah-dahn'yoh] *nm.* gain, profit; —**gni** [yee] *nf.* earnings, gains, profits, winnings (*pl.*).

Guadare [gwah-dah'ray] *vi.* to ford, wade.

Guado [gwah'doh] *nm.* ford.

Guai [gwah'ee] *int.* woe!

Guaina [gwah-ee'nah] *nf.* case, sheath; corset.

Guaio [gwah'ee-oh] *nm.* accident, mess, misfortune.

Guaire [gwah-ee'ray] *vi.* to whine, yelp. [cheek.

Guancia [gwahn'chah] *nf.*

Guanciale [gwahn-chah'lay] *nm.* pillow

Guantaio [gwahn-tah'yoh] *nm.* glover.

Guanto [gwahn'toh] *nm.* glove.

Guardaboschi [gwahr-dah-boss'kee] *nm.* forester.

Guardacaccia [gwahr-dah-kahch'chah] *nm.* gamekeeper.

Guardacoste [gwahr-dah-koss'tay] *nm.* coastguard.

Guarda/re [gwahr-dah'ray] *vt.* to consider, guard, look at, mind, protect, try; —**rsi** *vr.* to abstain from, beware of, forbear.

Guardaroba [gwahr-dah-roh'bah] *nf.* cloak-room, wardrobe.

Guardarobiera [gwahr-dah-roh-bee-ay'rah] *nf.* cloak-room attendant.

Guardasigilli [gwahr-dah-see-jeel'lee] *nm.* Lord Privy Seal. [guard, watch.

Guardia [gwahr'dee-ah] *nf.*

Guardiano [gwahr-dee-ah'noh] *nm.* keeper, watchman.

Guardingo [gwahr-deeng'goh] *a.* careful.

Guarentigia [gwah-ren-tee'jah] *nf.* guarantee.

Guari [gwah'ree] *ad. (poet.)* little.

Guaribile [gwah-ree'bee-lay] *a.* curable.

Guarigione [gwah-ree-joh'nay] *nf.* recovery.

Guarire [gwah-ree'ray] *vt.* to cure, heal; *vi.* to recover.

Guarnigione [gwahr-nee-joh'nay] *nf.* garrison.

Guarnire [gwahr-nee'ray] *vt.* to fortify, garnish, trim.

Guarnizione [gwahr-nee-tsee-oh'nay] *nf.* garnishing, trimming.

Guascone [gwah-skoh'nay] *nm. and a.* Gascon.

Guastafeste [gwah-stah-fess'tay] *nm.* spoil-sport, wet-blanket.

Guastamestieri [gwah-stah-mess-tee-ay'ree] *nm.* bungler.

Guasta/re [gwah-stah'ray] *vt.* to ruin, spoil; —**rsi** *vr.* to be spoilt, quarrel.

Guasto [gwah'stoh] *nm.* accident, break-down, damage; *a.* corrupt, decayed, spoilt.

Guatare [gwah-tah'ray] *vt.* to gaze, stare.

Guazza [gwaht'zah] *nf.* heavy dew.

Guelfo [gwell'foh] *nm. and a.* Guelf, Guelph.

Guercio [gwehr'choh] *a.* squint-eyed.

Guerra [gwehr'rah] *nf.* war.

Guerrafondaio [gwehr-rah-fon-dah'yoh] *nm.* warmonger.

Guerreggiare [gwehr-ray-djah'ray] *vi.* to carry on war, fight.

Guerresco [gwehr-ress'koh] *a.* (of) war, warlike.

Guerricciuola [gwehr-reech-choo-oh'lah] *nf.* local war, skirmishing.

Guerriero [gwehr-ree-ay'roh] *nm.* warrior; *a.* warlike.

Guerriglia [gwehr-reel'yah] *nf.* guerilla war.

Gufo [goo'foh] *nm.* owl.

Guglia [gool'yah] *nf.* spire.

Guida [gwee'dah] *nf.* guide, guidance, leadership, strip of carpet; **g. telefonica** [tay-lay-foh'nee-kah], telephone directory.

Guidare [gwee-dah'ray] *vt.* to drive (a car), etc., guide, lead.

Guiderdone [gwee-dehr-doh'nay] *nm.* recompense.

Guinzaglio [gweent-zahl'yoh] *nm.* lead, leash (for dogs).

Guisa [gwee'zah] *nf.* manner, way; **a** [ah] **g. di** [dee] *pr.* like.

Guizzare [gweet-zah'ray] *vi.* to dart, flash; **g. via** [vee'ah] to slip away.

Guizzo [gweet'zoh] *nm.* flare, flash.

Guscio [goo'shoh] *nm.* cover, pod, shell (of an egg).

Gustare [goo-stah'ray] *vt.* to enjoy, relish.

Gusto [goo'stoh] *nm.* enjoyment, flavour, liking, relish, taste, zest.

Gustosità [goo-stoh-see-tah'] *nf.* flavour, taste.

Gustoso [goo-stoh'soh] *a.* amusing, savoury, tasty.

Gutturale [goot-too-rah'lay] *a.* guttural.

I

I [ee] *art. m. (pl.)* the.

Iato [ee-ah'toh] *nm.* hiatus.

Iattanza [yaht-tahnt'zah] *nf.* boasting, bragging.

Iattura [yaht-too'rah] *nf.* misfortune.

Ibridismo [ee-bree-dees'moh] *nm.* hybridism.

Ibrido [ee'bree-doh] *a.* hybrid.

Iconoclaste [ee-koh-noh-klah'stay] *nm.* iconoclast.

Iddio [eed-dee'oh] *nm.* God.

Idea [ee-day'ah] *nf.* idea, notion.

Ideale [ee-day-ah'lay] *nm. and a.* ideal.

Idealismo [ee-day-ah-lees'moh] *nm.* idealism.

Idealista [ee-day-ah-lee'stah] *nm.* idealist.

Idealizzare [ee-day-ah-leed-zah'ray] *vt.* to idealise.

Idea/re [ee-day-ah'ray] *vt.* —**rsi** *vr.* to imagine, plan.

Identico [ee-den'tee-koh] *a.* identical.

Identificare [ee-den-tee-fee-kah'ray] *vt.* to identify.

Identificazione [ee-den-tee-fee-kah-tsee-oh'nay] *nf.* identification.

Identità [ee-den-tee-tah'] *nf.* identity.

Idillio [ee-deel'lee-oh] *nm.* idyll.

Idioma [ee-dee-oh'mah] *nm. (poet.)* language.

Idiosincrasia [ee-dee-oh-zeen-krah-tsee'ah] *nf.* idiosyncrasy.

Idiota [ee-dee-oh'tah] *nm. and f.* idiot; *a.* idiotic.

Idiotismo [ee-dee-oh-tees'moh] *nm.* idiom, idiomatic expression.

Idiozia [ee-dee-oh-tsee'ah] *nf.* idiocy.

Idolatrare [ee-doh-lah-trah'ray] *vt.* to adore, worship.

Idolatria [ee-doh-lah-tree'ah] *nf.* idolatry.

Idoleggiare [ee-doh-lay-djah'ray] *vt.* to idolise.

Idolo [ee'doh-loh] *nm.* idol.

Idoneità [ee-doh-nay-ee-tah'] *nf.* fitness, qualification.

Idoneo [ee-doh'nay-oh] *a.* fit, qualified.

Idra [ee'drah] *nf.* hydra.

Idro [ee-droh] scientific prefix, corresponding to English *hydro*.

Idrope [ee-droh'pay] *nm.* idropisia [ee-droh-pee-zee'ah] *nf. (med.)* dropsy.

Idropico [ee-droh'pee-koh] *nm.* dropsical patient; *a.* dropsical.

Iena [yay'nah] *nf.* hyena.

Ieri [ee-ay'ree] *ad.* yesterday; **i. l'altro** [lahl'troh] the day before yesterday.

Ietta/tore [yet-tah-toh'ray] *nm.* —**trice** [tree'chay] *nf.* bringer of ill-luck.

Iettatura [yet-tah-too'rah] *nf.* evil eye, misfortune.

Igiene [ee-jay'nay] *nf.* hygiene.

Igienico [ee-jay'nee-koh] *a.* [hygienic.

Ignaro [een-yah'roh] *a.* ignorant, unaware.

Ignavia [een-yah'vee-ah] *nf.* sloth.

Ignavo [een-yah'voh] *a.* slothful.

Igneo [een'yay-oh] *a.* igneous.

Ignizione [een-yee-tsee-oh'nay] *nf.* ignition.

Ignobile [een-yoh'bee-lay] *a.* ignoble.

Ignobilità [een-yoh-bee-lee-tah'] *nf.* ignobility.

Ignominia [een-yoh-mee'nee-ah] *nf.* ignominy.

Ignominioso [een-yoh-mee-nee-oh'soh] *a.* ignominious.

Ignorante [een-yoh-rahn'tay] *a.* ignorant, rude.

Ignoranza [een-yoh-rahnt'zah] *nf.* ignorance, rudeness.

Ignorare [een-yoh-rah'ray] *vt.* to be ignorant of, ignore.

Ignoto [een-yoh'toh] *nm. and a.* unknown.

Ignudo [een-yoo'doh] *a.* naked, unclothed.

Il [eel] *art. m.* the.

Ilare [ee'lah-ray] *a.* gay, hilarious.

Ilarità [ee-lah-ree-tah'] *nf.* gaiety, hilarity.

Illanguidire [eel-lahng-gwee-dee'ray] *vi.* to droop, flag, grow weak.

Illecito [eel-lay'chee-toh] *a.* illicit, unlawful.

Illegale [eel-lay-gah'lay] *a.* illegal, unlawful.

Illegalità [eel-lay-gah-lee-tah'] *nf.* illegality.

Illeggibile [eel-lay-djee'bee-lay] *a.* illegible.

Illegittimità [eel-lay-jeet-tee-mee-tah'] *nf.* illegitimacy, unlawfulness.

Illegittimo [eel-lay-jeet'tee-moh] *a.* illegitimate, unlawful.

Illeso [eel-lay'zoh] *a.* unhurt, uninjured.

Illetterato [eel-let-tay-rah'toh] *a.* illiterate, unlettered.

Illibatezza [eel-lee-bah-tet'zah] *nf.* chastity, purity.

Illibato [eel-lee-bah'toh] *a.* chaste, pure.

Illiberale [eel-lee-bay-rah'lay] *a.* illiberal.

Illimitato [eel-lee-mee-tah'toh] *a.* boundless, unlimited.

Illividire [eel-lee-vee-dee'ray] *vi.* to grow livid.

Illogico [eel-loh'jee-koh] *a.* illogical.

Illude/re [eel-loo'day-ray] *vt.* to deceive, delude; **—rsi** *vr.* to delude oneself.

Illumina/re [eel-loo-mee-nah'ray] *vt.* to enlighten, illuminate, light; **—rsi** *vr.* to light up.

Illuminazione [eel-loo-mee-nah-tsee-oh'nay] *nf.* illumination, lighting.

Illusione [eel-loo-zee-oh'nay] *f.* delusion, illusion.

Illusorio [eel-loo-zoh'ree-oh] *a.* deceptive, illusory.

Illustrare [eel-loo-strah'ray] *vt.* to explain, illustrate, make illustrious.

Illustrazione [eel-loo-strah-tsee-oh'nay] *nf.* illustration.

Illustre [eel-loo'stray] *a.* famous, illustrious.

Imbacucca/re [eem-bah-kook-kah'ray] *vt.* to muffle up, wrap up; **—rsi** *vr.* to muffle oneself.

Imbaldanzi/re [eem-bahl-dahn-tsee'ray] *vt.* to embolden; **—rsi** *vr.* to grow bold.

Imballaggio [eem-bahl-lah'djoh] *nm.* packing, wrapping.

Imballare [eem-bahl-lah'ray] *vt.* to pack, wrap.

Imbalsamare [eem-bahl-sah-mah'ray] *vt.* to embalm, stuff (animals).

Imbandierare [eem-bahn-dee-ay-rah'ray] *vt.* to beflag.

Imbandire [eem-bahn-dee'ray] *vt.* to prepare a gala meal.

Imbarazzare [eem-bah-raht-zah'ray] vt. to embarrass, perplex.

Imbarazzo [eem-bah-raht'zoh] nm. embarassment, perplexity.; i. di stomaco [dee stoh'mah-koh] indigestion.

Imbarcadero [eem-bahr-kah-day'roh] nm. landing-place, pier.

Imbarca/re [eem-bahr-kah'ray] vt. to put (take) on board, ship; —rsi vr. to embark, take ship.

Imbarcazione [eem-bahr-kah-tsee-oh'nay] nf. boat.

Imbarco [eem-bahr'koh] nm. embarkation, loading.

Imbastire [eem-bah-stee'ray] vt. to tack in (sewing).

Imbattersi [eem-baht'tehr-see] vr. to fall in with.

Imbavagliare [eem-bah-vahl-yah'ray] vt. to gag.

Imbecille [eem-bay-cheel'lay] nm. and f. and a. imbecile.

Imbellettarsi [eem-bell-let-tahr'see] vr. to paint one's face.

Imberbe [eem-behr'bay] a. beardless.

Imbestialire [eem-bess-tee-ah-lee'ray] vi. to grow furious.

Imbeve/re [eem-bay'vay-ray] vt. to imbue, steep; —rsi vr. to become imbued with.

Imbian/care [eem-bee-ahng-kah'ray], —chire [kee'ray] vt. to bleach, whiten, whitewash; —rsi vr. to turn white.

Imbianchino [eem-bee-ahng-kee'noh] nm. house-painter.

Imbizzarri/re [eem-beed-zahr-ree'ray] vi. —rsi vr. to grow furious, spirited (of horses).

Imboccare [eem-bock-kah'ray] vt. to enter (a street, etc.), feed, prompt; vi. to flow into.

Imbocco [eem-bock'koh] nm. entrance, mouth (of a river).

Imbosca/re [eem-boss-kah'ray] vi.—rsi vr. to hide, lie in wait.

Imboscata [eem-boss-kah'tah] nm. ambush.

Imbottigliare [eem-bot-teel-yah'ray] vt. to bottle.

Imbottire [eem-bot-tee'ray] vt. to pad, stuff.

Imbrattare [eem-braht-tah'ray] vt. to daub, dirty.

Imbrigliare [eem-breel-yah'ray] vt. to bridle, curb.

Imbroccare [eem-brock-kah'ray] vt. to guess right, hit the mark.

Imbroglia/re [eem-brohl-yah'ray] vt. to cheat, confuse, entangle, swindle; —rsi vr. to get confused.

Imbroglio [eem-brohl'yoh] nm. mess, tangle, trick.

Imbroglione [eem-brohl-yoh'nay] nm. cheat, swindler.

Imbronciare [eem-bron-chah'ray] vi. to be offended, sulk.

Imbru/nare [eem-broo-nah'ray], —nire [nee'ray] vi. to darken, grow dark.

Imbrutire: v. abbrutire.

Imbruttire [eem-broot-tee'ray] vt. to disfigure, make ugly; vi. to grow ugly.

Imbuca/re [eem-boo-kah'ray] vt. to post, put into a hole; —rsi vr. to creep into a hole.

Imburrare [eem-boor-rah'ray] vt. to butter, flatter.

Imbuto [eem-boo'toh] nm. funnel.

Imeneo [ee-may-nay'oh] nm. marriage. v. Matrimonio.

Imitare [ee-mee-tah'ray] vt. to copy, imitate, mimic.

Imitazione [ee-mee-tah-tsee-oh'nay] nf. copy, imitation, mimicry.

Immacolato [eem-mah-koh-lah'toh] a. immaculate, spotless.

Immagazzinare [eem-mah-gahd-zee-nah'ray] *vt.* to store up, warehouse.

Immagina/re [eem-mah-jee-nah'ray] *vt.* to devise, fancy, imagine; —**rsi** *vr.* to fancy, imagine, picture.

Immaginazione [eem-mah-jee-nah-tsee-oh'nay] *nf.* fancy, imagination.

Immagine [eem-mah'jee-nay] *nf.* image, picture.

Immane [eem-mah'nay] *a.* cruel, enormous, huge.

Immangiabile [eem-mahn-jah'bee-lay] *a.* uneatable.

Immantinente [eem-mahn-tee-nen'tay] *ad.* at once, immediately.

Immaturità [eem-mah-too-ree-tah'] *nf.* immaturity, unripeness.

Immaturo [eem-mah-too'roh] *a.* immature, unripe.

Immediato [eem-may-dee-ah'toh] *a.* immediate.

Immelmarsi [eem-mell-mah'see] *vr.* to get muddy.

Immemorabile [eem-may-moh-rah'bee-lay] *a.* immemorial.

Immemore [eem-may'moh-ray] *a.* forgetful, unmindful.

Immensità [eem-men-see-tah'] *nf.* immensity.

Immenso [eem-men'soh] *a.* immense, vast.

Immensurabile [eem-men-soo-rah'bee-lay] *a.* immeasureable.

Immerge/re [eem-mehr'jay-ray] *vt.* to dip, immerse, soak; —**rsi** *vr.* to immerse oneself, plunge.

Immersione [eem-mehr-see-oh'nay] *nf.* immersion.

Immigrante [eem-mee-grahn'tay] *nm. and f. and a.* immigrant.

Immigrare [eem-mee-grah'ray] *vi.* to immigrate.

Immigrazione [eem-mee-grah-tsee-oh'nay] *nf.* immigration.

Imminente [eem-mee-nen'tay] *a.* imminent, impending.

Imminenza [eem-mee-nent'zah] *nf.* imminence.

Immischia/re [eem-mees-kee-ah'ray] *vt.* to bring into, involve; —**rsi** *vr.* to interfere, meddle.

Immiserire [eem-mee-zay-ree'ray] *vt.* to impoverish; *vi.* to grow poor.

Immobile [eem-moh'bee-lay] *a.* immovable, motionless.

Immobilizzare [eem-moh-bee-leed-zah'ray] *vt.* to immobilise.

Immobilizzazione [eem-moh-bee-leed-zah-tsee-oh'nay] *nf.* immobilisation.

Immodestia [eem-moh-dess'tee-ah] *nf.* immodesty.

Immodesto [eem-moh-dess'toh] *a.* immodest.

Immolare [eem-moh-lah'ray] *vt.* to immolate, sacrifice.

Immolazione [eem-moh-lah-tsee-oh'nay] *nf.* immolation.

Immolla/re [eem-moll-lah'ray] *vt.* to wet; —**rsi** *vr.* to get wet.

Immondezza [eem-mon-det'zah] *nf.* uncleanness.

Immondizia [eem-mon-dee'tsee-ah] *nf.* garbage, sweepings (*pl.*).

Immondo [eem-mon'doh] *a.* impure, unclean.

Immorale [eem-moh-rah'lay] *a.* immoral.

Immoralità [eem-moh-rah-lee-tah'] *nf.* immorality.

Immortalare [eem-morr-tah-lah'ray] *vt.* to immortalise.

Immortale [eem-morr-tah'lay] *a.* immortal.

Immortalità [eem-morr-tah-lee-tah'] *nf.* immortality.

Immune [eem-moo'nay] a. exempt, free, immune.

Immunità [eem-moo-nee-tah'] nf. exemption, immunity.

Immutabile [eem-moo-tah'bee-lay] a. invariable, unalterable, unchanging.

Impacchettare [eem-pahk-ket-tah'ray] vt. to make up packets, pack.

Impaccia/re [eem-pahch-chah'ray] vt. to be in the way, embarass, encumber; —rsi vr. to meddle.

Impacciato [eem-pahch-chah'toh] a. awkward, embarassed.

Impaccio [eem-pahch'choh] nm. difficulty, encumbrance, obstacle.

Impadronirsi [eem-pah-droh-neer'see] vr. to master, seize, take possession of.

Impagabile [eem-pah-gah'bee-lay] a. extraordinary, invaluable.

Impaginare [eem-pah-jee-nah'ray] vt. (typ.) to make up (a book), page.

Impagliare [eem-pahl-yah'ray] vt. to cover with straw.

Impalcare [eem-pahl-kah'ray] vt. to board, plank.

Impalcatura [eem-pahl-kah-too'rah] nf. scaffolding.

Impallidire [eem-pahl-lee-dee'ray] vi. to turn pale.

Impalpabile [eem-pahl-pah'bee-lay] a. impalpable.

Impaluda/re [eem-pah-loo-dah'ray] vi. —rsi vr. to grow marshy.

Impancarsi [eem-pahng-kahr'see] vr. to presume, try.

Impappina/re [eem-pahp-pee-nah'ray] vt. to confuse, puzzle; —rsi vr. to become confused.

Imparare [eem-pah-rah'ray] vt. to learn.

Imparaticcio [eem-pah-rah-teech'choh] nm. amateur work.

Impareggiabile [eem-pah-ray-djah'bee-lay] a. incomparable.

Imparentarsi [eem-pah-ren-tahr'see] vr. to ally oneself by marriage, marry into.

Impari [eem'pah-ree] a. inadequate, odd, uneven.

Imparità [eem-pah-ree-tah'] nf. inequality, unevenness.

Imparruccarsi [eem-pahr-rook-kahr'see] vr. to put on a wig.

Impartire [eem-pahr-tee'ray] vt. to bestow, impart.

Imparziale [eem-pahr-tsee-ah'lay] a. impartial, unbiassed.

Impassibile [eem-pahs-see'bee-lay] a. impassible, impassive.

Impastare [eem-pah-stah'ray] vt. to knead, mix.

Impasto [eem-pah'stoh] nm. mixture.

Impastoiarsi [eem-pah-stoh-yahr'see] vr. to lose one's way (fig.).

Impauri/re [eem-pow-ree'ray] vt. to frighten, terrify; —rsi vr. to get frightened.

Impazientarsi [eem-pah-tsee-en-tahr'see] vr. to grow impatient.

Impaziente [eem-pah-tsee-en'tay] a. impatient.

Impazienza [eem-pah-tsee-ent'zah] nf. impatience.

Impazza/re [eem-paht-zah'ray], —zire [zee'ray] vi. to be crazy about, go mad.

Impeccabile [eem-peck-kah'bee-lay] a. impeccable.

Impeciare [eem-pay-chah'ray] vt. to pitch.

Impedimento [eem-pay-dee-men'toh] nm. hindrance, impediment, obstacle.

Impedire [eem-pay-dee'ray] vt. to hinder, obstruct, prevent.

Impegna/re [eem-payn-yah'ray] *vt.* to bind, engage, pledge; —**rsi** *vr.* to bind, engage oneself.

Impegno [eem-payn'yoh] *nm.* engagement, obligation.

Impellente [eem-pell-len'tay] *a.* driving.

Impenetrabile [eem-pay-nay-trah'bee-lay] *a.* impenetrable, inscrutable.

Impenitente [eem-pay-nee-ten'tay] *a.* impenitent.

Impenitenza [eem-pay-nee-tent'zah] *nf.* impenitence.

Impensabile [eem-pen-sah'bee-lay] *a.* inconceivable, unthinkable.

Impensieri/re [eem-pen-see-ay-ree'ray] *vt.* to make uneasy; —**rsi** *vr.* to grow uneasy.

Imperante [eem-pay-rahn'tay] *a.* ruling.

Imperare [eem-pay-rah'ray] *vi.* to rule (over).

Imperativo [eem-pay-rah-tee'voh] *nm. and a.* imperative.

Impera/tore [eem-pay-rah-toh'ray] *nm.* emperor; —**trice** [tree'chay] *nf.* empress.

Impercettibile [eem-pehr-chet-tee'bee-lay] *a.* imperceptible.

Imperdonabile [eem-pehr-doh-nah'bee-lay] *a.* unpardonable.

Imperfetto [eem-pehr-fet'toh] *nm.* (*gram.*) imperfect; *a.* imperfect, unfinished.

Imperfezione [eem-pehr-fay-tsee-oh'nay] *nf.* fault, flaw, imperfection.

Imperiale [eem-pay-ree-ah'lay] *a.* imperial.

Imperialismo [eem-pay-ree-ah-lees'moh] *nm.* imperialism.

Imperiosità [eem-pay-ree-oh-see-tah'] *nf.* imperiousness.

Imperioso [eem-pay-ree-oh'soh] *a.* domineering, imperious.

Imperizia [eem-pay-ree'tsee-ah] *nf.* lack of experience, lack of skill.

Impermalirsi [eem-pehr-mah-leer'see] *vr.* to get cross.

Impermeabile [eem-pehr-may-ah'bee-lay] *nm.* mackintosh; *a.* waterproof.

Impermeabilità [eem-pehr-may-ah-bee-lee-tah'] *nf.* impermeability.

Imperniare [eem-pehr-nee-ah'ray] *vt.* to hinge, pivot.

Impero [eem-pay'roh] *nm.* command, empire.

Impersonale [eem-pehr-soh-nah'lay] *a.* impersonal.

Imperterrito [eem-pehr-tehr'ree-toh] *a.* intrepid, unflinching.

Impertinente [eem-pehr-tee-nen'tay] *a.* impertinent, saucy.

Impertinenza [eem-pehr-tee-nent'zah] *nf.* impertinence.

Imperturbabile [eem-pehr-toor-bah'bee-lay] *a.* imperturbable.

Imperversare [eem-pehr-vehr-sah'ray] *vi.* to rage (of diseases, weather, etc.).

Impervio [eem-pehr'vee-oh] *a.* hard to reach, pathless.

Impeto [eem'pay-toh] *nm.* impetus, impetuousness, vehemence.

Impetrare [eem-pay-trah'ray] *vt.* to entreat; *vi.* to turn to stone.

Impetuoso [eem-pay-too-oh'soh] *a.* boisterous, impetuous, vehement.

Impiantare [eem-pee-ahn-tah'ray] *vt.* to establish, set up.

Impiantito [eem-pee-ahn-tee'toh] *nm.* floor.

Impianto [eem-pee-ahn'toh] *nm.* establishment, installation, plant (machinery).

Impiastrare [eem-pee-ah-strah'ray] *vt.* to daub, plaster, smear.

Impiastro [eem-pee-ah'stroh] *nm.* plaster. *(fig.)* bore.

Impiccagione [eem-peek-kah-joh'nay] *nf.* hanging (on the gallows).

Impicca/re, etc.: *v.* **Impacciare**, etc.

Impiccolire [eem-peek-koh-lee'ray] *vt.* to diminish, dwarf, lessen.

Impiega/re [eem-pee-ay-gah'ray] *vt.* to employ, spend, invest; —rsi *vr.* to get a post.

Impiegato [eem-pee-ay-gah'toh] *nm.* clerk, employee.

Impiego [eem-pee-ay'goh] *nm.* employment, job, position, use.

Impietosi/re [eem-pee-ay-toh-see'ray] *vt.* to move to pity; —rsi *vr.* to be touched.

Impietri/re [eem-pee-ay-tree'ray] *vi.* —rsi *vr.* to turn to stone.

Impigliare [eem-peel-yah'ray] *vt.* to entangle.

Impigrire [eem-pee-gree'ray] *vt. and i.* to make (grow) lazy.

Impingua/re [eem-peeng-gwah'ray] *vt.* to fatten; —rsi *vr.* to grow fat.

Impiombare [eem-pee-ombah'ray] *vt.* to cover with lead, stop (a tooth).

Impiombatura [eem-pee-om-bah-too'rah] *nf.* covering with lead, stopping (a tooth).

Impiumare [eem-pee-oomah'ray] *vi.* to grow feathers.

Implacabile [eem-plah-kah'bee-lay] *a.* implacable, relentless.

Implicare [eem-plee-kah'ray] *vt.* to implicate, imply, involve.

Implicazione [eem-plee-kah-tsee-oh'nay] *nf.* implication.

Implicito [eem-plee'chee-toh] *a.* implicit.

Implorare [eem-ploh-rah'ray] *vt.* to entreat, implore.

Impolitico [eem-poh-lee'tee-koh] *a.* impolitic.

Impoltronire [eem-poll-troh-nee'ray] *vt. and i.* to make (grow) lazy.

Impolverare [eem-poll-vay-rah'ray] *vt.* to cover with dust.

Imponente [eem-poh-nen'tay] *a.* imposing, impressive.

Imponenza [eem-poh-nent'zah] *nf.* impressiveness.

Imponibile [eem-poh-nee'bee-lay] *a.* chargeable, taxable.

Impopolare [eem-poh-poh-lah'ray] *a.* unpopular.

Impopolarità [eem-poh-poh-lah-ree-tah'] *nf.* unpopularity.

Impor/re [eem-porr'ray] *vt.* to impose; —rsi *vr.* to impose, impress, make oneself respected.

Importante [eem-porr-tan'tay] *nm.* main point; *a.* important, weighty.

Importanza [eem-porr-tahnt'zah] *nf.* importance.

Importare [eem-porr-tah'ray] *vt.* to import; *v. imp.* to be important, matter.

Importazione [eem-porr-tah-tsee-oh'nay] *nf.* import, importation.

Importo [eem-porr'toh] *nm.* amount.

Importunare [eem-porr-too-nah'ray] *vt.* to importune, tease.

Importunità [eem-porr-too-nee-tah'] *nf.* importunity.

Importuno [eem-porr-too'noh] *a.* importune, teasing.

Impossessarsi [eem-poss-sess-sahr'see] *vr.* to take possession of.

Impossibile [eem-poss-see'-bee-lay] *a.* impossible.
Impossibilità [eem-poss-see-bee-lee-tah'] *nf.* impossibility.
Imposta [eem-poss'stah] *nf.* shutter.
Imposta [eem-poh'stah] *nf.* duty, tax.
Impostare [eem-poh-stah'ray] *vt.* to set out (a problem), mail, post.
Impostazione [eem-poh-stah-tsee-oh'nay] *nf.* mailing, posting.
Impostore [eem-poh-stoh'ray] *nm.* impostor, swindler.
Impostura [eem-poh-stoo'rah] *nf.* imposture, swindle.
Impotente [eem-poh-ten'tay] *a.* impotent, powerless.
Impotenza [eem-poh-tent'zah] *nf.* impotence, powerlessness.
Inpoverimento [eem-poh-vay-ree-men'toh] *nm.* impoverishment.
Impoveri/re [eem-poh-vay-ree'ray] *vt.* to impoverish; —rsi *vr.* to grow poor.
Impraticabile [eem-prah-tee-kah-bee-lay] *a.* impracticable, not feasible.
Impratichirsi [eem-prah-tee-keer'see] *vr.* to gain practice.
Imprecare [eem-pray-kah'ray] *vt.* to curse, imprecate.
Imprecazione [eem-pray-kah-tsee-oh'nay] *nf.* imprecation.
Impregnare [eem-prayn-yah'ray] *vt.* to impregnate.
Impremeditato [eem-pray-may-dee-tah'toh] *a.* unpremeditated.
Imprendere [eem-pren'day-ray] *vt.* to begin, undertake.
Impresa [eem-pray'sah] *nf.* enterprise, undertaking.
Impresario [eem-pray-sah'-

ree-oh] *nm.* contractor impresario, undertaker.
Impressionabile [eem-press-see-oh-nah'bee-lay] *a.* impressionable.
Impressionante [eem-press-see-oh-nahn'tay] *a.* alarming, terrifying.
Impressiona/re [eem-press-see-oh-nah'ray] *vt.* to alarm, impress; —rsi *vr.* to be frightened.
Impressione [eem-press-see-oh'nay] *nf.* alarm, impression. **[tare**, etc.
Imprestare, etc.: *v.* imprestare.
Imprevedibile [eem-pray-vay-dee'bee-lay] *a.* not to be foreseen.
Imprevidente [eem-pray-vee-den'tay] *a.* improvident.
Imprevidenza [eem-pray-vee-dent'zah] *nf.* improvidence.
Imprevisto [eem-pray-vee'stoh] *nm.* something unexpected; *a.* unexpected, unforeseen.
Imprigionare [eem-pree-joh-nah'ray] *vt.* to imprison.
Imprimere [eem-pree'may-ray] *vt.* to engrave, impress, stamp.
Improbabile [eem-proh-bah'bee-lay] *a.* improbable, unlikely.
Improbabilità [eem-proh-bah-bee-lee-tah'] *nf.* improbability, unlikelihood.
Improbità [eem-proh-bee-tah'] *nf.* dishonesty.
Improbo [eem'proh-boh] *a.* dishonest.
Improduttività [eem-proh-doot-tee-vee-tah'] *nf.* unproductiveness.
Improduttivo [eem-proh-doot-tee'voh] *a.* unproductive.
Impronta [eem-pron'tah] *nf.* impression, mark, print, stamp.

Improperio [eem-proh-pay'-ree-oh] *nm.* abuse, abusive word.

Improprietà [eem-proh-pree-ay-tah'] *nf.* impropriety, inaccuracy.

Improprio [eem-proh'pree-oh] *a.* improper, inaccurate.

Improv(v)ido [eem-proh(v)'vee-doh] *a.* improvident, rash.

Improvvisare [eem-prov-vee-zah'ray] *vt.* to extemporise, improvise.

Improvvisata [eem-prov-vee-zah'tah] *nf.* surprise.

Improvvisa/tore [eem-prov-vee-zah-toh'ray] *nm.—* **trice** [tree'chay] *nf.* extemporiser, improviser.

Improvviso [eem-prov-vee'zoh] *a.* sudden, unexpected, unforeseen; **all'i.** [ahl] *ad.* suddenly.

Imprudente [eem-proo-den'tay] *a.* imprudent, rash.

Imprudenza [eem-proo-dent'zah] *nf.* imprudence, rashness.

Impudente [eem-poo-den'tay] *a.* impudent, shameless.

Impudenza [eem-poo-dent'zah] *nf.* impudence, shamelessness.

Impudicizia [eem-poo-dee-chee'tsee-ah] *nf.* lewdness, unchastity.

Impudico [eem-poo-dee'koh] *a.* lewd, unchaste.

Impugnare [eem-poon-yah'ray] *vt.* to attack, grip, impugn.

Impugnatura [eem-poon-yah-too'rah] *nf.* grip, hold.

Impulsione [eem-pool-see-oh'nay] *nf.* impulsion.

Impulsivo [eem-pool-see'voh] *a.* impulsive.

Impulso [eem-pool'soh] *nm.* impetus, impulse.

Impune [eem-poo'nay], **im-punito** [eem-poo-nee'toh] *a.* unpunished.

Impunità [eem-poo-nee-tah'] *nf.* impunity.

Impuntarsi [eem-poon-tahr'see] *vr.* to be stubborn.

Impurità [eem-poo-ree-tah'] *nf.* impurity.

Impuro [eem-poo'roh] *a.* impure.

Imputabile [eem-poo-tah'bee-lay] *a.* imputable.

Imputare [eem-poo-tah'ray] *vt.* to accuse, charge, impute.

Imputato [eem-poo-tah'toh] *nm.* accused, criminal; *a.* charged, imputed.

Imputazione [eem-poo-tah-tsee-oh'nay] *nf.* accusation, charge.

Imputridire [eem-poo-tree-dee'ray] *vi.* to putrefy, rot.

In [een] *pr.* in, into, on, to.

In- [een], negative prefix, corresponding usually to English *dis-, im-, in-, un-*.

Inabile [een-ah'bee-lay] *a.* incapable, unable, unfit.

Inabilità [een-ah-bee-lee-tah'] *nf.* inability, unfitness.

Inabilitazione [een-ah-bee-lee-tah-tsee-oh'nay] *nf.* disability, disqualification.

Inabissarsi [een-ah-bees-sahr'see] *vr.* to sink.

Inabitabile [een-ah-bee-tah'bee-lay] *a.* uninhabitable.

Inabitato [een-ah-bee-tah'toh] *a.* uninhabited.

Inaccessibile [een-ahch-chess-see'bee-lay] *a.* inaccessible.

Inaccettabile [een-ahch-chet-tah'bee-lay] *a.* unacceptable.

Inacerbire [een-ah-chehr-bee'ray] *vt.* to embitter.

Inadattabile [een-ah-daht-tah'bee-lay] *a.* unadaptable.

Inadatto [een-ah-daht'toh] *a.* improper, unfit, unqualified.

Inadeguato [een-ah-day-gwah'toh] *a.* inadequate, unfit.

Inadempimento [een-ah-dem-pee-men'toh] *nm.* non-performance, unfulfilment.

Inalbera/re [een-ahl-bay-rah'ray] *vt.* to hoist, raise; —**rsi** *vr.* to get angry.

Inalienabile [een-ah-lee-ay-nah'bee-lay] *a.* inalienable.

Inalterabile [een-ahl-tay-rah'bee-lay] *a.* unalterable.

Inamidare [een-ah-mee-dah'ray] *vt.* to starch.

Inammissibile [een-ahm-mees-see'bee-lay] *a.* inadmissible.

Inamovibile [een-ah-moh-vee'bee-lay] *a.* irremovable.

Inanimato [een-ah-nee-mah'toh] *a.* inanimate.

Inane [een-ah'nay] *a.* inane, vain.

Inanità [een-ah-nee-tah'] *nf.* inanity, vanity.

Inaridire [een-ah-ree-dee'ray] *vi.* to become arid, grow dry.

Inarrivabile [een-ahr-ree-vah'bee-lay] *a.* inimitable, unattainable.

Inarticolato [een-ahr-tee-koh-lah'toh] *a.* inarticulate.

Inaspettato [een-ah-spet-tah'toh] *a.* sudden, unexpected.

Inasprimento [een-ah-spree-men'toh] *nm.* embitterment, exacerbation.

Inaspri/re [een-ah-spree'ray] *vt.* to embitter, exacerbate; —**rsi** *vr.* to be embittered.

Inattaccabile [een-aht-tahk-kah'bee-lay] *a.* unassailable.

Inatteso [een-aht-tay'soh] *a.* unexpected.

Inattitudine [een-aht-tee-too'dee-nay] *nf.* inability, inaptitude. *(rare).* v. **Inabilità**.

Inattività [een-aht-tee-vee-tah'] *nf.* inactivity.

Inattivo [een-aht-tee'voh] *a.* inactive.

Inatto [een-aht'toh] *a.* unapt, unfit. *v.* Disadatto.

Inattuabile [een-aht-too-ah'bee-lay] *a.* impracticable, unreasonable.

Inaudito [een-ow-dee'toh] *a.* unheard-of.

Inaugurare [een-ow-goo-rah'ray] *vt.* to inaugurate, open.

Inaugurazione [een-ow-goo-rah-tsee-oh'nay] *nf.* inauguration, opening.

Inavvertenza [een-ahv-vehr-tent'zah] *nf.* inadvertence.

Inavvertito [een-ahv-vehr-tee'toh] *a.* uninformed, unobserved, unwarned.

Inazione [een-ah-tsee-oh'nay] *nf.* inaction.

Incagliarsi [een-kahl-yahr'see] *vr.* (naut.) to run aground.

Incalcolabile [een-kahl-koh-lah'bee-lay] *a.* incalculable.

Incallire [een-kahl-lee'ray] *vi.* to grow callous, harden.

Incalorire [een-kah-loh-ree'ray] *vt.* to heat.

Incalvire [een-kahl-vee'ray] *vi* to grow bald.

Incalzare [een-kahlt-zah'ray] *vt.* to chase, press, pursue.

Incammina/re [een-kahm-mee-nah'ray] *vt.* to set going, start; —**rsi** *vr.* to set out.

Incandescente [een-kahn-day-shen'tay] *a.* incandescent.

Incandescenza [een-kahn-day-shent'zah] *nf.* incandescence.

Incanta/re [een-kahn-tah'ray] *vt.* to charm, enchant; —**rsi** *vr.* to be enraptured, stop.

Incantesimo [een-kahn-tay'zee-moh] *nm.* charm, enchantment.

Incantevole [een-kahn-tay'voh-lay] *a.* enchanting.

Incanto [een-kahn'toh] *nm.* charm, enchantment, (*com.*) public sale; all' [ahl]ĩ *ad.* by auction.

Incantutire [een-kah-noo-tee'ray] *vi.* to grow grey.

Incapace [een-kah-pah'chay] *a.* incapable, unable.

Incapacità [een-kah-pah-chee-tah'] *nf.* incapacity.

Incarcerare [een-kahr-chay-rah'ray] *vt.* to imprison.

Incarica/re [een-kah-ree-kah'ray] *vt.* to charge, entrust; —rsi *vr.* to take upon oneself.

Incaricato [een-kah-ree-kah' toh] *nm.* agent, chargé d'affaires.

Incarico [een-kah-ree-koh]*nm.* appointment, commission, task.

Incarnare [een-kahr-nah' ray] *vt.* to embody, incarnate.

Incarnazione [een-kahr-nah-tsee-oh'nay] *nf.* embodiment, incarnation.

Incartamento [een-kahr-tah-men'toh] *nm.* correspondence, documents (*pl.*).

Incartare [een-kahr-tah-ray] *vt.* to wrap in paper.

Incassare [een-kahs-sah'ray] *vt.* to box, cash, embank, set.

Incasso [een-kahs'soh] *nm.* receipt, takings (*pl.*).

Incastonare [een-kah-stoh-nah'ray] *vt.* to set (jewels).

Incatenare [een-kah-tay-nah'ray] *vt.* to chain, fetter.

Incatenazione [een-kah-tay-nah-tsee-oh'nay] *nf.* chaining.

Incauto [een-kow'toh] *a.* incautious, rash.

Incavallare [een-kah-vahl-lah'ray] *vt.* to cross.

Incavare [een-kah-vah'ray] *vt.* to excavate, hollow.

Incavo [een-kah'voh] *nm.* cavity, hollow.

Incendia/re [een-chen-dee-ah'ray] *vt.* to set on fire; —rsi *vr.* to catch fire.

Incendiario [een-chen-dee-ah'ree-oh] *a.* incendiary.

Incendio [een-chen'dee-oh] *nm.* conflagration, fire.

Incenerire [een-chay-nay-ree'ray] *vt.* and *i.* to reduce (burn) to ashes.

Incensare [een-chen-sah'ray] *vt.* to incense, praise.

Incenso [een-chen'soh] *nm.* incense.

Incensurabile [een-chen-soo-rah'bee-lay] *a.* irreproachable.

Incentivo [een-chen-tee'voh] *nm.* and *a.* incentive.

Inceppare [een-chep-pah' ray] *vt.* to clog, jam.

Incerare [een-chay-rah'ray] *vt.* to (coat with) wax.

Incertezza [een-chehr-tet' zah] *nf.* irresolution, uncertainty.

Incerto [een-chehr'toh] *nm.* uncertainty; incerti (*pl.*) extra profit; *a.* doubtful, irresolute, uncertain.

Incessante [een-chess-sahn' tay] *a.* incessant, unceasing.

Incesto [een-chess'toh] *nm.* incest.

Incestuoso [een-chess-too-oh'soh] *a.* incestuous.

Incettare [een-chet-tah'ray] *vt.* (*com.*) to buy up, corner.

Inchiesta [een-kee-ess'tah] *nf.* inquest, inquiry.

Inchina/re [een-kee-nah'ray] *vt.* to bend, lower; —rsi *vr.* to bow, stoop.

Inchino [een-kee'noh] *nm.* bow, reverence.

Inchiodare [een-kee-oh-dah' ray] *vt.* to nail, rivet.

Inchiostro [een-kee-oss'troh] *nm.* ink.

Inciampare [een-chahm-pah' ray] *vi.* to meet with, stumble.

Inciampo [een-chahm'poh] *nm.* difficulty, stumbling-block.

Incidentale [een-chee-den-tah'lay] a. accidental, casual, incidental.

Incidente [een-chee-den'tay] nm. accident, incident.

Incidenza [een-chee-dent'zah] nf. incidence.

Incidere [een-chee-day-ray] vt. to engrave, incise.

Incinta [een-cheen'tah] a. (f.) pregnant.

Incipiente [een-chee-pee-en'tay] a. incipient.

Incipriare [een-chee-pree-ah'ray] vt. to powder.

Incisione [een-chee-zee-oh'nay] nf. incision, engraving, print.

Incisivo [een-chee-zee'voh] a. incisive.

Inciso [een-chee'zoh] nm. digression, parenthesis.

Incisore [een-chee-zoh'ray] nm. engraver, etcher.

Incitamento [een-chee-tah-men'toh] nm. incitement, instigation.

Incitare [een-chee-tah'ray] vt. to incite, spur, urge.

Incivile [een-chee-vee'lay] a. uncivil, uncivilised.

Incivilimento [een-chee-vee-lee-men'toh] nm. civilisation, refining.

Incivili/re [een-chee-vee-lee'ray] vt. to civilise, refine; —rsi vr. to become civilised, polite.

Inciviltà [een-chee-veel-tah'] nf. incivility.

Inclemente [een-klay-men'tay] a. inclement.

Inclemenza [een-klay-ment'zah] nf. inclemency.

Inclina/re [een-klee-nah'ray] vt. to bend, incline; vi. —rsi vr. to incline, lean, slope.

Inclinazione [een-klee-nah-tsee-oh'nay] nf. disposition, propensity, inclination, tendency.

Inclito [een'klee-toh] a. famous, illustrious.

Includere [een-kloo'day-ray] vt. to contain, comprise, include.

Inclusione [een-kloo-zee-oh'nay] nf. inclusion.

Inclusivo [een-kloo-zee'voh] a. inclusive.

Incoerente [een-koh-ay-ren'tay] a. incoherent.

Incoerenza [een-koh-ay-rent'zah] nf. incoherence.

Incognito [een-kohn'yee-toh] a. unknown.

Incollerirsi: v. adirarsi.

Incolpare [een-koll-pah'ray] vt. to accuse, inculpate.

Incolpevole [een-koll-pay'voh-lay] a. blameless, irreproachable.

Incolto [een-koll'toh] a. uncultivated, unkempt.

Incolume [een-koh'loo-may] a. safe, untouched.

Incolumità [een-koh-loo-mee-tah'] nf. safety.

Incombente [een-kom-ben'tay] a. impending.

Incombere [een-kom'bay-ray] vi. to impend.

Incominciare [een-koh-meen-chah'ray] vt. and i. to begin, commence.

Incomodare [een-koh-moh-dah'ray] vt. to inconvenience, disturb.

Incomodità [een-koh-moh-dee-tah'] nf. discomfort, inconvenience.

Incomodo [een-koh'moh-doh] nm. annoyance, disturbance; a. inconvenient, uncomfortable.

Incomparabile [een-kom-pah-rah'bee-lay] a. incomparable, matchless.

Incompatibile [een-kom-pah-tee'bee-lay] a. incompatible.

Incompetente [een-kom-pay-ten'tay] *a.* incompetent, unqualified.

Incompetenza [een-kom-pay-tent'zah] *nf.* incompetence, lack of qualifications.

Incompiuto [een-kom-pyoo'toh] *a.* unfinished.

Incompleto [een-kom-play'toh] *a.* incomplete.

Incomprensibile [een-kom-pren-see'bee-lay] *a.* incomprehensible.

Inconcepibile [een-kon-chay-pee'bee-lay] *a.* inconceivable.

Inconcludente [een-kong-kloo-den'tay] *a.* inconclusive.

Inconcluso [een-kong-kloo'zoh] *a.* unfinished.

Incongruente [een-kong-groo-en'tay] *a.* incongruous.

Incongruenza [een-kong-groo-ent'zah] *nf.* incongruency.

Incongruo [een-kong'groo-oh] *a.* inadequate.

Inconsapevole [een-kon-sah-pay'voh-lay] *a.* ignorant, unaware, unconscious.

Inconsapevolezza [een-kon-sah-pay-voh-let'zah] *nf.* ignorance, unawareness.

Inconscio [een-kon'shoh] *a.* unconscious.

Inconseguente [een-kon-say-gwen'tay] *a.* inconsequent.

Inconseguenza [een-kon-say-gwent'zah] *nf.* inconsequence.

Inconsideratezza [een-kon-see-day-rah-tet'zah] *nf.* inconsiderateness.

Inconsiderato [een-kon-see-day-rah'toh] *a.* inconsiderate, rash.

Inconsistente [een-kon-sees-ten'tay] *a.* inconsistent.

Inconsolabile [een-kon-soh-lah'bee-lay] *a.* inconsolable.

Inconsueto [een-kon-soo-ay'toh] *a.* unusual.

Incontentabile [een-kon-

ten-tah'bee-lay] *a.* exacting, insatiable.

Incontentabilità [een-kon-ten-tah-bee-lee-tah'] *nf.* insatiability.

Incontestabile [een-kon-tess-tah'bee-lay] *a.* indisputable, unquestionable.

Incontinente [een-kon-tee-nen'tay] *a.* incontinent.

Incontinenza [een-kon-tee-nent'zah] *nf.* incontinence.

Incontra/re [een-kon-traht'ray] *vt.* to come across, encounter, fall in with, meet; —rsi *vr.* meet.

Incontro [een-kon'troh] *nm.* encounter, meeting; *vr.* against, towards.

Inconveniente [een-kon-vay-nee-en'tay] *a.* inconvenient, unseemly.

Inconvenienza [een-kon-vay-nee-ent'zah] *nf.* inconvenience.

Inconvertibile [een-kon-vehr-tee'bee-lay] *a.* inconvertible.

Incoraggiamento [een-koh-rah-djah-men'toh] *nm.* encouragement.

Incoraggiare [een-koh-rah-djah'ray] *vt.* to animate, cheer, encourage.

Incorniciare [een-korr-nee-chah'ray] *vt.* to frame.

Incoronare [een-koh-roh-nah'ray] *vt.* to crown, wreathe.

Incoronazione [een-koh-roh-nah-tsee-oh'nay] *nf.* coronation.

Incorporare [een-korr-poh-rah'ray] *vt.* to embody, incorporate.

Incorruttibile [een-korr-root-tee'bee-lay] *a.* incorruptible.

Incorruzione [een-korr-roo-tsee-oh'nay] *nf.* incorruption.

Incostante [een-koh-stahn'tay] *a.* changeable, inconstant.

Incostanza [een-koh-stahnt'-zah] *nf.* inconstancy.

Incostituzionale [een-koh-stee-too-tsee-oh-nah'lay] *a.* unconstitutional.

Incredibile [een-kray-dee'-bee-lay] *a.* incredible, unbelievable.

Incredulità [een-kray-doo-lee-tah'] *nf.* incredulity, unbelief.

Incredulo [een-kray'doo-loh] *a.* incredulous, unbelieving.

Incremento [een-kray-men'-toh] *nm.* increase, increment.

Increscere: *v.* **rincrescere**.

Increscioso [een-kray-shoh'-soh] *a.* unpleasant.

Increspare [een-kress-pah'-ray] *vt.* to pleat, ruffle.

Incriminare [een-kree-mee-nah'ray] *vt.* to incriminate.

Incrocia/re [een-kroh-chah'-ray] *vt. and i.* to cross, cruise; —**rsi** *vr.* to cross, pass one another.

Incrociatore [een-kroh-chah-toh'ray] *nm.* (*naut.*) cruiser.

Incrollabile [een-kroll-lah'-bee-lay] *a.* immovable, unshakable.

Incrosta/re [een-kroh-stah'-ray] *vt.* to encrust, inlay; —**rsi** *vr.* to crust.

Incrudelire [een-kroo-day-lee'ray] *vt. and i.* to make (grow) cruel.

Incrudire [een-kroo-dee'ray] *vt. and i.* to make (grow) harsh, rough.

Incruento [een-kroo-en'toh] *a.* bloodless.

Incubazione [een-koo-bah-tsee-oh'nay] *nf.* incubation.

Incubo [een'koo-boh] *nm.* incubus, nightmare.

Incudine [een-koo'dee-nay] *nf.* anvil.

Inculcare [een-kool-kah'ray] *vt.* to engraft, implant, inculcate.

Incurabile [een-koo-rah'bee-lay] *nm. and f. and a.* incurable.

Incurante [een-koo-rahn'tay] *a.* careless, indifferent, neglectful.

Incuria [een-koo'ree-ah] *nf.* carelessness, neglect.

Incuriosire [een-koo-ree-oh-see'ray] *vt.* to make curious, rouse one's curiosity.

Incursione [een-koor-see-oh'nay] *nf.* incursion, inroad; *i.* **aerea** [ah-ay'ray-ah], air raid.

Incutere [een-koo'tay-ray] *vt.* to inspire.

Indagare [een-dah-gah'ray] *vt.* to inquire, investigate.

Indagine [een-dah'jee-nay] *nf.* inquiry, investigation.

Indarno: *v.* **invano**.

Indebitarsi [een-day-bee-tahr'see] *vr.* to get into debt.

Indebito [een-day'bee-toh] *a.* undeserved, undue.

Indeboli/re [een-day-boh-lee're] *vt.* to weaken; —**rsi** *vr.* to flag, grow weak(er).

Indecente [een-day-chen'tay] *a.* indecent.

Indecenza [een-day-chent'-zah] *nf.* indecency.

Indecisione [een-day-chee-zee-oh'nay] *nf.* hesitation, indecision.

Indecoroso [een-day-koh-roh'soh] *a.* indecorous, unseemly.

Indefesso [een-day-fess'soh] *a.* indefatigable.

Indefinibile [een-day-fee-nee'bee-lay] *a.* indefinable.

Indegnità [een-dayn-yee-tah'] *nf.* shame, worthlessness.

Indegno [een-dayn'yoh] *a.* undeserving, unworthy.

Indelicatezza [een-day-lee-kah-tet'zah] *nf.* indelicacy.

Indelicato [een-day-lee-kah'toh] *a.* indelicate, tactless.

Indemoniato [een-day-moh-nee-ah'toh] a. possessed.

Indennità [een-den-nee-tah'] nf. indemnity.

Indennizzo [een-dan-need'zoh] nm. indemnity.

Indennizzare [een-den-need-zah'ray] vt. to indemnify.

Indentro [een-den'troh] ad. inwards.

Indescrivibile [een-dess-kree-vee'bee-lay] a. indescribable.

Indeterminato [een-day-tehr-mee-nah'toh] a. indefinite, indeterminate, vague.

Indi [een'dee] ad. afterwards, hence, then.

Indiano [een-dee-ah'noh] nm. and a. Indian; fare l'i. [fah'ray een—] vi. to feign ignorance.

Indiavolato [een-dee-ah-voh-lah'toh] a. furious, terrible.

Indicare [een-dee-kah'ray] vt. to indicate, point out, show.

Indicato [een-dee-kah'toh] a. suitable.

Indicatore [een-dee-kah-toh'ray] nm. gauge, indicator.

Indicazione [een-dee-kah-tsee-oh'nay] nf. indication.

Indice [een'dee-chay] nm. forefinger, index, pointer.

Indicibile [een-dee-chee'bee-lay] a. ineffable, unspeakable.

Indietreggiare [een-dee-ay-tray-djah'ray] vi. to fall back, recoil.

Indietro [een-dee-ay'troh] ad. behind.

Indifferente [een-deef-fay-ren'tay] a. immaterial, indifferent.

Indifferenza [een-deef-fay-rent'zah] nf. indifference, unconcern.

Indigeno [een-dee'jay-noh] nm. native; a. home, indigenous.

Indigente [een-dee-jen'tay] nm. and f. **pauper**; a. indigent, needy.

Indigenza [een-dee-jent'zah] nf. indigence, need.

Indigeribile [een-dee-jay-ree'bee-lay] a. indigestible.

Indigestione [een-dee-jess-tee-oh'nay] nf. indigestion, surfeit.

Indigesto [een-dee-jess'toh] a. indigestible, tiresome.

Indigna/re [een-deen-ah'ray] vt. to make indignant; —rsi vr. to grow indignant.

Indignazione [een-deen-yah-tsee-oh'nay] nf. indignation.

Indimenticabile [een-dee-men-tee-kah'bee-lay] a. unforgettable.

Indipendente [een-dee-pen-den'tay] a. independent, self-reliant.

Indipendenza [een-dee-pen-dent'zah] nf. independence.

Indire [een-dee'ray] vt. to announce, call, fix.

Indiretto [een-dee-ret'toh] a. indirect.

Indirizza/re [een-dee-reet-zah'ray] vt. to address, direct; —rsi vr. to address oneself, have recourse to.

Indirizzo [een-dee-reet'zoh] nm. address.

Indiscernibile [een-dee-shehr-nee'bee-lay] a. indiscernible.

Indisciplinato [een-dee-shee-plee-nah'toh] a. undisciplined, unruly.

Indiscreto [een-dees-kray'toh] a. impertinent, indiscreet, inquisitive.

Indiscrezione [een-dees-kray-tsee-oh'nay] nf. impertinence, indiscretion.

Indiscutibile [een-dees-koo-tee'bee-lay] a. unquestionable.

Indispensabile [een-dees-pen-sah'bee-lay] a. indispensable, necessary.

Indispetti/re [een-dees-pet-tee'ray] *vt.* to vex; —**rsi** *vr.* to be angry, vexed.

Indisporre [een-dees-porr'-ray] *vt.* to indispose, turn against.

Indisposizione [een-dees-poh-zee-tsee-oh'nay] *nf.* indisposition.

Indisposto [een-dees-poss'-toh] *a.* indisposed, unwell.

Indisputabile [een-dees-poo-tah'bee-lay] *a.* indisputable.

Indissolubile [een-dees-soh-loo'bee-lay] *a.* indissoluble.

Indistinto [een-dees-teen'-toh] *a.* faint, indistinct, vague.

Indistruttibile [een-dees-troot-tee'bee-lay] *a.* indestructible.

Individuale [een-dee-vee-doo-ah'lay] *a.* individual.

Individualità [een-dee-vee-doo-ah-lee-tah'] *nf.* individuality.

Individuare [een-dee-vee-doo-ah'ray] *vt.* to identify, pick out.

Individuo [een-dee-vee'doo-oh] *nm.* fellow, individual.

Indivisibile [een-dee-vee-zee'bee-lay] *a.* indivisible.

Indiviso [een-dee-vee'zoh] *a.* undivided, whole.

Indizio [een-dee'tsee-oh] *nm.* indication, sign.

Indole [een'doh-lay] *nf.* character, disposition, temper.

Indolente [een-doh-len'tay] *a.* indolent, lazy, listless.

Indolenza [een-doh-lent'zah] *nf.* indolence, laziness.

Indolenzi/re [een-doh-lent-zee'ray] *vt.* to benumb, cramp; —**rsi** *vr.* to ache, get benumbed.

Indomani [een-doh-mah'nee] *ad.* morrow, next day.

Indomito [een-doh'mee-toh] *a.* unconquered, untamed.

Indorare [een-doh-rah'ray] *vt.* to gild.

Indossare [een-doss-sah'ray] *vt.* to put on, wear.

Indosso: *v.* addosso.

Indovinare [een-doh-vee-nah'ray] *vt.* to divine, guess.

Indovinazione [een-doh-vee-nah-tsee-oh'nay] *nf.* divination.

Indovinello [een-doh-vee-nell'loh] *nm.* conundrum, riddle.

Indovino [een-doh-vee'noh] *nm.* diviner, soothsayer.

Indubbio [een-doob'bee-oh], **indubitabile** [een-doo-bee-tah'bee-lay] *a.* undoubted.

Indugiare [een-doo-jah'ray] *vt.* to postpone; *vi.* to be long, delay, lag, linger, loiter.

Indugio [een-doo'joh] *nm.* delay.

Indulgente [een-dool-jen'tay] *a.* indulgent.

Indulgenza [een-dool-jent'zah] *nf.* fondness, indulgence.

Indulgere [een-dool'jay-ray] *vt.* to gratify, indulge.

Indumento [een-doo-men'-toh] *nm.* garment.

Indur/re [een-door'ray] *vt.* to induce; —**rsi** *vr.* to decide, resolve.

Industria [een-doos'tree-ah] *nf.* capacity, industry, manufacture.

Industriale [een-doos-tree-ah'lay] *nm.* manufacturer; *a.* industrial, manufacturing.

Industriarsi [een-doos-tree-ahr'see] *vr.* to do one's best, live from hand to mouth.

Industrioso [een-doos-tree-oh'soh] *a.* industrious.

Inebriante [een-ay-bree-ahn'tay] *a.* inebriating, intoxicating.

Inebria/re [een-ay-bree-ah'ray] *vt.* to intoxicate, make drunk; —**rsi** *vr.* to be enraptured, get drunk.

Ineccepibile [een-ehchchay-pee'bee-lay] a. unobjectionable.

Inedia [een-ay'dee-ah] nf. inanition, starvation.

Inedito [een-ay'dee-toh] a. unpublished.

Ineffabile [een-ef-fah'bee-lay] a. ineffable.

Ineffettuabile [een-ef-fet-too-ah'bee-lay] a. unrealisable.

Inefficace [een-ef-fee-kah'chay] a. ineffective, ineffectual.

Inefficacia [een-ef-fee-kah'chah] nf. inefficacy.

Ineguaglianza [een-ay-gwahl-yahnt'zah], **inegualità** [een-ay-gwah-lee-tah'] nf. inequality.

Ineguale [een-ay-gwah'lay] a. unequal, unlike.

Inelegante [een-ay-lay-gahn'tay] a. inelegant.

Ineleggibile [een-ay-lay-jee'bee-lay] a. ineligible.

Inenarrabile [een-ay-nahr-rah'bee-lay] a. unspeakable.

Inerente [een-ay-ren'tay] a. incidental to, inherent.

Inerme [een-ehr'may] a. defenceless, unarmed.

Inerte [een-ehr'tay] a. inert, limp, lifeless, sluggish.

Inerzia [een-ehr'tsee-ah] nf. inertness, lifelessness.

Inesattezza [een-ay-zaht-tet'zah] nf. inaccuracy, inexactness.

Inesatto [een-ay-zaht'toh] a. inaccurate, inexact.

Inesaudito [een-ay-zow-dee'toh] a. ungranted.

Inesauribile [een-ay-zow-ree'bee-lay] a. inexhaustible.

Inescusabile [een-ess-koo-zah'bee-lay] a. inexcusable, unjustifiable.

Ineseguito [een-ay-zay-gwee'toh] a. unperformed.

Inesistente [een-ay-zees-ten'tay] a. non-existent.

Inesorabile [een-ay-zoh-rah'bee-lay] a. inexorable, relentless.

Inesperienza [een-ess-pay-ree-ent'zah] nf. inexperience.

Inesperto [een-ess-pehr'toh] a. inexperienced, unskilled.

Inesplicabile [een-ess-plee-kah'bee-lay] a. inexplicable.

Inesplorato [een-ess-ploh-rah'toh] a. unexplored.

Inestimabile [een-ess-tee-mah'bee-lay] a. inestimable, invaluable.

Inettitudine [een-et-tee-too'dee-nay] nf. ineptitude.

Inetto [een-et'toh] a. inept, unfit.

Inevitabile [een-ay-vee-tah'bee-lay] a. inevitable, unavoidable. (trifle.

Inezia [een-et'zee-ah] nf.

Infallibile [een-fahl-lee'bee-lay] a. infallible, unfailing.

Infallibilità [een-fahl-lee-bee-lee-tah'] nf. infallibility.

Infamante [een-fah-mahn'tay] a. disgraceful, shameful.

Infama/re [een-fah-mah'ray] vt. to disgrace, bring shame upon; —rsi vr. to disgrace oneself.

Infame [een-fah'may] a. abominable, infamous.

Infamia [een-fah'mee-ah] nf. disgrace, infamy, shame.

Infangare [een-fahng-gah'ray] vt. to cover with mud.

Infanzia [een-fahnt'zee-ah] nf. infancy.

Infarinatura [een-fah-ree-nah-too'rah] nf. covering with flour, (fig.) smattering.

Infastidire [een-fah-stee-dee'ray] vt. to annoy, vex.

Infaticabile [een-fah-tee-kah'bee-lay] a. indefatigable.

Infatti [een-faht'tee] ad. in fact, really.

Infatua/re [een-fah-too-ah'ray] vt. to infatuate; —rsi vr. to become infatuated.

Infatuazione [een-fah-too-ah-tsee-oh'nay] *nf.* infatuation.

Infausto [een-fow'stoh] *a.* unlucky.

Infecondo [een-fay-kon'doh] *a.* barren, unfruitful.

Infedele [een-fay-day'lay] *nm.* and *f.* infidel; *a.* faithless, false.

Infedeltà [een-fay-dell-tah'] *nf.* faithlessness, infidelity.

Infelice [een-fay-lee'chay] *a.* unhappy, unlucky, unsuccessful.

Infelicità [een-fay-lee-chee-tah'] *nf.* unhappiness.

Inferiore [een-fay-ree-oh'ray] *nm.* and *a.* inferior; *a.* lower.

Inferiorità [een-fay-ree-oh-ree-tah'] *nf.* inferiority.

Infermarsi [een-fehr-mahr' see] *vr.* to become an invalid.

Infermeria [een-fehr-may-ree'ah] *nf.* infirmary.

Infermie/ra [een-fehr-mee-ay'rah] *nf.* nurse; — re [ray] *nm.* hospital attendant, male nurse.

Infermità [een-fehr-mee-tah'] *nf.* illness, infirmity.

Infermo [een-fehr'moh] *a.* ill, sick.

Infernale [een-fehr-nah'lay] *a.* hellish, infernal.

Inferno [een-fehr'noh] *nm.* hell.

Inferoci/re [een-fay-roh-chee'ray] *vt.* to make ferocious; *vi.* and —rsi *vr.* to become ferocious.

Inferriata [een-fehr-ree-ah'tah] *nf.* grating.

Infervora/re [een-fehr-voh-rah'ray] *vt.* to fill with fervour; —rsi *vr.* to be fervent.

Infestare [een-fess-tah'ray] *vt.* to infest.

Infesto [een-fess'toh] *a.* detrimental, harmful.

Infettivo [een-fet-tee'voh] *a.* catching, infectious.

Infetto [een-fet'toh] *a.* infected.

Infezione [een-fay-tsee-oh' nay] *nf.* infection.

Infiacchi/re [een-fee-ahk-kee'ray] *vt.* to enervate, weaken; —rsi *vr.* to grow weak.

Infiamma/re [een-fee-ahm-mah'ray] *vt.* to excite, inflame; —rsi *vr.* to grow excited, inflamed.

Infiammazione [een-fee-ahm-mah-tsee-oh'nay] *nf.* inflamation.

Infido [een-fee'doh] *a.* unfaithful, untrustworthy.

Infievoli/re [een-fee-ay-voh-lee'ray] *vt.* to weaken; —rsi *vr.* to grow weak.

Infilare [een-fee-lah'ray] *vt.* to slip on, string, thread.

Infiltrazione [een-feelt-trah-tsee-oh'nay] *nf.* infiltration.

Infilzare [een-feelt-zah'ray] *vt.* to pierce, run through, string.

Infimo [een'fee-moh] *a.* lowest, very low.

Infine [een-fee'nay] *ad.* after all, finally.

Infingardaggine [een-feeng-gahr-dah'djee-nay] *nf.* laziness, slothfulness.

Infingardo [een-feeng-gahr' doh] *a.* lazy, slothful.

Infingersi [een-feen'jehr-see] *vr.* to feign, simulate.

Infinità [een-fee-nee-tah'] *nf.* crowd, infinity, lot.

Infinito [een-fee-nee'toh] *nm.* and *a.* infinite; *a.* boundless, endless.

Infiorare [een-fee-oh-rah' ray] *vt.* to adorn (strew) with flowers.

Infischiarsi [een-fees-kee-ahr'see] *vr.* to laugh at, not care for.

Inflessibile [een-fless-see' bee-lay] *a.* inflexible.

Inflessione [een-fless-see-oh'nay] *nf.* inflexion.

Infliggere [een-flee'djay-ray] *vt.* to inflict.

Influente [een-floo-en'tay] *a.* influential.

Influenza [een-floo-ent'zah] *nf.* influence, influenza.

Influenzare [een-floo-ent-zah'ray] *vt.* to affect, bias, influence.

Influenzato [een-floo-ent-zah'toh] *a.* suffering from influenza.

Influire [een-floo-ee'ray] *vi.* to influence, persuade.

Influsso [een-floos'soh] *nm.* influx, influence.

Infocare [een-foh-kah'ray] *vt.* to excite, inflame, make hot; —rsi *vr.* to become hot, inflamed.

Infondere [een-fon'day-ray] *vt.* to infuse, instil.

Informare [een-forr-mah'ray] *vt.* to acquaint, let (someone) know, inform; —rsi *vr.* to be informed, inquire.

Informativo [een-forr-mah-tee'voh] *a.* informative.

Informatore [een-forr-mah-toh'ray] *nm.* informer; *a.* informing.

Informazione [een-forr-mah-tsee-oh'nay] *nf.* information, inquiry, intelligence.

Informe [een-forr'may] *a.* shapeless.

Informicolire [een-forr-mee-koh-lee'ray] *vt.* to cause a tickling sensation, pins and needles.

Informità [een-forr-mee-tah'] *nf.* shapelessness.

Infornata [een-forr-nah'tah] *nf.* batch, ovenful.

Infortunio [een-forr-too'nee-oh] *nm.* accident, misfortune.

Infra [een'frah] *pr.* among, between; *ad.* below.

Infradiciare [een-frah-dee-chah'ray] *vt.* —rsi *vr.* to drench, soak, wet.

Infrangere [een-frahn'jay-ray] *vt.* to break, shatter; —rsi *vr.* to break, be broken.

Infrascritto [een-frah-skreet'toh] *a.* undermentioned.

Infrattanto [een-fraht-tahn'toh] *ad.* meanwhile.

Infrazione [een-frah-tsee-oh'nay] *nf.* infraction, infringement.

Infreddarsi [een-fred-dahr'see] *vr.* to catch a cold.

Infreddatura [een-fred-dah-too'rah] *nf.* cold.

Infrequente [een-fray-kwen'tay] *a.* infrequent.

Infrequenza [een-fray-kwent'zah] *nf.* infrequency.

Infrigidire [een-free-jee-dee'ray] *vt.* to chill; *vi.* to grow chilly.

Infruttifero [een-froot-tee'fay-roh] *a.* unproductive.

Infruttuoso [een-froot-too-oh'soh] *a.* fruitless, unsuccessful.

Infuriare [een-foo-ree-ah'ray] *vi.* to rage; —rsi *vr.* to fly into a passion, lose one's temper.

Infusione [een-foo-zee-oh'nay] *nf.* infusion.

Ingaggiare [een-gah-djah'ray] *vt.* to engage, enlist.

Ingagliardire [een-gahl-yahr-dee'ray] *vt.* to invigorate, strengthen; —rsi *vr.* to grow strong(er).

Ingannare [een-gahn-nah'ray] *vt.* to appease, beguile, cheat, deceive; —rsi *vr.* to be mistaken.

Ingannevole [een-gahn-nay'voh-lay] *a.* deceitful, deceptive.

Inganno [een-gahn'noh] *nm.* deceit, fraud, trick.

Ingegnarsi [een-jayn-yahr'see] *vr.* to do one's best, manage.

Ingegnere [een-jayn-yay'ray] *nm.* engineer.

Ingegneria [een-jayn-yay-ree'ah] nf. engineering.

Ingegno [een-jayn'yoh] nm. genius, intellect, talent.

Ingegnosità [een-jayn-yoh-see-tah'] nf. ingeniousness, ingenuity.

Ingegnoso [een-jayn-yoh'soh] a. industrious, ingenious.

Ingelosi/re [een-jay-loh-zee'ray] vt. to make jealous; —rsi vr. to become jealous.

Ingenerare [een-jay-nay-rah'ray] vt. to cause, engender.

Ingente [een-jen'tay] a. enormous, huge.

Ingentili/re [een-jen-tee-lee'ray] vt. to civilise, refine;

—rsi vr. to become refined.

Ingenuità [een-jay-noo-ee-tah'] nf. ingenuousness.

Ingenuo [een-jay'noo-oh] a. ingenuous, simple.

Ingerenza [een-jay-rent'zah] nf. interference.

Ingeri/re [een-jay-ree'ray] vt. to swallow; —rsi vr. to interfere, meddle.

Ingessare [een-jess-sah'ray] vt. to (set in) plaster.

Inghiottire [een-ghee-ot-

Ingiustizia [een-joo-steet'tsee-ah] nf. injustice, unfairness.

Ingiusto [een-joo'stoh] a. unfair, unjust.

Ingoiare [een-goh-yah'ray] vt. to swallow (up).

Ingolfarsi [een-goll-fahr'see] vr. to plunge into.

Ingombrare [een-gom-brah'ray] vt. to encumber, obstruct.

Ingombro [een-gom'bron] nm. encumbrance, obstruction; a. encumbered, obstructed.

Ingommare [een-gom-mah'ray] vt. to gum, stick.

Ingordigia [een-gor-dee'jah] nf. greed(iness).

Ingordo [een-gorr'doh] a. covetous, greedy.

Ingranaggio [een-grah-nah'djoh] nm. (tech.) gearing, working.

Ingranare [een-grah-nah'ray] vt. (tech.) to put into gear; vi. to be in gear.

Ingranchire [een-grahng-kee'ray] vt. to benumb.

Ingrandimento [een-grahn-dee-men'toh] nm. enlargement.

Ingrandi/re [een-grahn-dee-

tee ray] *vt.* to engulf, swallow (up).

Ingiallire [een-jahl-lee-ray] *vt. and i.* to make (become) yellow.

Inginocchiarsi [een-jee-nock-kee-ahr'see] *vr.* to go on one's knees, kneel down.

Ingiunzione [een-joon-tsee-oh'nay] *nf.* injunction, order.

Ingiuria [een-joo'ree-ah] *nf.* affront, injury (of the weather), insult.

Ingiuriare [een-joo-ree-ah'ray] *vt.* to abuse, insult.

Ingiurioso [een-joo-ree-oh'soh] *a.* insulting, offensive.

Ingiustificabile [een-joo-stee-fee-kah'bee-lay] *a.* unjustifiable.

ray] *vt.* to amplify, enlarge, exaggerate, increase; —rsi *vr.* to grow larger, increase.

Ingrassare [een-grahs-sah'ray] *vt. and i.* to enrich (the soil), to make (grow) fat.

Ingraticciarsi [een-grah-teech-chahr'see] *vr.* to get tangled.

Ingratitudine [een-grah-tee-too'dee-nay] *nf.* ingratitude.

Ingrato [een-grah'toh] *a.* thankless, ungrateful, unpleasant.

Ingraziarsi [een-grah-tsee-ahr'see] *vr.* to ingratiate oneself.

Ingrediente [een-gray-dee-en'tay] *nm.* ingredient.

Innalzare [een-nahlt-zah'ray] *vt.* to heighten, raise; — **Innalzarsi** *vr.* to rise.

Innamorarsi [een-nah-moh-rah'ray] *vt.* to charm, —rsi *vr.*

rah'ray] *vt.* to fall in love.

Ingrossamento [een-gross-sah-men'toh] *nm.* enlargement, increase.

Ingrossare [een-gross-sah'ray] *vt.* to enlarge, increase.

Ingresso [een-gress'soh] *nm.* admittance, entrance.

Inoperosità [een-oh-pay-roh-see-tah'] *nf.* idleness, inactivity.

Inoperoso [een-oh-pay-roh' soh] *a.* idle, inactive.

Inopia [een-oh'pee-ah] *nf.* indigence, poverty, scarcity.

Inopinato [een-oh-pee-nah' toh] *a.* unexpected, unforeseen.

Inopportuno [een-op-porr-too'noh] *a.* inopportune, untimely.

Inoppugnabile [een-op-poon-yah'bee-lay] *a.* unquestionable.

Inorgoglire [een-orr-gohl-yee'ray] *vt.* to make proud; —rsi *vr.* to become proud.

Inorridire [een-orr-ree-dee' ray] *vt.* to horrify; *vi.* to be horrified.

Inospitale [een-oss-pee-tah' lay], **inospite** [een-oss'pee-tay] *a.* inhospitable.

Inquietare [een-kwee-ay-tah'ray] *vt.* to alarm, worry; —rsi *vr.* to grow alarmed, angry.

Inquietezza [een-kwee-ay-tet'zah] *nf.* uneasiness.

Inquieto [een-kwee-ay'toh] *a.* anxious, restless, uneasy.

Inquietudine [een-kwee-ay-too'dee-nay] *nf.* apprehension, restlessness, uneasiness.

Inquilino [een-kwee-lee'noh] *nm.* lodger, tenant.

Inquinare [een-kwee-nah' ray] *vt.* to pollute.

Inquirente [een-kwee-ren' tay] *a.* inquiring, investigating.

Inquisire [een-kwee-zee'ray] *vt.* to inquire, investigate.

Inquisitore [een-kwee-zee-toh'ray] *nm.* inquisitor.

Inquisizione [een-kwee-see-tsee-oh'nay] *nf.* inquisition.

Insaccare [een-sahk-kah'ray] *vt.* to put in sacks.

Insalata [een-sah-lah'tah] *nf.* salad.

Insalatiera [een-sah-lah-tee-ay'rah] *nf.* salad-bowl.

Insalubre [een-sah-loo'bray] *a.* unhealthy.

Insalubrità [een-sah-loo-bree-tah'] *nf.* unhealthiness.

Insania [een-sah'nee-ah] *nf.* insanity.

Insano [een-sah'noh] *a.* crazy, foolish, insane.

Insaponare [een-sah-poh-nah'ray] *vt.* to lather, soap.

Insaputa, all' [ahl-leen-sah-poo'tah] *ad.* unknown to.

Insaziabile [een-sah-tsee-ah'bee-lay] *a.* insatiable.

Inscrutabile [een-skroo-tah' bee-lay] *a.* inscrutable.

Insediare [een-say-dee-ah' ray] *vt.* to install; —rsi *vr.* to enter upon office, take possession.

Insegna [een-sayn'yah] *nf.* colours (*pl.*) flag, sign-board.

Insegnamento [een-sayn-yah-men'toh] *nm.* teaching, tuition.

Insegnante [een-sayn-yahn'tay] *nm. and f.* teacher; corpo [korr'poh] i. *nm.* teaching staff.

Insegnare [een-sayn-yah'ray] *vt.* to show, teach.

Inseguimento [een-say-gwee-men'toh] *nm.* chase, pursuit.

Inseguire [een-say-gwee'ray] *vt.* to pursue, run after.

Inselvatichire [een-sell-vah-tee-kee'ray] *vt. and i.* to make (grow) wild.

Insenatura [een-say-nah-too'rah] *nf.* inlet.

Insensato [een-sen-sah'toh] *a.* foolish, senseless.

Insensibile [een-sen-see'bee-lay] *a.* insensible, unfeeling.

Insensibilità [een-sen-see-bee-lee-tah'] *nf.* hard-heartedness, insensibility.

Inseparabile [een-say-pah-rah'bee-lay] *a.* inseparable.

Inserimento [een-say-ree-men'toh] *nm.* insertion.

Inserire [een-say-ree'ray] *vt.* to enclose, insert.

Inservibile [een-sehr-vee'-bee-lay] *a.* useless.

Inserzione [een-sehr-tsee-oh'nay] *nf.* advertisement, insertion.

Insetto [een-set-toh] *nm.* insect.

Insidia [een-see'dee-ah] *nf.* ambush, snare.

Insidiare [een-see-dee-ah'ray] *vt.* to lay snares for.

Insidioso [een-see-dee-oh'soh] *a.* insidious.

Insieme [een-see-ay'may] *nm.* whole; *ad.* at the same time, together.

Insigne [een-seen'yay] *a.* famous, notorious, signal.

Insignire [een-seen-yee'ray] *vt.* to award, confer (on), decorate.

Insinua/re [een-see-noo-ah'ray] *vt.* to insinuate, suggest; —rsi *vr.* to creep into, penetrate.

Insinuazione [een-see-noo-ah-tsee-oh'nay] *nf.* insinuation, suggestion.

Insipido [een-see'pee-doh] *a.* insipid, tasteless.

Insipienza [een-see-pee-ent'zah] *nf.* foolishness, ignorance.

Insistente [een-see-sten'tay] *a.* insistent, pressing, urgent.

Insistenza [een-see-stent'zah] *nf.* insistence.

Insistere [een-see'stay-ray] *vi.* to insist, persist.

Insoddisfatto [een-sod-dees-faht'toh] *a.* dissatisfied.

Insofferente [een-soff-fay-ren'tay] *a.* impatient, intolerant.

Insofferenza [een-soff-fay-rent'zah] *nf.* impatience, intolerance.

Insolazione [een-soh-lah-

tsee-oh'nay] *nf.* insolation, sun-stroke.

Insolente [een-soh-len'tay] *a.* insolent, pert.

Insolentire [een-soh-len-tee'ray] *vt. and i.* to abuse, speak insolently.

Insolenza [een-soh-lent'zah] *nf.* insolence, pertness.

Insolito [een-soh'lee-toh] *a.* unusual.

Insolubile [een-soh-loo'bee-lay] *a.* insoluble.

Insoluto [een-soh-loo'toh] *a.* unsolved.

Insolvente [een-soll-ven'tay] *a.* insolvent.

Insolvenza [een-soll-vent'zah] *nf.* insolvency.

Insomma [een-som'mah] *ad.* after all, in conclusion, in short; *int.* well!

Insonne [een-son'nay] *a.* sleepless.

Insonnia [een-son'nee-ah] *nf.* insomnia, sleeplessness.

Insopportabile [een-sop-porr-tah'bee-lay] *a.* insupportable, unbearable.

Insorgere [een-sorr'jay-ray] *vi.* to rebel, rise.

Insormontabile [een-sorr-mon-tah'bee-lay] *a.* insurmountable.

Insorto [een-sorr'toh] *nm.* rebel, rioter; *a.* risen.

Insospetti/re [een-soss-pet-tee'ray] *vt.* to make suspicious; —rsi *vr.* to grow suspicious.

Insostenibile [een-soss-tay-nee'bee-lay] *a.* excessive, untenable.

Insozzare [een-sod-zah'ray] *vt.* to soil, sully.

Insperato [een-spay-rah'toh] *a.* unhoped-for.

Inspirare [een-spee-rah'ray] *vt.* to inhale.

Instabile [een-stah'bee-lay] *a.* unstable, variable.

Instabilità [een-stah-bee-lee-

tah'] nf. unstability, variability.

Installa/re [een-stahl-lah'ray] vt. to install; **—rsi** vr. to install oneself, settle.

Installazione [een-stahl-lah-tsee-oh'nay] nf. installation.

Instaurare [een-stow-rah' ray] vt. to begin, initiate.

Instaurazione [een-stow-rah-tsee-oh'nay] nf. beginning, initiation.

Instillare [een-steel-lah'ray] vt. to infuse, instil.

Insù [een-soo'] ad. up-(wards).

Insuccesso [een-sooch-chess' soh] nm. failure.

Insufficiente [een-soof-fee-chen'ray] a. inadequate, insufficient.

Insufficienza [een-soof-fee-chent'zah] nf. insufficiency.

Insulare [een-soo-lah'ray] a. insular.

Insulsaggine [een-sool-sah'-djee-nay] nf. dullness, foolishness.

Insulso [een-sool'soh] a. dull, foolish.

Insultare [een-sool-tah'ray] vt. to abuse, insult.

Insulto [een-sool'toh] nm. affront, (med.) attack, insult.

Insuperabile [een-soo-pay-rah'bee-lay] a. insuperable.

Insuperbi/re [een-soo-pehr-bee'ray] vt. to elate, make proud; **—rsi** vr. to grow proud.

Insurrezionale [een-soor-ray-tsee-oh-nah'lay] a. insurrectionary.

Insurrezione [een-soor-ray-tsee-oh'nay] nf. insurrection, rising.

Insussistente [een-soos-see-sten'tay] a. non-existent.

Insussistenza [een-soos-see-stent'zah] nf. non-existence.

Intaccare [een-tahk-kah'ray] vt. to begin spending, corrode, injure, notch.

Intagliare [een-tahl-yah'ray] vt. to carve, engrave.

Intaglio [een-tahl'yoh] nm. carving, intaglio.

Intangibile [een-tahn-jee-bee'lay] a. intangible.

Intanto [een-tahn'toh] ad. meanwhile; **i. che** [kay] con. while.

Intarsiare [een-tahr-see-ah'ray] vt. to inlay.

Intarsio [een-tahr'see-oh] nm. inlay.

Intasa/re [een-tah-zah'ray] vt. to choke, obstruct, stop up; **—rsi** vr. to get stopped up.

Intascare [een-tah-skah'ray] vt. to pocket.

Intatto [een-taht'toh] a. intact, uninjured, unsullied.

Intavolare [een-tah-voh-lah' ray] vt. to begin, cover with planks, initiate.

Integerrimo [een-tay-jehr'ree-moh] a. honest, upright.

Integrale [een-tay-grah'lay] a. full, integral, whole.

Integrare [een-tay-grah'ray] vt. to complete, integrate.

Integrazione [een-tay-grah-tsee-oh'nay] nf. integration.

Integrità [een-tay-gree-tah'] nf. integrity, uprightness.

Integro [een'tay-groh] a. honest, upright.

Intelletto [een-tell-let'toh] nm. intellect, understanding.

Intellettuale [een-tell-let-too-ah'lay] a. intellectual.

Intelligente [een-tell-lee-jen'tay] a. clever, intelligent.

Intelligenza [een-tell-lee-jent'zah] nf. cleverness, intelligence, talent.

Intelligibile [een-tell-lee-jee'bee-lay] a. comprehensible, intelligible.

Intemerata [een-tay-may-rah'tah] nf. reproof.

Intemerato [een-tay-may-rah'toh] a. irreproachable.

Intemperante [een-tem-pay-rahn'tay] a. intemperate.

Intemperanza [een-tem-pay-rahn'zah] nf. intemperance.

Intemperie [een-tem-pay'ree-ay] nf. inclemency (climatic).

Intempestivo [een-tem-pess-tee'voh] a. unseasonable, untimely.

Intende/re [een-ten'day-ray] vt. to hear, intend, mean, understand; —rsi vr. to be a good judge of, come to an agreement with, understand (each other).

Intendimento [een-ten-dee-men'toh] nm. intention, purpose, understanding.

Intenditore [een-ten-dee-toh'ray] nm. connoisseur, judge.

Inteneri/re [een-tay-nay-ree'ray] vt. to move, soften; —rsi vr. to be moved, feel compassion.

Intensità [een-ten-see-tah'] nf. intensity.

Intenso [een-ten'soh] a. intense, violent.

Intento [een-ten'toh] nm. aim, intent(ion), purpose, view; a. intent.

Intenzionale [een-ten-tsee-oh-nah'lay] a. intentional.

Intenzione [een-ten-tsee-oh'nay] nf. intention, mind, wish.

Intercedere [een-tehr-chay'day-ray] vt. to intercede, to elapse (rare).

Intercessione [een-tehr-chess-see-oh'nay] nf. intercession.

Intercettare [een-tehr-chett-tah'ray] vt. to intercept.

Intercettazione [een-tehr-chett-tah-tsee-oh'nay] nf. interception.

Intercorrere [een-tehr-korr-ray-ray] vt. to elapse, happen, pass.

Interdetto [een-tehr-det'toh] nm. interdict; a. disqualified, dumbfounded, prohibited.

Interdire [een-tehr-dee'ray] vt. to disqualify, forbid, interdict.

Interdizione [een-tehr-dee-tsee-oh'nay] nf. disqualification, interdiction.

Interessamento [een-tay-ress-sah-men'toh] nm. concern, interest.

Interessante [een-tay-ress-sahn'tay] a. interesting.

Interessa/re [een-tay-ress-sah'ray] vt. to concern, interest; —rsi vr. to take an interest.

Interessato [een-tay-ress-sah'toh] a. keen on money, self-seeking.

Interesse [een-tay-ress'say] nm. interest.

Interinale [een-tay-ree-nah'lay] a. interim, temporary.

Interino [een-tay-ree'noh] a. provisional.

Interiora [een-tay-ree-oh'rah] nf. (pl.) entrails (pl.), intestines (pl.)

Interiore [een-tay-ree-oh'ray] nm. and a. inside, interior; a. inner.

Interlineare [een-tehr-lee-nay-ah'ray] vt. to interline; a. interlinear.

Interlocutore [een-tehr-loh-koo-toh'ray] nm. interlocutor.

Interloquire [een-tehr-loh-kwee'ray] vi. to put in a word, speak.

Intermediario [een-tehr-may-dee-ah'ree-oh] nm. and a. intermediary; nm. (com.) middle-man.

Intermezzo [een-tehr-med'zoh] nm. interval.

Interminabile [een-tehr-mee-nah'bee-lay] a. endless, interminable.

Intermissione [een-tehr

mees-see-oh'nay] *nf.* intermission.

Intermittente [een-tehr-meet-ten'day] *a.* intermittent.

Intermittenza [een-tehr-meet-tent'zah] *nf.* intermittence.

Interna/re [een-tehr-nah'ray] *vt.* to intern; —rsi *vr.* to enter into, penetrate.

Internato [een-tehr-nah'toh] *nm.* boarding-school, internee; *a.* interned.

Internazionale [een-tehr-nah-tsee-oh-nah'lay] *a.* international.

Interno [een-tehr'noh] *nm.* depth, inside, interior; ministero degli interni [mee-nees-tay'roh dayl'yee een-tehr'nee] *nm.* Home Office; *a.* inner, inside, interior, internal.

Intero [een-tay'roh] *nm.* whole; *a.* entire, whole.

Interpellanza [een-tehr-pell-lahnt'zah] *nf.* interpellation.

Interpellare [een-tehr-pell-lah'ray] *vt.* to ask, interpellate.

Interpor/re [een-tehr-porr'ray] *vt.* —rsi *vr.* to interpose, intervene.

Interposizione [een-tehr-poh-zee-tsee-oh'nay] *nf.* interposition, intervention.

Interpretare [een-tehr-pray-tah'ray] *vt.* to construe, interpret.

Interpretazione [een-tehr-pray-tah-tsee-oh'nay] *nf.* interpretation.

Interprete [een-tehr'pray-tay] *nm. and f.* interpreter.

Interrogare [een-tehr-roh-gah'ray] *vt.* to ask, inquire, interrogate, question.

Interrogatorio [een-tehr-roh-gah-toh'ree-oh] *nm.* (cross-) examination.

Interrogazione [een-tehr-roh-gah-tsee-oh'nay] *nf.* interrogation, question.

Interrompe/re [een-tehr-rom'pay-ray] *vt.* to break (off), interrupt; —rsi *vr.* to stop.

Interruttore [een-tehr-reet-toh'ray] *nm.* interrupter, (elec.) switch.

Interruzione [een-tehr-roo-tsee-oh'nay] *nf.* interruption.

Intersecare [een-tehr-say-kah'ray] *vt.* to cross, intersect.

Intervallo [een-tehr-vahl'loh] *nm.* interval, space.

Intervenire [een-tehr-vay-nee'ray] *vi.* to be present, happen, intervene.

Intervento [een-tehr-ven'toh] *nm.* entrance, interference, intervention, presence; i. chirurgico [kee-roor'jee-koh], operation.

Intervenzione [een-tehr-ven-tsee-oh'nay] *nf.* intervention.

Intervenuto [een-tehr-vay-noo'toh] *a.* present (at).

Intervista [een-tehr-vee'stah] *nf.* interview.

Intervistare [een-tehr-vee-stah'ray] *vt.* to interview.

Intesa [een-tay'sah] *nf.* agreement, understanding.

Intessere [een-tess'say-ray] *vt.* to weave.

Intesta/re [een-tess-tah'ray] *vt.* to enter, head, register; —rsi *vr.* to be obstinate.

Intestato [een-tess-tah'toh] *a.* obstinate, stubborn.

Intestazione [een-tess-tah-tsee-oh'nay] *nf.* heading, title.

Intestino [een-tess-tee'noh] *nm.* intestine; *a.* civil, intestine.

Intiepidi/re [een-tee-ay-pee-dee'ray] *vt.* to abate, cool, warm; —rsi *vr.* to cool down, warm up.

Intiero: *v.* intero.

Intimare [een-tee-mah'ray] *vt.* to enjoin, intimate, notify, order.

Intimazione [een-tee-mah-tsee-oh'nay] *nf.* notification, order, summons.

Intimidi/re [een-tee-mee-dee'ray] *vt.* to intimidate; —**rsi** *vr.* to be afraid.

Intimità [een-tee-mee-tah'] *nf.* intimacy.

Intimo [een'tee-moh] *nm.* heart, intimate (friend); *a.* intimate.

Intimorire [een-tee-moh-ree'ray] *vt.* to frighten.

Intingere [een-teen'jay-ray] *vt.* to dip, wet.

Intirizzi/re [een-tee-reed-zee'ray] *vt.* to (be)numb, stiffen; —**rsi** *vr.* to get benumbed.

Intisichire [een-tee-zee-kee'ray] *vt. and i.* to make (grow) consumptive.

Intitola/re [een-tee-toh-lah'ray] *vt.* to dedicate, entitle; —**rsi** *vr.* to bear the name of.

Intitolazione [een-tee-toh-lah-tsee-oh'nay] *nf.* dedication, title.

Intollerabile [een-toll-lay-rah'bee-lay] *a.* intolerable.

Intollerante [een-toll-lay-rahn'tay] *a.* intolerant.

Intolleranza [een-toll-lay-rahn'tzah] *nf.* intolerance.

Intonacare [een-toh-nah-kah'ray] *vt.* to plaster.

Intonaco [een-toh'nah-koh] *nm.* plaster.

Intona/re [een-toh-nah'ray] *vt.* to intone, strike up; —**rsi** *vr.* to be in tune (harmony) with, tone with.

Intonazione [een-toh-nah-tsee-oh'nay] *nf.* intonation, tone.

Intonti/re [een-ton-tee'ray] to amaze, stun; —**rsi** *vr.* to be amazed, stunned, become stupid.

Intoppo [een-top'poh] *nm.* hindrance, obstacle.

Intorbida/re [een-torr-bee-dah'ray] *vt.* to confuse, darken, make dirty, trouble; —**rsi** *vr.* to become confused, dirty, troubled, darken, grow dim.

Intorno [een-torr'noh] *ad. and vr.* about, (a)round, at.

Intossicare [een-toss-see-kah'ray] *vt.* to poison.

Intra [een'trah] *pr.* (*rare*) *v.* **Tra.**

Intraducibile [een-trah-doo-chee'bee-lay] *a.* untranslatable.

Intralciare [een-trahl-chah'ray] *vt.* to hinder, interfere with.

Intramettere: *v.* **intromettere.**

Intramezzare: *v.* **tramezzare.**

Intramezzo [een-trah-med'zoh] *nm.* partition.

Intransigente [een-trahn-see-jen'tay] *a.* intransigent, uncompromising.

Intransigenza [een-trahn-see-jent'zah] *nf.* intransigence.

Intraprendere [een-trah-pren'day-ray] *vt.* to enter (upon), undertake.

Intrapresa [een-trah-pray'sah] *nf.* enterprise, (old-fashion-ed) *v.* **Impresa.**

Intrattabile [een-traht-tah'bee-lay] *a.* intractable, unreasonable.

Intrattene/re [een-traht-tay-nay'ray] *vt.* to entertain; —**rsi** *vr.* to dwell on, linger, stop.

Intrattenimento [een-traht-tay-nee-men'toh] *nm.* entertainment.

Intrav(v)edere [een-trah(v)-vay-day'ray] *vt.* to catch a glimpse, have a hazy notion.

Intrecciare [een-trehch-chah'ray] *vt.* to entwine interlace, plait.

Intreccio [een-trehch'choh]

nm. interlacing, plot (of a play).

Intrepidezza [een-tray-pee-det'zah], **intrepidità** [een-tray-pee-dee-tah'] *nf.* intrepidity.

Intrepido [een-tray'pee-doh] *a.* fearless, intrepid.

Intrigante [een-tree-gahn'tay] *nm.* intriguer; *a.* intriguing.

Intriga/re [een-tree-gah'ray] *vt.* to entangle; *vi.* to intrigue; —**rsi** *vr.* to meddle.

Intrigo [een-tree'goh] *nm.* intrigue.

Intrinseco [een-treen'say-koh] *a.* intrinsic.

Intriso [een-tree'zoh] *nm.* mash, mixture; *a.* soaked.

Intristire [een-trees-tee'ray] *vt.* to become sad, droop.

Introdur/re [een-troh-door'ray] *vt.* to import, introduce, show in; —**rsi** *vr.* to get in, introduce oneself.

Introduzione [een-troh-doo-tsee'oh-nay] *nf.* beginning, importation, introduction.

Introitare [een-troh-ee-tah'ray] *vt.* (com.) to cash, get.

Introito [een-troh-ee'toh] *nm.* (eccl.) introit, (com.) returns (pl.), revenue.

Intromette/re [een-troh-met'tay-ray] *vt.* to insert, interpose, introduce; —**rsi** *vr.* to intervene, intrude, meddle.

Intromissione [een-troh-mees-see-oh'nay] *nf.* intervention, intrusion.

Intronare [een-troh-nah'ray] *vt.* to deafen, stun.

Intrusione [een-troo-zee-oh'nay] *nf.* intrusion.

Intruso [een-troo'zoh] *nm.* intruder; *a.* intruding.

Intuire [een-too-ee'ray] *vt.* to guess, imagine.

Intuito [een-too'ee-toh] *nm.* intuition.

Intuizione [een-too-ee-tsee-oh'nay] *nf.* intuition

Inuguale, etc.: *v.* **inegu-ale**, etc.

Inumanità [een-oo-mah-nee-tah'] *nf.* inhumanity.

Inumano [een-oo-mah'noh] *a.* barbarous, inhuman.

Inumidire [een-oo-mee-dee'ray] *vt.* to moisten, wet.

Inurbanità [een-oor-bah-nee-tah'] *nf.* incivility.

Inurbano [een-oor-bah'noh] *a.* rude, uncivil.

Inusato [een-oo-zah'toh] *a.* unused.

Inusitato [een-oo-zee-tah'toh] *a.* obsolete, unusual.

Inutile [een-oo'tee-lay] *a.* unnecessary, useless.

Inutilità [een-oo-tee-lee-tah'] *nf.* uselessness.

Invadente [een-vah-den'tay] *a.* pushing.

Invadere [een-vah'day-ray] *vt.* to break into, invade.

Invaghirsi [een-vah-gheer'see] *vr.* to fall in love with, take a liking to.

Invalidare [een-vah-lee-dah'ray] *vt.* to invalidate.

Invalidità [een-vah-lee-dee-tah'] *nf.* invalidity.

Invalido [een-vah'lee-doh] *a.* disabled, infirm, invalid.

Invano [een-vah'noh] *ad.* in vain, vainly.

Invariabile [een-vah-ree-ah'bee-lay] *a.* invariable.

Invariato [een-vah-ree-ah'toh] *a.* unchanged, unvaried.

Invasione [een-vah-zee-oh'nay] *nf.* invasion.

Invasore [een-vah-zoh'ray] *nm.* invader; *a.* invading.

Invecchia/re [een-vehk-kee-ah'ray] *vt.* to make old; *vi.* and —**rsi** *vr.* to grow old.

Invece [een-vay'chay] *pr.* instead; *ad.* instead, on the contrary.

Inveire [een-vay-ee'ray] *vi.* to inveigh, rail.

Inventare [een-ven-tah'ray] *vt.* to fabricate, find out, invent.

Inventario [een-ven-tah'ree-oh] *nm.* inventory.

Invenzione [een-ven-tsee-oh'nay] *nf.* contrivance, invention.

Inverdire [een-vehr-dee'ray] *vi.* to grow green.

Inverecondia [een-vay-ray-kon'dee-ah] *nf.* immodesty.

Inverecondo [een-vay-ray-kon'doh] *a.* immodest.

Invernale [een-vehr-nah'lay] *a.* winter, wintry.

Inverniciare [een-vehr-nee-chah'ray] *vt.* to varnish.

Inverniciatura [een-vehr-nee-chah-too'rah] *nf.* varnishing.

Inverno [een-vehr'noh] *nm.* winter.

Invero [een-vay'roh] *ad.* really, truly.

Inverosimiglianza [een-vay-roh-see-meel-yahnt'zah] *nf.* unlikelihood.

Inverosimile [een-vay-roh-see'mee-lay] *a.* improbable, unlikely.

Inversione [een-vehr-see-oh'nay] *nf.* inversion.

Inverso [een-vehr'soh] *a.* contrary, inverse, inverted.

Invertire [een-vehr-tee'ray] *vt.* to invert, reverse.

Investigare [een-vess-tee-gah'ray] *vt.* to inquire into, investigate.

Investigazione [een-vess-tee-gah-tsee-oh'nay] *nf.* inquiry, investigation.

Investimento [een-vess-tee-men'toh] *nm.* collision, investment.

Investi/re [een-vess-tee'ray] *vt.* to appoint, collide with, invest; —**rsi** *vr.* to collide, take a deep interest in.

Invetriata [een-vay-tree-ah'tah] *nf.* pane of glass.

Invettiva [een-vet-tee'vah] *nf.* invective.

Inviare [een-vee-ah'ray] *vt.* to send. [envy.

Invidia [een-vee'dee-ah] *nf.*

Invidiare [een-vee-dee-ah'ray] *vt.* to envy, grudge.

Invidioso [een-vee-dee-oh'soh] *a.* envious.

Invigilare [een-vee-jee-lah'ray] *vt.* to watch (over).

Invigori/re [een-vee-goh-ree'ray] *vt.* to invigorate, strengthen; —**rsi** *vr.* to grow stronger.

Invilupparle [een-vee-loop-pah'ray] *vt.* to envelop, hide, wrap up; —**rsi** *vr.* to wrap oneself up.

Invincibile [een-veen-chee'bee-lay] *a.* invincible.

Invio [een-vee'oh] *nm.* dispatch, sending.

Inviolabile [een-vee-oh-lah'bee-lay] *a.* inviolable.

Invisibile [een-vee-zee'bee-lay] *a* invisible.

Inviso [een-vee'zoh] *a.* disliked, hated.

Invitare [een-vee-tah'ray] *vt.* to ask, invite.

Invitato [een-vee-tah'toh] *nm.* guest; *a.* invited.

Invito [een-vee'toh] *nm.* call, invitation, request.

Invitto [een-veet'toh] *a.* undefeated.

Invocare [een-voh-kah'ray] *vt.* to appeal (to), invoke.

Invocazione [een-voh-kah-tsee-oh'nay] *nf.* invocation.

Invogliare [een-vohl-yah'ray] *vt.* to allure, induce, persuade.

Invola/re [een-voh-lah'ray] *vt.* to steal; —**rsi** *vr.* to elope, run away.

Involontario [een-voh-lon-tah'ree-oh] *a.* involuntary.

Involtare [een-voll-tah'ray] *vt.* to pack (up).

Involto [een-voll'toh] *nm.*

bundle, package; *a.* involved, wrapt up.
Involucro [een-voh'loo-kroh] *nm.* covering, envelope.
Invulnerabile [een-vool-nay-rah'bee-lay] *a.* invulnerable.
Inzolfare [een-zoll-fah'ray] *vt.* to sulphurate.
Inzuccherare [een-zook-kay-rah'ray] *vt.* to sugar.
Inzuppare [een-zoop-pah'ray] *vt.* to dip, drench, soak.
Io [ee'oh] *pn.* I.
Iodio [yoh'dee-oh] *nm.* iodine.
Ionico [ee-oh'nee-koh] *a.* Ionic.
Iosa, a [ah yoh'zah] *ad.* galore.
Iperbole [ee-pehr'boh-lay] *nf.* hyperbole.
Ipnotismo [eep-noh-tees'moh] *nm.* hypnotism.
Ipnotizzare [eep-noh-teed-zah'ray] *vt.* to hypnotise.
Ipocondria [ee-poh-kon-dree'ah] *nf.* hypochondria, spleen.
Ipocrisia [ee-poh-kree-zee'ah] *nf.* cant, hypocrisy.
Ipocrita [ee-poh'kree-tah] *nm. and f.* hypocrite; *a.* hypocritical.
Ipoteca [ee-poh-tay'kah] *nf.* hypothetic, mortgage.
Ipotecare [ee-poh-tay-kah'ray] *vt.* to mortgage.
Ipotesi [ee-poh'tay-zee] *nf.* hypothesis.
Ippico [eep'pee-koh] *a.* hippic, horse.
Ippocastano [eep-poh-kah-stah'noh] *nm.* horse-chestnut.
Ira [ee'rah] *nf.*, **iracondia** [ee-rah-kon'dee-ah] *nf.* anger, rage, wrath.
Iracondo [ee-rah-kon'doh] *a.* angry, choleric, wrathful.
Irascibile [ee-rah-shee'bee-lay] *a.* irascible, irritable, hot-tempered.
Irascibilità [ee-rah-shee-bee-lee-tah'] *nf.* irascibility.

Irato [ee'rah-toh] *a.* angry, in a rage.
Ire [ee'ray] *vi.* (*poet.*) to go.
Iride [ee'ree-day] *nf.* iris, rainbow.
Iridiscente [ee-ree-dee-shen'tay] *a.* irridescent.
Irlandese [eer-lahn-day'say] *nm. and f.* Irishman, -woman; *a.* Irish.   [irony.
Ironia [ee-roh-nee'ah] *n.*
Ironico [ee-roh'nee-koh] *a.* ironic(al).
Iroso [ee-roh'soh] *a.* angry.
Irradiare [eer-rah-dee-ah'ray] *vt. and i.* to (ir)radiate.
Irragionevole [eer-rah-joh-nay'voh-lay] *a.* absurd, irrational, unreasonable.
Irrazionale [eer-rah-tsee-oh-nah'lay] *a.* irrational.
Irreale [eer-ray-ah'lay] *a.* unreal.
Irreconciliabile [eer-ray-kon-chee-lee-ah'bee-lay] *a.* irreconcilable.
Irrecuperabile [eer-ray-koo-pay-rah'bee-lay] *a.* irrecoverable.
Irredento [eer-ray-den'toh] *a.* unredeemed.
Irredimibile [eer-ray-dee-mee'bee-lay] *a.* irredeemable.
Irreducibile [eer-ray-doo-chee'bee-lay] *a.* irreducible.
Irrefutabile [eer-ray-foo-tah'bee-lay] *a.* irrefutable.
Irregolare [eer-ray-goh-lah'ray] *a.* abnormal, irregular.
Irregolarità [eer-ray-goh-lah-ree-tah'] *nf.* irregularity.
Irreligioso [eer-ray-lee-joh'soh] *a.* irreligious.
Irremissibile [eer-ray-mees-see'bee-lay] *a.* impossible to remit.
Irremovibile [eer-ray-moh-vee'bee-lay] *a.* inflexible, irremovable.
Irreparabile [eer-ray-pah-rah'bee-lay] *a.* irreparable.

Irreperibile [eer-ray-pay-ree'bee-lay] a. not to be found.

Irreprensibile [eer-ray-pren-see'bee-lay] a. faultless, irreproachable.

Irrequietezza [eer-ray-kwee-ay-tet'zah] nf. restlessness.

Irrequieto [eer-ray-kwee-ay'toh] a. restless.

Irresistibile [eer-ray-see-stee'bee-lay] a. irresistible.

Irresolutezza [eer-ray-soh-loo-let'zah] nf. hesitation, irresolution.

Irresoluto [eer-ray-soh-loo'toh] a. hesitant, irresolute.

Irresponsabile [eer-ress-pon-sah'bee-lay] a. irresponsible.

Irrevocabile [eer-ray-voh-kah'bee-lay] a. irrevocable.

Irridere [eer-ree'day-ray] vt. to deride, laugh at.

Irriducibile [eer-ree-doo-chee'bee-lay] a. irreducible.

Irriflessivo [eer-ree-fless-see'voh] a. thoughtless.

Irrigare [eer-ree-gah'ray] vt. to irrigate.

Irrigidi/re [eer-ree-jee-dee'ray] vt. to benumb, make stiff; —rsi vr. to grow (stand) stiff.

Irrimediabile [eer-ree-may-dee-ah'bee-lay] a. irremediable.

Irrisione [eer-ree-zee-oh'nay] nf. derision, mockery.

Irrisorio [eer-ree-zoh'ree-oh] a. derisive, paltry.

Irritabile [eer-ree-tah'bee-lay] a. irritable.

Irrita/re [eer-ree-tah'ray] vt. to irritate, provoke; —rsi vr. to become angry, inflamed.

Irritazione [eer-ree-tah-tsee-oh'nay] nf. inflammation, irritation.

Irriverente [eer-ree-vay-ren'tay] a. irreverent.

Irrompere [eer-rom'pay-ray] vi. to break into.

Irruente [eer-roo-en'tay] a. impetuous, violent.

Irrugginire [eer-roo-djee-nee'ray] vt. and i. to make (grow) rusty.

Irruzione [eer-roo-tsee-oh'nay] nf. irruption.

Irsuto [eer-soo'toh] a. hairy, shaggy.

Irto [eer'toh] a. bristling, bushy, shaggy.

Iscritto [ee-skreet'toh] nm. member; a. entered, inscribed.

Iscrive/re [ee-skree'vay-ray] vt. to inscribe, record; —rsi vr. to enter for.

Iscrizione [ee-skree-tsee-oh'nay] nf. enrolment, entry, inscription.

Islandese [ees-lahn-day'say] nm. and f. Icelander; a. Icelandic.

Isola [ee'zoh-lah] nf. island, isle.

Isola/re [ee-zoh-lah'ray] vt. to insulate, isolate, separate; —rsi vr. to shun society.

Ispettorato [ees-pet-toh-rah'toh] nm. inspector's office, inspectorship.

Ispet/tore [ees-pet-toh'ray] nm. —trice [tree'chay] nf. inspector.

Ispezionare [ees-pay-tsee-oh-nah'ray] vt. to inspect.

Ispezione [ees-pay-tsee-oh'nay] nf. inspection.

Ispido [ees'pee-doh] a. bristling, rough, shaggy.

Ispira/re [ees-pee-rah'ray] vt. to infuse, inspire, instil; —rsi vr. to conform to, draw inspiration from.

Ispirazione [ees-pee-rah-tsee-oh'nay] nf. inspiration.

Issare [ees-sah'ray] vt. to hoist.

Istantanea [ee-stahn-tah'nay-ah] nf. snapshot.

Istantaneo [ee-stahn-tah'nay-oh] a. instantaneous.

Istante [ee-stahn'tay] *nm.* instant, moment.

Istanza [ee-stahnt'zah] *nf.* application, petition, request.

Isterico [ee-stay'ree-koh] *a.* hysteric(al).

Isterismo [ee-stay-rees'moh] *nm.* hysteria, hysterics (*pl.*).

Istesso: *v.* stesso.

Istigare [ee-stee-gah'ray] *vt.* to instigate.

Istigazione [ee-stee-gah-tsee-oh'nay] *nf.* instigation.

Istintivo [ee-steen-tee'voh] *a.* instinctive.

Istinto [ee-steen'toh] *nm.* instinct.

Istituire [ee-stee-too-ee'ray] *vt.* to appoint, found, institute.

Istituto [ee-stee-too'toh] *nm.* institute, school.

Istitu/tore [ee-stee-too-toh'ray] *nm.* founder, institutor; **—trice** [tree'chay] *nf.* governess.

Istituzione [ee-stee-too-tsee-oh'nay] *nf.* establishment, institution.

Istmo [eest'moh] *nm.* isthmus.

Istrice [ee'stree-chay] *nf.* porcupine.

Istrione [ee-stree-oh'nay] *nm.* bad actor, poor player.

Istrionico [ee-stree-oh'nee-koh] *a.* histrionic.

Istrui/re [ee-stroo-ee'ray] *vt.* to inform, instruct, teach; **—rsi** *vr.* to acquire knowledge, learn.

Istrumentale [ee-stroo-men-tah'lay] *a.* instrumental.

Istrumento [ee-stroo-men'toh] *nm.* instrument.

Istruttore [ee-stroot-toh'ray] *nm.* instructor, teacher; **giudice** [joo'dee-chay] i. examining magistrate.

Istruttoria [ee-stroot-toh'ree-ah] *nf.* examination, investigation.

Istruzione [ee-stroo-tsee-oh'nay] *nf.* education, instruction, learning, order, teaching; **ministero della pubblica** [mee-nee-stay'roh dell-lah poob'-blee-kah] i. *nm.* Board of Education.

Istupidire [ee-stoo-pee-dee'ray] *vt. and* i. to make (become) stupid.

Italianità [ee-tah-lee-ah-nee-tah'] *nf.* Italian feelings, Italian nationality.

Italiano [ee-tah-lee-ah'noh] *nm. and a.* Italian.

Iterare [ee-tay-rah'ray] *vt.* to iterate, repeat.

Iterazione [ee-tay-rah-tsee-oh'nay] *nf.* iteration, repetition.

Itinerario [ee-tee-nay-rah'ree-oh] *nm.* itinerary, route.

Itterizia [eet-tay-reet'zee-ah] *nf.* (*med.*) jaundice.

Iugero [yoo'jay-roh] *nm.* acre.

Iugoslavo [yoo-goh-slah'voh] *nm. and a.* Jugoslav.

Iuniore [yoo-nee-oh'ray] *a.* junior.

Iuta [yoo'tah] *nf.* jute.

Ivi [ee'vee] *ad.* there.

L

La [lah] *def. art. f.* the; *pr. f. and neut.* (*acc.*), her, it.

Là [lah] *ad.* there; al di [ahl dee] l. **(di)** [dee] *ad. and pr.* beyond.

Labbro [lahb'broh] *nm.* lip.

Labile [lah'bee-lay] *a.* weak.

Labirinto [lah-bee-reen'toh] *nm.* labyrinth, maze.

Laboratorio [lah-boh-rah-toh'ree-oh] *nm.* laboratory, work-room.

Laboriosità [lah-boh-ree-oh-see-tah'] *nf.* industry, laboriousness.

Laborioso [lah-boh-ree-oh'soh] *a.* industrious, laborious.

Laburista [lah-boo-ree'stah] *nm.* member of the Labour Party; *a.* Labour.

Laccio [lahch'choh] *nm.* noose, snare, shoe-lace, string, trap.

Lacera/re [lah-chay-rah'ray] *vt.* to lacerate, rend, tear (up); —**rsi** *vr.* to tear, get torn.

Lacerazione [lah-chay-rah-tsee-oh'nay] *nf.* laceration, rent.

Lacero [lah'chay-roh] *a.* in rags, rent, torn.

Laconico [lah-koh-nee-koh] *a.* laconic.

Laconismo [lah-koh-nees'moh] *nm.* laconism.

La/crim/a [lah'kree-mah], **-grima** ['gree-mah] *nf.* tear; scoppiare in [skop-pee-ah'ray een] **l—e** *vi.* to burst into tears.

Lacrimare [lah-kree-mah'ray] *vi.* to cry, shed tears, water, weep.

Lacrimoso [lah-kree-moh'soh] *a.* lachrymose, tearful, weeping.

Lacuna [lah-koo'nah] *nf.* blank, gap.

Laddove [lahd-doh'vay] *ad.* (there) where.

Ladro [lah'droh] *nm.* burglar, robber, thief.

Ladrone [lah-droh'nay] *nm.* highwayman, robber.

Ladroneria [lah-droh-nay-ree'ah] *nf.* burglary, robbery, theft.

Laggiù [lah-djoo'] *ad.* down there, there below.

Lagnanza [lahn-yahnt'zah] *nf.* complaint.

Lagnarsi [lahn-yahr'see] *vr.* to complain.

Lago [lah'goh] *nm.* lake, pool.

Lagrima, etc.: *v.* **Lacrima**, etc. [lagoon.

Laguna [lah-goo-nah] *nf.*

Laicato [lah-ee-kah'toh] *nm.* laity.

Laico [lah'ee-koh] *nm.* layman; *a.* lay.

Laidezza [lah-ee-det'zah] *nf.* foulness, obscenity.

Laido [lah'ee-doh] *a.* dirty, foul, obscene.

Lama [lah'mah] *nf.* blade; *nm.* Lama, llama.

Lambicca/re [lahm-beek-kah'ray] *vt.* to distil, refine; —**rsi il cervello** [eel chehr-vell'loh] *vr.* to cudgel one's brains.

Lambicco [lahm-beek'koh] *a.* alembic.

Lambire [lahm-bee'ray] *vt.* to lap, touch lightly.

Lamenta/re [lah-men-tah'ray] *vt.* to lament, mourn, regret; —**rsi** *vr.* to complain, mourn.

Lamento [lah-men'toh] *nm.* complaint, lament, mourning.

Lamiera [lah-mee-ay'rah] *nf.* plate, sheet iron.

Lamina [lah'mee-nah] *nf.* blade, thin plate (of metal).

Lampada [lahm'pah-dah] *nf.* lamp; **l. ad arco** [ahd ahr'koh], arc-lamp.

Lampadario [lahm-pah-dah'ree-oh] *nm.* chandelier, electric-light pendant.

Lampadina [lahm-pah-dee'nah] *nf.* electric bulb, small lamp.

Lampante [lahm-pahn'tay] *a.* clear, obvious.

Lampeggiare [lahm-pay-djah'ray] *vi.* to flash, lighten.

Lampionaio [lahm-pee-oh-nah'yoh] *nm.* lamp-lighter.

Lampione [lahm-pee-oh'nay] *nm.* head-lamp, street-lamp.

Lampo [lahm'poh] *nm.* flash, lightning.

Lampone [lahm-poh'nay] *nm.* raspberry.

Lampreda [lahm-pray'dah] *nf.* lamprey.

Lana [lah'nah] *nf.* wool; **di** [dee] **l.** *a.* wool(len).

Lanaiuolo [lah-nah-ee-oo-oh'loh] *nm.* wool-comber, wool-worker.

Lancetta [lahn-chet'tah] *nf.* hand (of watch or clock), lancet.

Lancia [lahn'chah] *nf.* lance. (*naut.*) launch.

Lancia/re [lahn-chah'ray] *vt.* to fling, launch, set, throw; —rsi *vr.* to fling (launch) oneself.

Lanciere [lahn-chay'ray] *nm.* lancer. [moor.

Landa [lahn'dah] *nf.* heath, moor.

Laneria [lah-nay-ree'ah] *nf.* woollens (*pl.*) woollen goods (*pl.*).

Languente [lahng-gwen'tay] *a.* drooping, languishing, pining.

Languidezza [lahng-gwee-det'zah] *nf.* languidness.

Languido [lahng'gwee-doh] *a.* languid, weak.

Languire [lahng-gwee'ray] *vi.* to be slack, droop, languish, pine.

Languore [lahng-gwoh'ray] *nm.* faintness, languor, weakness.

Lanifero [lah-nee'fay-roh] *a.* wool-producing.

Lanificio [lah-nee-fee'choh] *nm.* wool factory.

Lanterna [lahn-tehr'nah] *nf.* lantern, skylight; l. di sicurezza [dee see-koo-ret'zah], safety-lamp.

Lanugine [lah-noo'jee-nay] *nf.* down (on the skin).

Laonde [lah-on'day] *ad.* therefore, wherefore.

Lapidare [lah-pee-dah'ray] *vt.* to lapidate, stone.

Lapidazione [lah-pee-dah-tsee-oh'nay] *nf.* stoning.

Lapide [lah'pee-day] *nf.* memorial tablet, tomb-stone.

Lapis [lah'pees] *nm.* pencil.

Lappone [lahp-poh'nay] *nm.*

and f. Lapp, Laplander; *a.* Lapp.

Lardo [lahr'doh] *nm.* bacon.

Largheggiare [lahr-gay-djah'ray] *vi.* to be generous, liberal.

Larghezza [lahr-ghet'zah] *nf.* breadth, width; l. di mezzi [dee med'zee], wealth; l. di vedute [dee-vay-doo'tay], broad-mindedness.

Largire [lahr-jee'ray] *vt.* to give liberally.

Largizione [lahr-jee-tsee-oh'nay] *nf.* donation, gift.

Largo [lahr'goh] *nm.* breadth, width; farsi (fahr'see) l. *vi.* to make a way for oneself; *a.* broad, generous, large, wide.

Larice [lah'ree-chay] *nm.* larch(-tree).

Laringe [lah-reen'jay] *nf.* larynx.

Laringite [lah-reen-jee'tay] *nf.* (*med.*) laryngitis.

Larva [lahr'vah] *nf.* larva, phantom, sham.

Larvatamente [lahr-vah-tah-men'tay] *ad.* by innuendo.

Lasca [lah'skah] *nf.* roach.

Lasciapassare [lah-shah-pahs-sah'ray] *nm.* pass, permit.

Lascia/re [lah-shah'ray] *vt.* to abandon, desert, leave (out), let, permit, quit; l. cadere [kah-day'ray] vt. to drop; l. stare [stah'ray] vt. to let alone; —rsi *vr.* to allow (let) oneself.

Lascito [lah'shee-toh] *nm.* bequest, legacy.

Lascivia [lah-shee'vee-ah] *nf.* lasciviousness, wantonness.

Lascivo [lah-shee'voh] *a.* lascivious, wanton.

Lasso [lahs'soh] *nm.* lapse (of time), period; *a.* (*poet.*) unhappy, weary.

Lassù [lahs-soo'] *ad.* up there.

Lastra [lah'strah] *nf.* pane (of glass), plate, slab.

Lastricare [lah-stree-kah'ray] vt. to pave.

Lastrico [lah'stree-koh] nm. pavement; lasciare sul [lah-shah'ray sool] l. vt. to leave penniless.

Latebra [lah-tay'brah] nf. recess, secret place.

Latente [lah-ten'tay] a. concealed, latent.

Laterale [lah-tay-rah'lay] a. lateral, side.

Latifondo [lah-tee-fon'doh] nm. large landed estate.

Latino [lah-tee'noh] a. Latin.

Latitante [lah-tee-tahn'tay] a. absconding; rendersi [ren'dehr-see] l. vr. to abscond.

Latitudine [lah-tee-too'dee-nay] nf. latitude.

Lato [lah'toh] nm. side; a [ah] l. di [dee] pr. beside; dal [dahl] l. mio [mee'oh] ad. for my part.

La/tore [lah-toh'ray] nm. —trice [tree'chay] nf. bearer.

Latramento [lah-trah-men'toh] nm. barking.

Latrare [lah-trah'ray] vi. to bark.

Latrina [lah-tree'nah] nf. latrine, lavatory, w.c.

Latrocinio [lah-troh-chee'nee-oh] nm. larceny, theft.

Latta [laht'tah] nf. tin, tin can, tin plate.

Lattaio [laht-tah'yoh] nm. milkman.

Lattante [laht-tahn'tay] nm. child at the breast, suckling; a. sucking.

Lattare: v. **allattare**.

Latte [laht'tay] nm. milk.

Latteo [laht'tay-oh] a. milky.

Latteria [laht-tay-ree'ah] nf. dairy (farm or shop).

Latticinio [laht-tee-chee'nee-oh] nm. dairy product.

Lattivendo/la [laht-tee-ven'doh-lah] nf. milkwoman; —lo [loh] nm. milkman.

Lattuga [laht-too'gah] nf. lettuce.

Laudabile [low-dah'bee-lay] a. laudable, praiseworthy.

Laudano [low'dah-noh] nm. laudanum.

Laudativo [low-dah-tee'voh] a. laudatory.

Laude [low'day] nf. hymn of praise, laud.

Laurea [low'ray-ah] nf. degree (academic).

Laurea/re [low-ray-ah'ray] vt. to confer a degree on; —rsi vr. to take one's degree.

Laureato [low-ray-ah'toh] nm. Bachelor, Doctor.

Lauro [low'roh] nm. laurel.

Lautezza [low-tet'zah] nf. magnificence, sumptuousness.

Lauto [low'toh] a. large, magnificent, sumptuous.

Lava [lah'vah] nf. lava.

Lavabile [lah-vah'bee-lay] a. washable.

Lavabo [lah-vah'boh] nm. lavabo, wash-hand-basin.

Lavacro [lah-vah'kroh] nm. bath.,

Lavagna [lah-vahn'yah] nf. blackboard, slate.

Lavamano [lah-vah-mah'noh] nm. wash-stand.

Lavanda [lah-vahn'dah] nf. lavender, washing.

Lavandaia [lah-vahn-dah'yah] nf. laundress, washer-woman.

Lavanderia [lah-vahn-day-ree'ah] nf. laundry.

Lavandino [lah-vahn-dee'noh] nm. wash-basin.

Lava/re [lah-vah'ray] vt. —rsi vr. to wash.

Lavata [lah-vah'tah] nf. (fig.) dressing-down, reprimand, wash(ing).

Lavatura [lah-vah-too'rah] nf. wash(ing).

Lavorare [lah-voh-rah'ray] vt. and i. to labour, till, toil, work.

Lavora/tore [lah-voh-rah'-toh'ray] nm. —**trice** [tree'chay] nf. worker, workman, work-woman.

Lavorazione [lah-voh-rah-tsee-oh'nay] nf. make, manufacture, tillage, working.

Lavoro [lah-voh'roh] nm. labour, toil, work.

Le [lay] def. art. f. (pl.) the; pn. acc. f. (pl.) them; pn. dat. f. to her.

Leale [lay-ah'lay] a. fair, faithful, loyal, sincere, true.

Lealtà [lay-ahl-tah'] nf. fairness, loyalty, sincerity.

Lebbra [leb'brah] nf. leprosy.

Lebbroso [leb-broh'soh] nm. leper; a. leprous.

Leccare [leck-kah'ray] vt. to lick.

Leccio [lehch'choh] nm. holm-oak.

Leccornia [leck-korr'nee-ah] nf. dainty, titbit.

Lecito [lay'chee-toh] a. allowed, lawful, right.

Ledere [lay'day-ray] vt. to harm, injure, offend.

Lega [lay'gah] nf. alloy, league, union.

Legaccio [lay-gahch'choh] nm. band, string.

Legale [lay-gah'lay] nm. lawyer; a. lawful, legal.

Legalità [lay-gah-lee-tah'] nf. lawfulness, legality.

Legalizzare [lay-gah-leed-zah'ray] vt. to authenticate, legalise.

Legame [lay-gah'may] nm. bond, connection, link, tie.

Legare [lay-gah'ray] vt. to bind, fasten, tie (up).

Legatario [lay-gah-tah'ree-oh] nm. legatee.

Legatura [lay-gah-too'rah] nf. binding, fastening, ligature, tying.

Legazione [lay-gah-tsee-oh'nay] nf. legation.

Legge [lay'djay] nf. act (of Parliament), law.

Leggenda [lay-djen'dah] nf. legend. [to read.

Leggere [lay'djay-ray] vt.

Leggerezza [lay-djay-ret'zah] nf. levity, lightness, thoughtlessness.

Legge/ro [lay-djay'roh] a. frivolous, light, thoughtless; alla [ahl'lah] l. **-ra** [rah] ad. lightly, thoughtlessly; prendere [pren'day-ray] alla l—**ra** vt. to make light of.

Leggiadria [lay-djah-dree'ah] nf. grace.

Leggiadro [lay-djah'droh] a. graceful.

Leggibile [lay-djee'bee-lay] a. readable.

Leggio [lay-djee'oh] nm. lectern, music-stand, reading-desk. [legion.

Legione [lay-joh'nay] nf.

Legislatore [lay-jees-lah-toh'ray] nm. lawgiver, legislator.

Legislatura [lay-jees-lah-too'rah] nf. legislature.

Legislazione [lay-jees-lah-tsee-oh'nay] nf. legislation.

Legittimità [lay-jeet-tee-mee-tah'] nf. lawfulness, legitimacy.

Legittimo [lay-jeet'tee-moh] a. lawful, legitimate.

Legna [layn'yah] nf. wood; portare [porr-tah'ray] l. alla selva [ahl'lah sell'vah] vi. to carry coals to Newcastle.

Legnaiolo [layn-yah-ee-oh'loh] nm. joiner.

Legname [layn-yah'may] nm. timber.

Legno [layn'yoh] nm. wood; di [dee] l. a. wooden.

Legume [lay-goo'may] nm. vegetable.

Lei [lay'ee] pn. nom. and acc. (f.) she, her, **you** (polite form, m. and f.).

Lembo [lem'boh] *nm.* edge, hem, piece.

Lena [lay-nah] *nf.* breath, wind; **di buona** [dee boo-oh'nah] l. *ad.* willingly.

Lenire [lay-nee'ray] *vt.* to soften, soothe.

Lenitivo [lay-nee-tee'voh] *nm. and a.* lenitive; *a.* soothing.

Lente [len'tay] *nf.* eye-glass, lens.

Lentezza [len-tet'zah] *nf.* slowness, sluggishness.

Lenticchia [len-teek'kee-ah] *nf.* lentil.

Lentiggine [len-tee'djee-nay] *nf.* freckle.

Lento [len'toh] *a.* loose, slow, sluggish.

Lenza [lent'zah] *nf.* fishing-line, line.

Lenzuolo [lent-zoo-oh'loh] *nm.* (bed)sheet.

Leo/ne [lay-oh'nay] *nm.* lion; **—nessa** [ness'sah] *nf.* lioness.

Leopardo [lay-oh-pahr'doh] *nm.* leopard.

Lepidezza [lay-pee-det'zah] *nf.* facetiousness, pleasantry.

Lepido [lay'pee-doh] *a.* facetious, pleasant.

Lepre [lay'pray] *nf.* hare.

Lercio [lehr'choh] *a.* dirty, filthy, foul.

Lesina [lay'zee-nah] *nf.* awl.

Lesinare [lay-zee-nah'ray] *vi.* to be stingy; l. **sul prezzo** [sool pret'zoh], to haggle.

Lesione [lay-zee-oh'nay] *nf.* hurt, injury, lesion.

Leso [lay'zoh] *a.* hurt, injured, offended.

Lessare [less-sah'ray] *vt.* to boil.

Lessico [less'see-koh] *nm.* lexicon.

Lesso [less'soh] *nm.* boiled meat; *a.* boiled.

Lestezza [less-tet'zah] *nf.* agility, quickness, swiftness.

Lesto [less'toh] *a.* agile, quick, swift; *ad.* quickly.

Letale [lay-tah'lay] *a.* deadly, lethal.

Letame [lay-tah'may] *nm.* dung.

Letargia [lay-tahr-jee'ah] *nf.* **letargo** [lay-tahr'goh] *nm.* lethargy.

Letizia [lay-tee'tsee-ah] *nf.* gladness, joy.

Lettera [let'tay-rah] *nf.* letter; **alla** [ahl'lah] l. *ad.* literally; **belle lettere** [bell'lay let'tay-ray] (*pl.*) literature.

Letterario [let-tay-rah'ree-oh] *a.* literary.

Letterato [let-tay-rah'toh] *nm.* literary man, man of letters; *a.* lettered.

Letteratura [let-tay-rah-too'rah] *nf.* literature.

Lettiera [let-tee-ay'rah] *nf.* bedstead.

Lettiga [let-tee'gah] *nf.* litter, sedan-(chair).

Lettino [let-tee'noh] *nm.* crib, little bed.

Letto [let'toh] *nm.* bed; *a.* read.

Let/tore [let-toh'ray] *nm.* **—trice** [tree-chay] *nf.* reader.

Lettura [let-too'rah] *nf.* reading; **sala di** [sah'lah dee] l. reading-room.

Levante [lay-vahn'tay] *nm.* East; **vento di** [ven'toh dee] l. East wind; **il** [eel] **L.** the Levant.

Leva/re [lay-vah'ray] *vt.* to lift, raise, remove, take (away); **—rsi** *vr.* to get out of the way, get up, rise.

Levata [lay-vah'tah] *nf.* collection (postal), rising.

Levatrice [lay-vah-tree'chay] *nf.* midwife.

Levigare [lay-vee-gah'ray] *vt.* to smooth.

Levrie/re, **—ro** [lay-vree-ay'ray (-roh)] *nm.* greyhound.

Lezione [lay-tsee-oh'nay] *nf.* lesson.

Lezzo [led'zoh] *nm.* bad smell. [stink.

Lezzume [led-zoo'may] *nm.* foul heat.

Li [lee] *pn. m. acc. (pl.)* them.

Lì [lee] *ad.* there; giù di [joo dee] lì. *ad.* thereabouts; lì. per [pehr] lì *ad.* immediately; essere [ess'say-ray] lì. lì. per *vi.* to be within an ace of.

Libare [lee-bah'ray] *vt.* to make libation.

Libazione [lee-bah-tsee-oh'nay] *nf.* libation.

Libbra [leeb'brah] *nf.* pound (weight).

Libello [lee-bell'loh] *nm.* libel.

Libellula [lee-bell'loo-lah] *nf.* dragon-fly.

Liberale [lee-bay-rah'lay] *nm. and f. and a.* liberal.

Liberalismo [lee-bay-rah-lees'moh] *nm.* liberalism.

Liberalità [lee-bay-rah-lee-tah'] *nf.* generosity, liberality.

Libera/re [lee-bay-rah'ray *vt.* to free, liberate, set free; **—rsi** *vr.* to free oneself, get rid of.

Liberazione [lee-bay-rah-tsee-oh'nay] *nf.* deliverance, liberation.

Libero [lee'bay-roh] *a.* free.

Libertà [lee-behr-tah'] *nf.* freedom, liberty.

Libidine [lee-bee'dee-nay] *nf.* lust.

Libidinoso [lee-bee-dee-noh'soh] *a.* lustful.

Libraio [lee-brah'yoh] *nm.* bookseller.

Libra/re [lee-brah'ray] *vt.* to weigh; **—rsi** *vr.* to fly, soar.

Libreria [lee-bray-ree'ah] *nf.* bookcase, book-shop.

Liceale [lee-chay-ah'lay] *a.* of a classical school.

Licenza [lee-chent'zah] *nf.* certificate, liberty, license.

Licenziamento [lee-chen-tsee-ah-men'toh] *nm.* discharge, dismissal.

Licenzia/re [lee-chen-tsee-ah'ray] *vt.* to give (someone) the sack, discharge, dismiss; **—rsi** *vr.* to get one's diploma, resign.

Licenzioso [lee-chen-tsee-oh'soh] *a.* licentious.

Liceo [lee-chay'oh] *nm.* classical school.

Licitazione [lee-chee-tah-tsee-oh'nay] *nf. (jur.)* sale by auction.

Lido [lee'doh] *nm.* shore.

Lieto [lee-ay'toh] *a.* cheerful, glad, happy.

Lieve [lee-ay'vay] *a.* easy, light, slight.

Lievitare [lee-ay-vee-tah'ray] *vt.* to leaven; *vi.* to levitate, rise of bread, etc.).

Lievito [lee-ay'vee-toh] *nm.* leaven; l. di birra [dee beer'rah], yeast.

Ligio [lee'joh] *a.* faithful, obedient, observant.

Lignaggio [leen-yah'djoh] *nm.* lineage.

Ligustre [lee-goos'tray] *nm.* privet.

Lilla [leel'lah] *nm. or f.* lilac.

Lima [lee'mah] *nf. (mech.)* file.

Limaccioso [lee-mahch-choh'soh] *a.* miry, muddy.

Limare [lee-mah'ray] *vt.* to file, polish.

Limbo [leem'boh] *nm.* Limbo.

Limitare [lee-mee-tah'ray] *vt.* to confine, limit; *nm.* edge, threshold.

Limitazione [lee-mee-tah-tsee-oh'nay] *nf.* limitation.

Limite [lee'mee-tay] *nm.* bound, boundary, limit.

Limitrofo [lee-mee'troh-foh] *a.* adjacent, neighbouring.

Limo [lee'moh] *nm.* mire, mud.

Limonata [lee-moh-nah'tah] *nf.* lemonade.

Limone [lee-moh'nay] *nm.* lemon(-tree).

Limpidezza [leem-pee-det'zah] *nf.* clearness, limpidness.

Limpido [leem'-pee-doh] *a.* clear, limpid.

Linciare [leen-chah'ray] *vt.* to lynch. [neat.

Lindo [leen'doh] *a.* cleanly,

Linea [lee'nay-ah] *nf.* line.

Lineare [lee-nay-ah'ray] *vt.* to draw lines; *a.* lineal, upright.

Linfa [leen'fah] *nf.* lymph, sap.

Linfatico [leen-fah'tee-koh] *a.* lymphatic.

Lingua [leeng'gwah] *nf.* language, tongue.

Linguaggio [leeng-gwah'djoh] *nm.* language.

Linguista [leeng-gwee'stah] *nm.* linguist.

Linguistico [leeng-gwee'stee-koh] *a.* linguistic.

Linificio [lee-nee-fee'choh] *nm.* flax-spinning factory.

Lino [lee'noh] *nm.* flax, linen; seme di [say-may dee] l. linseed.

Liocorno [lee-oh-korr'noh] *nm.* unicorn.

Liquefa/re [lee-kway-fah'ray] *vt.* **—rsi** *vr.* to liquefy.

Liquidare [lee-kwee-dah'ray] *vt.* to liquidate, wind up.

Liquidazione [lee-kwee-dah-tsee-oh'nay] *nf.* liquidation, winding-up.

Liquido [lee'kwee-doh] *nm. and a.* liquid, ready (money).

Liquirizia [lee-kwee-ree'tsee-ah] *nf.* liquorice.

Liquore [lee-kwoh'ray] *nm.* liqueur, liquor.

Lira [lee'rah] *nf.* lira (Italian coin), (*mus.*) lyre.

Lirica [lee'ree-kah] *nf.* lyric, lyrical poem or poetry.

Lirico [lee'ree-koh] *nm.* lyric poet; *a.* lyrical.

Lisca [lee'skah] *nf.* fishbone.

Lisciamento [lee-shah-men'toh] *nm.* lisciatura [lee-shah-too'rah] *nf.* polishing, smoothing.

Lisciare [lee-shah'ray] *vt.* to polish, smooth.

Liscio [lee'shoh] *a.* smooth; *ad.* smoothly, without a hitch.

Lisciva [lee-shee'vah] *nf.* lye.

Lista [lee'stah] *nf.* bill, list, menu.

Listare [lee-stah'ray] *vt.* to border, list.

Listino [lee-stee'noh] *nm.* bill, list, price-list.

Litania [lee-tah-nee'ah] *nf.* litany.

Lite [lee'tay] *nf.* dispute, lawsuit, quarrel.

Litigante [lee-tee-gahn'tay] *nm.* disputant, litigant; *a.* disputing, quarrelling.

Litigare [lee-tee-gah'ray] *vi.* to dispute, quarrel.

Litigio [lee-tee'joh] *nm.* dispute, quarrel.

Litigioso [lee-tee-joh'soh] *a.* quarrelsome.

Litografare [lee-toh-grah-fah'ray] *vt.* to lithograph.

Litorale [lee-toh-rah'lay] *nm.* sea-board; *a.* coast.

Litro [lee'troh] *nm.* litre.

Liuto [lee-oo'toh] *nm.* (*mus.*) lute.

Livellare [lee-vell-lah'ray] *vt.* to level.

Livello [lee-vell'loh] *nm.* level; passaggio a [pahs-sah'djoh ah] l. level-crossing.

Livido [lee'vee-doh] *nm.* bruise; *a.* dismal, livid.

Lividore [lee-vee-doh'ray] *nm.* lividness.

Livore [lee-voh'ray] *nm.* hatred, rancour, spite.

Livrea [lee-vray'ah] *nf.* livery.

Lizza [leet'zah] *nf.* lists (*pl.*), tilt-yard.

Lo [loh] *def. art. m.* the; *pn. acc. m. and neut.* him, it.

Lobo [loh'boh] *nm.* lobe.

Locale [loh-kah'lay] *nm.* place, premises (*pl.*), room; *a.* local.

Località [loh-kah-lee-tah'] *nf.* locality.

Localizzare [loh-kah-leed-zah'ray] *vt.* to localise.

Locanda [loh-kahn'dah] *nf.* inn.

Locandie/ra [loh-kahn-dee-ay'rah] *nf.* —**re** [ray] *nm.* inn-keeper.

Locatario [loh-kah-tah'ree-oh] *nm.* lessee, tenant.

Locatore [loh-kah-toh'ray] *nm.* lessor.

Locazione [loh-kah-tsee-oh'nay] *nf.* lease.

Locusta [loh-koo'stah] *nf.* grasshopper, locust.

Lodare [loh-dah'ray] *vt.* to commend, praise.

Lode [loh'day] *nf.* commendation, praise.

Lodola [loh'doh-lah] *nf.* lark, skylark.

Logaritmo [loh-gah-reet'moh] *nm.* logarithm.

Loggia [loh'djah] *nf.* lodge, open-sided gallery or arcade.

Logica [loh'jee-kah] *nf.* logic.

Logico [loh'jee-koh] *nm.* logician; *a.* logical.

Loglio [loh'lyoh] *nm.* darnel.

Logora/re[loh-goh-rah'ray]*vt.* to exhaust, wear down, wear out; —**rsi** *vr.* to be worn out.

Logoro [loh'goh-roh] *a.* threadbare, worn down (out).

Lombaggine [lom-bah'djee-nay] *nf.* lumbago.

Lombata [lom-bah'tah] *nf.* loin (of meat).

Lombo [lom'boh] *nm.* loin (human).

Lombrico [lom-bree'koh] *nm.* earth-worm.

Londinese [lon-dee-nay'zay] *nm. and f.* Londoner; *a.* (of) London.

Longanime [long-gah'nee-may] *a.* forbearing, patient.

Longanimità [long-gah-nee-mee-tah'] *nf.* forbearance, patience.

Longevità [lon-jay-vee-tah'] *nf.* longevity.

Longevo [lon-jay'voh] *a.* long-lived.

Longitudinale [lon-jee-too-dee-nah'lay] *a.* longitudinal.

Longitudine [lon-jee-too'dee-nay] *nf.* longitude.

Lontananza [lon-tah-nahnt'zah] *nf.* distance; in [een] **l.** *ad.* at a distance.

Lontano [lon-tah'noh] *a.* distant, far; *ad.* far, far away; da [dah] **l.** *ad.* from a distance.

Lontra [lon'trah] *nf.* otter.

Lonza [lont'zah] *nf.* panther.

Loquace [loh-kwah'chay] *a.* loquacious, talkative.

Loquela [loh-kway'lah] *nf.* eloquence, language, way of speaking.

Lordare [lorr-dah'ray] *vt.* to dirty, soil.

Lordo [lorr'doh] *a.* dirty, soiled; peso [pay'zoh] **l.** *nm.* (*com.*) gross weight.

Lordura [lorr-doo'rah] *nf.* dirt, filth.

Loro [loh'roh] *pn. nom.* (*pl.*) you; *acc.* (*pl.*) you, them; *poss. a.* (*pl.*) your, their.

Losco [loss'koh] *a.* dubious, one-eyed, squint-eyed; figura [fee-goo'rah] **losca** *nf.* scoundrel.

Loto [loh'toh] *nm.* lotus, mire, mud.   [struggle.

Lotta [lott'tah] *nf.* fight,

Lottare [lot-tah'ray] *vi.* to contend, fight, struggle, wrestle.

Lotteria [lot-tay-ree'ah] *nf.* lottery, sweepstake.

Lotto [lot'toh] *nm.* lot, parcel; giuoco del [joo-oh'koh dell] l. lottery.

Lozione [loh-tsee-oh'nay] *nf.* lotion.

Lubricità [loo-bree-chee-tah'] *nf.* lewdness, lubricity.

Lubrico [loo'bree-koh] *a.* lewd; slippery.

Lubrificare [loo-bree-fee-kah'ray] *vt.* to grease, lubricate, oil.

Lucchetto [look-ket'toh] *nm.* padlock.

Lucciare [looch-chee-kah'ray] *vi.* to glitter, shine.

Luccichio [looch-chee-kee'oh] *nm.* glitter, sparkle.

Luccio [looch'choh] *nm.* pike (fish).

Lucciola [looch'choh-lah] *nf.* fire-fly, glow-worm.

Luce [loo'chay] *nf.* light.

Lucente [loo-chen'tay] *a.* shining, sparkling.

Lucentezza [loo-chen-tet'zah] *nf.* brightness, shine.

Lucere [loo'chay-ray] *vi.* to glitter, shine. *v.* Splendere.

Lucerna [loo-chehr'nah] *nf.* lamp.

Lucertola [loo-chehr'toh-lah] *nf.* lizard.

Lucidare [loo-chee-dah'ray] *vt.* to clean, glaze, polish.

Lucidezza [loo-chee-det'zah] *nf.* brightness.

Lucidità [loo-chee-dee-tah'] *nf.* clearness, lucidity.

Lucido [loo'chee-doh] *a.* bright, clear, lucid.

Lucignolo [loo-cheen'yoh-loh] *nm.* wick.

Lucrare [loo-krah'ray] *vt.* and *i.* to earn, make money.

Lucro [loo'kroh] *nm.* lucre.

Lucroso [loo-kroh'soh] *a.* lucrative, profitable.

Lucubrazione [loo-koo-brah-tsee-oh'nay] *nf.* lucubration.

Ludibrio [loo-dee'bree-oh] *nm.* laughing-stock, mockery, ridicule.

Lue [loo'ay] *nf.* (*med.*) syphilis.

Luglio [lool'yoh] *nm.* July.

Lugubre [loo'goo-bray] *a.* dismal, lugubrious.

Lui [loo'ee] *pn. m.* (*nom. and acc.*) he, him.

Lumaca [loo-mah'kah] *nf.* slug.

Lume [loo'may] *nm.* lamp, light; a questi lumi di luna [ah kwess'tee loo'mee dee loo'nah] *ad.* in these hard times.

Lumiera [loo-mee-ay'rah] *nf.* chandelier, lustre.

Luminare [loo-mee-nah'ray] *nm.* great man, luminary.

Luminaria [loo-mee-nah'ree-ah] *nf.* public illumination.

Luminoso [loo-mee-noh'soh] *a.* clear, luminous, shining.

Luna [loo'nah] *nf.* moon; l. di miele [dee mee-ay'lay] honeymoon; al lume di [ahl loo'may dee] l. *ad.* by moonlight.

Lunario [loo-nah'ree-oh] *nm.* almanac; sbarcare il [sbahr-kah'ray eel] l. *vi.* to make both ends meet.

Lunatico [loo-nah'tee-koh] *nm. and a.* eccentric.

Lunedì [loo-nay-dee'] *nm.* Monday.

Lunghesso [loong-ghess'soh] *pr.* along.

Lunghezza [loong-ghet'zah] *nf.* length.

Lungi [loon'jee] *ad.* far.

Lungo [loong'goh] *a.* long; *pr.* along; a [ah] l. *ad.* a long time; di gran [de grahn] l. *ad.* by far; a [ah] l. andare [ahn-dah'ray] *ad.* in the long run.

Luogo [loo-oh'goh] *nm.*

place, spot; l. comune [koh-moo'nay], commonplace.

Luogotenente [loo-oh-goh-tay-nen'tay] *nm.* lieutenant.

Lu/pa [loo'pah] *nf.* she-wolf; **—po** [poh] *nm.* wolf.

Luppolo [loop'poh-loh] *nm.* hop (plant).

Luridezza [loo-ree-det'zah] *nf.* dirtiness, filthiness.

Lurido [loo'ree-doh] *a.* dirty, filthy.

Lusinga [loo-zeeng'gah] *nf.* allurement, flattery.

Lusingare [loo-zeeng-gah'ray] *vt.* to allure, flatter.

Lusinghiero [loo-zeeng-ghee-ay'roh] *a.* alluring, flattering.

Lussare [loos-sah'ray] *vt.* (*med.*) to dislocate.

Lusso [loos'soh] *nm.* luxury.

Lussuoso [loos-soo-oh'soh] *a.* luxurious.

Lussureggiare [loos-soo-ray-djah'ray] *vi.* to be luxuriant, flourish, grow rank.

Lussuria [loos-soo'ree-ah] *nf.* lewdness, lust.

Lussurioso [loos-soo-ree-oh'soh] *a.* lewd, lustful.

Lustrare [loos-trah'ray] *vt.* to clean, polish.

Lustrascarpe [loos-trah-skahr'pay] *nm.* boots, shoeblack.

Lustratura [loo-strah-too'rah] *nf.* cleaning, polishing.

Lustro [loo'stroh] *nm.* lustre, lustrum (**5 years**); *a.* polished, shining.

Lutto [loot'toh] *nm.* mourning; **a** [ah] **l.** *ad.* in mourning.

Luttuoso [loot-too-oh'soh] *a.* mournful, sad.

M

Ma [mah] *con.* but; **macchè** [mahk-kay'] *int.* not at all.

Macabro [mah'kah-broh] *a.* macabre.

Macchero/ne, **—ni** [mahk-kay-roh'nay (-nee)] *nm.* (*sing. and pl.*) macaroni.

Macchia [mahk'kee-ah] *nf.* blot, spot, stain, bush, woodland; **alla** [ahl'lah] **m.** *ad.* clandestinely.

Macchia/re [mahk-kee-ah'ray] *vt.* to soil, spot, stain; **—rsi** *vr.* to disgrace oneself, get dirty.

Macchiaiolo [mahk-kee-ah-yoh'loh] *nm.* dishonest fellow, rogue.

Macchina [mahk'kee-nah] *nf.* engine, machine, (motor) car; **m. a vapore** [ah vah-poh'ray] steam-engine; **m. da scrivere** [dah skree'vay-ray] type-writer.

Macchinare [mahk-kee-nah'ray] *vt.* to plot.

Macchinario [mahk-kee-nah'ree-oh] *nm.* machinery.

Macchinazione [mahk-kee-nah-tsee-oh'nay] *nf.* machination, plot.

Macchinista [mahk-kee-nee'stah] *nm.* driver (*Amer.*) engineer.

Macellaio [mah-chell-lah'yoh] *nm.* butcher.

Macelleria [mah-chell-lay-ree'ah] *nf.* butcher's (shop).

Macello [mah-chell'loh] *nm.* massacre, slaughter-house, shambles.

Macera/re [mah-chay-rah'ray] *vt.* to macerate, soak; **—rsi** *vr.* to wear oneself out.

Macerie [mah-chay'ree-ay] *nf.* (*pl.*) remains, ruins (*pl.*).

Macero [mah'chay-roh] *nm.* macerating-vat.

Macigno [mah-cheen'yoh] *nm.* big stone.

Macilento [mah-chee-len'toh] *a.* emaciated, gaunt, lean.

Macina [mah'chee-nah] *nf.* mill-stone, presser.

Macinare [mah-chee-nah´ray] vt. to crush, grind, mill.

Macinatoio [mah-chee-nah-toh´yoh] nm. mill, press.

Macinino [mah-chee-nee´noh] nm. coffee-mill.

Maciullare [mah-chool-lah´ray] vt. to chew, crush.

Macula [mah´koo-lah] nf. spot.

Maculare [mah-koo-lah´ray] vt. to bruise, spot.

Madia [mah´dee-ah] nf. bread-bin, kneading-trough.

Madido [mah´dee-doh] a. damp, moist, wet.

Madornale [mah-dorr-nah´lay] a. enormous, gross, huge.

Madre [mah´dray] nf. dam (of animals), mother, (com.) counterfoil.

Madreperla [mah-dray-pehr´lah] nf. mother-of-pearl.

Madreselva [mah-dray-sell´vah] nf. honeysuckle.

Madrina [mah-dree´nah] nf. godmother.

Maestà [mah-ess-tah´] nf. majesty.

Maestra [mah-ess´trah] nf. (school)mistress, teacher.

Maestranza [mah-ess-trahnt´zah] nf. hands (pl.) workmen (pl.).

Maestrevole [mah-ess-tray´voh-lay] a. clever, masterly, skilful.

Maestria [mah-ess-tree´ah] nf. mastery, skill.

Maestro [mah-ess´troh] nm. (school)master, teacher; a. main, principal.

Magagna [mah-gahn´yah] nf. defect, fault, trouble, vice.

Magagnare [mah-gahn-yah´ray] vt. to damage, spoil, weaken.

Magari [mah-gah´ree] int. would to . . . ! ad. maybe, perhaps.

Magazzinaggio [mah-gahd-zee-nah´djoh] nm. cost of warehousing, storage.

Magazziniere [mah-gahd-zee-nee-ay´ray] nm. warehouse-man.

Magazzino [mah-gahd-zee´noh] nm. store, warehouse.

Maggio [mah´djoh] nm. May (month).

Maggiorana [mah-djoh-rah´nah] nf. marjoram.

Maggioranza [mah-djoh-rahnt´zah] nf. majority.

Maggiore [mah-djoh´ray] nm. ancestor, (mil.) major; a. bigger, elder, greater, high(er), larger, older, biggest, eidest, etc.; età [ay-tah´] m. nf. full age, majority.

Maggiorenne [mah-djoh-ren´nay] nm. major, person of full age; a. of age.

Magia [mah-jee´ah] nf. magic.

Magistero [mah-jee-stay´roh] nm. ingenuity, mastery, office, skill, teaching.

Magistrale [mah-jee-strah´lay] a. clever, masterly, skilful; istituto [ee-stee-too´toh] m. nm. training-school (for teachers).

Magistrato [mah-jee-strah´toh] nm. magistrate.

Maglia [mahl´yah] nf. link, mail, mesh, stitch jersey, vest; lavorare a. [lah-voh-rah´ray ah] m. nf. to knit.

Maglieria [mahl-ray-ree´ah] nf. hosiery, knitted goods (pl.).

Maglio [mahl´yoh] nm. hammer, mallet.

Magnanimità [mahn-yah-nee-mee-tah´] nf. magnanimity.

Magnanimo [mahn-yah´nee-moh] a. great-hearted, magnanimous.

Magnano [mahn-yah´noh] nm. locksmith.

Magnesia [mahn-yay´zee-ah] nf. magnesia.

Magnete [mahn-yay'tay] *nm.* magnet, magneto (in cars, etc.).

Magnetismo [mahn-yay-tees'moh] *nm.* magnetism.

Magnetizzare [mahn-yay-teed-zah'ray] *vt.* to magnetize.

Magnificare [mahn-yee-fee-kah'ray] *vt.* to extol, magnify.

Magnificenza [mahn-yee-fee-chent'zah] *nf.* grandeur, splendour.

Magnifico [mahn-yee'fee-koh] *a.* grand, magnificent, splendid.

Magniloquenza [mahn-yee-loh-kwent'zah] *nf.* grandiloquence.

Magno [mahn'yoh] *a.* great, illustrious, main.

Magnolia [mahn-yoh'lee-ah] *nf.* magnolia-tree.

Mago [mah'goh] *nm.* enchanter, sorcerer, wizard.

Magrezza [mah-gret'zah] *nf.* leanness, thinness.

Magro [mah'groh] *a.* lean, paltry, poor, thin; **giorno di** [jorr'noh dee] *nm.* day of abstinence.

Mai [mah'ee] *ad.* ever, never; **come** [koh'may] **m.?** how is that? **se** [say] **m.** *con.* in case.

Maiale [mah-ee-ah'lay] *nm.* pig, pork.

Maiolica [mah-ee-oh'lee-kah] *nf.* faience, majolica.

Maionese [mah-ee-oh-nay'say] *nf.* mayonnaise.

Maiuscolo [mah-ee-oos'koh-loh] *a.* capital (letter).

Malaccio [mah-lahch'choh] *nm.* dangerous disease.; **non c'è** [nonn chay] **m.** *int.* not too bad(ly).

Malaccorto [mah-lahk-korr'toh] *a.* imprudent, rash.

Malacreanza [mah-lah-kray-ahnt'zah] *nf.* ill-breeding, unmannerliness.

Malafatta [mah-lah-faht'tah] *nf.* defect (in materials).

Malafede [mah-lah-fay'day] *nf.* bad faith.

Malagevole [mah-lah-jay'voh-lay] *a.* difficult, hard.

Malagrazia [mah-lah-grah'tsee-ah] *nf.* awkwardness, bad grace.

Malandare [mah-lahn-dah'ray] *vi.* to go wrong, take a bad turn.

Malandato [mah-lahn-dah'toh] *a.* in bad repair, in poor health.

Malandrinaggio [mah-lahn-dree-nah'djoh] *nm.* robbery, robbers (*pl.*).

Malandrino [mah-lahn-dree'noh] *nm.* robber, scoundrel.

Malanno [mah-lahn'noh] *nm* disease, infirmity, misfortune, plague.

Malaparata [mah-lah-pah-rah'tah] *nf.* danger.

Malapena [a [mah-lah-pay'nah] *ad.* hardly, scarcely.

Malato [mah-lah'toh] *nm.* patient, sick person; *a.* ill, sick, sore.

Malattia [mah-laht-tee'ah] *nf.* disease, illness, malady.

Malaugurio [mah-low-goo'ree-oh] *nm.* ill-omen.

Malavita [mah-lah-vee'tah] *nf.* criminals (*pl.*), gangsters (*pl.*).

Malavvezzo [mah-lah-vet'zoh] *a.* ill-bred, unmannerly.

Malazzato [mah-laht-zah'toh] *a.* sickly.

Malcapitato [mahl-kah-pee-tah'toh] *a.* unfortunate, unlucky.

Malconcio [mahl-kon'choh] *a.* in a poor way, in tatters.

Malcontento [mahl-kon-ten'toh] *nm.* discontent, grievance, malcontent; *a.* discontented, dissatisfied.

Maldicenza [mahl-dee-chent'zah] *nf.* backbiting, scandal, slander.

Male [mah'lay] *nm.* disease, evil, harm, ill, illness, misfortune, trouble; **m. di denti** [dee den'tee], toothache; **m. di gola** [dee goh'lah], sorethroat; **m. di testa** [dee tess'tah], headache; **meno** [may'noh] **m.** *ad.* luckily; **non c'è** [nonn chay] **m.** pretty good; *ad.* badly; **restare** [ress-tah'ray] **m.** to be disappointed; **star** [stahr] **m.** to be ill.

Maledire [mah-lay-dee'ray] *vt.* to curse.

Maledizione [mah-lay-dee-tsee-oh'nay] *nf.* curse, ill-luck.

Malefico [mah-lay'fee-koh] *a.* evil, mischievous.

Malerba [mah-lehr'bah] *nf.* weed.

Malessere [mah-less'say-ray] *nm.* discomfort, indisposition, uneasiness.

Malevolenza [mah-lay-voh-lent'zah] *nf.* ill-will, malevolence.

Malfare [mahl-fah'ray] *vt.* evil-doing.

Malfattore [mahl-faht-toh'ray] *nm.* evil-doer, malefactor.

Malfermo [mahl-fehr'moh] *a.* poor, unsteady.

Malgoverno [mahl-goh-vehr'noh] *nm.* misgovernment, mismanagement.

Malgradito [mahl-grah-dee'toh] *a.* unwelcome.

Malgrado [mahl-grah'doh] *ad. and pr.* in spite of, notwithstanding.

Malìa [mah-lee'ah] *nf.* charm, enchantment, witchcraft.

Malignità [mah-leen-yee-tah'] *nf.* malignity, wickedness.

Maligno [mah-leen'yoh] *a.* evil, malicious, malignant.

Malinconia [mah-leen-koh-nee'ah] *nf.* melancholy, sadness.

Malinconico [mah-leen-koh'nee-koh] *a.* melancholy, sad.

Malincuore, a [ah mah-leen-kwoh'ray] *ad.* unwillingly.

Malinteso [mah-leen-tay'soh] *nm.* misunderstanding; *a.* misunderstood, wrong.

Malizia [mah-lee'tsee-ah] *nf.* cunning, malice, trick.

Malizioso [mah-lee-tsee-oh'soh] *a.* artful, malicious.

Mallevadore [mahl-lay-vah-doh'ray] *nm.* bail, surety.

Malle/veria [mahl-lay-vay-ree'ah, —vadoria [vah-doh'ree-ah] *nf.* bail, suretyship.

Malmenare [mahl-may-nah'ray] *vt.* to ill-treat, ill-use.

Malmesso [mahl-mess'soh] *a.* badly dressed.

Malo [mah'loh] *a.* bad, ill, wicked.

Malocchio [mah-lohk'kee-oh] *nm.* evil-eye; vedere di [vay-day'ray dee] **m.** *vt.* to dislike.

Malora [mah-loh'rah] *nf.* ruin.

Malore [mah-loh'ray] *nm.* sudden illness, indisposition.

Malsano [mahl-sah'noh] *a.* unhealthy, unwholesome.

Malsicuro [mahl-see-koo'roh] *a.* uncertain, unsafe, unsteady.

Maltalento [mahl-tah-lent'toh] *nm.* evil disposition, ill-will.

Maltempo [mahl-tem'poh] *nm.* bad weather.

Maltrattamento [mahl-traht-tah-men'toh] *nm.* ill-treatment.

Maltrattare [mahl-traht-tah'ray] *vt.* to ill-treat, ill-use.

Malumore [mah-loo-moh'ray] *nm.* discontent, ill-humour, spleen.

Malvagio [mahl-vah'joh] *a.* wicked.

Malvagità [mahl-vah-jee-tah'] *nf.* wickedness.

Malvolentieri [mahl-voh-len-tee-ay'ree] ad. unwillingly.

Malvolere [mahl-voh-lay'ray] vt. to dislike, hate.

Mamma [mahm'mah] nf. mother, mummie.

Mammella [mahm-mell'lah] nf. breast.

Mammola [mahm'moh-lah] nf. violet.

Manata [mah-nah'tah] nf. blow, handful, slap.

Manca [mahng'kah] nf. left-hand, left-hand side.

Mancanza [mahng-kahnt'-zah] nf. deficiency, faint, lack, want; **sentire la** [sen-tee'ray lah] m. di [dee] vt. to miss.

Mancare [mahng-kah'ray] vi. to be in want of, fail, lack, miss, want, be missing, be without; **mancano cinque minuti alle due** [mahng'kah-noh cheeng'kway mee-noo'tee ahl'lay doo'ay], it is five to two.

Mancia [mahn'chah] nf. gratuity, reward, tip.

Manciata [mahn-chah'tah] nf. handful.

Mancino [mahn-chee'noh] a. left-handed, treacherous.

Manco [mahng'koh] a. left; ad. less, not even.

Mandamento [mahn-dah-men'toh] nm. borough, district.

Mandante [mahn-dahn'tay] nm. instigator.

Mandare [mahn-dah'ray] vt. to forward, send.

Mandarino [mahn-dah-ree'noh] nm. mandarin, tangerine.

Mandata [mahn-dah'tah] nf. series, turning (of the key).

Mandato [mahn-dah'toh] nm. commission, mandate, order, warrant; a. sent.

Mandor/la [mahn'dorr-lah] nf. almond; —lo [loh] nm. almond-tree.

Mandra [mahn'drah], man-dria [mahn'dree-ah] nf. flock, herd.

Maneggevole [mah-nay-djay'voh-lay] a. easy to handle, manageable.

Maneggia/re [mah-nay-djah'ray] vt. to handle, manage, use; —rsi vr. to conduct oneself, manage.

Maneggio [mah-nay'djoh] nm. handling, horsemanship, management, riding-school, use.

Manesco [mah-ness'koh] a. ready with one's fists.

Manette [mah-net'tay] nf. (pl.) handcuffs.

Mangiare [mahn-jah'ray] vt. to eat.

Mangiatoia [mahn-jah-toh'yah] nf. crib, manger.

Mania [mah-nee'ah] nf. hobby, mania, passion.

Manica [mah'nee-kah] nf. channel, sleeve; **essere di** [ess'say-ray dee] m. larga [lahr'gah] vi. to be broad-minded; **un altro paio di maniche** [oon ahl'troh pah'yoh dee mah'nee-kay], nm. another pair of shoes.

Manico [mah'nee-koh] nm. handle.

Manicomio [mah-nee-koh'mee-oh] nm. (lunatic) asylum.

Manicotto [mah-nee-kot'toh] nm. muff, (mech.) clutch.

Maniera [mah-nee'rah] nf. manner, way; **in qualunque** [een kwah-loong'kway] m. ad. anyhow, somehow.

Manierato [mah-nee-ay-rah'toh] a. affected, mannered.

Manifattore [mah-nee-faht-toh'ray] nm. workman.

Manifattura [mah-nee-faht-too'rah] nf. make, manufacture.

Manifesta/re [mah-nee-fess-tah'ray] vt. to display, manifest, show; —rsi vr. to appear, reveal oneself.

Manifesto [mah-nee-fess'toh] *nm.* bill, manifesto, placard; *a.* clear, obvious.

Maniglia [mah-neel'yah] *nf.* handle.

Manigoldo [mah-nee-goll'doh] *nm.* knave, rascal.

Manipolare [mah-nee-poh-lah'ray] *vt.* to handle, manipulate, work.

Manipolazione [mah-nee-poh-lah-tsee-oh'nay] *nf.* handling, manipulation, working.

Maniscalco [mah-nee-skahl'koh] *nm.* farrier, shoeing-smith.

Manna [mahn'nah] *nf.* manna, sheaf.

Mannaia [mah-nah'yah] *nf.* axe.

Mano [mah'noh] *nf.* hand; **a portata di** [ah porr-tah'tah dee] **m.** *ad.* within reach; **fuori di** [foo-oh'ree dee] **m.** *ad.* out of reach, out of the way.

Manodopera [mah-noh-doh'pay-rah] *nf.* (manual) labour.

Manomettere [mah-noh-met'tay-ray] *vt.* to free, open, touch.

Manopola [mah-noh'poh-lah] *nf.* gauntlet, cuff.

Manoscritto [mah-noh-skreet'toh] *nm.* manuscript; *a.* hand-written.

Manovale [mah-noh-vah'lay] *nm.* labourer.

Manovra [mah-noh'vrah] *nf.* manœuvre, (*tech.*) shunting.

Manovrare [mah-noh-vrah'ray] *vt.* to manœuvre, shunt, work.

Mansione [mahn-see-oh'nay] *nf.* duty, function, office.

Mansuefare [mahn-soo-ay-fah'ray] *vt.* to subdue, tame.

Mansueto [mahn-soo-ay'toh] *a.* meek, mild, tame.

Mantello [mahn-tell'loh] *nm.* cloak, mantle.

Mantene/re [mahn-tay-nay'ray] *vt.* to hold, keep (up), maintain; **-rsi** *vr.* to keep (oneself).

Mantenimento [mahn-tay-nee-men'toh] *nm.* keeping, maintenance, preservation.

Mantice [mahn'tee-chay] *nm.* bellows (*pl.*), hood (of a car).

Manto [mahn'toh] *nm.* cloak, mantle.

Manuale [mah-noo-ah'lay] *nm.* hand-book, manual; *a.* manual.

Manubrio [mah-noo'bree-oh] *nm.* dumb-bell, handle(-bar).

Manufatto [mah-noo-faht'toh] *nm.* manufactured article; *a.* hand-made.

Manutengolo [mah-noo-teng'goh-loh] *nm.* accomplice, receiver of (stolen) goods.

Manutenzione [mah-noo-ten-tsee-oh'nay] *nf.* care, maintenance.

Manzo [mahnt'zoh] *nm.* beef, steer.

Maomettano [mah-oh-met-tah'noh] *nm. and a.* Mohammedan.

Mappamondo [mahp-pah-mon'doh] *nm.* map of the world.

Marachella [mah-rah-kell'lah] *nf.* naughtiness, trick.

Maraviglia, etc. *v.* **Meraviglia**, etc.

Marca [mahr'kah] *nf.* mark; **m. da bollo** [dah boll'loh], stamp; **m. di fabbrica** [dee fahb'bree-kah], trade-mark.

Marcare [mahr-kah'ray] *vt.* to mark.

Marche/sa [mahr-kay'zah] *nf.* marchioness; **—se** [zay] *nm.* marquis.

Marcia [mahr'chah] *nf.* march, (*med.*) pus.

Marciapiede [mahr-chah-pee-ay'day] *nm.* pavement, platform.

Marciare [mahr-chah'ray] *vi.* to march.

Marcio [mahr'choh] *a.* rotten, tainted.

Marcire [mahr-chee'ray] *vi.* to decay, go bad, rot, waste.

Marciume [mahr-choo'may] *nm.* rottenness, rotten things (*pl.*).

Marco [mahr'koh] *nm.* mark (coin).

Mare (mah'ray) *nm.* sea; in alto [een ahl'toh] m. *ad.* on the high seas; mal di [mahl dee] m. sea-sickness.

Marea [mah-ray'ah] *nf.* tide.

Mareggiata [mah-ray-djah'tah] *nf.* rough sea.

Margherita [mahr-gay-ree'tah] *nf.* daisy, pearl.

Marginale [mahr-jee-nah'lay] *a.* marginal.

Margine [mahr'jee-nay] *nm.* bank, border, edge, margin.

Marina [mah-ree'nah] *nf.* coast, navy, seascape (picture), seaside; regia [ray'jah] m. Royal Navy.

Marinaio [mah-ree-nah'yoh] *nm.* sailor, seaman.

Marino [mah-ree'noh] *a.* marine, (of the) sea.

Mariolo [mah-ree-oh'loh] *nm.* knave, rogue, swindler.

Marionetta [mah-ree-oh-net'tah] *nf.* marionette, puppet.

Maritabile [mah-ree-tah'bee-lay] *a.* marriageable.

Marita/re [mah-ree-tah'ray] *vt.* to give in marriage, marry; —rsi *vr.* to get married, marry.

Marito [mah-ree'toh] *nm.* husband.

Marittimo [mah-reet'tee-moh] *a.* marine, maritime, sea.

Marmista [mahr-mee'stah] *nm.* marble-cutter.

Marmitta [mahr-meet'tah] *nf.* kettle, saucepan.

Marmo [mahr'moh] *nm.* marble.

Marocchino [mah-rock-kee'noh] *nm.* marocco (-leather).

Maroso [mah-roh'soh] *nm.* billow, wave.

Marrone [mahr-roh'nay] *nm.* chestnut, gross mistake; *a.* brown, chestnut.

Martedì [mahr-tay-dee'] *nm.* Tuesday; m. grasso [grahs'soh], Shrove Tuesday.

Martellare [mahr-tell-lah'ray] *vt.* to beat, hammer, strike.

Martello [mahr-tell'loh] *nm.* hammer.

Martinicca [mahr-tee-neek'kah] *nf.* (*tech.*) drag, wheel-drag.

Martin pescatore [mahr-teen' pess-kah-toh'ray] *nm.* kingfisher.

Martire [mahr'tee-ray] *nm.* martyr.

Martirio [mahr-tee'ree-oh] *nm.* martyrdom.

Martirizzare [mahr-tee-reed-zah'ray] *vt.* to martyrize, torture.

Martora [mahr'toh-rah] *nf.* marten.

Martoriare [mahr-toh-ree-ah'ray] *vt.* to torment, torture.

Marzapane [mahrt-zah-pah'nay] *nm.* marzipan.

Marzo [mahrt'zoh] *nm.* March.

Marzocco [mahrt-zock'koh] *nm.* heraldic lion (of Florence).

Mascalzone [mah-skahlt-zoh'nay] *nm.* rascal, scoundrel.

Mascella [mah-shell'lah] *nf.* jaw.

Maschera [mah'skay-rah] *nf.* attendant (in a theatre), mask.

Maschera/re [mah-skay-rah'ray] *vt.* to camouflage, disguise, mask; —rsi *vr.* to disguise oneself.

Maschiezza [mah-skee-et'zah] *nf.* manliness.

Maschile [mah-skee'lay] *a.* male, manly, masculine.

Maschio [mah'skee-oh] *nm.* keep, prison, stronghold; *a.* male, masculine.

Mascolino [mahs-koh-lee'noh] *a.* male, masculine.

Masnada [mahs-nah'dah] *nf.* gang, set.

Masnadiere [mahs-nah-dee-ay'ray] *nm.* brigand, robber.

Massa [mahs'sah] *nf.* heap, majority, mass.

Massacrare [mahs-sah-krah'ray] *vt.* to massacre, slaughter.

Massacro [mahs-sah'kroh] *nm.* massacre, slaughter.

Massaggio [mahs-sah'djoh] *nm.* massage.

Massaia [mahs-sah'yah] *nf.* housewife.

Masseria [mahs-say-ree'ah] *nf.* farm.

Masserizie [mahs-say-ree'-tsee-ay] *nf.* (*pl.*) household goods (*pl.*), household utensils (*pl.*).

Massiccio [mahs-seech'choh] *nm.* massif; *a.* heavy, massive, stocky.

Massima [mahs'see-mah] *nf.* maxim, rule, saying.

Massimo [mahs'see-moh] *nm* maximum; *a.* best, greatest, highest, utmost.

Masso [mahs'soh] *nm.* big stone, block, boulder.

Massone [mahs-soh'nay] *nm.* mason, Freemason.

Massoneria [mahs-soh-nay-ree'ah] *nf.* Freemasonry.

Masticare [mahs-stee-kah'ray] *vt.* to chew, masticate, stammer; **m. una lingua** [oo'nah leeng'gwah] *vi.* to have a smattering of a language.

Mastino [mah-stee'noh] *nm.* mastiff.

Mastro [mah'stroh] *nm.* ledger, master. [skein.

Matassa [mah-tahs'sah] *nf.*

Matematica [mah-tay-mah'-tee-kah] *nf.* mathematics.

Materassa [mah-tay-rahs'-sah] *nf.* mattress.

Materia [mah-tay'ree-ah] *nf.* material, matter, subject, substance; **m. prima** [pree'mah] raw material.

Materiale [mah-tay-ree-ah'lay] *nm.* material; *a.* manual, material.

Maternità [mah-tehr-nee-tah'] *nf.* maternity, motherhood.

Materno [mah-tehr'noh] *a.* maternal, motherly, mother's.

Matita [mah-tee'tah] *nf.* pencil.

Matrice [mah-tree'chay] *nf.* matrix, mould, womb; registro a [ray-jees'troh ah] **m.** *nm.* (*com.*) counterfoil register.

Matricola [mah-tree'koh-lah] *nf.* register, roll.

Matricola/re [mah-tree-koh-lah'ray] *vt.*—**rsi** *vr.* to matriculate.

Matrigna [mah-treen'yah] *nf.* step-mother.

Matrimonio [mah-tree-moh'nee-oh] *nm.* marriage, match, wedding.

Mattacchione [maht-tahk-kee-oh'nay] *nm.* joker, wag.

Matti/na [maht-tee'nah] *nf.* —**no** [noh] *nm.* morning.

Mattinata [maht-tee-nah'tah] *nf.* forenoon, morning, (*theat.*) matinée.

Mattiniero [maht-tee-nee-ay'roh] *a.* early-rising.

Matto [maht'toh] *nm.* lunatic, madman; *a.* crazy, insane, mad; **scacco** [skahk'koh] **m.** check-mate (at chess).

Mattonaio [maht-toh-nah'yoh] *nm.* brick-maker.

Mattone [maht-toh'nay] *nm.* brick, (*fig.*) bore, nuisance.

Maturare [mah-too-rah'ray] *vt. and i.* to come to a head, mature, ripen.

Maturazione [mah-too-rah-tsee-oh'nay] *nf.* maturation, maturity, ripening.

Maturo [mah-too'roh] *a.* elderly, mature, ripe.

Mausoleo [mow-zoh-lay'oh] *nm.* mausoleum.

Mazza [maht'zah] *nf.* cane, cudgel, mallet, sledge-hammer.

Mazzo [maht'zoh] *nm.* bunch, nosegay, pack (of cards).

Mazzolino [maht-zoh-lee'noh] *nm.* posy, small bunch.

Me [may] *pn.* (*oblique case*) me, myself.

Meato [may-ah'toh] *nm.* channel, passage.

Meccanica [meck-kah'nee-kah] *nf.* mechanics (*pl.*).

Meccanico [meck-kah'nee-koh] *nm.* mechanic(ian); *a.* mechanical.

Meccanismo [meck-kah-nees'moh] *nm.* gear, mechanism, works.

Mecenate [may-chay-nah'tay] *nm.* Maecenas, patron.

Medaglia [may-dahl'yah] *nf.* medal.

Medaglione [may-dahl-yoh'nay] *nm.* medallion.

Medesimo [may-day'zee-moh] *a. and pn.* same, -self.

Media [may'dee-ah] *nf.* average; in [een] m. *ad.* on the average.

Mediante [may-dee-ahn'tay] *pr.* by means of.

Mediatore [may-dee-ah-toh'ray] *nm.* mediator, (*com.*) broker, middleman.

Mediazione [may-dee-ah-tsee-oh'nay] *nf.* mediation, (*com.*) brokerage.

Medicabile [may-dee-kah'bee-lay] *a.* curable, medicable.

Medicare [may-dee-kah'ray] *vt.* to dress, medicate, treat.

Medicastro [may-dee-kah'stroh] *nm.* quack.

Medicina [may-dee-chee'nah] *nf.* medicine, physic, remedy.

Medico [may'dee-koh] *nm.* doctor, physician.

Medio [may'dee-oh] *nm.* mean, medium, middle finger; *a.* average, middle, middling; scuola [skwoh'lah] m. *nf.* middle school.

Mediocre [may-dee-oh'kray] *a.* mediocre, second-rate.

Medioevo [may-dee-oh-ay'voh] *nm.* the Middle Ages (*pl.*)

Meditare [may-dee-tah'ray] *vt. and i.* to meditate, plan, think over.

Meditazione [may-dee-tah-tsee-oh'nay] *nf.* meditation.

Mediterraneo [may-dee-tehr-rah'nay-oh] *nm. and a.* Mediterranean.

Medusa [may-doo'zah] *nf.* jelly-fish, Medusa.

Meglio [mayl'yoh] *ad.* better, best.

Me/la [may'lah] *nf.* apple; —lo [loh] *nm.* apple-tree.

Melacotogna [may-lah-koh-tohn'yah] *nf.* quince.

Melagrana [may-lah-grah'nah] *nf.* pomegranate.

Melarancia [may-lah-rahn'chah] *nf.* orange.

Melassa [may-lahs'sah] *nf.* molasses.

Melenso [may-len'soh] *a.* sheepish, silly.

Mellifluo [mell-lee'floo-oh] *a.* honied, mellifluous, sweet.

Mellone [mell-loh'nay] *nm.* melon.

Melma [mell'mah] *nf.* mire, mud.

Melmoso [mell-moh'soh] *a.* miry, muddy.

Melodia [may-loh-dee'ah] *nf.* melody.

Membrana [mem-brah'nah] *nf.* membrane, web.

Membranoso [mem-brah-noh'soh] *a.* membranous.

Membro [mem'broh] *nm.* limb, member.

Membruto [mem-broo'toh] *a.* large-limbed, strong-limbed.

Memorabile [may-moh-rah'bee-lay] *a.* memorable, unforgettable.

Memore [may'moh-ray] *a.* grateful, mindful.

Memori/a [may-moh'ree-ah] *nf.* memory, remembrance, record; *a.* [ah] m. *ad.* by heart; —e [ay] (*pl.*) memoirs (*pl.*).

Menadito, a [ah may-nah-dee'toh] *ad.* perfectly, very well.

Menare [may-nah'ray] *vt.* to lead; m. calci [kahl'chee] to kick; m. un colpo [oon kohl'poh] to deal a blow; m. le mani [lay mah'nee] to fight; m. il can per l'aia [eel kahn pehr lah'ee-ah] to beat about the bush.

Menda [men'dah] *nf.* blemish, slight defect.

Mendace [men-dah'chay] *a.* deceitful, lying, mendacious.

Mendicante [men-dee-kahn'tay] *nm. and f.* beggar, mendicant; *a.* begging, mendicant.

Mendicare [men-dee-kah'ray] *vt. and i.* to beg.

Mendicità [men-dee-chee-tah'] *nf.* begging, beggary, beggars (*pl.*).

Mendico [men-dee'koh] *nm.* beggar, pauper.

Meno [may'noh] *ad.* less, least; fare a [fah'ray ah] m. di [dee] to do without; *a.* m. *ad.* cheaper; le due [lay doo'ay] m. cinque [cheeng'kway] 5 minutes to 2; *a.* less, fewer; *pr.* except; *a.* [ah] m. che non [kay nonn] *con.* unless.

Menomare [may-noh-mah'-

ray] *vt.* to diminish, impair, lessen.

Mensa [men'sah] *nf.* board, (*mil.*) mess, table, (*eccl.*) revenue.

Mensile [men-see'lay] *nm.* (month's) pay, wage; *a.* monthly.

Mensola [men'soh-lah] *nf.* bracket, console.

Menta [men'tah] *nf.* mint.

Mentale [men-tah'lay] *a.* mental, of the mind.

Mente [men'tay] *nf.* intellect, mind, understanding; *a.* [ah] m. *ad.* by heart.

Mentire [men-tee'ray] *vt.* to falsify, misrepresent; *vi.* to lie, tell lies.

Mento [men'toh] *nm.* chin.

Mentovare [men-toh-vah'-ray] *vt.* to mention.

Mentre [men'tray] *ad. and con.* while; in quel [een kwell] m. at that moment, meanwhile.

Menzionare [men-tsee-oh-nah'ray] *vt.* to mention.

Menzogna [ment-zohn'yah] *nf.* falsehood, lie, untruth.

Menzognero [ment-zohn-yay'roh] *a.* false, lying, untrue.

Meraviglia [may-rah-veel'yah] *nf.* astonishment, marvel, surprise, wonder; *a.* [ah] m. *ad.* wonderfully well.

Meraviglia/re [may-rah-veel-yah'ray] *vt.* to amaze, surprise; —rsi *vr.* to be amazed, wonder.

Meraviglioso [may-rah-veel-yoh'soh] *a.* amazing, marvellous, wonderful.

Mercante [mehr-kahn'tay] *nm.* dealer, merchant, trader.

Mercanteggiare [mehr-kahn-tay-djah'ray] *vi.* to bargain, deal, do business, haggle.

Mercanzia [mehr-kahn-tsee'ah] *nf.* merchandise, goods (*pl.*), wares (*pl.*).

Mercato [mehr-kah'toh] nm. market; **a buon** [ah boo'ohn] m. ad. cheap; **per sopra** [pehr soh'prah] m. ad. besides, moreover.

Mercatura [mehr-kah-too'rah] nf. trading.

Merce [mehr'chay] nf. goods (pl.), merchandise; **treno** [tray'noh] m. nm. goods train.

Mercè [mehr-chay'] nf. mercy; **sua** [soo'ah] m. thanks to him.

Mercede [mehr-chay'day] nf. pay, recompense, reward.

Mercenario [mehr-chay-nah'ree-oh] nm. and a. mercenary.

Merceri/a [mehr-chay-ree'ah] nf. haberdasher's shop; **—e** [ay] (pl.) haberdashery.

Mercia/io [mehr-chah'yoh] nm. —ia [yah] nf. draper, haberdasher, mercer.

Mercoledì [mehr-koh-lay-dee'] nm. Wednesday; m. **delle ceneri** [dell'lay chay'nay-ree], Ash-Wednesday.

Mercurio [mehr-koo'ree-oh] nm. mercury, quicksilver.

Merenda [may-ren'dah] nf. afternoon tea, light meal.

Meridiana [may-ree-dee-ah'nah] nf. sun-dial.

Meridionale [may-ree-dee-oh-nah'lay] a. south(ern).

Meriggio [may-reed'djoh] nm. midday, noon.

Merita/re [may-ree-tah'ray] vt. to be worth, deserve, merit, require; **—rsi** vr. to deserve.

Meritevole [may-ree-tay'voh-lay] a. deserving, worthy.

Merito [may'ree-toh] nm. desert, merit, worth; **in** [een] m. a [ah] pr. as regards, as to.

Merlettare [mehr-let-tah'ray] vt. to trim with lace.

Merlet/to [mehr-let'toh] nm. —ti [tee] (pl.) lace.

Merlo [mehr'loh] nm. blackbird (arch.) martlet, simpleton.

Merluzzo [mehr-loot'zoh] nm. cod(fish).

Mero [may'roh] a. mere, pure, simple.

Mescere [may'shay-ray] vt. to mix, pour (out).

Meschinità [mess-kee-nee-tah'] nf. mean dealing, meanness, poverty, stinginess.

Meschino [mess-kee'noh] a. mean, poor, shabby, stingy.

Mescita [may'shee-tah] nf. pouring out, wine-shop.

Mescolabile [mess-koh-lah'bee-lay] a. mixable.

Mescolamento [mess-koh-lah-men'toh] nm. mixing (up).

Mescola/re [mess-koh-lah'ray] vt. to blend, mingle, mix, shuffle (cards); **—rsi** vr. to blend, meddle, mix.

Mese [may'say] nm. month, month's pay.

Messa [mess'sah] nf. (eccl.) Mass; m. **in scena** [een shay'nah] (theat.) staging.

Messaggero [mess-sah-djay'roh] nm. **—ra** [rah] nf. forerunner, harbinger, messenger.

Messaggio [mess-sah'djoh] nm. message.

Messale [mess-sah'lay] nm. missal.

Messe [mess'say] nf. crop, harvest.

Messo [mess'soh] nm. legate, messenger; a. arranged, disposed, dressed.

Mestare [mess-tah'ray] vt. to mix, stir.

Mestierante [mess-tee-ay-rahn'tay] nm. tradesman.

Mestiere [mess-tee-ay'ray] nm. employment, occupation, profession, trade.

Mestizia [mess-tee'tsee-ah] nf. sadness.

Mesto [mess'toh] a. sad, sorrowful.

Mestola [mess'toh-lah] nf. ladle(ful), skimmer.

Mestruazione [mess-troo-]

ah-tsee-oh'nay] *nf.* menstruation.

Meta [may'tah] *nf.* aim, end, goal, purpose.

Metà [may-tah'] *nf.* half, middle; a. [ah] **m. prezzo** [pret'zoh] *ad.* half-price; a. [ah] **m. strada** [strah'dah] *ad.* half-way.

Metafisica [may-tah-fee'zee-kah] *nf.* metaphysics (*pl.*).

Metafora [may-tah'lee-koh] *nf.* metaphor.

Metallico [may-tah'lee-koh] *a.* metallic.

Metallo [may-tah'loh] *nm.* metal.

Metallurgia [may-tah-loor-jee'ah] *nf.* metallurgy.

Meteora [may-tay'oh-rah] *nf.* meteor.

Meteorologia [may-tay-oh-roh-loh-jee'ah] *nf.* meteorology.

Meticoloso [may-tee-koh-loh'soh] *a.* fussy, meticulous.

Metodico [may-toh'dee-koh] *a.* methodical.

Metodo [may'toh-doh] *nm.* custom, method, way.

Metrica [may'tree-kah] *nf.* prosody. [(measure).

Metro [may'troh] *nm.* metre

Metropoli [may-troh'poh-lee] *nf.* metropolis.

Mette/re [met'tay-ray] *vt.* to place, put, set; **—rsi** *vr.* to begin, set oneself.

Mettimale [met-tee-mah'lay] *nm.* mischief-maker.

Mezza [med'zah] *nf.* half-hour.

Mezzaluna [med-zah-loo'nah] *nf.* cleaver, crescent, half-moon.

Mezzanino [med-zah-nee'noh] *nm.* entresol.

Mezzano [med-zah'noh] *nm.* go-between; *a.* mean, middle.

Mezzanotte [med-zah-not'tay] *nf.* midnight.

Mezzo [med'zoh] *nm.* half,

means, middle; *a.* half; *ad.* almost, half; a. [ah] **m.** *ad.* by halves.

Mezzodi [med-zoh-dee'], **mezzogiorno** [med-zoh-jorr' noh] *nm.* midday, south.

Mezzombra [med-zom'bra] *nf.* half-tint.

Mezzotermine [med-zoh-tehr'mee-nay] *nm.* hint, innuendo.

Mi [mee] *pn. acc. and dat.* [to] me; *rf.* myself.

Miagolare [mee-ah-goh-lah'ray] *vi.* to mew.

Mica [mee'kah] *ad.* not, not at all, not in the least.

Miccia [meech'chah] *nf.* fuse (for explosives, etc.).

Micidiale [mee-chee-dee-ah'lay] *a.* deadly, killing.

Microbo [mee'kroh-boh] *nm.* microbe.

Microfono [mee-kroh'foh-noh] *nm.* microphone.

Microscopio [mee-kroh-skoh'pee-oh] *nm.* microscope.

Midolla [mee-doll'lah] *nf.* crumb (of bread), (*anat.*) marrow.

Midollo [mee-doll'loh] *nm.* marrow, pith.

Miele [mee-ay'lay] *nm.* honey.

Mietere [mee-ay'tay-ray] *vt.* to mow, reap.

Mieti/tore [mee-ay-tee-toh' ray] *nm.* **—trice** [tree'chay] *nf.* mower, reaper.

Mietitura [mee-ay-tee-too' rah] *nf.* mowing, reaping.

Miglia/io [meel-yah'yoh] *nm.* thousand; *a.* [ah] **m—ia** *ad.* by thousands.

Miglio [meel'yoh] *nm.* mile, millet.

Miglioramento [meel-yoh-rah-men'toh] *nm.* improvement.

Migliorare [meel-yoh-rah' ray] *vt. and i.* to improve, make (get) better.

Migliore [meel-yoh'ray] a. better, best.

Mignatta [meen-yaht'tah] nf. leech.

Mignolo [meen'yoh-loh] nm. little finger or toe; a. little.

Migrare [mee-grah'ray] vi. to migrate.

Migrazione [mee-grah-tsee-oh'nay] nf. migration.

Miliardo [mee-lyahr'doh] nm. milliard.

Milionario [mee-lee-oh-nah'ree-oh] nm. millionaire.

Milio/ne [mee-lee-oh'nay] nm. million; —**nesimo** [nay'zee-moh] a. millionth.

Militante [mee-lee-tahn'tay] a. militant.

Militare [mee-lee-tah'ray] vi. to militate, serve (in the army); nm. military man, soldier; a. military.

Milite [mee'lee-tay] nm. militiaman, soldier, warrior.

Milizia [mee-lee'tsee-ah] nf. army, militia.

Millantare [meel-lahn-tah'ray] vt. to boast of.

Millantatore [meel-lahn-tah-toh'ray] nm. boaster, braggart.

Millanteria [meel-lahn-tay-ree'ah] nf. boast(ing).

Mil/le [meel'lay] a. thousand; —**lesimo** [lay'zee-moh] a. thousandth.

Milza [meelt'zah] nf. milt, spleen.

Mimica [mee'mee-kah] nf. gestures (pl.), mimicry.

Mina [mee'nah] nf. bushel (measure), mine.

Minaccia [mee-nahch'chah] nf. menace, threat.

Minacciare [mee-nahch-chah'ray] vt. and i. to menace, threaten.

Minare [mee-nah'ray] vt. to injure, mine, undermine.

Minatore [mee-nah-toh'ray] nm. collier, miner.

Minatorio [mee-nah-toh'ree-oh] a. minatory, threatening.

Minerale [mee-nay-rah'lay] nm. mineral, ore; a. mineral.

Mineralogia [mee-nay-rah-loh-jee'ah] nf. mineralogy.

Minerario [mee-nay-rah'ree-oh] a. mining.

Minestra [mee-ness'trah] nf. soup.

Mingherlino [meeng-ghehr-lee'noh] a. lean, thin.

Miniare [mee-nee-ah'ray] vt. to illuminate (mss. etc.).

Miniatura [mee-nee-ah-too'rah] nf. miniature.

Miniera [mee-nee-ay'rah] nf. mine; m. di carbone [dee kahr-boh'nay], coal-mine.

Minimo [mee'nee-moh] nm. minimum; a. least, lowest, smallest.

Ministero [mee-nee-stay'roh] nm. board, department, function, ministry, office.

Ministrare [mee-nee-strah'ray] vt. to (ad)minister.

Ministro [mee-nee'stroh] nm. minister, secretary of state.

Minoranza [mee-noh-rahnt'zah] nf. minority.

Minorazione [mee-noh-rah-tsee-oh'nay] nf. diminution, handicap, maiming.

Minore [mee-noh'ray] a. less(er), lower, minor, smaller, younger, least, youngest, etc.

Minorenne [mee-noh-ren'nay] nm. minor; a. under age.

Minorità [mee-noh-ree-tah'] nf. minority (of age).

Minuscolo [mee-noos'koh-loh] a. minute, small.

Minuta [mee-noo'tah] nf. bill of fare, rough copy.

Minutezza [mee-noo-tet'zah] nf. smallness, thinness, trifle.

Minuto [mee-noo'toh] nm. minute; a. detailed, minute, small; al [ahl] m. ad. retail.

Minuzia [mee-noo'tsee-ah] nf. trifle.

Minuzioso [mee-noo-tsee-oh'soh] a. in detail, minute.

Minuzzolo [mee-noot'zoh-loh] nm. shred, small bit.

Mio [mee'oh] a. my; pn. mine; **i miei** [ee mee-ay'ee] (pl.) my family, my people.

Miope [mee'oh-pay] a. myopic, short-sighted.

Miopia [mee-oh-pee'ah] nf. short-sightedness.

Miosotide [mee-oh-zoh'tee-day] nf. forget-me-not.

Mira [mee'rah] nf. aim, end, object, purpose, sight.

Mirabile [mee-rah'bee-lay] a. admirable, wonderful.

Miracolo [mee-rah'koh-loh] nm. miracle, wonder.

Miracoloso [mee-rah-koh-loh'soh] a. miraculous, wonderful.

Miraggio [mee-rah'djoh] nm. illusion, mirage.

Mirare [mee-rah'ray] vt. to regard, gaze, look at; vi. to (take) aim at.

Miriade [mee-ree'ah-day] nf. myriad.

Mirra [meer'rah] nf. myrrh.

Mirtillo [mee-teel'loh] nm. bilberry.

Mirto [meer'toh] nm. myrtle.

Misantropia [mee-zahn-troh-pee'ah] nf. misanthropy.

Misantropo [mee-zahn'troh-poh] nm. misanthrope.

Miscela [mee-shay'lah] nf. blend, mixture.

Miscellanea [mee-shell-lah'nay-ah] nf. miscellany.

Mischia [mees'kee-ah] nf. fight, fray.

Mischia/re [mees-kee-ah'ray] vt. to mix, shuffle; —rsi vr. to mix (with).

Miscredente [mees-kray-den'tay] nm. and f. unbeliever; a. unbelieving.

Miscredenza [mees-kray-dent'zah] nf. unbelief.

Miscuglio [mees-kool'yoh] nm. medley, mixture.

Miserabile [mee-zay-rah'bee-lay] nm. pauper, wretch; a. destitute, vile, wretched.

Miserando [mee-zay-rahn'doh], **miserevole** [mee-zay-ray'voh-lay] a. pitiable, wretched.

Miseria [mee-zay'ree-ah] nf. distress, poverty, wretchedness.

Misericordia [mee-zay-ree-korr'dee-ah] nf. mercy, pity.

Misericordioso [mee-zay-ree-korr-dee-oh'soh] a. merciful.

Misero [mee'zay-roh] nm. poor fellow, wretch; a. mean, paltry, poor, wretched.

Misfatto [mees-faht'toh] nm. crime, misdeed.

Missionario [mees-see-oh-nah'ree-oh] nm. missionary.

Missione [mees-see-oh'nay] nf. mission.

Misterioso [mees-tay-ree-oh'soh] a. mysterious.

Mistero [mees-tay'roh] nm. mystery.

Misticismo [mees-tee-cheez'moh] nm. mysticism.

Mistico [mees'tee-koh] nm. and a. mystic.

Misto [mees'toh] nm. compound, mixture; a. mixed; **treno** [tray'noh] m. nm. train for passengers and goods.

Mistura [mees-too'rah] nf. mixture.

Misura [mee-zoo'rah] nf. gauge, measure(ment), moderation, proportion, size.

Misurabile [mee-zoo-rah'bee-lay] a. measurable.

Misura/re [mee-zoo-rah'ray] vt. to gauge, measure; —rsi vr. to measure oneself, try one's strength, vie. [meek, mild.

Mite [mee'tay] a. gentle,

Mitezza [mee-tet'zah] *nf.* gentleness, meekness, mildness.

Mitigare [mee-tee-gah'ray] *vt.* to allay, alleviate, mitigate.

Mito [mee'toh] *nm.* myth.

Mitologia [mee-toh-loh-jee'ah] *nf.* mythology.

Mitra [mee'trah] *nf.* mitre.

Mitraglia [mee-trah'lyah] *nf.* (*mil.*) grape-shot.

Mitragliatrice [mee-trahl-yah-tree'chay] *nf.* (*mil.*) machine-gun.

Mittente [meet-ten'tay] *nm. and f.* sender; *a.* forwarding, sending.

Mobile [moh'bee-lay] *nm.* piece of furniture; *a.* changeable, fickle, mobile, movable.

Mobilia [moh-bee'lee-ah] *nf.* furniture.

Mobilizzazione [moh-bee-leed-zah-tsee-oh'nay] *nf.* mobilization.

Moda [moh'dah] *nf.* fashion; di [dee] **m.** *ad.* fashionable.

Modalità [moh-dah-lee-tah'] *nf.* detail, modality.

Modellare [moh-dell-lah'ray] *vt.* to fashion, model, mould, shape.

Modello [moh-dell'loh] *nm.* model, pattern.

Modera/re [moh-day-rah'ray] *vt.* to abate, moderate, relax; —**rsi** *vr.* to check oneself, restrain oneself, retrench.

Moderazione [moh-day-rah-tsee-oh'nay] *nf.* moderation, temperance.

Modernità [moh-dehr-nee-tah'] *nf.* modernity.

Moderno [moh-dehr'noh] *a.* modern, new-fashioned, up-to-date.

Modestia [moh-dess'tee-ah] *nf.* moderation, modesty, simplicity.

Modesto [moh-dess'toh] *a.* moderate, modest, plain, simple.

Modico [moh'dee-koh] *a.* cheap, reasonable.

Modificare [moh-dee-fee-kah'ray] *vt.* to change, modify, vary.

Modificazione [moh-dee-fee-kah-tsee-oh'nay] *nf.* change, modification, variation.

Modista [moh-dees'tah] *nf.* milliner.

Modo [moh'doh] *nm.* manner, way; **ad ogni** [ahd ohn'yee] **m.** anyhow; **a.** [ah] **m.** *ad.* carefully, properly; *a.* well-bred.

Modulare [moh-doo-lah'ray] *vt.* to modulate.

Modulazione [moh-doo-lah-tsee-oh'nay] *nf.* modulation.

Modulo [moh'doo-loh] *nm.* (printed) form.

Mogano [moh'gah-noh] *nm.* mahogany.

Moggio [moh'djoh] *nm.* bushel.

Mogio [moh'joh] *a.* abashed, crest-fallen, quiet.

Moglie [moh'lyay] *nf.* wife.

Mola [moh'lah] *nf.* grindstone, millstone.

Molare [moh-lah'ray] *nm. and a.* molar.

Molcere [moll'chay-ray] *vt.* to caress, soothe.

Mole [moh'lay] *nf.* bulk, mass, size.

Molestare [moh-less-tah'ray] *vt.* to annoy, molest, tease, tire.

Molestia [moh-less'tee-ah] *nf.* annoyance, molestation.

Molesto [moh-less'toh] *a.* annoying, irksome, importunate, teasing.

Mol/la [moll'lah] *nf.* (*tech.*) spring; —**le** [lay] (*pl.*) tongs.

Mollare [moll-lah'ray] *vt.* to loose(n), relax, slacken; *vi.* to leave off, yield.

Molle [moll'lay] *a.* soft, wet;

tenere in [tay-nay'ray een] m. vt. to soak, steep.

Molletta [moll-let'tah] nf. hair-grip, small spring.

Mollezza [moll-let'zah] nf. effeminacy, feebleness, softness.

Mollica [moll-lee'kah] nf. crumb.

Molo [moh'loh] nm. breakwater, pier, quay.

Molosso [moh-loss'soh] nm. bull-dog.

Molteplice [moll-tay'plee-chay] a. manifold, multiple.

Moltiplica/re [moll-tee-plee-kah'ray] vt. —rsi vr. to multiply.

Moltiplicazione [moll-tee-plee-kah-tsee-oh'nay] nf. multiplication.

Moltiplicità [moll-tee-plee-chee-tah'] nf. multiplicity.

Moltitudine [moll-tee-too'dee-nay] nf. multitude.

Molto [moll'toh] nm. a lot, a good (great) deal, much; a. much; ad. greatly, much, very.

Momento [moh-men'toh] nm. importance, instant, moment, weight. [nun.

Monaca [moh'nah-kah] nf.

Monacale [moh-nah-kah'lay] a. monkish.

Monaco [moh'nah-koh] nm. monk.

Monade [moh'nah-day] nf. monad.

Monarca [moh-nahr'kah] nm. monarch.

Monarchia [moh-nahr-kee'ah] nf. monarchy.

Monarchico [moh-nahr'kee-koh] a. monarchic(al).

Monastero [moh-nah-stay'roh] nm. monastery.

Monco [mong'koh] a. maimed, mutilated, **one**-armed, one-handed.

Mondanità [mon-dah-nee-tah'] nf. worldliness.

Monda/no [mon-dah'noh] nm. worldling, worldly-minded person; a. mundane, worldly, worldly-minded; —na [nah] nf. prostitute.

Mondare [mon-dah'ray] vt. te clean, hull, peal, sift, winnow.

Mondiale [mon-dee-ah'lay] a. universal, world-wide.

Mondo [mon'doh] nm. earth, universe, world, mankind, men (pl.); a. clean, pure, spotless.

Monello [moh-nell'loh] nm. little rogue, street-boy, urchin.

Moneta [moh-nay'tah] nf. coin.

Monetare [moh-nay-tah'ray] vt. to coin, mint.

Monetazione [moh-nay-tah-tsee-oh'nay] nf. coining, minting.

Monile [moh-nee'lay] nm. ornament, trinket.

Monito [moh'nee-toh] nm. admonition, warning.

Monitore [moh-nee-toh'ray] nm. monitor, warner.

Monocolo [moh-noh'koh-loh] nm. monocle, one-eyed person; a. one-eyed.

Monografia [moh-noh-grah-fee'ah] nf. monograph.

Monologo [moh-noh'loh-goh] nm. monologue.

Monopolio [moh-noh-poh'lee-oh] nm. monopoly.

Monopolizzare [moh-noh-poh-leed-zah'ray] vt. to monopolise.

Monotonia [moh-noh-toh-nee'ah] nf. monotony, sameness.

Monotono [moh-noh'toh-noh] a. dull, monotonous.

Montagna [mon-tah'nyah] nf. mountain.

Montagnoso [mon-tahn-yoh'soh] a. mountainous.

Montanaro [mon-tah-nah'

roh] *nm.* highlander, mountaineer.

Monta/re [mon-tah'ray] *vt. and i.* to climb, excite, go up(stairs), mount, rise; **—rsi la testa** [lah tess'tah] *nf.* to listen to flattery.

Monte [mon'tay] *nm.* heap, hill, mount; **m. di pietà** [dee-pee-ay-tah']. pawnbroker's; **andare a** [ahn-dah'ray ah] **m.** *vi.* to come to nothing.

Montone [mon-toh'nay] *nm.* ram, wether.

Montuosità [mon-too-oh-see-tah'] *nf.* hilliness, steepness.

Montuoso [mon-too-oh'soh] *a.* hilly, steep.

Monumentale [moh-noo-men-tah'lay] *a.* monumental.

Monumento [moh-noo-men'toh] *nm.* monument.

Mora [moh'rah] *nf.* blackberry; negress; delay, respite.

Morale [moh-rah'lay] *nf.* lecture, morale, morals (*pl*), morality, reprimand; *a.* moral.

Moralità [moh-rah-lee-tah'] *nf.* morality.

Moralizzare [moh-rah-leed-zah'ray] *vt. and i.* to moralise.

Moratoria [moh-rah-toh'ree-ah] *nf.* moratorium.

Morbidezza [morr-bee-det'zah] *nf.* softness, tenderness.

Morbido [morr'bee-doh] *a.* soft, tender.

Morbillo [morr-beel'loh] *nm.* (*med.*) measles.

Morbo [morr'boh] *nm.* disease, plague.

Morbosità [morr-boh-see-tah'] *nf.* morbidness.

Morboso [morr-boh'soh] *a.* morbid.

Mordace [morr-dah'chay] *a.* biting, pungent, sarcastic.

Mordente [morr-den'tay] *nm.* corrosive; *a.* biting, mordent.

Mordere [morr'day-ray] *vt. and i.* to bite, sting.

Morello [moh-rell'oh] *a.* jet-black.

Morente [moh-ren'tay] *a.* dying, fading. [Moorish.

Moresco [moh-ress'koh] *a.*

Morfina [morr-fee'nah] *nf.* morphia, morphine.

Moria [moh-ree'ah] *nf.* high mortality rate.

Moribondo [moh-ree-bon'doh] *a.* dying, moribund.

Morigerato [moh-ree-jay-rah'toh] *a.* of good morals, of simple habits, temperate.

Morire [moh-ree'ray] *vi.* to die.

Mormorare [morr-moh-rah'ray] *vt. and i.* to disparage, murmur, whisper.

Mormorio [morr-moh-ree'oh] *nm.* murmur, rustling, whisper.

Moro [moh'roh] *nm.* mulberry-tree, **Moor**, negro (*pl*), black, dark-skinned.

Moroso [moh-roh'zoh] *a.* tardy.

Morsicare [morr-see-kah'ray] *vt.* to bite.

Morsicatura [morr-see-kah-too'rah] *nf.* bite, sting.

Morso [morr'soh] *nm.* bit, bite, morsel.

Mortaio [morr-tah'yoh] *nm.* mortar.

Mortale [morr-tah'lay] *nm. and a.* mortal; *a.* deadly, fatal.

Mortalità [morr-tah-lee-tah'] *nf.* mortality.

Morte [morr'tay] *nf.* death.

Mortella [morr-tell'lah] *nf.* myrtle.

Mortifica/re [morr-tee-fee-kah'ray] *vt.* to grieve, humilate, mortify; **—rsi** *vr.* to mortify oneself, to be mortified.

Mortificazione [morr-tee-fee-kah-tsee-oh'nay] *nf.* humiliation, mortification.

Morto [morr'toh] *nm.* dead man; *a.* dead, deceased.

Mosaico [moh-zah'ee-koh] *nm.* mosaic.

Mosca [moss'kah] *nf.* fly.

Moscatello [moss-kah-tell' loh] *nm.* muscatel grape.

Moscerino [moh-shay-ree' noh] *nm.* gnat, midge.

Moschea [moss-kay'ah] *nf.* mosque.

Moschetteria [moss-ket-tay-ree'ah] *nf.* musketry.

Moschettiere [moss-ket-tee-ay'ray] *nm.* musketeer.

Moschetto [moss-ket'toh] *nm.* musket, rifle.

Moscone [moss-koh'nay] *nm.* big fly, blue-bottle.

Mossa [moss'sah] *nf.* gesture, move(ment).

Mostarda [moss-tahr'dah] *nf.* French mustard.

Mosto [moss'toh] *nm.* must.

Mostoso [moss-toh'soh] *a.* full of must.

Mostra [moss'trah] *nf.* exhibition, ostentation, show, lapel (of a coat).

Mostra/re [moss-trah'ray] *vt.* to display, exhibit, prove, show; **—rsi** *vr.* to appear, show oneself.

Mostriciattolo [moss-tree-chaht'toh-loh] *nm.* ugly creature.

Mostro [moss'troh] *nm.* monster, prodigy.

Mostruosità [moss-troo-oh-see-tah'] *nf.* monstrosity.

Mostruoso [moss-troo-oh' soh] *a.* hideous, incredible, monstrous.

Mota [moh'tah] *nf.* mire, mud.

Motivare [moh-tee-vah'ray] *vt.* to give reasons for, justify, motivate.

Motivazione (moh-tee-vah-tsee-oh'nay] *nf.* citation.

Motivo [moh-tee'voh] *nm.* cause, motif, motive; *a.* [ah] **m. di** [dee] *pr.* on account of, owing to; *a.* motive.

Moto [moh'toh] *nm.* agitation, exercise, impulse, motion.

Moto/cicletta [moh-toh chee-klet'tah] *nf.* —ciclo [chee' kloh] *nm.* motor-cycle.

Motore [moh-toh'ray] *nm.* engine, motor.

Motteggiare [mot-tay-djah'ray] *vt. and i.* to banter, joke, make fun of.

Motto [mot'toh] *nm.* motto, saying, word.

Movente [moh-ven'tay] *nm.* cause, motive, reason; *a.* moving.

Movimento [moh-vee-men' toh] *nm.* gesture, motion, movement, traffic.

Mozione [moh-tsee-oh'nay] *nf.* motion.

Mozzo [mot'zoh] *nm.* cabinboy, lad, stable-boy, *(tech.)* wheel-hub; *a.* cropped, cut off, docked.

Mucca [mook'kah] *nf.* cow.

Mucchio [mook'kee-oh] *nm.* heap, pile.

Muco [moo'koh] *nm.* mucus.

Mudare [moo-dah'ray] *vi.* to moult.

Muffa [moof'fah] *nf.* mould, must.

Muffoso [moof-foh'soh] *a.* mouldy, musty.

Mugghiare [moog-ghee-ah' ray], **muggire** [moo-djee'ray] *vi.* to bellow, howl, low, roar.

Mugghio [moog'ghee-oh], **muggito** [moo-djee'toh] *nm.* bellowing, lowing, roaring.

Mughetto [moo-ghet'toh] *nm.* lily-of-the-valley.

Mugnaio [moon-yah'yoh] *nm.* miller.

Mugolare [moo-goh-lah'ray] *vi.* to whine, yelp.

Mulattiera [moo-laht-tee-ay'rah] *nf.* mule-track.

Mulattiere [moo-laht-tee-ay′ray] *nm.* muleteer.

Muliebre [moo-lee-ay′bray] *a.* feminine, womanly.

Mulinello [moo-lee-nell′loh] *nm.* whirlpool, whirlwind, (*tech.*) windlass.

Mulino [moo-lee′noh] **molino** [moh-lee′noh] *nm.* mill.

Mulo [moo′loh] *nm.* mule.

Multa [mool′tah] *nf.* fine.

Multare [mool-tah′ray] *vt.* to fine.

Multicolore [mool-tee-koh-loh′ray] *a.* many-coloured.

Multiforme [mool-tee-forr′may] *a.* multiform.

Multiplo [mool′tee-ploh] *a.* multiple.

Mummia [moom′mee-ah] *nf.* mummy (Egyptian).

Mummificare [moom-mee-fee-kah′ray] *vt.* to mummify.

Mungere [moon′jay-ray] *vt.* to exploit, milk.

Municipale [moo-nee-chee-pah′lay] *a.* municipal, of the town.

Municipio [moo-nee-chee′pee-oh] *nm.* borough, town council, town-hall.

Munificenza [moo-nee-fee-chent′zah] *nf.* generosity, munificence.

Munifico [moo-nee′fee-koh] *a.* generous, munificent.

Muni/re [moo-nee′ray] *vt.* to fortify, furnish, provide, supply; —rsi *vr.* to equip oneself.

Munizione [moo-nee-tsee-oh′nay] *nf.* (*mil.*) ammunition, munitions (*pl.*).

Muove/re [moo-oh′vay-ray] *vt.* —rsi *vr.* to move, stir.

Muraglia [moo-rah′lyah] *nf.* wall.

Murale [moo-rah′lay] *a.* mural.

Murare [moo-rah′ray] *vt.* to immure, wall (up).

Muratore [moo-rah-toh′ray] *nm.* bricklayer, mason.

Murena [moo-ray′nah] *nf.* sea-eel.

Muro [moo′roh] *nm.* wall.

Musa [moo′zah] *nf.* Muse.

Muschio [moos′kee-oh] *nm.* musk.

Musco [moos′koh] *nm.* moss.

Muscolo [moos′koh-loh] *nm.* muscle.

Muscoloso [moos-koh-loh′soh] *a.* muscular, wiry.

Muscoso [moos-koh′soh] *a.* mossy.

Museo [moo-zay′oh] *nm.* museum.

Museruola [moo-zay-roo-oh′lah] *nf.* muzzle.

Musica [moo′zee-kah] *nf.* band, music.

Musicale [moo-zee-kah′lay] *a.* harmonious, musical.

Musicante [moo-zee-kahn′tay] *nm. and f.* musician.

Musicista [moo-zee-chee′stah] *nm.* composer.

Muso [moo′zoh] *nm.* face (people), muzzle, snout (animals); **fare il** [fah′ray eel] **m.** to pout.

Mussare [moos-sah′ray] *vi.* to foam, froth.

Mussolina [moos-soh-lee′nah] *nf.* muslin.

Mussulmano [moos-sool-mah′noh] *nm. and a.* Mussulman.

Mustacchi [moos-tahk′kee] *nm.* (*pl.*) moustache.

Muta [moo′tah] *nf.* change, pack (of hounds).

Mutabile [moo-tah′bee-lay] *a.* changeable, variable.

Mutabilità [moo-tah-bee-lee-tah′] *nf.* changeableness, variableness.

Mutamento [moo-tah-men′toh] *nm.* alteration, change, variation.

Mutande [moo-tahn′day] *nf.* (*pl.*) drawers (*pl.*), knickers (*pl.*).

Muta/re [moo-tah'ray]. —rsi *vr.* to alter, change, vary.

Mutevole [moo-tay'voh-lay] *a.* changeable, variable.

Mutezza [moo-tet'zah] *nf.* muteness.

Mutilare [moo-tee-lah'ray] *vt.* to maim, mutilate.

Mutilazione [moo-tee-lah-tsee-oh'nay] *nf.* mutilation.

Mutismo [moo-tees'moh] *nm.* dumbness, muteness, taciturnity.

Muto [moo'toh] *a.* dumb, mute, silent, speechless.

Mutualmente [moo-too-ahl-men'tay] *a.* mutually.

Mutuante [moo-too-ahn'tay] *nm. and f.* lender, mortgagee; *a.* lending, loaning.

Mutuare [moo-too-ah'ray] *vt.* to borrow, lend, mortgage.

Mutuo [moo-too'oh] *nm.* loan; *a.* mutual, reciprocal.

N

Nacchere [nahk'kay-ray] *nf. (pl.)* castanets *(pl.).*

Nafta [nahf'tah] *nf.* naphtha, rock-oil.

Naiade [nah'yah-day] *nf.* naiad, water-nymph.

Nano [nah'noh] *nm.* dwarf; *a.* dwarf(ish).

Nappa [nahp'pah] *nf.* tassel, tuft.

Narciso [nahr-chee'zoh] *nm.* daffodil, narcissus.

Narcotico [nahr-koh'tee-koh] *nm. and a.* narcotic.

Narice [nah-ree'chay] *nf.* nostril.

Narrare [nahr-rah'ray] *vt.* to narrate, relate, tell.

Narrazione [nahr-rah-tsee-oh'nay] *nf.* narration, narrative, tale.

Nascente [nah-shen'tay] *a.* dawning, growing, rising.

Nascere [nah'shay-ray] *vi.* to be born, come into the world, originate, rise.

Nascita [nah'shee-tah] *nf.* birth; **fede di** [fay'day dee] *n.* birth-certificate.

Nasconde/re [nah-skon'day-ray] *vt.* to conceal, hide; —rsi *vr.* to hide oneself.

Nascondiglio [nah-skon-deel'yoh] *nm.* hiding-place, lair.

Nascosto [nah-skoss'toh] *a.* hidden, secret, underhand; **di** [dee] *n. ad.* secretly, stealthily.

Nasello [nah-sell'loh] *nm.* whiting (fish).

Naso [nah'soh] *nm.* nose; **a lume di** [ah loo'may dee] nah-tah'lee] *ad.* of humble guess-work.

Naspo [nah'spoh] *nm. (tech.)* reel, winder.

Nastro [nah-stroh] *nm.* band, ribbon, tape.

Natale [nah-tah'lay] *nm.* birthday, Christmas day; **di umili natali** [dee oo'mee-lee nah-tah'lee] *ad.* of humble birth, low-born.

Natalità [nah-tah-lee-tah'] *nf.* birth-rate.

Natalizio [nah-tah-lee'tsee-oh] *nm.* birthday; *a.* (of) Christmas, natal.

Natica [nah'tee-kah] *nf.* buttock.

Natio [nah-tee'oh] *a.* native.

Natività [nah-tee-vee-tah'] *nf.* nativity.

Nativo [nah-tee'voh] *nm.* native; *a.* native, natural.

Nato [nah'toh] *a.* born, risen, sprung up.

Natura [nah-too'rah] *nf.* kind, nature; **pagare in** [pah-gah'ray een] *n.* to pay in kind.

Naturale [nah-too-rah'lay] *a.* genuine, natural; *ad.* naturally, of course.

Naturalezza [nah-too-rah-let'sah] *nf.* naturalness.

Naturalizzare [nah-too-rah-leed-zah'ray] *vt.* to naturalise.

Naturalizzazione [nah-too-rah-leed-zah-tsee-oh'nay] *nf.* naturalisation.

Naufragare [now-frah-gah'ray] *vi.* to be (ship)wrecked.

Naufragio [now-frah'joh] *nm.* failure, (ship)wreck.

Naufrago [now'frah-goh] *nm. and a.* shipwrecked (man).

Nausea [now'zay-ah] *nf.* loathing, nausea, sickness; sentire [sen-tee'ray] n. to feel sick.

Nauseante [now-zay-ahn-tay] *a.* loathsome, nauseous.

Nauseare [now-zay-ah'ray] *vt.* to disgust, nauseate.

Nautica [now'tee-kah] *nf.* nautical science.

Nave [nah'vay] *nf.* ship, vessel.

Navicella [nah-vee-chell'lah] *nf.* bark, small ship.

Navigante [nah-vee-gahn'tay] *nm. and f.* passenger, voyager; *a.* navigating, sailing.

Navigare [nah-vee-gah'ray] *vt. and i.* to navigate, sail; n. in cattive acque [een kaht-tee'vay ahk'kway], to be badly off.

Navigato [nah-vee-gah'toh] *a.* experienced.

Navigazione [nah-vee-gah-tsee-oh'nay] *nf.* navigation.

Naviglio [nah-veel'yoh] *nm.* canal, craft, fleet.

Nazionale [nah-tsee-oh-nah'lay] *a.* home-grown, home-made, national.

Nazionalità [nah-tsee-oh-nah-lee-tah'] *nf.* nationality.

Nazione [nah-tsee-oh'nay] *nf.* nation.

Ne [nay] *pn.* (*oblique case*) of him, his, of her, hers; of it, its; of them, theirs; from there; any, some.

Nè [nay] *con.* neither, nor; ne . . . nè, neither . . . nor.

Nebbia [neb'bee-ah] *nf.* fog, mist.

Nebbioso [neb-bee-oh'soh] *a.* foggy, hazy, misty.

Nebulosità [nay-boo-loh-see-tah'] *nf.* haziness, nebulosity.

Nebuloso [nay-boo-loh'soh] *a.* hazy, nebulous.

Necessario [nay-chess-sah'ree-oh] *nm. and a.* (what is) necessary, needful.

Necessità [nay-chess-see-tah'] *nf.* necessity, need, poverty.

Necessitare [nay-chess-see-tah'ray] *vi.* to be in need of, in want of, lack.

Necrologia [nay-kroh-loh-jee'ah] *nf.* necrology, obituary.

Nefandezza [nay-fahn-det'sah] *nf.* abominableness.

Nefando [nay-fahn'doh] *a.* abominable, execrable.

Nefasto [nay-fah'stoh] *a.* fatal, ill-omened, unlucky.

Nefrite [nay-free'tay] *nf.* (*med.*) nephritis.

Negabile [nay-gah'bee-lay] *a.* deniable.

Negare [nay-gah'ray] *vt. and i.* to deny.

Negativa [nay-gah-tee'vah] *nf.* denial, negative.

Negato [nay-gah'toh] *a.* unfit, without talent for.

Negazione [nay-gah-tsee-oh'nay] *nf.* denial, negative, negation.

Neghittoso [nay-gheet-toh'soh] *a.* slothful.

Negletto [nay-glet'toh] *a.* neglected, untidy.

Negli [nayl'yee]=in gli *pr. and def. art. m.* (*pl.*) in the.

Negligente [nay-glee-jen'tay] *a.* careless, negligent, remiss.

Negligenza [nay-glee-jent'-sah] *nf.* carelessness, negligence.

Negligere [nay-glee'jay-ray] *vt.* to neglect. *v.* Trascurare.

Negoziabile [nay-goh-tsee-ah'bee-lay] *a.* negotiable.

Negoziante [nay-goh-tsee-ahn'tay] *nm.* dealer, shopkeeper, tradesman.

Negoziare [nay-goh-tsee-ah'ray] *vt.* to negotiate; *vi.* to bargain, deal, negotiate, traffic.

Negoziati [nay-goh-tsee-ah'-tee] *nm.* (*pl.*) negotiation(s).

Negozio [nay-goh'tsee-oh] *nm.* bargain, business, shop, transaction.

Negro [nay'groh] *nm.* negro, nigger.

Negromante [nay-groh-mahn'tay] *nm.* necromancer.

Negromanzia [nay-groh-mahn-tsee'ah] *nf.* necromancy.

Nei [nay'ee]=in i *pr.* and *def. art. m.* (*pl.*) in the.

Nel(lo) [nell'loh]=in il, in lo *pr.* and *def. art. m.* in the.

Nel(la) [nell'lah]=in la *pr.* and *def. art. f.,* —le [lay] (*pl.*) in the.

Nembo [nem'boh] *nm.* (storm-)cloud.

Nemico [nay-mee'koh] *nm.* adversary, enemy, opponent; *a.* enemy, hostile.

Nem/manco [nem-mahng'-koh], —**meno** [may'noh] *ad.* not even.

Nenia [nay'nee-ah] *nf.* dirge, plaintive song.

Neo [nay'oh] *nm.* blemish, mole (on the skin).

Neofito [nay-oh'fee-toh] *nm.* neophyte.

Neonato [nay-oh-nah'toh] *nm.* and *a.* newborn (child).

Neppure [nep-poo'ray] *ad.* not even.

Nequizia [nay-kwee'tsee-ah] *nf.* iniquity.

Nerastro [nay-rah'stroh], **nerognolo** [nay-rohn'yoh-loh] *a.* blackish.

Nerbo [nehr'boh] *nm.* best part, sinew, strength.

Nero [nay'roh] *nm.* and *a.* black, dark.

Nerume [nay-roo'may] *nm.* black, black things (*pl.*).

Nervatura [nehr-vah-too'rah] *nf.* nervature.

Nervo [nehr'voh] *nm.* energy, nerve, vigour; **avere i nervi** [ah-vay'ray eh nehr'vee] *vi.* to be in a bad temper.

Nervosità [nehr-voh-see-tah'] *nf.,* **nervosismo** [nehr-voh-sees-moh] *nm.* nerves, nervousness.

Nervoso [nehr-voh'soh] *a.* excitable, nervous, nervy.

Nespo/la [ness'poh-lah] *nf.* medlar; —**lo** [loh] *nm.* medlar-tree.

Nesso [ness'soh] *nm.* connection, link, nexus.

Nessuno [ness-soo'noh] *pn.* nobody, none, no one; *a.* any, no.

Nettare [net-tah'ray] *vt.* to clean, cleanse. [nectar.

Nettare [net'tah-ray] *nm.*

Nettezza [net-tet'sah] *nf.* cleanliness, cleanness; n. urbana [oor-bah'nah], dustmen (*pl.*).

Netto [net'toh] *a.* clean, distinct, exact, net.

Neutrale [nay-oo-trah'lay] *nm.* and *a.* neutral.

Neutralità [nay-oo-trah-lee-tah'] *nf.* neutrality.

Neutralizzare [nay-oo-trah-leed-zah'ray] *vt.* to neutralise.

Neutro [nay'oo-troh] *nm.* and *a.* neuter; *a.* neutral.

Neve [nay'vay] *nf.* snow.

Nevicare [nay-vee-kah'ray] *vi.* to snow.

Nevicata [nay-vee-kah'tah] *nf.* snow-fall, snow-storm.

Nevischio [nay-vee-'skee-oh] nm. sleet.

Nevoso [nay-voh'soh] a. snowy.

Nevralgia [nay-vrahl-jee'ah] nf. neuralgia.

Nevrite [nay-vree'tay] nf. (med.) neuritis.

Nevrosi [nay-vroh'zee] nf. (med.) neurosis.

Nibbio [neeb'bee-oh] nm. kite (bird).

Nicchia [neek'kee-ah] nf. niche, nook, recess.

Nicchiare [neek-kee-ah'ray] vi. to hesitate.

Nidiata [nee-dee-ah'tah] nf. brood, nestful.

Nidificare [nee-dee-fee-kah'ray] vi. to build a nest.

Nido [nee'doh] nm. haunt, nest.

Niente [nee-en'tay] nm. and pn. nothing.

Nientedimeno [nee-en-tay-dee-may'noh] avi. no less.

Ninfa [neen'fah] nf. nymph.

Ninfea [neen-fay'ah] nf. water-lily.

Ninna nanna [neen'nah nahn'nah] nf. lullaby.

Ninnolo [neen'noh-loh] nm. trifle, trinket.

Nipote [nee-poh'tay] nm. and f. grandson, granddaughter; nephew, niece.

Nitidezza [nee-tee-det'sah] nf. clearness.

Nitido [nee'tee-doh] a. clear, distinct. [neigh.

Nitrire [nee-tree'ray] vi. to

Nitro [nee'troh] nm. nitre, saltpetre.

Niuno [nee-oo'noh] pn. (poet.) no one.

Niveo [nee'vay-oh] a. snowy, snow-white.

No [noh] ad. no; se [say] no ad. otherwise; int. really?! [Nobile [noh'bee-lay] nm. and a. noble.

Nobiliare [noh-bee-lee-ah'ray] a. aristocratic.

Nobilitare [noh-bee-lee-tah'ray] vt. to ennoble.

Nobiltà [noh-bee-lee-tah'] nf. nobility, nobleness.

Nocca [nock'kah] nf. knuckle.

Nocchiere [nock-kee-ay'ray] nm. (naut.) pilot, steersman.

Noccio/la [nohch-choh'lah] nf. hazel-nut; —lo [loh] nm. hazel-tree.

Nocciolo [nohch'choh-loh] nm. kernel, (fig.) point, stone.

Noce [noh'chay] nf. walnut (-tree).

Nocevole [noh-chay'voh-lay]- nocivo [noh-chee'voh] a. harmful, hurtful.

Nodo [noh'doh] nm. difficulty, knot, lump (in the throat).

Nodosità [noh-doh-see-tah'] nf. knottiness.

Nodoso [noh-doh'soh] a. gnarled, knotty.

Noi [noh'ee] pn. we, us.

Noia [noh'yah] nf. boredom, trouble, vexation.

Noioso [noh-yoh'soh] a. boring, irksome, tedious.

Noleggiare [noh-lay-djah'ray] vt. to charter, hire.

Noleggio [noh-lay'djoh] nm. freight, hire.

Nolo [noh'loh] nm. hire; a [ah] n. ad. for (on) hire.

Nomade [noh'mah-day] nm. and f. nomad; a. nomadic.

Nome [noh'may] nm. name, noun.

Nomea [noh-may'ah] nf. renown, reputation.

Nomenclatura [noh-men-klah-too'rah] nf. nomenclature.

Nomignolo [noh-meen'yoh-loh] nm. nickname.

Nomina [noh'mee-nah] nf. appointment.

Nominare [noh-mee-nah'-

ray] *vt.* to appoint, elect, make mention, name.

Non [nonn] *ad.* not; **non che** [kay] *ad.* but, only.

Nonagenario [noh-nah-jay-nah'ree-oh] *nm.* and *a.* nonagenarian.

Noncurante [non-koo-rahn'tay] *a.* careless, heedless, indifferent.

Noncuranza [non-koo-rahn'sah] *nf.* carelessness, heedlessness.

Nondimeno [non-dee-may'noh] *ad.* nevertheless, still, yet.

Non/na [non'nah] *nf.* grandmother; **—no** [noh] *nm.* grandfather.

Nonnulla [non-nool'lah] *nm.* nothing, trifle.

Nono [noh'noh] *a.* ninth.

Nonostante [non-oss-tahn'tay] *pr.* in spite of, notwithstanding; *ad.* nevertheless.

Nonpertanto [non-pehr-tahn'toh] *ad.* nevertheless, still.

Nonsenso [non-sen'soh] *nm.* nonsense.

Non-ti-scordar-di-me [non-tee-skorr-dahr'dee-may'] *nm.* forget-me-not.

Nord [norrd] *nm.* north.

Nordico [norr'dee-koh] *nm.* Northerner; *a.* Northern.

Norma [norr'mah] *nf.* information, order, regulation, rule.

Normale [norr-mah'lay] *nm.* and *a.* normal.

Nosocomio [noh-zoh-koh'mee-oh] *nm.* hospital.

Nostalgia [noss-tahl-jee'ah] *nf.* home-sickness.

Nostalgico [noss-tahl'jee-koh] *a.* nostalgic.

Nostrale [noss-trah'lay], **nostrano** [noss-trah'noh] *a.* domestic, home, of one's own country.

Nostro [noss'troh] *poss. a.* and *pr.* our, ours; **i nostri** [ee noss'tree] (*pl.*) our family.

Nostromo [noss-troh'moh] *nm.*, (*naut.*) boatswain.

Nota [noh'tah] *nf.* list, mark, note.

Notabilità [noh-tah-bee-lee-tah'] *nf.* bigwig, notable.

Notaio [noh-tah'yoh] *nm.* notary.

Notare [noh-tah'ray] *vt.* to note, notice, observe; **farsi** [fahr'see] *n. vr.* to attract attention.

Notarile [noh-tah-ree'lay] *a.* notarial, notary's.

Notevole [noh-tay'voh-lay] *a.* considerable, notable, noticeable, remarkable.

Notificare [noh-tee-fee-kah'ray] *vt.* to notify.

Notificazione [noh-tee-fee-kah-tsee-oh'nay] *nf.* communication, notification.

Notizia [noh-tee'tsee-ah] *nf.* (piece of) news; **le notizie son buone** [lay noh-tee'tsee-ay sonn boo-oh'nay], the news is good.

Noto [noh'toh] *a.* famous, notorious, (well-)known.

Noto *nm.: v.* **nuoto.**

Notorietà [noh-toh-ree-ay-tah'] *nf.* notoriety.

Notorio [noh-toh'ree-oh] *a.* notorious, well-known.

Nottambulo [not-tahm'boo-loh] *nm.* sleep-walker, somnambulist; *a.* sleep-walking.

Nottata [not-tah'tah] *nf.* night; **fare** [fah'ray] *n. vi.* to sit up all night.

Notte [not'tay] *nf.* night; **di** [dee] *n. ad.* by night.

Nottetempo [not-tay-tem'poh] *ad.* by night, in the night.

Nottola [not'toh-lah] *nf.* bat.

Notturno [not-toor'noh] *nm.* (*mus.*) nocturne; *a.* night(ly), nocturnal.

Novan/ta [noh-vahn'tah] _a._ ninety; **—tenne** [ten'nay] 90-year-old; **—tesimo** [tay'zee-moh], ninetieth.

Nova/tore [noh-vah-toh'ray] _nm._ **—trice** [tree'chay] _nf._ innovator.

Nove [noh'vay] _a._ nine.

Novella [noh-vell'lah] _nf._ news, short story, tale.

Novellare [noh-vell-lah'ray] _vi._ to tell tales.

Novello [noh-vell'loh] _a._ new.

Novembre [noh-vem'bray] _nm._ November.

Noverare [noh-vay-rah'ray] _vt._ to count, number, reckon.

Novissimo [noh-vees'see-moh] _a._ quite new.

Novità [noh-vee-tah'] _nf._ latest news, newness, novelty, originality.

Noviziato [noh-vee-tsee-ah'toh] _nm._ apprenticeship, novitiate.

Novizio [noh-vee'tsee-oh] _nm._ apprentice, beginner, novice; _a._ inexpert, unskilled.

Nozione [noh-tsee-oh'nay] _nf._ idea, notion, rudiment.

Nozze [not'say] _nf._ (_pl._) marriage, wedding.

Nube [noo'bay] _nf._ cloud.

Nubifragio [noo-bee-frah'joh] _nm._ cloudburst, downpour.

Nubile [noo'bee-lay] _nf._ spinster; _a._ marriageable, unmarried.

Nuca [noo'kah] _nf._ nape (of the neck).

Nucleo [noo'klay-oh] _nm._ group, knot, nucleus.

Nudarsi [noo-dahr'see] _vr._ to strip. _v._ **Denudare.**

Nudità [noo-dee-tah'] _nf._ nakedness, nudity.

Nudo [noo'doh] _a._ bare, naked, nude. [nothing.

Nulla [nool'lah] _nm. and pn._

Nullità [nool-lee-tah'] _nf._ nullity, nothingness, worthlessness.

Nullo [nool'loh] _a._ null, void, worthless. [god.

Nume [noo'may] _nm._ deity.

Numerale [noo-may-rah'lay] _nm. and a._ numeral.

Numerare [noo-may-rah'ray] _vt._ to number.

Numerazione [noo-may-rah-tsee-oh'nay] _nf._ numbering.

Numerico [noo-may'ree-koh] _a._ numerical.

Numero [noo'may-roh] _nm._ number.

Numeroso [noo-may-roh'soh] _a._ numerous.

Numismatica [noo-mees-mah'tee-kah] _nf._ numismatics (_pl._).

Nunzio [noon'tsee-oh] _nm._ nuncio.

Nuocere [noo-oh'chay-ray] _vt._ to be harmful, injurious, harm, hurt.

Nuora [noo-oh'rah] _nf._ daughter-in-law.

Nuotare [noo-oh-tah'ray] _vi._ to swim; n. nell'oro [nell'loh'roh] _vi._ to roll in money.

Nuoto [noo-oh'toh] _nm._ swimming; passare a [pahs-sah'ray ah] n. _vt._ to swim across.

Nuova [noo-oh'vah] _nf._ (piece of) news.

Nuovo [noo-oh'voh] _nm._ newness, originality; _a._ new; di [dee] n. _ad._ again.

Nutrice [noo-tree'chay] _nf._ nurse, wet-nurse.

Nutriente [noo-tree-en'tay] _a._ nourishing, nutritious.

Nutrimento [noo-tree-men'toh] _nm._ nourishment.

Nutri/re [noo-tree'ray] _vt._ to feed, foster, nourish; **—rsi** _vr._ to feed (on).

Nutrizione [noo-tree-tsee-oh'nay] *nf.* feeding, nourishment, nutrition.

Nuvo/la [noo'voh-lah] *nf.* —lo [loh] *nm.* cloud. **Nuvolo** [noo'voh-loh], **nuvoloso** [noo-voh-loh'soh] *a.* cloudy.

Nuziale [noo-tsee-ah'lay] *a.* bridal, nuptial.

O

O [oh] *con.* or, or else; o . . . o, either . . . or, whether . . . or; o l'uno o l'altro [oh loo' noh oh lahl'troh] *pn.* either; *int.* oh!

Oasi [oh'ah-zee] *nf.* oasis.

Obbediente, etc.: *v.* ubbidiente etc.

Obbliga/re [ob-blee-gah'ray] *vt.* to bind, compel, force, oblige; —rsi *vr.* to bind oneself, undertake.

Obbligazione [ob-blee-gah-tsee-oh'nay] *nf.* obligation, (com.) bond, debenture.

Obbligo [ob'blee-goh] *nm.* duty, obligation.

Obbrobrio [ob-broh'bree-oh] *nm.* disgrace, infamy, opprobrium.

Obeso [oh-bay'zoh] *a.* corpulent, obese.

Obice [oh'bee-chay] *nm.* (mil.) howitzer.

Obiettare [ob-yet-tah'ray] *vt.* to object.

Obiettivo [ob-yet-tee'voh] *nm.* aim, objective, (tech.) object-lens; *a.* objective.

Obiezione [ob-yay-tsee-oh' nay] *nf.* objection.

Obla/tore [oh-blah-toh'ray] *nm.* —**trice** [tree-chay] *nf.* donor.

Oblazione [ob-blah-tsee-oh' nay] *nf.* donation, oblation.

Obliare [oh-blee-ah'ray] *vt* to forget.

Oblio [oh-blee'oh] *nm.* forgetfulness, oblivion.

Obliquità [oh-blee-kwee-tah'] *nf.* obliquity.

Obliquo [oh-blee'kwoh] *a.* ambiguous, oblique.

Obliterare [oh-blee-tay-rah'ray] *vt.* to obliterate.

Obolo [oh'boh-loh] *nm.* money.

Oca [oh'kah] *nf.* goose; pelle [pell'lay] d'o. gooseflesh.

Occasionale [ock-kah-zee-oh-nah'lay] *a.* casual, chance, fortuitous.

Occasione [ock-kah-zee-oh' nay] *nf.* chance, occasion, opportunity; d'o. *ad.* second-hand.

Occhiaia [ock-kee-ah'yah] *nf.* dark circle (under eye), eye-socket.

Occhiali [ock-kee-ah'lee] *nm.* (pl.) goggles (protective) (pl.), spectacles (pl.).

Occhiata [ock-kee-ah'tah] *nf.* glance.

Occhieggiare [ock-kee-ay-djah'ray] *vt.* to eye, ogle; *vi.* to glance.

Occhiello [ock-kee-ell'loh] *nm.* button-hole, eye-let.

Occhio [ock'kee-oh] *nm.* eye; colpo [koll'poh] d'o., view; tenere [tay-nay'ray] d'o. *vt.* to keep an eye on; ad [ahd] o. e. croce [ay kroh' chay] *ad.* roughly-speaking; a quattro occhi [ah kwaht'troh ock'kee] *ad.* privately.

Occidentale [och-chee-den-tah'lay] *a.* West(ern).

Occidente [och-chee-den' tay] *nm.* West.

Occorrente [ock-korr-ren' tay] *nm.* necessary, requisite; *a.* necessary, needful, required.

Occorrenza [ock-korr-ren' zah] *nf.* circumstance; all'o. *ad.* in case of need.

Occorrere [ock-korr'ray-ray] *v.imp.* to happen, need, want.

Occultare [ock-kool-tah'ray] *vt.* to conceal, hide, keep secret.

Occulto [ock-kool'toh] *a.* hidden, occult.

Occupante [ock-koo-pahn'tay] *nm.* and *f.* occupant, occupier; *a.* occupying.

Occupa/re [ock-koo-pah'ray] *vt.* to hold, occupy; —rsi *vr.* to attend to, be busy with, mind.

Occupato [ock-koo-pah'toh] *a.* busy, engaged.

Occupazione [ock-koo-pah-tsee-oh'nay] *nf.* employment, occupation.

Oceanico [oh-chay-ah'nee-koh] *a.* oceanic.

Oceano [oh-chay'ah-noh] *nm.* ocean.

Oculare [oh-koo-lah'ray] *nm.* (*tech.*) eye-piece; *a.* eye, ocular.

Oculatezza [oh-koo-lah-tet'sah] *nf.* cautiousness, circumspection, wariness.

Oculato [ock-koo-lah'toh] *a.* cautious, circumspect, wary.

Oculista [ock-koo-lee'stah] *nm.* eye-specialist, oculist.

Oculistica [ock-koo-lee'stee-kah] *nf.* ophthalmology.

Ode [oh'day] *nf.* ode.

Odiare [oh-dee-ah'ray] *vt.* to detest, hate.

Odierno [oh-dee-ehr'noh] *a.* contemporary, of to-day, to-day's.

Odio (oh'dee-oh) *nm.* hate, hatred, odium.

Odioso [oh-dee-oh'soh] *a.* hateful, odious.

Odissea [oh-dees-say'ah] *nf.* journey full of danger and difficulty, Odyssey.

Odorare [oh-doh-rah'ray] *vt.* and *i.* to scent, smell.

Odorato [oh-doh-rah'toh] *nm.* scent, (sense of) smell.

Odore [oh-doh'ray] *nm.* odour, perfume, scent, smell.

Offende/re [off-fen'day-ray] *vt.* to hurt, offend; —rsi *vr.* to be offended, take offence.

Offensiva [off-fen-see'vah] *nf.* offensive.

Offerente [off-fay-ren'tay] *nm.* and *f.* bidder, offerer; *a.* offering.

Offerta [off-fehr'tah] *nf.* bid, offer(ing), (*com.*) tender.

Offesa [off-fay'sah] *nf.* offence, wrong.

Officina [off-fee-chee'nah] *nf.* works, workshop.

Officio : *v.* ufficio.

Officioso [off-fee-choh'soh] *a.* unofficial.

Offri/re [off-free'ray] *vt.* to afford, bid, offer; —rsi *vr.* to offer oneself, present oneself.

Offusca/re [off-foo-skah'ray] *vt.* to darken, dim, obscure; —rsi *vr.* to grow dark, dim.

Oggetto [oh-djet'toh] *nm.* article, object, subject, thing.

Oggi [oh'djee] *ad.* to-day; *o. a otto* [ah ot'toh], to-day week.

Oggi/di [oh-djee-dee'] — **giorno** [jorr'noh] *ad.* nowadays.

Ogni [ohn'yee] *a.* each, every; *in* [een] *o. luogo* [loo-oh'goh] *ad.* everywhere; *in o. modo* [moh'doh] *ad.* anyhow; *o. tanto* [tahn'toh] *ad.* every now and then.

Ognissanti [ohn-yees-sahn'tee] *nm.* All-Saints' Day.

Ognora [ohn-yoh'rah] *ad.* always.

Ognuno [ohn-yoo'noh] *pn.* each, everybody, everyone.

Ohibò [oh-ee-boh'] *int.* oh, fie!

Ohimè [oh-ee-may'] *int.* alas!

Olà [oh-lah'] *int.* hallo!

Olandese [oh-lahn-day'say] *nm.* and *f.* Dutchman, Dutchwoman; *a.* Dutch.

Oleandro [oh-lay-ahn'droh] *nm.* oleander.

Oleoso [oh-lay-oh'soh] *a.* greasy, oily.

Olezzare [oh-led-zah'ray] *vt.* to smell sweet.

Olezzo [oh-led'zoh] *nm.* fragrance, sweet smell.

Olfatto [oll-faht'toh] *nm.* scent, (sense of) smell.

Oliera [oh-lee-ay'rah] *nf.* oil-cruet.

Oligarca [oh-lee-gahr'kah] *nm.* oligarch.

Oligarchia [oh-lee-gahr-kee'ah] *nf.* oligarchy.

Olimpico [oh-leem'pee-koh] *a.* Olympian, Olympic.

Olimpo [oh-leem'poh] *nm.* Olympus.

Olio [oh'lee-oh] *nm.* oil.

Oliva [oh-lee'vah] *nf.* olive; —vo [voh] *nm.* olive-tree.

Olivastro [oh-lee-vah'stroh] *a.* olive(-coloured).

Olivigno [oh-lee-veen'nyoh] *a.* olive(-coloured).

Oliveto [oh-lee-vay'toh] *nm.* olive-orchard.

Olmo [oll'moh] *nm.* elm.

Olocausto [oh-loh-kow'stoh] *nm.* holocaust, sacrifice.

Olografo [oh-loh'grah-foh] *nm.* holograph.

Oltraccio [oll-trahch-choh'] *ad.* besides.

Oltracotanza [oll-trah-koh-tahnt'sah] *nf.* arrogance, insolence.

Oltraggiare [oll-trah-djah'ray] *vt.* to insult, outrage.

Oltraggio [oll-trah'djoh] *nm.* insult, outrage, ravage.

Oltraggioso [oll-trah-djoh'soh] *a.* insulting, outrageous.

Oltranza [oll-trahnt'sah] *nf.* excess, extreme; ad [ahd] *o. ad.* to the death, to the last.

Oltre [oll'tray] *ad. and pr.* besides, beyond, longer than, more than, past; andare [ahn-dah'ray] *o. vi.* to proceed; più [pee-oo'] *o. ad.* further.

Oltremare [oll-tray-mah-

ray] *ad.* beyond the sea(s), overseas(s).

Oltremodo [oll-tray-moh'doh] *ad.* beyond measure, exceedingly.

Oltrepassare [oll-tray-pahs-sah'ray] *vt.* to exceed, go beyond, outstrip, surpass.

Oltretomba [oll-tray-tom'bah] *nm.* the Beyond.

Omaggio [oh-mah'djoh] *nm.* homage; copia in [koh'pee-ah een] *o.* presentation copy.

Omai [oh-mah'ee] *ad.* (*poet.*) now.

Ombelicale [om-bay-lee-kah'lay] *a.* umbilical.

Ombelico [om-bay-lee'koh] *nm.* navel.

Ombra [om'brah] *nf.* shade, shadow; all'o. *ad.* in the shade.

Ombreggiare [om-bray-djah'ray] *vt.* to shade.

Ombrella [om-brell'lah] *nf.* (*bot.*) umbel.

Ombrello [om-brell'loh] *nm.* sunshade, umbrella.

Ombrina [om-bree'nah] *nf.* grayling (fish).

Ombroso [om-broh'soh] *a.* shady (of places), nervous (of horses), suspicious (of people).

Omeopatia [oh-may-oh-pah-tee'ah] *nf.* homoeopathy.

Omero [oh'may-roh] *nm.* shoulder.

Omettere [oh-met'tay-ray] *vt.* to leave out, omit.

Omicida [oh-mee-chee'dah] *nm.* homicide (man); *a.* homicidal.

Omicidio [oh-mee-chee'dee-oh] *nm.* homicide (crime).

Omino [oh-mee'noh] *nm.* little man.

Omissione [oh-mees-see-oh'nay] *nf.* omission.

Omogeneo [oh-moh-jay'nay-oh] *a.* homogeneous.

Omologo [oh-moh'loh-goh] *a.* homologous.

Omonimo [oh-moh'nee-moh] *nm.* homonym; *a.* homonymous.

Oncia [on'chah] *nf.* ounce.

Onciale [on-chah'lay] *a.* uncial.

Onda [on'dah] *nf.* breaker, wave; **lunghezza** [loong-ghet'zah] **d'o.** [*rad.*] wave-length.

Onde [on'day] *ad.* from where, whence; *rel. pn.* by which, from which; *pr.* in order to.

Ondeggiamento [on-day-djah-men'toh] *nm.* hesitation, waving, wavering.

Ondeggiare [on-day-djah'ray] *vi.* to hesitate, wave, waver.

Ondoso [on-doh'soh] *a.* undulatory, waving.

Ondulare [on-doo-lah'ray] *vt.* to wave; *vi.* to undulate; —**rsi i capelli** [ee kah-pel'lee] *vr.* to wave one's hair.

Ondulazione [on-doo-lah-tsee-oh'nay] *nf.* hair-waving, undulation, waving.

Onere [oh'nay-ray] *nm.* burden, duty, load, tax.

Oneroso [oh-nay-roh'soh] *a.* burdensome, onerous.

Onestà [oh-ness-tah'] *nf.* honesty, uprightness.

Onesto [oh-ness'toh] *a.* fair, honest, upright.

Onice [oh'nee-chay] *nf.* onyx.

Onni/possente [on-nee-pos-sen'tay], —**potente** [poh-ten'tay] *a.* almighty, omnipotent.

Onniscienza [on-nee-shent'sah] *nf.* omniscience.

Onniveggente [on-nee-vay-djen'tay] *a.* all-seeing.

Onomastico [oh-noh-mah'stee-koh] *nm.* name-day.

Onoranza [oh-noh-rahnt'sah] *nf.* honour, solemnity.

Onora/re [oh-noh-rah'ray] *vt.* to be an honour to, honour; —**rsi** *vr.* to be proud of.

Onorario [oh-noh-rah'ree-oh] *nm.* fee, honorarium; *a.* honorary.

Onore [oh-noh'ray] *nm.* honour; **serata** [say-rah'tah] **d'o.** *nf.* (*theat.*) benefit-night.

Onorevole [oh-noh-ray'voh-lay] *a.* honourable, respectable.

Onorevolezza [oh-noh-ray-voh-let'sah] *nf.* honourableness.

Onorificenza [oh-noh-ree-fee-chent'sah] *nf.* dignity, honour, title.

Onorifico [oh-noh-ree'fee-koh] *a.* honorific.

Onta [on'tah] *nf.* disgrace, shame; *ad* [ahd] **o. di** [dee] *pr.* in spite of.

Ontano [on-tah'noh] *nm.* alder.

Opacità [oh-pah-chee-tah'] *nf.* opacity, opaqueness.

Opaco [oh-pah'koh] *a.* opaque.

Opale [oh-pah'lay] *nm.* opal.

Opera [oh'pay-rah] *nf.* action, labour, opera, work.

Operabile [oh-pay-rah'bee-lay] *a.* operable, workable.

Operaio [oh-pay-rah'yoh] *nm.* hand, workman; *a.* working.

Operare [oh-pay-rah'ray] *vt. and i.* to act, do, operate, work; **farsi** [fahr'see] **o.** *vi.* to undergo an operation.

Operativo [oh-pay-rah-tee'voh] *a.* operative.

Operatore [oh-pay-rah-toh'ray] *nm.* operating surgeon, operator.

Operazione [oh-pay-rah-tsee-oh'nay] *nf.* operation, (*math.*) sum, (*com.*) transaction.

Operosità [oh-pay-roh-see-tah'] *nf.* activity, industry.

Operoso [oh-pay-roh'soh] *a.* active, industrious.

Opificio [oh-pee-fee'choh] *nm.* factory, works.

Opinare [oh-pee-nah'ray] vi. to be of opinion, opine.

Opinione [oh-pee-nee-oh'nay] nf. opinion.

Oppio [op'pee-oh] nm. opium.

Opponente [op-poh-nen'tay] nm. adversary, opponent; a. opposing.

Oppor/re [op-porr'ray] vt. and **—rsi** vr. to object, oppose.

Opportunista [op-porr-too-nee'stah] nm. opportunist.

Opportunità [op-porr-too-nee-tah'] nf. expediency opportuneness, opportunity.

Opportuno [op-porr-too'noh] a. expedient, opportune, proper, suitable.

Opposizione [op-poh-zee-tsee-oh'nay] nf. opposition.

Opposto [op-poss'toh] nm. contrary, opposite; a. opposed, opposite.

Oppressione [op-press-see-oh'nay] nf. oppression, weight.

Oppressivo [op-press-see'voh] a. oppressive.

Oppresso [op-press'soh] a. oppressed, overwhelmed, weighed down.

Oppressore [op-press-soh'ray] nm. oppressor.

Opprimere [op-pree'may-ray] vt. to oppress, overwhelm.

Oppugnare [op-poon-yah'ray] vt. to attack, confute, oppose, refute.

Oppure [op-poo'ray] con. or (else).

Optare [op-tah'ray] vi. to choose, make one's option.

Opulento [oh-poo-len'toh] a. abundant, opulent, rich.

Opulenza [oh-poo-lent'sah] nf. abundance, opulence.

Opuscolo [oh-poo'skoh-loh] nm. leaflet, pamphlet.

Ora [oh'rah] nf. hour, time; che ore sono? [kay oh'ray soh'noh], what time is it? ad. at present, now; or ora, just now; ora che [kay] con. now that.

Oracolo [oh-rah'koh-loh] nm. oracle.

Orafo [oh'rah-foh] nm. goldsmith.

Orale [oh-rah'lay] nm. oral examination; a. oral, verbal.

Oramai [oh-rah-mah'ee] ad. by this time, now.

Orare [oh-rah'ray] vi. to pray.

Orario [oh-rah'ree-oh] nm. time-table; o. d'ufficio [doof-fee'choh], office hours; a. per hour; segnale [sayn-yah'lay] o. nm. time-signal.

Oratore [oh-rah-toh'ray] nm. orator, speaker, spokesman.

Oratoria [oh-rah-toh'ree-ah] nf. eloquence, oratory.

Orazione [oh-rah-tsee-oh'nay] nf. oration, prayer.

Orbene [orr-bay'nay] ad. well (now).

Orbita [orr'bee-tah] nf. eye-socket, limit, orbit.

Orbo [orr'boh] a. blind, bereaved.

Orca [orr'kah] nf. orc.

Orchestra [orr-kess'trah] nf. orchestra; direttore [dee-ret-toh'ray] d'o nm. conductor.

Orchidea [orr-kee-day'ah] nf. orchid.

Orco [orr'koh] nm. ogre.

Orda [orr'dah] nf. horde.

Ordigno [orr-deen'yoh] nm. implement; o. infernale [een-fehr-nah'lay] infernal machine.

Ordinamento [orr-dee-nah-men'toh] nm. arrangement, disposition, organization.

Ordinanza [orr-dee-nahnt'sah] nf. order, (mil.) orderly, ordinance.

Ordinare [orr-dee-nah'ray] vt. and i. to ordain, order, set in order, tidy.

Ordinario [orr-dee-nah'ree-oh] a. cheap, common, ordinary, vulgar, usual.

Ordinato [orr-dee-nah'toh] *a.* orderly, organized, tidy.

Ordinazione [orr-dee-nah-tsee-oh'nay] *nf.* order, ordination; **fatto su** [faht'toh soo] **o.** *a.* made to order.

Ordine [orr'dee-nay] *nm.* order, row.

Ordire [orr-dee'ray] *vt.* to plan, plot, weave.

Orditura [orr-dee-too'rah] *nf.* contriving, warping.

Orecchino [orr-reck-kee'noh] *nm.* ear-ring.

Orecchio [oh-reck'kee-oh] *nm.* ear; **a** [ah] **o.** *ad.* by ear; **duro** [doo'roh] **d'o.** hard of hearing.

Orefice [oh-ray'fee-chay] *nm.* goldsmith.

Oreficeria [oh-ray-fee-chay-ree'ah] *nf.* goldsmith's shop, things made of gold.

Orfa/na [orr'fah-nah] *nf.* —**no** [noh] *nm.* orphan.

Orfanotrofio [orr-fah-noh-troh'fee-oh] *nm.* orphanage.

Organico [orr-gah'nee-koh] *a.* organic.

Organino [orr-gah-nee'noh] *nm.* barrel-organ, small organ.

Organismo [orr-gah-nees'moh] *nm.* organism.

Organista [orr-gah-nee'stah] *nm.* organist.

Organizzare [orr-gah-need-zah'ray] *vt.* to organise.

Organizzazione [orr-gah-need-zah-tsee-oh'nay] *nf.* organization, preparation.

Organo [orr'gah-noh] *nm.* organ.

Orgasmo [orr-gahs'moh] *nm.* orgasm, violent excitement.

Orgia [orr'jah] *nf.* orgy.

Orgoglio [orr-gohl'yoh] *nm.* pride.

Orgoglioso [orr-gohl-yoh'soh] *a.* proud.

Orientale [oh-ree-en-tah'lay] *nm.* Oriental; *a.* East(ern), Oriental.

Orientamento [oh-ree-en-tah-men'toh] *nm.* bump of locality, orientation; **facoltà di** [fah-koll-tah'dee] **o.** *nf.* bump of locality.

Orienta/re [oh-ree-en-tah'ray] *vt.* to set, turn; —**rsi** *vr.* to find one's bearings or way.

Oriente [oh-ree-en'tay] *nm.* East, orient.

Originale [oh-ree-jee-nah'lay] *nm.* eccentric person, original; *a.* eccentric, original, queer.

Originalità [oh-ree-jee-nah-lee-tah'] *nf.* eccentricity, oddity, originality.

Origina/re [oh-ree-jee-nah'ray] *vt.* to give rise to, occasion, originate; *vi.* to originate, rise.

Originario [oh-ree-jee-nah'ree-oh] *a.* original, primary.

Origine [oh-ree'jee-nay] *nm.* beginning, birth, cause, origin, source.

Origliare [oh-reel-yah'ray] *vi.* to eavesdrop.

Origliere [oh-reel-yay'ray] *nm.* bolster.

Oriundo [oh-ree-oon'doh] *a.* born, native, of . . . descent.

Oriuolo: *v.* **orologio.**

Orizzontale [oh-reed-zon-tah'lay] *a.* horizontal.

Orizzonte [oh-reed-zon'tay] *nm.* horizon.

Orlare [orr-lah'ray] *vt.* to edge, hem.

Orlatura [orr-lah-too'rah] *nf.* edging, hemming.

Orlo [orr'loh] *nm.* border, brim, brink, edge, hem.

Orma [orr'mah] *nf.* footprint, mark, step, trace.

Ormai [orr-mah'ee] *ad.* by now.

Ormeggia/re [orr-may-djah'ray] *vt. and i.* and —**rsi** *vr.* to moor.

Ormeggio [orr-may'djoh] *nm.* mooring(s).

Ornamento [orr-nah-men'-toh] *nm.* ornament.

Orna/re [orr-nah'ray] *vt.* to adorn, beautify, ornament; —**rsi** *vr.* to deck oneself.

Ornitologia [orr-nee-toh-loh-jee'ah] *nf.* ornithology.

Ornitologo [orr-nee-toh'loh-goh] *nm.* ornithologist.

Oro [oh'roh] *nm.* gold; **farsi** [fahr'see] **d'o.** to get rich.

Orologiaio [oh-roh-loh-jah'-yoh] *nm.* clockmaker, watch-maker.

Orologio [oh-roh-loh'joh] *nm.* clock, watch.

Orrendo [orr-ren'doh], **orri-bile** [orr-ree'bee-lay] *a.* dread-ful, horrible.

Orrido [orr'ree-doh] *nm.* ravine; *a.* bristly, dreary, horrid. [horror, loathing.

Orrore [orr-roh'ray] *nm.*

Orso [orr'soh] *nm.* bear, *(fig.)* unsociable person.

Orsù [orr-soo'] *int.* come on!

Ortaggio [orr-tah'djoh] *nm.* vegetable.

Ortica [orr-tee'-kah] *nf.* nettle.

Orto [orr'toh] *nm.* kitchen-garden.

Ortografia [orr-toh-grah-fee'ah] *nf.* orthography, spell-ing.

Ortolano [orr-toh-lah'noh] *nm.* green-grocer market-gardener.

Ortopedia [orr-toh-pay-dee'-ah] *nf.* orthopaedy.

Orzaiolo [ord-zah-ee-oh'-loh] *nm.* sty, stye (on the eye-lid).

Orzata [ord-zah'tah] *nf.* barley-water.

Orzo [ord'zoh] *nm.* barley.

Osare [oh-zah'ray] *vt. and i.* to dare, venture.

Oscenità [oh-shay-nee-tah'] *nf.* indecency, obscenity.

Osceno [oh-shay'noh] *a.* immoral, indecent, obscene.

Oscillare [oh-sheel-lah'ray] *vi.* to hesitate, oscillate, swing.

Oscuramento [oss-koo-rah-men'toh] *nm.* black-out, dark-ening.

Oscura/re [oss-koo-rah'ray] *vt.* to blacken, darken, obscure; —**rsi** *vr.* to grow dark, dim.

Oscurità [oss-koo-ree-tah'] *nf.* darkness, obscurity.

Oscuro [oss-koo'roh] *a.* dark, doubtful, obscure; **essere all'o** [ess'say-ray ahl] to be ignorant of. [*nm.* hospital.

Ospedale [oss-pay-dah'lay]

Ospitale [oss-pee-tah'lay] *a.* hospitable.

Ospitalità [oss-pee-tah-lee-tah'] *nf.* hospitality.

Ospitare [oss-pee-tah'ray] *vt.* to entertain, give hospitality to, shelter.

Ospite [oss'pee-tay] *nm.* guest, host; *nf.* guest, hostess.

Ospizio [oss-pee'tsee-oh] *nm.* hospice; **o. di mendicità** [dee men-dee-chee-tah'] almshouse.

Osse/quente [oss-say-kwen'-tay] —**quioso** [kwee-oh'soh] *a.* obedient, respectful.

Ossequiare [oss-say-kwee-ah'ray] *vt.* to pay one's respects to.

Ossequio [oss-say'kwee-oh] *nm.* homage, obedience, re-spect; **i miei ossequi** [ee mee-ay'ee oss-say'kwee] (*pl.*) my regards, respects (*pl.*).

Osservanza [oss-sehr-vahnt'-sah] *nf.* obedience, observance.

Osservare [oss-sehr-vah'ray] *vt.* to keep, notice, observe, watch.

Osserva/tore [oss-sehr-vah-toh'ray] *nm.* —**trice** [tree'chay] *nf.* observer.

Osservazione [oss-sehr-vah-tsee-oh'nay] *nf.* observation, remark.

Ossessionare [oss-sess-see-oh-nah'ray] *vt.* to obsess.

Ossessione [oss-sess-see-oh'nay] *nf.* haunting fear, obsession.

Ossesso [oss-sess'soh] *nm.* demoniac, person possessed.

Ossia [oss-see'ah] *con.* or, that is. [oxide.

Ossido [oss'see-doh] *nm.*

Ossigeno [oss-see'jay-noh] *nm.* oxygen.

Osso [oss'soh] *nm.* bone; essere ridotto pelle e ossa [ess'say-ray ree-dot'toh pell' lay ay oss'sah] to be all skin and bone.

Ossuto [oss-soo'toh] *a.* big-boned, bony.

Ostacolare [oss-tah-koh-lah'ray] *vt.* to hinder, interfere with.

Ostacolo [oss-tah'koh-loh] *nm.* hindrance, obstacle.

Ostaggio [oss-tah'djoh] *nm.* hostage.

Oste [oss'tay] *nm.* host, innkeeper, landlord.

Osteggiare [oss-tay-djah'ray] *vt.* to be hostile to, oppose.

Ostentare [oss-ten-tah'ray] *vt.* to display, feign, show off.

Ostentazione [oss-ten-tah-tsee-oh'nay] *nf.* ostentation, pretence.

Osteria [oss-tay-ree'ah] *nf.* inn, tavern.

Ostetrica [oss-tay'tree-kah] *nf.* mid-wife.

Ostia [oss'tee-ah] *nf.* Host, victim, wafer.

Ostico [oss'tee-koh] *a.* difficult, hard, unpleasant.

Ostile [oss-tee'lay] *a.* adverse, hostile, sullen.

Ostilità [oss-tee-lee-tah'] *nf.* enmity, hostility.

Ostinarsi [oss-tee-nahr'see] *vr.* to insist, persist.

Ostinato [oss-tee-nah'toh] *a.* obstinate, stubborn.

Ostinazione [oss-tee-nah-

tsee-oh'nay] *nf.* obstinacy, persistence, stubbornness.

Ostracismo [oss-trah-chees'moh] *nm.* ostracism.

Ostrica [oss'tree-kah] *nf.* oyster.

Ostruire [oss-troo-ee'ray] *vt.* to obstruct, stop (up).

Ostruzione [oss-troo-tsee-oh'nay] *nf.* obstruction.

Otite [oh-tee'tay] *nf.* (*med.*) otitis.

Otre [oh'tray] *nm.* leather bag, leather bottle.

Ottan/ta [ot-tahn'tah] *a.* eighty; —tenne [ten'nay] *a.* 80-year-old; —tesimo [tay! zee-moh] *a.* eightieth; —tina [tee'nah] *nf.* about 80.

Otta/va [ot-tah'vah] *nf.* octave; —vo [voh] *nm.* eighth (part), octave; *a.* eighth.

Ottemperare [ot-tem-pay-rah'ray] *vi.* to comply with, obey.

Ottenebrare [ot-tay-nay-brah'ray] *vt.* to cloud, darken, obscure.

Ottenere [ot-tay-nay'ray] *vt.* to gain, get, obtain, reach.

Ottenibile [ot-tay-nee'bee-lay] *a.* obtainable.

Ottica [ot'tee-kah] *nf.* optics.

Ottico [ot'tee-koh] *nm.* optician; *a.* optic(al).

Ottimismo [ot-tee-mees'moh] *nm.* optimism.

Ottimo [ot'tee-moh] *nm.* best; *a.* excellent, very good.

Otto [ot'toh] *a.* eight.

Ottobre [ot-toh'bray] *nm.* October.

Ottocento [ot-toh-chen'toh] *nm.* the nineteenth century; *a.* eight hundred.

Ottomano [ot-toh-mah'noh] *nm. and a.* Ottoman.

Ottone [ot-toh'nay] *nm.* brass, brass instrument.

Ottundere [ot-toon'day-ray] *vt.* to (make) blunt. (*rare*).

Otturare [ot-too-rah'ray] *vt.* to obstruct, stop (a tooth, etc.).

Ottusità [ot-too-zee-tah'] *nf.* bluntness, obtuseness.

Ottuso [ot-too'zoh] *a.* blunt, dark, dull, obtuse.

Ovaia [oh-vah'yah] *nf.* ovary.

Ovale [oh-vah'lay] *nm.* oval; *a.* egg-shaped, oval.

Ovatta [oh-vaht'tah] *nf.* wadding.

Ovazione [oh-vah-tsee-oh'nay] *nf.* ovation.

Ove [oh'vay] *ad.* where; *con.* if, in case.

Ovest [oh'vest] *nm.* West.

Ovile [oh-vee'lay] *nm.* fold, sheep-fold.

Ovino [oh-vee'noh] *a.* ovine, (of) sheep; **ovini** [oh-vee'nee] *nm. (pl.)* sheep *(pl.)*.

Ovolo [oh'voh-loh] *nm.* a kind of mushroom.

Ovunque [oh-voong'kway] *ad.* anywhere, everywhere, wherever.

Ovvero [ov-vay'roh] *con.* or.

Ovviare [ov-vee-ah'ray] *vi.* to avoid, obviate.

Ovvio [ov'vee-oh] *a.* evident, obvious, plain.

Ozio [oh'tsee-oh] *nm.* idleness, leisure.

Ozioso [oh-tsee-oh'soh] *a.* idle, indolent, leisured.

P

Pacatezza [pah-kah-tet'sah] *nf.* calmness, placidity.

Pacato [pah-kah'toh] *a.* calm, placid.

Pacchetto [pahk-ket'toh] *nm.* packet, small parcel.

Pacco [pahk'koh] *nm.* package, packet, parcel.

Pace [pah'chay] *nf.* peace.

Pacie/re [pah-chay'ray] *nm.* —**ra** [rah] *nf.* peacemaker.

Pacificare [pah-chee-fee-kah'ray] *vt.* to appease, pacify, reconcile.

Pacificazione [pah-chee-fee-kah-tsee-oh'nay] *nf.* pacification, reconciliation.

Pacifico [pah-chee'fee-koh] *nm.* the Pacific; *a.* peaceable, peaceful, peace-loving.

Padella [pah-dell'lah] *nf.* bed-pan, frying-pan.

Padiglione [pah-deel-yoh'nay] *nm.* department, pavilion.

Padre [pah'dray] *nm.* father.

Padrino [pah-dree'noh] *nm.* god-father, second (in a duel).

Padronanza [pah-droh-nahnt'sah] *nf.* command, mastery; **p. di sè** [dee say] self-control.

Padronato [pah-droh-naht'toh] *nm.* ownership, possession.

Padro/na [pah-droh'nah] *nf.* landlady, mistress; —**ne** [nay] *nm.* landlord, master, owner, proprietor.

Padroneggiare [pah-droh-nay-djah'ray] *vt.* to command, master, rule; *vi.* to play the master. [marsh

Padule [pah-doo'lay] *nm.*

Paesaggio [pah-ay-zah'djoh] *nm.* landscape.

Paese [pah-ay'zay] *nm.* country (kingdom), district, village.

Paesista [pay-ay-zee'stah] *nm.* landscape-painter.

Paffuto [pahf-foo'toh] *a.* chubby, plump.

Paga [pah'gah] *nf.* pay, wages.

Pagabile [pah-gah-bee-lay] *a.* payable.

Pagamento [pah-gah-men'toh] *nm.* payment.

Pagano [pah-gah'noh] *nm. and a.* heathen, pagan.

Pagare [pah-gah'ray] *vt.* to pay.

Pagella [pah-jell'lah] *nf.* (school-) report.

Paggio [pah'djoh] *nm.* page (servant).

Pagina [[pah'jee-nah] *nf.* leaf, page (of a book).

Paglia [pahl'yah] *nf.* straw.

Pagliaccio [pahl-yahch'choh] *nm.* buffoon, clown.

Pagliaio [pahl-yah'yoh] *nm.* straw-rick.

Pagliericcio [pahl-yay-reech'choh] *nm* straw-mattress.

Pagnotta [pahn-yot'tah] *nf.* loaf.

Pago [pah'goh] *a.* content, satisfied. [pair.

Paio [pah'yoh] *nm.* couple.

Pala [pah'lah] *nf.* blade, shovel; **ruota a pale** [roo-oh'tah ah pah'lay] *nf.* (*tech.*) paddle-wheel.

Palafitta [pah-lah-feet'tah] *nf.* lake-dwelling, pile.

Palafreniere [pah-lah-fray-nee-ay'ray] *nm.* groom.

Palafreno [pah-lah-fray'noh] *nm.* palfrey.

Palagio [pah-lah'joh] *nm.* (poet.) palace.

Palatino [pah-lah-tee'noh] *nm.* and *a.* palatine.

Palato [pah-lah'toh] *nm.* palate.

Palazzo [pah-laht'soh] *nm.* mansion, palace (of the king), town-house

Palchetto [pahl-ket'toh] *nm.* shelf.

Palco [pahl'koh] *nm.* (theat.) box, flooring, platform, scaffold, stage, stand.

Palcoscenico [pahl-koh-shay'nee-koh] *nm.*(theat.) stage.

Palesa/re [pah-lay-zah'ray] *vt.* to disclose, reveal; —rsi *vr.* to show oneself, turn out to be.

Palese' [pah-lay'zay] *a.* clear, obvious.

Palestra [pah-less'trah] *nf.* gymnasium.

Paletta [pah-let'tah] *nf.* shovel.

Paletto [pah-let'toh] *nm.* bolt (of the door), pile.

Palio [pah-lee-oh] *nm.* prize, race, velvet cloak.

Palizzata [pah-leet-sah'tah] *nf.* fence, paling, palisade.

Palla [pahl'lah] *nf.* ball; **p. da cannone** [dah kahn-noh'nay] shell; **p. da fucile** [foo-chee'lay] bullet.

Palliare [pahl-lee-ah'ray] *vt.* to palliate.

Palliativo [pahl-lee-ah-tee'voh] *nm.* and *a.* palliative.

Pallido [pahl'lee-doh] *a.* faint, pale, pallid.

Pallone [pahl-loh'nay] *nm.* ball, balloon, football.

Pallore [pahl-loh'ray] *nm.* paleness, pallor.

Pallottola [pahl-lot'toh-lah] *nf.* bullet, pellet.

Palma [pahl'mah] *nf.* palm (-tree), palm (of the hand).

Palmeto [pahl-may'toh] *nm.* palm-grove.

Palmo [pahl'moh] *nm.* palm (of the hand, or measure).

Palo [pah'loh] *nm.* pile, pole, post; **saltare di** [sahl-tah'ray dee] **p. in frasca** [een frah'skah] *vi.* to ramble from the point.

Palombaro [pah-lom-bah'roh] *nm.* diver.

Palombo [pah-lom'boh] *nm.* dog-fish, wood-pigeon.

Palpabile [pahl-pah'bee-lay] *a.* palpable.

Palpare [pahl-pah'ray] *vt.* to feel, handle, (med.) palpate, touch.

Palpebra [pahl'pay-brah] *nf.* eyelid.

Palpitare [pahl-pee-tah'ray] *vi.* to palpitate, tremble, throb.

Palpito [pahl'pee-toh] *nm.* beat, throb. [coat.

Paltò [pahl-toh'] *nm.* (over-

Palude [pah-loo'day] *nf.* fen, marsh.

Paludoso [pah-loo-doh'soh], **palustre** [pah-loo'stray] *a.* marshy.

Panare [pah-nah'ray] *vt.* to cover with breadcrumbs.

Panca [pahng'kah] *nf.* bench, form.

Pancetta [pahn-chet'tah] *nf.* bacon, small paunch.

Panchetto [pahng-ket'toh] *nm.* footstool.

Pancia [pahn'chah] *nf.* belly, paunch.

Panciotto [pahn-chot'toh] *nm.* waistcoat.

Pane [pah'nay] *nm.* bread; chiamare [kee-ah-mah'ray] p. il [eel] **p.** *vi.* to call a spade a spade; rendere [ren'day-ray] **p. per focaccia** [pehr foh-kahch'chah] *vi.* to give tit for tat.

Panegirico [pah-nay-jee'ree-koh] *nm.* panegyric.

Panetteria [pah-net-tay-ree'ah] *nf.* baker's shop.

Panettiere [pah-net-tee-ay'ray] *nm.* baker. *v.* Fornaio.

Panico [pah'nee-koh] *nm.* panic.

Panico [pah-nee'koh] *nm.* bird seed, millet.

Paniere [pah-nee-ay'ray] *nm.* basket.

Panificio [pah-nee-fee'choh] *nm.* bakehouse, bakery.

Panino [pah-nee'noh] *nm.* roll of bread.

Panna [pahn'nah] *nf.* cream; p. montata [mon-tah'tah], whipped cream; (*aut.*) accident, breakdown.

Pannina [pahn-nee'nah] *nf.* woollen material.

Panno [pahn'noh] *nm.* cloth (*pl.* clothes).

Pannolino [pahn-noh-lee'noh] *nm.* diaper, sanitary towel.

Pantaloni [pahn-tah-loh'nee] *nm.* (*pl.*) trousers (*pl.*).

Pantano [pahn-tah'noh] *nm.* bog, fen.

Panteismo [pahn-tay-ees'moh] *nm.* pantheism.

Pantera [pahn-tay'rah] *nf.* panther.

Pantofola [pahn-toh'foh-lah] *nf.* slipper.

Papa [pah'pah] *nm.* Pope.

Papale [pah-pah'lay] *a.* papal.

Papato [pah-pah'toh] *nm.* papacy.

Papavero [pah-pah'vay-roh] *nm.* poppy.

Papiro [pah-pee'roh] *nm.* papyrus.

Pappa [pahp'pah] *nf.* pap.

Pappagallo [pahp-pah-gahl'loh] *nm.* parrot.

Parabola [pah-rah'boh-lah] *nf.* parable, parabola.

Paracadute [pah-rah-kah-doo'tay] *nm.* parachute.

Paracadutista [pah-rah-kah-doo-tee'stah] *nm.* parachutist, paratrooper.

Paracenere [pah-rah-chay'nay-ray] *nm.* fireguard.

Paradisiaco [pah-rah-dee-zee'ah-koh] *a.* heavenly, paradisiacal.

Paradiso [pah-rah-dee'zoh] *nm.* heaven, paradise.

Paradosso [pah-rah-dos'soh] *nm.* paradox.

Parafango [pah-rah-fahng'goh] *nm.* (*aut.*) mudguard.

Paraffina [pah-rahf-fee'nah] *nf.* oil, paraffin.

Parafrasi [pah-rah'frah-zee] *nf.* amplification, paraphrase.

Parafulmine [pah-rah-fool'mee-nay] *nm.* lightning-conductor.

Parafuoco [pah-rah-foo-oh'koh] *nm.* fireguard.

Paraggi [pah-rah'djee] *nm.* neighbourhood, parts (*pl.*).

Paragonabile [pah-rah-goh-nah'bee-lay] *a.* comparable.

Paragonare [pah-rah-goh-nah'ray] *vt.* to compare.

Paragone [pah-rah-goh'nay] *nm.* comparison.

Paragrafo [pah-rah'grah-foh] *nm.* paragraph, section.

Paralisi [pah-rah'lee-zee] *nf.* (*med.*) palsy, paralysis.

Paralitico [pah-rah-lee'tee-koh] *nm. and a.* paralytic.

Paralizzare [pah-rah-leed-zah'ray] *vt.* to paralyse.

Parallelo [pah-rahl-lay'loh] *nm. and a.* parallel.

Paralume [pah-rah-loo'may] *nm.* lampshade.

Parapetto [pah-rah-pet'toh] *nm.* parapet.

Parapiglia [pah-rah-peel'yah] *nm.* hurly-burly, scuffle.

Parare [pah-rah'ray] *vt. and i.* to avert, avoid, decorate, hinder, ornament, prepare, protect, shelter.

Parasole [pah-rah-soh'lay] *nm.* parasol.

Parassita [pah-rahs-see'tah] *nm.* parasite.

Parata [pah-rah'tah] *nf.* parade; **mala** [mah'lah] **p.** unlucky moment, ill plight.

Paratia [pah-rah-tee'ah] *nf.* (*naut.*) bulkhead.

Paravento [pah-rah-ven'toh] *nm.* (wind)screen.

Parco [pahr'koh] *nm.* park; *a.* frugal, moderate, sparing, temperate.

Parec/chio [pah-reck'kee-oh] *a.* a good deal of; *a.* a lot, much; **—chi** [kee] *a.* and *pn. m.* (*pl.*) **—chie** [kee-ay] *a.* and *pn. f.* (*pl.*) several.

Pareggiare [pah-ray-djah'-ray] *vt.* to balance, equal, equalise, level; **p. una scuola** [oo'nah skoo-oh'lah], to get a school officially recognised.

Pareggio [pah-ray'djoh] *nm.* balance, equalisation, levelling.

Parentado [pah-ren-tah'doh]

parentela [pah-ren-tay'lah] *nf.* kin (*pl.*), kindred, relations (*pl.*), relationship.

Parente [pah-ren'tay] *nm. and f.* relation, relative; **p. più stretto** [pee-oo' stret'toh] next-of-kin.

Parentesi [pah-ren'tay-zee] *nf.* brackets (*pl.*) parenthesis.

Parere [pah-ray'ray] *vi.* to appear, look like, seem, sound like, taste like; *nm.* advice, judgment, opinion.

Parete [pah-ray'tay] *nf.* wall (internal).

Pari [pah'ree] *nm.* (*sing. and pl.*), equal, like, peer; **camera dei** [kah'may-rah day'ee] **p.**, House of Lords; *nf.* par; *a.* equal, like, same.

Parificare *v.* pareggiare.

Pariglia [pah-reel'yah] *nf.* pair (of horses).

Parimenti [pah-ree-men'-tee] *ad.* also, likewise.

Parità [pah-ree-tah'] *nf.* equality, parity.

Parlamentare [pahr-lah-men-tah'ray] *vi.* to parley; *nm.* Parliamentarian; *a.* Parliamentary.

Parlamento [pahr-lah-men'-toh] *nm.* parley, Parliament.

Parlare [pahr-lah'ray] *vi.* to speak, talk; **p. chiaro** [kee-ah'roh], to be plain, speak one's mind.

Parmigiano [pahr-mee-jah'-noh] *nm.* Parmesan (cheese).

Parodia [pah-roh-dee'ah] *nf.* parody.

Parola [pah-roh'lah] *nf.* word; **p. d'ordine** [dorr'dee-nay] (*mil.*) pass-word.

Parolina [pah-roh-lee'nah] *nf.* honied word, sweet word.

Parossismo [pah-ross-sees'-moh] *nm.* paroxysm.

Parricida [pahr-ree-chee'-dah] *nm.* parricide (criminal); *a.* parricidal.

Parricidio [pahr-ree-chee'-dee-oh] *nm.* parricide (crime).

Parrocchia [pahr-rock'kee-ah] *nf.* parish.

Parrocchiano [pahr-rock-kee-ah'noh] *nm.* parishioner.

Parrucca [pahr-rook'kah] *nf.* wig.

Parrucchie/re [pahr-rook-kee-ay'ray] *nm.* **—ra** [rah] *nf.* hairdresser.

Parroco [pahr'roh-koh] *nm.* parish-priest, rector.

Parsimonia [pahr-see-moh'nee-ah] *nf.* parsimony, sparingness.

Parte [pahr'tay] *nf.* part, party, place, rôle, share, side; **la maggior** [lah mah'djorr] **p.** *nf.* the majority; **a** [ah] **p.** *ad.* extra; **da** [dah] **p.** *ad.* aside; **in** [een] **p.** *ad.* partly.

Partecipare [pahr-tay-chee-pah'ray] *vt.* to announce, inform, notify; *vi.* to be present, participate, take (a) part.

Partecipazione [pahr-tay-chee-pah-tsee-oh'nay] *nf.* announcement, notification, participation.

Partecipe [pahr-tay'chee-pay] *a.* informed, participating, sharing; **essere** [ess'say-ray] **p. di** [dee] *vi.* to share.

Parteggiare [pahr-tay-djah'ray] *vi.* to side with, take sides.

Partenza [pahr-tent'sah] *nf.* departure, start(ing), (*naut.*) sailing.

Particella [pahr-tee-chell'lah] *nf.* particle.

Participio [pahr-tee-chee'pee-oh] *nm.* participle.

Particolare [pahr-tee-koh-lah'ray] *nm.* detail, particular; *a.* particular, peculiar, private, special.

Partigiano [pahr-tee-jah'noh] *nm.* partisan, supporter; *a.* factious, partisan.

Parti/re [pahr-tee'ray] *vt.* to divide, separate; *vi.* to depart, leave, set out, start; **—rsi** *vr.* to depart, leave.

Partita [pahr-tee'tah] *nf.* game, match, party, (*com.*) lot.

Partito [pahr-tee'toh] *nm.* match (marriage), party (political), resolution; *a.* [ah] **p. preso** [pray'soh] *ad.* with mind made up.

Partizione [pahr-tee-tsee-oh'nay] *nf.* division, partition.

Parto [pahr'toh] *nm.* (child) birth, delivery.

Partorire [pahr-toh-ree'ray] *vt. and i.* to bring forth, cause, give birth to.

Parziale [pahr-tsee-ah'lay] *a.* biased, partial.

Parzialità [pahr-tsee-ah-lee-tah'] *nf.* bias, partiality.

Pasce/re [pah'shay-ray] *vt. and i.* **—rsi** *vr.*, **pascolare** [pahskoh-lah'ray] *vt. and i.* to feed, graze pasture.

Pascolo [pah'skoh-loh] *nm.* ground, pasture, food (fig.).

Pasqua [pah'skwah] *nf.* Easter; **contento come una** [kon-ten'toh koh'may oo'nah] **p.** *a.* as jolly as a sand-boy

Passaggio [pahs-sah'djoh] *nm.* crossing, passage, traffic; **diritto di** [dee-reet'toh dee] **p.** right of way; **p. a livello** [ah lee-vell'loh], level-crossing; **essere di** [ess'say-ray dee] **p.** *vi.* to pass through.

Passamano [pahs-sah-mah'noh] *nm.* braid, ribbon.

Passante [pahs-sahn'tay] *nm. and f.* passer-by.

Passaporto [pahs-sah-porr'toh] *nm.* passport.

Passa/re [pahs-sah'ray] *vt. and i.* to come in, elapse, pass, spend; **p. da** [dah] to call on; **—rsela** *vr.* to get on

Passata [pahs-sah'tah] *nf.* glance.

Passatempo [pahs-sah-tem'poh] *nm.* hobby, pastime.

Passeggero [pahs-say-djay'roh] *nm.* passenger, traveller; *a.* fleeting, passing, transient.

Passeggiare [pahs-say-djah'ray] *vi.* to (go for a) walk.

Passeggiata [pahs-say-djah'tah] *nf.* drive (by car, etc.), ride (on a cycle, etc.), walk.

Passeggio [pahs-say'djoh] *nm.* promenade, walk.

Passero [pahs'say-roh] *nm.* sparrow.

Passionato [pahs-see-oh-nah'toh] *a.* ardent. *v.* **Appassionato.**

Passione [pahs-see-oh'nay] *nf.* love, passion; **aver** [ah-vehr'] p. **per** [pehr] *vi.* to be very fond of.

Passività [pahs-see-vee-tah'] *nf.* (*com.*) liabilities (*pl.*), passiveness.

Passivo [pahs-see'voh] *nm. and a.* passive.

Passo [pahs'soh] *nm.* pace, passage, step, rate; a [ah] p. **d'uomo** [doo-oh'moh] *ad.* at a walking pace; **di pari** [dee pah'ree] p. *ad.* at the same rate; **tenere il** [tay-nay'ray eel] p. *vi.* to keep step.

Pasta [pahs'tah] *nf.* cake, dough, macaroni, paste; **avere le mani in** [ah-vay'ray lay mah'nee een] p. *vi.* to have a finger in the pie.

Pastello [pahs-stell'loh] *nm.* pastel.

Pasticca [pahs-steek'kah] *nf.* lozenge, tablet.

Pasticceria [pahs-steech-chay-ree'ah] *nf.* confectioner's, confectionery.

Pasticciere [pahs-steech-chay'ray] *nm.* confectioner.

Pasticcio [pahs-steech'choh] *nm.* bungled work, mess, pie, scrape.

Pastiglia [pah-steel'yah] *nf.* lozenge, pastille.

Pasto [pah'stoh] *nm.* meal.

Pastoia [pah-stoh'yah] *nf.* hobble, tether, encumbrance, impediment.

Pastorale [pah-stoh-rah'lay] *nm.* crozier; *nf.* pastoral letter; *a.* pastoral.

Pasto/re [pah-stoh'ray] *nm.* pastor, shepherd; **—rella** [rell'lah] *nf.* shepherdess.

Pastoso [pah-stoh'soh] *a.* mellow, palatable, soft.

Pastrano [pah-strah'noh] *nm.* (man's) overcoat.

Pastura [pah-stoo'rah] *nf.* pasturage, pasture.

Patata [pah-tah'tah] *nf.* potato.

Patema [pah-tay'mah] *nf.* anxiety, suffering, uneasiness.

Patente [pah-ten'tay] *nf.* licence; *a.* evident, obvious, plain.

Paternale [pah-tehr-nah'lay] *nm.* rebuke, scolding.

Paterno [pah-tehr'noh] *a.* paternal.

Patetico [pah-tay'tee-koh] *a.* lackadaisical, pathetic.

Patibolo [pah-tee'boh-loh] *nm.* gallows, gibbet.

Patimento [pah-tee-men'toh] *nm.* pain, suffering.

Patire [pah-tee'ray] *vt. and i.* to endure, suffer.

Patologia [pah-toh-loh-jee'ah] *nf.* pathology.

Patria [pah'tree-ah] *nf.* (one's own) country.

Patriarca [pah-tree-ahr'kah] *nm.* patriarch.

Patrigno [pah-treen'yoh] *nm.* step-father.

Patrimonio [pah-tree-moh'nee-oh] *nm.* estate, patrimony.

Patrio [pah'tree-oh] *a.* of one's own country or home.

Patriot(t)a [pah-tree-oh(t)'tah] *nm.* patriot.

Patriziato [pah-tree-tsee-ah'toh] *nm.* aristocracy, patrician order.

Patrizio [pah-tree'tsee-oh] *nm. and a.* patrician.

Patrocinare [pah-troh-chee-nah'ray] *vt.* to defend, patronize, plead, support.

Patrocinio [pah-troh-chee'nee-oh] *nm.* defence, patronage, support.

Patrono [pah-troh'noh] *nm.* defender, patron, protector, supporter.

Patronato [pah-troh-nah'toh] *nm.* patronage.

Patteggiare [paht-tay-djah'ray] *vt. and i.* to bargain, come to terms, negotiate.

Pattinaggio [paht-tee-nah'djoh] *nm.* skating.

Pattinare [paht-tee-nah'ray] *vi.* to skate.

Pattino [paht'tee-noh] *nm.* skate; p. a rotelle [ah roh-tell'lay] roller-skate.

Patto [paht'toh] *nm.* agreement, compact, condition, pact.

Pattuglia [paht-tool'yah] *nf.* (mil.) patrol.

Pattuire [paht-too-ee'ray] *vt. and i.* to agree (upon), fix, settle.

Paura [pah-oo'rah] *nf.* dread, fear, fright; aver [ah-vehr'] p. *vi.* to be afraid; far [fahr] p. *vi.* to frighten; per [pehr] p. che non [kay nonn] con. lest.

Pauroso [pah-oo-roh'soh] *a.* afraid, fearful, frightful.

Paventare [pah-ven-tah'ray] *vt. and i.* to be afraid, fear.

Pavesare [pah-vay-zah'ray] *vt.* to adorn, beflag.

Pavimento [pah-vee-men'toh] *nm.* floor.

Pavone [pah-voh'nay] *nm.* peacock.

Pazientare [pah-tsee-en-tah'toh] *vi.* to be patient, have patience.

Paziente [pah-tsee-en'tay] *nm. and f. and a.* patient.

Pazienza [pah-tsee-ent'sah] *nf.* patience; perdere la [pehr'day-ray lah] p. *vi.* to lose one's temper; *int.* all right, never mind.

Pazzia [paht-tsee'ah] *nf.* folly, insanity, madness.

Pazzo [paht'soh] *nm.* lunatic, madman; *a.* foolish, insane, mad.

Pecca [peck'kah] *nf.* blemish, defect, flaw.

Peccare [peck-kah'ray] *vi.* to be faulty, offend, sin.

Peccato [peck-kah'toh] *nm.* sin; che [kay] p.! *int.* what a pity!

Pecchia [peck'kee-ah] *nf.* (honey-)bee.

Pecchione [peck-kee-oh'nay] *nm.* drone.

Pece [pay'chay] *nf.* pitch.

Pecora [pay'koh-rah] *nf.* ewe, sheep.

Peculato [pay-koo-lah'toh] *nm.* peculation.

Peculiare [pay-koo-lee-ah'ray] *a.* peculiar, special.

Peculiarità [pay-koo-lee-ah-ree-tah'] *nf.* characteristic, peculiarity.

Pecunia [pay-koo'nee-ah] *nf.* money.

Pecuniario [pay-koo-nee-ah'ree-oh] *a.* pecuniary.

Pedaggio [pay-dah'djoh] *nm.* toll.

Pedagogo [pay-dah-goh'goh] *nm.* pedagogue.

Pedale [pay-dah'lay] *nm.* (tech.) pedal, treadle.

Pedana [pay-dah'nah] *nf.* dais, platform.

Pedante [pay-dahn'tay] *nm.* pedant; *a.* pedantic.

Pedanteria [pay-dahn-tay-ree'ah] *nf.* pedantry.

Pedata [pay-dah'tah] *nf.* footprint, kick.

Pedestre [pay-dess'tray] *a.* dull, foot, pedestrian, un-inspired.

Pediluvio [pay-dee-loo'vee-oh] *nm.* foot-bath.

Pedinare [pay-dee-nah'ray] *vt.* to follow, shadow.

Pedone [pay-doh'nay] *nm.* pedestrian.

Peggio [pay'djoh] *a.* and *ad.* worse, worst; alla [ahl'lah] p. *ad.* if the worst comes to the worst.

Peggiorare [pay-djoh-rah'ray] *vt.* and *i.* to make (grow) worse.

Peggiore [pay-djoh'ray] *a.* worse, worst.

Pegno [payn'yoh] *nm.* pawn, pledge, token; dare in [dah'ray een] p. *vt.* to pawn; giuoco dei [joo-oh'koh day'ee] pegni, forfeits (*pl.*).

Pelago [pay'lah-goh] *nm.* (open) sea.

Pela/re [pay-lah'ray] *vt.* to pare, peel, strip; —rsi *vr.* to go bald.

Pellame [pell-lah'may] *nm.* hides (*pl.*), skins (*pl.*).

Pelle [pell'lay] *nf.* hide (animals), peel, rind (fruit), skin (people).

Pellegrinaggio [pell-lay-gree-nah'djoh] *nm.* pilgrimage.

Pellegrinare [pell-lay-gree-nah'ray] *vi.* to wander.

Pellegrino [pell-lay-gree'noh] *nm.* pilgrim.

Pellicano [pell-lee-kah'noh] *nm.* pelican.

Pelliceria [pell-leech-chay-ree'ah] *nf.* furs (*pl.*), fur trade, furrier's shop.

Pelliccia [pell-leech'chah] *nf.* fur, fur coat.

Pellicciaio [pell-leech-chah'yoh] *nm.* furrier. [film.

Pellicola [pell-lee'koh-lah] *nf.*

Pellirossa [pell-lee-ross'sah] *nm.* and *f.* Redskin.

Pelo [pay'loh] *nm.* fur, hair, nap, pile (of stuff).

Peloso [pay-loh'soh] *a.* hairy, shaggy.

Peluria [pay-loo'ree-ah] *nf.* down (on the skin, etc.).

Pena [pay'nah] *nf.* pain, penalty, punishment; far (fahr) p. to move to pity; valere la [vah-lay'ray lah] p. *vi.* to be worth while; a mala [ah mah'lah] p. *ad.* hardly.

Penale [pay-nah'lay] *a.* criminal, penal.

Penalità [pay-nah-lee-tah'] *nf.* penalty.

Penare [pay-nah'ray] *vi.* to be hardly able, find it hard, suffer.

Pendaglio [pen-dahl'yoh] *nm.* pendant.

Pendente [pen-den'tay] *nm.* ear-ring; *a.* hanging, leaning.

Pendenza [pen-dent'sah] *nf.* incline, slope; avere una forte [ah-vay'ray oo'nah forr'tay] p. *vi.* to be very steep.

Pendere [pen'day-ray] *vi.* to be inclined, hang, lean.

Pendice [pen-dee'chay] *nf.* pendio [pen-dee'oh] *nm.* declivity, slope.

Pendola [pen'doh-lah] *nf.* clock.

Pendolo [pen'doh-loh] *nm.* pendulum.

Penetrare [pay-nay-trah'ray] *vt.* and *i.* to enter, penetrate, steal in.

Penetrativo [pay-nay-trah-tee'voh] *a.* penetrating.

Penetrazione [pay-nay-trah-tsee-oh'nay] *nf.* insight, penetration.

Peninsulare [pay-neen-soo-lah'ray] *a.* peninsular.

Penisola [pay-nee'soh-lah] *nf.* peninsula.

Penitente [pay-nee-ten'tay] *nm.* and *f.* and *a.* penitent.

Penitenza [pay-nee-tent′sah] *nf.* penitence, repentance.

Penna [pen′nah] *nf.* feather, pen, plume.

Pennacchio [pen-nahk′kee-oh] *nm.* bunch of feathers, plume.

Pennellare [pen-nell-lah′ray] *vt.* to paint.

Pennello [pen-nell′loh] *nm.* brush, paint-brush; a. [ah] p. ad. perfectly.

Penoso [pay-noh′soh] *a.* distressing, painful.

Pensante [pen-sahn′tay] *a.* thinking.

Pensare [pen-sah′ray] *vt. and i.* to think.

Pensiero [pen-see-ay′roh] *nm.* idea, intention, mind, thought.

Pensieroso [pen-see-ay-roh′soh] *a.* pensive, thoughtful.

Pensile [pen′see-lay] *a.* hanging, suspended.

Pensionare [pen-see-oh-nah′ray] *vt.* to pension (off).

Pensionato [pen-see-oh-nah′toh] *nm.* pensioner.

Pensione [pen-see-oh′nay] *nf.* boarding-house, pension.

Pensoso [pen-soh′soh] *a.* pensive, thoughtful.

Pentecoste [pen-tay-koss′tay] *nf.* Pentecost, Whit Sunday.

Pentimento [pen-tee-men′toh] *nm.* repentance.

Pentirsi [pen-teer′see] *vr.* to regret, repent.

Pentola [pen′toh-lah] *nf.* pot, saucepan.

Penuria [pay-noo′ree-ah] *nf.* lack, penury, scarcity.

Penzolare [pend-zoh-lah′ray] *vi.* to dangle, hang down.

Penzolo/ni [pend-zoh-loh′nee], —ne [nay] *ad.* dangling, hanging.

Pepe [pay′pay] *nm.* pepper.

Peperone [pay-pay-roh′nay] *nm.* capsicum, chilli.

Per [pehr] *pr.* at, by, for, on, through, to; on account of, owing to; to più [loh pee-oo′] *ad.* generally; p. l'appunto [lahp-poon′toh] *ad.* just so; un po' [oon poh] p. what with.

Pe/ra [pay′rah] *nf.* pear; —ro [roh] *nm.* pear-tree.

Percalle [pehr-kahl′lay] *nm.* cotton cambric.

Percentuale [pehr-chen-too-ah′lay] *nf.* percentage.

Percepire [pehr-chay-pee′ray] *vt.* to catch, get, perceive, receive.

Percettibile [pehr-chet-tee′bee-lay] *a.* perceptible.

Percezione [pehr-chay-tsee-oh′nay] *nf.* perception.

Perchè [pehr-kay′] *nm.* motive, reason; *con.* as, because, for, in order that, so that, that, why?

Perciò [pehr-choh′] *ad.* therefore, thus.

Percorrenza [pehr-kor-rent′sah] *nf.* distance, way.

Percorrere [pehr-kor′ray-ray] *vt.* to pass through, run along (through), travel over.

Percorso [pehr-korr′soh] *nm.* course, distance, way.

Percossa [pehr-koss′sah] *nf.* blow, stroke.

Percuotere [pehr-koo-oh′tay-ray] *vt.* to beat, hit, strike.

Percussione [pehr-koos-see-oh′nay] *nf.* percussion.

Perde/re [pehr′day-ray] *vt. and i.* to lose, miss, ruin; p. di vista [dee vee′stah] to lose sight of; —rsi *vr.* to get lost, go astray, vanish.

Perdita [pehr′dee-tah] *nf.* loss, waste; a [ah] p. d'occhio [dock′kee-oh] *ad.* as far as eye can see.

Perdizione [pehr-dee-tsee-oh′nay] *nf.* perdition.

Perdonabile [pehr-doh-nah′-

bee-lay] *a.* forgivable, pardonable.

Perdonare [pehr-doh-nah'ray] *vt. and i.* to excuse, forgive, pardon.

Perdono [pehr-doh'noh] *nm.* forgiveness, pardon.

Perdurare [pehr-doo-rah'ray] *vi.* to continue, last, persist.

Perdu/to [pehr-doo'toh] *a.* lost, ruined, undone; — **tamente** [tah-men'tay] *ad.* desperately, madly.

Peregrinare: *v.* **Pellegrinare**.

Peregrino [pay-ray-gree'noh] *a.* far-fetched, uncommon.

Perenne [pay-ren'nay] *a.* everlasting, perennial.

Perentorio [pay-ren-toh'ree-oh] *a.* peremptory.

Perfetto [pehr-fet'toh] *a.* complete, full, perfect.

Perfeziona/re [pehr-fay-tsee-oh-nah'ray] *vt.* to complete, improve, perfect; **—rsi** *vr.* to get a perfect knowledge of, perfect oneself.

Perfezione [pehr-fay-tsee-oh'nay] *nf.* perfection.

Perfidia [pehr-fee'dee-ah] *nf.* perfidy, wickedness.

Perfido [pehr'fee-doh] *a.* perfidious, treacherous, wicked.

Perfino [pehr-fee'noh] *ad.* even.

Perforare [pehr-foh-rah'ray] *vt.* to bore, perforate, pierce.

Pergamena [pehr-gah-may'nah] *nf.* parchment.

Pergamo [pehr'gah-moh] *nm.* pulpit.

Pergola [pehr'goh-lah] *nf.* arbour, trellis.

Pergolato [pehr-goh-lah'toh] *nm.* pergola.

Pericolante [pay-ree-koh-lahn'tay] *a.* in danger, tottering, unsafe, unsteady.

Pericolo [pay-ree'koh-loh] *nm.* danger, peril.

Pericoloso [pay-ree-koh-loh'soh] *a.* dangerous.

Periferia [pay-ree-fay-ree'ah] *nf.* boundary, outskirts (*pl.*) periphery.

Perifrasi [pay-ree'frah-zee] *nf.* periphrasis.

Periglio [pay-reel'yoh] *nm.* (*poet.*) danger.

Periodo [pay-ree'oh-doh] *nm.* period, (*gram.*) sentence.

Peripezia [pay-ree-pay-tsee'ah] *nf.* adventure, vicissitude.

Perire [pay-ree'ray] *vi.* to die, perish.

Periscopio [pay-ree-skoh'pee-oh] *nm.* periscope.

Peritarsi [pay-ree-tahr'see] *vr.* to hesitate.

Perito [pay-ree'toh] *nm. and a.* expert; *a.* skilful.

Perituro [pay-ree-too'roh] *a.* perishable.

Perizia [pay-ree'tsee-ah] *nf.* appraisement, dexterity, expert opinion, skill, survey.

Perla [pehr'lah] *nf.* pearl.

Perlustrare [pehr-loo-strah'ray] *vt.* to patrol, reconnoitre, scout.

Perlustrazione [pehr-loo-strah-tsee-oh'nay] *nf.* patrolling, reconnaissance.

Permaloso [pehr-mah-loh'soh] *a.* touchy.

Permanente [pehr-mah-nen'tay] *nf.* permanent-waving; *a.* permanent, standing.

Permanenza [pehr-mah-nent'sah] *nf.* permanence, permanency, stay.

Permeabile [pehr-may-ah'bee-lay] *a.* permeable.

Permesso [pehr-mess'soh] *nm.* leave, licence, permission, permit; *a.* allowed, permitted.

Permette/re [pehr-met'tay-ray] *vt.* to allow, permit; **—rsi** *vr.* to take the liberty;

p. il lusso [eel loos'soh] vi. to afford.

Permuta [pehr'moo-tah] nf. barter, exchange, permutation.

Permutare [pehr-moo-tah' ray] vt. to barter, exchange.

Pernice [pehr-nee'chay] nf. partridge.

Pernicioso [pehr-nee-choh' soh] a. pernicious.

Per/no [pehr'noh], **—no** [nee-oh] nm. pivot.

Pernottare [pehr-not-tah' ray] vi. to spend (stay) the night.

Però [pay-roh'] ad. and con. but, however, still.

Perorare [pay-roh-rah'ray] vt. and i. to plead.

Perpendicolare [pehr-pen-dee-koh-lah'ray] nf. and a. perpendicular.

Perpetrare [pehr-pay-trah' ray] vt. to commit, perpetrate.

Perpetua/re [pehr-pay-too-ah'ray] vt. to perpetuate; **—rsi** vt. to continue, last, persist.

Perpetuo [pehr'pay'too-oh] a. eternal, perpetual.

Perplessità [pehr-pless-see-tah'] nf. perplexity.

Perplesso [pehr-pless'soh] a. perplexed, puzzled.

Perquisire [pehr-kwee-zee' ray] vt. to search.

Perquisizione [pehr-kwee-zee-tsee-oh'nay] nf. search.

Persecutore [pehr-say-koo-toh'ray] nm. persecutor.

Persecuzione [pehr-say-koo-tsee-oh'nay] nf. persecution.

Perseguire [pehr-say-gwee' ray] vt. to follow, pursue.

Perseguitare [pehr-say-gwee-tah'ray] vt. to persecute.

Perseverante [pehr-say-vay-rahn'tay] a. persevering.

Perseverare [pehr-say-vay-rah'ray] vi. to persevere.

Persiana [pehr-see-ah'nah] nf. shutter, Venetian blind.

Persiano [pehr-see-ah'noh] nm. and a. Persian.

Persino [pehr-see'noh] ad. even.

Persistente [pehr-see-sten' tay] a. persistent, persisting.

Persistere [pehr-see'stay-ray] vi. to persist.

Persona [pehr-soh'nah] nf. body, figure, person.

Personaggio [pehr-soh-nah'djoh] nm. character (in a play), personage.

Personale [pehr-soh-nah'lay] nm. body, figure, person, personnel, staff; a. personal.

Personificare [pehr-soh-nee-fee-kah'ray] vt. to personify.

Personificazione [pehr-soh-nee-fee-kah-tsee-oh'nay] nf. embodiment, personification.

Perspicace [pehr-spee-kah' chay] a. perspicacious, shrewd.

Perspicacia [pehr-spee-kah' chah] nf. perspicacity, shrewdness.

Persuadere [pehr-swah-day' ray] vt. to convince, persuade.

Persuasione [pehr-swah-zee-oh'nay] nf. conviction, persuasion.

Persuasivo [pehr-swah-zee' voh] a. persuasive.

Pertanto [pehr-tahn'toh] ad. however, still.

Pertica [pehr'tee-kah] nf. perch, pole.

Pertinace [pehr-tee-nah' chay] a. pertinacious.

Pertinacia [pehr-tee-nah' chah] nf. pertinacity.

Pertinenza [pehr-tee-nent' sah] nf. pertinence, pertinency; **essere di** [ess'say-ray dee] p. vi. to belong; pertain; **non è di mia** [nonn ay dee mee'ah] p., it is not my business.

Perturbamento [pehr-toor-

bah-men'toh] *nm.* perturbation.

Perturbare [pehr-toor-bah'ray] *vt.* to disturb, perturb, trouble.

Pervenire [pehr-vay-nee'ray] *vi.* to arrive, reach.

Perversità [pehr-vehr-see-tah'] *nf.* wickedness.

Perverso [pehr-vehr'soh] *a.* immoral, wicked.

Pervertimento [pehr-vehr-tee-men'toh] *nm.* perversion.

Perverti/re [pehr-vehr-tee'ray] *vt.* to lead astray, pervert; —rsi *vr.* to go astray.

Pervicace [pehr-vee-kah'chay] *a.* obstinate.

Pervinca [pehr-veeng'kah] *nf.* periwinkle.

Pesante [pay-sahn'tay] *a.* heavy, wearisome, weighty.

Pesantezza [pay-sahn-tet'sah] *nf.* dullness, heaviness; p. di stomaco [dee-stoh'mah-koh], indigestion.

Pesare [pay-sah'ray] *vt.* and *i.* to weigh.

Pesatura [pay-sah-too'rah] *nf.* weighing.

Pes/ca [pess'kah] *nf.* peach; —co [koh] *nm.* peach-tree.

Pesca [pess'kah] *nf.* fishery, fishing.

Pescare [pess-kah'ray] *vt. and i.* to catch, find, fish.

Pescatore [pess-kah-toh'ray] *nm.* fisher(man).

Pesce [pay'shay] *nm.* fish; non sapere che pesci pigliare [nonn sah-pay'ray kay pay'shee peel-yah'ray] *vi.* to be at one's wits' end.

Pescecane [pay-shay-kah'nay] *nm.* shark, (*fig.*) profiteer.

Pescheria [pess-kay-ree'ah] *nf.* fish-market.

Peschiera [pess-kee-ay'rah] *nf.* fish-pond.

Pesciaiolo [pay-shah-ee-oh'loh], pescivendolo [pay-shee-

ven'doh-loh] *nm.* fishmonger.

Peso [pay'soh] *nm.* burden, load, weight.

Pessimismo [pess-see-mees'moh] *nm.* pessimism.

Pessimo [pess'see-moh] *a.* very bad, worst.

Pesta [pess-tah] *nf.* footprint, track; trovarsi nelle peste [troh-vahr'see nell'lay pess'tay] *vi.* to be in difficulties.

Pestare [pess-tah'ray] *vt.* to crush, pound, tread on.

Peste [pess'tay] *nf.* plague.

Pestello [pess-tell'loh] *nm.* pestle.

Pestifero [pess-tee'fay-roh], pestilenziale [pess-tee-len-tsee-ah'lay] *a.* plaguing, slanderous.

Pestilenza [pess-tee-lent'sah] *nf.* pestilence, plague.

Pestilenziale [pess-tee-len-tsee-ah'lay] *a.* pestilential.

Petalo [pay'tah-loh] *nm.* petal.

Petardo [pay-tahr'doh] *nm.* cracker (firework), petard.

Petizione [pay-tee-tsee-oh'nay] *nf.* petition, supplication.

Petrificare [pay-tree-fee-kah'ray] *vt.* to petrify, turn to stone.

Petrolio [pay-troh'lee-oh] *nm.* paraffin, petroleum.

Petroso [pay-troh'soh] *a.* stony.

Pettegolare [pet-tay-goh-lah'ray] *vi.* to gossip, tittle-tattle.

Pettegolezzo [pet-tay-goh-led'zoh] *nm.* gossiping, tittle-tattle.

Pettegolo [pet-tay'goh-loh] *nm.* tale-bearer, tatler; *a.* gossiping.

Pettinare [pet-tee-nah'ray] *vt.* to comb; —rsi *vr.* to do one's hair.

Pettine [pet'tee-nay] *nm.* comb.

Pettirosso [pet-tee-ross'soh] *nm.* robin(-redbreast).

Petto [pet'toh] *nm.* breast, chest; **mal di [mahl dee] p.** consumption.

Petulante [pay-too-lahn'tay] *a.* petulant, saucy.

Petulanza [pay-too-lahnt'sah] *nf.* petulance.

Pezza [pet'sah] *nf.* cloth, diaper, patch, piece; (*archaic*) time.

Pezzente [pet-sen'tay] *nm.* beggar.

Pezzo [pet'soh] *nm.* piece, time, while.

Pezz(u)ola [pet-soo-oh'lah] *nf.* kerchief (for the head).

Piacente [pee-ah-chen'tay] *a.* agreeable, attractive, pleasant.

Piacere [pee-ah-chay'ray] *vi.* to like, please; **questo mi piace [kwess'toh mee pee-ah'chay]** I like this; —*nm.* delight, favour, pleasure; **aver il [ah-vehr'eel] p. vi.** to be glad; **per [pehr] p. ad.** please.

Piacevole [pee-ah-chay'voh-lay] *a.* nice, pleasant, pretty.

Piacevolezza [pee-ah-chay-voh-let'sah] *nf.* agreeableness.

Piaga [pee-ah'gah] *nf.* calamity, evil, sore, wound.

Piaggia [pee-ah'djah] *nf.* (*poet.*) declivity, slope.

Piagnisteo [pee-ahn-nee-stay'oh] *nm.* wail(ing), whine.

Piagnucolare [pee-ahn-yoo-koh-lah'ray] *vi.* to whimper, whine.

Pialla [pee-ahl'lah] *nf.* (*tech.*) plane.

Piallare [pee-ahl-lah'ray] *vt.* (*tech.*) to plane.

Piana [pee-ah'nah] *nf.* level ground, plain.

Pianella [pee-ah-nell'lah] *nf.* brick, slipper.

Pianerottolo [pee-ah-nay-rot'toh-loh] *nm.* landing (on the stairs).

Pianeta [pee-ah-nay'tah] *nm.* planet.

Piangere [pee-ahn'jay-ray] *vt.* to lament, mourn; *vi.* to cry, weep.

Pianista [pee-ah-nee'stah] *nm. and f.* pianist.

Piano [pee-ah'noh] *nm.* floor, plan, plane, plain, storey; *a.* clear, easy, even, flat, level; *ad.* in a low voice, slowly, softly; *int.* softly.

Pianoforte [pee-ah-noh-forr'tay] *nm.* piano(forte).

Pianta [pee-ahn'tah] *nf.* map, plan, plant, sole (of the foot); **di sana [dee sah'nah] p. ad.** completely.

Piantagione [peen-ahn-tah-joh'nay] *nf.* plantation.

Pianta/re [pee-ahn-tah'ray] *vt.* to abandon, leave, place, plant, put, quit; —*rsi vi.* to plant oneself, take up one's position.

Pianterreno [pee-ahn-tehr-ray'noh] *nm.* ground floor.

Pianto [pee-ahn'toh] *nm.* tears (*pl.*), weeping. [plain.

Pianura [pee-ah-noo'rah] *nf.*

Piastra [pee-ah'strah] *nf.* plate (of metal).

Piattaforma [pee-aht-tah-forr'mah] *nf.* platform.

Piattino [pee-aht-tee'noh] *nm.* saucer.

Piatto [pee-aht'toh] *nm.* dish, plate, scale (of a balance); *a.* flat.

Piazza [pee-aht'sah] *nf.* square; **p. del mercato [deli mehr-kah'toh],** market-place; **p. d'armi [dahr'mee],** parade-ground; **fare [fah'ray] p. pulita [poo-lee'tah] vi.** to dismiss everyone, clear everything away.

Piazzale [pee-aht-sah'lay] *nm.* esplanade, large square.

Piazzare [pee-aht-sah'ray] *vt.* (*com.*) to sell.

Piazzista [pee-aht-see'stah] *nm.* (*com.*) agent.

Picca [peek'kah] *nf.* pique, spite; (*pl.*) spades (*pl.*) cards.

Piccante [peek-kahn'tay] *a.* cutting, piquant, stinging.

Picca/re [peek-kah'ray] *vt.* to irritate, prick, sting; —**rsi** *vr.* to insist on, set one's heart on.

Piccatto [peek-ket'toh] *nm.* picket, piquet.

Picchiare [peek-kee-ah'ray] *vt.* to beat, cudgel, hit, knock, strike.

Picchio [peek'kee-oh] *nm.* blow, knock.

Piccino [peech-chee'noh] *nm.* small boy; *a.* little, small, tiny.

Piccionaia [peech-choh-nah'-yah] *nf.* flat under the roof, pigeon-loft.

Piccione [peech-choh'nay] *nm.* pigeon; p. viaggiatore [vee-ah-djah-toh'ray], carrier-pigeon.

Picco [peek'koh] *nm.* peak, top; a [ah] p. *ad.* perpendicularly; andare a [ahn-dah'ray ah] p. *vi.* (*naut.*) to go to the bottom.

Piccolezza [peek-koh-let'sah] *nf.* meanness, smallness, trifle.

Piccolo [peek'koh-loh] *nm.* (small) boy; i piccoli [ee peek'koh-lee] *nm.* (*pl.*) the little ones (*pl.*); *a.* little, mean, petty, small.

Pidocchio [pee-dock'kee-oh] *nm.* louse.

Piede [pee-ay'day] *nm.* foot; a piedi [ah pee-ay'dee] *ad.* on foot; a piedi nudi [noo'dee], barefoot; stare in [stah'ray een] p. *vi.* to stand.

Piedistallo [pee-ay-dee-stahl'loh] *nm.* pedestal.

Piega [pee-ay'gah] *nf.* crease, fold, pleat, turn; prendere una brutta [pren'day-ray oo'nah broot'tah] p. *vi.* to take a bad turn.

Piegamento [pee-ay-gah-men'toh] *nm.* bending, flexion, folding.

Piega/re [pee-ay-gah'ray] *vt.* to bend, flex, fold (up), subdue; *vi.* to give way, submit, turn; —**rsi** *vr.* to bend, crease, submit.

Pieghevole [pee-ay-gay'voh-lay] *a.* folding, pliable, submissive.

Piena [pee-ay'nah] *nf.* abundance, crowd, flood, spate.

Pienezza [pee-ay-net'sah] *nf.* fullness, plenitude.

Pieno [pee-ay'noh] *a.* full; in [een] p. *ad.* completely.

Pietà [pee-ay-tah'] *nf.* devotion, mercy, piety, pity; monte di [monn-tay dee] p. *nm.* pawnbroker's.

Pietanza [pee-ay-tahnt'sah] *nf.* dish.

Pietoso [pee-ay-toh'soh] *a.* merciful, pitiful, wretched.

Pietra [pee-ay'trah] *nf.* stone.

Pietrificare [pee-ay-tree-fee-kah'ray] *vt.* to petrify.

Pietrina [pee-ay-tree'nah] *nf.* flint (for lighters).

Pievano [pee-ay-vah'noh] *nm.* curate, priest.

Pieve [pee-ay'vay] *nf.* parish-church (in the country)

Piffero [peef'fay-roh] *nm.* (*mus.*) fife.

Pigiama [pee-jah'mah] *nm.* pyjamas (*pl.*).

Pigia/re [pee-jah'ray] *vt.* to crush, press; —**rsi** *vr.* to crowd.

Pigione [pee-joh'nay] *nf.* rent.

Pigliare [peel-yah'ray] *vt.* to catch, seize, take.

Pigmeo [peeg-may'oh] *nm.* pygmy.

Pignorare [peen-yoh-rah'-ray] *vt.* to distrain.

Pigolare [pee-goh-lah'ray] vi. to chirp, peep (of birds).

Pigrizia [pee-gree'tsee-ah] nf. indolence, laziness.

Pigro [pee'groh] a. indolent, lazy, sluggish.

Pila [pee'lah] nf. heap, pile, (elec.) battery, pile.

Pilastro [pee-lah'stroh] nm. pillar.

Pillacchera [peel-lahk'kay-rah] nf. splash.

Pillola [peel'loh-lah] nf. pill.

Pilota [pee-loh'tah] nm. pilot.

Pilotaggio [pee-loh-tah'djoh] nm. pilotage.

Pimpinella [peem-pee-nell'lah] nf. pimpernel.

Pina [pee'nah] nf. (pine-)cone.

Pinacoteca [pee-nah-koh-tay'kah] nf. picture-gallery.

Pineta [pee-nay'tah] nf. pine-wood.

Pingue [peeng'gway] a. big, corpulent, fat.

Pinguedine [peeng-gway'dee-nay] nf. corpulence, fatness.

Pinguino [peeng-gwee'noh] nm. penguin.

Pinna [peen'nah] nf. fin.

Pinnacolo [peen-nah'koh-loh] nm. battlement, pinnacle.

Pino [pee'noh] nm. pine(-tree).

Pinze [peent'say] nf. (pl.) pincers (pl.).

Pinzimonio [peen-zee-moh'-nee-oh] nm. sauce made of oil, salt and pepper.

Pio [pee'oh] a. charitable, pious.

Pioggerella [pee-oh-djay-rell'lah] nf. drizzle, gentle rain.

Pioggia [pee-oh'djah] nf. rain.

Piombare [pee-om-bah'ray] vt. to lead, plumb, seal; vi. to fall, pounce, rush.

Piombatura [pee-om-bah-too'rah] nf. leading, plumbing, sealing.

Piombo [pee-om'boh] nm. lead (metal), plumb.

Pioniere [pee-oh-nee-ay'ray] nm. pioneer.

Pioppo [pee-op'poh] nm. poplar (tree).

Piota [pee-oh'tah] nf. sod, sole (of the foot).

Piovano: v. **pievano**.

Piovere [pee-oh'vay-ray] vi. to rain; p. a dirotto [ah dee-rot'toh], p. a catinelle [ah kah-tee-nell'lay], to pour.

Piovigginare [pee-oh-vee-djee-nah'ray] vi. to drizzle.

Pioviggginoso [pee-oh-vee-djee-noh'soh], **piovoso** [pee-oh-voh'soh] a. drizzling, rainy.

Pipa [pee'pah] nf. pipe (smoker's).

Pipistrello [pee-pee-strell'loh] nm. bat.

Pira [pee'rah] nf. pyre.

Piramide [pee-rah'mee-day] nf. pyramid.

Pirata [pee-rah'tah] nm. pirate.

Pirateria [pee-rah-tay-ree'ah] nf. piracy.

Pirica, polvere [poll'vay-ray pee'ree-kah] nf. gunpowder.

Piroscafo [pee-ross'kah-foh] nm. steamer, steamship.

Pirotecnica [pee-roh-teck'nee-kah] nf. fireworks (pl.), pyrotechnics.

Piscina [pee-shee'nah] nf. fish-pond, swimming-pond.

Pisello [pee-zell'loh] nm. pea.

Pisolino [pee-zoh-lee'noh] nm. doze, nap.

Pista [pee'stah] nf. course, race-course, track.

Pistillo [pee-steel'loh] nm. pistil.

Pistola [pee-stoh'lah] nf. pistol.

Pitoccheria [pee-tock-kay-ree'ah] nf. stinginess.

Pitocco [pee-tock'koh] nm. stingy man.

Pittima [peet'tee-mah] *nf.* (*fig.*) bore, (*med.*) plaster.

Pit/tore [peet-toh'ray] *nm.* —**trice** (tree-chay) *nf.* painter.

Pittura [peet-too'rah] *nf.* painting.

Pitturare [peet-too-rah'ray] *vt. and i.* to paint.

Più [pee-oo'] *ad.* longer, more, most; **mai** [mah'ee] p. never again; **sempre** [sem'pray] p. more and more; **per di** [pehr dee] p. moreover; **per lo** [loh] p. generally.

Piuma [pee-oo'mah] *nf.* feather, plume.

Piumino [pee-oo-mee'noh] *nm.* feather-cushion, powder-puff.

Piuolo [pee-oo-oh'loh] *nm.* peg; **scala a piuoli** [skah'lah ah pee-oo-oh'lee] *nf.* ladder.

Piuttosto [pee-oot-toss'toh] *ad.* rather. [(*pl.*).]

Piva [pee'vah] *nf.* bagpipes

Piviere [pee-vee-ay'ray] *nm.* plover.

Pizzicagnolo [peet-see-kahn'yoh-loh] *nm.* cheese-monger, pork-butcher.

Pizzicare [peet-see-kah'ray] *vt.* to chafe, itch, pluck.

Pizzico [peet'see-koh] *nm.* pinch.

Pizzo [peet'soh] *nm.* imperial (beard), lace.

Placa/re [plah-kah'ray] *vt.* to alleviate, appease, placate; —**rsi** *vr.* to be appeased, subside.

Placca [plahk'kah] *nf.* plate, tablet, spot (in the throat).

Placido [plah'chee-doh] *a.* peaceful, placid.

Plaga [plah'gah] *nf.* district, region.

Plagiario [plah-jah'ree-oh] *nm.* plagiarist.

Plagio [plah'joh] *nm.* plagiarism.

Planare [plah-nah'ray] *vi.*

(*avia.*) to glide down, volplane.

Planetario [plah-nay-tah'ree-oh] *nm.* planetarium; *a.* planetary.

Plasmare [plahs-mah'ray] *vt.* to form, mould.

Plastica [plah'stee-kah] *nf.* modelling, plastic art, plastic surgery.

Platano [plah'tah-noh] *nm.* plane-tree.

Platea [plah-tay'ah] *nf.* (*theat.*) pit; **posti di** [poss'tee dee] p. *nm.* (*pl.*) pit-seats, stalls.

Platinare [plah-tee-nah'ray] *vt.* to platinize.

Platino [plah'tee-noh] *nm.* platinum.

Plausibile [plow-zee'bee-lay] *a.* acceptable, reasonable.

Plauso [plow'zoh] *nm.* applause, approbation.

Plebaglia [play-bah'lyah] *nf.* mob, rabble.

Plebe [play'bay] *nf.* lower classes (*pl.*).

Plebiscito [play-bee-shee'toh] *nm.* plebiscite.

Plenario [play-nah'ree-oh] *a.* plenary.

Plenilunio [play-nee-loo'nee-oh] *nm.* full moon.

Plenipotenziario [play-nee-poh-ten-tsee-ah'ree-oh] *nm.* and *a.* plenipotentiary.

Pleurite [play-oo-ree'tay] *nf.* (*med.*) pleurisy.

Plico [plee'koh] *nm.* envelope, packet.

Plotone [ploh-toh'nay] *nm.* (*mil.*) platoon.

Plumbeo [ploom'bay-oh] *a.* dismal, dull, heavy, leaden.

Pluviale [ploo-vee-ah'lay] *a.* pluvial, rain.

Pneumatico [pnay-oo-mah'tee-koh] *nm.* tyre; *a.* pneumatic.

Po': *v.* poco.

Pochino [poh-kee'noh] *a.*

and *pn.* very little (*pl.* very few); un [oon] p. *ad.* rather, a little while.

Poco [poh'koh] *a.* and *pn.* little (*pl.* few); *ad.* (very) little, a little while; fra [frah] p. *ad.* soon; fa [fah] *ad.* not long ago; un po' per [oon poh'pehr] what with . . .

Podagra [poh-dah'grah] *nf.* (*med.*) gout.

Podere [poh-day'ray] *nm.* farm, field.

Poderoso [poh-day-roh'soh] *a.* mighty, powerful.

Podestà [poh-dess-tah'] *nf.* authority, power; *nm.* mayor, podestà.

Poema [poh-ay'mah] *nm.* long epic or narrative poem.

Poesia [poh-ay-zee'ah] *nf.* lyric, short poem, poetry.

Poeta [poh-ay'tah] *nm.* poet.

Poetare [poh-ay-tah'ray] *vi.* to write poetry.

Poetica [poh-ay'tee-kah] *nf.* poetics.

Poetico [poh-ay'tee-koh] *a.* poetical.

Poggiare [poh-djah'ray] *vt.* to place, put, rest; *vi.* (*fop*.) ascend, (*naut.*) run before the wind.

Poggio [poh'djoh] *nm.* hillock, knoll.

Poi [poh'ee] *ad.* afterwards, then; da ora in [da oh'rah een] p. from now on; da allora in [dah ahl-loh'rah een] p. from that time on; o prima o [oh pree'mah oh] p. sooner or later.

Poichè [poh-ee-kay'] *con.* after, as, for, since.

Polac/co [poh-lahk'koh] *nm.* —ca [kah] *nf.* Pole; *a.* Polish.

Polare [poh-lah'ray] *a.* polar.

Polemica [poh-lay'mee-kah] *nf.* controversy, polemic(s).

Polenta [poh-len'tah] *nf.* maize meal.

Poligamia [poh-lee-gah-mee'ah] *nf.* polygamy.

Poligamo [poh-lee'gah-moh] *nm.* polygamist; *a.* polygamous.

Poliglotta [poh-lee-glot'tah] *nm.* and *a.* polyglot.

Polipo [poh'lee-poh] *nm.* polyp, (*med.*) polypus.

Politecnico [poh-lee-teck'nee-koh] *nm.* polytechnic school; *a.* polytechnic.

Politica [poh-lee'tee-kah] *nf.* politics, policy.

Politico [poh-lee'tee-koh] *nm.* politician, statesman; *a.* politic(al).

Polizia [poh-lee-tsee'ah] *nf.* police; agente di [ah-jen'tay dee] p. *nm.* policeman.

Poliziotto [poh-lee-tsee-ot'toh] *nm.* detective, policeman.

Polizza [poh'leet-sah] *nf.* (*com.*) bill, pawn-ticket, policy; p. d'assicurazione [dahs-see-koo-rah-tsee-oh'nay], insurance-policy.

Pollaio [poll-lah'yoh] *nm.* hen-house, poultry-yard.

Pollame [poll-lah'may] *nm.* poultry.

Pollice [poll'lee-chay] *nm.* big toe, inch, thumb.

Polline [poll'lee-nay] *nm.* pollen. [fowl.

Pollo [poll'loh] *nm.* chicken,

Polmonare [poll-moh-nah'ray] *a.* of the lungs, pulmonary.

Polmone [poll-moh'nay] *nm.* lung.

Polmonite [poll-moh-nee'tay] *nf.* (*med.*) pneumonia.

Polo [poh'loh] *nm.* pole.

Polpa [poll'pah] *nf.* flesh (animals), pulp (fruit).

Polsino [poll-see'noh] *nm.* cuff (of dress, etc.).

Polso [poll'soh] *nm.* pulse, wrist; di [dee] p. *a.* energetic.

Poltiglia [poll-teel'yah] *nf.* mud, pap, slush.

Poltrona [poll-troh'nah] *nf.*
armchair, (*theat.*) stall.
Poltrone [poll-troh'nay] *nm.*
idler.
Poltroneria [poll-troh-nay-
ree'ah] *nf.* indolence, laziness.
Polvere [poll'vay-ray] *nf.*
dust, powder; **p. da fucile**
[dah foo-chee'lay], gun-
powder; **caffè in** [kahf-fay'
een] p. *nm.* ground coffee.
Polveriera [poll-vay-ree-ay'
rah] *nf.* powder-magazine.
Polverificio [poll-vay-ree-
fee'choh] *nm.* powder-factory.
Polverone [poll-vay-roh'nay]
nm. cloud of dust.
Polveroso [poll-vay-roh'soh]
a. dusty.
Pomeridiano [poh-may-ree-
dee-ah'noh] *a.* (in the) afternoon.
Pomeriggio [poh-may-reet'
djoh] *nm.* afternoon.
Pomice [poh'mee-chay] *nf.*
pumice(-stone).
Pomo [poh'moh] *nm.* apple
(-tree), head, knob.
Pomodoro [poh-moh-doh'
roh] *nm.* tomato.
Pompa [pom'pah] *nf.* pomp;
far [fahr] **p. di** [dee] *vi.* to
display, show off; (*tech.*)
pump; **p. da incendio** [dah
een-chen'dee-oh], fire-engine.
Pompare [pom-pah'ray] *vt.*
to pump (up).
Pompiere [pom-pee-ay'ray]
nm. fireman.
Pomposità [pom-poh-see-
tah'] *nf.* pompousness.
Pomposo [pom-poh'soh] *a.*
pompous.
Ponderare [pon-day-rah'
ray] *vt. and i.* to meditate,
ponder, think over.
Ponderazione [pon-day-
rah-tsee-oh'nay] *nf.* carefulness, circumspection.
Ponente [poh-nen'tay] *nm.*
West.

Ponte [pon'tay] *nm.* bridge,
(*naut.*) deck.
Pontefice [pon-tay'fee-chay]
nm. pontiff, pope.
Pontile [pon-tee'lay] *nm.*
landing-stage.
Pontone [pon-toh'nay] *nm.*
pontoon.
Popola/re [poh-poh-lah'ray]
vt. to people, populate; —**rsi**
vr. to become crowded, popu-
lated; *a.* popular.
Popolarizzare [poh-poh-
lah-reed-zah'ray] *vt.* to popu-
larize.
Popolazione [poh-poh-lah-
tsee-oh'nay] *nf.* people, popu-
lation.
Popolo [poh'poh-loh] *nm.*
nation, people.
Popoloso [poh-poh-loh'soh]
a. populous.
Popone [poh-poh'nay] *nm*
melon.
Poppa [pop'pah] *nf.*
(woman's) breast, (*naut.*) stern.
Poppare [pop-pah'ray] *vt.*
and i. to suck.
Porcellana [porr-chell-lah'
nah] *nf.* china, porcelain.
Porcheria [porr-kay-ree'ah]
nf. dirt, dirty trick.
Porcile [porr-chee'lay] *nm.*
(pig)sty.
Porco [porr'koh] *nm.* pig,
pork, swine.
Porcospino [porr-koh-spee'
noh] *nm.* hedgehog.
Porfido [porr'fee-doh] *nm.*
porphyry.
Porge/re [porr'jay-ray] *vt.*
to give, hand, offer, present,
tender; —**rsi** *vr.* to offer.
Poro [poh'roh] *nm.* pore.
Porosità [poh-roh-see-tah']
nf. porousness. [purple.
Porpora [porr'poh-rah] *nf.*
Porporato [porr-poh-rah'
toh] *nm.* cardinal.
Porporino [porr-poh-ree'
noh] *a.* purple, rosy.

Por/re [porr'ray] vt. to lay, place, put, set, suppose; senza por tempo in mezzo [sent'sah porr tem'poh een med'zoh] ad. without delay; —rsi vr. to put oneself, set oneself. [wart.

Porro [porr'roh] nm. leek.

Porta [porr'tah] nf. door, gate, goal (at football).

Portabagagli [porr-tah-bah-gahl'yee] nm. porter.

Portacenere [porr-tah-chay'nay-ray] nm. ash-tray.

Portafoglio [porr-tah-fohl'yoh] nm. pocket-book, portfolio.

Portalettere [porr-tah-let'tay-ray] nm. postman.

Portamento [porr-tah-men'toh] nm. bearing, carriage.

Portamonete [porr-tah-moh-nay'tay] nm. purse.

Portare [porr-tah'ray] vt. to bear, bring, carry, take, wear.

Portasigarette [porr-tah-see-gah-ret'tay] nm. cigarette-case.

Portata [porr-tah'tah] nf. capacity, course, dish, importance, range, (naut.) tonnage; a [ah] p. di mano [dee mah'noh] ad. (with)in reach; a. p. d'orecchio [doh-reck'kee-oh] ad. within hearing.

Porta/tore [porr-tah-toh'ray] —trice [tree'chay] nf. bearer.

Portavoce [porr-tah-voh'chay] nm. mouthpiece, speaking-trumpet, speaking-tube.

Portento [porr-ten'toh] nm. marvel, miracle, portent, prodigy.

Portico [porr'tee-koh] nm. arch, porch, portico.

Portiera [porr-tee-ay'rah] nf. door-curtain, door-keeper ('s wife).

Portiere [porr-tee-ay'ray] nm. door-keeper, goalkeeper, janitor, porter.

Porto [porr'toh] nm. harbour, haven, port, postage, (com.) carriage; p. franco [frahng'koh] ad. carriage free.

Portoghese [porr-toh-gay'zay] nm. and f. and a. Portuguese.

Porzione [porr-tsee-oh'nay] nf. part, portion, ration, share.

Posa [poh'sah] nf. attitude, pause, pose, rest, laying, placing, (phot.) exposure.

Posamine [poh-sah-mee'nay] nm. (naut.) mine-layer.

Posa/re [poh-sah'ray] vt. to lay, place, put, rest, set; vi. to pose, rest, stand; —rsi vr. to alight, land, place oneself, stand.

Poscia [poh'shah] ad. afterwards, then. v. Poi, Dopo.

Poscritto [poss-kreet'toh] nm. postscript.

Posdomani [poss-doh-mah'nee] ad. the day after tomorrow.

Positiva [poh-zee-tee'vah] nf. (phot.) positive.

Positivo [poh-zee-tee'voh] a. certain, matter-of-fact, positive.

Posizione [poh-zee-tsee-oh'nay] nf. position, situation.

Posporre [poss-porr'ray] vt. to postpone, set behind.

Possa [poss'sah] nf. power, strength.

Possedere [poss-say-day'ray] vt. to have, own, possess.

Possedimento [poss-say-dee-men'toh] nm. colony, dominion, possession, property. [powerful.

Possente [poss-sen'tay] a.

Possessione [poss-sess-see-oh'nay] nf. ownership, possession.

Possesso [poss-sess'soh] nm. possession, property.

Possessore [poss-sess-soh'ray] nm. owner, possessor.

Possibile [poss-see'bee-lay] *a.* possible; fare tutto il [fah'ray toot'toh eel] p. *vi.* to do all that lies in one's power.

Possibilità [poss-see-bee-lee-tah'] *nf.* possibility, power.

Possidente [poss-see-den'tay] *nm.* and *f.* landowner, man (woman) of property.

Posta [poss'tah] *nf.* mail, post (office), stake (bet), stall (for animals); a bella [ah bell'lah] p. *ad.* on purpose.

Postale [poss-tah'lay] *a.* post, postal; francobollo [frahng-koh-boll'loh] p. *nm.* postage stamp.

Postare [poss-tah'ray] *vt.* to place, station.

Posteggio [poss-tay'djoh] *nm.* rank, stand; p. di automobili di piazza [dee ow-toh-moh'bee-lee dee pee-aht'sah], taxi rank.

Posteri [poss'tay-ree] *nm.* (*pl.*) descendants (*pl.*), posterity.

Posteriore [poss-tay-ree-oh'ray] *a.* back, hind, posterior.

Posterità [poss-tay-ree-tah'] *nf.* posterity.

Posticcio [poss-teech'choh] *a.* artificial, fictitious.

Posticipazione [poss-tee-chee-pah-tsee-oh'nay] *nf.* delay, postponement.

Postilla [poss-teel'lah] *nf.* (marginal) note.

Postino [poss-tee'noh] *nm.* postman.

Posto [poss'toh] *nm.* employment, place, post, room, seat, spot; c'è [chay] p.? is there any room?

Postulante [poss-too-lahn'tay] *nm.* and *f.* applicant, petitioner.

Postumo [poss'too-moh] *a.* posthumous.

Potare [poh-tah'ray] *vt.* to lop, prune.

Potente [poh-ten'tay] *a.* influential, mighty, powerful.

Potenza [poh-tent'sah] *nf.* might, power, strength.

Potenziale [poh-ten-tsee-ah'lay] *a.* potential.

Potere [poh-tay'ray] *vi.* to be able (can), be allowed (may); *nm.* authority, power.

Povero [poh'vay-roh] *nm.* beggar, poor man; *a.* needy, poor, scanty, unhappy.

Povertà [poh-vehr-tah'] *nf.* poverty, want.

Pozione [poh-tsee-oh'nay] *nf.* draught, potion.

Pozzanghera [pot-sahng'gay-rah] *nf.* puddle.

Pozzo [pot'soh] *nm.* well.

Pranzare [prahnt-sah'ray] *vi.* to dine, have dinner.

Pranzo [prahnt'soh] *nm.* dinner; sala da [sah'lah dah] p. *nf.* dining-room; dopo [doh'poh] p. *nm.* and *ad.* (in the) afternoon.

Prateria [prah-tay-ree'ah] *nf.* grass-land, prairie.

Prati/ca [prah'tee-kah] *nf.* exercise, practice, training, affair, business, matter; religiose [kay ray-lee-joh'say] *nf.* (*pl.*) religious duties.

Praticare [prah-tee-kah'ray] *vt.* to practise; p. una persona [oo'nah pehr-soh'nah] *vt.* to be familiar with.

Pratico [prah'tee-koh] *a.* experienced, practical; essere [ess'say-ray] p. di [dee] *vi.* to know well.

Prato [prah'toh] *nm.* meadow.

Pratolina [prah-toh-lee'nah] *nf.* daisy.

Preambolo [pray-ahm'boh-loh] *nm.* preamble, preface.

Preavviso [pray-ahv-vee'soh] *nm.* forewarning, notice.

Precario [pray-kah'ree-oh] *a.* precarious.

Precauzione [pray-kow-tsee-oh'nay] *nf.* care, precaution.

Prece [pray'chay] *nf.* (*poet.*) prayer.

Precedente [pray-chay-den'tay] *nm.* precedent; *a.* preceding, previous.

Precedenza [pray-chay-dent'sah] *nf.* precedence, priority; **in** [een] **p.** *ad.* in advance.

Precedere [pray-chay'day-ray] *vt.* to go before, precede; *vi.* to come first, precede.

Precetto [pray-chet'toh] *nm.* maxim, obligation, order, precept.

Precipita/re [pray-chee-pee-tah'ray] *vt.* to fling down; *vi.* to crash, fall; **—rsi** *vr.* to rush, throw oneself.

Precipitazione [pray-chee-pee-tah-tsee-oh'nay] *nf.* fall (of rain, snow, etc.).

Precipizio [pray-chee-peet'-tsee-oh'nay] *nm.* precipice; *a.* [*p.*] *ad.* headlong.

Precipuo [pray-chee'poo-oh] *a.* chief, principal.

Precisare [pray-chee-zah'-ray] *vt.* to describe exactly, determine.

Precisione [pray-chee-zee-oh'nay] *nf.* accuracy, exactness, precision.

Preciso [pray-chee'zoh] *a.* accurate, exact, precise, punctual.

Precisato [pray-chee-zah'-toh] *a.* above-mentioned.

Preclaro [pray-klah'roh] *a.* noble, prominent.

Precludere [pray-kloo'day-ray] *vt.* to block, preclude.

Precoce [pray-koh'chay] *a.* early, precocious, premature.

Precocità [pray-koh-chee-tah'] *nf.* precociousness, prematureness.

Preconcetto [pray-kon-chet'toh] *nm.* preconception, prejudice.

Precursore [pray-koor-soh'-ray] *nm.* forerunner, harbinger, precursor.

Preda [pray'dah] *nf.* booty, prey.

Predare [pray-dah'ray] *vt.* to pillage, plunder, sack.

Predecessore [pray-day-chess-soh'ray] *nm.* ancestor, predecessor.

Predellino [pray-dell-lee'-noh] *nm.* foot-board, step (of carriage, etc.).

Predica [pray'dee-kah] *nf.* preaching, sermon.

Predicare [pray-dee-kah'ray] *vt.* and *i.* to preach; **p. al muro** [ahl moo'roh] to waste words.

Predicatore [pray-dee-kah-toh'ray] *nm.* preacher.

Prediletto [pray-dee-let'toh] *a.* darling, dearest, favourite.

Predilezione [pray-dee-lay-tsee-oh'nay] *nf.* partiality.

Prediligere [pray-dee-lee'jay-ray] *vt.* to like better, prefer.

Predire [pray-dee'ray] *vt.* to foretell, predict.

Predizione [pray-dee-tsee-oh'nay] *nf.* prediction.

Predominare [pray-doh-mee-nah'ray] *vt.* to (pre)-dominate.

Predone [pray-doh'nay] *nm.* marauder, plunderer.

Preesistenza [pray-ay-zees-tent'sah] *nf.* pre-existence.

Prefazione [pray-fah-tsee-oh'nay] *nf.* introduction, preface.

Preferenza [pray-fay-rent'-sah] *nf.* preference; **di** [dee] **p.** *ad.* preferably.

Preferire [pray-fay-ree'ray] *vt.* to like better, prefer.

Preferito [pray-fay-ree'toh] *a.* favourite.

Prefetto [pray-fet'toh] *nm.* prefect.

Prefettura [pray-fet-too'rah] *nf.* prefecture, prefect's office.

Prefiggersi [pray-fee'djehr-see] *vr.* to intend, purpose.

Prefisso [pray-fees'soh] *nm.* prefix; *a.* appointed, intended, proposed.

Pregare [pray-gah'ray] *vt. and i.* to ask, beg, invite, pray; **prego!** [pray'goh] *int.* not at all, don't mention it.

Pregevole [pray-jay'voh-lay] *a.* valuable.

Preghiera [pray-ghee-ay'rah] *nf.* entreaty, prayer, request.

Pregia/re [pray-jah'ray] *vt.* to appreciate, esteem, value; **—rsi** *vr.* to be honoured, have the honour.

Pregio [pray'joh] *nm.* good quality, merit, value.

Pregiudicare [pray-joo-dee-kah'ray] *vt.* to injure, prejudice.

Pregiudicato [pray-joo-dee-kah'toh] *nm.* jail-bird; *a.* prejudged, suspected.

Pregiudizio [pray-joo-dee'tsee-oh] *nm.* detriment, prejudice.

Pregno [prayn'yoh] *a.* full, impregnated, pregnant.

Pregustare [pray-goo-stah'ray] *vt.* to anticipate, foretaste, look forward to.

Preistorico [pray-ee-stoh'ree-koh] *a.* prehistoric.

Prelato [pray-lah'toh] *nm.* prelate.

Prelevare [pray-lay-vah'ray] *vt.* to deduct, take away, withdraw.

Prelibato [pray-lee-bah'toh] *a.* delicious, excellent.

Preliminare [pray-lee-mee-nah'ray] *nm. and a.* preliminary.

Preludio [pray-loo'dee-oh] *nm.* introduction, prelude.

Prematuro [pray-mah-too'roh] *a.* premature, untimely.

Premeditare [pray-may-dee-tah'ray] *vt.* to plan, premeditate.

Premere [pray'may-ray] *vt.* to press; *vi.* to be urgent, press, weigh.

Premessa [pray-mess'sah] *nf.* premise, premiss, previous statement.

Premettere [pray-met'tay-ray] *vt.* to premise, say first, state in advance.

Premiare [pray-mee-ah'ray] *vt.* to award a prize, reward.

Preminente [pray-mee-nen'tay] *a.* excelling, pre-eminent.

Premio [pray'mee-oh] *nm.* premium, prize, reward.

Premuni/re [pray-moo-nee'ray] *vt.* to fortify, strengthen; **—rsi** *vr.* to take precautions, protective measures.

Premura [pray-moo'rah] *nf.* attention, care, haste, kindness.

Premuroso [pray-moo-roh'soh] *a.* attentive, careful, kind.

Prendere [pren'day-ray] *vt.* to catch, seize, take.

Prenotare [pray-noh-tah'ray] *vt.* to book, engage.

Prenotazione [pray-noh-tah-tsee-oh'nay] *nf.* booking.

Preoccupare [pray-ock-loo-pah'ray] *vt.* to make anxious, preoccupy, trouble; **—rsi** *vr.* to be anxious about, mind, worry.

Preoccupato [pray-ock-koo-pah'toh] *a.* anxious, troubled, worried.

Preoccupazione [pray-ock-koo-pah-tsee-oh'nay] *nf.* anxiety, care, preoccupation.

Preordinare [pray-orr-dee-nah'ray] *vt.* to predetermine, pre-ordain.

Preparare [pray-pah-rah'

ray] *vt.* and —**rsi** *vr.* to get ready, prepare.

Preparativo [pray-pah-rah-tee'voh] *nm.* preparation.

Preparato [pray-pah-rah'toh] *nm.* patent medicine, preparation (chemical, medical, etc.).

Preparazione [pray-pah-rah-tsee-oh'nay] *nf.* preparation.

Preponderante [pray-pon-day-rahn'tay] *a.* predominant, prevailing.

Preporre [pray-porr'ray] *vt.* to prefer, put (place) before, set above.

Preposizione [pray-poh-zee-tsee-oh'nay] *nf.* preposition.

Preposto [pray-poss'toh] *nm.* (*eccl.*) rector, vicar.

Prepotente [pray-poh-ten'tay] *nm.* bully, tyrant; *a.* overbearing, tyrannical.

Prepotenza [pray-poh-tent'sah] *nf.* insolence, tyranny.

Prerogativa [pray-roh-gah-tee'vah] *nf.* prerogative.

Presa [pray'sah] *nf.* capture, hold, pinch, seizure, taking; essere alle prese [ess'say-ray ahl'lay pray'say] *vi.* to be struggling.

Presagio [pray-sah'joh] *nm.* omen, presage, presentiment.

Presagire [pray-sah-jee'ray] *vt.* to forebode, foresee, foretell, presage.

Presbite [press'bee-tay] *a.* long-sighted.

Prescegliere [pray-shell'yay-ray] *vt.* to choose, select.

Prescindere [pray-sheen'day-ray] *vi.* to leave out of account, prescind.

Prescritto [press-kreet'toh] *nm.* ordinance, prescript; *a.* fixed, obligatory, prescribed.

Prescrivere [press-kree'vay-ray] *vt.* to fix, prescribe.

Prescrizione [press-kree-

tsee-oh'nay] *nf.* command, ordinance, prescription.

Presenta/re [pray-zen-tah'ray] *vt.* to introduce, present; —**rsi** *vr.* to appear, arise offer, present oneself.

Presente [pray-zen'tay] *nm.* and *a.* present; tener [tay-nehr'] p. *vt.* to bear in mind.

Presentimento [pray-sen-tee-men'toh] *nm.* presentiment.

Presentire [pray-sen-tee'ray] *vt.* and *i.* to have a presentiment, presage.

Presenza [pray-zent'sah] *nf.* presence; p. di spirito [dee spee'ree-toh] presence of mind.

Presepio [pray-zay'pee-oh] *nm.* crib, manger.

Preservare [pray-sehr-vah'ray] *vt.* to preserve, save.

Preside [pray'see-day] *nm.* headmaster, principal.

Presidente [pray-see-den'tay] *nm.* chairman, president; *a.* presiding.

Presidiare [pray-see-dee-ah'ray] *vt.* to garrison.

Presidio [pray-see'dee-oh] *nm.* garrison.

Presiedere [pray-see-ay'day-ray] *vt.* and *i.* to act as chairman, preside.

Pressa [press'sah] *nf.* crowd, press. [*nf.* pressure.

Pressione [press-see-oh'nay]

Presso [press'soh] *pr.* at, beside, by, with; *ad.* close by, near; p. a poco [ah poh' koh] *ad.* approximately, nearly.

Pressochè [press-soh-kay'] *ad.* almost, nearly.

Prestabilire [press-tah-bee-lee'ray] *vt.* to establish beforehand, fix.

Prestante [press-tahn'tay] *a.* eminent, excellent, noble.

Presta/re [press-tah'ray] *vt.* to lend, pay (attention, etc.);

farsi [fahr'see] p. vt. to borrow;
—rsi vr. to be fit for, lend
oneself.

Prestigiatore [press-tee-jah-toh'ray] nm. conjurer,
juggler.

Prestigio [press-tee'joh] nm.
authority, influence, juggling,
prestige.

Prestito [press'tee-toh] nm.
loan; **avere** in [ah-vay'ray
een] p. vt. to borrow; **dare** a
[dah'ray ah] p. vt. to lend.

Presto [press'toh] ad. before
long, early, quickly, soon;
int. (be) quick!; far [fahr] p.
vi. to make haste; al più
[ahl pee-oo'] p. ad. as soon
as possible.

Presumere [pray-soo'may-ray] vi. to presume, suppose.

Presumibile [pray-soo-mee'-bee-lay] a. presumable.

Presuntuoso [pray-soon-too-oh'soh] a. conceited, pre-sumptuous.

Presunzione [pray-soon-tsee-oh'nay] nf. presumption.

Presupporre [pray-soop-porr'ray] vt. and i. to (pre)-suppose.

Presupposto [pray-soop-poss'toh] nm. presupposition;
a. presupposed.

Prete [pray'tay] nm. clergy-man, priest.

Pretendente [pray-ten-den'-tay] nm. applicant, claimant,
suitor; a. claiming.

Pretendere [pray-ten'day-ray] vt. to claim, want; vi. to
claim, pretend.

Pretensione [pray-ten-see-oh'nay] nf. pretension.

Pretesa [pray-tay'sah] nf.
claim, pretence, pretension;
senza **pretese** [sent'sah pray-tay'say] a. simple, un-pretentious.

Pretesto [pray-tess'toh] nm.
pretence, pretext.

Pretore [pray-toh'ray] nm.
judge, praetor.

Pretto [pret'toh] a. mere,
pure, real.

Prevalente [pray-vah-len'-tay] a. prevalent, prevailing.

Prevalenza [pray-vah-lent'-sah] nf. prevalence, supremacy.

Prevale/re [pray-vah-lay'-ray] vi. to prevail; —rsi vr.
to avail oneself, take advant-age of.

Prevedere [pray-vay-day'-ray] vt. to forecast, foresee.

Prevedibile [pray-vay-dee'-bee-lay] a. to be expected.

Preveggenza [pray-vay-djent'sah] nf. foresight.

Prevenire [pray-vay-nee'-ray] vt. to anticipate, avoid,
forestall, inform, precede, pre-vent, warn.

Preventivo [pray-ven-tee'-voh] nm. (com.) estimate.

Prevenzione [pray-ven-tsee-oh'nay] nf. bias, prejudice,
suspicion.

Previdente [pray-vee-den'-tay] a. provident.

Previdenza [pray-vee-dent'-sah] nf. foresight, providence,
prudence.

Previo [pray'vee-oh] a.
preceding, previous.

Previsione [pray-vee-zee-oh'nay] nf. expectation, fore-cast, prevision.

Preziosità [pray-tsee-oh-see-tah'] nf. costliness, preciosity,
preciousness.

Prezioso [pray-tsee-oh'soh]
a. costly, precious, valuable.

Prezzemolo [pret-say'moh-loh] nm. parsley.

Prezzo [pret'soh] nm. price.

Prigione [pree-joh'nay] nf.
gaol (jail), prison.

Prigionia [pree-joh-nee'ah]
nf. imprisonment.

Prigioniero [pree-joh-nee-ay'roh] nm. prisoner.

Prima [pree'mah] nf. (theat.) première; ad. before, earlier, first, formerly, once; **p. o poi** [oh poh'ee], sooner or later; **da** [dah] **p.** at first; **quanto** [kwahn'toh] **p.** very soon; pr. before; **p. che** [kay] con. before.

Primario [pree-mah-ree'oh] a. chief, head, primary.

Primaticcio [pree-mah-teech'choh] a. early.

Primato [pree-mah'toh] nm. pre-eminence, supremacy.

Primavera [pree-mah-vay'rah] nf. spring, springtime.

Primaverile [pree-mah-vay-ree'lay] a. (of the) spring, vernal.

Primeggiare [pree-may-djah'ray] vi. to be pre-eminent, excel.

Primiero [pree-mee-ay'roh] a. first, former, previous.

Primizia [pree-mee'tsee-ah] nf. early fruit or vegetable, novelty.

Primo [pree-moh] pn. first, former; a. first; **di prima mano** [dee pree'mah mah'noh] a. first-hand; **di prim'ordine** [dee preem-orr'dee-nay] first-rate.

Primogenito [pree-moh-jay'nee-toh] a. first-born.

Primordio [pree-morr'dee-oh] nm. beginning.

Primula [pree'moo-lah] nf. primrose.

Principale [preen-chee-pah'lay] nm. employer, manager, master; a. chief, main, principal.

Principato [preen-chee-pah'toh] nm. principality, supremacy, princedom.

Princi/pe [preen'chee-pay] nm. prince; —**pessa** [pess'sah] nf. princess.

Principiante [preen-chee-pee-ahn'tay] nm. and f.

beginner; a. beginning.

Principiare [preen-chee-pee-ah'ray] vt. to begin, commence, start.

Principio [preen-chee'pee-oh] nm. beginning, commencement, principle.

Priore [pree-oh'ray] nm. prior.

Privare [pree-vah'ray] vt. to deny, deprive, strip.

Privatista [pree-vah-tee'stah] nm. and f. external candidate (at exam.).

Privativa [pree-vah-tee'vah] nf. monopoly, tobacconist's.

Privato [pree-vah'toh] nm. private citizen; a. private.

Privazione [pree-vah-tsee-oh'nay] nf. (de)privation.

Privilegio [pree-vee-lay'joh] nm. privilege.

Privo [pree'voh] a. deprived, destitute, devoid, lacking in, wanting in.

Pro' [proh] nm. advantage, benefit, profit; **a che** [ah kay] **p.?** What is the use?; **il** [eel] **p. e il contro** [ay eel kon'troh] the pros and cons (pl.).

Probabile [proh-bah'bee-lay] a. likely, probable.

Probabilità [proh-bah-bee-lee-tah'] nf. chance, likelihood, probability.

Probità [proh-bee-tah'] nf. honesty, probity.

Probo [proh'boh] a. honest, upright.

Procaccia/re [proh-kahch-chah'ray] vt. to get, procure; —**rsi** vr. to earn, get, procure.

Procace [proh-kah'chay] a. provocative.

Procedere [proh-chay'day-ray] vi. to act, go on, proceed; nm. conduct, process, way of acting.

Procedimento [proh-chay-dee-men'toh] nm. conduct, course, dealing, proceeding.

Procedura [proh-chay-doo'rah] *nf.* practice, procedure.

Procella [proh-cheell'lah] *nf.* (*poet.*) storm.

Processare [proh-chess-sah'ray] *vt. and i.* (*leg.*) to prosecute, try.

Processo [proh-chess'soh] *nm.* process, (*leg.*) suit, trial.

Procinto, essere in [ess'say-ray een proh-cheen'toh] *vi.* to be on the point.

Proclama [proh-klah'mah] *nm.* proclamation.

Proclamare [proh-klah-mah'ray] *vt. and i.* to proclaim.

Proclive [proh-klee'vay] *a.* bent on, inclined.

Procrastinare [proh-krah-stee-nah'ray] *vt. and i.* to procrastinate.

Procreare [proh-kray-ah'ray] *vt. and i.* to generate, procreate.

Procura [proh-koo'rah] *nf.* power of attorney, procuration, proxy.

Procura/re [proh-koo-rah'ray] *vt.* to cause, get, manage, procure, try; —**rsi** *vr.* to get, procure.

Procuratore [proh-koo-rah-toh'ray] *nm.* attorney, proxy.

Prode [proh'day] *nm.* hero; *a.* bold, gallant, valiant.

Prodezza [proh-det'sah] *nf.* gallant deed, gallantry.

Prodigalità [proh-dee-gah-lee-tah'] *nf.* lavishness, prodigality.

Prodiga/re [proh-dee-gah'ray] *vt.* to lavish, pour out; —**rsi** *vr.* to do one's best.

Prodigio [proh-dee'joh] *nm.* marvel, miracle, prodigy.

Prodigo [proh'dee-goh] *nm. and a.* a prodigal; *a.* lavish.

Prodotto [proh-dot'toh] *nm.* produce, product.

Produr/re [proh-doo'ray] *vt.* to bear, bring in, cause, produce, yield; —**rsi** *vr.* to

appear in public, give oneself, happen.

Produttività [proh-doot-tee-vee-tah'] *nf.* productivity.

Produttore [proh-doot-toh'ray] *nm.* manufacturer, producer; *a.* producing.

Produzione [proh-doo-tsee-oh'nay] *nf.* manufacture, output, production.

Proemio [proh-ay'mee-oh] *nm.* introduction, preface.

Profanare [proh-fah-nah'ray] *vt.* to pollute, profane.

Profanazione [proh-fah-nah-tsee-oh'nay] *nf.* profanation.

Profano [proh-fah'noh] *nm.* bad judge (of); *a.* profane.

Proferire [proh-fay-ree'ray] *vt.* to utter.

Professare [proh-fess-sah'ray] *vt. and i.* to profess.

Professione [proh-fess-see-oh'nay] *nf.* calling, profession; **di** [dee] *p. ad.* by profession.

Professore [proh-fess-soh'ray] *nm.* professor (University), (school)master, teacher.

Profeta [proh-fay'tah] *nm.* prophet.

Profe/tare [proh-fay-tah'ray] —**tizzare** [teed-zah'ray] *vt. and i.* to prophesy.

Profezia [proh-fay-tsee'ah] *nf.* prophecy.

Proficuo [proh-fee'koo-oh] *a.* profitable, useful.

Profilassi [proh-fee-lahs'see] *nf.* (*med.*) prophylaxis.

Profilo [proh-fee'loh] *nm.* profile.

Profittare [proh-feet-tah'ray] *vi.* to make progress, profit.

Profitto [proh-feet'toh] *nm.* advantage, benefit, profit.

Profonde/re [proh-fon'day-ray] *vt.* to lavish, squander; —**rsi** *vr.* to be lavish.

Profondità [proh-fon-dee-tah'] *nf.* deepness, depth, profundity.

Profondo [proh-fon'doh] nm. depth; a. deep, profound.

Profugo [proh'foo-goh] nm. refugee; a. fugitive.

Profuma/re [proh-foo-mah'ray] vt. to perfume, scent; —rsi vr. to put on scent.

Profumeria [proh-foo-may-ree'ah] nf. perfumer's shop, perfumery.

Profumo [proh-foo'moh] nm. perfume, scent.

Profusione [proh-foo-zee-oh'nay] nf. abundance, profusion.

Progenie [proh-jay'nee-ay] nf. descendants (pl.), issue, progeny.

Progenitore [proh-jay-nee-toh'ray] nm. ancestor, forefather.

Progettare [proh-jet-tah'ray] vt. to plan.

Progetto [proh-jet'toh] nm. plan, project, scheme; p. di legge [dee lay'djay], bill (Parliamentary).

Prognosi [proh'nyoh-zee] nf. (med.) prognosis.

Programma [proh-grahm'mah] nm. program(me), prospectus, syllabus.

Progredire [proh-gray-dee'ray] vi. to advance, (make) progress.

Progresso [proh-gress'soh] nm. progress.

Proibire [proh-ee-bee'ray] vt. to forbid, prohibit, refuse.

Proibizione [proh-ee-bee-tsee-oh'nay] nf. prohibition, refusal.

Proiettile [proh-yet'tee-lay] nm. missile, projectile.

Proiezione [proh-yay-tsee-oh'nay] nf. projection, showing (of a film), slide.

Prole [proh'lay] nf. children, (pl.), issue.

Proletariato [preh-lay-tah-ree-ah'toh] nm. proletariat.

Proletario [proh-lay-tah'ree-oh] nm. and a. proletarian.

Prolissità [proh-lees-see-tah'] nf. prolixity.

Prolisso [proh-lees'soh] a. long-winded, prolix.

Prologo [proh'loh-goh] nm. prologue.

Prolunga/re [proh-loong-gah'ray] vt. to extend, prolong; —rsi vr. to continue, lay oneself out.

Prolusione [proh-loo-zee-oh'nay] nf. opening lecture.

Promessa [proh-mess'sah] nf. promise.

Promettere [proh-met'tay-ray] vt. and i. to promise.

Prominente [proh-mee-nen'tay] a. jutting (out), prominent.

Prominenza [proh-mee-nent'sah] nf. prominence.

Promiscuo [proh-mees'koo-oh] a. common, promiscuous.

Promontorio [proh-mon-toh'ree-oh] nm. headland, promontory.

Promozione [proh-moh-tsee-oh'nay] nf. promotion.

Promulgare [proh-mool-gah'ray] vt. to promulgate.

Promuovere [proh-moo-oh'vay-ray] vt. to cause, induce, open, promote.

Prono [proh'noh] a. prone.

Pronome [proh-noh'may] nm. pronoun.

Pronostico [proh-noss'tee-koh] nm. forecast, omen, prognostic.

Prontezza [pron-tet'sah] nf. promptitude, quickness, readiness.

Pronto [pron'toh] a. prompt, ready; int. halle!

Pronun/cia [proh-noon'chah], —zia [tsee-ah] nf. pronunciation.

Pronun/cia/re [proh-noon-chah'ray], —ziare [tsee-ah'ray] *vt.* to pronounce, utter —*rsi vr.* to express one's opinion, pronounce.

Propaga/re [proh-pah-gah'ray] *vt.* and —**rsi** *vr.* to propagate, spread.

Propaggine [proh-pah'djeenay] *nf.* outcrop (rock), layer (plant).

Propalare [proh-pah-lah'ray] *vt.* to divulge, spread.

Propendere [proh-pen'dayray] *vi.* to incline.

Propensione [proh-pen-seeoh'nay] *nf.* propensity.

Propenso [proh-pen'soh] *a.* inclined, ready.

Propinquo [proh-peeng'kwoh] *a.* near. *v.* Vicino.

Propizio [proh-pee'tsee-oh] *a.* favourable, propitious, right.

Proponimento [proh-pohnee-men'toh] *nm.* resolution, resolve.

Propor/re [proh-porr'ray] *vt.* to propose, propound, put; —**rsi** *vr.* to intend, purpose, resolve.

Proporzione [proh-porr-tseeoh'nay] *nf.* comparison, proportion.

Proposito [proh-poh'zee-toh] *nm.* aim, intention, object, plan, purpose; *a.* [ah] *p. ad.* by the by, by the way.

Proposta [proh-poss'tah] *nf.* proposal.

Proprietà [proh-pree-ay-tah'] *nf.* estate, property, propriety.

Proprio [proh'pree-oh] *nm.* (one's own) property; *a.* (one's) own, proper; *ad.* exactly, just, really.

Propugnare [proh-poon-nyar'ray] *vt.* to advocate, plead for, support.

Propugnazione [proh-poon-yah-tsee-oh'nay] *nf.* defence, support.

Prora [proh'rah] *nf.* (naut.) bow, prow.

Prorogare [proh-roh-gah'ray] *vt.* to delay, extend, postpone, put off.

Prorompere [proh-rom'pay-ray] *vi.* to break forth, break out.

Prosa [proh'zah] *nf.* prose.

Prosaico [proh-zah'ee-koh] *a.* prosaic.

Prosciogliere [proh-sholl'yay-ray] *vt.* to acquit, (set) free.

Prosciuga/re [proh-shoogah'ray] *vt.* to drain, dry, reclaim; *vi.* and —**rsi** *vr.* to dry (up).

Prosciutto [proh-shoot'toh] *nm.* ham.

Proscrivere [pross-kree'vay-ray] *vt.* to proscribe.

Proscrizione [pross-kree-tsee-oh'nay] *nf.* proscription.

Proseguimento [proh-say-gwee-men'toh] *nm.* continuation.

Proseguire [proh-say-gwee'ray] *vt.* and *i.* to continue, go on, pursue.

Proselito [proh-zay'lee-toh] *nm.* proselyte.

Prosodia [proh-zoh-dee'ah] *nf.* prosody.

Prosperare [pross-pay-rah'ray] *vi.* to prosper, thrive.

Prosperità [pross-pay-ree-tah'] *nf.* prosperity, wealth.

Prospero [pross'pay-roh] *a.* flourishing, happy, prosperous, thriving.

Prosperoso [pross-pay-roh'soh] *a.* florid, healthy, plump, thriving.

Prospettiva [pross-pet-tee'vah] *nf.* perspective, prospect, view.

Prospetto [pross-pet'toh] *nm.* plan, prospect, view.

Prossimità [pross-see-mee-tah'] *nf.* nearness, proximity, vicinity.

Prossimo [pross'see-moh] *nm.* neighbour; *a.* near, next;

in un [een oon] p. **avvenire** [ahv-vay-nee´ray] *ad.* in the near future.

Prostitui/re [pross-tee-too-ee´ray] *vt.* to prostitute; **—rsi** *vr.* to prostitute oneself, sell oneself.

Prostituta [pross-tee-too´tah] *nf.* prostitute.

Prostituzione [pross-tee-too-tsee-oh´nay] *nf.* prostitution.

Prostra/re [pross-trah´ray] *vt.* to exhaust; **—rsi** *vr.* to get exhausted.

Prostrazione [pross-trah-tsee-oh´nay] *nf.* exhaustion.

Protagonista [proh-tah-goh-nee´stah] *nm.* hero (of a book), chief character, protagonist.

Proteggere [proh-tay´djay-ray] *vt.* to defend, patronize, protect, support.

Protende/re [proh-ten´day-ray] *vt.* to hold out, stretch; **—rsi in avanti** [een ah-vahn´tee] *vr.* to lean forward.

Protervo [proh-tehr´voh] *a.* stubborn.

Protesta [proh-tess´tah] *nf.* protest(ation), remonstrance.

Protestare [proh-tess-tah´ray] *vt. and i.* to protest.

Protettore [proh-tet-toh´ray] *nm.* patron, protector.

Protezione [proh-tay-tsee-oh´nay] *nf.* patronage, protection.

Protocollo [proh-toh-koll´loh] *nm.* protocol, record.

Prototipo [proh-toh´tee-poh] *nm.* prototype.

Protrarre [proh-trahr´ray] *vt.* to defer, protract, put off.

Protrazione [proh-trah-tsee-oh´nay] *nf.* deferment, protraction.

Protuberante [proh-too-bay-rahn´tay] *a.* bulging, prominent, protuberant.

Prova [proh´vah] *nf.* evidence, proof, rehearsal, test, trial.

Prova/re [proh-vah´ray] *vt. and i.* to demonstrate, experience, feel, prove, rehearse, test, try (on); **—rsi** *vr.* to endeavour, try.

Proveniente [proh-vay-nee-en´tay] *a.* caused (by), coming (from).

Provenienza [proh-vay-nee-ent´sah] *nf.* origin, source.

Provenire [proh-vay-nee´ray] *vi.* to be caused (by), come (from), spring (from).

Provento [proh-ven´toh] *nm.* income, proceeds (*pl.*).

Provenzale [proh-vent-sah´lay] *nm. and f. and a.* Provençal.

Proverbio [proh-vehr´bee-oh] *nm.* adage, proverb.

Provetto [proh-vet´toh] *a.* experienced, skilled.

Provincia [proh-veen´chah] *nf.* district, province.

Provinciale [proh-veen-chah´lay] *nm. and f. and a.* provincial; **strada** [strah´dah] p. *nf.* highway, main road.

Provocante [proh-voh-kahn´tay] *a.* coquettish.

Provocare [proh-voh-kah´ray] *vt.* to cause, provoke, rouse, stir up.

Provocazione [proh-voh-kah-tsee-oh´nay] *nf.* provocation.

Provolone [proh-voh-loh´nay] *nm.* buffalo-milk cheese.

Provvede/re [prov-vay-day´ray] *vt.* to furnish, provide, supply; **—rsi** *vr.* to equip oneself.

Provvedimento [prov-vay-dee-men´toh] *nm.* measure, provision.

Provvidenza [prov-vee-dent´sah] *nf.* piece of luck, providence.

Provvido [prov've͞e-doh] a. provident, thrifty.

Provvigione [prov-vee-joh'nay] nf. (com.) commission, provision.

Provvisorio [prov-vee-zoh'ree-oh] a. provisional, temporary.

Provvista [prov-vee'stah] nf. supply.

Prua: v. prora.

Prudente [proo-den'tay] a. careful, prudent, wise.

Prudenza [proo-dent'sah] nf. prudence, wisdom.

Pru/gna [proon'yah] nf. plum; —gno [yoh] nm. plum-tree.

Pruno [proo'noh] nm. bramble, thorn.

Prurito [proo-ree'toh] nm. itch(ing).

Pseudonimo [psay-oo-doh'nee-moh] nm. pen-name, pseudonym.

Psicologia [psee-koh-loh-jee'ah] nf. psychology.

Pubblicare [poob-blee-kah'ray] vt. to edit, issue, publish.

Pubblicazione [poob-blee-kah-tsee-oh'nay] nf. (marriage), issue, publication.

Pubblicità [poob-blee-chee-tah'] nf. advertising, publicity.

Pubblico [poob'blee-koh] nm. audience, public; a. public.

Pudicizia [poo-dee-chee'tsee-ah] nf. modesty.

Pudico [poo-dee'koh] a. bashful, modest.

Pudore [poo-doh'ray] nm. decency, modesty.

Puerizia [poo-ay-ree'tsee-ah] nf. childhood.

Pugilato [poo-jee-lah'toh] nm. boxing.

Pugnale [poon-yah'lay] nm. dagger.

Pugno [poon'yoh] nm. blow, fist, handful; con un [konn oon] p. di mosche [dee moss'-]

kay] a. empty-handed; fare a pugni [fah'ray ah poon'yee] vi. to clash, fight.

Pulce [pool'chay] nf. flea.

Pulcino [pool-chee'noh] nm. chick(en).

Puledro [poo-lay'droh] nm. colt, foal.

Pulire [poo-lee'ray] vt. to clean, polish, wash.

Pulito [poo-lee'toh] a. clean, clear.

Pulizia [poo-lee-tsee'ah] nf. cleaning, cleanliness.

Pullulare [pool-loo-lah'ray] vi. to be full of, pullulate, swarm with.

Pulpito [pool'pee-toh] nm. pulpit.

Pulsare [pool-sah'ray] vi. to beat, pulsate, throb.

Pulsazione [pool-sah-tsee-oh'nay] nf. beat, pulsation, throb(bing).

Pungere [poon'jay-ray] vt. to prick, sting.

Pungiglione [poon-jeel-yoh'nay] nm. sting.

Pungolo [poon'goh-loh] nm. goad, spur.

Punire [poo-nee'ray] vt. to punish.

Punizione [poo-nee-tsee-oh'nay] nf. chastisement, punishment.

Punta [poon'tah] nf. end, headland, point, tip; in [een] p. di piedi [dee pee-ay'dee] ad. on tip-toe.

Puntare [poon-tah'ray] vt. to bet, direct, lay, level, ogle, point.

Punteggiatura [poon-tay-djah-too'rah] nf. punctuation.

Puntellare [poon-tell-lah'ray] vt. to prop, support.

Puntello [poon-tell'loh] nm. prop, support.

Puntiglio [poon-teel'yoh] nm. punctilio, spite.

Punto [poon'toh] nm. detail.

dot, mark, place, point, spot, stitch; *a.* any; **non** [nonn] . . . **p.** no, none; *ad.* at all; **in** [een] **p.** exactly; **di** [dee] **p. in bianco** [een bee-ahng'koh], point-blank.

Puntuale [poon-too-ah'lay] *a.* punctual.

Puntura [poon-too'rah] *nf.* injection, prick, sting.

Punzecchiare [poont-seck-kee-ah'ray] *vt.* to bite, goad, prick, sting, tease.

Pupilla [poo-peel'lah] *nf.* pupil (of the eye).

Pupil/lo [poo-peel'loh] *nm.* —**la** *nf.* ward.

Purchè [poor-kay'] *con.* on condition that, provided (that).

Pure [poo'ray] *ad.* also, too, however, yet.

Purezza [poo-ret'sah], **purità** [poo-ree-tah'] *nf.* purity.

Purga [poor'gah] *nf.* purge.

Purgante [poor-gahn'tay] *nm.* aperient, laxative, purge; *a.* laxative, purging.

Purgare [poor-gah'ray] *vt.* to expurgate, free, purify, purge.

Purgatorio [poor-gah-toh'-ree-oh] *nm.* Purgatory.

Purificare [poo-ree-fee-kah'ray] *vt.* to cleanse, purify.

Puro [poo'roh] *a.* clean, mere, pure.

Purtroppo [poor-trop'poh] *ad.* unfortunately.

Pusillanime [poo-zeel-lah'nee-may] *nm.* coward; *a.* cowardly, faint-hearted.

Putredine [poo-tray'dee-nay] *nf.* putridity, rottenness.

Putrefa/re [poo-tray-fah'ray] *vi.* and —**rsi** *vr.* to go bad, putrefy, rot.

Putrido [poo'tree-doh] *a.* putrid, rotten.

Putto [poot'toh] *nm.* (*arch.*) child's figure.

Puzzare [poot-sah'ray] *vi.* to smell bad, stink.

Puzzo [poot'soh] *nm.* bad smell, stench, stink.

Puzzola [poot'soh-lah] *nf.* pole-cat.

Puzzolente [poot-soh-len'tay] *a.* fetid, stinking.

Q

Qua (kwah) *ad.* here; **da quando in** (da kwahn'doh een) **q.?** since when?

Quaderno [kwah-dehr'noh] *nm.* exercise-book, quire.

Quadrangolo [kwah-drahng'goh-loh] *nm.* quadrangle.

Quadrante [kwah-drahn'tay] *nm.* dial, face, quadrant.

Quadrare [kwah-drah'ray] *vt.* to square; *vi.* to suit.

Quad/ro [kwah'droh] *nm.* picture, painting, view, description (*mil.*) cadre; —**dri** (dree) (*pl.*) diamonds (cards); **a** (ah) **quadri** checked (cloth, etc.).

Quaggiù [kwah-djoo'] *ad.* here below, in this world.

Quaglia [kwahl'yah] *nf.* quail.

Qualche [kwahl'kay] *a.* any, some; **q. cosa** [koh'sah] *pn.* anything, something; **in** [een] **q. luogo** [loo-oh'goh] *ad.* anywhere, somewhere.

Qualcosa [kwahl-koh'sah] *pn.* anything, something.

Qualcuno [kwahl-koo'noh] *pn.* anyone, anybody, someone, somebody; (*pl.*) some, some.

Quale [kwah'lay] *a.* and *pn.* what? which?; **il** [eel] **q.** *rel. pn.* la [lah] **q.** *rel. pn. f.* that, which, who.

Qualifica [kwah-lee'fee-kah] *nf.* name, qualification.

Qualifica/re [kwah-lee-fee-kah'ray] *vt.* to call, qualify; —**rsi** *vr.* to announce oneself.

Qualità [kwah-lee-tah′] *nf.* quality.

Qualora [kwah-loh′rah] *con.* if.

Qualsiasi [kwahl-see′ah-see] *a.* any, whatever, whichever.

Qualunque [kwah-loong′kway] *a.* any, whatever, whichever; **uomo** [oo-oh′moh] q. *nm.* the common man, man-in-the-street.

Qualvolta, ogni [ohn′yee kawhl-voll′tah] *con.* whenever.

Quando [kwahn′doh] *ad.* and *con.* when; da [dah] q. *con.* since; di [dee] q. in [een] q. *ad.* from time to time; **quand'anche** [kwahnd-ahng′kay] *con.* even if.

Quantità [kwahn-tee-tah′] *nf.* a good deal of, a lot of, quantity.

Quanto [kwahn′toh] *ad.* as (in comparisons), how (much); q. **prima** [pree′mah] *ad.* as soon as possible; **per** [pehr] q. *con.* though; *a.* and *pn.* as (much), how (much); **quanti** [kwahn′tee] (*pl.*) as (many), how many.

Quantunque [kwahn-toong′kway] *con.* (al)though.

Quaran/ta [kwah-rahn′tah] *a.* forty; **—tenne** [ten′nay] *a.* 40-year-old; **—tesimo** [tay′zee-moh] *a.* fortieth; **—tina** [tee′nah] *nf.* some forty.

Quaresima [kwah-ray′zee-mah] *nf.* Lent.

Quaresimale [kwah-ray-zee-mah′lay] *a.* Lenten.

Quartiere [kwahr-tee-ay′ray] *nm.* flat, quarter, (*mil.*) quarters (*pl.*); q. **generale** [jay-nay-rah′lay] (*mil.*) H.Q.

Quartino [kwahr-tee′noh] *nm.* pint (measure).

Quarto [kwahr′toh] *nm.* fourth, quarter; *a.* fourth.

Quasi [kwah′zee] *ad.* almost, nearly; *con.* as if.

Quassù [kwahs-soo′] *ad.* up here.

Quatto [kwaht′toh] *a.* cowering, crouching; **quatto** quatto *ad.* very quietly.

Quattordi/ci [kwaht-torr′dee-chee] *a.* fourteen; **—cenne** chen′nay] *a.* 14-year-old; **—cesimo** [chay′zee-moh] *a.* fourteenth.

Quattri/no [kwaht-tree′noh] *nm.* farthing; **—ni** [nee] (*pl.*) money.

Quattro [kwaht′troh] *a.* four.

Quattrocento [kwaht-troh-chen′toh] *nm.* the 15th century; *a.* four hundred.

Quegli [kwayl′yee] *pr.* the former.

Quel(lo) [kwell′loh] *dem. pn.* that man, that one, etc.; *a.* former (of 2), that; **quello** **che** [kay] *pn.* what.

Quercia [kwehr′chah] *nf.* oak(-tree).

Querela [kway-ray′lah] *nf.* complaint.

Querela/re [kway-ray-lah′ray] *vt.* (*leg.*) to proceed against, prosecute; **—rsi** *vr.* (*leg.*) to bring a complaint, take proceedings.

Questi [kwess′tee] *pn.* the latter.

Questionare [kwess-tee-oh-nah′ray] *vi.* to dispute, quarrel.

Questione [kwess-tee-oh′nay] *nf.* dispute, problem, quarrel, question.

Questo [kwess′toh] *dem. pn.* this man, this one, etc.; *a.* latter (of 2), this.

Questore [kwess-toh′ray] *nm.* superintendent of police.

Questua [kwess′too-ah] *nf.* collection (for charity).

Questura [kwess-too′rah] *nf.* police station.

Qui [kwee] *ad.* here; q. **vicino** [vee-chee′noh] close by; **fin** [feen] q. so far, till now.

Quietanza [kwee-ay-tahnt'-sah] *nf.* receipt.

Quieta/re [kwee-ay-tah'ray] *vt.* to quiet; —**rsi** *vr.* to quiet down.

Quiete [kwee-ay'tay] *nf.* calm, peace, quiet, rest.

Quieto [kwee-ay'toh] *a.* calm, quiet, still, tranquil.

Quindi [kween'dee] *ad.* hence, then, therefore.

Quindi/ci [kween'dee-chee] *a.* fifteen; —**cenne** [chen'nay] *a.* 15-year-old; —**cesimo** [chay'zee-moh] *a.* fifteenth.

Quindicina [kween-dee-chee'nah] *nf.* some fifteen; **una** [oo'nah] **q. di giorni** [dee jorr'nee] a fortnight.

Quinta [kween'tah] *nf.* (*theat.*) wing; **dietro le quinte** [dee-ay'troh lay kween'tay] *ad.* behind the scenes.

Quintale [kween-tah'lay] *nm.* quintal (100 kilos).

Quinto [kween'toh] *a.* fifth.

Quivi [kwee'vee] *ad.* here.

Quota [kwoh'tah] *nf.* (*avia.*) height, quota, share.

Quotare [kwoh-tah'ray] *vt.* (*com.*) to fix the price, quote.

Quotidiano [kwoh-tee-dee-ah'noh] *nm.* daily (paper); *a.* daily.

Quoziente [kwoh-tsee-en'tay] *nm.* quotient.

R

Rabarbaro [rah-bahr'bah-roh] *nm.* rhubarb.

Rabberciare [rahb-behr-chah'ray] *vt.* to botch, patch (up).

Rabbia [rahb'bee-ah] *nf.* anger, fury, wrath, hydrophobia, rabies.

Rabbino [rahb-bee'noh] *nm.* Rabbi.

Rabbioso [rahb-bee-oh'soh] *a.* furious, hot-tempered.

Rabboni/re [rahb-boh-nee'ray] *vt.* to calm, pacify; —**rsi** *vr.* to grow calm.

Rabbrividire [rahb-bree-vee-dee'ray] *vi.* to shiver, shudder.

Rabbuffo [rahb-boof'foh] *nm.* rebuke, reprimand.

Rabbuia/re [rahb-boo-yah'ray] *vi. and* —**rsi** *vr.* to grow dark.

Rabdomante [rahb-doh-mahn'tay] *nm.* dowser, water-diviner.

Raccapezza/re [rahk-kah-pet-sah'ray] *vt.* to collect, put together; —**rsi** *vr.* to find one's way, make out.

Raccapriccire [rahk-kah-preech-chee'ray] *vi.* to be horrified.

Raccapriccio [rahk-kah-preech'choh] *nm.* horror.

Raccattare [rahk-kaht-tah'ray] *vt.* to collect, pick up.

Racchetta [rahk-ket'tah] *nf.* racquet.

Racchiudere [rahk-kyoo'day-ray] *vt.* to contain, hold.

Raccoglie/re [rahk-koll'yay-ray] *vt.* to assemble, collect, gather, pick (up); —**rsi** *vr.* to collect one's thoughts.

Raccoglimento [rahk-koll-yee-men'toh] *nm.* concentration, gathering, meditation.

Raccol/ta [rahk-koll'tah] *nf.* collection, gathering; —**to** [toh] *nm.* crop, harvest.

Raccomanda/re [rahk-koh-mahn-dah'ray] *vt.* to recommend, register; —**rsi** *vr.* to commend oneself; **mi raccomando** [mee rahk-koh-mahn'doh] *int.* please.

Raccomandazione [rahk-koh-mahn-dah-tsee-oh'nay] *nf.* recommendation.

Raccomodare [rahk-koh-

moh-dah'ray] *vt.* to mend, repair.

Raccontare [rahk-kon-tah'-ray] *vt.* to narrate, relate, tell.

Racconto [rahk-kon'toh] *nm.* report, story, tale.

Raccorcia/re [rahk-korr-chah'ray] *vt.* to shorten; —rsi *vr.* to grow short(er), shrink.

Rachitide [rah-kee'tee-day] *nf. (med.)* rickets.

Racimolare [rah-chee-moh-lah'ray] *vt.* to collect, scrape together.

Rada [rah'dah] *nf. (naut.)* roads *(pl.)*, roadstead.

Raddolci/re [rahd-doll-chee'-ray] *vt.* to soften, soothe, sweeten; —rsi *vr.* to grow sweet.

Raddoppiare [rahd-dop-pee-ah'ray] *vt.* to (re)double.

Raddrizza/re [rahd-dreet-sah'ray] *vt.* to erect, make straight; —rsi *vr.* to draw oneself up.

Rade/re [rah'day-ray] *vt.* to raze, shave; —rsi *vr.* to shave (oneself).

Radiare [rah-dee-ah'ray] *vt.* to cancel, erase; *vi.* to beam, radiate.

Radica [rah'dee-kah] *nf.* briarwood, root.

Radicale [rah-dee-kah'lay] *nm. and a.* radical.

Radica/re [rah-dee-kah'ray] *vi. and* —rsi *vr.* to (take) root.

Radio [rah'dee-oh] *nf.* radio, wireless; *nm.* radium.

Radioso [rah-dee-oh'soh] *a.* beaming, radiant.

Rado [rah'doh] *a.* infrequent, rare, scattered, thin; *di* [dee] *r. ad.* seldom; *non di* r. *ad.* pretty often.

Raduna/re [rah-doo-nah'ray] *vt. and* —rsi *vr.* to assemble, gather. [glade.

Radura [rah-doo'rah] *nf.*

Rafano [rah'fah-noh] *nm.* horse-radish.

Raffermare [rahf-fehr-mah'-ray] *vt.* to renew, confirm.

Raffermo [rahf-fehr'moh] *a.* stale.

Raffica [rahf'fee-kah] *nf.* gust of wind, squall.

Raffigurare [rahf-fee-goo-rah'ray] *vt.* to represent.

Raffilare [rahf-fee-lah'ray] *vt.* to pare, sharpen, whet.

Raffinamento [rahf-fee-nah-men'toh] *nm.* refining.

Raffinare [rahf-fee-nah'ray] *vt.* to refine.

Raffinatezza [rahf-fee-nah-tet'sah] *nf.* distinction, refinement, subtlety.

Raffineria [rahf-fee-nay-ree'-ah] *nf.* refinery.

Rafforza/re [rahf-forrt-sah'-ray] *vt.* to re-inforce, strengthen; —rsi *vr.* to be strengthened.

Raffredda/re [rahf-fred-dah'-ray] *vt.* to chill, cool; —rsi *vr.* to cool, get cold, catch a cold.

Raffreddore [rahf-fred-doh'-ray] *nm.* cold.

Raffrenabile [rahf-fray-nah'-bee-lay] *a.* repressible.

Raffrena/re [rahf-fray-nah'-ray] *vt.* to check, curb, restrain; —rsi *vr.* to check oneself.

Raffrontare [rahf-fron-tah'-ray] *vt.* to compare.

Raffronto [rahf-fron'toh] *nm.* comparison.

Raganella [rah-gah-nell'lah] *nf.* rattle, tree-frog.

Ragazza [rah-gaht'sah] *nf.* girl, maid, spinster.

Ragazzo [rah-gaht'soh] *nm.* boy, fellow, lad.

Raggiante [rah-djahn'tay] *a.* radiant.

Raggio [rah'djoh] *nm.* beam, radius, ray, spoke (of a wheel).

Raggirare [rah-djee-rah'ray] *vt.* to cheat, swindle, trick.

Raggiro [rah-djee'roh] *nm.* trick.

Raggiungere [rah-djoon'-jay-ray] *vt.* to arrive, attain, get to, obtain, overtake, reach.

Raggiustare [rah-djoo-stah'-ray] *vt.* to mend, set in order.

Raggranellare [rahg-grah-nell-lah'ray] *vt.* to collect, scrape together.

Raggrinzire [rahg-greent-see'ray] *vt.* to wrinkle (up).

Raggruppamento [rahg-groop-pah-men'toh] *nm.* cluster, group(ing).

Raggruppa/re [rahg-groop-pah'ray] *vt.* to collect, set in groups; —rsi *vr.* to cluster, form groups.

Raggruzzolare [rahg-groot-soh-lah'ray] *vt.* to put together, save.

Ragguagliare [rahg-gwah-lyah'ray] *vt.* to compare, inform.

Ragguaglio [rahg-gwah'-lyoh] *nm.* comparison, information.

Ragguardevole [rahg-gwahr-day'voh-lay] *a.* considerable, important, notable.

Ragionamento [rah-joh-nah-men'toh] *nm.* argument, reasoning.

Ragionare [rah-joh-nah'ray] *vi.* to argue, discuss, reason, talk over.

Ragione [rah-joh'nay] *nf.* reason, right; aver [ah-vehr'] r. *vi.* to be right.

Ragioneria [rah-joh-nay-ree'ah] *nf.* accountancy, book-keeping.

Ragionevole [rah-joh-nay'-voh-lay] *a.* reasonable, reasoning, sensible.

Ragioniere [rah-joh-nee-ay'ray] *nm.* (chartered) accountant, book-keeper.

Ragliare [rahl-yah'ray] *vi.* to bray.

Raglio [rahl'yoh] *nm.* braying.

Ragnate/la [rahn-yah-tay'-lah] *nf.* —lo [loh] *nm.* spider's web.

Ragno [rahn'yoh] *nm.* spider.

Rallegramento [rahl-lay-grah-men'toh] *nm.* congratulation, rejoicing.

Rallegra/re [rahl-lay-grah'ray] *vt.* to cheer, make glad; —rsi *vr.* to be glad, congratulate, rejoice.

Rallentare [rahl-len-tah'ray] *vt.* to lessen, slacken; r. il passo [eel pahs'soh] to slacken one's pace; *vi.* to slow down.

Ramaiolo [rah-mah-yoh'loh] *nm.* ladle.

Ramanzina [rah-mahnt-see'nah] *nf.* lecture, reprimand, scolding.

Ramarro [rah-mahr'roh] *nm.* green lizard.

Rame [rah'may] *nm.* copper.

Ramifica/re [rah-mee-fee-kah'ray] *vi.* and —rsi *vr.* to branch (out), ramify.

Ramificazione [rah-mee-fee-kah-tsee-oh'nay] *nf.* branching, ramification.

Ramingo [rah-meeng'goh] *a.* roaming, wandering.

Ramino [rah-mee'noh] *nm.* kettle.

Rammaricarsi [rahm-mah-ree-kahr'see] *vr.* to be sorry, grieve, regret.

Rammarico [rahm-mah'ree-koh] *nm.* grief, regret.

Rammendare [rahm-men-dah'ray] *vt.* to darn, mend.

Rammendo [rahm-men'doh] *nm.* darn, mend.

Rammenta/re [rahm-men-tah'ray] *vt.* to recall, remind; —rsi *vr.* to recollect, remember.

Rammollimento [rahm-moll-lee-men'toh] *nm.* softening.

Rammolli/re [rahm-moll-

lee'ray] *vt.* to make effeminate, soften; —**rsi** *vr.* to grow effeminate, soft.

Ramo [rah'moh] *nm.* antler, arm, bough, branch, (*com.*) line.

Ramoscello [rah-moh-shell'loh] *nm.* spray, twig.

Rampicante [rahm-pee-kahn'tay] *a.* climbing, creeping.

Rampogna [rahm-pohn'yah] *nf.* rebuke, reproof.

Rampollo [rahm-poll'loh] *nm.* offspring, scion, shoot.

Rana [rah'nah] *nf.* frog.

Rancidezza [rahn-chee-det'-sah] *nf.* ranciditiness.

Rancido [rahn'chee-doh] *a.* rancid, rank.

Rancio [rahn'choh] *nm.* (*mil.*) mess.

Rancore [rahng-koh'ray] *nm.* grudge, rancour.

Randagio [rahn-dah'joh] *a.* stray, wandering.

Randello [rahn-dell'loh] *nm.* cudgel. [rank.

Rango [rahng'goh] *nm.* degree.

Rannicchiarsi [rahn-neek-kee-ahr'see] *vr.* to cower, crouch, huddle.

Rannuvola/re [rahn-noo-voh-lah'ray] *vt.* to cloud; —**rsi** *vr.* to cloud over, grow dark.

Ranoc/chia [rahn-nock'kee-ah] *nf.*—**chio** [kee-oh] *nm.* frog.

Rantolare [rahn-toh-lah'ray] *vi.* to have the death-rattle in one's throat.

Rantolo [rahn'toh-loh] *nm.* (death-)rattle.

Rapa [rah'pah] *nf.* turnip.

Rapace [rah-pah'chay] *a.* greedy, predatory, rapacious.

Rapacità [rah-pah-chee-tah'] *nf.* greed, rapaciousness.

Rapare [rah-pah'ray] *vt.* to crop one's hair.

Rapido [rah'pee-doh] *nm.*

express train; *a.* quick, rapid, speedy, swift.

Rapimento [rah-pee-men'toh] *nm.* rapture.

Rapina [rah-pee'nah] *nf.* rapine, robbery.

Rapire [rah-pee'ray] *vt.* to abduct, carry off, kidnap, ravish, seize.

Rappacificare [rahp-pah-chee-fee-kah'ray] *vt.* to pacify.

Rappezzare [rahp-pet-sah'ray] *vt.* to patch (up).

Rappezzo [rahp-pet'soh] *nm.* patch.

Rapporto [rahp-porr'toh] *nm.* connection, relation report, statement; **essere** in **buoni rapporti** [ess'say-ray een boo-oh'nee rahp-porr'tee] *vi.* to be on good terms.

Rappresaglia [rahp-pray-sahl'yah] *nf.* reprisal, retaliation.

Rappresentante [rahp-pray-zen-tahn'tay] *nm.* agent, deputy, representative.

Rappresentanza [rahp-pray-zen-tahnt'sah] *nf.* agency, deputation, representation.

Rappresentare [rahp-pray-zen-tah'ray] *vt.* (*theat.*) to perform, represent.

Rappresentazione [rahp-pray-zen-tah-tsee-oh'nay] *nf.* description, performance.

Rarefa/re [rah-ray-fah'ray] *vt. and* —**rsi** *vr.* to rarefy.

Rarità [rah-ree-tah'] *nf.* curiosity, rareness, rarity.

Raro [rah'roh] *a.* exceptional, rare, uncommon.

Rasa/re [rah-sah'ray] *vt.* to shave, smooth; —**rsi** *vr.* to shave.

Raschiare [rah-skee-ah'ray] *vt.* to scrape, scratch.

Raschio [rah-skee'oh] *nm.* irritation, scraping.

Rasentare [rah-zen-tah'ray] *vt.* to approach, go near.

Rasente [rah-zen'tay] *vr.* close to.

Raso [rah'soh] *nm.* satin.

Rasoio [rah-soh'yoh] *nm.* razor.

Raspare [rah-spah'ray] *vt.* to rasp, scrape.

Rassegna [rahs-sayn'yah] *nf.* review.

Rassegna/re [rahs-sayn-yah'ray] *vt.* to resign; —rsi *vr.* to accept, resign oneself, submit.

Rassegnazione [rahs-sayn-yah-tsee-oh'nay] *nf.* resignation, submission.

Rasserena/re [rahs-say-ray-nah'ray] *vt.* to brighten, calm; —rsi *vr.* to clear up, recover one's serenity.

Rassettare [rahs-set-tah'ray] *vt.* to mend, tidy.

Rassicura/re [rahs-see-koo-rah'ray] *vt.* to (re)assure, tranquillize; —rsi *vr.* to make sure, take courage.

Rassodare [rahs-soh-dah'ray] *vt. and i.* to consolidate, dry, harden, strengthen.

Rassomiglianza [rahs-soh-meel-yahnt'sah] *nf.* likeness, resemblance.

Rassomigliare [rahs-soh-meel-yah'ray] *vi.* to be like, resemble.

Rastrellare [rah-strell-lah'ray] *vt.* to rake, search.

Rastrelliera [rah-strell-lee-ay'rah] *nf.* crib, rack.

Rastrello [rah-strell'loh] *nm.* rake (tool).

Rata [rah'tah] *nf.* instalment.

Rateale [rah-tay-ah'lay] *a.* by instalments, partial.

Ratifica [rah-tee'fee-kah] *nf.* ratification.

Ratificare [rah-tee-fee-kah'ray] *vt.* to ratify.

Ratto [raht'toh] *nm.* abduction, kidnapping, rape.

Rattoppare [raht-top-pah'-
ray] *vt.* to mend, patch (up).

Rattrappire [raht-trahp-pee'ray] *vt. and i.* to contract.

Rattrista/re [raht-tree-stah'ray] *vt.* to sadden; —rsi *vr.* to grow sad.

Raucedine [row-chay'dee-nay] *nf.* hoarseness.

Rauco [row'koh] *a.* hoarse.

Ravanello [rah-vah-nell'loh] *nm.* small radish.

Ravvedersi [rahv-vay-dehr'see] *vr.* to mend one's ways, reform, repent.

Ravvedimento [rahv-vay-dee-men'toh] *nm.* reformation, repentance.

Ravviare [rahv-vee-ah'ray] *vt.* to (re)arrange, tidy.

Ravvicina/re [rahv-vee-chee-nah'ray] *vt.* to bring closer, compare, reconcile; —rsi *vr.* to draw closer.

Ravvisare [rahv-vee-zah'ray] *vt.* to recognise, see.

Ravviva/re [rahv-vee-vah'ray] *vt.* to animate, enliven, revive; —rsi *vr.* to cheer up, revive.

Ravvolgere, etc.: *v.* avvolgere, etc.

Raziocinio [rah-tsee-oh-chee'nee-oh] *nm.* reason(ing).

Razionale [rah-tsee-oh-nah'lay] *a.* rational.

Razione [rah-tsee-oh'nay] *nf.* allowance, portion, ration.

Razza [raht'sah] *nf.* breed, kind, race.

Razzia [raht-see'ah] *nf.* plundering expedition, raid.

Razziare [raht-see-ah'ray] *vt. and i.* to plunder, raid.

Razzo [raht'dzoh] *nm.* rocket (firework).

Razzolare [raht-soh-lah'ray] *vi.* to grub, scratch.

Re [ray] *nm.* king.

Reagire [ray-ah-jee'ray] *vi.* to react. [royal.

Reale [ray-ah'lay] *a.* real,

Realismo [ray-ah-lees′moh] *nm.* realism, reality.

Realista [ray-ah-lee′stah] *nm. and f.* realist, royalist.

Realizza/re [ray-ah-leed-zah′ray] *vt.* to realise; **—rsi** *vr.* to come true.

Realtà [ray-ahl-tah′] *nf.* reality.

Reame [ray-ah′may] *nm.* kingdom, realm.

Reato [ray-ah′toh] *nm.* crime.

Reazionario [ray-ah-tsee-oh-nah′ree-oh] *nm. and a.* reactionary.

Reazione [ray-ah-tsee-oh′nay] *nf.* reaction.

Recapitare [ray-kah-pee-tah′ray] *vt.* to deliver, hand.

Recapito [ray-kah′pee-toh] *nm.* address, delivery, office.

Reca/re [ray-kah′ray] *vt.* to bring, carry, cause, take; **—rsi** *vr.* to betake oneself, go.

Recedere [ray-chay′day-ray] *vi.* to recede, withdraw.

Recensione [ray-chen-see-oh′nay] *nf.* review (critical).

Recensire [ray-chen-see′ray] *vt.* to review.

Recente [ray-chen′tay] *a.* late, new, recent.

Recesso [ray-chess′soh] *nm.* recess.

Recidere [ray-chee′day-ray] *vt.* to cut off.

Recingere [ray-cheen′jay-ray] *vt.* to enclose, fence in.

Recinto [ray-cheen′toh] *nm.* enclosure.

Recipiente [ray-chee-pee-en′tay] *nm.* container, vessel.

Reciproco [ray-chee′proh-koh] *a.* mutual, reciprocal.

Reciso [ray-chee′zoh] *a.* concise, sharp.

Recita [ray′chee-tah] *nf.* performance, recital.

Recitare [ray-chee-tah′ray] *vt. and i.* to act, perform, play, recite.

Recitazione [ray-chee-tah-tsee-oh′nay] *nf.* acting, recitation.

Reclamare [ray-klah-mah′ray] *vt.* to ask for, claim; *vi.* to complain, protest.

Réclame [ray-klahm′] *nf.* advertisement.

Reclamo [ray-klah′moh] *nm.* complaint.

Reclusione [ray-kloo-zee-oh′nay] *nf.* imprisonment.

Reclusorio [ray-kloo-zoh′-ree-oh] *nm.* penitentiary, prison.

Recluta [ray′kloo-tah] *nf.* (*mil.*) recruit.

Reclutamento [ray-kloo-tah-men′toh] *nm.* recruiting.

Reclutare [ray-kloo-tah′ray] *vt.* to recruit.

Recondito [ray-kon′dee-toh] *a.* concealed, hidden, recondite.

Recriminare [ray-kree-mee-nah′ray] *vi.* to recriminate.

Recriminazione [ray-kree-mee-nah-tsee-oh′nay] *nf.* recrimination.

Recrudescenza [ray-kroo-day-shent′sah] *nf.* recrudescence.

Redarguire [ray-dahr-gwee′ray] *vt.* to reproach, scold.

Redarguizione [ray-dahr-gwee-tsee-oh′nay] *nf.* reproach, scolding.

Redattore [ray-daht-toh′ray] *nm.* compiler, journalist, writer.

Redazione [ray-dah-tsee-oh′nay] *nf.* compilation, editorial staff, editor's office.

Reddito [red′dee-toh] *nm.* income, revenue.

Redditizio [red-dee-tee′tsee-oh] *a.* paying, profitable.

Redento [ray-den′toh] *a.* freed, redeemed.

Redentore [ray-den-toh′ray] *nm.* redeemer; *a.* redeeming.

Redenzione [ray-den-tsee-oh′nay] *nf.* redemption.

Redigere [ray-dee′jay-ray] vt. to compile, compose, draw up.

Redimere [ray-dee′may-ray] vt. to free, redeem. [rein.

Redine [ray′dee-nay] nf.

Redivivo [ray-dee-vee′voh] a. new, risen from the dead.

Reduce [ray′doo-chay] nm. ex-service man, veteran; a. returning.

Refe [ray′fay] nm. thread.

Referenza [ray-fay-rent′sah] nf. information, reference, testimonial.

Refettorio [ray-fet-toh′ree-oh] nm. dining-hall, refectory.

Refezione [ray-fay-tsee-oh′nay] nf. light meal, refection.

Refrattario [ray-fraht-tah′ree-oh] a. fire-proof, refractory.

Refrigerare [ray-free-jay-rah′ray] vt. to refrigerate.

Refrigerio [ray-free-jay′ree-oh] nm. comfort, relief.

Refurtiva [ray-foor-tee′vah] nf. stolen goods (pl.).

Regalare [ray-gah-lah′ray] vt. to make a present of, present.

Regalo [ray-gah′loh] nm. gift, present.

Reggente [ray-djen′tay] nm. regent.

Reggenza [ray-djen′sah] nf. regency.

Regge/re [ray′djay-ray] vt. to bear, carry, govern, hold, rule, support; —rsi vr. to stand.

Reggia [ray′djah] nf. royal palace.

Reggimento [ray-djee-men′toh] nm. regiment.

Reggipetto [ray-djee-pet′toh] nm. brassière.

Regia [ray-jee′ah] nf. state monopoly; (theat.) produced by.

Regime [ray-jee′may] nm. diet, régime, regimen; **stare a** [stah′ray ah] r. vi. to be on a diet.

Regina [ray-jee′nah] nf. queen

Regio [ray′joh] a. royal.

Regione [ray-joh′nay] nf. district, region.

Regista [ray-jee′stah] nm. (theat.) producer.

Registrare [ray-jee-strah′ray] vt. (com.) to enter, record, register.

Registratore [ray-jee-strah-toh′ray] nm. register, registrar.

Registrazione [ray-jee-strah-tsee-oh′nay] nf. (com.) entry, registration.

Registro [ray-jee′stroh] nm. register.

Regnare [rayn-yah′ray] vi. to prevail, reign.

Regno [rayn′yoh] nm. kingdom, reign.

Regola [ray′goh-lah] nf. rule; **di** [dee] r. ad. as a rule.

Regolamento [ray-goh-lah-men′toh] nm. regulation, settlement.

Regola/re [ray-goh-lah′ray] vt. to regulate, settle; —rsi vr. to act, behave; a. regular.

Regolarità [ray-goh-lah-ree-tah′] nf. regularity.

Regolato [ray-goh-lah′toh] a. moderate, orderly, temperate.

Regolo [ray′goh-loh] nm. ruler (for lines); **r. calcolatore** [kahl-koh-lah-toh′ray] sliding-rule. [regress.

Regresso [ray-gress′soh] nm.

Reietto [ray-yet′toh] nm. castaway, outcast; a. abandoned, forsaken.

Reiezione [ray-yay-tsee-oh′nay] nf. rejection.

Reintegrare [ray-een-tay-grah′ray] vt. to reinstate.

Relatore [ray-lah-toh′ray] nm. narrator, reporter.

Relazione [ray-lah-tsee-oh′nay] nf. connection, relation, report; **aver molte relazioni**

[ah-vehr'moll'tay ray-lah-tsee-oh'nee] vi. to know many people.

Relegare [ray-lay-gah'ray] vt. to confine, relegate.

Religione [ray-lee-joh'nay] nf. religion.

Religioso [ray-lee-joh'soh] nm. member of a religious order; a. religious.

Reliquia [ray-lee'kwee-ah] nf. relic.

Relitti [ray-leet'tee] nm. (pl.) wreckage.

Remare [ray-mah'ray] vi. to paddle, row.

Reminiscenza [ray-mee-nee-shent'sah] nf. reminiscence.

Remissione [ray-mees-see-oh'nay] nf. remission.

Remissivo [ray-mees-see'voh] a. meek, submissive.

Remo [ray'moh] nm. oar.

Remoto [ray-moh'toh] a. distant, remote, secluded.

Rena [ray'nah] nf. sand(s).

Rende/re [ren'day-ray] vt. to make, render, return, yield; vi. to pay; —rsi vr. to become, make oneself; r. conto di [kon'toh dee] vi. to realise.

Rendiconto [ren-dee-kon'toh] nm. relation, report.

Rendimento [ren-dee-men'toh] nm. profit, reckoning.

Rendita [ren'dee-tah] nf. income, revenue.

Rene [ray'nay] nm. kidney.

Renna [ren'nah] nf. reindeer.

Reo [ray'oh] a. guilty.

Reparto [ray-pahr'toh] nm. department, (mil.) detachment, party.

Repellente [ray-pell-len'tay] a. repellent, repulsive.

Repentaglio [ray-pen-tahl'yoh] nm. danger, risk.

Repen/te [ray-pen'tay], —tino [tee'noh] a. sudden.

Reperibile [ray-pay-ree'bee-lay] a. to be found.

Reperire [ray-pay-ree'ray] vt. to find (again).

Repertorio [ray-pehr-toh'ree-oh] nm. collection, repertory.

Replica [ray'plee-kah] nf. repetition, reply, retort.

Replicare [ray-plee-kah'ray] vt. to repeat; vi. to reply.

Repressione [ray-press-see-oh'nay] nf. quelling, repression.

Reprimere [ray-pree'may-ray] vt. to check, quell, repress.

Reprobo [ray'proh-boh] nm. and a. reprobate.

Repubblica [ray-poob'blee-kah] nf. commonwealth, republic.

Repubblicano [ray-poob-blee-kah'noh] nm. and a. republican.

Reputare [ray-poo-tah'ray] vt. to consider, deem, think.

Reputazione [ray-poo-tah-tsee-oh'nay] nf. reputation.

Requie [ray'kwee-ay] nf. peace, rest.

Requisire [ray-kwee-zee'ray] vt. to requisition.

Requisitoria [ray-kwee-zee-toh'ree-ah] nf. accusation, charge.

Requisizione [ray-kwee-zee-tsee-oh'nay] nf. requisition.

Resa [ray'sah] nf. rendering, return, surrender.

Rescindere [ray-sheen'day-ray] vt. to annul, rescind.

Reseda [ray-say'dah] nf. mignonette.

Residente [ray-see-den'tay] nm. and f. resident; a. residing.

Residenza [ray-see-dent'sah] nf. residence, residency.

Residuo [ray-see'doo-oh] nm. balance, residue.

Resina [ray'zee-nah] nf. resin.

Resistente [ray-see-sten'tay] a. fast (of colours), resisting, strong.

Resistenza [ray-see-stent'...]

sah] *nf.* endurance, opposition, resistance.

Respingere [ress-peen'jay'ray] *vt.* to drive back, reject, repel, return.

Respirare [ress-pee-rah'ray] *vt. and i.* to breathe.

Respiro [ress-pee'roh] *nm.* breath, delay, respite.

Responsabile [ress-pon-sah'bee-lay] *a.* responsible.

Responsabilità [ress-pon-sah-bee-lee-tah'] *nf.* responsibility.

Responso [ress-pon'soh] *nm.* answer, decision, response.

Ressa [ress'sah] *nf.* crowd, throng.

Restare [ress-tah'ray] *vi.* to be left, remain, stay, stop.

Restaurare [ress-tow-rah'ray] *vt.* to re-establish, restore.

Restauro [ress-tow'roh] *nm.* repair, restoration.

Restio [ress-tee'oh] *a.* reluctant, unmanageable.

Restituire [ress-tee-too-ee'ray] *vt.* to give back, return.

Restituzione [ress-tee-too-tsee-oh'nay] *nf.* restitution, return.

Res/to [ress'toh] *nm.* change (money), remainder, residue, rest; —ti [tee] (*pl.*) remains (*pl.*); del [dell] r. *ad.* besides.

Restringe/re [ress-treen'jay-ray] *vt.* to contract, lessen, narrow, restrict; —rsi *vr.* to contract, narrow, retrench, shrink.

Restrizione [ress-tree-tsee-oh'nay] *nf.* restriction.

Retaggio [ray-tah'djoh] *nm.* heritage, inheritance.

Rete [ray'tay] *nf.* goal (football), net(work), snare.

Reticenza [ray-tee-chent'sah] *nf.* reticence.

Reticolato [ray-tee-koh-lah'toh] *nm.* barbed wire entanglement, cage (for prisoners).

Retorica [ray-toh'ree-kah] *nf.* rhetoric.

Retribuire [ray-tree-boo-ee'ray] *vt.* to (re)pay, reward.

Retribuzione [ray-tree-boo-tsee-oh'nay] *nf.* pay, retribution, reward.

Retrivo [ray-tree'voh] *a.* backward, behindhand.

Retrobottega [ray-troh-bot-tay'gah] *nf.* room at the back of a shop.

Retrocedere [ray-troh-chay'day-ray] *vt.* to degrade, reduce in rank; *vi.* to retreat, step back.

Retrogrado [ray-troh'grah-doh] *nm.* reactionary; *a.* backward, retrograde.

Retroscena [ray-troh-shay'nah] *nm.* behind the scenes, underhand dealing.

Retta [ret'tah] *nf.* charge, terms (*pl.*).

Rettificare [ret-tee-fee-kah'ray] *vt.* to adjust, rectify.

Rettificazione [ret-tee-fee-kah-tsee-oh'nay] *nf.* adjustment, rectification. [reptile.

Rettile [ret'tee-lay] *nm.*

Rettitudine [ret-tee-too'dee-nay] *nf.* honesty, uprightness.

Retto [ret'toh] *a.* honest, right, straight, upright.

Rettore [ret-toh'ray] *nm.* rector.

Reuma [ray'oo-mah] *nm.* (*med.*) rheumatic pain.

Reumatismo [ray-oo-mah-tees'moh] *nm.* rheumatism.

Revisione [ray-vee-zee-oh'nay] *nf.* revision; r. dei conti [day'ee kon'tee], audit.

Revoca [ray'voh-kah] *nf.* repeal, revocation.

Revocabile [ray-voh-kah'bee-lay] *a.* revokable.

Revocare [ray-voh-kah'ray] *vt.* to repeal, revoke.

Revolver [ray-voll'vehr] *nm.* revolver.

Revolverata [ray-voll-vay-rah'tah] *nf.* revolver-shot.

Rezzo [red'zoh] *nm.* coolness, shade.

Ri [ree]: common prefix to Italian verbs, meaning *again* or *back*; thus: richiudere, to shut again; ridare, to give back, etc. For verbs with prefix ri- not given below, see entries without prefix.

Riabilita/re [ree-ah-bee-lee-tah'ray] *vt.* to redeem, rehabilitate; —rsi *vr.* to regain one's good name.

Riabilitazione [ree-ah-bee-lee-tah-tsee-oh'nay] *nf.* rehabilitation.

Rialzare [ree-ahlt-sah'ray] *vt.* to heighten, lift up again.

Riassunto [ree-ahs-soon'toh] *nm.* summary, summing-up.

Riaversi [ree-ah-vehr'see] *vr.* to recover.

Ribadire [ree-bah-dee'ray] *vt.* to clench, clinch, fix, repeat.

Ribalderia [ree-bahl-day-ree'ah] *nf.* foul deed, knavish trick.

Ribaldo [ree-bahl'doh] *nm.* rascal, scoundrel; *a.* wicked.

Ribaltare [ree-bahl-tah'ray] *vi.* to capsize, overturn.

Ribassare [ree-bahs-sah'ray] *vt.* to lower, reduce.

Ribasso [ree-bahs'soh] *nm.* decline, fall, lowering, reduction.

Ribellarsi [ree-bell-lahr'see] *vr.* to rebel, rise (against).

Ribelle [ree-bell'lay] *nm.* rebel; *a.* rebel, rebellious.

Ribellione [ree-bell-lee-oh'nay] *nf.* rebellion.

Ribes [ree'bess] *nm.* currant.

Ribrezzo [ree-bred'zoh] *nm.* horror, loathing.

Ributtante [ree-boot-tahn'tay] *a.* revolting.

Ricadere [ree-kah-day'ray]

vi. to fall down, (have a) relapse.

Ricaduta [ree-kah-doo'tah] *nf.* relapse.

Ricamare [ree-kah-mah'ray] *vt.* to embroider.

Ricamatrice [ree-kah-mah-tree'chay] *nf.* embroideress.

Ricambiare [ree-kahm-bee-ah'ray] *vt.* to reciprocate, repay, return.

Ricambio [ree-kahm'bee-oh] *nm.* exchange, return; pezzo di [pet'soh dee] r. (*tech.*) spare (part).

Ricamo [ree-kah'moh] *nm.* embroidery.

Ricapitolare [ree-kah-pee-toh-lah'ray] *vt.* to recapitulate, sum up.

Ricattare [ree-kaht-tah'ray] *vt.* to blackmail.

Ricattatore [ree-kaht-tah-toh'ray] *nm.* blackmailer.

Ricatto [ree-kaht'toh] *nm.* blackmail(ing).

Ricavare [ree-kah-vah'ray] *vt.* to extract, gain, obtain.

Rica/vo [ree-kah'voh], —vato [vah'toh] *nm.* proceeds (*pl.*).

Ricchezza [reek-ket'sah] *nf.* riches (*pl.*), richness, wealth.

Riccio [reech'choh] *nm.* curl, lock, hedgehog.

Ricciuto [reech-choo'toh] *a.* curly. [wealthy.

Ricco [reek'koh] *a.* rich,

Ricerca [ree-chehr'kah] *nf.* demand, inquiry, research; alla [ahl'lah] r. di [dee] *ad.* in search of.

Ricercare [ree-chehr-kah'ray] *vt.* to inquire into, seek, search (for).

Ricercatezza [ree-chehr-kah-tet'sah] *nf.* affectation.

Ricetta [ree-chet'tah] *nf.* (*med.*) prescription, recipe.

Ricettacolo [ree-chet-tah'koh-loh] *nm.* receptacle.

Ricettare [ree-chet-tah'ray]

vt. to receive (stolen goods), reset.

Ricettazione [ree-chet-tah-tsee-oh'nay] *nf.* fencing, resetting.

Ricevere [ree-chay'vay-ray] *vt.* to meet with, receive, welcome.

Ricevimento [ree-chay-vee-men'toh] *nm.* reception.

Ricevitore [ree-chay-vee-toh'ray] *nm.* receiver.

Ricevuta [ree-chay-voo'tah] *nf.* receipt.

Richiamare [ree-kee-ah-mah'ray] *vt.* to (re)call, draw.

Richiamo [ree-kee-ah'moh] *nm.* admonition, call, warning.

Richiesta [ree-kee-ess'tah] *nf.* demand, request.

Richiesto [ree-kee-ess'toh] *a.* in demand, required, sought after.

Ricino, olio di [oll-yoh dee ree'chee-noh] *nm.* castor-oil.

Ricognizione [ree-kohn-yee-tsee-oh'nay] *nf.* (*mil.*) reconnaissance.

Ricolmare [ree-koll-mah'ray] *vt.* to fill, overload (with).

Ricolmo [ree-koll'moh] *a.* brim-full.

Ricompensa [ree-kom-pen'sah] *nf.* recompense, reward.

Ricompensare [ree-kom-pen-sah'ray] *vt.* to recompense, requite, reward.

Ricompor/re [ree-kom-porr'ray] *vt.* to reassemble, (re)compose; —rsi *vr.* to recover oneself.

Riconciliare [ree-kon-chee-lee-ah'ray] *vt.* to reconcile.

Riconferma [ree-kon-fehr'mah] *nf.* confirmation.

Riconoscente [ree-koh-noh-shen'tay] *a.* grateful, thankful.

Riconoscenza [ree-koh-noh-shent'sah] *nf.* gratitude.

Riconoscere [ree-koh-noh-

shay-ray] *vt.* to acknowledge, recognise.

Riconoscimento [ree-koh-noh-shee-men'toh] *nm.* acknowledgement, identification, recognition.

Ricoprire [ree-koh-pree'ray] *vt.* to cover, hide.

Ricordanza [ree-korr-dahnt'sah] *nf.* (*poet.*) recollection, remembrance.

Ricordare [ree-korr-dah'ray] *vt. and i.* to recall, recollect, remember, remind; —rsi *vr.* to recollect, remember.

Ricordo [ree-korr'doh] *nm.* memory, record, remembrance.

Ricorrenza [ree-korr-rent'sah] *nf.* anniversary, occasion, recurrence.

Ricorrere [ree-korr'ray-ray] *vi.* to apply, have recourse, recur.

Ricorso [ree-korr'soh] *nm.* complaint.

Ricostruzione [ree-koss-troo-tsee-oh'nay] *nf.* rebuilding, reconstruction.

Ricotta [ree-kot'tah] *nf.* buttermilk curd.

Ricovera/re [ree-koh-vay-rah'ray] *vt.* to (give) shelter, take in; —rsi *vr.* to find shelter.

Ricovero [ree-koh'vay-roh] *nm.* refuge, shelter.

Ricrea/re [ree-kray-ah'ray] *vt.* to recreate, refresh; —rsi *vr.* to find recreation.

Ricreazione [ree-kray-ah-tsee-oh'nay] *nf.* pastime, recreation.

Ricredersi [ree-kray'dehr-see] *vr.* to change one's mind.

Ricuperare [ree-koo-pay-rah'ray] *vt.* to make up for, recover.

Ricupero [ree-koo'pay-roh] *nm.* recovery, rescue.

Ricusare [ree-koo-zah'ray] *vt.* to deny refuse, reject.

Ridda [reed'dah] *nf.* confusion, medley.

Ridente [ree-den'tay] *a.* bright, laughing.

Ridere [ree'day-ray] *vi.* to laugh.

Ridicolo [ree-dee'koh-loh] *nm.* ridicule, ridiculousness; *a.* ridiculous.

Ridire, trovare da [troh-vah'ray dah ree-dee'ray] *vi.* to find fault.

Ridondare [ree-don-dah'ray] *vi.* to redound. (*rare*).

Ridosso, a [ah ree-doss'soh] *ad.* close by, very near.

Ridotta [ree-dot'tah] *nf.* (*mil.*) redoubt.

Ridurre [ree-door'ray] *vt.* to reduce.

Riduzione [ree-doo-tsee-oh'nay] *nf.* adaption, reduction.

Riempiere [ree-emp'yay-ray], **riempi/re** [ree-em-pee'ray] *vt.* to cram, fill, stuff; **—rsi** *vr.* to fill (oneself).

Rientrare [ree-en-trah'ray] *vi.* to return; **r. in sè.** [een say] to come to oneself.

Riepilogare [ree-ay-pee-loh-gah'ray] *vt.* to recapitulate.

Riepilogo [ree-ay-pee'loh-goh] *nm.* recapitulation.

Rifacimento [ree-fah-chee-men'toh] *nm.* remaking, restoration.

Rifa/re [ree-fah'ray] *vt.* to do again, (re)make; **—rsi** *vr.* to make up one's losses.

Rifatto [ree-faht'toh] *a.* done again, rebuilt, remade.

Riferi/re [ree-fay-ree'ray] *vt.* to relate, report, tell; **—rsi** *vr.* to refer, relate.

Rifiatare [ree-fee-ah-tah'ray] *vi.* to utter a word.

Rifinire [ree-fee-nee'ray] *vt.* to finish, give the last touch to.

Rifiuta/re [reef-yoo-tah'ray] *vt.* and *i.* and **—rsi** *vr.* to decline, deny, refuse, reject.

Rifiu/to [reef-yoo'toh] *nm.* refusal; **—ti** [tee] (*pl.*) refuse, scum.

Riflessione [ree-fless-see-oh'nay] *nf.* deliberation, reflection.

Riflettere [ree-flet'tay-ray] *vt.* to reflect; *vi.* to reflect on, think over.

Rifluire [ree-floo-ee'ray] *vi.* to ebb, flow back.

Riflusso [ree-floos'soh] *nm.* ebb(-tide), reflux.

Rifocilla/re [ree-foh-cheel-lah'ray] *vt.* to supply (with food and drink); **—rsi** *vr.* to supply oneself.

Rifondere [ree-fon'day-ray] *vt.* to melt again, refund.

Riforma [ree-forr'mah] *nf.* reform(ation).

Riformare [ree-forr-mah'ray] *vt.* to amend, reform; (*mil.*) to declare unfit for service, invalid out.

Riforni/re [ree-forr-nee'ray] *vt.* to provide, supply; **—rsi** *vr.* to take in a fresh supply.

Rifrangere [ree-frahn'jay-ray] *vt.* to refract.

Rifrazione [ree-frah-tsee-oh'nay] *nf.* refraction.

Rifugiarsi [ree-foo-jahr'see] *vr.* to hide oneself, take refuge.

Rifugio [ree-foo'joh] *nm.* haunt, refuge, shelter.

Rifulgere [ree-fool'jay-ray] *vi.* to become apparent, be resplendent, shine.

Riga [ree'gah] *nf.* line, parting (hair), row, stripe.

Rigaglie [ree-gahl'yay] *nf.* (*pl.*) giblets (*pl.*).

Rigagnolo [ree-gahn'yoh-loh] *nm.* brook, gutter.

Rigare [ree-gah'ray] *vt.* to rule (lines).

Rigattiere [ree-gaht-tee-ay'ray] *nm.* dealer in second-hand articles, old-clothes dealer.

Rigenera/re [ree-jay-nay-rah'ray] *vt. and* —**rsi** *vr.* to regenerate.

Rigenerazione [ree-jay-nay-rah-tsee-oh'nay] *nf.* regeneration.

Rigettare [ree-jet-tah'ray] *vt. and i.* to put out fresh shoots, eject, throw back, vomit.

Rigidezza [ree-jee-det'sah], **rigidità** [ree-jee-dee-tah'] *nf.* austerity, rigidity, strictness.

Rigido [ree'jee-doh] *a.* austere, rigid, severe, strict, very cold.

Rigira/re [ree-jee-rah'ray] *vt.* to trick, turn, twist; —**rsi** *vr.* to turn round.

Rigiro [ree-jee'roh] *nm.* shift, trick.

Rigo [ree'goh] *nm.* line.

Rigoglio [ree-gohl'yoh] *nm.* bloom, luxuriance.

Rigoglioso [ree-gohl-yoh'soh] *a.* luxuriant, rank.

Rigonfio [ree-gon'fee-oh] *a.* full, puffed up, swollen.

Rigore [ree-goh'ray] *nm.* rigour, severity, strictness; **a** [ah] **r. di termini** [dee tehr'mee-nee] *ad.* in the strict sense.

Rigorosità [ree-goh-roh-see-tah'] *nf.* rigorousness, strictness.

Rigoroso [ree-goh-roh'soh] *a.* rigorous, severe, strict.

Rigovernare [ree-goh-vehr-nah'ray] *vt.* to clean; *vi.* to wash up.

Riguardante [ree-gwahr-dahn'tay] *a.* regarding, concerning.

Riguarda/re [ree-gwahr-dah'ray] *vt.* to concern, look over, regard, revise; —**rsi** *vr.* to abstain from, beware of, take care of.

Riguardo [ree-gwahr'doh] *nm.* consideration, regard, respect.

Rigurgitare [ree-goor-jee-tah'ray] *vi.* to flow back, overflow, swarm with.

Rilasciare [ree-lah-shah'ray] *vt.* to give, grant, leave again, release.

Rilassa/re [ree-lahs-sah'ray] *vt. and* —**rsi** *vr.* to loosen, relax, slacken, weaken.

Rilegare [ree-lay-gah'ray] *vt.* to bind (again).

Rilegatore [ree-lay-gah-toh'ray] *nm.* bookbinder.

Rilevante [ree-lay-vahn'tay] *a.* considerable, heavy, important.

Rileva/re [ree-lay-vah'ray] *vt.* to draw, increase, point out, take away; —**rsi** *vr.* to get up again, recover, rise again.

Rilievo [ree-lee-ay'voh] *nm.* relief, remark.

Rilucere [ree-loo'chay-ray] *vi.* to glitter, shine.

Riluttante [ree-loot-tahn'tay] *a.* reluctant.

Rima [ree'mah] *nf.* rime, rhyme; **rispondere per le rime** [ree-spon'day-ray pehr lay ree'may] *vi.* to give as good as one gets.

Rimandare [ree-mahn-dah'ray] *vt.* to defer, postpone, put off, reject, send back.

Rimaneggiare [ree-mah-nay-djah'ray] *vt.* to alter, change, shuffle (in political sense).

Rimanente [ree-mah-nen'tay] *nm.* remainder; *a.* remaining.

Rimanenza [ree-mah-nent'sah] *nf.* remainder.

Rimanere [ree-mah-nay'ray] *vi.* to be left, be surprised, remain, stay, stop.

Rimare [ree-mah'ray] *vt. and i.* to rime, rhyme.

Rimasug/lio [ree-mah-sool'yoh] *nm.* remainder; —**li** [yee] (*pl.*) remains (*pl.*).

Rimatore [ree-mah-toh'ray] *nm.* rhymer.

Rimbalzo [reem-bahlt'soh] *nm.* rebound; di (*ger.*) r. ad. on the rebound.

Rimbambi(ni)re [reem-bahm-bee (nee)'ray] *vi.* to grow childish.

Rimbeccare [reem-beck-kah'ray] *vt.* to retort.

Rimbecco [reem-beck'koh] *nm.* retort.

Rimboccare [reem-bock-kah'ray] *vt.* to turn up, tuck in.

Rimbombare [reem-bom-bah'ray] *vi.* to roar, thunder.

Rimbombo [reem-bom'boh] *nm.* roar.

Rimborsabile [reem-borr-sah'bee-lay] *a.* repayable.

Rimborsare [reem-borr-sah'ray] *vt.* to reimburse, repay.

Rimborso [reem-borr'soh] *nm.* reimbursement, repayment.

Rimbrotto [reem-brot'toh] *nm.* rebuke, reproach.

Rimediare [reem-may-dee-ah'ray] *vt.* to make up for, (find a) remedy (for).

Rimedio [ree-may'dee-oh] *nm.* cure, remedy.

Rimembranza [ree-mem-brahn'tsah] *nf.* remembrance.

Rimeritare [ree-may-ree-tah'ray] *vt.* to recompense, reward.

Rimescola/re [ree-mess-koh-lah'ray] *vt.* to mingle, mix (up), shuffle (cards); —rsi *vr.* to be upset. [garage, shed]

Rimessa [ree-mess'sah] *nf.*

Rimesso [ree-mess'soh] *a.* meek, recovered (in health), submissive; r. a nuovo [ah noo-oh'voh] done up.

Rimestare [ree-mess-tah'ray] *vt.* to stir up.

Rimette/re [ree-met'tay-ray] *vt.* to do up, forgive, lose,

put back, refer, submit; —rsi *vr.* to recover, resume, set oneself again to.

Rimontare [ree-mon-tah'ray] *vt. and i.* to go back, mend, remount.

Rimorchiare [ree-morr-kee-ah'ray] *vt.* to tow.

Rimorchiatore [ree-morr-kee-ah-toh'ray] *nm.* (*naut.*) tug-boat.

Rimorchio [ree-morr'kee-oh] *nm.* tow(ing), trailer.

Rimorso [ree-morr'soh] *nm.* remorse.

Rimostranza [ree-moss-trahnt'sah] *nf.* complaint, protest, remonstrance.

Rimostrare [ree-moss-trah'ray] *vt.* to show again; *vi.* to remonstrate.

Rimozione [ree-moh-tsee-oh'nay] *nf.* removal.

Rimpatriare [reem-pah-tree-ah'ray] *vt. and i.* to repatriate.

Rimpetto: *v.* dirimpetto.

Rimpiangere [reem-pee-ahn'jay-ray] *vt.* to lament, regret.

Rimpianto [reem-pee-ahn'toh] *nm.* mourning, regret.

Rimpicciolire [reem-peech-choh-lee'ray] *vt. and i.* to lessen.

Rimprovera/re [reem-proh-vay-rah'ray] *vt.* to blame, reproach; —rsi *vr.* to blame oneself, repent.

Rimprovero [reem-proh'vay-roh] *nm.* rebuke, reproach.

Rimunerare [ree-moo-nay-rah'ray] *vt.* to remunerate, reward.

Rimuovere [ree-moo-oh'vay-ray] *vt.* to deter, remove.

Rinascere [ree-nah'shay-ray] *vi.* to be revived, come to life again, return, spring up again.

Rinascimento [ree-nah-shee-men'toh] *nm.* renaissance, rebirth, revival.

Rincalzare [reen-kahlt-sah´ ray] *vt.* to set (a plant), tuck in.

Rincantucciarsi [reen-kahn-tooch-chahr´see] *vr.* to cower, hide oneself.

Rincarare [reen-kah-rah´ ray] *vt.* to raise (prices); *vi.* to grow dearer.

Rincaro [reen-kah´roh] *nm.* rise in prices.

Rincasare [reen-kah-sah´ ray] *vi.* to return home.

Rinchiudere [reen-kee-oo´ day-ray] *vt.* to shut up.

Rincorrere [reen-korr´ray-ray] *vt.* to chase, pursue, run after.

Rincorsa [reen-korr´sah] *nf.* run.

Rincrescere [reen-kray´shay-ray] *v.imp.* to be sorry, regret.

Rincrescimento [reen-kray-shee-men´toh] *nm.* regret.

Rincrudire [reen-kroo-dee´ ray] *vt.* to aggravate, embitter; *vi.* to get worse.

Rinculare [reen-koo-lah´ray] *vi.* to draw back, recoil.

Rinfacciare [reen-fahch-chah´ray] *vt.* to cast in one's teeth, taunt.

Rinforzare [reen-fort-sah´ ray] *vt.* to make stronger, prop up, reinforce.

Rinforzo [reen-fort´soh] *nm.* reinforcement.

Rinfranca/re [reen-frahng-kah´ray] *vt.* to reanimate; —rsi *vr.* to pluck up courage, take heart again.

Rinfresca/re [reen-fress-kah´ ray] *vt.* to cool, refresh, restore; *vi.* to get cooler; —rsi *vr.* to take refreshment.

Rinfresco [reen-fress´koh] *nm.* refreshments (*pl.*).

Rinfusa, alla [ahl´lah reen-foo´zah] *ad.* higgledy-piggledy, in confusion.

Ringhiare [reeng-ghee-ah´ ray] *vi.* to growl, snarl.

Ringhiera [reeng-ghee-ay´ rah] *nf.* banisters (*pl.*), railing.

Ringiovanire [reen-joh-vah-nee´ray] *vt.* to make young(er), rejuvenate; *vi.* to grow younger.

Ringraziamenti [reen-grah-tsee-ah-men´tee] *nm.* (*pl.*) thanks (*pl.*).

Ringraziare [reen-grah-tsee-ah´ray] *vt.* to thank.

Rinnegamento [reen-nay-gah-men´toh] *nm.* denying, disowning.

Rinnegare [reen-nay-gah´ ray] *vt.* to deny, disown.

Rinnegato [reen-nay-gah´ toh] *nm.* renegade, traitor.

Rinnovabile [reen-noh-vah´ bee-lay] *a.* renewable.

Rinnovamento [reen-noh-vah-men´toh] *nm.* renewal, revival.

Rinnovare [reen-noh-vah´ ray] *vt.* to renew, renovate, renovate. [renewal.

Rinnovo [reen-noh´voh] *nm.*

Rinoceronte [ree-noh-chay-ron´tay] *nm.* rhinoceros.

Rinomanza [ree-noh-mahnt´ sah] *nf.* fame, renown.

Rinomato [ree-noh-mah´toh] *a.* famous, renowned.

Rinsanire [reen-sah-nee´ray] *vi.* to recover (one's health).

Rintanarsi [reen-tah-nahr´ see] *vr.* to hide, shut oneself up.

Rintoccare [reen-tock-kah´ ray] *vi.* to toll.

Rintocco [reen-tock´koh] *nm.* knell, stroke of (bell), tolling.

Rintracciare [reen-trahch-chah´ray] *vt.* to find (out), trace.

Rintronare [reen-troh-nah´ ray] *vt. and i.* to deafen, shake.

Rintuzzare [reen-toot-zah´ ray] *vt.* to abate, blunt.

Rinun/zia [ree-noon´tsee-ah]

—cia ['chah] *nf.* renunciation, retirement.

Rinun/ziare [ree-noon-tsee-ah'ray], —**ciare** [chah'ray] *vt. and i.* to give up, renounce.

Rinvenimento [reen-vay-nee-men'toh] *nm.* discovery, recovery.

Rinvenire [reen-vay-nee'ray] *vt.* to discover, find (out); *vi.* to recover one's senses.

Rinviare [reen-vee-ah'ray] *vt.* to adjourn, defer, postpone, put off.

Rinvigori/re [reen-vee-goh-ree'ray] *vt.* to make strong(er); —**rsi** *vr.* to grow strong(er).

Rinvio [reen-vee'oh] *nm.* adjournment, postponement.

Rio [ree'oh] *nm. (poet.)* brook; *a.* wicked.

Rione [ree-oh'nay] *nm.* part (of a town), quarter, ward.

Riordinare [ree-orr-dee-nah'ray] *vt.* to put in order, rearrange, reorganise.

Ripa [ree'pah] *nf.* bank, precipice.

Riparabile [ree-pah-rah'bee-lay] *a.* (that) can be mended, repaired.

Ripara/re [ree-pah-rah'ray] *vt.* to mend, protect, repair, shelter; *vi.* to make up for, remedy, take shelter; —**rsi** *vr.* to protect oneself.

Riparazione [ree-pah-rah-tsee-oh'nay] *nf.* reparation, repair; **esami di** [ay-zah'mee dee] r. *nm. (pl.)* second session (of examinations).

Riparo [ree-pah'roh] *nm.* cover, defence, shelter.

Ripartire [ree-pahr-tee'ray] *vt.* to distribute, divide, share; *vi.* to start again.

Ripartizione [ree-pahr-tee-tsee-oh'nay] *nf.* distribution, division.

Ripetere [ree-pay'tay-ray] *vt.* to repeat.

Ripetitore [ree-pay-tee-toh'ray] *nm.* coach, private teacher, repeater.

Ripetizione [ree-pay-tee-tsee-oh'nay] *nf.* coaching, private lesson, repetition.

Ripiano [ree-pee-ah'noh] *nm.* level place, plateau.

Ripicco [ree-peek'koh] *nm.* pique.

Ripido [ree'pee-doh] *a.* steep.

Ripiega/re [ree-pee-ay-gah'ray] *vt.* to fold (again); *vi.* to give ground, retire; —**rsi** *vr.* to become bent.

Ripiego [ree-pee-ay'goh] *nm.* expedient, remedy, shift.

Ripieno [ree-pee-ay'noh] *nm.* stuffing; *a.* full, stuffed (with).

Riporre [ree-porr'ray] *vt.* to conceal, hide, put away (back), set.

Riporta/re [ree-porr-tah'ray] *vt.* to bring again (back), (*com.*) carry forward, get, report; —**rsi** *vr.* to refer.

Riporto [ree-porr'toh] *nm.* (*com.*) balance forward.

Riposa/re [ree-poh-sah'ray] *vt.* to put down; *vi.* and *r.* to rest.

Ripostiglio [ree-poss-teel'yoh] *nm.* hiding-place, lumber-room, place to put things in.

Riprendere [ree-pren'day-ray] *vt.* to improve, resume, take again; *vi.* to begin again, reply, retort.

Ripresa [ree-pray'sah] *nf.* recovery, renewal, resumption, revival.

Ripristinare [ree-pree-stee-nah'ray] *vt.* to restore.

Riprodur/re [ree-proh-door'ray] *vt.* to reproduce; —**rsi** *vr.* to recur, return.

Riproduzione [ree-proh-doo-tsee-oh'nay] *nf.* reproduction.

Riprova [ree-proh'vah] *nf.* confirmation, new proof.

Riprovare [ree-proh-vah'ray] vt. to blame, experience again, try again.

Ripudiare [ree-poo-dee-ah'ray] vt. to reject, repudiate.

Ripugnanza [ree-poon-yahnt'sah] nf. aversion, reluctance.

Ripugnare [ree-poon-yah'ray] v.imp. to be repugnant.

Ripulsa [ree-pool'sah] nf. refusal, repulse.

Risaia [ree-sah'yah] nf. rice-field.

Risalire [ree-sah-lee'ray] vt. to ascend; vi. to go up, go back to, rise.

Risaltare [ree-sahl-tah'ray] vt. and i. to jump again; vi. to stand out.

Risalto [ree-sahl'toh] nm. relief, vividness; **dare** [dah'ray] **r.** vt. to lay stress, make stand out, show up.

Risanamento [ree-sah-nah-men'toh] nm. healing, reclamation, recovery, reformation.

Risanare [ree-sah-nah'ray] vt. to cure, heal, reclaim, reform.

Risarcimento [ree-sahr-chee-men'toh] nm. compensation, indemnification.

Risarcire [ree-sahr-chee'ray] vt. to compensate, heal, indemnify.

Risata [ree-zah'tah] nf. laugh(ter).

Riscaldamento [ree-skahl-dah-men'toh] nm. heating.

Riscalda/re [ree-skahl-dah'ray] vt. to heat, warm; —**rsi** vr. to get hot, warm.

Riscattare [ree-skaht-tah'ray] vt. to ransom, redeem.

Riscatto [ree-skaht'toh] nm. ransom, redemption.

Rischiara/re [ree-skee-ah-rah'ray] vt. to enlighten, illuminate, light up; —**rsi** vr. to brighten, clear up.

Rischiare [ree-skee-ah'ray] vt. to risk; vi. to run the risk. [risk.

Rischio [ree'skee-oh] nm.

Risciacquare [ree-shahk-kwah'ray] vt. to rinse.

Riscontrare [ree-skon-trah'ray] vt. to check, compare, find, notice.

Riscontro [ree-skon'troh] nm. comparison, draught.

Riscossa [ree-skoss'sah] nf. insurrection, recovery.

Riscuote/re [ree-skwoo-oh'tay-ray] vt. to draw (money), get, receive, rouse, shake; —**rsi** vr. to start, be startled.

Risentimento [ree-sen-tee-men'toh] nm. resentment.

Risenti/re [ree-sen-tee'ray] vt. to feel again, hear again, experience, feel, suffer; vi. to feel effect, show traces; —**rsi** vr. to come to oneself, wake up; —**rsi di** [dee] vr. to resent.

Risentito [ree-sen-tee'toh] a. angry, resentful.

Riserbo [ree-sehr'boh] nm. discretion, self-restraint.

Riserva [ree-sehr'vah] nf. reservation, reserve; **di** [dee] **r.** a. spare.

Riserva/re [ree-sehr-vah'ray] vt. to keep, lay by, reserve; —**rsi** vr. to reserve (to) oneself.

Riservatezza [ree-sehr-vah-tet'sah] nf. discretion, prudence.

Riservato [ree-sehr-vah'toh] a. confidential, private, reserved.

Riservista [ree-sehr-vee'stah] nm. reservist.

Risibile [ree-zee'bee-lay] a. laughable, ridiculous.

Risiedere [ree-see-ay'day-ray] vi. to reside.

Riso [ree'zoh] nm. laugh(ter).

Riso [ree'soh] nm. rice.

Risoluto [ree-soh-loo'toh] a. determined, resolute, resolved.

Risoluzione [ree-soh-loo-tsee-oh'nay] nf. resolution, solution.

Risolve/re [ree-soll'vay-ray] vt. to resolve, settle, solve; —rsi vr. to decide, end, make up one's mind.

Risonanza [ree-soh-nahnt'sah] nf. resonance, sound.

Risonare [ree-soh-nah'ray] vt. to ring again; vi. to echo, resound, ring.

Risorgere [ree-sorr'jay-ray] vi. to rise (again).

Risorgimento [ree-sorr-jee-men'toh] nm. renascence, revival.

Risorsa [ree-sorr'sah] nf. resource.

Risotto [ree-sot'toh] nm. boiled rice served with sauce, etc.

Risovvenirsi [ree-sov-vay-neer'see] vr. to remember.

Risparmiare [ree-spahr-mee-ah'ray] vt. to save, spare.

Risparmio [ree-spahr'mee-oh] nm. saving.

Rispettare [ree-spet-tah'ray] vt. to respect.

Rispettoso [ree-spet-toh'soh] a. respectful.

Risplendere [ree-splen'day-ray] vi. to glitter, shine.

Rispondere [ree-spon'day-ray] vt. and i. to agree with, answer, reply.

Risposta [ree-sposs'tah] nf. answer, reply. [fray]

Rissa [rees'sah] nf. brawl.

Ristabili/re [ree-stah-bee-lee'ray] vt. to re-establish, restore; —rsi vr. to recover one's health.

Ristampa [ree-stahm'pah] nf. (typ.) new impression; il libro è in [eel lee'broh ay een] r. the book is being reprinted.

Ristorante [ree-stoh-rahn'tay] nm. refreshment-room, restaurant.

Ristora/re [ree-stoh-rah'ray] vt. to refresh, restore; —rsi vr. to eat, refresh oneself, rest.

Ristoro [ree-stoh'roh] nm. refreshment, relief, rest.

Ristrettezza [ree-stret-tet'sah] nf. narrowness, shortness; r. di mezzi [dee med'zee] lack of means, straitened circumstances.

Ristretto [ree-stret'toh] a. limited, narrow, restricted.

Risucchio [ree-sook'kee-oh] nm. eddy, swirl.

Risultare [ree-sool-tah'ray] vi. to follow, result, spring from.

Risultato [ree-sool-tah'toh] nm. result.

Risurrezione [ree-soor-ray-tsee-oh'nay] nf. resurrection.

Risuscitare [ree-soo-shee-tah'ray] vt. and i. to return to life, resuscitate, revive.

Risveglia/re [ree-svayl-yah'ray] vt. to (a)wake, excite, rouse, stir up; —rsi vr. to wake up.

Risveglio [ree-svayl'yoh] nm. awakening, revival.

Ritaglio [ree-tahl'yoh] nm. clipping, cutting; ritagli di tempo [ree-tahl'yee dee tem'poh] (pl.) spare time.

Ritardare [ree-tahr-dah'ray] vt. to defer, delay, put off, retard; vi. to be late, delay.

Ritardatario [ree-tahr-dah-tah'ree-oh] nm. laggard, latecomer.

Ritardo [ree-tahr'doh] nm. delay; essere in [ess'say-ray een] r. vi. to be late.

Ritegno [ree-tayn'yoh] nm. reserve, restraint.

Ritene/re [ree-tay-nay'ray] vt. to keep back, withhold; vt. and i. to consider, hold, think; —rsi *vr.* to consider oneself, restrain oneself.

Ritenuta [ree-tay-noo'tah] *nf.* deduction.

Ritira/re [ree-tee-rah'ray] *vt.* to retract, take back, withdraw; —rsi *vr.* to retire, retreat, withdraw.

Ritirata [ree-tee-rah'tah] *nf.* closet, retreat, w.c.

Ritiro [ree-tee'roh] *nm.* retreat, withdrawal.

Ritmo [reet'moh] *nm.* measure, rhythm.

Rito [ree'toh] *nm.* custom, rite, usage.

Ritocco [ree-tock'koh] *nm.* (finishing) touch.

Ritornare [ree-torr-nah'ray] *vi.* to come (go) back, return.

Ritornello [ree-torr-nell'loh] *nm.* refrain.

Ritorno [ree-torr'noh] *nm.* recurrence, return; biglietto di andata e [beel-yet'toh dee ahn-dah'tah ay] r., return ticket; essere di [ess'say-ray dee] r. *vi.* to be back.

Ritrar/re [ree-trahr'ray] *vt.* to draw back, get, represent, reproduce; —rsi *vr.* to give up, withdraw.

Ritratta/re [ree-traht-tah'-ray] *vt.* to recall, retract, withdraw; —rsi *vr.* to withdraw one's words.

Ritratto [ree-traht'toh] *nm.* image, picture, portrait.

Ritroso [ree-troh'soh] *a.* bashful, coy, reluctant, shy; a [ah] r. *ad.* backwards.

Ritrova/re [ree-troh-vah'ray] *vt.* to find again, recover; —rsi *vr.* to be present, find oneself.

Ritrovo [ree-troh'voh] *nm.* haunt, meeting-place.

Ritto [reet'toh] *a.* erect, straight, upright.

Rituale [ree-too-ah'lay] *a.* customary, ritual.

Riunione [ree-oo-nee-oh'nay] *nf.* gathering, meeting.

Riuni/re [ree-oo-nee'ray] *vt.* to bring together, combine, gather, unite; —rsi *vr.* to be united, meet.

Riuscire [ree-oo-shee'ray] *vi.* to go out again; be able, be successful, manage, succeed.

Riuscita [ree-oo-shee'tah] *nf.* result, success.

Riva [ree'vah] *nf.* bank, shore.

Rivale [ree-vah'lay] *nm. and f. and a.* competitor, rival.

Rivalità [ree-vah-lee-tah'] *nf.* rivalry. [revenge.

Rivalsa [ree-vahl'sah] *nf.*

Rivedere [ree-vay-day'ray] *vt.* to correct, revise, see again; r. bozze [bot'say] to read proofs.

Rivelare [ree-vay-lah'ray] *vt.* to display, reveal, show.

Rivelazione [ree-vay-lah-tsee-oh'nay] *nf.* revelation.

Rivendere [ree-ven'day-ray] *vt.* to resell, retail.

Rivendicare [ree-ven-dee-kah'ray] *vt.* to claim, vindicate.

Rivendita [ree-ven'dee-tah] *nf.* resale, shop.

Riverbero [ree-vehr'bay-roh] *nm.* reflection, reverberation.

Riverente [ree-vay-ren'tay] *a.* respectful, reverent.

Riverenza [ree-vay-ren'tsah] *nf.* curtsey, reverence.

Riverire [ree-vay-ree'ray] *vt.* to pay one's respects to, respect, venerate.

Riversa/re [ree-vehr-sah'ray] *vt.* to pour (out), throw; —rsi *vr.* to flow, pour, rush.

Riversione [ree-vehr-see-oh'nay] *nf.* reversion.

Riverso [ree-vehr'soh] *a.* on one's back.

Rivestimento [ree-vess-tee-men'toh] *nm.* covering (external), lining (internal).

Rivestire [ree-vess-tee′ray] *vt.* to cover, dress again, line.

Riviera [ree-vee-ay′rah] *nf.* coast.

Rivincita [ree-veen′chee-tah] *nf.* return match, revenge.

Rivista [ree-vee′stah] *nf.* magazine, parade, review.

Rivo [ree′voh] (*poet.*) *nm.* brook, stream.

Rivolge/re [ree-voll′jay-ray] *vt.* to turn; r. la parola [lah pah-roh′lah] *vi.* to address; —rsi *vr.* to apply, turn.

Rivolgimento [ree-voll-jee-men′toh] *nm.* change, upheaval.

Rivolta [ree-voll′tah] *nf.* insurrection, rebellion, revolt.

Rivolta/re [ree-voll-tah′ray] *vt.* to disgust, revolt, turn (again), turn inside out; —rsi *vr.* to rebel, revolt, turn.

Rivoltella [ree-voll-tell′lah] *nf.* revolver.

Rivoluzionario [ree-voh-loo-tsee-oh-nah′ree-oh] *nm. and a.* revolutionary.

Rivoluzione [ree-voh-loo-tsee-oh′nay] *nf.* revolution.

Roba [roh′bah] *nf.* cloth, goods (*pl.*), material, things (*pl.*); r. da chiodi [dah kee-oh′dee] bad lot (*person*), rubbish (*thing*).

Robustezza [roh-boo-stet′sah] *nf.* robustness, strength.

Robusto [roh-boo′stoh] *a.* robust, strong, sturdy.

Rocca [rock′kah] *nf.* distaff, fortress, rock, stronghold.

Rocchetto [rock-ket′toh] *nm.* reel, (*eccl.*) surplice.

Roccia [rohch′chah] *nf.* cliff, rock.

Roccioso [rohch-choh′soh] *a.* rocky.

Roco [roh′koh] *a.* hoarse.

Rode/re [roh′day-ray] *vt.* to corrode, gnaw, nibble; —rsi *vr.* to be worried.

Rodimento [roh-dee-men′toh] *nm.* anxiety, gnawing, worry.

Rododendro [roh-doh-den′droh] *nm.* rhododendron.

Rogazioni [roh-gah-tsee-oh′nee] *nf.* (*pl.*) Rogation Days.

Rogna [rohn′yah] *nf.* mange, scab.

Rognone [rohn-yoh′nay] *nm.* kidney (animals).

Rogo [roh′goh] *nm.* fire, stake.

Romano [roh-mah′noh] *nm. and a.* Roman.

Romantico [roh-mahn′tee-koh] *nm.* romanticist; *a.* romantic.

Romanza [roh-mahnt′sah] *nf.* ballad, song.

Romanziere [roh-mahn-tsee-ay′ray] *nm.* novelist.

Romanzo [roh-mahnt′soh] *nm.* novel, romance.

Rombare [rom-bah′ray] *vi.* to roar. [thunder.

Rombo [rom′boh] *nm.* roar,

Romitaggio [roh-mee-tah′djoh] *nm.* hermitage.

Romito [roh-mee′toh] *a.* lonely, solitary.

Rompere [rom′pay-ray] *vt. and v.* to break.

Rompicapo [rom-pee-kah′poh] *nm.* puzzle, worry.

Rompicollo [rom-pee-koll′loh] *nm.* thoughtless person; a [ah] r. ad. headlong.

Rompighiaccio [rom-pee-ghee-ahch′choh] *nm.* icebreaker.

Roncola [rong′koh-lah] *nf.* pruning-knife.

Ronda [ron′dah] *nf.* (*mil.*) patrol, rounds.

Rondine [ron′dee-nay] *nf.* swallow.

Rondone [ron-doh′nay] *nm.* swift (bird).

Ronzare [ron-tsah′ray] *vi.* to buzz, hum.

Ronzino [ron-tsee′noh] *nm.* jade, worn-out horse.

Ronzio   [ron-tsee'oh] nm. buzzing, humming.

Rorido   [roh'ree-doh]   a. dewy. v. **Rugiadoso**.

Rosa   [roh'zah]   nf. rose; color [koh-lorr'] r. nm. pink.

Rosaio   [roh-zah'yoh]   nm. rose-bush, rose-tree.

Rosario   [roh-zah'ree-oh] nm. beads (pl.), rosary.

Roseo   [roh'zay-oh] a. rosy.

Roseto   [roh-zay'toh]   nm. rose-garden.

Rosicchiare   [roh-seek-kee-ah'ray] vt. to eat, gnaw, nibble.

Rosmarino   [ross-mah-ree'noh] nm. rosemary.

Rosolare   [roh-zoh-lah'ray] vt. to brown (the roast).

Rosolia   [roh-zoh-lee'ah] nf. (med.) German measles.

Rospo   [ross'poh]   nm. toad.

Rossastro   [ross-sahs'troh], **rossiccio** [ross-seech'choh] a. reddish.   [red.

Rosso   [ross'soh]   nm. and a.

Rossore   [ross-soh'ray]   nm. blush, flush, redness.

Rosticceria   [ross-teech-chay-ree'ah] nf. cook-shop.

Rostro   [ross'troh]   nm. dais, rostrum.

Rotaia   [roh-tah'yah] nf. rail.

Rotare   [roh-tah'ray]   vi. to revolve, rotate.

Rotazione   [roh-tah-tsee-oh'nay] nf. rotation.

Rotola/re   [roh-toh-lah'ray] vt. and i. to roll (up); —rsi vr. to roll, wallow.

Rotolo   [roh'toh-loh]   nm. roll; andare a rotoli [ahn-dah'ray ah roh'toh-lee] vi. to go to rack and ruin.

Rotolone   [roh-toh-loh'nay] nm. tumble.

Rotondare   [roh-ton-dah'ray] vt. to make round.

Rotondità   [roh-ton-dee-tah'] nf. roundness, rotundity.

Rotondo   [roh-ton'doh] a. plump, round, rotund.

Rotta   [rot'tah]   nf. course, disorderly retreat, rout; a [ah] r. di collo [dee koll'loh] ad. at breakneck speed.

Rotta/me   [rot-tah'may] nm. fragment; — mi [mee] (pl.) fragments (pl.), rubbish, ruins (pl.), wreck.

Rotto   [rot'toh]   a. broken.

Rottura   [rot-too'rah]   nf. break, breaking-off, rupture.

Rovente   [roh-ven'tay]   a. burning, red-hot, stinging.

Rovere   [roh'vay-ray]   nm. oak.

Rovescia/re   [roh-vay-shah'ray] v to overthrow, over-turn, pour, upset; —rsi vr. to be overturned, capsize, fall (down).

Rovescio   [roh-vay'shoh] nm. disaster, reverse, wrong side; a. (turned) inside-out, upside-down; a [ah] r. ad. inside-out, upside-down, the wrong way.

Rovina   [roh-vee'nah] nf. ruin.

Rovina/re   [roh-vee-nah'ray] vt. to ruin; vi. to fall with a crash; —rsi vr. to be ruined, spoilt.

Rovinìo   [roh-vee-nee'oh] nm. crash.

Rovinoso   [roh-vee-noh'soh] a. ruinous.

Rovistare   [roh-vee-stah'ray] vt. and i. to rummage, search.

Rovo   [roh'voh] nm. blackberry bush, bramble.

Rozzezza   [rod-zet'sah] nf. roughness, rudeness.

Rozzo   [rod'zoh] a. rough, rude.

Ruba, a   [ah roo'bah] ad. in great quantities.

Rubare   [roo-bah'ray] vt. to steal (from).

Rubicondo   [roo-bee-kon'doh] a. rubicund, ruddy.

Rubinetto   [roo-bee-net'toh] nm. tap.

Rubino [roo-bee'noh] *nm.* ruby.

Rublo [roo'bloh] *nm.* rouble.

Rubrica [roo-bree'kah] *nf.* address-book, column, rubric.

Rude [roo'day] *a.* coarse, cruel, rough, rude.

Ruderi [roo'day-ree] *nm.* (*pl.*) remains, ruins (*pl.*).

Rudimentale [roo-dee-men-tah'lay] *a.* rudimentary.

Rudimento [roo-dee-men'toh] *nm.* element, first principle, rudiment.

Ruffiano [roof-fee-ah'noh] *nm.* pander, procurer.

Ruga [roo'gah] *nf.* wrinkle.

Ruggine [roo'djee-nay] *nf.* blight, enmity, rust.

Rugginoso [roo-djee-noh'soh] *a.* rusty.

Ruggire [roo-djee'ray] *vi.* to roar.

Ruggito [roo-djee'toh] *nm.* roar(ing). [dew.]

Rugiada [roo-jah'dah] *nf.*

Rugiadoso [roo-jah-doh'soh] *a.* dewy.

Rugoso [roo-goh'soh] *a.* wrinkled.

Ruina, etc : *v.* **rovina**, etc.

Rullare [rool-lah'ray] *vi.* to roll. [rolling.]

Rullio [rool-lee'oh] *nm.*

Rullo [rool'loh] *nm.* cylinder, drum, roll.

Ruminare [roo-mee-nah'ray] *vt. and i.* to chew the cud, ponder, ruminate.

Ruminazione [roo-mee-nah-tsee-oh'nay] *nf.* rumination.

Rumore [roo-moh'ray] *nm.* noise.

Rumoreggiare [roo-moh-ray-djah'ray] *vi.* to make a noise, rumble, talk loudly.

Rumoroso [roo-moh-roh'soh] *a.* loud, noisy.

Ruolo [roo-oh'loh] *nm.* list, roll; di [dee] r. *a. and ad.* regular, on the staff.

Ruota [roo-oh'tah], **rota** [roh'tah] *nf.* wheel.

Rupe [roo'pay] *nf.* precipice, rock.

Rurale [roo-rah'lay] *nm.* countryman; *a.* rural.

Ruscello [roo-shell'loh] *nm.* brook.

Russare [roos-sah'ray] *vi.* to snore.

Russo [roos'soh] *nm. and a.* Russian.

Rustico [roo'stee-koh] *a.* rustic, unsociable.

Ruta [roo'tah] *nf.* rue (plant).

Ruvidezza [roo-vee-det'sah] *nf.* harshness, roughness.

Ruvido [roo'vee-doh] *a.* coarse, harsh, rough.

Ruzzare [rood-zah'ray] *vi.* to romp.

Ruzzolare [root-soh-lah'ray] *vi.* to roll, tumble down.

Ruzzolo/ne [root-soh-loh'nay] *nm.* fall, tumble; **—ni** [nee] *ad.* headlong.

S

Sabato [sah'bah-toh] *nm.* Saturday. [sand.]

Sabbia [sahb'bee-ah] *nf.*

Sabotaggio [sah-boh-tah'djoh] *nm.* sabotage.

Sabotare [sah-boh-tah'ray] *vt.* to sabotage, thwart.

Sacca [sahk'kah] *nf.* bag, (*mil.*) encircling movement.

Saccarina [sahk-kah-ree'nah] *nf.* saccharine.

Saccente [sahch-chen'tay] *nm.* wiseacre; *nf.* bluestocking; *a.* pedantic.

Saccheggiamento [sahk-kay-djah-men'toh] *nm.* pillaging, plundering.

Saccheggiare [sahk-kay-djah'ray] *vt.* to pillage, plunder, sack.

Saccheggio [sahk-kay'djoh] *nm.* plunder, sack.

Sacco [sahk'koh] *nm.* bag, sack; un [oon] s. di [dee] a lot of; mettere nel [met'tay-ray nell] s. *vt.* to outwit; vuotare il [voo-oh-tah'ray eel] s. *vi.* to speak one's mind.

Saccone [sahk-koh'nay] *nm.* straw mattress.

Sacerdote [sah-chehr-doh'tay] *nm.* priest.

Sacerdozio [sah-chehr-doh'tsee-oh] *nm.* priesthood.

Sacramentale [sah-krah-men-tah'lay] *a.* sacramental, solemn.

Sacramento [sah-krah-men'toh] *nm.* sacrament.

Sacrificare [sah-kree-fee-kah'ray] *vt. and i.* to devote, sacrifice.

Sacrifi/cio [sah-kree-fee'-choh], **—zio** [tsee-oh] *nm.* offering, privation, sacrifice.

Sacrilegio [sah-kree-lay'joh] *nm.* sacrilege.

Sacrilego [sah-kree'lay-goh] *a.* impious, sacrilegious.

Sacro [sah'kroh] *a.* holy, sacred.

Sacrosanto [sah-kroh-sahn'toh] *a.* indisputable, sacrosanct.

Saetta [sah-et'tah] *nf.* arrow, lightning, thunderbolt.

Saettare [sah-et-tah'ray] *vt.* to dart, shoot.

Saga [sah'gah] *nf.* legend, saga.

Sagace [sah-gah'chay] *a.* sagacious, shrewd, shrewd.

Saga/cia [sah-gah'chah], **—cità** [chee-tah'] *nf.* sagacity, shrewdness.

Saggezza [sah-djet'sah] *nf.* judiciousness, wisdom.

Saggiare [sah-djah'ray] *vt.* to test, try.

Saggio [sah'djoh] *nm.* essay (literary), example, pattern,

sample, specimen, test, trial; *a.* judicious, sage, wise.

Sagoma [sah'goh-mah] *nf.* mould, outline, shape.

Sagra [sah'grah] *nf.* annual feast (of patron saint).

Sagrato [sah-grah'toh] *nm.* hallowed ground (in front of church).

Sagrestano [sah-gress-tah'noh] *nm.* sexton.

Sagrestia [sah-gress-tee'ah] *nf.* sacristy, vestry.

Sala [sah'lah] *nf.* hall, room; s. d'aspetto [dah-spet'toh], waiting-room; s. da pranzo [dah prahnd'zoh] dining-room.

Salamandra [sah-lah-mahn'drah] *nf.* salamander.

Salame [sah-lah'may] *nm.* sausage.

Salare [sah-lah'ray] *vt.* to drysalt, salt.

Salariare [sah-lah-ree-ah'-ray] *vt.* to pay wages to.

Salario [sah-lah'ree-oh] *nm.* pay, wages.

Salasso [sah-lahs'soh] *nm.* blood-letting, extortion.

Saldare [sahl-dah'ray] *vt.* (*com.*) to settle; to solder, weld.

Saldezza [sahl-det'sah] *nf.* constancy, firmness, steadiness.

Saldo [sahl'doh] *nm.* (*com.*) balance, settlement; *a.* constant, firm, steady.

Sale [sah'lay] *nm.* salt, wit.

Salgemma [sahl-jem'mah] *nm.* rock-salt.

Salice [sah'lee-chay] *nm.* willow.

Saliente [sah-lee-en'tay] *nm.* (*mil.*) salient; *a.* salient, striking.

Saliera [sah-lee-ay'rah] *nf.* salt-cellar.

Salina [sah-lee'nah] *nf.* salt-mine, salt-pond.

Salire [sah-lee'ray] *vt. and i.*

to ascend, climb, go up, increase, mount, rise.

Saliscendi [sah-lee-shen'dee] *nm.* latch; finestra a [fee-ness'trah ah] *s. nf.* sash-window.

Salita [sah-lee'tah] *nf.* ascent, rise, slope.

Saliva [sah-lee'vah] *nf.* saliva.

Salma [sahl'mah] *nf.* corpse.

Salmista [sahl-mee'stah] *nm.* psalmist.

Salmo [sahl'moh] *nm.* psalm.

Salmone [sahl-moh'nay] *nm.* salmon.

Salnitro [sahl-nee'troh] *nm.* nitre, saltpetre.

Salone [sah-loh'nay] *nm.* hall, reception-room.

Salotto [sah-lot'toh] *nm.* drawing-room, sitting-room.

Salpare [sahl-pah'ray] *vi.* to (set) sail, weigh anchor.

Salsa [sahl'sah] *nf.* sauce.

Salsiccia [sahl-seech'chah] *nf.* sausage.

Saltare [sahl-tah'ray] *vt.* to clear, jump (over), skip; *vi.* to jump, leap, spring.

Salterellare [sahl-tay-rell-lah'ray] *vi.* to hop (about), skip (about).

Saltimbanco [sahl-teem-bahng'koh] *nm.* acrobat, tumbler.

Salto [sahl'toh] *nm.* bound, jump, leap; s. mortale [morr-tah'lay], somersault.

Salubre [sah-loo'bray] *a.* healthy, wholesome.

Salubrità [sah-loo-bree-tah'] *nf.* healthiness, wholesomeness.

Salumiere [sah-loo-mee-ay'ray] *nm.* pork-butcher.

Salutare [sah-loo-tah-ray] *vt.* to greet, salute, say good-bye to, welcome; *a.* moral, salutary.

Salute [sah-loo'tay] *nf.* health, safety, salvation; casa

di [kah'sah dee] s. nursing-home.

Saluto [sah-loo'toh] *nm.* greeting, salute; —ti [tee] (*pl.*) regards (*pl.*).

Salva [sahl'vah] *nf.* discharge, salvo, volley.

Salvacondotto [sahl-vah-kon-dot'toh] *nm.* safe-conduct.

Salvadanaio [sahl-vah-dah-nah'yoh] *nm.* money-box.

Salvagente [sahl-vah-jen'tay] *nm.* life-belt, (street-) island.

Salvaguardia [sahl-vah-gwahr'dee-ah] *nf.* protection, safeguard.

Salva/re [sahl-vah'ray] *vt.* to rescue, save; —rsi *vr.* to save oneself, take refuge.

Salvataggio [sahl-vah-taht'djoh] *nm.* rescue, salvage.

Salvatore [sahl-vah-toh'ray] *nm.* rescuer, saver, Saviour.

Salvazione [sahl-vah-tsee-oh'nay] *nf.* salvation.

Salvezza [sahl-vet'sah] *nf.* escape, safety, salvation.

Salvia [sahl'vee-ah] *nf.* sage (plant).

Salvo [sahl'voh] *a.* safe, secure; sano e [sah'noh ay] s. safe and sound; in [een] s. *ad.* in a safe place; *pr.* except, save.

Sambuco [sahm-boo'koh] *nm.* elder-tree.

San [sahn] *a.* Saint.

Sanare [sah-nah'ray] *vt.* to cure, heal, make healthy.

Sanatorio [sah-nah-toh'ree-oh] *nm.* sanatorium.

Sancire [sahn-chee'ray] *vt.* to decree, ratify, sanction.

Sandalo [sahn'dah-loh] *nm.* (naut.) hoy, sandal, sandal-wood.

Sangue [sahng'gway] *nm.* blood, extraction, family; s. freddo [fred'doh] composure.

Sanguinario [sahng-gweenah'ree-oh] a. bloodthirsty, sanguinary.

Sanguigno [sahng-gween'-yoh] a. (of) blood, blood-shot, sanguine.

Sanguinolento [sahng-gwee-noh-len'toh] a. bleeding, blood-stained.

Sanguinoso [sahng-gwee-noh'soh] a. bloody.

Sanguisuga [sahng-gwee-soo'gah] nf. leech, (fig.) extortioner.

Sanità [sah-nee-tah'] nf. health, sanity, soundness.

Sanitario [sah-nee-tah'ree-oh] nm. doctor; a. medical, sanitary.

Sano [sah'noh] a. healthy, sane, sound, wholesome.

Santificare [sahn-tee-fee-kah'ray] vt. to consecrate, hallow, sanctify.

Santità [sahn-tee-tah'] nf. holiness, sanctity. [a. holy.

Santo [sahn'toh] nm. saint;

Santuario [sahn-too-ah'ree-oh] nm. sanctuary, shrine.

Sanzionare [sahn-tsee-oh-nah'ray] vt. to authorize, sanction.

Sanzione [sahn-tsee-oh'nay] nf. ratification, sanction.

Sapere [sah-pay'ray] vt. and i. to be able (can), be acquainted with, get to know, hear, know (how to), learn, smell (of), taste (of); nm. knowledge, learning.

Sapiente [sah-pee-en'tay] nm. scholar; a. learned, well-informed, wise.

Sapienza [sah-pee-ent'sah] nf. learning, wisdom.

Sapone [sah-poh'nay] nm. soap.

Sapore [sah-poh'ray] nm. flavour, savour, taste.

Saporito [sah-poh-ree'toh], —roso [roh'soh] a. delicious, savoury.

Sarcasmo [sahr-kahs'moh] nm. sarcasm.

Sarcastico [sahr-kah'stee-koh] a. sarcastic.

Sarta [sahr'tah] nf. dressmaker

Sartie [sahr-tee'ay] nf. (pl.) (naut.) rigging, shrouds (pl.).

Sarto [sahr'toh] nm. tailor.

Sartoria [sahr-toh-ree'ah] nf. tailor's shop.

Sasso [sahs'soh] nm. stone; rimanere di [ree-mah-nay'ray dee] s. vi. to be astonished.

Satellite [sah-tell'lee-tay] nm. companion, follower, satellite.

Satira [sah'tee-rah] nf. lampoon, satire.

Satireggiare [sah-tee-ray-djah'ray] vt. to satirize.

Satollare [sah-toll-lah'ray] vt. to fill up, satiate.

Satollo [sah-toll'loh] a. full, overfed, satiated.

Saturare [sah-too-rah'ray] vt. to glut, saturate.

Saturo [sah'too-roh] a. saturated. [wisdom.

Saviezza [sah-vee-et'sah] nf.

Savio [sah'vee-oh] nm. sage; a. judicious, wise.

Sazia/re [sah-tsee-ah'ray] vt. to satiate, satisfy; —rsi vr. to get tired of.

Sazio [sah'tsee-oh] a. full, sated, satiated, tired.

Sbadato [sbah-dah'toh] a. careless, heedless, inattentive.

Sbadigliare [sbah-deel-yah'ray] vi. to gape, yawn.

Sbadiglio [sbah-deel'yoh] nm. gape, yawn.

Sbafo [sbah'foh] nm. scrounging.

Sbaglia/re [sbahl-yah'ray] vt. to mistake; s. strada [strah'dah] vi. to take the wrong turning; vi. and —rsi vr. to be mistaken, be wrong, make a mistake.

Sbaglio [sbahl'yoh] *nm.* blunder, error, mistake.

Sbalestrato [sbah-less-trah'toh] *a.* astray, lost.

Sballare [sbahl-lah'ray] *vt.* to unpack; *vi.* to tell lies, tell tall tales.

Sbalordire [sbah-lorr-dee'ray] *vt.* to amaze, astound, dumbfound; *vi.* to be amazed.

Sbalzare [sbahlt-sah'ray] *vt.* to cast out, dismiss, overthrow, remove.

Sbalzo [sbahlt'soh] *nm.* bound, leap, rush, sudden change; a sbalzi [ah sbahlt'see] *ad.* unevenly; by leaps.

Sbandare [sbahn-dah'ray] *vt.* to skid, break up, disband, disperse, (naut.) heel, list.

Sbaragliare [sbah-rahl-yah'ray] *vt.* to rout.

Sbaraglio [sbah-rahl'yoh] *nm.* defeat, risk, rout; allo [ahl'loh] s. *ad.* recklessly.

Sbarazza/re [sbah-raht-sah'ray] *vt.* to disembarass, rid; —rsi *vr.* to dispose of, get rid of.

Sbarcare [sbahr-kah'ray] *vt. and i.* to disembark, land; s. il lunario [eel loo-nah'ree-oh] *vi.* to make both ends meet.

Sbarco [sbahr'koh] *nm.* landing, unloading.

Sbarra [sbahr'rah] *nf.* bar.

Sbarrare [sbahr-rah'ray] *vt.* to bar, block up, obstruct, stop up; ad occhi sbarrati [ahd ock'kee sbahr-rah'tee] *ad.* with staring eyes.

Sbassamento [sbahs-sah-men'toh] *nm.* lowering.

Sbassare [sbahs-sah'ray] *vt.* to lower, reduce.

Sbatacchiare [sbah-tahk-kee-ah'ray] *vt.* to slam.

Sbattere [sbaht'tay-ray] *vt.* to fling, hurl, shake, toss, whip.

Sbiadire [sbee-ah-dee'ray] *vi.* to fade.

Sbieco [sbee-ay'koh] *a.* awry oblique; di [dee] s. *ad.* askance.

Sbigottimento [sbee-got-tee-men'toh] *nm.* discouragement, dismay.

Sbigottire [sbee-got-tee'ray] *vt.* to discourage, dismay.

Sbilancia/re [sbee-lahn-chah'ray] *vt.* to unbalance, unsettle; —rsi *vr.* to speak freely, spend beyond one's means.

Sbirciare [sbeer-chah'ray] *vt. and i.* to glance at, scan.

Sboccare [sbock-kah'ray] *vi.* to flow into, open into.

Sbocciare [sbohch-chah'ray] *vi.* to blossom, open.

Sbocco [sbock'koh] *nm.* mouth (of a river), outlet, way out.

Sbornia [sborr'nee-ah] *nf.* intoxication; prendere una [pren'day-ray oo'nah] s. *vi.* to get drunk.

Sborsare [sborr-sah'ray] *vt.* to disburse, lay out.

Sborso [sborr'soh] *nm.* disbursement, outlay, payment, to disburse, lay out.

Sbottona/re [sbot-toh-nah'ray] *vt.* to unbutton; —rsi *vr.* to unbutton one's clothes, unbosom oneself.

Sbozzare [sbot-sah'ray] *vt.* to rough out, shape roughly.

Sbraitare [sbrah-ee-tah'ray] *vi.* to bawl, shout.

Sbranare [sbrah-nah'ray] *vt.* to tear to pieces.

Sbriciola/re [sbree-choh-lah'ray] *vt.*—rsi *vr.* to crumble.

Sbriga/re [sbree-gah'ray] *vt.* to dispatch, finish; —rsi *vr.* to hurry up, make haste.

Sbrigliato [sbreel-yah'toh] *a.* lively, unbridled, wild.

Sbrogliare [sbrohl-yah'ray] *vt.* to disentangle, extricate.

Sbucare [sboo-kah'ray] *vi.* to come out, spring out.

...re [bocch-chah'ray] vi. to pare, peel, shell, skin.

...uffare [sboof-fah'ray] vi. to pant, puff.

Scabbia [skahb'bee-ah] nf. mange, scab, scabies.

Scabbioso [skahb-bee-oh'soh] a. scabby.

Scabroso [skah-broh'soh] a. difficult, rough, rugged, scabrous.

Scacchiera [skahk-kee-ay'rah] nf. chess-board, draughtboard.

Scacciare [skahch-chah'ray] vt. to dispel, drive out, expel.

Scac/co [skahk'koh] nm. check (at chess); —chi [kee] chess; a [ah] s. a. checked, chequered.

Scadente [skah-den'tay] a. inferior, of poor quality.

Scadenza [skah-den'sah] nf. (com.) maturity; a breve [in bray'vay] s. ad. in a short time.

Scadere [skah-day'ray] vi. (com.) to be due, expire, lose value, sink.

Scafandro [skah-fahn'droh] nm. diving apparatus.

Scaffale [skahf-fah'lay] nm. bookcase.

Scagionare [skah-joh-nah'ray] vt. to exculpate, justify.

Scaglia/re [skahl-yah'ray] vt. to fling, hurl, throw; —rsi vr. to hurl oneself, rush.

Scala [skah'lah] nf. ladder, staircase, stairs (pl.), scale.

Scalare [skah-lah'ray] vt. to scale, (com.) deduct.

Scalcinato [skahl-chee-nah'toh] a. seedy, shabby.

Scaldabagno [skahl-dah-bahn'yoh] nm. geyser.

Scalda/re [skahl-dah'ray] vt. to heat, warm; —rsi vr. to get excited, warm oneself.

Scaldavivande [skahl-dah-

vee-vahn'day] nm. chafingdish.

Scaldino [skahl-dee'noh] nm. hand-warmer, portable warming-pan.

Scalfire [skahl-fee'ray] vt. to graze, scratch.

Scalinata [skah-lee-nah'tah] nf. (flight of) steps.

Scalino [skah-lee'noh] nm. step.

Scalmanarsi [skahl-mah-nahr'see] vr. to get agitated, wear oneself out.

Scalo [skah'loh] nm. landing-place, stop; (rly.) s. merci [mehr-chee] goods station.

Scalpello [skahl-pell'loh] nm. chisel.

Scalpore [skahl-poh'ray] nm. ado, effect, excitement.

Scaltro [skahl'troh] a. artful, crafty, shrewd.

Scalzarsi [skahlt-sahr'see] vr. to take off shoes and stockings. [foot(ed).

Scalzo [skahlt'soh] a. bare-

Scambiare [skahm-bee-ah'ray] vt. to exchange, mistake.

Scambievole [skahm-bee-ay'voh-lay] a. mutual, reciprocal.

Scambio [skahm'bee-oh] nm. exchange; (rly.) points (pl.), switch.

Scampagnata [skahm-pahn-yah'tah] nf. country excursion.

Scampa/re [skahm-pah'ray] vt. to rescue, save; vi. to escape; —la bella [lah bell'lah] to have a narrow escape.

Scampo [skahm'poh] nm. escape, safety; shrimp (fish).

Scampolo [skahm'poh-loh] nm. remnant.

Scancellare: v. cancellare.

Scandagliare [skahn-dahl-yah'ray] vt. to sound.

Scandalizzare [skahn-dah-leed-zah'ray] vt. to scandalise, shock.

Scandalo [skahn'dah-loh] *nm.* scandal.

Scandaloso [skahn-dah-loh'soh] *a.* scandalous, shocking.

Scannare [skahn-nah'ray] *vt.* to butcher, cut someone's throat.

Scannellare [skahn-nell-lah'ray] *vt.* to channel.

Scanno [skahn'noh] *nm.* bench. seat.

Scansa/re [skahn-sah'ray] *vt.* to avoid, shun; **—rsi** *vr.* to get out of the way.

Scansia [skahn-see'ah] *nf.* bookcase, set of shelves.

Scantonare [skahn-toh-nah'ray] *vi.* to turn the corner.

Scapaccione [skah-pahch-choh'nay], **scappellotto** [skahp-pell-lot'toh] *nm.* slap, smack.

Scapestrato [skah-pess-trah'toh] *nm.* waster; *a.* dissolute, wasteful.

Scapigliare [skah-peel-yah'ray] *vt.* to ruffle.

Scapitare [skah-pee-tah'ray] *vi.* to lose.

Scapito [skah'pee-toh] *nm.* detriment, loss.

Scapolo [skah'poh-loh] *nm.* bachelor; *a.* unmarried (man).

Scappare [skahp-pah'ray] *vi.* to escape, run away.

Scappata [skahp-pah'tah] *nf.* escapade, escape, short call, trip.

Scarabeo [skah-rah-bay'oh] *nm.* beetle.

Scarabocchiare [skah-rah-bock-kee-ah'ray] *vt.* and *i.* to scrawl, scribble.

Scarabocchio [skah-rah-bock'kee-oh] *nm.* blot, scrawl.

Scarafaggio [skah-rah-fah'djoh] *nm.* beetle.

Scaramuccia [skah-rah-mooch'chah] *nf.* skirmish.

Scaraventa/re [skah-rah-ven-tah'ray] *vt.* to fling, hurl; **—rsi** *vr.* to rush out.

Scarcerare [skahr-chay-rah'ray] *vt.* to release (from prison).

Scarica [skah'ree-kah] *nf.* shower (of blows), discharge, volley.

Scaricare [skah-ree-kah'ray] *vt.* to discharge, unload.

Scarico [skah'ree-koh] *nm.* discharge, unloading; **tubo di** [too'boh dee] *s.* (*tech.*) exhaust-pipe; *a.* run down (of clock, etc.), unloaded.

Scarlattina [skahr-laht-tee'nah] *nf.* (*med.*) scarlet fever.

Scarlatto [skahr-laht'toh] *nm.* and *a.* scarlet.

Scarmigliare: *v.* **scapigliare.**

Scarno [skahr'noh] *a.* emaciated, lean, thin.

Scarpa [skahr-pah] *nf.* shoe.

Scarseggiare [skahr-say-djah'ray] *vi.* to be scarce, lack.

Scarsità [skahr-see-tah'] *nf.* dearth, lack, scarcity.

Scarso [skahr'soh] *a.* poor, scanty, scarce, short.

Scartare [skahr-tah'ray] *vt.* to cast aside, discard, reject.

Scarto [skahr'toh] *nm.* discard(ing), refuse; **di** [dee] *s. ad.* of inferior quality.

Scassinare [skahs-see-nah'ray] *vt.* to break in.

Scassinatore [skahs-see-nah-toh'ray] *nm.* burglar, house-breaker.

Scasso [skahs'soh] *nm.* house-breaking.

Scatena/re [skah-tay-nah'ray] *vt.* to cause, unchain; **—rsi** *vr.* to break loose, break out.

Scatola [skah'toh-lah] *nf.* box, tin.

Scattare [skaht-tah'ray] *vi.* to get angry, go off, spring up.

Scatto [skaht'toh] *nm.* explosion, outburst, spring.

Scaturire [skah-too-ree'ray] *vi.* to gush, spout, spring.

Scavalcare [skah-vahl-kah'-ray] vt. to climb over.

Scavare [skah-vah'ray] vt. to dig out, excavate.

Scavo [skah'voh] nm. excavation.

Scegliere [shell'yay-ray] vt. to choose, pick out, select.

Scellerato [shell-lay-rah'toh] nm. and a. wicked (man).

Scellino [shell-lee'noh] nm. shilling.

Scelta [shell'tah] nf. choice, selection.

Scelto [shell'toh] a. choice, picked, select(ed).

Scemare [shay-mah'ray] vt. to abate, diminish, lessen, reduce; vi. to decline, decrease, diminish, wane.

Scemo [shay-moh] nm. imbecile; a. foolish, stupid.

Scempio [shem'pee-oh] a. silly, single.

Scena [shay'nah] nf. scene; mettere in [met'tay-ray een] s. vt. (theat.) to produce, stage.

Scenario [shay-nah'ree-oh] nm. scenario, scenery.

Scendere [shen'day-ray] vt. and i. to come (go) down, descend.

Scenico [shay'nee-koh] a. scenic, stage.

Scernere [shehr'nay-ray] vt. to discern, distinguish.

Scervellarsi [shehr-vell-lahr'-see] vr. to cudgel (rack) one's brains.

Scettico [shet'tee-koh] nm. sceptic; a. sceptical.

Scettro [shet'troh] nm. sceptre.

Scevro [shay'vroh] a. exempt, free from.

Scheda [skay'dah] nf. card, form.

Scheggia [skay'djah] nf. splinter.

Scheggiare [skay-djah'ray] vt. —rsi vr. to splinter.

Scheletro [skay'lay-troh] nm. frame, skeleton.

Schema [skay'mah] nm. outline, plan, scheme, summary.

Scherma [skehr'mah] nf. fencing; -mo (moh) nm. screen (cinema, etc.).

Schermire [skehr-mee'ray] vi. to fence; —rsi vr. to defend oneself, parry.

Schernire [skehr-nee'ray] vt. to despise, flout, scoff at.

Scherno [skehr'noh] nm. derision, taunt.

Scherzare [skehrt-sah'ray] vi. to jest, joke, make fun.

Scherzo [skehrt'soh] nm. freak, jest, joke, trick.

Scherzoso [skehrt-soh'soh] a. facetious, joking, playful.

Schiaccianoci [skee-ahch-chah-noh'chee] nm. nutcrackers (pl.).

Schiaffeggiare [skee-ahf-fay-djah'ray] vt. to box one's ear, slap.

Schiaffo [skee-ahf'foh] nm. box on the ear, insult, slap.

Schiammazzare [skee-ah-maht-sah'ray] vi. to cackle, clamour squawk.

Schiantare [skee-ahn-tah'ray] vt. —rsi vr. to break.

Schiarimento [skee-ah-ree-men'toh] nm. clearing up, explanation.

Schiarire [skee-ah-ree'ray] vt. to clear up, explain; —rsi vr. to become clear, light, brighten, light up.

Schiatta [skee-aht'tah] nf. race, stock.

Schiavitù [skee-ah-vee-too'] nf. slavery.

Schiavo [skee-ah'voh] nm. -va [vah] nf. slave.

Schiena [skee-ay'nah] nf. back.

Schiera [skee-ay'rah] nf. band, group, rank.

Schiera/re [skee-ay-rah'ray] vt. —rsi vr. to draw up, side with.

Schiettezza [skee-ay-tet'sah] nf. frankness, sincerity.

Schietto [skee-et'toh] a. frank, genuine, plain, sincere.

Schifo [skee'foh] nm. disgust.

Schifoso [skee-foh'soh] a. disgusting, loathsome.

Schioppo [skee-op'poh] nm. gun.

Schiude/re [skee-oo'day-ray] vt. —rsi vr. to open.

Schiuma [skee-oo'mah] nf. dross, foam, froth, scum.

Schivare [skee-vah'ray] vt. and i. to avoid, shun.

Schivo [skee'voh] a. averse.

Schizzare [skeet-sah'ray] vt. to send out, sketch, squirt; vi. to gush out, squirt.

Schizzo [skeet'soh] nm. sketch, splash.

Scia [shee'ah] nf. track, wake.

Sciabola [shah'boh-lah] nf. sabre. [jackal.

Sciacallo [shah-kahl'loh] nm.

Sciacquare [shahk-kwah'ray] vt. to rinse.

Sciagura [shah-goo'rah] nf. disaster, misfortune.

Sciagurato [shah-goo-rah'toh] nm. wretch; a. unlucky, wretched.

Scialacquare [shah-lahk-kwah'ray] vt. to squander, waste.

Scialbo [shahl'boh] a. dim, faded, pale, wan.

Scialle [shahl'lay] nm. shawl.

Scialuppa [shah-loop'pah] nf. (naut.) launch.

Sciame [shah'may] nm. crowd, swarm.

Sciancato [shahng-kah'toh] nm. cripple; a. crippled, lop-sided. [scarf.

Sciarpa [shahr'pah] nf. sash,

Scibile [shee'bee-lay] nm. knowledge.

Scientifico [shen-tee'fee-koh] a. scientific.

Scienza [shent'sah] nf. knowledge, science.

Scienziato [shen-tsee-ah'toh] nm. scientist; a. learned.

Scimmia [sheem'mee-ah] nf. ape, monkey.

Scimmiottare [sheem-mee-ot-tah'ray] vt. to ape, mimic.

Scimunito [shee-moo-nee'toh] a. foolish, silly.

Scindere [sheen'day-ray] vt. to divide, separate, sever.

Scintilla [sheen-teel-lah] nf. spark, sparkle.

Scintillare [sheen-teel-lah'ray] vi. to scintillate, sparkle.

Sciocchezza [shock-ket'sah] nf. foolishness, nonsense, silly thing.

Sciocco [shock'koh] nm. fool; a. foolish, silly, tasteless.

Scioglie/re [sholl'yay-ray] vt. to dissolve, free, loosen(n), melt, release, undo, untie; —rsi vr. to dissolve, free oneself, melt.

Sciolto [sholl'toh] a. easy, free, loose, nimble; versi sciolti [vehr'see sholl'tee] nm. (pl.) blank verse.

Scioperare [shoh-pay-rah'ray] vi. to (go on) strike.

Scioperato [shoh-pay-rah'toh] nm. idle good-for-nothing.

Sciopero [shoh'pay-roh] nm. strike.

Scipito [shee-pee'toh] a. dull, insipid, tasteless.

Scirocco [shee-rock'koh] nm. South-East wind.

Sciroppo [shee-rop'poh] nm. syrup.

Scisma [shees'mah] nm. schism.

Scismatico [shees-mah'tee-koh] a. schismatic.

Scissione [shees-see-oh'nay] nf. division, split.

Sciupare [shoo-pah'ray] vt. to damage, ruin, spoil.

Sciupio [shoo-pee'oh] nm. waste.

Scivolare [shee-voh-lah'ray] vi. to glide, slide, slip.

Scodella [skoh-dell'lah] nf. bowl, soup-plate.

Scodinzolare [skoh-deent-soh-lah'ray] vi. to wag (the tail).

Scogliera [skoll-yay'rah] nf.

Scoglio [skoll'yoh] nm. reef, rock, stumbling-block.

Scoiattolo [skoh-yaht'toh-loh] nm. squirrel.

Scolare [skoh-lah'ray] vt. and i. to drain, drip.

Scola/ro [skoh-lah'roh] nm. pupil, schoolboy; —ra [rah] nf. schoolgirl.

Scollo [skoll'loh] nm. neck-opening.

Scolorire [skoh-loh-ree'ray] vt. to discolour; vi. to fade.

Scolpa/re [skoll-pah'ray] vt. to excuse, justify; —rsi vr. to apologise, justify oneself.

Scolpire [skoll-pee'ray] vt. to chisel, engrave, sculpture.

Scombinare [skom-bee-nah'ray] vt. to disarrange.

Scombussolare [skom-boos-soh-lah'ray] vt. to disturb, upset.

Scommessa [skom-mess'sah] nf. bet, wager.

Scommettere [skom-met'tay-ray] vt. to bet, wager.

Scemoda/re [skoh-moh-dah'ray] vt. to disturb, inconvenience, trouble; —rsi vr. to take the trouble.

Scomodo [skoh'moh-doh] a. inconvenient, uncomfortable.

Scompagnare [skom-pahn-yah'ray] vt. to disjoin, unmatch.

Scomparire [skom-pah-ree'ray] vi. to cut a poor figure, disappear, vanish.

Scompartimento [skom-pahr-tee-men'toh] nm. compartment.

Scompigliare [skom-peel-yah'ray] vt. to discompose, disorder, ruffle, upset.

Scompiglio [skom-peel'yoh] nm. bustle, confusion, fuss.

Scomunicare [skom-moo-nee-kah'ray] vt. to excommunicate.

Sconcertare [skon-chehr-tah'ray] vt. to baffle, disconcert.

Sconcio [skon'choh] a. indecent, nasty.

Sconfessare [skon-fess-sah'ray] vt. to disavow, disown.

Sconfiggere [skon-fee-djay'ray] vt. to defeat.

Sconfitta [skon-feet'tah] nf. defeat, discomfiture.

Sconforto [skon-forr'toh] nm. dejection, distress, sorrow.

Scongiurare [skon-joo-rah'ray] vt. to beseech, implore, remove.

Sconnettere [skon-net'tay-ray] vt. to disconnect.

Sconoscente [skoh-noh-shen'tay] a. ungrateful.

Sconosciuto [skoh-noh-shoo'toh] nm. and a. unknown.

Sconsigliare [skon-seel-yah'ray] vt. to advise against, dissuade.

Scontare [skon-tah'ray] vt. (com.) to deduct, discount; to atone for, expiate, pay for.

Scontento [skon-ten'toh] nm. discontent; a. disappointed, dissatisfied.

Sconto [skon'toh] nm. discount, payment, reduction.

Scontrino [skon-tree'noh] nm. check, receipt, ticket.

Scontro [skon'troh] nm. collision, encounter.

Scontroso [skon-troh'soh] a. sulky.

Sconveniente [skon-vay-nee-en'tay] *a.* improper, unseemly.

Sconvolgere [skon-voll'jay-ray] *vt.* to derange, overturn, upset.

Scopa [skoh'pah] *nf.* broom.

Scopare [skoh-pah'ray] *vi.* to sweep.

Scoperta [skoh-pehr'tah] *nf.* disclosure, discovery, revelation.

Scoperto [skoh-pehr'toh] *a.* bare, naked, open, unprotected.

Scopo [skoh'poh] *nm.* aim, end, object, purpose.

Scoppiare [skop-pee-ah'ray] *vi.* to burst (out), explode.

Scoppio [skop'pee-oh] *nm.* burst(ing), explosion, outbreak.

Scopri/re [skoh-pree'ray] *vt.* to detect, discover, find out, uncover, unveil; **—rsi** *vr.* to betray oneself, uncover oneself.

Scoraggiamento [skor-rahdjah-men'toh] *nm.* depression, discouragement.

Scorciare [skor-chah'ray] *vt.* to shorten.

Scorciatoia [skor-chah-toh'yah] *nf.* short-cut.

Scorda/re [skor-dah'ray] *vt.* **—rsi** *vr.* to forget, untune.

Scorgere [skorr'jay-ray] *vt.* to discern, perceive.

Scorno [skorr'noh] *nm.* disgrace, shame.

Scorpacciata [skorr-pahch-chah'tah] *nf.* bellyful.

Scorpione [skorr-pee-oh'nay] *nm.* scorpion.

Scorrazzare [skorr-rahtsah'ray] *vi.* to run about.

Scorrere [skorr'ray-ray] *vt.* to glance over, run over; *vi.* to elapse, flow, fly, glide.

Scorreria [skorr-ray-ree'ah] *nf.* incursion, raid.

Scorretto [skorr-ret'toh] *a.* improper, incorrect.

I.G.D.

Scorrevole [skorr-ray'voh-lay] *a.* flowing, fluent, gliding.

Scorsa [skorr'sah] *nf.* glance.

Scorso [skorr'soh] *a.* last, past.

Scorta [skorr'tah] *nf.* convoy, escort, supply.

Scortare [skorr-tah'ray] *vt.* to convoy, escort.

Scortecciare [skorr-tehch-chah'ray] *vt.* to bark, strip.

Scortese [skorr-tay'zay] *a.* discourteous, rude, uncivil.

Scortesia [skorr-tay-zee'ah] *nf.* rudeness, rude act.

Scorticare [skorr-tee-kah'ray] *vt.* to flay, fleece, skin.

Scorza [skord'zah] *nf.* bark, peel, rind, skin.

Scosceso [skoh-shay'soh] *a.* sloping, steep.

Scossa [skoss'sah] *nf.* shake, shock.

Scosso [skoss'soh] *a.* excited, moved, shaken.

Scosta/re [skoss-tah'ray] *vt.* to put aside, remove; **—rsi** *vr.* to get out of the way, stand aside.

Scostumato [skoss-too-mah'toh] *a.* dissolute.

Scottare [skot-tah'ray] *vt.* to burn, nettle, scald, scorch.

Scottatura [skot-tah-too'rah] *nf.* burn, scald.

Scovare [skoh-vah'ray] *vt.* to dislodge, rouse, find out.

Scozzese [skot-say'say] *nm. and f.* Scot; *a.* Scottish.

Screditare [skray-dee-tah'ray] *vt.* to discredit.

Scredito [skray'dee-toh] *nm.* discredit, disgrace.

Screpola/re [skray-poh-lah'ray] *vt.* **—rsi** *vr.* to chap, crack.

Screzio [skray'tsee-oh] *nm.* dispute, quarrel.

Scribacchiare [skree-bahk-kee-ah'ray] *vt. and i.* to scribble.

F

Scricchiolare [skreek-kee-oh-lah'ray] vi. to creak.

Scrigno [skreen'yoh] nm. jewel-case, safe, strong-box.

Scritta [skreet'tah] nf. inscription, notice.

Scritto [skreet'toh] nm. writing; a. written.

Scrit/tore [skreet-toh'ray] nm. —**trice** [tree'chay] nf. writer.

Scrittura [skreet-too'rah] nf. (hand-)writing.

Scritturare [skreet-too-rah'ray] vt. (theat.) to engage.

Scrivania [skree-vah-nee'ah] nf. (writing-)desk.

Scrivere [skree'vay-ray] vt. and vi. to write.

Scroccare [skrock-kah'ray] vt. to cheat, sponge.

Scrollare [skroll-lah'ray] vt. to shake, shrug.

Scrosciare [skroh-shah'ray] vi. to crash, pour, thunder.

Scrupolo [skroo'poh-loh] nm. scruple.

Scrupoloso [skroo-poh-loh'soh] a. scrupulous.

Scrutare [skroo-tah'ray] vt. to investigate, scan.

Scrutinare [skroo-tee-nah'ray] vt. to scrutinize.

Scrutinio [skroo-tee'nee-oh] nm. list of marks, scrutiny, voting.

Scucire [skoo-chee'ray] vt. to unsew.

Scuderia [skoo-day-ree'ah] nf. stable.

Scudiscio [skoo-dee'shoh] nm. lash, whip.

Scudo [skoo'doh] nm. protection, scutcheon, shield.

Scultore [skool-toh'ray] nm. sculptor.

Scultura [skool-too'rah] nf. carving, sculpture.

Scuola [skoo-oh'lah] nf. school.

Scuote/re [skoo-oh'tay-ray] vt. to excite, move, shake; —**rsi** vr. to rouse oneself, stir.

Scure [skoo'ray] nf. axe, hatchet.

Scuro [skoo'roh] nm. darkness, shutter; a. dark, dim, gloomy.

Scusa [skoo'zah] nf. apology, excuse, pretext.

Scusa/re [skoo-zah'ray] vt. to excuse, forgive, justify; —**rsi** vr. to apologise, justify oneself.

Sdebitarsi [sday-bee-tahr'see] vr. to pay off one's debts.

Sdegnare [sdayn-yah'ray] vt. to disdain, scorn.

Sdegno [sdayn'yoh] nm. disdain, indignation.

Sdegnoso [sdayn-yoh'soh] a. disdainful.

Sdraia/re [sdrah-yah'ray] vt. to stretch at full length; —**rsi** vr. to lie down, stretch oneself out.

Sdrucciolare [sdrooch-choh-lah'ray] vi. to slip.

Sdru/cire [sdroo-chee'ray], —**scire** [shee'ray] vt. to rend, rip, unstitch.

Se [say] con. if, whether; se no [naw], or else, otherwise.

Sè [say] rf. pn. (oblique case) oneself, himself, herself, itself, (pl.) themselves.

Sebbene [seb-bay'nay] con. although, though.

Secca/re [seck-kah'ray] vt. to bother, vex, dry, wither; —**rsi** vr. to dry (up), get tired.

Seccatura [seck-kah-too'rah] nf. nuisance, trouble.

Secchezza [seck-ket'sah] nf. dryness, thinness.

Secchia [seck'kee-ah] nf. bucket, pail.

Secco [seck'koh] a. dried, dry, thin.

Secolare [say-koh-lah'ray] nm. layman; a. lay, secular, that has stood for centuries.

Secolo [say'koh-loh] *nm.* age, century.

Secondare [say-kon-dah'ray] *vt.* to back up, second, support.

Secondo [say-kon'doh] *nm.* second; *a.* favourable, second; **di seconda mano** [dee say-kon'dah mah'noh]. second-hand; *pr.* according to; **s. me** [may], in my opinion; *int.* it depends!

Sedano [say'dah-noh]. *nm.* celery.

Sedare [say-dah'ray] *vt.* to appease, calm, put down.

Sede [say'day] *nf.* office, residence, seat, see.

Sedentario [say-den-tah'ree-oh] *a.* sedentary.

Sede/re [say-day'ray] *vi.* to sit; **—rsi** *vr.* to sit down, take a seat. [seat.

Sedia [say'dee-ah] *nf.* chair.

Sedicente [say-dee-chen'tay] *a.* pretended, self-styled, would-be.

Sedi/ci [say'dee-chee] *a.* sixteen; **—cenne** [chen'nay] 16-year-old; **—cesimo** [chay'zee-moh], sixteenth.

Sedizione [say-dsee-see-oh'nay] *nf.* sedition.

Sedizioso [say-dee-tsee-oh'soh] *a.* seditious.

Sedurre [say-door'ray] *vt.* to charm, corrupt, seduce.

Seduta [say-doo'tah] *nf.* meeting, sitting.

Seduttore [say-doot-toh'ray] *nm.* seducer.

Seduzione [say-doo-tsee-oh'nay] *nf.* charm, fascination, seduction.

Sega [say'gah] *nf.* saw.

Segale [say'gah-lay] *nf.* rye.

Segare [say-gah'ray] *vt.* to mow, saw.

Seggio [say'djoh] *nm.* chair, seat, see.

Seggiola: *v.* sedia.

Segnala/re [sayn-yah-lah'-ray] *vt.* to inform, signal; **—rsi** *vr.* to distinguish oneself.

Segnale [sayn-yah'lay] *nm.* signal.

Segna/re [sayn-yah'ray] *vt.* to enter, mark, note, score; **—rsi** *vr.* to cross oneself.

Segno [sayn'yoh] *nm.* mark, nod, note, sign, spot, vestige.

Sego [say'goh] *nm.* tallow.

Segregare [say-gray-gah'-ray] *vt.* to isolate, segregate.

Segreta/rio [say-gray-tah'-ree-oh] *nm.* **—ria** [ree-ah] *nf.* secretary.

Segreto [say-gray'toh] *nm. and a.* secret.

Seguace [say-gwah'chay] *nm. and f.* adherent, follower.

Seguire [say-gwee'ray] *vt.* to follow, take (advice, etc.); *vi.* to ensue, follow, result.

Seguitare [say-gwee-tah'ray] *vi.* to continue, go on, keep on.

Seguito [say'gwee-toh] *nm.* continuation, followers (*pl.*), retinue, sequel, series, succession; **di** [dee] *s. ad.* uninterruptedly; **in** [een] *s. ad.* later on; **in s. a** [ah] *pr.* owing to.

Sei [say'ee] *a.* six.

Seicento [say-ee-chen'toh] *nm.* 17th century; *a.* six hundred.

Selce [sell'chay] *nf.* flint (-stone).

Selciare [sell-chah'ray] *vt.* to pave.

Selciato [sell-chah'toh] *nm.* pavement, road surface.

Selezione [say-lay-tsee-oh'-nay] *nf.* selection.

Sella [sell'lah] *nf.* saddle.

Sellare [sell-lah'ray] *vt.* to saddle.

Seltz [selts] *nm.* soda-water.

Selva [sell'vah] *nf.* forest, wood.

Selvaggina [sell-vah-djee'-nah] *nf.* game.

Selvaggio [sell-vah'djoh] nm. savage; a. brutal, savage, uncultivated, wild.

Selvatico [sell-vah'tee-koh] a. uncultivated, wild.

Semaforo [say-mah'foh-roh] nm. semaphore, traffic-lights.

Sembianza [sem-bee-ahnt'sah] nf. appearance, look, mien.

Sembrare [sem-brah'ray] vt. and i. to appear look (like), seem, feel like, sound like, taste like.

Seme [say'may] nm. germ, seed.

Semestre [say-mess'tray] nm. half-year.

Semi- [say'mee] prefix. half-, semi-.

Semicupio [say-mee-koo'pee-oh] nm. hip-bath.

Seminare [say-mee-nah'ray] vt. to scatter, sow.

Seminario [say-mee-nah'ree-oh] nm. seminary.

Semola [say'moh-lah] nf. fine flour, freckles (pl.).

Sempiterno [sem-pee-tehr'noh] a. everlasting.

Semplice [sem'plee-chay] a. easy, mere, natural, plain, unaffected, unpretending; soldato [soll-dah'toh] s. nm. (mil.) private (soldier).

Semplicità [sem-plee-chee-tah'] nf. plainness, simplicity.

Semplificare [sem-plee-fee-kah'ray] vt. to simplify.

Sempre [sem'pray] ad. always; per [pehr] s. for ever; s. meno [may'noh] less and less; s. più [pee-oo'] more and more.

Senapa [say'nah-pah] nf. mustard.

Senato [say-nah'toh] nm. senate.

Senatore [say-nah-toh'ray] nm. senator.

Senile [say-nee'lay] a. senile.

Seniore [say-nee-oh'ray] nm. and a. senior; a. elder, older.

Senno [sen'noh] nm. judgment, sense, wisdom.

Seno [say'noh] nm. bosom, breast, cove, inlet.

Sensale [sen-sah'lay] nm. broker, middleman.

Sensato [sen-sah'toh] a. judicious, prudent, sensible.

Sensazione [sen-sah-tsee-oh'nay] nf. excitement, sensation.

Senseria [sen-say-ree'ah] nf. brokerage.

Sensibile [sen-see'bee-lay] a. feeling, notable, sensitive, tender-hearted.

Sensibilità [sen-see-bee-lee-tah'] nf. sensibility, sensitiveness.

Senso [sen'soh] nm. direction, feeling, meaning, sensation, sense.

Sensuale [sen-soo-ah'lay] a. sensual.

Sentenza [sen-tent'sah] nf. decision, decree, judgment, maxim.

Sentenziare [sen-ten-tsee-ah'ray] vt. to condemn, judge; vi. to talk sententiously.

Sentiero [sen-tee-ay'roh] nm. footpath, path(-way).

Sentimentale [sen-tee-men-tah'lay] a. mawkish, sentimental.

Sentimento [sen-tee-men'toh] nm. feeling, sentiment.

Sentinella [sen-tee-nell'lah] nf. (mil.) sentinel, sentry.

Senti/re [sen-tee'ray] vt. to feel, hear, learn, smell, taste; —rsi vr. to feel.

Senza [sent'sah] pr. without; senz'altro [sent-sahl'troh] ad. immediately, of course.

Separare [say-pah-rah'ray] vt. to divide, part, sever.

Separazione [say-pah-rah-tsee-oh'nay] nf. parting, separation.

Sepolcro [say-poll'kroh] *nm.* grave, sepulchre.

Sepoltura [say-poll-too'rah] *nf.* burial, funeral, grave.

Seppellimento [sep-pell-lee-men'toh] *nm.* burying.

Seppellire [sep-pell-lee'ray] *vt.* to bury, hide.

Seppia [sep'pee-ah] *nf.* cuttle-fish.

Sequela [say-kway'lah] *nf.* sequel, series.

Sequestrare [say-kwess-trah'ray] *vt.* to distrain, sequester, sequestrate.

Sequestro [say-kwess'troh] *nm.* distraint, sequestration.

Sera [say'rah] *nf.* evening.

Serata [say-rah'tah] *nf.* evening, evening party, (*theat.*) evening performance.

Serbare [sehr-bah'ray] *vt.* to keep, preserve.

Serbatoio [sehr-bah-toh'yoh] *nm.* reservoir, tank.

Serenità [say-ray-nee-tah'] *nf.* calmness, serenity.

Sereno [say-ray'noh] *a.* calm, cloudless, serene.

Sergente [sehr-jen'tay] *nm.* sergeant.

Serie [say'ree-ay] *nf.* series, set, succession.

Serietà [say-ree-ay-tah'] *nf.* earnestness, gravity, seriousness, trustworthiness.

Serio [say'ree-oh] *a.* earnest, grave, important, respectable, serious, trustworthy; **sui** [sool] *s. ad.* in earnest.

Sermone [sehr-moh'nay] *nm.* reproof, sermon.

Ser/pe [sehr'pay] *nf.* —**pente** [pen'tay] *nm.* serpent, snake.

Serpeggiare [sehr-pay-djah'ray] *vi.* to meander, spread, wind.

Serra [sehr'rah] *nf.* greenhouse, hothouse.

Serraglio [sehr-rah'lyoh] *nm.* menagerie.

Serra/re [sehr-rah'ray] *vt.* to clench, close, lock, shut; —**rsi** *vr.* to press upon, stand close.

Serva [sehr'vah] *nf.* maid, woman-servant.

Servente [sehr-ven'tay] *nm.* hospital orderly.

Servi/re [sehr-vee'ray] *vt.* to help (to), serve; *vi.* to be of use, serve; —**rsi** *vr.* to get, help oneself, (make) use (of).

Servitore [sehr-vee-toh'ray] *nm.* servant.

Servitù [sehr-vee-too'] *nf.* bondage, servitude, servants (*pl.*) staff.

Servizio [sehr-vee'tsee-oh] *nm.* favour, kindness, service; **di** [dee] *s. ad.* on duty; **fuori** [foo-oh'ree] *s. ad.* off duty; **donna di** [don'nah dee] *s. nf.* maid.

Servo [sehr'voh] *nm.* (man-)servant, slave.

Sessione [sess-see-oh'nay] *nf.* session.

Sesso [sess'soh] *nm.* sex.

Sessuale [sess-soo-ah'lay] *a.* sexual.

Sesto [sess'toh] *a.* sixth; *nm.* order; **mettere in** [met'tay-ray een] *s. vt.* to put in order, tidy.

Seta [say'tah] *nf.* silk.

Sete [say'tay] *nf.* eagerness, longing, thirst; **aver** [ah-vehr'] *s. vi.* to be thirsty.

Setola [say'toh-lah] *nf.* bristle, hair.

Setoloso [say-toh-loh'soh] *a.* bristly, hairy.

Setta [set'tah] *nf.* faction, sect.

Set/te [set'tay] *a.* seven; —**tenne** [ten'nay], seven-year-old.

Settecento [set-tay-chen'toh] *nm.* 18th century; *a.* seven hundred.

Settembre [set-tem'bray] *nm.* September.

Settentrionale [set-ten-tree-oh-nah'lay] *nm.* Northerner; *a.* north(ern), northerly.

Settentrione [set-ten-tree-oh'nay] *nm.* North.

Settimana [set-tee-mah'nah] *nf.* week.

Settimanale [set-tee-mah-nah'lay] *nm. and a.* weekly.

Settimo [set'tee moh] *a.* seventh; [sector.

Settore [set-toh'ray] *nm.*

Settuagenario [set-too-ah-jay-nah'ree-oh] *nm. and a.* septuagenarian.

Severità [say-vay-ree-tah'] *nf.* harshness, severity, strictness.

Severo [say-vay'roh] *a.* harsh, severe, strict.

Sevizie [say-vee'tsee-ay] *nf.* (*pl.*) cruelty, ill-treatment.

Sezionare [say-tsee-oh-nah'ray] *vt.* to cut up, dissect.

Sezione [say-tsee-oh'nay] *nf.* department, section.

Sfaccendare [sfahch-chen-dah'ray] *vi.* to do housework.

Sfaccendato [sfahch-chen-dah'toh] *nm.* idler, loafer.

Sfacchinare [sfahk-kee-nah'ray] *vi.* to drudge.

Sfacciato [sfahch-chah'toh] *a.* impudent, shameless.

Sfacelo [sfah-chay'loh] *nm.* breakdown, collapse, ruin.

Sfamare [sfah-mah'ray] *vt.* to appease someone's hunger.

Sfarzo [sfahrd'zoh] *nm.* luxury, pomp, splendour.

Sfarzoso [sfahrd-zoh'soh] *a.* gorgeous, sumptuous.

Sfavillare [sfah-veel-lah'ray] *vi.* to glare, glitter, sparkle.

Sfavorevole [sfah-voh-ray'voh-lay] *a.* adverse, unfavourable.

Sfera [sfay'rah] *nf.* circle, globe, sphere.

Sferico [sfay'ree-koh] *a.* spherical.

Sferza [sfert'sah] *nf.* lash, scourge, thong.

Sferzare [sfert-sah'ray] *vt.* to lash, scourge.

Sfiatarsi [sfee-ah-tahr'see] *vr.* to talk oneself hoarse.

Sfida [sfee'dah] *nf.* challenge, defiance.

Sfidare [sfee-dah'ray] *vt.* to brave, challenge, dare, defy; sfido! [sfee'doh] *int.* of course.

Sfiducia [sfee-doo'chah] *nf.* distrust, mistrust, want of confidence.

Sfilare [sfee-lah'ray] *vt.* to unstring, unthread; *vi.* to file (past).

Sfinge [sfeen'jay] *nf.* sphinx.

Sfinito [sfee-nee'toh] *a.* exhausted, worn out.

Sfiorare [sfee-oh-rah'ray] *vt.* to caress, graze, skim over, touch lightly.

Sfiorire [sfee-oh-ree'ray] *vi.* to decay, fade.

Sfoderare [sfoh-day-rah'ray] *vt.* to display, draw, show off, take out the lining.

Sfogare [sfoh-gah'ray] *vt.* to disclose, vent; —rsi *vr.* to give vent to one's feelings, speak frankly.

Sfoggiare [sfoh-djah'ray] *vt. and i.* to display, flaunt, show off.

Sfoggio [sfoh'djoh] *nm.* display, parade, show.

Sfogliare [sfoll-yah'ray] *vt.* to pick off leaves, run through (a book).

Sfogo [sfoh'goh] *nm.* eruption, outburst, vent.

Sfondare [sfon-dah'ray] *vt.* to break (down), knock the bottom out. [ground.

Sfondo [sfon'doh] *nm.* background.

Sfornare [sforr-nah'ray] *vt.* to take out of the oven.

Sfortuna [sforr-too'nah] *nf.* ill-luck, misfortune.

Sfortunato [sforr-too-nah'toh] *a.* unlucky.

Sforza/re [sfort-sah'ray] *vt.* to force, strain; **—rsi** *vr.* to strive, struggle, try.

Sforzo [sfort'soh] *nm.* attempt, effort, exertion.

Stracellare [strah-chell-lah'ray] *vt.* to shatter, smash.

Sfrattare [sfraht-tah'ray] *vt.* to expel, turn out.

Sfratto [sfraht'toh] *nm.* expulsion, notice to quit.

Sfrenato [sfray-nah'toh] *a.* dissolute, excessive, unbridled.

Sfruttare [sfroot-tah'ray] *vt.* to exhaust, exploit. [to escape.

Sfuggire [sfoo-djee'ray] *vi.*

Sfumare [sfoo-mah'ray] *vi.* to disappear, fade, vanish.

Sfumatura [sfoo-mah-too'rah] *nf.* nuance, shade.

Sgabello [sgah-bell'loh] *nm.* stool.

Sgangherare [sgahng-gay-rah'ray] *vt.* to unhinge.

Sgangherato [sgahng-gay-rah'toh] *a.* ramshackle, rickety, unhinged.

Sgarbato [sgahr-bah'toh] *a.* rude, unmannerly.

Sgar/beria [sgahr-bay-ree'ah] *nf.* **—bo** [boh] *nm.* offence, rudeness.

Sgelare [sjay-lah'ray] *vt. and i.* to melt, thaw.

Sghembo [sghem'boh] *a.* crooked, oblique, slanting.

Sgherro [sgherr'roh] *nm.* bravo, hired ruffian.

Sgobbare [sgob-bah'ray] *vi.* to drudge, toil, work hard.

Sgocciolare [shohch-choh-lah'ray] *vi.* to drip, trickle.

Sgomb(e)rare [sgom-bay-rah(brah)'ray] *vt.* (*mil.*) to abandon, clear, free up; to clear out, remove.

Sgomb(e)ro [sgom'bay-roh (broh)] *nm.* clearing, removal; *a.* clear, empty, free, tenantless.

Sgomentare [sgoh-men-tah'ray] *vt.* to dismay, frighten, terrify.

Sgomento [sgoh-men'toh] *nm.* dismay, fright; *a.* dismayed, frightened.

Sgominare [sgoh-mee-nah'ray] *vt.* to disperse, rout.

Sgonfiare [sgon-fee-ah'ray] *vt.* to deflate, empty, flatten.

Sgorbio [sgorr'bee-oh] *nm.* daub, scrawl, (*fig.*) ugly dwarf.

Sgorgare [sgorr-gah'ray] *vi.* to gush, spout (out).

Sgradevole [sgrah-day'voh-lay] *a.* disagreeable, unpleasant.

Sgrammaticato [sgrahm-mah-tee-kah'toh] *a.* ungrammatical.

Sgranchi/re [sgrahng-kee'ray] *vt.* **—rsi** *vr.* to stretch.

Sgravare [sgrah-vah'ray] *vt.* to lighten, relieve, unload.

Sgretolare [sgray-toh-lah'ray] *vt.* to crumble, grind, smash.

Sgridare [sgree-dah'ray] *vt.* to rebuke, scold.

Sgridata [sgree-dah'tah] *nf.* rebuke, scolding.

Sguaiato [sgwah-yah'toh] *a.* clumsy, ill-bred, noisy.

Sguardo [sgwahr'doh] *nm.* glance, look.

Sguarnire [sgwahr-nee'ray] *vt.* to untrim, (*mil.*) withdraw the garrison.

Sguatte/ra [sgwaht'tay-rah] *nf.* scullery-maid; **—ro** [roh] *nm.* scullery-boy.

Sguazzare [sgwaht-sah'ray] *vi.* to flounder, splash.

Sgusciare [sgoo-shah'ray] *vt.* to hull, husk, shell; *vi.* to slip away, steal away.

Si [see] *adj.* yes; dire di [dee'ray dee] s. *vi.* to agree.

Si [see] *rfl. pn.* oneself, himself, herself, itself, (*pl.*) themselves; *indef. pn.* one, people, they; *recip. pn.* each other, one another.

Sia . . . Sia [see'ah] *con.* whether . . . or; both . . . and.

Sibilare [see-bee-lah'ray] *vi.* to hiss, whizz.

Sibilo [see'bee-loh] *nm.* hiss, whistle, whizzing.

Sicario [see-kah'ree-oh] *nm.* hired assassin.

Sicchè [seek-kay'] *con.* so that.

Siccità [seech-chee-tah'] *nf.* drought, dryness.

Siccome [seek-koh'may] *ad.* and *con.* as.

Sicomoro [see-koh-moh'roh] *nm.* sycamore.

Sicurezza [see-koo-ret'sah] *nf.* certainty, safety, security; **s. di sè** [dee say]. self-possession.

Sicuro [see-koo'roh] *a.* certain, safe, secure, trusty; *int.* quite so! al [ahl] s. *ad.* in safety.

Sicurtà [see-koor'tah'] *nf.* guarantee, security.

Siepe [see-ay'pay] *nf.* hedge.

Siero [see-ay'roh] *nm.* serum, whey.   [such.

Siffatto [seef-faht'toh] *a.*

Sifilide [see-fee'lee-day] *nf.* (*med.*) syphilis.

Sifone [see-foh'nay] *nm.* siphon.

Sigaretta [see-gah-ret'tah] *nf.* cigarette.   [cigar.

Sigaro [see'gah-roh] *nm.*

Sigillare [see-jeel-lah'ray] *vt.* to seal.   [seal.

Sigillo [see-jeel'loh] *nm.*

Signifi/cante [seen-yee-fee-kahn'tay], —**cativo** [kah-tee'voh] *a.* expressive, significant.

Significare [seen-yee-fee-kah'ray] *vt.* to mean, signify.

Significato [seen-yee-fee-kah'toh] *nm.* meaning, purport, sense, significance.

Signo/ra [seen-yoh'rah] *nf.* lady, madam, Mrs.; —**re** [ray] *nm.* gentleman, Mr., sir; **vivere da** [vee'vay-ray dah] s. *vi.* to live like a lord.

Signoreggiare [seen-yoh-ray-djah'ray] *vt.* and *i.* to dominate, govern, master, rule.

Signoria [seen-yoh-ree'ah] *nf.* domain, Lordship, seigniory.

Signorile [seen-yoh-ree'lay] *a.* ladylike, lordly, like a gentleman (lady).

Signori/na [seen-yoh-ree' nah] *nf.* Miss, young lady; —**no** [noh] *nm.* young master.

Silenzio [see-len'tsee-oh] *nm.* silence.

Silenzioso [see-len-tsee-oh' soh] *a.* quiet, silent.

Sillaba [seel'lah-bah] *nf.* syllable.

Silurare [see-loo-rah'ray] *vt.* to torpedo.

Siluro [see-loo'roh] *nm.* cat-fish, torpedo.

Silvestre [seel-vess'tray] *a.* sylvan.

Simboleggiare [seem-boh-lay-djah'ray] *vt.* and *i.* to symbolize.

Simbolo [seem'boh-loh] *nm.* symbol.   [similar.

Similare [see-mee-lah'ray] *a.*

Simile [see'mee-lay] *nm.* fellow-creature, like; *a.* like, alike, such.

Similitudine [see-mee-lee-too'dee-nay] *nf.* simile, similitude.

Simmetria [seem-may-tree' ah] *nf.* symmetry.

Simpatia [seem-pah-tee'ah] *nf.* liking, sympathy, weakness.

Simpatico [seem-pah'tee-koh] *a.* agreeable, congenial, nice, pleasant, sympathetic.

Simpatizzare [seem-pah-teed-zah'ray] *vi.* to take a liking.

Simulacro [see-moo-lah'-kroh] *nm.* image, shadow.

Simulare [see-moo-lah'ray] *vt.* to feign, sham, simulate.

Simulazione [see-moo-lah-tsee-oh'nay] *nf.* shamming, simulation.

Simultaneo [see-mool-tah'-nay-oh] *a.* simultaneous.

Sinagoga [see-nah-goh'gah] *nf.* synagogue.

Sincerarsi [seen-chay-rahr'-see] *vr.* to make sure.

Sincerità [seen-chay-ree-tah'] *nf.* candour, sincerity.

Sincero [seen-chay'roh] *a.* candid, frank, sincere.

Sindacato [seen-dah-kah'-toh] *nm.* syndicate, trade union.

Sindaco [seen'dah-koh] *nm.* auditor, mayor, syndic.

Sinfonia [seen-foh-nee'ah] *nf.* symphony.

Singhiozzare [seeng-ghee-ot-sah'ray] *vi.* to sob.

Singhiozzo [seeng-ghee-ot'-soh] *nm.* hiccough, sob.

Singolare [seeng-goh-lah'-ray] *a.* eccentric, odd, peculiar, queer, singular.

Singolarità [seeng-goh-lah-ree-tah'] *nf.* oddness, singularity.

Singolo [seeng'goh-loh] *a.* each, individual, single.

Sinistra [see-nees'trah] *nf.* left (hand).

Sinistrare [see-nees-trah'-ray] *vt.* to damage, destroy.

Sinistrato [see-nees-trah'-toh] *a.* homeless.

Sinistro [see-nees'troh] *nm.* accident, mishap; *a.* left, ominous, sinister.

Sino : *v.* fino.

Sinodo [see'noh-doh] *nm.* synod.

Sinonimo [see-noh'nee-moh] *nm.* synonym; *a.* synonymous.

Sintassi [seen-tahs'see] *nf.* syntax.

Sintesi [seen'tay-zee] *nf.* synthesis.

Sintomo [seen'toh-moh] *nm.* symptom.

Sinuosità [see-noo-oh-see-tah'] *nf.* sinuosity.

Sinuoso [see-noo-oh'soh] *a.* sinuous, winding.

Sipario [see-pah'ree-oh] *nm.* (theat.) (drop) curtain.

Sirena [see-ray'nah] *nf.* hooter, siren, mermaid.

Siringa [see-reeng'gah] *nf.* (med.) syringe.

Sistema [sees-tay'mah] *nm.* system.

Sistemare [sees-tay-mah'-ray] *vt.* to arrange, settle.

Sitibondo [see-tee-bon'doh] *a.* thirsting (for), thirsty.

Sito [see'toh] *nm.* place, site, spot.

Situato [see-too-ah'toh] *a.* placed.

Situazione [see-too-ah-tsee-oh'nay] *nf.* condition, position, situation.

Slacciare [zlahch-chah'ray] *vt.* to unbind, undo, unlace, untie.

Slancia/re [zlahn-chah'ray] *vt.* to fling, hurl; —**rsi** *vr.* to be too daring, rush upon.

Slancio [zlahn'choh] *nm.* dart, enthusiasm, impulse, start.

Sleale [zlay-ah'lay] *a.* disloyal, unfair.

Slealtà [zlay-ahl-tah'] *nf.* disloyalty.

Slegare [zlay-gah'ray] *vt.* to unbind, untie.

Slitta [zleet'tah] *nf.* sledge, sleigh.

Slittare [zleet-tah'ray] *vi.* to skid, sledge, slip.

Slogamento [zloh-gah-men'toh] *nm.* dislocation.

Slogare [zloh-gah'ray] *vt.* to dislocate.

Sloggiare [zloh-djah'ray] *vt.* to dislodge, drive out; *vi.* to clear out, decamp.

Smacchiare [smahk-kee-ah'ray] *vt.* to clean, remove stains.

Smacco [smahk'koh] *nm.* humiliation, shame.

Smagliante [smah-lyahn'tay] *a.* dazzling, gaudy.

Smaltare [smahl-tah'ray] *vt.* to enamel, glaze.

Smaltire [smahl-tee'ray] *vt.* to digest, work off.

Smalto [smahl'toh] *nm.* enamel.

Smania [smah'nee-ah] *nf.* frenzy, restlessness, mania.

Smaniare [smah-nee-ah'ray] *vi.* to rave, toss about.

Smarrimento [smahr-ree-men'toh] *nm.* bewilderment, loss.

Smarri/re [smahr-ree'ray] *vt.* to lose, mislay; **—rsi** *vr.* to get confused, lose one's way, stray.

Smascherare [smah-skay-rah'ray] *vt.* to unmask.

Smembrare [smen-brah'ray] *vt.* to dismember.

Smemorato [smay-moh-rah'toh] *a.* absent-minded, forgetful, scatter-brained.

Smenti/re [smen-tee'ray] *vt.* to deny, disappoint, refute; **—rsi** *vr.* to eat one's words.

Smeraldo [smay-rahl'doh] *nm.* emerald.

Smerciare [smehr-chah'ray] *vt.* to sell (off). [sale.

Smercio [smehr'choh] *nm.*

Smettere [smet'tay-ray] *vt.* to give up, stop wearing; *vi.* to give up, leave off, stop.

Smilzo [smeelt'soh] *a.* slender, slim.

Smistare [smees-tah'ray] *vt.* (*rly.*) to shunt.

Smisurato [smee-soo-rah'toh] *a.* enormous, immeasurable.

Smobiliare [smoh-bee-lee-ah'ray] *vt.* to strip of furniture, unfurnish.

Smobilitare [smoh-bee-lee-tah'ray] *vt.* to demobilize.

Smo/dato [smoh-dah'toh], **—derato** [day-rah'toh] *a.* excessive, immoderate.

Smontare [smon-tah'ray] *vt.* to take down, take to pieces; *vi.* to alight, dismount, get out of.

Smorfia [smorr'fee-ah] *nf.* grimace, wry face.

Smorto [smorr'toh] *a.* pale, wan.

Smorzare [smort-sah'ray] *vt.* to abate, extinguish, quench, soften.

Smunto [smoon'toh] *a.* emaciated, exhausted, pale, wan.

Smuovere [smoo-oh'vay-ray] *vt.* to affect, deter, displace, remove, set in motion, stir.

Smussare [smoos-sah'ray] *vt.* to bevel, blunt, smooth.

Snaturare [snah-too-rah'ray] *vt.* to alter the nature of, misrepresent.

Snellezza [snell-let'sah] *nf.* agility, nimbleness, slimness.

Snello [snell'loh] *a.* agile, nimble, slim.

Snervare [snehr-vah'ray] *vt.* to enervate, exhaust.

Snodare [snoh-dah'ray] *vt.* to loosen, stretch, undo, unravel, untie, unwind.

Snudare [snoo-dah'ray] *vt.* to bare, unsheathe.

Soave [soh-ah'vay] *a.* mild, soft, sweet.

Soavità [soh-ah-vee-tah'] *nf.* softness, sweetness.

Sobbarcarsi [sob-bahrkahr'see] *vr.* to take on oneself. [suburb.

Sobborgo [sob-borr'goh] *nm.*

Sobillare [soh-beel-lah'ray] *vt.* to incite, instigate, stir up.

Sobrietà [soh-bree-ay-tah'] *nf.* sobriety, temperance.

Sobrio [soh'bree-oh] *a.* sober, temperate.

Soccombere [sock-kom'bay-ray] *vi.* to give in, succumb, yield.

Soccorrere [sock-korr'ray-ray] *vt.* to help, relieve, succour.

Soccorso [sock-korr'soh] *nm.* aid, help, relief.

Sociale [soh-chah'lay] *a.* social, (*com.*) of partnership; **ragion** [rah-john'] s. *nf.* (*com.*) style.

Socialismo [soh-chah-lees'moh] *nm.* socialism.

Società [soh-chee-ay-tah'] *nf.* community, society, (*com.*) company, partnership.

Socievole [soh-chay'voh-lay] *a.* companionable, sociable.

Socio [soh'choh] *nm.* associate, fellow, member, partner.

Sodalizio [soh-dah-lee'tsee-oh] *nm.* association, guild, society.

Soddisfacente [sod-dees-fah-chen'tay] *a.* satisfactory.

Soddisfare [sod-dees-fah'ray] *vt.* to comply with, fulfil, gratify, pay, satisfy.

Sodezza [soh-det'sah] *nf.* compactness, firmness, solidity.

Sodo [soh'doh] *a.* compact, firm, hard, solid, steady.

Sofà [soh-fah'] *nm.* sofa.

Sofferenza [sof-fay-rent'sah] *nf.* endurance, suffering, pain.

Soffermarsi [sof-fehr-mahr'see] *vr.* to linger over, stop a little.

Soffiare [sof-fee-ah'ray] *vt. and i.* to blow.

Soffice [sof'fee-chay] *a.* soft.

Soffietto [sof-fee-et'toh] *nm.* bellows (*pl.*), hood (of a car), puff (in a paper).

Soffio [sof'fee-oh] *nm.* blowing, breath, puff, whiff.

Soffitta [sof-feet'tah] *nf.* attic, garret. [ceiling.

Soffitto [sof-feet'toh] *nm.*

Soffocare [sof-foh-kah'ray] *vt.* to choke, extinguish, hush up, smother, stifle.

Soffrire [sof-free'ray] *vt. and i.* to bear, endure, put up with, suffer.

Sofisma [soh-fees'mah] *nm.* sophism.

Sofisticare [soh-fee-stee-kah'ray] *vt. and i.* to sophisticate.

Soggetto [soh-djet'toh] *nm.* subject, topic; *a.* liable, subject, subjected.

Soggezione [soh-djay-tsee-oh'nay] *nf.* awe, timidity, subjection.

Sogghignare [sog-gheen-yah'ray] *vi.* to jeer, sneer.

Soggiacere [soh-djah-chay'ray] *vi.* to be liable, be subject.

Soggiogare [soh-djoh-gah'ray] *vt.* to subdue subjugate.

Soggiornare [soh-djorr-nah'ray] *vi.* to sojourn, stay.

Soggiorno [soh-djorr'noh] *nm.* sojourn, stay; **permesso di** [pehr-mess'soh dee] *s.* permission to stay.

Soggiungere [soh-djoon'jay-ray] *vt.* to add, subjoin; *vi.* to remark, reply.

Soglia [sol'yah] *nf.* threshold. [throne.

Soglio [sol'yoh] *nm.* (*poet.*)

Sogliola [sol'yoh-lah] *nf.* sole (fish).

Sognare [sohn-yah'ray] *vt.* to dream of, imagine, long for.

Sogno [sohn'yoh] *nm.* dream, fancy.

Solaio [soh-lah´yoh] *nm.* loft.

Solcare [soll-kah´ray] *vt.* to furrow, plough.

Solco [soll´koh] *nm.* furrow, track, wrinkle.

Soldatesca [soll-dah-tess´kah] *nf.* soldiery.

Soldatesco [soll-dah-tess´koh] *a.* soldierly.

Soldato [soll-dah´toh] *nm.* soldier.

Soldo [soll´doh] *nm.* soldo (old Italian coin), pay, wages, money (general sense).

Sole [soh´lay] *nm.* sun(shine); **al** [ahl] **s.** *ad.* in the sun.

Soleggiare [soh-lay-djah´ray] *vt.* to sun; *vi.* to bask.

Solenne [soh-len´nay] *a.* solemn.

Solennità [soh-len-nee-tah´] *nf.* solemnity.

Solere [soh-lay´ray] *vi.* to be accustomed, be used, be wont, use.

Solerte [soh-lehr´tay] *a.* active, attentive, careful, enterprising, ingenious.

Solerzia [soh-lehr´tsee-ah] *nf.* activity, ingenuity.

Soletto [soh-let´toh] *a.* alone, lonely.

Sol/fare [soll-fah´ray], **—forare** [foh-rah´ray] *vt.* to sulphurate.

Solfato [soll-fah´toh] *nm.* sulphate.

Solidale [soh-lee-đah´lay] *a.* (com.) joint, loyal to.

Solidarietà [soh-lee-đah-ree-ay-tah´] *nf.* solidarity.

Solidità [soh-lee-dee-tah´] *nf.* compactness, firmness, solidity, steadiness, strength.

Solido [soh´lee-doh] *a.* compact, firm, solid, steady.

Soliloquio [soh-lee-loh´kwee-oh] *nm.* soliloquy.

Solingo [soh-leeng´goh] *a.* (poet.) lonely, solitary.

Solitario [soh-lee-tah´ree-oh] *nm.* hermit, solitary, solitaire (diamond); *a.* lonely, secluded, solitary.

Solito [soh´lee-toh] *a.* accustomed, customary, used, usual; **di** [dee] **s.** *ad.* as a rule, usually.

Solitudine [soh-lee-too´dee-nay] *nf.* seclusion, solitude.

Sollazzo [soll-laht´soh] *nm.* amusement, pastime, recreation.

Sollecitare [soll-lay-chee-tah´ray] *vt.* to hasten, request, urge.

Sollecito [soll-lay´chee-toh] *a.* early-rising, prompt, ready.

Sollecitudine [soll-lay-chee-too´dee-nay] *nf.* diligence, speed.

Solleone [soll-lay-oh´nay] *nm.* dog-days (pl.).

Solleticare [soll-lay-tee-kah´ray] *vt.* to excite, flatter, tempt, tickle.

Solleva/re [soll-lay-vah´ray] *vt.* to alleviate, lift, raise, relieve; **—rsi** *vr.* to rise.

Sollievo [soll-lee-ay´voh] *nm.* comfort, relief.

Solo [soh´loh] *a.* alone, only, sole; **da** [đah] **s.** by oneself; *ad.* but, only.

Solstizio [soll-stee´tsee-oh] *nm.* solstice.

Soltanto [soll-tahn´toh] *ad.* only, solely.

Solubile [soh-loo´bee-lay] *a.* soluble.

Solubilità [soh-loo-bee-lee-tah´] *nf.* solubility.

Soluzione [soh-loo-tsee-oh´nay] *nf.* solution.

Soma [soh´mah] *nf.* burden, load, weight.

Somaro [soh-mah´roh] *nm.* ass, donkey.

Somigliante [soh-meel-yahn´tay] *a.* like, resembling.

Somiglianza [soh-meel-yahnt'sah] *nf.* likeness, resemblance.

Somigliare [soh-meel-yah'ray] *vi.* to be like, look like, resemble.

Somma [somm'mah] *nf.* account, amount, sum.

Sommare [somm-mah'ray] *vt.* to add up; *vi.* to amount to.

Sommario [somm-mah'ree-oh] *nm.* abridgement, summary; *a.* brief, summary.

Sommerge/re [somm-mehr'-jay-ray] *vt.* to flood, submerge; —**rsi** *vr.* to dive, sink.

Sommergibile [somm-mehr-jee'bee-lay] *nm.* submarine; *a.* submergible.

Sommesso [somm-mess'soh] *a.* soft, subdued.

Somministrare [somm-mee-nees-trah'ray] *vt.* to administer, provide, supply.

Somministrazione [somm-mee-nees-trah-tsee-oh'nay] *nf.* administration, provision, supply.

Sommissione [somm-mees-see-oh'nay] *nf.* submission.

Sommità [somm-mee-tah'] *nf.* summit, top.

Sommo [somm'moh] *a.* high, very great.

Sommossa [somm-moss'sah] *nf.* riot, rising.

Sommuovere [somm-moo-oh'vay-ray] *vt.* to excite, rouse, stir up.

Sonaglio [soh-nahl'yoh] *nm.* bell, rattle.

Sonare: *v.* **suonare.**

Sondare [sonn-dah'ray] *vt.* to probe, sound.

Sonetto [soh-net'toh] *nm.* sonnet.

Sonnellino [sonn-nell-lee'noh] *nm.* doze, nap.

Sonno [sonn-noh] *nm.* sleep; aver [ah-vehr'] **s.** *vi.* to be sleepy.

Sonnolento [sonn-noh-len'toh] *a.* drowsy, sleepy.

Sonnolenza [sonn-noh-lent'sah] *nf.* drowsiness.

Sonorità [soh-noh-ree-tah'] *nf.* sonorousness.

Sonoro [soh-noh'roh] *a.* resonant, sonorous.

Sontuosità [sonn-too-oh-see-tah'] *nf.* sumptuousness.

Sontuoso [sonn-too-oh'soh] *a.* sumptuous.

Sopire [soh-pee'ray] *vt.* to calm.

Sopore [soh-poh'ray] *nm.* drowsiness, light sleep.

Soporifero [soh-poh-ree'fay-roh] *nm. and a.* soporific.

Soppiantare [sop-pee-ahn-tah'ray] *vt.* to oust, supplant.

Sopportabile [sop-porr-tah'bee-lay] *a.* bearable, endurable.

Sopportare [sop-porr-tah'ray] *vt.* to bear, endure, support, tolerate.

Soppressione [sop-press-see-oh'nay] *nf.* abolition, suppression.

Sopprimere [sop-pree'may-ray] *vt.* to abolish, suppress.

Sopra [soh'prah] *pr.* above, on, over; di [dee] **s.** *ad.* upstairs.

Soprabbondare, etc. : *v.* **sovrabbondare**, etc.

Soprabito [soh-prah'bee-toh] *nm.* overcoat.

Sopracciglio [soh-prahch-cheel'yoh] *nm.* eyebrow.

Sopraddetto [soh-prahd-det'toh] *a.* above-mentioned.

Sopraffare [soh-prahf-fah'ray] *vt.* to overcome, overwhelm.

Sopraggiungere [soh-prah-djoon'jay-ray] *vi.* to arrive, come up, happen.

Sopr(a)intendente [soh-pr(ah) een-ten-den'tay] *nm.* superintendent.

Sopraluogo [soh-prah-loo-oh'goh] *nm.* investigation on the spot.

Soprammobile [soh-prahm-moh'bee-lay] *nm.* nick-nack.

Soprannaturale [soh-prahn-nah-too-rah'lay] *nm. and a.* supernatural.

Soprano [soh-prah'noh] *nm.* soprano singer.

Soprappensiero [soh-prahp-pen-see-ay'roh] *ad.* sunk in thought.

Soprappiù [soh-prahp-pee-oo'] *nm.* extra.

Soprascritta [soh-prah-skreet'tah] *nf.* address, superscription.

Soprascritto [soh-prah-skreet'toh] *a.* above(-written).

Soprassalto [soh-prahs-sahl'toh] *nm.* start; di [dee] *s. ad.* with a start.

Soprastante [soh-prah-stahn'tay] *a.* impending, overhanging.

Soprattassa [soh-praht-tahs'sah] *nf.* surtax.

Soprattutto [soh-praht-toot'toh] *ad.* above all, especially.

Sopravanzare [soh-prah-vahnt-sah'ray] *vt.* to excel, surpass.

Sopravvenire [soh-prahv-vay-nee'ray] *vi.* to come up, happen, occur, supervene.

Sopravvento [soh-prahv-ven'toh] *nm.* advantage, superiority.

Sopravvivere [soh-prahv-vee'vay-ray] *vi.* to outlive, survive.

Sopruso [soh-proo'zoo] *nm.* abuse of power, insult, outrage.

Soqquadro [sock-kwah'droh] *nm.* confusion, disorder; a [ah] *s. ad.* topsy-turvy.

Sorbire [sorr-bee'ray] *vt.* to sip, swallow.

Sorcio [sorr'choh] *nm.* mouse.

Sordido [sorr'dee-doh] *a.* dirty, filthy.

Sordità [sorr-dee-tah'] *nf.* deafness.

Sordo [sorr'doh] *a.* deaf, deep, hollow.

Sordomuto [sorr-doh-moo'toh] *nm.* deaf-mute; *a.* deaf-and-dumb.

Sorella [soh-rell'lah] *nf.* sister.

Sorgente [sorr-jen'tay] *nf.* cause, fountain, origin, source, spring.

Sorgere [sorr'jay-ray] *vi.* to (a)rise, get up, rise up, stand up.

Sormontare [sorr-mon-tah'ray] *vt.* to overcome, surmount, surpass.

Sorpassare [sorr-pahs-sah'ray] *vt.* to excel, outdo, surpass.

Sorprendere [sorr-pren'day-ray] *vt.* to surprise.

Sorpresa [sorr-pray'sah] *nf.* astonishment, surprise.

Sorreggere [sorr-ray'djay-ray] *vt.* to support.

Sorridere [sorr-ree'day-ray] *vi.* to smile (at).

Sorriso [sorr-ree'zoh] *nm.* smile.

Sorso [sorr'soh] *nm.* draught, drop, sip.

Sorta [sorr'tah] *nf.* kind, sort.

Sorte [sorr'tay] *nf.* destiny, fortune, lot.

Sorteggiare [sorr-tay-djah'ray] *vt.* to draw by lot.

Sortire [sorr-tee'ray] *vt.* to be endowed with; *vi.* to come (go) out.

Sortita [sorr-tee'tah] *nf.* sally, witty remark.

Sorveglianza [sorr-vayl-yahnt'sah] *nf.* superintendence, supervision.

Sorvegliare [sorr-vayl-yah'ray] *vt.* to oversee, watch (over).

Sorvolare [sorr-voh-lah'ray] *vt.* to fly over, pass over.

Sospendere [soss-pen'day-ray] vt. to adjourn, defer, interrupt, stop, suspend.

Sospensione [soss-pen-see-oh'nay] nf. adjournment, suspension.

Sospeso [soss-pay'soh] a. hanging, in suspense, uncertain.

Sospettare [soss-pet-tah'ray] vt. and i. to suspect.

Sospetto [soss-pet'toh] nm. suspect, suspicion; a. suspect, suspicious.

Sospirare [soss-pee-rah'ray] vt. to long for, sigh for; vi. to sigh. [sigh

Sospiro [soss-pee'roh] nm.

Sossopra [soss-soh'prah] ad. topsy-turvy, upside-down.

Sosta [soss'tah] nf. halt, pause, respite, rest, stay.

Sostantivo [soss-tahn-tee'voh] nm. noun, substantive.

Sostanza [soss-tahnt'sah] nf. means, patrimony, substance; in [een] s. ad. altogether, on the whole.

Sostare [soss-tah'ray] vi. to pause, stay, stop.

Sostegno [soss-tayn'yoh] nm. support.

Sostene/re [soss-tay-nay'ray] vt. to bear, hold up, keep up, maintain, resist, stand, support; —rsi vr. to lean on, support oneself.

Sostentamento [soss-ten-tah-men'toh] nm. living, sustenance.

Sostentare [soss-ten-tah'ray] vt. to support.

Sostituire [soss-tee-too-ee'ray] vt. to replace, take the place of.

Sostituto [soss-tee-too'toh] nm. substitute.

Sostituzione [soss-tee-too-tsee-oh'nay] nf. change, exchange, replacement.

Sottaceti [sot-tah-chay'tee] nm. (pl.) pickles (pl.).

Sottana [sot-tah'nah] nf. (eccl.) cassock, (woman's) skirt.

Sottentrare [sot-ten-trah'ray] vi. to take the place of.

Sotterfugio [sot-tehr-foo'joh] nm. subterfuge.

Sotterra [sot-tehr'rah] ad. underground.

Sotterraneo [sot-tehr-rah-nay-oh] nm. basement, vault; a. subterranean, underground.

Sotterrare [sot-tehr-rah'ray] vt. to bury, hide.

Sottigliezza [sot-teel-yet'sah] nf. insight, subtlety.

Sottile [sot-tee'lay] a. sharp, slender, sly, subtle.

Sottilizzare [sot-tee-leed-zah'ray] vt. to subtilise.

Sottintendere [sot-teen-ten'day-ray] vt. to understand.

Sottinteso [sot-teen-tay'soh] nm. hidden meaning; a. understood.

Sotto [sot'toh] ad. and pr. below, beneath, under(neath); al di [dee] s. di pr. below.

Sottocchio [sot-tock'kee-oh] ad. before one's eyes.

Sottolineare [sot-toh-lee-nay-ah'ray] vt. to lay stress on, underline.

Sottomano, di [dee sot-toh-mah'noh] ad. by indirect means, from an illegal source.

Sottomarino [sot-toh-mah-ree'noh] nm. and a. submarine.

Sottomesso [sot-toh-mess'soh] a. respectful, submissive.

Sottomette/re [sot-toh-met'tay-ray] vt. to conquer, subdue, subject; —rsi vr. to give in, submit, yield.

Sottopassaggio [sot-toh-pahs-sah'djoh] nm. subway.

Sottopor/re [sot-toh-porr'ray] vt. to place under, submit; —rsi vr. to submit.

Sottoscrive/re [sot-toh-skree'vay-ray] vt. to sign, subscribe, underwrite; *vi.* to agree to, assent to; —**rsi** *vr.* to sign, subscribe.

Sottoscrizione [sot-toh-skree-tsee-oh'nay] *nf.* subscription.

Sottosopra [sot-toh-soh'prah] *ad.* topsy-turvy, upside-down.

Sottostare [sot-toh-stah'ray] *vi.* to be subject, give in to, lie below.

Sottosuolo [sot-toh-soo-oh'loh] *nm.* basement.

Sottotenente [sot-toh-tay-nen'tay] *nm.* 2nd lieutenant.

Sottovoce [sot-toh-voh'chay] *ad.* in a low voice, in an undertone.

Sottrar/re [sot-trahr'ray] *vt.* to deduct, conceal, deliver, embezzle, rescue, steal, subtract; —**rsi** *vr.* to escape from, evade.

Sottufficiale [sot-toof-fee-chah'lay] *nm.* non-commissioned officer.

Sovente [soh-ven'tay] *ad.* often.

Soverchiare [soh-vehr-kee-ah'ray] *vt.* to overcome, overwhelm, surpass.

Soverchio [soh-vehr'kee-oh] *a.* excessive, immoderate.

Sovra: *v.* sopra.

Sovrabbondanza [soh-vrahb-bon-dahnt'sah] *nf.* superabundance.

Sovrabbondare [soh-vrahb-bon-dah'ray] *vi.* to superabound.

Sovraccarico [soh-vrahk-kah-ree-koh] *nm.* additional burden or weight; *a.* overburdened; per [pehr] s. *ad.* in addition, moreover.

Sovranità [soh-vrah-nee-tah'] *nf.* sovereignty.

Sovrannaturale [soh-vrahn-nah-too-rah'lay] *nm. and a.* supernatural.

Sovrano [soh-vrah'noh] *nm. and a.* sovereign.

Sovrastare [soh-vrah-stah'ray] *vi.* to hang over, surpass, threaten.

Sovrumano [soh-vroo-mah'noh] *a.* superhuman.

Sovveni/re [sov-vay-nee'ray] *vt.* to assist, help; *vi.* to occur to; —**rsi** *vr.* to remember.

Sovvenzione [sov-ven-tsee-oh'nay] *nf.* subsidy, subvention.

Sovversione [sov-vehr-see-oh'nay] *nf.* overthrow, subversion.

Sovversivo [sov-vehr-see'voh] *a.* subversive.

Sovvertire [sov-vehr-tee'ray] *vt.* to overthrow, subvert.

Sozzo [sod'zoh] *a.* filthy, loathsome.

Sozzura [sod-zoo'rah] *nf.* filth.

Spaccalegna [spahk-kah-layn'yah] *nm.* wood-cutter.

Spaccapietre [spahk-kah-pee-ay'tray] *nm.* roadmender, stone-breaker.

Spaccare [spahk-kah'ray] *vt.* to cleave, split.

Spaccatura [spahk-kah-too'rah] *nf.* crack, split.

Spaccia/re [spahk-chah'ray] *vt.* to kill, make believe, spread, sell (off); —**rsi** *vr.* to give oneself out for.

Spaccio [spahch'choh] *nm.* sale, shop.

Spacco [spahk'koh] *nm.* cleft, split.

Spaccone [spahk-koh'nay] *nm.* boaster, braggart.

Spada [spah'dah] *nf.* sword.

Spagnuolo [spahn-yoo-oh'loh] *nm.* Spaniard; *a.* Spanish.

Spago [spah'goh] *nm.* string, twine.

Spaiare [spah-yah'ray] *vt.* to uncouple.

Spalancare [spah-lahng-

Spalancare [spah-lahn-kah'ray] *vt.* to open wide, throw open.

Spalla [spahl'lah] *nf.* back, shoulder.

Spalleggiare [spahl-lay-djah'ray] *vt.* to back, support.

Spalliera [spahl-lee-ay'rah] *nf.* back (of chair).

Spallina [spahl-lee'nah] *nf.* epaulet.

Spalmare [spahl-mah'ray] *vt.* to smear, spread.

Spalto [spahl'toh] *nm.* glacis.

Spandere [spahn'day-ray] *vt.* to scatter, shed, spread.

Spanna [spahn'nah] *nf.* span.

Sparare [spah-rah'ray] *vt. and i.* to discharge, fire, shoot.

Sparecchiare [spah-reck-kee-ah'ray] *vt.* to clear (away).

Spargere [spahr'jay-ray] *vt.* to scatter, shed, spread.

Sparire [spah-ree'ray] *vi.* to disappear, go away, vanish.

Sparizione [spah-ree-tsee-oh'nay] *nf.* disappearance.

Sparlare [spahr-lah'ray] *vi.* to speak ill of.

Sparo [spah'roh] *nm.* report, shot.

Sparpagliare [spahr-pahl-yah'ray] *vt.* to disperse, scatter, spread, squander.

Sparso [spahr'soh] *a.* loose, scattered.

Spartiacque [spahr-tee-ahk'kway] *nm.* watershed.

Spartire [spahr-tee'ray] *vt.* to distribute, divide, share.

Spartito [spahr-tee'toh] *nm.* (*mus.*) score.

Spartizione [spahr-tee-tsee-oh'nay] *nf.* distribution, division.

Sparuto [spah-roo'toh] *a.* gaunt, lean, thin.

Sparvie/re [spahr-vee-ay'ray], **-ro** [roh] *nm.* hawk.

Spasimare [spah-zee-mah'ray] *vi.* to long for, suffer terribly.

Spasimo [spah'zee-moh] *nm.* pang, (*med.*) spasm.

Spassarsi [spahs-sahr'see] *vr.* to amuse oneself, enjoy oneself.

Spassionato [spahs-see-oh-nah'toh] *a.* dispassionate, impartial.

Spasso [spahs'soh] *nm.* amusement, pastime; andare a [an-dah'ray ah] S. *vi.* to go for a walk.

Spatriare: *v.* **espatriare**.

Spauracchio [spow-rahk'kee-oh] *nm.* bugbear, scarecrow.

Spaurire [spow-ree'ray] *vt.* to frighten.

Spavaldo [spah-vahl'doh] *nm.* bold fellow, braggart; *a.* bold, defiant.

Spaventare [spah-ven-tah'ray] *vt.* to frighten, scare.

Spaventevole [spah-ven-tay'voh-lay] *a.* dreadful, frightful.

Spavento [spah-ven'toh] *nm.* fear, fright.

Spaziare [spah-tsee-ah'ray] *vi.* to soar.

Spazientirsi [spah-tsee-en-teer'see] *vr.* to lose one's patience.

Spazio [spah'tsee-oh] *nm.* distance, interval, room, space, time.

Spazioso [spah-tsee-oh'soh] *a.* broad, roomy, spacious.

Spazzacamino [spaht-sah-kah-mee'noh] *nm.* chimneysweep.

Spazzaneve [spaht-sah-nay'vay] *nm.* snowplough.

Spazzare [spaht-sah'ray] *vt.* to sweep.

Spazzatura [spaht-sah-too'rah] *nf.* sweeping.

Spazzino [spaht-see'noh] *nm.* dustman, sweeper.

Spazzola [spaht'soh-lah] *nf.* brush.

Spazzolare [spaht-soh-lah'ray] vt. to brush.

Specchiarsi [speck-kee-ahr'see] nr. to be reflected, look at oneself in the glass.

Specchiera [speck-kee-ay'rah] nf. looking-glass.

Specchio [speck'kee-oh] nm. looking-glass, mirror.

Speciale [spay-chah'lay] a. particular, special.

Specialità [spay-chah-lee-tah'] nf. patent medicine, peculiarity, speciality.

Specie [spay'chay] nf. kind, species, sort; far [fahr] s. vi. to amaze; in ispecie [een ee-spay'chay] ad. especially.

Specificare [spay-chee-fee-kah'ray] vt. to specify.

Specificazione [spay-chee-fee-kah-tsee-oh'nay] nf. specification.

Specifico [spay-chee'fee-koh] nm. and a. specific.

Specioso [spay-choh'soh] a. specious.

Speculare [spay-koo-lah'ray] vt. and i. to speculate.

Speculazione [spay-koo-lah-tsee-oh'nay] nf. speculation.

Spedale: v. **ospedale**.

Spedire [spay-dee'ray] vt. to dispatch, forward, send.

Speditezza [spay-dee-det'sah] nf. expedition, quickness.

Spedito [spay-dee'toh] a. prompt, quick, ready.

Spedizione [spay-dee-tsee-oh'nay] nf. dispatch, expedition, forwarding.

Spedizioniere [spay-dee-tsee-oh-nee-ay'ray] nm. forwarding agent, shipping agent.

Spegnere [spayn'yay-ray] vt. to blow out, extinguish, put out, quench switch off, turn out.

Spellare [spell-lah'ray] vt. to skin.

Spelonca [spay-long'kah] nf. cave, den.

Speme [spay'may] nf. (poet.) hope.

Spendere [spen'day-ray] vt. and i. to spend.

Spennare [spen-nah'ray] vt. to pluck (poultry).

Spensierato [spen-see-ay-rah'toh] a. light-hearted.

Spenzolo/ne [spend-zoh-loh'nay], —ni [nee] ad. dangling.

Sperabile [spay-rah-bee'lay] a. to be hoped for.

Speranza [spay-rahnt'sah] nf. expectation, hope.

Sperare [spay-rah'ray] vt. to expect, hope for.

Sperde/re [spehr'day-ray] vt. to disperse, scatter; —rsi vr. to get lost, go astray.

Spergiurare [spehr-joo-rah'ray] vi. to perjure oneself, swear falsely.

Spergiuro [spehr-joo'roh] nm. perjurer, perjury.

Sperimentale [spay-ree-men-tah'lay] a. experimental.

Sperimentare [spay-ree-men-tah'ray] vt. to experiment, test, try.

Sperone [spay-roh'nay] nm. spur.

Sperperare [spehr-pay-rah'ray] vt. to dissipate, squander, waste.

Sperpero [spehr'pay-roh] nm. dissipation, squandering.

Spesa [spay'zah] nf. cost, expenditure, expense.

Spesso [spess'soh] a. dense, thick; ad. frequently, often.

Spessore [spess-soh'ray] nm. thickness.

Spettacolo [spet-tah'koh-loh] nm. performance, sight, spectacle.

Spettanza. essere di [ess'say-ray dee spet-tahnt'sah] vi. to be the duty of, concern.

Spettare [spet-tah'ray] vi.

to be the duty of, be the turn of.

Spettatore [spet-tah-toh'ray] *nm.* bystander, on-looker, spectator.

Spettinato [spet-tee-nah'toh] *a.* dishevelled, unkempt.

Spettro [spet'troh] *nm.* ghost, spectre.

Speziale [spay-tsee-ah'lay] *nm.* apothecary, chemist.

Spezie [spay'tsee-ay] *nf.* (*pl.*) spices (*pl.*).

Spezzare [spet-sah'ray] *vt.* to break. [spy.

Spia [spee'ah] *nf.* informer.

Spiacente [spee-ah-chen'tay] *a.* sorry.

Spiacere: *v.* dispiacere.

Spiaggia [spee-ah'djah] *nf.* beach, shore.

Spianare [spee-ah-nah'ray] *vt.* to demolish, level, raze, smooth.

Spiantare [spee-ahn-tah'ray] *vt.* to ruin.

Spiantato [spee-ahn-tah'toh] *nm.* ruined man.

Spiare [spee-ah'ray] *vt.* to inquire into, spy upon, watch.

Spiccare [speek-kah'ray] *vt.* to be conspicuous, be different, stand out; **spiccare un salto** [—oon sahl'toh] to jump, leap, spring.

Spicchio [speek'kee-oh] *nm.* clove (of garlic), section, slice.

Spiccia/re [speech-chah'ray] *vt.* to dispatch, send off; —**rsi** *vr.* to hurry up, make haste.

Spicciolo [speech'choh-loh] *nm.* small coin (*pl.* change); *a.* small. [spit.

Spiedo [spee-ay'doh] *nm.*

Spiegabile [spee-ay-gah'bee-lay] *a.* explicable, justifiable.

Spiega/re [spee-ay-gah'ray] *vt.* to display, explain, justify, spread out, unfold; —**rsi** *vr.* to make oneself understood.

Spiegazione [spee-ay-gah-tsee-oh'nay] *nf.* explanation.

Spietato [spee-ay-tah'toh] *a.* pitiless, ruthless.

Spiffero [speef'fay-roh] *nm.* draught (of air).

Spiga [spee'gah] *nf.* ear (of corn).

Spigliatezza [speel-yah-tet'sah] *nf.* ease, nimbleness.

Spigliato [speel-yah'toh] *a.* easy, nimble.

Spigo [spee'goh] *nm.* lavender.

Spigolare [spee-goh-lah'ray] *vt.* to glean.

Spigolo [spee'goh-loh] *nm.* corner (of table, etc.).

Spilla [speel'lah] *nf.* brooch.

Spillare [speel-lah'ray] *vt.* to broach, tap.

Spillo [speel'loh] *nm.* pin.

Spilorcio [spee-lorr'choh] *nm.* miser, niggard; *a.* miserly, niggardly, stingy.

Spina [spee'nah] *nf.* thorn, (*elec.*) plug; **s. dorsale** [dorr-sah'lay] back-bone.

Spinaci [spee-nah'chee] *nm.* (*pl.*) spinach.

Spingere [speen'jay-ray] *vt.* to drive, induce, push, shove, thrust.

Spino [spee'noh] *nm.* thorn.

Spinoso [spee-noh-soh] *a.* (*fig.*) knotty, thorny, ticklish.

Spinta [speen'tah] *nf.* push, shove.

Spinto [speen'toh] *a.* excessive, immoderate, driven, pushed.

Spionaggio [spee-oh-nah'djoh] *nm.* espionage, spying.

Spiovere [spee-oh'vay-ray] *vi.* to stop raining.

Spira [spee'rah] *nf.* coil.

Spiraglio [spee-rahl'yoh] *nm.* air-hole, gleam (of light, etc.).

Spirale [spee-rah'lay] *nf. and a.* spiral.

Spirare [spee-rah'ray] *vi.* to blow, die, expire.

Spirito [spee'ree-toh] *nm.* courage, ghost, spirit, wit.

Spiritoso [spee-ree-toh'soh] *a.* alcoholic, witty.

Spirituale [speet'see-koh] *a.* spiritual. [pinch.

Spizzico [speet'see-koh] *nm.*

Splendente [splen-den'tay] *a.* bright, brilliant, shining.

Splendere [splen'day-ray] *vi.* to glitter, shine.

Splendido [splen'dee-doh] *a.* gorgeous, magnificent, splendid.

Splendore [splen-doh'ray] *nm.* grandeur, splendour.

Spodestare [spoh-dess-tah'-ray] *vt.* to dispossess, oust.

Spogl/ia [spoll'yah] *nf.* booty, spoil; —**ie** [yay] (*pl.*) remains (*pl.*).

Spoglia/re [spoll-yah'ray] *vt.* to despoil, plunder, undress; —**rsi** *vr.* to strip oneself, undress.

Spogliatoio [spoll-yah-toh'-yoh] *nm.* dressing-room.

Spogl/io [spoll'yoh] *nm.* selection; —**i** [yee] (*pl.*) cast-off clothes (*pl.*); *a.* bare, uncovered, undressed.

Spola [spoh'lah] *nf.* shuttle; fare la [fah'ray lah] **s.** *vi.* to go to and fro.

Spolpare [spoll-pah'ray] *vt.* to bleed white, despoil, remove flesh.

Spolverare [spoll-vay-rah'-ray] *vt.* to brush, dust.

Spolverata [spoll-vay-rah'-tah] *nf.* brush(ing), dust(ing).

Sponda [spon'dah] *nf.* bank, edge.

Sponsali [spon-sah'lee] *nm.* (*pl.*, *poet.*) wedding.

Spontaneità [spon-tah-nay-ee-tah'] *nf.* spontaneousness.

Spontaneo [spon-tah'nay-oh] *a.* spontaneous.

Spopolare [spoh-poh-lah'-ray] *vt.* to depopulate.

Sporcare [sporr-kah'ray] *vt.* to dirty, soil.

Sporcizia [sporr-chee'tsee-ah] *nf.* dirt, filth.

Sporco [sporr'koh] *a.* dirty, filthy.

Sporge/re [sporr'jay-ray] *vt.* to put out, stretch out; —**rsi** *vr.* to jut out, lean out.

Sporta [sporr'tah] *nf.* (shopping-)basket.

Sportello [sporr-tell'loh] *nm.* door (of carriage, etc.), window (of booking-office).

Sporto [sporr'toh] *nm.* jut, projection, shop-shutter; *a.* outstretched.

Sposa [spoh'zah] *nf.* bride, young wife; —**so** [zoh] *nm.* bridegroom.

Sposalizio [spoh-zah-lee'-tsee-oh] *nm.* marriage.

Sposa/re [spoh-zah'ray] *vt.* to marry, wed; —**rsi** *vr.* to get married.

Spossare [sposs-sah'ray] *vt.* to exhaust, wear out.

Spossatezza [sposs-sah-tet'-sah] *nf.* exhaustion, weariness.

Spossessare [sposs-sess-sah'-ray] *vt.* to dispossess.

Spostamento [sposs-tah-men'toh] *nm.* change, displacement, shifting.

Spostare [sposs-tah'ray] *vt.* to change, displace, shift.

Spranga [sprahng'gah] *nf.* bolt, (cross-)bar.

Sprazzo [spraht'soh] *nm.* flash, gleam.

Sprecare [spray-kah'ray] *vt.* to dissipate, squander, waste.

Spreco [spray'koh] *nm.* squandering, waste.

Sprecone [spray-koh'nay] *nm.* squanderer, waster.

Spregevole [spray-jay'voh-lay] *a.* despicable, mean.

Spregiare: *v.* sprezzare.

Spregio [spray'joh] nm. disdain, scorn.

Spregiudicato [spray-joo-dee-kah'toh] a. unbiased, unprejudiced.

Spremere [spray'may-ray] vt. to press (out), squeeze.

Spremuta [spray-moo'tah] nf. squash.

Sprezzare [spret-sah'ray] vt. to despise, disdain, scorn.

Sprigiona/re [spree-johnah'ray] vt. to give off, release, set free; —rsi vr. to exhale, spring out.

Sprizzare [spreet-sah'ray] vi. to spout, spring out.

Sprofonda/re [sproh-fondah'ray] vi. to founder, sink; —rsi vr. to be absorbed, sink.

Spronare [sproh-nah'ray] vt. to goad, spur, urge.

Sprone [sproh'nay] nm. spur.

Sproporzionato [sproh-porr-tsee-oh-nah'toh] a. disproportionate.

Sproposito [sproh-poh'zee-toh] nm. blunder, gaffe.

Sprovvedere [sprov-vay-day'ray] vt. to deprive.

Sprovvista, alla [ahl'lah sprov-vee'stah] ad. unawares, unexpectedly.

Sprovvisto [sprov-vee'stoh] a. lacking, unprovided with.

Spruzzare [sproot-sah'ray] vt. to spray, sprinkle.

Spruzzo [sproot'soh] nm. spray, sprinkle.

Spudorato [spoo-doh-rah'-toh] a. impudent, shameless

Spugna [spoon'yah] nf. sponge.

Spugnoso [spoon-yoh'soh] a. spongy.

Spuma [spoo'mah] nf. foam, froth.

Spuntare [spoon-tah'ray] vt. to blunt, cut off the end; vi. to appear, rise.

Sputacchiera [spoo-tahk-kee-ay'rah] nf. spittoon.

Sputare [spoo-tah'ray] vi. to spit.

Sputo [spoo'toh] nm. spitting, spittle.

Squadra [skwah'drah] nf. detachment, squad, square.

Squadrare [skwah-drah'ray] vt. to look over, square.

Squadriglia [skwah-dreel'yah] nf. squadron.

Squagliarsi [skwahl-yahr'see] vr. to make off, slip away.

Squallido [skwahl'lee-doh] a. wretched.

Squallore [skwahl-loh'ray] nm. squalor, wretchedness.

Squama [skwah'mah] nf. scale (of fish, etc.).

Squamoso [skwah-moh'soh] a. scaly.

Squarciare [skwahr-chah'ray] vt. to rend, tear asunder.

Squarcio [skwahr'choh] nm. gash, rent, tear; passage (of a book, etc.).

Squartare [skwahr-tah'ray] vt. to chop, quarter.

Squassare [skwahs-sah'ray] vt. to shake.

Squilibrato [skwee-lee-brah'toh] nm. and a. crazy, unbalanced (man).

Squilibrio [skwee-lee'bree-oh] nm. want of balance; s. mentale [men-tah'lay] madness.

Squilla [skweel'lah] nf. bell, sound of bell.

Squillante [skweel-lahn'tay] a. blaring, shrill.

Squillare [skweel-lah'ray] vi. to blare, ring, sound.

Squillo [skweel'loh] nm. blare, ring.

Squisito [skwee-zee'toh] a. exquisite.

Squittire [skweet-tee'ray] vi. to squeak.

Sradicare [srah-dee-kah'ray] vt. to eradicate, uproot.

Sregolatezza [sray-goh-lah-tet'sah] nf. disorder, dissoluteness, excess.

Sregolato [sray-goh-lah'toh] a. disorderly, dissolute, excessive.

Stabile [stah'bee-lay] a. firm, lasting, permanent, stable.

Stabilimento [stah-bee-lee-men'toh] nm. establishment, factory, branch, works, workshop.

Stabili/re [stah-bee-lee'ray] vt. to arrange, ascertain, decide, establish, fix, state; —rsi vr. to settle.

Stabilità [stah-bee-lee-tah'] nf. firmness, stability.

Stacca/re [stahk-kah'ray] vt. to detach, remove, separate; —rsi vr. to be different, become detached, break off, leave.

Stacciare [stahch-chah'ray] vt. to sieve, sift.

Staccio [stahch'choh] nm. sieve.

Stacco [stahk'koh] nm. difference, material; dress-length.

Stadera [stah-day'rah] nf. (tech.) steelyard.

Stadio [stah'dee-oh] nm. sports-ground, stadium.

Staffa [stahf'fah] nf. footboard, stirrup; perdere le staffe [pehr'day-ray lay stahf'fay] vi. to lose one's temper.

Staffiere [stahf-fee-ay'ray] nm. groom.

Staffilare [stahf-fee-lah'ray] vt. to lash, scourge.

Staffile [stahf-fee'lay] nm. scourge, whip.

Stagionare [stah-joh-nah'ray] vt. and i. to ripen, season.

Stagione [stah-joh'nay] nf. season.

Stagn/aio [stahn-yah'yoh] —ino (yee'noh) nm. tinker, tin-smith.

Stagnante [stahn-yahn'tay] a. stagnant.

Stagnare [stahn-yah'ray] vt. to solder, tin; vi. to stagnate.

Stagno [stahn'yoh] nm. pond, pool, tin.

Staio [stah'yoh] nm. bushel.

Stalla [stahl'lah] nf. cow-house, stable.

Stallaggio [stahl-lah'djoh] nm. stabling.

Stalliere [stahl-lee-ay'ray] nm. groom, stable-man.

Stallone [stahl-loh'nay] nm. stallion.

Sta/mane [stah-mah'nay], —mani [mah'nee], —mattina [maht-tee'nah] ad. this morning.

Stambugio [stahm-boo'joh] nm. cubby-hole, little dark room.

Stam/pa [stahm'pah] nf. press, print; —pe [pay] (pl.) printed matter.

Stampare [stahm-pah'ray] vt. to coin, engrave, print.

Stampella [stahm-pell'lah] nf. crutch.

Stamperia [stahm-pay-ree'ah] nf. printing-press.

Stampo [stahm'poh] nm. kind, mould, sort, stamp.

Stancare [stahng-kah'ray] vt. to bore, exhaust, tire.

Stanchezza [stahng-ket'sah] nf. tiredness, weariness.

Stanco [stahng'koh] a. tired, weary.

Stanga [stahng'gah] nf. bar, shaft (of carriage etc.).

Stangare [stahng-gah'ray] vt. to bar.

Stanotte [stah-not'tay] ad. last night, to-night.

Stante [stahn'tay] a. being; seduta [say-doo'tah] s. ad. during the sitting; at once.

Stantio [stahn-tee'oh] a. stale.

Stanza [stahnt'sah] nf.

room, stanza (poetry); **essere di** [ess'say-ray dee] **s.** *vi.* (*mil.*) to be stationed.

Stanziare [stahn-tsee-ah'ray] *vt.* to appropriate, set apart.

Stare [stah'ray] *vi.* to be, live, remain, stand, stay.

Starnutire [stahr-noo-tee'ray] *vi.* to sneeze.

Starnuto [stahr-noo'toh] *nm.* sneeze.

Stasera [stah-say'rah] *ad.* this evening, to-night.

Statale [stah-tah'lay] *a.* (of the) state; *nm.* civil servant.

Statista [stah-tee'stah] *nm.* statesman.

Stato [stah'toh] *nm.* condition, situation, state; **s. maggiore** [mah-djoh'ray] (*mil.*) staff. [statue.

Statua [stah'too-ah] *nf.*

Statuaria [stah-too-ah'ree-ah] *nf.* statuary.

Statura [stah-too'rah] *nf.* size, stature.

Statuto [stah-too'toh] *nm.* constitution, statute.

Stazionario [stah-tsee-oh-nah'ree-oh] *a.* stationary, unchanged.

Stazione [stah-tsee-oh'nay] *nf.* station; **s. climatica** [klee-mah'tee-kah] health-resort.

Stazzare [staht-sah'ray] *vt.* to gauge, measure; *vi.* (*naut.*) to have a tonnage of.

Stecca [steck'kah] *nf.* cue (billiards), false note (music), rib (umbrella), small stick.

Steccato [steck-kah'toh] *nm.* paling, rails (*pl.*).

Stecchino [steck-kee'noh] *nm.* toothpick.

Stecchito [steck-kee'toh] *a.* stiff and stark, very thin.

Stella [stell-lah] *nf.* star.

Stellato [stell-lah'toh] *a.* starry.

Stelo [stay'loh] *nm.* stalk, stem.

Stemma [stem'mah] *nm.* coat of arms.

Stemperare [stem-pay-rah'ray] *vt.* to dilute, melt.

Stendardo [sten-dahr'doh] *nm.* standard.

Stendere [sten'day-ray] *vt.* to draw up, lay out, spread, stretch.

Stenografare [stay-noh-grah-fah'ray] *vt.* to write in shorthand.

Stenografia [stay-noh-grah-fee'ah] *nf.* shorthand.

Stenogra/fo [stay-noh'grah-foh] *nm.* —**fa** [fah] *nf.* shorthand-writer, stenographer.

Stentare [sten-tah'ray] *vi.* to find it hard to.

Stento [sten'toh] *nm.* difficulty, privation, suffering; **a** [ah] **s.** *ad.* hardly, with difficulty.

Sterile [stay'ree-lay] *a.* barren, sterile, unproductive.

Sterilità [stay-ree-lee-tah'] *nf.* barrenness, sterility.

Sterlina [stehr-lee'nah] *nf.* pound (sterling).

Sterminare [stehr-mee-nah'ray] *vt.* to exterminate.

Sterminato [stehr-mee-nah'toh] *a.* boundless, unlimited.

Sterrare [stehr-rah'ray] *vt.* to dig up, excavate.

Stesso [stess'soh] *a. and pn.* same, self.

Stile [stee'lay] *nm.* style.

Stilla [steel'lah] *nf.* drop.

Stillare [steel-lah'ray] *vi.* to drip, ooze.

Stima [stee'mah] *nf.* consideration, esteem, estimation, valuation.

Stima/re [stee-mah'ray] *vt.* to appraise, consider, esteem, value; —**rsi** *vr.* to think oneself.

Stimolante [stee-moh-lahn'tay] *nm.* stimulant; *a.* stimulating.

Stimolare [stee-moh-lah'ray] vt. to drive, goad, stimulate, urge.

Stimolo [stee'moh-loh] nm. goad, spur, stimulus.

Stinco [steeng'koh] nm. shin, shin-bone.

Stipa/re [stee-pah'ray] vt. —rsi vr. to crowd, throng.

Stipendio [stee-pen'dee-oh] nm. salary, wages (pl.).

Stipite [stee'pee-tay] nm. (door-)post, stock (family).

Stipulare [stee-poo-lah'ray] vt. to arrange, draw up, stipulate.

Stipulazione [stee-poo-lah-tsee-oh'nay] nf. arrangement, stipulation.

Stiracchiare [stee-rahk-kee-ah'ray] vt. and i. to bargain, haggle.

Stira/re [stee-rah'ray] vt. to iron, stretch (out); —rsi vr. to stretch (oneself).

Stiro / ferro da [fehr'roh dah stee'roh] nm. iron.

Stirpe [steer'pay] nf. birth, descent, race.

Stitichezza [stee-tee-ket'sah] nf. constipation.

Stitico [stee'tee-koh] a. constipated.

Stiva [stee'vah] nf. (naut.) hold.

Stivale [stee-vah'lay] nm. boot.

Stivare [stee-vah'ray] vt. to stow.

Stizza [steet'sah] nf. anger.

Stizzirsi [steet-seer'see] vr. to fly into a passion, get angry.

Stizzoso [steet-soh'soh] a. ill-tempered, often angry.

Stoccafisso [stock-kah-fees'soh] nm. stockfish.

Stocco [stock'koh] nm. dagger.

Stoffa [stoff'fah] nf. matter, material, stuff.

Stoico [stoh'ee-koh] nm. stoic; a. stoical.

Stola [stoh'lah] nf. stole.

Stolidità [stoh-lee-dee-tah'] stolidezza [stoh-lee-det'sah] nf. stolidity, stupidity.

Stolido [stoh'lee-doh] a. stolid, stupid.

Stoltezza [stoll-tet'sah] nf. foolishness, folly.

Stolto [stoll'toh] nm. fool; a. foolish, silly.

Stomaca/re [stoh-mah-kah'ray] vt. to disgust, sicken; —rsi vr. to be disgusted with, be sick of.

Stomachevole [stoh-mah-kay'voh-lay] a. disgusting, loathsome.

Stomaco [stoh'mah-koh] nm. stomach.

Stonare [stoh-nah'ray] vi. to be out of place, out of tune.

Stoppa [stop'pah] nf. oakum, tow.

Stoppare [stop-pah'ray] vt. to stop with oakum (or tow).

Stoppia [stop'pee-ah] nf. stubble.

Stoppino [stop-pee'noh] nm. wick.

Storce/re [storr'chay-ray] vt. to distort, twist, wrench; —rsi vr. to twist, writhe.

Stordimento [storr-dee-men'toh] nm. dazed state, dizziness.

Stordire [storr-dee'ray] vt. to daze, stun, stupefy.

Storia [stoh'ree-ah] nf. history, story, tale.

Storico [stoh'ree-koh] nm. historian; a. historical.

Storione [stoh-ree-oh'nay] nm. sturgeon.

Stormire [storr-mee'ray] vi. to rustle.

Stormo [storr'moh] nm. flock, host, swarm; suonare a [soo-oh-nah'ray ah] s. vi. to sound the tocsin.

Stornare [storr-nah'ray] vt.

to deter, dissuade, turn away.

Stor/no [storr'noh], starling;
—**nello** [nell'loh] *nm.* starling.

Storpiare [storr-pee-ah'ray]
vt. to cripple, maim, spoil, twist.

Storpio [storr'pee-oh] *nm.*
cripple; *a.* crippled.

Storta [storr-tah] *nf.* sprain.

Storto [storr'toh] *a.* bandy,
crooked, wrong.

Stoviglie [stoh-veel'yay] *nf.*
(*pl.*) crockery.

Stra- [strah] *prefix,* over-.

Strabiliare [strah-bee-lee-
ah'ray] *vi.* to be amazed, be
astounded.

Strabismo [strah-beez'moh]
nm. squint, squinting.

Straboccare [strah-bock-
kah'ray] *vi.* to overflow.

Stracciare [strahch-chah-
ray] *vt.* to rend, tear.

Straccio [strahch'choh] *nm.*
rag, tatter; *a.* ragged, torn.

Strada [strah'dah] *nf.* road,
street, way; **s. facendo** [fah-
chen'doh] *ad.* on the way.

Stradone [strah-doh'nay]
nm. large street, main road.

Strafalcione [strah-fahl-
choh'nay] *nm.* blunder.

Strage [strah'jay] *nf.* havoc,
massacre, slaughter.

Strale [strah'lay] *nm.* arrow,
dart. *v.* Freccia.

Stralunare [strah-loo-nah'-
ray] *vt.* to open wide.

Stramazzare [strah-maht-
sah'ray] *vi.* to fall heavily.

Stramberia [strahm-bay-
ree'ah] *nf.* eccentricity, oddity.

Strambo [strahm'boh] *a.*
eccentric, queer, whimsical.

Strame [strah'may] *nm.*
litter, straw.

Strampalato [strahm-pah-
lah'toh] *a.* extravagant, illogical, queer.

Stranezza [strah-net'sah] *nf.*
oddness, strangeness.

Strangolare [strahng-goh-

lah'ray] *vt.* to choke, strangle,
throttle.

Straniero [strah-nee-ay'roh]
nm. foreigner; *a.* foreign.

Strano [strah'noh] *a.* funny,
odd, queer, strange.

Straordinario [strah-orr-
dee-nah'ree-oh] *a.* extraordinary, unusual; **edizione** [ay-
dee-tsee-oh'nay] **s.** -**a.** *nf.*
special edition (newspaper);
lavoro [lah-voh'roh] **s.** -**a.** *nm.*
overtime work.

Strapazza/re [strah-paht-
sah'ray] *vt.* to ill-treat, over-
tire, overwork; —**rsi** *vr.* to
overdo things.

Strapazzo [strah-paht'soh]
nm. excess, fatigue.

Strappa/re [strahp-pah'ray]
vt. to snatch, tear, wrench;
—**rsi** *vr.* to get torn, tear
oneself away.

Strappo [strahp'poh] *nm.*
jerk, rent, tear, wrench;
fare uno [fah'ray oo'noh]
s. alla regola [ah'lah ray'goh-
lah] *vi.* to make an exception.

Straripare [strah-ree-pah'-
ray] *vi.* to break the banks,
overflow.

Strascicare [strah-shee-kah'-
ray] *vt.* to drag, drawl, shuffle.

Strascico [strah'shee-koh]
nm. sequel, train.

Strategia [strah-tay-jee'ah]
nf. strategy.

Strato [strah'toh] *nm.*
coat(ing), layer, stratum.

Stravagante [strah-vah-
gahn'tay] *a.* extravagant, odd,
strange.

Stravaganza [strah-vah-
gahn'sah] *nf.* eccentricity,
extravagance, oddness.

Straviziare [strah-vee-tsee-
ah'ray] *vi.* to be intemperate.

Stravizio [strah-vee'tsee-oh]
nm. dissipation, excess.

Stravolto [strah-voll'toh] *a.*
convulsed, twisted.

Straziare [strah-tsee-ah´ray] vt. to rend, torture.

Strazio [strah´tsee-oh] nm. torment, torture.

Stre/ga [stray´gah] nf. witch; —**gone** [goh´nay] nm. wizard.

Stregare [stray-gah´ray] vt. to bewitch.

Stregua [stray´gwah] nf. standard, way.

Stremare [stray-mah´ray] vt. to exhaust.

Strenna [stren´nah] nf. Christmas box, gift.

Strenuo [stray´noo-oh] a. strenuous, vigorous.

Strepitare [stray-pee-tah´ray] vi. to make an uproar, shout.

Strepito [stray´pee-toh] nm. din, noise, uproar.

Stretta [stret´tah] nf. clasp, embrace, grasp, hold.

Strettezza [stret-tet´sah] nf. narrowness, strait.

Stretto [stret´toh] nm. straits (pl.); a. narrow, strict, tight.

Strettoio [stret-toh´yoh] nm. press.

Stricnina [streek-nee´nah] nf. strychnine.

Stridente [stree-den´tay] a. jarring, sharp, shrill, strident.

Stridere [stree´day-ray] vi. to creak, jar, screech.

Strido [stree-doh] nm. cry, screech.

Stridulo [stree´doo-loh] a. piercing, shrill.

Striglia [streel´yah] nf. curry-comb.

Strigliare [streel-yah´ray] vt. to curry, rebuke.

Strillare [streel-lah´ray] vi. to cry, shout, scream.

Strillo [streel´loh] nm. cry, shout, shriek.

Strillone [streel-loh´nay] nm. (news)paper-boy.

Stringa [streeng´gah] nf. (shoe-)lace.

Stringe/re [streen´jay-ray] vt. to grasp, press, tighten; —**rsi** vr. to press (against), shrug, squeeze.

Striscia [stree´shah] nf. strip, stripe.

Strisciare [stree-shah´ray] vt. to drag, graze, shuffle; vi. to crawl, creep.

Stritolare [stree-toh-lah´ray] vt. to crush.

Strizzare [street-sah´ray] vt. to squeeze, wring; s. l'occhio [lock´kee-oh] vi. to wink.

Strofa [stroh´fah] nf. strophe.

Strofinaccio [stroh-fee-nahch´choh] nm. duster, floor-cloth.

Strofinare [stroh-fee-nah´ray] vt. to dust, wipe.

Strombazzare [strom-baht-sah´ray] vt. to trumpet.

Stroncare [strong-kah´ray] vt. to break (off), criticise harshly.

Stropicciare [stroh-peech-chah´ray] vt. to drag, rub, scrub.

Strozza [strot´sah] nf. throat, throttle.

Strozzare [strot-sah´ray] vt. (fig.) to fleece, strangle, throttle.

Strozzino [strot-see´noh] nm. usurer.

Strugge/re [stroo´djay-ray] vt. to consume, distress, melt; —**rsi** vr. to be consumed, long (for), melt.

Strumento [stroo-men´toh] nm. implement, instrument, tool.

Strusciare [stroo-shah´ray] vt. to rub, wear (out).

Strutto [stroot´toh] nm. lard.

Struttura [stroot-too´rah] nf. structure.

Struzzo [stroot´soh] nm. ostrich.

Superbo [soo-pehr'boh] *a.* arrogant, proud, superb.

Superficie [soo-pehr-fee'chay] *nf.* area, surface.

Superfluo [soo-pehr'floo-oh] *a.* needless, superfluous, unnecessary.

Superiore [soo-pay-ree-oh'ray] *nm.* superior; *a.* higher, superior, upper.

Superiorità [soo-pay-ree-oh-ree-tah'] *nf.* superiority.

Superstite [soo-pehr-stee'tay] *nm.* survivor; *a.* surviving.

Superstizione [soo-pehr-stee-tsee-oh'nay] *nf.* superstition.

Superstizioso [soo-pehr-stee-tsee-oh'soh] *a.* superstitious.

Supino [soo-pee'noh] *a.* supine.

Suppellettili [soop-pell-let'tee-lee] *nf.* (*pl.*) equipment, fittings (*pl.*) furnishings (*pl.*).

Suppergiù [soop-pehr-joo'] *ad.* approximately, nearly, roughly.

Supplemento [soop-play-men'toh] *nm.* addition, extra, supplement.

Supplente [soop-plen'tay] *nm. and f.* substitute, temporary clerk, temporary teacher.

Supplenza [soop-plent'sah] *nf.* temporary post.

Supplica [soop'plee-kah] *nf.* entreaty, petition.

Supplicare [soop-plee-kah'ray] *vt.* to entreat, implore.

Supplire [soop-plee'ray] *vi.* to replace, substitute, take the place of.

Supplizio [soop-plee'tsee-oh] *nm.* punishment, torture.

Supporre [soop-porr'ray] *vt. and i.* to suppose.

Supposizione [soop-poh-zee-tsee-oh'nay] *nf.* supposition.

Suppurare [soop-poo-rah'ray] *vi.* to suppurate.

Supremazia [soo-pray-mah-tsee'ah] *nf.* supremacy.

Supremo [soo-pray'moh] *a.* extraordinary, greatest, highest, last, supreme.

Surrogare [soor-roh-gah'ray] *vt.* to replace, substitute.

Surrogato [soor-roh-gah'toh] *nm.* substitute.

Suscettibile [soo-shet-tee'bee-lay] *a.* easily offended, susceptible.

Suscettibilità [soo-shet-tee-bee-lee-tah'] *nf.* susceptibility, touchiness.

Suscitare [soo-shee-tah'ray] *vt.* to give rise to, provoke, rouse.

Susi/na [soo-see'nah] *nf.* plum; —no [noh] *nm.* plum-tree.

Susseguente [soos-say-gwen'tay] *a.* subsequent, successive.

Sussidiare [soos-see-dee-ah'ray] *vt.* to help, subsidize.

Sussidio [soos-see'dee-oh] *nm.* aid, dole, subsidy.

Sussiego [soos-see-ay'goh] *nm.* exaggerated dignity.

Sussistenza [soos-see-stent'sah] *nf.* existence, subsistence.

Sussistere [soos-see'stay-ray] *vi.* to exist, subsist.

Sussultare [soos-sool-tah'ray] *vi.* to start, tremble.

Sussurrare [soos-soor-rah'ray] *vi.* to murmur, mutter, whisper.

Sussurro [soos-soor'roh] *nm.* mutter, whisper.

Svagare [svah-gah'ray] *vt.* to amuse, distract someone's attention.

Svago [svah'goh] *nm.* amusement, recreation.

Svaligiare [svah-lee-jah'ray] *vt.* to steal everything from, strip.

Svalutare [svah-loo-tah'ray] vt. to depreciate.

Svanimento [svah-nee-men'toh] nm. vanishing, weakening. v. **svanire**.

Svanire [svah-nee'ray] vi. to be lost, disappear, vanish.

Svanito [svah-nee'toh] a. absent-minded, vanished.

Svantaggio [svahn-tah'djoh] nm. disadvantage, prejudice.

Svantaggioso [svahn-tah-djoh'soh] a. prejudicial, unfavourable.

Svaporare [svah-poh-rah'ray] vi. to evaporate, vanish.

Svariato [svah-ree-ah'toh] a. various.

Svedese [svay-day'zay] nm. and f. Swede; a. Swedish.

Sveglia [svayl'yah] nf. alarm clock, (mil.) reveille, waking (up).

Sveglia/re [svayl-yah'ray] vt. to (a)rouse, wake (up); —rsi vr. to wake (up).

Svegliatezza [svayl-yah-tet'sah] nf. quickness, readiness.

Sveglio [svayl'yoh] a. awake, quick-witted.

Svelare [svay-lah'ray] vt. to disclose, reveal.

Sveltezza [svell-tet'sah] nf. quickness, rapidity.

Sveltire [svell-tee'ray] vt. to make lively, nimble, quick, slender.

Svelto [svell'toh] a. nimble, quick(-witted), rapid, slender.

Svenimento [svay-nee-men'toh] nm. fainting-fit, swoon.

Svenire [svay-nee'ray] vi. to faint, swoon.

Sventare [sven-tah'ray] vt. to baffle, foil, thwart.

Sventato [sven-tah'toh] a. heedless, scatter-brained.

Sventolare [sven-toh-lah'ray] vt. to fan, wave.

Sventrare [sven-trah'ray] vt. to disembowel, destroy, rip up.

Sventura [sven-too'rah] nf. bad luck, misfortune, mishap.

Sventurato [sven-too-rah'toh] a. unfortunate, unlucky.

Svergognare [svehr-gohn-yah'ray] vt. to disgrace.

Svergognato [svehr-gohn-yah'toh] a. shameless.

Svernare [svehr-nah'ray] vi. to winter.

Svestire [svess-tee'ray] vt. to undress.

Sviamento [svee-ah-men'toh] nm. leading astray, turning aside.

Svignarsela [sveen-yahr'say-lah] vr. to slip away.

Sviluppa/re [svee-loop-pah'ray] vt. to develop, work out; —rsi vr. to break out, develop, grow.

Sviluppo [svee-loop'poh] nm. development, growth, increase.

Svincolare [sveeng-koh-lah'ray] vt. to clear, disengage, free.

Svisare [svee-zah'ray] vt. to disfigure, misrepresent.

Sviscerare [svee-shay-rah'ray] vt. to examine thoroughly.

Sviscerato [svee-shay-rah'toh] a. ardent, passionate.

Svista [svee-stah] nf. oversight, slip.

Svitare [svee-tah'ray] vt. to unscrew.

Svizzero [sveet'say-roh] nm. and a. Swiss.

Svogliatezza [svoll-yah-tet'sah] nf. listlessness.

Svogliato [svoll-yah'toh] a. lazy, listless.

Svolazzare [svoh-laht-sah'ray] vi. to flit, fly about.

Svolge/re [svoll'jay-ray] vt. to complete, display, unroll, unwind; —rsi vr. to happen, unfold, unroll.

Svolgimento [svoll-jee-men'toh] nm. course, development, treatment.

Svolta [svoll'tah] *nf.* turn, turning-point, winding.

Svoltare [svoll-tah'ray] *vi.* to turn.

Svoltola/re [svoll-toh-lah'ray] *vt.* to roll;—**rsi** *vr.* to roll about, wallow.

Svotare [svoh-tah'ray] *vt.* to empty.

T

Tabacca/io [tah-bahk-kah'-yoh] *nm.* —**ia** [yah] *nf.* to-bacconist.

Tabacchiera [tah-bahk-kee-ay'rah] *nf.* snuff-box.

Tabacco [tah-bahk'koh] *nm.* tobacco; **t. da naso** [da nah'-soh], snuff.   [cloak.

Tabarro [tah-bahr'roh] *nm.*

Tabella [tah-bell'lah] *nf.* list, schedule, table.

Tabernacolo [tah-behr-nah'-koh-loh] *nm.* shrine, tabernacle.

Tacca [tahk'kah] *nf.* defect, notch; **di mezza** [dee med'zah] **t.** a middle-class.

Taccagno [tahk-kahn'yoh] *a.* miserly, stingy.

Tacchino [tahk-kee'noh] *nm.* turkey.

Taccia [tahch'chah] *nf.* accusation, charge.

Tacciare [tahch-chah'ray] *vt.* to accuse of, charge with.

Tacco [tahk'koh] *nm.* heel (of a shoe).

Taccuino [tah-koo-ee'noh] *nm.* memorandum book, note-book.

Tacere [tah-chay'ray] *vt.* to leave out, omit; *vi.* to be silent, keep silence.

Tacito [tah'chee-toh] *a.* silent, tacit.

Taciturno [tah-chee-toor'-noh] *a.* sulky, taciturn.

Tafano [tah-fah'noh] *nm.* gad-fly.

Tafferuglio [tahf-fay-rool'-yoh] *nm.* brawl, fray.

Taglia [tahl'yah] *nf.* price on someone's head, ransom, tribute.

Tagliaboschi [tahl-yah-boss'-kee] *nm.* woodcutter, wood-man.

Tagliacarte [tahl-yah-kahr'-tay] *nm.* paper-cutter, paper-knife.

Tagliare [tahl-yah'ray] *vt.* to bar, cut (off), cut out.

Taglio [tahl'yoh] *nm.* cut, denomination (of notes, etc.), dress-length.

Tagli(u)ola [tahl-yee(oo)oh'-lah] *nf.* trap.

Talamo [tah'lah-moh] *nm.* nuptial couch.

Talco [tahl'koh] *nm.* talc, talcum powder.

Tale [tah'lay] *nm.* fellow; *a.* like, similar, such; **il** [eel] **t. dei tali** [day'ee tah'lee] *pn.* so-and-so.

Talento [tah-len'toh] *nm.* genius, intelligence, talent.

Talismano [tah-lees-mah'-toh] *nm.* talisman.   [heel.

Tallone [tahl-loh'nay] *nm.*

Talmente [tahl-men'tay] *ad.* so, so much, to such a degree.

Talora: *v.* **Talvolta.**

Talpa [tahl'pah] *nf.* mole.

Taluno [tah-loo'noh] *pn.* somebody, someone.

Talvolta [tahl-voll'tah] *ad.* sometimes.

Tamburino [tahm-boo-ree'-noh] *nm.* drummer.

Tamburo [tahm-boo'roh] *nm.* cylinder, drum.

Tampone [tahm-poh'nay] *nm.* (*med.*) dabber, tampon.

Tana [tah'nah] *nf.* den, hole, lair.

Tanaglia [tah-nahl'yah] *nf.* (*pl.*) nippers (*pl.*), pincers (*pl.*).

Tanfo [tahn'foh] *nm.* bad smell, stench.

Tanghero [tahng'gay-roh] nm. boor, bumbkin.

Tangibile [tahn-jee'bee-lay] a. tangible.

Tan/to [tahn'toh] ad. so, so long, so much; v. . . . quanto [kwahn'toh], as . . . as, both . . . and; a. and pn. as much; —ti [tee] a. and pn. (pl.) as many.

Tapino [tah-pee'noh] nm. wretch; a. miserable, wretched.

Tappa [tahp'pah] nf. halting-place, stage.

Tappa/re [tahp-pah'ray] vt. to cork, plug, stop (up); —rsi vr. to shut oneself up; t. gli orecchi [lyee oh-reck'kee] to stop one's ears.

Tappeto [tahp-pay'toh] nm. carpet, rug.

Tappezzare [tahp-pet-sah' ray] vt. to carpet, tapestry, upholster.

Tappezzeria [tahp-pet-say-ree'ah] nf. tapestry, upholstery.

Tappezziere [tahp-pet-see-ay'ray] nm. carpet-layer, upholsterer.

Tappo [tahp'poh] nm. cork, plug, stopper.

Tara [tah'rah] nf. reduction, tare.

Tarchiato [tahr-kee-ah'toh]. a. thickset.

Tardare [tahr-dah'ray] vi. to be late, be long, delay.

Tardi [tahr'dee] ad. late; far (fahr) t. vi. to be late.

Tardo [tahr'doh] a. dull, late, lazy, sluggish, tardy.

Targa [tahr'gah] nf. name-plate, number-plate.

Tariffa [tah-reef'fah] nf. tariff.

Tarlato [tahr-lah'toh] a. worm-eaten.

Tarlo [tahr'loh] nm. wood-worm.

Tarsia [tahr'see-ah] nf. inlaid work, marquetry.

Tartagliare [tahr-tahl-yah' ray] vi. to stammer, stutter.

Tartaglione [tahr-tahl-yoh' nay] nm. stammerer.

Tartaro [tahr'tah-roh] nm. tartar; nm. and a. Tartar.

Tartaruga [tahr-tah-roo'gah] nf. tortoise, turtle.

Tartassare [tahr-tahs-sah' ray] vt. to bully, harass, vex.

Tartufo [tahr-too'foh] nm. truffle.

Tasca [tah'skah] nf. pocket.

Tassa [tahs'sah] nf. fee (school, etc.), tax.

Tassare [tahs-sah'ray] vt. to assess, tax.

Tassativo [tahs-sah-tee'voh] a. definite, exact, positive.

Tasso [tahs'soh] nm. badger, rate (of interest), yew-tree.

Tastare [tah-stah'ray] vt. to feel, sound, touch.

Tastiera [tah-stee-ay'rah] nf. keyboard.

Tasto [tah'stoh] nm. key, subject.

Tastoni, (a) [ah tah-stoh' nee] ad. gropingly.

Tattica [taht'tee-kah] nf. tactics [pl.].

Tattico [taht'tee-koh] nm. tactician; a. tactical.

Tatto [taht'toh] nm. tact, touch.

Tatuaggio [tah-too-ah'djoh] nm. tattoo, tattooing.

Taumaturgo [tow-mah-toor' goh] nm. miracle-monger, miracle-worker.

Taverna [tah-vehr'nah] nf. public-house, tavern.

Tavola [tah'voh-lah] nf. board, plank, table.

Tavolino [tah-voh-lee'noh] nm. desk, small table.

Tavolozza [tah-voh-lot'sah] nf. palette. [mug.

Tazza [taht'sah] nf. cup, **Te** [tay] pn. (2nd pers. sing oblique case), you.

Tè [tay] *nm.* tea.

Teatrale [tay-ah-trah'lay] *a.* theatrical.

Teatro [tay-ah'troh] *nm.* stage, theatre.

Tecnica [teck'nee-kah] *nf.* technique.

Tecnico [teck'nee-koh] *nm.* technician; *a.* technical.

Tedesco [tay-dess'koh] *nm. and a.* German.

Tediare [tay-dee-ah'ray] *vt.* to bore, tire, weary.

Tedio [tay'dee-oh] *nm.* boredom, tedium, weariness.

Tedioso [tay-dee-oh'soh] *a.* irksome, tedious, tiresome.

Tegame [tay-gah'may] *nm.* pan.

Teglia [tayl'yah] *nf.* oven-pan.

Tego/la [tay'goh-lah] *nf.* —lo [loh] *nm.* brickbat, tile.

Teiera [tay-ee-ay'rah] *nf.* tea-pot.

Tela [tay'lah] *nf.* canvas (painter's), cloth, linen, picture.

Telaio [tay-lah'yoh] *nm.* frame, loom.

Teleferica [tay-lay-fay'ree-kah] *nf.* aerial railway.

Telefonare [tay-lay-foh-nah'ray] *vt. and i.* to ring up, telephone.

Telefono [tay-lay'foh-noh] *nm.* 'phone, telephone.

Telegrafare [tay-lay-grah-fah'ray] *vt. and i.* to cable, telegraph, wire.

Telegramma [tay-lay-grahm'mah] *nm.* cable, telegram, wire.

Telepatia [tay-lay-pah-tee'ah] *nf.* telepathy.

Teleria [tay-lay-ree'ah] *nf.* linen cloth; negoziante di telerie [nay-goh-tsee-ahn'tay dee tay-lay-ree'ay] *nm.* linen-draper.

Telescopio [tay-lay-skoh'pee-oh] *nm.* telescope.

Telo [tay'loh] *nm.* length, width (of material); (*poet.*) arrow.

Telone [tay-loh'nay] *nm.* (*theat.*) drop-curtain.

Tema [tay'mah] *nm.* subject, theme; *nf.* dread, fear.

Temerario [tay-may-rah'-ree-oh] *a.* foolhardy, rash.

Temere [tay-may'ray] *vt. and i.* to be afraid of, dread, fear.

Temerità [tay-may-ree-tah'] *nf.* rashness, temerity.

Tempera [tem'pay-rah] *nf.* distemper (painting), temper.

Temperamento [tem-pay-rah-men'toh] *nm.* disposition, mitigation, temper, temperament.

Temperanza [tem-pay-rahnt'sah] *nf.* moderation, temperance.

Temperare [tem-pay-rah'ray] *vt.* to mitigate, moderate, sharpen (pencil), temper.

Temperatura [tem-pay-rah-too'rah] *nf.* temperature.

Temperino [tem-pay-ree'noh] *nm.* pen-knife.

Tempesta [tem-pess'tah] *nf.* storm, tempest.

Tempestare [tem-pess-tah'ray] *vt.* to harass, vex; *vi.* to badger (with questions).

Tempestivo [tem-pess-tee'voh] *a.* opportune, seasonable, timely.

Tempia [tem'pee-ah] *nf.* forehead, temple.

Tempio [tem'pee-oh] *nm.* temple (building).

Tempo [tem'poh] *nm.* time, weather, (*gram.*) tense; che [kay] t. fa [fah]? What kind of weather is it?

Temporale [tem-poh-rah'-lay] *nm.* storm.

Temporaneo [tem-poh-rah'-nay-oh] *a.* temporary.

Temporeggiare [tem-poh-ray-djah'ray] *vi.* to temporise.

Tempra [tem'prah] *nf.*
mettle.

Temprare [tem-prah'ray] *vt.*
to inure, train.

Tenace [tay-nah'chay] *a.* constant, persevering, tenacious.

Tenacia [tay-nah'chah] *nf.*
constancy, tenacity.

Tenda [ten'dah] *nf.* awning,
curtain, tent.

Tendenza [ten-dent'sah] *nf.*
bent, disposition, inclination,
tendency.

Tendere [ten'day-ray] *vt.* to
hold out, stretch (out); **t. la
mano** [lah mah'noh] *vi.* to beg;
vi. to aim at, be inclined to,
tend to.

Tendina [ten-dee'nah] *nf.*
(window-)blind.

Tenebre [tay'nay-bray] *nf.*
(*pl.*) darkness.

Tenebroso [tay-nay-broh'-
soh] *a.* dark, obscure.

Tenente [tay-nen'tay] *nm.*
Lieutenant.

Tenere [tay-nay'ray] *vt.* to
hold, keep; **t. a** [ah] *vi.* to
be proud of, care for, like;
t. da [dah], to take after;
t. per [pehr], to side with;
—**rsi** *vr.* to consider oneself,
keep to.

Tenerezza [tay-nay-ret'sah]
nf. affection, tenderness.

Tenero [tay'nay-roh] *nm.*
weakness; *a.* loving, tender.

Tenia [tay'nee-ah] *nf.* tapeworm.

Tenore [tay-noh'ray] *nm.*
tenor; **t. di vita** [dee vee'tah],
standard of life, way of living.

Tensione [ten-see-oh'nay] *nf.*
strain, tension.

Tentacolo [ten-tah'koh-loh]
nm. tentacle.

Tentare [ten-tah'ray] *vt.* and
i. to attempt, (*med.*) probe,
tempt, try.

Tentativo [ten-tah-tee'voh]
nm. attempt, endeavour, trial.

Tenta/tore [ten-tah-toh'ray]
nm. tempter; —**trice** [tree'-
chay] *nf.* temptress.

Tentazione [ten-tah-tsee-oh'-
nay] *nf.* temptation.

Tentennamento [ten-ten-
nah-men'toh] *nm.* wavering.

Tentennare [ten-ten-nah'ray]
vi. to hesitate, stagger, waver.

Tenue [tay'noo-ay] *a.* fine,
slight, small, thin.

Tenuità [tay-noo-ee-tah'] *nf.*
fineness, smallness, thinness.

Tentoni [ten-toh'nee] *ad.*
gropingly.

Tenuta [tay-noo'tah] *nf.*
estate, property, uniform.

Tenzone [tent-soh'nay] *nf.*
tenzon, combat, argument.

Teologia [tay-oh-loh-jee'ah]
nf. theology.

Teologo [tay-oh'loh-goh] *nm.*
theologian.

Teorema [tay-oh-ray'mah]
nm. theorem.

Teoria [tay-oh-ree'ah] *nf.*
theory.

Teorico [tay-oh'ree-koh] *nm.*
theorist; *a.* theoretical.

Tepido [tay'pee-doh] *a.*
lukewarm, tepid, warm.

Tepore [tay-poh'ray] *nm.*
warmth.

Terapeutica [tay-rah-pay-
oo'tee-kah] *nf.* therapeutics
(*pl.*).

Tergere [tehr'jay-ray] *vt.*
to clean, polish, wipe (away).

Tergiversare [tehr-jee-vehr-
sah'ray] *vi.* to beat about the
bush, hesitate.

Tergiversazione [tehr-jee-
vehr-sah-tsee-oh'nay] *nf.* hesitation.

Tergo [tehr'goh] *nm.* back;
a [ah] **t.** *ad.* overleaf; **da** [dah]
t. *ad.* from behind.

Terme [tehr'may] *nf.* (*pl.*),
hot baths (*pl.*) hot springs (*pl.*).

Terminare [tehr-mee-nah'-
ray] *vt.* to finish; *vi.* to end.

Termine [tehr'mee-nay] *nm.* boundary, date, end, term; a rigor di termini [ah ree-gorr' dee tehr'mee-nee] *ad.* strictly speaking.

Termometro [tehr-moh'may-troh] *nm.* thermometer.

Terra [tehr'rah] *nf.* earth, ground, land.

Terraferma [tehr-rah-fehr'mah] *nf.* mainland.

Terraglia [tehr-rahl'yah] *nf.* earthenware, pottery.

Terrapieno [tehr-rah-pee-ay'noh] *nm.* bank, earthwork.

Terremoto [tehr-ray-moh'toh] *nm.* earthquake.

Terreno [tehr-ray'noh] *nm.* ground, soil; *a.* earthly, worldly; **pian** [pee-ahn'] **t.** *nm.* ground-floor.

Terrestre [tehr-ress'tray] *a.* earthly, terrestrial.

Terribile [tehr-ree'bee-lay] *a.* awful, frightful, terrible.

Terriccio [tehr-reech'choh] *nm.* mould.

Territorio [tehr-ree-toh'ree-oh] *nm.* territory.

Terrore [tehr-roh'ray] *nm.* fright, terror. [terse.

Terso [tehr'soh] *a.* cloudless,

Terziario [tehr-tsee-ah'ree-oh] *nm. and a.* tertiary.

Terzo [tehrt'soh] *nm.* third (party); *a.* third.

Tesa [tay'sah] *nf.* brim (of hat), net.

Teschio [tess'kee-oh] *nm.* skull. [thesis.

Tesi [tay'zee] *nf.* proposition,

Teso [tay'soh] *a.* strained, taut, tight.

Tesoreria [tay-zoh-ray-ree'ah] *nf.* treasury.

Tesoriere [tay-zoh-ree-ay'ray] *nm.* treasurer.

Tesoro [tay-zoh'roh] *nm.* treasure, treasury.

Tessera [tess'say-rah] *nf.* card, ticket.

Tesseramento [tess-say-rah-men'toh] *nm.* rationing.

Tesserare [tess-say-rah'ray] *vt.* to ration.

Tessere [tess'say-ray] *vt.* to weave.

Tessile [tess'see-lay] *nm. and a.* textile.

Tessi/tore [tess-see-toh'ray] *nm.* —**trice** [tree'chay] *nf.* weaver.

Tessitura [tess-see-too'rah] *nf.* weaving.

Tessuto [tess-soo'toh] *nm.* cloth, fabric, tissue, web.

Testa [tess'tah] *nf.* head.

Testamento [tess-tah-men'toh] *nm.* testament, will.

Testardo [tess-tahr'doh] *a.* headstrong, stubborn.

Testata [tess-tah'tah] *nf.* heading (newspaper).

Teste [tess'tay] *nm. and f.* witness.

Testè [tess-tay'] *ad.* a short time ago. (*poet.*) *v.* Dianzi.

Testicolo [tess-tee'koh-loh] *nm.* testicle.

Testimone [tess-tee-moh'nay] *nm. and f.* witness.

Testimonianza [tess-tee-moh-nee-ahnt'sah] *nf.* evidence, testimony, witness.

Testimoniare [tess-tee-moh-nee-ah'ray] *vt. and i.* to testify, witness.

Testo [tess'toh] *nm.* text.

Testuale [tess-too-ah'lay] *a.* exact, precise, textual.

Testuggine [tess-too'djee-nay] *nf.* tortoise, turtle.

Tetano [tay'tah-noh] *nm.* (*med.*) tetanus. [gloomy.

Tetro [tay'troh] *a.* dismal,

Tetto [tet'toh] *nm.* roof; **senza** [sent'sah] **t.** *a.* homeless.

Tettoia [tet-toh'yah] *nf.* penthouse, roof (of market, station), etc.

Tiara [tee-ah'rah] *nf.* diadem, tiara.

Tibia [tee'bee-ah] nf. (mus.) pipe, (anat.) shinbone.

Ticchio [teek'kee-oh] nm. caprice, whim.

Tiepidezza [tee-ay-pee-det'sah] nf. (fig.) lukewarmness.

Tiepido: v. **tepido.**

Tifo [tee-foh] nm. (med.) typhus.

Tifoide [tee-foh'ee-day] nf. (med.) typhoid fever.

Tifone [tee-foh'nay] nm. typhoon.

Tifoso [tee-foh'soh] nm. (fig.) fan (cinema, football, etc.), (med.) typhous patient.

Tiglio [teel'yoh] nm. fibre, lime(-tree).

Tiglioso [teel-yoh'soh] a. tough.

Tigna [teen'yah] nf. ringworm.

Tignola [teen-yoh'lah] nf. moth.

Tigrato [tee-grah'toh] a. striped, tabby.

Tigre [tee'gray] nm. tiger; nf. tigress.

Timbrare [teem-brah'ray] vt. to stamp.

Timbro [teem'broh] nm. stamp; t. postale [poss-tah'-lay], post-mark.

Timidezza [tee-mee-det'sah] nf. shyness, timidity.

Timido [tee'mee-doh] a. bashful, shy, timid.

Timo [tee'moh] nm. thyme.

Timone [tee-moh'nay] nm. (naut.) helm, rudder.

Timoniere [tee-moh-nee-ay'-ray] nm. (naut.) helmsman, steersman.

Timore [tee-moh'ray] nm. awe, fear.

Timpano [teem'pah-noh] nm. eardrum, (mus.) timbal.

Tinca [teeng'kah] nf. tench.

Tingere [teen'jay-ray] vt. to dye, paint.

Tino [tee'noh] nm. tub, vat.

Tinozza [tee-not'sah] nf. (bath-)tub.

Tinta [teen'tah] nf. colour, dye, hue, tint.

Tintinnare [teen-teen-nah'-ray] vi. to jingle, tinkle.

Tintore [teen-toh'ray] nm. dyer.

Tintoria [teen-toh-ree'ah] nf. dyer's, dye-works.

Tintura [teen-too'rah] nf. dyeing, tincture.

Tipico [tee'pee-koh] a. typical.

Tipo [tee'poh] nm. model, specimen, type; un bel [oon bell] t. a queer fellow.

Tipografia [tee-poh-grah-fee'ah] nf. printer's, typography.

Tipografico [tee-poh-grah'-fee-koh] a. typographical.

Tipografo [tee-poh'grah-foh] nm. printer, typographer.

Tiranneggiare [tee-rahn-nay-djah'ray] vt. to oppress, tyrannize; vi. to rule despotically.

Tiran/nide [tee-rahn'nee-day], —**nia** [nee'ah] nf. tyranny. **—no** [tee-rahn'noh] nm. tyrant.

Tirare [tee-rah'ray] vt. to drag, draw, (typ.) print, pull, throw; vi. to blow, shoot at; tira vento [tee'rah ven'toh], it is windy.

Tirata [tee-rah'tah] nf. draw, pull, tirade.

Tiratura [tee-rah-too'rah] nf. drawing, pulling (typ.) circulation, edition.

Tirchio [teer'kee-oh] nm. miser; a. miserly, stingy.

Tiro [tee'roh] nm. draught, fire, throw, trick; animale da [ah-nee-mah'lay dah] t. draught-animal.

Tirocinio [tee-roh-chee'nee-oh] nm. apprenticeship, training.

Tisi [tee´zee] *nf.* (med.) consumption.

Tisico [tee´zee-koh] *nm.* and *a.* consumptive.

Titillare [tee-teel-lah´ray] *vt.* to tickle.

Titolare [tee-toh-lah´ray] *nm.* owner, regular holder; *a.* regular, titular.

Tito/lo [tee´toh-loh] *nm.* name, qualification, right, title; **—li** [lee] (*pl. com.*) securities (*pl.*).

Titubante [tee-too-bahn´tay] *a.* hesitating, undecided.

Titubanza [tee-too-bahnt´-sah] *nf.* hesitation.

Titubare [tee-too-bah´ray] *vi.* to hesitate, waver.

Tizio [tee´tsee-oh] *nm.* fellow.

Tizzo [teet´soh], **tizzone** [teet-soh´nay] *nm.* (fire-)brand.

Toccare [tock-kah´ray] *vt.* (naut.) to call at, move, touch; *vi.* to be the duty of, be the turn of, be forced to, happen.

Tocco [tock´koh] *nm.* stroke, tolling, touch, one o'clock.

Toglie/re [toll´yay-ray] *vt.* to carry off, free, prevent, remove, take (away); **t. di mezzo** [dee med´zoh] to get rid of; **—rsi** *vr.* to get away, get out, take off.

Tollerante [toll-lay-rahn´tay] *a.* indulgent, tolerant.

Tolleranza [toll-lay-rahnt´-sah] *nf.* endurance, tolerance; **casa di** [kah´sah dee] **t.** brothel.

Tollerare [toll-lay-rah´ray] *vt.* to bear, endure, tolerate.

Tomba [tom´bah] *nf.* grave, tomb.

Tomo [toh´moh] *nm.* tome, volume.

Tonaca [toh´nah-kah] *nf.* (monk's) frock, (priest's) cassock, tunic.

Tonare [toh-nah´ray] *vi.* to thunder.

Tondere: *v.* tosare.

Tondino [ton-dee´noh] *nm.* small plate.

Tondo [ton´doh] *nm.* circle, plate, ring; *a.* round; **chiaro e** [kee-ah´roh ay] **t.** *ad.* plainly.

Tonfo [ton´foh] *nm.* splash.

Tonico [toh´nee-koh] *nm.* and *a.* tonic.

Tonnellaggio [ton-nell-lah´-djoh] *nm.* tonnage.

Tonnellata [ton-nell-lah´tah] *nf.* ton.

Tonno [ton´noh] *nm.* tunny.

Tono [toh´noh] *nm.* tone; **dare** [dah´ray] **t.** *vi.* to restore, revive.

Tonsura [ton-soo´rah] *nf.* tonsure.

Tonto [ton´toh] *a.* dense, dull, silly.

Topaia [toh-pah´yah] *nf.* hovel, rats' nest.

Topazio [toh-pah´tsee-oh] *nm.* topaz.

Topica [toh´pee-kah] *nf.* blunder, gaffe.

Topo [toh´poh] *nm.* mouse, rat; **t. di biblioteca** [dee bee-blee-oh-tay´kah] bookworm.

Topografia [toh-poh-grah-fee´ah] *nf.* topography.

Toppa [top´pah] *nf.* door-lock, lock, patch.

Torace [toh-rah´chay] *nm.* thorax.

Torba [torr´bah] *nf.* peat, turf.

Torbido [torr´bee-doh] *nm.* disorder, trouble; *a.* dim, gloomy, muddy, troubled, turbid.

Torbo: *v.* torbido (a).

Torcere [torr´chay-ray] *vt.* to twist, wring.

Torchio [torr´kee-oh] *nm.* press.

Torcia [torr´chah] *nf.* torch.

Torcicollo [torr-chee-koll´-loh] *nm.* stiff-neck.

Tordo [torr´doh] *nm.* thrush.

Torma [torr'mah] nf. crowd, swarm. (poet.) v. Folla.

Tormenta [torr-men'tah] nf. blizzard, snow-storm.

Tormenta/re [torr-men-tah'ray] vt. to harass, torment, torture, worry; —rsi vr. to be worried.

Tormento [torr-men'toh] nm. pain, torment, torture.

Tornaconto [torr-nah-kon'toh] nm. profit.

Tornare [torr-nah'ray] vi. to come (go) back, recur, return; to approve, suit; non mi torna [nonn mee torr'nah], I do not approve.

Torneo [torr-nay'oh] nm. tournament.

Tornio [torr'nee-oh] nm. (tech.) turning-lathe.

Tornire [torr-nee'ray] vt. (tech.) to turn.

Tornitore [torr-nee-toh'ray] nm. turner.

Torno [torr'noh] nm. period; torno torno ad. round and about.

Toro [toh'roh] nm. bull.

Torpedinare [torr-pay-dee-nah'ray] vt. to torpedo.

Torpedine [torr-pay'dee-nay] nm. torpedo.

Torpediniera [torr-pay-dee-nee-ay'rah] nf. torpedo-boat.

Torpido [torr'pee-doh] a. dull, sluggish, torpid.

Torpore [torr-poh'ray] nm. sluggishness, torpor.

Torre [torr'ray] nf. tower.

Torreggiare [torr-ray-djah'ray] vi. to loom, tower (above).

Torrente [torr-ren'tay] nm. flood, stream, torrent.

Torrone [torr-roh'nay] nm. nougat (sweet).

Torsione [torr-see-oh'nay] nf. twist.

Torso [torr'soh] nm. torso, trunk.

Torsolo [torr'soh-loh] nm. core (of fruit), stalk, stump, (fig.) lout.

Torta [torr'tah] nf. cake, pie, tart.

Torto [torr'toh] nm. fault, injustice, wrong; aver [ah-verr'] t. to be wrong; a [ah] t. ad. unjustly, wrongly.

Tortora [torr'toh-rah] nf. turtle-dove.

Tortuoso [torr-too-oh'soh] a. crooked, tortuous.

Tortura [torr-too'rah] nf. torture.

Torturare [torr-too-rah'ray] vt. to torture.

Torvo [torr'voh] a. grim, surly.

Tosare [toh-zah'ray] vt. to clip, cut one's hair, shear.

Tosatura [toh-zah-too'rah] nf. (sheep-)shearing.

Toscano [toss-kah'noh] nm. and a. Tuscan.

Tosse [toss'say] nf. cough.

Tossico [toss'see-koh] nm. poison; a. poisonous, toxic.

Tossire [toss-see'ray] vi. to cough.

Tostare [toss-tah'ray] vt. to roast (coffee), toast.

Tosto [toss'toh] a. hard; faccia [fahch'chah] tosta nf. impudence; a. immediately, soon; t. che [kay'] con. as soon as.

Totale [toh-tah'lay] nm. total; a. entire, total, whole.

Totalità [toh-tah-lee-tah'] nf. mass, totality, whole body.

Totano [toh'tah-noh] nm. cuttle-fish.

Tovaglia [toh-vahl'yah] nf. (table-)cloth.

Tovagliolo [toh-vahl-yoh'loh] nm. napkin, serviette.

Tozzo [tot'soh] nm. bit, crust, hunk, piece; a. squat, stocky, thickset.

Tra [trah] pr. among (more than two), between (two);

t, **poco** [poh'koh] *ad.* in a short time.

Traballare [trah-bahl-lah'ray] *vi.* to jolt, reel, shake, stagger, totter.

Trabiccolo [trah-beek'koh-loh] *nm.* bed-warmer, rickety vehicle.

Traboccare [trah-bock-kah'ray] *vi.* to brim over, overflow.

Trabocchetto [trah-bock-ket'toh] *nm.* trap.

Tracannare [trah-kahn-nah'ray] *vt.* to gulp down, swallow.

Traccia [trahch'chah] *nf.* mark, outline, trace, track, trail.

Tracciare [trahch-chah'ray] *vt.* to draw, mark out, sketch, trace.

Tracollo [trah-koll'loh] *nm.* breakdown, collapse, ruin.

Tracotante [trah-koh-tahn'tay] *a.* arrogant, overbearing.

Tracotanza [trah-koh-tahnt'sah] *nf.* arrogance.

Tradimento [trah-dee-men'toh] *nm.* betrayal, treachery, treason; a [ah] t. *ad.* treacherously.

Tradire [trah-dee'ray] *vt.* to be unfaithful, to betray, deceive.

Traditore [trah-dee-toh'ray] *nm.* betrayer, traitor; *a.* treacherous.

Tradizione [trah-dee-tsee-oh'nay] *nf.* tradition.

Tradurre [trah-door'ray] *vt.* to bring, take, translate; t. in pratica [een prah'tee-kah] to carry out.

Traduttore [trah-doot-toh'ray] *nm.* translator.

Traduzione [trah-doo-tsee-oh'nay] *nf.* translation.

Trafelato [trah-fay-lah'toh] *a.* breathless, panting.

Trafficante [trahf-fee-kahn'tay] *nm.* dealer, trafficker; *a.* dealing, trafficking.

Trafficare [trahf-fee-kah'ray] *vi.* to deal, trade, traffic.

Traffico [trahf'fee-koh] *nm.* trade, trading, traffic.

Trafiggere [trah-fee'djay-ray] *vt.* to pierce (through), wound.

Trafitta [trah-feet'tah] *nf.* pang, spasm.

Traforare [trah-foh-rah'ray] *vt.* to bore, perforate, pierce.

Traforo [trah-foh'roh] *nm.* boring, piercing, tunnelling.

Trafugare [trah-foo-gah'ray] *vt.* to carry off, hide, purloin.

Tragedia [trah-jay'dee-ah] *nf.* tragedy.

Traghetto [trah-ghet'toh] *nm.* ferry.

Tragico [trah'jee-koh] *nm.* tragedian, tragedy; *a.* tragic(al).

Tragittare [trah-jeet-tah'ray] *vt.* to cross, ferry.

Tragitto [trah-jeet'toh] *nm.* passage, way.

Trainare: *v.* **trascinare.**

Traino [trah'ee-noh] *nm.* load.

Tralasciare [trah-lah-shah'ray] *vt.* and *i.* to break off, cease, give up, omit.

Tralcio [trahl'choh] *nm.* vine-shoot.

Tralignare [trah-leen-yah'ray] *vi.* to degenerate.

Trama [trah'mah] *nf.* plot.

Tramandare [trah-mahn-dah'ray] *vt.* to hand down.

Tramare [trah-mah'ray] *vt.* and *i.* to plot.

Trambusto [trahm-boo'stoh] *nm.* bustle.

Tramestio [trah-mess-tee'oh] *nm.* agitation, confusion.

Tramezzare [trah-med-zah'ray] *vt.* to insert, partition off.

Tramezzo [trah-med'zoh] *nm.* partition.

Tramite [trah'mee-tay] *nm.*

way; per [pehr] t. di [dee]
pr. through.

Tramontana [trah-mon-tah'-
nah] nf. north wind.

Tramontare [trah-mon-tah'-
ray] vi. to fade, go down, set.

Tramonto [trah-mon'toh]
nm. end, setting, sunset.

Tramortire [trah-morr-tee'-
ray] vt. to stun; vi. to faint.

Trampolo [trahm'poh-loh]
nm. stilt.

Tramutare [trah-moo-tah'-
ray] vt. to alter, change,
transmute.

Tranello [trah-nell'loh] nm.
snare, trap.

Trangugiare [trahn-goo-
jah'ray] vt. to bolt, gulp,
swallow.

Tranne [trahn'nay] pr. but,
except, save.

Tranquillare [trahn-kweel-
lah'ray] vt. to tranquillize.

Tranquillità [trahn-kweel-
lee-tah'] nf. calm, tranquillity.

Tranquillo [trahn-kweel'loh]
a. calm, quiet, tranquil.

Transazione [trahn-sah-tsee-
oh'nay] nf. arrangement, composition, transaction.

Transigere [trahn-zee'jay-
ray] vi. to come to terms,
yield.

Transitare [trahn-see-tah'-
ray] vi. to pass across, pass
through.

Transito [trahn'see-toh] nm.
passage, transit.

Transitorio [trahn-see-toh'-
ree-oh] a. temporary, transi-
tory.

Transizione [trahn-see-tsee-
oh'nay] nf. transition.

Tranvai [trahn-vah'ee] nm.
tram (-car).

Tranviere [trahn-vee-ay'ray]
nm. tram-conductor, tram-
driver.

Trapanare [trah-pah-nah'-
ray] vt. to drill, (med.) trepan.

Trapano [trah'pah-noh] nm.
drill, (med.) trepanning.

Trapassare [trah-pahs-sah'-
ray] vt. to overstep, pierce,
run through; vi. to pass
(away).

Trapasso [trah-pahs'soh] nm.
death, passage, transfer.

Trapelare [trah-pay-lah'ray]
vi. to be divulged, escape,
leak out. [nm. trapeze.

Trapezio [trah-pay'tsee-oh]

Trapianta/re [trah-pee-ahn-
tah'ray] vt. to transplant;
—rsi vr. to emigrate, settle.

Trappola [trahp'poh-lah] nf.
snare, trap.

Trappolone [trahp-poh-loh'-
nay] nm. swindler.

Trapuntare [trah-poon-tah'-
ray] vt. to quilt.

Trar/re [trahr'ray] vt. to
draw, get, lead; —rsi vr. to
draw, get (out), stand (back)

Trasalire [trah-sah-lee'ray]
vi. to jump, start.

Trasandare [trah-sahn-dah'-
ray] vt. to neglect.

Trasandato [trah-sahn-dah'-
toh] a. careless, slatternly.

Trasbordare [trahs-borr-
dah'ray] vt. to transfer, trans-
ship.

Trascendere [trah-shen'day-
ray] vt. and i. to be beyond,
outstrip, surpass, transcend.

Trascinare [trah-shee-nah'-
ray] vt. to carry, drag, draw,
lead.

Trascorrere [trah-skorr'ray-
ray] vt. to pass, spend; vi. to
elapse, pass.

Trascorsi [trah-skorr'see]
nm. (pl.) past life.

Trascrivere [trah-skree'vay-
ray] vt. to transcribe.

Trascrizione [trah-skree-
tsee-oh'nay] nf. transcription.

Trascuranza [trah-skoo-
rahnt'sah] nf. carelessness,
negligence, slovenliness.

Trascurare [trah-skoo-rah′ray] *vt.* to disregard, neglect, omit, slight.

Trascurato [trah-skoo-rah′toh] *a.* careless, negligent.

Trasecolare [trah-say-koh-lah′ray] *vi.* to be amazed, startled.

Trasferimento [trah-sfay-ree-men′toh] *nm.* change, removal, transfer.

Trasferire [trah-sfay-ree′ray] *vt.* —**rsi** *vr.* to change, go, remove, transfer.

Trasferta [trah-sfehr′tah] *nf.* transfer.

Trasfigurare [trah-sfee-goo-rah′ray] *vt.* to transfigure.

Trasfigurazione [trah-sfee-goo-rah-tsee-oh′nay] *nf.* transfiguration.

Trasfondere [trah-sfon′day-ray] *vt.* to transfuse.

Trasformare [trah-sforr-mah′ray] *vt.* to transform.

Trasformazione [trah-sforr-mah-tsee-oh′nay] *nf.* transformation.

Trasfusione [trah-sfoo-zee-oh′nay] *nf.* transfusion.

Trasgredire [trah-sgray-dee′ray] *vt. and i.* to infringe, transgress.

Trasgressione [trah-sgress-see-oh′nay] *nf.* infringement, transgression.

Trasgressore [trah-sgress-soh′ray] *nm.* infringer, transgressor.

Traslato [trah-slah′toh] *nm.* metaphor; *a.* figurative, metaphorical.

Traslocare [trah-sloh-kah′ray] *vt.* to move; *vi.* to change one's address.

Trasloco [trah-sloh′koh] *nm.* removal.

Trasmettere [trah-smet′tay-ray] *vt.* to pass on, send, transmit; **t. per radio** [pehr rah′dee-oh] to broadcast.

Trasmissione [trah-smees-see-oh′nay] *nf.* broadcasting), transmission.

Trasmodare [trah-smoh-dah′ray] *vi.* to exaggerate, exceed.

Trasmodato [trah-smoh-dah′toh] *a.* excessive, immoderate.

Trasmutare [trah-smoo-tah′ray] *vt.* to transmute, transform.

Trasognare [trah-sohn-yah′ray] *vi.* to (day-)dream.

Trasognato [trah-sohn-yah′toh] *a.* day-dreaming, lost in reverie.

Trasparente [trah-spah-ren′tay] *a.* transparent.

Trasparire [trah-spah-ree′ray] *vi.* to appear (through), be evident; **lasciare** [lah-shah′ray] **t.** *vt.* to betray, reveal.

Traspirare [trah-spee-rah′ray] *vi.* to perspire.

Traspirazione [trah-spee-rah-tsee-oh′nay] *nf.* perspiration.

Trasportabile [trah-sporr-tah′bee-lay] *a.* transportable.

Trasportare [trah-sporr-tah′ray] *vt.* to carry, convey, transfer, transport.

Trasporto [trah-sporr′toh] *nm.* conveyance, enthusiasm, transfer, transport(ation).

Trastullarsi [trah-stool-lahr′see] *vr.* to amuse oneself, toy with.

Trastullo [trah-stool′loh] *nm.* amusement, game, play, toy, *(fig.)* laughing-stock.

Trasverso [trahs-vehr′soh] *a.* transverse.

Tratta [traht′tah] *nf. (com.)* draft, trade.

Trattabile [traht-tah′bee-lay] *a.* reasonable, tractable, that can be dealt with.

Trattamento [traht-tah-men′toh] *nm.* entertainment, reception, treatment.

Tratta/re [traht-tah'ray] *vt.* to deal, treat; *vi.* to deal with, speak of, treat of; **—rsi** *v.imp.* to be a question of.

Trattativa [traht-tah-tee'vah] *nf.* negotiation.

Trattato [traht-tah'toh] *nm.* tract, treatise, treaty.

Tratteggiare [traht-tay-djah'ray] *vt.* to describe, draw, outline, represent, sketch.

Trattene/re [traht-tay-nay'ray] *vt.* to hold, keep, hold, restrain; **—rsi** *vr.* to avoid, help, restrain oneself, stay, stop.

Trattenimento [traht-tay-nee-men'toh] *nm.* amusement, entertainment, party.

Tratto [traht'toh] *nm.* feature, stroke, way, way of treating; tutt'ad un [too'tahd-oon] t. *ad.* all of a sudden.

Trattoria [traht-toh-ree'ah] *nf.* eating-house, restaurant.

Travagliare [trah-vahl-yah'ray] *vt.* to torment, trouble; *vi.* to labour, toil.

Travaglio [trah-vahl'yoh] *nm.* anxiety, labour, toil.

Travasare [trah-vah-zah'ray] *vt.* to decant, pour off.

Trave [trah'vay] *nf.* beam.

Traversa [trah-vehr'sah] *nf.* cross-bar, side-street.

Traversale [trah-vehr-sah'lay] *a.* transversal.

Traversare [trah-vehr-sah'ray] *vt.* to cross.

Traversata [trah-vehr-sah'tah] *nf.* crossing, passage.

Traversìa [trah-vehr-see'ah] *nf.* misfortune, trouble.

Traverso [trah-vehr'soh] *a.* oblique, transverse; di [dee] t. *ad.* askance, wrong.

Travestire [trah-vess-tee'ray] *vt.* to disguise, travesty.

Traviamento [trah-vee-ah-men'toh] *nm.* depravity, going astray.

Travia/re [trah-vee-ah'ray] *vt.* to mislead, pervert; **—rsi** *vr.* to go astray.

Travicello [trah-vee-chell'loh] *nm.* joist.

Travisare [trah-vee-zah'ray] *vt.* to falsify, distort, misrepresent.

Travolgere [trah-voll'jay-ray] *vt.* to carry away, overcome, overwhelm, sweep away.

Travolgimento [trah-voll-jee-men'toh] *nm.* overthrow.

Trazione [trah-tsee-oh'nay]. *nf.* traction.

Tre [tray] *a.* three.

Trebbiare [treb-bee-ah'ray] *vt* to thrash, thresh.

Trebbiatrice [treb-bee-ah-tree'chay] *nf.* thresher, threshing-machine.

Trebbiatura [treb-bee-ah-too'rah] *nf.* threshing.

Treccia [trech'chah] *nf.* plait, pigtail, tress.

Trecentista [tray-chen-tee'stah] *nm.* painter or writer of the 14th century.

Trecento [tray-chen'toh] *nm.* 14th century. a. three hundred.

Tredi/ci [tray'dee-chee] *a.* thirteen; **—cenne** [chen'nay], thirteen-year-old; **—cesimo** [chay'zee-moh], thirteenth.

Tregua [tray'gwah] *nf.* respite, truce.

Tremare [tray-mah'ray] *vi.* to quake, shake, tremble.

Tremendo [tray-men'doh] *a.* awful, dreadful, tremendous.

Tremito [tray'mee-toh] *nm.* shaking, tremble, trembling.

Tremolare [tray-moh-lah'ray] *vi.* to quiver, tremble.

Tremolìo [tray-moh-lee'oh] *nm.* quivering, shaking, trembling.

Tremulo [tray'moo-loh] *a.* shaking, trembling, tremulous.

Treno [tray'noh] *nm.* train;

t. di vita [dee vee'tah] way of living.

Tren/ta [tren'tah] *a.* thirty; —**tenne** [ten'nay] thirty-year-old; —**tesimo** [tay'zee-moh] thirtieth; —**tina** [tee'nah] *nf.* some thirty.

Trepidare [tray-pee-dah'ray] *vi.* to be anxious, be in a flutter, tremble.

Trepidazione [tray-pee-dah-tsee-oh'nay] *nf.* anxiety, flutter, trepidation.

Trepido [tray'pee-doh] *a.* anxious, fluttering, trembling.

Treppiedi [trep-pee-ay'dee] *nm.* trivet, tripod.

Tresca [tress'kah] *nf.* intrigue.

Trespolo [tress'poh-loh] *nm.* rickety vehicle, trestle.

Triangolare [tree-ahng-goh-lah'ray] *a.* triangular.

Triangolo [tree-ahng'goh-loh] *nm.* triangle.

Tribolare [tree-boh-lah'ray] *vi.* to suffer, toil ; far [fahr] t. *v.* to vex.

Tribolazione [tree-boh-lah-tsee-oh'nay] *nf.* suffering, tribulation.

Tribo/lo [tree'boh-loh] *nm.* —**li** [lee] (*pl.*) suffering, tribulation.

Tribordo [tree-borr'doh] *nm.* (*naut.*) starboard [tribe.

Tribù [tree-boo'] *nf.* clan.

Tribuna [tree-boo'nah] *nf.* stand, tribune.

Tribunale [tree-boo-nah'lay] *nm.* (law) court, tribunal.

Tribuno [tree-boo'noh] *nm.* tribune.

Tributare [tree-boo-tah'ray] *vt.* to give, offer, pay.

Tributo [tree-boo'toh] *nm.* tax, tribute.

Tricolore [tree-koh-loh'ray] *nm. and a.* tricolour.

Tridente [tree-den'tay] *nm.* hay-fork, trident.

Triennale [tree-en-nah'lay] *a.* triennial.

Trifoglio [tree-foll'yoh] *nm.* clover, shamrock, trefoil.

Triglia [treel'yah] *nf.* mullet.

Trillo [treel'loh] *nm.* trill.

Trimestre [tree-mess'tray] *nm.* quarter, term.

Trina [tree'nah] *nf.* lace.

Trincea [treen-chay'ah] *nf.* trench.

Trinceramento [treen-chay-rah-men'toh] *nm.* entrenchment.

Trincera/re [treen-chay-rah'ray] *vt.* to entrench; —**rsi** *vi.* to take refuge.

Trinchetto, albero di [ahl'bay-roh dee treen-ket'toh] *nm.* (*naut.*) fore-mast.

Trinciare [treen-chah'ray] *vt.* to cut.

Trinità [tree-nee-tah'] *nf.* Trinity.

Trionfale [tree-on-fah'lay] *a.* triumphal.

Trionfante [tree-oh-fahn'tay] *a.* exultant, triumphal.

Trionfare [tree-on-fah'ray] *vi.* to be triumphant, triumph over.

Trionfo [tree-on'foh] *nm.* triumph.

Triplice [tree'plee-chay] *a.* threefold, treble, triple.

Triplo [tree'ploh] *nm.* triple the amount; *a.* triple.

Tripode [tree'poh-day] *nm.* tripod.

Trippa [treep'pah] *nf.* paunch, tripe.

Tripudiare [tree-poo-dee-ah'ray] *vi.* to exult.

Tripudio [tree-poo'dee-oh] *nm.* exultation.

Triste [tree'stay] *a.* sad, sorrowful.

Tristezza [tree-stet'sah] *nf.* sadness, sorrow.

Tristo [tree'stoh] *a.* wicked, wretched.

Tritare [tree-tah'ray] vt. to mince, pound.

Trito [tree'toh] a. commonplace, trite; minced.

Trittico [treet'tee-koh] nm. triptych.

Triunviro [tree-oon'vee-roh] nm. triumvir.

Trivella [tree-vell'lah] nf. (tech.) borer.

Trivellare [tree-vell-lah'ray] vt. (tech.) to bore.

Triviale [tree-vee-ah'lay] a. low, vulgar.

Trivialità [tree-vee-ah-lee-tah'] nf. coarseness, vulgarity, vulgar expression.

Trivio [tree'vee-oh] nm. cross-road(s).

Trofeo [troh-fay'oh] nm. trophy. [trough.]

Trogolo [troh'goh-loh] nm.

Troia [troh'yah] nf. sow.

Tromba [trom'bah] nf. bugle, horn, trumpet, tube.

Trombaio [trom-bah'yoh] nm. plumber.

Trombettiere [trom-bet-tee-ay'ray] nm. trumpeter.

Troncamento [trong-kah-men'toh] nm. cutting off, truncation.

Troncare [trong-kah'ray] vt. to break off, cut off, cut short, interrupt, truncate.

Tronco [trong'koh] nm. (tree)trunk; a. broken, truncated.

Tronfio [tron'fee-oh] a. conceited, puffed-up.

Trono [troh'noh] nm. throne.

Tropeolo [troh-pay'oh-loh] nm. nasturtium.

Tropico [troh'pee-koh] nm. tropic.

Trop/po [trop'poh] ad. too (much); a. and pn. too (much); —pi [pee] (pl.) too many.

Trota [troh'tah] nf. trout.

Trottare [trot-tah'ray] vi. to trot, walk fast.

Trottatore [trot-tah-toh'ray] nm. trotter.

Trotto [trot'toh] nm. trot.

Trottola [trot'toh-lah] nf. (whip-)top.

Trova/re [troh-vah'ray] vt. to catch, discover, find (out); andare a [ahn-dah'ray ah] t. to go and see; —rsi vr. to be, find oneself.

Trovata [troh-vah'tah] nf. contrivance, expedient, invention.

Trovatello [troh-vah-tell'loh] nm. foundling.

Trovatore [troh-vah-toh'ray] nm. finder, inventor, troubadour.

Trucca/re [trook-kah'ray] vt. to make up; —rsi vr. to make up one's face.

Trucco [trook'koh] nm. deceit, trick.

Truce [troo'chay] a. cruel, fierce, grim.

Trucidare [troo-chee-dah'ray] vt. to kill, murder.

Truciolo [troo'choh-loh] nm. chip, shaving.

Truculento [troo-koh-len'toh] a. truculent.

Truffa [troof'fah] nf. cheat, swindle.

Truffare [troof-fah'ray] vt. to cheat, swindle.

Truppa [troop'pah] nf. troops (pl.).

Tu [too] pn. thou, you (sing.); dare del [dah'ray dell] t. vi. to thou.

Tubercolare [too-behr-koh-lah'ray] a. (med.) tubercular.

Tubercolosi [too-behr-koh-loh'zee] nf. (med.) consumption, tuberculosis.

Tuberco/loso [too-behr-koh-loh'soh], —lotico [loh'tee-koh] nm. and a. consumptive.

Tubero [too'bay-roh] nm. tuber. [tube.]

Tubo [too'boh] nm. pipe.

Tubolare [too-boh-lah'ray] a. tubular.

Tuffa/re [toof-fah'ray] vt. to plunge; —**rsi** vr. to dive, plunge.

Tuffo [toof'foh] nm. dive, plunge.

Tugurio [too-goo'ree-oh] nm. (hovel.

Tulipano [too-lee-pah'noh] nm. tulip.

Tumido [too'mee-doh] a. tumid.

Tumore [too-moh'ray] nm. (med.) tumour.

Tumulare [too-moo-lah'ray] vt. to bury, inter.

Tumulo [too'moo-loh] nm. grave, tumulus.

Tumulto [too-mool'toh] nm. riot, tumult, uproar.

Tumultuoso [too-mool-too-oh'soh] a. riotous, tumultuous.

Tunica [too'nee-kah] nf. tunic.

Tuo [too'oh] poss. a. thy, your; poss. pn. thine, yours.

Tuono [too-oh'noh] nm. thunder.

T(u)orlo [too-orr'loh] nm. yolk (of egg).

Turacciolo [too-rahch'choh-loh] nm. cork, stopper.

Turare [too-rah'ray] vt. to bung, cork, stop.

Turba [toor'bah] nf. crowd, mob, rabble.

Turbante [toor-bahn'tay] nm. turban.

Turba/re [toor-bah'ray] vt. to disturb, trouble; —**rsi** vr. to be upset, get agitated.

Turbina [toor-bee'nah] nf. (tech.) turbine.

Turbinare [toor-bee-nah'ray] vi. to eddy, whirl.

Turbine [toor'bee-nay] nm. hurricane, whirl(-wind).

Turbinio (toor-bee-nee'oh] nm. whirling.

Turbolento [toor-boh-len'toh] a. troubled, turbulent.

Turchino [toor-kee'noh] nm. and a. dark blue.

Turco [toor'koh] nm. Turk; a. Turkish.

Turno [toor'noh] nm. turn; di (dee) t. ad. on duty.

Turpe [toor'pay] a. base, filthy, obscene.

Turpitudine [toor-pee-too'-dee-nay] nf. baseness, turpitude.

Tuta [too'tah] nf. mechanic's overall.

Tutela [too-tay'lah] nf. defence, guardianship, tutelage.

Tutelare [too-tay-lah'ray] vt. to defend, protect.

Tu/tore [too-toh'ray] nm. —**trice** [tree'chay] nf. guardian.

Tuttavia [toot-tah-vee'ah] ad. and con. nevertheless, still, yet.

Tut/to [toot'toh] a. all, whole; pn. all, everything; —**ti** [tee] (pl.) all, everyone; ad. completely, entirely, quite, wholly; del [dell] t. ad. quite t. ad un tratto [ahd oon traht'toh] ad. all of a sudden.

Tuttora [too-toh'rah] ad. still.

U

Ubbia [oob-bee'ah] nf. false idea, superstition, nonsense.

Ubbidiente [oob-bee-dee-en'tay] a. obedient.

Ubbidienza [oob-bee-dee-ent'sah] nf. obedience.

Ubbidire [oob-bee-dee'ray] vt. and i. to obey.

Ubertà [oo-behr-tah'] nf. fertility.

Ubertoso [oo-behr-toh'soh] a. fertile, fruitful.

Ubicazione [oo-bee-kah-tsee-oh'nay] nf. position, situation.

Ubiquità [oo-bee-kwee-tah'] *nf.* omnipresence, ubiquity.

Ubriaca/re [oo-bree-ah-kah'ray] *vt.* to intoxicate, make drunk; —**rsi** *vr.* to get drunk.

Ubria/catura [oo-bree-ah-kah-too'rah], —**chezza** [ket'sah] *nf.* drunkenness, intoxication.

Ubriaco [oo-bree-ah'koh] *a.* drunk, drunken, intoxicated.

Ubriacone [oo-bree-ah-koh'nay] *nm.* drunkard.

Uccellare [ooch-chell-lah'ray] *vi.* to go fowling.

Uccellatore [ooch-chell-lah-toh'ray] *nm.* fowler.

Uccello [ooch-chell'loh] *nm.* bird; **u.** di bosco [dee boss'koh] fugitive from the law.

Uccidere [ooch-chee'day-ray] *vt.* to kill.

Uccisione [ooch-chee-zee-oh'nay] *nf.* killing, murder.

Udienza [oo-dee-ent'sah] *nf.* audience, hearing; **dare** [dah'ray] **u.** *vi.* to receive.

Udire [oo-dee'ray] *vt.* to hear, listen to.

Udito [oo-dee'toh] *nm.* hearing (sense).

Udi/tore [oo-dee-toh'ray] *nm.* —**trice** [tree'chay] *nf.* hearer, listener.

Uditorio [oo-dee-toh'ree-oh] *nm.* audience, hearers (*pl.*).

Ufficiale [oof-fee-chah'lay] *nm.* officer; *a.* official.

Ufficiare [oof-fee-chah'ray] *vi.* to officiate.

Ufficio [oof-fee'choh] *nm.* duty, office; **d'u** *ad.* officially.

Ufficioso [oof-fee-choh'soh] *a.* unofficial.

Uffizio [oof-fee'tsee-oh] *nm.* office (religious).

Ufo, a [ah oo'foh] *ad.* in vain, to no purpose.

Uggia [oo'djah] *nf.* bore, dislike; avere in [ah-vay'ray eenj **u.** *vt.* to dislike.

Uggioso [oo-djoh'soh] *a.* annoying, dull, tiresome.

Ugonotto [oo-goh-not'toh] *nm.* Huguenot.

Uguaglianza [oo-gwahl-yahnt'sah] *nf.* equality, similarity.

Uguaglia/re [oo-gwahl-yah'ray] *vt.* to (be) equal (to); —**rsi** *vr.* to be(come) equal, claim equality.

Uguale [oo-gwah'lay] *nm. and f.* equal; *a.* equal, like, same.

Ugualità [oo-gwah-lee-tah'] *nf.* equality.

Uh! [oo] *int.* ah!

Ulcera [ool'chay-rah] *nf.* ulcer.

Uliva, etc.: *v.* **oliva**, etc.

Ulteriore [ool-tay-ree-oh'ray] *a.* further, ulterior.

Ultimamente [ool-tee-mah-men'tay] *ad.* lately, recently.

Ultimare [ool-tee-mah'ray] *vt.* to complete, finish.

Ultimo [ool'tee-moh] *a.* latest, last, utmost.

Ululare [oo-loo-lah'ray] *vi.* to howl.

Ululato [oo-loo-lah'toh], **ululo** [oo'loo-loh] *nm.* howl, howling.

Umanesimo [oo-mah-nay'zee-moh] *nm.* humanism.

Umanista [oo-mah-nee'stah] *nm.* humanist.

Umanità [oo-mah-nee-tah'] *nf.* humaneness, humanity, mankind.

Umanitario [oo-mah-nee-tah'ree-oh] *a.* humane, humanitarian.

Umano [oo-mah'noh] *a.* human(e), kind, sympathetic.

Umbelico: *v.* **ombelico**.

Umidità [oo-mee-dee-tah'] *nf.* dampness, moisture.

Umido [oo'mee-doh] *a.* damp, moist.

Umile [oo'mee-lay] *a.* humble, simple.

Umilia/re [oo-mee-lee-ah'ray] *vt.* to humble, humiliate, mortify; —rsi *vr.* to abase oneself, humble oneself.

Umiliazione [oo-mee-lee-ah-tsee-oh'nay] *nf.* humiliation, mortification.

Umiltà [oo-meel-tah'] *nf.* humility.

Umore [oo-moh'ray] *nm.* humour, mood, temper; **di buon** [dee boo-ohn'] **u.** *ad.* in a good humour.

Umorismo [oo-moh-rees'moh] *nm.* humour.

Umorista [oo-moh-ree'stah] *nm.* humorist.

Umoristico [oo-moh-ree'stee-koh] *a.* comic, funny, humorous.

Un–: *v.* **uno.**

Unanime [oo-nah'nee-may] *a.* unanimous.

Unanimità [oo-nah-nee-mee-tah'] *nf.* unanimity.

Uncinetto [oon-chee-net'toh] *nm.* crochet-hook. [hook.

Uncino [oon-chee'noh] *nm.*

Undi/ci [oon'dee-chee] *a.* eleven; —cenne [chen'nay], 11-year-old; —cesimo [chay'ree-moh], eleventh.

Ungere [oon'jay-ray] *vt.* to anoint (king, priest, etc.), grease, smear.

Ungherese [oong-gay-ray'say] *nm. and f. and a.* a Hungarian.

Unghia [oong'ghee-ah] *nf.* claw, hoof, nail.

Unguento [oong-gwen'toh] *nm.* ointment.

Unico [oo'nee-koh] *a.* only, single, sole; **u. nel suo genere** [nell soo'oh jay'nay-ray], unique (of one's kind).

Unificare [oo-nee-fee-kah'ray] *vt.* to unify.

Unificazione [oo-nee-fee-kah-tsee-oh'nay] *nf.* unification.

Uniforma/re [oo-nee-forr-mah'ray] *vt.* to conform, make uniform; —rsi *vr.* to comply with, conform to.

Uniforme [oo-nee-forr'may] *nf. and a.* uniform.

Unigenito [oo-nee-jay'nee-toh] *a.* only-begotten.

Unione [oo-nee-oh'nay] *nf.* harmony, union.

Unire [oo-nee'ray] *vt.* to join, unite.

Unisono [oo-nee'soh-noh] *nm.* harmony, unison.

Unità [oo-nee-tah'] *nf.* unit, unity.

Unito [oo-nee'toh] *a.* united; **tinta** [teen'tah] **unita** *nf.* uniform colour.

Universale [oo-nee-vehr-sah'lay] *a.* general, universal; **giudizio** [joo-dee'tsee-oh] **u.** *nm.* the Last Judgment.

Università [oo-nee-vehr-see-tah'] *nf.* university.

Universitario [oo-nee-vehr-see-tah'ree-oh] *nm.* university student; *a.* (of a) university.

Universo [oo-nee-vehr'soh] *nm.* universe.

Un/o [oon'oh] *indef. art.* a(n), one; *a.* one; *indef pn.* one; **l'uno e l'altro** [loo'noh ay lahl'troh] *pn.* both.

Unto [oon'toh] *nm.* grease, fat; *a.* dirty, greasy.

Untuoso [oon-too-oh'soh] *a.* greasy, oily, unctuous.

Unzione [oon-tsee-oh'nay] *nf.* unction.

Uomo [oo-oh'moh] *nm.* man.

Uopo [oo-oh'poh] *nm.* necessity, need; **essere** [ess'say-ray] **d'u** *v.imp.* to be necessary; **fare** [fah'ray] **all'u.** *vi.* to meet the case.

Uovo [oo-oh'voh] *nm.* egg.

Uragano [oo-rah-gah'noh] *nm.* hurricane.

Urango [oo-rang'goh] *nm.* orang-outang.

Urbanità [oor-bah-nee-tah'] *nf.* civility, courtesy, urbaneness.

Urbano [oor-bah'noh] *a.* civil, courteous, urban, urbane.

Urgente [oor-jen'tay] *a.* pressing, urgent.

Urgenza [oor-jent'sah] *nf.* urgency.

Urgere [oor'jay-ray] *vi.* to be pressing, be urgent.

Urina [oo-ree'nah] *nf.* urine.

Urlare [oor-lah'ray] *vi.* to howl, shout, shriek.

Urlo [oor'loh] *nm.* cry, howl, shout, shriek.

Urna [oor'nah] *nf.* ballot-box, urn; andare alle urne [ahn-dah'ray ahl'lay oor'nay] to go to the polls.

Urtare [oor-tah'ray] *vt.* to knock against, push, touch, (*fig.*) annoy, clash with.

Urto [oor'toh] *nm.* collision, push, shove; essere in [ess'say-ray een] u. *vi.* to be at variance, be on bad terms.

Usanza [oo-zahnt'sah] *nf.* custom, usage.

Usare [oo-zah'ray] *vt.* to employ, make use of, use; *vi.* to be accustomed, be wont, be fashionable.

Usato [oo-zah'toh] *a.* second-hand, usual, wonted.

Usciere [oo-shay'ray] *nm.* usher.

Uscio [oo'shoh] *nm.* door.

Uscire [oo-shee'ray] *vi.* to come (go) out, get out, leave.

Uscita [oo-shee'tah] *nf.* coming (going) out, exit, outlet, way out, sally, witty remark; via di [vee'ah dee] u. escape.

Usignuolo [oo-zeen-y(oo)-oh'loh] *nm.* nightingale.

Uso [oo'zoh] *nm.* custom, usage, wont; *a.* accustomed, used. (*rare*). v. **Avvezzo.**

Us/saro [oos'sah-roh], —**sero** [say-roh] *nm.* hussar.

Ustionare [oos-stee-oh-nah'ray] *vt.* to burn, scorch.

Ustione [oo-stee-oh'nay] *nf.* burn.

Usuale [oo-zoo-ah'lay] *a.* usual.

Usufruire [oo-zoo-froo-ee'ray] *vi.* to benefit by, take advantage of.

Usura [oo-zoo'rah] *nf.* usury.

Usuraio [oo-zoo-rah'yoh] *nm.* usurer.

Usurpare [oo-zoor-pah'ray] *vt.* to usurp.

Usurpazione [oo-zoor-pah-tsee-oh'nay] *nf.* usurpation.

Utensile [oo-ten-see'lay] *nm.* implement, tool, utensil.

Utero [oo'tay-roh] *nm.* (*med.*) uterus, womb.

Utile [oo'tee-lay] *nm.* benefit, profit, utility; *a.* useful; tempo [tem'poh] u. *nm.* time allowed.

Utilità [oo-tee-lee-tah'] *nf.* benefit, use, usefulness, utility.

Utilizzare [oo-tee-leed-zah'ray] *vt.* to make use of, turn to account, utilize.

Utilizzazione [oo-tee-leed-zah-tsee-oh'nay] *nf.* utilization.

Utopia [oo-toh-pee'ah] *nf.* chimerical project.

Uva [oo'vah] *nf.* grapes (*pl.*); u. spina [spee'nah] gooseberry.

Uzzolo [ood'zoh-loh] *nm.* longing, passion.

V

Vacante [vah-kahn'tay] *a.* vacant.

Vacanza [vah-kahnt'sah] *nf.* holiday, vacancy, (school) vacation.

Vacare [vah-kah'ray] *vi.* to be vacant.

Vacca [vahk'kah] *nf.* cow.

Vaccaro [vahk-kah'roh] nm. cowherd.

Vaccinare [vahch-chee-nah'ray] vt. to vaccinate.

Vaccinazione [vahch-chee-nah-tsee-oh'nay] nf. vaccination.

Vaccino [vahch-chee'noh] nm. vaccine. v. Vuoto.

Vacillante [vah-cheel-lahn'tay] a. hesitating, irresolute, tottering, wavering.

Vacillare [vah-cheel-lah'ray] vi. to be irresolute, hesitate, totter, waver.

Vacuità [vah-koo-ee-tah'] nf. emptiness, (rare). v. Vuoto.

Vacuo [vah'koo-oh] a. empty, vacuous, vain.

Vagabondaggio [vah-gah-bon-dah'djoh] nm. vagabondage, vagrancy, wandering.

Vagabondare [vah-gah-bon-dah'ray] vi. to roam, rove, wander.

Vagabondo [vah-gah-bon'doh] nm. tramp, vagabond, vagrant, wanderer; a. vagabond, wandering.

Vagare [vah-gah'ray] vi. to ramble, wander.

Vagheggia/re [vah-gay-djah'ray] vt. to cherish, long for, look lovingly at; —rsi vr. to look at oneself complacently.

Vaghezza [vah-ghet'sah] nf. beauty, longing.

Vagire [vah-jee'ray] vi. to whimper.

Vagito [vah-jee'toh] nm. whimper.

Vaglia [vahl'yah] nf. ability, merit, worth; v. postale [poss-tah'lay] nm. money order, postal order.

Vagliare [vahl-yah'ray] vt. to consider, sift, weigh (fig.).

Vaglio [vahl'yoh] nm. sieve.

Vago [vah'goh] a. eager, pretty, vague.

Vagone [vah-goh'nay] nm. (rly.) coach, truck, wagon.

Vainiglia [vah-ee-neel'yah] nf. vanilla.

Vaiolo [vah-ee-oh'loh] nm. (med.) small-pox.

Valanga [vah-lahng'gah] nf. avalanche.

Valdese [vahl-day'zay] nm. and f. and a. Waldensian.

Valente [vah-len'tay] a. clever, worthy.

Valentia [vah-len-tee'ah] nf. ability, cleverness, skill.

Valentuomo [vah-len-too-oh'moh] nm. working man.

Vale/re [vah-lay'ray] vi. to be worth; v. la pena [lah pay'nah] to be worth while; vale a dire [vah'lay ah dee'ray] that is to say; —rsi vr. to avail oneself, make use of.

Valetudinario [vah-lay-too-dee-nah'ree-oh] nm. and a. valetudinarian.

Valevole [vah-lay'voh-lay] a. available, efficacious.

Valicabile [vah-lee-kah'bee-lay] a. that can be crossed.

Valicare [vah-lee-kah'ray] vt. to cross, pass.

Valico [vah'lee-koh] nm. crossing, pass, passage.

Validità [vah-lee-dee-tah'] nf. validity.

Valido [vah'lee-doh] a. able, efficacious, valid.

Valigia [vah-lee'jah] nf. suit-case.

Valigiaio [vah-lee-jah'yoh] nm. trunk-maker.

Vallata [vahl-lah'tah] nf. plain, vale.

Valle [vahl'lay] nf. vale, valley. [valet.

Valletto [vahl-let'toh] nm.

Valligiano [vahl-lee-jah'noh] nm. dalesman, inhabitant of a valley.

Valore [vah-loh'ray] nm. courage, valour, value, worth.

Valorizzare [vah-loh-reed-zah'ray] *vt.* to employ to advantage, turn to account.

Valoroso [vah-loh-roh'soh] *a.* brave, valiant.

Valuta [vah-loo'tah] *nf.* money, value.

Valutare [vah-loo-tah'ray] *vt.* to appraise, value.

Valutazione [vah-loo-tah-tsee-oh'nay] *nf.* estimation, valuation.

Valva [vahl'vah] *nf.* valve.

Valvola [vahl'voh-lah] *nf.* (*elec.*) fuse, valve.

Valzer [vahlt'sehr] *nm.* waltz.

Vampa [vahm'pah] *nf.* flame, flush.

Vampare [vahm-pah'ray] *vi.* to blaze. *v.* **Divampare**.

Vampiro [vahm-pee'roh] *nm.* vampire.

Vanagloria [vah-nah-gloh'ree-ah] *nf.* arrogance, vain-glory.

Vanaglorioso [vah-nah-gloh-ree-oh'soh] *a.* vain-glorious.

Vandalismo [vahn-dah-lees'moh] *nm.* vandalism.

Vandalo [vahn'dah-loh] *nm.* vandal.

Vaneggiare [vah-nay-djah'ray] *vi.* to be delirious, rave.

Vanga [vahng'gah] *nf.* spade.

Vangare [vahng-gah'ray] *vt.* to dig.

Vangelo [vahn-jay'loh] *nm.* Gospel. [vanity.

Vanità [vah-nee-tah'] *nf.*

Vanitoso [vah-nee-toh'soh] *a.* conceited, vain.

Vano [vah'noh] *nm.* embrasure, opening, room; *a.* ineffectual, useless, vain.

Vantaggiare: *v.* **avvantaggiare**.

Vantaggio [vahn-tah'djoh] *nm.* advantage, profit.

Vantaggioso [vahn-tah-djoh'soh] *a.* advantageous, profitable.

Vantare [vahn-tah'ray] *vt.* to boast of; —**rsi** *vr.* to be proud of, boast.

Vanteria [vahn-tay-ree'ah] *nf.* boast(ing), brag(ging).

Vanto [vahn'toh] *nm.* honour, name, title.

Vanvera, a [ah vahn'vay-rah] *ad.* at random, nonsensically.

Vaporazione [vah-poh-rah-tsee-oh'nay] *nf.* evaporation.

Vapore [vah-poh'ray] *nm.* fume, steam, vapour; boat; mento a [bah-stee-men'toh ah] v. steamer; **macchina a** [mahk'kee-nah ah] v. *nf.* steam-engine.

Vaporoso [vah-poh-roh'soh] *a.* airy, filmy, vaporous.

Varare [vah-rah'ray] *vt.* to launch.

Varcare [vahr-kah'ray] *vt.* to cross, pass.

Varco [vahr'koh] *nm.* gate, passage, way; **aspettare al** [ah-spet-tah'ray ahl] v. *vt.* to lie in wait for.

Variabile [vah-ree-ah'bee-lay] *a.* changeable, unsettled, variable.

Variante [vah-ree-ahn'tay] *nf.* variant; *a.* varying.

Variare [vah-ree-ah'ray] *vt. and v.* to change, vary.

Variazione [vah-ree-ah-tsee-oh'nay] *nf.* change, variation.

Varicella [vah-ree-chell'lah] *nf.* (*med.*) chicken-pox.

Varietà [vah-ree-ay-tah'] *nf.* variety.

Vario [vah'ree-oh] *a.* different, several, various.

Variopinto [vah-ree-oh-peen'toh] *a.* many-coloured.

Varo [vah'roh] *nm.* launch(ing). [pool.

Vasca [vah'skah] *nf.* basin,

Vascello [vah-shell'loh] *nm.* ship, vessel.

Vaselina [vah-zay-lee'nah] *nf.* vaseline.

Vaso [vah'zoh] nm. pot, vase, vessel; v. da notte [dah not'tay], chamber(-pot).

Vassallo [vahs-sahl'loh] nm. vassal.

Vassoio [vahs-soh'yoh] nm. [dish, tray.

Vastità [vah-stee-tah'] nf. great extent, vast size, vastness.

Vasto [vah-stoh] a. vast, wide.

Vate [vah'tay] nm. (poet.) bard, poet, prophet.

Vaticinio [vah-tee-chee'nee-oh] nm. prophecy.

Vecchi/aia [veck-kee-ah'yah] —ezza [et'sah] nf. old age.

Vecchio [veck'kee-oh] a. old.

Veccia [vehch'chah] nf. tare, vetch.

Vece [vay'chay] nf. place, stead; in mia [een mee'ah] v. ad. in my stead; in v. di [dee] pr. instead of; fare le veci di [fah'ray lay vay'chee dee] vi. to act as.

Vedere [vay-day'ray] vt. to behold, see; farsi [fahr'see] v. rv. to appear, show oneself.

Vedetta [vay-det'tah] nf. look-out, sentinel, watch.

Vedo/va [vay'doh-vah], nf. widow; —vo [voh] nm. widower.

Vedovanza [vay-doh-vahnt'sah] nf. widow(er)hood.

Veduta [vay-doo'tah] nf. sight, view.

Veemente [vay-ay-men'tay] a. vehement.

Veemenza [vay-ay-ment'sah] nf. vehemence.

Vegetale [vay-jay-tah'lay] nm. and a. vegetable.

Vegetare [vay-jay-tah'ray] vi. to vegetate.

Vegetazione [vay-jay-tah-tsee-oh'nay] nf. vegetation.

Vegeto [vay'jay-toh] a. strong, thriving, vigorous.

Veggente [vay-djen'tay] nm. and f. seer; a. seeing.

Veglia [vayl'yah] nf. wake, waking, watch.

Vegliardo [vayl-yahr'doh] nm. old man.

Vegliare [vayl-yah'ray] vi. to be on the look-out, be awake, sit up, watch over.

Veicolo [vay-ee'koh-loh] nm. vehicle.

Vela [vay'lah] nf. sail; a gonfie vele [ah gon'fee-ay vay'lay] ad. swimmingly, very well.

Velato [vay-lah'toh] a. thick (voice), veiled.

Veleggiare [vay-lay-djah'ray] vi. and i. to sail.

Veleno [vay-lay'noh] nm. poison, venom.

Velenoso [vay-lay-noh'soh] a. poisonous, venomous.

Veliero [vay-lee-ay'roh] nm. sailing-boat.

Velina, carta [kahr'tah vay-lee'nah] nf tissue paper.

Velivolo [vay-lee'voh-loh] nm. aeroplane.

Velleità [vell-lay-ee-tah'] nf. foolish ambition, foolish idea.

Vello [vell'loh] nm. fleece.

Velluto [vell-loo'toh] nm. velvet.

Velo [vay'loh] nm. veil.

Veloce [vay-loh'chay] a. quick, rapid, swift.

Velocipede [vay-loh-chee'pay-day] nm. cycle.

Velocità [vay-loh-chee-tah'] nf. quickness, rapidity, speed, velocity.

Velodromo [vay-loh'droh-moh] nm. track for cycle-racing.

Veltro [vell'troh] nm. greyhound. v. **Levriere.**

Vena [vay'nah] nf. vein; essere in [ess'say-ray een] v. vi. to be in form.

Venale [vay-nah'lay] a. keen on money, venal.

Vendemmia [ven-dem'mee-

ah] *nf.* grape-gathering, vintage.

Vendemmiare [ven-dem-mee-ah'ray] *vi.* to gather grapes. [sell.

Vendere [ven'day-ray] *vt.* to

Vendetta [ven-det'tah] *nf.* revenge, vengeance.

Vendicare [ven-dee-kah'ray] *vt.* to avenge, revenge.

Vendicativo [ven-dee-kah-tee'voh] *a.* revengeful, vindictive.

Vendita [ven'dee-tah] *nf.* sale, shop.

Venditore [ven-dee-toh'ray] *nm.* —**trice** [tree'chay] *nf.* seller, vendor; **v. ambulante** [ahm-boo-lahn'tay] hawker, pedlar.

Venerabile [vay-nay-rah'bee-lay] *a.* venerable.

Venerazione [vay-nay-rah-tsee-oh'nay] *nf.* veneration, worship.

Venerdì [vay-nehr-dee'] *nm.* Friday; **gli manca un** [lyee mahng'kah oon] **v. he has a screw loose.**

Venereo [vay-nay'ray-oh] *a.* venereal. [don.

Venia [vay'nee-ah] *nf.* par-

Veniale [vay-nee-ah'lay] *a.* venial.

Venire [vay-nee'ray] *vi.* to come; **v. meno** [may'noh] to faint. [fan.

Ventaglio [ven-tahl'yoh] *nm.*

Ventata [ven-tah'tah] *nf.* puff of wind.

Venti [ven'tee] *a.* twenty; **—tenne** [ten'nay], 20-year-old; **—tesimo** [tay'zee-moh] twentieth; **—tina** [tee'nah] *nf.* a score.

Ventilare [ven-tee-lah'ray] *vt.* to ventilate, winnow.

Ventilatore [ven-tee-lah-toh'ray] *nm.* ventilator.

Ventilazione [ven-tee-lah-tsee-oh'nay] *nf.* ventilation.

Vento [ven'toh] *nm.* wind.

Ventoso [ven-toh'soh] *a.* windy.

Ventre [ven'tray] *nm.* belly.

Ventura [ven-too'rah] *nf.* chance, luck.

Venturo [ven-too'roh] *a.* to come, future, next.

Venustà [vay-noo-stah'] *nf.* beauty. **v. Bellezza.**

Venusto [vay-noo'stoh] *a.* beautiful. **v. Bello.**

Venuta [vay-noo'tah] *nf.* arrival, coming.

Venuto [vay-noo'toh] *nm.* comer; *a.* come.

Verace [vay-rah'chay] *a.* real, true, truthful.

Veracità [vay-rah-chee-tah'] *nf.* veracity.

Verbale [vehr-bah'lay] *nm.* minutes (*pl.*); *a.* oral, verbal.

Verbosità [vehr-boh-see-tah'] *nf.* prolixity, verbosity.

Verboso [vehr-boh'soh] *a.* prolix, verbose.

Verde [vehr'day] *nm. and a.* green; **essere al** [ess'say-ray ahl] **v.** *vi.* to be penniless.

Verdeggiante [vehr-day-djahn'tay] *a.* verdant.

Verdeggiare [vehr-day-djah'ray] *vi.* to be (grow) green.

Verdetto [vehr-det'toh] *nm.* sentence, verdict.

Verdura [vehr-doo'rah] *nf.* verdure, greens (*pl.*), vegetables (*pl.*).

Verecondia [vay-ray-kon'dee-ah] *nf.* bashfulness, modesty.

Verecondo [vay-ray-kon'doh] *a.* bashful, modest.

Verga [vehr'gah] *nf.* rod; **v. pastorale** [pah-stoh-rah'lay], (*eccl.*) crozier.

Verginale [vehr-jee-nah'lay] *a.* maidenly, virgin.

Vergine [vehr'jee-nay] *nf.* virgin.

Verginità [vehr-jee-nee-tah´] *nf.* virginity.

Vergogna [vehr-gohn´yah] *nf.* disgrace, shame, modesty.

Vergognarsi [vehr-gohn-yahr´see] *vr.* to be ashamed.

Vergognoso [vehr-gohn-yoh´soh] *a.* shameful, modest, timid.

Veridico [vay-ree´dee-koh] *a.* truthful, veracious.

Verifica/re [vay-ree-fee-kah´ ray] *vt.* to check, verify; —rsi *vr.* to come to pass, come true, happen.

Verificatore [vay-ree-fee-kah-toh´ray] *nm.* inspector.

Verificazione [vay-ree-fee-kah-tsee-oh´nay] *nf.* inspection, verification.

Verisimile, etc.: *v.* **vero-simile**, etc. [truth.

Verità [vay-ree-tah´] *nf.*

Veritiero [vay-ree-tee-ay´roh] *a.* truthful, veracious.

Verme [vehr´may] *nm.* worm.

Vermiglio [vehr-meel´yoh] *nm. and a.* vermilion.

Vernacolo [vehr-nah´koh-loh] *nm.* dialect, vernacular; *a.* dialectal.

Vernice [vehr-nee´chay] *nf.* glaze, paint, polish, varnish; una mano di [oo´nah mah´noh deej] *v.* a coat of paint.

Verniciare [vehr-nee-chah´ray] *vt.* to glaze, paint, varnish.

Verniciatore [vehr-nee-chah-toh´ray] *nm.* painter, varnisher.

Verniciatura [vehr-nee-chah-too´rah] *nf.* glazing, painting, varnishing.

Vero [vay´roh] *nm.* truth; dal [dahl] *v. ad.* from the life, from nature; *v. a.* real, true.

Verosimiglianza [vay-roh-see-meel-yahnt´sah] *nf.* likelihood, verisimilitude.

Verosimile [vay-roh-see´mee-lay] *a.* likely, probable.

Versamento [vehr-sah-men´toh] *nm.* payment.

Versante [vehr-sahn´tay] *nm.* side, slope, watershed; (*com.*) depositor, payer.

Versare [vehr-sah´ray] *vt.* to pay, pour, shed, spill; *vi.* to be, live, spill.

Versatile [vehr-sah´tee-lay] *a.* versatile.

Verseggiare [vehr-say-djah´ ray] *vt.* to turn into verse, versify; *vi.* to write verses.

Verseggiatore [vehr-say-djah-toh´ray] *nm.* versifier.

Versificazione [vehr-see-fee-kah-tsee-oh´nay] *nf.* versification.

Versione [vehr-see-oh´nay] *nf.* translation, version.

Verso [vehr´soh] *nm.* line, note, song, verse, sense, way; non c'è [nonn chay] *v.* it is impossible; *pr.* about, to, towards.

Vertente [vehr-ten´tay] *a.* pending.

Vertenza [vehr-tent´sah] *nf.* dispute, question.

Verticale [vehr-tee-kah´lay] *nf. and a.* vertical.

Vertice [vehr´tee-chay] *nm.* height, top, vertex.

Vertigine [vehr-tee´jee-nay] *nf.* —ni [nee] (*pl.*) dizziness, giddiness.

Vertiginoso [vehr-tee-jee-noh´soh] *a.* dizzy.

Veruno [vay-roo´noh] *pn.* (*poet.*) anyone, no one; *a.* any, no.

Vescica [vay-shee´kah] *nf.* bladder, blister, (*med.*) vesica.

Vescovado [vess-koh-vah´ doh] *nm.* bishopric, bishop's palace.

Vescovile [vess-koh-vee´lay] *a.* episcopal, of a bishop.

Vescovo [vess´koh-voh] *nm.* bishop.

Vespa [vess´pah] *nf.* wasp.

Vespaio [vess-pah'yoh] *nm.*
hornets' nest, wasps' nest,
(*med.*) mass of boils.
Vespero [vess'pay-roh] *nm.*
evening, evening star.
Vespro [vess'proh] *nm.* even-
song, vespers.
Vessare [vess-sah'ray] *vt.*
to molest, oppress.
Vessazione [vess-sah-tsee-
oh'nay] *nf.* injustice.
Vessillo [vess-seel'loh] *nm.*
flag, standard.
Vestaglia [vess-tahl'yah] *nf.*
dressing-gown.
Vestale [vess-tah'lay] *nf.*
vestal.
Ves/te [vess'tay] *nf.* dress,
guise; —ti [tee] (*pl.*) clothes
(*pl.*).
Vestibolo [vess-tee'boh-loh]
nm. hall, vestibule.
Vestigia [vess-tee'jah] *nf.*
trace, vestige.
Vesti/re [vess-tee'ray] *vt.* to
clothe, dress, wear; —rsi *vr.*
to dress.
Veterano [vay-tay-rah'noh]
nm. ex-service man, veteran.
Veterinaria [vay-tay-ree-
nah'ree-ah] *nf.* veterinary
surgery.
Veterinario [vay-tay-ree-
nah'ree-oh] *nm.* veterinary
surgeon; *a.* veterinary.
Veto [vay'toh] *nm.* veto.
Vetraio [vay-trah'yoh] *nm.*
glass-blower, glazier.
Vetrata [vay-trah'tah] *nf.*
glass door, (stained-) glass
window.
Vetreria [vay-tray-ree'ah] *nf.*
glass manufactory.
Vetrina [vay-tree'nah] *nf.*
glass case, shop-window, show-
case.   [*nm.* vitriol.
Vetriolo [vay-tree-oh'loh]
Vetro [vay'troh] *nm.* glass,
pane (of glass).   [top.
Vetta [vett'tah] *nf.* summit.
Vettovaglie [vet-toh-vahl'-

yay] *nf.* (*pl.*) provisions (*pl.*),
victuals (*pl.*).
Vettura [vet-too'rah] *nf.* cab,
carriage, coach.
Vetturino [vet-too-ree'noh]
nm. cabby, coachman, driver.
Vetusto [vay-too'stoh] *a.*
ancient, old. *v.* Antico.
Vezzeggiare [vet-say-djah'-
ray] *vt.* to fondle.
Vezzo [vet'soh] *nm.* (bad)
habit, necklace.
Vezzoso [vet-soh'soh] *a.*
charming, pretty.
Vi [vee] *pr.* (*acc. and dat.*) you,
to you; *ad.* there.
Via [vee'ah] *nf.* road, street,
way; v. di mezzo [dee med'-
zoh], half-measure.
Viadotto [vee-ah-dot'toh] *nm.*
viaduct.
Viaggiare [vee-ah-djah'ray]
vi. to journey, travel.
Viag/gio [vee-ah'djoh] *nm.*
journey, tour, voyage; —gi
[djee] (*pl.*) travels (*pl.*).
Viale [vee-ah'lay] *nm.* avenue.
Viandante [vee-ahn-dahn'-
tay] *nm.* passer-by, traveller.
Viavai [vee-ah-vah'ee] *nm.*
coming and going.
Vibrare [vee-brah'ray] *vt.*
to deal; *vi.* to quiver, vibrate.
Vibrazione [vee-brah-tsee-
oh'nay] *nf.* quiver, vibration.
Vicario [vee-kah'ree-oh] *nm.*
vicar.
Vicenda [vee-chehn'dah] *nf.*
event, vicissitude; a [ah] v.
ad. in turn, reciprocally.
Vicendevole [vee-chehn-day'-
voh-lay] *a.* mutual, reciprocal.
Vicinanza [vee-chee-nahn'-
sah] *nf.* closeness, nearness,
neighbourhood, vicinity.
Vicinato [vee-chee-nah'toh]
nm. neighbourhood, neigh-
bours (*pl.*).
Vicino [vee-chee'noh] *nm.*
neighbour; *a.* neighbouring;
ad. close by, near; v. a

[ah] *pr.* beside, close to, near.

Vicissitudine [vee-chees-see-too'dee-nay] *nf.* event, vicissitude.

Vicolo [vee'koh-loh] *nm.* alley, lane.

Vidimare [vee-dee-mah'ray] *vt.* to authenticate, visé.

Vieppiù [vee-ep-pee-oo'] *ad.* more (and more).

Vietare [vee-ay-tah'ray] *vt.* to forbid, prohibit.

Vigente [vee-jen'tay] *a.* in force.

Vigilante [vee-jee-lahn'tay] *a.* vigilant, watchful.

Vigilanza [vee-jee-lahnt'sah] *nf.* vigilance, watchfulness.

Vigilare [vee-jee-lah'ray] *vt.* to keep an eye on, watch over; *vi.* to be be on one's guard, be on the alert, keep watch.

Vigile [vee'jee-lay] *nm.* policeman; *a.* alert, vigilant, wary, watchful.

Vigilia [vee-jee'lee-ah] *nf.* eve, vigil.

Vigliacco [veel-yahk'koh] *nm.* coward; *a.* cowardly.

Vigna [veen'yah] *nf.* vigneto (veen-yay'toh) *nm.* vineyard.

Vigore [vee-goh'ray] *nm.* force, strength, vigour.

Vigoroso [vee-goh-roh'soh] *a.* strong, vigorous.

Vile [vee'lay] *nm.* coward; *a.* cowardly, low.

Vilipendere [vee-lee-pen'day-ray] *vt.* to despise, scorn.

Villa [veel'lah] *nf.* country-house.

Villaggio [veel-lah'djoh] *nm.* village.

Villania [veel-lah-nee'ah] *nf.* insult, rudeness.

Villano [veel-lah'noh] *nm.* boor, ill-bred fellow; *a.* rude, rough.

Villeggiare [veel-lay-djah'ray] *vi.* to spend one's summer holidays.

Villeggiatura [veel-lay-djah-too'rah] *nf.* holiday (in the country); luogo di [loo-oh'goh dee] *v. nm.* holiday-resort.

Viltà [veel-tah'] *nf.* cowardice, cowardly act.

Vimine [vee'mee-nay] *nm.* osier, withy; di vimini [dee vee'mee-nee] *a.* wicker.

Vince/re [veen'chay-ray] *vt.* to conquer, overcome, vanquish, win; —rsi *vr.* to master oneself.

Vincita [veen'chee-tah] *nf.* winning(s).

Vinci/tore [veen-chee-toh'ray] *nm.* —trice [tree'chay] *nf.* conqueror, winner.

Vincolare [veeng-koh-lah'ray] *vt.* to bind.

Vincolo [veeng'koh-loh] *nm.* bond, tie.

Vinicolo [vee-nee'koh-loh] *a.* wine-growing, wine-producing.

Vino [vee'noh] *nm.* wine.

Viola [vee-oh'lah] *nf.* (*mus.*) viol; *v.* del pensiero [dell pen-see-ay'roh], pansy.

Violacciocca [vee-oh-lahch-chock'kah] *nf.* stock, wall-flower.

Violare [vee-oh-lah'ray] *vt.* to violate.

Violento [vee-oh-len'toh] *a.* violent.

Violenza [vee-oh-lent'sah] *nf.* force, violence.

Violetta [vee-oh-let'tah] *nf.* violet.

Violinista [vee-oh-lee-nee'stah] *nm.* violinist.

Violino [vee-oh-lee'noh] *nm.* fiddle, violin.

Viottolo/la [vee-ot'toh-lah] *nf.* —lo [loh] *nm.* lane.

Vipera [vee'pay-rah] *nf.* viper.

Virare [vee-rah'ray] *vi.* (*naut.*) to tack, turn.

Virgola [veer'goh-lah] nf. comma; punto e [poon'toh ay] v. nm. semi-colon.

Virile [vee-ree'lay] a. manful, manly, virile.

Virilità [vee-ree-lee-tah'] nf. manhood, manliness, virility.

Virtù [veer-too'] nf. virtue.

Virtuoso [veer-too-oh'soh] a. virtuous.

Virulento [vee-roo-len'toh] a. virulent.

Visce/re [vee'shay-ray] nm. (anat.) vital organ; —ri [ree] (pl.) viscera (pl.); —re [ray] (pl. f.) bowels (fig.).

Vischio [vee'skee-oh] nm. bird-lime, mistletoe.

Visconte [vee-skon'tay] nm. viscount.

Viscoso [vee-skoh'soh] a. slimy, sticky, viscid.

Visibile [vee-zee-bee'lay] a. visible.

Visibilio [vee-zee-bee'lee-oh] nm. a lot; andare in [ahn-dah'ray een] v. vi. to go into raptures.

Visiera [vee-zee-ay'rah] nf. peak, visor.

Visionario [vee-zee-oh-nah'ree-oh] nm. and a. visionary.

Visione [vee-zee-oh'nay] nf. vision; prendere in [pren'day-ray een] v. vt. to examine.

Visita [vee'zee-tah] nf. visit; v. medica [may'dee-kah], medical examination.

Visitare [vee-zee-tah'ray] vt. to call on, visit, (med.) examine.

Visita/tore [vee-zee-tah-toh'ray] nm. —trice [tree'chay] nf. visitor.

Visivo [vee-zee'voh] a. of [ah] v. aperto [ah-pehr'toh] ad. frankly, openly.

Viso [vee'zoh] nm. face; a [ah] v. aperto [ah-pehr'toh] ad. frankly, openly.

Vispo [vee'spoh] a. brisk, lively.

Vista [vee'stah] nf. sight,

view; conoscere di [koh-noh'shay-ray dee] v. vt. to know by sight; far [fahr] v. di [dee] vi. to pretend.

Visto [vee'stoh] nm. visé; mettere il [met'tay-ray eel] v. vi. to visé; a. seen.

Vistoso [vee-stoh'soh] a. gaudy, large, showy.

Visuale [vee-zoo-ah'lay] nf. view; a. visual.

Vita [vee'tah] nf. life, living, livelihood, waist.

Vitalba [vee-tahl'bah] nf. traveller's joy, briony.

Vite [vee'tay] nf. vine, (tech.) screw.

Vitello [vee-tell'loh] nm. calf; carne di [kahr'nay dee] v. nf. veal.

Vittima [veet'tee-mah] nf. victim.

Vitto [veet'toh] nm. board, food, living.

Vittoria [veet-toh-ree-ah] nf. victory.

Vittorioso [veet-toh-ree-oh'soh] a. victorious.

Vituperare [vee-too-pay-rah'ray] vt. to vituperate.

Vituperio [vee-too-pay'ree-oh] nm. disgrace, insult, shame.

Vivace [vee-vah'chay] a. bright, lively, sprightly, vivacious.

Vivacità [vee-vah-chee-tah'] nf. brightness, vivacity.

Vivaio [vee-vah'yoh] nm. nursery (of fish or plants).

Vivanda [vee-vahn'dah] nf. dish. [living.

Vivente [vee-ven'tay] a.

Vivere [vee'vay-ray] vi. and i. to live; v. alla giornata [ahl'lah jorr-nah'tah] vi. to live from hand to mouth; nm. living.

Viveri [vee'vay-ree] nm. (pl.) provisions (pl.), supplies (pl.), victuals (pl.).

Vivido [vee'vee-doh] *a.* vivid.

Vivificare [vee-vee-fee-kah'ray] *vt.* to enliven, give life to, vivify.

Vivisezione [vee-vee-say-tsee-oh'nay] *nf.* vivisection.

Vivo [vee'voh] *a.* alive, bright, deep, great, lively, strong; **a viva voce** [ah vee'vah voh'chay] *ad.* orally; **toccare nel** [tock-kah'ray nell] *v. vt.* to pierce to the quick.

Viziare [vee-tsee-ah'ray] *vt.* to spoil, vitiate.

Viziato [vee-tsee-ah'toh] *a.* spoilt, vitiated.

Vizio [vee'tsee-oh] *nm.* bad habit, defect, vice.

Vizioso [vee-tsee-oh'soh] *a.* vicious.

Vizzo [veet'soh] *a.* withered.

Vocabolario [voh-kah-boh-lah'ree-oh] *nm.* dictionary, vocabulary.

Vocabolo [voh-kah'boh-loh] *nm.* term, word.

Vocale [voh-kah'lay] *nf.* vowel; *a.* vocal.

Vocazione [voh-kah-tsee-oh'nay] *nf.* calling, vocation.

Voce [voh'chay] *nf.* rumour, voice; **a** [ah] *v. ad.* orally; **ad alta** [ahd ahl'tah] *v.* loudly.

Vociferare [voh-chee-fay-rah'ray] *vi.* to rumour, shout, vociferate.

Vociferazione [voh-chee-fay-rah-tsee-oh'nay] *nf.* shouting, vociferation.

Voga [voh'gah] *nf.* fashion, vogue; **in** [een] *v. a.* fashionable.

Vogare [voh-gah'ray] *vi.* to row.

Voglia [voll'yah] *nf.* desire, wish, birthmark.

Voi [voh'ee] *pn.* [*nom. and oblique*], you.

Volante [voh-lahn'tay] *nm.* (*tech.*) (fly-)wheel; *a.* flying.

Volare [voh-lah'ray] *vi.* to fly.

Volata [voh-lah'tah] *nf.* flight, rush.

Volatile [voh-lah'tee-lay] *a.* volatile, winged.

Volenteroso [voh-len-tay-roh'soh] *a.* full of good will.

Volentieri [voh-len-tee-ay'ree] *ad.* willingly; **mal** [mahl] *v.* unwillingly.

Volere [voh-lay'ray] *vt. and i.* to be willing, like, require, take, want, wish.

Volgare [voll-gah'ray] *a.* coarse, vulgar.

Volge/re [voll'jay-ray] *vt. and i.* and **—rsi** *vr.* to turn.

Volgo [voll'goh] *nm.* common herd, lower classes.

Volo [voh'loh] *nm.* flight; **a** [ah], **di** [dee] *v. ad.* immediately.

Volontà [voh-lon-tah'] *nf.* will.

Volontario [voh-lon-tah'ree-oh] *nm.* volunteer; *a.* voluntary.

Volpe [voll'pay] *nf.* fox.

Volta [voll'tah] *nf.* time, turn; **una** [oo'nah] *v. ad.* once; **due volte** [doo'ay voll'tay] twice, (*arch.*) vault.

Voltaggio [voll-tah'djoh] *nm.* (*elec.*) voltage.

Voltata [voll-tah'tah] *nf.* turning.

Volteggiare [voll-tay-djah'ray] *vi.* to flutter (of birds), turn.

Volto [voll'toh] *nm.* countenance, face; *a.* turned.

Volubile [voh-loo'bee-lay] *a.* fickle, inconstant.

Volume [voh-loo'may] *nm.* bulk, mass, quantity, volume.

Voluminoso [voh-loo-mee-noh'soh] *a.* bulky, voluminous.

Voluttà [voh-loot'tah] *nf.* delight, pleasure, voluptuousness.

Vomere [voh'may-ray] *nm.* ploughshare.

Vomitare [voh-mee-tah'ray] *vt. and i.* to vomit.

Vongola [vong'goh-lah] *nf.* mussel.

Vorace [voh-rah'chay] *a.* greedy, voracious. [gulf.

Voragine [voh-rah'jee-nay] *nf.*

Vortice [vorr'tee-chay] *nm.* vortex, whirl(pool).

Vossignoria [voss-seen-yoh-ree'ah] *nf.* Your Honour, Your Lordship.

Vostro [voss'troh] *poss. a.* your; *poss. pn.* yours.

Votante [voh-tahn'tay] *nm.* voter; *a.* voting.

Vota/re [voh-tah'ray] *vt.* to approve, consecrate, offer, pass; *vi.* to vote; **—rsi** *vr.* to devote oneself.

Votazione [voh-tah-tsee-oh'nay] *nf.* voting.

Voto [voh'toh] *nm.* mark (at school), prayer, vote, vow.

Vulcano [vool-kah'noh] *nm.* volcano.

Vulnerabile [vool-nay-rah'-bee-lay] *a.* vulnerable.

Vuotare [voo-oh-tah'ray] *vt.* to empty.

Vuoto [voo-oh'toh] *nm.* empty space, vacuum, void; *a.* empty, vacant; andare a [ahn-dah'ray ah] *v. vi.* to fail.

Z

Zabaione [dsah-bah-yoh'nay] *nm.* eggs beaten up with sugar and wine.

Zafferano [dsahf-fay-rah'-noh] *nm.* saffron.

Zaffiro [dsahf-fee-roh] *nm.* sapphire.

Zaino [dsah-ee-noh] *nm.* knapsack, pack.

Zampa [tsahm'pah] *nf.* leg (of animals), paw.

Zampillare [dsahm-peel-lah'ray] *vi.* to gush, spring.

Zampillo [dsahm-peel'loh] *nm.* gush, jet.

Zampogna [dsahm-pohn'-yah] *nf.* bagpipes (*pl.*), reed-pipe.

Zampognaro [dsahm-pohn-yah'roh] *nm.* piper.

Zana [tsah'nah] *nf.* (*poet.*) cradle.

Zangola [tsahng'goh-lah] *nf.* churn, washing-up bowl.

Zanna [tsahn'nah] *nf.* fang, tusk.

Zanzara [dsahn-dsah'rah] *nf.* mosquito.

Zanzarie/ra [dsahn-dsah-ree-ay'rah] *nf.* **—re** [ray] *nm.* mosquito-net.

Zappa [tsahp'pah] *nf.* hoe.

Zappare [tsahp-pah'ray] *vt. and i.* to dig, hoe.

Zappatore [tsahp-pah-toh'ray] *nm.* digger, hoer, (*mil.*) pioneer.

Zattera [dsaht'tay-rah] *nf.* (*naut.*) lighter, raft.

Zavorra [dsah-vorr'rah] *nf.* (*naut.*) ballast.

Zazzera [tsaht'say-rah] *nf.* long hair.

Zecca [dseck'kah] *nf.* mint; nuovo di [noo-oh'voh dee] z. *a.* brand-new.

Zecchino [tseck-kee'noh] *nm.* sequin.

Zeffiro [dsef'fee-roh] *nm.* (*poet.*) zephyr.

Zelante [dsay-lahn'tay] *a.* zealous.

Zelo [dsay'loh] *nm.* zeal.

Zenit [dsay'neet] *nm.* zenith.

Zenzero [dsen'dsay-roh] *nm.* ginger.

Zeppo [tsep'poh] *a.* full; pieno [pee-ay'noh] z. crowded, packed.

Zerbinotto [dsehr-bee-not'toh] *nm.* beau, dandy.

Zia [tsee'ah] *nf.* aunt.

Zibellino [dsee-bell-lee'noh] *nm.* sable (animal and fur).

Zigomo [dsee'goh-moh] *nm.* cheek-bone. [robe.

Zimarra [dsee-mahr'rah] *nf.*

Zimbello [dseem-bell'loh] *nm.* decoy(-bird), laughing-stock.

Zinco [dseeng'koh] *nm.* zinc.

Zingaro [dseeng'gah-roh] *nm.* gypsy.

Zio [tsee'oh] *nm.* uncle.

Zittella [tseet-tell'lah] *nf.* maid, spinster.

Zittire [tseet-tee'ray] *vt. and i.* to hiss, hush, silence.

Zitto [tseet'toh] *a.* silent; stare [stah'ray] z. *vi.* to keep quiet.

Zizzania [dseed-dsah'nee-ah] *nf.* darnel, tare; seminare [say-mee-nah'ray] z. *vi.* to sow dissension.

Zoccolo [tsock'koh-loh] *nm.* clog, wooden shoe.

Zodiaco [dsoh-dee'ah-koh] *nm.* zodiac.

Zolfino [tsoll-fee'noh] *nm.* sulphur match.

Zolfo [tsoll'foh] *nm.* sulphur.

Zolla [dsoll'lah] *nf.* clod, lump, sod, turf.

Zona [dsoh'nah] *nf.* sphere, zone.

Zonzo, a [ah dson'dsoh] *ad.* idling, strolling.

Zoologia [dsoh-oh-loh-jee'ah] *nf.* zoology.

Zoologico [dsoh-oh-loh'jee-koh] *a.* zoological.

Zoppicare [tsop-pee-kah'ray] *vi.* to be lame halt, limp.

Zoppo [tsop'poh] *a.* halting, lame, limping.

Zotico [dsoh'tee-koh] *nm.* boor, rustic, *a.* boorish, rough, rude.

Zucca [tsook'kah] *nf.* gourd, pate (head), pumpkin.

Zuccheriera [tsook-kay-ree-ay'rah] *nf.* sugar-basin.

Zuccherificio [tsook-kay-ree-fee-'choh] *nm.* sugar-refinery.

Zucchero tsook'kay-roh *mn.*] sugar.

Zuffa [tsoof'fah] *nf.* brawl, scuffle.

Zufolare [dsoo-foh-lah'ray] *vi.* to whistle.

Zufolo [dsoo'foh-loh] *nm.* whistle.

Zuppa [tsoop'pah] *nf.* soup; z. inglese [eeng-glay'say) trifle (sweet).

Zuppiera [tsoop-pee-ay'rah] *nf.* (soup-)tureen.

Zuppo, fradicio [frah'dee-choh tsoop'poh] *a.* drenched, soaked.

GEOGRAPHICAL NAMES

Abissinia, *Abyssinia* ; abissino *n. and a., Abyssinian.*
Adriatico, *the Adriatic Sea.*
Africa, *Africa* ; africano *n. and a., African.*
Albania, *Albania* : albanese *n. and a., Albanian.*
Algeri, *Algiers;* algerino *n. and a., Algerian.*
Alpi, *the Alps.*
America, *America* ; americano *n. and a., American.*
Appennini, *The Apennines.*
Arabia, *Arabia* ; arabo *n. and a., Arab(ian).*
Argentina, *the Argentine* ; argentino *n. and a., Argentine.*
Armenia, *Armenia* ; armeno, *n. and a., Armenian.*
Asia, *Asia* ; asiatico *n. and a., Asiatic.*
Atene, *Athens* ; ateniese *n. and a., Athenian.*
Atlantico, *the Atlantic.*
Australia, *Australia* ; australiano *n. and a., Australian.*
Austria, *Austria* ; austriaco *n. and a., Austrian.*
Basilea, *Bâle.*
Belgio, *Belgium* ; belgo *n.,* belgico *a., Belgian.*
Birmania, *Burma* ; birmano *n. and a., Burmese.*
Borgogna, *Burgundy;* borgognano *n. and a., Burgundian.*
Brasile, *Brazil;* brasiliano *n. and a., Brazilian.*
Bretagna, *Brittany* , bretone *n. and a., Breton.*
Bulgaria, *Bulgaria* ; bulgaro *n. and a., Bulgarian.*
Canadà, *Canada* ; canadese *n. and a., Canadian.*
Caucaso, *Caucasus;* caucasiano *n. and a., Caucasian.*
Cecoslovachia, *Czechoslovakia;* cecoslovacco *n. and a., Czech.*
Cina, *China* ; cinese *n. and a., Chinese.*
Dalmazia, *Dalmatia* ; dalmato *n. and a., Dalmatian.*
Danimarca, *Denmark* ; danese *n. and a., Dane, Danish.*
Egitto, *Egypt* ; egiziano *n. and a., Egyptian.*
Europa, *Europe* ; europeo *n. and a., European.*
Fiandra, *Flanders* ; fiammingo, *n. and a., Fleming, Flemish.*
Finlandia, *Finland* ; finlandese *n. and a., Finn, Finnish.*
Firenze, *Florence* ; fiorentino *n. and a., Florentine.*
Francia, *France* ; francese *n. and a., French(man), etc.*
Galles, *Wales* ; gallese *n. and a., Welsh(man), etc.*
Germania, *Germany* ; tedesco *n. and a., German.*
Giappone, *Japan* ; giapponese *n. and a., Japanese.*
Ginevra, *Geneva.*
Gran Bretagna, *Great Britain;* britanno *a., British.*
Grecia, *Greece* ; greco *n. and a., Greek.*
Groenlandia, *Greenland;* groenlandese *n., Greenlander.*

352

Illiria, *Illyria*; illiro *n. and a.*, *Illyrian*.
India, *India*; indiano *n. and a.*, *Indian*.
Inghilterra, *England*; inglese *n. and a.*, *English*(man), *etc.*
Ionico, *the Ionian Sea*.
Irlanda, *Ireland*; irlandese *n. and a.*, *Irish*(man), *etc.*
Islanda, *Iceland*; islandese *n. and a.*, *Icelander, Icelandic*.
Isole Britanniche, *the British Isles*.
Italia, *Italy*; italiano *n. and a.*, *Italian*.
Lapponia, *Lapland*; lappone *n. and a.*, *Lapp*.
Lombardia, *Lombardy*; lombardo *n. and a.*, *Lombard*.
Londra, *London*; londinese *n. and a.*, *London*(er).
Lussemburgo, *Luxemburg*; lussemburghese *n. and a.*, *Luxemburgher*.
Marocco, *Morocco*; marocchino *n. and a.*, *Moroccan*.
Messico, *Mexico*; messicano *n. and a.*, *Mexican*.
Milano, *Milan*; milanese *n. and a.*, *Milanese*.
Mosca, *Moscow*; moscovito *n. and a.*, *Muscovite*.
Napoli, *Naples*; napolitano *n. and a.*, *Neapolitan*.
Norvegia, *Norway*; norvegese *n. and a.*, *Norwegian*.
Nuova Zelanda, *New Zealand*.
Olanda, *Holland*; olandese *n. and a.*, *Dutch*(man), *etc.*
Pacifico, *the Pacific*.
Parigi, *Paris*; parigino *n. and a.*, *Parisian*.
Persia, *Persia*; persiano *n. and a.*, *Persian*.
Perù, *Peru*; peruviano *n. and a.*, *Peruvian*.
Piemonte, *Piedmont*; piemontese *n. and a.*, *Piedmontese*.
Pirenei, *the Pyrenees*.
Polonia, *Poland*; polacco *n. and a.*, *Pole, Polish*.
Portogallo, *Portugal*; portoghese *n. and a.*, *Portuguese*.
Provenza, *Provence*; provenzale *n. and a.*, *Provencal*.
Prussia, *Prussia*; prussiano *n. and a.*, *Prussian*.
Roma, *Rome*; romano *n. and a.*, *Roman*.
Romania, *Roumania*; rumeno *n. and a.*, *Roumanian*.
Russia, *Russia*; russo *n. and a.*, *Russian*.
Sardegna, *Sardinia*; sardo *n. and a.*, *Sardinian*.
Sassonia, *Saxony*; sassone *n. and a.*, *Saxon*.
Savoia, *Savoy*; savoiardo *n.*, *Savoyard*.
Scozia, *Scotland*; scozzese *n. and a.*, *Scot, Scottish* (*Scotch*).
Sicilia, *Sicily*; siciliano *n. and a.*, *Sicilian*.
Spagna, *Spain*; spagnolo *n. and a.*, *Spaniard, Spanish*.
Stati Uniti, *the United States*.
Svezia, *Sweden*; svedese *n. and a.*, *Swede, Swedish*.
Svizzera, *Switzerland*; svizzero *n. and a.*, *Swiss*.
Tamigi, il, *The Thames*.
Terra Nuova, *Newfoundland*.

Tevere, il, *the Tiber.*
Toscana, *Tuscany*; toscano *n. and a.,* *Tuscan.*
Turchia, *Turkey*; turco, *n. and a.* Turk., *Turkish.*
Ucraina, *the Ukraine*; ucraino, *n. and a.,* *Ukrainian.*
Ungheria, *Hungary*; ungherese *n. and a.,* *Hungarian.*
Varsavia, *Warsaw.*
Venezia, *Venice*; veneziano *n. and a.,* *Venetian*

MEASURES, WEIGHTS AND MONEY

Italian Money

Notes: 1,000, 5,000, 10,000, 50,000, 100,000. Lire
Coins: 1, 2, 5, 10, 20, 50, 100, 500, 1,000.

Measures

I

un millimetro 1/1000 di metro	0 ·03937 inch
un centimetro 1/100 di metro	0 ·3937 inch
un decimetro 1/10 di metro	3 ·937 inches
un metro[1]	39 ·37 inches 3 ·28 feet
un decametro dieci metri	32 ·808 feet 10 ·936 yards
un chilometro mille metri	1093 ·633 yards 0 ·62138 miles
un miriametro dieci chilometri	10936 ·330555 yards 6 ·21382 miles

[1] Unit of lineal measure.

354

II

un millilitro 1/1000 di litro }	0·00176 pint.
un centilitro 1/100 di litro }	0·01760 pint.
un decilitro 1/10 di litro }	0·017607 pint.
un litro[1]	1·76077 pints.
un decalitro dieci litri }	{ 17·60773 pints. { 2·200966 gallons.
un ettolitro cento litri }	{ 176·077344 pints. { 22·009668 gallons.
un chilolitro mille litri }	{ 1760·77344 pints. { 220·09668 gallons.
un mirialitro dieci mila litri }	{ 17607·73440 pints. { 2200·96680 gallons.

III

una centiara	{ 1 square metre. { 1·196 square yards.
un'ara[2]	119·6033 square yards.
una decara dieci, are }	1196·0331 square yards.
un ettaro cento are }	11960·3313 square yards.
un decistero 1/10 di stero }	3·5317 cubic feet.
uno stero un metro cubo }	1·31 cubic yards.
un decastero dieci steri }	13·1 cubic yards.

Weights

un milligrammo 1/1000 di grammo }	0·015432 grain troy.
un centigrammo 1/100 di grammo }	0·154323 grain troy.
un decigrammo 1/10 di grammo }	1·543234 grains troy

[1] Unit of measure of capacity.
[2] Unit of superficial measure.

un grammo[1]	{ 15·432349 grains troy. or 0·03215 ounce troy.
un decagrammo dieci grammi }	{ 154·32349 grains troy. or 0·32150 ounce troy.
un ettogrammo cento grammi }	{ 1543·2349 grains troy. or 3·21507 ounces troy.
un chilogrammo mille grammi }	{ 2·205 pounds avoirdupois. or 2·68 pounds troy.
un quintale metrico cento chilogrammi }	{ 220·5 pounds avoirdupois. or 268 pounds troy.
una tonnellata maritima 1000 chilogrammi }	{ 2205·0 pounds avoirdupois. or 2680·0 pounds troy.

[1]Unit of weight

ABBREVIAZIONI

a.	aggettivo	*mat.*	matematica
archit.	architettura	*mecc.*	meccanica
art.	articolo	*med.*	medicina
av.	avverbio	*mil.*	militare
avia.	aviazione	*mus.*	musica
comm.	commercio	*n.*	nome
compl.	complemento	*naut.*	nautico
cong.	congiunzione	*pl.*	plurale
difett.	difettivo	*poet.*	poetico
elett.	elettrico	*pred.*	predicativo
f.	femminile	*prep.*	preposizione
famil.	famigliare	*pron.*	pronome
ferrov.	ferroviario	*prom. fran.*	pronunzia francese
fig.	figurato	*recipr.*	reciproco
geogr.	geografia	*rel.*	relativo
gram.	grammatica	*sing.*	singolare
impers.	impersonale	*tipogr.*	tipografica
interiez.	interiezione	*v.i.*	verbo intransivo
interr.	interrogativo	*v.rfl.*	verbo riflessivo
m.	maschile	*v.t.*	verbo transitivo

ENGLISH-ITALIAN DICTIONARY

A [é] *art. indeterm.* un(o), una.

Aback [ă-bèc'] *av.* (*naut.*) all'indietro; taken [tècn] a. a. sconcertato.

Abaft [ă-bèft'] *av. e prep.* (*naut.*) indietro, da poppa.

Abandon [ă-bèn'dŏn] *n.* abbandono; *v.t.* abbandonare, lasciare.

Abandonment [ă-bèn'dŏn-mĕnt] *n.* abbandono, slancio.

Abase [ă-bés'] *v.t.* abbassare, umiliare.

Abasement [ă-bés'mĕnt] *n.* umiliazione.

Abash [ă-bàs'] *v.t.* confondere.

Abate [ă-bét'] *v.t.* abbassare, diminuire; *v.i.* calmarsi, diminuire, indebolirsi.

Abatement [ă-bét'mĕnt] *n.* diminuzione, riduzione.

Abattoir [pron. fran.] *n.* ammazzatoio.

Abbess [ă'bĕs] *n.* badessa.

Abbey [ă'bi] *n.* badia.

Abbot [ă'bŏt] *n.* abate.

Abbreviate [ă-brí'vi-ét] *v.t.* abbreviare, accorciare.

Abbreviation [ă-brí-vi-é'sn] *n.* abbreviazione.

ABC [é bi si] *n.* abbicci.

Abdicate [èb'di-chét] *v.t. e i.* abdicare.

Abdomen [èb-dò'mĕn] *n.* addome.

Abduct [èb-dăct'] *v.t.* portar via, rapire.

Abduction [èb-dăc'sn] *n.* ratto.

Aberration [ă-be-ré'sn] *n.* aberrazione.

Abet [ă-bèt'] *v.t.* favoreggiare, incitare.

Abeyance [ă-bé'ĕns] *n.* sospensione.

Abhor [èb-hŏr'] *v.t.* aborrire, detestare.

Abhorrence [èb-hŏ'rĕns] *n.* odio, ripugnanza.

Abhorrent [èb-hŏ'rĕnt] *a.* contrario (a), ripugnante.

Abide [ă-baid'] *v.i.* dimorare, rimanere; a. by [bai] tener fede a.

Ability [ă-bĭ'li-tĭ] *n.* abilità, talento.

Abject [èb'gect] *a.* abbietto, reietto, vile.

Abjuration [èb-giu-ré'sn] *n.* abiura.

Abjure [èb-giu^r'] *v.t.* abiurare, ripudiare.

Ablaze [ă-bléz'] *a.* in fiamme, risplendente.

Able [é'bl] *a.* abile, capace, in grado di.

Ablution [ă-blu'sn] *n.* abluzione.

Abnegation [èb-nĭ-ghé'sn] *n.* abnegazione, rinunzia.

Abnormal [èb-nŏ^r'mĕl] *a.* annormale.

Aboard [ă-bo^rd'] *av. e prep.* (*naut.*) a bordo.

Abode [ă-bòd'] *n.* dimora, domicilio.

Abolish [ă-bó'liš] *v.t.* abolire, annullare.

Abolition [ă-bò-li'sn] *n.* abolizione, annullamento.

Abominable [ă-bŏm'i-năbl] *a.* abominevole.

Abominate [ă-bŏm'ĭ-nét] *v.t.* abominare, detestare.

Aboriginal [ă-bò-rĭ'ġĭ-nĕl] *a. e n.* aborigeno, indigeno.

Abortion [ă-bo˄r'ṡn] *n.* aborto.

Abound [ă-baund'] *v.i.* abbondare.

About [ă-baut'] *prep.* circa, di, intorno a, per; *av.* in giro, intorno, presso, qua e là; to be [bĭ] a. to, stare per.

Above [ă-băv'] *av. e prep.* al di sopra di, più (alto) che, lassù, più in alto, sopra.

Abrasion [ă-bré'ṡn] *n.* abrasione, scalfittura.

Abreast [ă-brĕst'] *av.* fianco a fianco.

Abridge [ă-brĭġ'] *v.t.* abbreviare, ridurre.

Abridg(e)ment [ă-brĭġ'ment] *n.* abbreviazione, compendio.

Abroad [ă-brôd'] *av.* all'estero, in giro.

Abrogate [ă'brò-ghét] *v.t.* abrogare.

Abrupt [ă-brăpt'] *a.* brusco, improvviso, ripido.

Abscess [ĕb'sĕs] *n.* ascesso.

Abscond [ĕb-scŏnd'] *v.i.* rendersi latitante.

Absence [ĕb'sĕns] *n.* assenza, mancanza; a. **of mind** [ŏf ma˄nd] distrazione.

Absent [ĕb'sĕnt] *a.* assente; to absent **oneself** [ĕb-sĕnt' uăn'sĕlf] *v. rfl.* allontanarsi, assentarsi.

Absentee [ĕb-sĕn-tĭ'] *n.* persona abitualmente assente dal suo domicilio.

Absinthe [ĕb'sĭnth] *n.* assenzio.

Absolute [ĕb'sò-liŭt] *a.* assoluto, completo, perfetto, puro.

Absolution [ĕb-sò-liŭ'ṡn] *n.* assoluzione.

Absolve [ĕb-zŏlv'] *v.t.* assolvere, perdonare.

Absorb [ĕb-so˄rb'] *v.t.* assorbire, inghiottire.

Absorption [ĕb-so˄rp'ṡn] *n.* assorbimento.

Abstain [ĕb-stén'] *v.i.* astenersi, essere astemio.

Abstemious [ĕb-stĭ'mĭ-ăs] *a.* astemio, moderato.

Abstention [ĕb-stĕn'ṡn] *n.* astensione.

Abstinence [ĕb'stĭ-nĕns] *n.* astinenza.

Abstinent [ĕb'stĭ-nĕnt] *a.* astinente, sobrio.

Abstract [ĕb'strĕct] *n.* compendio, estratto; *a.* astratto; [ĕb-strĕct'] *v.t.* astrarre, portar via, sottrarre.

Abstraction [ĕb-strĕc'ṡn] *n.* astrazione, distrazione.

Abstruse [ĕb-strŭs'] *a.* astruso, involuto, profondo.

Absurd [ĕb-se˄d'] *a.* assurdo, ridicolo.

Absurdity [ĕb-se˄r'dĭ-tĭ] *n.* assurdità.

Abundance [ă-băn'dĕns] *n.* abbondanza.

Abundant [ă-băn'dĕnt] *a.* abbondante.

Abuse [ă-bius'] *n.* abuso, cattivo uso, insulto, maltrattamento; [ă-biuz'] *v.t.* abusare di, far cattivo uso, insultare, maltrattare.

Abusive [ă-biu'sĭv] *a.* abusivo, illegale, ingiurioso.

Abyss [ă-bĭs'] *n.* abisso.

Academic [ă-că-dĕ'mĭc] *a. e n.* accademico.

Academician [ă-că-dĕ-mĭ'sĭĕn] *n.* accademico.

Academy [ă-că'dĕ-mĭ] *n.* accademia.

Accede [ĕc-sĭd'] *v.i.* accedere, assentire, consentire.

Accelerate [ĕc-sĕl'ĕ-rét] *v.t.* accelerare. [*n.* accelerazione.

Acceleration [ĕc-sĕl-ĕ-ré'ṡn] *n.*

Accent [ĕc'sĕnt] *n.* accento, tono; **accent** [ĕc-sĕnt'] accentuate [ĕc-sĕn'tiŭ-ét] *v.t.* accent(u)are.

Accentuation [èc-sĕn-tiŭ-é꞉ sh] *n.* accentuazione.

Accept [èc-sĕpt'] *v.t.* accettare, accogliere, approvare.

Acceptable [èc-sĕp'tà-bl] *a.* accetto, gradevole.

Acceptance [èc-sĕp'tĕns] *n.* accettazione, accoglienza.

Access [èc'sĕs] *n.* accesso.

Accessible [èc-sĕs'si-bl] *a.* accessibile.

Accession [èc-sĕs'sh'n] *n.* accessione, aggiunta.

Accessory [èc-sĕs'sŏ-ri] *n.* complice; *a.* e *n.* accessorio.

Accident [èc'sĭ-dent] *n.* accidente, caso, incidente; by [bai] *a.* per caso.

Accidental [èc-sĭ-dĕn'tĕl] *a.* casuale, fortuito.

Acclaim [à-clém'] *v.t.* acclamare. [acclamazione.

Acclamation [à-clà-mé'sh] *n.*

Acclimatize [à-clai'mà-ta'z] *v.t.* acclimatare.

Accommodate [à-có'mŏ-dét] *v.t.* accomodare, comporre, dare alloggio, fare una cortesia.

Accommodating [à-có'mŏ-dé-tĭn] *a.* arrendevole, cortese.

Accommodation [à-có-mŏ-dé꞉shn] *n.* accomodamento, addattamento, alloggio, sistemazione

Accompaniment [à-càm'pà-ni-ment] *n.* accompagnamento.

Accompanist [à-càm'pà-nist] *n.* accompa-tore (*m.*) -trice (*f.*).

Accompany [à-càm'pà-ni] *v.t.* accompagnare, scortare.

Accomplice [à-cŏm'plis] *n.* complice.

Accomplish [à-cŏm'plis̆] *v.t.* compiere, completare, finire.

Accord [à-cŏ'd'] *n.* accordo, consenso; *v.t.* accordare, concedere.

Accordance [à-cŏ'dĕns] *n.* accordo, conformità.

According to [à-cŏ'dĭn tŭ] *prep.* secondo.

Accordion [à-cŏ'dĭ-ŏn] *n.* (*mus.*) fisarmonica.

Accost [à-cost'] *v.t.* rivolgere la parola a.

Account [à-caunt'] *n.* conto, importanza, relazione; on a. of *prep.* a causa (motivo) di; on no [nŏ] a., a nessun patto.

Account [à-caunt'] *v.t.* considerare, stimare; v.i. (*semuto da* for), spiegare la ragione di.

Accountability [à-caun-tà-bi'li-tĭ] *n.* responsabilità.

Accountable [à-caun'tà-bl] *a.* responsabile.

Accountant [à-caun'tĕnt] *n.* contabile; chartered [cia̍r'te̍rd] a. ragioniere.

Accoutre [à-cu'te̍r] *v.t.* (*raro*) abbigliare.

Accredit [à-crĕ'dĭt] *v.t.* accreditare, fornire di credenziali, accreditare.

Accretion [à-crí'sn] *n.* accrescimento.

Accrue [à-cru'] *v.i.* derivare, provenire.

Accumulate [à-chiŭ-mŭ-lét] *v.i.* accumulare, ammassare; v.i. accumularsi.

Accumulation [à-chiŭ-miŭ-lé'sn] *n.* accumulamento, ammasso.

Accumulative [à-chiŭ'miŭ-là-tĭv] *a.* accumulativo.

Accumulator [à-chiŭ'miŭ-lé-te̍r] *n.* accumulatore [*radio*, ecc.].

Accuracy [à'chiŭ-rà-sí] *n.* accuratezza, precisione.

Accurate [à'chiŭ-rét] *a.* accurato, preciso.

Accursed [à-che̍rst'] *a.* infausto, maledetto.

Accusation [à-chiŭ-zé'sn] *n.* accusa.

Accusative [à-chiŭ'zà-tĭv] *a.* e *n.* accusativo.

Accuse [à-chiŭz'] *v.t.* accusare, incolpare.

Accustom [ă-căs'tăm] *v.t.* abituare; a. oneself [uăn'sèlf] *v. rfl.* abituarsi.

Ace [ès] *n.* asso; within [ui'thīn] an a. of, lì lì per.

Acerbity [ă-ser'bĭ-ti] *n.* acerbità, asprezza.

Ache [èc] *n.* dolore (fisico); *v.i.* dolere.

Achieve [ă-cīv'] *v.t.* compiere, condurre a termine, raggiungere.

Achievement [ă-cīv'ment] *n.* compimento, gesto, raggiungimento, successo.

Acid [ă'sĭd] *n.* acido; *a.* acido, aspro.

Acidify [ă-sĭ'dĭ-fai] *v.t* acidificare.

Acidity [ă-sĭ'dĭ-ti] *n.* acidità.

Acknowledge [èc-nó'lèg'] *v.t.* accusare (ricevuta), ammettere, riconoscere.

Acknowledg(e)ment [èc-nó'lèg-ment] *n.* ammissione, ricevuta, riconoscimento.

Acme [èc'mi] *n.* massimo, più alto punto.

Acolyte [ă'cò-la¹t] *n.* accolito.

Acorn [é'co²n] *n.* ghianda.

Acoustic [ă-cu'stic] *a.* acustico; -s, *n.* (*plur.*) acustica.

Acquaint [ă-quént'] *v.t.* avvertire, informare, mettere al corrente.

Acquaintance [ă-quén'tèns] *n.* conoscenza, conoscente.

Acquiesce [ă-qui-es'] *v.i.* accettare, acconsentire tacitamente.

Acquiescence [ă-qui-es'èns] *n.* acquiescenza.

Acquiescent [ă-qui-es'ènt] *a.* acquiescente, rassegnato.

Acquire [ă-quai²'] *v.t.* acquisire, acquistare.

Acquisition [ă-qui-sĭ'ăn] *n.* acquisizione, acquisto.

Acquit [ă-quit'] *v.t.* assolvere; a. oneself [uăn'sèlf] *v. rfl.* comportarsi.

Acquittal [ă-qui'tèl] *n.* assoluzione.

Acre [é'che²] *n.* acro (misura di superficie).

Acrid [ă'crid] *a.* acre, aspro.

Acrimonious [ă-cri-mò'nĭ-ăs] *a.* acrimonioso.

Acrimony [ă'cri-mŏ-nĭ] *n.* acrimonia.

Acrobat [ă'crŏ-bèt] *n.* acrobata.

Across [ă-cros'] *av. e prep.* attraverso, da un lato all'altro, dall'altra parte, in croce.

Acrostic [ă-crŏs'tic] *n.* acrostico.

Act [èct] *n.* atto, azione, fatto, opera; *v.t.* eseguire, fare, rappresentare, recitare; *v.i.* agire, comportarsi.

Acting [èc'tĭn] *n.* rappresentazione, modo di recitare.

Action [èc'ŏn] *n.* azione, combattimento, gesto, processo.

Actionable [èc-sò'nă-bl] *a.* passibile di azione giudiziaria.

Active [èc'tĭv] *a.* attivo, energico.

Activity [èc-tĭ'vĭ-ti] *n.* attività, energia.

Actor [èc'te²] *n. m.* attore; -tress [très] *n. f.* attrice.

Actual [èc'ciŭl] *a.* effettivo, reale.

Actuality [èc-ciŭ-ă'lĭ-ti] *n.* realtà.

Actually [èc-ciŭ'li] *av.* effettivamente, realmente.

Actuate [èc'ciŭ-èt] *v.t.* incitare all'azione, influenzare.

Acute [ă-chiŭt'] *a.* acuto, perspicace.

Acuteness [ă-chiŭt'nès] *n.* acutezza, perspicacia.

Adage [ă'dég] *n.* adagio, detto, proverbio.

Adamant [ă'dă-mènt] *a.* duro, inflessibile.

Adapt [ă-dèpt'] *v.t.* adattare, modificare.

Adaptability [ă-dèp-tă'bĭ'lĭ-ti] *n.* adattabilità.

Adaptable [ă-dèp'tă-bl] a. adattabile.

Adaptation [ă-dèp-té'ŝn] n. adattamento.

Add [èd] v.t. e i. aggiungere, soggiungere; **to a. up** [ăp] fare la somma.

Adder [è'dër] n. vipera.

Addict [ă'dict] n. persona dedita ad una droga; [ă-dict'] v.t. abituare, dedicare.

Addicted [ă-dict'ĭd] a. dedito (in senso cattivo).

Addle [èdl] v.t. confondere; v.i. guastarsi.

Addled [è'dld] a. confuso, guasto.

Address [ă-drès'] n. destrezza, discorso solenne, indirizzo; v.t. dirigere, indirizzare, rivolgere la parola o lo scritto a.

Addressee [ă-dres-si'] n. destinatario.

Adduce [ă-diùs'] v.t. addurre, citare.

Adept [ă-dèpt'] n. esperto; a. abile, capace.

Adequate [ă'dĕ-quĕt] a. adeguato, sufficiente.

Adhere [ăd-hie'r] v.i. aderire, attaccarsi.

Adherence [ăd-hie'rĕns] n. aderenza, adesione, attaccamento.

Adherent [ăd-hie'rĕnt] n. partigiano, seguace; a. aderente, attaccato.

Adhesive [ăd-hi'sĭv] a. adesivo, appiccicaticcio.

Adieu [ă-diù'] inter. e n. addio.

Adipose [ă'dĭ-pòs] a. adiposo.

Adjacency [ă-gé'sĕn-sĭ] n. adiacenza.

Adjacent [ă'gé'sĕnt] a. adiacente, attiguo.

Adjective [ă'gĕc-tiv] n. aggettivo.

Adjoin [ă-gioin'] v.i. essere attiguo.

Adjourn [ă-gër'n] v.t. aggior-

nare, rimandare; v.i. trasferirsi in un altro luogo.

Adjournment [ă-gër'n'ment] n. rinvio.

Adjudge [ă-giăg'] v.t. aggiudicare, assegnare.

Adjudicate [ă-giu'dĭ-chét] v.t. e i. giudicare.

Adjudication [ă-giu-dĭ-ché'ŝn] n. aggiudicazione, sentenza.

Adjunct [ă'giănct] n. aggiunta, aggiunto, appendice; a. aggiunto, congiunto.

Adjuration [ă-giu-ré'ŝn] n. lo scongiurare.

Adjure [ă-giu'r] v.t. implorare, scongiurare.

Adjust [ă-giăst'] v.t. adattare, aggiustare, regolare.

Adjustment [ă-giăst'mĕnt] n. adattamento.

Adjutant [ă'giu-tĕnt] n. aiutante, assistente.

Administer [ĕd-mĭ'nis-tĕr] v.t. amministrare, dare, somministrare; v.i. contribuire.

Administration [ĕd-mĭ-nis-tré'ŝn] n. amministrazione, somministrazione.

Administrator [ĕd-mĭ'nĭs-tré-tĕr] n. amministratore.

Admirable [èd-mĭ-ră-bl] a. ammirevole.

Admiral [ed'mĭ-rĕl] n. ammiraglio.

Admiralty [èd-mĭ-rĕl-tĭ] n. ammiragliato.

Admiration [èd-mĭ-ré'ŝn] n. ammirazione. [mirare.

Admire [èd-mai'er] v.t. ammirare.

Admirer [èd-mai're'] n. ammiratore, corteggiatore.

Admissible [èd-mĭs'ĭ-bl] a. ammissibile.

Admission [èd-mĭ'ŝn] n. ammissione.

Admit [èd-mĭt'] v.t. ammettere, riconoscere; a. **of** [ŏf] v.i. permettersi.

Admittance [èd-mĭ'tĕns] n. ammissione, ingresso.

Admonish [ĕd-mó'nĭš] *v.t.* ammonire.

Ado [ă-du'] *n.* affare, confusione, trambusto.

Adolescence [ă-dò-lĕs'ĕns] *n.* adolescenza.

Adolescent [ă-dò-lĕs'ĕnt] *a. e n.* adolescente.

Adopt [ă-dŏpt'] *v.t.* adottare.

Adoption [ă-dŏp'šn] *n.* adozione. [rabile.

Adorable [ă-dŏr'ă-bl] *a.* ado-

Adoration [ă-dŏr-é'šn] *n.* adorazione, venerazione.

Adore [ă-dŏr'] *v.t.* adorare, venerare.

Adorer [ă-dŏr'ĕʳ] *n.* adoratore.

Adorn [ă-dŏʳn'] *v.t.* abbellire, adornare.

Adornment [ă-dŏʳn'mĕnt] *n.* abbellimento, ornamento.

Adrift [ă-drĭft'] *av.* alla deriva.

Adroit [ă-drŏĭt'] *a.* abile, destro.

Adroitness [ă-drŏĭt'nĕs] *n.* abilità, destrezza.

Adulation [ă-diu-lé'šn] *n.* adulazione.

Adult [ă-dălt'] *a.* adulto.

Adulterate [ă-dăl'tĕ-rét] *v.t.* adulterare.

Adulteration [ă-dăl-tĕ-ré'šn] *n.* adulterazione.

Adulterer [ă-dăl'tĕ-rĕʳ] *n.* adultero; **-ress** [rĕs] *n.* adultera.

Adultery [ă-dăl'tĕ-rĭ] *n.* adulterio.

Adumbration [ă-dăm-bré'šn] *n.* adombramento.

Advance [ĕd-vans'] *n.* anticipo, avanzamento, marcia in avanti, progresso, rialzo (*di prezzi, ecc.*); *v.t.* anticipare, avanzare, presentare; *v.i.* avanzare, progredire, salire (*di prezzi, ecc.*).

Advancement [ĕd-vans'mĕnt] *n.* avanzamento, progresso, promozione.

Advantage [ĕd-van'téǧ] *n.* beneficio, vantaggio.

Advantageous [ĕd-văn-té'ǧiăs] *a.* conveniente, vantaggioso.

Advent [ĕd'vĕnt] *n.* avvento, venuta di Cristo.

Adventitious [ĕd-vĕn-tí'šiăs] *a.* avventizio, casuale.

Adventure [ĕd-vĕn'cĕʳ] *n.* avventura, impresa, rischio.

Adventurer [ĕd-vĕn'cĕ-rĕʳ] *n.* avventuriero, soldato di ventura.

Adventurous [ĕd-vĕn'cĕ-răs] *a.* impetuoso, rischioso.

Adverb [ĕd'vĕʳb] *n.* avverbio.

Adverbial [ĕd-vĕʳ'bi-ĕl] *a.* avverbiale.

Adversary [ĕd'vĕ-să-rĭ] *n.* antagonista, avversario.

Adverse [ĕd'vĕʳs] *a.* avverso, contrario, opposto.

Adversity [ĕd-vĕʳ'sĭ-tĭ] *n.* avversità, calamità.

Advertise [ĕd'vĕʳ-taiz] *v.t. e i.* fare della pubblicità per, mettere annunci, rendere noto.

Advertisement [ĕd-vĕʳ'tĭs-mĕnt] *n.* annuncio, avviso, inserzione.

Advertiser [ĕd'vĕʳ-tai-zeʳ] *n.* inserzionista.

Advice [ĕd-vais'] *n.* (*sing.*) consigli(o), opinione, parere.

Advisable [ĕd-vai'ză-bl] *a.* consigliabile, raccomandabile.

Advise [ĕd-vaiz'] *v.t.* avvertire, consigliare.

Advisedly [ĕd-vai'zĕd-lĭ] *av.* consideratamente, giudiziosamente. [siglier̄e.

Adviser [ĕd-vai'zeʳ] *n.* con-

Advisory [ĕd-vai'zŏ-rĭ] *a.* avente funzione consigliatrice.

Advocacy [ĕd'vŏ-că-sĭ] *n.* difesa, funzione di avvocato.

Advocate [ĕd'vŏ-chét] *n.* avvocato; *v.t.* consigliare, perorar̄e, sostenere.

Adze [ĕdz] *n.* ascia.

Aerate [é'rét] *v.t.* aerare, combinare con un gas.

Aerated [é°-ré'tĕd] a. gassoso.

Aerial [é-i'rì-ăl] n. (radio) antenna; a. aereo, etereo.

Aerodrome [é'rò-dròm] n. aerodromo.

Aeronaut [é'rò-nót] n. aeronauta.

Aeronautics [é-rò-nó'ties] n. aeronautica.

Aesthetic [ès-thé'tìc] a. estetico; -s n. estetica.

Afar [ă-fär'], a. off [ŏv] av. lontano, in lontananza; from a. da lontano.

Affable [ă'fà-bl] a. affabile.

Affability [ă-fà-bì'lì-tì] n. affabilità. [tura.

Affair [ă-fér'] n. affare, avventura

Affect [ă-fĕct'] v.t. colpire, commuovere, concernere, influire.

Affectation [ă-fĕc-té'šn] n. affettazione.

Affected [ă-fĕc'tĕd] a. affettato, artificioso, commosso.

Affection [ă-fĕc'šn] n. affetto, affezione.

Affectionate [ă-fĕc'sciò-nét] a. affettuoso.

Affidavit [ă-fì-dé'vìt]n.dichiarazione scritta e confermata con giuramento.

Affiliate [ă-fì'lì-ét] v.t. affiliare, associare.

Affiliation [ă-fì-lì-é'šn] n. affiliazione.

Affinity [ă-fì'nì-tì] n. affinità, parentela.

Affirm [ă-fĕrm'] v.t. affermare, confermare; v.i. asserire.

Affirmation [ă-fĕr-mé'šn] n. affermazione, asserzione.

Affirmative [ă-fĕr'mă-tìv] n. affermativa; a. affermativo.

Affix [ă-fìcs'] v.t. affiggere, apporre, attaccare.

Afflict [ă-flìct'] v.t. affliggere.

Affliction [ă-flìc'šn] n. afflizione.

Affluence [ă'flù-ĕns] n. abbondanza, affluenza.

Affluent [ă'flù-ĕnt] a. e n. affluente; a. agiate.

Afford [ă-fo'rd'] v.t. fornire, offrire, permettersi il lusso di.

Affranchise [ă-frèn'ciaiz] v.t. affrancare, liberare.

Affront [ă-frănt'] n. affronto, insulto; v.t. affrontare, insultare.

Afield [ă-fìld'] av. a distanza, lontano di casa.

Afloat [ă-flòt'] av. a galla, in circolazione, in mare.

Afoot [ă-fùt'] av. a piedi, in movimento.

Aforesaid [ă-fò'r'sèd] a. predetto.

Afraid [ă-fréd'] a. impaurito, pauroso; to be [bì] a. aver paura.

Afresh [ă-freš'] av. di nuovo, un'altra volta.

Aft [äft] av. (naut.) a poppa.

After [äf'tĕr] av., prep. e cong. dietro, dopo, in seguito, a imitazione di, dopo che; a. all [ól] in fin dei conti.

Aftermath [äf'tĕr-mäth] n. secondo taglio di fieno nella stagione; (fig.) conseguenze (pl.), risultati (pl.).

Afternoon [äf-tĕr-nūn'] n. pomeriggio.

Afterthought [äf'tĕr-thòt] n. riflessione, secondo pensiero.

Afterwards [äf'tĕr-ue'ds] av. dopo, più tardi.

Again [ă-ghén'] av. di nuovo, un'altra volta; a. and [ènd] a. ripetutamente; now [nau] and a. di quando in quando.

Against [ă-ghènst'] prep. contro, in opposizione a; per; cong. per quando; a. the grain [thì grén] (fig.) contro voglia.

Agape [ă-ghép'] a. e av. a bocca aperta.

Age [éğ] n. epoca, età, periodo; of [ŏv] a. maggiorenne; under [ăn'der] a. minorenne.

Age [éğ] v.t. e i. invecchiar(si).

Aged [é'gèd] *a.* in età avanzata, **vecchio**.

Agency [é'gèn-si] *n.* agenzia, opera, **rappresentanza**.

Agent [é'gènt] *n.* agente, rappresentante.

Agglomeration [ă-glò-mĕ-ré'šn] *n.* agglomerazione.

Aggrandisement [ă-grèn'-diz-mènt] *n.* aumento di potere o di ricchezza.

Aggravate [ă'gră-vét] *v.t.* aggravare, esasperare.

Aggravating [ă'gră-vé-tiñ] *a.* irritante, che fa perdere la pazienza.

Aggravation [ă-gră-vé'šn] *n.* aggravamento, aggravazione.

Aggregate [ă'gri-ghét] *a.* e *n.* aggregato; **in the a.** nel complesso.

Aggregation [ă-gri-ghé'šn] *n.* aggregazione.

Aggression [ă-grĕ'šn] *n.* aggressione.

Aggressive [ă-grĕ'siv] *a.* aggressivo, offensivo.

Aghast [ă-gàst'] *a.* stupefatto e terrorizzato.

Agile [ă'giail] *a.* agile.

Agility [ă-gi'li-ti] *n.* agilità.

Agitate [ă'gi-tét] *v.t.* agitare, dibattere, scuotere.

Agitation [ă-gi-té'šn] *n.* agitazione, commozione.

Ago [ă-gò'] *av.* fa.

Agog [ă-gòg'] *a. pred.* ansioso, desideroso; *av.* con ansia.

Agonize [ă'gò-na¹z] *v.t.* tormentare; *v.i.* agonizzare.

Agony [ă'gò-ni] *n.* agonia, angoscia.

Agrarian [ă-grè'ri-ĕn] *a.* agrario, agricolo.

Agree [ă-grî'] *v.i.* acconsentire, andare d'accordo, essere d'accordo, **accordarsi**, consentire.

Agreeable [ă-grî'ă-bl] *a.* piacevole, simpatico.

Agreeableness [ă-grî'ă-bl-nès] *n.* piacevolezza.

Agreement [ă-grî'mènt] *n.* accordo, contratto, patto.

Agricultural [ă-gri-căl'ciŭrél] *a.* agricolo.

Agriculture [ă'gri-căl-cĕr] *n.* agricoltura.

Aground [ă-graund'] *av.* (*naut.*) in secco; **to run** [rŭn] **a.** incagliarsi.

Ague [é'ghiŭ] *n.* febbre malarica.

Ahead [ă-hèd'] *av.* (in) avanti.

Aid [éd] *n.* aiuto, assistenza, sussidio; **first** [fe²st] **a.** pronto soccorso; *v.t.* aiutare.

Aide-de-camp [*pron. fran.*] aiutante di campo.

Ail [él] *v.i.* sentirsi male; *v.t.* affliggere.

Aileron [é'li-rŏn] *n.* (*avia.*) alerone.

Ailing [é'liñ] *a.* sofferente.

Ailment [é'lmènt] *n.* indisposizione, malattia.

Aim [ém] *n.* mira, proposito, scopo; *v.i.* aspirare, aver di mira, mirare; *v.i.* dirigere.

Aimless [ém'lès] *a.* senza scopo.

Air [é²] *n.* aria, aspetto, atmosfera, libero spazio; (*mus.*) aria, romanza.

Aircraft [é²'crèft] *n.* aereo, aerei (*pl.*); *a.* **carrier** [că'ri-ĕ²] nave porta-aerei.

Air force [é²² fo²s] *n.* aeronautica, aviazione.

Airily [é'ri-li] *av.* gaiamente, spensieratamente.

Airiness [é'ri-nès] *n.* leggerezza, spensieratezza.

Airing [é'riñ] *n.* esposizione all'aria o al fuoco, giretto all'aria aperta.

Airless [é²'lès] *a.* privo d'aria.

Air mail [é²'mél] *n.* posta aerea.

Airman [é²²'măn] *n.* (*avia.*) aviatore.

Air-pump [é°r'pămp] *n.* pompa pneumatica.

Air-raid [é°r'réd] *n.* incursione aerea.

Airship [é°r'scip] *n.* dirigibile.

Air-tight [é°r'ta¹t] *a.* impermeabile all'aria.

Airy [é°'rĭ] *a.* aereo, etereo, leggero, spensierato.

A¹sle [a¹l] *n.* navata.

Ajar [ă-gia°'] *av.* socchiuso (di porta).

Akimbo [ă-chìm'bò] *av.* le mani sui fianchi e i gomiti in fuori.

Akin [ă-chìn'] *a. pred.* affine, parente.

Alabaster [ă-lă-bă'stë°] *a. e .. [di]* alabastro.

Alacrity [ă-lă'crĭ-tĭ] *n.* alacrità.

Alarm [ă-la²m'] *n.* allarme; *v.t.* allarmare, spaventare.

Alarm-clock [clŏc'] *n.* (orologio a) sveglia.

Alas! [ă-lès'] *interiez.* ahimè!

Albanian [èl-bé'nĭ-ăn] *a. e n.* albanese.

Albatross [èl'bè-très] *n.* albatro.

Albeit [ôl-bi'ĭt] *cong.* quantunque.

Album [èl'băm] *n.* album.

Albumen [èl-biu'mèn] *n.* albume.

Alchemist [èl'chĭ-mĭst] *n.* alchimista.

Alchemy [èl'chĭ-mĭ] *n.* alchimia.

Alcohol [èl'cò-hŏl] *n.* alcool, spirito puro.

Alcove [èl'còv] *n.* alcova, recesso.

Alder [ôl'dë°] *n.* ontano.

Alderman [ôl'dër-măn] *n.* membro dell'amministrazione comunale, assessore.

Ale [él] *n.* birra; **a-house** [haus] birreria.

Alert [ă-lë°t'] *n.* allarme; *a.* vigilante; **on the a.** all'erta.

Alertness [ă-lë°t'něs] *n.* vigilanza.

Alexandrine [ă-lěc-zèn'drĭn] *n.* alessandrino (verso).

Alibi [ă'lĭ-ba¹] *n.* alibi.

Alien [é'lĭ-ĕn] *n.* forestiero, straniero; *a.* estraneo.

Alienate [é'lĭ-ĕ-nét] *v.t.* alienare.

Alienation [é-lĭ-ĕ-né'şn] *n.* alienazione.

Alight [ă-la¹t'] *a. pred.* acceso, infiammato; *v.i.* atterrare, posarsi, scendere, smontare.

Alike [ă-la¹c'] *a. pred.* (*pl.*) simili; *av.* parimenti.

Alimentary [ă-lĭ-mèn'tă-rĭ] *a.* alimentare, alimentario.

Alimentation [ă-lĭ-mèn-té'şn] *n.* alimentazione.

Alimony [ă'lĭ-mò-nĭ] *n.* (*legge*) alimenti (*pl.*). [vivo.

Alive [ă-la¹v'] *a. pred.* vivente.

All [ôl] *a.* tutto; *n. e pron.* tutto, tutti; *av.* completamente, del tutto; **not at** [et] **all!** niente affatto!

Allay [ă-lé'] *v.t.* alleviare, diminuire.

Allegation [ă-lĭ-ghé'şn] *n.* allegazione, asserzione.

Allege [ă-lèg'] *v.t.* allegare, asserire.

Allegiance [ă-lĭ'gèns] *n.* obbedienza (al sovrano, ecc.).

Allegorical [ă-lĭ-gò'rĭ-cl] *a.* allegorico.

Allegory [ă'lĭ-gŏ-rĭ] *n.* allegoria.

Alleviate [ă-lĭ'vĭ-ét] *v.t.* alleviare, mitigare.

Alliance [ă-la¹'ĕns] *n.* alleanza, unione.

Allied [ă-la¹d'] *a.* alleato, connesso.

Alliteration [ă-lĭ-tĕ-ré'şn] *n.* allitterazione.

Allocate [ă'lò-chét] *v.t.* assegnare, distribuire.

Allocation [ă-lò-ché'şn] *n.* assegnazione.

Allot [ă-lŏt'] *v.t.* assegnare (con autorità), dividere.

Allotment [ă-lŏt'mĕnt] *n.* assegnazione, parte assegnata, orto comunale, dove ogni cittadino ha il diritto di coltivare.

Allow [ă-lau'] *v.t.* ammettere, concedere, permettere.

Allowance [ă-lau'ĕns] *n.* assegno, indennità, riduzione, sconto.

Alloy [ă-loi'] *n.* lega (di metalli) mescolanza; *v.t.* attenuare, mescolare.

All-Saints' Day [ŏl séns de¹] *n.* ognissanti.

All-Souls' Day [ŏl sŏls de¹] *n.* giorno dei morti.

Allude [ă-liud'] *v.i.* accennare, alludere.

Allure [ă-liuʳ'] *v.t.* adescare, allettare.

Allurement [ă-liuʳ'mĕnt] *n.* allettamento, fascino.

Allusion [ă-liu'ẑn] *n.* allusione.

Alluvion [ă-liu'vi-ŏn] *n.* alluvione, terreno alluvionale.

Ally [ă-la¹'] *n.* alleato; *v.t.* alleare, collegare, unire.

Almanac [ŏl'mă-năc] *n.* almanacco.

Almighty [ŏl-ma¹'tĭ] *a.* onnipotente; [thē] *a.* Dio.

Almond [ĕl'mŏnd] *n.* mandorla; *a.*-tree [trī] mandorlo.

Almoner [ĕl'mò-nĕʳ] *n.* elemosiniere.

Almost [ŏl'mòst] *av.* quasi.

Alms [ăms] *n.* elemosina; *a.*-house [haus] ospizio di mendicità.

Aloft [ă-lŏft'] *av.* in alto.

Alone [ă-lòn'] *a. pred.* solo; to let a. lasciar stare.

Along [ă-loñ'] *av. e prep.* avanti, lungo, per; come [căm] a! su via!

Aloof [ă-luf'] *av.* a distanza, in disparte.

Aloud [ă-laud'] *av.* a voce alta, forte.

Alphabet [ĕl'fă-bĕt] *n.* [alfabeto.

Alpine [ĕl'pa¹n] *a.* alpino.

Also [ŏl'sò] *av.* anche, inoltre, pure.

Altar [ŏl'tĕʳ] *n.* altare; high [ha¹] a. altar maggiore.

Alter [ŏl'tĕʳ] *v.t.* alterare, cambiare; *v.i.* cambiarsi.

Alterable [ŏl'tĕ-ră-bl] *a.* mutabile.

Alteration [ŏl-tĕ-ré'ẑn] *n.* alterazione, modificazione.

Alternate [ŏl-tĕʳ'nĕt] *a.* alternato alterno; [ŏl'tĕʳ-nét] *v.t. e i.* alternar(si), avvicendar(si).

Alternation [ŏl-tĕʳ-né'ẑn] *n.* alternazione.

Alternative [ŏl-tĕʳ'nă-tiv] *n.* alternativa; *a.* alternativo.

Although [ŏl'thò] *cong.* sebbene, quantunque.

Altitude [ĕl'ti-tiŭd] *n.* altezza, altitudine.

Altogether [ŏl-tò-ghĕ'thĕʳ] *av.* completamente, nell'insieme.

Altruism [ĕl'tru-ism] *n.* altruismo.

Alum [ă'lăm] *n.* allume.

Aluminium [ă-liŭ-mi'ni-am] *n.* alluminio.

Always [ŏl'ués] *av.* sempre.

Amain [ă-mén'] *av.* (raro) con forza.

Amalgam [ă-mĕl'găm] *n.* amalgama.

Amalgamate [ă-mĕl'gă-mét] *v.t. e i.* amalgamar(si).

Amalgamation [ă-mĕl-gă-mé'ẑn] *n.* amalgamazione, fusione.

Amass [ă-măs'] *v.t.* accumulare, ammassare.

Amateur [ă'mĕ-tiuʳⁱ] *n.* dilettante.

Amaze [ă-méz'] *v.t.* meravigliare, stupire.

Amazement [ă-méz'mĕnt] *n.* meraviglia.

Annoy [ă-noi'] *v.t.* disturbare, irritare.

Annoyance [ă-noi'ĕns] *n.* fastidio, irritazione.

Annual [ĕn'iu-ĕl] *a.* annuale, annuo. [nualità.

Annuity [ĕn-iu'ĭ-tǐ] *n.* an-

Annul [ă-nŭl'] *v.t.* abolire, annullare.

Annunciation [ă-nŭn-sĭ-é'ăn] *n.* annunciazione.

Anodyne [ă'nŏ-da'ĭn] *a.* anodino.

Anoint [ă-noint'] *v.t.* consacrare, ungere.

Anomalous [ă-nŏm'ă-lăs] *a.* anomalo, irregolare.

Anomaly [ă-nŏm'ă-lǐ] *n.* anomalia, irregolarità.

Anon [ă-nŏn'] *av.* immediatamente, subito; ever and [ĕ've'ĕnd] *a.* di quando in quando.

Anonymous [ă-nŏn'ĭ-măs] *a.* anonimo.

Another [ă-ŏ'thĕr] *a. e pron.* (un) altro, (un) secondo; one [uăn] *a. pron. recipr.* l'un l'altro, sì.

Answer [ăn'sĕr] *n.* risposta; *v.t.* rispondere, corrispondere a, *v.i.* rispondere a, servire; to a. for, rispondere di.

Answerable [ăn'sĕ-rĕ-bl] *a.* responsabile.

Ant [ĕnt] *n.* formica.

Antagonism [ĕn-tĕ'gò-nĭsm] *n.* antagonismo.

Antagonist [ĕn-tĕ'gò-nĭst] *n.* antagonista.

Antarctic [ĕn-tĕr'tĭc] *a. e n.* antartico.

Antecedence [ĕn-tĭ-sĭ'dĕns] *n.* antecedenza.

Antecedent [ĕn-tĭ-sĭ'dĕnt] *a. e n.* antecedente.

Antechamber [ĕn'tĭ-cémbĕr] *n.* anticamera.

Antedate [ĕn-tĭ-dĕt'] *v.t.* anticipare, antidatare.

Antediluvian [ĕn-tĭ-dĭ-lŭ'vĭĕn] *a. e n.* antidiluviano.

Antelope [ĕn'tĭ-lòp] *n.* antilope.

Antemeridian [ĕn-tĭ-mĕ-rĭ'dĭ-ĕn] *a.* antimeridiano.

Antepenult [ĕn-tĭ-pĭ-nălt'] *a. e n.* antipenultimo.

Anteroom [ĕn'tĭ-rum] *n.* anticamera.

Anthem [ĕn'thĕm] *n.* antifona, inno.

Anthology [ĕn-thó'lò-gĭ] *n.* antologia.

Anthracite [ĕn'thră-sa'ĭt] *n.* antracite.

Anthropology [ĕn-thrò-pó'lò-gĭ] *n.* antropologia.

Anti-aircraft [ĕn'tĭ-é'er''crăft] *a.* anti-aereo.

Antic [ĕn'tĭc] *a.* (arcaic) bizzarro, grottesco; *n.* (quasi sempre *plur.*) atteggiamento ridicolo.

AntiChrist [ĕn'tĭ-cra'ĭst] *n.* anticristo.

Anticipate [ĕn-tĭ'sĭ-pét] *v.t.* aspettarsi, anticipare, prevenire.

Anticipation [ĕn-tĭ-sĭ-pé'ăn] *n.* anticipazione, anticipo, previsione.

Anticlimax [ĕn-tĭ-cla''mĕcs] *n.* gradazione discendente, conclusione banale.

Antidote [ĕn'tĭ-dòt] *n.* antidoto.

Antimacassar [ĕn-tĭ-mĕchĕs'sĕr] *n.* copridivano, copripoltrona.

Antipathy [ĕn-tĭ'pă-thǐ] *n.* antipatia avversione.

Antipodes [ĕn-tĭ'pò-dĭz] *n.* [pl.] antipodi [pl.].

Antipope [ĕn'tĭ-pòp] *n.* antipapa. [papa.

Antiquarian [ĕn-tĭ-qué'rĭ-ĕn] *n.* antiquario, studioso di cose antiche.

Antiquated [ĕn'tĭ-qué-tĭd] *a.* antiquato, fuori uso.

Antique [ĕn-tĭc'] *n.* oggetto di arte antica; *a.* antico, arcaico.

Antiquity [èn-tí'qui-tí] *n.* tempi antichi [*pl.*] antiquità.

Antiseptic [èn-ti-sěp'tic] *a. e n.* antisettico.

Antithesis [èn-tí'thi-sis] *n.* antitesi.

Antler [ènt'lěr] *n.* corno ramificato di cervo o di daino.

Anvil [èn'vil] *n.* incudine.

Anxiety [èn-za'i-tí] *n.* ansietà.

Anxious [ènc'sciàs] *a.* ansioso, preoccupato.

Any [è'ni] *a. (in frasi neg. e interrog.)* alcu-no, -ni, del, dei, qualche, un po' di; *(in frasi afferm.)* ogni, qualsiasi, qualunque; *pron.* alcuno, ne.

Any/body, -one [è'ni/bó-di, uǎn] *pron. (neg. e interrog.)* alcuno, qualcuno; *(afferm.)* chiunque.

Anyhow [è'ni-hau] *av.* in qualunque modo, in ogni caso, tuttavia.

Anything [è'ni-thínǧ] *pron. (neg. e interrog.)* qualche cosa, alcuna cosa; *(afferm.)* qualunque cosa.

Anywhere [è'ni-huěr] *av. (neg. e interrog.)* in alcun luogo, in qualche luogo; *(afferm.)* in qualsiasi luogo.

Apart [ă-pǎrt'] *av.* a parte, in disparte.

Apartment [ă-pǎrt'měnt] *n.* stanza; *(al pl.)* alloggio.

Apathetic [è-pǎ-thě'tic] *a.* apatico, indifferente.

Apathy [é'pǎ-thì] *n.* apatia, indifferenza.

Ape [êp] *n.* scimmia; *v.t.* imitare, scimmiottare.

Aperi/ent, -tive [ă-pě'rì-ěnt, -tìv] *n.* lassativo.

Aperitif [*pron. fran.*] *n.* aperitivo.

Apex [é'pěcs] *n.* apice, vertice.

Aphorism [ǎ'fó-rism] *n.* aforisma.

Apiary [é'piě-rì] *n.* apiario.

Apiece [ă-pís'] *av.* per ognuno, separatamente.

Apish [é'piš] *a.* scimmiesco.

Apocalypse [ă-pó'că-lips] *n.* apocalisse.

Apocryphal [ă-pó'crǐ-fěl] *a.* apocrifo, falso.

Apogee [ǎ'pó-ǧí] *n.* apogeo.

Apologetic [ă-pó-ló-ǧě'tic] *a.* apologetico.

Apologise [ă-pó'lò-ǧiaiz] *v.i.* scusarsi.

Apologue [ǎ'pò-lǒǧ] *n.* apologo.

Apology [ă-pó'lò-ǧì] *n.* apologia, giustificazione, scusa.

Apoplectic [ǎ-pò-plěc'tic] *a.* apoplettico.

Apoplexy [ǎ'pò-plěc-sì] *n.* apoplessia.

Apostle [ă-pós'l] *n.* apostolo.

Apostleship [ǎ-pós'l-scip] *n.* apostolato.

Apostolic [ă-pòs-tó'lic] *a.* apostolico.

Apostrophe [ă-pòs'trò-fì] *n.* apostrofe.

Apostrophize [ă-pos'trò-faiz] *v.t. e i.* apostrofare.

Apothecary [ă-pó'thì-cǎ-rì] *n. (arcaico)* farmacista.

Appal [ă-pól'] *v.t.* spaventare, terrorizzare.

Appalling [ă-pó'línǧ] *a.* spaventoso.

Apparatus [ǎ-pǎ-ré'tǎs] *n.* apparato, apparecchio.

Apparel [ă-pǎ'rěl] *n (arcaico)* abigliamento.

Apparent [ă-pè'rěnt] *a.* chiaro, manifesto; heir [ě'r] *a. n.* erede legittimo.

Apparition [ǎ-pǎ-rí'šn] *n.* fantasma, visione.

Appeal [ă-píl'] *n.* appello; *v.i.* appellarsi, fare appello, attrarre.

Appear [ă-pìěr'] *v.i* apparire, comparire manifestarsi, sembrare.

Appearance [ă-pìě'rěns] *n.*

apparenza, apparizione, a- spetto.

Appease [ă-pīz'] v.t. calmare, pacificare, placare.

Appellation [ă-pĕ-lé'śn] n. appello, titolo.

Append [ă-pĕnd'] v.t. aggiungere, appendere.

Appertain [ă-pĕr-tén'] v.t. appartenere, riferirsi.

Appetence [ă'pĭ-tĕns] n. brama.

Appetite [ă'pĭ-tait] n. appetito.

Appetising [ă'pĭ-ta'-ziń] a. appetitoso, succolento.

Applaud [ă-plód'] v.t. e i. applaudire.

Applause [ă-plóz'] n. applau/so, -si (pl.).

Apple [ă'pl] n. mela; a. -tree [tri] melo.

Appliance [ă-plắ'ăns] n. apparecchio, applicazione, strumento.

Applicable [ă'plĭ-că-bl] a. applicabile.

Applicant [ă'plĭ-chănt] n. candidato.

Application [ă-plĭ-ché'śn] n. applicazione, domanda, richiesta.

Apply [ă-pla'] v.t. e i. applicare, applicarsi, rivolgersi.

Appoint [ă-point'] v.t. destinare, nominare.

Appointment [ă-point'mĕnt] n. appuntamento, impegno, nomina, ufficio.

Apportion [ă-pŏr'śn] v.t. distribuire.

Apportionment [ă-pŏr'śn-mĕnt] n. ripartizione.

Apposite [ĕ'pò-zĭt] a. apposito, appropriato.

Appositeness [ĕ'pò-zĭt-nĕs] n. appropriatezza.

Apposition [ă-pò-zi'śn] n. apposizione, giustapposizione.

Appraisal [ă-pré'zĕl] n. stima, valutazione.

Appraise [ă-préz'] v.t. far la stima di, valutare.

Appreciate [ă-pri'sci-ét] v.t. apprezzare, tenere in giusto conto.

Appreciation [ă-pri-sci-é'śn] n. apprezzamento, giudizio, stima.

Apprehend [ă-pri-hĕnd'] v.t. arrestare, comprendere, temere.

Apprehension [ă-pri-hĕn'śn] n. apprensione, comprensione, arresto, timore.

Apprentice [ă-prĕn'tis] n. apprendista.

Apprenticeship [ă-prĕn'tis-scip] n. stato d'apprendista, tirocinio.

Apprise [ă-praiz'] v.t. informare.

Approach [ă-pròc'] n. accesso, approccio, avvicinamento; v.t. avvicinare; v.i. avvicinarsi, approssimarsi.

Approachable [ă-prò'ciă-bl] a. accessibile.

Approbation [ă-prò-bé'śn] n. approvazione, sanzione.

Appropriate [ă-prò'pri-ĕt] a. appropriato, proprio; [ă-prò'pri-ét] v.t. appropriarsi.

Appropriation [ă-prò-pri-é'śn] n. appropriazione.

Approval [ă-prù'vĕl] n. approvazione, sanzione.

Approve [ă-prù'v'] v.t. approvare, sanzionare.

Approximate [ă-prŏc'zi-mĕt] a. approssimativo; [ă-prŏc'zi-mét] v.t. e i. approssimar(si).

Approximation [ă-prŏc-zi-mé'śn] n. approssimazione.

Appurtenance [ă-pĕr'ti-nĕns] n. appendice, appartenenza.

Apricot [é'pri-cŏt] n. albicocca; a. -tree [tri] albicocco.

April [é'pril] n. aprile.

Apron [é'prŏn] n. grembiule.

Apropos [pron. fran.] av. a proposito.

Apt [èpt] a. adatto, atto; a. at [èt] bravo in; a. to [tu] avente tendenza a.

Aptitude [èp'tĭ-tiŭd] n. abilità, attitudine.

Aquarium [ă-qué'rĭ-ăm] n. acquario.

Aquatic [ă-quă'tĭc] a. acquatico.

Aqueduct [ă'qui-dăct] n. acquedotto.

Aquiline [ă'qui-lĭn] a. aquilino.

Arabesque [ă-ră-bĕsc'] a. arabesco.

Arab [ă'rèb] a. e n. arabo.

Arabic [ă'rè-bĭc] a. arabo.

Arable [ă'ră-bl] a. arabile.

Arbiter [ăr'bĭ-tĕr] n. arbitro, giudice.

Arbitrary [ăr'bĭ-tră-rĭ] a. arbitrario, dispotico.

Arbitrate [ăr'bĭ-trét] v.t. e i. arbitrare.

Arbitration [ă-bĭ-tré'śn] n. arbitrato.

Arbour [ăr'bĕr] n. pergolato.

Arc [ăr'c] n. arco; a. lamp [lèmp] lampado ad arco.

Arcade [ăr-chéd'] n. galleria, portico, portici (pl.).

Arch [ăr'c] n. arco, volta; a. furbo, matricolato, principale birichino.

Archaeological [ăr-chi-ŏ'lŏ-gist] n. archeologo.

Archaeology [ăr-chi-ŏ'lŏ-gi] n. archeologia.

Archaic [ăr-ché'ic] a. arcaico.

Archangel [ăr'chén-gĕl] n. arcangelo.

Archbishop [ăr'c-bi'sciŏp] n. arcivescovo.

Archbishopric [ăr'c-bi'sciŏp-rĭc] n. arcivescovado.

Archdeacon [ăr'c-dĭ'cŏn] n. arcidiacono.

Archduke [ăr'c'diŭc] n. arciduca.

Archer [ăr'cĕr] n. arciere.

Archery [ăr'cĕ-rĭ] n. tiro con l'arco.

Archetype [ăr'chĭ-ta'ĭp] n. archetipo.

Architect [ăr'chĭ-tĕct] n. architetto.

Architecture [ăr'chĭ-tĕc-cĕr] n. architettura.

Archives [ăr'chaivs] n. (pl.) archivio.

Archness [ăr'c'nĕs] n. aria birichina.

Archpriest [ăr'c'prĭst] n. arciprete.

Arctic [ăr'c'tic] a. e n. artico.

Ardent [ăr'dĕnt] a. ardente, fervido, zelante.

Ardour [ăr'dĕr] n. ardore, fervore, zelo.

Arduous [ăr'diŭ-ăs] a. arduo, difficile.

Area [é'rĭ-ĕ⁽ʳ⁾] n. area, zona.

Argentine [ăr'gĕn-ta'ĭn] a. argentino, d'argento; a. e n. (abitante) della Repubblica Argentina.

Argue [ăr'ghiù] v.t. e i. argomentare, discutere, disputare.

Argument [ăr'ghiù-mĕnt] n. discussione, ragionamento.

Argumentative [ăr'ghiù-mĕn'tă-tiv] a. amante della discussione.

Arid [é'rĭd] a. arido, nudo, sterile.

Aridity [e-rĭ'dĭ-tĭ] n. aridità, sterilità.

Aright [ă-ra'ĭt] av. bene, giustamente.

Arise [ă-ra'ĭs'] vi. aizarsi, sorgere.

Aristocracy [ă-rĭs-tŏ'cră-sĭ] n. aristocrazia.

Aristocrat [ă'rĭs-tŏ-crèt] n. aristocratico, nobile.

Aristocratic [ă-rĭs-tŏ-crè'tic] a. aristocratico.

Arithmetic [ă-rĭth'mĕ-tic] n. aritmetica.

Arithmetical [ă-rith-mĕ'ti-căl] *a.* aritmetico.

Ark [ā'c] *n.* arca.

Arm [ā'm] *n.* braccio, bracciuolo; (*comunemente usato al pl.* arms) arma, armi; *v.t. e i.* armar(si).

Armament [ā'r'mă-mĕnt] *n.* armamento.

Armchair [ā'm-cér'] *n.* poltrona.

Armful [ā'm'fŭl] *n.* bracciata.

Armistice [ā'r'mis-tis] *n.* armistizio.

Armlet [ā'm'lĕt] *n.* bracciale.

Armour [ā'r'mĕ'r] *n.* armatura, corazza.

Army [ā'r'mi] *n.* armata, esercito.

Around [ă-raund'] *av.* all'intorno, in ogni parte; *prep.* intorno a.

Arouse [ă-rauz'] *v.t.* (ri)svegliare, suscitare.

Arraign [ă-rén'] *v.t.* accusare, chiamare in giudizio.

Arrange [ă-réng'] *v.t.* accomodare, disporre, ordinare; (*mus.*) adattare; *v.i.* combinare, dare istruzioni, prendere accordi, stabilire.

Arrangement [ă-réng'mĕnt] *n.* accomodamento, accordo.

Arras [ā'răs] *n.* arazzo.

Array [ă-ré'] *n.* abbigliamento, numero imponente, orine.

Arrears [ă-riⁱᵉʳˢ'] *n.* (*pl.*) arretrati (*pl.*).

Arrest [ă-rĕst'] *n.* arresto, fermata; *v.t.* arrestare, fermare.

Arrival [ă-ra¹vĕl] *n.* arrivo.

Arrive [ă-ra¹v'] *v.i.* arrivare, giungere.

Arrogance [è'rò-ghĕns] *n.* arroganza, presunzione.

Arrogant [è'rò-ghĕnt] *a.* arrogante, presuntuoso.

Arrogate [è'rò-ghét] *v.t.* arrogarsi, pretendere.

Arrow [è'rò] *n.* freccia.

Arsenal [ā'r'si-nĕl] *n.* arsenale.

Arsenic [ā'r'sĕ-nic] *n.* arsenico.

Arson [ā'r'sĕn] *n.* incendio doloso.

Art [ā'rt] *n.* arte; fine [fa¹n] arts (*pl.*) belle arti (*pl.*).

Artery [ā'r-tĕ-ri] *n.* arteria.

Artful [ā'rt'fŭl] *a.* abile, astuto, ingannevole.

Arthritis [ā'r-thrai¹'tis] *n.* artrite. [carciofo.

Artichoke [ā'r'ti-ciòc] *n.*

Article [ā'rti-cl] *n.* articolo; leading [li'diñ] *a.* articolo di fondo; *v.t.* mettere come apprendista.

Articulation [ā'r-ti-chiŭ-le'śn] *n.* articolazione, giuntura.

Artifice [ā'r'ti-fis] *n.* artificio, astuzia.

Artificial [ā'r-ti-fi'śĕl] *a.* artificiale, artificioso.

Artificiality [ā'r-ti-fi-scià'li-ti] *n.* artificiosità.

Artillery [ā'r-ti'lĕ-ri] *n.* artiglieria.

Artilleryman [ā'r-ti'lĕ-ri-măn] *n.* artigliere.

Artisan [ā'r-ti-zăn'] *n.* artigiano.

Artist [ā'r'tist] *n.* pittore, scultore.

Artless [ā'rt'lĕs] *a.* ingenuo, semplice.

Artlessness [ā'r't'lĕs-nĕs] *n.* ingenuità, semplicità.

As [ès] *av.* come, nello stesso modo in cui; as . . . as così . . . come, tanto . . . quanto; as for, in quanto a; *pron. rel.* che, quale.

Ascend [ă-sĕnd'] *v.t. e i.* ascendere, salire.

Ascendency [ă-sĕn'dĕn-si] *n.* ascendente, influenza dominante.

Ascension [ă-sĕn'śŏn] *n.* ascensione.

Ascent [ă-sĕnt] *n.* ascesa, erta, salita.

Ascertain [ă-sĕr-tén'] v.t. accertarsi, scoprire.

Ascetic [ă-sĕ'tic] n. asceta; a. ascetico.

Ascribe [ă-scra¹b'] v.t. ascrivere, attribuire.

Ascription [ă-scrip'ŝn] n. l'essere ascritto.

Ash (tree) [ĕŝ'tri] n. frassino.

Ashamed [ă-ŝémd'] a. vergognoso; **to be** [bi] **a.** of, vergognarsi.

Ashen [ĕ'ŝĕn] a. cinereo, di frassino.

Ashes [ĕ'ŝĭs] n. (pl.) cenere, ceneri.

Ashore [ă-ŝiō'r] av. a riva, sulla spiaggia.

Aside [ă-sa¹d'] n. parole pronunziate a parte; av. a parte, in disparte.

Ask [ăsc] v.t. chiedere, domandare, invitare; v.i. (ri) chiedere, informarsi.

Askance [ă-schĕns'] av. obliquamente.

Asleep [ă-slĭp'] a. pred. addormentato; **to fall** [fól] **a.** addormentarsi.

Asparagus [ă-spĕ'ră-găs] n. asparagi (pl.).

Aspect [ă-spĕct'] n. apparenza, aspetto, esposizione (di case, ecc.).

Asperity [ă-spĕ'rĭ-ti] n. asperità, asprezza.

Asperse [ă-spĕrs'] v.t. aspergere, calunniare, denigrare.

Aspersion [ă-spĕr'ŝn] n. aspersione, calunnia.

Asphalt [ĕs'fĕlt] n. asfalto.

Aspirant [ĕs'pĭ-rănt] n. aspirante, candidato.

Aspirate [ĕs'pĭ-rét] v.t. aspirare.

Aspiration [ĕs-pĭ-ré'ŝn] n. aspirazione.

Aspire [ĕs-pa¹o'r] v.i. aspirare, bramare.

Aspiring [ĕs-pa¹e'rĭn] a. ambizioso.

Ass [ĕs] n. asino; **to make** [mĕc] **an a.** of oneself, rendersi ridicolo.

Assail [ă-sél'] v.t. assalire, attaccare.

Assailable [ă-sé'lă-bl] a. che può essere assalito.

Assailant [ă-sé'lĕnt] n. assalitore. [sino.

Assassin [ă-sĕ'sĭn] n. assas-

Assassinate [ă-sĕ'sĭ-nét] v.t. assassinare.

Assassination [ă-sĕ-sĭ-né'ŝn] n. assassinio.

Assault [ă-sólt'] v.t. assalire, assaltare.

Assemblage [ă-sĕm'blĭg] n. assemblea.

Assemble [ă-sĕm'bl] v.t. e i. riunir(si).

Assembly [ă-sĕm'bli] n. assemblea, riunione.

Assent [ă-sĕnt'] n. assenso, consenso; v.i. acconsentire, approvare.

Assert [ă-sĕrt'] v.t. asserire; rivendicare [un diritto, ecc.].

Assertion [ă-sĕr'ŝn] n. asserzione, rivendicazione.

Assess [ă-sĕs'] v.t. fissare, stimare.

Assessable [ă-sĕs'ă-bl] a. imponibile.

Assessment [ă-sĕs'mĕnt] n. (imposizione di) tassa, valutazione.

Assessor [ă-sĕ'sŏr] n. agente del fisco, assistente d'un giudice, assessore.

Assets [ĕ'sĕts] n. (pl.) (comm.) attività.

Assiduity [ĕs-ĭ-dĭū'ĭ-ti] n. assiduità, diligenza.

Assiduous [ĕ-sĭ'dĭū-ăs] a. assiduo, diligente.

Assign [ă-sa¹n'] v.t. assegnare, attribuire.

Assignee [ă-sa¹-ni'] n. (comm.) mandatario.

Assignment [ă-sa¹n'mĕnt] n. assegnazione, attribuzione.

Assimilate [ă-sĭ'mĭ-lét] v.t. assimilare, assorbire.

Assimilation [ă-sĭ-mĭ-lé'ŝn] n. assimilazione.

Assist [ă-sĭst'] v.t. aiutare, assistere.

Assistance [ă-sĭs'tĕns] n. aiuto, assistenza, sussidio.

Assistant [ă-sĭs'tĕnt] a. e n. aiutante, assistente.

Assize [ă-saĭz'] n. calmiere, processo; **assizes** [ă-saĭ'zĭs] (pl.) corte d'assise.

Associate [ă-sŏ'sci-ét] a. associato, socio; v.t. e i. associar(si).

Association [ă-sŏ-sci-é'ŝn] n. associazione.

Assort [ă-sŏ't'] v.t. assortire, raggruppare.

Assortment [ă-sŏ't'mĕnt] n. assortimento.

Assuage [ă-suég'] v.t. calmare, mitigare.

Assume [ă-siūm'] v.t. arrogarsi, assumere, presumere.

Assuming [ă-siū'mĭn] a. presuntuoso.

Assumption [ă-sămp'ŝn] n. assunzione, supposizione.

Assurance [ă-sciū'rĕns] n. assicurazione, certezza, fiducia in sé.

Assure [ă-sciū'ĕr] v.t. assicurare, rassicurare.

Asterisk [ĕs'tĕ-rĭsc] n. asterisco.

Astern [ă-stĕ'n] av. [naut.] a poppa.

Asthma [ĕsth'mĕ(r)] n. asma.

Astir [ă-stĕ'r] av. e a. pred. in moto.

Astonish [ĕs-tŏ'nĭŝ] v.t. sorprendere, stupire.

Astonishment [ĕs-tŏ'nĭŝmĕnt] n. sorpresa, stupore.

Astound [ă-staund'] v.t. stupefare.

Astray [ă-stre''] av. fuori della giusta via; **to go** [gò] a. sviarsi.

Astride [ă-straĭd'] av. a cavalcioni.

Astringent [ĕs-trĭn'gĕnt] a. e n. astringente.

Astrologer [ĕs-trŏ'lò-gĕr] n. astrologo.

Astrology [ĕs-trŏ'lò-gĭ] n. astrologia.

Astronomer [ĕs-trŏ'nò-mĕr] n. astronomo.

Astronomy [ĕs-trŏ'nò-mĭ] n. astronomia.

Astute [ă-stiūt'] a. astuto, sagace.

Asunder [ă-săn'dĕr] av. a pezzi, separatamente.

Asylum [ă-saĭ'lăm] n. asilo, manicomio.

At [ĕt] prep. a, da, di, in.

Atheism [é'thĭ-ĭsm] n. ateismo.

Atheist [é'thĭ-ĭst] n. ateo.

Athlete [ĕth'lit] n. atleta.

Athletics [ĕth-lĕ'tĭŝs] n. (pl.) atletica.

Atlantic [ĕt-lĕn'tĭc] n. oceano atlantico; a. atlantico.

Atlas [ĕt'lăs] n. atlante.

Atmosphere [ĕt'mŏs-fiĕr] n. atmosfera.

Atmospherics [ĕt-mŏs-fĕ'rĭcs] n. (pl.) suoni di disturbo della radio (pl.).

Atom [ĕ'tŏm] n. atomo.

Atomic [ĕ-tŏ'mĭc] a. atomico.

Atone [ă-tòn'] v.i. dare soddisfazione, fare ammenda.

Atonement [ă-tòn'mĕnt] n. espiazione, riparazione.

Atrocious [ă-trò'sciăs] a. atroce.

Atrocity [ă-trò'sĭ-tĭ] n. atrocità.

Atrophy [ă'trò-fĭ] n. atrofia.

Attach [ă-tĕ'c'] v.t. attaccare, attribuire, fissare; v.i. attaccarsi, aderire.

Attaché [pron. fran.] n. diplomatico, addetto ad un'ambasciata; a. **-case** [chĕs] valigetta.

Attached [ă-tĕc't'] a. affezionato.

Attachment [ă-tèć'mĕnt] n. affetto, attaccamento.

Attack [ă-tèć'] n. attacco, offensiva; v.t. assalire, attaccare.

Attain [ă-tēn'] v.t. conseguire, ottenere, raggiungere; v.i. arrivare.

Attainable [ă-te'nă-bl] a. conseguibile, reggiungibile.

Attainment [ă-tēn'mĕnt] n. conseguimento; -s (pl.) coltura.

Attaint [ă-tént'] v.t. privare dei diritti civili (per tradimento).

Attempt [ă-tĕmt'] n. attentato, tentativo; v.t. provare, tentare.

Attend [ă-tĕnd] v.t. accompagnare, frequentare; v.i. attendere a, prestar attenzione, dare assistenza, essere presente.

Attendance [ă-tĕn'dĕns] n. complesso delle persone presenti, servizio.

Attendant [ă-tĕn'dĕnt] n. cameriere, servente.

Attention [ă-ten'sñ] n. attenzione, premura; to pay [pe⁴] a. stare attento.

Attentive [ă-tĕn'tĭv] a. attento, premuroso.

Attenuation [ă-tĕ-niŭ-é'ñ] n. attenuazione, dimagramento.

Attenuate [ă-tĕ'niŭ-ét] v.t. attenuare.

Attest [ă-tĕst'] v.t. attestare; v.i. testimoniare.

Attestation [ă-tĕs-té'sñ] n. attestazione conferma.

Attic [ĕ'tic] n. soffitta, solaio.

Attire [è-ta¹ᵉʳ] n. (raro) abbigliamento.

Attitude [è'tĭ-tiŭd] n. atteggiamento, attitudine, posa.

Attorney [ă-tĕ'ʳnĬ] n. procuratore. [attrarre.

Attract [ă-trèct'] v.t. attirare,

Attraction [ă-trèc'sñ] n. attrazione.

Attractive [ă-trèc'tĭv] a. attraente, attrattivo.

Attribute [ă'trĬ-biŭt] n. attributo, qualità; [ă-trĬ'biŭt] v.t. attribuire.

Attrition [ă-trĬ'sñ] n. attrito.

Attune [ă-tiŭn] v.t. armonizzare.

Auburn [ó'bĕ'ʳn] a. color rame, ramato.

Auction [óc'sñ] n. asta, vendita all'incanto; v.t. vendere all'asta.

Auctioneer [óc-sciò-n¹ᵉʳ] n. banditore. [audace.

Audacious [ó-dé'sciăs] a.

Audacity [ó-dè'si-tĬ] n. audacia.

Audible [ó'dĬ-bl] a. udibile.

Audience [ó'dĬ-ĕns] n. pubblico, udienza.

Audit [ó'dĬt] n. controllo, verifica di conti; v.t. verificare ufficialmente i conti.

Auditor [ó'dĬ-tĕʳ] n. revisore (di conti), (legge) auditore.

Auger [ó'ghĕʳ] n. succhiello.

Aught [ót] pron. (arcaico) qualche cosa; a. per quello che.

Augment [óg-mĕnt'] v.t. aumentare; v.i. crescere.

Augmentation [óg-mĕn-té-sñ] n. aumento.

Augur [ó'ghĕʳ] n. augure; v.t. e i. predire, presagire.

Augury [ó'guĭ-rĬ] n. presagio, presentimento.

August [ó'găst] n. agosto.

August [ó-găst'] a. augusto, maestoso.

Aunt [ănt] n. zia.

Auspice [ó'spĬs] n. auspicio, previsione.

Auspicious [ó-spĬ'sciăs] a. di buon augurio.

Austere [ó-sti¹ᵉʳ] a. austero.

Austerity [ó-stĕ'rĬ-tĬ] n. austerità.

Authentic [ó-thĕn'tĬc] a. autentico.

Authenticate [ó-thĕn'ti-chét] *v.t.* autenticare.

Authentication [ó'thĕn-ti-ché'śn] *n.* autenticazione.

Authenticity [ó-thĕn-ti'śi-ti] *n.* autenticità.

Author [ó'thĕr] *n.* autore.

Authoritative [ó-thó'ri-tè-tiv] *a.* autorevole, autoritario.

Authority [ó-thó'ri-ti] *n.* autorità.

Authorization [ó-thó-ra¹-zé¹śn] *n.* autorizzazione.

Authorize [ó'thó-ra¹z] *v.t.* autorizzare.

Autobiography [ó-tò-ba¹-ó'gră-fi] *n.* autobiografia.

Autocrat [ó'tò-crĕt] *n.* autocrate.

Autograph [ó'tò-grèf] *n.* autografo; *v.t.* autografare.

Automatic [ó-tò-mè'tic] *n.* rivoltella; *a.* automatico.

Autonomy [ó-tò'nò-mi] *n.* autonomia.

Autopsy [ó-tòp'si] *n.* autopsia.

Autumn [ó'tăm] *n.* autunno.

Autumnal [ó-tăm'nĕl] *a.* autunnale, d'autunno.

Auxiliary [óg-zi'li-ă-ri] *n.* ausiliare; *a.* ausilio/rio, -re.

Avail [ă-vél'] *n.* (*raro*) utilità, vantaggio; *v.t.* essere utile, valere; **to avail oneself of** (*rifl*) valersi di.

Available [ă-vé'lă-bl] *a.* trovabile, valevole.

Avalanche [*pron. fran.*] *n.* valanga.

Avarice [ă'vă-rís] *n.* avarizia.

Avaricious [ă-vă-ri'sciús] *a.* avaro.

Avenge [ă-vĕng'] *v.t.* vendicare.

Avenger [ă-vĕn'gĕr] *n.* vendicatore, vindice.

Avenue [ă'vĕ-niú] *n.* viale.

Aver [ă-vĕr'] *v.t.* affermare, asserire.

Average [ă'vĕ-riġ] *n.* media; [*naut.*] avaria; *a.* di media

categoria medio: *v.t.* fare la media.

Averse [ă-vĕr's'] *a.* avverso, contrario.

Aversion [ă-vĕr'śn] *p.* antipatia.

Avert [ă-vĕr't'] *v.t.* allontanare, distogliere.

Aviary [é'vi-ĕ-ri] *n.* aviario.

Avid [ă'vid] *a.* avido.

Avidity [ă-vi'di-ti] *n.* avidità.

Avocation [ă-vò-ché'śn] *n.* occupazione, vocazione.

Avoid [ă-vo¹d'] *v.t.* evitare, schivare.

Avouch [ă-vauċ'] *v.t.* confessare, garantire.

Avow [ă-vau'] *v.t.* ammettere, confessare.

Avowal [ă-vau'ĕl] *n.* ammissione, confessione.

Await [ă-uét'] *v.t.* aspettare.

Awake [ă-uéc'] *a.* *pred.* sveglio, *v.t.* e i. svegliar(si).

Awakening [ă-uéc'ニ赿] *n.* risorgimento, risveglio.

Award [ă-uo^rd'] *n.* giudizio, *v.t.* aggiudicare, conferire.

Aware [ă-uér'] *a.* *pred.* conscio.

Away [ă-ué¹] *av.* lontano, via.

Awe [ó] *n.* timore misto a venerazione.

Awful [ó'fŭl] *a.* spaventoso, tragico.

Awfulness [ó'fŭl-nĕs] *n.* tragicità.

Awkward [óc'ue^rd] *a.* difficile, goffo, sgraziato.

Awkwardness [óc'ue^rd-nĕs] *n.* difficoltà, goffaggine.

Awl [ól] *n.* lesina.

Awning [ó'niñ] *n.* tenda.

Axe [ĕcs] *n.* ascia.

Axiom [ĕc'si'ăm] *n.* assioma.

Axis [ĕc'sis] *n.* asse.

Axle [ĕc'sĕl] *n.* asse (su cui girano le ruote).

Ay [a¹] *av.* si.

Aye [e¹] *av.* (*poet.*) sempre.

Azure [ă'jĕ'] *a.* azzurro.

B

Babble [bè'bl] *v.t.* balbettare, rivelare (un segreto); *v.i.* balbettare, parlare scioccamente.
Babbling [bè'blín] *n.* balbettio, discorso senza senso.
Babe [béb] *n.* (*poet.*) bimbo.
Baboon [bă-bun'] *n.* babbuino.
Baby [bé'bĭ] *n.* bimbo.
Babyhood [bé'bĭ-hŭd] *n.* prima infanzia.
Babyish [bé'bĭ-iš] *a.* bambinesco, infantile, puerile.
Bachelor [bè'cĕ-lĕr] *n.* celibe, scapolo, baccelliere.
Back [bèc] *n.* dorso, parte posteriore, schiena, schienale, spalle (*pl.*); spalliera; *a.* arretrato, posteriore.
Back [bèc] *av.* di dietro, di ritorno; be [bĭ] b. essere di ritorno; come [căm] b. ritornare.
Back [bèc] *v.t.* aiutare, spalleggiare; b. a horse [ho²s] puntare su un cavallo.
Backbite [bèc'ba²t] *v.t. e i.* calunniare.
Backbone [bèc'bòn] *n.* spina dorsale.
Background [bèc'graund] *n.* sfondo; (*fig.*) oscurità.
Backward [bèc'ue²d] *a.* arretrato, riluttante, tardivo.
Backwards [bèc'ue²dz] *av.* (all') indietro, a rovescio.
Bacon [bé'c'n] *n.* lardo affumicato, pancetta.
Bad [bèd] *a.* cattivo, colpevole, dannoso, grave, sfavorevole; to go [gò] b. andare a male.
Badge [bèg] *n.* distintivo, emblema.
Badger [bè'ge²] *n.* tasso (animale); [celiare.
Badinage [*pron. fran.*] *n.* il
Badness [bèd'nès] *n.* cattiveria, inferiorità (di qualità)

Baffle [bè'fl] *v.t.* impedire, rendere perplesso, rendere vano.
Bag [bèg] *n.* borsa, borsetta, sacco, carniera, pesci o selvaggina presi, corrispondenza; *v.t.* insaccare, prendere, rubare.
Bagatelle [bă-gă-tĕl'] *n.* bagatella.
Baggage [bè'ghíg] *n.* bagagli(o).
Bagpipe(s) [bèg'pa²ps] *n.* (*più comunem. al pl.*) cornamusa.
Bail [bél] *n.* cauzione, garanzia, garante; to go [gò] b. for, essere garante di; *v.t.* procurare la libertà provvisoria a, aggottare (una barca).
Bailiff [bé'lif] *n.* ufficiale civile alle dipendenze d'uno sceriffo, fattore di campagna.
Bait [bét] *n.* esca; *v.t.* esasperare, tormentare, fornire di esca; *v.i.* prendere cibo.
Bake [béc'] *v.t.* cuocere in forno; *v.i.* indurirsi per effetto del calore.
Bake-house [béc'haus], bakery [bé'chĕ-rĭ] *n.* forno.
Baker [bé'chĕr] *n.* fornaio.
Balance [bè'lèns] *n.* bilancio, equilibrio, armonia; (*comm.*) differenza, saldo; to lose one's [luz uăns] b. perdere il dominio di sè stesso; *v.t.* compensare, confrontare, controbilanciare, pesare; *v.i.* bilanciarsi.
Balance-sheet [bè'lèns-scìt] *n.* (*comm.*) bilancio.
Balcony [bèl'cō-ni] *n.* balcone.
Bald [bóld] *a.* calvo, nudo, (di stile) disadorno.
Baldness [bóld'nès] *n.* calvizie (*pl.*); nudità.
Bale [bél] *n.* (*poet. e arcaico*) distruzione, dolore; (*comm.*) balla; *v.t.* imballare.
Baleful [bèl'fŭl] *a.* distruttivo, infausto.
Balk [bóc] *n.* striscia di

terreno non arata, trave rozzamente digrossata; *v.t.* evitare, ostacolare; *v.i.* scoraggiarsi.

Ball [bôl] *n.* ballo, globo, sfera celeste, palla, pallottola.

Ballad [bè'lèd] *n.* poesia lirica di carattere popolare.

Ballast [bè'lèst] *n.* (*naut.*) zavorra.

Balloon [bè-lûn'] *n.* aerostato, pallone.

Ballot [bè'lŏt] *n.* scheda (di votazione), votazione segreta; *v.i.* votare segretamente.

Ballot-box [bè'lŏt-bŏcs] *n.* urna elettorale.

Balm [bäm] *n.* balsamo.

Balmy [bä'mi] *a.* balsamico, fragrante.

Balsam [bôl'săm] *n.* balsamo.

Balsamic [bôl'să-mic] *a.* balsamico, salubre.

Baluster [bè'lăs-tě^r] *n.* balaustro.

Balustrade [bè'lăs-tréd] *n.* balaustra(ta).

Bamboo [bèm-bū'] *n.* bambù.

Bamboozle [bèm-bū'zl] *v.t.* (*gergo*) ingannare, mistificare.

Ban [bèn] *n.* (sentenza di bando, maledizione, scomunica *v.t.* interdire, proibire; (*arcaico*) maledire.

Banal [bé'nèl] *a.* banale.

Band [bènd] *n.* banda, legame, striscia, (*arcaico*) promessa; *v.t.* legare insieme; *v.i.* unirsi.

Bandage [bèn'dîg] *n.* benda, fascia.

Bandbox [bènd'bŏcs] *n.* cappelliera.

Bandit [bèn'dît] *n.* bandito.

Bandolier [bèn-dò-li'er'] *n.* bandoliera.

Bandsman [bèns'măn] *n.* componente d'una banda.

Bandy [bèn'di] *a.* arcato, curvo, storto; *v.t.* gettare, mandare avanti e indietro, scambiare.

Bane [bén] *n.* rovina, veleno.

Baneful [bén'fûl] *a.* dannoso, velenoso.

Bang [bèn] *n.* colpo rumoroso, esplosione, fracasso; *v.t.* colpire rumorosamente, sbattacchiare.

Bangle [bèn'gl] *n.* braccialetto

Banish [bè'nîš] *v.t.* bandire, esiliare.

Banishment [bè'nîš-mènt] *n.* bando, esilio.

Banister [bè'nîs-tě^r] *n.* ringhiera (di scale).

Bank [bènc] *n.* argine, elevazione di terreno, riva, banca, banco; *v.t.* arginare, depositare in una banca.

Bank-bill [bènc'bîl] *n.* vaglia bancario.

Banker [bèn'chě^r] *n.* banchiere.

Bank-holiday [bènc-hŏ'lî-déⁱ] *n.* festa civile.

Banking [bèn'chîn] *n.* operazione bancaria; *a.* bancario.

Bank-note [bènc'nòt] *n.* banconota.

Bankrupt [bènc'răpt] *n.* fallito; *a.* fallito, insolvente; to go [go] b. far fallimento.

Bankruptcy [bènc'răpt-sî] *n.* fallimento.

Banner [bè'ně^r] *n.* bandiera, stendardo.

Banns [bèns] *n.* (*pl.*) pubblicazioni matrimoniali (*pl.*).

Banquet [bèn'quèt] *n.* banchetto; *v.i.* banchettare.

Banter [bèn'tě^r] *n.* il beffarsi; *v.t. e i.* prendere in giro, beffarsi.

Baptism [bèp'tîzm] *n.* battesimo.

Baptismal [bèp-tîz'mèl] *a.* battesimale.

Baptistery [bèp'tîs-trî] *n.* battistero.

Baptize [bèp'taⁱz] *v.t.* battezzare.

Bar [bă^r] *n.* barriera, limite, ostacolo, sbarra; the bar.

collegio degli avvocati penalisti; *v.t.* (s)barrare, escludere, ostacolare.

Barbarian [bar-bè'ri-ĕn] *a. e n.* barbaro.

Barbaric [bar-bè'ric] *a.* barbarico, incolto.

Barbarism [bar'bè-rìzm] *n.* barbarie, barbarismo.

Barbarity [bar'-bè'rì-tĭ] *n.* barbarie, crudeltà.

Barbarous [bar'bă-răs] *a.* barbaro.

Barbed [barbd] *a.* pungente, spinato; b. wire [uä'ier] n. filo di ferro spinato.

Barber [bar'bĕr] *n.* barbiere, parrucchiere. [vate.

Bard [bard] *n.* (*poet.*) bardo.

Bare [bèer] *a.* desolato, nudo, schietto, scoperto; *v.t.* denudare, scoprire.

Barefaced [bèer'fèst] *a.* impudente, sfrontato.

Barefoot(ed) [bèer'fŭt(id)] *a. e av.* a piedi nudi, scalzo.

Bareheaded [bèer-hè'did] *a. e av.* a testa scoperta.

Barely [bèer'lǐ] *av.* appena, a mala pena.

Bareness [bèer'nĕs] *n.* nudità.

Bargain [bar'ghĕn] *n.* affare, occasione; into the b. in aggiunta; *v.i.* contrattare, stiracchiare sul prezzo.

Barge [barg] *n.* (*naut.*) barca di parata, chiatta, lancia.

Baritone [bar'ri-tòn] *a. e n.* baritono.

Bark [bark] *n.* l'abbaiare dei cani; (*poet.*) barca, corteccia, scorza (d'albero); *v.t.* scorticare, **scorzare**; *v.i.* abbaiare.

Barley [bar'lǐ] *n.* orzo.

Barm [barm] *n.* fermento, lievito di birra.

Barn [barn] *n.* granaio; b.-yard [iard] aia, cortile di fattoria.

Barnacle [bar'nă-cl] *n.* cirripede.

Barometer [bă-rŏ'mì-tĕr] *n.* barometro.

Baron(ess) [bè'rŏn(ĕs)] *n.* barone(ssa).

Baronet [bè'rŏ-nĕt] *n.* baronetto.

Baroque [bă-ròc'] *a. e n.* barocco.

Barouche [bă-ruš'] *n.* (*arcaico*) carrozza.

Barrack [bè'rĕc] *n.* (*più comunem. al pl.*) caserma.

Barrage [bè'rǐg] *n.* (*mil.*) sbarramento.

Barrel [bè'rĕl] *n.* barile, canna (di fucile).

Barren [bè'rĕn] *a.* sterile.

Barrenness [bè'rĕn-nĕs] *n.* sterilità.

Barricade [bè-rì-chéd'] *n.* barricata.

Barrier [bè'rì-ĕr] *n.* barriera.

Barrister [bè'ris-tĕr] *n.* avvocato, penalista.

Barrow [bè'rò] *n.* carretta (a due ruote), carriola.

Barter [bar'tĕr] *n.* baratto; *v.t.* barattare, scambiare.

Barterer [bar'tĕ-rĕr] *n.* barattiere, trafficante.

Basalt [bă'sŏlt] *n.* basalto.

Base [bés] *n.* base, fondamento; *a.* basso, meschino, vile; *v.t.* basare, fondare.

Baseless [bés'lĕs] *a.* infondato, senza base.

Basement [bés'mĕnt] *n.* sottosuolo.

Baseness [bés'nĕs] *n.* bassezza, viltà. [vergognoso

Bashful [bèš'fŭl] *a.* timido, **Bashfulness** [bèš'fŭl-nĕs] *n.* timidezza, vergogna.

Basic [bé'sic] *a.* basilare, fondamentale.

Basil [bè'zil] *n.* basilico.

Basin [bé'sin] *n.* bacino, bacinella, catino.

Basis [bé'sis] *n.* base.

Bask [bask] *v.i.* godersi il caldo o il sole.

Basket [băs'chĕt] n. cesta, cesto, paniere.

Bas-relief [bè-rĭ-lĭf'] n. basso rilievo.

Bastard [bès'tĕªd] a. e n. bastardo.

Bastardy [bès'tĕª-dĭ] n. bastardaggine.

Baste [bést] v.t. arrosolare, imbastire, bastonare.

Bastion [bès'tĭ-ŏn] n. bastione.

Bat [bèt] n. grosso bastone, bastone per il giuoco del cricket, pipistrello.

Bate [bét] v.t. diminuire, ridurre.

Bath [bâth] n. bagno, tinozza; to take [téc] a. b. fare il bagno; v.t. e i. [far] fare il bagno.

Bathe [béth] n. bagno (di mare, ecc.); v.t. e i. bagnar(si), fare il bagno (nel mare, ecc.).

Bather [bé'dhĕª] n. bagnante.

Bathos [bé'thŏs] n. discesa dal sublime al ridicolo.

Batman [bèt'măn] n. (mil.) attendente.

Baton [bè'tn] n. bacchetta, bastone di comando.

Battalion [bè-tè'lĭ-ŏn] n. battaglione.

Batten [bè'tĕn] n. assicella, traversa in legno; v.t. rinforzare con legno; to b. down [daun] (naut.) chiudere in boccaporto.

Batter [bè'tĕª] n. piatto speciale ingl., a base di farina e uova; v.t. battere violentemente, cannoneggiare.

Battering-ram [bè'tĕ-rĭñ rěm] n. ariete.

Battery [bè'tĕ-rĭ] n. (mil., elettr.) batteria.

Battle [bè'tl] n. battaglia, combattimento; v.i. combattere, lottare.

Battlement [bè'tl-mĕnt] n. parapetto merlato.

Bauble [bô'bl] n. ornamento di poco valore, bastone dei buffoni.

Bawd [bôd] n. mezzana.

Bawl [bôl] v.i. gridare ad alta voce, schiamazzare.

Bay [bè¹] n. baia, insenatura del mare, lauro, recesso (d'una finestra, ecc.), latrato di grosso cane; to hold [hôld] at b. tenere a bada.

Bay [be¹] v.i. abbaiare, latrare.

Bayonet [bé'ŏ-nĕt] n. baionetta.

Bazaar [bă-zâª'] n. bazar.

Be [bĭ] v.i. e aus. essere, esistere, vivere, stare, andare, venire; to be to, dovere.

Beach [bĭć] n. lido, spiaggia.

Beacon [bĭ'cn] n. faro, fuoco (acceso come segnale).

Bead [bĭd] n. grano (di collana, ecc.), bolla, goccia (di liquidi, mira (di fucile); beads (pl.) rosario; v.t. ornare di grani; v.i. imperlarsi.

Beadle [bĭ'dl] n. bidello, sagrestano.

Beagle [bĭ'ghĕl] n. piccolo cane da caccia.

Beak [bĭc] n. becco, rostro (di uccello o di nave).

Beaker [bĭ'chĕª] n. coppa.

Beam [bĭm] n. trave, raggio (di luce), sorriso; v.i risplendere, sorridere.

Bean [bĭn] n. fagiolo, fava; full [fŭl] of beans (gergo), energico, vivace.

Bear [béeª] n. orso.

Bear [béeª] v.t. portare, sopportare, tollerare, partorire, produrre; v.i. dirigersi, inclinare; to b. oneself (rifl.) comportarsi.

Bearable [bé'ră-bl] a. sopportabile.

Beard [bĭeªd] n. barba.

Bearded [bĭeª'dĭd] a. barbuto.

Beardless [bĭeª'd'lès] a. imberbe. [portatore.

Bearer [bé'rĕª] n. latore

Bearing [bé⁰'riñ] n. condotta, portamento; -s (pl.) orientamento; [mecc.] cuscinetto.
Beast [bïst] n. animale, bestia.
Beastly [bïst'lï] a. bestiale; [gergo] orribile.
Beat [bït] n. battito, palpito, giro (di poliziotto o di sentinella); v.t. battere, vincere; v.i. battere, palpitare; to b. about the bush [bäš] menare il can per l'aia.
Beatification [bï-è'ti'fï-ché'šñ] n. beatificazione.
Beatify [bïé'ti-fa¹] v.t. beatificare.
Beating [bï'tïñ] n. azione del battere, busse (pl.); sconfitta.
Beatitude [bï-è'ti-tiûd] n. beatitudine.
Beauteous [biû'tï-äs] a. (poet.) bello.
Beautiful [biû'tï-fûl] a. bello.
Beautify [biû'tï-fa¹] v.t. abbellire.
Beauty [biû'tï] n. bellezza.
Beaver [bï'vě'] n. castoro, cappello fatto di pelo di castoro.
Becalm [bï-câm'] v.t. (naut.) fermare (di bonaccia).
Because [bï-côz'] cong. perchè.
Beck [bĕc] n. ruscello.
Beckon [bĕ'cn] v.t. e i. chiamare con un cenno.
Become [bï-câm'] v.i. accadere, divenire, diventare; v.t. convenire a, star bene a.
Becoming [bï-cǎ'mïñ] a. conveniente, che s'addice a.
Bed [bĕd] n. letto, giaciglio, alveo (di fiume).
Bedaub [bï-dôb'] v.t. imbrattare le tele, dare una mano di vernice a.
Bedding [bĕ'dïñ] n. materasso, coperte (pl.) ecc. da letto, lettiera (per bestiame).
Bedew [bï-diû'] v.t. irrorare.
Bedizen [bï-da¹'zn] v.t. (raro) vestire in modo sgargiante.

Bedlam [bĕd'lĕm] n. grande confusione, manicomio.
Bedouin [bě-dü-én'] n. beduino.
Bedraggle [bï-drè'gl] v.t. sporcare trascinando nel fango.
Bedridden [bĕd'rï-dn] a. allettato.
Bedroom [bĕd'rûm] n. camera (da letto).
Bedstead [bĕd'stĕd] n. fusto (del letto).
Bee [bï] n. ape; **b.-line** [la¹n] linea diretta.
Beech [bïč] n. faggio.
Beef [bïf] n. carne di bue, manzo; b. steak [stéc] bistecca.
Beehive [bï'ha¹v] n. alveare.
Beer [bïᵉʳ] n. birra; b. -house [haus] birreria.
Beet(root) [bït'rût] n. barbabietola.
Beetle [bï'tl] n. scarafaggio, mazzeranga.
Befall [bï-fôl'] v.t. accadere a, capitare a; v.i. succedere.
Befit [bï-fït'] v.t. essere adatto a, andar bene per.
Befitting [bï-fï'tïñ] a. adatto, conveniente.
Before [bï-foʳ'] av. avanti, davanti, prima; prep. davanti a, prima di; cong. prima che.
Beforehand [bï-foʳ'hĕnd] av. in anticipo.
Befriend [bï-frĕnd'] v.t. [aiutare.
Beg [bĕg] v.t. implorare, pregare, invitare; v.i. elemosinare, stendere la mano.
Beget [bï-ghĕt'] v.t. generare.
Beggar [bĕ'ghĕʳ] n. mendicante.
Beggarly [bĕ'ghĕʳ-lï] a. meschino, povero.
Beggary [bĕ'ghĕ-rï] n. estrema miseria, mendicità.
Begin [bï-ghïn'] v.t. e i. cominciare, iniziare, intraprendere, mettersi a.
Beginner [bï-ghï'nĕʳ] n. principiante.

Beverage [bĕ've-rĭg] n. bevanda.

Bevy [bĕ'vĭ] n. compagnia, stormo.

Bewail [bĭ-uél'] v.t. e i. deplorare, lamentar(si).

Beware [bĭ-uér'] v.i. (difett.) stare in guardia.

Bewilder [bĭ-uĭl'dĕr] v.t. confondere, rendere perplesso.

Bewilderment [bĭ-uĭl'dĕrmĕnt] n. confusione mentale.

Bewitch [bĭ-uĭc'] v.t. ammaliare, stregare.

Beyond [bĭ-iŏnd'] prep. av. e n. al di là (di); the back [bĕc] of b. il più remoto angolo della terra.

Bias [baì'ĕs] n. inclinazione, pregiudizio; on the b. per sbieco; v.t. far inclinare, influenzare.

Bib [bĭb] n. bavaglino.

Bible [baì'bl] n. bibbia.

Biblical [bĭ'blĭ-cl] a. biblico.

Bibliography [bĭ-blĭ-ò'grä-fĭ] n. bibliografia.

Bibliology [bĭ-blĭ-ò'lò-gĭ] n. bibliologia.

Bibliophile [bĭ'blĭ-ò-fĭl] n. bibliofilo.

Bicarbonate [baì-cä'r'bò-nét] n. bicarbonato.

Bicker [bĭ'chĕr'] v.i. becchettarsi, litigare.

Bicycle [baì'sĭ-cl] n. bicicletta.

Bid [bĭd] n. offerta (di prezzo), proposta; v.t. comandare, dire, offrire.

Bidder [bĭ'dĕr] n. offerente (in un'asta).

Bidding [bĭ'dĭñ] n. comando, offerta [di prezzo].

Bide [baìd] v.t. e i. [arcaico] aspettare, dimorare.

Biennial [baì-ĕ'nĭ-ĕl] a. biennale.

Bier [bĭer] n. bara.

Big [bĭg] a. grande, gravido, grosso, importante; **bigwig** [uĭg] (gergo) pezzo grosso.

Bigamist [bĭ'gä-mĭst] n. bigamo.

Bigamy [bĭ'gä-mĭ] n. bigamia.

Bilateral [baì-lè'tè-rĕl] a. bilaterale.

Bile [baìl] n. bile.

Bilge [bĭlg] n. (naut.) sentina.

Bilingual [baì-lĭñ'guĕl] a. bilingue.

Bilious [bĭ'lĭ-äs] a. biliare, bilioso.

Bill [bĭl] n. becco, conto, fattura, lista, nota, proposta di legge.

Billiards [bĭl'ĭĕ'dz] n. (pl.) biliardo.

Billow [bĭ'lò] n. flutto, maroso.

Billowy [bĭ'lò-ĭ] a. pieno di marosi, vaporoso.

Bin [bĭn] n. recipiente (per grano, carbone ecc.).

Binary [baì'nĕ-rĭ] a. binario.

Bind [baìnd] v.t. attaccare, fissare, (ri)legare, obbligare.

Binding [baìn'dĭñ] n. rilegatura; a. obbligatorio, costrittivo.

Bindweed [baìnd'uĭd] n. convolvolo.

Binocular [baì-nò'chiù-lĕr] a. binoccolo.

Biographer [baì-ò'grè-fĕr] n. biografo.

Biography [baì-ò'grè-fĭr] n. biografia. [logia.

Biology [baì-ò'lò-gĭ] n. bio-

Biped [baì'pĕd] a. e n. bipede.

Birch [bĕrc] n. betulla, sferza.

Bird [bĕrd] n. uccello.

Bird-lime [bĕrd'laìm] n. vischio.

Bird's eye view [bĕrds aì'viù] n. panorama a volo d'uccello.

Birth [bĕrth] n. nascita, origine, discendenza.

Birthday [bĕrth'deì] n. compleanno.

Birth-place [bĕrth'plés] n. luogo di nascita.

Birth-right [bẽ⁴th'ra⁴t] n. diritto di primogenito.

Biscuit [bĭs'chĭt] n. biscotto.

Bisect [ba⁴-sēct'] v.t. bisecare.

Bishop [bĭ'sciŏp] n. vescovo, alfiere [a scacchi].

Bishopric [bĭ'sciŏp-rĭc] n. vescovado.

Bismuth [bĭz'mŭth] n. bismuto.

Bit [bĭt] n. boccone, morso (di cibo o della briglia), pezzetto, breve spazio di tempo.

Bitch [bĭć] n. cagna, lupa, volpe femmina.

Bite [ba⁴t] n. morsicatura, morso, qualcosa da mangiare; v.t. mordere, pungere.

Biting [ba⁴tĭñ] a. pungente, sarcastico.

Bitter [bĭ'tẽʳ] n. amarezza, amaro (liquore): a. amaro, aspro.

Bitterness [bĭ'tẽʳ-nĕs] n. amarezza.

Bitumen [ba⁴-tiŭ'mĕn] n. bitume.

Bivouac [bĭ'vŭ-éc] n. bivacco.

Blab [blĕb] v.t. rivelare indiscretamente; v.i. chiacchierare.

Black [blĕc] a. e n. nero; a. minaccioso, oscuro, triste.

Blackberry [blĕc'bĕ-ri] n. mora.

Blackbird [blĕc'bẽʳd] n. merlo.

Blacken [blĕ'cn] v.t. annerire, diffamare.

Blackguard [blĕc'gaʳd] n. mascalzone.

Blacking [blĕ'chĭñ] n. crema per lucidare in nero le scarpe.

Blackish [blĕc'chĭš] a. nerastro.

Blackleg [blĕc'lĕg] n. crumiro.

Blackmail [blĕc'mél] n. ricatto; v.t. ricattare.

Blacksmith [blĕc'smĭth] n. fabbro-ferraio.

Bladder [blĕ'dẽʳ] n. vescica.

Blade [blĕd] n. filo (d'erba), lama.

Blain [blĕn] n. pustola.

Blame [blĕm] n. biasimo, censura, colpa; v.t. biasimare, censurare.

Blameless [blĕm'lĕs] a. innocente, irreprensibile.

Blanch [blĕnć] v.t. scolorire; v.i. impallidire. [ironico.

Bland [blĕnd] a. blando.

Blandishment [blĕn'dĭš-mĕnt] n. blandizia.

Blank [blĕnc] n. lacuna, spazio bianco.

Blanket [blĕn'chĕt] n. coperta di lana.

Blankness [blĕnc'nĕs] n. vuoto.

Blaspheme [blès-fĭm'] v.t. e i. bestemmiare.

Blasphemous [blès'fĭ-mäs] a. empio.

Blasphemy [blès'fĭ-mi] n. bestemmia.

Blast [blăst] n. esplosione, raffica, squillo; v.t. disseccare, inaridire, far saltare, maledire.

Blasting [blăs'tĭñ] a. distruttore.

Blaze [blèz] n. fiamma, vampata; v.i. divampare, fiammeggiare.

Blazon [blé'zĕn] n. blasone, stemma.

Blazonry [blé'zĕn-ri] n. araldica.

Bleach [blĭć] v.t. imbiancare.

Bleak [blĭc] a. esposto al vento, freddo, squallido.

Blear [blⁱeʳ] a. oscuro, turbato; b-eyed [a⁴d] dagli occhi cisposi.

Bleat [blĭt] v.i. belare.

Bleed [blĭd] v.i. sanguinare; v.t. salassare.

Blemish [blĕ'mĭš] n. macchia, difetto (morale o fisico).

Blench [blĕnć] v.i. indietreggiare.

Blend [blĕnd] n. miscela, miscuglio; v.t. e i. mescolar(si)

Bless [blĕs] *v.t.* benedire, consacrare.

Blessing [blĕ'sĭń] *n.* benedizione.

Blight [blaꞮt] *n.* malattia delle piante, influenza maligna; *v.t.* inaridire, esercitare un'influenza maligna su.

Blind [blaꞮnd] *n.* persiana, avvolgibile; *a.* cieco, senza apertura, senza discernimento; *v.t.* accecare.

Blindfold [blaꞮnd'fōld] *av.* ad occhi bendati.

Blindness [blaꞮnd'nĕs] *n.* cecità, mancanza di discernimento.

Blink [blĭnc] *n.* occhiata, sguardo rapido, guizzo di luce; *v.i.* battere gli occhi.

Bliss [blĭs] *n.* beatitudine.

Blissful [blĭs'fŭl] *a.* beato.

Blister [blĭs'tĕr] *n.* bolla, vescica; *v.t.* far venire vesciche a; *v.i.* coprirsi di vesciche.

Blithe [blaꞮth] *a.* giocondo.

Blitheness [blaꞮth'nĕs] *n.* giocondità.

Bloat [blōt] *v.t. e i.* gonfiar(si).

Block [blŏc] *n.* blocco, ceppo, gruppo di case, ostacolo; *v.t.* bloccare, ostacolare, fare opposizione a.

Blockade [blŏ-chéd'] *n.* assedio, blocco.

Blockhead [blŏc'hĕd] *n.* stupido.

Blockhouse [blŏc'haus] *n.* fortino isolato.

Blond(e) [blŏnd] *a. e n.* biondo.

Blood [blăd] *n.* sangue, discendenza, parentela.

Bloodhound [blăd'haund] *n.* segugio.

Bloodless [blăd'lĕs] *a.* esangue, pallido.

Bloodshed [blăd'scĕd] *n.* spargimento di sangue.

Bloody [blă'dĭ] *a.* sanguinario, sanguinoso.

Bloom [blūm] *n.* fiore, fioritura, incarnato; *v.i.* fiorire, sbocciare. [rente, fresco.

Blooming [blū'mĭń] *a.* flo-

Blossom [blŏ'săm] *n.* fiore, fioritura; *v.i.* fiorire.

Blot [blŏt] *n.* cancellatura, macchia, colpa, difetto; *v.t.* asciugare con carta assorbente, cancellare, macchiare.

Blotch [blŏč] *n.* macchia (sulla pelle), sgorbio; *v.t.* macchiare.

Blotting-paper [blŏ'tĭń pé'pĕr] *n.* carta assorbente.

Blouse [blauz] *n.* blusa, camicetta.

Blow [blō] *n.* colpo; *v.t.* soffiare, sonare (uno strumento a fiato); *v.i.* ansare, sibilare, soffiare, tirare (vento).

Blowzy [blau'zĭ] *a.* scapigliato.

Blubber [blă'bĕr] *n.* grasso di balena, pianto rumoroso; *v.i.* piangere rumorosamente.

Bludgeon [blă'gĕn] *n.* mazza ferrata.

Blue [blu] *a. e n.* azzurro, blu, celeste, turchino; *a.* nervoso, triste; to look [lŭc] b. (*gergo*) essere depresso.

Bluebell [blū'bĕl] *n.* giacinto selvatico.

Blue-book [blū'bŭc] *n.* rapporto parlamentare.

Bluebottle [blū'bŏ-tl] *n.* moscone.

Blue-stocking [blū'stŏ-chĭń] *n.* donna saputa.

Bluff [blăf] *a.* cordiale, sgarbato; *v.t.* ingannare.

Bluffness [blăf'nĕs] *n.* cordialità, sgarbatezza.

Bluish [blū'ĭš] *a.* azzurrognolo.

Blunder [blăn'dĕr] *n.* errore grossolano, svista, topica; *v.t. e i.* condurre maldestramente (un affare), fare un errore.

Blunderbuss [blăn'dĕr băs] *n.* vecchio fucile.

Blunt [blănt] *a.* insensibile, ottuso, spuntato, sgarbato; *v.t.* ottundere, rendere insensibile.

Bluntness [blănt'nĕs] *n.* ottusità, sgarbatezza.

Blur [blĕ'r] *n.* confusione, nebbia; *v.t.* annebbiare, fare confusione.

Blurt [blĕ't] *v.t.* dire indiscretamente, prorompere in.

Blush [blăsh] *n.* rossore; *v.i.* arrossire, vergognarsi.

Bluster [blăs'tĕ'] *n.* furia, minacce (*pl.*); *v.i.* infuriare rumoreggiando.

Blusterous [blăs'tĕ-răs] *a.* borioso, burrascoso.

Boar [bō'] *n.* cinghiale, verro.

Board [bō'd] *n.* asse, tavola, comitato, commissione, ministero, bordo (della nave), palcoscenico, pensione; *v.t.* e *i.* coprire di assi, dar pensione, tenere a pensione, salire a bordo.

Boarder [bō'r'dĕ'] *n.* convittore, pensionante.

Boarding-house [bō'r'dĭń haus] *n.* pensione; **b. -school** [scūl] convitto.

Boast [bōst] *n.* vanteria, vanto, impresa di cui uno va glorioso; *v.t.* e *i.* vantar(si).

Boastful [bōst'fŭl] *a.* millantatore.

Boat [bōt] *n.* barca, battello, vapore; **in the same** [sĕm] **b.** con gli stessi rischi.

Boatman [bōt'măn] *n.* barcaiuolo. [nostromo.

Boatswain [bō'sn] *n.* (*naut.*)

Bob [bŏb] *v.t.* tagliare corti (i capelli); *v.i.* fare inchini, muoversi in su e in giù, tornare a galla.

Bobbin [bŏ'bĭn] *n.* bobina, rocchetto.

Bode [bōd] *v.t.* e *i.* (*raro*) presagire, **promettere** (bene o male).

Bodice [bŏ'dĭs] *n.* corpetto attillato di abito femminile.

Bodiless [bŏ'dĭ-lĕs] *a.* incorporeo.

Bodily [bŏ'dĭ-lĭ] *a.* corporeo, fisico; *av.* completamente, tutt'insieme. [filanastri.

Bodkin [bŏd'chĭn] *n.* stiletto.

Body [bŏ'dĭ] *n.* corpo, entità; **in a b.** tutti insieme.

Bog [bŏg] *n.* palude, pantano.

Boggle [bŏ'gl] *v.i.* equivocare, esitare.

Boggy [bŏ'ghĭ] *a.* paludoso.

Bogie [bō'ghĭ] *n.* (*tec.*) carrello, carretto.

Boil [boĭl] *n.* (punto di) ebollizione, foruncolo; *v.t.* e *i.* (far) bollire, lessare.

Boiler [boĭ'lĕ'] *n.* bollitore, caldaia.

Boisterous [boĭ'stĕ-răs] *a.* impetuoso, turbolento.

Bold [bōld] *a.* ardito, baldo, temerario.

Boldness [bōld'nĕs] *n.* ardimento, temerità.

Bole [bōl] *n.* tronco (d'albero).

Bolster [bōl'stĕ'] *n.* cuscino, traversino.

Bolt [bōlt] *n.* bullone, catenaccio, spranga, freccia, fulmine; *v.t.* chiudere a catenaccio, inghiottire in fretta; *v.i.* darsela a gambe, prendere la mano.

Bomb [bŏm] *n.* bomba; *v.t.* e *i.* bombardare.

Bombard [bŏm-ba'd'] *v.t.* bombardare.

Bombardment [bŏm-ba'd'mĕnt] *n.* bombardamento.

Bombast [bŏm'bĕst] *n.* linguaggio ampolloso.

Bond [bŏnd] *n.* legame, vincolo, obbligazione; (*comm.*) deposito doganale.

Bondage [bŏn'dĭǵ] *n.* schiavitù, servitù.

Bone [bŏn] *n.* osso; *v.t.* disossare.

Boneless [bòn'lĕs] *a.* senz'osso.

Bonfire [bòn'faiᵉʳ] *n.* falò.

Bonnet [bó'nĕt] *n.* berretto scozzese, cappellino legato con nastri sotto il mento; (*aut.*) cofano.

Bonny [bó'ni] *a.* bello e allegro.

Bonus [bò'năs] *n.* compenso, gratificazione.

Bony [bò'ni] *a.* ossuto.

Booby [bü'bi] *n.* individuo sciocco.

Book [bŭc] *n.* libretto, libro, registro; *v.t.* mettere in lista, prenotare (un posto), registrare; *v.i.* fare un biglietto (ferroviario).

Book-binder [bŭc-baⁱn'dĕʳ] *n.* rilegatore di libri.

Booking [bŭ'chiñ] *n.* prenotazione.

Book-keeper [bŭc'chī-pèʳ] *n.* contabile.

Book-keeping [bŭc'chī-piñ] *n.* contabilità.

Bookseller [bŭc'sĕ-lĕʳ] *n.* libraio.

Bookshop [bŭc'sciŏp] *n.* libreria.

Boom [bũm] *n.* rimbombo, palo che tien tesa una rete, barriera galleggiante in un porto, improvviso aumento di attività commerciale; *v.i.* rimbombare, avere un improvviso aumento di attività.

Boon [bũn] *n.* dono, favore, vantaggio.

Boor [boʳ] *n.* tanghero, zotico.

Boorish [bo'riš] *a.* grossolano, zotico.

Boot [bŭt] *n.* stivale, ripostiglio per bagagli in una vettura.

Bootless [bŭt'lĕs] *a.* (*raro*) senza vantaggio.

Booth [bũth] *n.* banco sormontato da tenda.

Booty [bũ'ti] *n.* bottino.

Booze [bũs] *n.* (*famil.*) bevanda alcooliche (*pl.*); *v.i.* bere all'eccesso.

Borax [bò'rĕcs] *n.* borace.

Border [boʳ'dĕʳ] *n.* bordo, confine; *a.* di confine; *v.t. e i.* confinare (con), orlare, rasentare.

Borderer [boʳ'dĕ-rĕʳ] *n.* abitante di confine.

Bordering [boʳ'dĕ-riñ] *a.* di confine, limitrofo.

Bore [boʳ] *n.* buco, foro, calibro (di fucile), noia, seccatura, seccatore; *v.t.* (per)forare, seccare, stancare, tediare.

Boreal [bò'ri-ĕl] *a.* boreale.

Boredom [boʳ'dăm] *n.* tedio.

Boring [bo'riñ] *a.* seccante, tedioso.

Born [boʳn] *a.* nato; to be [bi] b. nascere.

Borough [bă'rò] *n.* città avente amministrazione autonoma, collegio elettorale, mandamento.

Borrow [bò'rò] *v.t.* prendere a prestito.

Bosom [bŭ'zăm] *n.* petto, seno; b. friend [frĕnd] amico intimo.

Boss [bós] *n.* borchia, ornamento in rilievo; (*gergo*) padrone.

Botanic [bŏ-tè'nic] *a.* botanico.

Botanist [bŏ'tă-nist] *n.* botanico.

Botany [bŏ'tă-ni] *n.* botanica.

Botch [bŏč] *v.t.* rappezzare inabilmente.

Both [bòth] *a. e pron.* ambedue, l'uno e l'altro; both . . and, tanto . . . quanto.

Bother [bŏ'thĕʳ] *n.* fastidi(o), noia; *v.t.* seccare; *v.i.* preoccuparsi.

Bottle [bó'tl] *n.* bottiglia; fascio di fieno; *v.t.* imbottigliare.

Bottom [bó'tm] *n.* fondo; at b. in fondo.

Bottomless [bŏ'tm-lĕs] *a.* senza fondo.

Bough [bau] *n.* ramo (d'albero).

Boulder [bōl'dĕr] *n.* masso roccioso.

Bounce [bauns] *n.* rimbalzo, salto; *v.i.* (rim)balzare.

Bound [baund] *n.* confine, limite, salto, scatto; *a.* legato; b. for, diretto a; *v.t.* limitare; *v.i.* saltare, scattare.

Boundary [baun'dĕ-rĭ] *n.* linea di confine.

Boundless [baund'lĕs] *a.* illimitato.

Bounteous [baun'tĭ-ăs] *a.* benefico, generoso.

Bounty [baun'tĭ] *n.* generosità, premio d'incoraggiamento. [d'acqua.

Bourn [bu°rn] *n.* piccolo corso

Bout [baut] *n.* accesso, colpo, partita.

Bow [bō] *n.* arco, nodo.

Bow [bau] *n.* inchino; *v.i.* inchinarsi, sottomettersi.

Bowel [bau'ĕl] *n.* budello; -s (*pl.*) budella (*pl.*); (*fig.*) teneri sentimenti.

Bower [bau'ĕr] *n.* (*poet.*) luogo ombroso, camera (di fanciulla).

Bowl [bōl] *n.* ciotola, vaschetta, recipiente, boccia, palla di legno; *v.t. e i.* giocare alle bocce, rotolare.

Bowsprit [bō'sprĭt] *n.* (*naut.*) compresso.

Box [bŏcs] *n.* cassetta, scatola, sedile di vetturino, cabina (di segnalazione), banco (dei testimoni); *v.t.* mettere in scatola; *v.i.* fare del pugilato.

Boxer [bŏc'sĕr] *n.* pugilatore.

Boxing [bŏc'sĭŋ] *n.* pugilato; b. -day [de¹] il 26 dicembre.

Box-office [bŏcs-ŏ'fĭs] *n.* botteghino del teatro.

Boy [boi] *n.* ragazzo.

Boyhood [boi'hŭd] *n.* adolescenza.

Boyish [boi'ĭš] *a.* fanciullesco, giovanile.

Boyishness [boi'ĭš-nĕs] *n.* fanciullaggine, spirito giovanile.

Brace [brēs] *n.* qualunque cosa che tiene unito, paio; -s (*pl.*) bretelle (*pl.*); *v.t.* assicurare strettamente.

Bracelet [brēs'lĕt] *n.* braccialetto.

Bracken [brĕ'cn] *n.* (specie di) felce.

Bracket [brĕ'chĕt] *n.* mensola, parentesi.

Brackish [brĕ'chĭš] *a.* salso (d'acqua).

Brag [brĕg] *n.* millanteria, vanteria; *v.i.* vantarsi.

Braggart [brĕ'ga°t] *n.* millantatore, spaccone.

Brain(s) [brēns] *n.* cervello, giudizio, intelligenza.

Brain [brēn] *v.t.* accoppare.

Brake [brēc] *n.* macchia di cespugli; (*mecc.*) freno; *v.t.* frenare.

Brakesman [brēcs'măn] *n.* frenatore. [rovo.

Bramble [brĕm'bl] *n.* pruno,

Bran [brĕn] *n.* crusca.

Branch [brānč] *n.* ramo, filiale.

Branching [brān'čĭŋ] *a.* ramoso.

Brand [brĕnd] *n.* marchio, spada, tizzone.

Brandish [brĕn'dĭš] *v.t.* brandire.

Brandy [brĕn'dĭ] *n.* acquavite, cognac.

Brass [brĕs] *n.* ottone; (*fig.*) sfrontatezza.

Brassy [brĕ'sĭ] *a.* d'ottone, sfrontato.

Brat [brĕt] *n.* bambino (spregiativo).

Brave [brēv] *a.* coraggioso; *v.t.* affrontare, sfidare.

Bravery [brē'vĕ-rĭ] *n.* coraggio.

Brawl [brôl] n. rissa; v.i. litigare rumorosamente.
Brawn [brôn] n. muscolo, forza muscolare, specie di gelatina di carne.
Brawny [brô'ni] a. forte, muscoloso.
Bray [brei] v.i. ragliare.
Brazen [brè'zn] a. d'ottone, impudente; b. -faced [fèsd] sfrontato.
Brazier [brè'zier] n. braciere.
Breach [brìć] n. breccia, rottura; v.t. far breccia in, rompere.
Bread [brèd] n. pane.
Breadth [brèdth] n. ampiezza, larghezza, altezza (di tessuti).
Break [brèc] n. interruzione, rottura; v.t. domare, interrompere, infrangere, rompere, spezzare; v.i. rompersi.
Breakage [brè'chiğ] n. rottura.
Break-down [brèc'daun] n. collasso, crollo, esaurimento nervoso, incidente.
Breakfast [brèc'fèst] n. (prima) colazione.
Breakwater [brèc'uò-tèr] n. molo.
Breast [brèst] n. mammella, petto, seno; v.t. affrontare, lottare con.
Breastplate [brèst'plèt] n. piastra anteriore della corazza.
Breath [brèth] n. fiato, respiro, soffio.
Breathe [brìth] v.t. emettere; v.i. prendere fiato, respirare.
Breathing [brì'thiñ] n. respirazione, respiro.
Breathless [brèth'lès] a. ansimante, senza fiato, afoso.
Breeches [brì'ćis] n. (pl.) calzoni corti (pl.).
Breed [brìd] n. discendenza, razza; v.t. e i. allevare, generare, partorire, (ri)prodursi, tenere un allevamento.
Breeding [brì'diñ] n. alleva-

mento, educazione, buone maniere (pl.).
Breeze [brìz] n. brezza, vento leggero.
Breezy [brì'zi] a. battuto dal vento, fresco.
Brethren [brè'thrèn] n. (pl.) confratelli (pl.).
Brevet [brè'vèt] n. documento che conferisce un privilegio, grado nell'esercito senza la paga corrispondente; brevetto.
Breviary [brè'vi-è-ri] n. breviario.
Brevity [brè'vi-ti] n. brevità, concisione.
Brew [brū] v.t. fabbricare (birra), tramare; v.i. essere in fermentazione, prepararsi.
Brewer [brū'èr] n. fabbricante (di birra).
Brewery [brū'è-ri] n. fabbrica (di birra).
Bribe [bra'ib] n. dono (per corrompere o influenzare); v.t. corrompere (per mezzo di doni).
Bribery [bra'i'bè-ri] n. corruzione.
Brick [brìc] n. mattone; a. di mattoni; to drop [dròp] a b. commettere un'indiscrezione.
Bridal [bra'i'dèl] n. festa nuziale; a. nuziale.
Bride [bra'id] n. sposa; b. -groom [grūm] sposo.
Bridesmaid [bra'idz'mèd] n. damigella d'onore della sposa.
Bridge [briğ] n. ponte, ponte di comando (d'una nave), giuoco di carte.
Bridle [bra'idl] n. briglia, freno.
Brief [brìf] n. (legge) riassunto; a. breve, conciso.
Briefness [brìf'nès] n. brevità.
Brier, briar [bra'ièr] n. rosa di macchia, rovo.
Brig [briğ] n. brigantino.
Brigade [bri-ghèd'] n. brigata.

Brigadier [bri-gă-dī'er'] n. generale di brigata.

Brigand [bri'ghẽnd] n. bandito, brigante.

Brigandage [bri'ghẽn-dĕǧ] n. brigantaggio.

Bright [bra¹t] a. brillante, luminoso, risplendente, gaio, vivace, vivo.

Brighten [bra¹tn] v.t. rallegrare, rendere più brillante; v.i. illuminarsi, rischiararsi.

Brightness [bra¹t'nĕs] n. splendore, vivacità.

Brilliancy [bril'iĕn-sI] n. splendore.

Brilliant [bril'iĕnt] n. brillante; a. brillante, splendido.

Brim [brim] n. ala, falda (di cappello), orlo (di tazza, ecc.); v.t. e i. colmar(si); **to b. over** [ò'vẽr'] traboccare.

Brimless [brim'lĕs] a. senza orlo, senz'ala (cappello).

Brindled [brin-dld] a. chiazzato.

Brine [bra¹n] n. acqua salata.

Bring [brĭŋ] v.t. portare, causare, indurre, procurare; **to b. up** [ǎp] educare.

Brink [brĭŋc] n. orlo (di burrone, ecc.), limite estremo.

Brisk [brisc] a. arzillo, attivo, vivace.

Briskness [brisc'nĕs] n. attività, vivacità.

Bristle [bri'sl] n. setola, pelo duro e rado.

Bristly [bris'lI] a. setoloso.

Britannic [bri-tè'nic] a. britannico, inglese.

British [bri'tîš] a. britannico, inglese.

Brittle [bri'tl] a. fragile.

Brittleness [bri'tl-nĕs] n. fragilità.

Broach [bròč] n. spiedo; v.t. aprire, spillare, cominciare (una discussione).

Broad [bród] a. ampio, largo, tollerante, volgare.

Broadcast [bród'căst] n. trasmissione radiofonica; v.t. trasmettere per radio; parlare alla radio.

Broaden [bró'dĕn] v.t. e i. allargar(si), estender(si).

Broadwise [bród'ua¹s] av. nel senso della larghezza.

Brocade [brò-chéd'] n. broccato.

Broil [bro¹l] n. lite, tumulto; v.t. arrostire sul carbone.

Broken [brò'cn] a. accidentato, frammentario, imperfetto.

Broker [brò'chẽr'] n. mediatore, sensale.

Bromide [brò'ma¹d] n. bromuro.

Bronchial [bro'chiĕl] a. bronchiale.

Bronchitis [broñ-ca¹'tis] n. bronchite.

Bronze [brŏnz] n. (oggetto di) bronzo; a. bronzeo, di bronzo; v.t. e i. abbronzar(si).

Brooch [brôč] n. spilla.

Brood [brûd] n. covata; v.t. e i. covare, meditare, preoccuparsi.

Brook [brŭc] n. ruscello.

Broom [brûm] n. ginestra, scopa.

Broth [bróth] n. brodo.

Brothel [brò'thĕl] n. bordello, casa di tolleranza.

Brother [bră-thẽr'] n. fratello; **b.-in-arms** [a¹ms], compagno d'armi; **b.-in-law** [ló] cognato.

Brotherhood [bră-thẽr'-hŭd] n. fratellanza, fraternità.

Brotherly [bră-thẽr'lI] a. fraterno.

Brow [brau] n. fronte, sommità di collina.

Browbeat [brau'bit] v.t. opprimere, vincere con la strontatezza.

Brown [braun] n. color marrone; a. marrone, bruciato dal sole; v.t. e i. rendere (divenire) marrone.

Brownish [brau'nĭš] a. marrognolo.

Browse [brauz] v.t. e i. brucare, leggere avidamente.

Bruise [brūz] n. contusione, livido; v.t. ammaccare.

Brunt [brănt] n. forza (d'un colpo), urto; **to bear** [be·er] **the b.** soportare il peso.

Brush [brăš] n. pennello, spazzola, coda (di volpe); v.t. spazzolare, sfiorare passando.

Brushwood [brăš'ŭŭd] n. macchia.

Brusque [brŭsc] a. brusco, rude.

Brutal [brū'tĕl] a. brutale.

Brutality [brū-tè'lĭ-tĭ] n. brutalità.

Brutalize [brū'tă-la'z] v.t. abbrutire.

Brute [brūt] n. bruto; a. brutale, irragionevole.

Brutish [brū'tĭš] a. bestiale, brutale.

Bubble [bă'bl] n. bolla (di liquido), progetto vano, rumore di liquido che bolle; v.i. essere effervescente, formare bolle.

Buccaneer [bă-că-nĭ·er'] n. pirata.

Buck [băc] n. daino, coniglio, leprotto, maschio di molti animali.

Bucket [bă'chĕt] n. secchia.

Buckle [bă'cl] n. fibbia; v.t. affibbiare, fermare.

Buckler [bă'clĕr] n. scudo rotondo; (fig.) protettore.

Bucolic [biù-cŏ'lĭc] a. bucolico, pastorale.

Bud [băd] n. bocciolo, gemma, germoglio; v.i. germogliare.

Budge [băj] v.i. fare un piccolo movimento, muoversi.

Budget [bă'jĕt] n. bilancio (preventivo); v.i. fare un bilancio preventivo.

Buff [băf] n. pelle di bufalo o di bue, pelle umana; a. di pelle.

Buffer [bă'fèr] n. respingente (di veicoli).

Buffet [bă'fĕt] n. credenza, ristorante (nella stazione, ecc.), schiaffo.

Buffoon [bă-fūn'] n. buffone.

Buffoonery [bă-fū'nĕ-rĭ] n. buffoneria.

Bug [băg] n. cimice; (gergo) **big** [bĭg] **b.** persona importante, [racchio.

Bugbear [băg'be·er] n. spau-

Bugle [biù'gl] n. bucina.

Bugler [biù'ghlĕr] n. sonatore di bucina.

Build [bĭld] n. costruzione, corporatura; v.i. costruire, edificare, fabbricare; v.i. costruirsi la propria casa, nidificare.

Builder [bĭl'dĕr] n. costruttore, impresario di costruzioni.

Building [bĭl'dĭñ] n. costruzione, edificio.

Bulb [bălb] n. bulbo, lampadina elettrica.

Bulbous [băl'băs] a. bulboso.

Bulge [bălj] n. gonfiore, protuberanza; v.t. gonfiarsi.

Bulk [bălc] n. massa, la maggior parte, volume; v.i. ammontare, essere voluminoso.

Bulkiness [băl'chĭ-nĕs] n. voluminosità.

Bulky [băl'chĭ] a. ingombrante, voluminoso.

Bull [bŭl] n. toro, bolla papale.

Bullet [bŭ'lĕt] n. pallottola.

Bulletin [bŭ'lĕ-tĭn] n. bollettino, notiziario.

Bullfinch [bŭl'fĭnč] n. ciuffolotto.

Bullion [bŭ'glĭòn] n. oro o argento in verghe.

Bullock [bŭ'lŏc] n. bue giovane.

Bully [bŭ'lĭ] n. prepotente, dominatore; v.t. opprimere, tiranneggiare.

Bulrush [bŭl'răš] n. specie di alto giunco.

Bulwark [bŭl'ue⁻c] n. baluardo, difesa.

Bum-boat [băm'bòt] n. battello di rifornimento viveri.

Bump [bămp] n. collisione, colpo, urto, bernòccolo, gonfiore; v.t. toccare, urtare; v.i. urtare contro qualcuno.

Bumpkin [bămp'chin] n. zotico.

Bun [băn] n. pasticcino, crocchia di capelli.

Bunch [băñc] n. fascio, mazzetto, mazzo.

Bundle [băn'dl] n. fagotto, fastello; v.t. affastellare, mandare via senza cerimonie.

Bung [băñ] n. tappo, grosso turacciolo.

Bungalow [băñ'gä-lò] n. casetta di costruzione leggera, a un piano.

Bungle [băñ'gl] n. errore grossolano, lavoro malfatto; v.t. e i. fare o aggiustare malamente.

Bunion [bă'gnŏn] n. gonfiore inflammato.

Buoy [bo¹] n. boa, gavitello.

Buoyant [bo¹ĕnt] a. allegro, elastico, che può galleggiare.

Burden [bŭr'dĕn] n. carico, fardello, onere, soma, ritornello; (naut.) tonnellaggio; v.t. caricare, gravare, tassare.

Burdensome [bŭr'dĕn-săm] a. gravoso, opprimente.

Burdock [bŭr'dŏc] n. (bot.) lappola.

Bureau [biū-rò'] n. scrittoio, (ufficio).

Burgess [bŭr'ğĕs] n. borghese, cittadino.

Burgher [bŭr'ğhĕr] n. (arcaico) cittadino.

Burglar [bŭr'ğlĕr] n. ladro, scassinatore.

Burglary [bŭr'ğlĕ-rī] n. furto mediante scasso.

Burgle [bŭr'ğl] v.t. scassinare.

Burial [bĕ'rī-ĕl] n. funerali (pl.).

Burke [be⁻c] v.t. evitare, mettere sotto silenzio.

Burlesque [bĕ⁻lĕsc'] n. caricatura, parodia; a. burlesco.

Burly [bĕ⁻lī] a. grosso e robusto.

Burn [bĕ⁻n] n. bruciatura, scottatura; (scoz.) ruscello; v.t. bruciare, dare alle fiamme; v.i. bruciare, essere in fiamme.

Burner [bĕ⁻'nĕ⁻] n. becco di lampada o di fornello a gas.

Burning [bĕ⁻'nīñ] n. conflagrazione, incendio; a. ardente, bruciante.

Burnish [bĕ⁻'nīsh] v.t. brunire, lustrare.

Burnt-offering [bĕ⁻nt ŏ'fĕrīñ] n. olocausto.

Burrow [bă'rò] n. tana; v.i. fare una tana, investigare.

Bursar [bĕ⁻'sĕ⁻] n. economo, tesoriere.

Bursary [bĕ⁻'sĕ-rī] n. borsa di studio.

Burst [bĕ⁻st] n. esplosione, scoppio; v.t. e i. (far) esplodere, (far) scoppiare, rompere.

Bury [bĕ'rī] v.t. seppellire; (fig.) dimenticare, nascondere alla vista.

Bus [băs] n. (abbrev. di omnibus) autobus.

Bush [băsh] n. cespuglio, macchia, regione selvaggia e incolta.

Bushel [bŭ'scĕl] n. misura di capacità.

Business [bīz'nĕs] n. affari (pl.) commercio, occupazione, azienda commerciale.

Buskin [băs'chin] n. (arcaico) coturno.

Bust [băst] n. busto (parte superiore del corpo).

Bustard [băs'tĕ⁻d] n. ottarda.

Bustle [băs'l] n. attività, disordinata, tramestio; v.i. agitarsi, frullare.

Busy [bī'zī] a. affaccendato, occupato.

Busybody [bi'zĭ-bŏ'dĭ] *n.* ficcanaso.

But [băt] *cong.* ma, soltanto, se non fosse che; *prep.* eccetto, tranne; *pron. rel. (neg.)* altro che.

Butcher [bŭ'čĕʳ] *n.* beccaio, macellaio.

Butchery [bŭ'čĕ-rĭ] *n.* macello, strage.

Butler [băt'lĕʳ] *n.* maggiordomo.

Butt [băt] *n.* cozzo (dato da un animale), barile, botte, calcio (di fucile), bersaglio, zimbello.

Butter [bă'tĕʳ] *n.* burro.

Buttercup [bă'tĕʳcăp] *n.* ranuncolo selvatico.

Butterfly [bă'tĕʳ-flaⁱ] *n.* farfalla.

Button [bă'tn] *n.* bottone.

Button-hole [bă'tn-hŏll] *n.* occhiello, fiore portato all'occhiello; *v.t.* attaccare un bottone a.

Buttress [bă'trĕs] *n.* contrafforte, sperone (in un muro).

Buxom [bă'csăm] *a.* grassoccio, prosperoso.

Buy [baⁱ] *v.t.* acquistare, comp[e]rare.

Buyer [baⁱ'ĕʳ] *n.* acquirente, compratore.

Buzz [băz] *v.i.* ronzare.

Buzzing [bă'zĭñ] *n.* brusìo, ronzìo.

By [baⁱ] *prep.* da, di, a fianco di, per, vicino a, non più tardi di; by the way [ueⁱ], by the by, by the by, a proposito; *av.* in diparte, vicino; to stand [stĕnd] by, stare vicino, parteggiare per, essere spettatore; to put [pŭt] by, metter via.

Bygone [baⁱ'gón] *a.* finito, passato.

Bye-law [baⁱ'lŏ] *n.* regolamento locale.

By-pass [baⁱ'păs] *n.* tratto

di strada nuova che congiunge due strade vecchie.

Byre [baⁱʳ] *n.* stalla (per buoi).

By-road [baⁱ'rŏd] *n.* strada secondaria.

Bystander [baⁱ'stĕn-dĕʳ] *n.* spettatore.

By-word [baⁱ'ueʳd] *n.* detto comune, oggetto di rimprovero.

Byzantine [baⁱ-zĕn'taⁱn] *a. e n.* bizantino.

C

Cab [chĕb] *n.* vettura pubblica da noleggio.

Cabal [că-bèl'] *n.* cabala, fazione.

Cabbage [chĕ'bĭg] *n.* cavolo.

Cabby [chĕ'bĭ] *n.* (gergo) fiaccheraio.

Cabin [chĕ'bĭn] *n.* cabina, capanna; c. -boy [boⁱ] mozzo (di nave).

Cabinet [chĕ'bĭ-nĕt] *n.* gabinetto, mobile per custodire oggetti di valore, stipo; c. -maker [mé'chĕʳ] stipettaio.

Cable [chĕ'bl] *n.* cavo, cablogramma; *v.i.* spedire un cablogramma.

Cabotage [chĕ'bŏ-tĕg] *n.* cabotaggio.

Cab-stand [chĕb'stĕnd] *n.* posteggio per vetture da noleggio.

Cackle [chĕ'chĕl] *v.i.* schiamazzare.

Caddy [chĕ'dĭ] *n.* scatola per custodire il tè.

Cadence [chĕ'dăns] *n.* cadenza.

Cadet [chè-dĕt'] *n.* cadetto.

Cage [chég] *n.* gabbia.

Caitiff [chè'tĭf] *n.* (arcaico) vigliacco.

Cajole [că-giòl'] *v.t.* persuadere con le moine.

Cajolery [că-giò'lĕ-rĭ] *n.* adulazione, persuasione.

Cake [chéc] *n.* dolce, pasticcino.

Calamitous [chè-lè'mĭ-tăs] *a.* accidentato, calamitoso.

Calamity [chè-lè'mĭ-tĭ] *n.* calamità, sventura.

Calculable [chèl'chiù-lă-bl] *a.* calcolabile.

Calculate [chèl'chiù-lét] *v.t. e i.* calcolare, pensare.

Calculation [chèl-chiù-lé'śn] *n.* calcolo, previsione.

Calculator [chèl'chiù-lé-tĕr] *n.* calcolatore, macchina calcolatrice.

Calculus [chèl'chiù-lăs] *n.* (*mat. e med.*) calcolo.

Calendar [chè'lĕn-dĕr] *n.* calendario, lista.

Calender [chè'lĕn-dĕr] *n.* [*mecc.*] cilindratoio.

Calends [chè'lĕns] *n.* (*pl.*) calende (*pl.*).

Calf [căf] *n.* vitello, pelle di vitello, piccolo di elefante e di altri mammiferi.

Calibro [chè'li-bĕr] *n.* calibro.

Call [cól] *n.* breve visita, chiamata, grido, invito; within [uith-in'] *a.* a portata di voce; *v.t. e i.* chiamare, gridare, invocare, fare una breve visita.

Calling [có'liñ] *n.* occupazione, professione, vocazione.

Callous [chè'lăs] *a.* calloso, insensibile.

Callow [chè'lò] *a.* imberbe, implume, inesperto.

Calm [căm] *n.* calma, serenità; *a.* calmo, sereno; *v.t.* calmare, tranquillare. [melano.

Calomel [chè'lò-mĕl] *n.* calo-

Caloric [chè'lŏ-ric] *a.* calorico.

Calumniate [chè-lăm'nĭ-ét] *v.t.* calunniare.

Calumnious [chè-lăm'nĭ-ăs] *a.* calunnioso.

Calumny [chè'lăm-nĭ] *n.* calunnia.

Calvinism [chèl'vĭ-nism] *n.* calvinismo.

Camber [chèm'bĕr] *n.* arco, leggera curvatura a volta, piccola darsena.

Cambric [chèm'bric] *n.* cambrì.

Camel [chè'mĕl] *n.* cammello.

Cameo [chè'mĭ-ò] *n.* cammeo.

Camera [chè'mĕ-rĕr] *n.* macchina fotografica.

Camomile [chè'mò-ma¹l] *n.* camomilla.

Camouflage [*pron. fran.*] *n.* camuffamento, mimetizzazione.

Camp [chèmp] *n.* accampamento, campo; *v.i.* accamparsi, attendarsi.

Campaign [chèm-pén'] *n.* (*mil.*) campagna.

Camphor [chèm'fĕr] *n.* canfora.

Can [chèn] *n.* brocca, scatola di latta per cibi conservati.

Can [chèn] *v.i.* difett. (*non ha infinito nè part. pass.*) essere in grado di, potere, sapere; *v.t.* mettere in scatola.

Canadian [chè-nè'dĭ-ĕn] *a. e n.* canadese.

Canal [chè-nèl'] *n.* canale.

Canary [chè-né'rĭ] *n.* canarino.

Cancel [chèn'sĕl] *v.t.* annullare, cancellare, sopprimere.

Cancellation [chèn-sĕl-é'śn] *n.* annullamento, soppressione.

Cancer [chèn'sĕr] *n.* cancro.

Candid [chèn'dĭd] *a.* franco, sincero.

Candidate [chèn'dĭ-dét] *n.* candidato.

Candidature [chèn'dĭ-dé-tiŭr] *n.* candidatura.

Candidness [chèn'dĭd-nĕs] *n.* franchezza.

Candied [chèn'dĭd] *a.* candito.

Candle [chèn'dl] *n.* candela.

Candlemas [chèn'dl-mĕs] *n.* Candelora.

Candlestick [chèn'dl-stic] *n.* candeliere.

Candour [chèn'dë^r] n. franchezza, sincerità.

Candy [chèn'di] n. candito, dolciumi (pl.).

Cane [chèn] n. bastone da passeggio, canna, mazza.

Canine [chè'na'in] a. canino.

Canister [chè'nis-të^r] n. barattolo di latta.

Canker [chèn'chë^r] n. cancro, brutto difetto, influenza corruttrice; v.t. e i. corromper(si).

Cankerous [chèn'chë-räs] a. cancrenoso, corruttore.

Cannibal [chè'nĭ-bël] n. cannibale.

Cannon [chè'nŏn] n. canno/ne, -ni (pl.).

Cannonade [chè-nò-néd'] n. bombardamento, cannoneggiamento.

Canon [chè'nŏn] n. canone, canonico.

Canonical [chè-nŏ'nĭ-cl] a. canonico.

Canonization [chè-nŏ-na'ĭ-zé! šn] n. canonizzazione.

Canonize [chè'nŏ-na'ĭz] v.t. canonizzare.

Canopy [chè'nò-pĭ] n. baldacchino.

Cant [chènt] n. gergo (d'un mestiere, ecc.), ipocrisia.

Cantankerous [chèn-kes' chë-räs] a. (famil.) intrattabile, litigioso.

Canteen [chèn-tîn'] n. boraccia da soldato, cantina militare, cassetta per posateria.

Canter [chèn'të^r] n. piccolo galoppo. [tico.

Canticle [chèn'tĭ-cl] n. cantico.

Cantilever [chèn'tĭ-lĭ-vë^r] n. mensola (che regge balconi, ecc.), modiglione.

Canton [chèn'tŏn] n. cantone (suddivisione d'un territorio).

Cantonal [chèn'tó-nël] a. cantonale.

Canvas [chèn'vès] n. canovaccio, tela, vele (pl.).

Canvass [chèn'vès] v.t. e i. sollecitare (voti, ordini, ecc.).

Canvasser [chèn'vè-së^r] n. [polit.] galoppino elettorale.

Cap [chèp] n. berretto, copricapo, cuffietta.

Capability [ché-pä-bĭ'lĭ-tĭ] n. abilità, capacità.

Capable [ché'pä-bl] a. abile, capace.

Capacious [ché-pé'-sciäs] a. spazioso, capace.

Capaciousness [chè-pé'sciäsnës] n. spaziosità.

Capacitate [chè-pè'sĭ-tét] v.t. rendere capace.

Capacity [chè-pè'sĭ-tĭ] n. capacità, competenza, ufficio.

Caparison [chè-pè'rĭ-sën] n. bardatura. [torio.

Cape [chép] n. capo, promontorio.

Caper [ché'pë^r] n. cappero, capriola, salto.

Capillary [chè-pĭ'lë-rĭ] a. capillare.

Capital [chè'pĭ-tël] n. capitale; (archit.) capitello, lettera maiuscola; a. capitale, eccellente, maiuscolo, principale.

Capitalist [chè'pĭ-tä-list] n. capitalista.

Capitalize [chè'pĭ-tä-la'ĭz] v.t. capitalizzare.

Capitular [chè-pĭ'tiù-lë^r] a. e n. capitolare.

Capitulate [chè-pĭ'tiù-lét] v.i. arrendersi, capitolare.

Capitulation [chè-vĭ-tiù-lé! šn] n. capitolazione, resa.

Capon [ché'pŏn] n. cappone.

Caprice [cä-prîs'] n. capriccio.

Capricious [cä-prî'sciäs] a. capriccioso, volubile.

Capsize [chèp-sa'ĭz'] v.t. e i. capovolger(si).

Capstan [chèp'stën] n. (naut.) argano.

Capsule [chèp'siùl] n. capsula.

Captain [chèp'tën] n. capitano, comandante.

Caption [chèp'śn] *n.* didascalia, titolo.

Captious [chèp'sciäs] *a.* capzioso, sofistico.

Captiousness [chèp'sciäsnès] *n.* capziosità.

Captivate [chèp'ti-vét] *v.t.* attrarre, cattivarsi.

Captive [chèp'tiv] *a. e n.* prigioniero.

Captivity [chèp-tiv'vi-ti] *n.* cattività.

Captor [chèp'tör] *n.* chi fa prigioniero.

Capture [chèp'cěr] *n.* arresto, cattura; *v.t.* catturare, far prigioniero.

Capuchin [chè'pŭ-cin] *n.* cappuccino (frate).

Car [car] *n.* automobile, carro.

Carabineer [chè-rä-bi-ni-er'] *n.* carabiniere.

Caracole [chè'rä-cōl] *v.i. o i.* (naut.) carenare.

Carat [chè'rèt] *n.* carato.

Caravan [chè-rä-vèn'] *n.* caravana, carrozzone.

Caravanserai [chè-rä-vèn'sè-rì] *n.* caravanserraglio.

Carbine [cär'baïn] *n.* carabina.

Carbolic [cär-bö'lic] *a.* fenico.

Carbon [cär'bön] *n.* carbonio.

Carbonate [cär'bö-nét] *n.* carbonato.

Carboniferous [cär-bò-ni'fè-räs] *a.* carbonifero.

Carbonize [cär'bò-naïz] *v.t.* carbonizzare.

Carburetor [cär-biù-rè'tör] *n.* carburatore.

Carcass [cär'chès] *n.* carcassa.

Card [cä'd] *n.* biglietto da visita, carta di giuoco, cartolina; *v.t.* cardare.

Cardboard [cä'd'bo'd] *n.* cartone.

Cardinal [cär'di-'nèl] *n.* cardinale; c. -ship [scip] cardinalato.

Care [chèr] *n.* ansietà, cura, premura, preoccupazione, sollecitudine; care of (nell'indirizzo), presso; *v.i.* importare; to care for, voler bene a, piacere.

Careen [chè-rin'] *v.t. e i.* (naut.) carenare.

Career [chè-rier'] *n.* carriera.

Careful [chèr'fùl] *a.* accurato, attento, premuroso.

Carefulness [chèr'fùl-nès] *n.* accuratezza, attenzione.

Careless [chèr'lès] *a.* negligente, trascurato.

Carelessness [chèr'lès-nès] *n.* negligenza, trascuratezza.

Caress [cä-rès'] *n.* carezza.

Caress [cä-rès'] *v.t.* accarezzare.

Cargo [cär'gò] *n.* carico (d'una nave).

Caricature [chè-ri-cä-tiùr'] *n.* caricatura; *v.t* caricaturare.

Caricaturist [chè-ri-cä-tiùt'rist] *n.* caricaturista.

Carmelite [cär'mi-laït] *a. e n.* carmelitano.

Carnage [cär'nig] *n.* carneficina, strage.

Carnal [cär'nèl] *a.* carnale, sensuale.

Carnation [cär-né'śn] *n.* garofano.

Carnival [cär'ni-vèl] *n.* carnevale.

Carnivorous [cär-nï'vö-räs] *a.* carnivoro.

Carol [chè'röl] *n.* carola, inno natalizio.

Carouse [chè-rauz'] *v.i.* far baldoria, gozzovigliare.

Carp [cä'p] *n.* carpione; c. at [èt] *v.i.* trovare sempre da ridire su.

Carpenter [cär'pèn-tör] *n.* carpentiere, falegname.

Carpentry [cär'pèn-tri] *n.* lavoro di falegname.

Carpet [cär'pèt] *n.* tappeto.

Carping [cär'ping] *a.* pieno di critiche.

Carriage [chè'rig] *n.* carro, carrozza, vettura, trasporto.

prezzo di trasporto, portamento.

Carrier [chè'rĭ-ĕʳ] n. corriere, imprenditore di trasporti, portapacchi (di bicicletta).

Carrion [chè'rĭ-ŏn] n. carogna.

Carrot [chè'rŏt] n. carota.

Carry [chè'rĭ] v.t. e i. portare (di peso), trasportare, sparare alla distanza di (di armi da fuoco); to carry oneself [ŭăn'sĕlf] v.i. rifl. comportarsi.

Cart [căʳt] n. calesse, carro; v.t. e i. trasportare (col carro).

Cartage [căʳ'tĭǵ] n. lavoro di trasporto col carro, prezzo di trasporto.

Carter [căʳ'tĕʳ] n. carrettiere.

Cartload [căʳt'lŏd] n. carrettata.

Cartoon [căʳ-tūn'] n. cartone (disegno), caricatura.

Cartridge [căʳ'trĭǵ] n. cartuccia.

Carve [căʳv] v.t. intagliare, scolpire, tagliare (carne, ecc.).

Carving [căʳ'vĭñ] n. scultura, arte di tagliare le vivande.

Cascade [chès-chéd'] n. cascata; v.i. scrosciare, spargliarsi.

Case [chés] n. astuccio, custodia, scatola; (tipogr.) cassa, avvenimento, caso, causa, processo.

Casemate [chés'mĕt] n. casamatta.

Casement [chés'mĕnt] n. finestra (a ganghieri).

Cash [chèš] n. cassa, contanti (pl.), danaro contante; v.t. incassare, prelevare.

Cashier [chè-sciʳ'] n. cassiere; v.t. destituire (ufficiali).

Cashmere [chès'miʳʳ] n. casimiro.

Cask [chèsc] n. barile.

Casket [chès'chét] n. cofanetto, scrigno.

Cassation [chè-sé'sʳn] n. cassazione.

Cassock [chè'sŏc] n. tunica portata dal clero anglicano.

Cast [càst] n. gettito, getto, lancio, stampo, forma; insieme degli attori in una rappresentazione; v.t. e i. gettare, lanciare, distribuire (parti agli attori).

Castenets [chès'tĕ-nĕts] n. (pl.) nacchere (pl.).

Castaway [chèst'à-ueʳ] n. naufrago, reietto.

Caste [càst] n. casta.

Castigate [chès'tĭ-ghét] v.t. castigare, punire.

Castigation [chès-tĭ-ghé'sʳn] n. castigo, punizione.

Casting [càs'tĭñ] n. forma, stampo.

Cast iron [càst'aiʳn] n. ghisa.

Castle [chès'l] n. castello, torre a scacchi.

Castor [chès'tĕʳ] n. castoro, piccola rotella al piede di mobili.

Castor oil [chès'tĕʳ oʳl] n. olio di ricino.

Castrate [chès'trét] v.t. castrare.

Castration [chès-tré'sʳn] n. castrazione.

Casual [chè'sciŭ-èl] a. accidentale, casuale, fortuito, impreveduto.

Casualty [chè'sciŭ-èl-tĭ] n. disgrazia, vittima; c. -list [list] lista degli uccisi, ecc. in guerra.

Casuist [chè'siŭ-ĭst] n. casista.

Casuistry [chè'siŭ-ĭs-trĭ] n. casistica.

Cat [chèt] n. gatto.

Cataclysm [chèt'à-clism] n. cataclisma.

Catacomb [chèt'à-còm] n. catacomba.

Catalepsy [chèt'à-lĕp-sĭ] n. catalessi.

Catalogue [chèt'à-lŏg] n. catalogo; v.t. catalogare.

Catapult [chèt'à-pàlt] n. catapulta, fionda.

Cataract [chèt'ă-răct] *n.* cateratta.

Catarrh [că-tār'] *n.* catarro.

Catastrophe [căt-ă'strŏ-fĭ] *n.* catastrofe.

Catch [chăč] *n.* cattura, preda, presa, guadagno fatto, paletto di porta; *v.t. e i.* acchiappare, afferrare, capire, prendere, essere contagioso.

Catching [chè'cĭn̄] *a.* contagioso.

Catchword [chĕč'ue'd] *n.* parola di richiamo, espressione in bocca a tutti.

Catechism [chĕt'ĕ-chism] *n.* catechismo.

Catechize [chèt'ĕ-cha¹z] *v.t.* catechizzare.

Categorical [chèt-ă-gŏ'rĭchĕl] *a.* categorico.

Category [chèt'tĕ²] *n.* categoria.

Cater [chè'tĕ²] *v.i.* provvedere cibo, procurare divertimenti.

Caterer [chè'tĕ-rĕ²] *n.* provveditore (di cibi, ecc.).

Caterpillar [chĕt'ĕ²-pĭ-lĕ²] *n.* bruco.

Cathedral [că-thī'drĕl] *n.* cattedrale, duomo.

Catholic [că'thò-lĭc] *a. e n.* cattolico.

Catholicism [că-thŏ'lĭ-sĭsm] *n.* cattolicismo.

Cattle [chè'tĭ] *n.* (*pl.*) bestiame.

Cauldron [cól'drŏn] *n.* caldaia.

Cauliflower [cŏ'lĭ-flau⁰²] *n.* cavolfiore.

Causal [cŏ'zĕl] *a.* causale.

Cause [cŏz] *n.* causa, motivo, movente, ragione; *v.t.* causare, produrre.

Causeway [cŏz'ue¹] *n.* strada rialzata.

Caustic [cóz'tic] *a. e n.* caustico.

Cauterize [có'tĕ-ra¹z] *v.t.* cauterizzare.

Cautery [có'tĕ-rĭ] *n.* cauterio.

Caution [có'śn] *n.* avvertimento, cautela, prudenza; *v.t.* mettere in guardia.

Cautious [có'sciăs] *a.* cauto, prudente.

Cautiousness [có'sciăs-nĕs] *n.* cautela.

Cavalcade [chè-vèl-chéd'] *n.* cavalcata.

Cavalier [chè-vè-lĭe²'] *n.* cavaliere; *a.* brusco, senza cerimonie.

Cavalry [chè'vèl-rĭ] *n.* cavalleria (soldati a cavallo).

Cave [chèv] *n.* caverna, tana.

Cavern [chè'vĕ²n] *n.* caverna.

Cavil [chè'vĭl] *n.* cavillo; *v.i.* cavillare.

Cavity [chè'vĭ-tĭ] *n.* cavità.

Caw [có] *v.i.* gracchiare.

Cease [sĭs] *v.t. e i.* cessare, fermarsi, finire.

Ceaseless [sĭs'lĕs] *a.* continuo, incessante.

Cedar [sĭ'dĕ²] *n.* cedro.

Cede [sĭd] *v.t.* cedere.

Ceiling [sĭ'lĭn̄] *n.* soffitto.

Celebrate [sĕ'lĭ-brét] *v.t.* celebrare.

Celebrated [sĕ'lĭ-bré-tĭd] *a.* celebre, famoso.

Celebration [sĕ-lĭ-bré'śn] *n.* celebrazione.

Celebrity [sĕ-lĕ'brĭ-tĭ] *n.* celebrità.

Celerity [sĕ-lĕ'rĭ-tĭ] *n.* celerità, rapidità.

Celery [sĕ'lĕ-rĭ] *n.* sedano.

Celestial [sĕ-lĕs'tĭ-ĕl] *a.* celeste, celestiale.

Celibacy [sĕ'lĭ-bĕ-sĭ] *n.* celibato.

Celibate [sĕ'lĭ-bét] *a. e n.* celibe.

Cell [sel] *n.* cella, (*biol.*) cellula; (*eletr.*) pila.

Cellar [sĕ'lĕ²] *n.* cantina.

Cellerer [sĕl'ĕ-rĕ²] *n.* cantiniere.

Cellular [sĕ'liù-lĕ²] *a.* cellulare.

Celtic [sĕl'tic] a. celtico.

Cement [sĕ-mĕnt'] n. cemento.

Cemetery sĕ'mĭ-tĕ-rĭ] n. cimitero.

Censer [sĕn'sĕʳ] n. incensiere, turibolo.

Censor [sĕn'sĕʳ] n. censore; c.ship (scip) censorato, censura.

Censorious [sĕn-sō'rĭ-ás] a. che critica severamente.

Censurable [sĕn'scĕ-rǎ-bl] a. censurabile.

Censure [sĕn'scĕʳ] n. censura, giudizio avverso; v.t. biasimare, censurare.

Census [sĕn'sás] n. censimento, censo.

Centaur [sĕn'tŏʳ] n. centauro.

Centenarian [sĕn-tĭ-nē'rĭ-ĕn] n. centenario, chi ha cent'anni.

Centenary [sĕn-tĭ'nē-rĭ] a. e n. centenario.

Centennial [sĕn-tĕ'nĭ-ĕl] a. centennale.

Centipede [sĕn'tĭ-pĭd] n. centogambe.

Central [sĕn'trĕl] a. centrale.

Centralization [sĕn-trĕ-la'zē'án] n. centralizzazione.

Centralize [sĕn'trĕ-la'z] v.t. centralizzare.

Centre [sĕn'tĕʳ] n. centro; v.t. e i. centrare, concentrar(si).

Centric [sĕn'tric] a. centrico.

Centrifugal [sĕn-trĭ'fiü-ghĕl] a. centrifugo.

Centuple [sĕn'tiü'pl] a. e n. centuplo.

Centurion [sĕn-tiü'rĭ-ĕn] n. centurione.

Century [sĕn'tiü-rĭ] n. secolo.

Ceramics [sĕ-rĕ'mĭcs] n. ceramica.

Cereal [sĭ'rĭ-ĕl] a. e n. cereale.

Cerebral [sĕ'rĭ-brĕl] a. cerebrale.

Ceremonial [sĕ-rĭ-mò'nĭ-ĕl] n. cerimoniale, etichetta; a. cerimoniale.

Ceremonious [sĕ-rĭ-mò'nĭ-ás] a. cerimonioso.

Ceremony [sĕ'rĭ-mò-nĭ] n. cerimonia; to stand [stĕnd] on c. fare complimenti.

Certain [sĕr'tĕn] a. certo, inevitabile, sicuro, for c. sicuramente.

Certainty [sĕr'tĕn-tĭ] n. certezza, sicurezza.

Certificate [sĕr-tĭ'fĭ-chĕt] n. certificato.

Certification [sĕr-tĭ-fĭ-ché'án] n. certificazione.

Certify [sĕr'tĭ-fa'] v.t. attestare, certificare.

Certitude [sĕr'tĭ-tiüd] n. certezza.

Cerulean [sĕ-rü'lĕ-ĕn] a. ceruleo.

Cessation [sĕ-sé'án] n. cessazione, pausa.

Cession [sĕ'án] n. cessione.

Cesspool [sĕs'pül] n. pozzo nero.

Cetacean [sĭ-té'sĭ-ĕn] n. cetaceo.

Chafe [céf] n. irritazione; v.t. e i. irritar(si) (la pelle); (fig.) impazientirsi, far arrabbiare.

Chaff [cĕf] n. pula, paglia.

Chaffer [cĕ'fĕʳ] v.i. e i. comprare (lesinando sul prezzo).

Chagrin [scĕ-grĕn'] n. cruccio.

Chain [cén] n. catena; v.t. incatenare.

Chair [cé'ʳ] n. sedia, seggio, cattedra; to take [téc] the c. assumere la presidenza.

Chairman [cé'ʳmán] n. presidente.

Chaise [scéz] n. (arcaico) carrozza.

Chalice [cĕ'lis] n. calice.

Chalk [cióc] n. creta, gesso; by a long [lòn] c. di gran lunga.

Chalky [ció'chi] a. cretoso, gessoso.

Challenge [cĕ'lĕnğ] n. domanda (della sentinella) sfida; v.t. sfidare, obbiettare.

Chamber [cém'bĕʳ] n. aula.

camera; c. -pot [pŏt] vaso da notte.

Chamberlain [cém'bĕr-lĕn] n. ciambellano.

Chamber-maid [cém'bĕr-méd] n. cameriera (d'albergo).

Chameleon [că-mi'li-ŏn] n. camaleonte.

Chamois [pron. fran.] camoscio; [sciâ'mi] pelle di camoscio.

Champagne [scèm'pén] n. sciampagna.

Champion [cèm'pi-ŏn] n. campione; c. ship [scip] campionato; (fig.) protezione.

Chance [ciâns] n. avvenimento fortuito, caso, occasione; by c. per caso; v.i. accadere.

Chancel [cèn'sĕl] n. coro (parte della chiesa).

Chancellor [cèn'sé-lŏr] n. cancelliere.

Chancery [cèn'sé-ri] n. cancelleria.

Chandelier [scèn-dé-li'er] n. lampadario.

Chandler [cènd'lĕr] n. negoziante in candele, olio, saponi, ecc.

Change [céng] n. alterazione, cambio, mutamento, danaro spicciolo, resto; v.t. e i. cambiar(si).

Changeable [cén'gé-bl] a. incostante, mutevole.

Changeableness [cén'gé-bl-nĕs] n. incostanza.

Changeless [céng'lĕs] a. costante, immutabile.

Channel [cè'nĕl] n. canale, (la) Manica, scanalatura.

Chant [ciânt] n. canto, recitativo monotono.

Chanty [cèn'ti] n. canto dei marinai.

Chaos [ché'ŏs] n. caos.

Chaotic [ché-ŏ'tic] a. caotico.

Chap [cèp] n. mascella, screpolatura; (famil.) amico, uomo.

Chap [cèp] v.t. e i. screpolar(si) (della pelle).

Chapel [cè'pl] n. cappella.

Chaperon [sciâ'pĕ-rón] n. signora o signorina anziana che accompagna una ragazza alle feste, ecc.

Chaplain [cèp'lén] n. cappellano.

Chaplaincy [cèp'lén-si] n. carica di cappellano.

Chaplet [cèp'lĕt] n. corona, ghirlanda.

Chapter [cèp'tĕr] n. capitolo.

Char(-woman) [ciâ'ùù-mân, n. donna di fatica.

Character [chè'rèc-tĕr] n. carattere, caratteristica, scrittura, attestato di servizio, individuo eccentrico, personaggio (di commedia, ecc.).

Characteristic [chè-rèc-tĕ-ri'tic] n. caratteristica; a. caratteristico.

Characterize [chè'rèc-tĕ-ra'z] v.t. caratterizzare.

Charade [pron. fran.] n. sciarada.

Charcoal [ciâr' còl] n. carbone (di legna).

Charge [ciâ'rg] n. carica, compito, dovere, cura, incarico, prezzo, spesa, accusa; v.t. caricare, esortare, accusare, mettere a un certo prezzo, addebitare; v.i. caricare.

Chargeable [ciâr'gé-bl] a. che si può addebitare.

Charger [ciâr'gĕr] n. destriero; (arcaico) vassoio.

Chariot [cè'ri-ŏt] n. carro, cocchio.

Charitable [cè'ri-tă-bl] a. caritatevole.

Charitableness [cè'ri-tă-bl-nĕs] n. filantropia.

Charity [cè'ri-ti] n. carità.

Charlatan [sciâr'lĕ-tên] n. ciarlatano.

Charm [ciâ'm] n. amuleto, ciondolo, attrattiva, fascino

incantesimo, incanto; *v.t.* affascinare, allettare, calmare, incantare.

Charming [cia^r'miñ] *a.* attraente, grazioso, incantevole.

Charnel-house [cia^r'nĕl haus] *n.* ossario.

Chart [cia^t] *n.* carta nautica, quadro statistico.

Charter [cia^r'tĕr] *n.* carta, documento; *v.t.* noleggiare con contratto.

Chartered accountant [cia^r'tĕ^d ă-caun'tĕnt] *n.* ragioniere collegiato.

Chase [cés] *n.* caccia, inseguimento, parco; *v.t.* cacciare, inseguire, cesellare, incidere.

Chasing [cé'siñ] *n.* cesellatura.

Chasm [chèsm] *n.* abisso, baratro.

Chaste [cést] *a.* casto, puro.

Chastise [cès-ta^iz'] *v.t.* castigare, correggere castigando.

Chastisement [cès'tiz-mĕnt] *n.* castigo, punizione.

Chastity [cès'ti-ti] *n.* castità, purezza.

Chat [cèt] *n.* chiacchierata; *v.i.* chiacchierare.

Chattels [cèt'ls] *n. (pl.)* beni mobili *(pl.).*

Chatter [cè'tĕr] *v.i.* chiacchierare stoltamente, battere (dei denti).

Chatterbox [cè'tĕr-bŏcs] *n.* chiacchierone.

Chauffeur [sciò'fĕr] *n.* autista.

Cheap [cip] *a. av.* a buon mercato.

Cheapen [ci'pn] *v.t.* diminuire il prezzo, menomare.

Cheapness [cip'nĕs] *n.* basso prezzo, buon mercato.

Cheat [cit] *n.* inganno, ingannatore, imbroglione; *v.t. e i.* barare, ingannare, truffare.

Check [cĕc] *n.* arresto improvviso, freno, controllò, impedimento, quadretto (su stoffa

o carta), scacco, scontrino; *v.t.* controllare, far arrestare, fermare.

Checkmate [cĕc'mét] *n.* scacco matto.

Cheek [cic] *n.* gota, guancia; *(gergo)* sfrontatezza.

Cheer [ci^er] *n.* applauso, disposizione d'animo, cibo, vivande *(pl.)*; *v.t. e i.* applaudire, incoraggiare, rallegrare.

Cheerful [ci^er'fŭl] *a.* allegro, di buon umore.

Cheerfulness [ci^er'fŭl-nĕs] *n.* allegria, buon umore.

Cheerless [ci^er'lĕs] *a.* triste.

Cheery [ci^e'ri] *a. (famil.)* allegro.

Cheese [ciz] *n.* formaggio.

Cheesemonger [ciz'măn-ghĕr] *n.* pizzicagnolo.

Chemical [chĕ'mi-chĕl] *a.* chimico.

Chemise [sci-miz'] *n.* camicia (da donna).

Chemist [chĕ'mist] *n.* chimico, farmacista.

Chemistry [chĕ'mis-tri] *n.* chimica.

Cheque [cĕc] *n.* assegno bancario.

Cherish [cĕ'riš] *v.t.* curare con affetto, tener caro.

Cherry [cĕ'ri] *n.* ciliegia; c. -tree [tri] ciliegio.

Cherub [cĕ'răb] *n.* cherubino.

Chess [cĕs] *n.* giuoco degli scacchi.

Chessboard [cĕs'bo^d] *n.* scacchiera.

Chessman [cĕs'măn] *n.* scacco.

Chest [cĕst] *n.* petto, torace, cassa, cassetta; c. of drawers [drô^ĕz] cassettone.

Chestnut [cĕs'nŭt] *n.* castagna; c. -tree [tri] castagno, ippocastano.

Chew [ciù] *v.t.* masticare; to c. the cud [căd] ruminare.

Chick [cic] n. pulcino.
Chicken [ci'chĕn] n. pollastro, pollo.
Chicken-pox [ci'chĕn pŏcs] n. varicella.
Chicory [ci'cŏ-rĭ] n. cicoria.
Chide [cia¹d] v.t. e i. rimproverare, sgridare.
Chief [cif] n. capo, condottiero; a. principale.
Chieftain [cif'tĕn] n. capo (di tribù barbara).
Chilblain [cil'blén] n. gelone.
Child [cia¹ld] n. bambino, figlio.
Childbirth [cia¹ld'be⁻rth] n. parto.
Childhood [cia¹ld'hŭd] n. infanzia.
Childish [cia¹l'dĭš] a. infantile, puerile.
Childless [cia¹l'dlĕs] a. senza figli.
Childlike [cia¹ld'la¹c] a. docile, infantile.
Chill [cil] n. sensazione di freddo, freddezza di modi; a. freddo, privo di cordialità; v.t. e i. raffreddar(si).
Chilly [ci'lĭ] a. freddoloso, piuttosto freddo.
Chime [cia¹m] n. scampanio armonioso; v.t. e i. battere, scampanare.
Chimney [cim'nĭ] n. camino, fumaiuolo; c. -corner [cŏr'nĕr] angolo del focolare.
Chimneysweep [cim'nĭ-suip] n. spazzacamino.
Chin [cin] n. mento.
China [cia'nǎ⁽ʳ⁾] n. porcellana.
Chine [cia¹n] n. spina dorsale, cresta (di montagna).
Chinese [cia¹nīz] a. e n. cinese.
Chink [cinc] n. crepa, fessura.
Chip [cip] n. frammento, scheggia, trucciolo; v.t. scheggiare, tagliare a piccoli pezzi.
Chiropodist [chi-ró'pò-dĭst] n. pedicure.

Chirp [chĕ⁻p] n. cinguettio; v.i. cinguettare.
Chisel [ci'zl] n. cesello, scalpello; v.t. cesellare.
Chit [cit] n. (famil.) ragazza, biglietto.
Chivalrous [ci'vĕl-rǎs] a. cavalleresco.
Chivalry [ci'vĕl-rĭ] n. cavalleria (senso fig.).
Chloral [cló'rĕl] n. cloralio.
Chloride [cló'ra¹d] n. cloruro.
Chlorine [cló-ra¹n] n. cloro.
Chloroform [cló'ró-fo⁻m] n. cloroformio.
Chocolate [ciŏ'cò-lét] n. cioccolata, cioccolatino.
Choice [ciŏ¹s] n. scelta; a. prelibato, scelto, squisito.
Choir [qua¹e⁻r] n. coro (specialmente di una chiesa).
Choke [ciòc] v.t. ingombrare, soffocare; v.i. soffocarsi, sentirsi soffocare.
Cholera [cò'lĕ-rǎ⁽ʳ⁾] n. colera.
Choleric [cò'lĕ-ric] a. collerico, irascibile.
Choose [ciůz] v.t. e i. scegliere.
Chop [ciŏp] n. colpo d'ascia, costoletta (di maiale o di montone), mascella; v.t. tagliare, tagliuzzare; v.i. vacillare.
Chopper [ciŏ'pĕr] n. eorta ascia, mannaia.
Choral [cò'rĕl] a. e n. corale.
Chord [eo⁻d] n. accordo (musicale), corda.
Choreography [cò-rĭ-ò'gră-fĭ] n. coreografia.
Chorister [cò'rĭs-tĕr] n. corista.
Chorus [cò'rǎs] n. coro.
Christen [crisn] v.t. battezzare.
Christendom [cris'n-dǎm] n. cristianità.
Christening [cris'nĭń] n. battesimo.
Christian [cris'ti-ĕn] a. e n. cristiano.
Christianity [cris-ti-è'nĭ-tĭ] n. cristianesimo.

Christianize [crìs'tĭ-ă-na¹z] *v.t.* convertire al cristianesimo.

Christmas [crìs'mès] *n.* Natale; **c. -box** [bòcs] mancia, strenna natalizia.

Chromatic [crò-mè'tĭc] *a.* cromatico.

Chronic [crŏ'nĭc] *a.* cronico.

Chronicle [crŏ'nĭ-cl] *n.* cronaca.

Chronicler [crŏ'nĭ-clĕr] *n.* cronista.

Chronology [crò-nŏ'lò-gĭ] *n.* cronologia.

Chronometer [crò-nŏ'mĭ-tĕr] *n.* cronometro.

Chrysalis [crĭ'sĕ-lĭs] *n.* crisalide.

Chrysanthemum [crĭ-sèn'thĭ-măm] *n.* crisantemo.

Chubby [ciă'bĭ] *a.* paffuto, (dal viso) tondo e grasso.

Chuckle [ciăc'l] *n.* riso soffocato; *v.i.* ridere di soppiatto.

Chum [ciăm] *n.* (*famil.*) amico intimo, compagno.

Chunk [ciănc] *n.* grosso pezzo, tozzo.

Church [cer'ć] *n.* chiesa.

Churchman [cer'ć'măn] *n.* ecclesiastico.

Churchyard [cer'ć'ia'rd] *n.* campo santo.

Churl [cer'l] *n.* zotico, uomo sgarbato o tirchio.

Churlish [cer'lĭs] *a.* rozzo, sgarbato, tirchio.

Churlishness [cer'lĭs-nĕs] *n.* sgarbatezza, tirchieria.

Churn [cer'n] *n.* zangola; *v.t. e i.* battere il latte dentro la zangola per farne burro.

Chute [sciùt] *n.* canale di scolo.

Cicatrize [sĭ'că-tra¹z] *v.t. e i.* cicatrizzare.

Cider [sa¹'dĕr] *n.* sidro.

Cigar [sĭ-gä'r] *n.* sigaro.

Cigarette [si-gă-rĕt'] *n.* sigaretta.

Cincture [sĭnc'cĕr] *n.* cintura.

Cinder [sĭn'dĕr] *n.* residuo di carbone o legna, bruciato solo in parte.

Cinema [sĭ'nĕ-mĕ⁽ʳ⁾] *n.* cinema(tografo).

Cinematography [sĭ-nĕ-mĕ-tŏ'gră-fĭ] *n.* cinematografia.

Cinnamon [sĭ'nă-mŏn] *n.* cannella, cinnamomo.

Cipher [sa¹'fĕr] *n.* cifra, cifrario.

Circle [ser'cl] *n.* cerchio, circolo, orbita; *v.t. e i.* andare intorno a, circolare, circondare.

Circlet [ser'clĕt] *n.* cerchietto.

Circuit [ser'chĭt] *n.* circuito, circoscrizione, giro.

Circuitous [ser-chiù'ĭ-tăs] *a.* indiretto. [circolare.

Circular [ser'chiù-lĕr] *a. e n.*

Circulate [ser'chiù-lĕt] *v.t. e i.* (far) circolare.

Circulation [ser-chiù-lĕ'śăn] *n.* circolazione.

Circumcise [ser'căm-sa¹z] *v.t.* circoncidere.

Circumcision [ser-căm-sĭ'śăn] *n.* circoncisione.

Circumference [ser-căm'fĕ-rĕns] *n.* circonferenza.

Circumflex [ser'căm-flĕcs] *a.* circonflesso.

Circumscribe [ser'căm-scra¹b] *v.t.* circoscrivere.

Circumspect [ser'căm-spĕc't] *a.* cauto, circospetto.

Circumspection [ser-căm-spĕc'śn] *n.* circospezione.

Circumstance [ser'căm-stĕns] *n.* circostanza, condizione.

Circumstantial [ser-căm-stĕn'śĕl] *a.* particolareggiato.

Circumvent [ser'-căm-vĕnt'] *v.t.* circonvenire, ingannare.

Circumvention [ser-căm-vĕn'śn] *n.* circonvenzione.

Circus [ser'căs] *n.* circo.

Cistern [sis'te'rn] *n.* cisterna, serbatoio.

Citadel [sì'tă-děl] *n.* cittadella, fortezza.

Cite [saìt] *v.t.* citare.

Citizen [sì'tì-zěn] *n.* cittadino; c. -ship [scìp] cittadinanza.

Citrate [sì'trét] *n.* citrato.

Citron [sì'trŏn] *n.* cedro.

City [sì'tì] *n.* città, centro d'una grande città.

Civic [sì'vìc] *a.* civico.

Civil [sì'vìl] *a.* civile, educato, gentile.

Civilian [sì-vì'lìěn] *n.* borghese (non militare).

Civilisation [sì-vì-la¹-zé'šn] *n.* civiltà, incivilimento.

Civility [sì-vì'lì-tì] *n.* cortesia, gentilezza.

Civilize [sì'vì-la¹z] *v.t.* incivilire.

Claim [clém] *n.* diritto, pretesa, reclamo, rivendicazione, terreno minerario concesso a qualcuno; *v.t.* pretendere, reclamare, rivendicare.

Claimant [clé'měnt] *n.* pretendente.

Clairvoyance [clér-vŏ'ěns] *n.* chiaroveggenza.

Clairvoyant [clér-vŏ'ěnt] *a.* e *n.* chiaroveggente.

Clam [clèm] *n.* mollusco bivalve; (*mecc.*) grappa, morsa.

Clamant [clè'měnt] *a.* insistente, rumoroso.

Clamber [clèm'bě²] *v.t.* arrampicarsi.

Clamminess [clè'mì-něs] *n.* viscosità.

Clammy [clè'mì] *a.* molliccio, viscoso.

Clamorous [clè'mŏ-rǎs] *a.* clamoroso.

Clamour [clè'mě²] *v.i.* chiedere clamorosamente, fare molte rumore.

Clamp [clèmp] *n.* (*mecc.*) grappa, morsa; *v.t.* tener fermo.

Clan [clèn] *n.* tribù, insieme di famiglie strettamente unite.

Clandestine [clèn-děs'tìn] *a.* clandestino.

Clang [clén] clangour [clèn'ě²] *n.* fragore.

Clang [clén] *v.t.* e *i.* far (risuonare con) fragore.

Glank [clénc] *n.* rumore quale di pesanti catene trascinate; *v.i.* fare rumore quale di catene ecc.

Clap [clèp] *n.* colpo, scoppio; *v.t.* e *i.* battere le mani, applaudire.

Clapper [clè'pě²] *n.* battaglio di campana.

Clarification [clè-rì-fì-ché'šn] *n.* chiarificazione.

Clarify [clè'rì-fa¹] *v.t.* chiarire, raffinare.

Clarinet [clè'rì-nět] *n.* (mus.) clari/no, -netto.

Clarity [clè'rì-tì] *n.* chiarezza.

Clash [clèš] *n.* collisione, scontro, conflitto, forte rumore, strepito; *v.t.* e *i.* urtar(si), fare strepito.

Clasp [clăsp] *n.* abbraccio, fermaglio, gancio, stretta di mano; *v.t.* abbracciare, afferrare, agganciare, stringere.

Class [clăs] *n.* classe; *v.t.* classificare.

Classic [clè'sìc] *a.* e *n.* classico.

Classical [clè'sì-cl] *a.* classico.

Classification [clè-sì-fì-ché'šn] *n.* classifica, classificazione.

Classify [clè'sì-fa¹] *v.t.* classificare.

Clatter [clè'tě²] *n.* rumore; *v.t.* e *i.* far rumore.

Clause [clóz] *n.* clausola, proposizione.

Claustral [cló'strěl] *a.* claustrale.

Claw [cló] *n.* artiglio; (*mecc.*) raffio; *v.t.* graffiare.

Clay [clé¹] *n.* argilla, creta.

Clean [clìn] *a.* netto, pulito, innocente, puro, completo; *v.t.* pulire.

Cleanliness [clĕn'li-nĕs] n. pulizia abituale.

Cleanse [clĕnz] v.t. purificare; (arcaico) pulire.

Clear [cli°ᵉʳ] a. chiaro, evidente, libero (da ostacoli); v.t. chiarire, liberare; v.i. schiarirsi.

Clearance [cli°ʳĕns] n. liquidazione.

Clearing [cli°rĭń] n. tratto di terreno di boscato per la coltivazione; c.-house [haus] (comm.) stanza di compensazione. [chiarezza.

Clearness [cli°ʳnĕs] n.

Cleavage [cli°vĭ] n. sfaldamento.

Cleave [cliv] v.t. fendere, spaccare; v.i. aderire, attaccarsi.

Cleaver [cli°vĕʳ] n. mannaia.

Clemency [clĕ'mĕ-si] n. clemenza.

Clement [clĕ'mĕnt] a. clemente, mite.

Clench [clĕnĉ] v.t. ribadire, stringere; (fig.) confermare.

Clergy [clĕ'gi] n. clero.

Clergyman [clĕ'gi-măn] n. pastore evangelico, ecclesiastico.

Cleric [clĕ'ric] n. ecclesiastico.

Clerk [clă'rc] n. commesso, impiegato d'ufficio, chierico.

Clever [clĕ'vĕʳ] a. abile, bravo, ingegnoso.

Cleverness [clĕ'vĕʳ-nĕs] n. abilità, bravura, ingegnosità.

Clew [clŭ] n. gomitolo (di) filo.

Click [clic] v.i. produrre un suono metallico breve e secco.

Client [cla'ĕnt] n. cliente.

Cliff [clif] n. rupe a picco.

Climate [cla'mĕt] n. clima.

Climatic [cla'mĕ'tic] a. climatico.

Climax [cla'mĕcs] n. culmine, punto culminante.

Climb [cla'm] v.t. e i. arrampicarsi, scalare.

Climber [cla'mĕʳ] n. alpinista, pianta rampicante; (fig.) arrivista. [regione.

Clime [cla'm] n. clima (poet.)

Clincher [clin'cĕʳ] n. argomento decisivo.

Cling [cliń] v.i. avviticchiarsi, essere fedele a.

Clinic [cli-nĭc] n. clinica.

Clink [clinc] n. tintinnio; (gergo) prigione; v.t. e i. (far) tintinnare.

Clip [clip] n. fermaglio, gancio, taglio, tosatura; v.t. tagliare, tosare.

Clipper [cli'pĕʳ] n. naviglio da trasporto veloce.

Clique [clic] n. cricca.

Cloak [clŏc] n. mantello; (fig.) pretesto.

Clock [clŏc] n. orologio da muro, pendola.

Clockwork [clŏc'uĕʳc] n. meccanismo d'orologeria.

Clod [clŏd] n. zolla (di terra).

Clog [clŏg] n. impedimento, zoccolo; v.t. impedire, impacciare, ostruire.

Cloister [clo'stĕʳ] n. chiostro, convento.

Close [clŏs] n. chiuso, recinto; a. chiuso, privo d'aria, rinchiuso, fitto, stretto, vicino; ad. (da) vicino; prep. vicino a.

Close [clŏz] n. conclusione, fine; v.t. chiudere, concludere, finire.

Closeness [clŏs'nĕs] n. prossimità, vicinanza, pesantezza (dell'aria).

Closet [clŏ'zĕt] n. gabinetto, salotto privato, studio.

Closure [clŏ'jĕʳ] n. chiusura, fine.

Clot [clŏt] n. coagulo, grumo; v.i. coagularsi, raggrumarsi.

Cloth [clŏth] n. stoffa, tela, tessuto, tovaglia.

Clothe [clŏth] v.t. (ri)vestire.

Clothes [clŏthz] n. (pl.) indumenti, vestiti (pl.).

Clothier [clò'thĭ-ĕʳ] *n.* commerciante in vestiti e stoffe.

Cloud [claud] *n.* nube, nuvola; *v.i.* rannuvolarsi.

Cloudless [claud'lĕs] *a.* senza nubi, sereno.

Cloudy [clau'dĭ] *a.* nuvoloso, oscuro.

Clove [clòv] *n.* chiodo di garofano.

Clover [clò'vĕʳ] *n.* trifoglio.

Clown [claun] *n.* buffone, pagliaccio.

Clownish [clau'nĭš] *a.* pagliaccesco, rustico.

Cloy [clò¹] *v.t.* nauseare, saziare.

Club [clăb] *n.* bastone, randello, circolo, fiori (a carte); *v.t.* bastonare; o c. together [tŭ-ghĕ'thĕʳ] pagare il proprio tributo.

Cluck [clăc] *v.i.* chiocciare.

Clue [clū] *n.* bandolo, indizio.

Clump [clămp] *n.* gruppo (d'alberi o di cespugli).

Clumsiness [clăm'zi-nĕs] *n.* goffaggine, mancanza di tatto.

Clumsy [clăm'zĭ] *a.* goffo, senza tatto.

Cluster [clăs'tŏʳ] *n.* grappolo, gruppo, sciame; *v.i.* crescere in grappoli, raccogliersi in gruppo.

Clutch [clăč] *n.* presa fortissima, stretta; **clutches** (*pl.*) artigli, grinfie (*pl.*).

Clutch [clăč] *v.t.* adunghiare, afferrare strettamente.

Clutter [clă'tĕʳ] *n.* confusione, massa confusa; *v.t.* e *i.* far confusione, ingombrare.

Coach [còč] *n.* carrozza, corriera, istitutore ripetitore, allevatore professionale di atleti; *v.t.* allenare, dare ripetizioni a.

Coach-house [còč'haus] *n.* rimessa per carrozze.

Coachman [còč'măn] *n.* cocchiere.

Coadjutor [cò-è'giù'tĕʳ] *n.* coadiutore.

Coagulate [còè·g'hiù-let] *v.t.* e *i.* coagulare, raggrumarsi

Coagulation [cò-è-ghiù-lé'šn] *n.* coagulazione.

Goal [còl] *n.* carbone.

Coalesce [cò-è-lĕs'] *v.i.* fondersi, unirsi.

Coalition [cò-è-li'šn] *n.* coalizione.

Coal-mine [còl'maɪ̈e] *n.* miniera di carbone.

Coarse [co²s] *a.* ruvido, rozzo, grossolano, volgare.

Coarseness [co²s'nĕs] *n.* ruvidezza, grossolanità.

Coast [còst] *n.* costa.

Coast-guard [còst'gaʳd] *n.* guardacoste.

Coat [còt] *n.* giacca, mantello, paltò, pastrano, intonaco, rivestimento di pelli o di penne (di animali).

Coat [còt] *v.t.* rivestire, verniciare.

Coating [cò'tĭn] *n.* rivestimento, strato.

Coat-of-arms [còt-ov-èʳms'] *n.* insegna, stemma.

Coax [còcs] *v.t.* persuadere con le moine.

Cob [còb] *n.* cavallo da tiro, cigno maschio, pannocchia di frumentone.

Cobalt [cò'bòlt] *n.* cobalto.

Cobble [còb'l] *v.t.* rabberciare, rattoppare, selciare con ciottoli.

Cobbler [còb'lĕʳ] *n.* ciabattino.

Cobweb [còb'uĕb] *n.* ragnatela.

Cocaine [cò-chén'] *n.* cocaina.

Cock [còc] *n.* gallo, maschio di uccelli, rubinetto, spina, mucchio di fieno, canna del fucile; *v.t.* e *i.* drizzar(si); *v.t.* ammucchiare (il fieno).

Cockade [cò-chéd'] *n.* coccarda.

Cockchafer [cŏc'cé-fĕ'] *n.* specie di grosso scarafaggio.

Cocker [cŏ'chĕ'] *n.* varietà di cane spagnolo; *v.t.* coccolare, trattare con indulgenza.

Cockerel [cŏc'ĕ-rĕl] *n.* galletto.

Cockle [cŏc'l] *n.* frutto marino bivalve, loglio.

Cockney [cŏc'nĭ] *a. e n.* londinese (spesso con senso spregiativo)

Cocoa [cò'cò] *n.* cacao; **c. -nut** [năt] noce di cocco.

Cocoon [cò-cūn'] *n.* bozzolo.

Cod [cŏd] *n.* merluzzo; *v.t.* (*gergo*) ingannare.

Coddle [cŏd'l], *v.t.* tenere con esagerati riguardi.

Code [còd] *n.* cifrario, codice.

Codeine [cò'dĕ-ĭn] *n.* codeina.

Codex [cò'dĕcs] *n.* codice.

Codicil [cŏ'di-sĭl] *n.* codicillo.

Codification [cò-di-fĭ-chè'ŝn] *n.* codificazione.

Codify [cò'di-fa'] *v.t.* codificare.

Coefficient [cò-ĕ-fĭ'scĕnt] *n.* coefficiente.

Coerce [cò-e'rs'] *v.t.* costringere.

Coercion [cò-ĕ'r'ŝn] *n.* coercizione.

Coercive [cò-ĕ'r'sĭv] *a.* coercitivo.

Coetaneous [cò-ĭ-té'nĭ-ăs], coeval [cò-ĭ'vĕl] *a.* coetaneo.

Coexistence [cò-ĕg-zis'tĕns] *n.* coesistenza.

Coffee [cŏ'fĭ] *n.* caffè; **c. -mill** [mĭl] macchinetta da caffè; **c. -pot** [pŏt] caffettiera.

Coffer [cŏ'fĕ'] *n.* cofano, scrigno.

Coffin [cŏ'fĭn] *n.* cassa da morto.

Cog [cŏg] *n.* (*mecc.*) dente (d'una ruota); *v.t.* (*mecc.*) dentare (una ruota).

Cogency [cò'gĕn-sĭ] *n.* forza, potenza.

Cogent [cò'gĕnt] *a.* convincente, potente.

Cogitate [cò'gi-tét] *v.t. e i.* cogitare, ponderare.

Cogitation [cò-gi-té'ŝn] *n.* cogitazione.

Cognate [cŏg'nét] *a. e n.* congiunto, parente.

Cognizable [cŏg'ni-zĕ-bl] *a.* conoscibile

Cognizance [cŏg'ni-sĕns] *n.* conoscenza sicura; (*arald.*) stemma.

Cohabit [cò-hè'bĭt] *v.i.* coabitare (dicesi di regola di coppia non coniugata).

Cohabitation [cò-hè-bĭ-té'ŝn] *n.* coabitazione.

Cohei/r [cò'é'] *n.* coerede (*m.*); **-ress** [rĕs] coerede (*f.*).

Cohere [cò-hi'e'] *v.i.* aderire, essere coerente.

Coherence [cò-hi'e'rĕnz] *n.* coerenza.

Coherent [cò-hi'e'rĕnt] *a.* coerente.

Cohesion [cò-hi'ŝn] *n.* coesione.

Cohesive [cò-hi'sĭv] *a.* coesivo.

Cohort [cò'hο'rt] *n.* coorte.

Coif [cο'f] *n.* (*arcaico*), cuffia, velo.

Coil [cο'l] *n.* molla, rotolo (di corda o di filo), spira (di serpe); (*elettr.*) bobina; *v.t.* arrotolare, avvolgere in spire.

Coin [cο'n] *n.* moneta; *v.t.* coniare.

Coinage [cο'nĭg] *n.* conio, sistema monetario.

Coincide [cò-ĭn-sa'd'] *v.i.* coincidere.

Coincidence [cò-ĭn'si-dĕnz] *n.* coincidenza.

Coincident [cò-ĭn'si-dĕnt] *a.* coincidente

Coke [còc] *n.* carbone coc.

Colander [că'lĕn-dĕ'] *n.* colino.

Cold [còld] *n.* freddo, infreddatura; *a.* freddo, raffreddato.

riservato; to be [bì] c. aver freddo; to catch [chèc] a c. infreddarsi.

Coldness [còld'něs] *n.* freddezza.

Colic [cŏ'lic] *n.* colica.

Collaborate [cŏ-lé'bŏ-rét] *v.i.* collaborare.

Collaboration [cŏ-lè-bŏ-ré'šn] *n.* collaborazione.

Collapse [cŏ-lèps'] *n.* caduta, crollo, prostrazione; (*med.*) collasso; *v.i.* crollare, avere un collasso.

Collar [cŏ'lěr] *n.* collare, colletto; *v.t.* arrestare, prendere per il collo.

Collate [cŏ-lét'] *v.t.* confrontare.

Collateral [cŏ-lè'tě-rěl] *a.* *n.* collaterale.

Collation [cŏ-lé'šn] *n.* collazione, confronto; (*arcaico*) pasto leggero.

Colleague [cŏ'lig] *n.* collega.

Collect [cŏ'lèct] *n.* colletta; [cŏ-lèct'] *v.t.* fare collezione di, mettere insieme, radunare; *v.i.* radunarsi; to c. oneself [ŭn'sèlf] *v.* *rifl.* radunare le proprie forze.

Collection [cŏ-lèc'šn] *n.* collezione, raccolta, questua (in chiesa).

Collective [cŏ-lèc'tĭv] *a.* collettivo.

Collector [cŏ-lèc'těr] *n.* collezionista, esattore.

College [cŏ'lĭg] *n.* collegio universitario.

Collide [cŏ-la'ĭd'] *v.i.* scontrarsi.

Collier [cŏ'lĭ-ěr] *n.* minatore, nave adebita al trasporto di carbone.

Collision [cŏ-lĭ'žn] *n.* collisione, scontro.

Collocate [cŏ'lŏ-chét] *v.t.* collocare.

Collocation [cŏ-lŏ-ché'šn] *n.* collocazione.

Colloquial [cŏ-lò'qu̇i-ěl] *a.* (usato nella conversazione) familiare.

Colloquy [cŏ'lò-qu̇i] *n.* colloquio.

Collusion [cŏ-lū'šn] *n.* collusione.

Colon [cŏ'lŏn] *n.* punto e virgola.

Colonel [chě'(r)'něl] *n.* colonello.

Colonial [cŏ-lò'nĭ-ěl] *a.* *e* *n.* coloniale.

Colonist [cŏ'lò-nĭst] *n.* abitatore di colonia, pioniere.

Colonization [cŏ-lò-na'ĭ-zé'šn] *n.* colonizzazione.

Colonize [cŏ'lò-na'ĭz] *v.t.* *e* *i.* colonizzare.

Colonnade [cŏ-lò-nèd'] *n.* colonnato.

Colony [cŏ'lò-nĭ] *n.* colonia.

Colossus [cŏ-lŏ'sǎs] *n.* colosso.

Colour [cǎ'lěr'] *n.* colore, colorito, tinta, apparenza, pretesto; colours (*pl.*) bandiera; *v.t.* colorire, tingere, dipingere; *v.i.* arrossire, colorirsi.

Colouring [cǎ'lě-rĭn] *n.* colorazione, coloritura.

Colt [cŏlt] *n.* puledro.

Column [cŏ'lǎm] *n.* colonna.

Comb [cŏm] *n.* pettine, cresta (di uccello o di onda), favo; *v.t.* pettinare, strigliare.

Combat [cŏm'bèt] *n.* combattimento, lotta; *v.t.* *e* *i.* combattere, lottare.

Combatant [cŏm'bǎ-tènt] *a.* *e* *n.* combattente.

Combination [cŏm-bi-né'šn] *n.* combinazione; -s (*pl.*) combinazione (capo di biancheria).

Combine [cŏm-ba'ĭn'] *v.t.* *e* *i.* combinar(si).

Combustible [cŏm-bǎs'tĭ-bl] *a.* *e* *n.* combustibile.

Combustion [cŏm-bǎs'tien] *n.* combustione.

Come [cǎm] *v.i.* venire, arrivare.

giungere; **to c. back** [bèc] ritornare; **to c. in**, entrare.

Comedian [cŏ-mī'dĭ-ĕn] *n.* attore, commediante.

Comedy [cŏ'mĕ'dĭ] *n.* commedia.

Comeliness [căm'lĭ-nĕs] *n.* avvenenza.

Comely [căm'lĭ] *a.* avvenente.

Comet [cŏ'mĕt] *n.* cometa.

Comfort [căm'fŏ't] *n.* agio, benessere materiale, conforto, consolazione; *v.t.* confortare, consolare.

Comfortable [căm'fŏ'-tĕ-bl] *a.* agiato, comodo.

Comic [cŏ'mĭc] *a.* buffo, comico.

Coming [că'mĭn] *n.* arrivo, venuta; *a.* venturo.

Comma [cŏ'mĕ(r)] *n.* virgola.

Command [cŏ-mènd'] *n.* comando, ordine, controllo; dominio *v.t. e i.* comandare, ordinare, controllare, dominare.

Commandeer [cŏ-mèn-dē'ᵉ'] *v.t.* requisire.

Commander [cŏ-mèn-dē'ᵉ] *n.* comandante.

Commandment [cŏ-mènd'mĕnt] *n.* comandamento.

Commemorate [cŏ-mě'mŏ-rét] *v.t.* commemorare.

Commemoration [cŏ-mĕ-mŏ-rē'sn] *n.* commemorazione.

Commence [cŏ-mènd'] *v.t. e i.* cominciare.

Commencement [cŏ-mènz'mĕnt] *n.* principio.

Commend [cŏ-mĕnd'] *v.t.* lodare, raccomandare.

Commendable [cŏ-mèn'dĕ-bl] *a.* lodevole.

Commendation [cŏ-mèn-dé'sn] *n.* elogio, raccomandazione.

Commensurable [cŏ-mĕn'scĕ-rĕ-bl] *a.* commensurabile.

Commensurate [cŏ-mĕn'scĕ-rét] *a.* adeguato, commisurato.

Comment [cŏ'mĕnt] *n.* commento; *v.i.* commentare, fare delle note critiche.

Commentary [cŏ'mĕn-tĕ-rĭ] *n.* commentario.

Commentator [cŏ'mĕn-tĕ-tēᵉ] *n.* commentatore, cronista radiofonico.

Commerce [cŏ'meᵉs] *m.* commercio.

Commercial [cŏ-mēᵉ'scĕl] *a.* commerciale.

Commination [cŏ-mĭ-né'sn] *n.* comminazione.

Commingle [cŏ-mĭń'gl] *v.i.* mescolarsi a.

Commiserate [cŏ-mĭ'sĕ-rét] *v.t.* compiangere.

Commiseration [cŏ-mĭ-sĕ-ré'sn] *n.* pietà.

Commissariat [cŏ-mĭ-sé'rĭ-ĕt] *n.* (*mil.*) commissariato.

Commission [cŏ-mĭ'sn] *n.* commissione, autorità, mandato; *v.t.* incaricare, dare una carica a, armare, equipaggiare (una nave).

Commissioner [cŏ-mĭ'sciŏ-nēᵉ] *n.* commissario.

Commit [cŏ-mĭt'] *v.t.* commettere, affidare, consegnare, mandare in prigione.

Committal [cŏ-mĭ'tĕl] *n.* consegna, il mandare in prigione.

Committee [cŏ-mĭ'tĭ] *n.* commissione, commitato.

Commode [cŏ-mŏd'] *n.* cassettone.

Commodious [cŏ-mŏ'dĭ-ăs] *a.* spazioso.

Commodity [cŏ-mŏ'dĭ-tĭ] *n.* cosa utile, genere di prima necessità, merce.

Common [cŏ'mŏn] *n.* territorio di proprietà comune; *a.* comune, pubblico, usuale, volgare. [popolano.

Commoner [cŏ'mŏ-nēᵉ] *n.*

Commonplace [cŏ'mŏn-plés] *n.* luogocomune; *a.* banale, comune.

Commons [cŏ'mŏns] n. (pl.) popolo; House [haus] of C. Camera dei Comuni; cibo, razioni (pl.); short [scioᵉt] c. scarse razioni (pl.)

Commonwealth [cŏ'mŏn-uëlth] n. repubblica (storia inglese), unione di domini.

Commotion [cŏ-mŏ'śn] n. agitazione, trambusto.

Communal [cŏ'miû-nël] a. comunale.

Commune [cŏ'miû-niun] v.i. comunicare, discutere.

Communicate [cŏ-miû'ni-chét] v.t. e i. comunicar(si).

Communication [cŏ-miû-ni-ché'śn] n. (mezzo di) co-municazione.

Communicative [cŏ-miû'ni-că-tiv] a. comunicativo.

Communion [cŏ-miû'ni-ŏn] n. comunione, comunità che professa la stessa fede, intima partecipazione.

Communism [cŏ'miû-nism] n. comunismo. [comunista.

Communist [cŏ'miû-nist] n.

Community [cŏ-miû'ni-ti] n. comunità.

Commutation [cŏ-miû-té'śn] n. commutazione.

Commute [cŏ-miût'] v.t. commutare.

Compact [cŏm'pèct] n. accordo, patto, trattato.

Compact [cŏm-pèct'] a. compatto, conciso.

Compactness [cŏm-pèct'nës] n. compattezza, concisione.

Companion [cŏm-pè'gnŏn] n. compagno, socio, dama di compagnia; c.ship [scip] n. amicizia, compagnia.

Companionable [cŏm-pè'gnŏn-ë-bl] a. socievole.

Company [căm'pă-ni] n. compagnia, associazione, società.

Comparable [cŏm'pè-ră-bl] a. paragonabile.

Comparative [cŏm-pè'ră-tiv] a. e n. comparativo, relativo.

Compare [cŏm-péᵉr'] v.t. e i. comparare, confrontare, sostenere il confronto.

Comparison [cŏm-pè'ri-săn] n. comparazione, paragone, raffronto.

Compartment [cŏm-paᵉt'mënt] n. scompartimento.

Compass [căm'pès] n. area, circonferenza, spazio, estensione, bussola; v.t. andare intorno a, compiere, ideare.

Compasses [căm'pès-is] n. (pl.) compasso.

Compassion [cŏm-pè'śn] n. compassione, pietà.

Compassionate [cŏm-pè'śiŏ-nét] a. che prova compassione; v.t. compassionare.

Compatible [cŏm-pè'ti-bl] a. compatibile.

Compatibility [cŏm-pè-ti-bi'li-ti] n. compatibilità.

Compatriot [cŏm-pè'tri-ŏt] n. compatriota.

Compeer [cŏm-piᵉr'] n. (raro) associato, eguale.

Compel [cŏm-pël'] v.t. costringere, forzare.

Compendious [cŏm-pën'di-ăs] a. compendioso.

Compensate [cŏm'pën-sét] v.t. e i. compensare, ricompensare.

Compensation [cŏm-pën-sé'śn] n. compensazione, compenso, indennità. [petere.

Compete [cŏm-pit'] v.i. com-

Competence [cŏm'pi-tëns] n. competenza, capacità.

Competent [cŏm'pi-tënt] a. competente, capace.

Competition [cŏm-pi-ti'śn] n. competizione, concorso, gara.

Competitive [cŏm-pë'ti-tiv] a. di competizione, di concorso.

Competitor [cŏm-pë'ti-tëᵉr] n. competitore, concorrente.

Compilation [cŏm-pĭ-lé'ŝn] n. compilazione.

Compile [cŏm-paıl'] v.t. compilare.

Complacence [cŏm-plé'sĕns] n. compiacenza, compiacimento.

Complacent [cŏm-plé'sĕnt] a. compiaciuto.

Complain [cŏm-plén'] v.i. amentarsi.

Complaint [cŏm-plént'] n. lagnanza, malattia.

Complaisance [cŏm-plé'sĕns] n. compiacenza, cortesia.

Complaisant [cŏm-plé'sĕnt] a. compiacente, cortese.

Complement [cŏm'plĭ-mĕnt] n. complemento.

Complete [cŏm-plít'] a. completo, intero, perfetto; v.t. completare, finire.

Complex [cŏm'plĕcs] n. complesso; a. complesso, complicato.

Complexion [cŏm-plĕc'ŝn] n. aspetto, carnagione.

Compliance [cŏm-plaı'ĕns] n. condiscendenza; in c. with, d'accordo con.

Compliant [cŏm-plaı'ĕnt] a. accondiscendente.

Complicate [cŏm'plĭ-chét] v.t. complicare.

Complication [cŏm-plĭ-ché'ŝn] n. complicanza, complicazione.

Compliment [cŏm'plĭ-mĕnt] n. complimento; v.t. congratularsi con.

Comply [cŏm-plaı'] v.i. accondiscendere, consentire.

Comport [cŏm-po't'] **oneself** [uàn sélf] v.i. rifl. comportarsi; to c. with, accordarsi con.

Compose [cŏm-pòz'] v.t. comporre, calmare.

Composed [cŏm-pòzd'] a. calmo, composto.

Composer [cŏm-pò'zĕr] n. compositore.

Composite [cŏm'pò-zĭt] a. composto, composito.

Composition [cŏm-pò-zĭ'ŝn] n. composizione, concordato, stile.

Compositor [cŏm-pò'sĭ-tĕr] n. (tipogr.) compositore.

Composure [cŏm-pò'jĕr] n. calma, compostezza.

Compound [cŏm'paund] a. composto; [cŏm-paund'] v.t. comporre; v.i. venire ad un accomodamento.

Comprehend [cŏm-prĭ-hĕnd] v.t. comprendere, includere.

Comprehensible [cŏm-prĭ-hĕn'sĭ-bl] a. comprensibile, intelligibile.

Comprehension [cŏm-prĭ-hĕn'ŝn] n. comprensione.

Comprehensive [cŏm-prĭ-hĕn'sĭv] a. comprensivo.

Compress [cŏm'prĕs] n. compressa.

Comprise [cŏm-praız'] v.t. comprendere, includere.

Compromise [cŏm'prò-maız] n. compromesso; v.t. accomodare, sistemare, compromettere.

Compulsion [cŏm-păl'ŝn] n. costrizione.

Compunction [cŏm-pănc'ŝn] n. compunzione.

Compute [cŏm-piùt'] v.t. computare.

Comrade [cŏm'réd] n. camerata, compagno.

Concave [cŏn'chév] a. concavo, a volta. [nascondere.

Conceal [cŏn-sìl'] v.t. celare.

Concealment [cŏn-sìl'mĕnt] n. nascondimento, nascondiglio.

Concede [cŏn-sìd'] v.t. ammettere, concedere.

Conceit [cŏn-sìt'] n. concetto piacevole, idea ricercata, opinione, presunzione.

Conceited [cŏn-sì'tĭd] a. presuntuoso.

Conceivable [cŏn-sī'vĕ-bl] *a.* concepibile.

Conceive [cŏn-sīv'] *v.t.* concepire.

Concentrate [cŏn'sĕn-trét] *v.t. e i.* concentrar(si).

Concentration [cŏn-sĕn-tré'-śn] *n.* concentramento, concentrazione.

Conception [cŏn-sĕp'śn] *n.* concezione.

Concern [cŏn-sĕr'n] *n.* ansietà, faccenda, azienda, ditta, riferimento; *v.t.* avere a che fare con, concernere, riguardare.

Concert [cŏn'sĕr̃t] *n.* concerto, accordo, unione.

Concert [cŏn-sĕr̃t'] *v.t.* concertare.

Concession [cŏn-sĕ'śn] *n.* concessione.

Conciliate [cŏn-sī'lī-ét] *v.t. e i.* (ri)conciliar(si).

Conciliatory [cŏn-sī'lī-à-tŏ-rī] *a.* conciliativo.

Concise [cŏn-saı͡s'] *a.* breve, conciso. [cisione.

Concision [cŏn-sī'śn] *n.* con-

Conclave [cŏn'clév'] *n.* conclave.

Conclude [cŏn-clūd'] *v.t. e i.* concludere, finire.

Conclusion [cŏn-clū'śn] *n.* conclusione, fine, giudizio.

Conclusive [cŏn-clū'sĭv'] *a.* conclusivo, convincente.

Concoct [cŏn-cŏct'] *v.t.* concuocere, preparare, tramare.

Concoction [cŏn-cŏc'śn] *n.* storia inventata.

Concomitance [cŏn-cŏ'mĭ-tĕns] *n.* concomitanza.

Concord [cŏn'cŏr̃d] *n.* armonia, concordia; (*mus.*) accordo.

Concordance [cŏn-cŏr̃'dĕns] *n.* accordo, indice alfabetico di parole in un libro.

Concordant [cŏn-cŏr̃'dĕnt] *a.* armonioso, concorde.

Concourse [cŏn'cŏr̃s] *n.* affluenza, concorso.

Concrete [cŏn'crīt] *a. e n.* concreto.

Concretion [cŏn-crī'śn] *n.* concrezione.

Concubinage [cŏn-chiù'bĭ-niǵ] *n.* concubinato.

Concubine [cŏn'chiù-ba̍ın] *n.* concubina.

Concur [cŏn-chĕr'] *v.i.* accordarsi, concorrere.

Concurrence [cŏn-că'rĕns] *n.* concorrenza (di linee), consenso.

Concussion [cŏn-că'śn] *n.* concussione.

Condemn [cŏn-dĕm'] *v.t.* condannare, biasimare.

Condemnation [cŏn-dĕm-né'śn] *n.* condanna, biasimo.

Condensation [cŏn-dĕn-sé'śn] *n.* condensazione.

Condense [cŏn-dĕns'] *v.t. e i.* condensar(si).

Condescend [cŏn-dī-sĕnd'] *v.i.* (ac)condiscendere, degnarsi.

Condescending [cŏn-dī-sĕn'dĭn] *a.* affabile, condiscendente.

Condescension [cŏn-dī-sĕn'śn] *n.* affabilità, condiscendenza.

Condign [cŏn-da̍ın'] *a.* adeguato.

Condiment [cŏn'dĭ-mĕnt] *n.* condimento.

Condition [cŏn-dĭ'śn] *n.* condizione, patto.

Conditional [cŏn-dĭ'scé-n ĕl] *a. e n.* condizionale.

Condole [cŏn-dòl'] *v.i.* fare le condoglianze. [condoglianza.

Condolence [cŏn-dò'lĕns] *n.*

Condone [cŏn-dòn'] *v.t.* condonare, perdonare.

Conduce [cŏn-diùs'] *v.i.* condurre (ad un risultato), contribuire.

Conducive [cŏn-diù'sĭv'] *a.* contribuente, tendente.

Conduct [cŏn'dăct] *n.* condotta, direzione; [cŏn-dăct'] *v.t.* condurre, dirigere.

Conductor [cŏn-dăc'tĕr] *n.* conduttore, guida, fattorino, (del tram, ecc.), direttore d'orchestra.

Conduit [cŏn'dĭt] *n.* condotto.

Cone [cŏn] *n.* cono, pina.

Confectioner [cŏn-fĕc'sciŏ-nĕr] *n.* pasticciere.

Confectionery [cŏn-fĕc'sciŏ-nĕ-rĭ] *n.* dolci, pasticceria.

Confederacy [cŏn-fĕ'dĕ-ră-sĭ] *n.* confederazione.

Confederate [cŏn-fĕ'dĕ-rĕt] *a. e n.* alleato, confederato.

Confer [cŏn-fĕr'] *v.t. e i.* conferire.

Conference [cŏn'fĕ-rĕns] *n.* abboccamento, conferenza.

Confess [cŏn-fĕs'] *v.t. e i.* confessar(si).

Confession [cŏn-fĕ'sn] *n.* confessione, professione.

Confessional [cŏn-fĕ'sciŏ-nĕl] *a. e n.* confessionale.

Confessor [cŏn-fĕ'sĕr] *n.* confessore.

Confidant(e) [cŏn-fĭ-dănt'] *n.* confidente.

Confide [cŏn-faɪd'] *v.t. e i.* confidare.

Confidence [cŏn'fĭ-dĕns] *n.* confidenza, presunzione; self-c. sicurezza di sè.

Confident [cŏn'fĭ-dĕnt] *a.* fiducioso, presuntuoso.

Confidential [cŏn-fĭ-dĕn'scĕl] *a.* confidenziale, privato.

Configuration [cŏn-fĭ-ghiù-rĕ'sn] *n.* configurazione.

Confine [cŏn'faɪn] *n.* (usato di regola al plurale) confine, limite; [cŏn-faɪn'] *v.t. e i.* confinare, mandare al confino, rinchiudere.

Confinement [cŏn-faɪn'mĕnt] *n.* confino, reclusione, parto.

Confirm [cŏn-fĕrm'] *v.t.* con-fermare, ratificare, cresimare.

Confirmation [cŏn-fĕr-mé'sn] *n.* conferma, confermazione, cresima.

Confiscate [cŏn'fĭs-chét] *v.t.* confiscare.

Confiscation [cŏn-fĭs-ché'sn] *n.* confisca.

Conflagration [cŏn-flă-gré'sn] *n.* conflagrazione.

Conflict [cŏn'flĭct] *n.* conflitto, lotta, urto; [cŏn-flĭct']*v.i.* lottare, urtarsi.

Confluence [cŏn'flù-ĕns] *n.* confluenza.

Confluent [cŏn'flù-ĕnt] *a. e n.* confluente.

Conform [cŏn-fo'm'] *v.t. e i.* conformar(si).

Conformity [cŏn-fo'mĭ-tĭ] *n.* conformità.

Confound [cŏn-faund'] *v.t.* confondere, mandare in rovina; confound it ! *(interjec.)* accidenti !

Confounded [cŏn-faun'dĭd] *a.* confuso, sconcertato; *(famil.)* maledetto.

Confraternity [cŏn-fră-tĕr'nĭ-tĭ] *n.* (con)fraternità.

Confront [cŏn-frănt'] *v.t.* affrontare, confrontare.

Confuse [cŏn-fiùz'] *v.t.* confondere, sconcertare.

Confused [cŏn-fiùzd'] *a.* confuso, disorientato.

Confusion [cŏn-fiù'sn] *n.* confusione, disordine, imbarazzo.

Confutation [cŏn-fiù-té'sn] *n.* confutazione.

Confute [cŏn-fiùt'] *v.t.* confutare.

Congeal [cŏn-gìl'] *v.t. e i.* congelar(si).

Congealment [cŏn-gìl'mĕnt] *n.* congelamento.

Congenial [cŏn-gì'nĭ-ĕl] *a.* affine, degli stessi gusti.

Congenital [cŏn-gĕ'nĭ-tĕl] *a.* congenito.

Congestion [cŏn-gĕs'tiŏn] n. congestione.

Conglomerate [cŏn-glŏ'mĕrĕt] a. e n. conglomerato.

Conglomerate [cŏn-glŏ'mĕrĕt] v.t. e i. conglomerar(si).

Congratulate [cŏn-grä'tiŭlĕt] v.t. congratularsi con, rallegrarsi con.

Congratulation [cŏn-grä-tiŭ-lē'šn] n. congratulazione, rallegramento.

Congregate [cŏń'grĭ-ghĕt] v.t. e i. congregare, unirsi.

Congregation [cŏn-grĭ-ghĕ'šn] n. congregazione, insieme dei fedeli.

Congress [cŏń'grĕs] n. congresso.

Congruous [cŏń'grŭ-ăs] a. congruo.

Conjectural [cŏn-gĕc'ciŭ-rĕl] a. congetturale.

Conjecture [cŏn-gĕc'cẽr] n. congettura; v.t. e i. congetturare, immaginarsi.

Conjoin [cŏn-gio'n'] v.t. e i. congiunger(si).

Conjoint [cŏn-gio'nt'] a. congiunto, unito.

Conjugal [cŏn'giŭ-ghĕl] a. coniugale.

Conjugate [cŏn'giŭ-ghĕt] v.t. e i. coniugar(si).

Conjugation [cŏn-giŭ-ghĕ'šn] n. coniugazione.

Conjunction [cŏn-giănc'šn] n. congiunzione, unione.

Conjunctive [cŏn-giănc'tiv] a. e n. congiuntivo.

Conjuncture [cŏn-giănc'cẽr] n. congiuntura.

Conjuration [cŏn-giŭ-rē'šn] n. scongiuro, solenne invocazione.

Conjure [căn'gẽr] v.i. e i. evocare (spiriti), far giuochi di prestigio; [cŏn-giŭ'ẽr] scongiurare.

Conjurer [căn'gĕ-rẽr] n. prestigiatore.

Connect [cŏ-nĕct'] v.t. e i. collegar(si), connetter(si).

Connection, **connexion** [cŏ-nĕc'šn] n. collegamento, connessione, parente.

Connivance [cŏ-na¹'vẽns] n. connivenza.

Connive [cŏ-na¹v'] v.i. essere connivente.

Connoisseur [cŏ-nĕ-sẽr'] n. conoscitore, critico (d'arte, ecc.).

Connubial [cŏ-niŭ'bĭ-ĕl] a. coniugale.

Conquer [cŏń'chẽr] v.t. e i. conquistare, vincere.

Conqueror [cŏń'chĕ-rẽr] n. conquistatore. [quista.

Conquest [cŏń'quĕst] n. con-

Consanguineous [cŏn-sĕn̄-guĭ'nĭ-ăs] a. consanguineo.

Conscience [cŏn'scĕns] n. coscienza.

Conscientious [cŏn-sci-ĕn'sciăs] a. coscienzioso.

Conscious [cŏn'sciăs] a. consapevole, conscio, cosciente.

Consciousness [cŏn'sciăs-nĕs] n. consapevolezza, coscienza, sensi (pl.).

Conscript [cŏn'script] a. e n. coscritto.

Conscription [cŏn-scrip'šn] n. coscrizione.

Consecrate [cŏn'sĭ-crĕt] v.t. consacrare, dedicare.

Consecration [cŏn-sĭ-crē'šn] n. consacrazione, dedica.

Consecutive [cŏn-sĕ'chiŭ-tiv] a. consecutivo.

Consent [cŏn-sĕnt'] n. accordo, consenso; v.i. acconsentire, essere d'accordo.

Consequence [cŏn'sĭ-quĕnz] n. conseguenza, effetto, importanza.

Consequent [cŏn'sĭ-quĕnt] a. e n. conseguente.

Consequential [cŏn-sĭ-quĕn'scĕl] a. presuntuoso, pomposo.

Conservative [cŏn-sẽr'vä-

tiv] _a. e n._ conservatore.
Conservatory [cŏn-sẽr've-tŏ-rĭ] _n._ serra.
Conserve [cŏn-sẽrv'] _n._ conserva; _v.t._ conservare.
Consider [cŏn-sĭ'dẽr'] _v.t. e i._ considerare, riflettere.
Considerable [cŏn-sĭ'dĕ-rĕ-bĭ] _a._ considerevole, grande.
Considerate [cŏn-sĭ'dĕ-rĕt] _a._ riguardoso dei sentimenti altrui.
Consideration [cŏn-sĭ-dĕ-rĕ'şn] _n._ considerazione, importanza, ricompensa.
Consign [cŏn-sa'n'] _v.t._ consegnare, mandare.
Consignee [cŏn-sa'-nĭ'] _n._ (_comm._) destinatario.
Consignor [cŏn-sa'nẽr'] _n._ (_comm._) mittente.
Consignment [cŏn-sa'n'mĕnt] _n._ consegna; (_comm._) partita di merci; [sĭstere.
Consist [cŏn-sĭst'] _v.i._ con-
Consistence [cŏn-sĭs'tĕns] _n._ consistenza, densità.
Consistent [cŏn-sĭs'tĕnt] _a._ coerente, fedele ai principî.
Consolation [cŏn-sŏ-lĕ'şn] _n._ consolazione.
Console [cŏn-sŏl'] _v.t._ confortare, consolare.
Consolidate [cŏn-sŏ'lĭ-dĕt] _v.t. e i._ consolidar(si).
Consolidation [cŏn-sŏ-lĭ-dĕ'şn] _n._ consolidamento.
Consols [cŏn-sŏls] _n._ (_pl._) titoli del debito pubblico consolidato (_pl._).
Consonant [cŏn'sŏ-nĕnt] _a._ armonioso, in accordo (con).
Consort [cŏn'sŏ't] _n._ compagno, consorte; (_comm._) ._v.i._ accompagnar(si).
Conspicuous [cŏn-spĭ'chiŭ-ăs] _a._ cospicuo, preminente.
Conspiracy [cŏn-spĭ'rĕ-sĭ] _n._ congiura, cospirazione.
Conspirator [cŏn-spĭ'ra-tẽr] _n._ cospiratore.

Conspire [cŏn-spa'er'] _v.t. e i._ cospirare, tramare.
Constable [căn-stă'bl] _n._ guardia, poliziotto.
Constancy [cŏn'stĕn-sĭ] _n._ costanza, perseveranza.
Constant [cŏn'stĕnt] _a._ costante, fedele.
Constellation [cŏn-stĕ-lĕ'şn] _n._ costellazione.
Consternation [cŏn-stẽr-nĕ'şn] _n._ costernazione.
Constipate [cŏn'stĭ-pĕt] _v.t._ costipare.
Constipation [cŏn-stĭ-pĕ'şn] _n._ stiticezza.
Constituency [cŏn-stĭ'tiŭ-ĕn-sĭ] _n._ collegio elettorale.
Constituent [cŏn-stĭ'tiŭ-ĕnt] _n._ membro d'un collegio elettorale; _a. e n._ constituente.
Constitute [cŏn'stĭ-tiŭt] _v.t._ costituire.
Constitution [cŏn-stĭ-tiŭ'şn] _n._ costituzione, legge.
Constitutional [cŏn-stĭ-tiŭ-sciŏ-nĕl] _n._ passeggiata igienica; _a._ costituzionale.
Constrain [cŏn-strĕn'] _v.t._ costringere, forzare.
Constraint [cŏn-strĕnt'] _n._ costrizione, repressione, modo imbarazzato.
Constrict [cŏn-strĭct'] _v.t._ comprimere, contrarre.
Constriction [cŏn-strĭc'şn] _n._ contrazione, costrizione.
Construct [cŏn-străct'] _v.t._ costruire, fare.
Construction [cŏn-străc'şn] _n._ costruzione.
Constructive [cŏn-străc'tĭv] _a._ costruttivo.
Construe [cŏn-strŭ'] _v.t._ analizzare (_gram._) interpretare.
Consul [cŏn'săl] _n._ console.
Consulate [cŏn'siŭ-lĕt] _n._ consolato.
Consult [cŏn-sălt'] _v.t. e i._ consultar[si].
Consultation [cŏn-săl-tĕ'şn]

n. consultazione, consulto.

Consume [cŏn-siûm′] *v.t e i.* consumar(si).

Consummate [cŏn-să′mĕt] *a.* consumato, perfetto.

Consummate [cŏn-să-mét′] *v.t.* compiere, consumare.

Consummation [cŏn-să-mé′ṣn] *n.* consumazione.

Consumption [cŏn-sămp′ṣn] *n.* consumo, (*med.*) consunzione, tisi.

Consumptive [cŏn-sămp′tiv] *a. e n.* tisico.

Contact [cŏn′tèct] *n.* contatto.

Contagion [cŏn-té′gĕn] *n.* contagio.

Contagious [cŏn-té′giăs] *a.* contagioso.

Contain [cŏn-tén′] *v.t.* contenere, includere, reprimere.

Contaminate [cŏn-tè′mi-nét] *v.t.* contaminare, infettare.

Contamination [cŏn-tè-mi-né′ṣn] *n.* contaminazione.

Contemn [cŏn-tèm′] *v.t.* disprezzare.

Contemplate [cŏn′tèm-plét] *v.t.* contemplare, meditare.

Contemplation [cŏn-tèm-plé′ṣn] *n.* contemplazione.

Contemplative [cŏn′tèm-plé-tiv] *a.* contemplativo, meditativo.

Contemporaneous [cŏn-tèm-pô-ré′ni-ăs] *a.* contemporaneo.

Contemporary [cŏn-tèm-pô-rà-ri] *a. e n.* contemporaneo.

Contempt [cŏn-tèmpt′] *n.* dispregio, disprezzo.

Contemptible [cŏn-tèm′ti-bl] *a.* disprezzabile.

Contemptuous [cŏn-tèm′tiû-ăs] *a.* sprezzante.

Contend [cŏn-tènd′] *v.i.* contendere, lottare.

Content [cŏn′tènt] *n.* contentezza, contento; *a.* contento, soddisfatto; *v.t.* accontentare, soddisfare.

Contented [cŏn-tèn′tid] *a.* contento.

Contents [cŏn-tènz′] *n.* [*pl.*] contenuto.

Contest [cŏn′tèst] *n.* competizione; [cŏn′tèst′] *v.t.* contestare, disputare. [testo.]

Context [cŏn′tècst] *n.* contesto.

Contiguous [cŏn-ti′ghiû-ăs] *a.* contiguo.

Continent [cŏn′ti-nènt] *n.* continente; *a.* casto, continente, moderato.

Continental [cŏn-ti-nèn′tĕl] *a. e n.* continentale.

Contingency [cŏn-tin′gĕn-si] *n.* contingenza.

Contingent [cŏn-tin′gĕnt] *a. e n.* contingente.

Continual [cŏn-ti′niû-ĕl] *a.* continuo.

Continuation [cŏn-ti-niû-é′ṣn] *n.* continuazione, seguito.

Continue [cŏn-ti′niû] *v.t. e i.* continuare, persistere, proseguire.

Continuity [cŏn-ti-niû′i-ti] *n.* continuità.

Continuous [cŏn-ti′niû-ăs] *a.* continuo, ininterrotto.

Contort [cŏn-to*t′] *v.t.* contorcere.

Contortion [cŏn-to*′ṣn] *n.* contorsione.

Contour [cŏn′tû*] *n.* contorno (*geogr.*).

Contraband [cŏn′trà-bènd] *a. e n.* (di) contrabbando.

Contract [cŏn′trèct] *n.* appalto (*comm.*); contratto, patto; [cŏn-trèct′] *v.t.* appaltare (*comm.*) contrarre, contrattare.

Contraction [cŏn-trèc′ṣn] *n.* contrazione.

Contractor [cŏn-trèc′tè*] *n.* appaltatore, imprenditore.

Contradict [cŏn-trà-dict′] *v.t.* contraddire.

Contradiction [cŏn-trà-dic′ṣn] *n.* contraddizione.

Contradictory [cŏn-trā-dĭc'tō-rĭ] *a.* contradditorio.

Contrariety [cŏn-trā-ra'ĭ-tĭ] *n.* contrarietà, opposizione.

Contrary [cŏn'trā-rĭ] *n.* contrario; *a.* contrario, opposto, sfavorevole.

Contrast [cŏn'trăst] *n.* contrasto; (cŏn-trăst') *v.t.* mettere in contrasto, confrontare; *v.i.* contrastare.

Contravene [cŏn-trā-vīn'] *v.i.* contravvenire.

Contravention [cŏn-trā-vĕn'ŝn] *n.* contravvenzione.

Contribute [cŏn-trĭ'bĭŭt] *v.t.* contribuire; *v.i.* collaborare.

Contribution [cŏn-trĭ-bĭŭ'ŝn] *n.* contributo, collaborazione.

Contributor [cŏn-trĭ'bĭŭ-tĕr] *n.* donatore, collaboratore.

Contrite [cŏn'traĭt] *a.* contrito. [contrizione.

Contrition [cŏn-trī'ŝn] *n.*

Contrivance [cŏn-trā'ĭ'vĕns] *n.* congegno, invenzione.

Contrive [cŏn-traĭv'] *v.t.* effettuare, inventare; *v.i.* fare in modo.

Control [cŏn-trōl'] *n.* autorità, influenza, controllo, freno; *v.t.* controllare, dominare, frenare.

Controversial [cŏn-trŏ-vĕr'sĭ-ĕl] *a.* controverso.

Controversy [cŏn'trŏ-vĕr-sĭ] *n.* controversia.

Controvert [cŏn'trŏ-vĕrt] *v.t.* controvertere.

Contumacious [cŏn-tĭŭ-mé'sciăs] *a.* contumace.

Contumacy [cŏn'tĭŭ-mè-sĭ] *n.* contumacia, ostinazione.

Contuse [cŏn-tĭŭz'] *v.t.* ammaccare, contundere.

Contusion [cŏn-tĭŭ'ŝn] *n.* contusione.

Conundrum [cŏ-năn'drăm] *n.* indovinello.

Convalesce [cŏn-vè-lĕs'] *v.i.* rimettersi in salute.

Convalescence [cŏn-vè-lĕs'sĕns] *n.* convalescenza.

Convalescent [cŏn-vè-lĕs'sĕnt] *a. e n.* convalescente.

Convene [cŏn-vīn'] *v.t.* convocare.

Convenience [cŏn-vī'nĭ-ĕns] *n.* comodità, convenienza, vantaggio materiale.

Convenient [cŏn-vī'nĭ-ĕnt] *a.* comodo, conveniente.

Convent [cŏn'vĕnt] *n.* convento.

Conventicle [cŏn-vĕn'tĭ-cl] *n.* conventicola.

Convention [cŏn-vĕn'ŝn] *n.* convenzione.

Conventional [cŏn-vĕn'sciŏnĕl] *a.* convenzionale.

Conventual [cŏn-vĕn'tĭŭ-ĕl] *a.* conventuale.

Converge [cŏn-vĕrg'] *v.i.* convergere.

Convergent [cŏn-vĕr'gĕnt] *a.* convergente.

Conversable [cŏn-vĕr'sä-bl] *a.* di piacevole conversazione, socievole.

Conversant [cŏn'vĕr-sĕnt] *a.* versato (in), bene informato.

Conversation [cŏn-vĕr-sé'ŝn] *n.* conversazione.

Converse [cŏn'vĕrs] *a. e n.* converso, contrario, opposto; (cŏn-vĕrs') *v.i.* conversare.

Conversion [cŏn-vĕr'ŝn] *n.* conversione.

Convert [cŏn'vĕrt] *n.* convertito; [cŏn-vĕrt'] *v.t.* convertire.

Convex [cŏn'vĕcs] *a.* convesso.

Convey [cŏn-vé'] *v.t.* esprimere, portare, trasportare, trasmettere.

Conveyance [cŏn-vé'ĕns] *n.* mezzo di trasporto.

Convict [cŏn'vĭct] *n.* ergastolano; (cŏn-vĭct') *v.t.* dichiarare colpevole.

Conviction [cŏn-vĭc'ŝn] *n.* condanna, convinzione.

Convince [cŏn-vĭns'] v.t. convincere.

Convivial [cŏn-vĭ'vĭ-ĕl] a. conviviale.

Convocation [cŏn-vò-ché'śn] n. assemblea, convocazione.

Convoke [cŏn-vòc'] v.t. convocare.

Convoy [cŏn'voı'] n. convoglio, scorta; [cŏn-voı'] v.t. convogliare, scortare.

Convulse [cŏn-vǎls'] v.t. agitare, mettere in convulsioni.

Convulsion [cŏn-vǎl'śn] n. convulsione.

Convulsive [cŏn-vǎl'sĭv] a. convulsivo.

Coo [cû] v.i. tubare.

Cook [cûc] n. cuo/co, -ca; v.t. e i. cucinare, cuocere.

Cooker [cû'chĕr] n. fornello (a gas, ecc.).

Cookery [cû'chĕ-rĭ] n. arte culinaria.

Cool [cûl] n. fresco; a. fresco, calmo, indifferente, impudente; v.t. e i. rinfrescar(si).

Cooler [cû'lĕr] n. recipiente per tenere in fresco.

Cooling [cû'lĭñ] a. rinfrescante.

Coolness [cûl'nĕs] n. fresco, sangue freddo.

Coop [cûp] n. barile, stia.

Co-operate [cò-ŏ'pĕ-rét] v.i. cooperare.

Co-operation [cò-ŏ-pĕ-ré'śn] n. cooperazione.

Co-operative [cò-ŏ'pĕ-rǎ-tĭv] a. cooperativo.

Co-operator [cò-ŏ'pĕ-ré-tĕr] n. cooperatore.

Co-ordinate [cò-ŏr'dĭ-nét] v.t. coordinare.

Co-ordination [cò-ŏr-dĭ-né'śn] n. coordinazione.

Copartner [cò-pa'rt'nĕr] n. socio (comm.).

Cope [cŏp] n. cappa di ecclesiastico; c. with (uuith) v.i. far fronte a, lottare contro.

Coping [cò'pĭñ] n. tetto in muratura.

Copious [cò'pĭ-ǎs] a. abbondante, copioso.

Copiousness [cò'pĭ-ǎs-nĕs] n. abbondanza.

Copper [cŏ'pĕr] n. rame, caldaia; -s (pl.) moneta spicciola.

Coppice [cŏ'pĭs] n. bosco ceduo.

Copulate [cò'pĭu-lét] v.i. congiungersi sessualmente.

Copy [cŏ'pĭ] n. copia, trascrizione; v.t. e i. copiare, imitare, trascrivere.

Copyright [cŏ'pĭ-raıt] n. diritti d'autore (pl.), proprietà letteraria.

Coquet [cò-chĕt'] v.i. civettare.

Coquette [cò-chĕt'] n. civetta (donna).

Coral [cŏ'rĕl] n. corallo; a. di corallo, rosso corallo (colore).

Cord [cŏrd] n. corda, funicella; v.t. legare con una corda.

Cordial [cŏr'dĭ-ĕl] a. e n. cordiale.

Cordiality [cŏr-dĭ-è'lĭ-tĭ] n. cordialità.

Corduroy [cŏr'dĭu-rŏ-ı] n. frustagno.

Core [cŏr] n. torsolo (di frutta); (fıg.) midollo.

Cork [cŏrc] n. sughero, tappo, turacciolo; v.t. tappare, turare.

Corkscrew [cŏr'c'scrû] n. cavatappi.

Corn [cŏrn] n. grano, callo.

Corner [cŏr'nĕr] n. angolo, canto, cantuccio, posizione difficile, svolta; c. -stone [stŏn] pietra angolare.

Cornet [cŏr'nĕt] n. cartoccio fatto a cono; (mus.) cornetta.

Cornflower [cŏr'n'flau-er'] n. fiordaliso.

Cornice [cŏr'nĭs] n. cornicione.

Coronation [cŏ-rò-né'śn] n. incoronazione.

Coroner [cŏ'rŏ-nĕᵣ] *n.* magistrato che fa inquisizioni intorno ai casi di morti accidentali o sospette.

Coronet [cŏ'rŏ-nĕt] *n.* corona nobiliare, diadema.

Corporal [cŏ'r-pŏ-rĕl] *n.* caporale; *a. e n.* corporale; *a.* corporeo.

Corporate [cŏ'r-pŏ-rĕt] *a.* costituito.

Corporation [cŏr-pŏ-rē'śn] *n.* corporazione; (*famil.*) pancia.

Corporeal [cŏr-pŏ'ri-ĕl] *a.* corporeo, materiale.

Corps [cŏᵣ] *n.* (*mil.*) corpo (di truppe).

Corpse [cŏᵣps] *n.* cadavere.

Corpulence [cŏ'r-piū-lĕns] *n.* corpulenza.

Corpulent [cŏ'r-piū-lĕnt] *a.* corpulento.

Corpuscle [cŏ'r-păs-l] *n.* corpuscolo.

Correct [cŏ-rĕct'] *a.* accurato, corretto; *v.t.* correggere.

Correction [cŏ-rĕc'śn] *n.* correzione, punizione.

Correctness [cŏ-rĕct'nĕs] *n.* correttezza.

Correspond [cŏ-rĕs-pŏnd'] *v.i.* corrispondere.

Correspondence [cŏ-rĕs-pŏn'dĕns] *n.* corrispondenza.

Correspondent [cŏ-rĕs-pŏn'dĕnt] *a. e n.* corrispondente.

Corridor [cŏ'ri-dōᵣ] *n.* corridoio.

Corroborate [cŏ-rŏ'bŏ-rĕt] *v.t.* corroborare.

Corroboration [cŏ-rŏ-bŏ-rē'śn] *n.* conferma, corroborazione; [corroder(si).

Corrode [cŏ-rŏd'] *v.t. e i.*

Corrosive [cŏ-rŏ'sïv] *a. e n.* corrosivo.

Corrugate [cŏ'riŭ-ghĕt] *v.t. e i.* corrugar(si).

Corrupt [cŏ-răpt'] *a.* corrotto, depravato; *v.t. e i.* corromper(si).

I.G.D.

Corruption [cŏ-răp'śn] *n.* corruzione.

Corsair [cŏr'seᵣ] *n.* corsaro.

Corset [cŏr'sĕt] *n.* busto (da donna); c. -maker (mē'chĕᵣ) bustaia.

Cosmetic [cŏz-mĕ'tïc] *a. e n.* cosmetico.

Cosmic [cŏz'mïc] *a.* cosmico.

Cosmogony [cŏz-mŏ'gŏ-ni] *n.* cosmogonia.

Cosmography [cŏz-mŏ'grä-fï] *n.* cosmografia.

Cosmopolitan [cŏz-mò-pŏ'lï-tĕn] *a. e n.* cosmopolita.

Cosmos [cŏz'mŏs] *n.* cosmo.

Cossack [cŏ'sĕc] *n.* cosacco.

Cost [cŏst] *n.* costo, prezzo; costs (*pl.*) spese processuali (*pl.*); *v.t.* costare; (*comm.*) fissare il prezzo.

Costermonger [cŏs'tĕr-măn-ghĕᵣ] *n.* venditore ambulante di frutta o pesce.

Costive [cŏs'tïv] *a.* stitico.

Costiveness [cŏs'tïv-nĕs] *n.* stitichezza.

Costliness [cŏst'lï-nĕs] *n.* costosità.

Costly [cŏst'lï] *a.* costoso.

Costume [cŏs'tiūm] *n.* costume, completo, foggia di vestito.

Cot [cŏt] *n.* (*poet.*) capanna, culla.

Coterie [cŏ'tĕ-rï] *n.* circolo.

Cottage [cŏ'tĭǵ] *n.* casetta di campagna.

Cotton [cŏ'tn] *n.* cotone, tela di cotone; *a.* di cotone; c. wool (ūl) cotone idrofilo.

Couch [cauč] *n.* specie di divano, giaciglio; *v.t.* esprimere (un pensiero); (*med.*) togliere una cateratta; *v.i.* giacere.

Cough [cŏf] *n.* tosse; *v.i.* tossire.

Council [caun'sïl] *n.* concilio, consiglio.

Councillor [caun'sï-lĕᵣ] *n.*

H

consigliere, membro d'un consiglio.

Counsel [caun'sĕl] n. consiglio(o), parere, consulente legale.

Counsellor [caun'sĕ-lĕr] n. consigliere.

Count [caunt] n. Conte, conto, (legge) capo d'accusa; v.t. contare, enumerare.

Countenance [caun'ti-nĕns] n. aspetto, fisionomia, viso; v.t. approvare, incoraggiare.

Counter [caun'tĕr] n. gettone, banco (in un negozio); av. contro, in opposizione.

Counteract [caun-tĕr-ect'] v.t. agire in opposizione a, neutralizzare.

Counterfeit [caun'tĕr-fĭt] n. cosa falsa; a. contraffatto, falso, imitato; v.t. contraffare, falsificare; v.t. e i. fingere.

Counterfoil [caun'tĕr-fŏil] n. madre (in un registro).

Countermand [caun-tĕr-mènd'] v.t. disdire, revocare.

Countermarch [caun'tĕr-mãrc] v.i. fare una contromarcia. [n. copriletto.

Counterpane [caun'tĕr-pén]

Counterpoise [caun'tĕr-pŏiz] v.t. controbilanciare.

Counterpoison [caun-tĕr-po''zèn] n. antidoto.

Countersign [caun'tĕr-sa¹n] v.t. aggiungere la propria firma a un documento già firmato.

Counterweight [caun'tĕr-ue¹t] n. contrappeso.

Countess [caun'tĕs] n. contessa.

Counting-house [caun'tĭn-haus] n. ufficio.

Countless [caunt'lĕs] a. innumerevole.

Country [cȧn'trĭ] n. campagna, paese [nel senso di stato], patria; c. man [măn] n. campagnuolo, contadino.

County [caun'tĭ] n. contea.

Couple [cȧ'pl] n. coppia, paio; v.t. e i. accoppiar(si); (ferrov.) agganciare.

Coupon [cũ'pŏn] n. cedola, tagliando.

Courage [cȧ'rĭǧ] n. coraggio.

Courageous [cȧ-ré'ǧiàs] a. coraggioso.

Courier [cũ'rĭ-ĕr] n. corriere, messaggero.

Course [cõrs] n. tratto, corso, direzione, pista, portata (in un pranzo).

Court [cõrt] n. corte, tribunale; v.t. corteggiare.

Courteous [chĕr'tĭ-às] a. cortese.

Courteousness [chĕr'tĭ-àsnĕs] n. cortesia.

Courtezan [cõr-tĭ-zèn'] n. cortigiana, prostituta.

Courtesy [chĕr'tĭ-sĭ] n. cortesia, eleganza di modi.

Courtier [cõr'tĭ-ĕr] n. cortigiano.

Courtly [cõrt'lĭ] a. cerimonioso, cortigianesco.

Courtship [cõrt'scĭp] n. corte, corteggiamento.

Cousin [cȧ'zĭn] n. cugi/no, -na.

Cove [cŏv] n. insenatura, piccola baia.

Covenant [cȧ'vĭ-nènt] n. convenzione, patto; v.t. e i. fare una convenzione, pattuire.

Covenanter [cȧ'vĭ-nèn-tĕr] n. chi aderisce ad una convenzione.

Cover [cȧ'vĕr] n. copertina, copertura, coperto, nascondiglio, riparo; v.t. coprire, nascondere, rivestire, raccontare (giornalismo).

Covering [cȧ'vĕ-rĭn] n. copertura.

Coverlet [cȧ'vĕ-lĕt] n. coperta, piumino.

Covet [cȧ'vĕt] v.t. bramare.

Covetous [cȧ'vĕ-tàs] a. avaro, avido.

Covey [că'vi] n. stormo (di uccelli).

Cow [cau] n. vacca (femmina di altri mammiferi); v.t. intimidire.

Coward [cau'ĕ'rd] n. codardo.

Cowardice [cau'ĕr-dis] n. codardia.

Cowardly [cau'ĕrd-li] a. codardo.

Cower [cau'ĕr] v.i. accasciarsi (per timore).

Cowl [caul] n. cappuccio.

Coxcomb [côcs'côm] n. damerino presuntuoso.

Coxswain [côcs'n] n. timoniere, sottuffiale comandante della nave in assenza degli ufficiali.

Coy [coi'] a. modesto, ritroso.

Coyness [coi'nĕs] n. modestia, ritrosità.

Crab [crĕb] n. granchio, gru (macchina).

Crabbed [crĕ'bĕd] a. ruvido, sgarbato, indecifrabile (di scrittura).

Crack [crĕc] n. scoppio, spaccatura, percossa; a. di prim'ordine, ottimo; v.t. e i. spaccar(si).

Cracker [crĕ'chĕr] n. biscotto, petardo.

Crackle [crĕc'l] v.i. crepitare.

Crackling [crĕc'lín] n. crepitio, pelle croccante del maiale arrostito.

Cracknel [crĕc'nĕl] n. biscotto croccante.

Cradle [crĕ'dl] n. culla, apparecchio per un arto spezzato.

Craft [crăft] n. abilità, arte, furberia, inganno, piccola imbarcazione.

Craftiness [crăf'ti-nĕs] n. furbizia.

Craftsman [crăfts'măn] n. artigiano; c. -ship [scip] arte dell'artigiano.

Crafty [crăf'ti] a. furbo, ingannevole.

Crag [crĕg] n. picco, roccia scoscesa.

Craggy [crĕ'ghi] a. pieno di picchi.

Cram [crĕm] v.t. e i. rimpinzar(si); (famil.) preparar(si) ad un esame.

Cramp [crĕmp] n. crampo; v.t. impacciare; cagionare crampi a.; impedire nei movimenti.

Crane [crĕn] n. gru; v.t. e i. allungare il collo.

Cranium [crĕ'ni-ăm] n. cranio.

Crank [crĕnc] n. manovella; (fig.) individuo eccentrico.

Cranny [crĕ'ni] n. fessura.

Crape [crĕp] n. crespo, gramaglie (pl.).

Crash [crĕsì] n. fracasso; v.i. crollare con fracasso, precipitare (di velivolo).

Crass [crĕs] a. crasso, grossolano.

Crate [crĕt] n. gabbietta da imballaggio.

Crater [crĕ'tĕr] n. cratere.

Cravat [cră-vĕt'] n. cravatta.

Crave [crĕv] v.t. e i. bramare, implorare.

Craven [crĕ'vn] a. e n. codardo.

Craving [crĕ'vín] n. brama, voglia.

Crawl [crŏl] v.i. strisciare, andare carponi.

Crayfish [crĕ'fìs] n. gambero (d'acqua dolce).

Crayon [crĕ'ón] n. matita colorata.

Craze [crĕz] n. mania, pazzia.

Craziness [crĕ'zi-nĕs] n. follia, instabilità d'un edificio.

Crazy [crĕ'zi] a. folle, pazzo, instabile.

Creak [cric] n. cigolio; v.i. cigolare, scricchiolare.

Cream [crim] n. panna.

Crease [cris] n. grinza, piega; v.t. e i. sgualcir(si).

Create [crī-èt'] *v.t.* creare.
Creation [crī-é'śn] *n.* creato, creazione.
Creator [crī-é'tĕr] *n.* creatore.
Creature [crī'cĕr] *n.* creatura.
Credence [crē'dèns] *n.* [raro] credenza, fede.
Credentials [crī-dĕn'scèls] *n.* (pl.) credenziali (pl.).
Credible [crē'di-bl] *a.* credibile.
Credit [crē'dit] *n.* credito, fiducia, reputazione, stima; *v.t.* accreditare a, credere, prestar fede a.
Creditable [crē'di-tă-bl] *a.* degno di fede, di stima, che torna all'onore di.
Creditor [crē'di-tĕr] *n.* creditore.
Credulity [crē-diū'li-ti] *n.* credulità.
Credulous [crē'diū-lǎs] *a.* credulo.
Creed [crīd] *n.* credo, somma degli articoli di fede.
Creek [crīc] *n.* cala, piccola baia.
Creep [crīp] *v.i.* arrampicarsi (di piante), insinuarsi, rabbrividire, strisciare.
Creeper [crī'pĕr] *n.* pianta rampicante.
Cremate [crī-mét'] *v.t.* cremare.
Creole [crī-òl'] *a. e n.* creo/lo, -la.
Crescent [crē'sĕnt] *n.* fila di case in semicerchio; *a.* crescente.
Cress [crēs] *n.* crescione.
Crest [crēst] *n.* cresta, ciuffetto, criniera; c. -fallen [fól'n] *a.* abbattuto.
Crevasse [crī-vès'] *n.* crepaccio.
Crevice [crē'vis] *n.* crepatura, fessura.
Crew [crū] *n.* ciurma, equipaggio (d'una nave).
Crib [crib] *n.* lettino per bimbo, mangiatoia, presepio;

v.t. confinare in uno spazio ristretto, copiare senza discernimento.
Cricket [crī'chĕt] *n.* grillo, nome d'un giuoco molto comune nella Gran Bretagna.
Crier [cra'ĕr] *n.* banditore.
Crime [cra'm] *n.* delitto, misfatto.
Criminal [crī'mi-nĕl] *n.* criminale, delinquente; *a.* criminale.
Crimp [crimp] *v.t.* arricciare (i capelli), far arrolare con inganno (soldati e marinai).
Crimson [crim'zn] *a. e n.* cremisi.
Cringe [crinġ] *v.i.* contrarsi (di muscoli), comportarsi servilmente.
Cripple [crī'pl] *a. e n.* sciancato, zoppo; *v.t.* azzoppare; (fig.) diminuire la capacità di.
Crisis [cra'sis] *n.* crisi.
Crisp [crisp] *a.* crespo, croccante, frizzante (aria), sicuro (stile).
Criterion [cra-ti'ri-ŏn] *n.* criterio.
Critic [crī'tic] *n.* critico.
Critical [crī'ti-chĕl] *a.* critico, difficile, minuzioso.
Criticism [crī-ti'sism] *n.* critica, giudizio critico.
Criticize [crī'ti-sa'z] *v.t.* criticare, fare la critica a; (fig.) fare il critico.
Croak [cròc] *v.i.* gracchiare, gracidare; (fig.) predire malanni.
Crockery [crŏ'chĕ-ri] *n.* terraglie (pl.).
Crocodile [crŏ'cò-da'l] *n.* coccodrillo.
Crocus [crŏ'cǎs] *n.* croco.
Croft [crŏft] *n.* piccolo appezzamento di terreno coltivato unito ad una casetta.
Crone [cròn] *n.* [raro] vecchia rugosa.
Crony [crŏ'nî] *n.* (famil.) vecchio amico.

Crook [crŭc] *n.* ricurvatura, bastone da pastore; (*gergo*) malvivente; *v.t. e i.* curvar(si).

Crooked [crŭ'chĕd] *a.* curvo, storto, disonesto.

Crookedness [crŭ'chĕd-nĕs] *n.* curvatura, disonestà.

Croon [crūn] *v.i.* canticchiare sotto voce.

Crop [crŏp] *n.* raccolto, gozzo (d'uccello), frusta, moda dei capelli corti; *v.t.* brucare, mietere, raccogliere, tagliare corto.

Crosier [crŏ'jĭer] *n.* pastorale (di vescovo, ecc.).

Cross [crŏs] *n.* croce, incrocio, tribolazione; *a.* obliquo, trasversale, di cattivo umore; *v.t.* attraversare, incrociare, segnare con una croce; *v.i.* incrociarsi.

Crossing [crŏ'sĭn] *n.* crocicchio, incrocio, traversata.

Cross-roads [crŏs'rŏds] *n.* (*pl.*) crocevia.

Cross-word [crŏs'uĕrd] *n.* cruciverba.

Crochet [crŏ'chĕt] *n.* nota musicale equivalente ad una semiminima, mania; (crŏ'sci) lavoro ad uncinetto.

Crouch [crauč] *v.i.* accucciarsi.

Croup [crŭp] *n.* groppa; (*med.*) crup.

Crow [crŏ] *n.* cornacchia, corvo; *v.i.* cantare (del gallo), emettere gridetti gioiosi, trionfare.

Crowd [craud] *n.* folla, massa; *v.t. e i.* affollar(si).

Crown [craun] *n.* corona, parte superiore del trono, (*old*) moneta inglese (= cinque scellini); *v.t. e i.* (in)coronare.

Crucifix [crū'sĭ-fĭcs] *n.* crocifisso.

Crucifixion [crū-sĭ-fĭc'šn] *n.*

Crucify [crū'sĭ-fai] *v.t.* crocifiggere.

Crude [crūd] *a.* crudo, immaturo, primitivo.

Cruel [crū'ĭl] *a.* crudele.

Cruelty [crū'ĭl-tĭ] *n.* crudeltà.

Cruet [crū'ĭt] *n.* ampolla, ampollina; **c. -stand** [stĕnd] ampolliera.

Cruise [crūz] *n.* crociera; *v.i.* andare in crociera, incrociare.

Cruiser [crū'zĕr] *n.* incrociatore.

Crumb [crăm] *n.* briciola di pane, molica.

Crumble [crăm'bl] *v.t. e i.* sbriciolar(si), sgretolar[si].

Crumple [crăm'pl] *v.t. e i.* raggrinzar(si), sgualcir(si).

Crunch [crănč] *v.t.* schiacciare rumorosamente.

Crusade [crū-sĕd'] *n.* crociata.

Crusader [crū-sĕ'dĕr] *n.* crociato.

Crush [crăš] *n.* compressione, schiacciamento, calca; *v.t.* annientare, sgualcire, schiacciare.

Crust [crăst] *n.* crosta, incrostazione; *v.t. e i.* incrostar(si)

Crustiness [crăs'tĭ-nĕs] *n.* irascibilità. [irritabile.

Crusty [crăs'tĭ] *a.* irascibile,

Crutch [crăč] *n.* gruccia, stampella.

Cry [crai] *n.* grido, richiamo, urlo, pianto; *v.i.* gridare, piangere.

Crypt [cript] *n.* cripta.

Cryptic [crip'tic] *a.* misterioso, nascosto.

Crystal [crĭ'stĕl] *n.* cristallo; *a.* di cristallo.

Crystalize [crĭ'stè-laiz] *v.t. e i.* cristallizzar(si).

Cub [căb] *n.* piccolo di cert animali selvaggi (orso, leone, ecc.).

Cube [chiūb] *n.* cubo.

Cubit [chiū'bĭt] *n.* cubito.

Cuckold [că'chĕld] *n.* becco.

Cuckoo [cŭ'cū] *n.* cuculo; (*gergo*) mezzo scemo.

Cucumber [chiŭ'căm-bĕʳ] n. cetriolo.

Cud [căd] n. cibo riportato dallo stomaco in bocca per la ruminazione.

Cuddle [cä'dl] v.t. (famil.) abbracciare stretto.

Cudgel [că'gĕl] n. clava, randello; v.t. picchiare con la clava, randellare; to c. one's brains [brèns] scervellarsi.

Cue [chiū] n. ultime parole nel discorso d'un attore, via da seguire, stecca (da bigliardo).

Cuff [căf] n. polsino, cagno, scapaccione; v.t. percuotere, picchiare.

Cuirass [chiŭ-rès'] n. corazza.

Cull [căl] v.t. (poet.) cogliere, raccogliere.

Culminate [căl'mi-nét] v.i. culminare.

Culmination [căl-mi-né'śn] n. acme, culminazione.

Culpable [căl'pă-bl] a. colpevole. [imputato.

Culprit [căl'prit] n. colpevole,

Cultivate [căl'ti-vét] v.t. coltivare.

Cultivation [căl-ti-vé'śn] n. coltivazione, cultura.

Culture [căl'cĕʳ] n. cultura.

Cultured [căl'cĕʳd] a. colto.

Cumber [căm'bĕʳ] v.t. impacciare, ingombrare.

Cumbersome [căm'bĕʳ-săm] a. ingombrante, poco maneggevole.

Cumulative [chiū'miŭ-lĕ-tiv] a. cumulativo.

Cunning [că'niŭ] n. astuzia, abilità; a. astuto, abile, ingegnoso.

Cup [căp] n. tazza, calice, coppa; (fig.) benedizioni (pl.), tribulazioni (pl.).

Cupboard [că'bĕʳd] n. armadio.

Cupidity [chiū-pi'di-ti] n. cupidigia.

Cur [chĕʳ] n. cane bastardo.

Curable [chiū'rĕ-bl] a. guaribile. [di curato.

Curacy [chiū'rĕ-si] n. ufficio

Curate [chiū'rĕt] n. curato.

Curator [chiū-ré'tĕʳ] n. sovrintendente.

Curb [chĕʳb] n. costrizione, freno, bordo di marciapiede; v.t. frenare, soggiogare.

Curds [chĕʳdz] n. (pl.) latte accagliato.

Curdle [chĕʳ'dl] v.t. agghiacciare; v.i. accagliare, agghiacciarsi.

Cure [chiūeʳ] n. cura, guarigione, rimedio; v.t. guarire, affumicare (pesce, ecc.).

Curfew [chĕʳ'fiŭ] n. coprifuoco.

Curiosity [chiŭe-ri-ŏ'si-ti] n. curiosità.

Curious [chiŭe'ri-ăs] a. curioso, raro, singolare.

Curl [chĕʳl] n. arricciamento, ricciolo; v.t. arricciare; v.i. arricciarsi, sollevarsi in onde, in spire.

Curly [chĕʳ'li] a. ricciuto.

Currant [că'rĕnt] n. ribes, uva sultanina.

Currency [că'rĕn-si] n. circolazione, moneta circolante.

Current [că'rĕnt] a. e n. corrente.

Currier [că'ri-ĕʳ] n. conciapelli.

Curry [că'ri] n. salsa (fatta di spezie e di aromi); v.t. stufare (con aromi, ecc.), conciare (pelli), strigliare (cavalli).

Currycomb [că'ri-còm] n. striglia.

Curse [chĕʳs] n. imprecazione, maledizione, sventura, tormento; v.t. e i. bestemmiare, maledire; (al passivo) essere afflitto.

Cursed [che'ʳst] a. maledetto, odioso.

Cursory [chĕr'sŏ-ri] *a.* frettoloso, rapido.
Curt [chĕ't] *a.* asciutto, brusco.
Curtail [chĕr'tél'] *v.t.* abbreviare, accorciare.
Curtain [chĕr'tin] *n.* cortina, tenda, sipario.
Curtsey [chĕrt'si] *n.* inchino riverenza (di donna).
Curve [chĕrv] *n.* curva; *v.t.* e *i.* curvar(si).
Cushion [cū'scin] *n.* cuscino; (*mecc.*) cuscinetto.
Custard [cặs'tĕrd] *n.* crema.
Custody [cặs'tò-di] *n.* custodia, imprigionamento.
Custom [cặs'tăm] *n.* abitudine, uso, clientela; (*al plurale*) dazio, dogana.
Customary [cặs'tŏ-mĕ-ri] *a.* abituale, consueto.
Customer [cặs'tŏ-mĕr] *n.* avventore, cliente.
Cut [cặt] *n.* fetta, taglio, affronto, riduzione (di paga, ecc.), incisione; *v.t.* tagliare, trinciare, ridurre (prezzi, ecc.), togliere il saluto a, alzare (carte).
Cuticle [chiū'ti-cl] *n.* cuticola.
Cutlass [cặt'lès] *n.* arma da taglio (usato dai marinai).
Cutler [cặt'lĕr] *n.* coltellinaio.
Cutlery [cặt'lĕ-ri] *n.* coltelli (*pl.*).
Cutlet [cặt'lĕt] *n.* cotoletta.
Cutter [cặt'tĕr] *n.* tagliatore; (*naut.*) cottro.
Cutting [cặ'tiñ] *n.* taglio, ritaglio; *a.* tagliente, offensivo.
Cycle [sai'cl] *n.* ciclo, bicicletta; *v.i.* andare in bicicletta.
Cyclist [sai'clist] *n.* ciclista.
Cyclone [sai'clòn] *n.* ciclone.
Cylinder [si'lin-dĕr] *n.* cilindro.
Cynic [si'nic] *n.* cinico.
Cynical [si'ni-chĕl] *a.* cinico.
Cynicism [si'ni-sism] *n.* cinismo.

Cypress [sai'près] *n.* cipresso.
Cyst [sist] *n.* ciste.

D

Dab [dĕb] *n.* pezzettino, pillacchera.
Dabble [dè'bl] *v.i.* sguazzare; 'o d. in, fare una cosa senza darci peso.
Dad, Daddie [dèd'(i)] *n.* (*famil.*) babbo, babbino.
Daffodil [dè'fò-dil] *n.* narciso.
Daft [dèft] *a.* pazzerello.
Dagger [dè'ghĕr] *n.* daga, pugnale.
Daily [dé'li] *n.* quotidiano; *a.* giornaliero, quotidiano.
Daintiness [dén'ti-nès] *n.* delicatezza, difficoltà nei gusti.
Dainty [dén'ti] *n.* leccornia; *a.* delicato, difficile nei gusti.
Dairy [dĕ'ri] *n.* caseificio, cascina, latteria.
Dais [dé'is] *n.* pedana.
Daisy [dé'zi] *n.* margherita, pratolina.
Dale [dél] *n.* vallata.
Dally [dè'li] *v.i.* perdere tempo oziando o giocando.
Dam [dèm] *n.* argine, diga, madre (di animali); *v.t.* arginare.
Damage [dè'migi] *n.* danno, -ni (*pl.*); perdita; *v.t.* danneggiare.
Damask [dè'mèsc] *n.* damasco.
Dame [dém] *n.* dama, nobildonna.
Damn [dèm] *v.t.* dannare; *v.i.* maledire.
Damnation [dèm-né'śn] *n.* dannazione.
Damned [dèmd] *a.* dannato, maledetto; *avv.* (*gergo*) molto.
Damp [dèmp] *n.* umidità; *a.* umido; *v.t.* inumidire; (*fig.*) scoraggiare.
Dampness [dèmp'nès] *n.* umidità.

Damsel [dèm'zĕl] *n.* (*poet.*) donzella.

Damson [dèm'zĕn] *n.* specie di susina.

Dance [dàns] *n.* ballo, danza; *v.i.* ballare, danzare.

Dancer [dàn'sĕr] *n.* balleri/no, -na.

Dandle [dèn'dl] *v.t.* tenere sulle braccia (un bimbo), vezzeggiare.

Dandruff [dèn'drăf] *n.* forfora.

Dandy [dèn'dĭ] *n.* bellimbusto, damerino.

Dane [dén] *n.* danese.

Danger [dén'ġĕr] *n.* pericolo, rischio.

Dangerous [dén'ġĕ-răs] *a.* pericoloso.

Dangle [dèn'gl] *v.t.* e *i.* (far) dondolare.

Dangling [dèn'ghlĭn] *a. predic.* e *av.* penzoloni.

Danish [dé'nĭš] *a.* danese.

Dank [dènc] *a.* umido e freddo.

Dapper [dè'pĕr] *a.* arzillo, spocchioso.

Dapple [dè'pl] *v.t.* macchiettare.

Dare [dé'ĕr] *v.i.* osare; I daresay [aɪ déĕr'seɪ] forse, probabilmente.

Daring [dé'rĭŋ] *n.* audacia; *a.* audace, intrepido.

Dark [dàrc] *n.* oscurità, tenebre (*pl.*); *a.* buio, (o)scuro, tenebroso.

Darken [dàr'cĕn] *v.t.* e *i.* oscurar(si).

Darkness [dàr'c'nĕs] *n.* oscurità, tenebre (*pl.*).

Darling [dàr'lĭn] *n.* prediletto; *a.* amatissimo, diletto.

Darn [dàrn] *n.* rammendo; *v.t.* rammendare.

Dart [dàrt] *n.* dardo, balzo, movimento rapido; *v.i.* dardeggiare, lanciare; *v.i.* balzare, slanciarsi.

Dash [dèš] *n.* colpo, crollo goccia, ostentazione, scroscio, tonfo, tocco, lineetta; *v.t.* distruggere, mandare in pezzi, sbattere violentemente; *v.i.* infrangersi, slanciarsi.

Dashing [dè'šĭn] *a.* impetuoso, sgargiante.

Dastard [dès'tĕrd] *n.* codardo, vile.

Dastardliness [dès'tĕrd-linĕs] *n.* viltà.

Date [dét] *n.* dattero, data, termine; out [aut] of d. antiquato; up [ăp] to d. aggiornato; *v.t.* e *i.* datare.

Daub [dŏb] *n.* pittura grossolana; *v.t.* imbrattare, spalmare.

Daughter [dó'tĕr] *n.* figlia; d.-in-law (lō) nuora.

Daunt [dónt] *v.t.* scoraggiare, spaventare.

Dauntless [dónt'lĕs] *a.* intrepido.

Dawdle [dó'dl] *v.i.* bighellonare.

Dawn [dŏn] *n.* alba, aurora, inizio; *v.i.* albeggiare, cominciare ad apparire.

Day [deɪ] *n.* giorno, giornata, dì.

Day-boy [deɪ'boɪ] *n.* mezzo convittore.

Daybreak [deɪ'bréc] *n.* alba.

Day-labourer [deɪ-lé'bĕ-rĕr] *n.* lavoratore a giornata.

Daylight [deɪ'laɪt] *n.* (luce del) giorno.

Dazzle [dè'zl] *v.t.* abbagliare.

Deacon [dī'cn] *n.* diacono.

Dead [dĕd] *a.* morto, defunto; *av.* interamente, profondamente; at d. of night [naɪt] nel cuor della notte.

Deaden [dĕ'dn] *v.t.* ammortire, smorzare.

Deadly [dĕd'lĭ] *a.* mortale.

Deadness [dĕd'nĕs] *n.* ammortimento, stato di torpore.

Deaf [dĕf] *a.* sordo.

Deafen [dĕf'n] *v.t.* assordare, stordire.

Deaf-mute [dĕf'miùt] n. sordomuto.

Deafness [dĕf'nĕs] n. sordità.

Deal [dìl] n. affare, trattativa, distribuzione di carte (da giuoco), legno di pino o d'abete, quantità; a good [gūd] d. [ðl] molto; si usa solo con i nomi coliettivi; v.t. distribuire; v.i. commerciare, trattare, comportarsi.

Dealer [dì'lĕr] n. commerciante, negoziante.

Dealing [dì'lǐn] n. trattativa.

Dean [dìn] n. arciprete, decano.

Dear [dìⁱʳ] a. caro, costoso; dear me [mǐ]! interiez. Dio mio!

Dearness [dìⁱʳ'nĕs] n. alto prezzo, carezza.

Dearth [dĕrth] n. carestia, scarsità.

Death [dĕth] n. morte.

Debar [dǐ-bäʳ'] v.t. escludere.

Debase [dǐ-bĕs'] v.t. abbassare.

Debate [dǐ-bĕt'] n. dibattito, discussione; v.t. e i. dibattere, discutere.

Debauch [dǐ-bóć'] n. crapula, orgia; v.t. pervertire.

Debauchery [dǐ-bó'ćĕ-rǐ] n. pervertimento, scostumatezza.

Debenture [dĕ'bĕn-ćĕʳ] n. obbligazione (finanziaria).

Debilitate [dĕ-bǐ'lǐ-tĕt] v.t. debilitare.

Debility [dĕ-bǐ'lǐ-tǐ] n. debolezza, languore.

Debit [dĕ'bǐt] n. [comm.] debito; v.t. addebitare.

Debt [dĕt] n. debito.

Debtor [dĕ'tĕʳ] n. debitore.

Debut [pron. fran.] n. debutto.

Decade [dĕ'chĕd] n. decade, decennio.

Decadence [dĕ'că-dĕns] n. decadenza.

Decadent [dĕ'că-dĕnt] a. e n. decadente.

Decalogue [dĕ'că-lòg] n. decalogo.

Decamp [dǐ-chĕmp'] v.i. andarsene improvvisamente, levar le tende.

Decant [dǐ-chĕnt'] v.t. versare, travasare.

Decanter [dǐ-chĕn'tĕʳ] n. caraffa.

Decapitate [dǐ-chè'pǐ-tĕt] v.t. decapitare.

Decay [dǐ-che'] n. decomposizione, decadenza, rovina; v.i. decadere, decomporsi, deperire.

Decease [dǐ-sìs'] v.i. decadere, morire.

Deceased [dǐ-sìst'] a. e n. defunto, fu.

Deceit [dǐ-sìt'] n. falsità, frode, inganno.

Deceitful [dǐ-sìt'fūl] a. falso, ingannevole.

Deceitfulness [dĕ-sìt'fūl-nĕs] n. doppiezza, falsità.

Deceive [dǐ-sìv'] v.t. deludere, ingannare.

December [dǐ-sĕm'bĕʳ] n. dicembre.

Decency [dǐ'sĕn-sǐ] n. decenza, decoro.

Decent [dǐ'sĕnt] a. decente, decoroso, onesto, per bene.

Deception [dǐ-sĕp'sⁿ] n. inganno, insidia.

Deceptive [dǐ-sĕp'tǐv] a. ingannevole.

Decentralize [dǐ-sĕn'trĕ-laⁱz] v.t. decentrare.

Decide [dǐ-saⁱd'] v.t. e i. decidere.

Decided [dǐ-saⁱ'dǐd] a. deciso, risoluto.

Deciduous [dǐ-sǐ'dǐù-ăs] a. caduco, deciduo.

Decimal [dĕ'sǐ-mĕl] a. e n. decimale.

Decimate [dĕ'sǐ-mét] v.t. decimare.

Decimation [dĕ-sǐ-mé'sⁿ] n. decimazione.

Decipher [dǐ-saⁱ'fĕʳ] v.t. decifrare.

Decision [dĭ-sĭ′ẓn] n. conclusione, decisione.

Decisive [dĭ-sa′sĭv] a. decisivo, deciso.

Deck [dĕc] n. (naut.) coperta, ponte (della nave), tolda; v.t. coprire, rivestire, ornare.

Declaim [dĭ-clēm′] v.t. e i. declamare.

Declamation [dĕ-clĕ-mé′ṣn] n. declamazione.

Declamatory [dĕ-clĕ′mă-tō-rĭ] a. declamatorio.

Declaration [dĕ-clă-ré′ṣn] n. dichiarazione, proclamazione.

Declare [dĭ-clêr′] v.t. asserire, dichiarare, proclamare; v.i. dichiararsi.

Declension [dĭ-clĕn′ṣn] n. decadenza, declinazione (gram.) declino.

Decline [dĭ-cla′n] n. declino, inclinamento, ribasso (di prezzi), consunzione, tisi; v.t. e i. declinare, rifiutare.

Declivity [dĭ-clĭ′vĭ-tĭ] n. declivio.

Decoction [dĭ-cŏc′ṣn] n. decozione.

Decompose [dĭ-cŏm-pòs′] v.t. e i. decomporre, decomporsi, scomporre, scomporsi.

Decomposition [dĭ-cŏm-pò-sĭ′ṣn] n. decomposizione.

Decontrol [dĭ-cŏn-tròl′] v.t. togliere i controlli a.

Decorate [dĕ′cŏ-rét] v.t. adornare, ornare.

Decoration [dĕ-cŏ-ré′ṣn] n. ornamento, [roso.

Decorous [dĕ′cŏ-răs] a. decoroso.

Decorum [dĕ-có′răm] n. decoro.

Decoy [dĭ-co′] n. trappola, uccello da richiamo; v.t. allettare, attirare (specialm. con inganni).

Decrease [dĭ-crīs′] n. diminuzione; v.t. e i. diminuire.

Decree [dĭ-crī′] n. decreto; v.t. decretare.

Decrepit [dĭ-crĕ′pĭt] a. decrepito.

Decry [dĭ-cra′] v.t. deprezzare.

Dedicate [dĕ′dĭ-chét] v.t. dedicare.

Dedication [dĕ-dĭ-ché′ṣn] n. dedica, dedicazione.

Deduce [dĭ-diũs′] v.t. dedurre, desumere.

Deduct [dĭ-dăct′] v.t. dedurre, sottrarre.

Deduction [dĭ-dăc′ṣn] n. deduzione. [impresa.

Deed [dĭd] n. atto, fatto,

Deem [dĭm] v.t. e i. giudicare, pensare.

Deep [dĭp] n. abisso, (poet.) mare; a. alto, profondo; av. molto, profondamente.

Deepen [dĭ′pn] v.t. e i. approfondir(si).

Deepness [dĭp′nĕs] n. profondità.

Deer [dĭer] n. cervo, daino.

Deface [dĭ-fés′] v.t. sfigurare, defalcare.

Defalcate [dĭ′fĕl-chét] v.i. defalcare.

Defalcation [dĭ-fèl-ché′ṣn] n. appropriazione indebita, defalco.

Defame [dĭ-fém′] v.t. calunniare, diffamare.

Default [dĭ-fólt′] n. contumacia, difetto, mancanza; v.t. e i. render(si) contumace, mancare di pagare.

Defaulter [dĭ-fól′tĕr] n. debitore moroso, imputato contumace.

Defeat [dĭ-fìt′] n. disfatta, sconfitta; v.t. sconfiggere.

Defect [dĭ-fĕct′] n. difetto, imperfezione.

Defection [dĭ-fĕc′ṣn] n. defezione, rivolta.

Defective [dĭ-fĕc′tĭv] a. difettoso, imperfetto; mentally [mĕn′tè-lĭ] d. infermo di mente.

Defence [dĭ-fĕns′] n. difesa.

Defenceless [dĭ-fĕns′lĕs] a. indifeso.

Defend [dĭ-fĕnd'] *v.t.* difendere, proteggere.

Defendant [dĭ-fĕn'dènt] *n.* (*legge*) accusato.

Defensive [dĭ-fĕn'sĭv] *n.* difensiva, ; *a.* difensivo.

Defer [dĭ-fö'r'] *v.t.* differire, ritardare.

Deterence [dĕ'fė-rëns] *n.* deferenza.

Deferent [dĕ'fė-rënt] *a.* deferente.

Defiance [dĭ-faì'ëns] *n.* provocazione, sfida.

Deficiency [dĭ-fĭ'scën-sĭ] *n.* deficienza, disavanzo, insufficienza.

Deficient [dĭ-fĭ'scënt] *a.* deficiente, difettoso, insufficiente.

Deficit [dĕ'fĭ-sĭt] *n.* disavanzo.

Defile [dĭ-faì'l] *n.* gola (di montagna), stretto passaggio; [dĭ-faìl'] *v.t.* insozzare, violare; *v.i.* procedere in fila, sfilare.

Defilement [dĭ-faì'lmënt] *n.* insudiciamento, violazione.

Define [dĭ-faì'n'] *v.t.* definire, determinare.

Definition [dĕ-fĭ-nĭ'śn] *n.* definizione.

Deflate [dĭ-flét'] *v.t.* deflazionare (*finanz.*), sgonfiare (pallone, ecc.).

Deflect [dĭ-flĕct'] *v.t. e i.* (far) deflettere.

Deflection [dĭ-flĕc'śn] *n.* deviazione.

Deform [dĭ-fo'rm'] *v.t.* deformare.

Deformed [dĭ-fo'rmd'] *a.* deforme.

Deformity [dĭ-fo'rmĭ-tĭ] *n.* deformità.

Defraud [dĭ-frŏd'] *v.t.* defraudare, togliere con inganno.

Defray [dĭ-fre'] *v.t.* pagare, sostenere (le spese).

Defunct [dĭ-fănct'] *a. e n.* defunto, morto.

Defy [dĭ-faì'] *v.t.* sfidare.

**presentare insormontabili difficoltà.

Degenerate [dĭ-gĕ'nĕ-rĕt] *n.* degenerato; *a.* degenere; *v.i.* degenerare.

Degradation [dĕ'grä-dé'śn] *n.* degradazione.

Degrade [dĭ-gréd'] *v.t.* degradare.

Degree [dĭ-grì'] *n.* grado, laurea.

Deify [dĭ'ĭ-faì] *v.t.* deificare.

Deign [dén] *v.i.* degnarsi.

Deism [dĭ'izm] *n.* deismo.

Deity [dĭ'ĭ-tĭ] *n.* deità, divinità.

Deject [dĭ-gĕct'] *v.t.* deprimere, scoraggiare.

Dejection [dĭ-gĕc'śn] *n.* scoraggiamento.

Delay [dĭ-le'] *n.* indugio, ritardo; *v.t.* differire, ritardare; *v.i.* indugiare.

Delectable [dĭ-lĕc'tă-bl] *a.* delizioso, dilettevole.

Delegacy [dĕ'lė-ghè-sĭ] *n.* delegazione.

Delegate [dĕ'lė-ghét] *n.* delegato; *v.t.* delegare.

Delete [dĭ-lìt'] *v.t.* cancellare.

Deleterious [dĕ-lĭ-tĕ'rĭ-ăs] *a.* deleterio.

Deliberate [dĭ-lĭ'bĕ-rĕt] *a.* cauto, deliberato, misurato; *v.t. e i.* deliberare.

Deliberation [dĭ-lĭ-bĕ-ré'śn] *n.* deliberazione, ponderatezza.

Delicacy [dĕ'lĭ-chè-sĭ] *n.* delicatezza, leccornia.

Delicate [dĕ'lĭ-chét] *a.* delicato.

Delicious [dĭ-lĭ'sciăs] *a.* delizioso, squisito.

Deliciousness [dĭ-lĭ'sciăsnès] *n.* squisitezza.

Delight [dĭ-laìt'] *n.* diletto, gioia; *v.t. e i.* dilettar(si), divertir(si).

Delightful [dĭ-laìt'fŭl] *a.* dilettevole, piacevole, simpatico.

Delightfulness [dĭ-la¹t'fúl-nĕs] n. piacevolezza.

Delineate [dĭ-lĭ'nĭ-ét] v.t. delineare.

Delineation [dĭ-lĭ-nĭ-é'śn] n. delineazione.

Delinquency [dĭ-lĭń'quĕn-sĭ] n. delinquenza.

Delinquent [dĭ-lĭń'quĕnt] a. colpevole, delinquente.

Delirious [dĭ-lĭ'rĭ-ăs] a. delirante.

Delirium [dĭ-lĭ'rĭ-ăm] n. delirio.

Deliver [dĭ-lĭ'vĕʳ] v.t. consegnare, liberare, salvare, pronunziare, sgravare (una partoriente).

Deliverance [dĭ-lĭ'vĕ-rĕns] n. liberazione.

Deliverer [dĭ-lĭ'vĕ-rĕʳ] n. liberatore, salvatore.

Delivery [dĭ-lĭ'vĕ-rĭ] n. consegna, distribuzione (di posta), parto, modo di parlare (d'un oratore).

Dell [dĕl] n. conca, valletta.

Delude [dĭ-lĭud'] v.t. deludere, ingannare.

Deluge [dĕ'lĭüg] n. diluvio.

Delusion [dĭ-lĭü'śn] n. allucinazione, illusione.

Delusive [dĭ-lĭü'sĭv] a. ingannevole.

Delve [dĕlv] v.t. (poet.) scavare, zappare.

Demagogue [dĕ'mă-gŏg] n. demagogo.

Demand [dĭ-mănd'] n. domanda, richiesta; v.t. domandare, esigere, richiedere.

Demean oneself [dĭ-mĭn¹ uăn'sĕlf] v.i. (rifl.) comportarsi.

Demeanour [dĭ-mĭ'nĕʳ] n. comportamento.

Dement [dĭ-mĕnt'] v.t. far impazzire.

Demented [dĭ-mĕn'tĭd] a. demente, pazzo.

Demise [dĭ-ma¹z'] n. morte, trasferimento (di beni, ecc.).

Demobilization [dĭ-mò'bĭ-la¹-zé'śn] n. smobilitazione.

Demobilize [dĭ-mò'bĭ-la'z] v.t. smobilitare.

Democracy [dĭ-mó'cră-sĭ] n. democrazia.

Democrat [dĕ'mò-crĕt] n. democratico.

Democratic [dĕ-mò-crĕ'tĭc] a. democratico.

Demolish [dĭ-mó'lĭś] v.t. demolire.

Demon [dĭ'mŏn] n. demonio, spirito maligno.

Demoniac [dĭ-mò'nĭ-ĕc] n. indemoniato; a. demoniaco.

Demonstrate [dĕ'mŏn-strét] v.t. e i. dimostrare.

Demonstration [dĕ-mŏn-stré'śn] n. dimostrazione, espansione.

Demonstrative [dĭ-mŏn-stré'tĭv] a. espansivo.

Demoralization [dĭ-mŏ-ră-la¹-zé'śn] n. demoralizzazione.

Demoralize [dĭ-mŏ'ră-la'z] v.t. demoralizzare.

Demur [dĭ-mĕʳ'] n. esitazione, irresolutezza; v.i. esitare, obiettare.

Demure [dĭ-mĭü'ĕʳ] a. modesto (spesso in modo affettato).

Demureness [dĭ-mĭü'ĕʳnĕs] n. modestia.

Den [dĕn] n. covo, tana; (fig.) stanza in cui si studia.

Denationalize [dĭ-nĕ'sćĕ-nĕ-la¹z] v.t. privare dei diritti nazionali.

Denial [dĭ-na¹ĕl] n. diniego, rifiuto.

Denizen [dĕ'nĭ-zĕn] n. (raro) abitante.

Denominate [dĭ-nŏ'mĭ-nét] v.t. denominare.

Denomination [dĭ-nŏ-mĭ-né¹śn] n. denominazione, setta, taglio (di banconote).

Denote [dĭ-nòt'] v.t. denotare, indicare.

Denounce [dǐ-nauns´] *v.t.* denunciare.

Dense [dĕns] *a.* denso, spesso, ottuso.

Density [dĕn´sǐ-tǐ] *n.* densità, stupidità

Dent [dĕnt] *n.* incavo, intaccatura; (*mecc.*) dente; *v.t.* produrre un'intaccatura; (*mecc.*) dentare.

Dentist [dĕn´tist] *n.* dentista.

Denture [dĕn´cĕr] *n.* dentiera.

Denude [dǐ-niûd´] *v.t.* denudare.

Denunciation [dǐ-nănsǐ-é´śn, *n.* denuncia.

Deny [dǐ-naí´] *v.t.* negare, rifiutare.

Depart [dǐ-part´] *v.i.* partire.

Department [dǐ-part´mĕnt] *n.* dipartimento.

Departure [dǐ-pār´cĕr] *n.* partenza, direzione (di azione, ecc.)

Depend [dǐ-pĕnd´] *v.i.* dipendere, contare su.

Depen/dant, -dent [dǐ-pĕn´dĕnt] *n.* dipendente.

Dependence [dǐ-pĕn´dĕns] *n.* dipendenza, fiducia.

Dependent [dǐ-pĕn´dĕnt] *a.* dipendente.

Depict [dǐ-pǐct´] *v.t.* descrivere minutamente, dipingere.

Depilatory [dǐ-pǐ´lĕ-tǒ-rǐ] *a.* e *n.* depilatorio.

Deplete [dǐ-plīt´] *v.t.* esaurire, vuotare.

Deplorable [dǐ-plǒ´rǎ-bl] *a.* deplorevole.

Deplore [dǐ-plo˕r´] *v.t.* deplorare.

Deploy [dǐ-ploí´] *v.t.* e *i.* dispiegar(si).

Deponent [dǐ-pǒ´nĕnt] *n.* deponente, testimone.

Depopulate [dǐ-pǒ´pǐü-lét] *v.t.* spopolare.

Deport [dǐ-po˕rt´] *v.t.* deportare, esiliare.

Deportment [dǐ-po˕rt´mĕnt] *n.* portamento.

Depose [dǐ-pòz´] *v.t.* deporre, togliere di carica.

Deposit [dǐ-pǒ´zǐt] *n.* deposito; *v.t.* depositare.

Depositary [dǐ-pǒ´zǐ-tĕ-rǐ] *n.* depositario.

Deposition [dǐ-pò-zǐ´śn] *n.* deposizione.

Depositor [dǐ-pǒ´zǐ-tĕr] *n.* depositante.

Depository [dǐ-pǒ´zǐ-tǒ-rǐ] *n.* deposito.

Depravation [dǐ-prè-vé´śn] *n.* corruzione, depravazione.

Deprave [dǐ-prév´] *v.t.* corrompere, depravare.

Depravity [dǐ-prĕ´vǐ-tǐ] *n.* depravazione, pervertimento morale.

Deprecate [dĕ´prǐ-chét] *v.t.* deprecare.

Deprecation [dĕ-prǐ-ché´śn] *n.* deprecazione.

Depreciate [dǐ-prǐ´scǐ-ét] *v.t.* deprezzare; screditare; *v.i.* diminuire di valore.

Depreciation [dǐ-prǐ-scǐ-é´śn] *n.* deprezzamento.

Depredation [dĕ-prǐ-dé´śn] *n.* depredazione.

Depress [dǐ-prĕs´] *v.t.* deprimere.

Depressing [dǐ-prĕ´sǐń] *a.* deprimente.

Depression [dǐ-prĕ´śn] *n.* depressione.

Deprivation [dĕ-prǐ-vé´śn] *n.* privazione.

Deprive [dǐ-praí´v´] *v.t.* privare.

Depth [dĕpth] *n.* profondità; d. -charge [ciä˕g] bomba di profondità.

Deputation [dĕ-pǐü-té´śn] *n.* deputazione.

Depute [dǐ-pǐüt´] *v.t.* deputare.

Deputy [dĕ´pǐü-tǐ] *n.* delegato, deputato, rappresentante.

Derail [dǐ-rél´] *v.t.* far deragliare.

Derailment [dǐ-rél´mĕnt] *n.* deragliamento.

Derange [dĭ-rénğ'] v.t. disorganizzare, scombussolare.

Derelict [dĕ'rĭ-lĭct] n. relitto; a. abbandonato, derelitto.

Deride [dĭ-ra̤ĭd'] v.t. deridere.

Derision [dĭ-rĭ'ẑn] n. derisione, sarcasmo.

Derisive [dĭ-ra̤ĭ'sĭv] a. sarcastico.

Derivation [dĕ-rĭ-vé'ẑn] n. derivazione.

Derivative [dĭ-rĭ'vĕ-tĭv] a. e n. derivato.

Derive [dĭ-ra̤ĭv'] v.t. e i. derivare.

Derogate [dĕ'rò-ghét] v.i. derogare.

Derogation [dĕ-rò-ghé'ẑn] n. deroga.

Derogatory [dĕ-rŏ'ghĕ-tŏ-rĭ] a. derogatorio.

Derrick [dĕ'rĭc] n. (mecc.) sorta di gru.

Descend [dĭ-sĕnd'] v.i. derivare, discendere.

Descen/dant n. -dent n. [dĭ-sĕn'dĕnt] discendente.

Descent [dĭ-sĕnt'] n. discesa, discendenza, china, pendio, invasione.

Describe [dĭs-cra̤ĭb'] v.t. descrivere.

Description [dĭs-crĭp'ẑn] n. descrizione, genere, specie.

Descriptive [dĭs-crĭp'tĭv] a. descrittivo.

Descry [dĭs-cra̤ĭ'] v.t. discernere, scorgere.

Desecrate [dĕ'sĭ-crét] v.t. profanare.

Desecration [dĕ-sĭ-cré'ẑn] n. profanazione.

Desert [dĭ-zĕ̤'t] n. merito.

Desert [dĕ'zĕ̤t] n. deserto; [dĭ-zĕ̤'t] v.t. e i. disertare.

Deserter [dĭ-zĕ̤'tĕ̤'] n. disertore.

Deserve [dĭ-zĕ̤'v'] v.t. meritare.

Deserving [dĭ-zĕ̤'vĭñ] .. degno, meritevole.

Desiccate [dĕ'sĭ-chét] v.t. essiccare.

Design [dĭ-za̤ĭn'] n. disegno; v.t. designare, disegnare.

Designate [dĕ'zĭg-nét] v.t. designare.

Designation [dĕ-zĭg-né'ẑn] n. designazione.

Designer [dĭ-za̤ĭ'nĕ̤'] n. disegnatore, modellista.

Designing [dĭ-za̤ĭ'nĭñ] a. astuto, intrigante.

Desirable [dĭ-za̤ĭe'rĕ̤-bl] a. desiderabile.

Desire [dĭ-za̤ĭe'r'] n. desiderio, preghiera; v.t. augurare, desiderare, pregare.

Desirous [dĭ-za̤ĭe'rĕs] a. desideroso.

Desist [dĭ-zĭst'] v.i. desistere.

Desk [dĕsc] n. banco (di scuola) scrittoio.

Desolate [dĕ'sò-lĕt] a. desolato.

Desolation [dĕ-sò-lé'ẑn] n. desolazione, distruzione.

Despair [dĕs-pé̤e'r'] n. disperazione; v.i. disperar(si).

Desperate [dĕs'pĕ-rĕt] a. disperato, furioso.

Desperation [dĕs-pĕ-ré'ẑn] n. disperazione.

Despicable [dĕs'pĭ-chĕ-bl] a. spregevole.

Despise [dĭs-pa̤ĭs'] v.t. disprezzare.

Despite [dĭs-pa̤ĭt'] n. dispetto; prep. a dispetto di.

Despoil [dĭs-po̤ĭl'] v.t. derubare, spogliare.

Despond [dĭs-pònd'] v.i. scoraggiarsi.

Despondency [dĭs-pòn'dĕn-sĭ] n. abbattimento, scoraggiamento.

Despondent [dĭs-pòn'dĕnt] a. abbattuto, scoraggiato.

Despot [dĕs'pŏt] n. despota.

Despotic [dĕs-pŏ'tĭc] a. dispotico.

Despotism [dĕs'pò-tizm] n. dispotismo.

Dessert [dĭ-zĕʳt'] n. dolci e frutta (serviti alla fine del pasto) (pl.).

Destination [dĕs-tĭ-né'śn] n. destinazione.

Destine [dĕs'tĭn] v.t. destinare.

Destiny [dĕs'tĭ-nĭ] n. destino, fato.

Destitute [dĕs'tĭ-tiŭt] a. bisognoso, privo di mezzi.

Destitution [dĕs-tĭ-tiŭ'śn] n. destituzione, miseria.

Destroy [dĭs-tro¹'] v.t. distruggere, rovinare.

Destroyer [dĭs-tro¹'ĕʳ] n. distruttore, cacciatorpediniere (nave).

Destruction [dĭs-trăc'śn] n. distruzione, rovina.

Destructive [dĭs-trăc'tĭv] a. dannoso, distruttivo.

Desultory [dĭ'săl-tò-rĭ] a. saltuario, sconnesso.

Detach [dĭ-tĕc'] v.t. (di)staccare, separare.

Detachment [dĭ-tĕc'mĕnt] n. distacco; (mil.) distaccamento.

Detail [dĭ'tél] n. dettaglio, particolare minuzioso; (dĭ-tél') v.t. dettagliare; (mil.) distaccare (truppe).

Detain [dĭ-tén'] v.t. detenere, trattenere. [svelare.

Detect [dĭ-tĕct'] v.t. scoprire,

Detective [dĭ-tĕc'tĭv] n. agente di polizia.

Detention [dĭ-tĕn'śn] n. detenzione, ritardo.

Deter [dĭ-tĕr'] v.t. distogliere, scoraggiare.

Deteriorate [dĭ-ti'rĭ-ô-rét] v.t. e i. deteriorar(si).

Deterioration [dĭ-ti-rĭ-ô-ré'śn] n. deteriorazione.

Determinate [dĭ-tĕr'mĭ-nĕt] a. deciso, definito.

Determination [dĭ-tĕr-mĭ-né'śn] n. determinazione, risolutezza.

Determine [dĭ-tĕr'mĭn] v.t. decidere, determinare; v.i. decidersi.

Detest [dĭ-tĕst'] v.t. detestare.

Detestable [dĭ-tĕs'tĕ-bl] a. detestabile.

Detestation [dĭ-tĕs-té'śn] n. avversione, odio.

Dethrone [dĭ-thròn'] v.t. detronizzare.

Detonate [dĕ'tò-nét] v.t. e i. (far) detonare.

Detonation [dĕ-tò-né'śn] n. detonazione.

Detour [dĭ-tuᵉʳ'] n. deviazione, giravolta.

Detract [dĭ-trĕct'] v.t. e i. detrarre, sottrarre.

Detraction [dĭ-trĕc'śn] n. detrazione, diffamazione.

Detractor [dĭ-trĕc'tĕʳ] n. detrattore, diffamatore.

Detriment [dĕ'trĭ-mĕnt] n. danno, detrimento.

Detrimental [dĕ-trĭ-mĕn'tĕl] a. dannoso.

Deuce [diŭs] n. diavolo, malanno, (nel giuoco di dadi, ecc.) due, (al tennis) quaranta pari.

Devastate [dĕ'vĕs-tét] v.t. devastare.

Devastation [dĕ-vĕs-té'śn] n. devastazione.

Develop [dĭ-vĕ'lŏp] v.t. sviluppare, svolgere; v.i. svilupparsi.

Development [dĭ-vĕ'lŏp-mĕnt] n. sviluppo.

Deviate [dĭ'vĭ-ét] v.t. e i. (far) deviare.

Deviation [dĭ-vĭ-é'śn] n. deviazione.

Device [dĭ-va's'] n. artificio, espediente, progetto, stratagemma, aggeggio.

Devil [dĕ'vĭl] n. diavolo.

Devilish [dĕ'vĭ-lĭś] a. diabolico. [voleria.

Devilry [dĕ'vĭl-rĭ] n. diavoleria.

Devious [dĭ'vĭ-ăs] a. indiretto, serpeggiante.

Devise [dǐ-vaɪz'] v.t. escogitare, progettare, lasciare (per testamento); v.i. fare un piano.
Devoid [dǐ-voɪd'] a. privo.
Devolution [dě-vò-liū'šn] n. devoluzione.
Devolve [dǐ-vòlv'] v.t. devolvere; v.i. cadere.
Devote [dǐ-vòt'] v.t. consacrare, dedicare.
Devoted [dǐ-vò'tĭd] a. affezionatissimo, devoto.
Devotee [dě-vò-tī'] n. bigotto, devoto.
Devotion [dǐ-vò'šn] n. devozione.
Devotional [dǐ-vò'scio-něl] a. di devozione.
Devour [dǐ-vauɜr'] v.t. divorare.
Devout [dǐ-vaŭt'] a. divoto, pio.
Devoutness [dǐ-vaŭt'něs] n. religiosità.
Dew [diū] n. rugiada.
Dewy [diū'ǐ] a. rugiadoso.
Dexterity [děc-stě'rĭ-tǐ] n. destrezza.
Dexterous [děc'stě-răs] a. abile, destro.
Diabetes [daɪ-ĕ-bī'tǐs] n. (med.) diabete.
Diabolic [daɪ-ĕ-bò'lǐc] a. diabolico.
Diadem [dàɪ'ĕ-děm] n. diadema.
Diagnose [daɪ-ĕg-nòz'] v.t. diagnosticare.
Diagnosis [daɪ-ĕg-nò-sǐs] n. diagnosi.
Diagonal [daɪ-è'go-něl] a. e n. diagonale.
Diagram [daɪ'ĕ-grĕm] n. diagramma.
Dial [daɪ'ĕl] n. meridiana, quadrante (d'orologio, ecc.).
Dialect [daɪ'ĕ-lĕct] n. dialetto.
Dialogue [daɪ'ĕ-lòg] n. dialogo.
Diameter [daɪ-è'mǐ-tĕr] n. diametro.

Diamond [daɪ'ă-mǒnd] n. diamante; (geom.) rombo; -s (pl.) quadri (carte).
Diaper [daɪ'ă-pěr] n. diaspro, pannolino, pezza.
Diaphanous [daɪ-è'fè-năs] a. diafano.
Diaphragm [daɪ'ă-frèm] n. diaframma.
Diary [daɪ'ă-rǐ] n. diario.
Dice [daɪs] n. (pl. di die).
Dictate [dǐc-tét'] v.t. e i. dettare.
Dictation [dǐc-té'šn] n. dettatura, comando.
Dictator [dǐc-té'tĕr] n. dittatore, chi detta.
Dictatorship [dǐc-té'tĕr-scip] n. dittatura.
Diction [dǐc'šn] n. dizione.
Dictionary [dǐc'scio-nè-rǐ] n. dizionario, vocabolario.
Didactic [daɪ-dĕc'tǐc] a. didattico.
Die [daɪ] n. dado, stampo (per monete, ecc.); v.i. morire; to d. out [aut] scomparire.
Diet [daɪ'ět] n. dieta, regime; v.t. mettere a dieta, a regime.
Differ [dǐ'fěr] v.i. differire, dissentire.
Difference [dǐ'fè-rěns] n. differenza, contesa.
Different [dǐ'fè-rěnt] a. differente, diverso.
Differential [dǐ'fè-rěn'scěl] a. differenziale.
Difficult [dǐ'fǐ-călt] a. difficile.
Difficulty [dǐ'fǐ-căl-tǐ] n. difficoltà, ostacolo.
Diffidence [dǐ'fǐ-děns] n. sfiducia in sè, timidezza.
Diffident [dǐ'fǐ-děnt] a. modesto, timido.
Diffuse [dǐ-fiūs'] a. diffuso; v.t. e i. diffonder(si).
Diffusion [dǐ-fiū'šn] n. diffusione.
Dig [dǐg] v.t. e i. lavorare la terra, scavare, vangare.
Digest [daɪ'gěst] n. digesto:

(da¹-gĕst') *v.t.* e *i.* assimilare, digerire.

Digestible [dĭ-gĕs'tĭ-bl] *a.* digeribile.

Digestion [dĭ-gĕs'tĭ-ĕn] *n.* digestione.

Digestive [dĭ-gĕs'tĭv] *a.* digestivo.

Digger [dĭg'hĕr] *n.* scavatore.

Dignified [dĭg'nĭ-fa¹d] *a.* composto, dignitoso.

Dignify [dĭg'nĭ-fa¹] *v.t.* investire di dignità.

Dignitary [dĭg'nĭ-tă-rĭ] *n.* dignitario.

Dignity [dĭg'nĭ-tĭ] *n.* dignità.

Digress [da¹-grĕs'] *v.i.* fare delle digressioni.

Digression [da¹-grĕ'śn] *n.* digressione.

Dike [da¹c] *n.* diga.

Dilapidation [dĭ-lè-pĭ-dé'śn] *n.* dilapidazione.

Dilate [da¹-lét'] *v.t.* e *i.* dilatar(si).

Dilatory [dĭ'lă-tŏ-rĭ] *a.* dilatorio.

Diligence [dĭ'lĭ-gĕns] *n.* diligenza.

Diligent [dĭ'lĭ-gĕnt] *a.* diligente.

Dilute [da¹-lіűt'] *v.t.* diluire.

Dilution [da¹-lіű'śn] *n.* diluzione.

Dim [dĭm] *a.* indistinto, oscuro, vago; *v.t.* e *i.* offuscar(si), oscurar(si).

Dimension [dĭ-mĕn'śn] *n.* dimensione.

Diminish [dĭ-mĭ'nĭś] *v.t.* e *i.* diminuire.

Diminution [dĭ-mĭ-nіű'śn] *n.* diminuzione.

Diminutive [dĭ-mĭ'nіű-tĭv] *a.* e *n.* diminutivo.

Dimness [dĭm'nĕs] *n.* oscurità.

Dimple [dĭm'pl] *n.* fossetta.

Din [dĭn] *n.* frastuono, rumore assordante.

Dine [da¹n] *v.i.* pranzare.

Dinginess [dĭn'gĭ-nĕs] *n.* scoloritura, sudiciume.

Dingy [dĭn'gĭ] *a.* scolorito, sporco.

Dining-room [da¹'nĭñ-rūm] *n.* sala da pranzo.

Dinner [dĭ'nĕr] *n.* desinare, pranzo.

Dint [dĭnt] *n.* forza, potere; by d. of, *prep.* a forza di.

Diocese [da¹'ŏ-sĭs] *n.* diocesi.

Dip [dĭp] *n.* immersione, inclinazione, candela di sego; *v.t.* e *i.* immerger(si), tuffar(si).

Diphtheria [dĭf-thī'rĭ-ĕ⁽ʳ⁾] *n.* difterite.

Diphthong [dĭf'thŏn] *n.* dittongo.

Diplomacy [dĭ-plò'mè-sĭ] *n.* diplomazia.

Diplomatic [dĭ-plò-mè'tĭc] *a.* diplomatico.

Diplomatist [dĭ-plò'mè-tĭst] *n.* diplomatico.

Dire [da¹ᵉʳ] *a.* spaventoso, terribile.

Direct [da¹-rĕct'] *a.* diretto; *av.* immediatemente; *v.t.* avviare, dirigere, indirizzare.

Direction [da¹-rĕc'śn] *n.* direzione, indicazione, indirizzo.

Directive [da¹-rĕc'tĭv] *a.* direttivo.

Director [da¹-rĕc'tĕr] *n.* direttore.

Directory [da¹-rĕc'tŏ-rĭ] *n.* direttorio, elenco telefonico, guida.

Direful [da¹ᵉʳ'fūl] *a.* spaventoso, terribile.

Dirge [dĕr'ǵ] *n.* canto funebre, nenia.

Dirt [dĕrt] *n.* sporcizia, sudiciume.

Dirtiness [dĕr'tĭ-nĕs] *n.* l'essere sporco, sporcizia.

Dirty [dĕr'tĭ] *a.* sporco, sudicio; *v.t.* insudiciare, sporcare.

Disability [dĭs-è-bĭ'lĭ-tĭ] *n.* incapacità, invalidità.

Disable [dis-é'bl] *v.t.* inabilitare, rendere incapace.

Disabled [dis-é'bld] *a.* incapace, invalido.

Disabuse [dis-è-biûz'] *v.t.* disingannare.

Disadvantage [dis-èd-vèn'tíg] *n.* svantaggio.

Disadvantageous [dis-èd-vèn-té'giǎs] *a.* svantaggioso.

Disagree [dis-à-gri'] *v.i.* discordare, dissentire, non andar d'accordo, non essere confacente.

Disagreeable [dis-à-gri'à-bl] *a.* antipatico, sgradevole.

Disagreement [dis-à-gri'mènt] *n.* disaccordo, dissenso.

Disallow [dis-à-lau'] *v.t.* non ammettere, respingere.

Disappear [dis-à-pi'er] *v.i.* scomparire, svanire.

Disappearance [dis-à-pi'e-rèns] *n.* scomparsa.

Disappoint [dis-à-po'nt'] *v.t.* deludere.

Disappointment [dis-à-po'nt'mènt] *n.* delusione, disappunto.

Disapproval [dis-à-prû'vèl] *n.* disapprovazione.

Disapprove [dis-à-prûv'] *v.t.* disapprovare.

Disarm [dis-a'rm] *v.t. e i.* disarmare.

Disarrange [dis-è-rén'g'] *v.t.* disorganizzare, scombussolare.

Disarray [dis-à-re'] *n.* disordine, scompiglio.

Disarray [dis-à-re'] *v.t. (raro)* scompigliare.

Disaster [di-zès'tèr] *n.* disastro.

Disastrous [di-zès'trǎs] *a.* disastroso.

Disavow [dis-è-vaǔ'] *v.t.* disconoscere, sconfessare.

Disavowal [dis-è-vaǔ'èl] *n.* disconoscimento.

Disband [dis-bènd'] *v.t. e i.* sbandar(si).

Disbelief [dis-bi-lif'] *n.* incredulità.

Disbelieve [dis-bi-liv'] *v.t.* non credere a.

Disburden [dis-bër'dn] *v.t.* alleggerire d'un peso.

Disburse [dis-bërs'] *v.t.* sborsare.

Disbursement [dis-bërs'mènt] *n.* sborso.

Discard [dis-ca'd'] *v.t. e i.* scartare.

Discern [di-sër'n'] *v.t.* discernere.

Discerning [di-sër'níŋ] *a.* acuto, penetrante.

Discernment [di-sër'n'mènt] *n.* discernimento, acutezza di giudizio.

Discharge [dis-cia'g'] *n.* emissione, liberazione, pagamento, scari/ca, -co; *v.t.* compiere (un dovere), emettere, congedare, licenziare, scaricare; *v.i. (med.)* mandar fuori pus.

Disciple [di-sa'pl] *n.* discepolo.

Disciplinarian [di-sa-pli-né'ri-ën] *n.* chi mantiene una rigida disciplina.

Disciplinary [di'si-pli-në-ri] *a.* disciplinare.

Discipline [di'si-plin] *n.* disciplina.

Disclaim [dis-clém'] *v.t.* negare, ripudiare.

Disclose [dis-clòs'] *v.t.* dischiudere, rivelare.

Disclosure [dis-clò'jër] *n.* rivelazione.

Discolour [dis-cǎ'lër] *v.t.* scolorire.

Discomfit [dis-cǎm'fit] *v.t. (raro)*, sconfiggere, sconcertare.

Discomfiture [dis-cǎm'fi-cër] *n.* sconfitta, scoraggiamento.

Discomfort [dis-cǎm'fë't] *n.* disagio, mancanza di comodità.

Disconcert [dis-cön-së't] *v.t.* sconcertare.

Disconnect [dĭs-cŏ-nĕct'] v.t. sconnettere.

Disconsolate [dĭs-cŏn'sŏ-lét] a. sconsolato, triste.

Discontent [dĭs-cŏn-tĕnt'], discontentment [dĭs-cŏn-tĕnt'mĕnt] n. scontento.

Discontinuance [dĭs-cŏn-tĭ'nū-ĕns] n. cessazione, interruzione.

Discontinue [dĭs-cŏn-tĭ'nū] v.t. cessare, interrompere.

Discord [dĭs'cor̄d] n. discordia, lotta; (mus.) disaccordo.

Discordance [dĭs-cor̄'dĕns] n. discordanza.

Discount [dĭs'caunt] n. sconto, tara; (dĭs'caunt) v.t. scontare, fare la tara a.

Discourage [dĭs-cŭ'rĭg̃] v.t. dissuadere, scoraggiare.

Discouragement [dĭs-cŭ'rĭg̃-mĕnt] n. scoraggiamento.

Discourse [dĭs'co'r̄s] n. discorso; (dĭs-co'r̄s)v.i.discorrere.

Discourteous [dĭs-chĕr'tĭ-ăs] a. scortese.

Discover [dĭs-cŭ'vĕr̄] v.t. scoprire.

Discoverer [dĭs-cŭ'vĕ-rĕr̄] n. scopritore.

Discovery [dĭs-cŭ'vĕ-rĭ] n. scoperta.

Discredit [dĭs-crĕ'dĭt] n. discredito; v.t. screditare.

Discreditable [dĭs-crĕ'dĭ-tĕ-bĭl] a. vergognoso.

Discreet [dĭs-crĭt'] a. circospetto, giudizioso.

Discrepancy [dĭs-crĕ'pĕn-sĭ] n. discrepanza.

Discretion [dĭs-crĕ'ṣn] n. discrezione, prudenza, libertà di scelta.

Discriminate [dĭs-crĭ'mĭ-nét] v.t. discriminare.

Discrimination [dĭs-crĭ-mĭ-né'ṣn] n. discriminazione.

Discursive [dĭs-chĕr'sĭv] a. digressivo, saltuario.

Discuss [dĭs-căs'] v.t. discutere.

Discussion [dĭs-că'ṣn] n. discussione.

Disdain [dĭs-dén'] n. (di) sdegno; v.t. disdegnare.

Disdainful [dĭs-dén'fŭl] a. sdegnoso.

Disease [dĭ-zĭz'] n. malattia.

Diseased [dĭ-zĭzd'] a. malato, affetto da malattia.

Disembark [dĭs-ĕm-ba'r̄c'] v.t. e i. sbarcare.

Disengage [dĭs-ĕn-gég'] v.t. disimpegnare, liberare.

Disentangle [dĭs-ĕn-tĕn'gl] v.t. districare, sbrogliare.

Disfavour [dĭs-fé'vĕr̄] n. disistima.

Disfigure [dĭs-fĭ'ghĕr̄] v.t. deformare.

Disgorge [dĭs-go'r̄g'] v.t. e i. buttar fuori.

Disgrace [dĭs-grés'] n. disonore, vergogna, disgrazia; v.t. disonorare, far cadere in disgrazia.

Disgraceful [dĭs-grés'fŭl] a. disonorante, vergognoso.

Disguise [dĭs-gha'ĭz'] n. maschera, travestimento; v.t. mascherare, travestire.

Disgust [dĭs-găst'] n. disgusto; v.t. disgustare.

Disgusting [dĭs-găs'tĭñ] a. disgustoso.

Dish [dĭsh] n. piatto, piatto di portata, vassoio; v.t. mettere nel piatto, servire.

Dishearten [dĭs-ha'r̄tn] v.t. scoraggiare. (gliare.

Dishevel [dĭ-scĕ'vĕl] v.t. scapi-

Dishonest [dĭs-ŏ'nĕst] a. disonesto.

Dishonour [dĭs-ŏ'nĕr̄] n. disonore; (comm.) mancato pagamento; v.t. disonorare; (comm.) rifiutarsi di pagare.

Dishonourable [dĭs-ŏ'nŏ-ră-bl] a. disonorevole.

Disinclination [dĭs-ĭn-clĭ-né'ṣn] n. antipatia, disinclinazione.

Disincline [dìs-in-clai'n'] *v.t.* rendere avverso a.

Disinfect [dìs-in-fèct'] *v.t.* disinfettare.

Disinfectant [dìs-in-fèc'tènt] *n.* disinfettante.

Disinherit [dìs-in-hè'rit] *v.t.* diseredare.

Disintegrate [dìs-in'tì-grèt] *v.t.* e *i.* disintegrar(si).

Disinterested [dìs-in'tè-rès-tid] *a.* disinteressato, imparziale.

Disjointed [dìs-gioi'n'tid] *a.* incoerente, sconnesso.

Disjunction [dìs-giànc'sn] *n.* disgiunzione, separazione.

Disk [dìsc] *n.* disco.

Dislike [dìs-lai'c'] *n.* antipatia; *v.t.* sentire antipatia per; I dislike it, non mi piace.

Dislocate [dìs-lò-chèt'] *v.t.* dislocare, slogare.

Dislocation [dìs-lò-chè'sn] *n.* dislocazione, slogatura.

Dislodge [dìs-lóg'] *v.t.* e *i.* sloggiare.

Disloyal [dìs-loi'èl] *a.* infedele, sleale.

Disloyalty [dìs-loi'èl-ti] *n.* infedeltà, slealtà.

Dismal [dìz'mèl] *a.* cupo, malinconico, triste.

Dismantle [dìs-mèn'tl] *v.t.* smantellare.

Dismay [dìs-me'i'] *n.* costernazione, sbigottimento; *v.t.* costernare, sbigottire.

Dismember [dìs-mèm'bèr] *v.t.* smembrare.

Dismiss [dìs-mìs'] *v.t.* bandire (dalla mente, ecc.), licenziare, mandar via.

Dismissal [dìs-mì'sèl] *n.* licenziamento.

Dismount [dìs-maunt'] *v.i.* smontare.

Disobedience [dìs-ò-bì'dièns] *n.* disobbidienza.

Disobedient [dìs-ò-bì'diènt] *a.* disobbidiente.

Disobey [dìs-ò-be'i'] *v.t.* e *i.* disobbidire (a).

Disoblige [dìs-ò-bla'ig'] *v.t.* offendere, rifiutare un favore a.

Disorder [dìs-o'r'dèr] *n.* confusione, disordine, indisposizione; *v.t.* disordinare, far ammalare.

Disorganization [dìs-o'r-ghèna'i-zè'sn] *n.* disorganizzazione.

Disorganize [dìs-o'r'ghè-na'iz] *v.t.* disorganizzare.

Disown [dìs-òn'] *v.t.* rinnegare, ripudiare.

Disparage [dìs-pè'rìg'] *v.t.* denigrare, deprezzare.

Disparagement [dìs-pè'rìg'mènt] *n.* denigrazione.

Dispatch [dìs-pèc'] *n.* spaccio, spedizione, prontezza, sollecitudine; *v.t.* sbrigare, spacciare, spedire.

Dispel [dìs-pèl'] *v.t.* dissipare, scacciare. [dispensario.

Dispensary [dìs-pèn'sè-ri] *n.*

Dispensation [dìs-pèn-sè'sn] *n.* dispensa, dispensazione.

Dispense [dìs-pèns'] *v.t.* dispensare, distribuire.

Dispersal [dìs-pèr'sèl] *n.* dispersione.

Disperse [dìs-pèrs'] *v.t.* diffondere, decomporre [luce], disperdere *v.i.* disperdersi.

Dispersion [dìs-pèr'sn] *n.* dispersione, decomposizione (della luce).

Displace [dìs-plès'] *v.t.* sostituire, spostare.

Display [dìs-plé'i'] *n.* esibizione, ostentazione *v.t.* esporre, ostentare, spiegare.

Displease [dìs-plìs'] *v.t.* far arrabbiare, offendere.

Displeasure [dìs-plè'jèr] *n.* collera, scontento.

Disposal [dìs-pò'zèl] *n.* disposizione, ordine; at your [èt iô'r] d. a sua disposizione.

Dispose [dìs-poz'] *v.t.* e *i.* disporre, disfarsi, vendere.

Disposition [dìs-pò-z'-'sn] n. carattere, temperamento.

Dispossess [dìs-pò-zès'] v.t. privare, spossessare.

Disproportion [dìs-prò-po'-sn] n. sproporzione.

Disprove [dìs-prùv'] v.t. mostrare la falsità di.

Dispute [dìs-piùt'] n. dibattimento, discussione, disputa.

Dispute [dìs-piùt'] v.t. e i. disputare.

Disqualification [dìs-quó-li-fi-chè'sn] n. (causa di) squalifica.

Disqualify [dìs-quó'li-fa¹] v.t. inabilitare, squalificare.

Disquiet [dìs-qua¹²ët] n. inquietudine; a. inquieto; v.t. rendere inquieto.

Disregard [dìs-rì-ga'd'] n. indifferenza, noncuranza; v.t. trascurare, trattare con noncuranza.

Disreputable [dìs-rè'più-tä-bl] a. di cattiva riputazione, non rispettabile.

Disrespect [dìs-rìs-pèct'] n. mancanza di rispetto, sgarbatezza.

Disruption [dìs-räp'sn] n. violenta scissione.

Dissatisfaction [dì-sè-tìs-fèc'sn] n. malcontento.

Dissatisfied [dì-sè'tìs-fa¹d] a. insoddisfatto, scontento.

Dissatisfy [dì-sè'tìs-fa¹] v.t. non soddisfare la.

Dissect [dì-sèct'] v.t. sezionare; (fig.) criticare.

Dissection [dì-sèc'sn] n. dissezione.

Dissemble [dì-sèm'bl] v.t. e i. dissimulare, nascondere, simulare.

Disseminate [dì-sè'mi-nét] v.t. disseminare, diffondere.

Dissension [dì-sèn'sn] n. dissensione, discordia.

Dissent [dì-sènt'] n. dissenso, dissentimento; v.i. dissentire.

Dissenter [dì-sèn'tè'] n. dissidente.   [dissimile.

Dissimilar [dì-sì'mi-lè'] a.

Dissimilarity [dì-sì-mi-lè'ri-ti] n. disparità.

Dissipate [dì'sì-pét] v.t. e i. dissipar(si).

Dissipated [dì'sì-pé-tìd] a. dissoluto.

Dissipation [dì-sì-pé'sn] n. dissipazione, dispersione.

Dissoluble [dì'sò-liù-bl] a. dissolubile.

Dissolute [dì'sò-liùt] a. dissoluto, sregolato.

Dissolution [dì-sò-liù'sn] n. dissoluzione, scioglimento.

Dissolve [dì-zòlv'] v.t. e i. discioglier(si), dissolver(si).

Dissuade [dì-suéd'] v.t. dissuadere.

Distaff [dì'stäf] n. conocchia.

Distance [dì'stèns] n. distanza.

Distant [dì'stènt] a. distante, remoto; (fig.) freddo, riservato.

Distaste [dìs-tést'] n. ripugnanza.

Distasteful [dìs-tést'fùl] a. ripugnante, sgradevole.

Distemper [dìs-tèm'pè'] n. tempera, indisposizione, malattia dei cani.

Distemper [dìs-tèm'pè'] v.t. dipingere a tempera; turbare nelle funzioni fisiche o mentali.

Distend [dìs-tènd'] v.t. e i. distender(si).

Distil [dìs-stil'] v.t. distillare; v.i. stillare.

Distillation [dìs-stì-lé'sn] n. distillazione.

Distillery [dì-stì'lè-ri] n. distilleria.

Distinct [dìs-tìnct'] a. ben definito, distinto, diverso.

Distinction [dìs-tìnc'sn] n. distinzione.

Distinguish [dì-stìn'guìś] v.t. e i. differenziare, distinguere.

Distort [dìs-tò't'] v.t. deformare (fatti, ecc.) distorcere.

Distortion [dĭs-tŏr'sn] n. deformazione, distorsione.

Distract [dĭs-trĕct'] v.t. distrarre, far impazzire.

Distracted [dĭs-trĕc'tĭd] a. pazzo, perplesso.

Distrain [dĭs-trén'] v.t. e i. sequestrare, fare un sequestro.

Distress [dĭs-trĕs'] n. dolore, rammarico, sventura; v.t. affliggere.

Distribute [dĭs-trĭ'bĭŭt] v.t. distribuire.

Distribution [dĭs-trĭ-bĭŭ'sn] n. distribuzione.

District [dĭs'trĭct] n. distretto.

Distrust [dĭs-trăst'] n. diffidenza, sfiducia; v.t. diffidare di.

Distrustful [dĭs-trăst'fŭl] a. diffidente, sospettoso.

Disturb [dĭs-tĕrb'] v.t. disturbare.

Disturbance [dĭs-tĕr'bĕns] n. agitazione, interruzione, tumulto. [sunione.

Disunion [dĭs-iŭ'nĭĕn] n. di-

Disuse [dĭs-iŭs'] n. disuso.

Ditch [dĭč] n. fossa, fossato.

Ditto [dĭt'tò] n. lo stesso, come sopra.

Ditty [dĭt'tĭ] n. canzone popolare (di regola tradizionale).

Divan [dă'vĕn] n. divano.

Dive [dă'v] v.i. immergersi, tuffarsi; (avia.) scendere in picchiata.

Diver [dă'vĕr] n. palombaro, tuffatore.

Diverge [dă'vĕrg'] v.i. divergere.

Divergen/ce, -cy [dă'vĕr'gĕns (sĭ)] n. divergenza.

Divergent [dă'vĕr'gĕnt] a. divergente.

Divers [dă'vĕrz] a. (pl. arcaico) alcuni, diversi (pl.).

Diverse [dă'vĕrs'] a. diverso.

Diversify [dă'vĕr'sĭ-fă'] v.t. diversificare, variare.

Diversion [dă'vĕr'sn] n. diversione.

Divert [dă'vĕrt'] v.t. stornare, mutare la direzione di, divertire.

Divest [dă'vĕst'] v.t. spogliare, svestire.

Divide [dĭ-vă'd'] v.t. e i. divider(si).

Dividend [dĭ'vĭ-dĕnd] n. (comm.) dividendo.

Dividers [dĭ-vă'dĕrs] n. (pl.) sorta di compasso.

Divine [dĭ-vă'n] n. teologo; a. divino; v.t. e i. indovinare.

Divinity [dĭ-vĭ'nĭ-tĭ] n. divinità, teologia.

Division [dĭ-vĭ'žn] n. divisione.

Divorce [dĭ-vors'] n. divorzio; v.t. divorziare da.

Divulge [dĭ-vălg'] v.t. divulgare, rivelare.

Dizziness [dĭ'zĭ-nĕs] n. capogiro, vertigine.

Dizzy [dĭ'zĭ] a. che ha il capogiro, vertiginoso.

Do [dŭ] v.t. fare, compiere, eseguire, cucinare; (gergo) ingannare; v.i. fare, comportarsi; (famil.) ridurre; v.i. entrare in porto (di una nave).

Docile [dŏ'să'l] a. docile.

Docility [dŏ-sĭ'lĭ-tĭ] n. docilità.

Dock [dŏc] n. bacino; d. -yard [iă'd] arsenale; v.t. mozzare; (famil.) ridurre; v.i. entrare in porto (di una nave).

Doctor [dŏc'tĕr] n. dottore, medico.

Doctrine [dŏc'trĭn] n. dottrina.

Document [dŏ'chiŭ-mĕnt] n. documento.

Dodge [dŏg] v.t. eludere, schivare; v.i. muoversi qua e là, schivare.

Doe [dò] n. femmina del coniglio, del cervo, e di altri animali di caccia.

Doff [dŏf] v.t. (raro) togliere (gli abiti).

Dog [dŏg] n. cane; d. -days

[de¹s] (*pl.*) la canicola; *v.t.* seguire (e spiare) costantemente.

Dogged [dŏ'ghĭd] *a.* ostinato, tenace.

Doggerel [dŏ'ghĕ-rĕl] *n.* versi zoppicanti, senza valore (*pl.*).

Dogmatize [dŏg'mă-ta¹z] *v.t. e i.* dogmatizzare.

Dole [dŏl] *n.* distribuzione caritatevole; **the d.** sussidio dato ai disoccupati; *v.t.* distribuire in piccole quantità.

Doleful [dŏl'fŭl] *a.* malinconico, triste.

Doll [dŏl] *n.* bambola.

Dollar [dŏ'lĕr] *n.* dollaro.

Dolphin [dŏl'fĭn] *n.* delfino.

Dolt [dŏlt] *n.* individuo ottuso, stolto.

Domain [dŏ-mén'] *n.* dominio, proprietà terriera.

Dome [dŏm] *n.* cupola.

Domestic [dŏ-mĕs'tĭc] *n.* domesti/co, -ca; *a.* casalingo, domestico, non forestiero.

Domicile [dŏ'mĭ-sa¹l] *n.* domicilio.

Dominate [dŏ'mĭ-nét] *v.t. e i.* dominare.

Domination [dŏ-mĭ-né'šn] *n.* dominazione, dominio.

Domineer [dŏ-mĭ-nĭ°r'] *v.i.* spadroneggiare, tiranneggiare.

Dominican [dŏ-mĭ'nĭ-chĕn] *e. e n.* domenicano.

Dominion [dŏ-mĭ'nĭĕn] *n.* dominio.

Don [dŏn] *v.t.* (*raro*) mettersi (i vestiti).

Donate [dŏ-nét'] *v.t.* donare.

Donation [dŏ-né'šn] *n.* donazione.

Donkey [dŏñ'chĭ] *n.* asino, somaro; **d. -engine** [ĕn'gĭn] macchina per sollevare pesi sulla coperta d'una nave.

Donor [dŏ'nĕr] *n.* dona/tore, -trice.

Doom [dŭm] *n.* condanna, destino, sorte; *v.t.* condannare.

Doomsday [dŭmz'dé¹] *n.* giorno del giudizio.

Door [dŏ°r] *n.* porta; **d. -way** [ué¹] vano della porta.

Dormitory [dŏr'mĭ-tŏ-rĭ] *n.* dormitorio. [ghiro.

Dormouse [dŏr'maus] *n.*

Dorsal [dŏr'sĕl] *a.* dorsale.

Dose [dŏs] *n.* dose; *v.t.* dare una medicina a, adulterare (liquori).

Dot [dŏt] *n.* macchia, punto, puntino, piccolo segno.

Dotage [dŏ'tĭĝ] *n.* rimbambimento.

Dotard [dŏ'tĕrd] *n.* vecchio rimbambito.

Dote [dŏt] *v.i.* essere infatuato.

Double [dă'bl] *a.* doppio, duplicato; *a.* doppio, finto; *av.* due volte; *v.t.* (rad)doppiare, passar intorno a; *v.i.* (rad)doppiare, voltare improvvisamente.

Doubt [daut] *n.* dubbio, incertezza, sospetto; *v.t.* dubitare di; *v.i.* dubitare, essere incerto.

Doubtful [daut'fŭl] *a.* ambiguo, dubbioso.

Doubtless [daut'lĕs] *avv.* indubbiamente, senza dubbio.

Dough [dŏ] *n.* pasta.

Doughty [dau'tĭ] *a.* forte, valoroso.

Dove [dăv] *n.* colombo.

Dowager [dau'ĕ-ĝĕr] *n.* vedova (che ha un titolo o un patrimonio ereditato dal marito).

Down [daun] *n.* landa, lanugine, peluria, piumino; *a.* depresso; *prep.* in basso, giù per; *av.* giù, in basso, in giù; **d. with . . .** *interiez.* abbasso; *v.t.* (*famil.*) abbattere, gettare a terra.

Downcast [daun'căst] *a.* abbattuto.

Downfall [daun'fŏl] *n.* rovina, rovescio di fortuna.

Downhill [daun'hil] *n.* discesa; *a.* discendente; *av.* in discesa.

Downpour [daun'pô⁰] *n.* forte scroscio di pioggia.

Downright [daun-ra¹t'] *a.* brusco, chiaro; *av.* in termini chiari.

Downstairs [daun-ste⁰rs'] *a.* del (al) piano di sotto; *av.* giù dalle scale.

Downward [daun'ue³rd] *a.* discendente, inclinato; -s *av.* dall'alto al basso, in discesa.

Dowry [dau⁰ri] *n.* dote (di sposa).

Doze [dòz] *n.* sonnellino; *v.i.* sonnecchiare.

Dozen [dä'zn] *n.* dozzina.

Drab [drèb] *n.* prostituta; *a.* incolore.

Draft [dráft] *n.* abbozzo (di documento), brutta copia, assegno, tratta; (*mil.*) distaccamento; *v.t.* mandare in distaccamento, redigere.

Drag [drèg] *n.* carrozza a quattro cavalli, ostacolo, peso; *v.t.* trascinare, dragare.

Dragon [drè'gòn] *n.* drago(ne); d. -fly (fla¹) libellula.

Dragoon [drè-gûn'] *n.* (*mil.*) dragone.

Drain [dre¹n] *n.* canale, fogna, tubo di scarico, tubo per drenaggio; *v.t.* prosciugare per drenaggio, scolare, bere fino in fondo; *v.i.* prosciugarsi, scolare.

Drainage [dre¹'nig] *n.* drenaggio. [maschio.

Drake [dre¹c] *n.* anitra

Drama [drä'mè⁽r⁾] *n.* dramma.

Dramatic [drä-mè'tic] *a.* drammatico.

Dramatist [drè'mä-tist] *n.* drammaturgo.

Drape [dre¹p] *v.t.* coprire, drappeggiare.

Draper [dré'pê⁰] *n.* merciaio, negoziante in tessuti.

Drapery [dré'pè-ri] *n.* commercio in tessuti, drappeggio.

Drastic [drès'tic] *a.* drastico, violento.

Draught [draft] *n.* bevanda, corrente d'aria, dose di medicinale; (*naut.*) pescaggio d'una nave, trazione, forza di trazione.

Draughts [drafts] *n.* (*pl.*) dama (giuoco).

Draughtsman [drafts'män] *n.* disegnatore.

Draughty [draf'ti] *a.* pieno di correnti d'aria.

Draw [drô] *v.t.* attrarre, tirare, trascinare, abbozzare, disegnare, tirare a sorte.

Drawback [drô'bèc] *n.* inconveniente, svantaggio.

Drawbridge [drô'brig] *n.* ponte levatoio.

Drawer [drô'ê⁰] *n.* cassetto, chi disegna, tira, ecc.; -s (*pl.*) mutande (*pl.*).

Drawing [drô'iñ] *n.* disegno, sorteggio, tiro, tiraggio; d. -room (rûm) salotto.

Drawl [drôl] *v.i.* parlare in modo lento e affettato.

Dray [dre¹] *n.* carro pesante.

Dread [drèd] *n.* terrore; *v.t.* temere.

Dreadful [drèd'fûl] *a.* terribile.

Dreadnought [drèd'nôt] *n.* (*naut.*) supercorazzata.

Dream [drim] *n.* sogno; *n. e i.* sognare.

Dreary [dri'èri] *a.* desolato, triste.

Dredge [drèǵ] *v.t.* dragare, coprire di farina, zucchero, ecc.

Dregs [drègs] *n.* (*pl.*) feccia, sedimento.

Drench [drènč] *v.t.* imbevere, inzuppare.

Dress [drès] *n.* abito, vestito, modo di vestirsi; *v.t.* vestire; (*mil.*) allineare, medicare (una ferita), cucinare; *v.i.* vestirsi.

Dresser [drĕ'sĕr] *n.* assistente chiurgo, cameriera (d'attrice), specie di credenza per cucina.

Dressing [drĕ'sĭṅ] *n.* abbigliamento, benda per medicazione, salsa.

Dressing-gown [drĕ'sĭṅ gaun] *n.* vestaglia.

Dressmaker [drĕs'mé-chĕr] *n.* sarta.

Dribble [drī'bl] *v.i.* cadere a piccole gocce, sbavare.

Drift [drift] *n.* corrente, deriva, corso, proposito, scopo, cumulo (di neve, ecc.), detrito; *v.i.* andare alla deriva, lasciarsi trasportare.

Drill [dril] *n.* (*mecc.*) perforatrice, trapano; (*mil.*) esercitazioni (*pl.*); *v.t.* perforare, far esercitare; *v.i.* fare esercitazioni.

Drink [drĭṅc] *n.* bevanda, intemperanza nel bere; *v.t. e i.* bere.

Drinkable [drĭṅ'că-bl] *a.* bevibile, potabile.

Drip [drip] *n.* gocciolamento, stillicidio; *v.i.* gocciolare.

Drive [draiv] *n.* passeggiata in carrozza o in auto, viale carrozzabile; *v.t.* condurre, guidare, costringere a fare, trasportare; *v.i.* andare in carrozza, in auto.

Drivel [drī'vĕl] *v.i.* parlare da sciocco, sbavare.

Driver [drai'vĕr] *n.* autista, conducente, vetturino.

Drizzle [drī'zl] *n.* pioggerella; *v.i.* piovigginare.

Droll [drōl] *n.* buffone; *a.* buffo, divertente. [neria.

Drollery [drò'lĕ-rĭ] *n.* buffoneria.

Dromedary [drŏ'mĭ-dă-rĭ] *n.* dromedario.

Drone [drōn] *n.* bordone (di cornamusa), fuco; *v.i.* ronzare, parlare con tono monotono.

Droop [drūp] *v.i.* abbattersi, languire.

Drop [drŏp] *n.* goccia, caduta, decadenza, ribasso (prezzi), abbassamento (di temperatura) *v.t.* lasciar cadere; *v.i.* cadere, diminuire (di prezzi).

Dropper [drŏ'pĕr] *n.* contagocce.

Dropsy [drŏp'sĭ] *n.* (*med.*) idropisia.

Dross [drŏs] *n.* scoria, rifiuto.

Drought [draut] *n.* siccità, sete.

Drove [drōv] *n.* branco, gregge, mandra, folla.

Drover [drò'vĕr] *n.* mandriano.

Drown [draun] *v.t. e i.* affogare, annegare.

Drowse [drauz] *v.i.* assopirsi, sonnecchiare.

Drowsiness [drau'zĭ-nĕs] *n.* sonnolenza.

Drowsy [drau'zĭ] *a.* sonnolento.

Drudge [drăǵ] *n.* schiavo, servo, chi fa un lavoro aspro.

Drudge [drăǵ] *v.i.* compiere un lavoro umile e faticoso.

Drudgery [dră'gĕ-rĭ] *n.* lavoro umile e faticoso.

Drug [drăǵ] *n.* droga, articolo che non trova compratori.

Druggist [dră'ghist] *n.* farmacista.

Drum [drăm] *n.* tamburo, timpano (dell'orecchio); (*mecc.*) rullo; *v.i.* tambureggiare, tamburellare (con le dita).

Drunk [drăṅc], **drunken** [drăṅ'cn] *a.* ubriaco.

Drunkard [drăṅ'chĕrd] *n.* ubriacone.

Drunkenness [drăṅ'cn-nĕs] *n.* ubriachezza.

Dry [drai] *a.* asciutto, arido, secco, disseccato, privo d'interesse; *v.t.* asciugare, esaurire, seccare; *v.i.* evaporare completamente, seccarsi.

Dryness [drai'nĕs] *n.* aridità, secchezza.

Dubiety [diŭ-ba'ĭ-tĭ] n. senso di dubbio.

Dubious [diŭ'bĭ-ăs] a. dubbio, incerto.

Ducat [dă'chĕt] n. ducato (moneta).

Duchess [dă'cĕs] n. duchessa.

Duchy [dă'cĭ] n. ducato.

Duck [dăc] n. anitra; v.t. e i. immerger(si), tuffar(si); v.i. abbassare il capo improvvisamente.

Duckling [dăc'lĭñ] n. anatroccolo.

Duct [dăct] n. canale, tubo, vaso (di animale o di pianta).

Dudgeon [dă'ğĕn] n. risentimento.

Due [diŭ] n. diritto, tassa; a. adeguato, debito, dovuto; to be [bĭ] d. dover arrivare, scadere.

Duel [diŭ'ĕl] n. duello.

Duet [diŭ-ĕt'] n. duetto.

Duke [diŭc] n. duca.

Dukedom [diŭc'dăm] n. ducato.

Dull [dăl] a. monotono, triste, duro, lento, smorto (colori), sordo (suoni); v.t. intorpidire, rattristare.

Dullard [dă'lĕʳd] n. individuo ottuso.

Dullness [dăl'nĕs] n. durezza, lentezza, mancanza di vita, monotonia, ottusità.

Dumb [dăm] a. muto, taciturno.

Dumbfound [dăm'faund] v.t. stupefare.

Dumbness [dăm'nĕs] n. mutezza.

Dummy [dă'mĭ] n. fantoccio, uomo di paglia.

Dump [dămp] n. luogo adibito allo scarico dei rifiuti; (mil.) deposito di munizioni; v.t. buttare giù con un tonfo, scaricare.

Dumpy [dăm'pĭ] a. tarchiato, tozzo.

Dun [dăn] n. creditore importuno e noioso.; a. grigio scuro; v.t. domandare insistentemente (il pagamento).

Dunce [dăns] n. individuo lento nell'imparare.

Dune [diŭn] n. duna.

Dung [dăñ] n. letame, sterco di animali.

Dungeon [dăn'ğĕn] n. prigione sotterranea.

Dupe [diŭp] n. credulone, gonzo; v.t. gabbare, ingannare.

Duplicate [diŭ'plĭ-chĕt] a. e n. duplicato; [diŭ'plĭ-chĕt] v.t. duplicare.

Durable [diŭ'ʳă-bl] a. durabile, durevole.

Durability [diŭ'ʳă-bĭ'lĭ-tĭ] n. durabilità.

Duration [diŭ-ré'ăn] n. continuazione, durata.

During [diŭ'rĭñ] prep. durante.

Dusk [dăsc] n. crepuscolo.

Dusky [dăs'chĭ] a. piuttosto scuro.

Dust [dăst] n. polvere, spazzatura; v.t. spolverare, impolverare.

Duster [dăs'tĕʳ] n. cencio da spolverare.

Dusty [dăs'tĭ] a. polveroso.

Dutch [dăč] a. olandese.

Dutiful [diŭ'tĭ-fŭl] a. ubbidiente.

Duty [diŭ'tĭ] n. dovere, ubbidienza, rispetto, servizio militare, imposta, tassa.

Dwarf [duo'f] a. e n. nano; v.t. rimpicciolire.

Dwell [duĕl] v.i. dimorare, abitare, fermare l'attenzione, il discorso, su.

Dwelling [duĕl'ĭñ] n. abitazione, dimora.

Dwindle [duin'dl] v.i. consumarsi, rimpicciolirsi.

Dye [da'ĭ] n. tintura, materia colorante; v.t. tingere; v.i. tingersi, prendere il colore di.

Dyer [da'ĕʳ] n. tintore.

Elastic [i-lès'tic] *a. e n.* elastico.

Elasticity [i-lès-ti'si-ti] *n.* elasticità.

Elate [i-lét'] *v.t.* esaltare, rendere fiero.

Elation [i-lé'sn] *n.* esaltazione, orgoglio.

Elbow [èl'bò] *n.* gomito; e. -room [rūm] ampio spazio.

Elder [èl'dër] *n.* sambuco; *a.* (*comp. di* old) più vecchio, maggiore (di età); *n.* maggiore (di età).

Elect [i-lèct'] *a.* eletto, scelto; *v.t. e i.* eleggere, scegliere.

Election [i-lèc'sn] *n.* elezione.

Elector [i-lèc'tër] *n.* elettore.

Electorate [i-lèc'tö-rèt] *n.* elettorato, elettori (*pl.*).

Electric [i-lèc'tric] *a.* elettrico.

Electrician [i-lèc-tri'scën] *n.* elettricista.

Electricity [i-lèc-tri'si-ti] *n.* elettricità.

Electrification [i-lèc-tri-fi-ché'sn] *n.* elettrificazione.

Electrify [i-lèc'tri-fa¹] *v.t.* elettrificare, elettrizzare.

Elegance [è'li-ghèns] *n.* eleganza.

Elegant [è'li-ghènt] *a.* elegante.

Elegy [è'li-gi] *n.* elegia.

Element [è'li-mènt] *n.* elemento.

Elemental [è-li-mèn'tël] *a.* degli elementi, fondamentale.

Elementary [è-li-mèn'të-ri] *a.* elementare, rudimentale.

Elephant [è'li-fènt] *n.* elefante.

Elevate [è'li-vét] *v.t.* elevare, innalzare.

Elevation [è-li-vé'sn] *n.* elevazione.

Elevator [è'li-vé-tër] *n.* ascensore, elevatore.

Eleven [i-lè'vn] *a. e n.* undici; -th *a. e n.* undicesimo.

Elf [èlf] *n.* folletto, gnomo.

Elicit [i-li'sit] *v.t.* cavare, dedurre, tirar fuori.

Eligibility [è-li-gi-bi'li-ti] *n.* eleggibilità.

Eligible [è'li-gi-bl] *a.* desiderabile, eleggibile.

Eliminate [i-li'mi-nét] *v.t.* eliminare.

Elimination [i-li-mi-né'sn] *n.* eliminazione.

Elision [i-li'jën] *n.* elisione.

Elk [èlc] *n.* alce.

Ellipse [è-lips'] *n.* ellisse.

Ellipsis [è-lip'sis] *n.* ellissi.

Elm [èlm] *n.* olmo.

Elocution [è-lò-chiū'sn] *n.* elocuzione.

Elope [i-lòp'] *v.i.* fuggire, scappare (con l'amante).

Elopement [i-lòp'mènt] *n.* fuga di amanti.

Eloquence [è'lò-quèns] *n.* eloquenza.

Eloquent [è'lò-quènt] *a.* eloquente.

Else [èls] *a.* altro; *av.* altrimenti.

Elsewhere [èls'huër] *avv.* altrove.

Elucidate [i-liū'si-dét] *v.t.* chiarire.

Elucidation [i-liū-si-dé'sn] *n.* schiarimento.

Elude [i-liūd'] *v.t.* eludere.

Elusive [i-liū'siv] *a.* elusivo.

Emaciate [i-mé'sci-ét] *v.t.* emaciare, far dimagrire.

Emaciation [i-mé-sci-é'sn] *n.* macilenza.

Emanate [è'mǎ-nét] *v.t. e i.* emanare.

Emanation [è-mǎ-né'sn] *n.* emanazione.

Embalm [èm-bām'] *v.t.* imbalsamare.

Embankment [èm-bènc'mènt] *n.* argine, diga.

Embargo [èm-ba²'gò] *n.* embargo.

Embark [ĕm-bà̱ŕc'] v.t. e i. imbarcar(si); (fig.) impegnarsi, mettersi.

Embarcation [ĕm-bà̱r-ché̱šn] n. imbarcazione.

Embarrass [ĕm-bè̱rĕs] v.t. imbarazzare.

Embarrassment [ĕm-bè̱rĕs-mĕnt] n. imbarazzo.

Embassy [ĕm'bà̱-si] n. ambasciata. [abbellire.

Embellish [ĕm-bĕ'li̱š] v.t.

Embellishment [ĕm-bĕ'li̱š-mĕnt] n. abbellimento.

Ember [ĕm'bĕŕ] n. (special. al pl.) brace, ceneri ardenti (pl.); e. days [dé̱s] i tre giorni di digiuno delle quattro Tempora.

Embezzle [ĕm-bĕ'zl] v.t. appropriarsi fraudolentemente.

Embezzlement [ĕm-bĕ'zl-mĕnt] n. appropriazione indebita.

Embitter [ĕm-bi̱'tĕŕ] v.t. amareggiare, inasprire.

Emblem [ĕm'blĕm] n. emblema, simbolo.

Embody [ĕm-bŏ'di̱] v.t. incorporare, personificare, includere.

Embolden [ĕm-bŏl'dĕn] v.t. rendere baldanzoso, incoraggiare.

Embolism [ĕm'bò̱-lizm] n. (med.) embolia.

Emboss [ĕm-bŏ̱s'] v.t. ornare con rilievi.

Embrace [ĕm-brés'] n. abbraccio; v.t. abbracciare.

Embrasure [ĕm-brè̱'jĕŕ] n. feritoia per cannone, parte interna inclinata d'un muro, accanto ad una porta finestra, vano (d'una finestra).

Embroider [ĕm-brŏ̱'dĕŕ] v.t. ricamare.

Embroidery [ĕm-brŏ̱'dĕ-ri̱] n. (arte del) ricamo.

Embroil [ĕm-brŏ̱'l'] v.t. coinvolgere in una contesa.

Embryo [ĕm'bri̱-ò̱] n. embrione; a. embrionale.

Emerald [ĕ'mĕ-rĕ̱ld] n. smeraldo.

Emerge [i-mĕ̱'g] v.i. emergere.

Emergency [i-mĕ̱r'gĕn-si̱] n. emergenza.

Emery [ĕ'mĕ-ri̱] n. smeriglio.

Emetic [i-mĕ'tic] a. e n. emetico.

Emigrant [ĕ'mi̱-grĕnt] a. e n. emigrante.

Emigrate [ĕ'mi̱-grét] v.i. emigrare.

Emigration [ĕ-mi̱-gré'šn] n. emigrazione.

Eminence [ĕ'mi̱-nĕns] n. eminenza.

Eminent [ĕ'mi̱-nĕnt] a. eminente.

Emit [i-mi̱t'] v.t. emettere.

Emollient [i-mŏ̱'li̱-ĕnt] a. e n. emolliente.

Emolument [i-mŏ̱'li̱ŭ-mĕnt] n. emolumento.

Emotion [i-mò̱'šn] n. commozione, emozione.

Emperor [ĕm'pĕ-rĕŕ] n. imperatore.

Emphasis [ĕm'fà̱-si̱s] n. enfasi.

Emphasize [ĕm'fà̱-sa̱'z] v.t. dare enfasi a, mettere in rilievo.

Emphatic [ĕm-fè̱'tic] a. enfatico.

Empire [ĕm'pa̱ier] n. impero.

Emplacement [ĕm-plé̱s'mĕnt] n. collocamento; (mil.) piazzuola.

Employ [ĕm-plŏ̱'i'] v.t. impiegare, dare impiego a, tenere occupato, adoperare, usare.

Employee [ĕm-plŏ̱'i-i'] n. impiega/to, -ta.

Employer [ĕm-plŏ̱'i'ĕŕ] n. datore di lavoro, padrone (d'un'azienda).

Employment [ĕm-plŏ̱'i'mĕnt] n. impiego, occupazione.

Emporium [ĕm-pó'rĭ-ăm] *n.* emporio.

Empower [ĕm-pau⁰ʳ'] *v.t.* autorizzare.

Empress [ĕm'prĕs] *n.* imperatrice.

Emptiness [ĕmp'tĭ-nĕs] *n.* condizione di vuoto, vacuità.

Empty [ĕmp'tĭ] *n.* fusto vuoto; *a.* vuoto, vacuo; *v.t. e i.* vuotar(si).

Emulate [ĕ'mĭŭ-lĕt] *v.t.* emulare. [emulazione.

Emulation [ĕ-mĭŭ-lĕ'ŏn] *n.*

Enable [ĕ-né'bl] *v.t.* mettere in grado, permettere.

Enact [ĕ-nèct'] *v.t.* mettere in atto, rappresentare.

Enactment [ĕ-nèct'mĕnt] *n.* sanzione, termine, legge.

Enamel [ĕ-nè'mĕl] *n.* nichelatura, smalto.

Enamel [ĕ-nè'mĕl] *v.t.* nichelare, smaltare.

Enamour [ĕ-nè'mĕʳ] *v.t.* (*raro*) innamorare.

Encamp [ĕn-chèmp'] *v.t. e i.* accampar(si).

Encampment [ĕn-chèmp'mĕnt] *n.* accampamento.

Enchant [ĕn-ciànt'] *v.t.* incantare.

Enchanter [ĕn-ciàn'tĕʳ] *n.* incantatore, mago.

Enchantment [ĕn-ciànt'mĕnt] *n.* incantesimo, incanto.

Enchantress [ĕn-ciàn'trĕs] *n.* incantatrice, maga.

Encircle [ĕn-sĕʳ'cl] *v.t.* accerchiare.

Enclose [ĕn-clòz'] *v.t.* accludere, rinchiudere.

Enclosure [ĕn-clò'jĕʳ] *n.* allegato, recinto.

Encompass [ĕn-căm'pĕs] *v.t.* contenere, circondare.

Encounter [ĕn-caun'tĕʳ] *n.* incontro, combattimento; *v.t. e i.* incontrar(si), lottare.

Encourage [ĕn-că'rĭg] *v.t.* incoraggiare.

Encouragement [ĕn-că'rĭg'mĕnt] *n.* incoraggiamento.

Encroach [ĕn-crŏc'] *v.i.* intromettersi illegalmente, usurpare i diritti altrui.

Encroachment [ĕn-crŏc'mĕnt] *n.* intromissione abusiva, usurpazione.

Encumber [ĕn-căm'bĕʳ] *v.t.* gravare, ingombrare.

Encumbrance [ĕn-căm'brĕns] *n.* impedimento, ingombro.

Encyclopædia [ĕn-saⁱ-clò-pĭ'dĭ-ĕⁿ] *n.* enciclopedia.

End [ĕnd] *n.* fine, scopo, morte; *v.t. e i.* finire.

Endanger [ĕn-dén'gĕʳ] *v.t.* mettere in pericolo.

Endear [ĕn-dĭⁱʳ'] *v.t.* rendere (più) caro.

Endearment [ĕn-dĭⁱʳ'mĕnt] *n.* carezza, parola affettuosa.

Endeavour [ĕn-dé'vĕʳ] *n.* sforzo, tentativo; *v.i.* sforzarsi, tentare.

Ending [ĕn'dĭⁿ] *n.* conclusione, termine; (*gramm.*) desinenza.

Endive [ĕn'dĭv] *n.* indivia.

Endless [ĕnd'lĕs] *a.* eterno, senza fine.

Endorse [ĕn-do⁰s'] *v.t.* firmare, girare, confermare, sanzionare.

Endow [ĕn-daù'] *v.t.* dotare.

Endowment [ĕn-daù'nfĕnt] *n.* dotazione, dote.

Endurance [ĕn-dĭŭ⁰'rĕns] *n.* pazienza, sopportazione.

Endure [ĕn-dĭŭ⁰ʳ'] *v.t.* sopportare, tollerare.

Enemy [é'nĭ-mĭ] *a. e n.* nemico.

Energetic [ĕ-nĕʳ-gé'tĭc] *a.* energico, vigoroso.

Energy [ĕ'nĕʳ-gĭ] *n.* energia.

Enervate [é'nĕʳ-vét] *v.t.* snervare.

Enfeeble [ĕn-fí'bl] *v.t.* indebolire.

Enforce [ĕn-fō'rs'] *v.t.* imporre con la forza, far osservare (la legge).

Enforcement [ĕn-fō'rs'mĕnt] *n.* imposizione.

Enfranchise [ĕn-frĕn'cia¹z] *v.t.* affrancare, liberare.

Enfranchisement [ĕn-frĕn'cia¹z-mĕnt] *n.* affrancamento, liberazione.

Engage [ĕn-ghég'] *v.t.* impegnare, prenotare, assumere in servizio; *v.i.* impegnarsi.

Engagement [ĕn-ghég'mĕnt] *n.* impegno, obbligo, fidanzamento.

Engender [ĕn-gĕn'dĕr] *v.t.* generare, produrre. [motore.

Engine [ĕn'gin] *n.* macchina.

Engineer [ĕn-gi-ni°r'] *n.* ingegnere, macchinista; (*mil.*) soldato del Genio.

Engineer [ĕn-gi-ni°r'] *v.t.* dirigere la costruzione di; (*famil.*) organizzare, combinare.

Engineering [ĕn-gi-ni°'rĭñ] *n.* ingegneria.

English [ĭñ'gliš] *a.* inglese.

Engrave [ĕn-grév'] *v.t.* incidere; (*fig.*) imprimere.

Engraving [ĕn-gré'vĭñ] *n.* incisione.

Engross [ĕn-gròs'] *v.t.* monopolizzare, esprimere in forma legale.

Enhance [ĕn-hĕns'] *v.t.* aumentare, intensificare.

Enigma [i-nĭg'mĕr'] *n.* enigma.

Enjoin [ĕn-gio¹n'] *v.t.* e *i.* ingiungere, ordinare.

Enjoy [ĕn-gio¹'] *v.t.* divertirsi a, godere.

Enjoyment [ĕn-gio¹'mĕnt] *n.* divertimento, godimento.

Enlarge [ĕn-lä²g'] *v.t.* espandere, estendere, ingrandire; *v.i.* allargarsi.

Enlargement [ĕn-lä²g'mĕnt] *n.* aumento, ingrandimento.

Enlighten [ĕn-la¹'tn] *v.t.* illuminare (*senso fig.*).

Enlightenment [ĕn-la¹'tn-mĕnt] *n.* spiegazione, schiarimento. [lar(si).

Enlist [ĕn-list'] *v.t.* e *i.* arro-

Enlistment [ĕn-list'mĕnt] *n.* arrolamento.

Enliven [ĕn-la¹'vn] *v.t.* ravvivare.

Enmity [ĕn'mĭ-ti] *n.* inimicizia, ostilità.

Ennoble [ĕ-nò'bl] *v...* conferire un titolo, nobilitare.

Ennui [*pron. fran.*] *n.* noia.

Enormity [i-nŏr'mĭ-ti] *n.* enormità.

Enormous [i-nŏr'mŭs] *a.* enorme, molto grande.

Enough [i-nắf'] *n.* quanto basta, sufficienza; *a.* sufficiente *av.* abbastanza, sufficientemente.

Enrage [ĕn-rég'] *v.t.* far arrabbiare, imbestialire.

Enrich [ĕn-rič'] *v.t.* arricchire.

Enrol[l] [ĕn-rōl'] *v.t.* iscrivere, registrare.

Enrolment [ĕn-ròl'mĕnt] *n.* iscrizione, registrazione.

Enshrine [ĕn-śra¹n'] *v.t.* custodire come cosa sacra.

Ensign [ĕn'sa¹n] *n.* bandiera, insegna; (*arcaico*) portabandiera.

Enslave [ĕn-slév'] *v.t.* asservire, fare schiavo.

Enslavement [ĕn-slév'mĕnt] *n.* asservimento, schiavitù.

Ensnare [ĕn-snér'] *v.t.* irretire, prendere al laccio.

Ensue [ĕn-siŭ'] *v.i.* accadere, seguire (come risultato).

Entail [ĕn-tél'] *n.* possedimento su cui grava un vincolo dell'inalienabilità; *v.t.* rendere necessario, lasciare in eredità col vincolo dell'inalienabilità.

Entangle [ĕn-tèñ'gl] *v...* aggrovigliare, mettere nei guai.

Entanglement [ĕn-tĕn'gl-mĕnt] n. aggrovigliamento, imbroglio.

Enter [ĕn'tẽr] v.t. entrare in, cominciare, intraprendere, registrare; **to e. into** (fig.) entrare in, iniziare.

Enterprise [ĕn'tẽr-praiz] n. impresa, intrapresa.

Entertain [ĕn-tẽr-tén'] v.t. divertire, intrattenere, ricevere ospitalmente, nutrire (sospetti ecc.).

Entertainment [ĕn-tẽr-tén'mĕnt] n. divertimento, trattenimento.

Enthusiasm [ĕn-thiũ'zi-ĕzm] n. entusiasmo.

Enthusiastic [ĕn-thiũ-zi-ĕs'tic] a. entusiastico.

Entice [ĕn-taïs'] v.t. adescare, allettare.

Enticement [eĕ-taïs'mĕnt] n. allettamento, lusinga.

Entire [ĕn-taïẽr'] a. completo, intero.

Entitle [ĕn-taï'tl] v.t. autorizzare, intitolare.

Entity [ĕn'ti-ti] n. entità.

Entomb [ĕn-tũm'] v.t. inumare.

Entombment [ĕn-tũm'-mĕnt] n. inumazione.

Entrails [ĕn'tre-ls] n. (pl.) intestini, viscere (pl.).

Entrance [ĕn'trĕns] n. entrata, ingresso; **e. -fee** [fi] tassa d'iscrizione.

Entrap [ĕn-trĕp'] v.t. intrappolare; (fig.) imbrogliare.

Entreat [ĕn-trit'] v.t. implorare, supplicare.

Entreaty [ĕn-tr.'ti] n. preghiera, supplica.

Entrench [ĕn-trĕnč'] v.t. trincerare; v.i. intromettersi con usurpazione.

Entrenchment [ĕn-trĕnč'mĕnt] n. trinceramento.

Entrust [ĕn-trãst'] v.t. affidare, confidare.

Entry [ĕn'tri] n. entrata, ingresso, iscrizione; [legge] presa di possesso.

Entwine [ĕn-tuã'n] v.t. intrecciare.

Enumerate [i-niũ'mĕ-rét] v.t. enumerare.

Enunciate [i-nãn'si-ét] v.t. enunciare.

Enunciation [i-nãn-si-é'sn] n. enunciazione.

Envelop [ĕn-vĕ'lŏp] v.t. avvolgere; (mil.) accerchiare.

Envelope [ĕn'vĕ-lŏp; ŏn'vlŏp] n. busta, fascia.

Enviable [ĕn'vi-ä-bl] a. invidiabile.

Envious [ĕn'vi-ãs] a. invidioso.

Environment [ĕn-vaï'rŏn-mĕnt] n. ambiente.

Environs [ĕn-vaï'rŏns] n. (pl.) dintorni (pl.); vicinato.

Envoy [ĕn'vo] n. inviato, ministro plenipotenziario.

Envy [ĕn'vi] n. invidia.

Envy [ĕn'vi] v.t. invidiare.

Epaulet [ĕ'pŏ-lĕt] n. (mil.) spallina.

Epic [ĕ'pïc] n. epica; a. epico.

Epidemic [ĕ-pï-dĕ'mic] n. epidemia.

Epigram [ĕ'pï-grĕm] n. epigramma.

Epigraph [ĕ'pï-grĕf] n. epigrafe.

Epilepsy [ĕ-pï-lĕp'sï] n. epilessia.

Epileptic [ĕ-pï-lĕp'tic] a. e n. epilettico.

Epilogue [ĕ'pï-lŏg] n. epilogo.

Epiphany [i-pi'fã-ni] n. epifania, befana.

Episcopacy [i-pïs'cŏ-pä-sï] n. episcopato.

Episcopal [i-pïs'cŏ-pĕl] a. episcopale.

Episode [ĕ'pï-sŏd] n. episodio.

Epistle [i-pïs'l] n. epistola.

Epitaph [ĕ'pï-tĕf] n. epitaffio.

Epithet [ĕ'pï-thĕt] n. epiteto.

Epitomise [i-pi'tò-ma¹z] *v.t.* compendiare, riassumere.

Epoch [i'pòc] *n.* epoca.

Epopee [e'pò-pi] *n.* epopea.

Equable [e'quâ-bl] *a.* equo.

Equal [i'qual] *a. e n.* uguale; *v.t.* essere uguale a, uguagliare.

Equality [i-quò'li-ti] *n.* uguaglianza.

Equalize [i'quâ-la¹z] *v.t.* uguagliare.

Equanimity [i-quâ-ni'mi-ti] *n.* equanimità.

Equation [i-qué'śn] *n.* equazione.

Equator [i-qué'tě²] *n.* equatore.

Equerry [e'quě-ri] *n.* (*arcaico*) scudiero.

Equestrian [i-quès'tri-ěn] *n.* cavaliere, cavallerizzo; *a.* equestre.

Equilibrium [i-qui-li'bri-ăm] *n.* equilibrio.

Equinox [e'qui-nòcs] *n.* equinozio.

Equip [i-quip'] *v.t.* equipaggiare.

Equipage [e'qui-pěg] *n.* equipaggio.

Equipment [i-quip'mènt] *n.* equipaggiamento.

Equitable [e'qui-tă-bl] *a.* equo, giusto.

Equity [e'qui-ti] *n.* equità.

Equivalent [i-qui'vă-lènt] *a. e n.* equivalente.

Equivocal [i-qui'vò-chěl] *a.* ambiguo, equivoco, sospetto.

Equivocate [i-qui'vò-chét] *v.i.* giocare sull'equivoco, usare inganni.

Era [i²'rě⁽ʳ⁾] *n.* era.

Eradicate [i-ré'di-chét] *v.t.* sradicare.

Erase [i-rés'] *v.t.* cancellare, raschiar via.

Erasure [i-ré'jě²] *n.* cancellatura.

Ere [é²] *prep. e av.* (*raro*) prima di, prima che.

Erect [i-rěct'] *a.* eretto, ritto. *v.t.* erigere, innalzare.

Erection [i-rěc'śn] *n.* elevazione, erezione.

Ermine [ě'min] *n.* ermellino.

Erode [i-ród'] *v.t.* consumare, erodere.

Erosion [i-ró'śn] *n.* erosione.

Err [ě²] *v.i.* errare, sbagliare.

Errand [ě'rănd] *n.* commissione, incarico.

Errant [ě'rănt] *a.* errante.

Erratic [ě-rè'tic] *a.* irregolare.

Erroneous [ě-ró'ně-ăs] *a.* erroneo, scorretto.

Error [ě'rě²] *n.* colpa, errore, sbaglio.

Erudite [ě'rū-da¹t] *a.* erudito.

Erudition [ě-ru-di'śn] *n.* erudizione.

Eruption [i-răp'śn] *n.* eruzione, scoppio.

Erysipelas [ě-ri-si'pi-lès] *n.* (*med.*) erisipela.

Escalator [ěs'că-lé-tě²] *n.* scala mobile.

Escapade [ěs-că-péd'] *n.* scappata.

Escape [ěs-chép'] *n.* fuga, scampo, scappamento.

Escape [ěs-chép'] *v.t.* evitare, sfuggire a; *v.i.* [s]fuggire.

Eschew [ěs-ciù'] *v.t.* astenersi da.

Escort [ěs'cò²t] *n.* scorta; [ěs-cò²t'] *v.t.* scortare.

Especial [ěs-pě'sčěl] *a.* particolare, speciale.

Espionage [ěs'pi-ŏ-něg] *n.* spionaggio.

Esplanade [ěs-plă-néd'] *n.* passeggiata lungo mare, spianata.

Espouse [ěs-pauz'] *v.t.* (*raro*) sposare.

Espy [ěs-pa¹'] *v.t.* discernere.

Esquire [ěs'qua¹eʳ] *n.* (*arcaico*) scudiero, signore (usato sempre abbrev. Esq. negli indirizz., dopo il nome di casato).

Essay [ĕ'se¹] n. saggio (letterario) ; (ĕ-se¹') v.t. (raro) tentare.

Essence [ĕ'sĕns] n. essenza.

Essential [ĕ-sĕn'scĕl] a. e n. essenziale.

Establish [ĕs-tè'blĭš] v.t. fondare, istituire, stabilire.

Establishment [ĕs-tè'blĭš-mĕnt] n. casa, casa commerciale, istituto, istituzione.

Estate [ĕs-tét'] n. condizione, grado, patrimonio, proprietà, tenuta.

Esteem [ĕs-tím'] n. considerazione, stima; v.t. considerare, stimare.

Estimable [ĕs'ti-mă-bl] a. stimabile, degno di stima.

Estimate [ĕs'ti-mét] v.t. stimare, valutare.

Estimation [ĕs-ti-mé'šn] n. stima, valutazione.

Estrange [ĕs-trénǵ'] v.t. alienare.

Estuary [ĕs'tiŭ-ĕ-rĭ] n. estuario.

Etch [ĕč] v.t. incidere all'acquaforte.

Etching [ĕ'čĭṅ] n. acquaforte.

Eternal [ĭ-tė'rnĕl] a. eterno.

Eternity [ĭ-tė'rnĭ-tĭ] n. eternità.

Ether [í'thĕr] n. etere.

Ethics [ĕ'thĭcs] n. (pl.) etica.

Etiquette [ĕ'tĭ-chĕt] n. etichetta.

Etymology [ĕ-tĭ-mŏ'lò-ġĭ] n. etimologia.

Eucharist [iŭ'că'rĭst] n. eucarestia.

Eulogy [iŭ'lò-ġĭ] n. elogio.

Eunuch [iŭ'năc] n. eunuco.

Euphony [iŭ'fò-nĭ] n. eufonia.

European [iŭᵉ-rò-pí'ĕn] a. e n. europeo.

Evacuate [i-vé'chiŭ-ét] v.t. evacuare, sfollare, sgombrare; (mil.) ritirare.

Evacuation [i-vè-chiŭ-é'šn]

n. evacuazione sfollamento, sgombero; (mil.) ritiro.

Evade [ĭ-véd'] v.t. eludere, sfuggire a. [n. evanescenza.

Evanescence [ĕ-vă-nĕ'sĕns,

Evaporate [š-vé'pò-rét] v.t. e i. (far) evaporare.

Evaporation [ĭ-vè-pò-ré'šn] n. evaporazione.

Evasion [ĭ-vé'šn] n. evasione, sotterfugio.

Eve [ĭv] n. vigilia.

Even [í'vĕn] n. (poet.) sera; a. pari uguale, piatto, uniforme; av anche, perfino; v.t. uguagliare, uniformare.

Evening [ĭv'nĭṅ] n. sera.

Evenness [í'vĕn-nĕs] n. uguaglianza, uniformità.

Event [i-vĕnt'] n. avvenimento, evento.

Eventful [i-vĕnt'fŭl] a. emozionante, pieno di avvenimenti.

Eventide [í'vĕn-ta¹d] n sera.

Eventual [i-vĕn'tiŭ-ĕl] a. eventuale, finale; -ly [lĭ] av. finalmente.

Ever [ĕ'vĕᵣ] av. continuamente, mai, (per) sempre.

Evergreen [ĕ'vĕᵣ-grĭn] a. e n. sempreverde.

Everlasting [ĕ-vĕᵣ-làs'tĭṅ] n. eternità; a. eterno.

Every [ĕ'vĕ-rĭ] a. ogni; e. now [naŭ] and then [thĕn] av. di quando in quando; e. other day [ă'thĕᵣ de¹] un giorno sì e un giorno no.

Everybody, **-one** [ĕ'vĕ-rĭ bŏ'dĭ, uăn] pron. ognuno, tutti (pl.).

Everyday [ĕ'vĕ-rĭ de¹] a. di ogni giorno, quotidiano.

Everything [ĕ'vĕ-rĭ-thĭṅ] pron. ogni cosa, tutto.

Everywhere [ĕ'vĕ-rĭ-huĕᵣ] av. in ogni luogo, ovunque.

Evict [i-vĭct'] v.t. espellere; (legge) sfrattare.

Eviction [i-vɪc'šn] n. espulsione, sfratto.

Evidence [ĕ'vĭ-dĕns] n. evidenza, prova, testimonianza.

Evident [ĕ'vĭ-dĕnt] a. chiaro, evidente.

Evil [ĭ'vĕl] n. male; a. cattivo, dannoso, funesto; av. male.

Evince [ĭ-vĭns'] v.t. manifestare, mostrare.

Evolution [ĭ-vŏ-liū'śn] n. evoluzione, svolgimento.

Evolve [ĭ-vŏlv'] v.t. e v. evolver(si).

Ewe [iū] n. pecora [fem.].

Ewer [iū'ẽr] n. [raro] brocca.

Exact [ĕg-zĕct'] a. esatto, preciso.

Exact [ĕg-zĕct'] v.t. esigere.

Exacting [ĕg-zĕc'tĭñ] a. esigente.

Exaction [ĕg-zĕc'śn] n. esazione, estorsione.

Exactitude [ĕg-zĕc'tĭ-tiūd] **exactness** [ĕg-zĕct'nĕs] n. esattezza, precisione.

Exaggerate [ĕg-zĕ'gĕ-rēt] v.t. esagerare.

Exaggeration [ĕg-zĕ-gĕ-rē'śn] n. esagerazione.

Exalt [ĕg-zŏlt'] v.t. esaltare.

Exaltation [ĕg-zŏl-tē'śn] n. esaltazione.

Examination [ĕg-zĕ-mĭ-nē'śn] n. esame.

Examine [ĕg-zĕ'mĭn] v.t. esaminare.

Examiner [ĕg-zĕ'mĭ-nẽr] n. esaminatore.

Example [ĕg-zĕm'pl] n. esempio.

Exasperate [ĕg-zĕs'pĕ-rēt] v.t. esasperare.

Exasperation [ĕg-zĕs-pĕ-rē'śn] n. esasperazione.

Exceed [ĕc-sĭd'] v.t. e i. eccedere, superare.

Excel [ĕc-sĕl'] v.t. eccedere, eccellere su, essere superiore a; v.i. eccellere.

Excellence [ĕc'sĕ-lĕns] n. eccellenza, superiorità.

Excellency [ĕc'sĕ-lĕn-sĭ] n. (titolo) eccellenza.

Excellent [ĕc'sĕ-lĕnt] a. eccellente.

Except [ĕc-sĕpt'] prep. eccetto, eccettuato, ad eccezione di, tranne; v.t. eccettuare; v.i. fare obiezioni.

Exception [ĕc-sĕp'śn] n. eccezione, obiezione.

Exceptional [ĕc-sĕp'scĕ-nĕl] a. eccezionale.

Excess [ĕc-sĕs'] n. eccesso; e. fare [fe^r] differenza in più (su un biglietto ferroviario).

Exchange [ĕc-s-cēnǵ'] n. Borsa, cambio, scambio; (tel.) centrale telefonica; v.t. (s)cambiare.

Exchequer [ĕc-s-cĕ'chĕr] n. scacchiere, tesoro.

Excise [ĕc-sa^ız'] n. imposta indiretta, dazio sul consumo interno.

Excite [ĕc-sa^ıt'] v.t. eccitare, promuovere.

Excitement [ĕc-sa^ıt'mĕnt] n. agitazione, eccitazione.

Exclaim [ĕc-s-clĕm'] v.i. esclamare.

Exclamation [ĕc-s-clă-mē'śn] n. esclamazione.

Exclude [ĕc-s-clūd'] v.t. escludere.

Exclusion [ĕc-s-cĭū'śn] n. esclusione.

Excommunicate [ĕc-s-cŏ-mĭū'nĭ-chĕt] v.t. scomunicare.

Excursion [ĕc-s-chĕr'śn] n. escursione, gita.

Excuse [ĕc-s-chĭūs'] n. discolpa, giustificazione, scusa; (ĕc-s-chĭūz') v.t. perdonare, scusare, dispensare da.

Execrable [ĕc'sĭ-cră-bl] a. esecrabile.

Execrate [ĕc'sĭ-crĕt] v.t. esecrare.

Execute [ĕc'sĭ-chĭūt] v.t. eseguire, mettere in esecuzione, giustiziare.

Execution [ĕc-si-chiū'ṣn] *n.* esecuzione, sequestro.

Executioner [ĕc-si-chiū'scĕ-nẽr] *n.* boia, carnefice, esecutore.

Executive [ĕg-sĕ'chiū-tiv'] *n.* potere esecutivo; *a.* esecutivo.

Exemplar [ĕg-zĕm'plẽr] *n.* esemplare, modello.

Exempt [ĕg-zĕmpt'] *a.* esente *v.t.* esentare.

Exemption [ĕg-zĕm'ṣn] *n.* esenzione.

Exercise [ĕc'sẽr-sa'is] *n.* esercizio, esercitazione; *v.t.* e *i.* esercitar(si).

Exert [ĕg-zẽr't'] *v.t.* compiere, esercitare; **to e. oneself** [ŭan'sĕlf'] *v. rifl.* sforzarsi.

Exertion [ĕg-zẽr'ṣn] *n.* azione, sforzo.

Exhalation [ĕc-sá-lé'ṣn] *n.* esalazione.

Exhale [ĕc-sél'] *v.t.* esalare.

Exhaust [ĕg-zŏst'] *n.* (*mecc.*) scarico di vapori; *v.p.* esaurire, vuotare completamente.

Exhaustion [ĕg-zŏs'cẽn] *n.* esaurimento.

Exhibit [ĕg-zi'bit] *n.* oggetto mandato ad un'esposizione; *v.t.* esibire, mettere in esposizione.

Exhibition [ĕg-zi-bi'ṣn] *n.* esibizione, esposizione, mostra, borsa di studio.

Exhilarate [ĕg-zi'lă-rét] *v.t.* esilarare.

Exhort [ĕg-zŏr't] *v.t.* esortare.

Exhortation [ĕg-zor-té'ṣn] *n.* esortazione.

Exigency [ĕc'si-gĕn-si] *n.* esigenza.

Exigent [ĕc'si-gĕnt] *a.* esigente.

Exile [ĕg'za'il] *n.* esilio, esule; *v.t.* bandire, esiliare.

Exist [ĕg-zist'] *v.i.* esistere.

Existence [ĕg-zis'tĕns] *n.* esistenza.

Exit [ĕc'sit] *n.* uscita.

Exonerate [ĕg-zŏ'nĕ-rét] *v.t.* esonerare.

Exoneration [ĕg-zŏ-nĕ-ré'ṣn] *n.* esonero.

Exorbitant [ĕg-zŏr'bi-tĕnt] *a.* esorbitante.

Exorcize [ĕc'sŏr-sa'iz] *v.t.* esorcizzare.

Exotic [ĕg-zŏ'tic] *n.* **pianta** esotica; *a.* esotico.

Expand [ĕc-spĕnd'] *v.t.* e *i.* espander(si), sviluppar(si).

Expansion [ĕc-spĕn'.n] *n.* espansione, estensione.

Expatiate [ĕc-spé'sci-ét] *v.t.* diffondersi, spaziare.

Expatriate [ĕc-spè'tri-ét] *v.t.* espatriare.

Expect [ĕc-spĕct'] *v.t.* aspettar(si), sperare.

Expectation [ĕc-spĕc-té'ṣn] *n.* aspettativa, speranza.

Expectorate [ĕc-spĕc'tŏ-rét] *v.i.* espettorare.

Expediency [ĕc-spi'di-ĕn-si] *n.* convenienza, opportunità.

Expedient [ĕc-spi'di-ĕnt] *n.* espediente, mezzo ingegnoso; *a.* conveniente, espediente.

Expedite [ĕc'spi-da'it] *v.t.* accelerare, sbrigare.

Expedition [ĕc-spi-di'ṣn] *n.* impresa, spedizione, prontezza.

Expel [ĕc-spĕl'] *v.t.* espellere.

Expend [ĕc-spĕnd'] *v.t.* consumare, spendere.

Expenditure [ĕc-spĕn'di-cĕr] *n.* spesa.

Expense [ĕc-spĕns'] *n.* spesa.

Expensive [ĕc-spĕn'siv] *a.* costoso, dispendioso.

Experience [ĕc-spi'ri-ĕns] *n.* esperienza; *v.t.* provare, sperimentare.

Experiment [ĕc-spĕ'ri-mĕnt] *n.* esperienza, esperimento, prova; *v.i.* fare esperienze, sperimentare.

Expert [ĕc'spĕrt] *n.* perito, specialista; (ĕc-spĕr't') *a.* abile, esperto.

Expiate [ĕc'spi-ét] v.t. espiare.
Expiation [ĕc-spi-é'sn] n. espiazione.
Expiration [ĕc-spi-ré'sn] n. espirazione, termine.
Expire [ĕc-spaier'] v.i. spirare, spegnersi.
Explain [ĕc-splén'] v.t. spiegare.
Explanation [ĕc-splă-né'sn] n. spiegazione.
Explicit [ĕc-spli'sit] a. chiaro, esplicito.
Explode [ĕc-splòd'] v.t. esplodere; (fig.) rivelare la falsità di; v.i. esplodere, scoppiare.
Exploit [ĕc'splo¹t] n. fatto d'armi, gesto; [ŭc-splo¹t'] v.t. sfruttare, utilizzare.
Exploitation [ĕc-splo¹-té'sn] n. sfruttamento, utilizzazione.
Explosion [ĕc-splò'sn] n. esplosione, scoppio.
Explosive [ĕc-splò'siv] a. e n. esplosivo.
Exponent [ĕc-spò'něnt] n. esponente, interprete.
Export [ĕc'spo't] n. esportazione, genere esportabile; [ĕc-spo't'] v.t. esportare.
Expose [ĕc-spòz'] v.t. esporre, rivelare.
Expostulate [ĕc-spŏs'tiu-lét] v.i. fare rimostranze.
Expostulation [ĕc-spŏs-tiu-lé'sn] n. rimostranza.
Exposure [ĕc-spò'jěr] n. esposizione; (fotogr.) posa.
Expound [ĕc-spaund'] v.t. commentare, spiegare.
Express [ĕc-sprĕs'] n. espresso (lettera), direttissimo (treno); a. apposito, espresso; v.t. esprimere.
Expression [ĕc-sprĕ'sn] n. espressione.
Expressive [ĕc-sprĕ'siv] a. espressivo.
Expropriate [ĕc-sprò'pri-ét] v.t. espropriare.

Expulsion [ĕc-spŭl'sn] n. espulsione. [(es)purgare.
Expurgate [ĕc'spĕr-ghét] v.t.
Exquisite [ĕc'squi-zit] a. squisito.
Exquisiteness [ĕc'squi-zit-nĕs] n. squisitezza.
Ex-service [ĕcs-sĕr'vis] a. che ha prestato servizio militare; e. -man [măn] n. ex-combattente.
Extant [ĕc-stĕnt'] a. esistente ancora.
Extemporary [ĕc-stĕm'pŏ-ră-ri] a. estemporaneo, improvvisato.
Extemporize [ĕc-stĕm'pŏ-ra¹z] v.t. improvvisare.
Extend [ĕc-stĕnd'] v.t. distendere, (e)stendere, prolungare; v.i. estendersi.
Extension [ĕc-stĕn'sn] n. estensione, prolungamento.
Extensive [ĕc-stĕn'siv] a. esteso, largo.
Extent [ĕc-stĕnt'] n. distesa, estensione, grado.
Extenuate [ĕc-stĕ'niŭ-ét] v.t. attenuare, scusare.
Extenuation [ĕc-stĕ-niŭ-é'sn] n. attenuazione.
Exterior [ĕc-stī'rī-ĕr] n. esterno; a. e n. esteriore.
Exterminate [ĕc-stĕr'mi-nét] v.t. sterminare.
External [ĕc-stĕr'nĕl] a. esterno. [spento.
Extinct [ĕc-stínct'] a. estinto.
Extinction [ĕc-stínc'sn] n. estinzione.
Extinguish [ĕc-stíń'guis] v.t. estinguere.
Extinguisher [ĕc-stíń'gui-scĕr] n. spegnitoio.
Extirpate [ĕc'stĕr-pét] v.t. estirpare.
Extirpation [ĕc-stĕr-pé'¡n] n. estirpazione. [estollere.
Extol [ĕc-stòl'] v.t. esaltare,
Extort [ĕc-stô't'] v.t. cavare, estorcere.

Extortion [ĕc-stor'śn] *n.* estorsione.

Extra [ĕc'strĕ^(r)] *n.* aggiunta, supplemento; *a.* extra, straordinario; *av.* extra, in più.

Extract [ĕc'strĕct] *n.* estratto; (ĕc-strĕct') *v.t.* estrarre, fare degli estratti, strappare.

Extraction [ĕc-strĕc'śn] *n.* estrazione, origine.

Ex.radition [ĕc-strä-dī'śn] *n.* estradizione.   [estraneo.

Extraneous [ĕc-strē'ni-ăs] *a.*

Extraordinary [ĕc-stro''di-nă-rĭ] *a.* eccezionale, straordinario.

Extravagance [ĕc-strĕ'vă-ghĕns] *n.* prodigalità, stravaganza.

Extravagant [ĕc-strĕ'vă-ghĕnt] *a.* prodigo, stravagante.

Extreme [ĕc-strīm'] *a.* e *n.* estremo.

Extremity [ĕc-strĕ'mi-tĭ] *n.* estremità, punto estremo.

Extricate [ĕc'stri-chĕt] *v.t.* districare.   [estrinseco.

Extrinsic [ĕc-strin'sic] *a.*

Exuberance [ĕg-ziū'bĕ-rĕns] *n.* esuberanza.

Exuberant [ĕg-ziū'bĕ-rĕnt] *a.* esuberante.

Exult [ĕg-zălt'] *v.i.* esultare.

Exultation [ĕg-zăl-tē'śn] *n.* esultanza.

Eye [aⁱ] *n.* occhio, sguardo; *v.t.* guardare, osservare.

Eyeball [a^{i'}ból] *n.* globo dell'occhio.   [ciglio.

Eyebrow [a^{i'}braŭ] *n.* soprac-

Eyelash [a^{i'}lĕš] *n.* ciglio.

Eyelid [a^{i'}lid] *n.* palpebra.

Eyesight [a^{i'}saⁱt] *n.* vista, potere visivo.

F

Fable [fē'bl] *n.* favola.

Fabric [fĕ'bric] *n.* tessuto, edifizio, struttura.

Fabricate [fĕ'bri-chēt] *v.t.* inventare, fabbricare (*senso fig.*).

Fabrication [fĕ-bri-chē'śn] *n.* bugia, invenzione, costruzione.

Fabulous [fĕ'biù-lăs] *a.* favoloso.

Façade [fă-sēd'] *n.* facciata.

Face [fēs] *n.* faccia, viso; *v.t.* affrontare, fronteggiare, guardare verso.

Facet [fĕ'sĕt] *n.* faccetta.

Facetious [fă-sī'sciăs] *a.* faceto, gioviale.

Facetiousness [fă-sī'sciăs-nĕs] *n.* giovialità.

Facial [fē'sī-ĕl] *a.* facciale.

Facile [fĕ'sil] *a.* docile, facile.

Facilitate [fă-sī'li-tĕt] *v.t.* facilitare.

Facility [fă-sī'li-tĭ] *n.* agevolazione, facilità.

Fact [fĕct] *n.* fatto, realtà.

Faction [fĕc'śn] *n.* fazione.

Factious [fĕc'sciăs] *a.* fazioso.

Factor [fĕc'tĕ^r] *n.* fattore.

Factory [fĕc'tŏ-rĭ] *n.* fabbrica, manifattura.

Faculty [fĕ'căl-tĭ] *n.* facoltà.

Fad [fĕd] *n.* mania.

Fade [fēd] *v.i.* appassire, dileguarsi, sbiadire, svanire.

Fag [fĕg] *n.* lavoro faticoso, seccatura; (*gergo*) sigaretta.

Fag(g)ot [fĕ'gŏt] *n.* fascina, fascio (di legna).

Fail [fēl] *n.* fallo; *v.t.* abbandonare, mancare a; *v.i.* fallire, mancare, essere insufficiente, bocciare (ad un esame); (*comm.*) fallire.

Failing [fē'liń] *n.* debolezza, difetto, mancanza.

Failure [fēl'iĕ^r] *n.* fallimento, fiasco, insuccesso, mancanza.

Fain [fēn] *a. predic.* costretto a, disposto a; *av.* volentieri.

Faint [fĕnt] *n.* svenimento; *a.* debole, pallido (di colori); *v.i.* svenir(si).

Faintness [fĕnt'nĕs] *n.* debo-

lezza, scarsità (di colore o di luco).

Fair [féᵉʳ] *n.* fiera, mercato; *a.* bello, biondo, buono, giusto, leale, onesto, puro, sereno; *av.* bene, diritto, onestamente.

Fairy [féᵉriⁱ] *n.* fata; f. **-tale** (tél) fiaba.

Faith [féth] *n.* fede, religione.

Faithful [féth′fŭl] *a.* coscienzioso, degno di fiducia, fedele, leale.

Faithless [féth′lĕs] *a.* falso, miscredente, sleale.

Fake [féc] *n.* articolo manipolato, notizia falsa.

Falcon [fŏl′chĕn] *n.* falcone.

Fall [fŏl] *n.* caduta, abbassamento, ribasso, crollo, decadenza, cascata, precipitazione (atmosferica); *v.i.* cadere, decadere, cedere alle tentazioni.

Fallacious [fă-lé′sciăs] *a.* fallace.

Fallacy [fè′lă-sⁱ] *n.* errore, sofisma.

Fallible [fè′lⁱ-bl] *a.* fallibile.

Fallow [fè′lo] *a.* e *n.* giallo; maggese.

False [fŏls] *a.* falso, finto, ingannevole.

Falsehood [fŏls′hŭd] *n.* bugia, falsità.

Falsify [fŏl′sⁱ-fai] *v.t.* falsificare.

Falter [fŏl′tĕʳ] *v.i.* balbettare, essere irresoluto, vacillare.

Fame [fém] *n.* fama.

Familiar [fă-mⁱ′lⁱ-ĕʳ] *a.* e *n.* familiare.

Familiarity [fă-mⁱ-lⁱ-è′rⁱ-tⁱ] *n.* familiarità.

Familiarize [fă-mⁱ′lⁱ-ă-raⁱz] *v.t.* familiarizzare.

Family [fè′mⁱ-lⁱ] *n.* famiglia.

Famine [fè′mⁱn] *n.* carestia.

Famish [fè′mⁱsh] *v.t.* affamare; *v.i.* morire di fame.

Famous [fé′măs] *a.* famoso.

Fan [fèn] *n.* ventaglio, ventilatore; (*gergo*) tifoso (d'uno sport, ecc.); *v.t.* sventolare, ventilare.

Fanatic [fă-nè′tⁱc] *a.* e *n.* fanatico.

Fanaticism [fă-nè′tⁱ-sizm] *n.* fanatismo.

Fanciful [fèn′sⁱ-fŭl] *a.* capriccioso, fantasioso, irreale.

Fancy [fèn′sⁱ] *n.* capriccio, fantasia, supposizione; *v.t.* creare con la fantasia, immaginare, desiderare.

Fane [fén] *n.* [*poet.*] tempio.

Fang [fèng] *n.* zanna.

Fantastic [fĕn-tès′tⁱc] *a.* fantastico.

Fantasy [fèn′tă-sⁱ] *n.* fantasia, immaginazione.

Far [fäʳ] *a.* lontano, remoto; *avv.* a grande distanza, di gran lunga, molto; so [sò] f. finora, fin qui.

Farce [fäʳs] *n.* buffonata, farsa.

Farcical [fäʳsⁱ-chĕl] *a.* farsesco.

Fare [féᵉʳ] *n.* cibo, nutrimento, prezzo (del viaggio, ecc.), passeggero (di veicolo da noleggio); *v.i.* andare (bene o male), tirare avanti, viaggiare, nutrirsi.

Farewell [féᵉr-uèl′] *n.* (*raro*) addio.

Far-fetched [fäʳ′féćt] *a.* esagerato, ricercato.

Farm [fäʳm] *n.* fattoria, podere; f. **-yard** [iaʳd] aia; *v.t.* coltivare, prendere in appalto; *v.i.* fare l'agricoltore.

Farmer [fäʳ′mĕʳ] *n.* agricoltore, affittavolo.

Farrier [fè′rⁱ-ĕʳ] *n.* maniscalco.

Farther [fäʳ′thĕʳ] (*comp. di* far) *a.* più lontano; *av.* anche, inoltre, più a lungo.

Farthing [fäʳ′thiⁿ] *n.* (*old*) moneta inglese (quarta parte di un penny).

Fascinate [fè'sĭ-nét] *v.t.* affascinare.

Fascination [fè-sĭ-né'šn] *n.* fascino.

Fashion [fè'scĕn] *n.* moda, modello, modo, stile; *v.t.* fare, foggiare, creare secondo un modello.

Fashionable [fè'scĕ-nǎ-bl] *a.* alla moda, di moda.

Fast [fàst] *n.* digiuno; *a.* fermo, fisso, saldo, dissipato, leggero (*senso morale*), rapido, veloce; *avv.* rapidamente, fermamente, saldamente; *v.i.* digiunare.

Fasten [fàs'n] *v.t.* assicurare, attaccare, fissare; *v.i.* attaccarsi.

Fastening [fàs'nĭn] *n.* chiusura, fermatura.

Fastidious [fès-tĭ'dĭ-ǎs] *a.* di gusti difficili.

Fastidiousness [fès-tĭ'dĭ-ǎs-nĕs] *n.* l'essere di gusti difficili.

Fasting [fàs'tĭn] *n.* digiuno; *a.* a digiuno.

Fat [fèt] *n.* grasso; *a.* corpulento, grasso.

Fatal [fé'tǎl] *a.* funesto, mortale.

Fatality [fé-tè'lĭ-tĭ] *n.* fatalità, sventura, vittima.

Fate [fét] *n.* destino, fato.

Fated [fé'tĭd] *a.* destinato.

Father [fà'thĕr] *n.* padre; f.-in-law (ló) suocero.

Fatherhood [fà'thĕr-hŭd] *n.* paternità.

Fatherless [fà'thĕr-lĕs] *a.* orfano (di padre.)

Fatherly [fà'thĕr-lĭ] *a.* paterno.

Fathom [fè'thǒm] *n.* misura di profondità (metri 1, 83 circa); *v.t.* scandagliare; (*fig.*) capire.

Fathomless [fè'thǒm-lĕs] *a.* incommensurabile.

Fatigue [fǎ-tíg'] *n.* fatica; *v.t.* affaticare, stancare.

Fatness [fèt'nĕs] *n.* grassezza, grossezza.

Fatten [fè'tn] *v.t.* e *i.* ingrassare.

Fatty [fè'tĭ] *a.* adiposo, grasso.

Fatuity [fǎ-tiú'ĭ-tĭ] *n.* fatuità.

Fatuous [fè'tiŭ-ǎs] *a.* fatuo.

Fault [fôlt] *n.* colpa, difetto, fallo; to a f. all'eccesso.

Faultless [fôlt'lĕs] *a.* irreprensibile, perfetto.

Faulty [fôl'tĭ] *a.* colpevole, difettoso.

Faun [fôn] *n.* fauno.

Favour [fé'vĕr] *n.* favore, parzialità, pegno; *v.t.* favorire; (*famil.*) somigliare.

Favourable [fé'vǒ-rǎ-bl] *a.* favorevole, propizio.

Favourite [fé'vǒ-rĭt] *a.* e *n.* favorito.

Fawn [fôn] *n.* cerbiatto; *a.* bruno-giallastro; *v.i.* adulare.

Fealty [fĭ'àl-tĭ] *n.* fedeltà, giuramento di fedeltà.

Fear [fíer] *n.* paura, timore; *v.t.* temere; *v.i.* aver paura.

Fearful [fíer'fûl] *a.* pauroso, spaventoso, timoroso.

Fearless [fíer'lĕs] *a.* ardimentoso, impavido, intrepido.

Feasible [fĭ'zĭ-bl] *a.* fattibile, possibile.

Feast [fĭst] *n.* banchetto, festa [religiosa]; *v.t.* festeggiare; *v.i.* banchettare.

Feat [fĭt] *n.* atto eroico, prodezza.

Feather [fĕ'thĕr] *n.* penna, piuma.

Feature [fĭ'cĕr] *n.* fattezza (*di solito pl.*), lineamento, configurazione (*geogr.*); caratteristica.

February [fĕ'brŭ-ǎ-rĭ] *n.* febbraio.

Feckless [fĕc'lĕs] *a.* inefficiente.

Fecund [fé'cŭnd] *a.* fecondo.

Fecundity [fĕ-cŭn'dĭ-tĭ] *n.* fecondità.

Federal [fĕ'dĕ-rĕl] a. federale.

Federate [fĕ'dĕ-rĕt] a. (con)-federato.

Federation [fĕ-dĕ-ré'śn] n. (con)federazione.

Fee [fī] n. onorario (di professionista), quota (d'iscrizione), tassa (d'esame, ecc.); v.t. pagare un onorario a.

Feeble [fī'bl] a. debole.

Feed [fīd] v.t. e i. nutrir(si).

Feeding [fī'dĭñ] n. alimentazione, nutrimento.

Feel [fīl] v.t. e i. sentir(si), avere la sensazione di, percepire.

Feeler [fī'lĕr] n. antenna, tentacolo; (fig.) osservazione lanciata per sondare l'animo degli altri.

Feeling [fī'lĭñ] n. sentimento, sensazione, tatto; a. sensibile.

Feign [fēn] v.t. e i. fingere, simulare.

Feint [fēnt] n. finta; (mil.) finto attacco.

Felicitate [fĕ-li'sĭ-tét] v.t. congratularsi con.

Felicitation [fĕ-li-sĭ-té'śn] n. congratulazione; [felice.

Felicitous [fĕ-li'sĭ-tăs] a.

Felicity [fĕ-li'sĭ-ti] n. felicità.

Feline [fī'la¹n] a. e n. felino.

Fell [fĕl] n. collina brulla, pelle, vello; a. (poet.) crudele; v.t. abbattere, far cadere.

Fellow [fĕ'lò] n. individuo, camerata, compagno, socio; -ship [ścĭp] cameratismo, compagnia.

Felon [fĕ'lŏn] n. fellone.

Felonious [fĕ-lò'ni-ăs] a. criminale.

Felony [fĕ'lò-nĭ] n. fellonia, infrazione alla legge.

Felt [fĕlt] n. feltro.

Female [fī'mél] n. donna, femmina; a. femminile, di sesso femminile.

Feminine [fĕ'mi-nĭn] a. femminile.

Fen [fĕn] n. terreno acquitrinoso.

Fence [fĕns] n. recinto, steccato, ricettatore; v.t. chiudere con un recinto, ricettare; v.i. schermire, tirar di scherma.

Fencing [fĕn'sĭñ] n. scherma.

Fend [fĕnd] v.t. parare (un colpo, ecc.); v.i. provvedere, fare le provviste.

Fender [fĕn'dĕr] n. riparo in metallo davanti al camino.

Ferment [fĕr'mĕnt] n. fermento; (fĕr-mĕnt') v.t. e i. (far) fermentare.

Fermentation [fĕr-mĕn-té'śn] n. fermentazione.

Fern [fĕrn] n. felce.

Ferocious [fĕ-rò'sciăs] a. feroce.

Ferocity [fĕ-rŏ'sĭ-ti] n. ferocia.

Ferret [fĕ'rĕt] n. furetto; f. out (aut) v.t. scoprire (segreti).

Ferrule [fĕ'rĕl] n. ghiera.

Ferry [fĕ'rĭ] n. traghetto; v.t. trasportare su nave traghetto, tra₁ hettare.

Fertile [fĕr'ta¹l] a. fertile.

Fertility [fĕr-tĭ'lĭ-tĭ] n. fertilità.

Fertilize [fĕr'tĭ-la¹z] v.t. fertilizzare.

Fervent [fĕr'vĕnt] a. fervente.

Fervid [fĕr'vĭd] a. fervido.

Fervour [fĕr'vĕr] n. fervore.

Fester [fĕs'tĕr] v.i. suppurare.

Festival [fĕs'tĭ-vĕl] n. festa, festino, serie di rappresentazioni musicali, ecc.

Festive [fĕs'tĭv] a. festivo, gioioso.

Festivity [fĕs-tĭ'vĭ-tĭ] n. festa.

Festoon [fĕs'tŭn] n. festone; v.t. adornare con festoni.

Fetch [fĕć] v.t. andare a prendere, essere venduto per.

Fetching [fĕ'cĭñ] a. (famil.) attraente.

Fetid [fĕ'tĭd] a. fetido.

Fetish [fĭ'tĭš] n. feticcio.

Fetlock [fĕt'lŏc] n. ciuffo di capelli nella parte posteriore del piede d'un cavallo.

Fetter [fĕ'tĕʳ] n. catena; -s (pl.) ceppi (pl.); v.t. mettere in ceppi, intralciare.

Feud [fĭûd] n. faida, feudo.

Feudal [fiû'dĕl] a. feudale.

Feudalism [fiû'dă-lĭzm] n. feudalismo.

Fever [fĭ'vĕʳ] n. febbre.

Feverish [fĭ'vĕ-rĭš] a. febbricitante, febbrile, inquieto.

Few [fiû] a. e pron. (pl.) pochissimi, quasi punti; a f. alcuni, un certo numero; the f. la minoranza.

Fib [fĭb] n. (famil.) piccola bugia.

Fibre [fa'bĕʳ] n. fibra.

Fibrous [fa'brăs] a. fibroso.

Fickle [fĭ'cl] a. incostante, volubile.

Fickleness [fĭ'cl-nĕs] n. incostanza, volubilità.

Fiction [fĭc'šn] n. romanzi (pl.), finzione, invenzione.

Fictitious [fĭc-tĭ'sciăs] a. fittizio.

Fiddle [fĭ'dl] n. (famil.) violino; v.t. e i. (famil.) suonare il violino, perdersi in sciocchezze, gingillarsi.

Fidelity [fa'-dĕ'lĭ-tĭ] n. fedeltà.

Fidget [fĭ'gĭt] n. irrequietezza; v.i. essere irrequieto, trovarsi a disagio.

Fidgety [fĭ'gĭ-tĭ] a. irrequieto.

Fie! [fa'] interiez. vergogna!

Field [fĭld] n. campo.

Fiend [fĭnd] n. demonio, spirito maligno.

Fiendish [fĭn'dĭš] a. demoniaco.

Fierce [fĭeʳs] a. feroce, violento.

Fiery [fa'-ĕ-rĭ] a. focoso, infiammato.

Fife [fa'f] n. piffero.

Fifteen [fĭf'tĭn] a. e n.

quindici; -th a. e n. quindicesimo, decimo quinto.

Fifth [fĭfth] a. e n. quinto.

Fifty [fĭf'tĭ] a. e n. cinquanta; -tieth [tĭ-ĕth] a. e n. cinquantesimo. [di] fico.

Fig [-tree] [fĭg'trĭ] n. (pianta

Fight [fa't] n. battaglia, combattimento; v.t. e i. combattere, lottare.

Figment [fĭg'mĕnt] n. finzione, invenzione.

Figure [fĭ'ghĕʳ] n. cifra, figura; v.t. figurarsi, raffigurare; v.i. far calcoli, figurare; f. -head [hĕd] uomo di paglia.

File [fa'l] n. (mil.) fila, filza, lima; v.t. archiviare, ordinare, limare; (mil.) mettere in fila; v.i. andare in fila.

Filial [fĭ'lĭ-ĕl] a. filiale.

Filibuster [fĭ-lĭ-băs'tĕʳ] n. filibustiere.

Filigree [fĭ'lĭ-grĭ] n. filigrana.

Fill [fĭl] v.t. riempire, rifornire, occupare (un posto), otturare (un dente) v.i. riempirsi.

Fillet [fĭ'lĕt] n. nastro (da portare intorno al capo), filetto, fetta (di pesce).

Fillip [fĭ'lĭp] n. buffetto (colpo), stimolo.

Filly [fĭ'lĭ] n. puledra.

Film [fĭlm] n. film, pellicola, patina, velo (che si forma sull'occhio).

Filmy [fĭl'mĭ] a. filamentoso, velato, vaporoso.

Filter [fĭl'tĕʳ] n. filtro; v.t.e i. filtrare.

Filth [fĭlth], **filthiness** [fĭl'thĭ-nĕs] n. sudiciume, oscenità.

Filthy [fĭl'thĭ] a. sudicio, osceno.

Filtrate [fĭl'trĕt] v.t. filtrare.

Fin [fĭn] n. pinna.

Final [fa'-nĕl] n. finale; a. conclusivo, decisivo, finale.

Finance [fa'-nèns'] n. finanza.

Financial [fĭ-nèn'scĕl] a. finanziario.

Financier [fĭ-nèn'sĭᵉʳ] n. finanziere.

Finch [finč] n. fringuello.

Find [faɪnd] n. ritrovamento, scoperta; v.t. trovare; f. out [aʊt] scoprire.

Fine [faɪn] n. multa; a. bello, delicato, fine, fino, penetrante; v.t. multare.

Fineness [faɪn'nĕs] n. bellezza, finezza, sottigliezza.

Finery [faɪ'nĕ-rĭ] n. abiti delle feste (pl.), fronzoli (pl.).

Finesse [fĭ-nĕs'] n. finezza, sottigliezza.

Finger [fiɲ'ghĕʳ] n. dito; v.t. tastare, toccare delicatamente.

Finical [fĭ'nĭ-cl] a. affettato.

Finish [fĭ'nĭš] n. rifinitura, ultimo tocco, fine; v.t. e i. finire, perfezionare.

Finite [faɪ'naɪt] a. definito, limitato.

Finn [fin] n. finlandese.

Finnish [fĭ'nĭš] a. finlandese.

Fir [-tree] [fĕʳ'trī] n. abete.

Fire [faɪᵉʳ] n. fuoco, incendio, sparo; v.t. incendiare, sparare. **Fire-arms** [faɪᵉʳ'ã'rms] n. (pl.) armi da fuoco (pl.).

Fire-brigade [faɪᵉʳ bri-ghéd'] n. corpo dei pompieri.

Firefly [faɪᵉʳ'flaɪ] n. lucciola.

Fireman [faɪᵉʳ'män] n. pompiere.

Fire-place [faɪᵉʳ'plés] n. caminetto, camino.

Fire-proof [faɪᵉʳ'prŭf] a. incombustibile.

Fireside [faɪᵉʳ'saɪd] n. focolare.

Fire-stone [faɪᵉʳ'stòn] n. pietra refrattaria.

Fire-wood [faɪᵉʳ'ŭũd] n. legna da ardere.

Fire-work [faɪᵉʳ'ŭĕʳc] n. fuoco d'artifizio.

Firing [faɪᵉ'rĭɲ] n. combustibile, scarica, sparo; f. party [pã'rtĭ] (mil.) plotone d'esecuzione.

Firm [fĕʳm] n. ditta; a. fermo, saldo, stabile.

Firmament [fĕʳ'mă-mĕnt] n. firmamento.

Firmness [fĕʳm'nĕs] n. fermezza, stabilità.

First [fĕʳst] a e n. primo; av.á prima, in primo luogo.

Firth [fĕʳth] n. estuario (scozzese).

Fish [fiš] n. pesce; v.t. e i. pescare.

Fisher[man] [fĭ'scĕʳ-män] n. pescatore.

Fishery [fĭ'scĕ-rĭ] n. peschiera.

Fishmonger [fĭš'män-ghĕʳ] n. pescivendolo.

Fish-pond [fĭš'pònd] n. vasca per pesci.

Fishy [fĭ'scĭ] a. di pesce; (fig.) dubbio, equivoco.

Fissure [fĭš'iŭʳ] n. crepa, fessura.

Fist [fĭst] n. pugno; (famil.) scrittura.

Fit [fĭt] n. accesso, attacco, colpo (apopletico, ecc.); a. adatto, appropriato, conveniente, idoneo, in buona salute; v.t. e i. adattare, preparare, mettere a prova, convenire, star bene.

Fitful [fĭt'fŭl] a. impulsivo, irregolare, lunatico.

Fitness [fĭt'nĕs] n. opportunità, buona salute.

Fitting [fĭ'tĭɲ] n. prova (d'un vestito); -s (pl) infissi (pl.); a. adatto, convenevole.

Five [faɪv] a. e n. cinque.

Fix [fĭcs] n. (famil.) dilemma, difficoltà; v.t. assicurare, fissare, definire, stabilire.

Fixture [fĭcs'cĕʳ] n. infisso, data fissata per un avvenimento sportivo.

Fizz [fĭz] n. (gergo) spumante.

Fizzle [fĭz'l] v.i. frizzare, sibilare.

Flabbergast [flĕ'bĕʳ-ghèst] v.t. (famil.) sbalordire.

Flabbiness [flè'bi-něs] n. flaccidezza.

Flabby [flè'bi] a. cascante, floscio.

Flaccid [flèc'sid] a. flaccido.

Flag [flèg] n. bandiera, iride (fiore), giaggiolo; v.i. perdere le forze.

Flagon [flé'gŏn] n. bottiglione.

Flagrant [flé'grěnt] a. flagrante.

Flail [fiél] n. coreggiato, flagello.

Flair [flé'er] n. fiuto, intuizione.

Flake [flèc] n. fiocco, lamina, scaglia.

Flaky [flè'chi] a. fioccoso, frollo (di pasta).

Flam [flèm] n. (gergo) inganno, racconto falso.

Flamboyant [flèm-bo'ěnt] a. fiammeggiante, sgargiante.

Flame [flèm] n. fiamma; v.i. fiammeggiare.

Flange [flènğ] n. bordo, costa, flangia.

Flank [flènc] n. fianco; v.t. fiancheggiare.

Flannel [flè'něl] a. e n. (di) flanella.

Flap [flèp] n. battito (di ala, ecc.), trabocchetto; v.t. agitare, sbattere; v.i. muoversi.

Flare [flé'r] n. chiarore intenso, fiammata improvvisa (aviaz.) razzo; v.i. brillare di luce viva, avvampare.

Flash [flès] n. baleno, lampo, vampata; v.t. lanciare; v.i. balenare, sfavillare.

Flashy [flè'sci] a. (famil.) sgargiante, vistoso.

Flask [flàsc] n. fiasco.

Flat [flèt] n. appartamento, pianura; a. piano, piatto, monotono, uniforme, reciso.

Flatness [flèt'něs] n. l'essere piatto, monotonia, uniformità.

Flatten [flè'tn] v.t. appiattire.

Flatter [flè'těr] v.t. adulare, lusingare.

Flattering [flè'tě-rin] a. adulatorio.

Flattery [flè'tě-ri] n. adulazione.

Flatulent [flè'tiu-lěns] n. flatulenza.

Flaunt [flŏnt] v.t. ostentare.

Flavour [flév'ěr] n. aroma, gusto, sapore; v.t. dare il gusto a.

Flaw [flŏ] n. difetto, pecca.

Flax [flècs] n. lino.

Flaxen [flèc'sěn] a. di lino, giallognolo (colore).

Flay [fle'] v.t. scorticare, scuoiare.

Flea [fli] n. pulce.

Fleck [flěc] n. lentiggine, macchietta, particella.

Fledge [flěğ] v.i. mettere le ali.

Fledgling [flěğ'lin] n. uccellino appena uscito dal nido.

Flee [fli] v.i. fuggire.

Fleece [flis] n. vello; v.t. (gergo) pelare, spogliare (di danaro, ecc.).

Fleecy [fli'si] a. lanoso, velloso.

Fleet [flit] n. flotta; a. (poet.) agile, veloce.

Fleeting [fli'tin] a. fugace, transitorio.

Fleetness [flit'něs] n. agilità.

Fleming [flé'min] n. fiammingo.

Flemish [flé'mis] a. fiammingo.

Flesh [flěs] n. carne.

Flexibility [flěc-si-bi'li-ti] n. flessibilità.

Flexible [flěc'si-bl] a. flessibile, pieghevole.

Flicker [fli'chěr] n. barlume, tremolio, vibrazione; v.i. tremolare, vacillare, vibrare.

Flight [fla·t] n. fuga, rampa (di scale), volo.

Flighty [fla'ti] a. capriccioso, mutevole, poco serio.

Flimsiness [flim'zi-něs] n. frivolezza, tenuità.

Flimsy [flim'zi] a. debole, frivolo, tenue.

Flinch [flínć] *v.i.* indietreggiare, ritirarsi.

Fling [flín] *n.* getto, lancio, godimento completo; *v.t.* gettare, lanciare.

Flint [flint] *n.* pietra focaia, selce, qualunque cosa di durezza eccezionale.

Flinty [flín'ti] *a.* di selce, crudele, duro.

Flip [flip] *v.t.* mandare avanti con buffetti.

Flippancy [fli'pèn-si] *n.* leggerezza, mancanza di serietà.

Flippant [fli'pènt] *a.* leggero, irrispettoso.

Flirt [flë't] *n.* ragazza civettuola, damerino; *v.t.* agitare; *v.i.* civettare.

Flirtation [flër-té'śn] *n.* corteggiamento senza intenzioni serie.

Flit [flit] *v.i.* emigrare, passare rapidamente, svolazzare.

Float [flòt] *n.* galleggiante, specie di carretta bassa; *v.t.* disincagliare, far galleggiare, lanciare (una società); *v.i.* disincagliarsi, galleggiare.

Flock [flòc] *n.* branco, gregge, bioccolo, fiocco (di lana); *v.i.* riunirsi a stormi.

Floe [flò] *n.* lastra di ghiaccio galleggiante. [frustare.

Flog [flòg] *v.t.* frustigare,

Flood [flåd] *n.* diluvio, inondazione; *v.t.* inondare, sommergere.

Floor [flór] *n.* pavimento, piano (di casa); *v.t.* pavimentare; (*gergo*) ridurre al silenzio.

Flop [flòp] *v.i.* camminare (sedersi) goffamente; (*gergo*) far fiasco.

Floral [fló'rël] *a.* floreale.

Florid [fló-rid] *a.* florido, prosperoso.

Florin [fló'rin] *n.* florino (in Inghilterra, moneta che valeva due scellini).

Florist [fló'rist] *n.* floraio, floricultore.

Flotilla [flò'ti'lè(r)] *n.* flottiglia.

Flotsam [flòt'săm] *n.* relitti (*pl.*); merci ritrovate galleggianti sul mare (*pl.*).

Flounce [flaünz] *n.* falpalà; *v.t.* ornare di volani; *v.i.* dimenarsi, muoversi in modo agitato.

Flounder [flaün'dër] *n.* sorta di pesce; *v.i.* condurre una cosa male, fare errori.

Flour [flauer] *n.* fior di farina.

Flourish [flå'riś] *n.* fioritura, squillo (di trombe); *v.i.* fiorire; (*fig.*) prosperare.

Flout [flaüt] *v.t.* insultare, schernire.

Flow [flò] *n.* abbondanza, facilità nel parlare, corrente, flusso; *v.i.* fluire, scorrere.

Flower [flauer] *n.* fiore, f. -bed [bëd] aiuola; *v.i.* fiorire, produrre fiori.

Flowery [flaue'ri] *a.* florito.

Fluctuate [flåc'tiü-ét] *v.i.* fluttuare.

Flue [flù] *n.* conduttura d'un camino, tubo.

Fluency [flü'ën-si] *n.* prontezza, rapidità (di parole).

Fluent [flü'ënt] *a.* corrente, eloquente, facile (di modo di parlare).

Fluff [flåf] *n.* lanugine, peluria.

Fluid [flü'id] *a.* e *n.* fluido.

Fluke [flûc] *n.* (*famil.*) vantaggio inaspettato, colpo di fortuna.

Flunkey [flån'chi] *n.* servo in livrea.

Flurry [flå'ri] *n.* fretta nervosa, improvviso colpo di vento, o scroscio di pioggia.

Flush [flåś] *n.* rossore, afflusso di sangue al volto; *v.t.* sciacquare (con acqua abbondante). *v.i.* arrossire.

Fluster [flås'tër] *n.* agitazione.

eccitazione; *v.t.* agitare, rendere nervoso.

Flute [flūt] *n.* flauto.

Flutter [flŭ'tẽr] *n.* agitazione, svolazzamento; (*gergo*) speculazione; *v.t.* agitare; *v.i.* agitarsi, svolazzare.

Fly [flai] *n.* mosca; *v.t. e i.* [far] volare.

Flyer, flier [flai'ẽr] *n.* aviatore, volatore.

Foal [fōl] *n.* puledro.

Foam [fōm] *n.* schiuma, spuma; *v.i.* schiumare, spumeggiare.

Fodder [fŏ'dẽr] *n.* foraggio.

Foe [fō] *n.* avversario, nemico.

Fog [fŏg] *n.* nebbia fitta, nebbione.

Foggy [fŏ'ghi] *a.* nebbioso.

Foible [foi'bl] *n.* lato debole.

Foil [foil] *n.* foglia sottile di metallo, cosa che serve a guarnire; *v.t.* far fallire, frustrare, far perdere (le tracce).

Foist [foist] *v.t.* introdurre di nascosto, far accettare con un trucco.

Fold [fōld] *n.* piega, spira, ovile; (*fig.*) Chiesa; *v.t.* piegare, abbracciare, incrociare (le braccia).

Foliage [fō'li-ĕg] *n.* fogliame.

Folk [fōc] *n.* gente, popolo; (*famil.*) la propria famiglia.

Follow [fŏ'lō] *v.t.* seguire, imitare, inseguire; *v.i.* conseguire, derivare, seguire.

Folly [fŏ'li] *n.* follia, scemenza.

Foment [fŏ-mĕnt'] *v.t.* fomentare.

Fomentation [fŏ-mĕn-tē'sn] *n.* fomentazione, fomento.

Fond [fŏnd] *a.* affezionato, appassionato; to be [bi] f. of, voler bene a; piacere.

Fondle [fŏn'dl] *v.t.* accarezzare.

Fondness [fŏnd'nĕs] *n.* affettuosità indulgente.

Font [fŏnt] *n.* fonte battesimale.

Food [fūd] *n.* cibo, alimento, nutrimento.

Fool [fūl] *n.* buffone (di corte), idiota, sciocco; *v.t.* imbrogliare, ingannare; *v.i.* fare lo sciocco.

Foolery [fū'lĕ-rī] *n.* atto di pazzia, buffonata.

Foolhardy [fūl'här-di] *a.* temerario. [stolto.

Foolish [fū'liš] *a.* sciocco.

Foolishness [fū'liš-nĕs] *n.* sciocchezza, stoltezza.

Foot [fūt] *n.* piede; (*col verbo al pl.*) fanteria, misura lineare (corrispondente a 30, 5 circa).

Football [fūt'bôl] *n.* calcio, pallone per il calcio.

Foot-bridge [fūt'brig] *n.* ponte per soli pedoni.

Footing [fū'tin] *n.* appoggio; (*fig.*) condizioni (in cui uno si trova rispetto agli altri) (*pl.*).

Footman [fūt'män] *n.* servo in livrea.

Footstep [fūt'stĕp] *n.* passo, suono di passi.

Footstool [fūt'stūl] *n.* sgabello.

For [fŏr] *prep.* per, a, di; *conj.* perchè.

Forage [fŏ'rig] *n.* foraggio.

Foray [fŏ'rē'] *n.* incursione, scorreria.

Forbear [fŏr'bĕer] *n.* antenato. [fŏr-bĕer'] *v.t.* sopportare, trattenersi da; *v.i.* pazientare.

Forbearance [fŏr-bĕer'rĕns] *n.* pazienza, sopportazione.

Forbearing [fŏr-bĕer'rin] *a.* paziente.

Forbid [fŏr-bid'] *v.t.* proibire, vietare.

Forbidding [fŏr-bi'din] *a.* di aspetto poco invitante.

Force [fŏrs] *n.* forza, vigore (legge); -s (*pl.*) truppe (*pl.*); *v.t.* costringere, forzare.

Forceps [fŏr'sĕps] *n.* (*pl.*) pinze chirurgiche (*pl.*), forcipe.

Forcible [for'si-bl] *a.* impetuoso, violento.

Ford [fo'd] *n.* guado; *v.t. e i.* passare a guado.

Fordable [for'dĕ-bl] *a.* guadabile.

Fore [for] *n.* davanti, parte anteriore; *a.* anteriore.

Fore-arm [for'ă'm] *n.* avambraccio.

Forecast [for-căst'] *v.t.* predire; *v.i.* far previsioni.

Forecastle [fōc'sl] *n.* (*naut.*) castello di prua.

Forefather [for'fā-thĕr] *n.* antenato.

Foreground [for'graund] *n.* primo piano (in un quadro, ecc.).

Forehead [for'(h)ĕd] *n.* fronte (della testa).

Foreign [fŏ'rĭn] *a.* estero, estraneo, straniero.

Foreigner [fŏ'rĭ-nĕr] *n.* straniero, forestie/re.

Foreman [for'măn] *n.* capo operaio, presidente d'una giuria.

Foremost [for'mòst] *a.* primo, il più avanzato; *av.* in avanti.

Forenoon [for'nūn] *n.* mattino

Forerunner [for'rǎ-nĕr] *n.* precursore.

Foresee [for-sī'] *v.t.* prevedere.

Foresight [for'saĭt] *n.* previsione, prudenza.

Forest [fŏ'rĕst] *n.* foresta; *a.* forestale.

Forestall [for-stól'] *v.t.* anticipare; (*comm.*) fare incetta.

Forester [fŏ'rĕs-tĕr] *n.* guardia forestale.

Foretaste [for'te'st] *n.* anticipazione, pregustazione.

Foretell [for-tĕl'] *v.t.* predire, presagire.

Forethought [for'thót] *n.* previdenza.

Forewarn [for-uo'n'] *v.t.* (pre)avvertire.

Forfeit [for'fĭt] *n.* multa,

pegno, perdita; *v.t.* demeritare, perdere il diritto a, dover pagare.

Forfeiture [for'fĭ-ciŭᵉr] *n.* multa, penalità.

Forge [fo'ǵ] *n.* bottega del fabbro ferraio, fucina; *v.t.* foggiare, contraffare, inventare; *v.i.* fare contraffazioni; to f. ahead [ă-hĕd'] avanzare.

Forger [for'ǵĕr] *n.* falsificatore.

Forgery [for'ǵĕ-rĭ] *n.* contraffazione, documento falso, firma falsa.

Forget [for-ghĕt'] *v.t. e i.* dimenticare.

Forgetful [for-ghĕt'fŭl] *a.* dimentico, distratto, immemore.

Forgetfulness [for-ghĕt'fŭl-nĕs] *n.* facilità a dimenticare, oblio.

Forgivable [for-ghĭ'vĕ-bl] *a.* perdonabile.

Forgive [for-ghĭv'] *v.t.* perdonare.

Forgiveness [for-ghĭv'nĕs] *n.* perdono, remissione.

Fork [fo'c] *n.* forca, forchetta; *v.i.* biforcarsi.

Forlorn [for-ló'n'] *a.* abbandonato, infelice.

Form [fo'm] *n.* forma, modulo, scheda, banco di scuola, classe, covo di lepre; *v.t. e i.* formar(si).

Formal [for'mĕl] *a.* cerimonioso, formale.

Formality [for-mè'li-tĭ] *n.* formalità.

Formation [for-mé'šn] *n.* formazione.

Former [for'mĕr] *a.* precedente, primo; *pron.* quegli, il primo (di due persone).

Formerly [for'mĕr-lĭ] *av.* già, un tempo.

Formidable [for'mĭ-dĕ'bl] *a.* formidabile.

Forsake [for-séc'] *v.t.* abbandonare.

Forswear [for-suér'] v.t. (raro) abiurare.

Fort [fort] n. forte, fortezza.

Forth [forth] av. (in) avanti, fuori, via.

Forthcoming [forth-că'mïn] a. prossimo, vicino, vicino alla pubblicazione.

Fortification [for-tĭ-fĭ-ché'šn] n. fortificazione.

Fortify [for'tĭ-fa¹] v.t. fortificare.

Fortitude [for'tĭ-tiŭd] n. forza d'animo.

Fortnight [fort'na¹t] n. due settimane (pl.).

Fortress [for'trĕs] n. fortezza (luogo fortificato), roccaforte.

Fortuitous [for-tiŭ'ĭ-tăs] a. casuale, fortuito.

Fortunate [for'tiŭ-nét] a. favorevole, fortunato.

Fortune [for'tiŭn] n. fortuna.

For/ty [for'tĭ] a. e n. quaranta; -tieth ['tĭ-ĕth] a. e n. quarantesimo.

Forward [for'uĕ'd] a. spinto; av. (in) avanti, in poi; v.t. far proseguire, spedire, promuovere.

Fossil [fŏ'sĭl] a. e n. fossile.

Fossilize [fŏ'sĭ-la¹z] v.t. e i. fossilizzar(si).

Foster [fŏs'tĕr] v.t. allevare, nutrire, incoraggiare.

Foul [faŭl] a. sporco, sudicio, osceno, (di giuoco) irregolare.

Foulness [faŭl'nĕs] n. sporcizia, oscenità.

Found [faŭnd] v.t. fondare, fondere; v.i. fondarsi.

Foundation [faŭn-dé'šn] n. fondazione, fondamenta (pl.), istituzione.

Founder [faŭn'dĕr] n. fondatore, fonditore.

Founder [faŭn'dĕr] v.t. affondare, azzoppare (un cavallo); v.i. affondare, sprofondarsi.

Foundling [faŭnd'lĭn] n. trovatello.

Fount [faŭnt] n. (poet.) fonte, sorgente.

Fountain [faŭn'tĕn] n. fontana, fonte.

Four [fōr] a. e n. quattro; -th a. e n. quarto.

Fourfold [fō'fōld] a. quadruplo.

Fourteen [fō'-tín'] a. e n. quattordici; -th a. e n. quattordicesimo.

Fowl [faŭl] n. pollo, uccello.

Fox [fŏs] n. volpe.

Fraction [frĕc'šn] n. frazione.

Fractious [frĕc'sciăs] a. di cattivo umore, litigioso.

Fracture [frĕc'cĕr] n. frattura; v.t. e i. fratturar(si).

Fragile [frĕ'gia¹l] a. fragile.

Fragment [frĕg'mĕnt] n. frammento. [grante.

Fragrant [fré'grĕnt] a. fragrant.

Frail [frél] n. cestello; a. fragile, incapace di resistere alle tentazioni.

Frailty [frél'tĭ] n. fragilità.

Frame [frém] n. cornice, forma, struttura; v.t. incorniciare, servire da cornice a, dar forma a, inventare.

Franc [frĕnc] n. franco (moneta).

Franchise [frĕn'cia¹z] n. diritti di voto (pl.), franchigia.

Franciscan [frĕn-sis'chĕn] a. e n. francescano.

Frank [frĕnc] a. aperto, franco, schietto.

Frankness [frĕnc'nĕs] n. franchezza, schiettezza.

Frantic [frĕn'tic] a. fuori di sè.

Fraternal [fră-tĕr'nĕl] a. fraterno.

Fraternize [frĕ'tĕr-na¹z] v.i. fraternizzare.

Fratricide [frĕ'trĭ-sa¹d] n. fratrici/da, -dio.

Fraud [frŏd] n. frode.

Fraudulent [frŏ'diŭ-lĕnt] a. fraudolento.

Fray [freⁱ] *n.* combattimento, rissa.

Freak [frīc] *n.* capriccio, prodotto anormale della natura, aborto.

Freakish [frī'chīs] *a.* capriccioso.

Freckle [frē'cl] *n.* lentiggine; *v.t. e i.* macchiar(si) di lentiggini.

Free [frī] *a.* libero, liberale; *v.t.* emancipare, liberare.

Freedom [frī'dǎm] *n.* libertà, familiarità fuori luogo con le persone.

Freemason [frī'mé-sn] *n.* frammassone.

Freemasonry [frī'mé-sn-rĭ] *n.* frammassoneria.

Freethinker [frī'thǐn-chĕr] *n.* libero pensatore, razionalista.

Freeze [frīz] *v.t. e i.* congelar(si), gelare, irrigidir(si).

Freight [freⁱt] *n.* nolo, carico (di nave, treno, ecc.); *v.t.* caricare (una nave), noleggiare.

French [frēnć] *a.* francese.

Frenzy [frēn'zĭ] *n.* frenesia.

Frequency [frī'quĕn-sĭ] *n.* frequenza.

Frequent [frī'quĕnt] *a.* frequente; (frī-quĕnt') *v.t.* frequentare.

Fresh [frēš] *a.* fresco, inesperto, nuovo, (di acqua) dolce.

Freshen [frēš'n] *v.t. e i.* rinfrescar(si), rinvigorir(si).

Freshness [frēš'nĕs] *n.* freschezza.

Fret [frēt] *n.* agitazione, irritazione, greca (ornato); *v.t.* agitare, irritare, fregare, rodere; *v.i.* impazientirsi.

Fretful [frēt'fŭl] *a.* irritabile.

Fretwork [frēt'uĕrc] *n.* lavoro d'intaglio, lavoro a greca.

Friar [fraⁱ'ĕr] *n.* frate.

Friction [frīc'sn] *n.* attrito, frizione.

Friday [fraⁱ'deⁱ] *n.* venerdì.

Friend [frēnd] *n.* amico, quacchero.

Friendless [frēnd'lĕs] *a.* senz' amici.

Friendliness [frēnd'lĭ-nĕs] *n.* amichevolezza.

Friendly [frēnd'lĭ] *a.* amichevole, da amico.

Friendship [frēnd'scĭp] *n.* amicizia.

Frieze [frīz] *n.* fregio.

Frigate [frī'ghĕt] *n.* fregata.

Fright [fraⁱt] *n.* spavento, timore, spauracchio.

Frighten [fraⁱt'n] *v.t.* spaventare.

Frightful [fraⁱt'fŭl] *a.* spaventoso.

Frigid [frī'gĭd] *a.* frigido.

Frill [frĭl] *n.* frangia, gala increspata.

Fringe [frĭnğ] *n.* bordo, frangia, frangetta; *v.t.* ornare di frangia.

Frisk [frĭsc] *v.i.* far salti, salterellare.

Frisky [frĭs'chĭ] *a.* saltellante, vivace.

Fritter [frī'tĕr] *n.* frittella, frammento; *v.t.* suddividere in frammenti, sciupare (tempo).

Frivolous [frī'vŏ-lǎs] *a.* frivolo.

Frizzle [frī'zl] *v.t. e i.* arricciar(si).

Fro [frò] *av.* indietro; to (tǔ) and t. avanti e indietro.

Frock [frŏc] *n.* tonaca (da frate), vestito (da donna o da bambina).

Frog [frŏg] *n.* rana, ranocchio, alamaro.

Frolic [frŏ'lĭc] *n.* scherzo, spasso; *v.i.* far salti, scherzare.

Frolicsome [frŏ'lĭc-sǎm] *a.* allegro, gaio. [per.

From [frŏm] *prep.* da, fin da.

Front [frǎnt] *n.* fronte, facciata, parte anteriore; *a.* di fronte, davanti; *v.t.* essere di fronte a.

Frontal [frăn'tĕl] *a. e n.* frontale.

Frontier [frăn'tiᵉʳ] *a. e n.* (di) frontiera.

Frontispiece [frăn'tis-pīs] *n.* frontespizio.

Frost [frŏst] *n.* gelo, gelata; (*gergo*) fiasco.

Frostbite [frŏst'ba'ᵗ] *n.* cancrena prodotta dal freddo.

Frosty [frŏs'tĭ] *a.* gelato, gelido.

Froth [frŏth] *n.* schiuma, spuma, chiacchierata vuota.

Frothy [frŏ'thĭ] *a.* schiumoso, spumoso, vuoto.

Frown [fraŭn] *n.* aggrottamento delle ciglia, cipiglio; *v.i.* aggrottare le ciglia.

Frowzy [fraŭ'zĭ] *a.* sciatto, di cattivo odore.

Fructify [frăc'tĭ-fa'] *v.i.* fruttificare.

Frugal [frü'ghĕl] *a.* frugale.

Fruit [früt] *n.* frutto, frutta (*pl.*).

Fruiterer [frü'tĕ-rĕʳ] *n.* commerciante in frutta, fruttivendolo.

Fruitful [früt'fŭl] *a.* fruttifero, produttivo, fecondo.

Fruitless [früt'lĕs] *a.* senza frutto, non proficuo.

Frump [frămp] *n.* donna vestita di abiti fuori moda.

Frustrate [frăs'trét] *v.t.* frustrare.

Frustration [frăs-tré'sn] *n.* delusione, scacco.

Fry [fra'] *n.* fritto, frittura; (*gergo*) small [smŏl] *i* bambini (*pl.*); *v.t. e i.* friggere.

Frying-pan [fra'ĭñ-pĕn] *n.* padella.

Fuddle [fă'dl] *v.t.* far ubbriacare.

Fuel [fiŭ'ĕl] *n.* combustibile; (*fig.*) esca.

Fugitive [fiŭ'gĭ-tiv] *a. e n.* fuggitivo.

Fugue [fiŭg] *n.* [*mus.*] fuga.

Fulfil [fŭl-fĭl'] *v.t.* compiere, eseguire.

Fulfilment [fŭl-fĭl'mĕnt] *n.* compimento, esecuzione.

Full [fŭl] *a.* pieno; *av.* completamente, perfettamente, in pieno; *v.t.* follare, gualcare.

Fuller [fŭ'lĕʳ] *n.* follatore.

Ful(l)ness [fŭl'nĕs] *n.* abbondanza, pienezza, colmo.

Fulminate [făl'mĭ-nét] *v.t. e i.* fulminare.

Fulsome [fŭl'săm] *a.* disgustoso, nauseante.

Fumble [făm'bl] *v.t. e i.* frugare, maneggiare senza abilità, stroppicciare nervosamente.

Fume [fiŭm] *n.* fumo, vapore, accesso di rabbia; *v.t.* sottoporre a vapori chimici; *v.i.* emettere vapori, essere in collera.

Fumigate [fiŭ'mĭ-ghét] *v.t.* fumigare.

Fumigation [fiŭ-mĭ-ghé'sn] *n.* fumigazione.

Fun [făn] *n.* allegria, divertimento, svago.

Function [fănc'sn] *n.* funzione.

Fund [fănd] *n.* fondo (*finanz.*).

Fundamental [făn-dă-mĕn'tĕl] *a.* fondamentale.

Funeral [fiŭ'nĕ-rĕl] *n.* funerale; *a.* funebre, funereo.

Fungus [făn'gŭs] *n.* fungo.

Funicular [fiŭ-nĭ'chiŭ-lĕʳ] *a. e n.* funicolare.

Funk [fănc] *n.* (*gergo*) panico, timore, codardo.

Funnel [fă'nĕl] *n.* imbuto, ciminiera (di nave).

Funny [fă'nĭ] *a.* buffo, comico, strano.

Fur [fĕʳ] *n.* pelliccia, pelo, incrostazione, patina.

Furbish [fĕʳ'bĭs] *v.t.* forbire, rinnovare.

Furious [fiŭᵉʳĭ-ăs] *a.* furioso, violento.

Furl [fĕ'l] *v.t.* ammainare, chiudere.

Furlough [fĕ'lò] *n.* (*mil.*) licenza, permesso.

Furnace [fĕ'nis] *n.* fornace, caldaia di termosifone.

Furnish [fĕ'ni-ʃ] *v.t.* fornire, riformire, ammobiliare.

Furniture [fĕ'ni-cĕr] *n.* mobilia, mobili (*pl.*).

Furrier [fă'ri-ĕr] *n.* pellicciaio.

Furrow [fă'rò] *n.* solco, ruga, traccia; *v.t.* solcare.

Further [fĕ'rhĕr] *a.* addizionale, ulteriore, *av.* oltre, più avanti; *v.t.* favorire, promuovere.

Furtive [fĕ'tiv] *a.* furtivo.

Fury [fiŭ'rĭ] *n.* furia.

Furze [fĕ'z] *n.* ginestra spinosa.

Fuse [fiŭz] *n.* spoletta; (*elettr.*) valvola; *v.t. e i.* fonder(si).

Fuselage [fiŭ'zĕ-līg] *n.* (*avia.*) fusoliera.

Fusillade [fiŭs-zĭ-lĕd'] *n.* scarica di fucili.

Fusion [fiŭ'ʃn] *n.* fusione.

Fuss [fă's] *n.* brontolìo, trambusto.

Fussy [fă'sĭ] *a.* brontolone, di difficile contentatura.

Fustian [făs'tĭ-ĕn]*n.*frustagno.

Fusty [făs'tĭ] *a.* ammuffito, che sa di muffa.

Futile [fiŭ'taĭl] *a.* futile.

Future [fiŭ'cĕr] *a. e n.* futuro.

Futurity [fiŭ-tiŭ'rĭ-tĭ] *n.* avvenire.

G

Gabble [ghè'bl] *v.t.* pronunciare in modo inarticolato o confuso; *v.i.* parlare indistintamente.

Gable [ghé'bl] *n.* porzione di edificio che sovrasta al cornicione ed è compresa fra i due spioventi del tetto ed il cornicione stesso.

Gad [ghĕd] *n.* il bighellonare; on the g. in giro.

Gad-fly [ghĕd'flaĭ] *n.* tafano.

Gaelic [ghe'lĭc] *a.* gaélico.

Gag [ghĕg] *n.* bavaglio; (*gergo*) battuta improvvisata da un attore; *v.t.* imbavagliare; *v.i.* (*gergo*) introdurre battute non contenute nel copione.

Gage [ghég] *n.* pegno.

Gaiety [ghé'ĭ-tĭ] *n.* gaiezza.

Gain [ghén] *n.* guadagno; *v.t.* guadagnare; *v.i.* andare avanti (dell'orologio).

Gainsay [ghén'sé] *v.t.* (*raro*) contraddire, negare.

Gait [ghét] *n.* andatura.

Gaiter [ghé'tĕr] *n.* ghetta.

Galaxy [ghĕl'lăc-sĭ] *n.* Galassia; (*fig.*) assemblea brillante.

Gale [ghél] *n.* bufera (di)vento.

Gall [gôl] *n.* fiele, galla; (*fig.*) malignità; *v.t.* irritare, scorticare.

Gallant [ghè'lĕnt] *n.* fine cavaliere; *a.* intrepido, valoroso, galante.

Gallantry [ghè'lĕn-trĭ] *n.* valore, galanteria.

Gallery [ghè'lĕ-rĭ] *n.* galleria; (*teatr.*) loggione.

Galley [ghè'lĭ] *n.* galea; (*naut.*) cucina (d'una nave).

Gallivant [ghè-lĭ-vènt'] *v.i.* andare a zonzo.

Gallon [ghè'lĕn] *n.* gallone (misura inglese di capacità = litri 4·543).

Gallop [ghè'lŏp] *n.* galoppo; *v.t. e i.* (far) galoppare.

Gallows [ghè'lŏz] *n.* (*pl.*) forca.

Galore [gă-lo'r] *av.* a bizzeffe.

Galvanize [ghèl'vă-naĭz] *v.t.* galvanizzare.

Gamble [ghèm'bl] *v.t. e i.* giocare d'azzardo, speculare rischiosamente.

Gambler [ghèm'blĕr] *n.* giocatore d'azzardo, speculatore.

Gambling [ghèm'blĭń] *n.* giuochi d'azzardo (*pl.*); g. -house [haus] bisca.

Game [ghém] *n.* giuoco, partita, caccia, selvaggina.

Game-keeper [ghém'chi-pĕr] *n.* guardacaccia.

Gammon [ghè'mĕn] *n.* parte più bassa d'un prosciutto; (*fig.*) inganno.

Gamut [ghè'mŭt] *n.* gamma, serie completa.

Gander [ghèn'dĕr] *n.* oca maschio.

Gang [ghèń] *n.* banda, squadra (di operai).

Ganglion [ghèn'ghlĭ-ŏn] *n.* ganglio.

Gangrene [ghèn'grìn] *n.* cancrena.

Gangster [ghèn'stĕr] *n.* membro d'una banda di delinquenti.

Gangway [ghèn'uĕ¹] *n.* corridoio, passaggio, passerella, pontile (di sbarco).

Gaol [gél] *n.* prigione.

Gaoler [gé'lĕr] *n.* carceriere.

Gap [ghép] *n.* breccia, fenditura; (*fig.*) divergenza, lacuna.

Gape [ghép] *n.* sbadiglio; *v.i.* sbadigliare, spalancare la bocca (per meraviglia).

Garage [ghè'rĭǵ] *n.* autorimessa.

Garb [gärb] *n.* (*raro*) abbigliamento.

Garbage [gär'bĭǵ] *n.* rifiuti (*pl.*).

Garble [gär'bl] *v.t.* falsificare (una storia).

Garden [gär'dn] *n.* giardino; *v.i.* lavorare di giardinaggio.

Gardener [gär'd'nĕr] *n.* giardiniere.

Gardening [gär'd'nĭń] *n.* giardinaggio.

Gargle [gär'gl] *n.* gargarismo; *v.i.* fare gargarismi.

Gargoyle [gär'go¹l] *n.* cariatide, figura grottesca.

Garish [ghé'rĭš] *a.* abbagliante, sgargiante.

Garland [gär'lènd] *n.* ghirlanda.

Garlic [gär'lĭc] *n.* aglio.

Garment [gär'mĕnt] *n.* articolo di vestiario, indumento.

Garner [gär'nĕr] *v.t.* immagazzinare.

Garnish [gär'nĭš] *n.* guarnizione, contorno (a una pietanza); *v.t.* guarnire, ornare.

Garret [ghè'rĕt] *n.* abbaino, soffitta.

Garrison [ghè'rĭ-sĕn] *n.* guarnigione; *v.t.* fornire di guarnigione.

Garrulity [gä-rŭ'lĭ-tĭ] *n.* loquacità.

Garrulous [ghè'rŭ-läs] *a.* garrulo, loquace.

Garter [gär'tĕr] *n.* giarrettiera.

Gas [ghès] *n.* gas; (*gergo abbrev. di* gasolene) benzina.

Gash [ghès] *n.* squarcio; *v.t.* fare uno squarcio.

Gasp [gäsp] *n.* anelito, sforzo estremo per respirare; *v.t. e i.* boccheggiare, pronunziare affannosamente.

Gassy [ghè'sĭ] *a.* gassoso.

Gastritis [ghès-tra¹'tĭs] *n.* (*med.*) gastrite.

Gate [ghét] *n.* cancello, porta (di città).

Gather [ghè'thĕr] *v.t.* (rac)cogliere, radunare, fare le pieghe; *v.i.* radunarsi; (*med.*) venire a suppurazione.

Gathering [ghè'thĕ-rĭń] *n.* adunata, assemblea; (*med.*) gonfiore purulento.

Gaudy [gó'dĭ] *a.* sfarzoso e di cattivo gusto.

Gauge [ghéǵ] *n.* apparecchio misuratore, misura base, stima; *v.t.* misurare con esattezza; (*fig.*) formarsi un concetto di.

Gaunt [gönt] *a.* macilento, sparuto.

Gauntness [gônt'něs] n. macilenza.

Gauntlet [gónt'lět] n. grosso guanto che copre il polso; (arcaico) guanto di armatura.

Gauze [gôz] n. garza, velo.

Gay [ghe'] a. allegro, gaio, a colori vivaci, dedito alla vita galante.

Gaze [ghéz] n. sguardo fisso; v.i. guardare fisso.

Gazelle [gă-zěl'] n. gazzella.

Gazette [gă-zět'] n. gazzetta.

Gazetteer [ghě-zě-ti'er'] n. dizionario geografico.

Gear [ghi'er] n. equipaggiamento; (mecc.) congegno, ingranaggio, meccanismo.

Gelatin(e) [gě'lă-tin] n. gelatina.

Geld [ghěld] v.t. castrare.

Gem [gěm] n. gemma, gioiello.

Gender [gěn'děr] n. genere, sesso.

Genealogy [gĭ-nĭ-ĕ'lŏ-gĭ] n. genealogia.

General [gě'ně-rěl] a. e n. generale; -ship [scip] abilità militare, strategia, guida.

Generalize [gě'ně-ră-la'z] v.t. e i. generalizzare.

Generate [gě'ně-rét] v.t. generare.

Generation [gě-ně-ré'šn] n. generazione.

Generative [gě'ně-ră-tĭv] a. generativo, produttivo.

Generosity [gě-ně-rŏ'sĭ-tĭ] n. generosità.

Generous [gě'ně-răs] a. generoso.

Genial [gĭ'nĭ-ěl] a. amabile, piacevole, mite (clima).

Geniality [gĭ-nĭ-ě'lĭ-tĭ] n. amabilità.

Genitive [gě'nĭ-tĭv] a. e n. genitivo.

Genius [gĭ'nĭ-ăs] n. genio, talento, essere dotato di potere intellettuale superiore al normale.

Genteel [gěn-tĭl'] a. (spesso ironico) compito, elegante (di modi).

Gentle [gěn'tl] a. delicato, dolce, mite, nobile.

Gentlefolk [gěn'tl-fòc] n. gente che appartiene alle classi elevate.

Gentleman [gěn'tl-măn] n. gentiluomo, signore.

Gentlemanlike [gěn'tl-măn-la'c] a. da gentiluomo, signorile.

Gentleness [gěn'tl-něs] n. delicatezza, dolcezza, mitezza.

Gentlewoman [gěn'tl-uŭ-măn] n. gentildonna, signora.

Gentry [gěn'trĭ] n. piccola nobiltà.

Genuine [gě'nĭŭ-ĭn] a. genuino.

Genuineness [gě'nĭŭ-ĭn-něs] n. genuinità.

Geodesy [gĭ-ŏ'dě-sĭ] n. geodesia.

Geography [gĭ-ŏ'gră-fĭ] n. geografia. [logia.

Geology [gĭ-ŏ'lŏ-gĭ] n. geometria.

Geometry [gĭ-ŏ'mě-trĭ] n. geometria.

Germ [gěrm] n. germe.

German [gěr'măn] a. e n. tedesco; a. germanico.

Germinate [gěr'mi-nét] v.i. germinare.

Gerund [gě'rănd] n. gerundio.

Gestation [gěs-té'šn] n. gestazione.

Gesticulate [gěs-tĭ'chiŭ-lét] v.i. gesticolare.

Gesticulation [gěs-tĭ-chiŭ-lé'šn] n. il gesticolare.

Gesture [gěs'cěr] n. gesto.

Get [ghět] v... ottenere, ricevere, guadagnare, prendere, persuadere; v.i. arrivare, raggiungere, divenire.

Gewgaw [ghiŭ'gô] n. ninnolo.

Geyser [ghé'sěr] n. sorgente calda, apparecchio scaldabagno.

Ghastliness [gȧst'lĭ-nĕs] n. apparenza spettrale.

Ghastly [gȧst'lĭ] a. spettrale.

Gherkin [ghĕr'chĭn] n. specie di cetriolo.

Ghost [gòst] n. apparizione, fantasma, spettro, anima; **The Holy** [hò'lĭ] **G.** lo Spirito Santo.

Ghostly [gòst'lĭ] a. spettrale, spirituale.

Giant [giȧ'ĕnt] a. e n. gigante; **-ess** [giȧ'ĕn-tĕs] n. gigantessa.

Gibber [gĭ'bĕr] v.i. parlare rapidamente e senza senso.

Gibberish [gĭ'bĕ-rĭš] n. parole senza senso.

Gibbet [gĭ'bĕt] n. forca.

Gibe [giȧ¹b] n. beffa, scherno; v.t. e i. beffar(si) schernire.

Giblets [gĭb'lĕts] n. (pl.) rigaglie (pl.).

Giddiness [ghĭ'dĭ-nĕs] n. vertigine, incostanza.

Giddy [ghĭ'dĭ] a. in preda a vertigini, incostante.

Gift [ghĭft] n. dono, donazione.

Gig [ghĭg] n. leggero veicolo a due ruote; (naut.) leggera e stretta imbarcazione.

Gigantic [giȧ¹-ghĕn'tĭc] a. gigantesco.

Giggle [ghĭ'gl] v.i. ridere scioccamente.

Gild [ghĭld] v.t. (in)dorare.

Gilding [ghĭl'dĭñ] n. doratura.

Gill [ghĭl] n. misura di capacità liquida (litri .0142).

Gillyflower [gĭ'lĭ-flau⁹r] n. violacciocca.

Gilt [ghĭlt] n. doratura; a. dorato.

Gimcrack [gĭm'crĕc] n. cianfrusaglia; a. appariscente e di nessun valore.

Gimlet [gĭm'lĕt] n. succhiello.

Gin [gĭn] n. gin (bevanda), trappola.

Ginger [gĭn'ghĕr] n. zenzero.

Gipsy, gypsy [gĭp'si] n. zinga/ro, -ra.

Giraffe [gĭ-rĕf'] n. giraffa.

Gird [ghĕrd] v.t. cingere, circondare; v.i. beffare.

Girder [ghĕr'dĕr] n. (mecc.) trave (maestra).

Girdle [ghĕr'dl] n. cintura; v.t. recingere, chiudere con una cintura.

Girl [ghĕrl] n. ragazza, fanciulla.

Girlhood [ghĕrl'hŭd] n. adolescenza (di una ragazza).

Girlish [ghĕrl'ĭš] a. di (da) ragazza.

Gist [gĭst] n. punto essenziale, reale essenza.

Give [ghĭv] v.t. e i. dare.

Gizzard [ghĭz'zĕrd] n. ventriglio (di uccello).

Glacial [glè'sĭ-ĕl] a. glaciale.

Glacier [glè'sĭ-ĕr] n. ghiacciaio.

Glad [glĕd] a. contento, lieto.

Glade [glĕd] n. radura.

Gladness [glĕd'nĕs] n. contentezza.   [maga.

Glamour [glè'mĕr] n. fascino, fascino.

Glance [glȧns] n. occhiata, sguardo; v.i. dare un'occhiata, gettare uno sguardo.

Gland [glĕnd] n. glandola.

Glanders [glĕn'dĕrs] n. (pl.) cimurro (dei cavalli).

Glare [glĕⁱr] n. bagliore, sguardo furibondo; v.i. risplendere di luce abbagliante, guardare con rabbia.

Glass [glȧns] n. vetro, vetri (pl.); bicchiere, cristallo, specchio, barometro, telescopio; **-es** (pl.) occhiali (pl.).

Glaucous [glô'cȧs] a. glauco.

Glaze [glĕz] n. smalto, vernice; v.t. fornire di vetri, smaltare, verniciare.

Glazier [glè'zĭ-ĕr] n. vetraio.

Gleam [glīm] n. barlume, debole raggio di luce; v.i. emettere barlumi di luce.

Glean [glīn] v.t. e i. spigolare, raccogliere.

Gleaning [glī'niń] *n.* spigolatura.

Glebe [glīb] *n.* gleba.

Glee [glī] *n.* giubilo, composizione musicale per tre o più voci.

Glen [glēn] *n.* valletta.

Glib [glīb] *a.* fluente, pronto (di discorso).

Glide [glīd] *v.i.* scivolare, passare impercettibilmente.

Glimmer [glī'mĕr] *n.* luce debole e incerta; *v.i.* mandare una luce fioca.

Glimpse [glimps] *n.* rapida visione; *v.t.* intravedere.

Glitter [glī'tĕr] *n.* scintillio; *v.i.* scintillare.

Gloaming [glō'miń] *n.* crepuscolo.

Gloat [glōt] *v.i.* guardare con gioia perversa.

Globe [glōb] *n.* globo.

Gloom [glūm] *n.* tenebre (*pl.*), tristezza.

Gloomy [glū'mi] *a.* fosco, tetro, triste.

Glorification [glō-ri-fi-ché'śn] *n.* glorificazione.

Glorify [glō'ri-fa¹] *v.t.* glorificare.

Glorious [glō'ri-ăs] *a.* glorioso, magnifico.

Glory [glō'ri] *n.* gloria, splendore; *v.i.* esultare, gloriarsi.

Gloss [glŏs] *n.* chiosa, glossa, lucidezza, lucicchio; *v.t. e i.* chiosare, glossare, lucidare.

Glossary [glŏ'sĕ-ri] *n.* glossario.

Glossy [glŏ'si] *a.* lucente, lucido.

Glove [glăv] *n.* guanto.

Glow [glō] *n.* ardore, incandescenza, splendore; *v.i.* ardere, essere incandescente.

Glow-worm [glō'uĕ²m] *n.* lucciola (che non vola).

Glower [glau'ĕ²] *v.i.* guardare con cipiglio.

Gloze [glŏz] *v.t.* coprire, nascondere con discorsi speciosi.

Glue [glū] *n.* colla; *v.t.* incollare.

Glum [glăm] *a.* accigliato, taciturno.

Glut [glăt] *n.* saturazione (d'un mercato), sazietà.

Glutton [glă'tn] *n.* ghiottone.

Gluttonous [glă'tĕ-năs] *a.* ghiotto, goloso.

Gluttony [glă'tĕ-ni] *n.* golosità, ingordigia.

Glycerine [gli'sĕ-rin] *n.* glicerina.

Gnarled [nă²ld] *a.* nodoso, pieno di nodi.

Gnash [nĕs] *v.t.* digrignare (i denti).

Gnat [nĕt] *n.* moscerino.

Gnaw [nô] *v.t.* rodere, rosicchiare.

Gnome [nòm] *n.* gnomo.

Go [gō] *v.i.* andare.

Goad [gōd] *n.* pungolo, stimolo; *v.t.* mandar avanti col pungolo, stimolare.

Goal [gōl] *n.* mèta, porta (nel giuoco del calcio).

Goat [gōt] *n.* capra; -herd [hĕ²d] capraio.

Gobble [gō'bl] *v.t.* ingoiare a grossi bocconi.

Goblet [gō'blĕt] *n.* calice, coppa.

Goblin [gō'blin] *n.* folletto, spirito maligno.

God [gŏd] *n.* Dio, Iddio, idolo.

Goddess [gŏ'dĕs] *n.* dea.

Godfather [gŏd'fă-thĕr] *n.* padrino (al battesimo).

Godhead [gŏd'hĕd] *n.* divinità.

Godless [gŏd'lĕs] *a.* ateo, empio.

Godlessness [gŏd'lĕs-nĕs] *n.* ateismo, empietà.

Godliness [gŏd'li-nĕs] *n.* devozione, religiosità.

Godly [gŏd'li] *a.* devoto, religioso.

Godmother [gŏd'mă-thĕ'] n. madrina.

Codson [gŏd'sán] n. figlioccio.

Goggle [gŏ'gl] v.i. stralunare.

Goitre [goi'tĕ'] n. gozzo.

Gold [gŏld] n. oro; a. aureo, d'oro.

Golden [gŏl'dn] a. aureo, d'oro, dorato.

Goldfinch [gŏld'fíné] n. cardellino.

Goldsmith [gŏld'smith] n. orefice.

Golosh [gŏ-lŏś'] n. soprascarpa di gomma.

Good [gŭd] a. buono.

Good-bye [gŭd-ba'i'] interiez. addio, arrivederci.

Goodly [gŭd'lĭ] . bel.o, considerevole (di quantità).

Good-natured [gŭd-né'cĕ'd] a. di buon carattere.

Goodness [gŭd'nĕs] n. bontà, generosità.

Goods [gŭds] n. (pl.) merci (pl.).

Goose [gūs] n. oca.

Gooseberry [gūz'bĕ-rĭ] n. uva spina.

Gorge [go'g] n. strozza, gola (di montagna).

Gorgeous [go'gĭăs] a. sfarzoso, vistoso.

Gorgon [go'ghĕn] n. gorgona.

Gorse [go's] n. ginestra spinosa.

Gory [gŏ'rĭ] a. insanguinato.

Gosling [gŏz'lĭn] n. giovine oca, paperotto.

Gospel [gŏs'pĕl] n. vangelo.

Gossamer [gŏ'să-mĕ'] n. sottile filo di ragnatela, velo finissimo.

Gossip [gŏ'sĭp] n. chiacchiera, pettegolezzo, individuo pettegolo; v.i. pettegolare.

Gothic [gŏ'thĭc] a. gotico.

Gouge [gŭg] n. sgorbia; v.t. fare una scanalatura con la sgorb.a, far venire fuori a forza.

Gourd [gu'd] n. zucca.

Gout [gaŭt] n. gotta.

Gouty [gaŭ'tĭ] a. gottoso.

Govern [gă'vĕ'n] v.t. e i. governare.

Governable [gă'vĕ'-nă-bl] a. docile.

Governess [gă'vĕ'-nĕs] n. istitutrice.

Government [gă'vĕ'n-mĕnt] n. governo.

Governor [gă'vĕ'-nĕ'] n. governatore; (gergo) padre.

Gown [gaŭn] n. toga, veste, vestito.

Grab [grĕb] v.t. afferrare, impadronirsi con la violenza di.

Grace [grés] n. grazia, favore; v.t. favorire.

Graceful [grés'fŭl] a. aggraziato, grazioso.

Gracefulness [grés'fŭl-nĕs] n. grazia.

Gracious [gré'sciăs] a. condiscendente, grazioso.

Gradation [gră-dé'śn] n. gradazione.

Grade [gréd] n. grado; v.t. classificare, graduare.

Gradient [gré'dĭ-ĕnt] n. gradiente, pendenza.

Gradual [gré'diŭ-ĕl] a. e n. graduale.

Graduate [gré'diŭ'ĕt] n. laureato, [gré'diŭ-ét] v.t. graduare; v.i. laurearsi.

Graft [grăft] n. innesto; v.t. e i. innestare, fare innesti.

Grain [grén] n. grano, grana.

Gram(me) [grĕm] n. grammo.

Grammar [grĕ'mĕ'] n. grammatica.

Grammarian [grè-mé'rĭ-ĕn] n. grammatico.

Grammatical [gră-mè'tĭ-cl] a. grammaticale.

Gramophone [grè'mŏ-fòn] n. gramofono.

Granary [grè'nĕ-rĭ] n. granaio.

Grand [grènd] a. grande, grandioso, imponente, maestoso, principale.

Grandchild [grèn'cia'ld] *n.* nipote, nipoti/no, -na.

Grandeur [grèn'dë^r] *n.* magnificenza, splendore.

Grand/father [grèn'fä-thë^r] *n.* nonno; **-mother** [mä-thë^r] nonna.

Grange [gréng] *n.* fattoria, casa signorile di campagna.

Granite [grè'nit] *n.* granito.

Grant [gränt] *n.* concessione, dono; *v.t.* ammettere, concedere.

Grape [grép] *n.* (acino d') uva; [*mil.*] carica di mitraglia.

Graph [gräf] *n.* grafico.

Grapnel [gräp'nél] *n.* ancoretta, uncino.

Grapple [grä'pl] *n.* ancoretta, rampone, lotta corpo a corpo; *v.t.* assicurare con l'ancoretta; *v.i.* venire alle prese.

Grasp [gräsp] *n.* presa, stretta, comprensione; *v.t.* afferrare.

Grasping [gräs'piñ] *a.* avaro, avido.

Grass [gräs] *n.* erba.

Grasshopper [gräs'hŏ-pë^r] *n.* cavalletta.

Grassy [grä'sI] *a.* erboso.

Grate [grét] *n.* grata, griglia, inferriata; *v.t.* munire di grata, grattugiare; *v.i.* irritare.

Grateful [grét'fŭl] *a.* grato, riconoscente.

Grater [gré'të^r] *n.* grattugia.

Gratification [grè-ti-fi-ché'-sñ] *n.* gratificazione, soddisfazione.

Gratify [grè'ti-fa'] *v.t.* gratificare.

Grating [grè'tiñ] *n.* grata, inferriata; *a.* irritante, stridente.

Gratitude [grè'ti-tiüd] *n.* gratitudine, riconoscenza.

Gratuitous [grä-tiü'i-täs] *a.* gratuito, inutile.

Gratuity [grä-tiü'i-ti] *n.* gratificazione, mancia.

Grave [grév] *n.* tomba; *a.* austero, grave, serio; *v.t.* imprimere nella mente.

Gravel [grè'vël] *n.* ghiaia; *v.t.* ricoprire di ghiaia; (*gergo*) rendere perplesso.

Gravestone [grév'stòn] *n.* pietra sepolcrale.

Graveyard [grév'iä^rd] *n.* camposanto.

Gravitate [grè'vi-tét] *v.i.* gravitare.

Gravitation [grè-vi-té'śn] *n.* gravitazione.

Gravity [grè'vi-ti] *n.* gravità, solennità.

Gravy [gré'vi] *n.* sugo di carne.

Gray: *v.* **Grey.**

Graze [gréz] *n.* abrasione; *v.t.* escoriare, scalfire, sfiorare; *v.i.* pascere, pascolare.

Grease [gris] *n.* grasso, unto, materia lubrificante; *v.t.* lubrificare, ungere.

Greasy [gri'sI] *a.* grasso, unto, untuoso.

Great [grét] *a.* grande, nobile.

Greatness [grét'nès] *n.* grandezza.

Greed [grid] *n.* bramosia, cupidigia.

Greediness [gri'di-nès] *n.* avidità, golosità.

Greedy [gri'di] *a.* ghiotto, goloso, avido.

Greek [gric] *a.* e *n.* greco.

Green [grin] *n.* verde, verzura; *a.* [*pl.*] erbaggi (*pl.*); *a.* verde.

Greenery [gri'né-ri] *n.* piante verdi (*pl.*); verdura.

Greengrocer [grin'grò-së^r] *n.* erbivendolo, ortolano.

Greenhouse [grin'haus] *n.* serra.

Greet [grit] *v.t.* salutare (all'arrivo).

Greeting [gri'tiñ] *n.* saluto.

Grenade [grè-néd'] *n.* granata (ordigno esplosivo).

Grenadier [grè-nä-di^{er}] *n.* granatiere.

Grey, Gray [grei] a. e n. grigio.

Greyhound [grei'hàund] n. levriero.

Greyness [grei'nës] n. grigiore.

Grief [grif] n. afflizione, dolore.

Grievance [grì'vëns] n. (motivo di) lagnanza.

Grieve [griv] v.t. e i. addolorar(si), affligger(si).

Grievous [grì'vàs] a. doloroso, penoso, grave, serio.

Griffin [grì'fin] n. grifone.

Grill [gril] n. (vivanda alla) griglia; v.t. arrostire alla griglia, sottoporre ad un severo interrogatorio; v.i. esser tormentato (dal caldo).

Grim [grim] a. fosco, spaventoso, senza pietà.

Grimace [gri-mës'] n. smorfia.

Grime [grà'm] n. sudiciume.

Grimy [grà'mi] a. sudicio.

Grin [grìn] n. sogghigno; v.i. sogghignare.

Grind [grà'nd] n. lavoro faticoso e ingrato; v.t. arrotare, macinare; (fig.) opprimere; v.i. sgobbare.

Grinder [grà'n'dër] n. arrotino, macina, dente molare.

Grip [grip] n. presa, stretta, controllo, impugnatura, capacità di fermare l'attenzione; v.t. afferrare, tenere fermo.

Gripe [grà'p] v.t. afferrare, causare dolori al ventre.

Grisly [griz'li] a. orribile, spaventoso.

Grist [grist] n. grano da macinare, malto preparato per la fabbricazione della birra.

Gristle [gri'sl] n. cartilagine.

Grit [grit] n. grana, sabbia; (famil.) forza di carattere.

Grizzled [gri'zld] a. brizzolato, grigio, dai capelli grigi.

Groan [gròn] n. gemito, lamento; v.i. gemere, lamentarsi.

Grocer [grò'sër] n. droghiere.

Grocery [grò'së-ri] n. (generi di) drogheria.

Grog [gròg] n. (famil.) bevanda alcoolica calda.

Groin [gròn] n. inguine; (archit.) sesto acuto, ogiva.

Groom [grūm] n. stalliere; v.t. strigliare.

Groove [grūv] n. scanalatura, solco; v.t. scanalare, solcare.

Grope [gròp] v.i. andare tentoni, brancolare.

Groping(ly) [grò'pìń-li] av. (a) tentoni.

Gross [gròs] n. blocco, grossa; a. grossolano, volgare, lordo, totale.

Grossness [gròs'nës] n. grossolanità, volgarità.

Grotesque [grò-tësc'] a. e n. grottesco.

Grotesqueness [grò-tësc'nës] n. aspetto grottesco.

Ground [gràund] n. terra, terreno, suolo, base, motivo, sfondo; v.t. basare, fondare, istruire bene; v.i. incagliarsi, -s (pl.) deposito, fondi (pl.).

Groundfloor [gràund'flò'r] n. pianterreno.

Groundless [gràund'lës] a. infondato.

Groundwork [gràund'uë'c] n. base, fondamento.

Group [grūp] n. gruppo; v.t. e i. raggruppar(si).

Grouse [gràus] n. specie di uccello gallinaceo; v.i. (gergo) brontolare.

Grove [gròv] n. boschetto.

Grovel [grò'vël] v.i. strisciare a terra, umiliarsi.

Grow [grò] v.i. crescere, aumentare, svilupparsi, divenire; v.t. coltivare.

Grower [grò'ër] n. coltivatore.

Growl [gràul] n. borbottio rabbioso; v.i. brontolare, borbottare irosamente.

Growler [gràu'lër] n. brontolone; (arcaico) carrozza a quattro ruote.

Grown-up [gròn'ăp] *a. e n.* adulto.

Growth [gròth] *n.* crescita, sviluppo, progresso; (*med.*) escrescenza morbosa, tumore.

Grub [gràb] *n.* larva di tarma o di altri insetti; (*gergo*) cibo; *v.i.* occuparsi in lavori faticosi, scavare superficialmente.

Grubby [grà'bi] *a.* sporco.

Grudge [gràg] *n.* astio, rancore; *v.t.* concedere, dare, permettere a malincuore, invidiare.

Gruesome [grū'săm] *a.* orribile, orripilante.

Gruff [gràf] *a.* burbero, laconico, sgarbato.

Gruffness [gràf'nĕs] *n.* burbanza.

Grumble [gràm'bl] *v.i.* borbottare, brontolare.

Guarantee [ghè-răn-tī'] *n.* garanzia, garante; *v.t.* garantire, essere garante per.

Guard [gä'd] *n.* guardia; *v.t.* custodire, proteggere, sorvegliare.

Guardian [gä''dĭ-ĕn] *n.* guardiano, tutore; **-ship** [scĭp] protezione, tutela.

Guess [ghĕs] *n.* congettura, supposizione; *v.i. e t.* congetturare, indovinare, supporre.

Guest [ghĕst] *n.* ospite.

Guidance [gha''dĕns] *n.* guida (nel senso di direzione, norma).

Guide [ghaĭd] *n.* guida, cicerone; *v.t.* dirigere, guidare.

Guild [ghĭld] *n.* corporazione, associazione di scambievole aiuto.

Guile [ghaĭl] *n.* artificio, astuzia, inganno.

Guileless [gha'l'lĕs] *a.* ingenuo, semplice.

Guilt [ghĭlt] *n.* colpa, colpevolezza.

Guiltless [ghĭlt'lĕs] *a.* innocente.

Guilty [ghĭl'tĭ] *a.* colpevole.

Guinea [ghĭ'nĭ] *n.* ghinea (moneta inglese antica, che valeva ventun scellini).

Guineafowl [ghĭ'nĭ-faŭl] *n.* gallina faraona.

Guineapig [ghĭ'nĭ-pĭg] *n.* porcellino d'india, cavia.

Guise [ghaĭz] *n.* apparenza, foggia, guisa.

Guitar [ghĭ-tä''] *n.* chitarra.

Gulf [gălf] *n.* abisso, golfo, vortice.

Gull [găl] *n.* gabbiano; *v.t.* gabbare, ingannare.

Gullet [gă'lĕt] *n.* esofago, gola.

Gully [gă'lĭ] *n.* burrone.

Gulp [gălp] *n.* atto dell'inghiottire, quantità inghiottita in una volta; *v.t.* inghiottire voracemente, trangugiare.

Gum [găm] *n.* gomma, gengiva; *v.t.* ingommare.

Gun [găn] *n.* cannone, fucile, arma da sparo in genere.

Gunboat [găn'bòt] *n.* (*naut.*) cannoniera.

Gunner [gă'nĕr] *n.* artigliere.

Gunnery [gă'nĕ-rĭ] *n.* arte del maneggiare cannoni.

Gunshot [găn'sciòt] *n.* portata di un'arma da fuoco.

Gunsmith [găn'smith] *n.* armaiolo.

Gurgle [ghĕr'gl] *n.* gorgoglio; *v.i.* gorgogliare.

Gush [găsˌ] *n.* flotto, zampillo, effusione sentimentale; *v.i. e i.* sgorgare in gran copia, zampillare, fare esagerate effusioni.

Gushing [gă'scin] *a.* zampillante, che si profonde in effusioni.

Gust [găst] *n.* raffica, colpo (di vento), scoppio (di rabbia, ecc.).

Gusto [gă'stò] *n.* entusiasmo.

Gusty [gă'stĭ] *a.* burrascoso.

Gut [găt] *n.* budello, minugia; *v.t.* sbudellare, sventrare; **-s** (*pl.*) budella (*pl.*); (*gergo*) fegato.

Gutter [gă'tĕʳ] n. cunetta, grondaia.

Guttural [gă'tĕ-rĕl] a. gutturale.

Guy [ghaⁱ] n. (mecc.) cavo, figura grottesca, spauracchio.

Guzzle [gă'zl] v.t. e i. trangugiare.

Gymnasium [gǐm-né'zǐ-ăm] n. palestra, ginnasio (sul continente).   [nasta.

Gymnast [gǐm'nèst] n. ginnasta.

Gymnastics [gǐm-nès'tǐcs] n. (pl.) ginnastica.

Gyve [giaⁱv] n. catena, ceppo.

H

Haberdasher [hè'bĕʳ-dè-scĕʳ] n. merciaio.

Haberdashery [hè'bĕʳ-dè-scĕ-rǐ] n. (articoli di) merceria.

Habit [hè'bǐt] n. abitudine; (arcaico) abito.

Habitable [hè'bǐ-tă-bl] a. abitabile.

Habitation [hè-bǐ-té'śn] n. abitazione.

Habitual [hă-bǐ'tiǔ-èl] a. abituale.

Habituate [hă-bǐ'tiǔ-ét] v.t. abituare.

Hack [hèc] n. intaccatura, taglio, cavallo da nolo, individuo sfruttato in un lavoro gravoso; v.t. intaccare, tagliare v.i. adoperare cavalli da nolo, condurre una vita faticosa facendo lavori mal retribuiti.

Hackney cab [hèc'nǐ chèb] n. vettura da nolo.

Haddock [hè'dŏc] n. pesce (specie di merluzzo).

Haemorrhage [hè'mŏ-rĕġ] n. emorragia.

Haft [hàft] n. elsa, manico.

Hag [hèg] n. donna vecchia e brutta, strega.

Haggard [hè'gă'd] a. magro, sparuto.

Haggle [hè'gl] v.i. disputare, lesinare sul prezzo.

Hail [hél] n. grandine, grido, saluto; v.i. grandinare; v.t. chiamare a gran voce.

Hair [hé'eʳ] n. capel/lo, -li (pl.), pelo.

Hairdresser [hé'ʳdrè-sĕʳ] n. parucchie/re, -ra.

Hairless [hé'ʳlès] a. calvo, senza peli.

Hairy [hé'ʳǐ] a. peloso.

Halcyon [hèl'sǐ-ĕn] n. alcione; a. calmo.

Hale [hél] a. robusto, sano, vigoroso.

Half [hàf] n. metà, mezzo; a. mezzo; av. a metà, (a) mezzo; **half-brother** [hàf'brà-thĕʳ] n. fratellastro; **half-way** [hàf'uéⁱ] a. e av. a mezza strada; **half-witted** [hàf-uǐ'tǐd] a. corto d'intelletto; **half-yearly** [hàf-ïéeʳ'lǐ] a. semestrale; av. due volte all'anno.

Halfpenny [hé'pè-nǐ] n. mezzo penny (moneta).

Hall [hŏl] n. aula, salone, sala di ricevimento, vestibolo.

Hallucination [hè-liū-sǐ-né'śn] n. allucinazione.

Halo [hé'lŏ] n. alone, aureola.

Halt [hŏlt] n. alt (mil.); fermata; a. (raro) storpio, zoppo; v.i. fare una sosta, fermarsi, esitare, zoppicare.

Halter [hŏl'tĕʳ] n. capestro, cavezza.

Halve [hàv] v.t. dimezzare, dividere in due metà.

Ham [hèm] n. prosciutto, coscia.

Hamlet [hèm'lèt] n. piccolo villaggio.

Hammer [hè'mĕʳ] n. martello, cane (del fucile); v.t. martellare; (famil.) ficcare in testa.

Hammock [hè'mŏc] n. amaca.

Hamper [hèm'pĕʳ] n. cesta; v.t. impedire, ostacolare.

Hamster [hĕm'stĕʳ] n. criceto.
Hand [hènd] n. mano, lancetta (d'orologio) spanna, carte distribuite ad un giocatore; v.t. consegnare, porgere.
Hand-barrow [hènd'bé-rò], -cart (cáʳt) n. carretto a mano.
Handbill [hènd'bil] n. volantino.
Handcuff [hènd'cǎf] v.t. mettere le manette a.
Handful [hènd'fǔl] n. manata, pugno; (famil.) ragazzo discolo.
Handicap [hèn'dì-chèp] n. corsa a ostacoli; (fig.) impedimento, svantaggio.
Handicraft [hèn'dì-cräft] n. arte, lavoro dell'artigiano.
Handiwork [hèn'dì-uéʳc] n. lavoro (a mano).
Handkerchief [hèn'chèʳ-cif] n. fazzoletto.
Handle [hèn'dl] n. manico, maniglia; (fig.) occasione; v.t. maneggiare, manipolare.
Handsome [hèn'sǎm] a. bello ben proporzionato.
Handwriting [hènd'ra¹-tiñ] n. calligrafia, scrittura.
Handy [hèn'dì] a. abile, destro, a portata di mano.
Hang [hèñ] n. piombo [d'un vestito], filo (d'un racconto); v.t. appendere, attaccare, impiccare; v.i. dipendere, pendere. [messa.
Hangar [hèñ'gàʳ] n. aviorimessa.
Hanger-on [hèñ'éʳ-ôn] n. parassita (uomo).
Hangman [hèñ'mǎn] n. boia.
Hanker [hèñ'chèʳ] v.i. bramare.
Hansom [cab] [hèn'sǎm chèb] n. (arcaico) leggera vettura a due posti.
Hap [hèp] n. (arcaico) caso, fortuna.
Hap-hazard [hèp²-hè-zéʳd] n. puro caso; av. a caso.
Hapless [hèp'lès] a. sfortunato.

Happen [hè'pn] v.i. accadere, avvenire.
Happiness [hè'pì-nès] n. felicità.
Happy [hè'pì] a. felice, propizio.
Harangue [hă-rèñ'] n. arringa; v.t. arringare.
Harass [hè'ràs] v.t. seccare, tormentare.
Harbinger [hàʳ'bìn-gèʳ] n. precursore.
Harbour [hàʳ'bèʳ] n. porto, rifugio; v.t. accogliere, albergare; (fig.) nutrire.
Hard [hàʳd] a. compatto, difficile, duro; av. molto.
Harden [hàʳ'dn] v.t. indurire, rendere insensibile; v.i. indurirsi, diventare insensibile.
Hardihood [hàʳ'dì-hŭd] n. ardimento, arditezza.
Hardly [hàʳd'lì] av. appena, a mala pena, scarsamente.
Hardness [hàʳd'nès] n. compatezza, durezza.
Hardship [hàʳd'scìp] n. avversità, disagio, privazione.
Hardware [hàʳd'uéʳ] n. ferramenta (pl.).
Hardy [hàʳ'dì] a. ardito, resistente.
Hare [héʳ] n. lepre; v.i. correre.
Haricot [hè'rì-cót] n. fagiolino.
Hark! [hàʳc] interiez. ascolta(te)!
Harlequin [hàʳ'lì-quin] n. arlecchino.
Harlot [hàʳ'lèt] n. prostituta.
Harm [hàʳm] n. danno, male; v.t. danneggiare, far male a.
Harmful [hàʳm'fŭl] a. dannoso, nocivo.
Harmless [hàʳm'lès] a. innocuo.
Harmonics [hàʳ-mǒ'nìcs] n. (pl.) armonia.
Harmonious [hàʳ-mò'nì-ǎs] a. armonioso.

Harmonize [hãr'mŏ-na'z] v.t. e i. armonizzare.

Harmony [hãr'mŏ-nĭ] n. armonia.

Harness [hãr'nĕs] n. bardatura, finimenti (pl.); v.t. bardare; (fig.) utilizzare.

Harp [hãrp] n. arpa; v.i. insistere fino ad annoiare.

Harpoon [hãr-pūn'] n. fiocina; v.t. fiocinare.

Harpy [hãr'pĭ] n. arpia; (fig.) donna rapace.

Harrow [hĕ'rō] n. erpice; v.t. erpicare; (fig.) straziare.

Harry [hĕ'rĭ] v.t. saccheggiare, tormentare.

Harsh [hãrš] a. aspro, crudele, severo.

Harshness [hãrš'nĕs] n. asprezza, severità.

Hart [hãrt] n. cervo, daino.

Harum-scarum [hĕ'răm-schĕ'răm] a. avventato, irresponsabile.

Harvest [hãr'vĕst] n. messe, raccolto; v.t. mietere, raccogliere.

Harvester [hãr'vĕs-tĕr] n. mietitrice.

Hash [hĕš] n. specie di ragù; (fig.) pasticcio; v.t. ricuocere; (fig.) fare un pasticcio (fig.).

Hasp [hĕsp] n. fermaglio (di lucchetto), matassa (di filato).

Hassock [hĕ'sŏc] n. grosso cuscino usato come inginocchiatoio.

Haste [hēst] n. fretta, furia.

Hasten [hēs'n] v.t. e i. affrettar(si).

Hastiness [hĕs'tĭ-nĕs] n. fretta, impetuosità, irritabilità.

Hasty [hĕs'tĭ] a. frettoloso, impetuoso, irritabile.

Hat [hĕt] n. cappello; h. -box (bŏcs) cappelliera.

Hatch [hĕč] n. mezza porta; (naut.) boccaporto, covata; v.t. covare, macchinare (un piano); v.i. schiudersi (di uova), nascere.

Hatchet [hĕ'čĕt] n. accetta.

Hate [hēt], **hatred** [hē'trĕd] n. odio.

Hate [hēt] v.t. odiare.

Hateful [hēt'fŭl] a. odioso.

Hatter [hĕ'tĕr] n. cappellaio.

Haughtiness [hŏ'tĭ-nĕs] n. arroganza, superbia.

Haughty [hŏ'tĭ] a. arrogante, superbo.

Haul [hŏl] n. retata, tirata; (fig.) guadagno; v.t. tirare, trascinare, rimorchiare.

Haunch [hŏnč] n. anca, coscia.

Haunt [hŏnt] n. luogo di ritrovo; v.t. frequentare, ossessionare, seguire insistentemente, visitare spesso.

Have [hĕv] v.t. e aus. avere, ricevere, fare; h. to, dovere.

Haven [hē'vn] n. porto, rifugio.

Haversack [hĕ'vĕr-sĕc] n. tascapane.

Havoc [hĕ'vŏc] n. devastazione, distruzione.

Hawk [hŏc] n. falco; v.t. portare in giro (merci) per la vendita; v.i. cacciare col falco.

Hawker [hŏ'chĕr] n. venditore ambulante.

Hawse [hŏz] n. (naut.) parte della prua.

Hawser [hŏ'zĕr] n. (naut.) gomena, piccolo cavo.

Hawthorn [hŏ'thŏrn] n. biancospino.

Hay [hē] n. fieno.

Hay/cock [hē'cŏc], **-stack** [stĕc] n. mucchio di fieno.

Hazard [hĕ'zĕrd] n. azzardo, rischio; v.t. arrischiare, azzardare. [rischioso.]

Hazardous [hĕ'zĕr-dŭs] a.

Haze [hēz] n. nebbia, nebbiolina; (fig.) confusione di mente.

Hazel [hē'zl] n. noccio/lo, -la.

Hazy [hē'zĭ] a. nebbioso, indistinto, vago.

He [hi] *pron.* egli, esso.

Head [hĕd] *n.* capo, testa; *v.t.* capeggiare, intestare; *v.i.* dirigersi; h. -master [mä'stĕʳ] direttore di scuola, preside.

Headache [hĕd'ec] *n.* mal di capo, emicrania.

Heading [hĕ'diñ] *n.* intestazione, titolo.

Headland [hĕd'lènd] *n.* capo, promontorio.

Headless [hĕd'lĕs] *a.* senza capo.

Headlong [hĕd'lŏñ] *a.* impetuoso, precipitoso; *av.* (a) capofitto.

Headmost [hĕd'mòst] *a.* più avanzato.

Head-quarters [hĕd-quŏ'ʳtĕʳs] *n.* (*pl.*) quartier generale (*comunem. abbrev.* H.Q.).

Headstrong [hĕd'strŏñ] *a.* ostinato, testardo.

Heal [hil] *v.t. e i.* guarire, sanare.

Health [hĕlth] *n.* salute.

Healthful [hĕlth'fŭl] *a.* salubre, sano.

Healthy [hĕl'thi] *a.* salubre, sano, salutare.

Heap [hip] *n.* cumulo, mucchio; *v.t.* accumulare, ammucchiare.

Hear [hiᵉʳ] *v.t.* ascoltare; *v.t. e i.* sentire, udire, sapere.

Hearing [hiᵉ'rñ] *n.* (senso di) udito, udienza, ascolto; within [uith'in] h. a portata di voce.

Hearken [hä'ʳcn] *v.i.* (*arcaico*) ascoltare.

Hearsay [hĕʳ'seᵢ] *n.* diceria, voce.

Hearse [hĕʳs] *n.* carro funebre.

Heart [häʳt] *n.* cuore.

Heart-broken [häʳt'brò-cn] *a.* straziato.

Heartburn [häʳt'bĕʳn] *n.* (*med.*) fortore.

Hearten [häʳ'tn] *v.t.* incoraggiare, rincorare.

Hearth [häʳth] *n.* focolare.

Hearty [häʳ'ti] *a.* cordiale, vigoroso.

Heat [hit] *n.* ardore, calore, caldo, prova (alle corse); *v.t.* infiammare, riscaldare.

Heater [hi'tĕʳ] *n.* calorifero, stufetta elettrica.

Heath [hith] *n.* brughiera, erica.

Heathen [hi'thĕn] *a. e n.* pagano.

Heather [hĕ'thĕʳ] *n.* erica.

Heave [hiv] *n.* spinta, conato di vomito; *v.t.* alzare con fatica; (far) sollevare; *v.i.* ansimare, sollevarsi.

Heaven [hĕ'vn] *n.* cielo.

Heavenly [hĕ'vn-li] *a.* celes/te, -tiale, divino.

Heaviness [hĕ'vǐ-nĕs] *n.* pesantezza, oppressione, sonnolenza.

Heavy [hĕ'vi] *a.* pesante, opprimente, violento.

Hebrew [hi'brû] *a. e n.* ebraico, ebreo.

Hectic [hĕc'tic] *a.* (*med.*) etico, tisico; (*gergo*) agitato, febbrile.

Hedge [hĕǵ] *n.* siepe; h. -hog [hŏg] porcospino, riccio.

Heed [hid] *n.* attenzione; *v.t.* osservare attentamente, fare attenzione a, ubbidire a.

Heedful [hid'fŭl] *a.* attento, cauto. [sattento.

Heedless [hid'lĕs] *a.* disattento.

Heel [hil] *n.* calcagno, tacco, tallone; (*naut.*) sbandamento; *v.t.* mettere i tacchi a; *v.i.* (*naut.*) sbandare.

Hefty [hĕf'ti] *a.* forte, vigoroso, piuttosto pesante.

Hegemony [hĕ'ǵi-mä-ni] *a.* egemonia.

Heifer [hĕ'fĕʳ] *n.* giovenca.

Height [haᵢt] *n.* altezza, altura, culmine.

Heighten [haᵢ'tn] *v.t.* esagerare, intensificare.

Heinous [hé'näs] *a.* atroce, odioso.

Heir [é^{er}] *n.* erede: **heiress** [é^{er}rĕs] ereditiera.

Heirloom [é^{er}lūm] *n.* oggetto di valore tramandato di generazione in generazione.

Hell [hĕl] *n.* inferno.

Helm [hĕlm] *n.* (*naut.*) timone.

Helm[et] (hĕl'mĕt) *n.* elmo, elmetto.

Helmsman [hĕlmz'măn] *n.* timoniere.

Help [hĕlp] *n.* aiuto, assistenza, rimedio, via d'uscita; *v.t.* aiutare, soccorrere, evitare, servire (cibo a tavola).

Helpful [hĕlp'fŭl] *a.* servizievole, utile.

Helping [hĕl'pĭn] *n.* porzione (di cibo).

Helpless [hĕlp'lĕs] *a.* impotente.

Helpmate [hĕlp'mét] *n.* compa/gno, -gna (generalm marito o moglie).

Helter-skelter [hĕl'tĕr-schĕl'tĕr] *n.* disordine frettoloso; *av.* alla rinfusa.

Hem [hĕm] *n.* orlo (d'indumento); *v.t.* fare un orlo a, orlare.

Hemisphere [hĕ'mĭs-fī^{er}] *n.* emisfero.

Hemlock [hĕm'lŏc] *n.* cicuta.

Hemp [hĕmp] *n.* canapa.

Hen [hĕn] *n.* gallina, femmina di vari uccelli.

Hence [hĕns] *av.* da qui, perciò, quindi.

Henceforth [hĕns'fŏ'th] *av.* d'ora in avanti.

Her [hĕr] *pron. pers. femm. compl.* lei, la, le; *a. poss. femm.* (il) suo, di lei; **hers** *pron. poss. femm.* (il) suo, di lei; **herself** [hĕr'sĕlf] *pron. femm.* (*rifl. o enf.*) lei stessa, si, se stessa.

Herald [hĕ'rĕld] *n.* araldo; *v.t.* annunciare, proclamare.

Horaldry [hĕ'rĕl-drĭ] *n.* araldica.

Herb [hĕrb] *n.* erba aromatica.

Herbalist [hĕr'bă'lĭst] *n.* erborista.

Herculean [hĕr-chiū'lĭ-ĕn] *a.* erculeo.

Herd [hĕrd] *n.* branco, gregge, mandra; *v.t.* custodire (bestiame); *v.i.* formare gregge.

Herdsman [hĕrdz'măn] *n.* mandriano.

Here [hi^{er}] *av.* qui, costì.

Hereabout(s) [hi^{er}'ră-bauts] *av.* all'intorno, qui vicino.

Hereafter [hi^{er}-răf'tĕr] *n.* avvenire, stato futuro; *av.* d'ora in poi.

Hereditary [hĕ-rĕ'di-tă-rĭ] *a.* ereditario. [eredità].

Heredity [hĕ-rĕ'dĭ-ti] *n.*

Heresy [hĕ'rĕ-sĭ] *n.* eresia.

Heretic [hĕ'rĕ-tĭc] *a. e n.* eretico.

Herewith [hi^{er}-uĭth] *av.* con questo, qui accluso.

Heritage [hĕ'rĭ-tĕĝ] *n.* eredità.

Hermit [hĕr'mĭt] *n.* eremita.

Hermitage [hĕr'mĭ-tĕĝ] *n.* eremitaggio.

Hero [hi^{er}'rŏ] *n.* eroe, protagonista.

Heroic[al] [hĕ-rŏ'ĭ-cl] *a.* eroico.

Heroine [hĕ'rŏ-ĭn] *n.* eroina.

Heroism [hĕ'rŏ-ĭzm] *n.* eroismo.

Heron [hĕ'rĕn] *n.* airone.

Herring [hĕ'rĭn] *n.* aringa.

Hesitate [hĕ'zĭ-tét] *v.i.* esitare.

Hesitation [hĕ-zĭ-té'şn] *n.* esitazione.

Heterogeneous [hĕ-tĕ-rŏ-ĝĭ'nĭ-ăs] *a.* eterogeneo.

Hew [hiū] *v.t.* abbattere, spaccare.

Hibernate [hai'bĕr-nét] *v.i.* svernare, passare l'inverno in letargo.

Hiccup, hiccough [hĭ'căp] *n.* singhiozzo.

Hide [ha'ĭd] *n.* pelle (d'animale) *v.i. e t.* nasconder(si), celar(si).

Hidebound [ha'ĭd'baŭnd] *a.* retrogrado.

I.G.D.

I

Hideous [hĭ'dĭ-ăs] *a.* mostruoso, ripugnante.

Hideousness [hĭ'dĭ-ăs-nĕs] *n.* mostruosità.

Hiding [ha¹'dĭṅ] *n.* nascondiglio, fustigazione.

Hie [ha¹] *v.i.* (*poet.*) affrettarsi.

Hierarchy [ha¹ᵉ'rä'-chĭ] *n.* gerarchia.

Higgledy-piggledy [hĭ'glĭ-dĭ-pĭ'gĕ-dĭ] *av.* alla rinfusa, in gran confusione.

High [ha¹] *a.* alto.

Highland [ha¹'lĕnd] *n.* paese montuoso; *a.* montanaro.

Highness [ha¹'nĕs] *n.* altezza (titolo).   [maestra.

High road [ha¹'rŏd] *n.* strada

High water [ha¹'uó-tĕ'] *a.* alta marea.

Highway [ha¹'uĕ¹] *n.* strada pubblica.

Hill [hĭl] *n.* colle, collina.

Hilliness [hĭ'lĭ-nĕs] *n.* natura collinosa.   [poggio.

Hillock [hĭ'lŏc] *n.* collinetta,

Hilly [hĭ'lĭ] *a.* collinoso.

Hilt [hĭlt] *n.* elsa, impugnatura.

Him [hĭm] *pron. pers. masch. compl.* lui, lo, gli; **himself** [hĭm-sĕlf'] *pron.* (*rifl. e enfat.*) esso stesso, proprio lui, si, se stesso.

Hind [ha¹nd] *n.* cerva, daina, garzone di fattoria; *a.* posteriore.

Hinder [ha¹n'dĕr] *a.* posteriore (hǐn'dĕr) *v.t.* impedire, ostacolare.

Hindrance [hĭn'drĕns] *n.* impedimento, ostacolo.

Hinge [hĭṅg] *n.* cardine; *v.t.* munire di cardini; *v.i.* dipendere.

Hint [hĭnt] *n.* allusione, accenno; *v.t. e i.* alludere, accennare.

Hip [hĭp] *n.* anca, fianco; h. -bath [băth] semicupio.

Hippopotamus [hĭ-pò-pŏ'tä-mäs] *n.* ippopotamo.

Hire [ha¹ᵉʳ] *n.* nolo; (*arcaico*) salario; *v.t.* affittare, noleggiare; (*arcaico*) salariare.

Hireling [ha¹ᵉʳlĭṅ] *n.* mercenario.

His [hĭs] *a. e pron. poss. masch.* [il] suo, di lui.

Hiss [hĭs] *n.* fischio, sibilo; *v.t. e i.* fischiare, sibilare.

Historian [hĭs-tŏ'rĭ-ĕn] *n.* storico.

Historical [hĭs-tŏ'rĭ-chĕl] *a.* storico.

History [hĭs'tŏ-rĭ] *n.* storia.

Histrionic [hĭs-trĭ-ŏ'nĭc] *a.* istrionico.

Hit [hĭt] *n.* colpo, successo, tentativo fortunato; *v.t.* colpire.

Hitch [hĭč] *n.* nodo, impedimento, ostacolo.

Hither [hĭ'thĕr] *a.* il più vicino di due, citeriore; *av.* (*arcaico*) qua, qua, qui.

Hitherto [hĭ-thĕr-tū'] *av.* finora.

Hive [ha¹v] *n.* alveare.

Hoar [hŏᵉr] *a.* canuto, grigio; h. -frost [frŏst] *n.* brina.

Hoard [hŏᵉrd] *n.* ammasso, cumulo, tesoro; *v.t. e i.* ammassare, accumulare, fare incetta di.

Hoarding [hŏᵉr'dĭṅ] *n.* assito, impalcatura.

Hoarse [hŏᵉrs] *a.* rauco.

Hoarseness [hŏᵉrs'nĕs] *n.* raucedine.

Hoary [hŏᵉ'rĭ] *a.* canuto, venerabile.

Hoax [hòcs] *n.* inganno, tiro scherzoso; *v.t.* ingannare.

Hob [hŏb] *n.* sporgenza ai lati del focolare su cui si mettono le cose da tenersi caldo.

Hobble [hŏ'bl] *n.* andatura incerta e zoppicante, cavezza; *v.t.* legare (un cavallo, ecc.); *v.i.* arrancare.

Hobbledehoy [hŏ'bl-dĭ-hoi'] *n.* adolescente goffo.

Hobby [hŏ′bĭ] *n.* occupazione favorita, passione.

Hobnail [hŏb′nél] *n.* chiodo per suola di scarpe.

Hock [hŏc] *n.* garretto, vino del Reno.

Hoe [hō] *n.* zappa; *v.t. e i.* zappare.

Hog [hŏg] *n.* maiale, porco.

Hogshead [hŏgz′héd] *n.* grossa botte della capacità di galloni 52½ (= litri 238,5).

Hoist [ho′ĭst] *n.* montacarico; *v.t.* innalzare, sollevare.

Hold [hŏld] *n.* presa, stretta, luogo fortificato; (*naut.*) stiva; *v.t.* contenere, tenere, trattenere, usare; *v.i.* tenere [duro].

Holder [hŏl′dĕʳ] *n.* detentore, possessore.

Holding [hŏl′dĭŋ] *n.* possesso, tenuta.

Hole [hŏl] *n.* buca, buco, cavità, tana; (*gergo*) situazione difficile.

Holiday [hŏ′lĭ-de¹] *n.* giorno festivo, vacanza.

Holiness [hŏ′lĭ-nĕs] *n.* santità.

Hollow [hŏ′lō] *n.* bacino, depressione, valletta; *a.* cavo, vuoto; (*fig.*) falso; *v.t.* scavare.

Hollowness [hŏ′lō-nĕs] *n.* cavità, falsità.

Holly [hŏ′lĭ] *n.* agrifoglio.

Holm [hŏm] *n.* leccio.

Holster [hŏl′stĕʳ] *n.* fondina (di pistola).

Holy [hŏ′lĭ] *a.* sacro, santo.

Homage [hŏ′mĕʤ] *n.* omaggio.

Home [hŏm] *n.* casa propria, focolare domestico, patria; *a.* domestico, familiare, nazionale.

Homeless [hŏm′lĕs] *a.* senza tetto, senza patria.

Homely [hŏm′lĭ] *a.* casalingo, insignificante, semplice.

Home-made [hŏm′méd] *a.* fatto in casa.

Home-sick [hŏm′sĭc] *a.* sofferente di nostalgia.

Homicide [hŏ′mĭ-sa¹d] *n.* omicida, omicidio.

Hone [hŏn] *n.* cote.

Honest [ŏ′nĕst] *a.* onesto, leale.

Honesty [ŏ′nĕs-tĭ] *n.* onestà, lealtà.

Honey [hă′nĭ] *n.* miele.

Honeycomb [hă′nĭ-còm] *n.* favo.

Honeymoon [hă′nĭ-mūn] *n.* luna di miele.

Honeysuckle [hă′nĭ-să-cl] *n.* caprifoglio.

Honorary [ŏ′nŏ-ră-rĭ] *a.* onorario.

Honour [ŏ′nĕʳ] *n.* onore, onoranza, (titolo) Eccellenza; *v.t.* onorare.

Honourable [ŏ′nĕ-ră-bl] *a.* onorevole.

Hood [hŭd] *n.* cappuccio, mantice di carrozza; *v.t.* incappucciare.

Hoodwink [hŭd′uĭŋc] *v.t.* ingannare.

Hoof [hūf] *n.* zoccolo (di animale).

Hook [hŭc] *n.* amo, gancio, uncino; *v.t.* agganciare, prendere all'amo.

Hooked [hŭct] *a.* adunco.

Hoop [hūp] *n.* cerchio (di metallo).

Hooping-cough [hŭ′pĭŋ cŏf] *n.* tosse cavallina.

Hoot [hūt] *n.* grido (della civetta, o di derisione); *v.i.* gridare, sonare il klaxon; *v.t.* deridere.

Hooter [hū′tĕʳ] *n.* sirena (di fabbrica, ecc.).

Hop [hŏp] *n.* balzo, salto (su un piede), luppolo; *v.i.* saltare su un piede.

Hope [hŏp] *n.* speranza; *v.t. e i.* sperare.

Hopeful [hŏp′fŭl] *a.* speranzoso, ottimista.

Hopeless [hŏp′lĕs] *a.* disperato, senza rimedio, senza speranza.

Hopper [hŏˈpĕʳ] *n.* raccoglitore di luppolo, saltatore, insetto che salta.

Horde [hŏˈɛʳd] *n.* orda.

Horizon [hŏ-raˈɪˈzn] *n.* orizzonte.

Horizontal [hŏ-rĭ-zŏnˈtĕl] *a.* orizzontale.

Horn [hŏˈn] *n.* corno, klaxon (di automobile), antenna (di insetto).

Hornet [hŏˈnĕt] *n.* calabrone.

Horoscope [hŏˈrŏ-scŏp] *n.* oroscopo.

Horrible [hŏˈrĭ-bl] *a.* orribile.

Horrid [hŏˈrĭd] *a.* odioso.

Horrify [hŏˈrĭ-faˈ] *v.t.* far inorridire.

Horror [hŏˈrĕʳ] *n.* orrore.

Horse [hŏˈs] *n.* cavallo, cavalleria (*col verbo al pl.*).

Horseback [hŏˈsˈbĕc] *n.* groppa; on h. *av.* a cavallo, in sella.

Horse/man [hŏˈsˈmăn] *n.* cavaliere; -woman [ˈuˈ-măn] amazzone.

Horsemanship [hŏˈsˈmănscĭp] *n.* equitazione.

Horticulture [hŏˈtĭ-cŭl-cĕʳ] *n.* orticultura.

Hose [hŏz] *n.* tubo flessibile per annaffiare; (*pl.*) calze (*pl.*).

Hosier [hŏˈzĭˈˈbĕc] *n.* calzettaio.

Hosiery [hŏˈzĭˈˈrĭ] *n.* maglieria.

Hospice [hŏˈpĭs] *n.* ospizio.

Hospitable [hŏˈpĭ-tă-bl] *a.* ospitale.

Hospital [hŏˈpĭ-tĕl] *n.* (o)spedale.

Hospitality [hŏs-pĭ-tèˈlĭ-tĭ] *n.* ospitalità.

Host [hŏst] *n.* ospite (che ospita), albergatore, oste, moltitudine, schiera, ostia.

Hostage [hŏsˈtĕg] *n.* ostaggio.

Hostess [hŏsˈtĕs] *n.* padrona di casa, ostessa.

Hostile [hŏsˈtaˈl] *a.* ostile.

Hostility [hŏs-tĭˈlĭ-tĭ] *n.* ostilità.

Hot [hŏt] *a.* caldo, ardente, veemente.

Hotel [hŏ-tĕl] *n.* albergo.

Hound [haŭnd] *n.* cane da caccia; *v.t.* inseguire, incitare.

Hour [aˈɛʳ] *n.* ora.

Hourly [aˈɛʳˈlĭ] *a.* e *av.* (di)ogni ora.

House [haŭs] *n.* casa.

Housebreaker [haŭsˈbrécĕʳ] *n.* scassinatore.

Household [haŭsˈhŏld] *n.* famiglia, compresi i domestici; *a.* di (da) famiglia.

Householder [haŭsˈhŏl-dĕʳ] *n.* capofamiglia.

Housekeeper [haŭsˈchi-pĕʳ] *n.* governante, massaia.

Housekeeping [haŭsˈchi-píŋ] *n.* governo della casa.

Housewife [haŭsˈuăˈf] *n.* massaia; [hăˈzĭf] astuccio da lavoro tascabile.

Hovel [hŏˈvĕl] *n.* casupola, tugurio.

Hover [hŏˈvĕʳ] *v.i.* librarsi sulle ali, aggirarsi.

How [haŭ] *av.* come, quanto.

However [haŭ-ĕˈvĕʳ] *av.* e *conj.* comunque, però, per quanto.

Howitzer [haŭˈĭt-sĕʳ] *n.* obice.

Howl [haŭl] *n.* ululato, urlo; *v.i.* lamentarsi, ululare.

Hub [hăb] *n.* (*mecc.*) mozzo di ruota; (*fig.*) punto centrale.

Hubbub [hăˈbăb] *n.* suono confuso, tumulto.

Huddle [hăˈdl] *n.* folla disordinata; *v.t.* ammucchiare confusamente; *v.i.* accoccolarsi, affollarsi, mettersi addosso in fretta.

Hue [hiù] *n.* colore, tinta, clamore.

Hug [hăg] *n.* (*famil.*) abbraccio, stretta; *v.t.* (*famil.*) abbracciare stretto, tenersi vicino a.

Huge [hiùg] *a.* enorme.

Hugeness [hiŭg'nĕs] n. grandezza esagerata.

Hugger-mugger [hă'ghĕr-mă'ghĕr] av. confusamente.

Hulk [hălc] n. (naut.) carcassa, grosso individuo fannullone.

Hull [hăl] n. (naut.) scafo, baccello.

Hum [hăm] n. ronzio; v.i. ronzare, canticchiare a labbra chiuse; (famil.) essere in grande attività. [umano.

Human [hiŭ'mĕn] a. e n.

Humane [hiŭ-mén'] a. umano, umanitario, benevolo.

Humanism [hiŭ'mă-nizm] n. umanesimo.

Humanist [hiŭ'mă-nist] n. umanista.

Humanity [hiŭ-mè'ni-ti] n. umanità.

Humble [hăm'bl] a. umile; v.i. umiliare; to eat (ĭt) h. pie [pā'] scusarsi umilmente.

Humbug [hăm'băg] n. (famil) inganno, ipocrisia, impostore, ipocrita; sciocchezze.

Humid [hiŭ'mĭd] a. umido.

Humidity [hiŭ-mĭ'di-ti] n. umidità.

Humiliate [hiŭ-mĭ'lĭ-ét] v.t. umiliare.

Humiliation [hiŭ-mĭ-lĭ-é'śn] n. umiliazione.

Humility [hiŭ-mĭ'lĭ-ti] n. umiltà.

Humorist [hiŭ'mŏ-rist] n. umorista.

Humorous [hiŭ'mŏ-răs] a. umoristico, spiritoso.

Humour [hiŭ'mĕr] n. umore, umorismo, vena; v.t. adattarsi agli umori di.

Hump [hămp] n. gobba, protuberanza; (fig.) malumore.

Hump-backed [hămp'bĕct] a. gibboso, gobbo.

Hunch [hănć] n. gobba, protuberanza. [cento.

Hundred [hăn'drĕd] a. e n.

Hundredfold [hăn'drĕd-fòld] n. cento volte tanto; a. centuplicato.

Hundredweight [hăn'drĕd-uét] n. (abbr. cwt.) misura di peso di 112 libbre (chili 50,800).

Hunger [hăn'ghĕr] n. fame; v.i. bramare.

Hungry [hăn'gri] a. affamato, desideroso; be [bi] h. aver fame.

Hunt [hănt] n. caccia, gruppo di cacciatori; v.t. e i. cacciare.

Hunter [hăn'tĕr] n. cacciatore.

Hunting [hăn'tin] n. caccia.

Huntsman [hăntz-măn] n. cacciatore.

Hurdle [hĕr'dl] n. graticcio, siepe mobile.

Hurdy-gurdy [hĕr'di-ghĕr'di] n. organetto a manovella.

Hurl [hĕrl] v.t. scagliare.

Hurly-burly [hĕr'li'bĕr'li] n. mischia, tumulto.

Hurricane [hă'ri-chén] n. ciclone, uragano.

Hurry [hă'ri] n. fretta, premura; v.t. e i. affrettar(si).

Hurt [hĕrt] n. danno, ferita, male; v.t. danneggiare, far male a, nuocere a, v.i. far male.

Hurtful [hĕrt'fŭl] a. dannoso, nocivo.

Husband [hăz'bănd] n. marito; v.t. amministrare con parsimonia risparmiare.

Husbandman [hăz'bănd-măn] n. agricoltore.

Husbandry [hăz'băn-dri] n. agricoltura, amministrazione oculata.

Hush [hăś] n. immobilità, silenzio; v.t. e i. (far) stare zitto; h. -money [mo'ni] prezzo del silenzio.

Husk [hăsc] n. buccia.

Husky [hăs'chi] a. pieno di bucce, [di voce] rauco, secco.

Hussar [hă-zăr'] n. ussaro.

Hussy [hă'zl] n. civetta, donna leggera.

Hustle [hă'sl] n. spinta, trambusto; v.t. spingere; v.i. affrettarsi.

Hut [hăt] n. capanna, (mil.) baracca.

Hutch [hăč] n. capanna, gabbia (per conigli).

Hyacinth [ha'ă-sinth] n. giacinto.

Hybrid [hĭ'brĭd] a. e n. ibrido.

Hydrate [ha'drét] n. idrato.

Hydrogen [ha'drŏ-gĕn] n. idrogeno.

Hyena [ha-ĭ'nĕ⁽ʳ⁾] n. iena.

Hygiene [ha'i'gĭn] n. igiene.

Hygienic [ha¹-gĭ'nĭc] a. igienico.

Hymn [hĭm] n. inno.

Hyphen [hĭ'fĕn] n. lineetta, tratto d'unione.

Hypnotism [hĭp'nò-tĭzm] n. ipnotismo.

Hypnotize [hĭp'nò-ta'z] v.t. ipnotizzare.

Hypocrisy [hĭ-pŏ'crĭ-sĭ] n. ipocrisia.

Hypocrite [hĭ'pŏ-crĭt] n. ipocrita.

Hypothec [ha'-pŏ'thĕc] n. ipoteca.

Hypothecate [ha¹-pŏ'thĭ-chĕt] v.t. ipotecare.

Hysteria [hĭs-tĭ'e⁽ʳ⁾-ĕ⁽ʳ⁾] n. isterismo.

Hysterical [hĭs-tĕ'rĭ-cl] a. isterico.

Hysterics [hĭs-tĕ'rĭcs] n. accesso d'isterismo.

I

I [a¹] pron. io.

Ice [a¹s] n. ghiaccio, gelato.

Iceberg [a's'bĕ'g] n. massa di ghiacci galleggianti.

Ice-cream [a's'crĭm] n. gelato

Icelander [a's'lĕn-dĕ'] n. islandese.

Icelandic [a's'lĕn-dĭc] a. islandese.

Icicle [a''sĭ-cl] n. ghiacciolo.

Icy [a''sĭ] a. gelato, gelido, di ghiaccio.

Idea [a'dĭ'ĕ⁽ʳ⁾] n. idea.

Ideal [a'-dĭ'ĕl] a. e n. ideale.

Idealism [a¹-dĭ'ă-lĭzm] n. idealismo. [lista.

Idealist [a¹-dĭ'ă-lĭst] n. idea-

Identic(al) [n¹-dĕn'tĭ-chĕl] a. identico.

Identify [a¹-dĕn'tĭ-fa¹] v.t. identificare.

Identity [a¹-dĕn'tĭ-tĭ] n. identità.

Ideology [a¹-dĭ-ŏ'lŏ-gĭ] n. ideologia.

Idiocy [ĭ'dĭ-ŏ-sĭ] n. idiozia, sciocchezza.

Idiom [ĭ'dĭ-ŏm] n. idiotismo, espressione idiomatica.

Idiomatic [ĭ-dĭ-ŏ-mé'tĭc] a. idiomatico.

Idiot [ĭ'dĭ-ŏt] n. idiota.

Idiotic [ĭ-dĭ-ó'tĭc] a. idiota.

Idle [a¹'dl] a. inutile, ozioso, inutile, vano; v.i. oziare.

Idleness [a¹'dl-nĕs] n. indolenza, ozio.

Idol [a¹'dŏl] n. idolo.

Idolator [a¹-dŏ'lă-tĕ'] n. idolatra.

Idolatry [a¹-dŏ'lă-trĭ] n. idolatria.

Idolize [a''dŏ-la'z] v.t. idolatrare.

Idyl(l) [a¹'dĭl] n. idillio.

If [ĭf] con. se, in caso che.

Ignoble [ĭg-nŏ'bl] a. ignobile.

Ignominious [ĭg-nò-mĭ'nĭ-ăs] a. ignominioso.

Ignominy [ĭg'nò-mĭ-nĭ] n. ignominia.

Ignoramus [ĭg-nò-ré'măs] n. individuo ignorante.

Ignorance [ĭg'nò-rĕns] n. ignoranza.

Ignorant [ĭg'nò-rĕnt] a. ignorante.

Ignore [ĭg-nó'er'] v.t. far finta di non sentire, di non vedere ecc.; ignorare.

Ill [il] *n.* danno, male, sfortuna; *a.* (am)malato, dannoso, malefico; *av.* male.

Illegal [i-li'ghèl] *a.* illegale.

Illegality [i-li-ghè'li-ti] *n.* illegalità. [gibile.

Illegible [i-lé'gi-bl] *a.* illeg-

Illegitimacy [i-li-gi'ti-mà-si] *n.* illegittimità.

Illegitimate [i-li-gi'ti-mèt] *a.* illegittimo.

Illiberal [i-li'be-rèl] *a.* illiberale, tirchio.

Illicit [i-li'sit] *a.* illecito.

Illiterate [i-li'tè-rèt] *a.* analfabeta.

Illness [il'nès] *n.* malattia.

Illogical [i-lò'gi-chèl] *a.* illogico.

Illuminate [i-liù'mi-nét] *v.t.* illuminare.

Illumination [i-liù-mi-né'sn] *n.* illuminazione.

Illusion [i-liù'sn] *n.* allucinazione, illusione.

Illusive [i-liù'siv] *a.* illusorio.

Illustrate [i'làs-trét] *v.t.* illustrare.

Illustration [i-làs'tri- às] *n.* illustrazione.

Illustrious [i-làs'tri-às] *a.* illustre.

Image [i'mig] *n.* immagine; *v.t.* raffigurare, rispecchiare, ritrarre.

Imagery [i'mig-ri] *n.* immagini (*pl.*); figure retoriche.

Imaginable [i-mè'gi-nà-bl] *a.* immaginabile.

Imaginary [i-mè'gi-nà-ri] *a.* immaginario.

Imagination [i-mè-gi-né'sn] *n.* immaginazione.

Imaginative [i-mè'gi-nà-tiv] *a.* fantasioso.

Imagine [i-mè'gin] *v.t.* immaginare, supporre.

Imbecile [im'bi-sil] *a. e n.* imbecille.

Imbibe [im-ba'ib'] *v.t.* assimilare, assorbire, bere.

Imbue [im-biù'] *v.t.* imbevere, saturare.

Imitate [i'mi-tét] *v.t.* imitare.

Imitation [i-mi-té'sn] *n.* imitazione.

Immaculate [i-mè'chiù-let] *a.* immacolato.

Immaterial [i-mà-ti'e'ri-èl] *a.* immateriale, di nessun'importanza.

Immature [i-mà-tiù°r'] *a.* immaturo.

Immeasurable [i-mè'jù-rà-bl] *a.* immensurabile.

Immediate [i-mi'di-èt] *a.* immediato.

Immemorial [i-mi-mo°'ri-èl] *a.* immemorabile.

Immense [i-mèns] *a.* immenso.

Immensity [i-mèn'si-ti] *n.* immensità.

Immerse [i-mè°s'] *v.t.* immergere.

Immersion [i-mè°'sn] *n.* immersione.

Immigrant [i'mi-grènt] *a. e n.* immigrante.

Immigrate [i'mi-grét] *v.i.* immigrare.

Immigration [i-mi-gré'sn] *n.* immigrazione.

Imminent [i'mi-nènt] *a.* imminente.

Immobilize [i-mò'bi-la'iz] *v.t.* immobilizzare.

Immoderate [i-mò'dè-rèt] *a.* immoderato, smodato.

Immodest [i-mò'dèst] *a.* immodesto, impudico.

Immolate [i'mò-lét] *v.t.* immolare. [mor...le.

Immoral [i-mò'rèl] *a.* immorale.

Immorality [i-mò-rè'li-ti] *n.* immoralità.

Immortal [i-mo°'tèl] *a. e n.* immortale.

Immortality [i-mo°-tè'li-ti] *n.* immortalità.

Immortalize [i-mo°'tà-la'iz] *v.t.* immortalare.

Immovable [i-mŭ'vă-bl] *a.* inamovibile.

Immune [i-miŭn'] *a.* immune.

Immunity [i-miŭ'ni-ti] *n.* immunità.

Immure [i-miŭ^{er}] *v.t.* imprigionare, rinchiudere.

Immutable [i-miŭ'tă-bl] *a.* immutabile.

Imp [imp] *n.* diavoletto.

Impact [im'pĕct] *n.* collisione, impressione, urto.

Impair [im-pé^{er}'] *v.t.* danneggiare, menomare.

Impalpable [im-pĕl'pă-bl] *a.* impalpabile.

Impart [im-pä't'] *v.t.* comunicare, impartire.

Impartial [im-pä'scĕl] *a.* imparziale.

Impartiality [im-pä'sci-ĕ'li-ti] *n.* imparzialità.

Impassible [im-pè'si-bl] *a.* impassibile.

Impassioned [im-pè'scĕnd] *a.* appassionato, eloquente.

Impassive [im-pè'siv] *a.* impassibile.

Impatience [im-pé'scĕns] *n.* impazienza.

Impatient [im-pé'scĕnt] *a.* impaziente.

Impeach [im-pié'] *v.t.* accusare di alto tradimento.

Impeachment [im-pié'mĕnt] *n.* processo per alto tradimento.

Impeccable [im-pè'că-bl] *a.* impeccabile.

Impecunious [im-pi-chiŭ'ni-ăs] *a.* senza danaro.

Impede [im-pid'] *v.t.* impedire, ostacolare.

Impediment [im-pè'di-mĕnt] *n.* impedimento, ostacolo.

Impel [im-pĕl'] *v.t.* costringere, spingere.

Impend [im-pĕnd'] *v.i.* essere sospeso; (*fig.*) sovrastare minacciosamente.

Impenetrable [im-pè'ni-tră-bl] *a.* impenetrabile.

Impenitent [im-pè'ni-tĕnt] *a.* impenitente.

Imperative [im-pè'ră-tiv] *a. e n.* imperativo; *a.* imperioso.

Imperfect [im-pĕr'fĕct] *a. e n.* imperfetto.

Imperfection [im-pĕr-fĕc'sn] *n.* imperfezione.

Imperial [im-pi'ĕ'ri-ĕl] *n.* imperiale, pizzetto; *a.* imperiale.

Imperialism [im-pi'ĕ'ri-ă-lizm] *n.* imperialismo.

Imperil [im-pè'ril] *v.t.* mettere in pericolo.

Imperious [im-pi'ĕ'ri-ăs] *a.* imperioso.

Imperishable [im-pè'ri-sciă-bl] *a.* imperituro.

Impermeable [im-pĕr'mi-ă-bl] *a.* impermeabile.

Impersonal [im-pĕr'sŏ-nĕl] *a.* impersonale.

Impersonate [im-pĕr'sŏ-nét] *v.t.* assumere il carattere di, impersonare.

Impertinence [im-pĕr'ti-nĕns] *n.* impertinenza.

Impertinent [im-pĕr'ti-nĕnt] *a.* impertinente.

Imperturbable [im-pĕr-tĕr'bă-bl] *a.* imperturbabile.

Impervious [im-pĕr'vi-ăs] *a.* impervio; (*fig.*) sordo.

Impetuous [im-pè'tiŭ-ăs] *a.* impetuoso.

Impetus [im'pi-tăs] *n.* impeto.

Impiety [im-pa'i-ti] *n.* empietà.

Impinge [im-ping'] *v.i.* venire a contatto con.

Impious [im'pi-ăs] *a.* empio.

Implacable [im-plè'că-bl] *a.* implacabile.

Implant [im-plănt'] *v.t.* impiantare, instillare.

Implement [im'pli-mĕnt] *n.* arnese, strumento, utensile; *v.t.* adempiere a.

Implicate [im'pli-chét] *v.t.* implicare.

Implicit [im-pli'sit] *a.* implicito.

Implore [im-plo^er'] *v.t.* implorare.

Imply [im-plaⁱ'] *v.t.* implicare, insinuare, significare.

Impolite [im-pò-laⁱt'] *a.* scortese, sgarbato.

Impolitic [im-pò'li-tic] *a.* imprudente, impolitico.

Import [im'po^et] *n.* (articolo di) importazione, importanza, significato; [im-po^et'] *v.t.* importare; (*arcaico*) premere a.

Importance [im-po^er'tèns] *n.* importanza.

Important [im-po^er'tènt] *a.* importante.

Importation [im-po^er-té'šn] *n.* importazione.

Importunate [im-po^er'tiù-nèt] *a.* importuno, insistente.

Importune [im-po^er'tiùn] *v.t.* importunare, sollecitare.

Impose [im-pòz'] *v.t.* appioppare, imporre; *v.i.* ingannare, costringere.

Imposition [im-pò-zi'šn] *n.* imposizione, imposta, inganno.

Impossibility [im-pò-si-bi'li-ti] *n.* impossibilità.

Impossible [im-pò'si-bl] *a.* impossibile.

Impostor [im-pòs'tè^r] *n.* impostore.

Imposture [im-pòs'tiù^er] *n.* impostura, inganno.

Impotence [im'pò-tèns] *n.* impotenza.

Impotent [im'pò-tènt] *a.* impotente.

Impound [im-paùnd'] *v.t.* confiscare, sequestrare.

Impoverish [im-pò'vè-riš] *v.t.* impoverire, ridurre alla miseria.

Impracticable [im-prèc'ti-cà-bl] *a.* impraticabile, intrattabile.

Impregnable [im-prèg'nà-bl] *a.* inespugnabile.

Impregnate [im-prèg'nèt] *v.t.* impregnare, saturare.

Impress [im-près'] *v.t.* imprimere, impressionare, arrolare forzatamente.

Impression [im-prè'šn] *n.* impressione, impronta, edizione, ristampa.

Impressionable [im-prè'šcè-nà-bl] *a.* impressionabile.

Impressive [im-prè'siv] *a.* impressionante, solenne.

Imprint [im-print'] *v.t.* imprimere, stampare.

Imprison [im-pri'žen] *v.t.* imprigionare.

Imprisonment [im-pri'žèn-mènt] *n.* prigionia.

Improbable [im-prò'bà-bl] *a.* improbabile, inverosimile.

Improper [im-prò'pè^r] *a.* improprio, sconveniente, scorretto.

Impropriety [im-prò-praⁱ'i-ti] *n.* improprietà, sconvenienza.

Improve [im-prùv'] *v.t. e i.* migliorare.

Improvement [im-prùv'mènt] *n.* miglioramento, progres(so, -si (*pl.*).

Improvidence [im-prò'vi-dèns] *n.* imprevidenza.

Improvident [im-prò'vi-dènt] *a.* imprevidente.

Improvise [im'prò-vaⁱz] *v.t.* improvvisare.

Imprudence [im-prù'dèns] *n.* imprudenza.

Imprudent [im-prù'dènt] *a.* imprudente.

Impudence [im'più-dèns] *n.* impudenza, sfacciataggine.

Impudent [im'più-dènt] *a.* birichino, impudente, sfacciato.

Impulse [im'påls] *n.* impulso.

Impulsive [im-pål'siv] *a.* impulsivo.

Impunity [im-più'ni-ti] *n.* impunità.

Impure [im-più^er'] *a.* impuro.

Impurity [ĭm-piŭ′rĭ-ti] *n.* impurità.

Imputation [ĭm-piŭ-té′śn] *n.* imputazione.

Impute [ĭm-piŭt′] *v.t.* attribuire, imputare.

In [ĭn] *prep.* a, in, entro; *av.* dentro, in casa.

Inability [ĭn-ă-bĭ′lĭ-ti] *n.* inabilità.

Inaccessible [ĭn-ĕc-sĕ′sĭ-bl] *a.* inaccessibile.

Inaccuracy [ĭn-è′chiŭ-ră-sĭ] *n.* inaccuratezza.

Inaccurate [ĭn-è′chiŭ-rĕt] *a.* inaccurato.

Inaction [ĭn-èc′śn] *n.* inattività.

Inactive [ĭn-èc′tĭv] *a.* inattivo.

Inadequate [ĭn-è′dĭ-quĕt] *a.* inadeguato, insufficiente.

Inadmissible [ĭn-èd-mĭ′sĭ-bl] *a.* inammissibile.

Inadvertence [ĭn-èd-vĕr′tĕns] *n.* inavvertenza, disattenzione, svista.

Inadvertent [ĭn-èd-vĕr′tĕnt] *a.* negligente, non fatto apposta.

Inane [ĭn-én′] *a.* inane, sciocco, vacuo.

Inanimate [ĭn-è′nĭ-mĕt] *a.* inanimato, senza vita.

Inanity [ĭn-è′nĭ-ti] *n.* inanità, vacuità.

Inappropriate [ĭn-ă-prò′prĭ-ĕt] *a.* inadatto, inappropriato.

Inapt [ĭn-èpt′] *a.* inadatto, inatto.

Inarticulate [ĭn-ă′-tĭ′chiŭ-lĕt] *a.* inarticolato, indistinto.

Inasmuch as [ĭn-èz-măc′èz] *con.* inquantoché.

Inattention [ĭn-ă-tĕn′śn] *n.* disattenzione, distrazione.

Inattentive [ĭn-ă-tĕn′tĭv] *a.* distratto.

Inaudible [ĭn-ó′dĭ-bl] *a.* inaudibile.

Inaugurate [ĭn-ó′ghiŭ-rét] *v.t.* inaugurare.

Inborn [ĭn′bò′n] *a.* innato.

Incandescence [ĭn-chĕn-dĕ′sĕns] *n.* incandescenza.

Incandescent [ĭn-chĕn-dĕ′sĕnt] *a.* incandescente.

Incantation [ĭn-chĕn-té′śn] *n.* incantesimo, parole magiche.

Incapable [ĭn-ché′pă-bl] *a.* incapace, inetto.

Incapacitate [ĭn-că-pè′sĭ-tĕt] *v.t.* rendere inabile, incapace.

Incapacity [ĭn-că-pè′sĭ-ti] *n.* inabilità, incapacità.

Incarcerate [ĭn-cà′sĕ-rĕt] *v.t.* incarcerare.

Incarceration [ĭn-cà′-sĕ-ré′śn] *n.* incarcerazione.

Incarnate [ĭn-cà′nĕt] *a.* incarnato; [ĭn-cà′nét] *v.t.* incarnare.

Incautious [ĭn-có′sciăs] *a.* incauto.

Incendiary [ĭn-sĕn′dĭ-ă-rĭ] *a. e n.* incendiario.

Incense [ĭn′sĕns] *n.* incenso; *v.t.* incensare; [ĭnsĕns′] *v.t.* far arrabbiare.

Incentive [ĭn-sĕn′tĭv] *n.* incentivo, motivo.

Incessant [ĭn-sĕ′sĕnt] *a.* continuo, incessante.

Incest [ĭn′sĕst] *n.* incesto.

Incestuous [ĭn-sĕs′tiŭ-ăs] *a.* incestuoso.

Inch [ĭnĉ] *n.* pollice (misura lineare = cm. 2,54).

Incidence [ĭn′sĭ-dĕns] *n.* incidenza.

Incident [ĭn′sĭ-dĕnt] *n.* avvenimento, episodio, incidente; *a.* incidente, inerente.

Incidental [ĭn-sĭ-dĕn′tĕl] *a.* casuale, fortuito.

Incision [ĭn-sĭ′śn] *n.* incisione.

Incisive [ĭn-sa′sĭv] *a.* incisivo, acuto, penetrante.

Incite [ĭn-sa′t′] *v.t.* incitare, stimolare.

Incitement [ĭn-sa′t′mĕnt] *n.* incitamento, stimolo.

Incivility [ĭn-sĭ-vĭ′lĭ-ti] *n.* scortesia.

Inclemency [in-clĕ'mĕn-si] n. inclemenza.

Inclement [in-clĕ'mĕnt] a. inclemente.

Inclination [in-cli-né'śn] n. disposizione, inclinazione, propensità.

Incline [in-cla'n'] n. pendío, piano inclinato; v.t. e i. inclinare, essere incline.

Include [in-clūd'] v.t. includere.

Inclusion [in-clū'śn] n. inclusione.

Inclusive [in-clū'śiv] a. completo, inclusivo.

Incoherence [in-cō-hi'rĕns] n. incoerenza.

Incoherent [in-cō-hi'rĕnt] a. incoerente. [entrata.

Income [in'căm] n. reddito, entrata.

Incommode [in-cō-mōd'] v.t. incomodare, recar disturbo a.

Incomparable [in-cŏm'pă-ră-bl] a. incomparabile.

Incompatible [in-cŏm-pè'ti-bl] a. incompatibile.

Incompetence [in-cŏm'pi-tĕns] n. incompetenza.

Incompetent [in-cŏm'pi-tĕnt] a. incompetente.

Incomplete [in-cŏm-plit'] a. incompleto.

Incomprehensible [in-cŏm-pri-hĕn'si-bl] a. incomprensibile.

Inconceivable [in-cŏn-si'vă-bl] a. inconcepibile.

Inconclusive [in-cŏn-clū'siv] a. inconcludente.

Incongruous [in-cŏn'grū-ăs] a. incongruo.

Inconsequent [in-cŏn'si-quĕnt] a. illogico, inconseguente.

Inconsiderable [in-cŏn-si'dĕ-ră-bl] a. di poca entità.

Inconsistent [in-cŏn-sis'tĕnt] a. incompatibile, inconsistente.

Inconsolable [in-cŏn-sò'lă-bl] a. inconsolabile.

Inconspicuous [in-cŏn-spi'chiŭ-ăs] a. incospicuo, modesto.

Inconstancy [in-cŏn'stăn-si] n. incostanza.

Inconstant [in-cŏn'stănt] a. incostante.

Incontinent [in-cŏn'ti-nĕnt] a. incontinente.

Incontinently [in-cŏn'ti-nĕnt-li] av. immediatamente, incontinentemente.

Inconvenience [in-cŏn-vi'ni-ĕns] n. disturbo, inconveniente, disagio.

Inconvenient [in-cŏn-vi'ni-ĕnt] a. incomodo, scomodo.

Inconvertible [in-cŏn-vĕr'ti-bl] a. inconvertibile.

Incorporate [in-cŏr'pò-rét] v.t. incorporare.

Incorporeal [in-cŏr-pò'ri-ĕl] a. immateriale, incorporeo.

Incorrect [in-cō-rĕct'] a. inesatto, scorretto.

Incorrectness [in-cō-rĕct'nĕs] n. inesattezza, scorrettezza.

Incorruptible [in-cō-răp'ti-bl] a. incorruttibile.

Incorruption [in-cō-răp'śn] n. incorruttibilità.

Increase [in'cris] n. aumento, incremento; (in-cris') v.t. e i. aumentare, (far) crescere.

Incredible [in-crĕ'di-bl] a. incredibile.

Incredulity [in-cri-diŭ'li-ti] n. incredulità.

Incredulous [in-crĕ'diŭ-lăs] a. incredulo.

Increment [in'cri-mĕnt] n. guadagno, incremento.

Incubate [in'chiŭ-bét] v.t. e i. covare. [inculcare.

Inculcate [in'căl-chét] v.t. inculcare.

Inculpate [in'căl-pét] v.t. incolpare.

Incumbent [in-căm'bĕnt] n. titolare d'un beneficio ecclesiastico; a. incombente, obbligatorio.

Incur [in-chër'] v.t. incorrere in.

Incurable [in-chiû°'rä-bl] a. incurabile.

Incursion [in-chër'sn] n. incursione.

Indebted [in-dè'tid] a. indebitato, grato.

Indecency [in-dì'sën-si] n. indecenza, spudoratezza.

Indecent [in-dì'sënt] a. indecente, spudorato.

Indecision [in-dì-sì'sn] n. indecisione.

Indecisive [in-dì-sa''siv] a. indeciso, non decisivo.

Indecorous [in-dè'cö-räs] a. indecoroso, sconveniente.

Indecorum [in-dì'co°-räm] n. indecoro, sconveniente.

Indeed [in-dìd'] av. davvero, infatti, in realtà.

Indefatigable [in-dì-fè'ti-gä-bl] a. instancabile.

Indefensible [in-dì-fèn'si-bl] a. indifendibile.

Indefinite [in-dè'fi-nit] a. indefinito. [delebile.

Indelible [in-dè'li-bl] a. in-

Indelicacy [in-dè'li-cä-si] n. indelicatezza.

Indelicate [in-dè'li-chèt] a. indelicato.

Indemnify [in-dèm'ni-fa¹] v.t. indennizzare, risarcire.

Indemnity [in-dèm'ni-ti] n. indennità, risarcimento.

Indent [in'dènt] n. dentellatura, contratto, documento, requisizione; [in-dènt'] v.t. e i. dentellare, frastagliare, stendere un documento in due copie, requisire.

Indenture [in-dèn'tiû°r] n. tentellatura, insenatura, contratto stipulato.

Independence [in-di-pèn'dèns] n. indipendenza.

Independent [in-dì-pèn'dènt] a. indipendente.

Indescribable [in-dis-cra¹'bä-bl] a. indescrivibile.

Indestructible [in-dis-träc'ti-bl] a. indistruttibile.

Indeterminate [in-dì-tër'mi-nët] a. indeterminato.

Index [in'dècs] n. indice.

Indian [in'di-ën] a. e n. indiano.

Indicate [in'di-chét] v.t. indicare.

Indication [in-dì-ché'sn] n. indicazione, segno, sintomo.

Indicator [in-dì-ché-të°'] n. indicatore, tabella.

Indict [in-da¹t'] v.t. accusare.

Indictment [in-da¹t'mènt] n. accusa, imputazione.

Indifference [in-dì'fë-rëns] n. indifferenza.

Indifferent [in-dì'fè-rënt] a. indifferente, mediocre.

Indigence [in'dì-gëns] n. indigenza, miseria.

Indigenous [in-dì'gë-näs] a. indigeno.

Indigent [in'dì-gënt] a. indigente, povero.

Indigestible [in-dì-gës'ti-bl] a. indigeribile, indigesto.

Indigestion [in-dì-gës'ti-ën] n. indigestione.

Indignant [in-dìg'nènt] a. indignato, sdegnato.

Indignation [in-dig-né'sn] n. indignazione, sdegno.

Indignity [in-dìg'ni-ti] n. offesa, trattamento indegno.

Indirect [in-dì-rèct'] a. indiretto.

Indiscernible [in-dì-zër'ni-bl] a. indiscernibile.

Indiscreet [in-dis-crìt'] a. imprudente, indiscreto.

Indiscretion [in-dis-crè'sn] n. imprudenza, indiscrezione.

Indiscriminate [in-dis-cri'mi-nët] a. che non fa distinzioni, promiscuo.

Indispensable [in-dis-pèn'sä-bl] a. indispensabile.

Indispose [in-dis-pöz'] v.t. indisporre, rendere avverso a.

Indisposition [ĭn-dĭs-pò-zĭ'-shn] n. indisposizione.

Indisputable [ĭn-dĭs'pū-tă-bl] a. indiscutibile, sicuro.

Indissoluble [ĭn-dĭ'sō-lĭŭ-bl] a. indissolubile.

Indistinct [ĭn-dĭs-tĭnct'] a. confuso, indistinto.

Indite [ĭn-daĭt'] v.t. comporre, redigere.

Individual [ĭn-dĭ-vĭ'dĭŭ-ĕl] n. individuo; a. individuale.

Individuality [ĭn-dĭ-vĭ-dĭŭ-ĕ'lĭ-tĭ] n. individualità.

Indivisible [ĭn-dĭ-vĭ'zĭ-bl] a. indivisibile. [dolenza.

Indolence [ĭn'dō-lĕns] n. in-

Indolent [ĭn'dō-lĕnt] a. indolente.

Indoor [ĭn'doer] a. che ha luogo in casa, da eseguirsi in casa; **indoors** [ĭn-doers'] av. dentro, in casa.

Indubitable [ĭn-dĭŭ'bĭ-tă-bl] a. indubitabile.

Induce [ĭn-dĭŭs'] v.t. indurre.

Inducement [ĭn-dĭŭs'mĕnt] n. allettamento, motivo.

Induction [ĭn-dăc'sn] n. induzione, investitura.

Indulge [ĭn-dălg'] v.t. indulgere, lasciar libero corso a; v.i. indulgere, abbandonarsi.

Indulgence [ĭn-dăl'gĕns] n. indulgenza, soddisfazione.

Industrial [ĭn-dăs'trĭ-ĕl] a. industriale.

Industrious [ĭn-dăs'trĭ-ăs] a. attivo, operoso.

Industry [ĭn'dăs-trĭ] n. industria, attività.

Inebriate [ĭn-ĭ'brĭ-ĕt] v.t. inebriare, ubriacare.

Inedited [ĭn-ĕ'dĭ-tĭd] a. inedito.

Ineffable [ĭn-ĕ'fă-bl] a. ineffabile.

Ineffective [ĭn-ĕ-fĕc'tĭv] a. inefficace, di scarso effetto.

Ineffectual [ĭn-ĕ-fĕc'tĭŭ-ĕl] a. inefficace, vano.

Inefficacy [ĭn-ĕ'fĭ-că-sĭ] n. inefficacia.

Inefficient [ĭn-ĕ-fĭ'scĕnt] a. inefficiente, poco capace.

Inept [ĭn-ĕpt'] a. inetto.

Inequality [ĭn-ĭ-quó'lĭ-tĭ] n. inuguaglianza.

Inert [ĭn-ĕrt'] a. inerte.

Inertness [ĭn-ĕrt'nĕs] n. inerzia.

Inevitable [ĭn-ĕ'vĭ-tă-bl] a. fatale inevitabile.

Inexact [ĭn-ĕg-zĕct'] a. inesatto.

Inexcusable [ĭn-ĕc-schiŭ'ză-bl] a. imperdonabile.

Inexhaustible [ĭn-ĕg-zŏ'stĭ-bl] a. inesauribile.

Inexorable [ĭn-ĕc'sŏ-ră-bl] a. inesorabile.

Inexperience [ĭn-ĕc-spĭ'rĭ-ĕns] n. inesperienza.

Inexperienced [ĭn-ĕc-spĭ'rĭ-ĕnst] a. inesperto, novellino, senza esperienza.

Inexpert [ĭn-ĕc-spĕrt'] a. inabile, inesperto.

Inexpressible [ĭn-ĕc-sprĕ'sĭ-bl] a. inesprimibile.

Inexpressive [ĭn-ĕc-sprĕ'sĭv] a. inespressivo.

Infallibility [ĭn-fè-lĭ-bĭ'lĭ-tĭ] n. infallibilità. [fallibile.

Infallible [ĭn-fè'lĭ-bl] a. in-

Infamous [ĭn'fă-măs] a. infame.

Infamy [ĭn'fă-mĭ] n. infamia.

Infancy [ĭn'făn-sĭ] n. infanzia.

Infant [ĭn'fănt] n. bim/bo, -ba, infante; a. infantile.

Infantry [ĭn'făn-trĭ] n. fanteria.

Infatuate [ĭn-fè'tĭŭ-ĕt] v.t. infatuare.

Infatuation [ĭn-fè-tĭŭ-ĕ'sn] n. infatuazione.

Infect [ĭn-fĕct'] v.t. infettare.

Infection [ĭn-fĕc'sn] n. infezione.

Infectious [ĭn-fĕc'sciăs] a. infettivo.

Infer [ĭn-fê͡r'] v.t. accennare, dedurre.

Inference [ĭn'fê-rĕns] n. conclusione, deduzione.

Inferior [ĭn-fî'rĭ-ê͡r] a. e n. inferiore.

Inferiority [ĭn-fî'rĭ-ŏ'rĭ-tĭ] n. inferiorità.

Infernal [ĭn-fê͡r'nĕl] a. infernale.

Infertile [ĭn-fê͡r'taĭl] a. improduttivo, non fertile.

Infest [ĭn-fĕst'] v.t. infestare.

Infidel [ĭn'fĭ-dĕl] a. e n. infedele, miscredente.

Infidelity [ĭn-fĭ-dĕl'ĭ-tĭ] n. infedeltà.

Infiltrate [ĭn-fĭl'trĕt] v.t. e i. infiltrar(si).

Infinite [ĭn'fĭ-nĭt] a. e n. infinito.

Infinitive [ĭn-fĭ'nĭ-tĭv] n. infinito, infinitivo.

Infinity [ĭn-fê'm'] n. infinità.

Infirm [ĭn-fê'm'] a. debole, infermo, irresoluto.

Infirmary [ĭn-fê͡r'mă-rĭ] n. infermeria.

Infirmity [ĭn-fê͡r'mĭ-tĭ] n. infermità, irresolutezza.

Inflame [ĭnflêm'] v.t. infiammare.

Inflammable [ĭn-flè'mă-bl] a. infiammabile.

Inflammation [ĭn-flă-mé'sn] n. infiammazione.

Inflammatory [ĭn-flè'mă-tŏ-rĭ] a. infiammatorio.

Inflate [ĭn-flét'] v.t. e i. gonfiare.

Inflation [ĭn-flé'sn] n. gonfiamento, inflazione.

Inflect [ĭn-flĕct'] v.t. inflettere.

Inflexion [ĭn-flĕc'sn] n. inflessione.

Inflexible [ĭn-flĕc'sĭ-bl] a. inflessibile, rigido.

Inflict [ĭn-flĭct'] v.t. infliggere.

Infliction [ĭn-flĭc'sn] n. inflizione.

Influence [ĭn'flŭ-ĕns] n. ascendente, influenza, influsso; v.t. influenzare.

Influential [ĭn-flŭ-ĕn'scĕl] a. autorevole, influente.

Influenza [ĭn-flŭ-ĕn'zĕ͡r] n. (med.) influenza.

Influx [ĭn'flăcs] n. afflusso, flusso.

Inform [ĭn-fo'm'] v.t. informare.

Informal [ĭn-fo'mĕl] a. semplice, senza formalità, irregolare.

Informant [ĭn-fo'mĕnt] n. informatore.

Information [ĭn-fo'r-mé'sn] n. informazio/ne, -ni (pl.), accusa.

Infrequent [ĭn-frĭ'quĕnt] a. infrequente, raro.

Infringe [ĭn-frĭng'] v.t. trasgredire.

Infringement [ĭn-frĭng'mĕnt n. infrazione, trasgressione.

Infuse [ĭn-fiûz'] v.t. infondere, instillare, mettere in infusione; v.i. stare in infusione.

Infusion [ĭn-fiû'sn] n. infusione, infuso.

Ingenious [ĭn-gĭ'nĭ-ăs] a. ingegnoso.

Ingenuity [ĭn-gĭ-nĭŭ'ĭ-tĭ] n. abilità inventiva, ingegnosità.

Ingenuous [ĭn-gĕ'nĭŭ-ăs] a. ingenuo; i./ness n. ingenuità.

Ingle [ĭn'gl] n. angolo del camino.

Inglorious [ĭn-glŏ'rĭ-ăs] a. inglorioso.

Ingrate [ĭn'grét] n. (raro) ingrato.

Ingratiate [ĭn-gré'scĭ-ét] v.t. ingraziarsi.

Ingratitude [ĭn-grè'tĭ-tiŭd] n. ingratitudine.

Ingredient [ĭn-grĭ'dĭ-ĕnt] n. ingrediente.

Inhabit [ĭn-hè'bĭt] v.t. abitare, occupare.

Inhabitable [ĭn-hè'bĭ-tă-bl] a. abitabile.

Inhabitant [in-hè'bi-tènt] *n.* abitante.

Inhale [in-hél'] *v.t.* aspirare.

Inhere [in-hi⁰ʳ'] *v.i.* essere inerente.

Inherent [in-hi⁰'rènt] *a.* inerente, innato.

Inherit [in-hè'rìt] *v.t. e i.* ereditare.

Inheritance [in-hè'ri-tèns] *n.* eridità, retaggio.

Inhibit [in-hi'bìt] *v.t.* inibire, impedire.

Inhospitable [in-hòs'pi-tà-bl] *a.* inospitale.

Inhuman [in-hiù'màn] *a.* barbaro, inumano.

Inhumanity [in-hiù-mè'ni-ti] *n.* inumanità.

Inimical [in-i'mi-chèl] *a.* nemico, ostile.

Inimitable [in-i'mi-tà-bl] *a.* inimitabile.

Iniquity [in-i'qui-ti] *n.* iniquità.

Initial [in-i'scèl] *a. e n.* iniziale; *v.t.* firmare con le sole iniziali.

Initiate [in-i'sci-èt] *n.* iniziato; (in-i'sci-ét) *v.t.* iniziare.

Initiative [in-i'sci-è-tiv] *n.* iniziativa.

Inject [in-gèct'] *v.t.* iniettare.

Injection [in-gèc'ʃn] *n.* iniezione.

Injudicious [in-giù-di'sciàs] *a.* sconsiderato, che manca di giudizio.

Injunction [in-giànc'ʃn] *n.* ingiunzione.

Injure [in'gèʳ] *v.t.* danneggiare, ferire, nuocere a.

Injury [in'gè-ri] *n.* danno, ferita, torto.

Injustice [in-giàs'tìs] *n.* ingiustizia.

Ink [ínc] *n.* inchiostro; **-stand** [stènd] calamaio.

Inkling [ínc'lìn] *n.* leggero accenno, vaga idea.

Inland [in'lènd] *a. e n.* interno

(d'un paese); *av.* nell'interno, verso l'interno.

Inlay [in'le¹] *n.* intarsio; *v.t.* intarsiare.

Inlet [in'lèt] *n.* insenatura, piccolo braccio di mare.

Inmate [in'mét] *n.* inquilino, paziente (in un manicomio).

Inmost [in'mòst] *a. (superl.)* il più interno, profondo.

Inn [in] *n.* albergo, locanda.

Innate [i-nét'] *a.* innato, istintivo.

Inner [i'nèʳ] *c. (comp.)* interiore, interno.

Innocence [i'nò-sèns] *n.* innocenza.

Innocent [i'nò-sènt] *a. e n.* innocente.

Innocuous [i-nò'chiù-às] *a.* innocuo.

Innovate [i'nò-vét] *v.t.* innovare.

Innovation [i-nò-vé'ʃn] *n.* innovazione.

Innuendo [i-niù-èn'dò] *n.* allusione, insinuazione.

Inoculate [in-ò'chiù-lét] *v.t.* inoculare.

Inoculation [in-ò-chiù-lé'ʃn] *n.* inoculazione.

Inoffensive [in-ò-fèn'siv] *a.* inoffensivo.

Inopportune [in-ò-voʳ-tiùn'] *a.* inopportuno, intempestivo.

Inordinate [in-oʳ'di-nét] *a.* immoderato.

Inquest [in-quèst] *n.* inchiesta.

Inquire [in-quà¹eʳ] *v.t.* domandare; *v.i.* indagare, informarsi, fare ricerche (*pl.*).

Inquiry [in-quà¹e'ri] *n.* investigazione, ricerca d'informazioni.

Inquisition [in-qui-zi'ʃn] *n.* inquisizione.

Inquisitive [in-qui'zi-tiv] *a.* curioso, inquisitorio.

Inquisitor [in-qui'zi-tèʳ] *n.* inquisitore.

Inroad [in'ròd] *n.* incursione ostile.

Insane [in-sén'] *a.* folle, pazzo.

Insanity [in-sè'ni-ti] *n.* follia, pazzia.

Insatiable [in-sé'scì-ă-bl] *a.* insaziabile.

Inscribe [in-scra¹b'] *v.t.* i(n)-scrivere.

Inscription [in-scrìp'sn] *n.* i(n)scrizione.

Inscrutable [in-scrū'tă-bl] *a.* inscrutabile.

Insect [in'sèct] *n.* insetto.

Insecure [in-sì-chiū°r'] *a.* malsicuro.

Insecurity [in-sì-chiū°'ri-ti] *n.* mancanza di sicurezza.

Insensible [in-sèn'si-bl] *a.* inconscio, insensibile, privo di sensi.

Inseparable [in-sè'pă-ră-bl] *a.* inseparabile.

Insert [in-sèrt'] *v.t.* inserire.

Insertion [in-sè°'rsn] *n.* aggiunta, inserzione.

Inside [in'sa¹d] *n.* interno, parte interna; *a.* interiore, interno; *av.* nell'interno; *prep.* dentro; **i. out** [aut] interno a rovescio (abito).

Insidious [in-sì'dì-ăs] *a.* insidioso.

Insight [in'sa¹t] *n.* penetrazione, potere psicologico.

Insignificance [in-sig-nì'fì-chèns] *n.* scarsa importanza.

Insignificant [in-sig-nì'fì-chènt] *a.* insignificante.

Insincere [in-sin-sì°r'] *a.* falso, insincero.

Insincerity [in-sin-sè'ri-ti] *n.* falsità, mancanza di sincerità.

Insinuate [in-sì'niù-ét] *v.t.* insinuare, introdurre.

Insinuation [in-sì-niù-é'sn] *n.* insinuazione.

Insipid [in-sì'pi̯d] *a.* insipido, insulso.

Insipidity [in-sì-pì'di̯-ti] *n.* insulsaggine.

Insist [in-sìst'] *v.i.* insistere.

Insistence [in-sìs'tèns] *n.* insistenza, perseveranza.

Insolence [in'sò-lèns] *n.* insolenza.

Insolent [in'sò-lènt] *a.* insolente.

Insoluble [in-sò'liù-bl] *a.* insolubile.

Insolvable [in-sòl'vă-bl] *a.* insolvibile.

Insolvency [in-sòl'vèn-si] *n.* insolvenza.

Insolvent [in-sòl'vènt] *a.* insolvente.

Inspect [in-spèct'] *v.t.* ispezionare.

Inspection [in-spèc'sn] *n.* ispezione.

Inspector [in-spèc'tè°r] *n.* controllore, ispettore.

Inspiration [in-spi-ré'sn] *n.* ispirazione.   [rare.

Inspire [in-spä¹°r'] *v.i.* ispi-

Instability [in-stă-bì'li̯-ti] *n.* instabilità.

Install [in-stòl'] *v.t.* insediare, installare.

Instalment [in-stòl'mènt] *n.* puntata, rata.

Instance [in'stăns] *n.* esempio, istanza.

Instant [in'stănt] *n.* attimo, istante; *a.* corrente, urgente.

Instantaneous [in-stăn-tè'ni-ăs] *a.* istantaneo.

Instantly [in'stănt-li] *av.* immediatamente.

Instead [in-stèd'] *avv.* e *prep.* invece (di).

Instep [in'stèp] *n.* collo del piede.

Instigate [in'sti-ghét] *v.i.* istigare.

Instigation [in-sti-ghé'sn] *n.* istigazione.

Instil(1) [in-stil'] *v.t.* instillare.

Instinct [in'stin̄ct] *n.* istinto; *a.* pieno.

Instinctive [in-stin̄c'tiv] *a.* istintivo.

Institute [in'stĭ-tiŭt] institution [in-stĭ-tiŭ'ṡn] n. istituto,
istituzione.
Institute [in'stĭ-tiŭt] v.t.
istituire.
Instruct [in-străct'] v.t.
istruire, informare.
Instruction [in-străc'ṡn] n.
istruzione (comunen. al pl.)
disposizione, ordine.
Instructor [in-străc'tĕr] n.
istruttore.
Instrument [in'strŭ-mĕnt] n.
(i)strumento.
Insubordinate [in-să-bo'r'dĭ-
nĕt] a. insubordinato, di-
subbidiente.
Insufficient [in-să-fĭ'scĕnt] a.
inadeguato, insufficiente.
Insular [in'siŭ-lĕr] a. insulare.
Insult [in'sălt] n. insulto;
(in-sălt') v.t. insultare.
Insuperable [in-siŭ'pĕ-ră-bl]
a. insuperabile.
Insurance [in-sciŭ'e'rĕns] n.
(comm.) assicurazione.
Insure [in-sciŭ'er'] v.t. assicurare (contro i danni, ecc.).
Insurgent [in-sĕr'gĕnt] n.
insorto; a. e n. ribelle.
Insurmountable [in-sĕr-
maŭn'tă-bl] a. insormontabile.
Insurrection [in-să-rĕc'ṡn] n.
insurrezione.
Intact [in-tĕct'] a. intatto,
intero.
Intake [in'tĕc] n. immissione,
tratto di brughiera, ecc. resa
coltivabile.
Integer [in'tĭ-ghĕr] n. numero
intero.   [integrale.
Integral [in'tĭ-grĕl] a. e n.
Integrity [in-tĕ'grĭ-tĭ] n. integrità.
Intellect [in'tĕ-lĕct] n. intelletto.
Intellectual [in'tĕ-lĕc'tiŭ-ĕl]
a. e n. intellettuale.
Intelligence [in-tĕ'lĭ-gĕns] n.
intelligenza, informazioni, notizie (pl.).

Intelligent [in-tĕ'lĭ-gĕnt] a.
intelligente.
Intemperance [in-tĕm'pĕ-
rĕns] n. intemperanza.
Intend [in-tĕnd'] v.t. e i. in-
tendere, proporsi.
Intended [in-tĕn'dĭd] n.
fidanza/to, -ta.
Intensify [in-tĕn'sĭ-fa¹] v.t.
e i. intensificar(si).
Intensive [in-tĕn'sĭv] a. in-
tensivo.
Intent [in-tĕnt'] n. intento,
scopo; a. attento, intento.
Intention [in-tĕn'ṡn] n. intenzione, proposito.
Inter [in-tĕr'] v.t. interrare,
seppellire.
Intercede [in-tĕr-sĭd'] v.i.
intercedere.
Intercept [in-tĕr-sĕpt'] v.t.
intercettare.
Interchange [in-tĕr-cĕng'] n.
scambio reciproco; v.t. e i.
scambiar(si).
Interchangeable [in-tĕr-
cĕn'giă-bl] a. scambievole.
Intercourse [in'tĕr-cōrs] n.
comunicazione, rapporto,
rapporti sessuali (pl.).
Interdict [in-tĕr-dĭct] n. interdetto (papale); (in-tĕr-dĭct')
v.t. interdire, vietare.
Interdiction [in-tĕr-dĭc'ṡn] n.
divieto, interdizione.
Interest [in'tĕ-rĕst] n. interesse, -si (pl.), interessamento; v.t. interessare.
Interesting [in'tĕ-rĕs-tĭn] a.
interessante.
Interfere [in-tĕr-fīer'] v.i. intervenire, intromettersi, ostacolare.
Interference [in-tĕr-fī'e'rĕns]
n. ingerenza; (tec.) interferenza.
Interior [in-tī'rĭ-ĕr] a. interiore, interno.
Interject [in-tĕr-gĕct'] v.t. e i.
interporre.
Interjection [in-tĕr-gĕc'ṡn] n.
interiezione.

Interlace [ĭn-tĕr-lés'] v.t. intrecciare.
Interleave [ĭn-tĕr-lĭv'] v.t. interfogliare.
Interloper [ĭn'tĕr-lò-pĕr] n. intruso.
Interlude [ĭn'tĕr-liŭd] n. interludio, intermezzo.
Intermediate [ĭn-tĕr-mĭ'dĭ-ĕt] a. intermedio.
Interment [ĭn-tĕr'mĕnt] n. inumazione.
Intermingle [ĭn-tĕr-mĭn'gl] v.t. e i. inframmischiar(si).
Intermission [ĭn-tĕr-mĭ'sn] n. intervallo, sospensione.
Intern [ĭn-tĕrn'] v.t. internare.
Internal [ĭn-tĕr'nĕl] a. interno.
International [ĭn-tĕr-né'scĕnĕl] a. e n. internazionale.
Internment [ĭn-tĕr'nmĕnt] n. internamento.
Interpellation [ĭn-tĕr-pĕ-lé'sn] n. interpellanza.
Interpolate [ĭn-tĕr'pŏ-dĕt] v.t. interpolare.
Interpose [ĭn-tĕr-pòz'] v.t. e i. interpor(si).
Interpret [ĭn-tĕr'prĕt] v.t. interpretare; v.i. fare da interprete.
Interpreter [ĭn-tĕr'prĭ-tĕr] n. interprete.
Interrogate [ĭn-tĕ'rŏ-ghĕt] v.t. e i. interrogare.
Interrogation [ĭn-tĕ-rŏ-ghĕ'sn] n. interrogazione.
Interrogatory [ĭn-tĕ-rŏ'gă-tŏ-rĭ] a. e n. interrogatorio.
Interrupt [ĭn-tĕ-răpt'] v.t. interrompere.
Interruption [ĭn-tĕ-răp'sn] n. interruzione.
Intersect [ĭn-tĕr-sĕct'] v.t. e i. intersecar(si).
Intersection [ĭn-tĕr-sĕc'sn] n. intersecazione.
Intersperse [ĭn-tĕr-spe's'] v.t. inframmezzare.
Intertwine [ĭn-tĕr-tuă'n'] v.t. e i. intrecciar(si).

Interval [ĭn'tĕr-vĕl] n. intervallo.
Intervene [ĭn-tĕr-vĭn'] v.i. intervenire, intromettersi.
Intervention [ĭn-tĕr-vĕn'sn] n. intervento.
Interview [ĭn'tĕr-viŭ] n. abboccamento, intervista; v.t. intervistare.
Intestate [ĭn-tĕs'tĕt] a. (legge) chi muore senza fare testamento, intestato.
Intestine [ĭn-tĕs'tĭn] n. (comunem. al pl.) intestino.
Intimacy [ĭn'tĭ-mă-sĭ] n. intimità.
Intimate [ĭn'tĭ-mĕt] a. intimo; (ĭn'tĭ-mĕt) v.t. annunciare, comunicare, accennare a.
Intimation [ĭn-tĭ-mé'sn] n. annuncio, accenno.
Intimidate [ĭn-tĭ'mĭ-dĕt] v.t. intimidire.
Intimidation [ĭn-tĭ-mĭ-dé'sn] n. intimidazione.
Into [ĭn'tŭ] prep. in.
Intolerable [ĭn-tŏ'lĕ-ră-bl] a. intollerabile.
Intolerance [ĭn-tŏ'lĕ-rĕns] n. intolleranza.
Intonation [ĭn-tŏ-né'sn] n. intonazione, tono.
Intone [ĭn-tòn'] v.t. intonare.
Intoxicate [ĭn-tòc'sĭ-chĕt] v.t. inebriare, ubriacare.
Intoxication [ĭn-tòc-sĭ-ché'sn] n. ebbrezza, ubriachezza.
Intransigent [ĭn-trăn'sĭ-gĕnt] a.e n. intransigente.
Intrepid [ĭn-trĕ'pĭd] a. intrepido.
Intrepidity [ĭn-trĕ-pĭ'dĭ-tĭ] n. intrepidità.
Intricacy [ĭn'trĭ-că-sĭ] n. complicazione, groviglio, viluppo.
Intricate [ĭn'trĭ-chĕt] a. intricato, involuto.
Intrigue [ĭn-trĭg'] n. intrigo, macchinazione; v.i. intrigare, macchinare; v.t. (gergo) stuzzicare la curiosità di.